William Grunert

History of the One Hundred and Twenty-ninth Regiment Illinois Volunteer Infantry

containing the marches, events and battles of the army commanded by Gen. Sherman, from the commencement of the campaign against Atlanta, Georgia, to the arrival at Wash

William Grunert

History of the One Hundred and Twenty-ninth Regiment Illinois Volunteer Infantry
containing the marches, events and battles of the army commanded by Gen. Sherman, from the commencement of the campaign against Atlanta, Georgia, to the arrival at Wash

ISBN/EAN: 9783337293635

Printed in Europe, USA, Canada, Australia, Japan

Cover: Foto ©Andreas Hilbeck / pixelio.de

More available books at **www.hansebooks.com**

HISTORY

OF THE

One Hundred and Twenty-Ninth

REGIMENT ILLINOIS VOLUNTEER INFANTRY,

CONTAINING THE

MARCHES, EVENTS AND BATTLES OF THE ARMY COMMANDED BY GEN. SHERMAN, FROM THE COMMENCEMENT OF THE CAMPAIGN AGAINST ATLANTA, GEORGIA, TO THE ARRIVAL AT WASHINGTON, D. C.;

ALSO,

THE RETURN OF THE REGIMENT FROM WASHINGTON TO CHICAGO, ILLS., AND EVENTS ON THE ROUTE AND IN CHICAGO,

BY

WILLIAM GRUNERT.

WINCHESTER, ILL.

PRINTED BY R. B. DEDMAN.

1866.

HISTORY OF THE
ONE HUNDRED AND TWENTY-NINTH.

President LINCOLN had scarcely issued his call for three hundred thousand volunteers in the year 1861, when the loyal hearts of the inhabitants of Scott county, Illinois, were moved and filled with enthusiasm. Every one that could leave his loved ones hastened to be mustered in, thinking that his country needed his services in the pending danger more than father, mother, wife or children. The love of country caused the farmer to leave his plow, the mechanic to change his implements of peace with implements of war, to take part in the great work of suppressing the rebellion. Many of our friends and acquaintances had set a good example and gone to the field of battle before us; many had already shed their blood in the defence of the country, while others were lying ill in the hospitals. It was the duty of every loyal, upright man to assist in saving the country from ruin, and in consequence of the call of the President for volunteers, a company was raised and organized under the care of the later Col. HENRY CASE, in Winchester, Scott Co., Ill., in July, 1862. In a few days the company was full, nevertheless more volunteers came and offered their services. During the same month a second company was raised by Captain (later Lieut. Colonel) THOMAS H. FLYNN. On the 5th day of August, 1862, we left our homes and friends and dear ones, for how long a period no one could tell, to command a halt to the enemy that grew bolder and more daring every day. Early in the morning of the above day we entered the wagons of our friends who wished to do this last act of kindness and bring us to the next railroad station. It is almost needless to say, that tears glistened in many eyes when the parting farewell was said! At noon, on the 5th of August, we reached Jacksonville, and after the last friends had bid us adieu and wished us a speedy and safe return, cheers were given, hats waved and the locomotive steamed with us towards the State Capital, Springfield. There we remaided until 9 o'clock, P. M., when we again entered a train of open cars, while a heavy drenching rain saturated every thread of our clothing, and a few hours before daybreak on the 6th of August we reached Pontiac, Ill., where we went into camp. The next day was also a rainy one, and our barracks offered us but very poor shelter. As a matter of course, this new mode of life did not suit us exactly, until we became more accustomed to it. Bad as our barracks were, we began to be satisfied with them, after we had stood guard for several hours, and wind and rain made this part of the service rather unpleasant. When not on guard, we went to town, after procuring a pass, where we were well received and kindly treated by the citizens. A company of volunteers was also being organized here, which afterwards became the first company of our regiment. Three weeks passed quickly, during which time we did guard duty with clubs. By this time the requisite number of ten companies for the regiment were full and had arrived, and now we received uniforms and muskets and the drilling was done with more exactness. On the 8th of September we were sworn in for three years, unless sooner discharged, and received two months' pay in advance and twenty-five dollars bounty; after which we moved nearer to the enemy's country. The "iron horse" brought the 129th Illinois volunteer regiment to Jeffersonville, Ind. The regimental officers were Col. SMITH, Lt. Col. HENRY CASE, and Maj. CROPSEY. Here we remained a short time after our arrival, and then crossed the Ohio river to Louisvlle, Ky. This was at the time when BRAGG threatened Louisville, and was only a few miles distant. When one day some cannon shots were heard, we supposed the enemy was making an attack, our camp was alarmed and the regiment posted into line—but no enemy appeared.

We had been in camp near Louisville two weeks, done guard duty and improved in drilling, when one morning at 3 o'oclock we were ordered to "fall in" line of battle. We were told to be ready at a moment's notice, though the day of our march had not been fixed. We were of course all very anxious to know the time and direction of our march or "tramp," but could get no positive information. So we packed up our knapsacks every day anew, in order to leave nothing behind, until finally some had such a heavy load that it was an impossibility for them to march, much less run after the flying rebels. On the first day of marching, blankets, overcoats, socks, &c., &c., were thrown away in all directions and the knapsacks lightened. The day for our departure had come at last. On the 3d of October, 1862, we turned our backs to the city of Louisville, after having received sixty cartridges, and after many a "parting bumper" had been taken. The sun was tremendously hot, and as the water in our canteens gave out, no springs or creeks on our way, the knapsacks overloaded and heavy, it may be imagined that this our first day's "tramp" was anything but pleasant. The sun had long departed and it was dark, and yet we were on our march toward Shelbyville, Ky. Every one that was with us this night, will never forget the scene when by the light of the moon a small spring, half dry, was discovered close by the road. The confusion that followed this discovery is indescribable. Every body rushed to the water, quenched his thirst and returned to his former place—no company there— the different companies were completely intermingled—from all sides the cry: "Where is my company?"

was heard—the officers sought their men, and the men their officers. The officers strove in vain to bring some order in this confused mass of human beings, until some of the men, tired and worn out, threw themselves down on the ground to rest and sleep, despite the entreaties and commands of the company officers. The part of the regiment not so tired followed the officers, and when we halted at two o'clock, near a small creek, I counted not more than eight of my company. Although we were hungry, we were too tired and worn out to cook anything, but stretched ourselves on the ground and were soon asleep.

October 4th, 1862. Before sunrise a good many of the sleepers left behind had rejoined us. Some of my comrades, hungry as they were, shot a hog in a corn field close by, cut a few slices off and roasted them over the camp-fires on bayonets or sticks of wood. We missed the necessary salt very much. Many had just arisen from their sleep, when the signal was given to fall in, and many had to march the second day also with an empty stomach. This day's march was, nevertheless, not as severe on the men as the day before, and there were less sore feet. We had to march only thirteen miles this day, and reached Shelbyville, Ky., long before sunset, where we went into camp and remained until the seventh of October.

October 7th, 1862 The bugle called us up rather early and we were told, that a march of twenty-two miles would be our day's work. We were all right again and the tramp was not so hard, although several sick members of the regiment had to be left in Shelbyville. Evening approached, but as on the third, there were no prospects of going into camp. We were told that the enemy was at Frankfort, Ky., and that we would have to reach that city before morning yet. The whole column moved along silently, and without a word being spoken, resting a little now and then, until midnight, when we rested two hours near a small creek. Those two hours seemed to us to be but as many minutes, and scarcely had we closed our eyes, when the command to "fall in," tore us from our slumber. No march has ever been so tiring to me as this one, being hardly able to remain in the column. Many of the men left the column and laid down by the road to sleep and rest.

October 8th. Before day-break we had reached Frankfort, the Capital of Kentucky, but too late nevertheless, as the enemy had fled. Our advance guard of cavalry had a skirmish with the enemy at the bridge over the Kentucky river, while the latter were endeavoring to demolish the bridge. The enemy had to flee with the loss of several wounded and killed. Blood-spots were to be seen on the walls of a house up to nearly eight feet from the ground, where some wounded rebel had laid his bleeding hands. The enemy had been successful in destroying part of the bridge, and we had to remain on the other side of the river until the repairs could be made. This was done a few hours after sunrise, and, marching over the bridge, we saw three of our killed cavalrymen lying there; several wounded had been brought to the hospital. We remained upon our arrival in the city on the streets, where part of the men laid down on the hard pavement, another part prepared breakfast, and a third went to the citizens for something to eat. The sun was scorchingly hot, and it was with the greatest difficulty that some of the men, when the bugler blew forward, could be brought to move, and kept in line. We did not march but a mile south of town, where we were stationed as guard on a high hill to protect some guns stationed there. After we had rid ourselves of our knapsacks and muskets, most of the men went to the river to bathe and cool and refresh the aching and worn out limbs. We were enjoying ourselves finely, when the report of a cannon and the buglars called us under arms again. We were posted in line of battle and were expecting an attack from the enemy; but in vain, no enemy appeared. Near Frankfort we remained for three days, but on

October 11*th*, the tramp commenced again; nothing of importance, however, appeared until

October 13*th*. It was some time after sunset, when we arrived near the small town of Rough and Ready, with a large force of rebels but a short distance from our front. As we were unacquainted with the country and the night a very dark one, it was impossible for us to move on, and we remained in front of the town on the road, where every one made himself as comfortable a resting place as the road would permit. Early on

October 14*th*, we were awakened and commanded to get ready for a move; what this new move was to be no one knew or could find out just then. We soon found out that we were reconnoitering and were marching with great caution several miles east of the town, when the command to load was given, after which we again moved forward very quietly and with great caution. Finally we found tracks of the rebels, who appeared to have been a whole brigade of cavalry, as in every fence corner the leavings of the horse fodder were seen. The rebels had fled on hearing of our approach. We advanced about five miles from Rough and Ready, when the pursuit was given up. After having partaken of a scanty breakfast, consisting of coffee, pork and crackers, we returned to the city, where we remained during the day.

October 15*th*. We were aroused at four o'clock in the morning, and after marching ten miles reached Lawrenceburg, where we encamped.

October 16. After another march of ten miles we reached Harrodsburg and camped.

October 17. We reached Danville, after having marched twenty miles, where we pitched our tents.

October 18. A march of fifteen miles brought us

to the town of Harrisport, where we remained over night.

October 19. We struck tents at eight o'clock A. M., and reached Crab Orchard after having marched twenty miles. The place assigned us for camp ground was so covered with briars and brush, that we had to cut these before we could commence to pitch tents. We took some corn stalks from a cornfield close by, belonging to an arch rebel, for which crime (thanks to our contemptible General) we had to drill for two hours with knapsacks. Here we remained for eight days, when we received marching orders for Lebanon. As I cared but little for keeping a diary from here, I cannot give the exact date of our departure from Crab Orchard. Our march to Lebanon brought us again to Danville, thence to Harrodsburg, where we camped. When the sun arose the next morning, we were already on the march which we continued until we had reached Danville and the sun disappeared. As there was not water enough for the horses and men, we were compelled to march five miles further to a creek. Hundreds of the men did not reach the creek on account of being too tired and having sore feet. The road from Danville to the creek was covered with stragglers and sick soldiers, while in every fence corner one or more sleepers could be seen. Myself and my comrades H. D. and H. F. belonged to the worn-out men, and without thinking of supper, stretched ourselves in the cool grass of a meadow to sleep, and let the others who chose to endeavor to follow their officers in order to get to the creek.

The next morning, after taking coffee, pork and crackers, we packed our "things," and went towards the creek in search of our regiment. The regiment, however, had left, and we were compelled to continue the march alone. We reached the regiment just after the dinner was over, and had scarcely taken our places, when the order to move on was given. We reached Perryville after a march of eight miles at five o'clock P. M., and went into camp. But a few days had passed after the battle between BRAGG's and BUELL's command, and this was the first battle-field we had ever seen. The houses were riddled by bullets and inhabited or rather filled with the wounded of both armies. The inhabitants were gone, either to the rebel or to the Union army. The dead had been interred but lightly, and here and there a leg or hand was protruding out the ground, or lying unburied. The devastating effects of war were but too plainly to be seen. Here we remained but one night, and continued our march early the next morning. Despite the stony and sandy road, that frequently led through the bottom of a creek, we made twenty-four miles that day, and camped only a few miles from Lebanon. As our place of destination was Lebanon, we commenced our march the next day later than usual and reached Lebanon about noon. I had kept my diary very accurately till now, but lost all pleasure in its continuation in consequence of the hardships we passed through. The wish to continue the diary, arose again on Christmas, 1863, and from there I did not stop with it until my safe return home. If I remember right, we remained at Lebanon but one or two days, when we were ordered to Bowling Green, Ky. Here we were for some time, and at one time Gen. ROSECRAN's held review. Our time was spent in drilling and doing guard duty. We were then ordered to Mitchellsville, Tennessee, where we also remained a longer period, until part of the regiment was ordered to Buck's Lodge, a station on the Louisville-Nashville Railroad. Our chief duty now was to keep the rebels and guerrillas from the road between Gallatin and Mitchellsville, which we did with a good will. The hiding places of the guerrillas were soon known to us, and no accidents happened on that part of the road under our control, as long as we remained there. The guerrillas were completely powerless. We did not see anything of them until Christmas

1863. This was at the time when the two great armies under Rosecrans and Bragg were confronting each other at Murfreesboro, Tenn., and fighting the battle on Stone River. In times when the great armies were lying idle, the bushwhackers generally remained quiet, but were very troublesome when these were making some move or fighting, in order to prevent the transportation of provisions, ammunition, etc. But all their efforts were of no avail. As mentioned above, the 129th Ills. regt. was stationed at Buck's Lodge, six miles above Gallatin, at a water tank of the Louisville-Nashville Railroad, when we heard of the approach of a strong band of guerrillas, whose object seemed to be to steal on us, attack us suddenly and then destroy the road, bridges, water tanks, etc. But our officers and men were on the alert. Christmas night, when the news came that the neighborhood was full of rebels, we were under arms. The guards were reinforced and instructed to keep quiet, strong patrols went up and down the road, while the balance of the regiment was under arms in camp. From 2 o'clock until sunrise we waited and watched patiently, a grave-like silence reigned, but no enemy appeared. As the danger seemed past, we stacked arms to satisfy the cravings of our stomachs by a hearty breakfast. Great prudence was nevertheless necessary, and the men were allowed to leave the camp only in large numbers. Several companies were now sent to Fountain Head, several miles north of us, where they did guard duty for some time, while we spent our time in drilling and trench work. Sometimes we would scour the neighborhood in search of guerrillas and forage "for man and beast."

The bi-monthly muster and review took place on the 31st of December, 1863.

January 1, 1864. The day was beautiful. We were busy digging trenches. The trains had come very irregular and for several days no mail had arrived. Nothing of importance happened until the 3d of January, when two trains ran into each other near our camp. Both trains came from Louisville, and the first had been delayed. The locomotive of the last train was totally destroyed, several cars were smashed to pieces and two persons badly wounded.

January 5th. I was on picket duty; the day was very pleasant. We received good news from the army of the Potomac. The next day passed without anything of importance.

January 7th. The day was clear and pleasantly cold. Myself and several comrades went several miles from camp, where we found a German family, the first in the neighborhood. We were well received and kindly treated. In the afternoon we worked on the trenches

January 8th. I was again on picket duty on this cold and rainy day. My place was in a deep hollow near the railroad. The night was dark, and rain and snow coming down in an unpleasant way.

January 9th. Two members of our company, JORDAN H. WHITEHURST and JOHN MIKLES died to-day. Three trains with rebel prisoners passed north. A rebel captain was brought in a prisoner by our scouts. The night was very rainy.

January 10, 1863. The whole day was rainy and cold.

January 11, 1863. The day was very cold and I had the pleasure of doing picket duty.

January 12, 1863. Another cold day—everything was very quiet. We received a very large mail.

January 13, 1863. A negro that had been shot by his master, but not fatally wounded, came to us and offered his services, "to live and die with us," he said. Several companies had to go to Buck's Lodge to reinforce the part of the regiment stationed there.

January 14, 1863. I was again doing picket duty. The morning was very rainy, and turned afterwards to snowing and became so cold that I could hardly move a limb.

January 15, 1863. A snow of five inches, accompanied by great cold fell. On arising we found our blankets frozen tight to the ground and covered with sleet. It is hardly necessary to say that we froze very much.

January 16, 1863. Despite the chilling blast and snow I had to stand guard, but as permission had been given to kindle a fire, I liked the day better than the day before in camp. A number of volunteers were demanded to-day to go in search of a gang of guerrillas. They left the camp in the evening.

January 17. The cold weather continued. The road was out of order and no trains passed. A company was ordered to go in search of the volunteers that went on a guerrilla hunt. We had heard nothing from them since they left. Both detachments soon returned, without having seen a trace of the enemy.

January 18. A strong detail was sent out foraging with wagons and returned well loaded before nightfall.

January 19. The unpleasant duty of standing guard in a very heavy rain was my lot to-day, and wet to the skin I returned to camp the next morning.

January 20. Another cold day; all quiet in camp.

January 21. Since standing guard the last time I felt sick and broken down in consequence of getting wet. A friend thought I would have to go to the hospital.

January 22. I felt decidedly better to-day, well enough to go along with a foraging party. The negro mentioned above, shot by his master, was our guide, and led us immediately to the house of his (former) master, where we confiscated everything that we could use. The negro took a couple of blankets along, and under his lead we returned with our well loaded wagons towards evening into camp.

January 23. Although not entirely well, I went

on picket duty again. Three men of Morgan's command surrendered to-day. Fifteen men on horseback, under command of our (then) Colonel SMITH scoured the country in order to confiscate all serviceable horses of the rebels. Part of our regiment was to be mounted to clear the surrounding country of rebels.

January 24. We received another mail to-day and the trains are running regular again. We had much fun to-day and spent the time with music and singing until we went to bed.

January 25. The day was rainy; nevertheless we were inspected by a staff officer of Gen. WARD, and our drill and general looks were perfectly satisfactory to Col. SMITH, as well as to the inspecting officer. This satisfaction was a hint that we were sufficiently posted in tactics and rules of warfare to be sent to the front.

January 26. In the forenoon we received firewood for a couple of days. In the afternoon I was detailed with several others to guard some female prisoners, among them the wife of the noted and feared guerrilla chief PETTICORD, in a neighboring house. It rained hard the whole day.

January 27. News was received that a large quantity of salt was to be smuggled by the rebels close by, and a number of men, among which myself, under command of Capt. FLYNN and Lieutenant HALDEMAN were ordered to capture it. All mounted, and with a faithful guide, we left camp immediately after breakfast, and rode in full gallop to our place of destination. Evening came, and we were yet without any positive information of the whereabouts of the smuggler. As night came on and we were unacquainted with the country, we resolved to go to a neighboring mill for information and then seek a shelter for the night. The mill was not far from Franklin, Ky., and soon reached. But unfortunately we were separated from it by a creek very high in conseqeunce of the heavy rains and over which no bridge could lead us to the mill. To swim through seemed impossible and too hazardous. The miller was called, and asked about the narrowest and shoalest place of the creek. The place was shown us, but the miller thought that the current would be too strong for us to cross. The feeling of finding our reward in the mill, however, overpowered every other consideration. Lieutenat HALDEMAN kneeled on his horse, led it to the water, and although only after great exertions and danger, the horse reached the other side of the creek. We followed the example, fastened our muskets and cartridge-boxes around our necks as well as we could, so they could not get wet, and in a few minutes joined our lieutenant on the other side of the creek. The mill and neighboring houses were thoroughly searched, but all labor was in vain; our swim through the creek had been for nought and we were obliged to swim the creek another time, in order to find a shelter for the night and to attend to our jaded horses. The sun had long disappeared, darkness reigned everywhere, and the cold had given the ground a hard surface. As we all got more or less wet, it may be imagined that our situation on horseback was not a very enviable one. We would rather have camped in the bushes close by, but our commander, Capt. FLYNN, would not listen to such a proposition, until about ten o'clock we reached a well filled corn crib and a large farm-house. The inhabitants were at first very much frightned at this armed visit at night, but were soon pacified on being told whence we came and what our object was. A couple of negroes took charge of our horses, after which we went to the house, where shortly after we were invited to a substantial supper. After supper beds were prepared and guards posted. The beds we refused, because our clothes were too wet, and because it was not advisable to "strip." We laid down around a roaring chimney fire on the floor of a room, where we slept soundly the next morning, better than in a feather bed.

January 28. Before daybreak we were up again, and after having taken a substantial breakfast and our horses a sufficient quantity of corn and hay, we intended to confiscate horses in the neighborhood, doubting the successful accomplishment of the object of our expedition, the capture of the salt smugglers. The horses were completely worn out, and the horses of the neighboring farmers were not much better, the good ones having been confiscated already. We determined to send three men back to the camp, over twenty miles distant, and fetch fresh horses. At this moment we heard the noise of gallopping horses and our guards cry "halt." Our frightened commander gathered his small and scattered force as quickly as possible, when several "blue jackets" hastily rode up and made ready for firing. The officer of the party now demanded of us who we were and what we were after. Satisfactory answers having been given, we learned that we had been pursued by Union troops. The miller, to whom we had paid a visit the night before, had immediately after our departure sent word to the commanding officer of the Union troops at Franklin, that what he supposed to be a fact, "guerrillas in Union uniforms had been at his mill." This officer immediately sent half a regiment of cavalry in our pursuit. This mutual explanation caused a good deal of merriment, and the cavalry returned to Franklin, while three of our men returned to the camp. The others scoured the country for horses, and succeeded in finding and bringing away eleven very fine horses.

January 29. A detail was sent to Gallatin, Tenn., as escort of a train for provisions. The guerrilla chief PETTICORD sent a flag of truce which was admitted into camp, with the following propositions:

1. The return of all property confiscated by our men, to its rightful owner; 2. this done, to surren-

der; 3. in case of refusal of these propositions to prepare to smell powder. The last proposition we were willing to accept. The flag of truce, however, was not allowed to leave the camp again. We received additional ammunition, and towards evening one hundred men on foot and twenty mounted men were sent out to see if there really was danger, while the remainder of the regiment staid in camp under arms. The night passed as peaceably as the former.

January 30. Our detail returned without having found a trace of the enemy.

January 31. A number of rebel prisoners were sent to Gallatin, Tenn., among them the bearer of PETTICORD's flag of truce.

February 1. The day was rainy, and nothing of importance happened. The general subject of conversation was our pending move, as we had received marching orders the day before.

February 2. On arising we received orders to be ready for marching immediately. At 7 o'clock we left the camp at Fountain Head and repaired to the South Tunnel, two miles north of Gallatin, where we arrived at 12 o'clock and went into camp. During the whole day it was very cold.

February 3. A better and more suitable place for camping was selected, tents erected, &c. It was very cold.

February 4. The day was spent in making the tents more comfortable. I had the honor of standing in the cold on guard. A deep snow fell.

February 5. A very cold and snowy day. A messenger from Mitchelsville brought the news that a train with clothes had been attacked by guerrillas, and fifty men were detached to assist the garrison there. The detail were met on the way by a second messenger, who reported that the guerrillas had been compelled to retreat, whereupon our men returned to camp, as it was very cold.

February 6 and 7. Everybody that could made the camp and tent more commodious and pleasant.

February 8. The whole regiment was busy to-day digging ditches around our camp.

February 9. The whole day rain; was on guard.

February 11. A beautiful warm day. Two soldiers that were buried near our camp, were disinterred and sent north to their friends. Both corpses were in an advanced stage of putrefaction.

February 12. Was sick.

February 13. Half sick I went on guard, and reported myself at the doctor sick, when I got worse.

February 14. Was sick a-bed until February 23.

February 23. Went to do guard duty again for the first time. The corpse of another soldier that had lain two months, was disinterred.

February 25. Early in the morning at three o'clock the camp was alarmed, as our pickets had been fired upon. In ten minutes the regiment stood in line of battle, awaiting an attack. It was found out afterwards that a certain captain of our regiment had only tried us, and wishing the disturber of our night's rest all ill, we retired to sleep again. The afternoon brought us a heavy rain, nevertheless we had an inspection of arms.

February 27. Was on guard again; in camp the inspection was continued.

February 28. The bi-monthly muster took place to-day; in the afternoon we had rain again.

March 1. The day was a very beautiful one, nothing of any importance happened.

March 2. A company of mounted men were sent off, as we had received news of the notorious guerrilla chief PETTICORD.

March 3. During the night the long sought for guerrilla chief PETTICORD was captured and placed under guard. When caught he was at a house in the neighborhood, taking his supper. At the sight of our "boys in blue," he endeavored to escape, and ran through a back door, away from our men. When a few "blue beans" were sent whistling about his ears, however, he surrendered and begged for life. On his arrival in camp, he became very insolent, but trusty men were placed to guard and soon quieted him.

March 5. It was very cold, accompanied by a heavy snow storm.

March 6. A rainy day; nevertheless several companies were sent out foraging. This was a rather difficult task to be accomplished in the neighborhood of our camp, and the party had to go about twenty miles with the wagons before they succeeded in getting corn. We got the corn at a large plantation that was well stored and stocked with corn, cattle, &c., and as night was near it was impossible for us to return to camp, but we remained on the plantation. The inhabitants of the house treated us kindly and gave us a hearty supper. The night passed quietly.

March 7. Early we went to work to load our wagons, which caused the smiling face of our landlord to change to a very sour and angry one, because we were not satisfied with supper and lodging. The family no noubt considered us very impudent, but such is war; and we did not provoke it. After we had filled about half a dozen wagons with oats and corn, perhaps compelled a hog or chicken to go with us, we started on our return. The day was very rainy and the roads worse than bottomless, and the drivers could with the greatest difficulty only compel the animals to pull. The camp was reached at last about eight o'clock. During the night one of our pickets shot a horse, that did not understand the meaning of the command: "halt," and the picket not being able to see whether the horse was riderless or not.

March 10. The day was very rainy.

March 12. Myself with several comrades were in the country to get some fresh meat. Our cavalry captured twenty-six prisoners to-day. We were ordered to sleep on our arms, because it was feared that the friends of PETTICORD intended to pay us a visit. The night passed quietly however.

March 13. The prisoners were taken to Gallatin by a guard of honor.

March 14. I was on guard; the day was fine.

March 15. All our "duds" were inspected minutely and to the satisfaction of the officers.

March 16. At the usual battallion drill, during the pause, we laid our arms on the ground, when one gun that was left loaded imprudently, went off and the ball entered the right foot of a sergeant of co. I. The wounded man was taken to the hospital, where the surgeon removed some bone splinters from the wound. The sergeant became forever unfit for duty.

March 17. On gaurd to-day; nothing new happened.

March 19. The passenger train from Nashville was this evening attacked by a band of guerrillas near Richland station, Tenn., where companies A. and K. of our regiment were stationed. The train was stopped by tearing up the track, while the guerrillas were in bushes near by, and a briggadier general, several colonels, the mail and all goods on the train captured by the enemy. Companies A. and K., however, always on the look out, attacked the rebels, a small skirmish took place, and the guerrillas lost one dead, several wounded, horses and guns, and also the prisoners, mail and provisions. The train was soon put back on the track, and went on. We received orders to be on our guard, and ten men, reinforcements, were sent to the two companies. They returned, however, on hearing on the way that all danger was past. The night passed quietly.

March 20. Was on picket duty during a heavy thunder storm, accompanied by incessant rain the whole day. The prisoners taken yesterday were to day brought in.

March 21. The day was cloudy and cool.

March 22. It was Sunday, and we had inspection of arms and dress, and in the evening, dress parade. The day was cloudy and rainy.

March 23. Incessant rain; a foraging expedition was sent out to-day.

March 24. Was on guard; it rained again day and night.

March 25. The weather was cold and cloudy, sometimes an occasional fall of snow. We had to keep our arms loaded and ready on hand, as the neighborhood had become unsafe.

March 26. The day was beautiful, and a number of men were sent foraging; five men from each company were detailed to act as escort.

March 27. Companies A. and B. were again troubled by guerrillas and had to be on their guard.

March 28. I was on picket; a heavy thunder storm, accompanied by torrents of rain fell upon us durng the night, and everybody got wet to the skin. Three of MORGAN's men were captured by our cavalry to-day. They were well armed and fired four times on our men, before they surrendered. It was reported that the passenger train had run off the track, and six men been killed. The report was afterwards corrected, that a freight train had been demolished at a bridge below Gallatin, while in motion. Three soldiers were killed and several others crippled; seventy head of cattle were burnt with the fragments of the cattle cars.

March 29. Inspection took place to-day. The cavalry at Gallatin were driven back to-day by 400 rebels.

March 30. Our camp was moved to a high mountain, and consequently our line of pickets could be reduced.

March 31. I was on guard to-day; the day was

fine, in the night a deep snow fell, accompanied by a heavy wind.

April 1. We made improvements in our camp; had battallion drill in the afternoon.

April 2. The trains came very irregular; our picket line was reinforced during the night; had company drill in the afternoon.

April 3. The day was clear and cold; drilled in the fore and afternoon

April 5. Had inspection and in the afternoon a visit from Gen. PAINE, staff and daughters, who were well satisfied with our discipline and state of health. Towards evening dress parade. The day was cloudy.

April 6 and 7. We drilled the principal part of both days.

April 8. Two men were shot to-day through the carelessness of another, who was cleaning his loaded gun. The bullet went through the breast of one and the head of the other. As we intended to remain at South Tunnel for some time yet, we commenced the erection of small buildings, in order to live more comfortable.

April 9. We made several improvements in our camp; a detachment of cavalry captured two of MORGAN's guerrillas.

April 10. We had general inspection, and the inspecting officers were well satisfied.

April 11. It was Sunday, and the inspection of our "duds" was continued. A larger portion of the regiment was sick to-day than usual. The weather was dark and cold.

April 23. A negress that had been maltreated by her mistress, came into camp crying and begging for admission into camp and protection. It was granted, and she was set to work in the hospital.

April 14. A dispatch from Franklin, Ky., reported that a large band of guerrillas had shown itself near there with the intention of destroying the railroad. A strong detachment of our regiment was sent off to

Franklin, but before the men reached their destination they learned that the guerrillas had withdrawn without accomplishing their object, and our men returned to camp.

April 15 A detail of men was sent to Gallatin to escort the paymaster to us; after having received our money we made preparations to send it home. The day was rainy.

April 17. A foraging party was sent out to-day.

April 19. Inspection of arms was ordered, but the rain prevented it. A member of company I deserted last night, and cavalry was sent after him, but in vain. At night dress parade.

April 27. When the drum beat for roll-call this morning, and the men were taking their places, the gun of a member of company C went off and the bullet wounded him on the right hand. His wife, who was with him at the time, became very excited, but was soon pacified.

April 28 *and* 29. Had battallion drill this as well as the next day.

April 30. The bi-monthly muster took place to-day; there was much talk about marching orders.

May 1, 1863 Company D left South Tunnel and went to a station fifteen miles further North, called Richland, where three companies were stationed already.

May 2. We reached Richland station and erected our tents and camp according to order. We chopped wood for houses, which we finished on the third and fourth day of the month.

May 6. It rained the whole day. In the evening one of our pickets shot at a person stealing on him; the person escaped, but was captured half an hour later by our cavalry returning from a scout. The prisoner was placed in the guard-house under a strong guard, where several of his captive friends were enjoying themselves.

May 7. The day was very rainy, and many of our men went home on a furlough.

May 9. We dug ditches near our quarters; the war news received to-day was not very pleasing.

May 10. Five men were detached from each company to go to Gallatin, and assist Gen. PAINE in arresting several disloyal persons that had acted the traitor to the Union cause. A number of them were sent beyond our lines. In the evening dress parade.

May 11. Twenty-five men infantry and a detachment of cavalry went off on a scout to-night.

May 12. To-day a dinner was brought us by a neighboring Union family. After dinner dancing took place, and speeches were made by Col. CASE, and other officers, which were well received by the Union family and by our men. The report that Richmond had been taken, reached our camp the third time.

May 13. The report came in that sixty guerrillas, in Federal uniforms, had shown themselves at Woodburn station, near Franklin, Ky., and were destroying the road property. A detachment of infantry and cavalry was sent from here, but came too late, and returned without accomplishing anything.

May 14. Our whole camp was fortified and the trees around it cut down. Part of our cavalry went after guerrillas. In the afternoon drill.

May 15. A party went foraging, but were in great danger on account of bushwhackers that had been reinforced and were becoming bolder.

May 16. To-night a number of bushwhackers fired on one of our pickets, but, as the man was standing behind a tree, not harmed. The guerrillas were kept back by our pickets and retreated. We were in line of battle from 12 o'clock until daybreak, but nothing occurred. One rebel was taken prisoner.

May 17. Had inspection of arms and towards evening dress-parade.

May 18. Several shots were fired during the night, but the camp was not alarmed. One of the pickets had in the darkness shot a calf for a rebel.

May 20. Inspection of arms, cartridge boxes, and

ammunition; in the afternoon drill. The necessary water began to get scarce and we commenced digging a well.

May 22. The digging of the well was continued incessantly.

May 23. The report was received that one thousand rebels had crossed the Cumberland river and driven in part of our cavalry that was out on a scout. The report was not believed by many.

May 25. Several of our officers had arranged a ball, but during the dancing some jovial fellows fired a couple of shots, and the enjoyment of the officers had an end.

May 26. All wagons and twenty mounted men went out foraging, who, in order to get forage faster, divided off into small parties, and intended to return as soon as possible. One party arrived at a plantation, where corn, &c., was in the field, and as they needed an axe one man went to the house to get it. When near the house this messenger saw several armed men there, and immediately made a retrogade movement; but too late, the armed men had seen him, and went in pursuit. A race took place and five shots fired at the fleeing man, until the supposed rebels reached the wagons, where it was found that our own party had pursued our messenger, which caused a good deal of merriment.

May 27. A regiment of cavalry passed by here to-day en route for Murfreesboro. Many of our men off on a furlough, returned to-day. Received the report as a fact that Vicksburg had been taken.

May 28. It rained the whole day; nothing of importance happened.

May 29. The day was dark and sultry. There was a good deal of talk about marching orders having been received.

May 31. Company A received marching orders, and had to go to Gallatin to night yet.

June 1. It was announced that an inspection of

arms would take place, but afterwards we were ordered to be ready for marching. It turned out finally, that companies F and C had marching orders, and that companies D and K would remain.

June 3. Company K received marching orders, and left for Gallatin on the 8 o'clock train.

June 4. In the forenoon we had target shooting, and were served a substantial dinner in the afternoon, for the second time, by a Union lady living near. Lieut. HALDEMAN and Corporal CLARK, both of company D, went about twilight to the house of a widow lady near, where they were by treachery surprised by guerrillas. CLARK escaped, but HALDEMAN, according to CLARK's testimony, taken prisoner and shot. During the night a scout of mounted men was sent out to learn something definite of the fate of Lieut. HALDEMAN, and, if possible, rescue him. As the scout remained absent so long, another detachment was sent out after the first, and, as we supposed, captured one.

June 5. Ten more men were sent out after the two detachments sent out before, of whom no news had as yet been received. There were now but few men left in camp, and as the bushwhackers were aware of this, they showed themselves openly and often, but did not venture an attack, knowing that we were well fortified and always prepared for them. About 7 o'clock in the evening the long expected men returned from their troublesome and dangerous ride. They had made inquiries about Lieut. HALDEMAN, giving his description to several citizens and received the answer that they had seen a wounded Federal officer on a mule between some Confederate soldiers, and had given our men the direction the party went. But all was in vain, and being convinced that Lieut. HALDEMAN was in the enemy's hands, they returned to camp, after a ride of more than fifty miles. This evening, sufficient proof having been given that HALDEMAN had been captured through the treachery of the widow lady, her house was set on fire by Colonel CASE and several men, and the woman ordered beyond our lines.

June 6. The whole company was again on duty, The guerrillas had heard that Gen. PAINE was going on a furlough, we had to patrol the road and prevent its destruction. In the afternoon we were reinforced by two companies of the 106th Ohio regiment. Towards evening nine men of Capt. FLYNN's company, under command of a corporal, were posted at a place where a road crosses the track, which road was much used by the bushwhackers. The men were well posted behind trees and very quiet. About 10 o'clock they heard the clatter of horses' feet, and soon two riders came in sight. When near enough the command to halt was given, but scarcely was this uttered, when the two horsemen turned their horses to flee. Faster than I can write this the reports of nine guns were heard, but alas! but one bullet hit the aim. One of the horsemen staggered in the saddle, but as he had strength enough to hold himself, both horsemen escaped. As the shots were fired, the whole camp was alarmed, and all men were under arms until they learned that there was no danger of an attack.

June 7. A foraging party, sent out to-day, found the hat of the guerrilla shot last night on the road. The guerrilla was found dead in a house in Mitchellsville, and was buried by our men in the later part of the day.

June 8. When we returned from our foraging tour, we found the whole camp deserted, excepting by the men that had been on guard the night before. The guerrillas were very troublesome, and attacked the trains very frequently; our "garrison" had to guard a train to Bowling Green, Ky., and did not return till late in the afternoon.

June 9 Our company D received marching orders and went to Gallatin on a train at night, where the whole regiment was once more united—the first time for a long while. A member of company A drowned in the Cumberland river while bathing.

June 10. We received two months' pay to-day. A young lady, dressed in men's clothes, was taken prisoner and put under guard. A great excitement was in camp to-night in consequence of the report, that a large force of rebels were approaching town. All our cavalry, not otherwise on duty, were sent out on the main roads, and stationed at the entrance of the roads into the city, wagons were placed as barricades, and all the regiments of infantry posted in line of battle. The night passed without any attack, and it was doubted very much the next day, whether there really had been any danger.

June 11. A rainy day; nothing of importance happened.

June 12. We had to drill in the forenoon.

June 13. News had come in from Lieut. HALDEMAN's place of captivity and a detail ordered to rescue him. On arriving at the house described, it was found that he had been removed by the guerrillas. A freight train was burnt by guerrillas near Elizabethtown, Ky. From now until the 20th everything remained quiet in camp and neighborhood, the service however became more arduous on account of having to patrol the principal roads, outside our picket lines, every night.

June 20. A tremendous excitement existed last night, as it was generally believed that an attack would be made by the enemy. Reports had come in contniually that the rebels were gathering around us, of which smaller or larger squads had been seen by our scouts, and our cavalry had to patrol all roads leading to the city, as on a former occasion; the regiments of infantry were posted in line of battle to await the attack of the enemy. But again we were unnecessarily robbed of our sleep, and the morning dawned without an enemy having appeared in sight.

June 21. It was generally reported that the rebel Gen. Morgan, with eight thousand men, was moving against us to attack Gallatin. No man was permitted to leave camp without permit, from which we drew the conclusion that the report was believed at headquarters. We received marching orders to-day. Morgan, who had the night before attacked Alexandria, had been beaten back by the Union troops.

June 22. Another dreadful night. Nobody doubted an attack of the enemy that had the day before been seen in numerous large squads by our scouts, and we knew that Morgan was close on hand with a large force. All our tents, whose erection and commodious arrangement had caused us so much trouble, had to be struck, so that the enemy should not see our exact strength and position from a distance. The whole 129th regiment marched to Fort Thomas, near the camp, as we could defy the enemy better there. After all preparations had been made, the necessary caution taken, plenty of ammunition given out, and the silence of the grave reigned everywhere, we swore "never to surrender Fort Thomas as long as a cartridge was left us." In vain we listened, but no report of a single shot was heard from our picket line, and when morning came, and no enemy had appeared yet, we left our guns, went to the camp, and commenced erecting our tents again.

June 23. Many of our men went on a furlough; we had inspection of arms.

June 24. Twenty-five men were sent to a plantation eight miles from Gallatin, confiscated by the Government, with a number of negroes, to protect them in harvesting the wheat on the field against an attack of the guerrillas. Rain set in and prevented the work to-day, and the men were compelled to remain on the plantation over night.

June 25. It rained the whole day.

June 26. Thunderstorm and rain the whole day.

June 27. Another day of rain; a foraging party was sent out after the most necessary things.

June 28. Rain the whole day.

June 29. Storm and rain during the day; a detachment of cavalry met twenty rebels, several shots were fired but nobody hurt; the rebels escaped.

June 30. It rained again. The bi-monthly muster took place to-day. The 106th Ohio regiment that took our place at Richland station, was attacked by eighty rebels. Fifteen of the "rebs" were taken prisoners and several killed; no loss on our side.

July 1. This was the first clear day since the 23d of June.

July 2. Another party was sent to a confiscated plantation, to protect the negroes working there against an attack of guerrillas. The party returned on the 3d of July.

July 4. The day was foggy; everything was quiet until noon, when thirty-two guns were fired in Fort Thomas in honor of the day. The locomotives that passed here were completely covered by the stars and stripes. In the afternoon speeches were made by Col. CASE, Lieut. Col. CRORSEY, and others. The rebel Gen. MORGAN was fighting in Kentucky. The telegraph wires were in disorder.

July 5. Another fight in Kentucky; we could plainly hear the roar of the cannons. No trains to-day. A heavy rain set in towards night.

July 6. Another hard rain. A train was taken by guerrlllas between here and the border of Kentucky. The guard of the train was paroled, mail and other valuables taken, passengers, etc., taken off the train and the train set in motion again.

July 7. More rain. The track had been destroyed somewhere, as the trains did not run. We got new uniforms to-day.

July 8. Received the news that Vicksburg had surrendered on the Fourth. A negro regiment was organized here and many of our men applied for officers' posts in the same. No train to-day—more rain.

July 9. Received the news that MORGAN had gone to Indiana with his gang, and that preparations were made there to capture him. A train was expected.

July 10. Beautiful and very warm weather.

July 11. One hundred and twenty men infantry and some cavalry were ordered to be ready for a scout, under command of Lieut. Col. CROPSEY and Maj. FLYNN. According to the testimony of some loyal citizens there were about two hundred rebels near a place called Cottontown, situated near Gallatin, which robbed and plundered and threatened the Union men. At half past 11 o'clock the expedition was ready, and started. We soon reached the Red River Pike, leading to the place named, our cavalry taking the lead, and about the dawn of day we arrived at Cottontown, where we halted. The infantry was brought in position, while the cavalry, led by a trusty guide, approached the camping ground of the rebels. A citizen of the town, however, had acted the spy and reported to the rebels the fact of our arrival and our strength, whereupon the rebs fled. The spy did not escape, was taken prisoner and his property burnt.

July 12. As we had missed the object of our yesterday's expedition in consequence of treason, it was resolved to search the neighborhood further and more thoroughly. We started again, but the country, a continuous changing of high mountains and deep valleys, with roads almost bottomless in consequence of the heavy rain, presented such obstacles that we could advance only with great trouble and very slowly. We were about twenty-five miles from camp, in a country, offering every facility to guerrilla warfare, and frequently we saw the traces of these gangs of rebels. Our men were divided now, all by-roads and houses searched, and frequently men captured, who were afraid of Yankees, but in their hearts good Union men. The more we advanced, the more impassable the country became, and as our small stock of provisions was giving out we were compelled to return to camp, which we reached about dusk, after having been thoroughly drenched by a heavy shower of rain.

July 13. Col. HENRY CASE received the first authentic news about the whereabouts of Lieut. HALDEMAN in a letter from his mother. She stated that he was in Richmond, Va., in prison, and that he had been wounded when captured, because he refused to surrender, when demanded to do so.

July 14. The pay rolls were signed and some time afterwards we received two months' pay. It rained heavily the whole day.

July 18. Several Union families were admitted in our lines, because their lives had been threatened by guerrillas. This afternoon a dress parade took place.

July 19. Several of our men were punished very severely to-day, by deductions being made from their pay, and the men themselves put under arrest for months.

July 23. Inspection of our arms, uniforms, tents and kitchens took place to-day.

July 24. We received new tents to-day and the camp was moved to a higher piece of ground.

July 25. The day was rainy and the men busy in making the camp commodious.

July 26. Part of our cavalry, that was always on a scout, came across a gang of rebels that as usually fled on the approach of the Union troops. Several rebels were wounded by our boys.

July 27. The work on the camp continued, although there was a good deal of talk about marching orders, and many stopped working in consequence.

July 28. Drill in the forenoon and afternoon.

July 31. One of the Union men, admitted into camp a few days ago, asked for an escort to his farm, where he had some harvesting to do. His wish was granted, and, although the party had to suffer much from the enemy, they returned to camp in safety.

August 1. The day was very hot, and during inspection and review many men left their places, others drilled until they fell down. Generally speaking the drill was satisfactory.

August 2. The train that left Gallatin at 9 o'clock P. M., was attacked by guerrillas between this place and Bowling Green, Ky. As the train was not off the track and the conductor supposed the track to be torn up, the train returned to Gallatin. The behavior of every soldier in camp and on duty was put down in writing every day, and the whole report read at the end of every week on dress parade in front of the whole regiment. A scout of 150 men infantry was sent out to-day.

August 3. The scout sent out yesterday, returned. They had killed one guerrilla and taken several others prisoners.

August 4. The day was very hot.

August 5. Thunder storm and rain, the lightning felled one man of company A in camp to the ground, without injuring him otherwise much.

August 8. Inspection of arms to-day.

August 9. Many of our boys went off on a furlough; inspection of arms and dress took place again.

August 10. A number of horses were taken to Nashville by our cavalry.

August 11. A rebel deserter came in our lines; the day was made interesting by thunder storms and rain.

August 12. Company D received a new recruit.

August 13. To-day a year ago we left Pontiac, Ill., for the three years' service. In the afternoon drill.

August 14. Drill.

August 15. Inspection.

August 16. Tremendous heat and rain.

August 17. The second Lieutenant of our company, BURCH, received his commission as Captain. In the afternoon dress parade.

August 18. One hundred men infantry were sent off again on a scout.

August 19. Inspection; the scout returned with several rebel prisoners.

August 20. We received marching orders.

August 21. We packed up and at 4 o'clock P. M., turned our backs upon Gallatin. Five miles west of the city, on the Nashville Pike, we halted and camped for the night.

August 22. Left camp at 5 o'clock A. M., and as the sun was very hot we did not continue our march longer than 9 o'clock, when we rested near a creek. At 5 o'clock we resumed our march and camped 5 miles from Nashville for the night.

August 23. We struck our tents at 4½ o'clock and reached the Cumberland River at 8 o'clock; we rested some time before we crossed. At 12 o'clock we were on the ground assigned us for camping, between Fort Negley and the Murfreesboro Pike, near the eastern part of the city.

August 24. The ground assigned us for camp, was so covered with stones, wood, etc., that but a small part of the regiment had been able to erect tents the evening before, and it required the hardest work of every man to get everything fixed and right.

August 25. Worked on our tents again. One man of the regiment was tied to a tree for bad behavior; he broke loose, however, and escaped, but was afterwards recaptured and tied again. We delivered up our old Springfield muskets and received Enfield rifles in their stead. Got another new recruit in company D.

August 29. Had brigade drill for the first time under command of Gen. WARD.

August 30. Inspection of arms and dress.

August 31. Gen. WARD's brigade had parade

before Gen. R. S. GRANGER; the bi-monthly muster took place.

September 1. Brigade drill in the forenoon and company drill in the afternoon.

Sept. 2. Part of the 129th went as escort on the trains to Stevenson, Ala.; brigade drill in the afternoon.

Sept. 3. Another escort went with the trains to Stevenson, 113 miles from here.

Sept. 5. Company drill and dress parade.

Sept. 6. Another escort went to Stevenson, Ala.

Sept. 7. On our return from Stevenson, when near Nashville, one of our men jumped out the car, while the car was in motion and crossing a bridge, which the man could not see in consequence of the darkness. The poor fellow was badly hurt and carried to camp.

Sept. 10. On the 9th we went to Stevenson again. On our return on the 10th, the locomotive of our train ran off the track near Andersonville station in the Cumberland Mountains, and as the engine could not be brought on the track again, we had to remain over night on a switch close by.

Sept. 11. About twenty miles from the place where the locomotive had run off the track, another like mishap befell us, and all endeavors to bring the locomotive on the track again were fruitless. As our cars were on a switch, other trains were not stopped by our disaster. Afterwards we took another train, as we were beginning to feel hungry, and the country being hardly able to feed the bushwhackers, much less us half-starved Yankees.

Sept. 13. Our orderly sergeant, WILLIAM LEMON, died to-day in the hospital with the flux. The whole regiment mourned the loss of this much-liked, brave soldier, but all mourning could not recall him to life. A few hours after his death he was buried with the usual military honors, the customary salutes fired over the body of the brave man now resting in the cool sod, and slowly and mournfully the regiment returned to camp.

Sept. 14. Inspection of arms, equipments, etc., was announced, and everything prepared for it.

Sept. 15. In consequence of the rain no inspection was held.

Sept. 16. Rain and heavy storms.

Sept 17. The inspection announced for the 14th, took place to-day.

Sept. 19. The paymaster arrived here, and we received pay for two months.

Sept. 20. A detail of our men were ordered to guard the negroes working for the Government near the city on the Cumberland river.

Sept 21. The unpaid part of the regiment was paid off to-day. The guard sent out yesterday, returned.

Sept 22. Company and battallion drill.

Sept 23. Inspection took place again; fire-wood was received; in the afternoon battallion drill.

Sept 24. Four hundred wounded from ROSE-CRAN's army were brought to Nashville.

Sept 25. Many Eastern regiments passed through here for ROSECRAN's army; in the afternoon brigade drill.

Sept 26. In the fore and afternoon company drill.

Sept. 27. Had company drill twice.

Sept. 28. Brigade drill in the afternoon.

Sept. 29. Part of ZOLLIKOFFER's large building in the city, which served as a prison for rebel soldiers, caved in, over two hundred prisoners were crippled and six killed.

Sept. 30. A rainy day; inspection was announced, but did not take place.

October 2. Inspection took place to-day, and in the afternoon brigade drill. Sergeant HOWARD of company H died in the hospital.

Oct. 3. Company drill in the forenoon and dress parade in the afternoon.

Oct. 4. Inspection and dress parade.

Oct. 5. The regiment received marching orders. The rebels burned a bridge near Murfreesboro, Tenn. All the camps had been alarmed, and all regiments near Nashville, had hereafter to be in line of battle from 3 o'clock A. M. to daybreak.

Oct 7. To-night at 10 o'clock the camp was alarmed again. The order came to our regiment to draw rations for two days and be ready for marching. The order was promptly obeyed, everything packed up, and shortly after we marched to the Chattanooga depot, where a train was awaiting us to take us to Franklin, Tenn., which place was threatened by the enemy and contained but a small Union garrison.

Oct 9. A sergeant of the regiment, on guard at the time of the departure to Franklin, got into a difficulty while in company this evening, and was wounded slightly on the hand by a pistol ball.

Oct. 10. The regiment returned from Franklin, without the loss of a man; the enemy had kept away from the place.

Oct. 12. The day was very cold. One hundred rebels came to Nashville with horses, accoutrements and arms, and surrendered.

Oct. 13. An escort was sent again with a train to Stevenson, Ala.; JAMES HILL, a member of company D, died in the hospital, and was buried with military honors.

Oct. 15. Inspection of the regiment took place.

Oct. 16. A rainy day.

Oct. 19. Company and battallion drill in the forenoon, and brigade drill in the afternoon.

Oct 20. Spent the day with drilling, as yesterday.

Oct. 21. Companies A and D had to do picket duty. Gen. GRANT came through Nashville to take command of Gen. ROSECRANS' army; Gen. ROSECRANS was called to Washington.

Oct. 22. Company and battallion drill in the forenoon, and brigade drill in the afternoon.

Oct. 23. A cold and rainy day, in consequnence of which no drill took place.

Oct. 25. Received the news that the escort of the train, sent off a few days ago, had been taken prisoners and the train burned. The report was not believed. In the evening inspection of the regiment took place. Another party was detailed as train guard, but as no trains were running, the men returned to camp.

Oct. 26. A member of company H was buried with military honors. The detail again went to the depot, but returned again, as no trains were running.

Oct. 28. Battallion drill in the forenoon and brigade drill in the afternoon.

Oct. 29. Battallion drill in the afternoon.

Oct 30. Company D was detailed as train guard, and left camp at 6 o'clock P. M., had to remain at the depot the whole night, and did not leave Nashville until the next morning.

November 1. Nothing particularly unpleasant happened on our trip to Stevenson, excepting that we had to wait several times rather long for trains bound North. We did not reach Stevenson until 10 o'clock at night.

Nov 2. Company D had to remain in Stevenson, because the next train would not leave before tomorrow.

Nov 3. At five o'clock A. M., the train with company D and a number of disabled horses left Stevenson; between Smyrna station and Nashville two cars with horses were thrown off the track and several horses slightly hurt. Reached Nashville at 8 o'clock.

Nov. 4. In the afternoon company drill.

Nov. 5. Rainy and cold weather; no drill took place.

Nov. 7. A foraging party was sent 18 miles from the city after hay.

Nov. 8. Inspection and dress parade.

Nov. 9. Cold weather; brigade drill in the afternoon.

Nov. 10. Battallion drill in the forenoon and dress parade towards evening. Company D was again detailed as train guard.

Nov. 11. The report was current that we would be paid off to-day.

Nov. 12. Company D returned from Stevenson.

Nov. 13. Company drill in the forenoon; brigade drill and practice in firing in the afternoon.

Nov. 14. Were paid off for two months.

Nov 16. Between the hours of 3 and 4 o'clock, a fire broke out in the city; but one building burned down.

Nov. 17. General inspection and dress parade. A corporal of company C was stabbed by an Irish storekeeper, and died afterwards in the hospital; the Irishman escaped.

Nov. 18. Battallion drill in the afternoon.

Nov. 19. A number of men were arrested for firing their guns in the camp which had been prohibited; they were, however, not severely punished. In the afternoon the following regiments had brigade parade before Gen's. WARD and GRANGER; the 129th, 105th, 102d Illinois, 79th Ohio, 13th Wisconsin and 70th Indiana; also, a regiment of cavalry. The parade was the finest we ever had, and both Generals were well satisfied. The day was sultry and dark.

Nov. 20. A foraging party was sent out again, but as a heavy rain set in, the party was compelled to return to camp, without having accomplished their object.

Nov. 21. A large part of the regiment went as train guards to Stevenson and Chattanooga.

Nov 23. The men returned from Stevenson; a good many of the boys got furlough.

Nov. 24. The boys went off on a furlough.

Nov. 25. Kitchens were erected by the regiment, brigade drill the afternoon. There was an alarm of fire in the city.

Nov. 26. In the evening dress parade.
Nov. 27. In the afternoon brigade drill.
Nov. 28. It was cold and rainy, and no drill took place.
Nov. 29. A large part of the regiment was again detailed as train guard for to-morrow's trains. Dress parade in the evening.
Nov. 30. The train gaards left the camp at 3 o'clock A. M., but did not reach Stevenson until December 1.
December 2. One hundred and eighty rebel officers were escorted by the train guard from Stevenson to Nashville; among them was a son of the rebel Gen. BRECKINRIDGE.
Dec. 3. Drill in the forenoon and afternoon; no passes to the city were issued, on account of the small-pox raging there.
Dec. 4. Battallion drill in the afternoon.
Dec. 5. Dress parade in the afternoon.
Dec. 7. All regiments of infantry, some cavalry and artillery were reviewed by Gen's. ROSSEAU, WARD, GRANGER and PAINE. The day was cool and suited for the occasion.
Dec. 9. The small-pox broke out in the regiment. There was talk about marching orders to Gallatin. General inspection was announced.
Dec. 10. The regiment was inspected and passed review before Gen. HUNTER.
Dec. 14. In honor of the victories won by the armies of the Cumberland, large bonfires were kindled; Generals HUNTER, GRANGER and WARD were present.
Dec 15. Firewood was received by the regiment. A member of company B shot at the captain of his company this evening, but missed him; he was put under guard.
Dec 16. The day was rainy and cold. A number of men were sent out to catch negroes, who were to unload the steamboats.

Dec 17. A strong detail was sent out to guard a number of wagons dispatched after some timber for a new powder magazine.

Dec. 18. Brigade drill in the afternoon; the day was very cold.

Dec. 19. Dress parade towards evening. A member of company D who had imbibed too much, was robbed of his watch when returning to camp.

Dec. 20. Company inspection in the forenoon, and in the evening dress parade.

Dec 21. It was the general talk that we were ordered back to Gallatin. Brigade drill in the afternoon. The provost guard shot a soldier through the head, who refused to stop when ordered to do so.

Dec 23. Brigade drill in the afternoon.

Dec. 24. Christmas eve shots were fired in every direction.

Dec. 25. A beautiful day. The officers of the regiment took their men to a neighboring brewery, and treated them to several barrels of beer.

Dec. 26. A rainy day; except guard duty we had nothing to do.

Dec. 27. It rained day and night.

Dec. 28. Company and regiment inspection.

Dec. 29. We drilled twice to-day. During the night heavy rain.

Dec. 30. Brigade drill in the afternoon.

Dec. 31. Muster for pay; rain and snow fell.

January 1, 1864. New Year's day; very cold and frosty; snow fell more abundantly.

Jan. 2. It snowed the whole day and turned very cold, so that those out with passes returned.

Jan 4. The report came that our Doctor Johns who went along with a boat guard several hundred miles up the Cumberland river, had been shot by guerrillas. The guard returned and reported that the Doctor had been shot through his coat tail; otherwise "nobody hurt" nor killed.

Jan. 6. Very cold weather.

Jan. 9. Company K was called to the city on duty. Col. HARRISON, of the 70th Indiana regiment, took command of our brigade provisionally, our former commander, Gen. WARD, having assumed command of the first division of the eleventh army corps.

Jan 10. Company inspection; the day was very cold.

Jan. 11. As the inspecting officer was not satisfied yesterday, another inspection took place to-day.

Jan 13. It commenced thawing. Several citizens from Scott county, Ill., in order (perhaps) to escape the draft at home, came to Nashville to offer their services to the Government.

Jan. 15. It was reported that certain parties tried to persuade the whole brigade to re-enlist, in case the Government would permit.

Jan. 16. Inspection of the regiment in the afternoon.

Jan 17. A heavy rain night and day.

Jan. 18. Snow, rain and frost.

Jan. 21. Gen. ROSSEAU received orders to hold all troops in Nashville ready for marching at any moment.

Jan 22. A warm and clear day.

Jan. 23. Inspection of the regiment in the afternoon.

Jan 24. A beautiful and pleasant day. Dress parade in the evening.

Jan. 25. Got the news that the guerrilla chief JOHN MORGAN had escaped from prison; everybody was angry about the prison-keeper of MORGAN's place of confinement.

Jan. 26. The day was hot; drilled in the afternoon.

Jan. 27. Company drill in the forenoon; received marching orders.

Jan. 28. All necessaries were packed up, and all unnecessaries boxed up to be left here.

Jan. 29. Had brigade drill; the time fixed for

our departure was Sunday morning at 6 o'clock.

Jan. 30. A rainy day; we got shelter tents.

Jan. 31. Delivered up our old tents; had general inspection in the afternoon.

February 1. Guards were again sent out as usual, and the talk was that we would remain until further orders.

Feb. 2. A number of men went off on a furlough; the order came that we would remain but three days longer. In the night all pickets were drawn in, and yet the report was that we would not move.

Feb. 3. The tents were again erected and the camp made as commodious as possible.

Feb. 4. Firewood was received, and many of the men commenced erecting houses, and worked generally as though we would spend the balance of our time of enlistment in Nashville.

Feb. 5. The pay rolls were signed as we were to be paid off the next day.

Feb. 6. The weather was very cold to-day; to-morrow was fixed for pay day.

Feb. 7. Received two months pay.

Feb. 9. Inspection was afterwards countermanded; had brigade drill instead.

Feb. 10. Battallion drill in the afternoon.

Feb. 11. Company drill in the forenoon and afternoon.

Feb. 12. Brigade drill in the afternoon; the weather was cool; many soldiers got permission to go to the theater to-night.

Feb. 13. General inspection in the afternoon.

Feb. 14. Our regiment had to guard the new powder magazine. A sergeant of the 105th Ill. regt. was murdered to-day near our camp; his scull had been split and the body thrown across the track where it was found the next morning.

Feb. 15. Furloughs were granted again.

Feb. 16. Our regiment had many sick members

who were brought to the hospitals; the weather was cold; brigade drill in the afternoon.

Feb. 17. Battallion drill in the afternoon.

Feb. 18. Intensely cold weather to-day.

Feb. 19. Half the regiment was on duty; as laborers were wanting the soldiers had to help; the other half of the regiment was free from duty.

Feb. 20. The other half of the regiment had to assist in unloading the boats.

Feb. 21. A number of men, anxious to make a little, went to the landing to assist in unloading the boats. The day was beautiful. In the evening dress parade. At 12 o'clock at night the regiment again received marching orders.

Feb. 22. Our things were unpacked for the second time, and things drawn when the last marching orders came, were offered to the citizens for sale for almost nothing. We were not allowed to take them along, and could not send them home. We were permitted to have in our knapsacks 1 shirt, 1 pair of drawers, 1 pair of socks, a woollen blanket and an oil cloth.

Feb. 23. The time for our departure had been fixed at to-morrow morning 5 o'clock and to-day was the last day that we were here. No one had any idea that the whole company, regiment or brigade would ever return. The men, therefore, amused themselves highly, because they know that with them garrison duty had an end now, and that hereafter fighting had to be done,—and also because no one knew whether he would return alive or as a cripple, that had to live off the small starving penny, called pension, the balance of his days.

Feb. 24. We were awakened at 5 o'clock, and everything packed up, while our cooks were preparing the breakfast of coffee, crackers and meat for the last time in our kitchens. After breakfast we "fell into line" immediately, and at 8 o'clock the whole brigade, consisting of the 79th Ohio, 70th Indiana,

102d, 129th and 105th Illinois regiments, was assembled on the Murfreesboro Pike. Many of the citizens, with whom we had become intimately acquainted during our six months' stay in Nashville, accompanied us to the suburbs of the city, until the command "forward" was given, and the band of the 79th Ohio played a beautiful march, we turned our backs to Nashville, the friends we had won there, and our own sick in the hospitals. The day was pleasant for marching, but soon in the afternoon the brigade camped near Lavergne, a station on the Nashville and Chattanooga rail road, about 10 miles from the former place. The camp was in the field of a rebel, and in order to have a good remembrance we burned a considerable number of fence rails in the camp fires, which kept us warm.

Feb. 25. We left camp at 6 o'clock and reached Lavergne at 8. The weather was very hot, the road dusty, and in consequence of this we camped at 12 o'clock M. already.

Feb. 26. Broke camp before sunrise and reached the battlefield of Murfreesboro about 10 o'clock. Here we rested and visited the graves of the brave Union defenders, quietly sleeping beneath the sod. Here and there bones were bleaching in the sun. The trees near the battlefield were nearly all withered, others shot down or at least robbed of their crowns and branches by bullets and balls. Shells, canister shot and rifle balls were scattered about, in pieces or entire, in every direction. We were yet looking on these to us unwonted things, when the bugle called us to return. We had several miles to march to the city, and at 12 o'clock we were treading the streets of Murfreesboro, delighted by the music of the 79th Ohio. We camped on the south side of the place, near the Shelbyville road.

Feb. 27. We left Murfreesboro early in the morning. The march was more fatiguing than the day before. Had to cross several creeks without bridges, which caused much loss of time. The road was either covered with several inches of dust, or led through a rocky, hilly country, and as we had rations for several days, sixty cartridges and a full knapsack to carry, many a drop of sweat was squeezed out of us. We marched 13 miles and camped in a fenced field of a rebel; the fence rails of which were of course confiscated and used.

Feb. 28. We commenced our march early, and reached Shelbyville at 12 o'clock M. After passing through the city we crossed to the south side of Dog river, and stopped near by half an hour, for dinner. The afternoon was rainy, and we continued three miles, when we camped, after a march of 15 miles.

Feb. 29. As usual we left our camp early. It had rained during the whole night before and rained to-day, the weather was disagreeably cold, nevertheless we marched to Tullahoma, 15 miles distant. Some of our baggage wagons reached camp to-day, while others, after sticking in the mud every now and then, did not reach us until morning. Our camping ground became a regular sea during the night, and only those who were fortunate enough to be encamped upon high ground found rest; the others could choose between a drenching in the shelter tents, or have the rain outside from the first hand, and freeze too.

March 1, 1864. The rain continued, the roads had become bottomless, and in consequence we were unable to advance.

March 2. The sky had cleared off, and although the roads had by no means improved, we broke camp and left Tullahoma. The sappers had to place wood and fence rails for miles on the road, in order to get the wagons along. Early in the afternoon we reached Elk river, which we crossed, and camped after a march of 10 miles.

March 3. The weather was beautiful, the roads

had dried off remarkably and the marching went in a fine style. At noon we reached Orchard station and soon after Cowan station, when we camped at the foot of the Cumberland mountains, after a march of 10 miles.

March 4. Soon we were up, climbing the mountains. Our regiment was detailed to-day to guard the train of wagons against an attack of guerrillas and to help them along through the mountains,— three or four men to each wagon. We got along slowly during the day, and as the last wagons were several miles behind the brigade, (which had marched on,) the situation became critical. The darkness was impenetrable, many wagons ran against trees, stumps and rocks, and had to remain in that position until daylight; the others were drawn together on an open place, where they remained.

March 5. We were under way soon, and as the roads were in better condition, we soon reached the brigade camp, but the brigade had gone on. We went into camp early, after having made a march of 12 miles in the last two days.

March 6. We reached Andrew station, and camped 2 miles north of Stevenson, Ala.

March 7. Passed through Stevenson, and stopped, after a march of 12 miles, at Bridgport, Tenn.

March 8. Remained in camp and spent the day washing our clothes.

March 9. Left Bridgport, crossed the Tennessee river twice on pontoons, and had dinner at Bellefont station, where we visited a large cave. We went further until we reached a valley, entirely surrounded by high mountains, where we camped during the following, very rainy night.

March 10. We had to wait for the wagons that lagged behind, and did not resume our march until 9 o'clock The country was mountainous. At noon we reached Whiteside station and about sunset the Lookout Valley, after passing through immense hollows and passes. This last day and the bad roads had cost us many mules. During the night it rained heavily, accompanied by thunder and lightning:

March 11. A camping ground was found at last for the brigade. The weather was fine.

March 12 Inspection was ordered, but did not take place. We chopped wood for houses and preparations made to draw clothes.

March 13 Inspection of the company took place. Major General HOOKER was introduced to-day. It was currently reported that the 11th army corps would be ordered to Virginia.

March 14. The regiment was on picket, for the first time, since our arrival, and for 48 hours at that.

March 16 We were relieved from picket duty by a detachment of Zuaves; the day was windy and cold.

March 17. More cold weather. Many drummers and fifers, not having been mustered in as such, were sent to their respective companies on duty. Received the news that JAMES MONDAY, of company H, who had become sick at Stevenson, had died there. A train with $15,000 and the mail, was attacked, robbed and burned near Tullahoma by guerrillas.

March 18. A grand parade took place; the whole brigade was inspected by its commander, Gen. HARRISON We got new clothes.

March 19 The parade announced took place to-day. At 8 o'clock the brigade assembled and marched to the parade ground two miles distant, where the regiments were posted according to their number, and had to await the arrival of the commanding General. At the appointed hour some cannon shots announced the arrival of Major Generals HOOKER and HOWARD, who, after having passed along the front and rear of the column, took their places, and the column moved forward, delighted by the excellent music of the 33d Massachusetts regiment. The parade went off fine, and both Generals seemed well pleased with the manoeuvers of the brigade. The day was very cold. A member of the 79th Ohio fell from the top of the Lookout, 100 feet, and was killed.

March 20. Company inspection and muster for pay took place; in the evening, dress parade.

March 21. It was very cold; fire-places were built by the whole regiment. Major FLYNN was appointed lieutenant colonel.

March 22. We remained in our bunks under the blanket nearly the whole day, in order to keep warm.

March 23. The day was milder, and in order not to be compelled to remain a-bed again during the day, the fire-places were completed.

March 24. The whole camp was cleaned; a heavy snow fell in the night.

March 25. It rained the whole day.

March 26. A brigade hospital was erected.

March 27. In consequence of the continuous change of weather, there were many men on the sick report.

March 28. Company and battallion drill; in the afternoon heavy rain.

March 29. We got the first bread from our newly erected brigade bakery; trees were dug out in camp.

March 30. Company and battallion drill in the forenoon; brigade drill in the afternoon. The weather was fine, and the camp was decorated by planting budding trees therein.

March 31. Company and battallion drill in the forenoon, and brigade drill in the afternoon; inspection was announced for to-morrow.

April 1. Inspection of the regiment in the afternoon; the day was rainy.

April 2. A rainy day; a number of men went fishing; company drill in the afternoon.

April 3. Inspection and dress parade; the day was fine, but in the night, thunderstorm and rain.

April 4. As it rained the whole day, no other than guard duty was performed.

April 5. The camp was cleaned and inspected by our brigade commander, HARRISON, in the afternoon.

April 6. Company and battallion drill in the forenoon and brigade drill in the afternoon. Some more decorations were added to the camp of company D, but not so generally as would have been the case, if the report had not been current that we had marching orders again.

April 8. Gen. HOOKER was expected in camp, but the rain in the latter part of the day prevented his coming.

April 9. A beautiful day; no duty to do.

April 10. Inspection of the regiment took place in the forenoon and dress parade toward evening; the day was rainy.

April 11. A great many troops went to the front, and the report of an advance on our part, was current again.

April 12. Rain the whole day.

April 13. The day was beautiful. Gen. HOOKER arrived, and a parade before Gen. THOMAS was announced.

April 14. The parade announced yesterday took place to-day. At 8 o'clock the brigade marched to the parade ground, and soon after Gen. THOMAS appeared. Gens. HOOKER, WARD, BUTTERFIELD, &c. were present. The parade was one of the finest we had ever witnessed.

April 15. Gen. BUTTERFIELD was expected in the camp, but did not come; in the morning we had company and battallion drill, in the afternoon brigade drill.

April 16. Inspection was announced for to-morrow; company drill in the afternoon. Large portals were erected at the entrance of every company's street, and our camp was one of the finest now of all the camps around, and presented a handsome and pleasing appearance.

April 17. Inspection of the regiment in the afternoon. As it was Sunday, there being no duty to do, many of the men went to the the top of Lookout and to Sommerville, near there, whence Chattanooga and the whole surrounding country with its camps and soldiers could be seen distinctly. In the evening dress parade. Gen. WARD again assumed command of the brigade, and his provisional successor, Col. HARRISON, again assumed command of his, the 70th Indiana regiment. Gen. BUTTERFIELD assumed command of the division. The 4th and 12th army corps were consolidated and called the 20th. Our division, formerly the first in the 11th army corps, became the 3d in the 20th. Many of our men were sent fishing every day, and the fish divided among the regiment.

April 18. More decorations were fixed through the camp. Brigade drill took place in the afternoon in the presence of Gen. THOMAS and other strange officers. Gen. THOMAS inspected our camp after the drill. The day was rainy and cool.

April 19. Company and battallion drill in the forenoon; brigade drill in the afternoon.

April 20. Company and battallion drill again in the forenoon; inspection was announced for the afternoon, but did not take place, but brigade drill took place in its stead. We received the news of the surrender of fort Pillow, and the barbarous treatment of the union soldiers after the surrender on the part of the rebels under FOREST.

April 21. The parade ground was made more level and cleared of the shrubs and rocks. The men not at work had to drill in the afternoon. General BUTTERFIELD drilled his division for the first time to-day. Below Chattanooga, in the neighborhood of Ringgold, our pickets met the enemy, and a considerable skirmish took place. Everything quiet in the front. The enemy, under Gen. JOHNSON, lay behind his entrenchments near Dalton and Buzzard Roost. A bloody spring campaign was expected, and from all signs and orders we could begin to believe that the "dance of war" would soon begin. The trooqs, now under the command of Gens. SHERMAN and THOMAS, were "full of fight" and in the best condition.

April 22. Company drill and skirmish drill by signals; brigade drill in the afternoon. The band of music of the 33d Massachusetts, which regiment belonged to the 3d brigade of our division, serenaded our brigade commander and all the regiments to-night. The evening was spent joyfully and merrily. It was reported for certain that we would have to leave our beautiful camp in a few days, the erection of which had cost us so much labor, and to commence the campaign against the enemy. As yet we had no marching orders, and all these reports were to be believed but half.

April 23. We had no marching orders yet, nevertheless the report of our advance became more positive.

April 24. Inspection of company and dress parade in the afternoon; the weather was rainy.

April 25. Company and battallion drill in the forenoon and brigade drill in the afternoon.

April 26. Brigade drill in the afternoon; weather warm.

April 27. Company drill in the forenoon and battallion drill in the afternoon.

April 28. Division drill and practice in firing in the afternoon. Two members of company I, of our regiment deserted to-night, after having borrowed revolvers and watches from several men. Preparations to capture them were made, but not a word was heard of the successful accomplishment of this object.

April 29. The weather was excessively warm;

brigade drill in the presence of Gen BUTTERFIELD; a heavy rain fell during the night.

April 30. Inspection and muster for pay in the forenoon; the weather was very hot.

May 1. This morning at last we received the long expected marching orders, to be ready for the tramp to-morrow morning early. Rations for three days were drawn, and all things more than the prescribed baggage, which had been taken along from Nashville, were put in chests and left. The officers had to leave their writing desks, paper, ink &c. Hereafter we were to be loaded down by provisions, cooking utensils, ammunition, etc. The last dress parade took place towards evening, in Lookout valley, by the 1st brigade of the 3d division of the 20th army corps. In order to be ready early in the morning, we slept early and soundly—for the last time at the foot of the grand Lookout, whose peak towers high toward heaven.

May 2. We were awakened at 4 o'clock by the roll of the drums. After roll call a hasty breakfast was prepared and taken and the haversacks filled with bread, meat etc. for three days. The hour for the march was set at 7 o'clock; this hour approaching the dog or shelter tents used as roofs on our houses, were taken down, rolled up and buckled to our knapsacks. The bunks were searched once more to see if everything had been taken out that the rebels in the neighborhood might make use of. It was seven, the drummers gave the signal to fall in to line and soon we were on the march to the drill ground, where the brigade was to rendezvous, and every regiment took its place in the line. With unpleasant feelings of regret we left our comfortable and commodious camp, where we had spent so many happy hours. The 1st and 2d division of our corps had left camp before we did, and as both were far enough ahead of us, no impediments were in our way to Chattanooga. Passing to the right of the city, we moved over Missionary Ridge to the Chickamauga battle-field. The battlefield looked very much like that of Murfreesboro, except that there was more wood here which had been riddled by thousands of bullets and was either withering or had withered already. We marched over the battlefield without halting. A little while before sunset we reached Chickamauga creek, and camped near Gordon's mill, after having marched 15 miles. We received a big mail to-night.

May 3. According to orders we remained quiet to-day in order to give the regiments that had been here before us time to pack up and move on. We drilled in the afternoon. The day was very hot. Another mail came.

May 4. Early in the morning we struck our tents and marched on to the front. The march became more unsafe, as the enemy's cavalry, knowing that the Yankee army was in motion, displayed much agility and harassed us wherever it could be done. In order not to be surprised by the enemy or lose men unnecessarily, several regiments of one brigade had to throw out flankers; but no enemy appeared where the 20th army corps was marching. At 3 o'clock in the afternoon we reached the 14th army corps, or at least a part of it, near Ringgold, Ga. Here we camped in the woods, after a march of 12 miles, near the front. The pickets were instructed to be very cautious, as a nightly attack was at least possible, if not certain. The night passed quietly.

May 5. We remained in camp and in consequence of this lying idle, the fighting spirit of the men gave way to still and silent thoughts about the impenetrable future, or about the strength of the enemy in our front, estimated at 80,000 men. Letters were written to our friends and relatives at home to let them know that we were well. Although all knew that many a one would have to lose his life, or be wounded on the battlefield, or peraps be crippled for life, yet a stern resolution was fixed in all hearts of those brave men to fight and perhaps die for the country. Such a spirit can only arise from a pure and holy love of the cause of our glorious Union! Our officers were equally brave and to be trusted, and we were certain of the final victory. We drew rations to-day for three days, and the regiment had dress parade. Several of our scouts were taken prisoner to-day.

May 6. We commenced our march early on the road from Ringgold to Dalton Southward. As nothing impeded our progress, we advanced rapidly and went into camp early in the afternoon. Our regiment was ordered on picket duty, the principal part posted on the brow of a high mountain, the balance in the valley below. From the mountain we could see tents at a considerable distance, but it was impossible to say whether they belonged to the Union or the rebel army. The night passed quietly. We were near the celebrated Nicka Jack Gap.

May 7. Before daybreak our pickets were called in and after remaining on the Dalton road preparing and eating breakfast, until the balance of the brigade came up, we marched in the advance forward. Our march to-day was not a pleasant one, over, narrow, dusty, or rocky roads, although the enemy did not harass us. The weather was intolerably hot, and the necessary fresh water was wanting. When we rested in the afternoon for a couple of hours in a field, we quenched our thirst in a milky, dirty creek, in which higher up some were bathing, others washing their feet. But all these minor considerations were nothing, we could at least quench our thirst and rest a couple of hours. We left our dusty resting place and went into camp after sunset, after having marched 20 miles. At Buzzard Roost we heard some fighting; Gen's. HOOKER. SICKLES and BUTTERFIELD were with the brigade the principal part of the day. Gen. KILLPATRICK with his cavalry was continually in our front or at our flanks. Everything went off quiet.

May 8. We lay quiet to-day, but had orders to be ready at any moment to advance. A horse, saddle and bridle which the adjutant of the regiment had brought from Louisville, Ky., yesterday, was presented to Col. CASE. The present was made to Col. CASE by the whole regiment. The Colonel was deeply touched by the love of his men, and thanked them sincerely. Later in the day we were ordered to be ready for marching, but to leave all baggage behind under the care of some guards.

May 9. The 2d division of our army corps under Gen. GEARY met the enemy unexpectedly to-day near Buzzard Roost and immediately got in the heavy fire of the enemy's guns. Several attempts were made to dislodge the enemy from his strong entrenchments, but in vain. The division lost about 500 dead and wounded who were brought past our camp in ambulances. We remained quiet, although under marching orders since noon. It was expected that our division would be sent to Buzzard Roost, but we remained during the night. Heavy firing was heard in our front in the afternoon. We drew rations for three days.

May 10. A rainy day; we were still lying in the bush, though under orders again to be ready for an advance at any moment. A glorious time was in camp on the reception of the news that the rebel army had been badly whipped at Richmond after a bloody four days' fight, and that the much longed for peace was near. The news was too glorious and but half believed, as the strong inimical force in our front did not much give room to the thought of the conclusion of an early peace. On the contrary, the enemy in our front seemed more determined than ever. Gen. McPHERSON, with the 11th corps went to the road to Dalton, in order, if possible, to shut up the enemy in Dalton, or to take such positions that the enemy would become an easy prey to our cannons. The report of guns was heard during the whole day; the night brought us a thunder storm and rain.

May 11. We were awakened from our slumber before day-break, and left the main road for small by-roads and paths, sometimes even on paths cut by our pioneers. The march lasted without interruption until evening, when we remained near the Wall Gap over night.

May 12. We remained quiet until noon; the roads which had become in bad condition in consequence of the many wagons passing over them, were repaired during that time, our guns put in the best order, as now there could be no doubt of meeting the enemy. After twelve o'clock we moved forward, but only three miles, where we went into camp at Snake Creek, and remained for the night. Heavy firing the whole day at Dalton and Buzzard Roost.

May 13. Remained on our camping ground until 3 o'clock P. M., when, after drawing a large quantity of ammunition, we advanced. It was generally believed that to-day we would have a first chance at the enemy. After a short and slow march we halted in a forest of beautiful oak trees, while skirmishing was going on in our immediate front; we could, however, see no enemy. The firing became less audible, a sign that the enemy had to retreat before our cavalry, whereupon we advanced again in the immediate rear of our pickets, not in column, but in line of battle, prepared for any attack the enemy might make. Our advancing was slow and cautious through the woods, in search of the enemy; the country changed with hill and valley. We had not long to search for the enemy; on our arrival at the foot of a tolerably high hill some well aimed rifle shots told us of the presence of the enemy, whose determined refusal to retreat brought on a skirmish. Our pickets and the enemy vied with each other in rapid and well aimed firing, but our continual advance and the sure marksmen in our ranks brought the enemy to retreat at last.

The rebel pickets once on the retreat, could not be brought to a stand, as our pickets advanced as the enemy retreated, and were compelled to return to their principal force, and until evening came on and the darkness prevented a continuation of the murderous play. We were nearer to Reseca now than to Dalton, and when we camped at night on a hill on the opposite site of that occupied by the enemy, and were talking over the events of the day and preparing supper, we were not more than ½ mile distant from the enemy's main force. The most part of the night we kept awake, the knapsack packed and the gun on hand; but few hours sleep were allowed us, for at 2 o'clock A. M.,

May 14, we again advanced for new slaughter work. Early in the morning shots were exchanged, but ere this our brigade was up and in line of battle, ready for any attack. The firing of the pickets became more rapid and violent at sunrise, now and then the enemy fired a cannon shot, while ours were brought into position, the positions of the infantry improved and reinforcements came to our aid. For three days we remained quiet in our place, tolerably well protected against the enemy's cannons; we did not lose a single man of our regiment, as the enemy's balls went whizzing over our heads. The 102d Illinois, which was on picket during the day made several attempts to drive the enemy back further; but all attacks were without avail and only caused loss to the regiment. In the evening company D of our regiment, and companies from other regiments, went to relieve the 102d Illinois that had stood the enemy's fire the whole day. When we arrived the firing had ceased, but when we were posted occasional shots would come flying past us, while we watched and listened to the enemy. Gen. HOWARD took Buzzard Roost; Gen. KILLPATRICK was wounded to-day.

May 15. As yesterday, so to-day, shots were fired early, but having taken positions behind trees, we were safe from such shots, and exposed only to the bullets of the rebel sharpshooters posted in trees. No one, however, of our regiment or brigade was killed or wounded while on picket. After some skirmishing of two hours we were relieved by other (strange) troops, and we were told that our brigade had left its position and moved off early in the morning. This seemed strange, as a regiment or brigade never leaves its positions without drawing in the pickets first. As it was so, however, we supposed that the brigade had been ordered away in a hurry to a place where its services were needed. A staff officer had remained to draw in the pickets and guide them to the brigade.. As we had not had anything to eat the evening before, nor early in the morning, and as we were in no particular hurry to find the brigade, which, was no easy matter, we took our time in marching. After many inquiries on the part of the staff officer as to the whereabouts of the division, we at last found it four miles to the right of our former camp in the woods, where Gen. PALMER's men had been stationed heretofore. We went to our respective regiments and took our places. Along the whole line there was fighting going on, and in the distance we heard distinctly the deafening yells of an attacking party, which a few seconds later were drowned by the dreadful roar of cannon and musket fire and exploding shells. Here a picket line advanced towards the enemy in his rifle pits, who continually fired on the advancing line; there ambulances were hurrying off and past with their loads of groaning and crying wounded. Everywhere the awful reality of war and battle stared in our faces; everywhere the fight was raging, except in our own front. But we should not long remain idle, and soon have the pleasure of testing the enemy. The enemy had a fort with three guns in our front and attempts to take it had been unsuccessful, on account of the terrific fire with shot, shell and canister. Another attempt was to be made by our division, our brigade leading, to take the fort; we knew nothing of the object of our being here, until we were in the fire. As said before, the first brigade was commanded by Gen. WARD, and led the attack; the third followed, while the second took position to our right. Each brigade marched by regiments in line of battle, 35 feet apart. Having taken our position we were ordered to unbuckle our knapsacks and leave them on the spot we then occupied, and which were to be guarded by some sick members of each regiment. The bayonets were fixed and the command "forward march" was given, which was promptly obeyed. The way from here to the fort was covered with underbrush and almost impenetrable, and only with the greatest difficulty could one regiment follow the other; the tapes of the haversacks and canteens of many tore, but the men had to leave them and advance—there was no time now for mending such things The fort was situated on a slight elevation, and although we had advanced quite a distance, yet we could see nothing of the fort. The regiments remained in pretty good line, despite the brush, and everything went on well until we came to the border of an open space, where a most murderous fire of the enemy unexpectedly saluted us. This unexpected fire, that had killed several of our men, caused some confusion in our ranks, some companies were completely disorganized, while here and there parts of regiments stood dispirited. The command "lay down" brought all down on the ground. After remaining there several seconds, during which the enemy's fire slackened, the command to arise was given and obeyed, when the enemy again opened on us and causing the loss of many valuable lives. We advanced some distance and again threw ourselves on the ground. Our first line, however, was completely broken and when we arose again after a short while, nothing but the broken ranks of our former line were seen rushing toward the enemy, which they reached, as the distance was but short. Gen's. HOWARD and BUTTERFIELD, who had observed our movements from a neighboring hill, gave the men up for lost, as they had seen no regular line advance, but merely a confused mass of dare-devils. Both Generals erred. The men, maddened by the excitement of the moment, knew no fear; they rushed fighting, shooting, stabbing on the enemy, encouraged by the words of Gen. WARD; "Go in, boys, give them the devil,"—until our beloved and courageous commander, who had placed himself at the head of the brigade, was wounded by a grape shot in the shoulder. The enemy began to stagger—the fort was ours! with the three cannons, all in good order, as the enemy in his fright left them. After the fort had been taken, the enemy was not pursued, and the slaughter began to cease; now and then a rebel sharpshooter would send a bullet to us, but as soon as pickets were posted, this fire also ceased, and the regiments retreated a short distance to gather again. The enemy in our front had been completely whipped, but not without considerable loss on our side. Many a fine fellow who but a few hours ago, in hopeful and joyful spirits, was at our side in the ranks and fought gallantly was stretched, a cold corpse, on mother earth. Others, wounded, unable to go to the hospitals, lay bleeding on the ground, an unspeakable thirst drying their lips, waiting with patience until help could be rendered. And help did come! The roar of the cannons had ceased, we went out to assist the wounded, embraced our unfortunate comrades, and carried or helped them along to the hospital. Now, after the fight had closed, we could get some idea as to the number of bullets and balls fired. The brush was riddled, branches and leaves shot off; here and there a solid shot or a shell had plowed up the ground, and the battlefield was covered with blankets, haversacks, canteens, hats, guns, equipments, etc. The flag of our regiment was riddled by seventy-five bullets, and the ensign, although wounded at the commencement of the fight, nevertheless carried the flag on, not heeding his wound, to the fort, where he proudly and defiantly raised and waved it, when he was shot through the head, and sank down a corpse. As night approached, our wounded were brought to the field hospitals and cared for as well as could be expected, our position was attended to and guarded against a surprise, our knapsacks were gotten and we went to sleep, satisfied with our dearly bought victory. At 12 o'clock P. M. we were awakened by a heavy musket fire, accompanied a few seconds later by the deep bass of our cannon. The enemy tried to retake his fort and guns, but our boys would not assent, and soon the horde of butternuts were sent back in double quick whence they came; not even taking their dead and wounded along. Soon after everything was quiet again, and, satisfied with the victory of Resaca, we laid down awaiting the events of the next day.

May 16 The enemy had been attacked yesterday along his whole line almost, and lost nearly all his entrenchments. While we kept the enemy busy behind his entrenchments, McPHERSON continually advanced in his rear and sought to cut off his retreat. The enemy hearing this, and considering McPHERSON's plan probable, considered prudence the better part of valor and fled in the night. To-day we could find but dead or wounded rebels, a number by no means small; the chivalrous and hale rebels had given leg bail. We were thereby enabled to give our fallen comrades a befitting funeral. The grave of the fallen heroes of our brigade was dug on an elevation, the corpses wrapped in blankets and laid along side of each other to sleep "the sleep that knows no waking." Some green twigs were put over the dead, several chaplain's addressed the listeners, the grave was closed up, and a board, bearing as an inscription the name, number of brigade, regiment and company of the dead, was placed at the head of each corpse. It was late in the afternoon when the burial ceremonies had ended, and the greater part of the army had gone in pursuit of the enemy; but we had to march during the night in order to catch up to them. The brigade had lost, since yesterday morning, 315 men, and did not assemble until sunset, as those not engaged at the burial, had to gather the guns of the dead, or bring the wounded rebels away, and others moved the cannons a distance of several miles to Resaca. After sunset we commenced our march, passed several dead rebels, lying unburied, and marched the whole night without camping.

May 17. We stopped only long enough to prepare and eat a hasty breakfast, when we again went on our march until noon. We stopped 1½ hour to prepare and eat dinner and to wait for our men that had taken the captured cannons to Resaca. At 2 o'clock we continued our march with as great haste as in the morning; many of the men gave out, remained behind, or were taken along in wagons. The rebels must have been very hasty in their retreat, or else our advance guard would have seen something of the rebel rear guard. The inhabitants of the country swore they had never seen Yankees, and particularly not these "horny figures." They either had expected a different result of the battle, or else they had not the means to flee. And although we convinced them that we had no "horns," we although convinced them that we wanted all their things with or without horns that were of any service to the army—in fact that we were carrying out the confiscation act. We did not go into camp until 9 o'clock P. M.

May 18. A beautiful spring morning; early we were on the road again pursuing the retreating enemy, to whom we got nearer and were close at his heels. Our cavalry was continually fighting his rear guard and took many prisoners. The day was tremendously hot, and many of our men had been completely worn out and sank to the ground, we therefore stopped oftener than we would have done if the day had been cooler. The enemy, however, was harassed everywhere by our cavalry and got no rest whatever, until we compelled him towards evening to make a stand. Our men were very tired and the further we marched the less men remained in ranks; we would rather have thrown ourselves behind the first tree to rest for the night. Suddenly and unexpectedly we heard some heavy firing in our front, and with double quick, worn out as we were, albeit, we rushed there. The enemy had stopped his retreat and posted a strong line of pickets against our cavalry, in order that his main force could continue the retreat a couple of miles. On reaching our cavalry, we assumed our positions in front of the enemy, and being late we went into camp; but few shots were fired in the night, during which the enemy again fled.

May 19. We could find the enemy without hunting for him, for after a march of a few miles, when near the place, Cassville, we found him and exchanged shots with him immediately. After our first mutual salutations, not knowing the strength and position of the enemy, we halted and erected a kind of breastworks, behind which we placed ourselves, until the numbers, position, &c., of the enemy could be found out. This done we made a movement to the right, which the enemy found out, however, and made his preparations accordingly, so that our men found the enemy's pickets everywhere. Till now our brigade had not a member on the line of pickets, which consisted of troops strange to us whom we had supported; but as these were relieved now, our brigade was called upon, and the 129th Illinois had to advance. We assembled in an open field, bordered by brush, in which the enemy lay hidden. We advanced expecting a heavy fire, but the enemy had disappeared and retreated to a stronger position further back in the woods, and we had marched some distance before some wild scattered shots told us of the presence of the enemy. The resistance of the enemy was but a timid one, caused perhaps in consequence of commands, certainly though partly in consequence of fear, as the wild, scattered and ill-aimed shooting proved conclusively; and soon the enemy had been driven back three miles. We had been ordered to drive the enemy to his works, and as these were seen, we halted, and cavalry was sent out to draw the fire of the enemy. Scarcely had our cavalry shown itself, when a shower of shot and shell saluted them, but one of our batteries that had been brought in position in the mean time, soon silenced the enemy's guns by well aimed shots. After sundown, still lying in the picket line, the second brigade of our division rushed on our right with terrific yells against the town, Cassville, which was taken after a weak resistance. Great joy spread through the whole division, and the hurrahs must have struck terror in the hearts of the enemy as they again had been whipped in a position chosen by himself and driven him out of it. We camped around the town for the night, during which the enemy retreated again.

May 20. We remained quiet in camp to-day, near Cassville; of the enemy nothing could be seen and in consequence no firing took place. Our yesterday's loss in taking the town was but small, our brigade did not lose a single member. We received a very large mail to-night, and as a mail was to leave again, many letters were written home in the course of the day.

May 21. We remained idle another day, and the report was that we were to remain here three days. Rations were drawn and new clothes sent after. Everything was quiet.

May 22. Had inspection of arms and clothes; the division was lauded by Gen. BUTTERFIELD for the bravery shown on the 19th inst.

—5

May 23. We continued our advance, and left camp at 4 o'clock already in the direction of Kingston, Ga. The day was very hot and many men were sunstruck. We were commanded to put fresh leaves in our hats, to protect head and brains against the burning rays of the sun. Several scouts of the enemy were seen; some distance on our right heavy cannon firing was heard, though we marched on unmolested by the enemy. About sundown we camped on the south side of a river and remained there during the night.

May 24 We broke camp early, and, as yesterday, had to suffer very much from the sun. Our advance met the enemy after a march of ten miles who fired hastily at our men. We were ordered to halt, and camped for the night, during which it rained, while we built entrenchments. Many of our men had suffered so much from the sun and heat that they could not assist at the work, but threw themselves down on the cold ground to sleep and rest, not caring even for any supper. This was the first night we camped in the Altoona mountains; the enemy disappeared during the night.

May 25. We commenced our march early in order to make use of the cool morning hours in marching a couple of miles, for the heat became more oppressive every day, while every day the number of our men became smaller. Despite of the heat we continued our march with but few and short rests until 5 o'clock P. M. During the whole day we had not been troubled by the enemy, until after 5 o'clock we suddenly saw staff officers and dispatch bearers gallop in every direction, troops were drawn together, and everything betrayed a bloody evening. Our division, the third, was formed near the road where we had halted, while the troops of the 1st and 2d divisions, who had heretofore been in our rear, moved past us against the enemy. The regiments of the two divisions were scarcely past and had barely taken their assigned position, when a terrible fire of musketry and cannon was heard—the bloody battle at Dallas or Burnt Hickory had commenced. Our own division now advanced again, and after many flank movements approached the battle-field; many wounded, able to help themselves, met us and sought shelter or went to the hospitals. We were acting as support in the rear of the 1st and 2d divisions of our corps, but were as much exposed to the enemy's fire as the men in the front, and consequently lost many men. The bullets continually tore holes in our ranks, or whizzed over our heads. The firing did not slacken until after hard fighting of two hours and darkness commenced setting in. Fresh troops had arrived in the mean time, our lines were re-established and entrenchments built on our outer lines. When this work was commenced with, the enemy's picket resumed firing, and continued during the whole night, although a heavy rain had commenced falling. Forming as we did the second line, we were not allowed to leave the ranks, but remain in the rain, with the face on the ground and the knapsack on the back, the whole night.

May 26. Amid heavy firing of the pickets the entrenchments on the front line were finished, in which work we took no part, as we relieved the front line in the evening, and took our places behind the new works. The enemy lay silent behind his works during the day, but night had scarcely set in, when we heard hundreds of axes a twork felling trees; the enemy was either building new works, or strengthening those already built.

May 27. Earth and breastworks had been erected along our whole line, and our guns, after being placed in position, began to play on the enemy, who still remained silent, (as had been the case since the 25th.) Our guns began their thunderous music early in the morning and our pickets, safely placed behind trees and logs. were harassing the enemy very much, while our main force was safely stationed behind our works. Our bombardment did not elicit an answer from the enemy to our great surprise—his guns continued silent. What was the cause?? was everybody's question. To save power or lead, could not be the cause. It was the intention of the enemy to remain silent until we advanced to an attack, and then butcher us by the hundred. But they were mistaken. Gen. SHERMAN pondered over ways and means to whip the enemy without perhaps uselessly sacrificing thousands of valuable lives, he understood flank movements and get in the enemy's rear. He had men enough to confront the enemy everywhere, and he had the men who were willing to do anything to whip the rebels. At 12 o'clock at noon we advanced a few hundred steps to draw the enemy from his works, but as he believed we were advancing to an attack, he remained behind his works; his pickets and sharpshooters, however, opened a merciless fire on our column, by which our regiment lost one killed and thirteen wounded. As we had not been ordered to attack the enemy, we went as close to him as possible, and entrenched ourselves in broad daylight almost under his nose. The 102d Illinois regiment had taken one of the enemy's batteries yesterday, but could not hold it on account of the murderous fire of musketry, being situated between the two picket lines. The enemy did not think it prudent, however, to retake the battery, which was afterwards shivered by our artillery fire. The enemy now made an attack on our first division, but got the worst of it and fled, leaving all his dead and wounded behind. Gen. SHERMAN inspected our lines. There was an incessant picket fire going on during the whole day, and the loss of the brigade was larger to-day than yesterday. As night approached the fire slackened, and the night passed quietly.

May 28. Our brigade was relieved at the front and went to the rear; but as we were posted near one of our batteries, at which the enemy's guns were firing to-day continually, every moment a shell exploding over or near us and cutting off the branches of the trees, our present position was a more dangerous one than the one in the front line. The enemy, under JOHNSTON, had received reinforcements from Richmond, and the report was that JOHNSTON had sent a flag of truce to SHERMAN demanding his surrender, or else he would come with his mighty army—five to our one—compel us to surrender and play the d—l generally. It did not seem as though the enemy was going to do all this at once, and that SHERMAN did not expect it either, for large foraging parties were sent out in the neigbborhood.

May 29. During the day the pickets continued their firing, which was now and then intermingled with the deep bass voices of the cannons. Our loss, therefore, was less to-day than yesterday. Our men had become accustomed to the continual firing of musketry and the thunder of the cannons and were in excellent spirits, heightened on the reception of a mail from home. We saw thereby that the road behind us was clear and that we could write to our parents, relatives and friends the news of our victories; aud also, alas! the sad news of the death of many a brave and noble fellow in behalf of our glorious country. We received letters in return with news from home, encouraging us in our work of the restoration of our country, telling us of the doings of the Copperheads in the North, etc. The day was pleasant, but the night hrought the more trouble. Several hours after sundown the enemy made an attack on our lines, and advanced, several lines of hattle, with a terrific yell towards us. But the rebs. had calculated too surely, without consulting us, on a victory. They were received by a well directed fire of musketry and canister that made them stagger; another volley made them flee in thick confusion, leaving their dead and wounded behind them. The fire must have been an effective one and the enemy suffered severely; but as the firing was continued now the principal part of the night, we also lost a number of men killed, who should no more behold the light of the sun, or wounded, who were to lie in the hospitals for months, and be discharged, perhaps, as cripples for life.

May 30. There was an incessant roar of the cannons, intermingled with the rattle of musketry. The enemy attacked the pickets on our left and drove them back; many of our pickets were surprised and taken prisoner and afterwards shot or killed by a blow with the musket in a most fiendish manner. An attack the enemy made on our right proved unsuccessful for him, and he lost some 1800 men in the attempt. There was fighting going on at our left, but the loss could not be ascertained. During the pauses, when the firing ceased for a few moments, the signal bugles of the enemy could be distinctly heard, and sometimes we even heard the enemy's officers curse the Yankees.

May 31 The 129th had to go on picket to-day. Early in the morning there was not much firing going on, but after a gang of rebel sharpshooters had taken possession of a house between the two lines and began to fire on us from the upper story, the firing became more lively, but all our firing at the rebels in the house was of no effect. To stop the annoying and dangerous fire of these sharpshooters, two of our guns were placed in the picket line, and a few shots from them stopped the mad firing of the rebels. Hereafter the firing was continued from behind the trees and ditches and pits, and even words were exchanged, but it was not very prudent to show one's head, as a bullet was sure to be sent on the appearance of a head. During the night the rebels were again very busy felling trees; on our right heavy firing was going on.

June 1, 1864. After being relieved from picket duty and having joined our brigade, we remained in our old position until noon. In our front there was but little firing going on, but on our left the firing was very lively. In the afternoon we received orders to be ready to march, and a short while afterwards the whole division marched a few miles further to the left of our former position, where, when night came on, we took our place behind the 14th army corps as supports. The night passed quietly.

June 2. During the night a heavy rain had commenced to fall which became worse, streaming on us in torrents, after we had packed up and were ready for marching. Wet to the skin, we waded through the morass further to our left, and reached the extreme flank in the afternoon. On approaching our new position we heard heavy firing going on, a number of wounded met us on their way to the hospital, while here and there a corpse was stretched on the ground. We took our place in an open field in line of battle and had scarcely shown ourselves when the enemy began to fire shells at us, wounding and killing several. Doctor POTTER, of the 105th Illinois, who was washing in a creek far behind the division, was shot by a ball of the enemy in the head, and instantly killed. The firing continued during the balance of the day, but slackened during the night until morning.

June 3. A brigade of the 23d army corps and the 1st and 2d brigade of our division of the 20th army corps, went further to the left; the enemy noticing this, after we had marched but a short distance, fired several shells at us, without doing any harm, however. A few hours before sundown we camped near Big Shanty station in the forest. No firing during the night.

June 4. Heavy rain in the forenoon and rapid firing on our right. We remained quiet until noon, when we went behind breastworks and remained there during the night. No firing in our front. The enemy retreated a short distance towards Lost mountain.

June 5. A rainy day, and in conseqence of this we were quiet; the enemy was retreating. Our music bands began to play again, the first time for a long while,

June 6. We moved nearer to Big Shanty station, but our advance soon met the pickets of the enemy, who began to fire. The position of the rebels was soon discovered, but as we had no order to advance further, we erected light breastworks, and remained for the night. A heavy rain fell afterwards.

June 7. We remained still and had inspection in the forenoon. The weather was very hot, and the enemy quiet. A music band of the brigade, sent after long ago, arrived at last. We received a large mail.

June 8. We still remained quiet; nothing was heard of the enemy.

June 9. We still remained quiet; a member of the 1st brigade, found guilty of theft, was drummed through our lines.

June 10. We received marching orders, but as the 14th army corps marched off before us, the roads were blocked, and we remained; the 129th Illinois went on picket for the night. Heavy firing was going on in the afternoon. Rain and sunshine changed.

June 11. Our pickets were relieved; it rained incessantly during the day and the roads were in a most wretched condition. Firing was heard throughout the day. We had received marching orders.

June 12. The rain continued and no movements were made.

June 13. Big Shanty station fell in our hands after hard fighting, and the Railroad trains followed immediately to the station. It rained again, and heavy firing was going on at our right. We remained quiet.

June 14. The rain stopped at last; heavy artillery

fire in the afternoon. We remained quiet and drew rations.

June 15. Early in the morning we began our pursuit after the enemy, who was again on the retreat; skirmishing between our advance and the enemy's rear took place continually. During the forenoon we marched by the flank, but in the afternoon, being nearer to the main force of the enemy, in line of battle. amid continual fire of the enemy. We lost our second ensign and several other men. Although near the enemy's works, we had not yet reached our destination. We advanced and drove the enemy's pickets behind the entrenchments; these we approached to about one hundred yards. amidst a most murderous fire of the rebel artillery We laid down on the ground, with the face downward, while the hilly elevations somewhat protected us. Yet, many had been killed and wounded, and their number was steadily increasing. After the fire of the enemy had slackened somewhat and the night set in, we were ordered to erect breastworks, which we did as quickly as possible by placing logs and branches of trees in piles, covering them with earth. Scarcely done with this we again received orders to advance, while the 3d brigade of our division moved in our place behind our breastworks. Having formed a line, we climbed over our entrenchments and advanced, despite the murderous fire the enemy opened on us. The object of our advance was to protect the brigade that had taken our place in finishing the works, and until they offered good shelter against the enemy's balls and attacks. We approached the enemy ten to twelve steps, when we again laid down to evade the blue beans that were whizzing around our ears. While lying down the enemy's fire became more violent, and as our position offered no protection whatever, causing the loss of many a life, the whole regiment, misunderstanding a command, rose to the feet and retreated behind the breastworks, despite the endeavors of the company officers to stop the men. Even if this retreat had not been caused by a misunderstanding, nobody could blame the regiment for seeking shelter from such a shower of lead and iron behind breastworks, principally erected by itself, losing thereby 18 wounded and 2 killed. Even the men behind the works did not blame us for seeking shelter, although many of them were knocked down and trodden upon in the scramble over the breastworks. They themselves thought it wrong to take us away from our breastworks, that we had to a great extent erected with such hard work and amid such danger. During the night we were ordered to a position on the left, where we again built entrenchments. Of course no one slept a minute that night.

June 16. The firing commenced early in the morning, particularly annoying were the rebel sharpshooters, who could do us no harm behind the breastworks, but our pickets were in continual danger. Later in the day our cannons opened on the enemy, who did not answer with his artillery until evening, when he sent some shell and solid shot against our breastworks. The shells either exploded on the ground before our breastworks or behind us, cutting off branches from the trees, and doing us no harm. Provisions were very scarce, as the roads were too bad and had to be repaired before the wagons could reach us.

June 17. The night passed quietly and without much firing, and even the day was not ushered in by the usual picket fire; it seemed as if the pickets were tired of shooting at each other. The rebel pickets satisfied themselves saying f.om their rifle pits,; "we have taken JOE HOOKER and staff prisoner last night;" our men gave them the lie and asked why they had left Dalton and Resaca so quickly, how far it was to Atlanta, etc., the rebs refusing every positive answer to these questions. Some time afterwards we found out that the enemy had fled and left the pickets to mask his retreat, and who now also beat a hasty retreat. Curiosity led us to the enemy's works to take a look at them. They had been built a great deal better than ours. Here and there the upper part had been shot away, and stains of blood near by proved that our artillery fire had been very exact, more so than the enemy's against ours. Our cavalry was soon at the heels of the enemy, and as the shells the enemy fired at the cavalry exploded near us, he cannot have been far when our men caught up to him. We soon went on after the enemy, and 1½ miles further we approached him from an open field and halted. Our brigade was in the reserve to-day. A number of cannons were placed in the front line, who assisted the enemy in "getting along." Our cannons barked incessantly at the enemy who continued to retreat until dusk, when again a courageous notion caused him to stop and answer every shot. A continuous thunder of cannon shots filled the air until late at night, when the whole surrounding country was thickly filled with the sulphurous smoke, and the lateness of the hour stopped all operations and the noise.

June 18. As it always had happened after a heavy cannonade, so to-day again a hard rain set in, becoming more intense as the day advanced, and giving no room whatever for the hope of an early clearing up. Despite this rain the fighting seemed to become more fierce than on the day before; the roar of the cannons was almost insufferable; reverberating in the mountains and thereby becoming more frightful. Here and there the deafening cheers of the attacking columns were heard, followed by a continual rattle of musketry. Our brigade still remained in the reserve, and we were thereby enabled to observe the better the movements and fighting during the day. Where the roar of the artillery was the loudest and where the rattle of musketry was the hardest, there our men made an attempt to cross a creek.

But all attempts were for naught, as the enemy was too strong and determined to resist and prevent our our crossing over. Although during the forenoon the fight was going on incessantly, yet during the afternoon, instead of increasing in violence, it became more quiet. A brigade of rebels was taken prisoner to-day.

June 19. Yesterday's slaughter took place on the right side of the Kenesaw mountains, and to-day we marched 1½ miles further to the right of the mountain, through bottomless morass and in the heaviest showers of rain. The enemy had to be driven part of the way, before we could get close enough to his entrenchments. By this work we frequently got in a rather unpleasant fire, particularly when in the woods, supporting our line of pickets and making movements of every sort. Two of our men were badly wounded and the horse of Col. CASE that had been in all the battles and violent fires, was wounded under its rider. To our left, near the Kenesaw, a heavy cannonade was frequently heard. We again erected breastworks in the night and had but an hour's sleep. The night passed with but very little firing.

June 21. During the forenoon we remained in our pl ace, strengthening our breastworks In the afternoon we protected the 23d army corps that advanced a short distance for a better position. After having returned to our breastworks, we had to advance again in order to form a staight line with the corps mentioned, and had to erect new breastworks again; of course we got but very little sleep. The hay was rainy and on our left heavy firing going on.

June 22. The enemy sent us several feelers to-day in the shape of shells, that exploded harmlessly in our front and rear. Gen. HOOKER climbed up a tree in front of our regiment to get a better view of the enemy and the surrounding country. Soon after we got the order to advance, and drove the enemy from

Lost mountain amid heavy skirmishing. The enemy halted at the edge of the forest, with an open field in front, and as our pickets could not drive the rebels further, the second brigade of our division was sent to assist, and brought the enemy to stagger, though it cost many valuable lives. Our brigade, on the left of the second, had to cross the field also and was fired upon by the enemy, losing a considerable number; our own regiment losing four members. When we had advanced far enough, we built breastworks at the foot of a hill held by the rebels, who fired at us continually, having a plain view of us and our work. The shots, however, nearly all went over our heads, and soon our new breastworks afforded us shelter against rifle balls. In the afternoon, while yet busy at our breastworks, the enemy made an attack on our right on the first division of the 20th corps and part of the 23d corps, in order to regain the ground lost to-day. The first division had just gotten a firm hold of their new position when the rebels, half drunk, came from their hiding place and rushed like madmen upon the Yankees. But as on former occasions the rebels again lost their courage when our men gave them the first salute at very short range. Many a rebel bit the dust and our shots riddled the rebel lines. A panic seized them and they turned and fled; but before all had begun to flee several pieces of cannon opened on them with grape and canister, reducing their numbers by hundreds of killed and wounded which were left behind. All the rebels now fled panic-stricken, not thinking any more of recovering the lost ground. The fire on the enemy continued until night, and at dusk our "tender regards" were reciprocated and elicited frequent replies, doing but little damage, however.

June 23. Early in the morning we were relieved in our position on ground, taken away from the enemy by us, by other troops and we marched to the right wing, where yesterday the enemy had attacked a part of the 23d army corps, and where the rebel dead were lying in every direction. Here our division and troops of the 23d army corps were gathered to make an attack on the enemy. After everything had been prepared for the undertaking, the advance was delayed, perhaps in order to find out more about the enemy before the movement was made. The undertaking seemed too costly a one, and we were divided along the line, whereupon our cannons opened on the enemy. The fire at the rebels on the Kenesaw was a spirited one, as were the "tit for tat" answers of the enemy. Our pickets during the night were advanced toward the enemy without meeting with any resistance.

June 24. Half of our company D of our regiment was on picket. We were at a point to which the line had advanced the night before and had ntrentrenced ourselves in an open field. When the morning dawned and the rebels saw our new works they gathered in crowds to take a look at the wonderful works; to assist them in looking and convince them that our works were inhabited, we soon opened our fire on them, whereupon the crowd disappeared. Curiosity had been awakened on the part of the rebels, and every now and then a head became visible, was shot at and disappeared, until one rebel was seen to fall. The rebels tried to carry the fallen one away, but as they were fired upon they thought the job too hazardous and quit. The enemy advanced his pickets to the place where the one shot had fallen, and we were fired on in return. This mutual gratulation continued throughout the day despite the almost melting heat. One of our pickets at our right was killed by a ball through the head. After sunset we were relieved and went to our regiment. The night was a restless one; no thought of sleep.

June 25. The weather was very hot and we remained quiet. The picket firing in our front continued, intermingled with cannon shots from the Kenesaw.

June 26. The weather was very hot, and firing going on at our right and left and skirmishing in our front.

June 27. The first division at our left, which had been further back, advanced until it got into a straight line with us. This was a hot work for the division as it had to drive back a strong line of the enemy's pickets, who seemed determined to keep the division back and keep their own places. At such advances the artillery generally assists, as it did to-day, and as the division went to work with a heart and a will, the enemy was soon compelled to withdraw after a hard struggle. The firing continued until night when the whole field was completely covered with a thick and heavy smoke. Our brigade was behind its entrenchments, awaiting an attack. During the night we strengthened our breastworks and in camp every regiment was on guard until the work was done.

June 28. During the entire day heavy firing took place; in the night a rebel patrol came too close to our pickets and was received with shots; the whole camp became alarmed and every regiment was placed in line of battle until the firing ceased and we could find out what had happened.

June 29. No firing of any consequence took place in our front, but heavy musketry fire was occasionally heard from Kenesaw. The enemy made a night attack on our left, which must have been a determined one, as the firing continued very long and violent; later news reported that the enemy had been whipped.

June 30. But very little firing along the line. Gen BUTTERFIELD started for New York, and our brigade commander, Gen. Ward assumed command of the division. Col. HARRISON assumed command of the brigade. Muster for pay in the afternoon.

July 1. But little firing going on between the pickets. Uniforms had arrived and were distributed among the regiments, many a member of whom was barefooted or ragged. Several members off on a furlough returned; one member of our regiment was wounded. We were to-day behind the first line of entrenchments, and towards evening we went to the second line.

July 2. Before daybreak we were awakened and placed in line of battle behind our works, as the 23d corps had been selected for a flanking movement around the enemy's left flank. In our front, in order to engage his attention, a tremendous cannonade was opened on the enemy. The pickets were pushed forward, and the enemy expecting an attack from our direction, was deceived and his left outflanked. The object of the 23d corps must have been successful as we noticed the enemy making preparations to-day for a retreat, and as we received orders at 9 P. M., to be ready for marching at daybreak.

July 3. The rebels had been outflanked and during the night had given up Kenesaw mountain and the town of Marietta. We found his pickets only the next morning. As had been ordered, we commenced the pursuit of the enemy early, whom we reached early in the forenoon. The enemy, expecting immediate pursuit, had left a considerable force at the point where we overtook him, in order to stop our progress, until his main force with the train of wagons and cannons had retreated to the Chattahoochee river, there to await our approach. The enemy's rear guard was seen in an open field, too powerful for a mere line of pickets, a section of artillery began to play on the enemy, who immediately answered from a larger number of cannons than ours. Our brigade had taken position in the rear of our cannons, with our pieces on the ground, while the enemy's shells exploded in front, behind and over us. We were in a dangerous position, but every man remained at his post. One shell of the rebel gun exploded over us and a piece struck a member of company A on the head, scattering his brains in every direction on the men; several others were slightly wounded. Another shell exploded and the pieces struck a gunner who had always faithfully performed his duty, tore one of his legs off, wounded the other, tore off an arm, the nose and part of the chin. The unfortunate man lived until night, when death ended his sufferings. The enemy's fire became more violent and accurate, and as one of our guns had become unserviceable, a second battery came to our assistance; but ere this could begin its work, the enemy had packed up and fled. The road from here to Marietta was now examined by our regiment to see if it was clear of rebels, while the remainder kept the position until we retuned. We took five rebels prisoners in the forest, and brought them along. The number of rebel prisoners taken to-day amounted to about 15,000. In the afternoon we again went in pursuit of the enemy, overtook his rear guard several times, built breastworks, and again advanced. During the night we camped at the right wing of the army.

July 4. We remained quiet until 2 o'clock in the afternoon when we again advanced without opposition of the enemy. In the direction of the breastworks built by us yesterday afternoon, a cannonade was heard, and the enemy used his artillery heavily against SCHOFIELD's 23d army corps. Our music bands played delightful this evening and merriment and hurrahs abounded in camp. Rebel deserters frequently came into our lines.

July 5. The enemy was still on the retreat and we marched the whole day without meeting any resistance; towards evening, when near the Chattahoochie river, we reached the enemy and light skirmishing took place.

July 6. We lay quiet until noon when we went

to the left wing, and in the night we commenced skirmishing with the enemy in the front line.

July 7. Very hot weather. The enemy had given way again and our pickets advanced 1½ miles before catching up to the enemy. During the day no firing took place—a kind of treaty of peace having been concluded to that effect—and the rebels sold sonthern papers to our men for coffee. The men weree quite conversational until our men were relieved, when the firing commenced again and was continued until morning.

July 8. The weather was hot—we remained quiet, except clearing up a little in camp, as it was believed that we would remain for a longer period. No firing took place.

July 9. From a high mountain the houses of Atlanta were to be seen, but also the intermediate forts and camps of the enemy; and it seemed not, as though the enemy would allow our early entrance into that city. We received orders to pack up and support the line of skirmishers—we remained in camp, however. Heavy cannon firing on our right and left, and insufferable heat. A shell exploding in one of our ammunition wagons, wounded the driver and killed five mules.

July 10. At 2 o'clock A. M. we received orders to be ready by sunrise; at the appointed time we marched a couple of hundred steps, when we halted, remained quiet some time, and again returned to our old camps. A rebel major with 1,400 men was captured near the river, while the balance of the enemy's forces were crossing from the north to the south side of the river. In the night we drew rations.

July 11. A member of our regiment while upon picket duty was shot by the rebels—the bullet went through his head and he fell dead. We still remained in our camp; the day was very hot and but little firing on the picket line.

July 12. The camps were cleaned again and we had no prospect of an early move. In the afternoon rain.

July 13. We remained quiet yet—the heat was very great. Drew rations.

July 14. A rainy afternoon; a cannonade was heard sometimes in the day, and sometimes in the night.

July 15. Cool and dark weather; we remained quiet.

July 16. Our pickets were now on the north side and the enemy's pickets on the south side of the Chattahoochie river. Not a single shot was fired by the pickets of our brigade at the rebels, or by those at us, but the rebels were prohibited from speaking a single word to our men and would not allow them to go into the water. Our men generally were out of tobacco and continually asked the rebels for some, who did not answer, but now and then tied a piece of tobacco on a stone, and threw it over the river. Cannonade on our left.

July 17. At 3 o'clock in the afternoon we left our camp and marched until late at night in an easterly direction, whereupon we crossed over the river pontoons ready there, without resistance from the enemy. We continued our march in an easterly direction without stopping, until we were abot four miles from the river, when we camped for the night.

July 18. Again we commenced our march at 3 o'clock in the afternoon, principally in line of battle, as we were near the enemy, and whose pickets had to be driven ahead frequently after slight resistance. Late in the evening we reached our camping ground, and erected breastworks during the night. Trees were being felled in every direction, despite the darkness, and a member of the 102d Illinois regiment, feeling ill, laid down under a tree, and had his skull crushed by a falling tree while asleep. Senseless and dying the wounded man was taken to the hospital.

July 19. We remained quiet and made our breastworks stronger—the heat was intolerable. Heavy cannonading and skirmishing was going on near us. Gen. HOOD had relieved Gen. JOHNSTON in the command of the rebel army, the latter having declared his inability to keep Atlanta from the Yankees' grasp.

July 20. To judge from all preparations and movements in camp it seemed, as though the day would not pass by as former days, but that an attack would be made on the enemy. All the sick were taken from the doctors' hands and placed in wagons, or wherever there was room for them. Men were detailed and sent with ladders to the regiments to be on hand in time for carrying off the wounded and dead. Everything betokened a bloody day. Early in the day we had received orders to pack up and immediately after breakfast we left our camp for the bloody work. The commencement was at hand, as our advance immediately commenced exchanging shots with the enemy. The firing sometimes increased and then again decreased. At noon, the sun burning almost insufferably, we reached a creek, Peach Tree creek, which was very high, although there had been but little rain of late. A dyke had been erected by the rebels below our positon, in order to prevent our crossing. We crossed, however, without any obstacles, as a bridge had been built over the creek and the 14th army corps had driven the enemy back. After crossing the creek, we reached an open field, where we halted, but where the rifle ball of the enemy reached, without doing any damage, however. The 17th corps was on our right, and the 14th on our left in position, while we remained in the open field. The centre was a gap between the two corps, destined to be our position, but was not filled because the supposition was general that the enemy would again retreat without much fighting. This did not seem to be the case, and all attacks of our pickets were of no use, but seemed to make the enemy the more determined on resistance. We arose again and marched to the right until we reached the right wing of the 17th army corps. Thus the gap was filled, and we were stationed at the foot of a hill in our front; here we stacked arms. Our orders were not to go too far from our guns, as orders for an advance were expected. As the noon sun was very hot, we went in the shade of a neighboring thorny thicket, others went after water for the dinner coffee. We had scarcely seated ourselves, and long before the thirsty ones could get their coffee ready, a tremendous roar of musketry in our front was heard, coming nearer every second. In a few minutes our pickets were driven in, who reported that the enemy was coming, three lines of battle strong and was approaching fast. As soon as the firing had commenced, every one rushed for his gun, and before the enemy, who approached in double quick time, could open his fire on us, we were on the top of the hill, meeting them, and thereby preventing a surprise. The rebels, being thus unexpectedly confronted by a line of Yankees, lost some of their courage, and instead of rushing on us, they stretched themselves behind a rail fence on the top of the hill, waiting until we had advanced to within ten steps of them. The fire between the two armies now became most violent and no member of our regiment who expected death on that day, will ever in his life forget the slaughter, while the powder smoke rose slowly up to heaven between the fighting parties,—where one gallant lad after another was snatched from our side! He will never forget, how after a short continuation of this wholesale butchery, on our left, cheers were given, like a prairie-fire leaping to the right, and all our men rushed on the enemy with the bayonet, like so many devils! The scene was a bloody one, but glorious one after all to the Union heart! The rebel lines behind the fence, not accustomed to such bravery, rose to their feet and ran away as fast as their legs could carry them. Now our harvest had come and we paid back the enemy in the same coin they had given us. Every man now aimed at an enemy running in his front, who went down before such a fire as the ripe wheat before the scythe of the mower. The enemy ran about 300 or 400 steps and then gathered and began to return our fire again, thereby endangering his own wounded in our front. The fire, which commenced at 2 o'clock P. M., continued until night; but as we were protected somewhat by the fence, our loss was smaller than at the beginning. While we were thus fighting with the enemy, the troops on our right and left had to do the same thing, as the rebels under HOOD were trying their best to whip the Yankees, and had attacked our whole line. Both wings had to give way to the enemy several times, who had even taken several cannons from them, when they again rallied, until the enemy had been whipped everywhere. Although the rebels can say "at Peach Tree creek we did good work," yet they cannot say that the work was a master-piece. They had no master-workman in HOOD as we did in SHERMAN, and where the "boss" is of no account, what can you expect from the "jours" and boys? Our loss on this day was large, smaller however than the loss of the enemy. All our wounded were collected during and after the fight, and cared for in the hospitals as well as possible. Our regiment lost 10 killed, but many of the wounded died afterwards in the hospitals. Our division took seven flags from the enemy, (one of which was taken by our regiment;) the bearers of three had to be killed before the flags were taken. The rebel wonuded, by no means a small number, were collected after dark and cared for. They were very thankful for our care, and as they were well provided with tobacco, which our men were in want of, they willingly divided with us. As our own wounded were very numerous, best little medical aid could be rendered the rebel wounded during the night. We had but little sleep, as we were busy erecting breastworks, for which, however, we had no use, as the rebels made no attack in the night

July 21. We buried our own dead and some of the enemy's, whereby most of the day was spent. Gen. Hooker rode along our line as we were collecting the enemy's dead, and as the General was a favorite of the men, cheers were repeatedly given. He stopped a while and looked at the staring dead, and was soon surrounded by our men. He could not, however, control his feelings, tears came in his eyes, and he rode off. The enemy retreated quite a distance during the night, to make another stand around Atlanta. The 14th corps, which formed our left wing, swung around, thereby approaching our destination, Atlanta. During this manoeuver there was frequent heavy firing on the left. We remained for the night on the battle-field.

July 22. Without taking breakfast we left the bloody field in pursuit of the flying enemy, to avenge our fallen comrades and the losses we had sustained, determined not to rest until the rebels had been completely whipped. In the afternoon, about $1\frac{1}{2}$ miles from Atlanta, we found the enemy's pickets and saw the rebels busy perfecting their fortifications. We pressed as near to the enemy as possible, until our pickets could advance no further without suffering loss. We stopped and entrenched ourselves. The enemy gave us time for this work until night, when he began his artillery fire; by this time our breastworks afforded us good shelter. Our left wings, having pushed forward yesterday, had to fight with the enemy and whipped him again, as on the 20th.

We suffered an irreparable loss in the death of Gen. McPherson, who was killed by a rebel ball.

July 23. The enemy opened a heavy fire on us in the forenoon and compelled us to seek shelter behind our breastworks. A shell struck our breastworks in front of company A and exploded, doing, however, no other damage than throwing the earth up high in the air. At noon our pickets were driven some distance by the enemy, being in too close proximity to him; but when our pickets advanced again, the enemy retreated and our men resumed their old position. The night was rest and sleepless, the enemy's fire continued, while we were in the ditches behind our breastworks.

July 24. Artillery and musketry fire as yesterday. Two negroes were struck by pieces of a shell, and instantly killed. Gen. Sherman demanded the surrender of Atlanta, but was refused by Hood; after which we made preparations to bombard the town and compel the enemy to surrender. Many women who had fled from the horrors of the war and had been in the woods heretofore, prepared to come into our lines instead of those of the enemy, and were admitted. A false alarm robbed us of our sleep again to-night, and we had to remain on guard behind our breastworks, even after the cause or no cause of the alarm had been found out.

July 25. During the forenoon we remained behind our entrenchments, in consequence of the enemy's fire. In the afternoon, the firing having subsided somewhat, a second line of breastworks was built closer to the enemy's lines. The rebels now thought of preventing our work by a continual fire, particularly by sharpshooters; but of no avail. To hear the bullets whistle, our soldiers had become used to, and on account of the loss of a few wounded it would not be prudent to stop such a work, which was therefore continued amid jokes and jests, and the works became stronger and safer every hour, nearing completion. Having picket firing in the night.

July 26. More improvements were made to our works, but on account of being under marching orders, we did not advance to them. The rebel pickets and sharpshooters did more damage than yesterday, as a number of men were wounded. A member of the 70th Indiana lost his life by his own carelessness. He was relieving his man and in the act of stepping in the skirmish pit, when the cock of his gun caught on a root, the gun went off and the ball passed through the breast of the man, who fell down dead. The enemy's cannon's were more quiet than usual, but our artillery opened on the enemy frequently.

July 27. Our whole brigade was relieved last night from its position, and marched further to the right, where we took position behind breastworks. Our pickets that had been sent out on the evening before, were left in their position, and brought to us the next morning by a staff officer. The pickets, before reaching us, had to pass through an open field, where they were within easy range of the enemy's balls, that were sent to them. A soldier of the 79th Ohio was shot in the hip and disabled from reaching the hospital. His comrades, unwilling to leave him, had hard work in carrying the wounded man off, before they got out of reach of the enemy's bullets that continued to fly about them faster than before. The fire along the picket line was very violent to-day, as the enemy's pickets were driven back at several points.

July 28. Heavy fighting was going on at our right wing; we had marching orders to go there in case of necessity. About 10 o'clock we left our breastworks, and immediately fired at by the enemy who had noticed our movement. After having marched several miles we received orders to return, as the enemy had been completely whipped and our troops were able to withstand the enemy in their front. We returned to our former position, but with the order, not to make ourselves too comfortable there. Maj. Gen. HOOKER gave up the command of the 20th army corps to go North. The men were not well pleased with this change, as all loved and adored him as a prudent and good General.

July 29. The whole third division went to the extreme right. Our army led past yesterday's battlefield, on which the rebel dead and wounded were scattered in every direction yet. To judge from the balls lodging in the trees yet standing and fallen down, the fight must have been a hard one. The troops stationed there were in the best humor, standing and sitting, jesting and laughing between wounded and dead rebels, talking of the events of the day just passed—how the enemy had approached and afterwards the slaughter, in which the enemy suffered severely, where, after the rebels had given leg bail in the most amusing manner. These men belonged to the 17th army corps which had suffered heavy losses too, but which the men did not mind, as their wounded were cared for, and as they themselves had been victorious. At night our division formed the extreme right flank and erected breastworks on all four sides to be protected against attacks by cavalry and infantry. The night passed quiet.

July 30. In the forenoon we remained quiet, and in the afternoon we pressed on further to the right and the gap thus occasioned filled by other troops immediately. We had scarcely marched a mile ere we met the enemy, when a slight firing commenced and the division halted and was formed in a hollow space, whereupon we again entrenched ourselves. During the night slight firing commenced occasionally, but not sufficient to cause alarm and prepare for battle.

July 31. A division of the 14th army corps, under command of JEFF. C. DAVIS, had to do duty as an inspecting patrol and approach the Macon and Atlanta Railroad as near as possible. We remained quiet, but had orders to be ready to march to DAVIS' assistance, in case he should come in contact with the enemy. Towards evening DAVIS returned with his men; he had lost some men by the enemy's balls, but no attack had been made. They reported that the road, the only one the enemy had left, had been strongly fortified and was well guarded. The trains the enemy had running were heard distinctly in the night. We remained in our hollow square to-night. The weather was rainy.

August 1, 1864. The enemy moved his pickets nearer to our southern side several times, seemingly thinking of making an attack. Perhaps he feared that we would gradually come closer to his last road, whence it would have been difficult to drive us, after we had entrenched ourselves there and gotten a firm hold. All roads leading to us were barricaded with trees and the trees around us were felled, in order to make the task of reaching us the more dangerous for the enemy. Our breastworks, hastily and irregularly erected, were strongly fortified, and now every man desired the enemy to approach. The rebels did not deem it prudent to attack, and there was no other firing but slight skirmishing on our southern front. On our left heavy firing was going on. In the evening an inspection of arms took place.

August 2. Our division was relieved by the 23d army corps, which now held the right wing, and we returned to the left, where the 1st and 2d division of our corps were. We went into the front line of the position of the corps on the right of the Chattanooga road and relieved the troops placed there yesterday evening, that had erected entrenchments in the night, and were now taken away to be disposed of somewhere else.

August 3. In the forenoon, when behind the entrenchments and the enemy not over eight hundred steps from us, was firing very heavily, we lost a member of the regiment who was busy with the others in fastening branches of trees for shade on our breastworks; in the afternoon we lost two more men the same way. In the night another line of entrenchments was erected closer to the enemy; the work went on incessantly, and the enemy troubled us but little in the night, and while erecting breastworks.

August 4. The new line of entrenchments, which already afforded us some shelter, we finished, amid the enemy's most rigid fire. The fire on the picket line was very heavy, particularly that of the enemy. At 12 o'clock at night we went behind our new works, the enemy not knowing anything about it; we thereby came closer to the enemy, though the distance was but a short one.

August 5. Shortly after the enemy had been driven from the Chattahoochie river, the building of a bridge was commenced with for the Railroad. The bridge was done now and to-day the first train reached the front before Atlanta. The locomotive was received with tremendous cheers by our soldiers, and the shrill whistle must have sounded defiantly to the rebels. As provisions had become scanty, we were glad at the arrival of the iron horse, as sufficient quantities could now reach us, despite of the guerrillas.

August 8. The city had been bombarded for several days, and the fire to-day was more rapid than before. Siege guns had arrived yesterday and been brought into position immediately. We could hear plainly, particularly at night, when the shells struck a house and exploded inside—the sound of which resembled the crash of a falling building, followed by the tremendous explosion in the upper story or cellar. The inhabitants of the city, as we read in the Atlanta papers (which we exchanged from the rebel pickets for coffee,) fled to the most distant parts of the city, or sought refuge in cellars, or dug caves in the ground, where they remained during the bombardment and only left their hiding places, when compelled to by hunger or thirst. The war is a scene of horror, and it was particularly so the case with Atlanta, full as the city was with refugees from the neighborhood all around. What would the enemy have cared for the women and children, if the reverse had been the case and the city of Atlanta in Union hands, besieged by rebels? How did the rebels act towards the women and children in Pennsylvania and Maryland? And what cared the rebel bushwhackers for women and children, or the passenger trains, when they tore up the rails and hurried hundreds of them to an untimely grave and death, and even robbing them of the little they had left. Not so did SHERMAN act. As the surrender of the city had been refused by HOOD, SHERMAN had told him to order the women and children out of the city. HOOD did not fulfill this request, hoping thereby to compel SHERMAN to forego the bombardment, a foolish supposition indeed. SHERMAN had done everything to prevent loss of life and cannot be called cruel, as has been done by the rebels for the bombardment of Atlanta—HOOD is to blame and to be held responsible for every innocent life sacrificed there, as he knew of SHERMAN's purpose,—to him the spirits of the innocent, the cripple now begging in the South, must be held responsible and accused of murder, of wantonly sacrificing the lives of his men.

July 7. The rebel pickets and sharpshooters were very annoying again, and endeavored to kill the men at our guns; but all efforts were useless, as our cannon barked most lustily. A member of company K of our regiment was badly wounded, and died afterwards in the hospital.

August 8. Rain and heavy picket fire. A member of company I of our regiment was badly wounded in the evening at guard mounting.

August 9. Every one of our cannon along our whole line had to fire fifty shots during the day at the town. The enemy answered very lively, but was soon made to hush by a few shells. Our shots were principally directed at the town. Several cannon balls struck our breastworks, but did no damage, as they were bomb proof.

August 19 Capt. BURCH wounded in the head at Peach Tree Creek, had recovered and again assumed command of his company D. There was much talk of introducing Henry Rifles in our regiment. Very little firing to-day.

August 11 The enemy's pickets fired incessantly at our pickets who had received orders to remain quiet; now and then, however, one of our pickets could not control himself and fired a shot. On both sides a heavy cannonade was going on. About 10 o'clock P. M., when everything was quiet in our lines, a tremendous artillery and musketry fire commenced, and soon we were in line of battle, not knowing whether the enemy would actually dare an attack or not. From all appearances the enemy made an attack, some distance on our right, as the firing approached our lines, and gradually grew fainter until it ceased entirely.

August 12. Heavy picket and artillery fire on both sides. All firing had of late had but little or no result. We were as close to the enemy's lines as we could get, to outflank him, seemed impossible here; but no attack on his forts or works was made, and the soldiers of both armies shot at each other whenever there was a chance—each day demanded its sacrifice, but we did not gain what we wanted, Atlanta. However, we did not grieve very much about this, Atlanta would be taken we all knew, and that Gen. SHERMAN was plotting ways and means to take this, to the rebels, very important position, there could be no doubt. The enemy's road from Atlanta to Macon was yet open for him, and he believed no doubt that we were afraid to drive him out of his entrenchments, or considered the capture of Atlanta an impossibility. A member of the 105th Illinois was shot while on picket to-day. During the night heavy firing was going on.

August 13 The brush that was between us and the enemy before the fighting around Atlanta commenced, had been shot away or crippled by the musket balls and shells, whereby the enemy gained a clear view at our works at many points, and whenever our men showed themselves at such points and kept not close behind the breastworks, they were fired upon by the enemy. The rebels had become very good marksmen and but seldom the balls went overhead, but hit either the works or the men behind at work or cooking; wounding or killing them. To prevent any further losses we hightened the breastworks several inches; while at work we again lost one man of our regiment, who was shot through the abdomen; Lieut. FISHER, of the 195th Illinois regiment, was also shot when on picket duty. The bombardment of the city still continued and several times houses had been set afire by our shells—the alarms could be distinctly heard by us—but the fire was quenched by the military and citizens before it could make much headway.

August 14. The enemy's fire in our front slackened somewhat, our artillery was the busier in bombarding the city. The enemy made another attack on the 17th corps on our right, and tried very hard to break through our lines. He had to give up his efforts, after a loss of 500 killed and wounded, and 400 prisoners. During the night heavy firing was again going on at our right. Close to our left a fort was built, opposite an enemy's fort. The weather was rainy.

August 15. In the morning a heavy cannonade was going on, as well as occasional picket fire. We drew new clothes. Our pickets were again advanced a little, and as this was done very quietly the enemy did not know anything about it until new rifle pits were being dug, when the enemy sent a shot occasionally to the spot whence the noise of digging emanated.

August 17. Early in the day our pickets saw rebel regiments and brigades marching to and fro, and the general belief was that the enemy was preparing to break through our lines. An attack was desired by every one as we had good breastworks, and many rebels would have been killed before they could have reached the main works. We had driven poles in the ground with sharp points and this with the brush made an approach to our breastworks very difficult and dangerous. But the enemy seemed to know the strength of our fortifications as well as we did, as he did not come, and we waited for him in vain. The pickets were the busier in firing at us and we lost five men of our regiment. During the night the fire slackened.

August 18. Before daybreak the enemy opened a most dreadful fire from all his guns, the shells went howling over our heads and exploding further back without doing any damage, however, excepting tearing holes in the ground. In a moment our men were under arms behind the entrenchments, as each firing was generally the commencement of an attack, and we were prepared for the worst. The game of the enemy should not last long and our artillery was preparing to make the "erring brethren" hush. They commenced and soon the enemy cooled down, while our artillery continued as long as they pleased. On our right heavy firing was heard. Gen. KILLPATRICK, with his cavalry was in the enemy's rear, destroying railroads and other valuable rebel property, south of Atlanta.

August 19. The enemy was very lively in the early morning hours, but became quiet after a few well aimed shots of our artillery. The pickets on both sides did not cease firing for one minute throughout the day and we had to remain quiet behind the entrenchments, in order not to suffer unnecessary loss. Our commissary sergeant was shot through the right hand. The weather was rainy.

August 20 In consequence of the rain, the pickets were kind enough to remain unusually quiet to-day. Our men were busy writing letters.

August 21. It seemed as no inimical feeling existed between the two armies, for not a cannon was fired, except toward the city, which fire was stopped but seldom even at night. But little picket firing was going on, and we could leave our breastworks for hours, without danger of the enemy's bullets.

August 22 The bombardment of the city continued without interruption, but the picket fire was very light. Several houses in the city were again set afire by our shells.

August 23 Part of our army retreated to-day, but was not compelled to by the enemy—it retreated in consequence of SHERMAN's own orders. The 97th Ohio regiment of our brigade marched back to the Chattahoochie river, there to build fortifications, and we took the place of this regiment behind the breastworks, at the same time each brigade had to stretch out a little, so that we stood but one man deep on some points, in order to fill the gap. Not a shot was fired in our front, as the enemy had not noticed the movement, and as only such troops were moved that could without being noticed by the enemy. It had been determined upon to move the 20th army corps, that was stationed on the right and left of the Chattanooga-Atlanta Railroad, in a direct line back to the Chattahoochie river, to make the enemy believe that the whole army had retreated. At the same time the five other army corps were to fall back a distance and thence approach the Atlanta-Macon Railroad. The retreat of our division was commenced as soon as it became dark, the brigade music band was to give the signal by playing, as usual, the customary marches and finishing with the Yankee Doodle. As soon as the enlivening notes of the Yankee Doodle were

—7

heard, our regiment formed and marched without making the least noise to its destination. Our pickets were to remain in front of the enemy and then to retreat slowly in our wake. Our siege guns had been moved the night previous, and as they were quiet the entire day, the enemy must have thought it rather queer; and when even towards evening an unexampled quietness reigned in his front, the enemy must have come to the conclusion that we had retreated. The enemy seemed certain that our whole army had retreated and called to our few pickets left: "Never mind, Yankee, we'll find you again in the morning!" The retreat was made very slowly, sometimes we lay still for long periods, and did not reach the river until 4 o'clock A. M.

August 26. Major General Slocum assumed command of our corps, and presented himself to the troops. The 1st and 2d division went to the south side of the river, and took position on the right and left side of the Railroad, and built breastworks Our division, destined to take position on the north bank of the river, remained quietly on his southern shore. Heavy cannonade was heard in the direction of our main army.

August 27. We felled wood in front of the 1st division that was busy building entrenchments. In the afternoon our division went over the river and took possession of the works of the enemy, of whom nothing was to be seen, and who must have followed our main army.

August 28. We erected tents and put branches of trees up, in order to protect ourselves a little more against the burning rays of the sun. The fifer major of our regiment drowned in the river while bathing. Part of our troops was skirmishing with the enemy, without suffering much loss.

August 29 In consequence of the scorching sun we remained quiet. No news from our main army.

August 30. We remained quiet, awaiting patiently news from the other corps.

August 31. Gen. SLOCUM inspected our camp; we were mustered for pay. Everything quiet.

September 1. 1864   We got the news that the rebels had left Atlanta and that our army had overtaken them at Jonesboro and whipped them soundly. This happy news created the wildest excitement and the whole day nothing but songs and cheers were heard. Gen. WARD, with two brigades, the second and third of our division, moved to town, which we entered, without molestation. Our brigade was under marching orders; we remained in our old places during the night, however.

Sept. 2.   We received further news about the fight at Jonesboro between our troops and the rebel army. The army under HOOD, according to the report, had been split in two, and had been compelled to leave its dead and wounded behind, and was still pursued by SHERMAN and THOMAS. In the city many rebel wounded were found, and a number of prisoners had been captured, consisting principally of such men that had left the army with the firm belief that the rebel cause was lost, and had left the sinking ship in time to save themselves. All siege guns which the enemy had used against us in his fortification, fell in our hands, though they had been spiked and made useless for the present. The arsenal from which the whole rebel army had been supplied, had been blown up by the enemy. A large number of railroad cars, filled with ammunition, guns, &c., had been set afire by the enemy, as they could not be moved on account of SHERMAN taking part of the road before the rebels were aware of it. The town itself resembled a building having passed through a gale and threatening to tumble down every minute. In the northern part of the city not a house was left uninjured and many either leveled to the ground entirely or completely riddled, and nothing but a skeleton of the former stately mansion left standing. The streets were a complete morass, here and there plowed up by shells or solid shot. The inhabitants looked shy and frightened from their shattered dwellings at the victorious Yankees, coming in by the thousands, receiving them, of course, not as friends, and never believing until it became reality, that *such men could take Atlanta!* The wealthy and arch rebels had fled with the rebel army, taking their light and movable property along with them, but leaving their homes and firesides and "last ditch," for, and in which, they were going to die so gloriously as—rank traitors to the Union! The goods from the stores had principally been moved, but nevertheless some things been left, which were being stolen before our army arrived. Here and there old women or children were seen with small parcels, kegs, baskets, &c., hurrying through the streets to take the captured things to their homes in some remote corner or cavern. We never found out what the armed rebels thought about the loss of their stronghold, Atlanta, but many of the inhabitants believed firmly that "their men" would take the city again in about ten days, and had retreated merely to get in our rear, then to return and starve us out. Such suppositions and threats were laughed at by such men as Sherman had in his army. Atlanta will remain in our hands, and if it should be evacuated, there will be nothing left of it but a heap of ashes! These were our answers to such impertinent remarks of the haughty enemy. To strive is not fashionable in an inimical state like Georgia, and if our communication with the North is cut off, we have learned to forage, was another answer. To subjugate us by powder and lead requires courage, and this we have shown at Dalton, Reseca, Marietta, &c., on the 20th of July, while your men lost the last bit of courage at Atlanta and Jonesboro, were the remarks of our boys. The more angry the men became with the Copperheads in the North, of whose doings we learned by letters, and threats were uttered frequently with the expectation of calling the rebel sympathisers in the

North to an account some day. At noon we had garrisoned Atlanta, and reached the object of the campaign.

Sept. 3. Our brigade yet remained behind the old entrenchments on the Chattahoochie, guarding both bridges leading over the river here, and a large quantity of supplies that had arrived and been deposited here. Atlanta had been taken but a few days ago, and here was the nearest and most suitable place for a depository of supplies, &c. The enemy, having recovered from his whipping at Jonesboro, gathered his scattered forces and had retreated towards Macon, there to await, what our next move would be. The enemy's cavalry was principally in our rear, tearing up railways, burning bridges and trains, laden with supplies for our army, and tried their best generally to cut off our communication with the North, hoping thereby to compel us to evacuate Atlanta. The report came in to-day that the rebel cavalry were between here and Marietta, and the report must have been true, as no trains arrived as usual. We were on our guard, in order not to be surprised, but the enemy moved Northward.

Sept. 4. The hospital of our division that had till now been here at the river, was moved to the city. The weather was cloudy and rainy.

Sept 5 The damage the enemy had done to the track must have been considerable, as no trains had come in yet.

Sept. 6. The weather was again rainy and chilly; no news of any importance.

Sept. 7 Everything was quiet here; no trains had reached us, and we heard nothing from other points, as not only the track but also the telegraph had been demolished by the enemy. Our main army had left Jonesboro and camped around Atlanta.

Sept 8. The general talk was that all Illinois troops were to be sent home for the Presidential election, but very little faith was placed in the report.

Sept. 9. Several trains arrived and the commissary stores here were moved to Atlanta. The track of the Louisville-Nashville Railroad had been destroyed by WHEELER's cavalry on several places, and we had not received any letters for some time. We also received the news that the guerrilla chief JOHN MORGAN had been taken prisoner by a private of the 13th Tennessee cavalry in Kentucky, and shot. The weather was very hot.

Sept. 10. A member of our company, wounded on the 20th of July, died on the 24th of August in Kingston, Ga.; we received the news of his decease to-day.

Sept. 11. We received new clothes and looked like respectable men again, and not like ragged beggars. The weather was windy and warm.

Sept. 12. An address from the President and Lieut. Gen. GRANT was read to us, thanking the army under SHERMAN for the deeds of valor done during the campaign. In honor of the capture of Atlanta and the troops that captured it, 100 minute guns were fired in all the Northern cities and from all the forts by order of the President. An order was issued that each flag of the army having participated in the capture of Atlanta, should have the inscription, "Atlanta," affixed on it. The weather was very warm to-day.

Spt. 13. Guerrillas were doing mischief in our neighborhood and persons were frequently attacked and robbed on the road from here to Atlanta.

Sept 14. A few days ago the report was current that furloughs were being granted, in consequence of which a number of our men applied, but were all refused, as we were to remain at Atlanta but a short while, and then commence a new campaign. We received marching orders to-day for Atlanta; five men of each company had to pack up in the night and march to the destined place.

Sept. 16. The hour for marching was fixed at 6

A. M. We assembled punctually and marched to the North side of the Chattahoochee, where the brigade was assembling, crossed the river then, and at 7 o'clock we passed over a part of the battlefield of the 20th of July. About 8 o'clock we reached our former entrenchments in front of Atlanta, passed the graves of the fallen dear comrades, that were "sleeping the sleep that knows no waking," and many of us could not resist the silent tear at the thought of the many pleasant hours, privations and sufferings, enjoyed and endured in company with the fallen heroes, now slumbering beneath the silent sod! They had fallen in defence of our glorious country—peace to their ashes, and may the memory of those days fill us with new love of our Republic and its glorious freemen! We halted and remained for some time, although under quite different circumstanbes as formerly, when we were in continual danger of the enemy's shells, balls and bullets, and nothing was heard but the roar of artillery and the rattle of musketry. A solemn silence reigned to-day, not disturbed by the howl of shells, the moans of the wounded, nor the last yells of the dying! The thoughts of our men there now, I do not dare to describe, or even suppose! We continued our march and at 10 o'clock we reached the ruined city with its (formerly) inimical fortifications, passed straight through the city and went in camp about 1½ mile farther South. The day was excessively hot and the roads covered with dust several inches deep. After we had been dismissed, a number of our men went to the enemy's former works on the South side of the city. They were very strong and in their erection every modern invention in the art of war had been added—but all of no avail—the doom of rebellion had been sealed!

Sept. 18 A more suitable camping ground was selected to-day and cleared of the dirt and brush piled there. Received the first mail again for some time. During the night a heavy rain commenced

Beautiful and valuable deserted frame houses in the neighborhood, that had been riddled by bullets and balls, were torn down and doors, lumber and even shingles taken and used in erecting tenements in camp, in order to be as comfortable as possible while we remained here. The timber was carried from a distance of sometimes more than half a mile, as the houses in our immediate neighborhood had been "appropriated" by troops before our arrival. But we were satisfied with what we received and in case of necessity were willing to do our share in burning down what we had so laboriously erected.

Sept. 19. Our camp was divided off by Col. CASK and FLYNN, and each company got its own ground, which every four or five men were allotted a space of eight feet in width and twelve feet in length, to enjoy themselves in a glorious and noble style—in a straight line with the rest of the company, of course. With the erection of the buildings we were not long at work; to lay a safe and sure foundation, was not necessary, aye, very superfluous, as this was not destined to be our "final resting place." At every corner of the "lot" allowed us, pillars" were erected in the ground, bearing no particular Corinthian or Dorian ornament, and the boards, gathered up as they were, were made to fit some way or other and nailed to the "pillars," whereby a kind of a box or cage for wild animals, without a roof, was formed. The rafters and spars, if such were on hand, were put on next, or otherwise our shelter tents formed the roof, and the "noble mansion", stood there. The lack of furniture was not felt very severely, where such could not be gotten from the houses near, a board was taken, four holes bored in the ends, sticks put in, and our chair, stool, lounge, settee, sofa, etc., was done. The beds were made the same way, and branches of trees made a splendid "spring mattress," and did good service. Or forks of trees were cut down, boards nailed across, and covered with straw, leaves, grass,

&c., and the "bed" was fixed for the night. Rubber blankets and woollen blankets formed the "featherbed" covering and our knapsacks the pillars. Windows we needed none, as the roof—either entirely or partially missing—afforded no obstacle to light, and besides we received light through the opening left, generally called door, in civilized life. With such work the day was spent; the hammering, knocking, splicing was as deafening as the rattle of the musketry and the roar of cannon in battle. A looker on was reminded involuntarily of an ant-hill—here a party went after building materials, there a party returned loaded down with such, while others sawed, hammered, nailed and fitted As everybody was at work, nails, hammers, saws, &c., were in great demand, hunted, hooked, confiscated, stolen, or robbed and cries of "Jake, give me that hammer," "Jim, hand me that saw," "who stole my nails?' resounded on every side. Others, having finished their work, or being worn out, laid down and rested and slept and dreamed about the dear ones at home, about a battle, about a falling comrade shot through the heart!

Sept. 19. Those that had not finished building yesterday, continued to-day, and some, not being satisfied with their "bed' tore it apart and slept on the ground.

Sept. 20. Several of our men who had left camp had gone to the city, and had commenced demolishing houses there, were arrested by the provost guard. A heavy rain commenced at sunset, and lasted the whole night.

Sept. 21. The rain continued as heavy as last night, despite of this the slow builders and joiners in our camp finished their work; the streets between the company grounds were cleaned. Review was announced for to-morrow, in consequence of which new clothes were drawn, guns and dress cleaned and our quarters put in order and cleaned up.

Sept. 22. At 12 o'lclock M. the parade announced

yesterday was to commence, but as a sudden rain set in the order was not executed, and the parade postponed. We drew new tents and haversacks. Old clothes were condemned by the brigade inspector.

Sept. 23. The weather changed from rain to thunderstorm and to rain again. Ditches were dug along the company streets in order to keep them free of water.

Sept. 24. Early in the morning a heavy rain continued, afterwards the sun shone uncomfortably warm. More clothes were sent after, as the whole army had not been supplied, and as there was talk of the commencement of another campaign.

Sept. 25. Company inspection in the forenoon, and brigade inspection in the afternoon. The weather was very chilly. The road had been interrupted again by the enemy's cavalry, and no trains were running. We suffered nothing, however, as we had pleanty of provisions.

Sept. 26. The parade announced for thr 22d took place to-day. At 11½ o'clock A. M. the brigade assembled and marched to the headquarters of the division, where the division was assembling and where we were received by the delightful music of the 33d Massachusetts regiment. Thence the division moved with music to the parade ground, northwest from the city, where we arrived at 1 o'clock P. M. The parade was before Gen. SLOCUM, the first one held before him. Gen. SLOCUM was well satisfied with our movements, although they were not as they would have been on even ground; the ground was very uneven and stony, and not in the least suitable for a parade ground. Late in the evening we returned to our camp.

Sept. 27. Lieut. SMITH, of company A, and a private of company I were discharged on account of disability. A captain of our regiment was discharged for not obeying orders.

Sept. 28. The 17th army corps, commanded by

F. P. BLAIR, had a fight with the enemy; the wounded were brought to town. An engineer regiment, heretofore stationed at Chattanooga, arrived and camped next to us.

Sept. 29. Had a drill for the first time since the commencement of the campaign—company drill in forenoon, and battallion drill in the afternoon. In the evening rations were drawn, among which sourkrout and onions something unusual and quite a delicacy with some.

Sept. 30. We spent the day drilling. A perfect flood of rain came down upon us in the night, inundating everything, as our camp was situated low, and as the shelter tents on our houses offered little or no resistance to such rain, and were in the water up to the knees.

Oct. 1, 1864. At sunrise the day promised fine weather, in consequence a great part of the men went to the ditch, close to camp, in order to wash the clothes completely covered with mud and dirt by the rain. We had been told that no work was to be done by us, and that we could wash to our hearts' contents. Some of the men had commenced the work of washing, while others were preparing to commence, when orders for marching came, and to be ready in an hour. This caused a general dissatisfaction, and the wet clothes had to be stowed in the knapsack. All grumbling did not alter the situation, and a short while afterwards we were on the tramp to town, through which we passed and went in the direction of the Chattahoochee river, 10 miles from Atlanta. This was about the time when Hood made his last march to Chattanooga and Nashville, and our brigade was ordered to the river to protect the bridges, and prevent the rebels from getting in our rear. At the commencement of the march we suffered very much from the heat, but afterwards thick and dark clouds darkened the sky, and before we had come half way to our destined point, a thunder storm and rain broke upon us, threatening to drown us. The roads were inundated and at places we marched knee dep in the water. On such days a soldier wishes himself far away from his regiment, to his home, and don't see much fun in "soldiering" then But the rascally rebels were the cause of all our trouble and privations, and we knew that we would not find rest until they were subjugated. Tired, worn out and completely saturated to the skin we reached the river after dark and very late. Company D of the 129th Illinois regiment was ordered to remain on the south side of the river on picket duty, while the balance of the brigade crossed the swollen river, that was rising very rapidly. Lieut. Col. FLYNN of our regiment remained with company D during the night and selected a hill for our resting place. After having stationed the necessary guard our men hunted boards in the darkness from the creacuated rebel camps, while some erected the shelter tents, and all things done we sought rest. The night continued rainy, illuminated now and then by a flash of lightning, and we fell asleep amid the rushing sound of the rising river. About midnight we were awakened by a tremendous noise and crash.

Oct. 2. In the night both the railroad bridge and the bridge for wagons had been swept away by the river; we were thus compelled to remain in our place on the south side of the river until a bridge could be erected again. Our provision wagons were on the other side, and provisions had to be brought to us in skiffs. In the afternoon a pontoon bridge had been made and we returned to our regiment. Scarcely arrived at our place we heard a heavy artillery fire in a westerly direction; afterwards we heard that KILPATRICK had surprised the enemy at Sweetwater creek and had a fight with him. Preparations for a new railroad bridge were made, and laborers were brought from Atlanta. Gen. ROUSSEAU, who was stationed at a creek between Tullahoma and Murfreesboro, had to retreat to the latter place as the enemy's cavalry was threatening him with superior numbers. It was reported that Gen. LEE was retreating from Richmond.

Cc'. 3. A division of mounted insantry arrived on the way to reinforce KILPATRICK. We made our camp more commodious and many men pitched their tents, while others felled trees for log cabins. In the afternoon we erected breastworks, while the rain was drenching us.

Oct. 4. Gen. SHERMAN arrived here to look at the position of our brigade; from him we received orders to pack up and move to the south side of the river, and entrench ourselves. Large bodies of troops left Atlanta for the north, to prevent HOOD from cutting off our communication. The 20th army corps under Gen. SLOCUM remained and held Atlanta and the river. The work on the fortifications went on incessantly, as the report was that LEE was marching from Richmond to Atlanta with a very large force.

Oct. 5. Long trains of wagons with ammunition and provisions passed north, stragglers sought their regiments as they passed by yesterday, and from morning until night the road was covered with wagons and with men. Our brigade continued to build houses, as the cold weather was approaching and as our common "pup tents" became too cold without a fire. The report was that Big Shanty station, between Dalton and Marietta, had been taken by the enemy, and that the main rebel force was in the Allatoona mountains, 40 or 50 miles in our rear.

Oct. 5. Danger must be near as we received orders to finish our breastworks quickly and to hold this place at all hazards. The "duds" we left at Lookout mountain had arrived a few days ago and were given to the owners to-day; some of the owners were dead, others in the hospitals wounded. The work on the railroad bridge progressed finely. A report was current that 900 rebels had been surprised in the act of tearing up the railroad in our rear, and captured, and compelled to build the road again by our men.

Oct. 7. The enemy had injured the road very much and the last few days no trains had arrived from Chattanooga, and those that had come did not return but brought lumber to Atlanta, and from Marietta to the river. We had learned from a bearer of dispatches from THOMAS to SHERMAN that the former had met the enemy under HOOD on the 5th in the mountains, and had whipped him again and compelled him to run away. The chief of artillery of SHERMAN's army had been killed in this fight. Our loss had been smaller than that of the enemy. We were working on our fort; new and more clothes were drawn, as the whole army was to be clothed anew before a move could be made. The pickets of the 105th Illinois regiment, the only one on the north side of the river, were fired at by guerrillas.

Oct. 8. We erected another line of breastworks, and were now enabled to hold this place against a superior inimical force. Shoes were drawn. The weather was cold. The report was that we were to remain here during the winter, which report others doubted, as SHERMAN would not allow the enemy to build new entrenchments that we would have to take in the spring; something would be done this winter that would break the enemy's neck, and Charleston and Mobile would be the next points from which to drive the rebels. A courier from Marietta brought the news that the enemy was coming to the river in strong force, between here and Marietta. The wagons sent to that place returned, and we got ready for the enemy but waited in vain.

Oct. 9. It was Sunday and the first actual day of rest we had seen for some time.; the weather was cold. The railroad bridge over the river was finished and a locomotive tried the strength of same towards evening. Major HOSKINS left us and went on a furlough. The first mail was sent off to-day.

Oct. 10 A courier of our brigade, sent to Atlanta with orders, was surprised by guerrillas on his return, robbed of his arms and horse and shot by guerrillas. His friends found the corpse lying on the road. Since the capture of Atlanta the bushwhackers had had become very numerous and bold, and even showed themselves in daylight along our picket line, or they would attack our provision wagons, kill the driver and steal the mules. The work on our fortifications was continued and our regiment worked by reliefs the whole day.

Oct. 11. A strong detail of members of our regiment and the 102d Illinois was sent to Marietta to-day. The road had been in disorder for some time and we could not get anything that way. The cattle the army used near Atlanta, had to come afoot from Chattanooga and perhaps further yet. A lot of cattle for our boys near Marietta was driven to the river by our men. The cattle, perhaps formerly fat and sleek had become so lean and poor in consequence of the long march and of the lack of food, that there was nothing left of those who had gotten so far safely and not died on the road, but skin and bones. Nevertheless they were butchered, and divided among the regiments, who, if they did not get meat, at any rate got bones! It was reported in camp for certain that Richmond had been taken—a wish whose fulfillment all desired—but unfortunately most thought it to be but a camp rumor.

Oct. 12. The days became colder and fire-places were erected in our huts both for cooking and heating purposes, so that hereafter we could have warm rooms.

Oct. 14. Our camp became continually safer and

stronger against an attack. Trees were cut down, the branches left in their places, and the trees placed in position with the branches extending from us. It was quite a task to climb through the branches and reach us, and an attack would have cost the rebels hundreds of men, before they could have reached us, in case they had ventured it. Sixteen miles of railroad track were torn up by the enemy, who had also taken Stevenson, Ala. We received the first mail to-day for many days.

Oct. 15. The trains did not leave here and no mail matter was received. We drew whisky and for five days rations. Were very anxious for news from Gen. Thomas, but as the telegraph had been destroyed, con'd get none, and but seldom heard of what transpired be'ween him and the enemy.

Oct. 16. As we had nothing to do, the day was spent as everybody pleased. The company commanders delivered over the muskets of the dead and wounded.

Oct 18 Four hundred mules, brought from Atlanta and neighborhood to the river to the pasture; had been guarded day and night by detachments of a regiment of *pontoniers*. They were surprised by the rebels, and nearly all the mules taken away from them. The men must have been very careless, as seven of them were taken prisoner; otherwise it would la e been imposs.bl for the enemy to get away with his booty, as our line of pickets was not more than five hundred steps distant from the pasture. Had the guard given the alarm in time, there would have been help on hand soon enough to prevent the capture of the men and mules. Our regiment was ordered to be ready for a scout and foraging expedition in the morning. As the scout was to be out for several days, we drew rations for five days and got forty cartridges extra. The general talk was that pay day would soon be on hand, a time hoped for, as most of the men were out of money, and us their families in the North with needed money very much. Signs of rain were plenty.

Oct. 19. We were awakened at four o'clock A. M., prepared a hasty breakfast, packed up everything we needed, and at seven o'clock we commenced our march. We were accompanied by a large number of wagons, that were to be filled with rebel property. This foraging expedition was the first since the commencement of the campaign, and we knew that nothing could be found within twenty miles of the railroad on either side, everything having either been taken by the rebels or our men, or been destroyed by both in order to starve the other out. We calculated on a day's tramp of twenty-five miles before we could commence foraging. We crossed the river and went along its northern shore upward in an easterly direction to the neighborhood of Rossville, about twenty miles from our camp, where it was said there was a good deal of corn left, and where we could remain for the night. We had no hindrances on our march excepting the bad roads; there could be no doubt that rebels had been near, but they did not annoy us but let us move on without resistance. Tracks of the enemy were to be seen frequently. At a house where we rested for half an hour for dinner, a skull was found; and in the afternoon we passed the ruins of a cotton mill, burnt by KILPATRICK, where formerly hundreds of laborers found their daily bread. The larger part of the inhabitants of Rossville had not yet fled, but this unexpected visit on our part frightened most of them who fled; very seldom a man was found at home, but women and children the more, who informed us that there were many armed rebels near, to be upon our guard, etc., but wished in their hearts that we were with the devil or somewhere else, and who would, if possible, act treasonable to us. After posting a strong line of pickets, eating supper, we retired to rest. The night passed without alarm.

Oct. 20. A short distance from our quarters, which we left very early in the morning, while our pickets remained at their posts, we found corn, and commenced filling our wagons. We did not inquire about the proprietor of the corn, as the rebels did not ask our permission when they tore up the track over which our corn was carried. Without any trouble we loaded our wagons with the products and property of the slave barons, and with filled wagons we commenced our return at 2 o'clock P. M. We were told that a brigade of rebel infantry, having learned our whereabouts, was preparing to cut off our retreat. Whether this was true or not, we did not find out, as we did not return the same way we came, but used a better though circumferous road to Marietta. About dusk we arrived safely to within about two miles of the city with our booty, without having seen a single rebel, where we camped for the night. Our arrival near Marietta and the Kenesaw had created quite an excitement and to some extent fear, as our troops stationed there could see our numerous camp fires without being able to tell who we were. The troops in town had to remain behind the entrenchments, guards were doubled, signals went up from the Kenesaw every moment, while we were making merry over our booty, ate a hearty supper, and laid down to sleep, giving the garrisons at the two above mentioned places permission to guard us.

Oct. 21. Early in the morning we took breakfast, marched to the city, where they had found out by that time who we were. We went straight through and pursued our way to the river. Between Marietta and the river we passed a place, where the night before a train from Atlanta had been thrown off the track, robbed and set afire. Two soldiers had been killed and buried near the spot where they were overtaken by death, while others had been wounded. The locomotive had been completely shattered and several of the cars were burning yet when we passed. In the same night another train was fired upon by the rebels, but passed through safely, as the rebels did not get time to tear up the track before the arrival of the train. About four o'clock P. M. we reached our camp at the river, where everybody was surprised at our speedy and safe return.

Oct. 22. We received a large mail, that had passed here yesterday for Atlanta. The weather was rough and windy and we remained most of the day in our huts around the fire. There was a rumor that two companies of our regiment would be ordered to Vininy station, btween the river and Marietta, to guard the track—but the rumor was without foundation.

Oct. 23. We were busy writing letters; a foraging party was ordered to be ready to-morrow morning for another "trip to the country." The paymaster had arrived, and we were to be paid off tomorrow.

Oct. 24. Although the much hoped for payday had come, yet the men, selected from the various regiments for the foraging party, broke up and went in the direction of Rossville again. Our regiment was paid off in the afternoon—for the first time after our departure from Nashville.

Oct. 25. Those indebted to their comrades paid them off and preparations were made to send the principal part of the money received yesterday home. Had nothing to do besides this.

Oct. 26. It rained day and night. The foraging party, sent out day before yesterday, returned; they had been fired at several times by the enemy, but suffered no loss, and brought three young rebs, of 17 or 18 years, along as prisoners.

Oct. 27. The rain continued. As we were not allowed to go home to vote, we had a mock election to-day in the regiment. LINCOLN received a large majority of the votes, and McClellan a minority.

Oct. 28. The track had been repaired and trains were running regular to Chattanooga. To prevent further destruction of the track, we had to patrol the track day and night half way from here to Atlanta. This was a very dangerous piece of business, but the track remained undisturbed. We received orders to pack up all unnecessary things and be ready for marching at any moment. We did not know our place of destination, but from rumor we learned that our tramp would not be northward, but southward— deeper into the heart of rebeldom. A larger number of men from our regiment and other regiments of our brigade were ordered to be ready for another foraging tour. From this order we came to the conclusion that our march to the south had been postponed, as a foraging party could not return in less than three days.

Oct. 29. At 5½ o'clock we went on our foraging tour the same way as the first time, and reached Rossville before dark. Here we camped, confiscated pork, chickens, geese, flour, honey etc., on the plantations near, for our supper, that vanished in our hungry mouths in a good style. Afterwards we retired to rest, having made a march of 20 miles.

Oct. 30. In the neighborhood of our camp we found plenty of forage for man and beast; the wagons were filled with corn, calves, geese, hogs, chickens, turkeys etc., to such an extent that the drivers were fearful of not being able to return to camp with such a load. The wagon-masters could hardly prevent the men from putting a still heavier load on. Cows and oxen were tied to wagons and taken along, while the men carried a load of chickens, turkeys or geese, and stuffed the haversack with eggs, apples or potatoes. After we had loaded twenty government wagons, each one drawn by six mules, we commenced our retreat and camped 9¼ miles from Marietta, near Bush mountain.

129TH ILLINOIS INFANTRY REGIMENT. 117

Nov. 1, 1864. After we had lightened our haversacks by taking therefrom a substantial breakfast, we started and reached Marietta at 10 o'clock A. M. Our march in the morning had been very rapid, though the day was hot, the officer commanding us (belonging to the 26th Wisconsin) had not allowed us the necessary rest, and in consequence of these circumstances we marched slow in the afternoon, and did not reach the river until late at night.

Nov. 2. The day was rainy and cold. The evacuation of Atlanta was continued briskly; all the cannons captured there were sent north. The talk was, that our next promenade would be to Savannah, Ga., and the sea coast.

Nov. 3. Rainy and cold. Atlanta had not been yet evacuated.. Trains of wagons, belonging to the 15th army corps, stationed at Marietta and Kenesaw, were ordered to Atlanta and there to load with ammunition and provisions for our expedition.

Nov. 4. All superfluous clothing, such as we could do without on the march (nobody knew where to except our generals), had to be packed up to-day and sent north, as "we would get to a warmer country." Everything being done, we were ready for the promenade, and the day of our departure was fixed for Monday the 6th. Our corps, the 20th, formerly belonging to the army of the Cumberland, was now attached to the army of the Tennessee.

Nov. 5. We received special notice to be ready to-morrow at an early hour, and all things from the smallest to the largest to be taken along, were packed up. Several persons had, before getting this order, even packed up their tents, expecting to use them again at some future time; but for the coming night they were shelterless and got along badly. The 70th Indiana regiment belonging to our brigade, heretofore stationed at Landtown, had been ordered here and arrived towards evening, to go along with us on the promenade. Everything and everybody was ready for the march, and we laid down for the last time in our bunks, warmed by the blazing fires in our fireplaces, and intending to spend the last night by a glorious sleep. At 12 o'clock at night we received orders not to march to-morrow, but to await further orders; the cause of this postponement we could not find out, but supposed that Atlanta had not been evacuated sufficiently, and that the town would be burnt entirely before the army left it. Guards were detailed for the morrow, when we went to rest and slept until awakened by the reville of the drummers.

Nov. 6. Another part of the wagon train of the 15th corps went to Atlanta, and as troops and wagons were coming and going to Atlanta troughout the whole day we began to doubt that our destination would be southward. The evacuation of Atlanta was continued, however; trains left empty and returned heavy laden, a sure sign that the evacuation of the city was progressing in earnest.

Nov. 7. Two government wagons on the road between the river and Atlanta, with but a small guard, were attacked and taken by the guerrillas. The latter jumped from the brush, stopped the mules and took them and two soldiers along. This happened but a short distance from our picket line. Another attack took place shortly after, on a single picket on the Atlanta road. The picket belonged to the 79th Ohio and was stationed behind a tree, and did not see the guerrillas until ordered by them to surrender. He refused and fired at the rebels who in return fired at him; when assistance came, the man had been shot in the abdomen and robbed of his gun and ammunition. The shots fired at the flying guerrillas killed one of their horses, without hurting one of the enemy. The wounded man was brought into the hospital and a strong patrol under Lieut. Col. **Flynn** was sent after the guerrillas, but it was useless; they had got too far ahead before our men left, who could not find the daring enemy. The report was that the enemy was 30,000 strong between Atlanta and Stone Mountain, but the report was not believed, as Hood was too far in the rear with his army, and the report that LEE was coming from Richmond had proved untrue. Strong guerrilla bands might have been there. The weather was rainy.

Nov. 8. Rebels showed themselves again between the river and the city, but the men sent after them could not find them. All was anxiety about the result of the election in the North, though we did not doubt that President LINCOLN would be re-elected. Atlanta had not been emptied yet, and trains were arriving continually with freight from there, which was sent north. All the inhabitants left had to leave town, many went north, but most of them south, swearing that they had no friends in the north.

Nov. 9. We were alarmed by a heavy cannonade in the direction of Atlanta, which commenced between 8 and 9 o'clock A. M. and at first we believed that the evacuation had been completed and the burning of the town, blowing up of the forts &c., had commenced. This was not so, but the enemy, 15,000 strong, had attacked the 1st and second divisions and the two brigades of the 3d, stationed there, and quite unexpectedly at that. They had heard enough of the existence of this force in the neighborhood, but never credited the report until convinced of its truth to-day. The enemy had approached from the south side, where our former entrenchments were, but as pickets had been posted a good distance from the fortifications, was given in time, that our men could shoulder their arms, form and take their position, before the pickets were driven in and the enemy make an attack. Our artillery and infantry was ready for the enemy, who lost all courage after having made three desperate attempts to take Atlanta, losing many men every time. Our men said they took it as playwork to keep the enemy back. The rebel loss was 500 killed and wounded, all falling in our hands, while our own loss amounted to scarcely 100. The enemy, seeing the foolishness of his attempt, retreated and we expected him at the river; no enemy came in sight. The day for our departure was fixed to-day on the 15th of November, and we were ordered to have in our haversacks on that day the following provisions: Coffee for 10 days, sugar for 5, salt for 10, bread for 2, and meat for 2 days. Every man was to have 60 cartridges. Our knapsacks to contain 1 shirt, 1 pair of drawers. 1 pair of socks, 1 woollen and 1 India rubber blanket and the shelter tent. If a person took more and the bundle became too heavy, and the person was found tired and resting, the knapsack was to be searched by the provost guard following every brigade, and everything except the things allowed to be thrown away.

Nov. 10. We could hear nothing from the enemy, not even a guerrilla showed himself on the road to Atlanta. Neverless the wagons going to and coming from Atlanta were strongly guarded.

Nov. 11. Two wagons going to Atlanta and guarded by 12 men, attacked by 6 bushwhackers, and the mules taken. How this was done I dare not say, but suppose that the guard (that did not belong to our regiment,) lost the courage and that the rebels were regulur devils, or else they could not have got away with 12 mules, guarded by 12 men In camp everything was quiet and everybody patching and repairing his clothes for the march.

Nov. 13. The telegraph brought the news of the re-election of ABRAHAM LINCOLN to the Presidency of the United States for the next four years. In consequence there was general rejoicing, but seldom a man could be seen with a bowed head, angry because Little Mack had been beaten by Old Abe! The destruction of the railroad from the river to Marietta was commenced with, the track taken up and the wood work placed in piles and set afire, the iron rails were put across the pile and soon the heat soon softened the centre and the rails became crooked. The fires as far as the road run straight and as far as the eye could see, created a fine sight for the looker on, and filled the air with smoke. It was said that Marietta and Rome had been burned. Guerrillas came forward again, but did no damage.

Nov. 13 The army of the Tennessee, our corps excepted, began to move; part of the 15th and 17th corps passed by us during the day on the way to Atlanta. We remained quiet but received orders to be ready to-morrow. The new built railroad bridge was set afire to-day, but the fire had to be quenched again to prevent the pontoon bridge from burning up too. The railroad on the South side of the river was destroyed by our brigade, the same road that we had captured, protected and partly built ourselves. The road could be of no further use to us, particularly after the burning of Atlanta, but the rails could have been used in repairing the roads that we were going to destroy on our promenade to the sea coast. We burned the wood and iron, and made destruction complete. The day was on hand for our departure, and we were to go to Atlanta first, where the 20th, 14th, 15th and 17th army corps were assembling; the 4th and 23d corps that had been with us in our summer campaign, were to go to Gen. THOMAS and assist in whipping HOOD out of Tennessee. At 9 o'clock we had left our work and at 10 stood ready for the march, after having set fire to our quarters and huts— all burnt down with their contents. At 5 o'clock P. M. we reached Atlanta and camped on our old place. The city burned and smoked for several days, and the flames finished what the shells, shot and bullets had left undone. One foot after another was blown up with a tremendous noise; also many large brick buildings. In the evening we drew the prescribed provisions, whereupon we sought rest.

Nov. 15. The 14th army corps had arrived and the hour for marching been fixed at 9 o'clock A. M., and until then we assisted in the work of destruction. Thick volumes of smoke rested over the city, now and then wafted aside by the wind, and the roar and thunder of the explosions, of the falling timber, &c., struck every one with awe at the grand scene of destruction. The following further orders had been given before 9 o'clock: 1. Every army corps had to pursue its own road, that the army could advance the quicker. 2. The different divisions had to change daily in the lead of the corps; for instance, if the 1st division led the corps to-day; the 2d had to to-morrow; and the next day, the third. 3. The 2d brigade of the leading division had to do guard duty for the whole corps in the night; every brigade thus knew, when it was its turn to do guard and picket duty. Every soldier was allowed to take along what pleased him, but had to remain in the line, and was punished if he left the line to go plundering on his own hook. Mills and manufactories were to be destroyed by designated persons or foraging parties. Foraging parties had to start daily to the right and left of each corps and fetch provisions for man and beast, whereby rebels in the distance suffered as well as those near the line of march of the different corps. These parties were at liberty to fetch along cattle, sheep, hogs, horses, mules, and everything that could be of any service to the enemy's army. Gen. SHERMAN assured us in his order that the march would perhaps be a troublesome and dangerous one, but that the victory was sure, as the enemy would thereby receive a blow that would destroy all his hopes and insure us an early peace. Nine o'clock was past after all these orders had been read to us and three cheers given for Gen. SHERMAN, and about 11 o'clock we turned back to the ruins of Atlanta. Our corps took the road from Atlanta to Decatur, with the first division leading, followed by the second, while ours, the 3d, was the last, and made but slow progress, as the first two divisions had not stretched out yet, and as their wagon trains were in our front and got along very slowly. As our advances was slow and the night very damp, several deserted houses along our route were burned, the men came and moved, or slept, until the wagons got ahead apiece and we could advance again. Late at night we reached the small town of Decatur. The inhabitants, at that time quite numerous, seemed to sleep, as all houses were dark and not a sound or voice was heard. Just as our brigade was passing through town a halt was made, and several hours elapsed before we went on. During this halt we cooked coffee and here and there a voice called to the dark houses: "Why don't you come and see who is here?" As every army, so ours too had its bad members, who, in cooking their coffee, kindled the fire as near to the seemingly deserted frame houses as possible, until they caught afire and the frightened and lamenting inhabitants fled from them. Some of our men were softened by the entreaties and assisted in extinguishing the fire, but as fast as it was put out at one corner, another corner commenced to burn until the whole was wrapped in a sheet of flame and became a prey to the devouring element. Several houses were thus burnt down, until guards were stationed through town, who stopped this unnecessary incendiarism. About 12 o'clock at night we left town again, and in the darkness two men were shot by bushwhackers or inhabitants. In the morning it became very cold, and we would have frozen, if the fence on both sides of our route had not been fired and burned by those ahead of us. On several places the heat became so intense that our ambulance wagons had to take to the field. To fulfill Gen. SHERMAN's order to the letter, several cotton presses and gins and mills were fired during the night, and along the whole route to Atlanta the sky was red, while an occasional explosion indicated, that the fire was still raging there We marched and it rained the whole night without stopping, until the sun arose and we halted at a creek.

Nov. 16. We prepared our breakfast, but had hardly time to eat it, before the signal sounded a renewal of the march; tired and worn out as we were, we had to fall in and march. The second division took the lead and the 1st found the rear, with the 3d in the center. The country through which we passed was filled with brush and not inhabited, and we could do but little in consequence. Our advance was slow, because we had no rest the night before, and many fell asleep as soon as a halt was made. We reached Stone Mountain about noon, and a river, called South or Yellow River, in the afternoon. which we crossed and camped for the night in its neighborhood on the road to Social Circle.

Nov. 17. We commenced our march at 5 o'clock A. M., our division in the advance. The marching was quicker and more pleasant, because we had some rest the night previous. The country began to look better, and edibles we found whatever we wanted along our route. From the calves and hogs which we killed by a shot or by the bayonet, we ate only the hindquarters, the balance we left to rot, or for the dogs or buzzards. The inhabitants at home we found in their houses, and not with the militia, not having had time to escape or hide, and as they had never expected a visit from us. Kitchens and cellars were opened and everything of any use to us taken therefrom, without taking notice of the wry faces of the rebels. The houses were left unharmed, as they were principally inhabited, but barns filled with tobacco and cotton, add hay presses and fences, were burned. A member of company A, of our regiment, was shot to-night in the dark, after we had driven a fine drove of hogs from their resting places. The wounded man died in the night, but the soldier that had fired the fatal shot immediately withdrew and could not be punished. At 8 o'clock we camped near Social Circle.

Nov. 18. At F. A. M. we left our camping ground and reached Social Circle at 10 o'clock; as also the railroad building from Atlanta to Augusta to Atlanta and other points. The report of our movement had spread, many inhabitants were gone as well as the goods from the stores. Many of the fugitives, escaping to the right or left fell into the hands of the 15th or 17th corps. Only those escaping to Augusta got off safely. Much property was destroyed here, among which the railroad depot and the railroad track, over which the last trains had come but yesterday and taken the inhabitants to Augusta. The town was plundered completely by our division that remained during the dinner hour and took dinner there. The weather during the day was very hot and the roads dusty. We went into camp at 10 o'clock P. M.

Nov. 17. We left camp as early as usual, and went along the railroad, tearing up the track at the same time, in the direction of Madison. The country through which we passed yesterday and to-day, was poorly provided with water and with the greatest trouble only we got sufficient water for cooking purposes, to say nothing of quenching our thirst. The wells were nearly all dry and where one with water was found it was immediately surrounded by hundreds, not half of whom got the water they wanted. A very large amount of cotton, cotton factories and bridge timber was burned along the railroad. Horses, mules and cattle were brought in by our foraging parties by the dozen. As a general thing we found more edibles to-day than we had expected. A number of rebels that had followed us from Atlanta, attacked our rear guard, but were repulsed with a loss of 5 killed and 13 wounded, while our men lost but 1 killed and 4 wounded. The entire loss of our brigade since its departure from Atlanta amounted to 20 men, mostly stragglers or foragers. Negroes, both male and female, came to us to-day in masses, having heard near and far of our arrival. As their masters and mistresses had set the good example of running away, they followed suit and came to the saving Yankees, loaded down with bundles and babies. At 1 o'clock we reached the beautiful town of Madison, where the blacks welcomed us most kindly and sincerely. Having heard that a world of blue jackets was coming they had come to town and lined both sides of the road, slapping their hands and one "God bless you!" followed the other from the mouth of our recipients. After we had arrived in the center of the town a hollow square was formed by our brigade, around the court house, and our band began to play. The negroes, and even whites, came flocking to us now, and in such numbers as to rob us of the "look" at the contents of the stores and court house. The negroes, music-loving creatures as they were, commenced dancing and jumping and shouting, saying "God bless the Yankees," and swearing that this was the happiest day of their life. They saw that the Yankees carried no horns as had been told them, and that they did not have holes through their shoulders and hitch them as oxen to a government wagon, but that they treated them more kindly than their masters did. They got over these lies of their masters very quick, and according to them there were no better men living than the Yankees. While resting here, the depot, railroad and a negro prison, (where negroes were tied to a bank and lashed in a most unmerciful manner,) were given to the flames. Many other houses were burned or demolished more or less, After these buildings had been burned, we proceeded $3\frac{1}{2}$ miles further, burned a good deal of cotton outside of the town, and went into camp about 9 o'clock P M. The day had been rainy, and the night was dark and very rainy; but we enjoyed a nice sleep after having had a hearty supper, kindling a fire in front of our tents, and making a bed of leaves.

Nov. 20. We left at 7 o'clock, while the rain continued to pour down and saturated all our things; besides this the road was very bad, so that the march to-day was a disagreeable one. The country was mountainous and inhabited less than around Madison. As our brigade was in the advance and foraging parties were not allowed to go ahead of our line, we got plenty of chickens, honey, &c., for our supper and breakfast, and edibles were plenty and good, and the opposite of the right kind. As the marching was slow in consequence of the bad roads, we halted half an hour for dinner, and went into camp at 3 o'clock P. M., two miles from the town of Eatonton, which place our cavalry occupied during the night. The male inhabitants had all fled, and the females put on no smiles at our approach. We passed one house, in front of which a number of ladies were standing and waved their handerchiefs, as we defiled past them. Whether they were actually glad, or whether they only showed gladness to save their property, we never learned. About dark we heard artillery firing going on in the distance, and we supposed that either in or near Milledgeville we would come in contact with the enemy. The reports went that Milledgeville had been fortified and strongly garrisoned, that reinforcements were arriving there daily, and that Gov. BROWN was gathering the militia there, determined to hold the place as long as he could. In the afternoon the rain had ceased, but commenced again about dusk and continued throughout the night.

Nov 21. At six o'clock we broke camp and reached Eatonton, where we were received by the black inhabitants with great enthusiasm. Their joy had no bounds when we burned their prison, and "God bless you all" was heard on every side. They came to us, shook our hands and burst into tears when they saw the flames rise from their house of torture. The depot and the railroad from Gordon to Eatonton was destroyed by us and the troops on our right. The bridges and water tanks along the road suffered the same fate, as we had everything our own way. The roads were in a worse condition than ever before, and in some places actually bottomless. The afternoon was fine and the marching became more pleasant, until at 4 o'clock we had tramped 10 miles and camped on a field of a rebel quartermaster. Our brigade was camped near the plantation villa. The plantation was well stocked with hogs, geese, chickens, turkeys, etc., but all became a ready prey to the hungry Yankees. In the house we found flour, molasses, meat and salt; in fact everything to make us feel comfortable and "at home." In a few hours the beautiful, well stocked plantation had been completely ruined, while the Yankees were busy in camp cooking, roasting and baking the rebel quartermaster's property, using for their fires the fence rails they found very handy. The distance from here to Milledgeville is only 40 miles, and we expected to reach that place and fight there to-morrow. We camped on the Oconee River.

Nov. 22 We broke camp later than usual, as we had to cross the river, the bridge of which had been burnt. A pontoon bridge was ready at 8 o'clock in the morning. We crossed at 10 o'clock, as we formed the center of the corps to-day. The day being rather chilly the marching went fine and quickly through the mountainous country. We did not take time to prepare dinner, but rested occasionally. As we neared the city and heard no firing we supposed that our advance had taken the place and that the enemy had again given "leg bail." We approached the capital of Georgia rapidly and soon reached the newly erected but evacuated rebel fortifications. From the first house of the city a white flag, the signal of surrender, was flying. We marched through the city by the music of our bands to the South side, and camped on the Northern shore of the Oconee river. In the city great stores of guns, lances ammunition were found which the retreating enemy had left behind, not being able to take it along. Many of the guns were burnt by us, or with the ammunition thrown into the river. The state prison was torn down and the men sent there on account of their loyalty, set free. Most of the white inhabitants had gone off with Gov. Brown and his brave militia, and many of the stoutest and healthiest negroes had been dragged along. Among those that remained there was a general rejoicing and all were willing to divide everything with us. With the negroes left here by their masters to starve some of our boys divided their last cracker. The night was very cold, and we missed the fence rails very much, that had until now been always "so handy."

Nov 23. We remained in our camp and looked in town and neighborhood for provisions, which we found plenty. Many valuable things, dug away in the ground by the owners, were disinterred and taken along or destroyed. Houses whose inhabitants treated us well and showed no rebel spirit, were protected and as a general thing, Milledgeville suffered less than any of the towns we had visited, but all things, that could be of any use to the enemy, were destroyed, The day was clear but cold.

Nov 24. We left Milledgeville early in the morning, and crossed the Oconee river for the second time, but this time on the regular wagon bridge, left unimpaired by the retreating enemy. The bridge was burned after our last wagon had crossed. On the Southern shore we remained for some time in order to let the 14th corps that had gotten on our road, pass by. This corps took another route sometime in the afternoon, and thus each corps had its own road again. As we were getting into the swampy part of Georgia, our progress became very slow, passing as it seemed from one swamp to the other. As the bridges had been destroyed by the enemy we had to build new ones, by which much time was lost. Our pioneers had to build the bridges on what was left of the burnt ones, or build pontoons. Where wood for the bridges could not be gotten we had to wade through the swamps, sometimes up to our knees. The men were completely disgusted with such state of the country, but all wishes brought no relief. On the contrary, the situation became worse, as the swamps increased and the provisions decreased. A short distance from Milledgeville the pineries commenced, and the ground was either covered with long grass or the needles from the pine. Here the inhabitants had gathered pitch in Summer season by taking the bark off on the sunniest side, cut a hole near the roots, whence issued the pitch made fluid by the sun. Many of the trees, where the pitch had collected and become hard, were set afire by us, both to give us light and to keep us warm when we halted. After having spent the first night in the swamps, every man wished it to have been his last there, and persons who have been in that country will agree with me when I say that this wish was based on a good reason.

Nov. 25. We remained in our position until 11 o'clock A. M., because several bridges had to be erected before we could advance. The day was cold and marching quite a task, as we had to pass through swamps or cross them on bridges; and as a consequence our advance was very slow. We marched in a straight line towards Augusta, although we were yet a good distance from that city. The enemy believed, as we did also, and as the rebel papers reported, that Augusta was to be besieged, and all preparations were made there to make it very strong. All able bodied slaves, not cut off from Augusta or Savannah, were ordered there to work on the fortifications. The families, who had fled there for safety, were again threatened by new dangers from the never resting Yankees. At 3 o'clock P. M. we reached a river, not bordered by high banks as other rivers, but by swamps, filled with brushwood, or cypress trees, and standing water. The road on which we were was dry, though it led through the swamp, and we would have no trouble, if the Georgia State militia and Wheeler's cavalry had not burned the bridge over the stream. The enemy was hidden on the other side, fired on our advance, and then fled again. Six of our men were wounded. We had to halt and await our pontoon train; night, however, commenced, and we remained in our position after the bridge was done. The 14th corps that had again gotten on our road, passed by us during the night and crossed, in order to get out of our way. A heavy cannonade was heard on our right and we learned afterwards, that the 15th and 17th corps had met quite a resistance in their endeavors to cross the stream.

Nov. 26. At 7 o'clock we crossed the stream, our brigade formed the rear guard of the corps. After the whole corps had crossed we had to wait until the pontoon bridge had been taken up again and the train got in motion ahead of us, before we started. The obstacles were very numerous, the rebels had not only destroyed the bridges in the country, becoming more swampier as we advanced, but had thrown trees across the road at places where the bordering swamps were deep. We were compelled to clear away these obstructions before we could advance. The enemy awaited us behind these obstructions, and as soon as our cavalry or advance guard of infantry came in sight, shots were fired, and more or less men killed or wounded. Thus we worked our way along very slowly and advanced but a few miles before dark, while our advance guard was continually skirmishing with the enemy, and sometimes had great trouble in driving the daring enemy from his dangerous hiding place. We were on our way to Sandersville, and only a few miles distant from it, but did not expect to reach it, in case the obstructions should be as numerous in the afternoon as they had been in the morning. Our first division had lost several men by the enemy's shots. As we approached Sandersville, the country became higher, the swamps less numerous and the road more dry, so that our men could pass round the obstructions, or the trees could be cut away from the side to make room for the wagons to pass. The enemy had retreated to the the town to make another halt there. We reached Sandersville about 5 o'clock P. M., sometime after our advance guard, that had quite a skirmish with the rebels, losing two men. The enemy had fled, after the meeting house, in which he had lodged himself, had been completely riddled by the balls of our men. We camped here for the night. The inhabitants had fled, taking all the property with them they could, as the armed rebels had told them that we would hang all the citizens and burn the property, but this was only partly true, as we hung no citizens, but only those that were trying to hang us. We only burned the houses that were deserted or whose inhabitants had betrayed us, or murdered our men. Edibles were scarce around Sandersville (water, however, plenty,) but what we did find was carried along. We were forced to do this, and it was also Gen. SHERMAN's intention, to take everything from those rich slavocrats, and to let them know the consequence of war. They did not expect us, or else HOOD would not have gone to Tennessee.

Nov. 27. Before we broke camp at 8 o'clock, an event caused the loss of a member of our regiment. A member of company A had a rusty rebel musket and thrown the same into the fire, not supposing it to be loaded. The shot went off and wounded a memmember of company F, in the leg just below the knee. The wounded man limped a little and then fell down, and was carried to the hospital train, after the surgeon had exmained the wound and stated that the shin bone was hurt but little. The bullet wounded another member of the 2d brigade slightly. The country through which we passed to-day was level and sandy, but very seldom interspersed with swamps. Our road was but seldom obstructed by the enemy, and our march was faster than yesterday, however. We had to do great work yet before sundown. After reaching the Savannah and Macon Railroad we destroyed a good portion of it on our right and left, while the corps further on our right did the same, as also the 14th on our left. After we had burned as much of the road as possible, we continued our march to Davisboro, several miles distant. The trees along our to-day's march presented a different appearance from those we had seen heretofore. The pines, with their needles, had disappeared mostly, and trees with beautiful large foliage were seen, every branch or twig bedecked with the so-called Spanish moss, hanging down from some a yard or more long. The trees looked very romantic and presented a view entirely new and very interesting to us After sundown we reached Davisboro, and camped. The country around here was very even and clear, and as the night was very dark the thousands of camp-fires presented an interesting sight, surrounded as they were by thousands of men holding pans, coffee pots, or other cooking utensils in their hands, and preparing their supper. Everything wore a pleasant aspect and as the troops were in the best humor, enlivened as they were by the music of the various bands and the cheers and jokes of the men, the looker on would not have supposed that these men were in the midst of the enemy's country, surrounded by countless dangers by swamps and enemies. The camping ground of our brigade was close to the Canuchee river.

Nov. 28. We left camp at 7 A. M., and as the sun was very hot, the marching in the deep sand was very difficult and troublesome. We had with us a number of rebel prisoners, among them a rebel Colonel and quartermaster. In the afternoon we reached the Ogeechee river, where our advance guard was fired at by the enemy, who had burned the bridge before our arrival. We were compelled to go into camp here, while the enemy was being driven from the other shore, and the pontoons put down before night commenced.

Nov. 29   Our division formed the rear, and in consequence our turn to march did not come until 1 o'clock P. M. The first and second divisions passed by, but their advance was slow as eight bridges beyond the river had been destroyed by the enemy, and had to be repaired again; the swampy road also caused a good deal of delay. After we had crossed, the pontoons had to be taken up, and our brigade had to wait until this was done. It was reported that a strong force of rebel cavalry was threatening our pontoon, and we marched a good distance from the bridge to keep the enemy back, while the bridge was being taken up. Our regiment had to stand picket in the direction from which the enemy was expected; half the regiment remained in reserve. We were all stationed behind large trees, about 10 paces apart, kneeling or standing, looking watchfully in the direction the enemy was to come. Not a word was spoken and the only noise heard was the shaking and rustling of the leaves and branches of the trees overhead; what were the thoughts of those silent watches? At such moments the reflections and thought take man's mind as by a storm. The sun had long gone down behind the trees and hills, and still we were watching, in vain expecting the enemy. The pontoon bridge had been taken up, we left our posts and returned to our brigade, already in motion, and went after the balance of the corps ahead of us, and which by this time must have been in camp resting. The night was very dark and the country become more swampy as we advanced, until at 8 o'clock we reached a place we might properly have termed "father of swamps." We had to pass through, though it would have taken the whole night to do it, as we could not remain in the place where we were, feeling, as we did, our way along by the roots of the trees. The trees thrown in by the column ahead of us had disappeared below water and mud, and not a bit of them was to be seen. Those fellows who unfortunately missed trees and sunk down between the logs, were indeed to be pitied, but on account of the darkness nobody could help them, and they had to get out the best way they could, assisted by their muskets or a club kindly handed them by a passing comrade. Luckily many of us had hatchets or axes, and we cut pieces from a dry pine, using them as torches, when we got along a little better. We reached the end of the swamp at last, though our clothes did no longer look blue but had pounds of the Georgia swamp-mud and water on them. But the end of our march was not here, much as we desired it, and though it was after 10 o'clock, we reached Louisville about 11 o'clock, and we could see despite the darkness, that the place had been partly burned by our cavalry. We continued our march for several miles, when we found the balance of the corps encamped in front of a large swamp. Bridges had to be erected ere we could advance. We went into camp about 12 o'clock, desiring a little rest after the "promenade" we had made that day. Our provisions were rather scanty to-day, and many a fellow went to sleep without eating supper, either because he had nothing to eat, or else because he was too tired to prepare something to eat. Our foragers had returned for the last days as empty-handed as they had gone out. The swamps and neighboorhood contained nothing for the subsistence of an army. Our provision wagons contained provisions for but a few days, and we would have to make them last until we could reach Savannah. And even after reaching Savannah, we did not know how soon we could get close enough to Fort Pulaski, to get provisions from there. Four of our men were taken prisoner to-day, and shot by the enemy.

Nov. 30. As announced yesterday we remained in our position near Louisville, Ga., and many of our boys preferred to go to town, and look after provisions, as to remaining in camp and cleanse their clothes. But the efforts of these provision hunters were mostly fruitless, as but a few returned with a half starved, lean cow or hog; flour or potatoes were not to be found, having either been taken along by the flying inhabitants or destroyed. The rebels thought they could thus starve us in the swamps, by preventing our rapid progress by burning the bridges, and by destroying the necessaries of life. And it did look a little that way, and our situation was by no means a pleasant one. The men were hungry, very hungry and begged the quartermasters continually for food, but these were rather stingy with the provisions, hoping that the country contained enough subsistence. But this hope did not satisfy the craving stomachs of our men, who now went to the Colonel's and higher officers for food, and even threatened to take the bread and meat from the wagons, if withheld from them. The threats became more numerous until at last we received rations for three days with the order to make them last ten days. More than one Illinoisian now wished himself back to the flesh-pots of Egypt. The day was hot and the work on the road through the swamp in our front was carried on with vigor, so that by night part of our corps could cross to the other side of the swamp. We remained quiet. Near Louisville there was some firing going on, and some said that our men had found some cattle or hogs, others said that skirmishing with the enemy's cavalry was going on

December 1, 1864. We left camp at 11 o'clock A. M., and went into the direction of the railroad running from Augusta to Millen where it forms a junction with the railroad from Savannah to Macon. This was the only road upon which reinforcements could be brought from Richmond to Georgia to stop our advance to Savannah. As we supposed that there would be fighting to do on that road in case the enemy had received reinforcements from Richmond, we hurried as fast as possible in order to prevent the enemy from getting a firm hold before our arrival. Cannon shots were heard occasionally, fired by our cavalry in front at the enemy, who refused to let our men cross the swamps. The day was very hot and the swamps were as frequent as ever, besides this the heavy clouds threatened with rain, so that our situation became anything but pleasant. We crossed the Cedar swamp to-day, meeting less difficulties than we had expected; the swamp was well filled with water. Several members of the 102d Illinois regiment of our brigade, were sent out to hunt horses, which the inhabitants had commenced hiding in the swamps; some of the men were taken prisoners at a house, by rebels dressed in Federal uniforms. The rest escaped. Several members of our regiment were found missing at night. We got some provisions from the neighborhood, and the hope dawned, that, with the sweet potatoes and hams of the rebels in the neighborhood, and our rations of three days (which had to do us for ten, and which had decreased in an astonishing style in the last two days) we would not starve at least for the present.

Dec. 2. We broke camp at 6½ o'clock. The greater part of the 14th army corps and a large number of KILPATRICK's wagons was with us, and our division had to guard them. The 14th corps had given us the guard of its train to enable it to move the faster. This corps advanced to 20 miles from Augusta, threatened the city and compelled the enemy to bring reinforcements from Savannah. Our troops then turned and went in the direction of Savannah, but before the enemy had time to return the reinforcements to Savannah on the same road, the track had been destroyed in the mean time by the other corps. Swamps we encountered as ever, and also the usual obstructions, but we had become accustomed to all this somewhat. Our provisions began to fall off in a frightful manner, and fortunately the country through which we marched to-day, was inhabited but little.

Dec 3. We broke up our camp at 6½ o'clock A. M. The whole army was drawn together closer as we neared the above mentioned railroad, and were expecting some fighting. Our road had been blocked on many places and we were compelled to drive the enemy from behind the obstructions before we could advance. These small fights always caused loss on our side, as the enemy always had in a sure mark at our men and never fired, until they got within easy range. Where the rebels did not impede our progress, the deep sand did, and the march to-day was very troublesome and annoying. Houses had been burnt more or less every day as we had advanced, particularly in the afternoon and towards night, and in looking to the right (where the 15th and 17th corps were marching,) or to the left, (where the 14th corps was marching,) the pillars of smoke arising high, told us where those corps were, and whether we were ahead of or behind them. At noon we reached a large and, from all appearances, well stocked plantation, where we halted for dinner and where our brigade received orders to go to the railroad, a mile distant, and commence the work of destruction. The inhabitants of the plantation consisted of negresses who informed us that their master had fled with his male slaves, victuals, &c , several days ago, without leaving them anything to eat, and that they were left to starve and knew not what to do, not having a bit to eat. We found about fifty bushels of pea nuts that had till now served the negresses as nourishment, but were now mostly taken by our famished men. The smithing and wagon shops, with contents, were burned up, as well as the dwelling house of the proprietor, before we left the place After leaving the plantation our brigade went to the left, while the other two brigades of our division went to the right, to points on the road, to commence burning and tearing up the track, until the brigades would meet each other. We reached the road at 3 o'clock P. M., without meeting any resistance. Having stacked arms and posted pickets some distance from the road, we went to work; half of the regiment remaining at our arms, while the other half was at the work of destruction. As soon as a few rods of the road had been destroyed, the party at work was relieved by the party guarding the arms. Fence rails were set afire and the iron rails laid across, whereby the latter soon became bent and unserviceable. The road had been repaired by the rebels but a few days before, as we saw from the newly made ditches on both sides of the track, not supposing that we would be there so soon. After we had destroyed our part of the road, we left in the direction of Milan, until we reached the main road to Statesboro, leaving Milan, where our pioneers were bothered very much, on our right. The troops on our right moved through Milan, burning it more or less. Night approached, and in vain we looked for our camp; our men were completely worn out, not having had enough to eat, and were hardly able to keep in the ranks. The march was continued, though many, not being able to go further, fell by the road and in the hands of the enemy, or died in the swamp. The march continued until 12 o'clock P. M., when we reached the camp of the first and second division, but had to go a distance further for a dry camping ground. More than half of the members of our regiment had remained behind in the swamps, completely worn out, and did not come up until the next morning, shaking and trembling, barely able to stand straight, much less to prepare food. They fell down on their arrival, to rest and sleep, but had scarcely laid down when rain set in and those of us able to do it, went off after some branches of trees to cover our things with and protect us from the rain. Some of our men, more wise than others, after feeling the first drops of rain, looked at the clouds, and being satisfied that "the rain would not last long" went to sleep again, and had the pleasure the next day of carrying and wearing their wet clothes and blanket.

Dec. 4. At 4 o'clock A. M. we were awakened, and at 6 we turned our backs on our short resting place, hoping that to-day's march would bring less difficulties and hardships. We felt something like men just recovered from a severe illness, who have to rest and gather strength very frequently. Forming the advance guard, we were the first to go into camp, it is true, but also, in case we met the enemy, the first to get the fire, requiring, perhaps, more strength than we had, to drive the enemy away. Shortly after we left, heavy firing was heard on our left, in the direction of Waynesboro, where the greater part of KILPATRICK's cavalry and the 14th corps were, and where we had learned the enemy was entrenched. The 14th corps made no attack on the enemy, but in stead, passed to the left of the city, and was only harassed by the enemy's cavalry, exchanging rifle and cannon shots only with him in order to compel him to "go along." We approached nearer to the Savannah river, and the black population, that always took our part, informed us that the rebels were srongly entrenched there. We did not believe it to be Sherman's objct to attack the enemy where it was unnecessary to do so, as the wounded and sick could not, on a march like ours, receive the necessary aid and comfort, and as every fight reduced our ranks, and as every mile of march brought us deeper and further into rebeldom. Our communication with the North was cut off, and if our friends at home placed confidence in the reports of the rebel papers, prophesying the sure and certain destruction of the Yankee corps in Georgia, which reports must have given especial pleasure to the Copperheads—then indeed we would have been lost. At noon we reached a river, swelling at so rapid a rate that it was impossible to cross on pontoons, and had to remain there for about three hours. The corps on our left had caused this inundation by destroying a mill and dam above, not knowing that thereby our advance was stopped, until we could lay our pontoons and cross. Neither enemy nor swamps were as troublesome to-day as the sand, through which we had to march. We saw beautiful pineries, and as the day was very hot it was a pleasure to stretch out in the shade of the pines and rest for a short while. The inhabitants had all fled. Victuals we got more to-day than on the day before, particularly sweet potatoes and sugar; sometimes we quenched our thirst with the sugar cane growing there. Seven members of the 70th Indiana were taken prisoner when out foraging. We went into camp at 8 o'clock P. M., after a long march in the sand and heat.

Dec. 5. At 5 o'clock we left camp on the way to our destination. The day was clear and promised to become hot. The country was level and sandy, adorned by beautiful pineries, with high grass covering the ground. To-day we reached the first rice plantation, but the rice, yet in the straw, had been burnt. We found rice, however, in the houses of the blacks, and hereafter rice and sweet potatoes was to be our main nourishment and food. It was reported that 3,000 rebel cavalry was in our rear, endeavoring to destroy our trains, and catch our foragers at work in the neighboring houses. Not satisfied with capturing them, the rebels would hang or shoot them, or cut their throats and leave the dead corpses lie unburied on the ground. Such horrible deeds were continually committed, although we treated the rebel prisoners well; yea, they were better treated than our own men, for while these had to be satisfied with crackers and pork, the rebel prisoners in Nashville and Chattanooga had wheat bread and fresh meat for food! Some of our men who had strayed from the ranks, were even driven back into the swamps to starve there! The inhabitants had all fled, endeavoring to escape the just punishment for their rebellion against the best government in the world, and those few that were captured testified that most of the rebels had despaired of their cause as lost, but did not intend to give up as long as they had one man left to fight. The enemy cannot have had a great deal of spunk, as we noticed in all the skirmishes and fights, in which they generally retreated soon after the commencement, leaving the dead and wounded in our hands. Each defeat or retreat of the rebels gave us new courage, and we went into battle sure of victory. About 3 o'clock we encamped near Springfield, 8 miles from the Savannah river.

Dec. 6. We left our camp at 5½ o'clock A. M., and advanced rapidly through the sand, the day being cool and pleasant, and rested but seldom in the high and inviting grass under the beautiful trees. The march in the afternoon was slower, as the road had been blocked by trees which had to be cut away before we could advance. At 4 o'clock our to-day's march ended and we camped about 35 miles from Savannah. Fighting was expected on the morrow, as the enemy was between Springfield and Savannah, and as we expected to reach his first entrenchments. The sooner we got to these entrenchments the less time the enemy got to fortify himself, and the easier was the task of taking the works. Rice we found but little, meat none at all, and as we had none in our haversacks, we had to get along as well as we could, hoping to get some to-morrow.

Dec. 7. We left camp at 7½ o'clock A. M., having drank coffee, but without eating anything. After marching several miles we came to a large swamp, called by the negroes Abonesor swamp. The bridges in places where a road could not be made had been burnt, and trees felled across, making it impossible to pass but through the water, or to cut away the trees. We had a sufficient number of pioneers and laborers to do the latter work quickly, enabling us to follow our cavalry, that had gotten through the water. Our brigade was the first of infantry that had to cross, and our position not a safe one, as the cavalry had reported the enemy in force in front, and had had a sharp skirmish with the rebels. The enemy would no doubt make a stand at Springfield, a few miles distant. But we were always ready to "do good to our enemies," and after we had passed the dangerous spot, we examined our guns, put them in good order and loaded. The road became more passable now, though on both sides the swamp continued, until at once we were again stopped by a blockade of the rebels. At a place more dangerous than any former one, they had burned the bridge, and felled trees across every way, so that there was nothing else possible for us but to go through the water. The trees obstructed our way for about a quarter of a mile, and we could not see whether the rebels were on the other side of the blockade or not, but supposed they were. Our situation was most critical as we had to advance, and if the enemy lay in wait for us we must fall an easy prey to his shots, it being impossible in such places to keep in order. Our officers proposed to go through the swamp, and our men obeyed readily, knowing that the officers would die with and for the men, who had the greatest confidence in them. We got into the water and mud nearly up to our waists, and haversacks and cartridge boxes became wet, but after we had passed the first bad spot, the walking became better, and soon we were on dry land again. Not a shot was fired at us, but instead of this the town of Springfield was in our immediate front, the court house but a few steps distant. We marched to the court house and gave three hearty cheers for the Union, stacked our arms, and went on a hunt "for something to eat." Geese and chickens were found in abundance and confiscated without "a show of law." For catching chickens we generally used our ramrods—everywhere men were seen chasing the screaming birds, or here and there a soldier was seen tumbling in his endeavors to catch "the derned things," amid the laughter of his more lucky comrade who returned to his mess with a load of fowl. Many of the inhabitants had hidden their valuables in the swamps, these we found and either taken along or destroyed. The men found hidden were taken to headquarters. The country around Springfield is very level. On our right heavy firing was heard. We camped in the place, 27 miles from Savannah, and 12 miles from the first rebel fortification in our road. The night was rainy and cool.

Dec. 8. Our marching hour had been fixed at 9 o'clock A. M., but as the 14th army corps and the two first divisions of our corps had to pass us, we remained quiet. The weather was very warm and we had great trouble to keep in the shade, as we had been forbidden to enter the houses. Early in the morning a heavy firing commenced on our right, and in our front the fire became very rapid at noon; from this and from the slow advancing of the troops defiling past us we supposed that there "was something the matter." Edibles were very scarce, all chickens had been eaten, and nothing else been found. Some little rice we found in the husk, and which we ground in self-made wooden mortars, with clubs, and let the wind blow the husks away; this was all we got. A lot of government mules and horses that had become unserviceable, were killed to-day so that the rebels should not get them and use them again. We left camp at 7 o'clock P. M., prepared for an unpleasant night's march, knowing that such marches were very tiresome, even on a level road, on account of the many missteps in the darkness. We marched a couple of hundred steps and then halted, as the troops ahead of us had done. Another march of a few hundred steps, and another halt took place. The men became restless and demanded either to sleep or to march; and some left the ranks in search of food. The houses of Springfield became less with every halt; at first the near houses were set afire, then those further off, until finally a guard was sent out to put a stop to this incendiarism. We marched a few hundred paces again and again kindled fires but now with fence rails. While resting here, cavalry which had till now been in our rear, hurried past us in such numbers that we thought there would be no end of it. Cannon firing was going on in our front continually, and we were now certain that the enemy was the cause of all this delay. We commenced the march again and advanced some distance into a swamp, where the horrors of the night commenced. Two army corps with their trains were ahead of us and had made the roads literally bottomless, in some places trees had to be felled across and fence rails thrown in the road to make it passable. The night was "wrapped up in darkness," the enemy a few miles ahead, behind his entrenchments, from which we were to drive him in the morning,—no provisions were on hand, nor was there any sign that to-morrow there would be some,—instead of getting out of the swamps on dry land and hurrying to our destination, we were here "stuck in the mud," and getting in deeper as we advanced,—the night march and the last "fast days" had enervated and weakened us:—in fine, it seemed, as though every thing had conspired our destruction just at the time of reaching our resting place, Savannah.

Dec. 9. At 7 o'clock A. M. we reached the camp of our advance, where we prepared breakfast, consisting of nothing but coffee. The provisions on our wagons were "done for," and we were told that there was no bread for us, nor would be until we had reached Savannah and had opened communications. This was poor consolation for our empty stomachs, as hunger is unpleasant even without such hardships and marching, and doubly so with them. But all grumbling could not alter the case. After a rest of half an hour we proceeded, protecting the train of the entire corps, while the first and second division went on by roads to outflank the enemy entrenched on the main road. In consequence of the swampy country our advance was very slow again, and the necessary fodder for the mules was wanting, as well as the food for the men. Our foragers returned without a single ear of corn, or piece of straw. The cannonade in our front commenced early in the morning, became very heavy about noon, but decreased gradually until it ceased entirely. At 7 o'clock P. M. we again got into a swamp, but as there was "plenty of water," we camped. We laid down without supper, but were awakened afterwards and got sweet potatoes and pork for breakfast. The swamps had became less in the afternoon, but as the country was as level as a floor, we knew that we had not passed through the last one yet. We encamped 17 miles from Savannah, and immediately after we had gone into camp, signal rockets went up several times on our right, and were answered from headquarters. The night was cold.

Dec. 10. We left camp at 6 o'clock with the intention either to take Savannah to-day, or else get close enough to put an end to our daily marching. The blockade of trees had been removed principally during the night, and soon we reached the fort, whence the enemy had been driven yesterday, and whence had proceeded the heavy firing heard for the last few days. Here our division halted again, in order to let the other two divisions that had returned to the main road, defile past us. About noon we reached the Charleston and Savannah railroad; the destruction of which was commenced without molestation. Our division did not participate in this work this time but went on straight towards the city, after having found a good road. Not long afterwards we heard the enemy's cannon bark at our advance and saw on our road a rebel fort. The enemy opened on us with shell from the fort and batteries on the right and left of the fort, doing but little injury and not in the least affecting our steady advance. Finally, we halted and the regiments, that had heretofore marched by the flank were drawn in line of battle, and perhaps it was the object of our commander to make an attack on the city immediately, as the enemy's force could not be a large one. Our prisoners had been brought from Milan to Savannah and compelled to work on the entrenchments and even to shoulder a musket against their old flag—it was our purpose to liberate these. Our regiment, under Col. CASE, was ordered forward as skirmishers and to advance until further orders. The order was obeyed with alacrity, and soon we moved forward through thick underbrush and thorns in the pines, without a single shot being fired at us by rebel infantry. We could not explain this any other way than that the enemy's intention was to get us within easy range, and then pepper away at us to kill as many as possible. We expected this and were prepared for it. We advanced until a swamp prevented all further progress, from the other side of which the enemy stationed there now opened on us. The enemy, being secure behind the swamps, answered three or four times to our shots, but all balls went overhead, as at Atlanta. An attempt to wade through the swamp was not made, and would have been foolish and hazardous, as we afterwards found out on measuring the depth of the water. As a further advance was impossible without any "further orders," the line of battle behind us was withdrawn out of range of the enemy's balls, and went in camp. Our regiment remained on picket duty until 8 o'clock p. m., when we were relieved by other troops, and spent a rainy night, expectant of the things tomorrow.

Dec. 11. The weather was rainy and cool Early in the morning the cannon of the enemy opened on us, and several 32-pound shells had the audacity to fall down in the midst of our camp, bury themselves in the ground and explode, without, however, doing any damage. A bloody day was expected, but as the order to advance did not come we remained in camp the entire day. The first division of our corps, being near the Savannah river, destroyed a rebel transport boat. The enemy's armed vessels, defending the city, commenced to shell our troops lying nearest to the river, in a most unmerciful manner. but did no damage as our men protected themselves from all shots. But few rifle shots were exchanged, as our pickets had been prohibted to fire without seeing an object worthy to fire at. Our food consisted of rice cooked in water without salt, and tasted excellently, as an empty stomach is not very particular, and as coffee, sugar and rice were the only things we had. The communication with Fort Pulaski could not be opened as long as the rebels held Fort McAllister, between us and Fort Pulaski, and before we could get victuals, so much needed by us.

Dec. 12. The day was very cold. Preparations were made to construct a road to Fort Pulaski, and to capture Fort McAllister. A trial was made to lay pontoons, over which provisions could be brought from South Carolina, but rebel vessels prevented it. One of the rebel vessels that had got too close to our land batteries, in the endeavor to destroy our pontoons, was compelled to surrender with crew and arms. As we expected an attack we had to be prepared for it; but the rebels seemed indisposed to cross the swamp and visit us, supposing no doubt that they would have to pay their visit as dearly as we would if we crossed. We began to fell trees and erect breastworks during the enemy's inactivity.

Dec. 13. The enemy had filled the swamp in our front with water, and even inundated the road through the same, by cutting the river dam, and thus put an attack by assault out of question. The water was very deep, on some places 6—7 feet, besides this torpedoes had been put in, so that, had we ventured in, we would not only have been in danger of the canister and grape shot of the enemy, but also of the torpedoes and rifle balls. The swamp extended away to our right, and it was as impossible for the other corps to cross, as it was for ours. Nevertheless the building of a bridge across the swamp was commenced with after sundown in our front. The enemy heard the chopping and felling of trees between the two picket lines, and opened a heavy fire on our pioneers; but the swamp was low and the balls went mostly overhead of our workmen; nevertheless they were glad when, a little after 6 o'clock, the enemy's canister fire ceased, and when they could continue the work with less danger. In camp we were busy with our breastworks and had the pleasure of smelling several shells, which were fired very accurately at our campfires; the shells did no harm, as the rustling in the tree-tops gave us sufficient warning to put our heads behind the works, until the howling shell had became quiet after the explosion. The fire along the whole line was livelier in the afternoon than in the forenoon, not only the artillery fire, but also the fire of the pickets. In the night we could hear plainly the rumbling noise of wagons passing through the streets of Savannah and the clocks striking, so that it seemed as though everything was going on the accustomed way in the city, and that it was not besieged by one hundred thousand Yankees. We did not care about the capture of the city at present, we cared more for something to eat, knowing that if we got that soon, the city would also soon be ours. We could then starve the enemy out, as all communications with the country had been cut off, and as his stores cannot have been large, After 10 o'clock the night became quiet. Our cannon that could hardly be brought in position on account of the low and wooded country, had kept quiet to-day. There was talk about the erection of a fort in our front, opposite the enemy's fort.

Dec. 14. The enemy went to work at day-break with the best will with his muskets and artillery, and bullets and balls and shells whistled, howled and screamed all around us. Every shot was accompanied by a yell of the rebel troops, that consisted principally of Georgia militia, and we believed that some good lies had been told them to make them feel brave and persevering, while we kept very quiet. But all shots were waste of powder, only making holes in the air, but not in the Yankee ranks. Communication had been opened yesterday afternoon about 4 o'clock with Fort Pulaski, after Fort McAllister had fallen, and everybody was glad on account of getting something to eat and to wear on the morrow. The fort named had been taken by assault, by part of the 15th army corps, which had done the work so well that fort with garrison, arms, ammunition, &c. had been captured. This blow the rebels in our front must have felt severely, as the firing and yelling ceased almost entirely in the afternoon. We were the merrier in anticipation of something to eat and wear, and that our march to the sea coast—filled with privations and hardships though it had been—had been crowned by success. New zeal inspired our men, who felt able to whip the whole Confederate army, provided their stomachs were satisfied first.

Dec. 15. The train of wagons sent to Fort Pulaski after provisions which was expected back to-day, did not arrive, on account of the bad roads and of the half starved mules drawing the wagons. Unpleasant as it was, it could not be remedied, knowing that the provisions would reach us by and by. We had taken possession of a rice mill on the river, and of the rice we found on a large island in the river. Our whole brigade was busy grinding and eating rice, a dish they always had put aside at Nashville and other places, preferring to buy their victuals than to eating "such stuff." The construction of the bridge across the swamp was continued to-day, as the enemy could nos injure the workmen. The enemy kept quiet until the afternoon, when he again commenced his usual waste of powder and lead; our men had become so accustomed to hear the bullets whistle that they no longer minded them. A member of the 102d Illinois regiment was wounded badly yesterday when on picket, on account of his carelessness for not hiding in his rifle pit. A member of our regiment was slightly wounded in the arm. The firing, generally speaking, was very light. A number of men sent out foraging a few days ago, had not returned yet, and it was supposed that they had been captured by the rebel cavalry in our rear. This cavalry endeavored to catch such parties, and destroy our wagon trains, whenever the train guard was sufficiently small for them. Foragers going too far from camp, were captured frequently, or driven back to camp. A rumor was current that the job of taking the fort in our front by an assault would be ours in a few days, but we could get no positive information from our officers, who either knew no more than we did ourseves, or else were ordered to keep silent. Many of the men considered a successful assault of the fort an impossibility on account of the depth of the water, and did not intend to obey when ordered to advance. The first mail arrived at the headquarters of Gen. SLOCUM, commanding the 20th and 14th corps, and was expected at the brigade headquarters to-morrow.

Dec. 16. From the papers that some of the men had received yesterday, we received the first news from THOMAS and HOOD's armies, since our depaarture from Atlanta. With the greatest joy we learned that HOOD's army had become demoralized and been cut to pieces in the battles at Nashville and Franklin, Tenn. This news caused great joy in camp and it became evident that the Confederate cause was sinking rapidly—that our government was becoming stronger in the North, while its armies were marching through rebeldom, to break the enemy's neck. The news not only gave us joy, but also the assurance that soon we could leave the bloody fields and return to our families—that soon the war, that had robbed so many mothers of their sons, so many wives of their husbands, would be over. A brigade of the first division crossed the Savannah river into South Carolina to keep the rebels there in check, and also to advance far enough so that the city could be besieged from the South Carolina side, or to draw the enemy from the city in this way. But very light firing along the picket line, and the enemy's guns remained quiet until between 8 and 10 o'clock a couple of shells were sent to us, without doing any injury. We were yet busy on our breastworks without being interrupted by the enemy; the building of the bridge was also continued, and the continued silence caused to suppose that the enemy had either retreated or was meditating an attack Neither the one no the other was the case. The enemy supposed perhaps, that we might finish the bridge, useless as it would be for us us long as he remained so close to the water, and could be reinforced at any moment.

Dec. 17. The provisions had not yet arrived and the men began to lose their patience. We spent our time improving our works and camp. Not expecting an early surrender of the city, we made everything as strong and comfortable as on former occasions, when resting on one place for some time; there was nothing wanting but provisions to make us feel comfortable in front of the rebel works on the other side of the swamp. The underbrush was cut away, and only the shade trees left standing, as the days had been warm and even hot. The ground was made level and swept clean with branches of trees; the tents were erected in rows by companies. The enemy did not like this, and sent several shells across to us. We received the first large mail near Savannah, and almost every one got 3—4 letters from friends in the North, who never expected that the letters would reach the address at Savannah. Many letters found no owners who had died in our front or in the hospitals, or fallen in the hands of the enemy. Many of the brave fellows had always stood in our front line and were stretched out by the fire of the rebels. Others were languishing in rebel prisons, gradually approaching the gate of death—hastened on more or less by such murderers as Wirz, of the like of which the rebel army was full, who took especial delight in torturing the helpless prisoners and to make them suffer. How different was our treatment of the rebel prisoners, who fattened on good bread, coffee and fresh beef, to enable them to shoulder the musket again against the very men who provided for them, as soon as they were exchanged. The rebels did everything to drive the workmen from the bridge, and one shell followed the other, but in vain. The night was quiet.

Dec. 18. The weather was very hot and everybody that had time sought a place under a shade tree. The artillery fire of the rebels had hushed entirely, and the picket fire was light. The men were busy writing letters home to their friends, and to let the Copperheads know that all sympathies for the dying rebellion were vain and useless, as we were daily drawing the rope tighter around the rebels' throats, and that we would not return North until the rebellion had been put down and until we were enjoying a lasting peace. A number of volunteers examined the depth of the swamp about 9 o'clock P. M., getting in the water and morass up to their arms, and did not yet get to the deepest places, but returned, satisfied with the examination, and before the water went over their heads. The night was quiet, and we enjoyed a good night's rest.

Dec 19 The weather was hot in the day, but the nights were cool without frost. Letters were sent off to-day. We were busy with our breastworks and camp. Another party volunteered to go into the swamp and were sent out to-night to examine the depth of the same in several places; they returned with the same report as the first party; that the water was too deep to wade through. Thus it seemed as if our Generals meditated an attack through the swamp, as the orders to examine the depth of the water came from them. No firing took place, not even between the pickets who had made peace and were talking, laughing and joking with each other. A suitable place for the erection of a fort was selected by some artillery officers, and to-morrow the work was to begin. The place selected was immediately in the rear of our line of pickets, on the road that we had approached towards Savannah, and where we had seen the fort, opposite which our fort was to be erected. It seemed to be the intention of the commanding officers, that the infantry should go through the swamp and attack the enemy's fort while our artillery opened a most furious fire on the same. This plan would have been successful on dry land, but to cross the swamp (an undertaking to be done but very slow.) when the water went up to and over the shoulder, wetting everything but the top of the head, must necessarily be done slowly, while we were exposed to the enemy's musket balls, shells, torpedoes, canister and grape shot from all sides in our front. The undertaking would have been a fool-hardy one, its success be very doubtful, and hundreds of lives would have been spent in vain in case of its unsuccessfulness. But the attack through the swamp had not been ordered, nor could it be until the fort had been built.

Dec. 20 The enemy used his cannon again and the pickets had commenced their fire again, so that a walk beyond the rifle pits became rather hazardous and dangerous. As our pickets answered every fire very promptly, it was equally dangerous for the enemy to venture from behind his works. A shell exploded where the second division was posted, and ten men were wounded or killed, the shell exploded among the group as it fell, and the pieces flew in every direction. The work on the fort was commenced early in the morning. Negroes were busy doing the earthwork, while our pioneers felled trees and got them ready for use. Another line of breastworks was commenced, for which the trees were felled at dusk. From this we supposed that the idea of taking the enemy's works by assault, had been given up, and that we were to approach the enemy as near as possible, after which our artillery could do its work better and surer. Our wagons returned from Fort Pulaski with provisions and ammunition, and we got the first piece of bread since the 30th November. The general talk was about an assault to be made to-morrow on the rebel works. Some even said that they had heard the order, and the reason for not being communicated to the regiments was that an order had so commanded it, that the regiments would not hear the order until standing at the edge of the swamp, and were ordered to go forward. The enemy ceased his fire at short intervals during the day, but after sundown the cannonade became more violent as the hours passed. The whole swamp seemed afire from the constant flashes of the enemy's artillery. This horrible noise lasted until after 1 o'clock, while the pickets remained quiet during that time and afterwards. At the hour named the silence of the grave reigned, and were very anxious to know the cause of it.

Dec. 21. The greater part of company D of our regiment was sent on picket last night and I was among the men sent. As long as the enemy fired during the night, we remained in our rifle pits. As soon as the fire ceased, one or two of the pickets, consisting of 3, 4 or five men each, were permitted to sleep in the pits for one hour, while the others watched. At last my turn for a nap had come, and I laid down on the bare ground, the root of a tree served as a pillow, and tired as I was, I would not have exchanged my place for a feather bed and a warm room. I was awakened by the sergeant at 4 o'clock, thereby losing half of my allotted time for sleep, and we were ordered to pack up immediately for an advance. We were now certain that an assault on the works would take place, and we expected to be the first ones ordered in the swamp, and draw the first and worst enemy's fire. The whole line of pickets was moved to the road, and here—judge our surprise!—we had to advance, but not through the swamp, but on the road through the same, to a small extent only covered with water. The enemy had fled! We soon reached the enemy's works, from which but a few hours previous a continued spitting of fire was going on, in order to prevent us from noticing the retreat too soon, and to prevent us from hearing the noise of the moving wagons and cannons. In the enemy's fort we found two large siege guns, spiked and unfit for present use. A lot of ammunition had been thrown into the water. The guns found in the fort were not the only ones captured; we found others, small and large, standing in every direction—a certain sign that the enemy did not even take time in his hasty retreat to destroy them, in order to save himself. The entire works with contents were in our hands, and right glad we were that we got possession of them without the expected bloodshed. The city was our next point, three miles distant, and we stopped but a short time in the works. The pickets of the 2d division of our corps were ahead of us, and the first that reached Savannah; we followed after them and reached there about 6 o'clock A. M. Our joy was great, as we had expected a bloody day, but instead we were here safe and sound. The joy of the foreigners and blacks in Savannah was great, and on all sides we heard them say, "Welcome, welcome, we have prayed for you!" Invitations were extended to us by them to go with them to breakfast, and mostly accepted. Where an invitation was refused, it was renewed with another soldier, until some one went along with the good hearted man. Of course there were plenty of others in the city who would rather have chopped a finger off than give to a Union soldier to eat or drink. But we cared little for such fellows, and took what we wanted. About 400 cannons in and near the city fell into our hands, a large amount of cotton, 15 locomotives, (most of them serviceable) and many other valuable things. While we were in the city, our brigade had gone into camp a short distance west of the city, and as we had nothing particular to do here, we went out and joined our commands. A short time afterwards we were ordered to guard behind the same rebel entrenchments at the swamp, where the night before the enemy had been firing at us on the other side of the swamp. The enemy had taken the road to South Carolina, and his rear guard was crossing the bridge, when our advance entered the city. Our advance immediately went to the bridge, hoping to save the same and cut off the retreat of the rebel stragglers in town, but they found they had destroyed it after they had crossed. A number of our prisoners had made use of the confusion which reigned among the rebels, and escaped from their guards, and remained hidden in houses until they heard the enlivening strains of our brass bands in the streets. A number of rebel soldiers, not wishing to go with the retreating army, had remained, were arrested and put under guard. Many of the inhabitants, mostly of the poorer class, had not been able to earn a livelihood for the last few weeks, and broke into several stores the night before, and helped themselves to the provisions.

Dec. 22. The weather was very cold and windy, and as our camp ground was in an open field, which offered no protection from wind and cold, many of our boys went into the city, partly to warm themselves, and partly to see what the rebels had left. Througout the day men could be seen returning with bags of rice, boxes of tobacco, bottles of wine and whisky, clothes and other things, to divide with their comrades in camp. Others had gone to the city, visited families, and talked with them on the present state of rebeldom. They were of course invited to dinner and the political conversation was continued in the afternoon. Our boys spoke of our next march through South Carolina, and said that if the enemy did not surrender before the march was commenced, the whole state of South Carolina would be laid waste and burned, because this state had been the first cause of all the bloodshed and murders. Several vessels of the enemy were compelled to surrender, but our ships could not yet get to the city, on account of the blockade and the torpedoes in the water. The locations of the torpedoes were found out, and red and white flags placed there as a warning for our ships.

Dec. 23. The weather was again very cold, and as we had nothing to do, we went to the city again to have a chat with the citizens, or to get some more provisions. Some of the boys commenced tearing down deserted houses near the city, as at Atlanta, carried the boards to camp, where the erection of buildings was begun, as we found it rather cold here. The inhabitants accused us northerners of being the cause of the cold, as they had never before had such cold weather here. The 15th corps had parade before Gen. SHERMAN and other generals. But the most joyful of all on such occasions were the blacks. Only those that were eye witnesses can form a correct idea about the capers the darkies cut. The sounds of the distant music called the negro from his hut, leaving everything behind them, slapping the hands and dancing as the music approached. In the mean time the music had stopped to draw breath, while the column went steadily forward. Like pillars the astonished darkies stood, sometimes breaking out in a terrible laughter, such as only darkies can, surprised at the regular step of the men and the regularity of the endless column, seeing as far as the eye could reach nothing but glittering bayonets. The music commenced again, and like a flock of frightened sheep, the black crowd rushed after the music, dancing, hopping and slapping their hands. Not knowing what to do after they had caught up to the music, they stopped but those in the rear pushed those in front, who were thus pushed towards the music band. A cramming and jamming commenced, laughter, grins and curses became loud until the city guard interfered, and the frightened darkies dispersed as fast as they had come, being afraid of the glittering bayonets..

Dec. 24. Gen. GEARY, commander of the second division of the 20th army corps, commanding the city, had issued orders prohibiting the soldiers from visiting the city without passes from the commanders of their regiments, signed by by the brigade commander. Only such on duty in the city were permitted to go. This order put a damper on the expectations of many of our men, desirous of spending Christmas Eve in the city, as the members of the 2d division took great delight in arresting members of the other divisions, cherishing angry feelings against them. Another order forbade the soldier to enter the private houses. A good many difficulties were the consequence of this last order between the guards stationed at the houses, and the soldiers visiting the city. The guards had to obey their orders and were punished for disobedience if they did not. But this only increased the hatred against the 2d division, not only of the two other divisions of our corps, but also of every corps at Savannah. We had expected more of a Christmas Eve than we got. The present, Savannah, we got, and thanked GOD for getting it without fording the deep swamps; but we had not yet had time to make jolly over our good luck. So we managed to get up as good a Christmas party as we could, gathered around the camp fire, and one man commenced relating the events of the last year, while we listened attentively, and finishing with an eloquent appeal for our fallen comrades. This was our programme, but scarcely had the speakers began talking, when shots were heard in the direction of the road we had crossed over a few days ago. The officers, supposing an attack on our pickets, called us to arms, and in a few moments we were posted in line of battle. Although many of us laughed at these unnecessary preparations, as no one believed the enemy spunky enough to return, still we were kept in position nearly an hour, until some bright minded commander came to the conclusion that it was Christmas Eve, and the 14th corps was having a little spree in shooting from behind the former enemy's works. Satisfied that we would not be surprised, we returned to our tents, threw our guns away, but our Christmas Eve programme could not be carried through now.

Dec. 25. The men generally were busy building huts with boards, partly taken from houses, and partly furnished to the various regiments. Nails had been collected from houses or taken out of the stores, and nothing prevented us from having more commodious quarters than the pup tents. The hammering, sawing and digging lasted throughout the entire day; how long we were to enjoy the huts after their erection, we could not tell, as rumors of another advance were current, and as it generally had been the case that soon after the completion of the huts we had received marching orders. But as the weather was very cold, we intended to enjoy the huts at least as long as we were here; but few huts would have been built, as every one knew that Sherman could not remain long on one place, if it had not been so unusually cold. A member of our division got in possession of $10,000 in silver to-day, and sold it for paper money, getting $20,000 for it. The man said he had gotten it in the city, but where and how he got it, neither officers nor men enquired. That man made money by the war.

Dec. 23 The weather was cloudy and rainy and the work on our huts continued. We commenced to drill again, and only such men were excused from drilling, as had not been able to work yesterday on account of lack of tools or on account of duty. There was much talk about an early move and many of the men did not resume the work on their huts, after they returned from drilling, placing too much belief in the reports. The rumor became verified by receiving orders to quit the work, and be ready for marching. Neither day nor hour was fixed. The men that had finished the huts after arduous and long labor, were thunderstruck; not being able to comprehend the fact, that all the labor had been done for only two nights' rest in the huts. As they had scarcely drawn breath in Savannah, been at work while there, with tattered clothes and without provisions—all this gave them the consoling thought that the march would be but a short one, and perhaps we would remain here for a couple of weeks yet.

Dec. 27. The principal part of the day was spent with drilling, marching by company and flank, as a grand parade was expected to take place before our departure. There was but little talk about our march-

—11

ing to-day, but we heard that our march would go through South Carolina. It was reported that 5000 of HARDEE's rebel army had been taken prisoner by Gen. FOSTER. It will be recollected that HARDEE commanded in Savannah before our arrival, and retreated to South Carolina; FOSTER moved from Beaufort Southward, cut the number mentioned off, and took them prisoner, although HARDEE was hiding in the swamps most of the time. The news received to-day were very good generally. A flag of truce came in to-day, proposing an exchange of captive officers; the result we did not learn. The Lieut. Colonel of the 70th Indiana was promoted to the Colonency of said regiment, and gave to the officers of the brigade a supper. The citizens of the city held a meeting to deliberate the necessary steps for a return to the old flag. A newspaper, edited by a loyal editor, was issued to-day for the first time. The weather was warm during the day, but in the night cold and rainy. Many of the men resumed the work on their huts, expecting to remain until New Year.

Dec. 28. A thunder-storm commenced, followed by a heavy rain that lasted the entire day. The talk of our march was renewed, and it was generally agreed, that we would attack Charleston by land, take it, and march to Wilmington, N. C., thence to Richmond and compel it too to surrender after a four years' struggle. If this was the plan, the work was by no means a small one, particularly as South Carolina was full of swamps, and as the enemy would endeavor to molest our march and impede our progress as much as possible by blocking the roads and skirmishing, burning the bridges over creeks and rivers, &c. But we had the officers to make the plans and the men to do the work, and were confident of success. We also knew that the whole rebel army, excepting that under LEE at Richmond, was discouraged and could not offer much resistannce. And if LEE had come with his whole army, we could have entrenched ourselves and held our position, until reinforcements could reach us from GRANT's army, following up, if it would be the case, LEE's army as fast as it could advance. Besides this we wanted to get out of the swamps before the Summer heat created swamp fever and decimated our ranks. Such were the rumors, suppositions and propositions on the eve of every move or fight. The rain stopped in the afternoon and the drilling commenced again, in order to get some exercise; we had among us men to be found everywhere that would not move until compelled to, and unless such men were compelled they would not move for hours. After the thunder storm the weather became hot.

Dec. 29. The camp was cleaned and the bits of lumber and branches of trees removed, the company streets swept and ditches dug for the water. The men not busy with this, cleaned their muskets and clothes, as a parade had been announced for to-morrow. In the afternoon some drilling for the parade took place. A rebel transport from England, freighted with clothes for the rebel army, ran the blockade at Fort Pulaski, (the crew not having heard of the capture of Savannah,) and brought us a load of English "neutrality." The crew was taken prisoners. They did not find out that things had changed until they saw at Fort Jackson, (several miles below the river,) the stars and stripes flying from every prominent house and steeple; but it was too late then to return. A number of members of our regiment, I among the number, were sent as guard to the rebel works at the swamp, where the cannon had been left and where the fishing for torpedoes had continued. The night was chilly, but as we were allowed to have fires, we felt tolerably comfortable.

Dec. 30. The morning was clear and cold. The 20th corps had parade before Gen. SHERMAN and other Generals in the streets of Savannah. Everybody able to carry a musket had to participate, and only such as were on picket or other duty were excused. An early move was expected now, as we heard that the parade to-day had been the only thing to keep us back. The fishing for torpedoes along our picket line was continued by men that understood the business. A number of negroes, that had helped in the erection of the works, came to us, and told the cruel treatment they and our prisoners had received from the enemy during the building of the works. The prisoners and negroes had been set to work where our fire was the most violent. They were guarded by rebel scoundrels, and if they became frightened by bullets or shells whizzing, howling or exploding near them, and the work was not done in time, they received 30—50 lashes, and had to go to work again with wounded and sore backs. Our prisoners i. e. captive Union soldiers, half starved, had to work from morning until night despite the insufferable heat, and were guarded by brutal rebels who threatened to shoot or bayonet them if they refused or fainted from weakness. Only those of them that shouldered muskets and promised to fight for the rebels. received better treatment and food. Nevertheless they were guarded, as the enemy knew that the prisoners cared nothing for the rebel cause and would escape the first opportunity they would get. We were aware of this brutal treatment of our prisoners on the part of the rebels, and a negro and an eye witness of these cruelties confirmed these reports, at the same time wishing the slaveholders a place in the deepest pool of perdition. About three o'clock we were relieved from picket, and our relief told us that our division would commence the march to-morrow. In camp no one knew anything about this, and no order to that effect had as yet been published. The 14th corps was still busy cleaning up its camp.

Dec. 31. The noisy sounds of the drums awoke us early, several hours before daybreak, in consequence of the marching orders. After roll call we were ordered to prepare a hasty breakfast, pack up and remain ready for the march. Such sudden order and such unexpected marching made the men in bad humor, and they very reasonably thought, that the marching orders could have been issued a day or two previous, so that the men could get everything in better readiness for the tramp. But the men knew that a soldier has to be ready for any service at any time, and that it looks bad for him to grumble or resist orders. As we had been ordered to discontinue the work on our huts, we could but expect such an order at any moment. The bad humor was soon dispelled and the men went to work preparing breakfast and packing up. Many of the boys gave the assurance never to build any more huts. At 6 o'clock we were ready, and many of the men were about to set fire to their huts, as they had always done, but this was forbidden, expecting that other troops would take our quarters. It was a certainty now, that none but our division was ordered forward, for we had scarcely left our quarters when men of the first division and of the 14th corps, took possession of the huts, who told us that they had not yet received marching orders. This was somewhat consoling, as consequently our march could not be a long one. From camp we marched to the headquarters of the division in the city, stopped a short while, and then went to the river, which we crossed. We crossed the island, about two miles wide, and came to the main channel of the Savannah river, where we halted. No bridge being there we had to wait until one had been erected. The day was windy and cold, and it was feared that by such wind a bridge could not be constructed, it became utterly impossible after the flood of the sea had set in. The work was commenced and continued, until the pontooniers met unexpected hindrances, and had to stop. The enemy had appeared on the other side, seen our work, and fired rapidly until our pontooniers stopped. **A member of** the 105th Illinois was badly wounded. The rebels were protected by the houses on the other side, the stream was very wide, and our bullets could not penetrate the thick boards of the houses. A cannon was now placed close to the shore, and a few well-aimed shells accomplished what we wanted; the rebels fled, and did not return, as our cannon remained in position. A sufficient number of men of the 102d Illinois, armed with Spencer rifles, went across the river in skiffs, and kept the rebels back. The work on the bridge was commenced again, but the wind became more violent, the water commenced rising and white capped waves became frequent, so that all efforts to lay the bridge proved fruitless. As the river could not be crossed to-day, we had the consolation of crossing on the day after, and that we would remain on the island for the night. The following night no one on the rice field there will forget. The ground was loose and swampy; the wind threatened to blow everything away, camp-fires were not allowed, tents were blown down by the storm, and the cold wind threatened to freeze every one's life blood. We have spent many a night in front of the enemy, before and after the battle, more comfortable than this night in the "Sunny South." With all our hearts we greeted the morning sun, as he to some extent at least dispelled the cold, and saved us from freezing to death.

January 1, 1865. Another effort was made to lay the bridge, but the gale made all labor fruitless. We returned to the city where our brigade went on board of a steamer and was dispatched to the main stream, landing on the South Carolina side. From here we advanced four miles in the interior, where we halted on a plantation, and camped. The usual obstructions were found on this short march, trees had been felled across the road in places where it was difficult to remove them, and the bridges over swamp ditches had been burned, many of them were still burning as we moved past them. This proved to us that the enemy was but a few hundred steps ahead of us, and after dark our march was continued prudently and carefully, as our brigade was the first and only one in the State of South Carolina, then as we did not know how large a force the enemy had in our front. During the whole march not a word was spoken, nor a shot fired. The night was as cold as the one before, but we could protect us now by tearing down fences and old houses for fuel, and by making a warm bed of the Spanish moss. We learned here that our march through South Carolina would not be an easy task, as we had but just left Savannah and already met obstructions, that would increase as we advanced. And although all the rebel troops that could be sent against us could not stop our advance, they could at least compel us to move slowly.

Jan 2 We remained quietly on the plantation, the second and third brigades of the division were on the other side of the river, awaiting the completion of the bridge. Many of our men not on duty went around in the neighborhood in search of provisions. It is true, we were at the time not in want of them, but the plundering was continued, as it was our intention not to spare this State. The inhabitants of the interior, the very ones that had commenced and brought on the war, but had hitherto not felt the effects of their own work, were to be punished for their rebellion against the best Government in the world, and made to "feel like war." The work of tearing down the deserted houses was commenced here, the inhabitants had fled, leaving the crippled and very old slaves behind them. These were in a very bad situation indeed, a small quantity of rice had been left them, and sometimes not even that, but their masters had told them that they would now "soon become free." Some of our men got sight at some of the enemy's scouts who took to their heels as soon as the boys in blue appeared, our boys followed them a short distance and then returned to camp. The rebels now turned on their pursuers in stronger numbers, but when our boys halted they kept back beyond the range of our bullets, and when a stronger force went out against the rebels, they fled again. At another point the rebels approached our pickets until fired at, when they ran away. The bridge across the river had been finished, and Gen. WARD, with the third brigade of our division, reached us in the evening. The night was frosty and cold.

Jan. 3 The enemy had appeared in stronger numbers in our neighborhood during the night, so that he could resist small parties sent against him. One and a half mile from our front a rebel fort had been built several years ago, and was now without a garrison. The rebels in our front generally sought shelter there when pursued, as it was more difficult to drive him away from there. As the enemy appeared in our front again, company D of our regiment, was ordered to take possession of the fort (on HARDEE's plantation.) Under the command of Capt. BURCH, we went forward, part of the company on the road, and the other part along its sides. We soon found the rebels and gave him a salute, which they answered and commenced to retreat. We reached the fort without any loss, though fired at continually. We camped near the enemy's works until evening, when several companies of reinforcements came up. The reinforcements were posted as pickets while we went to the mansion, where we quartered in the rooms, using the shingles of an out-house for fire wood. We prepared supper and slept on the floor, half of the company standing guard while the other half slept. On the walls our (Northern) Generals were pictured off in most ridiculous figures, and mottoes and inscriptions under it, that "they would bet a thousand to one that the Yankees would be driven back to Atlanta the same way they had come in double quick, and that they would soon all be dead or in hell." This might have been possible, if our ammunition had not compelled the enemy to advance backwards.

Jan. 4. An expedition, consisting of the right wing of the 129th Illinois, two companies of the 102d Illinois and all pickets on duty, was sent out on the main road to Hardeesville, that was in the hands of the enemy. We moved slowly along the road, some distance behind our pickets, advancing on both sides of the road in the bushes. We halted several times and advanced again cautiously, but no enemy appeared; several horses, however, shot at by our pickets were found dead in the road. We advanced with the hope of meeting and seeing the enemy somewhere to-day. Atter marching some distance we did come near the enemy, to a swamp, the bridges of which had been destroyed or blocked. We heard the enemy felling trees and talking on the other side of the swamp, but could not see him. It was impossible to cut away the trees, as we had no tools, and the water was too deep and dangerous and full of underbrush to wade through. We allowed the enemy this time the pleasure of supposing that he had kept us back, and returned to camp at 1 o'clock P. M. As the sun was hot, we pitched our tents. Late in the afternoon a heavy cannonade was heard in the direction of Charleston, and it was supposed that the 15th and 17th corps, sent to Beaufort, S. C., by water, had met the enemy. Our whole brigade had advanced to the fort on HARDEE's plantation in the forenoon, while the other brigade of our division remained in the old camp ground, where they erected comfortable quarters.

Jan. 5. A number of men of our regiment were sent foraging, met the enemy and commenced firing; the enemy retreated but answered every shot. No one on our side was hurt. Several members of our division were taken prisoners. They had left the camp alone, gone off too far, and were captured by the rebel scouts that lay in wait for them. The men in camp were busy writing letters, others, expecting a longer stay, commenced improving their quarters. We received no mail nor news from Savannah. The night was rainy.

Jan 6. The day was rainy, we drew rations for several days, but no sugar nor coffee. There was a rumor, though disbelieved generally, that our corps would remain in or near Savannah, as a garrison. Our wagons, till now, on the other side of the river, arrived to-day.

Jam. 7. At 8 o'clock A. M., twelve men, under command of a sergeant, were sent to the river to confiscate all skiffs not confiscated. The object was to bring provisions from the river by way of the canal to us. The canal was navigable for small craft, and the proprietors of he plantations along its shore shipped their rice in this way to the river. In consequence of the loose and swampy soil our wagons and mules could bring but very light loads. But all skiffs, so plenty when we crossed the river, had been confiscated, and all hunting was useless. Part of the men got permission from the sergeant to return to camp, while he and the rest of the men remained to renew their hunt for skiffs in the morning. We quartered in a log cabin near the river where we slept soundly until awakened by the hot rays of the sun falling in our faces.

Jan 8 Our hunt for skiffs again proved fruitless, and we had to return to camp without them. There was much talk in camp about marching orders. Several attempts had been made to draw clothes, but in vain, as "the other corps have to be dressed first." These words strengthened our belief that our corps would remain, as our corps needed clothes as much as any one. Many of our men went barefooted, and their clothes were too tattered to commence another campaign in.

Jan. 9. A number of men of our regiment were sent out to catch fresh oysters; in order to get them they had to pass down the Savannah river, that was full of torpedoes to near fort Pulaski, where the oysters were left on the land by the tide. They left camp amid wishes for their success. The rumor that our corps was to remain in Savannah, was again current, and believed by those tired of marching; but the majority were dissatisfied with the climate, and wanted to get out of the swamps into a healthier country, before the summer season set in.

Jan. 10. Our camp was moved and logs for houses brought. Many of the men were rather slow to go to work on the huts, as they had been fooled at Savannah, and as it generally had been the case that soon after the completion of the huts we were ordered away. We received some paper, envelopes, religious books, tracts, thread &c. from the Christian Commission, things much in demand, but very seldom distributed. The weather was rainy and cool. Rations were drawn for three days.

Jan. 11. The erection of our huts was continued slowly, as but little faith was placed in the report that we were to remain. New clothes arrived but not near enough. Some of our prisoners had escaped from the enemy and approached our pickets, and one of them was shot in the supposition that they were rebels. When the others made themselves konwn they were admitted in our lines. A mistake like this, fatal though it became, could easily happen, as none of our men were beyond our lines at that hour unless by permission of the pickets, who of course could but believe the new comers to be rebels. The weather was cold.

Jan. 12. The day was beautiful, clear and warm. In the forenoon the work on the huts was continued. Others were busy cleaning the rice in a confiscated wooden mortar of its husks that were afterwards fanned away by the wind. Many gave a negro some coffee, meat or a finger ring, for which he did this by no means easy work the whole day; and besides the darky also wanted to show his gratitude to the men that freed him from his bondage. In the afternoon the building was stopped, and the camp cleaned and ammunition drawn. The men returned with sixty bushels of oysters, that were in the skiffs and had to be brought to camp in wagons. We were delighted in anticipation of a good oyster supper to-morrow evening. In the city the preparations for a move were commenced hurriedly, and all troops clothed, and the wagons loaded with provisions and ammunition. Our corps needed new clothing very much, ere it could start through South Carolina, where perhaps for months we would not be able to draw anything in that line. KILPATRICK's cavalry had a parade before Gen. SHERMAN in the the city, and many of our men went there with passes, to see it.

Jan. 13. In the forenoon company drill took place, and in the afternoon the haversacks, knapsacks, canteens and shelter tents were inspected by the brigade inspector and the old ones condemned. We received another mail and the news of lietenant HALDEMAN's death. It will be remembered that he was taken prisoner on the 4th of June, 1863, near Richland station, Tenn.; he was kept in prison in Richmond, Charleston and Columbia, S. C. At his last place of confinement he made an attempt to escape, after having erred about in the swamps for several days, he was captured by the enemy, in search of him. The maltreatment and privations were the cause of his death This unexpected news caused sorrow among us, as we all had loved him. The country and the men under his command lost a patriot and a friend. Peace to his ashes! A ship load of women, whose husbands were in the rebel service, and who did not like our presence, was sent to Charleston, considering it the safest place. In our opinion it had been a safe place long enough! Another detail was sent after oysters. The day was clear and beautiful..

Jan. 14. We got firewood for the regiment, and every company had to get its own wood to camp, so that the wagons would be but a short while beyond our line of pickets. We went to a house half torn down to get dry wood, with our wagons. A short distance from the house we espied several butternuts sitting, who as soon as they saw us, snatched up their guns and ran away. They had been reading letters, and were in such a hurry that they left these behind. Not supposing that there were more than three rebels near, we loaded our wagons with wood from the house, and returned to camp unmolested. In camp the rumors of an early move were current again, others said that our corps was to remain. Some were certain that we would move on the 17th inst.

Jan. 15. Another beautiful day. More clothes arrived but not near enough yet. In the afternoon an inspection of all our things took place. Nobody believed that we would remain, but everybody opined that we would move on the 17th.

Jan. 16. A rainy day. We received marching orders for to morrow morning at 8 o'clock. Cavalry crossed the river and moved with the 2d division of our corps to the right of the river. The detail returned with one hundred bushels of oysters, and we had a fine supper. In the evening we drew our rations and clothes for the march to Hardeesville, 10 miles distant.

Jan. 17. We packed up early and left our camp on HARDEE's plantation at seven o'clock, to look around in South Carolina, and see how far the enemy's scouts, of which nothing had been perceived in the last few days, had retreated. Our road was clear and dry, and although leading through swamps, no obstructions had been placed in our way. The men were all carrying a heavy load, their clothes, cooking utensils &c., not wishing to leave them, and as our to-day's march was but a short one. At four oclock P. M. we reached Hardeesville, but the march of only 10 miles had tired us more than many other marches of double that distance. Our utensils did us good service after we had gone into camp. The town was entirely deserted—but one poor family had remained. Towns thus deserted were never spared as the desertion was the best evidence of the sympathies of the inhabitants for the rebels, and had fled from the well deserved punishment due to them. As soon as we had stacked our arms one house after the other was torn down. No fire was needed, but fire could not have consumed the houses faster than we made them tumble. Every house was full of Yankees from top to bottom, engaged in the work of destruction, and every one hurried to get a board to lie down on for the night. The houses reserved for officers quarters alone were spared. The family that had remained were not troubled in the least. A church containing a good many boards was first taken hold of, the sides taken away, the pillars chopped through, and the roof came down with a tremendous crash, amid the yells of the bystanders. In a few minutes not a board of the building was left. Rank treason had been preached from the pulpit in that church! The noise did not cease until late in the evening.

Jan. 18. The Charleston and Savannah railroad, passing but a short distance from Hardeesville, had been torn up completely by the enemy, thereby saving us the trouble of doing it. The rails had been put on other roads, and we were angry only at this for we would not only have destroyed the ties but, also the rails, and made them unfit for use. In the afternoon inspection of our arms and accoutrements took place. The leather had been so often saturated by water since our mustering in, that it had been completely worn out, and was condemned. In the afternoon another camp ground was shown us, and we were busy in making our quarters comfortable. A foraging party sent out returned with but a small amount of provisions, as the rebels had either taken everything along, or destroyed it.

Jan. 19. Salutes were fired in Savannah upon the reception of the news of the capture of fort Fisher, near Wilmington, N. C.. We received the news quite unexpectedly, as Gen. BUTLER had considered the capture of the place an impossibility, and had withdrawn his troops. Since then no further news had been received. Such news had a good effect upon the men, and was the subject of the conversation during the day. If the enemy was not even able to hold such places as fort Fisher, we could most assuredly take Charleston and Augusta. A foraging party was sent out, as we had heard that a considerable quantity of rice had been left in the neighborhood. We started at 7 o'clock A. M. and reached the destined place, about 5 miles distant, and found the rice, sweet potatoes and several head of cattle—the latter were slaughtered on the spot. There lived a family near the place where we got our wood, whose condition would have moved even a heart of stone. The husband and wife were mulattos, though the latter's complexion was but a shade darker than that of any white woman. Both were free and had gathered a pretty good crop for the winter, but everything had been taken by the enemy, with whom and with whose cause they had no sympathy, but were friends to the Union cause. The rough household furniture, mostly made by the husband, had principally been destroyed by the rebels, and nothing was left uninjured but the roof. Two children, the oldest not more than six years of age, belonged to the family, and begged their mother with tearful eyes for bread; but not a crumb of bread had she to give, and all she could do was to endeavor to soothe them by kissing the tears away. The poor ones were left in this condition for the purpose of starving them. Fortunately we had taken our dinner of crackers, meat and coffee along from camp, and we gave some to the starving children, who greedily commenced to gnaw the hard tack. The mother commenced to weep the more, but tears of joy were now flowing, because we had saved her little ones from starvation! She could hardly express her thanks to us, tears suffocated her voice! But we had no time to remain, and left for our wagons, telling the man to come to camp, make his wants known, and he would be assisted readily by our boys officers, as any one of them would readily have divided his rations with the sufferers. He promised to come the next day, but for some reason we never saw the man again. About 2 o'clock P. M. we reached camp and a rain set in, lasting throughout the balance of the day and night.

Jan. 20. The day was very rainy. The third brigade of our division was encamped on rather low ground and the camp was entirely surrounded by water. Empty wagons only, could move on the road, and fence rails and wood had to be put down for the loaded wagons. Nevertheless there was much talk of an early move; as this was the general talk of the day, we began to believe it, as such rumors were generally the forerunner of an advance, and also as it seemed to be the general desire (and the wish is the father of the thought,) to get away from an unpleasant situation. Such days as these always compelled us to remain in our tents, and as it was cold, the situation was by no means an agreeable one.

Jan. 21. The rain had slackened somewhat, and from time to time we could venture in the open air. Our camp was completely under water, even some tents, situated on low ground were inundated. To drain the water to some extent, we dug ditches.

Towards evening the rain ceased. It was reported for certain, that we would advance either to-morrow or the next day, and as we drew rations for five days in the evening, the reports seemed to be confirmed, as we generally drew rations for only three days. It was, also reported that LEE intended another invasion of the North. We hoped that this would be the case, knowing that his departure from the forts about Richmond would be a heavy blow to the rebellion.

Jan. 22 The day was rainy and cool. Many of the sick, that had been left in the hospitals since our departure from Chattanooga, having recovered, returned to our brigade to-day. We received mail, and, as always on such days, there was a good deal of news told about the camp from the "neighborhood of home." About the entire day was rainy and our stay in camp compulsory. The night also was rainy.

Jan. 23. The rain continued, and an advance had now become impossible on account of the state of the roads, which on many places presented the appearance of a lake, making it impossible for man or beast to venture in the water without danger of drowning. The roads were made higher and ditches dug on each side, but as the country was very level, the ditches were soon filled and the water could not flow off. We were very desirous of getting away from here, so we were sworn in as soldiers and not as marines or sailors. As of old the "dry land disappeared," and dry land is the great consideration for an army, having no resting place, like SHERMAN'S. We received more new clothes, but not near enough for a promenade of several months' duration. A rumor was current, that men were to return to Savannah. The night was cold.

Jan 24. The rain had ceased and the air was cold and rough. A foraging party was sent out on horse back, provided with two days' rations, as it was rather problematic whether and where they would find provisions, and as the chief object was to find

—12

out where the rebels had gone to. The men belonged to all regiments and were mounted on the pack horses and mules of the companies, that carried the cooking utensils when the army was moving. Many of them, like the riders, had become so lean in consequence of the imaginary dinners and suppers that the riders were afraid they would return muleless. We received another mail and orders to make ourselves "perfectly comfortable and at home"—in the mud! This encouraging order was no doubt given to make us have something to do and to give us exercise, and to make us overlook the "pleasantness of the situation." Of course nobody believed or even desired that we would remain here.

Jan 25. A beautiful and warm day. A continual rattle of hammers, saws and axes was going on in camp. Our tents were taken away and cabins erected of pines. The men did not know whether they would be able of ever finishing the cabins, but preferred to do something than be idling about; in case we were to remain a while here, then the work would not have been for nought. The foraging party sent out yesterday returned with few provisions; they had not been able to advance very far, as the enemy had shown himself too often, with whom they had exchanged several shots. There was a camp rumor current that the enemy was leaving Charleston and fortifying Columbia and the main roads to Augusta. In the afternoon brigade drill took place before Col. CASE, who commanded a brigade for the first time to-day, Lieut. Col. FLYNN commanded the regiment.

Jan. 26. The day was cold and windy. As a number of men frequently left camp and remained away for a good while, an order for roll-calls five times in the day was issued, and the absentees to be punished. The order was a timely one, and we supposed that marching orders were expected at any moment, and that this frequent roll call would keep the men in camp. Many of the men were busy with their cabins.

Jan 27 We received marching orders for to-morrow, the pioneers started to-day to clear the roads of the trees felled across them by the rebels. The cabins were all done, and the men would rather have remained and enjoyed their work for a few days longer. "Nothing new under the sun,"—we again received marching orders immediately after we had finished the by no means easy task of building cabins. "The good of the country" was our only consolation. Towards evening another order was issued that threw a damper on all our speculations about the new campaign, and caused some to suppose that we were to remain for a couple of days yet. Instead of fixing the hour for marching we received orders to drill in the fore and afternoon, and have our guns ready for inspection every noon. But as our pioneers had left with their tools, we could but suppose that if we did not advance to-morrow we would the day after, and that the march to-morrow had been impeded by something not expected, and had only been postponed.

Jan. 28. Early in the morning we received a large mail, mostly letters that had long been on the way. The weather was rough and cold, and in order to spend at least one night warmly in the quarters we erected fire places. Inspection of arms took place at precisely 12 o'clock at the roll call. Company drill took place in the afternoon. In the evening orders came to be ready at 8 o'clock A. M. to-morrow, for the march, and our expectations were thus verified. We believed this order, as we had desired it, and packed everything after supper.

Jan. 29. We were in ranks at 7 o'clock, ready for the new promenade through South Carolina. The orders of Gen. SHERMAN were read to us, informing us that the march would be a long and dangerous one, but that we would be victorious, and that this campaign would break the neck of the rebellion completely They could be fired only by persons designated for this purpose. A little after 7 o'clock we left camp and marched the whole day very rapidly through a bushy and swampy country, but little cultivated. The few houses along our route, deserted as they were, were burned down by the men designated. After a tramp of 19 miles we camped near Robertsville.

Jan 30. We left camp at 7 o'clock A. M. a wet and swampy one it had been,) reaching Robertsville at noon where we camped. Robertsville was mostly deserted, and but little harm was done as long as our brigade remained, as we did not want to build cabins, expecting that the promenade had commenced in earnest. WHEELER's cavalry had been in the place and was driven out by our advance, capturing one man. The neighborhood of the town was higher and more dry than we were used to; but when we went out in the afternoon after provisions, we had to wade in water up to our ankles, and did not find anything else than water. From here our last letters went by way of Savannah river.

Jan. 31. We remained quiet at Robertsville, making the necessary preparations for our march. Some men, not satisfied with our report that the country contained nothing but water, went out, found water and brought several pounds of beef of half-starved cattle. As there was nothing to do in camp and as we were not allowed to go beyond the guards, most of us were idling about, hoping that the next day would give us something to do.

February 1, 1865. The day seemed to become a quiet one for us, as no arrangements for the march were made; and as we had no orders to remain we supposed that we would, as it had happened before, commence the march towards evening. This supposition kept our men together, and when the provision wagons were unloaded and we received three days' rations, we knew that we were to remain. Company drill took place in the afternoon, and our company D marched and drilled to Robertsville, and there we quenched our thirst with cold water, and returned to camp the same day. The camp ground was cleared of the underbrush, in order to keep the men busy. Late in the afternoon we heard heavy canonnading in the direction of Charleston, though it seemed to proceed from a place close by.

Feb. 2 We left camp near Robertsville early in the morning, moved through the town in a northerly direction, until we halted at a cross-road about noon, where we took dinner. Till here our road had been good, the country being high, but here it seemed to become lower and more swampy, and our pioneers went ahead of us, felling trees in the road for our wagons. The road had been left unobstructed by the enemy, but as we advanced in the swamp, we not only found obstructions, in some places three to four hundred feet wide, but we saw from the blazing fires that the rebels were in our immediate front, and had but just left. The continual galloping to and fro of the orderlies and staff officers, the frequent looking through spy glasses, told us that danger was near. The road the pioneers had repaired for us led in a westerly direction to the town of Lordensville, and as we advanced the obstructions became more frequent, and in consequence our advance the slower. We found more cultivated land between the swamps than near Robertsville and Hardeesville. The male inhabitants had all fled, and only the women and children been left, expecting thereby to save their property from destruction. This expectation was not wrong, as no house was injured, and but seldom one burned, unless the women showed too unbearable a rebel spirit. Nothing was taken from houses where the women and children either ran away frightened or offered everything, except what was absolutely wanted by us. But many of these so-called South

Carolina ladies used worse language and more obscene words to our boys, when they took some provisions, than the roughest and most brutal soldier ever used! On asking some of these females what they thought about the rebellion now, whether they had ever expected us here, and how strong the enemy in our front was, they would answer, that they would never give up, and in case of necessity shoulder a gun themselves to destroy SHERMAN's army, and that the enemy in our front was strong enough for us—in fact, had we believed these members of the "tender sex," it was folly to advance, and we ought to have returned, to escape a certain and most horrid death! But we did not rely much on such talk of the female chivaliers of South Carolina! When we ridiculed and laughed at such nonsense, the females became almost crazy, and to avoid the sight of clenched fists, or hearing of the shameful epithets, we left. They would never, under any consideration, return to Yankee allegiance. Supposing that our Northern ladies would at least have shown the same resolute spirit (of course without clothing their sentiments in such elegant South Carolina language) if the rebels had come to Illinois, we pardoned them in some degree, and hoped that these Southern females would soon form different ideas and learn better manners! While these talks were being held with the "ladies," the road had been repaired, and we advanced again to Lordensville, of which place we were but a few miles distant. We reached higher country again, but as the marching continued as slowly as through the swamps, and as the deserted rebel camps became yet more frequent, we came to the conclusion that our advance was close to the enemy's heels. We soon found out the cause of the delay. Behind the fence to the right of the road, we found the regiments ahead of us in line of battle, and now and then a shot was heard in our front, as they had thrown out pickets, who began to feel the enemy by shots. Our regiment took position to the left of the road and remained quietly behind a fence until the firing became more distant and the enemy's position been found out somewhat. We advanced again about two o'clock, P. M., in the direction of the town, but the more we advanced, the livelier the fire became, a sign that the enemy intended to make a stand this time, and not run as usual. We halted again until plans for driving the enemy had been adopted, who was posted at the edge of a heavy underbrush and swamp, with an open field in front, and who seemed determined to dispute our advance. The artillery opened on the rebels, as the 105th Illinois advanced to join the pickets already skirmishing on the right. Our regiment advanced as support of the 105th Illinois. After we had taken our position behind the latter regiment, while the brigade was posted a short distance back, our ever-ready and courageous Lieutenant Colonel FLYNN gave the the command: "Forward march," and the pickets and we advanced toward the enemy, several hundred steps distant, who had opened a lively fire on us. The artillery continued firing as we advanced, and the enemy gave us a general salute and disappeared in the thicket. We went in pursuit, over ditches and through swamps, sometimes wading knee-deep in water and mud, following the fire of the invisible enemy, until he again lodged at the edge of an open field behind some barricades of fence rails, which we did not notice until but a short distance from them. Our pickets advanced, and receiving a salute from the enemy, we answered, and were masters of the barricades. One rebel, shot in the leg, and not able to follow his comrades, was left and taken prisoner. But the prisoner appeared to be as spunky as ever, stating that he had a Yankee ball in his leg, and being asked if he was tired of the war now, he answered: "No!—himself and comrades would never give it up, and that he would commence hostilities again as soon as his leg permitted him, until the Northern government had been tumbled down."

As the bones were shattered, the leg was amputated on the following night. The firing ceased here, as the rebels had retreated behind the town, of which we took possession, and stopped the pursuit. About dusk the enemy again appeared, when we retreated, in order to draw him after us, and joined our brigade at the swamp. During the night the rebels retreated, too, to a place where he could dream safely of the events of the day. Rebel prisoners and wounded informed us that the enemy in our front was CLAYBOURNE's cavalry, 8,000 strong. Our loss was ten killed and wounded, one from the 129th, four from the 105th, and five from the 102d Illinois regiments. The night was quiet.

Feb. 3d. We left camp about 10 o'clock, A. M., amid heavy rain, that lasted throughout the day. As we had been but three-quarters of a mile from Lordensville, we soon reached this town. The town must have been a wretched one even before the war, consisting of but few houses, either entirely deserted, or inhabited by old, half starved negroes. The enemy had knocked the windows out of many of the houses, and in some of which traces of blood of wounded rebels was visible; no wounded, however, were found. The first division led to-day. The country through which we passed in the forenoon was high, and our march would have been pleasant if the rain had not made the roads muddy and slippery. The houses were inhabited only by females and negroes, the white males being either in the army or had fled. Deserted houses, and beautiful ones among them, containing mostly all the furniture, and stables, fences, farming implements cotton mills and other buildings were burned, and provisions for man and beast confiscated in large quantities. We got everything we wanted, and crackers did no longer suit us; from flour we baked buscuit, that made the crackers unnecessary—instead of pickled pork we ate good hams—instead of resting on rocks and stumps, that had so often made our limbs sore, we slept on downy cotton, better and sounder than any prince in a feather bed. In consequence of the continual rain, we marched but ten miles, and camped in the field of an arch traitor and rebel. As the night continued rainy and as our shelter tents were not on hand, most of our things got wet.

Feb. 4th. After breakfast we started at 7 o'clock, but to our great enjoyment we had to carry our clothes, made heavy by the rain, and as the day commenced clear and beautiful, a long march was to be expected. Many of the men hung their wet blankets and tents around them, in order to dry them in the air; but they soon quit the experiment, as both continually slipped from their shoulders, holding, as they did, in one hand the flour, and in the other the gun. Our division took a side road, to prevent the enemy from making an attack on the balance of the corps and train of wagons. The enemy tried yesterday to get in our rear, but was not cautious enough, and came in contact with the 17th corps, losing ten dead and wounded and ninety prisoners. It was expected that the attempt would be renewed, but the enemy had either got enough by his first attempt, or else he considered it an impossibility to get between us and the 14th corps, that was marching in a straight line with us without being seen. He kept in our front, supposing that we would certainly not leave many provisions in our rear, besides this we continued the practice of burning the bridges as soon as we had passed them. The enemy remained in our front, no doubt to have the first pick of the chickens, turkeys, hams, &c., and to let his sympathizers know what to hide from us. The country was more swampy, and we freqently waded in water and mud up to our ankles. In the forenoon we passed but few and poor looking cabins, where provisions were scarce and where poorly clad women and children were lamenting their misfortune. In the afternoon the country became higher and wealthier, large two and three story buildings, fashionably built, were seen, but almost invariably deserted. These were fired, after the provisions had been taken from them. We were apparently in the most flourishing part of the State, that had never seen the effects of war; but after our column had passed, and each brigade been foraging, it seemed as if a whirlwind had passed over the spot, leveling and destroying everything in its course. In the evening we came in with the 17th corps, and went into camp, after a march of fifteen miles, beyond a small place called Symrna. After an excellent supper of the many confiscated provisions, we went to sleep around the high, blazing fires of fence rails.

Feb. 5th. A quarter after 7 o'clock we were ready for the tramp. The 1st divisions was again in the advance, and it took sometime before it could stretch itself out with the train, and before our turn came. In our camp we could see that we had no lack of meat at present, but which was left behind, knowing that we would get more during the day, and that the country would not be left untouched. The day was cloudy, and the march pleasant; we hurried on to a place fifteen miles distant, where the enemy were said to be entrenched. Foragers, many of them on horseback, were sent out on both sides of the road, as soon as we started, to scour the country for provisions. The plantations near the road were cleared of everything by the columns. A number of houses, filled with cotton, were found and fired, and only those dwellings were left untouched that were inhabited. We reached the rebel works about 4 o'clock, P. M , but the enemy had been driven away before our arrival, by the 15th corps, and we passed the works unmolested. At six o'clock we encamped at Randebee, or sometimes called Rumby River, were we had reached our foragers, that were well loaded with provisions of all kinds, and had captured some horses and cattle.

Feb. 6. At seven o clock we started, and went

through a swamp of a mile in length, on a high and dry road, before we crossed the river. The bridge over the river had been burnt, and a kind of an excuse of a bridge been built across. Close to the opposite shore were the remains of the formerly flourishing Rushfordbridge-village. Whether the town had been set afire by the inhabitants or not we did not learn, as the fire was almost out when our boys arrived there; these could not have been the cause of it. We found two lines of breastworks that could easily have been defended, if the enemy had had any courage and perhaps not been afraid of being outflanked. The swamps in front prevented any other approach than by the road, and this could have been defended easily. Here we remained quiet for a while, and then proceeded, destroying the deserted houses, cotton factories and other buildings as we went along. We saw nothing of the enemy; a division of the 15th corps, however, had a slight skirmish with the fugitive rebels. In the evening, the weather became rainy and cold, and we camped at seven o'clock.

Feb. 7th. We commenced our tenth day's march at half-past seven o'clock, expecting to reach the Charleston and Augusta railroad and the enemy. Shortly after our promenade had commenced, we crossed a very large swamp, sinking sometimes up to our knees in the morass. To make our situation the more glorious, a rain set in, and we were wetted from above as from below. Many of our wagons stuck fast very frequently, and a flood of lashes rained on the poor mules, that were deeper in the mud than the lightly loaded wagons, and could not move until assisted by human hands. Late in the afternoon we came to a line of breastworks built by the 15th corps, and to judge from the bullet marks on the trees and brush, this corps must have met a severe resistance. Here we crossed another swamp, but the road had been repaired by the men in our front, and our troubles were less than we had expected. A couple of hours after sunset we reached the railroad, from which the enemy had been driven, and on which the last rebel trains had left Charleston to-day. Here we went into camp, wet, worn and muddy, after the severest day's march we had so far made in South Carolina. Rebel prisoners that had been captured, had not yet learned that their cause was lost, but still cherished the greatest hopes.

Feb. 8th. We left camp early, expecting great work, but encouraged by the certainty that every step we advanced brought the end of the rebellion nearer. Our work was to destroy all communications of the enemy, and our march to the seacoast was commenced for this object. After a breakfast of hardcrackers (our "better" provisions that we had been accustomed to for the last few days, had given out,) we were ordered to leave our equipments in camp, (each company piling the things together,) station a guard over it, and to commence the work of destruction on the road. We had scarcely left camp wen an order came countermanding the first, and ordering us to take everything along. We complied, and again moved forward with picks and axes, with which to cut the heads of the iron spikes holding the rails on the ties. We then piled ten or twelve together and set them on fire. Afterwards we laid the rails across. The rails became heated in the centre, and commenced to bend, thereby being unfit for use. In order to make the destruction more complete, some of the rails we twisted, some we even saw twisted around trees—of course this was only done for fun, and not according to order. One member of Company C, of our regiment, was badly wounded by a spike being carelessly thrown and striking his head. All the other corps were busy at the same work, and after we had thus destroyed about two miles of road, we reached Graham's Station, where we pitched tents and had dinner, to go to work again at one o'clock. The day was beautiful, and the work easy, as we knew the rebels would be injured by it, and that it would ruin him by and by. When we went to work again, we left our things behind, excepting our trusty guns, that had saved many a one of us his life, and finished many a rebel since our departure from Chattanooga. We could not find a place for our brigade to fall in and commence the destruction, and went over four miles in the direction of Augusta, but everywhere other troops were busy, and no room for us. Suddenly we were ordered to return, and we supposed that we would return to camp and remain for the night. On reaching there we were ordered to pack up, and despite of all vain talking and protesting we returned the same way, and camped about nine o'clock several miles further toward Augusta. It was so dark that one could see neither bush nor water, and the men preparing supper did not get done with their work until midnight. The night was rainy and unpleasant, and we used the damp ground for a bed.

Feb. 9th. At half-past seven o'clock we intended to commence destroying the road, but found the work done, either by KILPATRICK's cavalry or our infantry. After a march of several miles, we left the road and took a nearer route to Blacksville, on the same road, which we reached at one o'clock, P. M. KILPATRICK's cavalry had left the place a short time before our arrival, and destroyed several miles of road in the direction of Augusta. The rebel cavalry had told the inhabitants that the Yankees were coming to destroy their town. Our first brigade had been away from the division since yesterday, and we were the first infantry that reached Blackville, where we went into camp to await the arrival of the balance of the division. Our right wing had a fight with the enemy as Branchville, on the same road, but the rebels got worsted, and had to fly, losing cannons, amunition, &c. A part of the Branchville and Wilmington Railroad was destroyed. The only road now open for the rebels in Charleston was the Charleston and Florence Railroad, and as this could remain open but a short while, the rebels in Charleston would be surrounded, unless they made use of the only route left for them to escape on. The inhabitants of Blackville were very accommodating. Myself and other members of the regiment were entertained by a handsome young lady, who played the piece: "When This Cruel War is Over," for us on the piano, and accompanied it with her sweet voice. The town was not destroyed, as foretold by the rebels, but a few houses and the depot were burned, and the inhabitants had no cause of complaint. Patrols went around the city day and night, and arrested every one found plundering or tearing down houses. Late in the evening we received a large mail, that had been brought by the second division of our corps. This division had been in Savannah, and since its departure most of the time with KILPATRICK's cavalry. The distance from here to Augusta is forty-seven miles, to Branchville, twelve, and to Charleston, sixty miles.

Feb. 10th. We left camp at seven o'clock, not knowing whether the march or the destruction of the road would be continued. We went in the direction of Augusta until we reached Willas Station, where the work of destroying the road commenced again, and was continued until night, when we went into camp with the satisfactory thought of having done injury to the rebels. KILPATRICK had a fight on the 8th of this month, and whipped the rebels, keeping them as far as possible from our front, and thus preventing an interruption in our advance. Our loss, therefore, consisted only of men, who left the column to plunder on their own hook, contrary to strict orders. These men were frequently gobbled up by the enemy. It seemed to-day as if our campaign in South and North Carolina would have a happy result. The enemy seemed indisposed to try his luck in battle another time—his army being smaller than ours, and JOHNSTON not a general like SHERMAN. This last assertion had been proven satisfactorily at Dalton, Resaca, Marietta, Atlanta and other points, when the rebel army was strong in numbers yet, behind their own entrenchments, and on a ground chosen by themselves for battle. We were not afraid about the result of the campaign, as in the spring of 1864; the only requisites were provisions and marches that would not break us down. The men had not been able to carry all the hams, chickens, geese, turkeys, molasses, flour, &c., and had pressed negroes to assist them in carrying the provisions to camp. Others had found old wagons and buggies, and came driving to camp with a full load, and were welcomed by their comrades. A picket fired at a man endeavoring to sneak up to him, but the man escaped after the shot had been fired. In the direction of Augusta single shots were heard in the night.

Feb. 11th. The morning was as beautiful a spring morning as any one could desire. We broke camp at half-past eight, left the railroad and our former direction towards Augusta, and moved towards the capital of the State, Columbia. Our division took a side road and moved rapidly forward, not being troubled by many wagons, and the roads being high and dry. About noon it became very warm, and the marching unpleasant. Heavy artillery fire and musketry was heard early in the morning on our left, and we supposed that perhaps we would get hold of the rebels to-day, having been informed that rebel cavalry had been sent from Richmond against us. KILPATRICK had a fight with them. At three o'clock P. M., we reached the Yellow Stone River, that could more properly be called a swamp than a river. The bridge had been burnt, and we were compelled to remain in camp until a new bridge had been built. Our camp was situated on a high hill—the country was more broken than formerly, though the swamps had not disappeared entirely. On looking round from our camp upon the surrounding country, a scene presented itself to our view as grand as it was awful. In every direction large clouds of smoke were seen ascending, pillar-like towards heaven, and every minute the number of these smoke pillars increased in every direction, turning day almost into night. Thus is war! We had burned but little to-day, having passed through a country not much cultivated, containing but few poor-looking houses and no provisions. Of these, however, we had plenty, not having thrown the surplus of yesterday's foraging away, and lived as well to-day as yesterday, and had sufficient left for several days more. The camp of the divisions was full of fun and music until sleep put an end to it. Two members of our cavalry wounded, had died and were buried to-day.

Feb. 12th. Our fifteenth day's march commenced very unpleasantly. The bridge had not been finished entirely, (as it would have required too long time to do this,) and the water was too shallow for pontoons. We had to wade two hundred to three hundred steps through water from two and a half to three feet deep, but cold as ice, and it seemed as though the water would cut our legs. The faces of our boys became dark, and many a one wished South Carolina in the deepest pool of perdition. We reached dry land without any accident, and set a fence on fire, to dry our wet clothes a little and warm ourselves. Five miles further we reached the Dean Swamp, and a small town whose name we could not learn, as no inhabitants were there to give us information. We got further news about yesterday's fight on our left. KILPATRICK had whipped the enemy gloriously, and taken a good many prisoners. KILPATRICK had lost many wounded that were mostly brought to our hospital train. One member of the regiment had learned while foraging that horses were hidden in a swamp, and went with several other foragers after them. They got the track of the horses and the informant went in the thicket, while the others awaited his return. Shortly after a shot was heard and the men, when calling the name of the informant, got no answer. They supposed him dead, returned to the regiment and related the affair, whereupon a detail was sent out to bring the wounded or dead man back. They soon found the lost one sound who told them, that he had fired at a man in the thicket who had run away, but that it had been impossible for him to get the horses out of the thorny brush alone and his comrades had left him. We reached our regiment, when at dinner, close to the swamp in the forest. We went into camp at 7 o'clock, after a march of 15 miles, on a dusty field, whence we had to go three-fourths of a mile for water. The night was cold, but blazing fires of fence rails kept us warm.

Feb. 13. We left camp at 8 o'clock. Several members of the regiment had been missing for several days, and must have been taken prisoner. After a march of two miles we reached a river, behind which the enemy was said to be, who seemed indisposed to continue his retreat any longer. Although it was not our turn to take the advance, yet we were ordered forward; while the other regiments made way for us to pass. We reached the river, and found several regiments and wagons and artillery were ahead of us, but these paused too, while we advanced. About half a mile from the river the enemy fired, retreated a short distance and then halted again. A strong line of skirmishers was sent out to protect our flanks, and advanced steadily amid heavy firing towards the enemy, who was compelled to give way. Thus we drove the enemy until noon when we were ordered to go into camp. A number of foragers were daring enough to go foraging in the rear of the enemy, knowing that the rebels would not leave much behind them. They might have been taken prisoner or even lost their life, but it seemed as though our men knew not the meaning of danger when going after provisions. They were not as fortunate this time as they had been always; the enemy had discovered them, and they escaped capture only by means of their horses, and came gallopping into camp, some without hats, and some even without guns. They were heartily laughed at, when relating about their hasty retreat. Several rebels in Union officers' uniforms approached our pickets, and questioned them about their instructions, but escaped when they became known. A number of prisoners captured said they belonged to Early's forces, with whom we had the fight in the morning. They showed themselves brave enough here, but would no doubt have been braver, if Phil. Sheridan had not frightened them before!

Feb. 14. The march was commenced by our brigade at 2 o'clock P. M., as it was in the rear to-day. We expected another night march, but after a march of six miles, we found the corps in camp. The enemy had opposed us in the day, and was close in our front at night, wherein was quiet, but heavy firing was going on at our right and left. Several rebels were captured to-day. Several mounted orderlies and members of the body guard of Gen. Williams had gone too far beyond our skirmishing line, and were surrounded by the enemy, but cut their way through to our camp without any loss. A staff officer of Gen. Williams was taken prisoner. The rebels were becoming more numerous everywhere; from all corps the reports informed us that the enemy's resistance was becoming more determined, and that many foragers had been taken prisoner. We were on the road to Livingston C. H., and expected to reach there to-morrow, unless the enemy resisted. The night was rainy, and the ground an unpleasant resting place. We had to fell trees and split wood for fire for supper.

Feb. 15. We commenced our march at 8½ o'clock, but shortly afterwards our advance met the enemy, that retreated only when it was high time for him to do so. The rebels were driven back amid continual firing until 2 o'clock P. M., when they made a stand behind a swamp, and fired at every one of our men on showing himself. The enemy had to be driven hence by assault, our advance being thereby one killed and two wounded. Not only in our front was a continual firing going on, but also on our right and left, occasionally intermingled with the bass voice of cannon; we judged from this that not merely cavalry was in our front, but also infantry. But the enemy had to retreat, despite of his resistance, and we advanced steadily though slowly towards the capital of the State, where we expected a larger rebel force. We left Lexington on our left, taking a nearer route to Columbia, expecting to reach it on the morrow. We lost a good deal of time in the swamp, but towards evening the country became higher and the roads more dry, and had at least a dry camp ground, when we went into camp at 6 o'clock.

Feb. 16 We left camp at 6¾ o'clock A. M., our regiment had the advance of the whole corps. As the enemy was soon discovered in our front, we advanced as skirmishers. We expected a hot work before reaching Columbia, but the enemy was on his guard and had escaped in time to get out of the way of the 15th corps; had he remained in our front but a few hours longer, he would either have been cut to pieces or taken prisoner. The 15th corps marched on our right, on a nearer road, towards Columbia and crossed our road a few miles South of town, and must therefore have come to the crossing before our advance. The enemy had found this out in time to escape being surrounded. When we reached the 15th corps, it was in position and busy firing at the enemy. The river prevented an immediate attack and we were compelled to go into camp without firing a single shot at the enemy entrenched on the other side. We camped on an elevation, overgrown with brush, whence we could overlook the whole city, presenting a very inviting view. The rebels suffered much from the artillery fire of the 15th and 17th corps, and had to be driven a distance back, so that our pontoons could be laid. This could not be done in day-time, and consequently we could not gain possession of the city immediately. Our 2d division erected entrenchments in our rear during the night, expecting an attack from that direction But the night passed quiet. Foraging parties were sent out, but the men returned with tired limbs, though without provisions, after taking a good look at the country. The inhabitants along our route to-day had all fled, and their houses and property became a prey to the flames. Every body had fled to the "safe place" Columbia but now no longer safe as to-morrow's sun was to see us in possession of it.

Feb. 17. We left camp at 10½ o'clock A. M., foragers were sent out immediately after breakfast. The whole corps returned on the same road we had come, then took a road leading right, and reached the river after a march of six miles. A pontoon bridge had been built here the night before and crossed by the 14th corps. KILPATRICK's cavalry was just crossing as we approached the river, and we had to wait until they had passed. We crossed late at night. KILPATRICK seemed to have been pressed by the enemy under CHEATHAM, that was in his rear, and got to our front by forced marches. Columbia was taken possession of by our right wing in the forenoon, and the greater part of the city burned. All endeavors to extinguish the flames were fruitless, as they received fresh nourishment by the firing of other houses and the strong wind aided the work of destruction. Gen. SHERMAN was compelled by the flames several times to move his headquarters. Many of the poor inhabitants thus became the victims of the rich traitors, whose houses were fired. The anger of the Great Judge was poured out upon the city of the wealthy traitors, punishing them for the infamous rebellion against a good and just Government. Lexington had been visited by our cavalry and laid in ashes yesterday. The night was restless. Shots were fired continually, and there could be no longer any doubt, that the rebels were in our rear.

Feb. 18. We left camp at 9 o'clock and crossed Congaree river; on the North side of the river several regiments of the first division erected entrenchments to protect the pontoon bridge. Our brigade had to halt on the North side of the river and wait until everybody had passed and the pontoons been taken up. We did not start again until in the afternoon. The day was warm and the marching unpleasant and slow, the country becoming low and swampy again. A good many men and cattle (the latter was always driven along under control of the brigade butcher) became sick suddenly; the physician ascribed the cause to the water that had been poisoned. We camped about 9 o'clock, and a fuss took place among the men about some fence rails. We had received the news from the rebels that Charleston was in possession of the Union troops.

Feb. 19. We left camp at 6½ o'clock A. M., our brigade taking the lead of the corps. The country became higher and more dry, making the marching easier. Although the neighborhood was inhabited more, yet but few provisions were found. We were told to-day, particularly, that there were provisions, meat and bread, but for four days in the wagons, and that these would have to last during the campaign of forty days yet before us, and that we should be very saving. After a march of four miles we came to the 14th corps, that was crossing a river. We were compelled to go into camp, although it was not later than noon; as we had no orders to remain for the night, we supposed that we would follow the 14th corps as soon as it had crossed. We would have remained, had our leaders not made a mistake. Our division (with our brigade in the advance) was leading the corps and got on the wrong road, where the two other divisions did not follow, but took the right route. The mistake was not found out until in the afternoon; when we immediately formed and returned part of the way back, then went to the left until two hours afterwards we got on the right road, despite the brush, swamps and fence rails, in our way. We got to the balance of the corps when it had camped for the night at a river, for which a bridge had to be constructed before crossing. We camped for the night.

Feb. 20. An order of Gen. SHERMAN was read, ordering a lightening of our baggage wagons particularly of the many small and large tents of the officers, so that our wagons could be loaded with provisions from the country through which we passed, and that we were prepared when coming through a country where no provisions could be found. Foraging parties were detailed whose only duty was to scour the country along both sides of the road for provisions, catch and use horses for their use, if not wanted by the marching column, and who were free from all labor as long as they did their work faithfully. Whatever they brought in the evening was delivered to the quartermasters and by them distributed among the men; the surplus was put on the wagons and saved until needed. Although we had been but a short while in the advance yesterday, we formed the rear now, and instead of a day's march we had a night's march. We remained in camp until after sundown and our other men had crossed over the river, and as usual had to remain on the other side until the bridge had been taken up, and the pontoon train been put in motion ahead of us. This night march was by no means pleasant. The night was cloudy and dark and the road for a good way swampy or wet. The guard of the train made a little light by lanterns, so that the wagons could avoid the worst and deepest mud, while we tramped our way along in the dark, sometimes getting in the deepest morass. We did not reach camp until 3 o'clock A. M., on the road to Winsboro, where we got a few hours rest.

Feb. 21. We commenced our tramp early in the morning, although we would rather have had a day of rest, this being the twenty-fifth day of our march. Nearly all men complained of such continuous marching, yet we were in a better condition now than while marching in Kentucky, Tennessee or Georgia, and we had less men with sore feet than ever before. The country to-day was hilly and rocky, but well settled, and contained plenty of provisions and good water. At 12 o'clock M., we reached Winsboro, a good sized town, and halted a short distance from it to take dinner. The 2d division, in the advance to-day, showed some of the old hatred against the other divisions and corps, wherever it could. They allowed no forager of the other corps to come to the city, so that the members of their own division might swallow everything. Foragers from the other divisions, were robbed of their provisions and placed under arrest. The men of the 14th corps were treated the same way. But we swore to repay them in the same coin some day and play "eye for eye, tooth for tooth." To keep our men together while here roll call was had every half hour. After an hour's rest we marched by company front and parading through town, we camped two miles further in a pinery on a hill. It was reported for certain that Gen. THOMAS had marched through East Tennessee, and was at Charlotte C. H to-day, there to unite with us, but that LEE had left Richmond to prevent this union. We believed this report, not knowing how matters stood in the North, and as we were expecting LEE; should he have left Richmond, we knew that GRANT's army would follow him on his heels.

Feb. 22. At 7 o'clock the bugles sounded the commencement of the 25th days' march. Our division was in front and our foragers had the pleasure of gathering the principal and best portion of the provisions, before the 2d division in the rear, that had taken everything at Winsboro, could get hold of any. The country was again hilly and rocky, but well settled and well provided with provisions. Negroes were pressed into service to assist in bringing the provisions to camp. Many of them awaited the column at the road, loaded with hams, flour, &c., threw their burden into the wagons, and then went off again like bees after more. The forests we passed through to-day were indeed beautiful and it was delightful to rest under the trees in the shade. The pineries that we had constantly been in since our departure from Chattanooga, were becoming scarce, and we were glad of it, as the continual smell of pitch had become unpleasant and the smoke given us a negro-like complexion. We began to hope of getting our "fair complexion" again. Our road led to Rocky Mount, which place we expected to reach to-day, in case we should not take a side road again. At 12 o clock we reached a house, where a member of our advance had been shot by the enemy hidden there. The country was full of rebel scouts, the foraging business had become dangerous, and our foragers were surprised frequently. We seemed to be the objects of Gen. SHERMAN's especial regard, as he was with us throughout the day. He was reported to have said, that he feared no danger, if he could cross the Catawba river without resistance. This river could only be crossed on the main road from Rocky Mount to Lancaster, at all other points the shores were so high and steep that our pontoons could not be laid. At this point, we had learned, the bridge had been burned, and the enemy on the other side strongly entrenched. To avoid this we turned to the right where at the crossing the bridge had been burned, and the enemy would be in wait for us, as we expected. We reached the river about sundown, but found no rebels there, a bridge was quickly constructed, after strong details had crossed in skiffs and were guarding the other shore, and by midnight our brigade was in the mountains and valleys of the Northern shore. We marched a distance farther to make room for the other troops and train, and at 2 o'clock A. M., we camped on a hill, and rested the remainder of the night.

Feb. 23. We were awakened before daybreak and were ordered forward without breakfast, with the assurance, however, that the march would be but a short one. We advanced but five miles, but those five miles were severe on us, not having had sufficient rest the night before, nor any breakfast in the morning. We erected tents in a large forest, just before the rain set in. The enemy had been outflanked completely yesterday, and did not show himself until late in the afternoon, when he made several fruitless attempts to demolish our bridge, and then continued firing at our men. Gen. SHERMAN assured us that the darkest day of our campaign had passed in crossing the river safely, and that in three months he would be with us on the way to Washington.

Feb. 24. The rain had continued yesterday and during the night, and even to-day we had occasional showers; the roads became bad, particularly after the wagons had passed over them. We had expected that no movements would take place, as all our men had not yet crossed the river, and as the morning was rainy. At 10 o'clock we received marching orders and at 11 o'clock we advanced 2½ miles, to make room for the men that were following; the 14th corps crossed here too. We were now 15 miles in a straight line from the border of North Carolina and 25 miles from Charlotte C. H. Seventeen of our men were murdered by the rebels a few days ago, and retaliatory measures were said would be adopted. The night was rainy and dark.

Feb. 25. The pickets were drawn in early, and soon the merry bugles sounded the advance. When everything was ready, orders were received to remain until further orders. The pickets had scarcely been sent out again when a heavy rain set in and prevented any further movement. The rain continued the whole day and night accompanied by heavy thunderstorms.

Feb. 26. The rain had not ceased yet, but the time for our rest was past, despite the threatening sky. We knew that a hard day's march was in store for us, but circumstances did not permit us to care for rain or bad roads, as the loss of a single day gave the enemy new strength, and power to impede our progress, and cause us more losses. We left the camp about 6½ o'clock. We advanced a short distance, and until the deep morass and mud and the continued rain compelled our wagons to halt until the roads had been repaired. We had not made 5 miles yet, and from here every foot of the road had to be paved with fencerails for our wagons, whereby our pioneers and front regiments were kept busy. Our road led to Lancaster, but late in the afternoon we took a side road to the right of the city. At a crossing we found one of our men lying dead, whose throat had been cut by the rebels, who had left him there as a warning to others, knowing that we would find him. About 1 o'clock P. M. we went into camp on a battlefield of the revolution, Hanging Rock, near Lancaster. Close to our camp we found several bales of cotton hidden in the swamp, that furnished fine beds for the night. The rain had ceased and the night was clear and beautiful.

Feb. 27. No signals to advance were given, and we supposed, as other troops continued to move past us, that we would form the rear, it being the turn of our division. Many of our men left camp, others commenced to wash, and yet others went foraging, to clear the country. About noon we were informed that we were to remain, and could use the day for a washing day. We were glad of this, not having had an opportunity to wash since we left Hardeesville, and in a few hours the camp presented quite a novel appearance with the drying clothes flying in the breeze in every direction, many of which had formerly ornamented rebels, but now graced Yankee bodies. Our foragers returned in the afternoon empty-handed. We remained in camp during the night, preparing for an early march on the morrow.

Feb. 28. The day commenced with rain again, and we could tell from that, what we would find on the march. The time we generally commenced our march was past, and we were still in camp, though ready for the "excursion in the country." At 10 o'clock the bugles sounded, and half an hour later we left our camp at Hanging Rock, our division forming the rear of the column. To march in the rear is an unpleasant job in any kind of weather. If the roads are dry, the rear gets the most of the dust; if wet, the thousands of feet and the large number of wagons ahead of you, plow the road up and make it almost bottomless. The marching went very slow, and when we went into camp at 6 o'clock P. M., we had made but 8 miles, but were more tired than if we had marched 18 or 20 miles on a good road. Our foragers made use of a mill, having gathered wheat and corn, and afterward burned it up. The country became less settled and poorer with regard to provisions, but the swamps ceased, hills and mountains and vales appeared, with plenty of clear spring water. We camped in the rain, and expected another unpleasant march on the morrow.

March 1. 1865. We left camp 7 o'clock A. M., our

brigade in the rear of the division, which formed the centre of the corps. The march was not quite as unpleasant as yesterday, as the roads were becoming more solid and were able to stand more rain. We advanced much faster, and were not compelled as often to stop to repair the roads before advancing farther. The country was more settled but the inhabitants had all fled, mostly to the thickest part of the woods, taking with them everything they wanted to save. A negro's information, however, soon set our foragers on the track of the fugitives, and they found more provisions in the woods than in the houses. But on such occasions the foragers were in danger of the rebels, who endeavored to protect their property, and were frequently wounded. An accident of this kind occurred to-day. A party of foragers suddenly came up to rebels, who fired at them, wounding two of our men badly with fine shot. The others pounced like tigers on the rascals, took two of them prisoner and took what they wanted and destroyed the balance. The two rebels were taken to head quarters. Such scenes occurred frequently, but as a general thing the rebels got the worst of the encounter, as our men knew that if they were taken prisoner by the rebels, they would surely be murdered in some cruel and brutal manner, particularly if captured in houses. But all these dangers could not frighten our foragers, who went as far as they pleased, no matter how dangerous the road might be, if provisons were to be had. The night was rainy.

March 2. We moved forward at 7 o'clock in a heavy rain, in the direction of Chesterfield, 15 miles distant. We marched five miles in the greatest hurry, then camped until dark, during which time a bridge over a large swamp was being erected. For us logs had been thrown in, and took several hours to cross, and was by no means an easy task in the darkness, as nearly every one slipped once at least from the logs into the water, about 1 to three feet in depth. All of us got more or less wet. The march was continued on the wet road, as the rain had continued, until 11 o'clock P. M., when we went into camp with the order to be ready at 6½ o'clock the next morning for the march.

March 3. After a few hours rest we were awakened to commence our 34th day's march. Our brigade formed the advance of the division, and frequently we had to lay our arms aside and go to work repairing the roads. The enemy had not shown himself for some time, nor had he blocked the road; the only hindrances were the burnt bridges, that we soon repaired, however, in a rather rude style. We expected to meet the enemy at the Great Pedee river, on to-morrow, if possible. Our neighboring corps also seemed to be unmolested, as neither artillery nor musketry fire was heard at our right or left. We reached Chesterfield at 1 o'clock P. M., a place entirely deserted; our first division had reached the town yesterday. We went into camp here. A forager of our regiment belonging to company C, had been taken prisoner several days ago by the rebels. Wearing cavalry clothes, he passed himself off for one of KILPATRICK's men, and as a few days afterwards an exchange was effected of an equal number of WHEELER's and KILPATRICK's prisoners, our comrade luckily got out of the rebel clutches, and returned to our regiment to-day. A few hours after he had been captured he was taken to WHEELER's headquarters and questioned about our strength &c. Of course he answered the questions his own way. He also stated that a member of company F, of whom no trace had been found for several days, had been with him when he was captured. He had run, and all cries of the enemy to surrender, had only increased his speed, until a bullet was sent through his head and he fell down dead. The rebels left the corpse lying where it fell, without taking further notice of it. Rebel prisoners stated that there were 35,000 rebels in our front, commanded by Gen. JOE JOHNSTON; we did not believe this, as an army of that size would not have allowed us to advance without showing some resistance.

March 4. We left Chesterfield at 7 o'clock A. M., had a fine road when a few miles from the town, without meeting any resistance. At 12 o'clock we stepped over the border of South Carolina into North Carolina, and went into camp at 2 o'clock P. M., in a forest of young pines. The town of Cheraw, distant 8 miles, was taken possession of by the 17th corps, under Gen. HOWARD yesterday, after a slight skirmish. The enemy lost a number of prisoners and cannons, and was driven into North Carolina, over the Great Pedee river. Gen. HOWARD commanded the right wing of Gen. SHERMAN's army. It was reported that we would have three days rest here, but as it was mere camp rumor, not much confidence could be reposed in it.

March 5. We remained in camp, busy washing our clothes; others scoured the country for provisions, although we could not say that we had suffered much from want of provisions in South Carolina. As to-day was the day for the bi-monthly muster, the officers or their clerks commenced making out the muster rolls. In the direction of Cheraw a continual thunder was heard, and we supposed that the fortifications there were being blown up, or the town laid waste.

March 6. The explosions in the direction of Cheraw continued, and at 10 o'clock we broke camp to approach that place. We had to return to South Carolina, and marched along the border until we were near our point of destination, when we camped for supper. We had received order not to prepare for a night's rest, in order to cross the Great Pedee river as soon as possible. Nevertheless we got a few hours rest and at 12 o'clock P. M. we marched through the half burnt town, the darkness preventing a good view at the place, and reached the south side of the river a short while before sunrise.

March 7. After we had crossed the river, we advanced on Rockingham and Fayettville road, and camped in an open field to prepare breakfast. After this our brigade was detailed as guard of the wagon train. The day was warm and the road sandy, but we moved quickly forward and went into camp, after a march of 17 miles, in the neighborhood of the Lawrenceburg and Wilmington railroad. The rebels had in no wise obstructed the road, but here and there a broken vehicle of a fugitive citizen was found in the road.

March 8. We left camp at 9 o'clock and continued our march for Fayetteville. The country was much more thinly settled than yesterday. Immense pineries, with tremendous trees stretched everywhere, here and there diversified by a turpentine factory. There was much talk about opening communication at Fayetteville, by way of Cape Fear river with Wilmington, that was now in the hands of Union troops, according to reports of rebel prisoners. We were anxious to reach that place, expecting to remain for some time, but according to information received from negroes the place was strongly fortified. Be this as it may, we were bound to have the place, if necessary, with hard fighting; the latter we did not expect, knowing that the rebels were disheartened, and gave up their cause as lost, and that it was impossible for such troops to withstand the determined attacks of our boys. Along our route to-day incendiarism was all the rage, no houses were burned, for there were few or none about, but the pitch pine pines. The pitch had collected at the foot of some pines to the height of sometimes 8 or 10 feet, and hardened; a burning coal or match set the column of pitch afire very rapidly, and many of the trees were killed thereby. We also found houses, where the pitch was distilled into turpentine, which were also burned. The volumes of smoke thereby created, were seen everywhere, and became so thick as almost to darken the light of the sun. The tramping through these smoky and burning woods was more difficult than through swamps and morass; we could hardly open our eyes, that were continually filled with tears and the smoke pregnant with pitch settled on our faces and hands, so that our friends in the North would sooner have thought us to be negroes than white men, had they seen us in our "glorious condition" in those pineries. Close to the road where we halted in the afternoon, a man with a wagon and box was chased. In the box we found clothes and a large package of love letters, that gave us a good deal of merriment. We also found a number of hams and a barrel of molasses, that did us good service. The clothes were all female apparel and we left them to the proprietor who had been allowed to escape without molestation. The horse was confiscated. The afternoon and night were rainy, and we went into camp about forty miles from Fayetteville.

March 9. We left camp at 6 o'clock on our march to Fayetteville. The country was still thinner settled than yesterday, but all turpentine distilleries we found were set afire as well as the pitch pines. We looked like negroes and it did not make any difference whether the smoke of one or two days had settled on our skins. We heard for certain to-day that Wilmington was in possession of the Union troops, and also Fayetteville; the latter proved to be a mere rumor and untrue. We marched rapidly despite of the heavy rain, and did not go into camp until evening, when a swamp in our front compelled us to halt. When we camped we did not have a dry thread on our clothes, and we became more wet still as we were compelled to get the fire-wood out of the water, sometimes knee deep. Those with us that night will hardly forget it.

March 10. We commenced our march at 6 o'clock, and had to endure hardships at the start that tested the constitution of many a soldier, causing sickness either immediately or afterwards, of which but few recovered entirely, and many have died in consequence of it We were at a swamp that bordered both sides of the Lumber river, a river like all South Carolina rivers with low shores. A bridge had been erected over the river, but we had to wade through the cold, knee deep water of the swamp. Our clothes had scarcely become dry, and were again saturated at the start this morning, and were very slowly dried by the air. But this was not the case to-day, as we had to cross six smaller swamps behind the first large one, all more or less filled with water. It was not considered worth the trouble or time to erect bridges over these swamps. The further we advanced, the worse the road became, the pioneers alone could no longer repair the roads fast enough, and the brigade had to furnish men to assist them; our company furnished twenty men. The order was obeyed with alacrity in order to get out of this land of swamps the sooner. Three Union prisoners, captured in front of Petersburg, Va., by the rebels, and held in confinement in Salisbury, N. C., had escaped from there, and were taken prisoner by our men, as they were dressed in rebel uniforms, and as their assurances of being Union soldiers were not believed. Even our cominander at first thought them to be rebels, though they had told him that they had used the rebel uniforms only in order to effect their escape the better. As they had neither arms nor other equipments, and on bringing good proof that they were Union soldiers, they were finally believed and got the same liberties that we enjoyed. They had heard from the Union prisoners in Salisbury, where they had arrived but a short while before their escape, that SHERMAN was penetrating into North Carolina, and would perhaps advance to Richmond, and considered this a

—14

good opportunity to get back to Petersburg to escape. In a very dark night they had effected their escape, but were in continual danger from armed rebels near them, and were for three weeks in the swamps where they received food and nourishment from the negroes. About noon the ground became so loose that the horses sank knee-deep along the road and could be freed with the greatest difficulty only. Cattle that had to be driven along side of the roads, sank down and many were seen with nothing but the head above ground and had to be left to die there. Almost every step of our road had to be covered with trees before we could advance. The day was cloudy. We went into camp 25 miles from Fayetteville. KILPATRICK was surprised in camp this morning by two divisions of rebel cavalry and lost a large number of men, but as the enemy commenced to plunder the tents he was overpowered at last and made to suffer for his audacity.

March 11. We broke camp at 6 o'clock and neared the town, being able to reach it by rapid marches; but it was not our intention to promenade 25 miles to-day. Everywhere the men were complaining of tired and sore legs and feet, our ambulance wagons were filled with men whose legs and feet did not allow them to continue the promenade, and this number increased every day. Particularly in the morning, after a rest on the damp ground, it seemed as though we could not march a mile with our baggage; but when resolved on a walk and once in motion, we found that we could stand more privations than we thought we could, and generally felt better in the evening than in the morning. Many preferred to take their cold victuals while on the march, and rest during dinner time, with the knapsack under the head, under the shade of some beautifully leaved tree. Of such pleasant rests we were to see nothing to-day. Immediately after breaking camp, we moved rapidly forward past the first division, and took the lead. The day was beautiful and the road dried rapidly, nevertheless we were compelled frequently to repair it. We had advanced on a side road from Cheraw to Fayetteville, while the 14th corps advanced on the main road that was in a great deal better condition than our road through swamps and morasses. In the afternoon we reached the main road, and were but about 8 miles distant from the city. As this road was high and dry, the 14th corps had gotten ahead of us and the advance of this corps must have been in town by this time, but no firing was heard. It was the intention of our Generals as well as our own desire, to reach town to-day yet, we increased our speed, and arrived at Fayetteville, on the Cape Fear river, at 7 o'clock P. M., after a march of 25 miles. The city was strongly fortified, but the main force of the rebels had fled, and the foragers of the different corps found some cavalry only to drive away. A division of the 14th corps quartered in the city for the night.

March 12. We remained quiet in our by no means comfortable camp, shade trees and fire wood were wanting; but we were satisfied, hoping to receive a better camp ground, if we should remain here longer. A boat came up Cape Fear river from Wilmington and brought us news, the first we had received since we had left Robertsville, S. C. The same boat took a large mail from here along. The inhabitants of the town commenced hoisting the stars and stripes and seemed glad at our arrival and gave the Confederate cause up for lost. They believed that the war could last but a short while longer in case SHERMAN should advance directly towards Richmond, which they did not doubt. They said that SHERMAN had gone during the last year wherever he pleased and where he could do the most harm, and that no power of the rebels could now stop him. The children, boys as well as girls, went around the streets, crying: " Hurrah for SHERMAN and his boys;"

such were treated kindly by our men, who would have divided everything with them. But these Union inhabitants were a minority, compared to the arch-traitors of the town, whose faces showed the rebel spirit within, who kept their houses closed from our boys, but who would readily have butchered a fat calf for a rebel soldier, had he come and said: "I am an arch-traitor, and despise the infernal Yankees."

March 13. Marching orders were announced and the time for rest was past, not merely to move the camp, but to take up the line of march for Goldsboro, where we had communication and could get provisions from the North. We left camp on the South side of the city, marched by company front through Fayetteville and passed review of Generals SHERMAN, SLOCUM, HOWARD, and others. At 4 o'clock recrossed Cape Fear river on pontoons; both shores were lined by large numbers of negroes, of both sexes, principally those that had followed us from Georgia and South Carolina, and for which no work could be found here. We supposed that these poor half starved, and half naked figures were waiting there to be transported to Wilmington, where they might perhaps get work, After a march of two miles from the river we went into camp, in line of battle before we stacked arms, as danger was supposed to be near. The enemy was in force but two miles ahead of us. Foragers of our and the 17th corps had come up to him and been driven back by artillery fire, whereby several had been killed and wounded. An artillery man was carried past us dead, before we went into camp, killed by a grape shot. A rebel captain was taken prisoner by our company.

March 14. We remained quiet in camp, but two miles from Cape Fear river and Fayetteville. Our foragers had taken possession of a mill and were grinding corn fit for use. A number of prisoners and a rebel cannon fell into our hands to-day. The weather was beautiful in the forenoon, but rainy afterwards. The main force of the rebels had retreated a short distance, but the country a short distance from our camp was full of rebel foragers and scouts, and part of our men returned for reinforcements, not being allowed to go to a plantation where provisions were plenty. Our 2d brigade went out, drove the rebels off, but nearly all the provisions had been removed. We expected a severe fight between here and Goldsboro, as it was easily perceived now that the rebels in our front were strong, consisting of all those we had driven from Savannah, Augusta and Charleston. EARLY had so sent part of his men here.

March 14. We left camp at 6½ o'clock A. M., the 1st and 3d division of our corps taking a side road, while the 2d division with the train went to our right on a better road with the train, that had to be guarded well now, as danger was ahead. On our road we found many barricades, held by the enemy yesterday, but evacuated to-day. About noon we came to a line of entrenchments, also evacuated. From all movements we judged that the enemy was close in our front, and did not feel much like giving way; but all these suppositions were kept to ourselves and not much talked about. We advanced until 3 o'clock when we went into camp, as the country began to become lower and more swampy. The day was threatening with rain, and we had scarcely stacked arms and gotten rid of our knapsacks, when the rain commenced and continued until night. Before we had stacked arms and thrown down our knapsacks, the greater part of KILPATRICK's cavalry gallopped past us, accompanied by the commander and staff; a short while afterwards shots were fired that increased for a while, but slacked towards night. We were certain that the strength of the enemy was known, or else we would not have gone into camp so early in the day. Two members of WHEELER's escort were taken prisoner. Our foragers found out particularly that the enemy began to show resistance, and several parties were taken prisoner, others escaped with the loss of their horses, mules and guns. We heard for certain that quite a number of our regiment had been captured.

March 16. We left our camp, 10 miles from Averysboro, at 6½ o'clock, and marched in the direction of the town. Our road was over very loose and wet ground and had become a morass by the rain, and in consequence our advance was very slow; but we never stopped to repair the road, as we had but a few headquarter wagons with us. Our cavalry was playing with the enemy again, and shot followed shot, a short time afterwards intermingled with loud cannon reports. We knew now what was ahead of us to-day, and our yesterday's suppositions were verified. KILPATRICK seemed in danger and we were ordered forward in double quick, until we got close to the scene of conflict, where we left our wagons and mules and prepared for the work in store for us. The place where the enemy was entrenched was low and well provided with water and mud, and it was very difficult to get to the proper points. The enemy based his hopes and expectations on this, much more than we would have done, had we been in his place. Our brigade took position to the right of the road, and a short distance to our right the enemy had been attacked; here the officers left their horses, and the intention was to advance. Suddenly an order came to our brigade to move to the left and seek the enemy's right flank. While we moved forward cautiously through morass and water and brush, the first and the remainder of our division took our place and awaited our flank attack. The enemy fired during this time like a set of madmen, expecting an attack in front, and considered his right flank entirely safe, as not a single shot was fired at us during our move. Although we were but a short distance from the enemy, yet we were not seen by him, as the thick brush prevented any view, and as we moved very quietly. It was difficult for us to find the end of the rebel lines without exposing ourselves, but that sly fox, our Lieut. Col. FLYNN, every now and then looked, when we continued our march slowly and cautiously. We had continued our march for several miles in search of the end of the enemy's works, while the fire to our right had become very rapid, the enemy becoming bolder as the hours went by, until we suddenly fronted. Our pickets, with the brigade in the immediate rear, went at the enemy, a terrific yell was raised, accompanied by a no less terrific fire; the enemy, so safely lodged behind his works, fled panic-stricken without firing a shot, like so many frightened birds, leaving cannons, knapsacks, guns, horses, the killed and wounded behind him. The balls our boys sent after the fugitives halted many a one forever! The rebels could beat us running, and before we had reached his second line of entrenchments they had gathered again, and opened on us with guns and musketry fire, compelling us to halt, as we had lost all communication with our right and left. Thus far our regiment had not lost a single member. The cannon captured from the enemy were turned, and as our gunners had enough to do with their own guns, we compelled several rebel artillerymen to load and fire them, after they had been sighted by one of our sergeants. Our line had been re-established, and the enemy made an attempt to give us a flank fire, and bullets and balls went thick as hailstones over our heads, wounding several of our men. In a moment our front was changed, and the enemy driven back. After arrangements had been made to prevent an attack on the flanks, and after part of the 14th corps had joined our left, we received order to advance again, but no order to attack the enemy in his works that stretched a good way farther to our left (the enemy's right) than the works taken by us. We had scarcely commenced our advance, when the enemy opened a most furious fire, causing a loss of twenty men of our regiment, among them several killed. The buglers sounded the advance several times, but not to attack, and as soon as we showed ourselves, a rain of bullets and balls came flying at us, compelling us to remain on the ground; nevertheless we suffered some whenever we advanced. Finally, the fire became continuous, as the enemy knew he was doing us harm. Never before had we been exposed to such a fire of shells and grape, as in that afternoon at the battle of Averysboro. The grape balls struck everywhere, above, below, in front and behind us; we remained alive only by remaining quietly on the ground. We did not advance, but we kept our ground, and after dark we erected breast-works amid a brisk fire. A heavy firing was going on at our right during the afternoon as well as in our front. Rebel soldiers had fled in the morass between the two lines of works, after we had captured the first line and sent a shower of balls after the flying rebels; then begged our men to draw them out of the swamp, but it lasted some time before we could relieve them and place them under guard with other prisoners. The rebels in our front were artillery men from Charleston, but had to handle a musket here. Our wounded were brought to neighboring houses, taken care of as well as possible; we prepared our supper amid a heavy rain that had set in, and spent the night mostly awake. The rebels fled during the night, pursued by our cavalry.

March 17. We went to the rebel works before sunrise and prepared our breakfast. Scouts were sent out to see if the enemy was still in the neighborhood, and did not go very far when they were fired at by the rebels who demanded to know what they wanted, retreating at the same time. We did not commence to advance until 8 o'clock A. M., and although the enemy was still in our front in small parties, yet our advance was in no way hindered, and the rebels managed to keep beyond the rage of our guns. We were on the way to Averysboro, but three miles distant from the battlefield in a southerly direction. The road was strewn with rebel dead, and ambulances, that had not been able to get away fast enough, the horses had been unhitched and the wagons left. We found the greater part of the wounded in the frame-houses on both sides of the road, all alone and without attendants, medicine, or provisions; they had been left to their fate until our surgeons took pity and attended to their wounds. In one of the ambulances we found a wounded rebel, almost dead, whom a shot had struck in the forehead, the brain oozed out of the wound over his eyes, and a few faint groans were all the poor fellow could utter. The enemy had perhaps thought him to be too far gone, to take the trouble of bringing him to a neighboring house. If the rebels acted thus towards their own comrade and messmate, what must be the tortures our poor prisoners in the rebels' hands must have suffered! Nobody will ever be able to prove that the rebels were innocent of all such barbarities and abuse, and if they escape their just due here, they will have to answer before a higher Judge for all these cruelties! We reached Averysboro at 11 o'clock A. M., where we found more rebel wounded, quartered in the deserted houses of the citizens, but under the treatment of a surgeon. Many of them were but slightly wounded and cursed their cause, Jeff. Davis and his assistants We camped near the town. Our foragers had another set-to with the enemy, and took a number of prisoners and ammunition wagons, which they destroyed.

March 18. At 6½ o'clock we left camp, and returned part of the way, passing the wounded rebel in the ambulance wagon, who was now dead, then took a road to the left, and marched in an easterly direction. We had to wade on the West side of Black river, through very deep water, before we reached the bridge. The day was clear and warm, and our clothes soon dried again; but as we continued to march through a swamy country, they soon became wet again. The country was not inhabited, but full of rebel cavalry, which KILPATRICK kept clear of us. Two of our wounded of company H, died in the hospital to-day. We got no sleep and but one hour for supper, and then continued our march until 5 o'clock the next morning.

March 19. We left camp at 8 o'clock and had marched but a short distance, when the roar of artillery was heard in our front that gradually drew away, and finally ceased altogether. The whole 14th corps was in our front and had to do the bloody work, if such should become necessary. The roads became better and the country more thickly settled, and was better cultivated than it had been for the last few days. Provisions were not found, as the enemy had taken all away. But our foragers had gathered sufficiently for us, so that we had not wanted the provisions taken along from Savannah. But as a regiment of very hungry Yankees makes quite a reduction even of the largest pile of provisions, and as our foragers had not been able during the last few days to replenish our stock, it was time for us to reach Goldsboro. Our clothes were becoming tattered too, and many of our men could not be distinguished from rebels, being often taken for such by their own comrades and by the rebels, and thereby got out of scrapes frequently. But if a Yankee in rebel uniform was discovered to be such by the rebels, his treatment was a doubly severe one. The afternoon of our to-day's march brought more events than the forenoon, and seemed to end like the 16th of March. We had advanced briskly, although we had not had an hour's rest the night before, in order to keep up with the 14th corps, as it seemed that this corps would need our help yet, on account of the large rebel force in our front. Our forced march by double-quick, told us plainly of the events ahead of us, and the pack-mules and horses of the 14th corps, that were not allowed to follow their brigades any more, confirmed our belief. The roar of the cannons became more violent and we saw a brigade of the 1st division, that had reached the battlefield before we did, drawn up in line of battle, marching courageously, like a solid phalanx with a steady step against the enemy, who were saluting our boys with volleys of lead. Several batteries were posted behind and to the right of this brigade, and others galloped up and were in position in a few moments. All this betokened danger and an attack from the enemy, as we had heretofore always taken our own time and measures, and had commenced the battle ourselves. Our brigade had formed the rear of the division and reached the battlefield at last, joined the left of the 2d brigade, forming the extreme left of our army. None but some of KIPATRICK's cavalry was in the woods beyond us, to give us timely notice in case the enemy should attack our flank. After we had taken our positions and stacked arms, we were ordered to throw up breastworks, as an attack on our flank was expected. Pickets were sent out, and we went to work in earnest, and soon had our works sufficiently strong to keep double our number back. Suddenly the deafening cries of thousands, sounding as though all the demons of Hell had been let loose, were heard, followed by the terrible rattle of musketry, for the time overpowering the cries—cannons assisted to increase the noise, until it gradually slackened. The enemy had raised these yells while making an attack on the 14th corps and our 1st division, and had thus been compelled to retreat with the loss of his killed and wounded. But this first repulse did not satisfy the enemy. He gathered again, the same noise and roar and rattle of artillery and musketry was heard, so loud that we had to yell to make our nearest neighbors understand us, while the ground trembled under our feet. But our troops, who we could see plainly from our position, stood like a solid wall, not moving an inch and compelled the enemy to beat another retreat, with the loss of his killed and wounded. This did not satisfy the enemy yet, and could not convince him of his inability to break through our lines, for he renewed the attempt six times during the afternoon and was repulsed every time. Our men seemed able to brave every danger, and if LEE had come from Richmond, even, we were in the fighting spirit to keep him back. Prisoners and deserters told us that the enemy in our front numbered 50,000, and that HARDEE had sworn to break through our lines or lose the last man. The 15th and 17th corps moved on the right towards Goldsboro. We hoped for an attack behind our works during the night, and were on guard by reliefs, but nothing occurred, and but few shots were fired along the picket line. The battle occurred near Bentonville, a small place in North Carolina, and we named the battlefield accordingly. Our loss was great, but small compared to that of the enemy, who made bayonet charges and only used his cannons when retreating and gathering again.

March 20. It was generally supposed that the attack would be renewed to-day, and as the attacks were generally made before daybreak, we were drawn in line of battle at 4 o'clock, in order not to let the enemy gain any advantage. In fact, we *hoped* he would come, but he did not make his appearance, and at sunrise we saw that the enemy had retreated a distance from his former position. Our line of pickets was pushed forward, and the right wing of our regiment, a company of the 79th Ohio, and one of the 102d Illinois were ordered forward as support, in case of danger. After we had advanced a distance we saw the enemy in a field, and retreated to draw him after us. But in vain, the rebels remained where they were. The enemy then fell back, perhaps to draw us on, and we accordingly advanced, drove him about 500 steps, killed one rebel and took one prisoner, and then retreated again to see if we could not coax the enemy to advance against us. But the enemy remained in his old position. We had scarcely retreated the second time when the whole brigade moved up, we advanced until the brigade had taken its position, where we rejoined it, and erected breastworks. The rebel cannons opened on us occasionally, while ours remained quiet. At our right wing a heavy cannonade was going on, and we supposed that the advance on Goldsboro was being made. We drew rations as some wagons were emptied to make room for wounded, that were to be brought back to Kingston. The night was quiet.

March 21. We were ordered to be ready at 5½ o'clock A. M. for the march, and received fresh cartridges. Our brigade was the only one that had received marching orders At the appointed time we were ready, but no bugle sounded the advance. It was at first believed the enemy had fled, but he was in his old position, and at 3 o'clock we fell back behind our old entrenchments, built on the 19th, where we pitched our tents. Afterwards we again advanced to our former entrenchments, although a heavy rain had commenced. Rebel cavalry was in our rear, but KILPATRICK was watching it, and prevented an attack on our wagon train. But little firing was going on in our front. We received the news that Gen. TERRY had taken Goldsboro on the 19th inst. Our wagons with wounded were sent there, and with them we expected provisions on their return. The night was dark, rainy and very unpleasant.

March 22. At 1 o'clock A. M. we received order to be ready, all pack horses were to be brought to the rear, and that we were to be in line of battle at daybreak. We could assign no other cause for this order than an advance, and camp rumor went that the main force of the enemy had retreated yesterday, and only a line of pickets was in our front. At the appointed hour we arose from our miserable resting places, prepared a hasty breakfast, and when the day dawned we were ready, awaiting the command to advance. But this order did not come. The sun sent his rays smilingly on us, as though he would tell that we were again the victors and conquerors. Several rebels came to us and surrendered themselves, and and brought the news that the enemy had fled. We now marched off in the direction of Goldsboro, hoping there to get the much needed rest. A number of rebel wounded were taken along. Some of them cherished the queer idea that the North would get the finishing blow now, and the South be victorious in the end. After a march of 12 miles we went into camp near the Neuse river, which we had reached after a laborious tramp of 8 miles over miserable roads. Nothing was seen or heard of the enemy.

March 23. We advanced towards Goldsboro at 7 o'clock A. M. The day was beautiful and pleasant for marching, but we advanced slowly, as a river had to be crossed, which always causes a good deal of delay. It was 1 o'clock P. M. before we crossed the Neuse river. The bridge formerly over the stream, called Cox's bridge, had been burned by the rebels. In the afternoon we reached Gen. SCHOFIELD's head quarters and the old 23d army corps, that had taken part in the campaign from Chattanooga to Atlanta, and had returned to Nashville, when HOOD advanced to that city, and had been driven back in glorious style by the 4th and 23d corps. Our joy was great when our brve companions, whose weather-beaten faces spoke volumes, rushed to us to grasp our hands. The joy of those glorious men was no less on meeting their companions of SHERMAN's army, of which they had not seen any trace nor heard of it; they were glad, tattered and lame as we were, from our long march and the many privations, that we were nevertheless "all right" yet. Such feelings are only felt by soldiers, who have suffered, bled and hungered with each other! The music bands commenced to play, and joy was depicted on every face, that we almost forgot that we were in the enemy's country; our joy would not have been greater, if peace had been declared that day. The marching was no longer tiresome, and we advanced rapidly until we camped at 6 o'clock.

March 24. At 2 o'clock A. M. some rebel shots brought us in line of battle, and we remained in this position until 7 o'clock. We left camp on our 55th day's tramp from Hardeesville, it should be our last one before reaching Goldsboro. We passed a place where a slight skirmish had taken place yesterday, and one of our killed was being buried as we passed. At 12 o'clock at noon we entered the city; our route passed SHERMAN'S head-quarters, and we paraded past with all music bands playing. Our beloved leader stood bareheaded as we passed, and returned thanks. We marched 4 miles further, in a northeasterly direction, where we camped, and immediately commenced erecting our tents, and to make everything as commodious as possible, in the expectation of remaining here at least a month. Foragers were sent out, but found more rebels than provisions, and firing was heard in every direction. Not unfrequently our men found one of our solders killed on the road, or wounded crying for help, and it seemed as though the enemy killed the men as quick as he captured them. Our campaign was ended, for the present at least, and our boys in butternut uniforms would soon be properly uniformed, as it was positively asserted, that we would not advance until the whole army had been clothed anew.

March 25. Thanks were tendered us by Gen. SHERMAN for our indefatigable marching through

Georgia, South Carolina and North Carolina, through swamps, morass, forests and valleys, by day and by night, sometimes even without any food. He also thanked us for the bravery shown in the fights, and assured us that now we might have some rest after our march of five hundred miles. There was enough work to do in camp, relying on the promise of our commander that we would stop awhile here, and the erection of cabins was commenced to-day. These could not be built of boards, as at Savannah and other places, because we were four miles from Goldsboro, and no houses near our camp that we might "appropriate." But we had excellent timber and wherever there was a mill to build, there the work was commenced to erect comfortable quarters. Many of our men went in search of a hog or chicken, but came back empty handed, as the enemy had taken everything fit to eat. A number of our men were found shot or hung up on the trees, and a determination fixed in our hearts, hereafter not to take any more prisoners, but to do to them, as they were doing to our men. The commander of our division, Brig. Gen. WARD, was promoted to the post of Major General.

March 26. The erection of cabins were continued and preparations made to draw clothes, and cooking utensils, camp kettles, mess pans, &c., were sent after. We received the first mail since our departure from Blackville, S. C. Major HOSKINS, absent on furlough since we left the Chattahoochie river, Ga., returned to-day to our regiment.

March 27. The erection of the cabins was continued. Another mail arrived, and letters were written and sent off. New clothes arrived this evening and were distributed, and it seemed as though Gen. SHERMAN did not intend to remain long, as the rumor of an advance was current. Many of our men were pleased with this prospect, desiring to serve their time out with marching rather than to lie idle. Experience had taught us that marching was by far healthier, for since we had camped, nearly all complained of something, of weakness and stiffness of the limbs, while on the march they had complained merely of being tired, and "used up."

March 28. The weather was sultry and dark. A good many of the cabins were done, while others approached completion. A number of men went to the city, where a good many traders and suttlers had arrived.

March 29. The officers and clerks were busy making out the pay rolls and other papers. The day was beautiful The rumor of an early advance was current again, but we did not place much credit in it.

March 30. We received another mail, and from the letters we learned that LEE had left Richmond. This was believed, and the troops were full of joy, while the music bands played half the night.

March 31. The camp was full of peace rumors, that LEE had been whipped out of Richmond by GRANT, the latter losing 2500 men. As we had nothing definite or positive, these rumors were believed but half.

April 1, 1865. The topic of our yesterday's conversation was again talked about, and so much believed that GRANT was fighting hard and trying his best to take that impenetrable city. This the papers told us, but did not mention that the work had been done, and LEE been whipped or driven out of Richmond.

April 2. The camp had quieted down somewhat, as also the talk about peace had ceased, but everybody was anxious to hear further news, and we eagerly awaited the next mail. In the afternoon we had dress parade for the first time for a long while.

April 3. The whole regiment was ordered to get fodder for the horses and mules, but we did not know where to find it, supposing that the enemy had even taken this along. We left camp early in the morning
—15

in a westerly direction, and advanced about two miles, when we found corn and fodder sufficient, and returned to camp in the forenoon. One of our pickets was surprised at a house where he was on his post, and killed before he could fire his gun; the rebels took the gun and escaped. Gen. MOWER took command of our, the 20th corps, and we expected a parade. Our corps and the 14th, commanded by Maj. Gen. SLOCUM, now formed the Army of Georgia. We received another heavy mail, but we could get no information about the affairs between GRANT and LEE, as the news from the Virginia seat of war was old. All rumors and exciting tales failed, and everybody was anxiously awaiting something definite and true.

April 4. Arms and clothing was cleansed for the inspection that took place in the afternoon.

April 5. Everything was on the tip-toe in our camp, as the cheering of the troops in town was frequently heard, and we expected that some glad news had arrived, that we could place confidence in. But we waited in vain to hear anything.

April 6. Unexpectedly we were told to-day that a parade would take place before Gen. MOWER. We prepared and at 10 o'clock marched to the parade ground, where the column, consisting only of our division, was moving by regiments. Gen. MOWER soon appeared and the parade commenced. All went very well, although everybody was excited and did not think much about the movements, on account of the cheering and yells, that we heard to proceed from camp. At 1 o'clock the parade was over, and on our return to camp we learned, that it was true, Richmond had been taken, and although LEE had escaped with most of his men, yet GRANT was close at his heels, and would soon compel the former to surrender his army, stores and arms. This news was received by three cheers, and prophecies of an early peace became current everywhere. JOHNSTON, it was said, could not fight, if LEE surrendered; but if the two armies of these Generals were to unite, one more bloody battle would have to be fought, in which we would again be victorious, and which would finish the rebellion. This last battle (if one was to take place) we expected with pleasure, for we would thereby get an opportunity to take revenge on the enemy, who would not seize the proffered rope to save him from sinking, which was his settled fate. If another battle is fought, and the enemy does not surrender, we will kill every rebel that falls in our hands, were the words of our men. The officers and leaders of the rebels were threatened most; JEFF. DAVIS and consorts could not have got past a single regiment in SHERMAN's army, without getting a sufficient number of balls in them. Of course, we also heard the excuse of cruelty, and that DAVIS, BRECKINRIDGE, &c., ought to be imprisoned for life-time, and receive such treatment as did our prisoners in Andersonville and other places, there to meditate over their crimes. But most of the men were unwilling to try this experiment, and give the rebel friends an opportunity to assist these leaders in escaping. But all these propositions were but desires and suppositions; the arch-traitors and prime movers of the war were still at large and not yet captured, and it was very doubtful whether they ever would get in our hands, and that they would not escape their just deserts in the end, we hoped most sincerely. Other regiments were more noisy in their joy, loaded and fired their guns, filled bottles and canteens with powder and set them off, cheered GRANT and SHERMAN, threw their hats high in the air, danced, hopped and jumped, and whipped each other, until they became tired and squatted down around the camp fires for a talk. The air was filled with music until late in the night, now and then intermingled by a loud explosion or shot, until the noise gradually ceased, like a lamp without oil, and everything became quiet and sought rest.

April 7. But very little was talked about the fall of Richmond, that had caused so much joy yesterday, so that one should have supposed the whole story to be but a camp rumor. The camps became more lively in the afternoon, now and then a shot was fired and music bands commenced to play, the troops began to cheer again. Amid all this excitement we heard that the rebels had left all the heavy siege guns behind them, that GRANT had taken 2500 rebels prisoner, and that the town had been fired in several places by the enemy, but that the fire had after hard labor of our troops been extinguished by them. From the enemy in our front, we heard only, that he was still in possession of Raleigh, but did not fortify it; it seemed therefore not to be JOHNSTON's intention to defend the place. The last rumors, or latest grape vines as they were called, of the day were about an early advance from Goldsboro, to prevent a junction of LEE's and JOHNSTON's armies. A great many believed that LEE would now lose a great many men by desertion, and also by being killed or captured by GRANT, and as the same was the case with JOHNSTON, either of them would not have been a great help for the other. It was JOHNSTON's intention, according to the talk of the rebel prisoners, in case of necessity, to disband his army and organize them in guerrilla bands. If he should do this, he might rely on it that every rebel captured would have been treated as an outlaw, i. e. to a blue pill. The enemy would have been exterminated gradually but completely, should he attempt to continue the war in this manner, and his whole property of every description been laid waste.

April 8. We received the news that JEFF. DAVIS had been captured near Irvington, Ga., while endeavoring to make his escape in petticoats, by federal cavalry. As the petticoats were not made for him and too short, they did not cover his boots and spurs; he was recognized and taken prisoner. This news caused merriment and anger; anger because DAVIS had been allowed to take off his wife's dress alive, and because he had not been made to suffer the just punishment for his crimes on the spot. Many expressed their belief, that this blood-dripping traitor would now escape the bullet or the rope. The reward of $100,000 seemed to have been offered uselessly and to be money expended for nothing, and the future will show, that our suppositions were right, and that the leniency shown JEFF. DAVIS and the other leaders of the rebellion, will only tend to expose the Union to new dangers, and may yet cost us many valuable lives of true-hearted patriots and Union men, as in the years just passed.

April 9. It was asserted for certain that we would leave our present position in a few days to advance against JOHNSTON and Raleigh. A number of wounded of the different brigades that had recovered, were expected prior to our departure. In camp everything was quiet and the men were busy writing to their friends and relatives the events of the last days and hoped that soon we would commence our last march against the armed rebels.

April 10. We received orders to be ready at daybreak the next day for our advance. These preparations occupied our time to-day, and we drew rations for three days. It was reported that a strong rebel force was in position six miles from Goldsboro, on the road to Smithfield, and as this was the road our corps, the 20th, was to take, we would perhaps get another opportunity to frighten the enemy. The recovered sick and wounded arrived to-day from Wilmington, N. C.; quite a number belonged to our regiment, and had a good deal to say about their journey from Nashville, Tenn., and about the battles at Franklin and Nashville, in which some of them had participated.

April 11. Our drummers gave the signal at 4½ o'clock A. M., to get ready, after we had prepared and eaten our breakfast. Soon in every direction blazing camp fires were seen, and our boys around them busy cooking, while the others packed up. This could be done in an hour, but we generally got two hours to do it in. This morning new leather equipments, &c., were distributed among the men in need of it. At 6 o'clock the signal was given to break up, the knapsacks were buckled, the gun shouldered, and we were now ready to advance. We returned to Goldsboro, where a member of company D of our regiment had just arrived, that had been wounded and taken prisoner by the rebels while foraging some three weeks ago. The man had been taken to Smithfield and was closely guarded at first, but escaped when a good opportunity offered, and came from Smithfield to Goldsboro, 25 miles on his crutches. Here he was sent to the hospital, as his wounds had become worse in consequence of his flight. He testified of having heard from rebels, that nearly the whole force of the enemy had left Raleigh, and moved to Greensboro and neighborhood. We left the city at noon in a southwesterly direction until near the Neuse river, then we moved westward along the river over a swampy, wet road. The first division led the corps to-day. At a creek, the bridge of which had been burned, our advance met the enemy, and had a brisk skirmish, but drove the rebels back. A bridge had to be built, and we did not go into camp until 11 o'clock P. M., between Smithfield and Goldsboro, wet to the skin. The rain continued during the night, and we had great trouble to get wood for supper, and to get the wet wood to burn.

April 12. We were awakened at 3 o'clock A. M., and advanced at daybreak. The enemy, consisting of cavalry, had retreated, and we met no resistance, but the bad roads and the bridgeless streamlets prevented our rapid advance. The day was very hot and many men were compelled to leave the ranks, and follow as soon as they were able to. We reached

Smithfield about sundown and went into camp. We advanced the next day at 6 A. M., marched through Smithfield and crossed the Neuse river on pontoons, as the enemy had burned the railroad bridge. While marching through town we got the news that LEE had surrendered to GRANT, near Appomatox C. H., Va. This news created the greatest joy, and when we halted a few miles west of Smithfield, in an open field to rest and to await the train and rear, (we had the advance to-day,) we heard the news officially, and "three times three" were freely and heartily given. the hats went up into the air, and wild enthusiasm was seen everywhere. In our rear we heard continual shouting and cheering, as our rear passed through Smithfield and received the news, intermingled by the music of the bands. We were sure now that JOHNSTON would follow LEE's example immediately, and our wish was that this would happen soon and without further bloodshed. We left the field in the best humor, and although the day was hot and the march continued very quick, yet no murmurs were heard, not even from those hardly able to remain in the ranks. The country between Smithfield and Raleigh, although low, was dry and beautiful, but in places too sandy to make the marching a pleasure. The woods consisted mostly of pines, and the shady reposes under them, when we halted, were quite a luxury. We went into camp early in the afternoon, being but 10 miles from Raleigh. Rebel cavalry was in our front and on our left throughout the day, but did us no harm. Our cavalry, under Gen. KILPATRICK, was continually skirmishing with the enemy, whom no time was given to get a firm foothold, but was always driven back. After we had gone into camp, part of our brigade had to assist our cavalry to drive the enemy further back. When the enemy saw the infantry and cavalry advancing, it needed no order on our part to make him retreat; our cavalry advanced as far as it chose to, and the infantry returned to camp. KILPATRICK captured 60 ammunition wagons from the enemy. The night was quiet and pleasant.

April 13. We left camp at 6 o'clock A. M., expecting either a bloody or a joyful day. We supposed the latter, for if the enemy knew that LEE had surrendered, and had a bit of sense left, he would not dispute our entrance in Raleigh. It seemed as though the enemy considered "prudence the mother of wisdom," and we advanced rapidly without meeting resistance, until we could see the church steeples of the city, when a couple of rapidly fired cannon shots on our right seemed to convince us of the contrary. We now supposed that we would have to take the city, but all firing ceased, and the nearer we approached the city the firmer the conviction became that no resistance would be offered. At 2 o'clock P. M., we camped near Raleigh, N. C., the city had been surrendered by the Mayor to KILPATRICK; nevertheless, a few rebels had dared to fire on our troops, these were pursued, captured and punished for their perfidy as they deserved. Later in the day the town was garrisoned by infantry, while the cavalry cleared the surrounding country of rebels, but met a decided resistance a few miles from town, the fire being brisk and continuous. Raleigh was not injured in the least and we had leave to go to town without a pass, but found a guard at every house to prevent our entrance, and that nothing was taken without permission of the proprietor. The inhabitants, although mostly rebels, that would have given their all to place us in the situation of their friends, were friendly and mild to us. The arch rebels could hardly be gotten to talk about the present situation of the rebel armies, and sought seclusion when we told them how we had driven the rebels before us, and that LEE had been compelled to surrender and that JOHNSTON, KIRBY SMITH, and others would soon have to follow LEE's example; that they would have to acknowledge the hated Yankee regime after fruitless endeavors for four years to overthrow it.

Such food was too wholesome for the soured rebel stomachs, but no replies were made. But aside from these there were many inhabitants that hated the rebellion and were really glad at the victory of the Union troops, and who hoped that the war would soon terminate. They proved their words by actions, were kind and friendly to us, gave us such things as we needed for building cabins most readily, and visited us in camp to have a chat with us. We received the news that LEE's men had been paroled immediately, and were allowed to return home, and that JOHNSTON's main force was at Hillsboro, N. C.

April 14. We remained in camp, while other corps moved their camps north of the city. A number of our men went to town and broke into some stores, but the provost guard stopped them. The lunatic asylum, where a number of sick soldiers were lying, was surrounded by a guard and nobody admitted. Rumors were "thick as bees" about JOHNSTON's surrender. Some said that the surrender had taken place, while others thought that JOHNSTON had refused to surrender and intended to continue the war on his own hook. Others again opined that JOHNSTON was personally in Raleigh to arrange matters for the surrender. But these were all rumors, and nobody but the commander and his immediate neighborhood knew what was going on.

April 15. We got marching orders, packed up, and paraded through the streets, but a rain prevented our move, and we remained in camp. In our front, north of Raleigh, a heavy cannonade was heard, and as no news came in we supposed that KILPATRICK had again found the enemy. In town JOHNSTON's arrival was looked for, and many of our men, anxious to see this great rebel, went to the depot, but waited in vain. Foraging, burning or demolishing houses or fence rails, was prohibited by an order of Gen. SHERMAN, until further orders. We judged from this that JOHNSTON intended to surrender, and that all hostilities were to be suspended. We did not receive any positive news, and everybody was as "anxious as a granny" to "learn all about it."

April 16. Not much talking was going on, but anxiety was depicted on every face. These were trying times, such as we had expected, and which were now about to commence. The men were no longer quieted by mere say-so's, but all wished to know the truth, the whole truth, and nothing but the truth from SHERMAN himself. A train arrived from the front with a number of rebel officers, and a short while afterwards the neighboring camps showed life, while ours remained quiet. A rumor was that JOHNSTON had capitulated, and the manifestations of joy increased as the time flew by. One cheer followed the other, the firing was as brisk as in a fight, the music bands were compelled to play, and the air was filled with all kinds of noises and tunes. We remained quiet as we wanted to hear a certainty, something about an accomplished fact, and not merely a "grape-vine." A number of our men at last went to the brigade headquarter, but Col. CASE knew no more than we did ourselves, but that the news would soon come if there was any truth in it; the brigade band was ordered to play, in case the reports should be confirmed. We anxiously awaited the first notes of our band, and our situation became very unpleasant; but all waiting was in vain. By and by the noise and music ceased in the neighboring camps, and we learned that the whole report was a hoax, and without foundation: our expectations, though not our hopes, were verified.

April 17. Our camp-ground had to be cleaned after breakfast, as it was expected that our stay here would be prolonged. Some of the men, not busy, went to town to learn something about the truth or untruth of JOHNSTON's surrender, but all returned with the most conflicting reports. Gen. SHERMAN had gone to JOHNSTON's head-quarters in company with several officers, and his return was anxiously looked for. At 7 o'clock the general returned, but nothing became public in regard to the course pursued, and we had to content ourselves by hoping the best. To crown the depressed feeling of the men, rumors of an assassination of President LINCOLN became current, but this seemed too awful for belief. Yet it was evident that something must have transpired, as Secretary SEWARD had been wounded, as well as his son. Deserters of JOHNSTON's army and paroled men of LEE's army continued to arrive. The former knew nothing about the surrender of the army, the latter were tired of the war, and expressed the hope that JOHNSTON and KIRBY SMITH would act as sensibly as LEE had done, and thereby prevent the further unnecessary slaughter of their men.

April 18. Gen. SHERMAN again went to the headquarters of JOHNSTON. The particulars of the assassination of President LIMCOLM, while in the theatre in Washington on the 14th inst., was published in the "Raleigh Progress" to-day. We could not believe the astounding, yea, stunning news, yesterday, but as the papers confirmed the report, we had to believe it. The effect this news of the assassination of such a beloved man as LINCOLN had upon the men under SHERMAN, is an impossibility to describe. Everything else was forgotten, and both officers and soldiers swore vengeance on the rebels, who had robbed the nation of its dearest and best citizen; they hoped that JOHNSTON would not surrender and that SHERMAN would advance immediately against him, and punish the murderer's abettors as they had well deserved. A rebel near Raleigh, expressing his satisfaction at this horrible deed, was killed instantly by our men. The least expression on the part of the rebels, was sufficient to make our men mark them as they deserved. If JEFF DAVIS had been here, he would have been sent to the deepest pool of perdition, where this arch traitor, the abettor and assistant of cowardly assassins, belonged. It was not doubted that LEE and some of his officers knew about the premeditated assassination, and had also assisted in its execution. All the leaders of the gigantic rebellion that had cost the nation thousands of valuable lives, would have been executed had they but been in our midst. Everybody mourned over the loss of our beloved, honest president, the flags waved at half mast, and the bands played melancholy airs in memory of the good and true man that had stood for four years at the helm of the ship of state, when lashed by the furious waves of rebellion and copperheadism! When the light of peace began to dawn upon the nation, he was re-elected to his high station, as the people were satisfied that a patriot and a good man held the reins of government, despite the infamous accusations of the rebels and their northern sympathizers, the copperheads. And this good man fell by the hand of a cowardly assassin! Col. CASE intended to deliver a speech in memory of the murdered president, but later and contradicting reports caused him to postpone it until to-morrow.

April 19. The papers published further particulars about the assassination, and there could be no longer any doubt about its truth, much as we disliked to be forced to such a belief. Gen. HARRISON, who returned from his furlough, during which he had been promoted to general, took command of our brigade. In the evening he made a speech during which he expressed his doubt that we would get an opportunity to take revenge as armed soldiers on the enemy for the loss he had caused the northern people. The enemy, he said, knows too well that henceforward he cannot longer expect clemency, or be spared, in case he does not discontinue his hostilities. The speaker expressed the hope of the whole army when he said, he hoped that JOHNSTON would not accept SHERMAN'S terms of surrender, that we might get a chance to tame the enemy, who had given a terrible blow to the army by this foul murder,—and that we might subdue the enemy, and drive the last remains of rebel spirit out of him. Cols. CASE, DUSTIN and DOHN spoke next, (DOSTON formerly commanded the 105th Ills. regt., but now the 2d brigade of our division,) encouraged the men and bewailed the death of the president, who would remain in grateful memory of the nation, as long as the republic existed. The assembly did not disperse until late at night, anxious to learn the events of the next day.

April 20. Everything and everybody wore a mournful aspect, and all merriment had fled. Even in town, where all kinds of rumors were in circulation generally, nothing else was talked about but the murder of the president in FORD's theater. No one wanted to know anything about the surrender of JOHNSTON, but everyone desired to advance, to avenge the foul murder, to avenge the sufferings of our prisoners, to avenge our fallen comrades—the fathers of families, and to punish the rebels for their crimes and cruelties. All wanted peace, but not until the enemy had been subdued, and was at our feet, begging for mercy and pardon! We knew that in such a manner only a lasting peace could be secured, and that all our prayers that the "erring brethren" would return to loyalty, had made them more stiff-necked, and that all our sacrifices would be vain if our terms were less. Gen. SHERMAN assured us in an order that we would be on our way to Washington in a few days, but caused very little satisfaction thereby. We judged from this that JOHNSTON either had accepted the conditions of surrender, or was about to accept them. We had too much confidence in our commander to believe that his conditions would lead to anything but a lasting peace; but we would rather have given the enemy a lesson, to show him that his enormities and cruelties had created a powerful, revengeful spirit within us! The camps were cleaned again but the building of cabins was neglected, in the expectation that it "would not pay." It was said that a grand parade would take place before we left Raleigh.

April 21. A grand parade was announced for to-morrow before Gen. SHERMAN. The order added that the regiments would have to appear on the parade-ground in heavy fighting order, in the expectation that this would be the last time. A heavy rain set in in the afternoon. Among the chit-chats of camp the route we would take from here to Washington formed a conspicuous part of the conversation. Most of the men were of the opinion that we would have to tramp it, as SHERMA's army seemed destined to march through the whole rebel territory, as we had heretofore done amid hard and continual fighting. Our leaders would no doubt think that as we had marched thus far, we might foot the distance to Washington too. Others thought differently and that the enemy had been the cause of our marching, and that the government would now take pity on us, let us return to Newbern, and thence ship to Washington. Many feared this, knowing that when soldiers are sent by water they are generally packed like herrings, and be in want of the necessary exercise and water and food. Such were the chats in camp while the men cleaned, scoured and brushed for the parade on the morrow.

April 22. We fell in rank early, as the parade was to take place in the forenoon, and marched to town, leaving our knapsacksacks and other things except the guns and equipments in camp. The parade took place in the streets of Raleigh, where a large number of lookers-on from other corps, (our corps alone was parading to-day,) of citizens of both sexes, and paroled rebel soldiers had come to be eye witness of the scene. The streets were kept clear by guards, so that one regiment after the other could advance by company front to the court house, where Gens. SHERMAN, SLOCUM and others were scrutinizing the movements of the troops. The streets were rather rough for the parade, but as our loads were light everything passed off satisfactorily, and by noon the whole regiment was back in camp. A rumor was current in camp that we would leave next Tuesday for Richmond and Washington. This report was not believed, as no confirmation of JOHNSTON's surrender had been received, and as we could not leave until the rebel army had been compelled to surrender. Paroled soldiers arrived daily on the way to their homes.

April 23. Nothing to do in camp and no "grape vines" current. Nothing positive was as yet known about the surrender of JOHNSTON, and we were surprised that all transactions were kept so secret. We could not believe that JOHNSTON intended to continue the war on his own hook, as SHERMAN had been to the rebel head-quarter several times, and would have advanced if such would be the case, and compell him to surrender. We relied on SHERMAN's order and promise that we would be on the march to Washington in a few days, but could not comprehend the propriety of keeping the terms of surrender secret, knowing as we did that SHERMAN would offer such terms only, as would secure a lasting peace. The weather was cold.

April 24. The regiment received orders to go foraging, and immediately after breakfast, a number of wagons were packed for the expedition, that would last several days, as all provisions had vanished in the neighborhood of the city, and as we would have to go many miles before getting any. As I had attended to the "writing business" of the company for the captain, since we left our place between Chesterfield and Cheraw, I was free from duty, excepting when danger was nigh. I remained in camp, busy making out the papers, necessary to expedite the business of making out the muster-rolls. The men idling about the camp, were speculating on the day of their discharge, and how they intended to meet their wives, children and friends, and the speeches they intended to make to them, in case they should get home safe. Many doubted that they would be recognized by their relatives. The beloved wife or child of one or the other had died, and they went home less cheerful than others, but all the heads of families were anxious to return to support their families again, as in former years. Such were the conversation, until, when suddenly an order of Gen. SHERMAN put a stop to them. Our neighboring regiments had received marching orders, and soon after an order came to our regimental headquarters that we would start to-morrow morning early, but not for Washington, but against JOHNSTON. The feeling of revenge again arose in the breasts of the men, because JOHNSTON had not surrendered, and all thoughts about an early discharge were soon forgotten. Several couriers were sent after our regiment that must have been a good way from camp by this time, and the regiment returned shortly after midnight. While the men were ridding themselves of their guns, &c., many promises were made that every rebel captured should be shot, if he did not surrender, as the enemy had compelled us again to commence the slaughter. Rumors became current that the Government and GRANT had refused to sanction SHERMAN's terms of surrender to JOHNSTON, and that SHERMAN would be superseded by MEADE. As we knew nothing about the terms we could not say anything as regards the justice of this step, but knew that the deposition of SHERMAN would have been a terrible if not fatal blow to our army, more so than the murder of President LINCOLN. As a general thing we considered the report untrue, knowing that a man like SHERMAN, who hated the rebellion from the bottom of his heart, could not be guilty of a crime to justify such a step, after having led his army victoriously through Georgia, Alabama, South Carolina and North Carolina. Nobody cared about any sleep in the night, but prepared for the bloody conflict on the morrow.

April 25. As usually when on the march we were awakened early, and soon we were ready to recommence hostilities. For some reason or other we did not start until 8½ o'clock, when we left Raleigh and marched in a southwesterly direction towards Pittsboro. After the first and second divisions ahead of us had stretched out, we advanced rapidly, though it was very severe on account of the scorching rays of the sun. Neither enemy nor obstructions prevented our march, as heretofore in North and South Carolina. As usually one man after the other left the ranks to sit down on the road side to rest, and then continue the trot as soon as the limbs permitted. We advanced until nearly sunset, after having made 13 miles, when we camped in the bush near the road. We met many paroled rebel soldiers, on their way to Raleigh, who spread the report that JOHNSTON had been shot by one of his own men for ordering every straggler and deserter shot. Others said that JOHNSTON had left the army and sought safety in flight. These reports were not believed and proved to be untrue in the evening. The night was very noisy, and the noise of the cannons robbed us of a good deal of our sleep.

April 26. We remained quiet for some reason unknown to us. Foragers were detailed to scour the country for provisions and fodder, and commenced their work to-day, but nearly all returned empty-handed. The day was very warm. Deserters from JOHNSTON's army contradicted all reports of yesterday in regard to that army, that was at Greensboro, 85 miles from here. They doubted that another fight would take place, as JOHNSTON's men were tired of the war and were deserting by hundreds and leaving for their homes.

—16

April 27. We remained quiet, without any prospect of an early move. From all appearances it seemed more likely that JOHNSTON had surrendered, and that we would return to Raleigh. This seemed to be confirmed, as the 105th Illinois regiment, belonging to our brigade, was ordered to pack up immediately, and escort the division wagon-train back to Raleigh, and there to resume their former camping ground. The other regiments of the brigade had not received any order to return, but the return of the provision and ammunition train seemed to indicate that we would follow, perhaps to-morrow already. It was certain that JOHNSTON had surrendered, and we expected the particulars about this event.

April 28. At a quarter before six we left camp for Raleigh; the weather was as warm as it had been on the day of our departure from there. Yet we performed the march more rapidly than on the 25th, at 12 o'clock M, we were at our former camping ground. Soon after our arrival it became clear that we would have to foot our way to Washington, and commence perhaps in a few days, as the camp commanders received order to make out the descriptive rolls of all sick and disabled, and hand them to the regiment surgeon, so that arrangements could be made to send the men North. With their descriptive rolls it was not necessary for them to await our arrival in New York or Washington, but could be mustered out as soon as they had been paid off, and leave for their homes. In the afternoon the pay rolls were made out, and the 30th of April (Monday) fixed as the day of our departure from here. We were to march via Richmond and Alexandria to Washington. About the surrender of JOHNSTON we could gain no particulars, and we supposed from this that SHERMAN must have made a mistake, as his army had not been officially notified of the surrender of the enemy, that we had driven through Georgia, whom we had compelled to leave Savannah, assisted his speed through the Carolinas, and whom we had whipped on the 16th and 19th of last month at Averysboro and Bentonville, and whom we had tamed.

April 29. The regiment had inspection of arms and clothes, and the pay rolls were completed, although we did not expect to be paid off until we had reached Washington. We had to give up fifteen of the forty cartridges we had always had to carry with us, but a good many men thought it unnecessary to carry surplus weight and reduced the number of their cartridges yet more. Our sick and wounded and lame left Raleigh this evening for Newbern, whence they were transported by water. The morrow was fixed for our departure, while the 23d corps and KILPATRICK's cavalry remained for a while as a garrison, and to keep the returned rebels quiet and in order.

April 30. We started early on our march to the North and our homes that we had left some three years ago. Before leaving an order of Gen. SHERMAN was read to us, that roll call would be held three times a day, and all absentees without leave punished. Plundering, destroying or robbing rebel property was prohibited and severely punished. The divisions had to be three to five miles apart while on the march; the marching was to be done slowly, so that every soldier could get along without becoming tired. We were assured finally, that we would be mustered out in Washington, and would soon be at home with our friends. We left at 7 o'clock, paraded through town with music, stopped at the edge of the town until 9, and then advanced. At 8 o'clock P. M. we reached the Neuse river, the bridges had broken down, and we were compelled to halt and eat our supper. Two men were killed by the breaking down of the bridge. The night was rainy, but we enjoyed a good sleep after a march of 15 miles, through a country but little inhabited. All the houses were deserted.

May 1, 1865. We commenced our second day's

march and crossed the river at 7 o'clock on a bridge, erected in the night, and then moved ahead rapidly to get closer to the two divisions ahead of us. The weather was warm, but the marching pleasant, as the country was more thickly settled, and the inhabitants no longer afraid and shy, but treated us kindly, and were delighted when our bands played, while passing their houses. The blacks could not content themselves with grinning, but some louder manifestations of joy were necessary for them; they came in droves, hopped and danced around the bands, until they had accompanied us several miles, when they disappeared as suddenly as they had come. After a march of 17 miles we went into camp; the night was cool and clear.

May 2. We did not leave camp until 8 o'clock, as our regiment formed the rear of the division. The day was cool and the promenading as pleasant and easy as yesterday. The country was well inhabited and the inhabitants (particularly the female part) were, at least outwardly, friendly, came from their houses to look at the Yankee army that had caused them so much trouble and whipped their armies continually. They came from their houses that could not be visited any more on account of Sherman's order, and viewed us until some one of our boys made an insulting remark, when they turned their backs disdainfully to us. Females of the poorer class thought of doing us and themselves a favor by bringing tobacco in baskets to us and selling it for greenbacks; but these were as great a scarcity as tobacco; they had to take their loads home again, unless they took pity on us and gave part of the load away. In the morning we marched in the direction of Oxford, but left the place on our left without touching it, and camped after a march of 15 miles, being distant from Richmond 117 miles. When in camp, our thoughts turned a year back, when we left our splendid and commodious camp in Lookout Valley and commenced our first day's march against the enemy behind his works at

Dalton and Reseca. Then every one's life was in jeopardy, not knowing whether it was the will of the Almighty to allow him to be with his comrades in the evening; to-day we were on our way to our homes, with the hope of soon enjoying a lasting peace. Then most of our regiments were full. at least the rebel balls had not decimated them, now numerous graves of the fallen members spotted the route from Chattanooga through Georgia and the two Carolinas. The regiments had become small and slender. and in looking over the original company roll, many names were seen, whose bearers were either sleeping beneath the quiet sod, or who had been mustered out on account of disability. In those days the rebels and JEFF. DAVIS considered themselves unconquerable and all offers of peace were disdainfully rejected,—the States just named had not seen the devastation of war and consequences of the rebellion,—but now all the rebel armies. with the exception of a small one West of the Mississippi, had surrendered, JEFF. DAVIS was a prisoner in Fort Monroe, and Georgia and the Carolinas had gotten their full share of the evil effects of war.

May 3. As it was our intention to-day to reach the Roanoak river and cross, we started earlier than usual on our promenade of twenty miles. We were awakened at 3 o'clock A. M., and started at 5. About 7 we got up with the first and second division, that had been several miles ahead, but getting on the wrong road, we met them just as they were getting on the right road again. We were compelled to halt until the divisions with train had gotten out of our way. At 9 o clock we reached Williamsboro, a small town, through which we passed with music. The negroes came flocking to us, attracted by the sound of music, and as they saw one regiment after the other pass without insulting them, they showered the "God-bless-you's" upon us. But few white inhabitants showed themselves, whether they had fled or whether they kept away from hatred we did not learn. At 2½ o'clock we stepped over the border of North Carolina into Virginia, when we took the lead of the column, and reached Roanoak river, 7 miles from the border, before sundown. We went into camp a mile beyond the river, after a march of 25 miles. From here we had but 92 miles to Richmond. But few murmurs were heard about this rapid marching, but on the contrary all men seemed anxious to get to Washington as soon as possible, and to march even 25 or 30 miles a day to get there. The only murmur was heard about the provisions, for we had received but half rations since our departure from Raleigh, and tonight we had nothing but bread, but no meat. We were told that but a small quantity was left on the wagons, and with it we would have to be as saving as possible. The men grumbled badly and said that they could not march 25 miles a day, with no other food than coffee and crackers; they intended to go foraging on their own hook, if not provided with the proper rations.

May 4. We left camp at 4½ o'clock A. M., and moved in the direction of Boydston, but left this place on our right and took the road to Saffold's bridge, over the Newbern river. Our brigade led the division, and we moved through a country but little cultivated. The inhabitants were kind to us, and consisted mostly of poor families, that were, as they told us themselves, not treated better than slaves. The road was very rocky and narrow, and the men had to pass through the brush frequently and be careful about sore feet. Nevertheless we advanced rapidly, and at noon we reached the Newbern river, which we crossed on the so-called Saffold's bridge. One mile north of the river we went into camp, after having made 21 miles. The men complained a good deal about sore feet and being worn out, many became disabled from walking, while others stepped from the ranks and got along as well as they could. The country North of the river had been visited by troops that had assisted in penning JOHNSTON, after the surrender of LEE, and left their traces everywhere. The weather was excessively hot, but a short rain cooled the air somewhat, and the night was pleasant.

May 5. We left camp amid a heavy thunderstorm and rain at 5 o'clock A. M., and could not move as fast as formerly, as the roads were muddy and had to be repaired in many places before our wagons could pass. Several hours later the rain ceased, the day became clear and hot, and the roads dried gradually, enabling us to move faster. At noon we took a main road for Petersburg, and made 10 miles in 3 hours. It was our intention to reach Black and White station on the Petersburg and Lynchburg R. R. and camp there; but when 8 miles from the station the 14th corps got on our road, and we were compelled to camp, after a march of 20 miles, at 2 o'clock P. M. The rapid advance and the hot weather had disqualified many of the men from marching and compelled them to leave the column, the ambulances were crowded by sick and such, whose legs would no longer perform their duty. Many had been allowed to move along at their own pleasure, with nothing but their musket, and from 2 o'clock until evening these poor fellows continued to come in limping on their feet, covered with blisters. They assured us that no march had ever worn them out to such a degree as this one. The whole blame was thrown on our leaders, and with justice, as they did not heed SHERMAN's order at all to let the men march slowly, but did the contrary. Gen. SHERMAN was not with us, but had left Raleigh for Charleston, and our leaders had everything their own way. The men grumbled at Gen. MOWER who was the cause of this senseless hurrying, and said as there was no longer any danger of being killed by balls, they did not want to kill themselves by marching, but take their own time hereafter.

May 6. We left camp at 5 o'clock and reached Black and White station at 9. Here we found the first troops of the Eastern army, belonging to the 6th corps and guarding the Railroad track. We marched through the place and rested a few miles further to rest. The weather was very hot again, and many left the ranks, reported themselves sick to the surgeon, or gave up their baggage, or rested under some shade tree until able to advance again. Some, hating the epithet "straggler," compelled negroes to carry their baggage for a couple of hours, or for the balance of the day. After we had marched 14 miles, we went into camp 10 miles Southwest of the Appomatox river. The number of sick and disabled increased and all complained of being worn out, as we marched almost daily 15—20 miles until noon or early in the afternoon. If we had made the marches in the whole day, and if we had rested a couple of hours at noon during the hottest part of the day, the men would not have complained and compelled the half-starved mules and horses to drag them along in wagons. To make such marches day for day without halting, was enough to wear out the stoutest, and proved conclusively that our commander did not care for his men.

May 7. We were awakened at 2 o'clock A. M. by the signal, left camp at 4 and had made several miles by sunrise, before the heat commenced. Like many of my comrades I was disqualified to march, for the first time since entering the service, but ridding myself of baggage and gun managed to get along a little at least. Fortunately, the marching went slower, as the road leading to the river became lower and prevented a more rapid advance. Perhaps the thought had struck our leaders, that by slow and steady marching we could get along better than by rapid marching—a pity, that such common sense ideas seize great men's brains generally too late. At 9 o'clock A. M. we reached a line of works near the Appomatox river, that had partly been torn or fallen down.

Behind the works we saw that we were on a battlefield, each tree having bullet marks, some with branches and crowns shot off, while some had been completely shattered. The ground was covered with rotting uniforms, knapsacks, canteens, &c., and sometimes a broken carbine was seen. A short distance from here a house was visible, with a hospital flag waving from it, where we found 5 of SHERIDAN's men that had been wounded at the fight several weeks ago. We could learn no particulars about the fight, but that the rebels made a determined stand and that the Union troops suffered greatly, before the enemy retreated. We crossed the river at 11 o'clock on pontoons, and advanced through a bushy, hilly country, until near Cloverhill, where we camped after a march of 15 miles near a coal mine.

May 8. We left camp at 4½ o'clock, marched through Cloverhill, a place of a few houses, and approached Richmond on a narrow bushy road, that had been but seldom used. The day became very hot, but I determined to carry my baggage and resume my place in the ranks. After vainly trying to get along after a march of 5 miles, I had to sit down, and when the brigade had passed, several of my comrades, in the same unfortunate condition with myself, came limping up to me. After we had rested awhile, we continued our march, until our failing strength again compelled us to rest. Thus we forced our wearied limbs along, until we found the regiment at 1 o'clock P. M, about going into camp. But the regiment advanced again, and I took my place in the company, and at 2 o'clock we camped at Falling Creek or Falling Water, with the order to remain here for several days. We were but 7 miles from Richmond, and could have reached the shores of the James river, if we had continued to march until night, and not cared for the sick and lame. But we found out that it was not the proper attention for the sick that made us rest, but that we had arrived here several days too soon, and had to wait until Gen. SHERMAN would rejoin us, before we could enter Richmond and continue our march to Washington. With to-day's march the greatest suffering since entering the service ended, and which had disabled more men than the four months' campaign of last Summer from Chattanooga to Atlanta.

May 9. Excruciating pain in my breast and limbs compelled me to take medicine, something I had done but very seldom since entering the service, and then only with the greatest dread. I was compelled to report myself sick, for if I had attempted to march, the weight of the baggage would have broken me down immediately. Fortunately for our regiment our surgeon was a man who had a heart and feeling for his fellow-men, and did everything in his power, while we were on our march, for the sick and broken down soldiers. The number of men seeking his assistance to-day was by no means small, and he had enough to do to get means of transportation for those not able to walk, and to write permits for those able to march, but unable to carry their baggage. Every sick soldier received a pass to-day, as we expected to receive orders to resume our march for a better camp ground. The expectation became verified, and at 9 o'clock we marched 2 miles closer to the city where we camped again, being but 5 miles from Richmond. Inspection was announced for 5 o'clock P. M., and the men kept busy thereby (except the sick) in preparing for it. We also received orders to parade through the streets of Richmond, and supposed from this that Gen. SHERMAN had returned from Charleston, and would accompany us to Washington. As the parade was to take place to-morrow, preparations were made to give all the sick transportation by water. The sick of the different regiments (among whom myself) were called around the regimental surgeon, and other names put down, whereupon the sick of our brigade were ordered to the division hospital. It was my first time to leave the regiment for a longer period and did not expect to rejoin it before reaching Alexandria or Washington. I was very sorry for not being able to take part in the parade and the march to Washington, but it was an utter impossibility for me to do so. The division head-quarter was also used as the division hospital, and on our way there passed the head-quarter of the 3d brigade just as an orderly had fired a pistol shot at a staff officer, wounding him badly but without doubt intending to kill him. The orderly fled, but the report of the pistol had attracted a crowd, who took charge of the wounded and went in pursuit of the assassin, and captured him soon. When caught the fellow commenced to hollow and cry, professing his innocence and that his pistol had gone off without his intention; his cries "for God's sake, don't let them kill me," were indeed pitiful. He was placed under arrest, to await his punishment for his attempted murder.

May 10. We got a poor breakfast in the hospital, consisting of beefsteak soup with crackers. The sick of the division were again examined, and those able to march got permission to return to their regiments. But as one night's rest was not very apt to restore strength and health to the sick, but few went. We left the hospital at 9 o,clock and went to Manchester, opposite Richmond, a part on foot and the other part in wagons, and reached there at 11 o'clock. We moved through town as fast as our strength permitted, crossed the river and entered Richmond, that had cost many a brave union soldier his life, and was now to some extent burnt down. We did not get the pleasure to take a more minute view of the rebel capital, as we were ordered not to leave the shore, as the boat was ready to take us to Alexandria. We had a close view of the Libby prison and castle Thunder, where many union soldiers had been tortured to death; we passed both prisons on our march. All union soldiers had left the cell, and rebel soldiers taken their places, guarded by union soldiers. We would like to have seen the interior, but our entrance was prohibited by the guard. After having been in Richmond for several hours, a steamer came to take us on board. We found the sick of the 2d division on board, and could hardly find room to put down our knapsacks, much less to sit down. As our and this division never agreed, quarrels and even fights soon threatened to break out, when the commanding officer, a major, seeing such an inimical feeling among the men, ordered the sick of the 3d division from the steamer, that started immediately afterwards, full enough without us. After remaining on shore several hours longer, another steamer took us on board, where we had room enough now, and left at 6 o'clock P. M. In consequence of our late departure, we lost the hoped for look at the entire rebel works along the James river. Nevertheless we got a good distance from Richmond before it became quite dark, and saw the rebel forts but a short distance apart, along the shore. The guns were yet in position, and some forts were guarded by our troops. The river was full of torpedoes, but their position was marked by little red flags; nevertheless the pilot had great trouble to avoid them, as the least touch would have blown us to atoms. The darkness prevented our seeing the works at and near City Point, and we sought rest.

May 11. We had remained at City Point until after midnight and were near Newport News when we awoke. The day was beautiful and warm, the shores lined with woods, interspersed here and there by a plantation, bearing visible marks either of the war or the idleness of its proprietor, as the fields were desolate and empty. Several steamers, loaded with cattle, hay, railroad wagons and machinery, passed our boat bound for Richmond. We reached

Fort Monroe at 2 o'clock P. M., where we stopped a short while to take some provisions on board. We saw several armed vessels here. When we left the tide had set in the Chesapeake bay, and soon the land disappeared on one side. The wind being favorable, the sails were set, whereby the speed of our steamer was increased. At 4 P. M. we lost sight of all land, but it soon re-appeared on one side. At 8 o'clock P. M. a storm arose, accompanied by thunder and lightning, and rain, and though the sails were fastened, many of the men became sea-sick in consequence of the plunging of the steamer. After the sails had been reefed, the steamer went ahead more steadily, and we could seek rest on the deck without running danger of rolling overboard. The storm began to abate, but dark clouds moved along the heavens, and lightning flashes for a moment illuminated the sky, while the grumbling thunder told us that the danger had not passed yet. Nevertheless we sought rest, but had scarcely fallen asleep when heavy drops of rain fell in our faces, and compelled us to hide under our oil-cloths. We were thus protected from the rain, but the water soon ran under the sides and soaked our blanket, cloak and other things, serving us as a bed. Some preferred now to take the rain standing, but when we got to the mouth of the Potomac, the weather had become so cold that they sought shelter again under their oil cloths.

May 12. With day-break the cold became more intense, and we could feel plainly that we had gotten out of the "sunny South." We felt the cold the severer on account of receiving nothing but cold meat and crackers yesterday; the same we got to-day, but hoped to reach Alexandria at noon, and then get a warm dinner. We reached Cedar Point at 7 o'clock A. M., the country was beautiful and romantic, and on the Virginia side only the deserted houses and desolated fields told us of the existence of war. As we approached Washington, the scenes became more lovely aud beaatiful, we saw the men at work in the fields on the Maryland shore, and others fishing. We saw the men throw out their nets and wink at our pilot to the right and left to avoid their nets. These scenes caused us a good deal of pleasure, as we had years ago left our peaceable vocations, had been continually on the way, principally through deserted regions where we had always to be on the look out for the enemy, death or captivity. Then all thoughts of peace had fled the hearts of our men, but these scenes revived their love of peace and peaceful vocations, and they would willingly have assisted the fishermen or farmers. Our conversation now naturally turned to what we would do on our return home; this one intended to go back on the farm, the other at his trade and set up a shop for himself with the money he had saved, and some even thought of marrying! Amid such pleasant chats we steamed up the Potomac, until we reached fort Washington at 3 o'clock P. M., where the glistening guns and the thick walls of the fort attracted our attention, and we continued to gaze at it until it disappeared from view. Soon afterward the steeples of Washington appeared in sight, and at 5 P. M. we landed at Alexandria, Va. We left the boat immediately and marched through the town, all draped in mourning for the assassination of president LINCOLN, to the "Soldier's Rest," where our names were put down, and where we received a good supper. There we found over 8,000 men of SHERMAN's army, and every steamer brought more sick and disabled soldiers from Raleigh. After supper we retired, and found the first quiet and good rest for some time.

May 13. At 3 o'clock A. M. we were awakened by the loud speaking of soldiers just arrived, and it was impossible to go to sleep again. We left our resting place, and soon after our breakfast was ready, whereupon roll call was held. We then marched to convalescent camp, a mile from town, where we had to await the arrival of the main army. We found several men of our regiment, who had left us at Savannah on account of sickness, and also one member, whose whereabouts we had lost some time ago. He had been taken prisoner in North Carolina, and was paroled after a short captivity, and had been ordered by the military authorities at Alexandria to await the arrival of the regiment at the convalescent camp. We made ourselves as comfortable as possible, were divided off in companies and battallions, and frequently a corporal or sergeant commanded a company, and a lieutenant a regiment. We drew rations for several days, and after supper we chatted awhile about the army, until sleepiness put the finishing touch to our conversation.

May 14. We had to leave our camp place and move into some wall tents, four or five men in each tent where they could "make themselves at home." Provisions were plenty, as were also the common commodities, but as we were guarded by members of the Potomac army, who had received orders to allow no one to leave camp, we could not enjoy any liberty. Quarrels between our men and the guards were frequent on this account, but the guards could not be blamed for it, as they had to obey orders, much as they perhaps disliked it. Finally we were allowed to leave camp in day time, but not in the night. In the evening we saw, a great distance off, rockets go up, and believed them to be signals of the army that seemed to be several day's marches from us.

May 15. We had nothing to do and no news, as we did not get to those that could tell us any. We were in camp all day.

May 16. We remained in camp, and received no news. Our thoughts turned to the events of the past year, when to-day a year ago we buried our brave comrades after the bloody battle of Resaca, and went after the retreating enemy in the evening. We heard that our army would perhaps arrive by to-morrow, and we were glad to get to our regiments every one being tired of the place and situation.

May 17. As the day was very hot and no shade trees in camp, we had to remain in our tents the whole day, where most of us wrote letters. The 15th army corps camped four miles from here, but the other corps were further back, but were all expected here to-morrow. There was a rumor that we would have to march to Baltimore, but this was to be but little believed.

May 18. Gen. SLOCUM, commander of the left wing of SHERMAN's army, arrived at Alexandria with staff—the army being but a few miles from the city. As part of the army had taken a nearer route to Washington, but part of right wing was to pass through Alexandria. The morning was very hot, but in the afternoon a steady rain filled our tents several inches, compelling us to bail the water out with tin cups, and to throw all our things up in a heap. We had to sleep on the wet ground, but on right and left matters were still worse, and although the men deepened the ditches, yet the water increased so fast that the men were compelled to leave the tents until the rain was past and the tents could be moved. Of course we got but little rest on our soaked ground and wet blankets and clothes.

May 19. A large number of our men were sick again and compelled to take medicine. They complained about head-ache, catarrh and stiffness of the limbs, and the pains increased as the hours advanced, so that the surgeons had their hands full to do. I also felt worse, my pain in the breast had increased, compelling me again, much as I dreaded it, to take medicine, that was given me by the Christian Commission. We also received clothes we needed from the Christian Commission for nothing, as well as victuals. In case any one needed paper, pen or ink, he could go to the commission, where he could get these articles every afternoon.

May 20. Many of the convalescents left camp without order or permission to go to their regiments, encamped, as they said, but a few miles distant. The guards could not prevent this escape *en masse*, as our men were determined to leave, whether with or without permission; they met but weak resistance. I received a present from the Christian Commission, consisting of a small bag, containing the following articles: Firstly, a little prayer-book for soldiers; secondly, a very adaptable spool of cotton; thirdly, a needle-cushion with needles, and fourthly, (by no means the latest) a letter of the lady donor, which I read with delight, and learned therefrom that the friend of the soldier and donor lived at Farmington, N. Y. The day was cloudy and rainy, and we expected the order to join our regiments hourly, being dissatisfied with the convalescent camp. The 15th corps reached here at noon and marched through the town. At 5 o'clock all members of the 20th corps received order to pack up and prepare for the march to our respective regiments, but as the marching orders did not come the men gathered and left, without any resistance by the officers, in order to reach their regiments before dark. We had learned the direction from which our division was coming, and after crossing fields and creeks and climbing over fences, we found the wagon train, where we learned the position of the various brigades, and soon after the men of the 129th Illinois had reached the regiment about 7 o'clock P. M. The division camped 4 miles west of Alexandria, on the road leading to the Bull Run battlefield.

May 21. The rain continued to pour down in torrents, and prevented our movements. We had the greatest trouble in preparing our meals, got wet to the skin, and had to remain in the tents until more favorable weather commenced. We received a large mail, the first since we had left Raleigh, and all men in tents somewhat water tight were busy answering the letters, telling their friends that they would be home at latest in July, then to lay aside the armor and pursue the former peaceful vocation. Threats were again uttered against the copperheads, and in the plainest language possible they were told that their doom was sealed and that hereafter they would stand disgraced and covered with infamy in the eyes of every soldier and true union man. Whenever a train had been thrown off the track and soldiers had been killed, the cries for vengeance in the army arose anew, and we vowed, if the choice was left us between the open rebels in the field and the cowardly copperheads at home, the latter would have to answer first for their crimes! It was announced that a grand parade, our last, would take place in the streets of Washington on the 24th of May. Endeavors were made to draw new clothes for occasion, but few of the men took the clothes offered them, not considering it necessary to draw clothes for the short remainder of their time of service.

May 22. Those that did not draw new clothes repaired and cleaned their old uniforms, while the others received the new dresses desired. Guns and equipments were polished, and preparations made generally, to appear in a proper condition on the parade. Some said the parade was to take place on the old Bull Run battle field. The weather was very warm during the day, but the night was cool.

May 23. The army of the Potomac passed a review in the streets of Washington to-day, and many citizens were there witnessing it and awaiting the parade to-morrow. As inspection had been announced for the afternoon, every stain was removed from our uniforms and guns, as we had to clean everything and show it to the company commander until it was in a proper condition. The weather was excessively hot to march through the streets of Washington, as did the army of the Potomac, where a cool draft of air could but seldom be felt. We hoped that the morrow would be cooler and better fit for the parade than to-day, as many of our men had not yet recovered entirely and would become worse at the least exertion.

May 24. We commenced our march towards Washington at 5 o'clock A. M., where thousands of persons, young and old, of both sexes, anxiously expected the army that had moved through a great portion of the West, fighting their way to the seacoast, that had compelled the rebels to surrender Vicksburg, Savannah, Atlanta and other strongholds, and that had shown to the states of Georgia and the Carolinas the effects of a war they themselves had provoked. We threw our knapsacks and haversacks on piles by companies, so that many could participate who otherwise could not. We left Alexandria to our right and took a nearer route to the Long Bridge that crosses the Potomac at Washington. On the way we passed Fort Richardson and other strong works. The sun became hot and our thirst, the more felt in consequence of pickeled pork, almost insufferable, but many springs along our route eased it somewhat. The marching went slow and we rested frequently, as the parade was not to commence before 9 o'clock, and our corps would not be reviewed before 10 o'clock, the 15th and 17th corps being ahead of us. We reached the river at 7 o'clock and had the National Capital in all its glory and grandeur before our eyes. Before we crossed we rested on the former property of Gen. LEE, but a short distance from the palace of this great rebel, where partly hidden by the trees and foliage a flag was waving at half mast. At 9 o'clock a few cannon shots from the neighborhood of the White House informed us of the commencement of the parade, when we crossed over and were most of us for the first time, in the National Capital. We were received in a most delightful and pleasing manner by little girls and boys, when we approached the White House, where the parade was to commence. They cheered and saluted us and brought us bouquets of flowers and water; several ventured close to our column, gave the men their hands and commenced a conversation. Our feelings were indiscribable and a heart of stone would have been melted by such love of the little ones, of which none of us had seen anything for the last three years of slaughter and murder. We had been received everywhere by treason and treachery and treated disdainfully by all but the negroes. We were compelled to cruelty, in order to compel the rebels to treat us right and as human beings. The little boys and girls wanted to know all about our campaign, where we had been, &c., and surely we could not force these dear little ones away by any harsh words. We saw that their parents were true to the union, or else the children would not have been kind to union soldiers. We halted at the White House that was shrouded in mourning drapery, where we stacked arms, awaiting our turn to "fall in." We had to halt some time, as the second division occupied the street, and the first began to move when we formed. Further ahead and in other parts of the city the music of the bands of the other corps were heard, and also the continual cheering of the lookers on. Finally the signal was given for us to fall in and the parade commenced for us. We had never seen such number of witnesses at any parade, than were in Washington that day. The divisions were about 150 steps apart, so that no interruption in the parade could take place, in case something should happen to impede the progress of a division ahead. Our brigade was the first of our division, and we could see plainly that the cavalry guard had great trouble to keep the spectators in their places and out of our way, as a continual pushing and crowding was going on, and as everybody wanted "to see something." Hats and pocket handkerchiefs were waved, and a continual cheering saluted the brigades in our front. We were asked for name and number of the regiment, and if friends or acquaintances were among the bystanders, cheers were given by them with a good will. We could not join the cheering, much as we felt like it, but continued to march along steadily. The further we advanced the more numerous the lookers on became, not only the streets were lined, but all windows and even house tops were crowded. Innumerable flags waved from all houses and windows. One large and beautiful flag particularly attracted our attention, waving in a street we had to pass through, and bearing the inscription: "All hail to our Western Heroes," and the names of the various towns captured by them, Vicksburg, Atlanta and Savannah for instance. We were so overcome by this reception that we did not feel the heat of the sun, nor care for the thirst that commenced again. The deepest gratitude filled our hearts for these manifestations on the part of strangers to show their appreciation of our services. Amid continual cheering we proceeded steadily, now and then a bouquet was thrown to us and the officer's horses were decorated with flowers and flags. Near the mansions of high officers the command to shoulder arms was given, and as we passed hats and handkerchiefs and flags waved. At 12 o'clock we came to a point where President Johnson, Gens. Grant, Sherman and other high officers had their places in an arbor of flowers and flags. For a quarter of a mile from this point the number of the bystanders was so great that we could scarcely force our way through by company front, but after getting through this crowd the number of spectators gradually decreased. Many of the men were too fatigued to remain in rank, and as the "fun" was mostly over they were allowed to seek a place of rest. The little boys and girls (God bless them!) now came forward again and handed us water, milk and other beverages that were eagerly drank with thanks to the dear little ones. About 3 o'clock we reached the end of the city. Many of us did not refuse the glass of ice water or milk, offered us by a fair hand, although we knew that it would do us more harm than good. Nevertheless we appreciated the good intentions of the donors and were filled with a deep sense of gratitude towards the citizens of Washington for this truly enthusiastic reception. We camped for the night four miles from the city, near Fort Lincoln.

May 25. In consequence of the parade and ice water of yesterday and the coldness of the night myself and many others were compelled to seek the assistance of the surgeon again, who gave no medicine and ordered us to remain quietly in our tents. Baltimore papers, that were read close to my tent, in speaking of yesterday's parade, stated that although the Potomac army had looked cleaner than SHERMAN'S, yet the slender, sun-burnt and ragged-looking army of SHERMAN had been applauded by the spectators more than the former, and that it had kept a better line and moved more regularly, despite of the heat and the thirst, than the Potomac army. As we had not seen the parade on the 22d, we could not judge for ourselves; but it seemed doutful than an army but little used up by a march of a few hundred miles, should not be able to beat a tired army that had marched through a greater part of the West and South. The heat was very great, but we had shade trees to protect us from the rays of the sun. There was no duty to do, and those that could not stand idleness commenced to clean up the camping ground. We received some refreshments from the Christian Commission, among them peaches in cans that were very welcome to the sick

May 26. My situation became worse, a continual headache and pain in the breast caused me to sigh frequently, yet I did not go to the doctor, as the medicine yesterday had done no good. Despite of my appetite I was falling off continually, and it seemed as though I would be thrown on a sick bed for a long while, and would have to suffer for the privations and hardships of the campaigns now happily ended. But I thought as long as I had good appetite my constitution would help itself. The day was rainy, and we were compelled to remain in our tents. The only desire the men now had was to be mustered out of the service, and hours began to seem as long as days, and days as long as months, as we had nothing to do whatever. We did not expect to remain here long at the expense of the government, and that the mustering out would commence as soon as the necessary papers had been made out. An order to prepare the pay rolls caused much joy, as all of us were out of greenbacks that we could have used very well. It was said to our great satisfaction, that we would be mustered out of the U. S. service in Washington, and then sent to the capitals of our respective States, to be paid off there. Many prophecied that they would be home by the 25th of June. As the members of Sherman's army had free access to the White House during certain hours of the day, during which the business of the departments was suspended, some of our men intended to pay a visit there to-morrow. As I felt a great deal better towards evening, it was my intention to commence making out the pay rolls in the morning.

May 27. My condition had improved somewhat, and I commenced to make out the pay rolls. For this purpose we used the empty artillery quarters at Fort Lincoln, as the day was rainy and the camp not suited for such work. A number of our men went to Washington immediately after breakfast to see the White House with its ornaments and antiquities; others went to the river with hooks and bait to fish; yet others made improvements in their tents, raised these with poles so that they could enter and leave without crawling on the ground,—they raised their beds several inches from the ground to avoid the dampness arising therefrom, and to protect their health. When I had completed the pay rolls necessary for the present, my pains in breast and head commenced again, and worse than before, so that I was compelled to go to the regimental surgeon, who gave me medicine. I went to bed, and the exhaustion soon made me fall asleep, until I awoke at 12 o'clock at night, when I felt a great deal easier and better. We received several kinds of fruit from the Sanitary Commission.

May 28. My condition was worse to-day than in the night previous, and I had to go to the surgeon again. The medicine I got was effectless on me, and it was impossible for me to attend to making out rolls, that became necessary, the day of mustering out approaching; I could leave my bed with the greatest difficulty only. The weather was hot, and many of the men went to Washington to see the sights.

May 29. The work of making out the muster out rolls was commenced, but I could not assist in consequence of the pains, much as I desired to. In the afternoon my condition became better, and I hoped soon to be able to attend to the work again that I had to neglect for several days past. The Sanitary Commission distributed canned fruit and potatoes, as well as shirts, drawers, socks and handkerchiefs. But as these things were not sufficient for every member of the company, each company arranged a raffle, whereby many of the men got things they did not need at all, while others who needed a shirt or a pair of socks did not get them. Many exchanged the articles thus gotten for luxuries women offered for sale in our camp. The officers decided now, to give the articles to those in need of them only, and then, if any were left, to raffle for them. But the majority of the men protested against this, as the men in need of clothes could draw them from the government, but of course had to pay for them as well as the others, who did not care for a couple of dollars for warm and clean clothes. The officers could not contradict this argument, as every man received the same pay that the others did, and could buy as many clothes as others, if he chose to, and return to the West equally well dressed.

May 30. As I felt a great deal better, though somewhat weak yet, I continued to make out the muster out papers. About dusk I became so weak that I had to seek my bed for rest. Being busy thus, I learned nothing about the rumors or news. The day was clear and warm, the night cool.

May 31. We continued our work on the papers, as we could not be discharged until these were made out. We received orders to have the papers ready by to-morrow, but as this was an impossibility with every company of the regiment, we paid little attention to the order. All trains that left Washington were crowded with discharged soldiers on their way home. The cheering of these men, as they passed with lightning speed the neighboring camps, could be heard distinctly by us, though we were quite a distance from the railroad; the cheering made a deep impression on our men. They could scarcely await the time when the "iron horse" would take them also to their homes, but the prospects for this event were rather poor for several days to come yet. It was no longer to be doubted that we would not be paid off in Washington, as all returning troops were sent to their respective States without pay, and only such soldiers, in possession of their descriptive rolls, and lying sick in the hospitals at Washington or elsewhere, were paid off and sent to the station nearest their homes. As the Illinois troops were sent to Chicago or Springfield to be paid off, the question, to which one of these two towns we would be sent to, created lively discussions. All the men, except those from Rock Island county, preferred Springfield, being the nearest place to their homes. The weather was very warm.

June 1, 1865. As our papers had to be ready by the 3d at farthest, we commenced to work on them early and with a good will for the whole day. Gen. SHERMAN issued his farewell order to his troops to-day, thanking them for their love for the union, for their fidelity to him, for enduring so bravely the privations and hardships, for their bravery in the fights, &c. He desired earnestly that no soldier would disgrace his hard earned good name by unlawful and degrading actions when at home, but that he would resume his peaceful vocation in life, to support the country in every respect, as he had assisted to suppress the rebellion, and thereby gain honor at home as he had gained laurels on the battle field. He reminded his men not to spend their hard earned savings for luxuries, but that they could appear with their old blouses and torn shirts, that had covered them on many a bloody battle field, before every good union man and woman, and would be received with higher honors than if dressed in fine and costly clothes, that were not becoming a soldier. For this well meant and timely order we gave three hearty cheers for our estimable and beloved general, and we vowed, that should necessity again occur we would again shoulder our arm, and fight under BILLY SHERMAN, and under no other general.

June 2. The mustering out papers, or discharge lists were completed, and it became evident that we would be mustered out of the service day after to-morrow. No news were received.

June 3. As the muster out rolls had not been examined yet, it was impossible for us to be mustered out to-morrow. Thousands of soldiers left Washingington daily, and every one desired his turn to come next. We had no duty to do, and our men were not accustomed to remain idling about the camps; they were willing to change their guns for the mechinist's tools and the plows, and quit "soldiering." Our brigade headquarter was discontinued, and the staff officers sent to their various regiments. The day was very warm again, but the night was unusually cool.

June 4. It war Sunday and no work whatever was to be done. The 102d Illinois regiment of our brigade was mustered out to-day, and expected to get transportation to Chicago day after to-morrow. The day was very warm.

June 5. A very tiresome day, as I had nothing more to do. The day was very hot. Gen. WARD, commander of our division, intended to take leave in an address this evening, but as he had imbibed too much "strong drink" words as well as sense were wanting or but half understood, and could not properly be called a farewell address. The listeners interrupted him several times, compelling him to hush, shook hands and turned their backs on him laughing; they were flooded by blessings or curses, or both at the same time. Brig. Gen. HARRISON and Col. DOHN of the 79th Ohio also made short speeches, dwelt on the privations, hardships and fights, and were interrupted frequently by stormy applause. The 102d Illinois prepared to go to Washington in the morning to get transportation to Chicago.

June 6. Our comrades of the 102d Illinois commenced their march to Washington early, and most of us were asleep and were awakened by the "good byes" of our fellow soldiers. Our pay rolls were examined to-day, and the officers supposed that we would be mustered out day after to-morrow. The 105th Illinois was mustered out to-day, and intended to leave for the west to-morrow. The weather was cool.

June 7. At 2 o'clock P. M. our regiment was mustered out of the United States service by Capt. BEECHER, mustering officer of our division, after a service of 2 years and 9 months (lacking one day,) having entered the service on the 8th of September, 1862. All were glad that the long hoped for hour had come, when we would become free citizens again. Prepations were made immediately for our departure for our homes. Col. CASE sought for and received transportation for the morrow. All the men who had to serve a year or more longer, or who were but recruits, were taken away to serve out their time in some regiment of their choice. Our men joined the 16th Illinois, at the time in Kentucky, and where they were sent shortly after our departure from Washington. At 5 o'clock we received order to be ready to march to Washington at 6 o'clock the next morning. Most of us had been deceived in our expectations, for we got transportation to Chicago instead of to Springfield, Ill., the nearest place to our homes. But as most of us had never seen Chicago, and as we would find those regiments of our brigade there that had left us in the last few days, (one of which left to-day) we consoled ourselves with such thoughts. Most of us were in a good humor and could scarcely await the dawn of the next morning that would see us on our way to the West; nevertheless a depressed feeling pervailed somewhat, in consequence of the order that we would carry our arms along quite unnecessarily, for which we had no further use, and which we could have left in Washington just as well. It is true these arms had been our true and constant companions on all our marches, in all our fights, had frightened the rebel frequently and decimated their ranks often enough, but we could see no propriety in taking the arms to Chicago. The weather was pleasantly cool, but the night frosty.

June 8. We left camp at 6 o'clock, bidding our companions of the 79th Ohio and 70th Indiana, (the only regiments now left of our brigade, and that had to remain for several days yet,) an affectionate farewell. We were provided with provisions for our trip, but left our pans, kettles and other things which we could do without, moving to the Baltimore railroad depot, where we arrived at about 8 o'clock A.

M. Our regiment was not alone here, but the whole neighborhood of the depot was crowded with troops, that had been left on yesterday and during the night in consequence of the insufficient means of transportation. Other regiments were arriving continually, so that we began to doubt whether we would be able to get transportation or not. The trains were coupled almost continually, and almost hourly empty trains arrived from Baltimore, were filled with troops, and left amid the cheering of those that were left awaiting their turn. We had been waiting several hours in the hot sun, when we were told that we would leave in the afternoon; as the hour was not fixed, we could not leave the depot for a great distance. Our time while waiting was pleasantly occupied with conversation with the women and girls that offered refreshments to the boys, but not, as on the 24th or May, free, but as high prices as possible, seemingly to take the last picayune out of our pockets, if one was left. As most of the men were entirely out of money, they had to content themselves with chatting and joking with the females, and trying all sorts of ways to "confiscate" in a way unknown to the owner. The ire of the Washington peddlers was aroused frequently when they found a hand in their baskets, while some of the boys entertained them interestingly, and words not at all becoming the "delicate sex" were showered on the men, who answered the curses and epithets with roars of laughter. Several of these women were arrested by the provost guard for giving strong drink to the men, contrary to orders. But few of the men got anything of the luxuries offered by the women, and most of them had to be satisfied with a watery mouth. At 3 o'clock the train began to move amid the waving of hats and handkerchiefs on the part of the citizens and soldiers. As all the troops that had left before us were in freight cars, in which benches had been placed for the men, uncomfortable as the seats were, it did not lessen our joy, knowing that the whole United States did not contain a sufficient number of passenger wagons to transport such numbers of troops in so short a time to the various parts of the country. We were satisfied with being under shelter, and as each farm-house we passed was decorated with flags and their owners waving hats and handkerchiefs our good humor remained. In all towns along the road we were received with enthusiasm. When we reached Baltimore at 6 o'clock P. M., we were well and friendly received, but not with such manifestations of love as at Washington. We were compelled to march through part of the city to reach the Harrisburgh depot, where we arrived after dark. We got into the wagons, but the departure was delayed for some reason, and most of us went to sleep. I did not wake until the train stopped next morning at York, Pa.

June 9. The reception in York was a pleasant one, ladies and gentlemen welcomed us, but to make the moment a more pleasant one, greenbacks were necessary, an article not in our possession. We had not taken a regular meal since we had left camp yesterday morning, and here we had neither the time nor the utensils to prepare a breakfast, and could not satisfy the cravings of our stomachs with anything else than crackers and pork, the latter somewhat raw. Women came again and offered us meat, coffee and other victuals, but as we were out of money they did but a small business, and our watery mouths were not satisfied. We reached Harrisburgh, Pa., at 7 o'clock, remained a short while, and then went arrow-like through a mountainous though thickly settled country. The inhabitants of every hamlet and town had gathered in the yard and at the depots, and saluted us by waving flags and handkerchiefs and by cheers. About dark we reached Altoona, and remained here until 10 o'clock

P. M. We got time here to prepare supper, though but few kettles and pots were on hand, and much less wood for the fire; nevertheless, every one got at least a cup of warm coffee. It had been published in the Washington papers, and we had relied on this statement, that the Christian Commission would have victuals in readiness wherever we stopped, but thus far we had been grossly deceived. After 10 o'clock the train got in motion again and sped towards Pittsburg, stopping but a few times.

June 10. At 6 o'clock A. M. we arrived at Pittsburg, where we were well received. Immediately after our arrival we were told that a table had been set at the City Hall, but before we went there we took possession of another train, leaving our baggage and guns there under guard, and then passed through the principal part of the city to City Hall. Here we got a breakfast prepared by the U. S. Sanitary Commission, and such a one as only hungry men as we were could enjoy and appreciate. We could see that the meal had been prepared by true union men for union soldiers, though we knew that it would be the last meal we would get before reaching Chicago, where, in our own native state, we had a right to expect at least as good a reception and as good a meal. No one doubted this. After breakfast we returned to our train, and soon after steamed towards the border of Pennsylvania. The train passed through a great part of the city in slow motion, and from every house cheers and flags and hats and handkerchiefs saluted us, bidding us welcome and good-bye. To the honor of Pittsburg be it said that we were treated like its own sons, and the citizens proved that they were true union men and humane to the union soldiers. The scholars were taken to the road by their teachers, and hearty cheers saluted us as we passed these crowds of little union children, whose hurrahs for SHERMAN,s army and for the union soldiers, made a lasting impression on our minds. May they never leave the cause of our free, glorious country! As the train moved slowly we had a good chance to take a close view at these manifestations of joy and enthusiasm, but after we had crossed the Alleghany river the train moved faster for several hours along the shores of "the beautiful river," the Ohio. At 10½ o'clock we crossed the border of Pennsylvania and entered Ohio; here also along our road the manifestations of patriotism were equally enthusiastic as in Pennsylvania. We only stopped when the water and coals had given out, and passed through a country whose beauty could have been excelled only by Paradise. Here and there we saw the farmer and his family busy in the gardens, while the waving fields of rye and wheat were visible in every direction. We here saw the peaceable husbandman at work amid his gilding grain, while but a few months ago we had seen nothing but the effects of war and desolation in the Southern states. We reached the small but handsome town of Mansfield about 6 o'clock P. M., where we stopped a short while, and then moved on to Crestline, Ohio, where we intended to stop for a longer time. We got to Crestline half an hour later. The inhabitants of Forest City must have been notified of our arrival, as we had not expected what happened here, owing to the lateness of the hour. (Forest City was the name of the next town we reached after leaving Crestline.) Here a large number of beautiful young ladies had been awaiting our arrival for some time, everyone of them holding a bouquet of flowers in her hand, to which was attached a card or slip of paper, containing the name of the donor and some patriotic words, expressing the feelings of the young lady towards the union soldiers. They also gave expression to their feelings in words that made us feel happy, coming as they did from such beautiful lips and such true and faithful union hearts. No one can appreciate such welcome but he that returns from battle fields, and after suffering hardships and privations in every shape and form, grim death staring in his face continually, and is welcomed on his return in such a manner. It was hard for us to leave this place of true union ladies, but the shrill whistle of the locomotive compelled us to mount the cars, and all we could do was to cheer the lovely donors, whose memory will ever remain fresh in our minds. May God bless them for what they did for the 129th Illinois regiment on the 10th of June 1865. At the next town the inhabitants had also gathered at the depot, particularly the fair ladies, who came with refreshments for the sick. Here we stopped but a few minutes, and the ladies distributed their presents among those standing nearest to them. Our train went ahead rapidly, but we were kept all awake by the unevenness of the road, as it was dangerous to sleep on the benches. About midnight we crossed from Ohio into Indiana, passed Fort Wayne and Plymouth at night, and when the sun arose we were but 80 miles from Chicago, the place of our destination.

June 11. Every hour brought us nearer to our native State and every body was speaking about the enthusiasm with which we would be received in Chicago. Most of the men cared less for the enthusiasm and for the cheers, of which they had heard enough for the last few days, than for a good substantial breakfast, of which we were certain on our arrival at Chicago, and of which we all stood in need in consequence of our inability to prepare even a cup of coffee. We had crossed the small strip of Indiana, which the Pittsburg, Ft. Wayne & Chicago Railroad runs, and were now on the level, wide and green prairies of Illinois, moving along as fast as an arrow. The country became lovelier and more beautiful as we advanced, our hearts beat expectantly, while our eyes were straining to see the church steeples of Chicago in the distance. Soon our eys were satisfied and in a few minutes the city with all its splendor and wealth was in full view. At 10½ o'clock we left the cars, taking knapsacks and guns along, formed and stacked arms to await what the future had in store for us and where we were to camp. Before Col. Case had found this out several hours had passed, and we were compelled to remain near the depot, on the street, exposed to the rays of a burning sun, and it seemed as though our expectations would not be verified. For so far not one handkerchief, flag or hat was seen saluting us, and bidding us welcome in our native State, so that it seemed as though we ought even to ask permission to enter the city. We resumed our march, but not to beefsteak but to Camp Fry, three miles from Chicago. The loss of the breakfast, expected with certainty, caused a good deal of excitement among the men, and many swore not to leave the spot before having prepared a breakfast. The continual coaxing and ordering of the officers, however, forced them to enter the ranks and come along. But what a different reception was this from that at Pittsburg! We were wrong in expecting something from Chicago, what other and strange towns had done for us. Not a single cheer greeted us as we passed through the streets, and but seldom a handkerchief was waved, but so faintly that it was apparent the owner had to force himself to this external show of patriotism. Bouquets were not offered us, nay, not even a drink of water. If we had been treated the same way by the citizens of Ohio and Pennsylvania, the insult of the Chicagonians would have been felt less, but as we marched to Camp Fry, hungry and thirsty, many vowed to pay the citizens back in the same way. With sad and angry hearts we reached Camp Fry, where we were received by our old companions of the 102d and 105th Illinois with hearty and enthusiastic cheers, which we answered the same way. We stacked arms and threw down our knapsacks, and were asked by our comrades about our reception in Chicago. We related everything that had transpired on our way from Washington, and what we had rightfully expected from Chicago, and how we had been received. The men of the 102d Illinois assured us that they had been treated the same way, but those of the 105th Illinois (this regiment had been organized near the city) had not only been treated the same way, but stated that the police had ordered the men off the pavement, it having been laid for citizens only, and not for the soldiers! The excitement of these two regiments was great and our words only inflamed them the more; the city was to be punished for this coldness towards the men that had fought the battles of the country, and that had given its vote for McCLELLAND, and showed too plainly that it hated the soldiers of the Union. The men went to the barracks to think about the best mode of punishing the citizens. We had to wait in Camp Fry until 2 o'clock P. M., until the barracks had been cleared for us, but which we had to clear off the filth and dirt, before we could take possession. We had scarcely moved in our quarters when a noise was heard of breaking windows and doors. We hurried to the scene and saw a great crowd of citizens and soldiers collected around the saloon near the camp, taking freely of the saloon keeper's liquors without paying for them. We saw immediately that the whole fuss was an act of revenge, but could not just at the moment find out the immediate cause. All doors of the saloon had been broken open, empty wine bottles came flying through the windows and were sent back by the outsiders, the barrels were taken out of the cellar, the heads knocked in and the wine, beer or whisky poured out on the ground, or filled in canteens. Boys and girls that had been attracted by the noise, were seen busy filling some vessel with the contents of the barrel, to drink or hurry off with it; many had imbibed too much already and were tumbling about regardless of the direction. Curses upon curses were heaped on the citizens and the police of Chicago—more drinks were taken, whereby the men became the more incensed. Citizens that had come out in the horse-cars, looked on in surprise at the scene, were surrounded by soldiers who told them in no mild tone that they (the citizens) were the cause of this scene. The citizens professed their innocence and laid the blame on the Christian Commission, whose duty it was to give us a proper reception and provisions, the citizens having given them money for this purpose. We now learned the immediate cause of the quarrel. The officer commanding in Chicago, Gen. SWEET, whom we knew, from Gallatin, Tenn., had issued an order, prohibiting the saloon keepers to give any spirituous liquors to the soldiers. This was a difficult matter to do for the keeper of the house near our camp, as he sold his liquors to the citizens and had to refuse them to soldiers, although they asked him for it. He had called several policemen to protect him, whereby the rage of the soldiers was increased. The saloon keeper could not stand much from the soldiers, and considered himself superior to them. He lost his temper in consequence of the frequent begging for a drink, and unluckily for him, he gave vent to his political ideas, declaring that he would not have anything to do with such traitors as SHERMAN or his men. This was too much for our boys, some of them tried to jump over the counter to take hold of the barkeeper, but were prevented by the policemen and maltreated. This noise attracted other soldiers who took the part of their comrades, the policemen got thrashed and carried away senselessly, while the saloon keeper and his assistants ran away through a back door. The noise continued to attract more soldiers, and the work of demolishing commenced. This disgraceful scene continued until night, nobody interfered, as loss of life would have been the consequence, and words did no good. Some of the men were not satisfied yet and offered themselves as leaders to go to the city to take revenge; but no one went, though it was not considered a crime to do so. Several companies of armed soldiers had been moved to the city from another camp, as an attack was expected by the frightened Chicagonians.

June 12. A good many got up with a heavy head, and those that had laid in a supply of liquor, did not get over their spree for several days. The regiment delivered up the guns and equipments, and we were awaiting our pay in order to turn our back to this by no means agreeable place. A number of men went to the city to the Sanitary Fair building, where every soldier had free admission. We were assured there that no one had known anything about the arrival of the regiment, and that no preparations for the reception could therefore have been made; and as the fair was occupying every one, it was impossible to pay attention to anything else. But all these subterfuges could not appease the anger of the men. Maj. Gen. HOOKER visited our camp this afternoon, and was received with tremendous cheers by all troops, especially those that had served under him in the 20th corps on the march from Chattanooga to Atlanta. He was recognized immediately and touched by the reception he received in camp, so that it was some time before he could talk and express his thanks for the attachment and bravery of our boys, shaking hands with every one who came forward to do so. The weather was cool and pleasant.

June 13. The day was cloudy, and interspersed by showers of rain. Gen. SHERIDAN arrived in town where several shots apprised us of his arrival. Gov. OGLESBY appeared in camp and made a speech this afternoon. He begged the men to forget their hatred against Chicago, and to become peaceable citizens. A Chicagonian spoke after the governor, endeavoring to defend the city in regard to our "noble reception," that no one had known anything about the arrival of any Illinois troops. But when the soldiers understood what the Chicagonian was after, cries arose and the speaker had to retire amid hisses and groans, and with the assurance that he did not cure the wound the insulting reception had made. Whether the Chicagonians really did not know the arrival of Illinois troops, I will not say; but certain it is, that every newspaper in the country published the fact that the Illinois troops would be sent to Chicago or Springfield, and remain in camp there until paid off and returning to their homes. It seems queer that everybody else should know this fact but the Chicagonians. The soldiers could not be convinced of the contrary, but believed rightly that it was lack of patriotism and Union feeling not to give the soldier, who had fought the battles of his country, a proper reception. Gen. SHERMAN, who was present in Chicago, made a speech in the Sanitary Fair building, and was loudly applauded, especially by the soldiers.

June 14. The 102d Illinois regiment, our companions on the promenade through Georgia, the Carolinas and Virginia, was paid off to-day, and most of the members of this regiment left immediately a city so filled with "patriots." Most of our men were in town all day, where the 96th Illinois had arrived. This regiment was received somewhat better than those who had arrived here before. Nevertheless, the inspiring, soul-stirring, warm-hearted enthusiasm that leaves a lasting impression on the returning soldier's heart, which we found in Pennsylvania and Ohio, was wanting. The regiment received a meal from the Christian Commission, was shown the Sanitary Fair building, and then marched to the camp. We expected to be paid off day after to-morrow. The day was rainy.

June 15. Part of the 105th Illinois regiment was paid off and went home. One of the men, who had not remained with his comrades and had perhaps imbibed too much "spirit," was found dead at the

Rock Island depot, and robbed of his money. It became very unsafe for the soldiers to venture singly on the streets; they were robbed of their money in daytime and at night, and were frequently found insensible in the street. When walking, some "friend" would come to them, advise them not to take "that dangerous street," or invite them into a beer cellar where strong drink was drugged, and soon made them insensible. The troops were paid off very slow, as the paymaster in camp paid but two and three companies a day, and we were compelled to remain in a city whose mere name made us sick and of which we were tired. A scene occurred that seemed to prolong our stay. The paymaster was driven out of camp by troops that he had paid off in money the Chicago merchants refused to receive. It was said that he had exchanged the money he had received to pay off the troops with for torn and mutilated bills, or for bills of broken banks, putting the premium thus made in his own pocket. This was merely a supposition, but founded on the fact that we had never before been paid off in mutilated bills or uncurrent money, and we could not believe that the paymaster had received such money to pay the soldiers with. He was ordered out of camp, and not to return, except with better money. Several men of our regiment who had the means went home for several days; relatives of others who had found out our hereabouts came on a visit to our camp. The weather was rainy.

June 16. We signed the pay rolls, hoping that payment would follow to-morrow. The balance of the 105th Illinois was paid off, not in camp, but in town. The fuss in camp had brought other and good money and the mutilated bills had disappeared; the Chicago merchants no longer refused to take our money, but on the contrary tried all means to get as much of it as possible. The 82d Illinois, or HECKER-regiment, arrived in the city to-day, and was well received.

June 17. Company A of our regiment was paid off and most of the members went off for home immediately. Other regiments continued to arrive daily to be paid off, and were well received and fed in the Sanitary Fair building, and then quartered in Camp DOUGLAS or FRY. The Chicagonians tried to make amends for their past sins, and were defended warmly by some of the troops that had lately arrived. Speeches were made continually and the troops lauded for their bravery; nevertheless all agreed that the reception was not as warm and glorious as those in Pennsylvania and Ohio. All those troops that had been here for several days desired their money, to get away from Chicago and to get home to forget that place entirely. The day was rainy.

June 18. It was Sunday and we were compelled to remain another day for our pay. To-morrow, however, if it suited Mr. paymaster, was our turn, we made preparations to leave as soon as possible after the reception of the pay. We had been to the stores, bought suits of clothes ready or made, to get them as soon as we were paid off. Everybody was in good humor in expectation of the money and an early return home. Many of us from Livingston county were thinking about the beloved wife or children or parents, whom we had left three years ago, not knowing whether we would ever see them alive again. Many of us intended to arrive home unexpectedly, in case some spy had not betrayed our presence in Chicago. For the last time, but in the best humor, we took possession of our hard beds, consisting of rough boards, and slept as soundly and sweetly as a prince in down.

June 19. Two companies, our company D and C,

Anonymous

Historical and Commercial Philadelphia Handsomely Illustrated

With supplement of the World's Columbian Exposition

Anonymous

Historical and Commercial Philadelphia Handsomely Illustrated
With supplement of the World's Columbian Exposition

ISBN/EAN: 9783337386481

Printed in Europe, USA, Canada, Australia, Japan

Cover: Foto ©ninafisch / pixelio.de

More available books at **www.hansebooks.com**

Historical and Commercial Philadelphia

SECOND EDITION

Handsomely Illustrated

1892

With Supplement of the World's Columbian Exposition.

Published by
A. F. Parson's Publishing Company,
149 & 151 Church St.
· N · Y ·

GENERAL INDEX.

Adams, John, Wood Mantels, Wardrobes, etc. 282
Adams, William S., Cigars. 257
Addis, John A., Undertaker and Embalmer. 202
Albion Dye and Bleach Works, G. J. Littlewood & Co., Proprs 129
Aldine Hotel, The, S. Murray Mitchell, Propr. 113
Aldine Livery Stables and Riding Academy, T. Riddle & Co., Proprs. 184
Alexander, S. N., Manfr. Stained Glass 244
Allebach, M. B., Watchmaker, etc. 187
Allen, Henry, & Co., Bankers and Brokers. 123
Althouse, Wm. D., William Penn Hotel and Sale Stables. 131
American Manfg. Co., M. F. Maguire & Co., Props... 243
American Marine and Canal Propeller Co., The. 259
American Trust, Loan and Guaranteed Investment Company, ... 155
Anderson, Robt., Real Estate, etc. 219
Andreykovicz & Dunk, Aniline Dyes, etc. 257
Arch Street House, Theo. K. Batt, Prop. 237
Archambault, V. E. & Son, Fine Carpetings. 155
Ardis, Albert A., Jr., Bricklayer and Builder. 216
Armstrong, The J. M., Company 171
Ashland Hotel, Oliver Sproul, Propr. 183
Atkinson, J. J., Wholesale Commission Merchant, Fruit and Produce 213
Atlantic Works, Berry & Orton Company, Proprs. ... 135
Avil Printing Company 123
Axford, James, Furniture, Stoves, etc. 238

Bailey, Lewis L. & Co., Manfrs. Ladies' and Children's Cloaks. 176
Baily & Truscott, Architects 203
Baker, John E., Grain, Feed, etc. 225
Baker, Geo. W. C. & Co., Real Estate, etc. 186
Baker, Householder & Leonard, Engineers and Machinists. 132
Ballantine, C. H., M.D., Pharmacy. 245
Baltimore & Philadelphia Steamboat Co. 165
Barry, Wm., Guilder. 235
Beck, Theodore, Manfg. Jeweler. 218
Beckett, George W., Sanitary Plumber. 132
Beitel & Kinsler, Manfg. Jewelers. 254
Benner, Edwin, Plate Printer, etc. 255
Benner, Harry D., Acme Market. 227
Benners, William J. & Sons, Hard Wood Lumber, etc. 151

Berger, Wm., Marble Works. 214
Berry & Orton Company, Atlantic Works, Manfrs. Wood Working Machinery. 135
Betz, Charles, Carriage and Wagon Builder. 210
Betz, H. M., Jeweler. 178
Bew, Jas. W., House Furnishing Goods, ... 248
Bewley's Boarding and Livery Stable 239
Bichy, Wm., Apothecary. 195
Bickham, Stephen A., Leaf Tobacco. 188
Biddle, C. J., Drugs. 191
Biles, Walter K., Wall Paper, etc. 194
Bird Bros., Wholesale and Retail Grocers. 174
Bissinger, M. & Son, Importers of Tailors' Trimmings 144
Blackwood, Russel T., Druggist. 228
Blankley Bros. & Co., Manfrs. Machinery Castings, etc. 196
Blitzstein, M. L. & Co., Money Exchange. 221
Blood, John, & Co., Manfrs. Hosiery and Jerseys ... 269
Blum, Andrew, Tailor. 242
Boerner, A. W., Florist. 231
Bonner, John W., Agent, Manfr. Shirts. 189
Bonsall Bros., Conveyancers. 146
Bonsall's, Wm. S., Sons, Metal and Slate Roofers. .. 216
Boothby, Wm., Oysters. 256
Borcky, D. K., Copper, Tin and Sheet Iron Worker... 173
Borda, E. & Son, Coal. 226
Borgner, Cyrus, Manfr. Fire Brick and Clay Retorts .. 123
Bosanko, The Dr., Medicine Company. 132
Boston Laundry, Thomas F. Houston, Propr. 263
Bovard, M. M. & Son, Jewelers. 198
Bowen, David H. & Son, Undertakers. 225
Bowen, Jos. E. & Son, Commission Merchants in Produce, etc. 171
Bowker, George C., Real Estate, etc. 205
Bowman, A. A., Livery Stables 227
Boyce Bros., Grocers. 223
Bradway & Jocher, Insurance Agents and Brokers... 150
Branson, Geo. & Co., Manfrs. Hosiery. 121
Brant, Josiah, House and Sign Painter. 180
Brobst, C. A., Paints, Oils, Glass, etc. 248
Bronson & Co., Commission Merchants and Dealers in Broom Corn, etc. 248
Brossmann, Chas., Boarding Stable. 177
Brown, Dr. B. L., St. Cloud Pharmacy. 206
Brown, D. V., Wholesale and Manufacturing Optician. 162
Brown, Geo. P., Butter, Eggs, etc. 186

GENERAL INDEX.

Brown, Michael J., Wool.................. 182
Brown, Samuel W. & Co., Platinum Enlargements by Electric and Solar Light.................... 185
Buck, Thomas, & Co., Manfrs. Hosiery............. 253
Bull's Head Horse and Mule Bazaar, Weber & Sullivan, Props..................... 280
Bureau Brothers, Bronze Statuary, etc................ 132
Burk & McFetridge, Printers, etc..................... 111
Burns, Albert E., Agent for The Trenton Lamp Co... 224
Burns, Charles M., Architect................. 152
Butterworth, George, Beamer of Warps........... 217
Butterworth, G. W., Wholesale Fruit & Vegetables.... 203

CALLOWHILL BEEF CO., H. A. Wood, Manager...... 253
Calver, John W. & Co., Manfrs. Bonnet and Hat Frames..................... 153
Cambria Iron Company.................. 107
Camden, Robt. L. M., Jr., & Bro., Artists............. 175
Canby & Costello, Philadelphia Supply Co........... 178
Cantrell, Dr. J. H., Druggist.................. 236
Careless, Geo., Manfr. Fine Silver Plated Ware....... 142
Carey & Co., Carriage Lamps.................... 237
Catanach & Peterson, Real Estate, etc................ 223
Caton, J. H., Manfr. Barrels.................. 253
Centennial National Bank.................... 116
Central Boarding and Sales Stables, The, R. S. Reeve, Mgr..................... 261
Central Cycle Company, Frank R. Evans, Mgr........ 206
Chandler, W. S., Tobacco Commission Merchant,.... 184
Chapman Decorative Co., The (Limited).............. 104
Chicago Varnish Company, F. S. Gellatly, Resident Manager..................... 134
Chipman, Charles, & Son, Manfrs. Hosiery and Underwear..................... 128
Christman, Geo. M., Coal Yard.................. 212
Church, W. Harry, Butter, Eggs, Poultry............ 231
Clapp & Mattis, Meats and Provisions 213
Clark, W. E. & Co., Fine Furniture................ 207
Cleveland Baking Powder Co., Chas. F. Warner, Mgr. 223
Clower, Wm. L., Germantown Market House......... 251
Clyde Steamship Co.................. 267
Coates, Henry C., Printer.................. 235
Coates & Mathias, Quaker City Whisk Broom Works.. 167
Collins, Wm. W., Dry Goods.................... 233
Collisson, Wm. H., Plumbing, etc.................. 188
Comfort, Thos. & Son, Manayunk Brass Foundry..... 240
Compound Spring Power Company, The, Incorporated. 108
Conaway & Co., Butter, Eggs, Game, etc............. 249
Connecticut Mutual Life Insurance Co., The, H. O. Chapman, Gen'l Agt.................. 96
Conner, George P., Continental Pharmacy............ 106
Conradt Art Metal Industry, Charles Conradt, Propr... 197
Cooley & Geiger, Pharmacists.................. 220
Cooper, H. L., Wool.................. 256
Coöperative Nickel Plating Co., W. H. Lentz & Co... 179
Corbin, L. P. & Co., Produce Commission Merchants, etc..................... 221
Cramp, B. H. & Co., Brass Founders................ 84
Cramp, Wm. & Sons. Ship and Engine Building Company, The.................... 82, 83
Crane Iron Company.................. 100

Cranston, S. P., Real Estate and Fire Insurance....... 209
Craven & Dearnley, Yarns.................... 272
Crawford, Charles, Florist.................... 234
Cressman, Milton A. & Co., Produce Commission Merchants..................... 142
Cresson, Geo. V., Company, Manfrs. Power Transmitting Machinery, etc.................... 235
Creutzburg, Geo. F. & Son, Importers, Manfrs., and Dealers in Cutlery.................... 140
Croft & Allen Co., Manfg. Confectioners............ 129
Crouch, Geo. W., Horse Collar Manfr. and Dealer in Neat's Foot Oil.................... 163
Cundey, Elijah, Wood Turning Mills................ 225
Cushing, William A., Real Estate Broker............ 156

DAISY SUSPENDER CO., THE.................... 219
Dale, Thomas B., Plumber, etc.................. 205
Daugherty Bros., Oysters, Clams, etc................ 258
Davey, Philip, Photographer on Wood............. 212
Davis, The F. A., Company, Medical Publishers 157
Davis & Galt, Silversmiths.................... 220
Dawson & Adams, Real Estate and Mortgage Brokers. 176
Decatur Coal Company.................... 92
De Kieffer & Canning, Drugs and Druggists' Specialties 148
Delahunty, Thomas, Marble and Granite Works....... 87
Delaplaine & Co., Hatters' Goods.................... 148
Delker, Dr. Wm., Druggist.................... 229
Depuy, Thomas, Carpetings, Matting. Oil Cloth, etc... 154
Devine, William, Agent, Manfr. Window Shading. Wall Papers, etc..................... 156
Devinny, Geo. W., Masonic Marks and Society Badges 140
Devlin & Brother, Oakdale Oil Works................ 205
Devlin, C. J., Upholstery.................... 236
Diamond Electric Company.................... 138
Diamond Glass Company.................... 252
Dickinson, Justus D., Manfr. Harness................ 193
Dilks, Jas., Musical Instruments, etc................ 232
Dingee, James E., Brick Manufacturer............ 124
Ditson, J. E. & Co., Sheet Music, etc................ 258
Dittess, Chas. J. & Co., Power Printers............. 255
Dixey, Wm. B., Plumber, etc..................... 195
Doerle, P. H., Real Estate.................... 193
Doflein, Ph., Manfr. Soap and Bottle Molds........... 219
Dohan & Taitt, Tobacco.................... 271
Donaldson Iron Company.................... 152
Dorey, Daniel, Hat and Cap Leathers, etc 190
Dorfner, John, Steam Dyeing and Scouring Establishment..................... 80
Dougherty, H. D. & Co., Wholesale Bedding.......... 219
Dougherty's, J. A., Sons, Distillers................ 179
Douglass, J. Walter, Patents and Patent Causes....... 149
Dunlap & Co., Hats.................... 104
Dunmore, R. S., Grocer.................... 159
Dunshee, E. S., Photographer.................... 235
Duquesne Coal Company.................... 260
Dyer, Peleg A., Boarding Stables 197

EASTON & McMAHON TRANSPORTATION CO., THE . 260
Eaton & Reaney, Printers.................... 255
Ebel, Charles A., Teamster.................... 191
Eberle, Chas. L., Pharmacist.................... 236

GENERAL INDEX.

Edison's Mimeograph, W. M. Abbey, Agt............ 226
Edwards, Frank, Wools, Mohair, etc................. 283
Elliott, Andrew G., Stoves, etc..................... 217
Ellis, W. G. & Co., Manfrs. Star Seamless Hosiery.... 128
Emack, John D., Slate Blackboards................ 119
Engard, Abraham, Confectionery.................... 225
English, B., & Sons, Ladies' Cloaks, Suits, Furs, etc.. 103
English, John A., Oysters........................... 183
Enterprise Dyeing and Finishing Works, Joseph Hanson, Agent..................................... 153
Enterprise Plating and Silverware Manufacturing Co., F. H. Hyde, Propr.............................. 204
Equitable Life Assurance Society, Reginald L. Hart, Mgr... 97
Estey, Bruce & Co., Pianos and Organs 207
Etting, Edward J., Iron Broker and Commission Merchant.. 180
Evans, Geo. & Co., Tailors 278
Evanson, John E. & Son, Plumbers................. 263
Eynon, T. J. & Son, Saw and Planing Mill......... 201

Fadin, Edward, Fruit and Produce................ 190
Fairlamb, P. H. & Co., Cement..................... 186
Farmers' New Hay Market Hotel, Jos. M. Jones, Propr. 148
Faunce, Taylor, Auditor and Public Accountant 145
Faussett, H. S., Wholesale Dry Goods............... 156
Ferris, M. A., Flour, Feed, etc..................... 198
Finnerty, McClure & Co., Wholesale Druggists...... 243
Fiske, Louis S. & Co., Commission Wool Merchants.. 247
Flagg, Stanley G. & Co., Malleable Iron, Gray Iron and Steel Founders............................. 268
Flanagan, William A., Wool, Hair, Wool Waste, Woolen Rags, etc................................ 147
Fleming, Geo. R. & Co., Piano and Organ Warerooms 262
Flick, Geo. L., Manfr. Steamship Ranges, etc 183
Fling, Thomas W. & Bro., Manfrs. Hosiery......... 281
Ford, John G., Real Estate, Mortgage and Fire Insurance Broker...................................... 151
Forner, Henry C., Real Estate 192
Foster, E. & R. G., Ranges and Heaters............. 234
Foster, Fred. L. & Sons, Boot and Shoe Makers and Rubber Shoe Brokers............................. 176
Frank Bros. & Co., Manfrs. Fine Clothing........... 159
Frank, H. N. & Co., Standard Cloak Company...... 155
Frankford Real Estate and Safe Deposit Company.... 149
Frankford Mutual Fire Insurance Company of the County of Philadelphia........................... 131
Freas, H. & Son, Grocers............................. 194
Fredericks, Charles, Hatters' Specialties............. 204
Freshell, Geo., Druggist 167
Furbush, M. A. & Son Machine Co.................. 143

Gadd, S. W., M.D., Druggist....................... 250
Gallager & Feusht, Granite and Marble Works...... 227
Gallagher, Alex., Manfr. Stonecutters' Tools 192
Garden, C. H. & Co., Hats, Caps, Furs, Straw and Millinery Goods................................. 190
Gardiner, Samuel E., Real Estate................... 197
Garrett & Buchanan, Paper........................ 200
Gemmi Bros., Manfrs. Pearl and Vegetable Ivory Buttons... 124

Genth, Dr. F. A., Chemist, etc.................... 255
Gentzsch, A. & Sons, Paper Box Manfrs............ 258
Germantown Woolen Mills, Chas. H. Topham, Propr. 144
Germantown Real Estate, Deposit and Trust Company. 145
Ghriskey, Chas. M., Hardware..................... 217
Gilbert, T. W. & Co., Carriage Goods, Saddlery Specialties, Wagon Hardware, and Wheel Stock...... 132
Gilbert, J. & Son, Gents' Furnishers............... 216
Glendinning, Robert, & Co., Bankers and Brokers... 118
Glenmore Worsted Company (Limited) 153
Glenn, J. Temple, Jobbing Bricklayer............... 122
Glover & Reep, Paper Hangings, etc 213
Glover Bros., Iron Founders, etc.................... 114
Godshall, Wm. H., Carriage Builder................ 190
Godwin, Harold, Architect and Engineer........... 184
Goldner, Henry, Machine and Boiler Works and Blacksmithing....................................... 146
Goldsmith, A. & Sons, Summer Clothing............. 224
Goodman & Brother, Produce Commission Merchants. 254
Goodman, S. W., Printing House................... 187
Greaves, Thomas, Manfr. Cardigan Jackets 136
Greaves' Machinery Depot, Textile Machinery........ 185
Greenhalge & Wadsworth, Plush Manfrs............ 184
Greenlund, B. N., Jeweler........................... 164
Greer, Benjamin W., Bellevue Worsted Mills........ 80
Griendling's, J., Sons, Barbers' Chairs, Supplies, etc.. 185
Griffin, Nicholas J., Manfr. Alcohol and Cologne Spirits 163
Griffin, Graham & Co., Importers and Retailers of Fine Carpetings................................. 157
Grigg, Thomas H., Drug Store Fixtures............. 210
Groben, Edward A., Fish............................ 234
Groves', G. P., Sons, Furniture, Stoves, etc 241
Guarantee Trust and Safe Deposit Co............... 138
Guarantee Company of North America, The, A. F. Sabine, Resident Secretary...................... 127
Guenther, F., Upholsterer, etc 169
Gumpert, A. H., Belmont Laundry.................. 234
Gutekunst, F., Clayton S. Harris, Mgr., Photographer. 88
Gutekunst, F., Photogravure, Phototype Specialties... 204

Haas, Albert, Gents' Furnishing Goods........... 218
Haenchen, C. E., Pharmacy........................ 242
Hagen, Harry R., Real Estate, etc.................. 195
Hagen, Arthur, & Co., Agents for Tobacco.......... 168
Hagy, Geo. & Bro., Patent Lime, etc............... 212
Haines, C. H., Fruit and Produce 220
Haines, William A., Manfr. Fancy Leather Goods.... 135
Haley & Baker, Blank Book Manfrs. and Paper Rulers 132
Hall & Carpenter, Importers of Tin Plate and Metals.. 117
Hall, Wm. & Co., Manfrs. Shoddy................ 165
Hamell, P. E. & Co., Rope and Twine Manfrs...... 161
Hammer, John B., Range Works 214
Hance Brothers & White, Manfg. Chemists and Pharmaceutists...................................... 172
Hancock, The John, Mutual Life Ins. Co........... 228
Hanson Bros., Electrotypers........................ 87
Harkness & Dering, Teas, Coffees and Spices....... 262
Harley, J. M. & Co., Oils.......................... 153
Harold, Mrs. Mary A., Dry Goods................. 248
Harris, Fuller & Smith, Stock Brokers.............. 174
Harrison Safety Boiler Works...................... 254

GENERAL INDEX.

Hartel, Geo. Merchant Tailor.... 219
Hartford Steam Boiler Inspection and Insurance Co.,
    Corbin & Goodrich, General Agts................ 200
Hastings Truss Co., The 128
Hawkins, Thomas, Manfr. Ornamental, Cut, Stained
    and Leaded Glass............................. 172
Hayhurst, Henry T., Pharmacist.... 217
Heacock, H. F., Grocers', Butchers' and Confectioners'
    Fixtures..................................... 211
Heermann, Fred. W., Wines and Liquors..... 186
Heid, E., Maker of Cloth Hats and Caps............ 102
Heins, Frank B., Plumber........................ 232
Helffrich, J. W., Boarding Stables.................. 249
Henry, Bayard & Co., Lumber.................... 178
Henson Brothers, Manfrs. Knit Goods.............. 122
Hepworth, John W. & Co., Manfrs. Knitting Machinery 146
Herkness, Alfred M. & Co., Horse and Carriage Bazaar 143
Hertsch, B. A. & Co., Manfg. Chemists, etc......... 129
Hess, J. M., Manfr. of Stoves, etc.................. 177
Hewitt, G. W. & W. D., Architects................. 177
Hexter Brothers, Manfrs. Summer Clothing......... 105
Heyser, George, Clothing......................... 250
Hirst, Charles S., Jeweler........................ 224
Historical Publishing Company................... 81
Hobensack's, Dr., Medical Institute............... 166
Hoffer, David, Wholesale Dressed Beef.............. 142
Hoffman, J. W. & Co., Iron and Steel............... 277
Hoffmann, Jacob, & Son, Manfrs. Pearl Buttons and
    Novelties.................................... 134
Hohenadel, John, Brewer........................ 177
Holmes, Archibald, Manfr. Carpetings............. 124
Hongler & Bready, Cotton and Wool............... 253
Hoppe, F., Real Estate Broker.................... 212
Hoser, Chas. F., Printer.......................... 244
Hotel Waverley, T. J. Victory, Propr............... 223
Hover Ink Company............................. 158
Howe, Arthur W., Iron Commission Merchant....... 129
Howe Scale Company, The 118
Howell & Bros. (Limited), Manfrs. Wall Papers...... 112
Howell, Chas. H. & Co., Paint Makers............. 203
Huey & Christ, Wines and Liquors................ 261
Huff, C. L. & Co., Paper, Twine, etc................ 242
Huggard, John, Linens, etc....................... 192
Hughs, Cook & Co., Hides and Tallow............. 133
Humbert, Alfred, The National Watch Case and Jewelry
    Manufacturing Co............................ 113
Hunter & Dickson, Pipe Fittings, etc............... 217
Hutchison, T. F., Tin Roofing, etc................. 192
Hyde, Joseph, Plumber, etc...................... 206

IFILL, SAMUEL, Livery and Boarding Stables........ 246
Integrity Title Insurance, Trust and Safe Deposit Co.. 167
International Navigation Company, The.........100, 101
Ireland, William P., Fruit and Produce Commission
    Merchant.................................... 255

JACKSON, J. T. & Co., Real Estate................. 107
Jaeger, Geo., Photographer....................... 227
Jaeger's, Dr., Sanitary Woolen System Company,
    Samuel C. Hancock, Mgr....'................. 133
Jamison, John, Commission Merchant.............. 181

Johns, H. W., Manufacturing Co., Philadelphia Branch 113
Johnson, T. S., Tin, Slate and Gravel Roofing........ 237
Johnson, John D. & Co., Manfrs. and Dealers in Plumbers' Supplies................................. 212
Jones, J. & W., Dyers and Scourers................ 245
Jones, J. H., Manfr. Sash, Door, and Mill Work..... 182
Jordan, John L., Butter, Eggs, etc................. 182

KALBACHER, CHAS. S., Bottler of Beer............. 209
Kanouse, H. W., Groceries....................... 221
Kaupp, J. M., Printer............................ 165
Kehrweider Co., Studio.......................... 238
Keller, Ferdinand, Antique Furniture, etc........... 251
Keller, A. R., Company, Publishers and Printers..... 86
Kelley, Geo. W., Marble and Granite Works........ 144
Kelly, J. C., Carriage Builder..................... 143
Kelly, Henry, Public Accountant.................. 126
Kennedy, John H., Contractor and Practical Furniture
    Finisher..................................... 185
Kennelly, John S., Undertaker.................... 241
Kerr, James, Whiskeys, Brandies, etc.............. 183
Kerr, Alex., Bro. & Co., Salt...................... 130
Keystone Knitting Machine Manfg. Co............. 270
Keystone Horseshoe Company.................... 90
Kimely & Seidle, Wholesale Fruits................. 237
King, Wm. & Co., Wholesale Grocers.............. 168
Kinkerter, Jos. L., Hardware..................... 239
Kirk & Nice, Undertakers........................ 197
Klaisz, Edward F., Ornamental Painter............ 197
Koenig, J. & Co., Manfrs. Musical and Mathematical
    Instrument Cases............................. 156
Kolb, Wm., Feed Mills........................... 232
Kolb, J. H., Gents' Furnisher and Clothier.......... 193
Kram, Henry E. & Co., Wholesale Grocers.......... 263
Kraus, S. C., Real Estate, Insurance, etc............ 219
Krell, F. B., M.D., Druggist...................... 213
Kulp, G. & Son, Hardware, etc.................... 229
Kurtz, W. W. & Co., Bankers and Brokers.......... 112

LAIR, WILLIAM H., Ornamental Glass Cutter........ 202
Lamb, D. L. & Son, Butter, Eggs, etc............... 255
Lammer, Francis J., Apothecary................... 239
Landell, Chas. W., Glazed Kid Maker.............. 163
Lang, Bernheimer & Co., Distillers and Wholesale
    Whiskey Dealers............................. 160
Latimer, Robert L. & Co., Bolting Cloth and Flour
    Mill Supplies................................ 180
Laurent, A. G., Druggist......................... 258
Lawrence, Charles P., Sailmaker.................. 187
Lee, J. B. & Son, Dry Goods, Notions, etc 170
Lefevre, H., Jr., Paints, etc....................... 264
Lehman House Sale and Exchange Stables, Eli Kindig,
    Jr., Propr................................... 273
Lelar, William D., Real Estate and Collection Agency 109
Lenhert, S. B., Livery and Boarding Stable......... 245
Lentz, W. H. & Co., Coöperative Nickel Plating Company.. 179
Levis, Henry, & Co., Engineers, etc................ 92
Lewis, Walter L., Paper Hangings, Frescoing, etc.... 177
Lewis, John C., Stoves, etc....................... 232

GENERAL INDEX.

Leyboldt, F. W., Manfr. Scarificators, Spring Lancets and Patent Button Hole Cutters... 145
Lindley, Geo., Machinist... 228
Lindsay, J. G. & Co., Iron and Steel Factors, etc... 261
Lindsay, Mines & Co., Iron, Steel, etc... 115
Link-Belt Engineering Company, The... 91
Littlewood, G. J. & Co., Albion Dye and Bleach Works... 129
Liveright, Greenewald & Co., Manfrs. Clothing... 136
Livezey, J. J. & G. F., Painting and Painters' Supplies... 241
Lloyd, Wm. J., Manfg. Co... 211
Lockhart, Isaac, Manfr. Standard Ingrain Carpets... 137
Loesch, William, Druggist... 145
Long Valley Coal Company... 166
Loose, Daniel W., Sign Painter... 255
Louchheim, Joseph, & Co., Manfrs. Clothing... 155
Loughney, James A., Plumber, etc... 191
Lovatt, Thomas B., Auctioneer... 210
Luburg Manufacturing Company, Bicycles, Children's Carriages, etc... 105
Luckman, Geo. H., Carpets... 232
Lutner Bros., Wagon Builders... 192
Lynch, John, & Bro., Flour Commission Merchants... 108
Lyon, Lichten & Co., Manfrs. Glazed Kid... 249

MACLEAN, GEO., Agent, Stained Glass, etc... 224
MacNeece, Wm., Manfr. Art Furniture... 146
Maene, E., Sculptor... 178
Magee Art Company, Manfrs. Art Novelties... 174
Manayunk National Bank... 141
Manayunk Steam Laundry, M. & J. Metzler, Props... 221
Manayunk Trust Company... 111
Mander, Geo., Builder, etc... 220
Mann, John F., & Bro., Veal... 235
Manning, Geo. W., Sewing Machines... 231
Mansfield Bros., Printers... 216
Maris, Robert W., Apothecary... 166
Markle, S. C., Undertaker... 236
Markley, A. H., Wood Engraver... 215
Marshall Bros., Bobbin and Spool Makers... 140
Martin, Otto, & Co., Manfrs. Lithographic Printing Inks... 156
Martin, Thos. J., Jr. & Bro., Attorneys at Law... 119
Mason, Geo. C. & Son, Architects... 244
Mathieu Brothers & Co., Produce Commission Merchants... 264
Matthias, Chas. & Co., Manfrs. Horse Collars... 211
Mayberry, Samuel H., Grocer... 235
McCann, F. H., Real Estate... 211
McCauley, Matthew, Boots and Shoes... 248
McCollin, Thos. H. & Co., Photographic Supplies... 192
McCowan & Longaker, Safety Lighting Devices... 263
McCurdy & Hallowell, Conveyancers, Real Estate and Insurance Brokers... 174
McFarland, A., Packing Box Manufacturer... 253
McGarrigle, P., Flour, Grain, Feed, etc... 228
McGettigan, Edward, Importer of Wines, etc... 185
McGirr, Thomas, Painter... 238
McGlenn, W. R., Marble and Brownstone Works... 140
McGrane, Jas. A., Hardware, etc... 212
McKay & Kahler, Terra Cotta Sewer Pipe, Vitrified Paving Brick, etc... 176

McKeaige & McComb, Poultry, Eggs, etc... 184
McKee, Joseph, Chemist... 249
McLeod, John A. R., Harness... 210
McMahen, Wm. H., Wholesale Bedding... 221
McMenamin, David B., Agent for Soaps... 194
McNally, Chas. S., Paints, etc... 230
McNamara, Frank, Fashionable Hatter... 163
McNicholl, Samuel, Harness... 231
McWilliams, John, Tailoring... 197
Meadows, John, Electro Plater... 233
Medicke, J. H., Manfr. Heaters and Ranges... 189
Meeks, Edward, Publisher... 130
Merchants' Trust Company... 147
Merino, A. & Co., Wholesale Wines and Liquors... 242
Methodist Episcopal Book Room, F. B. Clegg, Agt... 196
Meyer, Louis J., Gilder and Electro Silver Plater... 197
Meyer, Wm., Steam Packing Box Manufacturer... 260
Miller & Melville, Printers... 238
Miller, Christian, Importer and Bottler of all Kinds of Malt Liquors... 191
Miller, The John C., Brewing Company... 92
Miller, Nathan, Manfr. Ingrain Carpets... 156
Milner, Dr. Jas. P., Pharmacist... 225
Mitton, Job G., Jr., Manfr. Stonecutters' Tools... 122
Mohr, J. J., Pig Iron, etc... 112
Moll, Ezra, House Furnishing Goods... 242
Mollenkof, George, Undertaker and Embalmer... 193
Montgomery, R. W., Fruit and Produce Commission Merchant... 174
Moore & White Company, The, Paper Mill Machinery etc... 196
Moore, Kelly & Co., Coal... 187
Morell & Bro., Commission Merchants in Butter, Eggs and Poultry... 210
Morgan, William C. & Co., General Stock Brokers... 110
Moroney, James, Wholesale Liquors... 168
Morris & Richter, Electricians, Hardware and Electrical Supplies... 261
Morris, Tasker & Co. (Incorporated), Iron Founders, etc... 110
Morrison Plumbing Co... 238
Morse, H. B., Druggist... 227
Moshannon Coal Company... 153
Moyer, J. P. & Co., Produce Commission Merchants... 171
Mühe, J. S., Paper Hangings... 233
Mulligan, Edward, Whiskeys... 244
Murray, B. J., M.D., Druggist... 151
Murrow, Robert H., Boot and Shoe Store... 193
Murtha, D. Chas., Brick Manfr... 182
Mutual Fire Insurance Co., The, of Germantown and its Vicinity... 121
Myers, F. D. & Co., Fruit and Produce... 257
Myers, Theo. & Co., Stock Brokers... 104

NARAMORE, G. H., Agent, Importer of Tailors' Trimmings... 207
Nassau, James, Manfr. Varnishes, Japans, etc... 119
National Bank of Germantown... 173
National Law and Collection Ass'n, D. H. Showers & Co., Gen'l Mgrs... 221
National Metal Edge Box Company... 151
Newell, R. & Son, Photographers... 159

GENERAL INDEX.

Newell & Ridgway, Wines, Liquors, etc... 114
New Philadelphia Planing Mill Co., W. H. Kline, Proprietor... 282
Nilson, P. A., Pianos and Organs... 215
Nolan, H. C. & Co., Manfrs. Cigars... 217
Nonpareil Cement Co., The (Incorporated)... 283
Nonpareil Vest Manufacturing Company, M. J. Cohen, Mgr... 170
North, Jos. C. & Sons, Coal... 210
Nuttall, R. & Son, Hardware, etc... 230
Nye & Tredick, Manfrs. Plain and Circular Rib Knitting Machinery... 150

O'BRIEN, JOHN, Coal... 201
O'Malley & Walsh, Coal... 233
O'Rourke, John J., Undertaker... 241
Ogden, Henry, & Son, Company (Ltd.), Furniture... 225
Ogden, John, & Co., Apothecaries... 189
Ott & Nicoud, Pharmacists... 197
Otto, George Wm., Agent, Bottler and Manfr. Soda Waters, etc... 142
Owens Bros., Manfrs. Hats and Caps... 125

PAIGE, ARTHUR E., Mechanical Expert... 149
Palmer, John T., Printer... 249
Palmer, John S., Manfr. Paper Boxes... 149
Pancoast, S. R., Building Stone... 189
Paris, Edgar P. & Co., Apothecaries... 232
Parker's, Joseph, Sons, "Combination Stores"... 114
Patton, G. W. & Co., Wool... 124
Paxon, Comfort & Co., Funeral Supplies... 175
Pedrick & Ayer, Manfrs. Universal Milling Machines, etc... 98, 99
Pennsylvania Optical Co. (Limited)... 178
Pennsylvania Salt Manfg. Company... 100
Pennsylvania Steel Company... 80
People's Five Year Benefit Order... 121
Péquignot, Z. J., Diamonds, Watches, etc... 117
Pessano, John D., Real Estate Broker... 126
Pflaum, Christian, Jr., Confectioner... 170
Philadelphia Supply Co. (Canby & Costello), Manfrs. Steam and Hydraulic Packing, etc... 178
Philadelphia Storage and Upholstering Co., The, Lewis King, Propr... 189
Philadelphia Knitting Mills Company... 114
Philadelphia Marble Company... 131
Phillips, Edw. A., Burial Casket and Coffin Manfr... 186
Pinkstone, R., Jewelry... 213
Piper, W. H. & Co., Coal and Coke... 220
Platt, E. M., Druggist... 209
Poehlmann, W., Groceries... 228
Poole, C. P. & Co., Manfrs. Tin Cans... 257
Potter, Joseph, Manfr. Straw Goods... 117
Potter & Seymour, Real Estate and Conveyancing... 173
Potts, Horace T. & Co., Iron and Steel... 252
Powell, G. Washington, Real Estate... 104
Power, Maurice H., Printer... 214
Price, Geo. C., Watchmaker...
Priest, Jas. S., Manfr. Tin, Sheet Iron and Copper Ware 221
Procter, Wm., Jr., Co., Apothecaries... 212
Provident Bond and Investment Company... 54

Prudential Insurance Co., H. R. Raiguel, Jr., Supt... 130
Pulaski, F. & Co., Manfrs. and Dealers in Picture Frames... 241

QUAKER CITY WHISK BROOM WORKS, Coates & Mathias, Proprs... 107
Quaker City Watch Case Co., Louis A. Buchy, Propr... 222
Quay, Lewis H., Frescoing, Paper Hanging, etc... 240
Quirk, J. S. & Co., Designers and Engravers on Wood. 256

RAIGUEL, H. R., Jr., Supt. Prudential Insurance Co... 130
Ramsey, Jas. B. & Son, Paper Manfrs... 214
Randolph, Wm. C., Manfr. Bone Rings... 208
Rauch, Ruetschlin & Co., Wholesale Grocers, etc... 144
Rausenberger, J. F., Bee Hive Meat Market... 284
Rawson Manfg. Co., The, Manfrs. Rawson Step Ladder Chair, etc... 260
Raynor, Thomas C., Veterinary Surgeon... 228
Read, Chas E., Manfr. Gents' and Boys' Footwear... 209
Read & Stanton Co., The (Limited), Spices, Mustards, etc... 284
Reading Paper Mills... 110
Reading Rolling Mill Company, The... 265
Redifer, Albert A. & Bro., Manfrs. Lasts... 252
Redles, George, Manfr. Bobbins and Spools... 144
Redstone Oil, Coal and Coke Company... 134
Reed, R. S., Real Estate... 140
Reese, Chas. P. & Co., Wholesale Meat... 234
Reese, John, Ship Chandler and Grocer... 230
Reformed Church Publication House, Rev. Chas. G. Fisher, D.D., Propr... 157
Reger, Albert P., Agent for Sheet Brass, etc... 224
Reichner, Samuel K., Real Estate, etc... 222
Reifsneider Bros., Manfrs. Furniture, etc... 253
Reuss, Dr. Wm., Druggist... 215
Rhodes, Wm. S. & Co., Street Railway Supplies and Builders' Iron Work... 181
Rice, C. J., Butter, Eggs, etc... 104
Ridgway House... 226
Rieser, A. F., Specialist in Butter, etc... 161
Robbins, H. J., Paper Hanger, etc... 154
Robbins, Chas. S., Hatter...
Roberts & Andrews, Produce Commission Merchants.. 158
Roberts, Enoch T., Coal, Flour and Feed... 174
Roberts, Owen D., Real Estate... 144
Robertson, Jas., Manfr. Gloves... 222
Robinson, Wm., Men's and Boys' Clothing... 236
Roehm, John, Brewer... 180
Rogers, Francis P. & Son, Tin, Iron and Copper Ware Manfrs... 252
Rogers, T. A. & Son, Oysters... 250
Rohner, Henry, Groceries... 106
Rohrman, J. Hall, & Son, Tinwares... 130
Rosatto, Frank, Manfr. Billiard and Pool Tables... 213
Rowan & Parker, Wholesale Liquor Dealers... 218
Rowbotham, Geo. S. & Sons, Dry Goods, etc... 242
Rowley, F. C., Wholesale Sea Food, etc... 262
Rubenstone, Jacob, Diamond Setter, etc... 162
Ruff, John G., Carpenter and Builder... 215
Ruffner, Daniel B., Coal, Lime, Cement, etc... 143
Ruffner & Dunn, Manfrs. Nut Locks and Tube Cleaners 143

GENERAL INDEX.

Rulon, J. W. & Sons, Importers East India Goods.... 137
Rumpp, Chas., Manfr. Fancy Leather Goods........ 224
Ruth, George H. & Co., Manufacturers' Agents...... 199
Rutherford & Barclay, Miners and Manfrs. Rutherford's Metallic Paint............................ 100
Rutherford, H., Manfr. Heaters and Ranges......... 220

Sabin, F., Ranges, Stoves, Heaters, etc............. 206
Saving Fund Society of Germantown and its Vicinity, The.. 139
Sawyer, C., Manfr. Sewing Machines 209
Sawyers & Co., Fruit and Produce................... 105
Scattaglia, L. C. & Co., Artists and Decorative Painters 103
Schelder, John H., Custom Tailor.................... 216
Schenck, Albert, Importer China and Glassware..... 199
Schoelgens, Wm., Wines and Brandies............... 203
Schoell, Chas. F., Tailor............................ 204
Schuler, John G., Carpenter and Builder............ 248
Schumacher, C. W., Wall Paper and Window Shades.. 239
Schwarz, G. A., Toys, Fancy Goods, etc.............. 179
Sciple, H. M. & Co., Boilers, Engines, etc........... 85
Scott, John H., Real Estate, etc..................... 226
Scott, Thomas, & Co., Grocers....................... 226
Scott Paper Co. (Limited).......................... 140
Scott & Williams, Builders of Knitting Machinery.... 279
Searle, Vanueman & Co., Hosiery, White Goods, etc.. 125
Second National Bank of Philadelphia, The, at Frankford.. 79
Seidel, R. B., Philadelphia Black Lead Crucible Works, 122
Seitter, Chas. F., Hardware.......................... 218
Sexennial Printing House........................... 233
Sharp, John, & Son, Wholesale Grocers............... 175
Sharpless, John M. & Co., Manfrs. Dye Stuffs........ 230
Shaw, Thomas, Mechanical Engineer, Manfr. Engineers' Special Appliances, etc.................... 130
Sheppard, Isaac A. & Co., Excelsior Stove Works.... 89
Sheppard, J. B. & Sons, Curtains, Linens, etc........ 104
Sheridan's Canton Tea Store......................... 109
Shermer, Lemuel Z., Manfr. Harness and Horse Collars.. 205
Sherry, F. P., Painters' Supply House................ 245
Shetzline, R. A. & Sons, Wholesale Fruit and Produce Dealers and Shippers............................. 170
Schoenewald & Stillman, Manfrs. Brass Goods,..... 163
Shore, James, & Co., Plumbing and Heating......... 227
Shore, Thomas, & Son, Hosiery Press and Pump Works.. 102
Shultz Belting Company............................ 243
Sickel, W. V., Pension and Claim Attorney.......... 205
Sidebotham & Lever, Fire Insurance and Real Estate Brokerage.. 205
Sidle, John W., Optician............................ 238
Silver King Mining and Milling Co.................. 90
Simpson, Wm. A. & Son, Insurance.................. 182
Sixth National Bank................................ 157
Smith, Wm. & Co., Fruit and Produce............... 234
Smith, Henry A. W., Plumber, Steam and Gas Fitter.. 211
Smith & Pyle, Lapidists............................. 193
Smith, Edmund D. & Co., Iron and General Commission Merchants................................... 96
Smith, The Geo. A., Machinery Co................... 134

Smith, Franklin A., Yellow Pine Flooring............ 133
Smith, C. R. & Son, Jewelers........................ 203
Smith's, J. L., Map Establishment 130
Snyder, M. L., Rubber Goods........................ 168
Sorber, George T., Real Estate...................... 217
Southwark Ice Co, John R. Carpenter, Prop........ 220
Southwark Paint Works, Joseph Lawless, Proprietor.. 156
Sowden, Wm., Meat Market........................ 154
Spaeth, Krautter & Hess, Anchor Brewery........... 281
Sperry, J., Bookbinder's Stamp and Letter Engraver.. 239
Spoerhase, Louis, Jeweler............................ 229
Stafford, James, Star Woolen Mills.................. 142
Stamm, S. & Co., Manfrs. of Pantaloons............. 214
Standard Sewing Machine Company, T. D. Brown, Mgr.. 126
Stanger, J. B. & Bros., Furnishing Undertakers 143
Stanton, Frank W. & Co., Fruits.................... 168
Stanton & Lewis, General Blacksmiths.............. 189
Star and Crescent Mills Co., Manfrs. Turkish Towels, etc.. 275
Star Engraving and Printing Company, The (Limited). 178
Star Woolen Mills, James Stafford, Propr........... 142
Stark, E. C. & Co., Memorial Cards................ 137
St. Cloud Pharmacy, Dr. B. L. Brown................ 206
Stephen, H. & Co., Iron and Steel................... 214
Stetson, John B., Company, Manfrs. Hats, ... .94, 95
Stockley, Wm. K., Commission Sales Stables........ 229
Stratton Ice Works.................................. 180
Straub, A. W. & Co., Manfrs. Grinding Mills........ 162
Streeper, Frank P., Druggist....................... 170
Stroup, J. H. & Co., Druggists 230
Struse, Charles O., Coal, Wood and Builders' Supplies. 128
Stuckert, J. F., Architect........................... 154
Stutz, Henry, Jr., Contractors' Supplies............. 133
Sullivan, J. P., Real Estate 250
Sullivan, Photographer.............................. 254
Summers, J. J., Dry Goods.......................... 249
Sunderland, Geo. W., Real Estate................... 251
Supplee Hardware Company........................ 111
Sutter Bros., Importers and Packers Leaf Tobacco... 159
Swain, Harry, Druggist............................ 184
Sweeney, B. M. & E., Wholesale Liquors........... 231
Sweeny, J. F. & Sons, Engravers of Signs in Brass, etc. 185

Taylor, B. F. & Co., Lumber and Millwork.......... 146
Taylor & Co., Coal................................. 192
Teller Bros., Leaf Tobacco......................... 160
Textile Machine Co. (Ltd.)......................246, 247
Thomas, Banner, Manfr. Cotton and Linen Netting, etc. 116
Thomas, Robert, & Son, Lumber Merchants......... 199
Thomas the Tailor................................. 239
Thomas, Wm. H. & Co., Jobbers in Dry Goods Specialties....................................... 232
Thompson, Foust & Co., Manfrs'. Agents for Hosiery, etc.. 207
Thompson, Thos., Sons & Co., Upholstery Goods.... 112
Thurwanger, H. J., Manfr. Signs.................... 208
Todd, J. Chas., Druggist........................... 233
Tomlin, N. F., Real Estate, Insurance, etc.......... 218
Townsend, Isaac, Manfr's Agent for Steam Packing, and Sash Cord.................................... 250

GENERAL INDEX.

Tracy Worsted Mills Company, The.................. 108
Treichler, L. A., Apothecary........................ 248
Trumbauer, J. & Son, Produce Commission Merchants. 257
Tryon, Harrison, Photographer of Machinery......... 241
Tyndale & Mitchell Company, China, Glass, Pottery, etc.. 137

Union Central Life Ins. Co. of Cincinnati, O., J. W. Woods, Agent........................... 107
Union National Bank................................ 161
United Firemen's Insurance Co...................... 108
United States Credit System Co. (Incorporated), Wm. A. Whittick, General Agent..................... 102

Van Gunden, W. F., Marble and Granite............. 186
Vanier, A., House, Sign and Fresco Painting, etc.... 191
Valdivia, J. H., Leaf Tobacco 219
Van Sciver, Samuel, Conveyancer and Penman........ 206
Vasey's, E. M., West Philadelphia Model Stables..... 93

Walker, Robert J., Star Finishing Works............ 160
Walker Bros. & Co., Founders and Machinists........ 182
Walkup, A. M., Carpenter and Builder............... 244
Walmsley, W. H. (Limited), Opticians, etc 190
Walsh's, John F., Sons, Wall Paper, etc............. 189
Wampole's Tasteless Preparation of Cod Liver Oil... 264
Warden Manufacturing Co., The..................... 274
Wareham, Robt., Manfr. Engineers' and Surveyors' Instruments....................................... 165
Warrington, Jos., Builder of Carriages.............. 118
Waters, Wm. T. & Co., Steam Broom and Whisk Works.. 161
Watson, Parker & Co., Foreign Fruits and Produce... 183
Watson & Robinson, Wood Working Mill............. 194
Watson, Thos. S., Agent, Manfr. Iron and Wire Work. 204
Weaver, Henry M., & Son, Manfrs. Cigars........... 250
Weber & Petzoldt, Continental Carpet Mills......... 115
Weed & Jesson, Machinists', Die and Press Tool Makers, etc..................................... 251
Weil & Taws, Importers and Dealers in Drawing and Artists' Materials and Mathematical Instruments.. 159
Weinert, Wm. & Co., Fruit and Produce.............. 247
Welden, A. G. C., Butter, Eggs, Poultry............. 200
Wells, C. F. & Son, Carpenters, Contractors and Builders.. 141
Welsh & Naulty, Funeral Directors and Embalmers... 234
Wendell, Edward, Manfr. of Mouldings, Mirrors, etc.. 240
Wenderoth, J. G., Boot, Shoe and Trunk House...... 154
Werner, August, Maker of Fine Shoes................ 188
Wescoat, T. E., Fruit Commission Merchant.......... 171
West, Geo. H. & Sons, Boots and Shoes.............. 190
West End Drug Store................................ 227

West Philadelphia Bank............................. 150
West Philadelphia Real Estate Agency, The, Clayton W, Peirson, Propr............................. 121
Wetherill, Geo. D. & Co., Drugs, etc............... 110
Wheeler, Wm. C., Printer........................... 210
Whelen, Townsend, & Co., Bankers and Brokers..... 124
White, A. & Son, Flour and Feed.................... 201
White, Hentz & Co., Sole Proprietors "Trimble" Whiskeys...................................... 198
White, The S. S., Dental Manufacturing Company... 141
Whitehill, Edward, Household Goods, etc............ 231
Why, John Jr., & Bro., Bicycles and Accessories.... 210
Wigmore, Wm. H., Manfr. Surgical Instruments..... 112
Wilde's, Robert, Sons, Carpet Yarn Manufacturers... 153
Wiley & Wallace Co., Manfrs. Pharmaceutical Specialties.. 235
Willard, T. Newton, Druggist....................... 241
William Penn Hotel and Sale Stables, Wm. D. Althouse, Propr... 131
Williams, De Witt C., Photographer................. 220
Williamson Bros., Engineers, Machinists, etc....... 118
Wilson & Rogers, Boneless Meats, etc............... 259
Wilson, William D., General Insurance Broker...... 134
Wilson Brothers & Co., Civil Engineers, Architects, etc. 106
Wilson Biscuit Works............................... 116
Wilson, James L., Painting 187
Wilson & Raughley, Flour, Feed, etc................ 245
Wilson, John C., Cracked Corn and Feed, etc....... 240
Wiltberger, D. S., Wholesale Druggist and Dealer in Paints, Oils, etc................................. 126
Windolph, Jacob, Flour, Feed, etc.................. 231
Wister, L. & R. & Co., Brokers and Commission Merchants... 159
Wolf, Isaac, Insurance............................. 113
Wolf Bros., Manfrs. Paper Envelopes............... 207
Wollenberger, R., Merchant Tailor.................. 245
Woltemate Brothers, Florists....................... 164
Woodcock Bros., Manfrs. Hosiery and Knit Goods.... 114
Woodruff, David S., Provision Dealer............... 170
Woods, Wilson, & Bro., Upholsterers............... 240
Woodside, Geo. D. & Co., Milk, Butter, Eggs, Poultry, etc... 204
Wotherspoon, E. & Son, House Furnishing Goods, etc 240
Wrigley Manufacturing Company, The................ 127

Young, Wm., Real Estate Agent..................... 207

Zane, Charles E., Importer Kid Gloves, Fabric Gloves and Silk Mitts.................................. 170
Zentmayer, Jos., Optician, etc..................... 255
Zinn, Wm. T., Wood Engraver, etc.................. 223
Zook, J. M., Real Estate........................... 204
Zurn, O. F. & Co., Oils............................ 270

HISTORICAL AND COMMERCIAL Philadelphia PENN.

EVERYTHING IN LIFE is said to be relative. And as effects cease not always with the causes in which they have their origin, so also may the events of the dead past bear closely upon the affairs of the present.

Thus, while the scope of this work comprehends, primarily, live matters of interest pertaining to Philadelphia of today—its institutions, resources, material wealth and prosperity—there is so much that is distinctly notable in the history of the settlement, growth and progress of the "City of Brotherly Love" germane to the subject matter hereinafter presented, that a review thereof from the earliest period seems eminently fitting by way of a prologue to the chapters that follow. For, though vast and of surpassing importance her manufacturing, mercantile and financial interests, she stands preëminent in her relations with the destinies of the nation in "the times that tried men's souls." Indeed, Philadelphia may be said to occupy a niche in historic associations with the epoch which gave civil and political liberty to the American people preëminently her own. The Birth-place of the Republic; the Capital up to 1800; the Metropolis of the Western world for many years; and the first place on earth to proclaim and put into practical application the sublime doctrine of the Brotherhood of Man and the Fatherhood of God; Philadelphia may justly be called the most noted city in the country. Here, too, was printed the first American newspaper; the first Colonial Congress met here, likewise, and the city maintained commercial supremacy until the opening of the Erie Canal, when New York became the great *entrepôt* for inland and maritime traffic.

The early history of the Quaker City is replete with stirring incidents, and the story of the rise and progress of Philadelphia for two hundred and ten years presents an epitome of human interest unsurpassed in the annals of nations. No lust of conquest impelled hither the man to whom it owes its name and its origin. The very antithesis was, in fact, the *raison d'état*. His object in founding it William Penn announced thus: "I took charge of the province of Pennsylvania for the Lord's sake. I wanted to afford an asylum for the good and oppressed of every nation, and to frame a government which might be an example. I desired to show men as free and happy as they could be: and I had kind views to the Indians." For similar reasons he selected its name; the original site of the city was called by the Indians, Coaquenaku, said to mean "the grove of tall pines," which may be regarded as doubtful, as the Indians called the Delaware River by the same name. The colony was vigorous from the start; for in 1682 not less than twenty-three ships arrived with settlers, almost all of whom were Friends. Legislation began the year next succeeding, and in 1684 there were 300 houses and a population of 2,500 in the embryo city. In 1699 the number of houses had increased to 700, and the place boasted 4,500 inhabitants.

Before his final departure Penn incorporated the city, in 1701. Scarcely, however, had the great philanthropist departed from the scene in which his presence was an all-powerful factor, with an abiding faith in Providence and the hand of destiny, than dissentions arose, not among the Friends, but between them and those in authority in the affairs of state. And for three-quarters of a century following the history of Philadelphia exhibits the most glaring contradiction of its name; for it is simply a record of discords growing out of the conflicting views of the Quaker settlers and the governors of the Province on military and financial matters. During the war of England with France and Spain the governor, alive to the dangers threatening the colony, created a militia in 1704, a measure particularly obnoxious to the disciples of Fox, whom he sought to enlist in its favor by stratagem. On the Fair day, 1706, a messenger arrived from New Castle with the news that the enemy's ships were in the river and approaching the city. The governor, on horseback, with sword drawn, urged the people to take up arms for the public defense. A panic ensued: the ships were placed out of reach of danger; the people hid their valuables and fled; but the Quakers remained calm, and could neither be frightened nor coaxed into the movement. The fraud was discovered, however, and the governor promptly displaced. When Lewes, on the Delaware, was plundered by the French privateers in 1709, Governor Gookin's demand for a grant of £4,000, to aid the Queen in the invasion of Canada, was refused by the Assembly.

In 1732 Thomas Penn, son of the founder of the colony, arrived here, the city at this period having attained considerable importance as a trading and commercial center.

In 1739 Governor Thomas, in the quarrel between England and Spain, issued letters of marque and reprisal. Less than a decade later Benjamin Franklin, by the timely publication of his "Plain Truth," roused a spirit of military enthusiasm among the people, which eventuated in an armed force of 10,000. He also promoted the erection of a battery below the city, which, in 1750, mounted fifty pieces of cannon, and occupied the site of the present United States Navy Yard.

HISTORICAL AND COMMERCIAL PHILADELPHIA.

In 1744 Whitfield became a central figure in Philadelphia, and in his preaching was notably successful.

In 1755 a militia bill was passed, and Benjamin Franklin was colonel of the city regiment.

From 1765 to 1774 this city was active and prominent in resisting British aggression. The first Continental Congress met at Carpenter's Hall, September 5, 1774; the second May 10, 1775, in the State House.

Here, on June 15, 1775, Colonel George Washington, of Virginia, was appointed general, and commander-in-chief of the armies of the United States. The Declaration of Independence was adopted in the State House July 4, and proclaimed July 8, 1776. The British held possession of the city from September, 1777, to June, 1778. The battle of Germantown was fought on October 4, 1777. Philadelphia was the capital of Pennsylvania (except during the British occupation) until 1799, and the seat of the federal government from 1790 to 1800.

EDWIN SIDNEY STUART.

In the war with Great Britain, 1812 to 1814, the city exhibited much martial spirit and patriotism.

The construction of the steam water-works at Fairmount was commenced in 1812. The same year yellow fever prevailed. In 1832 the Philadelphia, Germantown and Norristown Railroad was completed. During the summer of that year Asiatic cholera made its dread appearance, and from July 5 to October 4, caused 935 deaths. Riots disturbed the city in 1834, and 1835, and again in 1838, 1840 and 1844. Gas was introduced in 1836. In 1837 specie payment was suspended, and the failure of the Bank of the United States, two years later, for a time prostrated the commerce of the city.

The establishment of the first telegraph lines dates from April 27, 1846. The charter of the city (March 11, 1789) being merely an adaptation of the original Act of Incorporation to the political changes of the period, the suburbs, in the course of time, were created districts, with independent organizations; the inconvenience of the system led ultimately to the Consolidation Act, in 1854, which abolished the suburban municipalities and made the city coextensive with the county of Philadelphia.

In the cause of the Union the city lavished its treasure in men and money, and the First Regiment of National Guards stands eminent for services throughout the late war. The great Sanitary Fair was held in 1864, in Logan Square, and netted upward of $1,000,000. The Centenary of American Independence was duly celebrated in 1876, the World's Fair marking a notable epoch in the history of Philadelphia and the United States.

In subsequent chapters the Centennial and all other features of interest connected with the city in the past and the present are presented in a concise and exhaustive manner.

A PAGE FROM EARLY HISTORY.

Although the site of the city where now move, live and have their being, upward of a million of people, was a veritable wilderness and the abode of primitive man, traversed only by the bear, the wolf and the child of the forest, at the advent of William Penn, there had already been established on the banks of the Delaware some straggling white settlements. It is a matter of historical record, that even before Penn was born Gustavus Adolphus, King of Sweden, had conceived the idea of planting a colony on this very spot. The design of the Swedish monarch would seem to even have anticipated the purposes of the noble Quaker almost in their entirety, for it is said he made plans to found a "state absolutely free, an asylum for the oppressed of every creed, where every man should enjoy the fruits of his own labor." It was further proposed by him that "the land should be fairly bought from the wild peoples," that no slavery of any kind should be permitted, and that the truths of the Christian religion should be taught these same "wild peoples." It was not until many years later, however, that the project could be put into execution. An expedition was fitted out, in 1637, to plant the "New Sweden."

The Swedish settlers occupied a narrow strip of ground along the rivers, on the edge of the forest in that section of the city known as Southwark. In the meantime a number of Dutch settlers had arrived in the vicinity. So that when Penn first set foot in the New World, he was met by a friendly people and received hearty greeting. The first civilized man who visited Delaware Bay was Capt. Henry Hudson, and he came in 1609. About a year prior to this, however, the mouth of the bay was accidentally discovered by Lord De la Warr, in honor of whom the river and bay were named. The Dutch, in 1623, took possession of the whole territory between the South River, (Delaware) and the North River, (Hudson), and held it until 1664, when the English assumed control. It was subsequently recovered by the Dutch, and reverted to British rule in 1674. The first actual European settlement in this region was Fort Nassau, near Gloucester, in New Jersey, and the first Dutch settlers were murdered by the Indians. The Swedes, who followed in 1638 and settled on the west bank of the Delaware, were more successful, but their success involved them in trouble with the Dutch, to whom they finally succumbed.

In 1681 a charter for the territory twelve miles north of New Castle to 43° northeast, bounded east by the Delaware River, and to extend west 5° in longitude to the same degree of latitude, was granted to William Penn. The whole region was then an unbroken wilderness, for the Swedish and Dutch settlers had made no effort toward changing the primeval aspect of the district. The former lived in caves, dressed in sheepskins, and barely tilled the ground enough to furnish the means of subsistence, while the latter devoted themselves almost entirely to trading with the Indians. The Swedes were nowise averse to the Quakers settling in the neighborhood, but they were not over-kindly disposed toward the Dutch, who claimed the soil as their own. The Swedish settlers, too, had established friendly relations with the natives; in fact, the utmost good feeling had existed between them and the children of the forest for fully half a century before Penn's famous treaty with the Indians was entered into. And when William Penn came among them he declared the Swedes to be more sober and industrious than the people of other nations. There was very much in common between these colonists and the Quaker settlers. They were patient, hopeful and virtuous, and were extremely simple in their habits. They neither murmured at the fate that had driven them from home to seek an abode amid such uninviting surroundings, nor made the forest resound with hallelujahs, but applied themselves diligently to the task of creating a new order of things on this earth, viz.: the building up of a community where all could live in peace and harmony, in accordance with the teachings of the founder of Christianity. Theirs was to be an ideal commonwealth, where perfect freedom of conscience, religious liberty and equal rights were to be the corner stones of the moral and social fabric—the first practical attempt in this direction, in all probability, in the history of the race. And here, too, came those who were persecuted for their religious opinions, not only in the Old World countries, but also in some of the colonies in the New. Here the different sects lived in brotherly love, the pastors of the various denominations evincing their friendliness toward each other by appearing occasionally in each others' pulpits. But little progress, in a material way,

The Summer House.

VIEW IN FAIRMOUNT PARK

was made up to the time of the arrival of the English immigrants. The Swedish colonists had, however, abandoned the caves and now lived in rude log huts, caulked with mud and lighted by holes cut in the walls; but there was scarcely any stir in the community. The new arrivals from England settled down in a spot near the Delaware, close by the Swedes, and at that point the city remained for nearly a century. From this period onward there were signs of activity, and the place soon after could boast of houses built of brick, although they were very unpretentious structures.

The implements, tools and utensils in use, while they were a great improvement on those doing service hitherto, were still of the crudest character. The furniture was of the plainest, and the clothing worn by the people was for the most part of the coarsest material.

One of the earliest English settlers, Gabriel Thomas, soon after landing, wrote that the only vehicles in the community, in addition to William Penn's calash, were thirty carts. He says further that laboring men were paid three times as much wages as in England. Women's wages he declares to be "exorbitant—from £5 to £10 per annum." And there are "no begars, nor olde maydes, neither lawyers nor doctors, with lycence to kill and make mischeef."

At long intervals there came to the settlement men of means, cadets of respectable families, driven from England by persecution, or emigrants from the Barbadoes, bringing their slaves or household goods along with them; and thus the population continued to increase.

WILLIAM PENN.

The founder of the colony of Pennsylvania, the renowned Quaker and philanthropist, William Penn, was born at Tower Hill, London, on October 14, 1644. He was the son of Sir William Penn, an eminent English admiral. His mother's name was Margaret Jaspar. His early days were spent partly in Essex, and partly in Ireland, where his father had several estates. He went to school at Chigwell, near his home in Essex, and studied at Christ Church, Oxford, where he was converted to Quakerism by the preaching of a disciple of George Fox, named Thomas Loe. His enthusiasm for his new faith assumed a pugnacious form. Not only did he object personally to attend the services of the Church of England, and to wear the surplice of a student—both of which he considered eminently papistical—but, along with some companions, who had also become Quakers, he attacked several of his fellow-students and tore the obnoxious robes from their backs. For this unseemly procedure Penn was expelled from the university. His father was so excessively annoyed at his conduct that he gave Penn a severe beating and turned him out of doors; but he soon after mollified and sent his son to travel on the Continent, in the hope that the change of scene and the gayety of French life would alter the bent of his mind. This failed, however, to produce the desired effect, but the youth certainly acquired a grace and suavity of address that he did not before possess.

William served for several days on the staff of his father, now a great commander, and was by him sent back in April, 1665, to Charles II., with dispatches.

Returning after the naval victory off Lowestoft, in June, Admiral Penn found that, probably from the effect upon his mind of the awful outbreak of the plague, his son had become settled in seriousness and Quakerism.

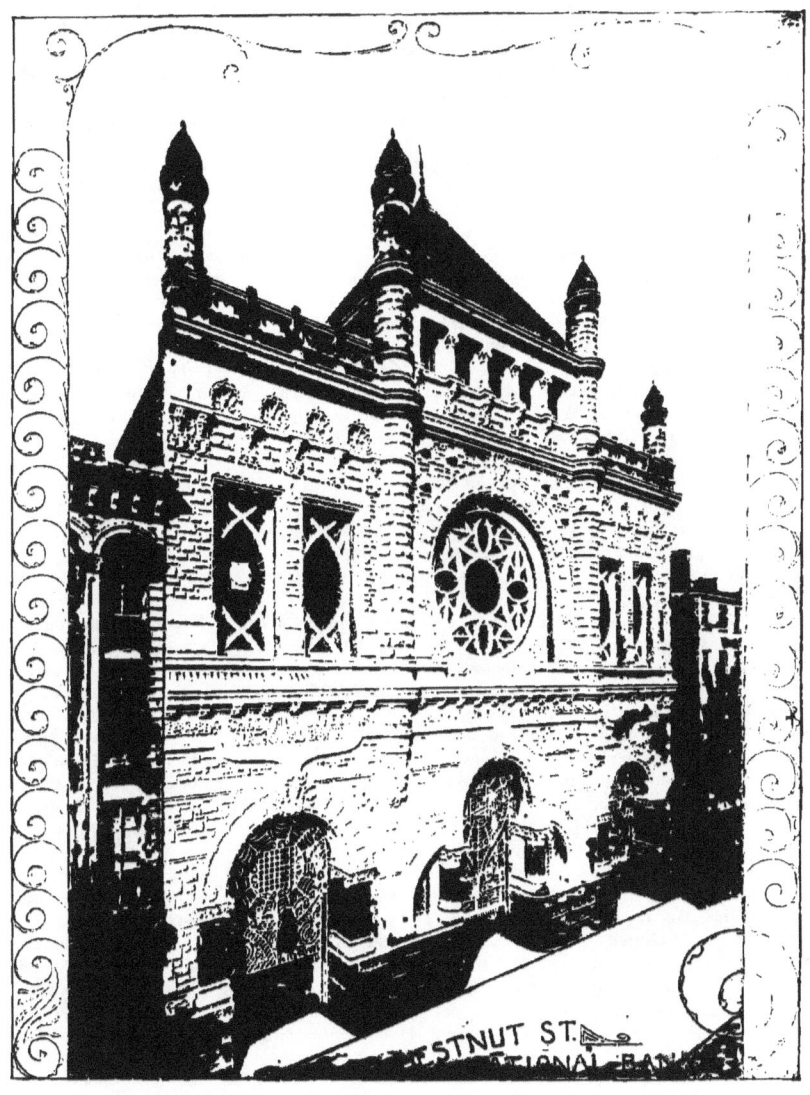

In 1666 the admiral sent him to Ireland to look after his estates in the county of Cork, which he did to the complete satisfaction of his father; for in matters of business he was as practical as in religion he was an out-and-out mystic. In the city of Cork, however, he again fell in with Thomas Loe, and soon became involved in difficulty.

On September 3, 1667, while attending a meeting of Quakers in Cork, Penn assisted in expelling a soldier who had disturbed the proceedings, and for this he was, along with others, imprisoned by the mayor, but was immediately released upon appealing to the lord president of the council of Munster, who was personally acquainted with him. He then returned to London an avowed believer in the doctrines enunciated by George Fox and an advocate of these tenets. Again he and his father quarreled, because the conscience of the former would not allow him to take off his hat to anybody, not even to the king, the Duke of York, or the admiral himself. Once more he was turned out of doors by his, perhaps testy, but assuredly provoked parent. His mother, however, stepped in and smoothed matters so far that Penn was permitted to return home, and his father even exerted his influence with the government to wink at his son's attendance at the illegal conventicles of the Quakers, which nothing could induce him to give up.

Penn now became a minister of the persuasion he professed, and at once entered upon controversy and authorship. His first public discussion was with Thomas Vincent, a Presbyterian preacher of London, who had reflected on the "damnable" doctrines of the Quakers. In this he appears to have acted as second to George Whitehead. The imputations upon his opinions and good citizenship, made, as well by dissenters as by the Church, he repelled with vigor. In 1688 he was thrown into the Tower, on account of a publication entitled "The Sandy Foundation Shaken," in which he attacked the ordinary tenets of the Trinity, God's "satisfaction" in the death of Christ and justification by the imputation of Christ's righteousness. While in prison William Penn wrote the most famous and popular of his books "No Cross, No Crown" and "Innocency with her Open Face," a vindication of himself, which contributed to his liberation, which was obtained through the interference of the Duke of York.

In 1670 Admiral Penn died, leaving his son an estate of £1,500 a year, together with claims upon the government for £16,000.

Early in 1671 Penn was again arrested for preaching in Wheeler Street meeting-house, by Sir J. Robinson, the lieutenant of the Tower, formerly lord mayor, and known as a brutal and bigoted churchman. Refusing to take the oath at his trial, Penn was committed to Newgate for six months. During his imprisonment he wrote several works, the most important being "The Great Cause of Liberty of Conscience," a noble defense of complete toleration. After regaining his freedom, he visited Holland and Germany, in the company of Fox and Barclay, for the purpose of disseminating the doctrines of his sect. Upon his return home, in the spring of 1672, Penn married Gulielma, Maria Springett, daughter of Sir William Springett, and for some years thereafter continued to devote himself to the propagation of the Quaker faith, which he did, both by preaching and writing. During the year last mentioned he published the "Treatise on Oaths and England's Present Interest Considered."

In the year 1673 Penn was still more active. He secured the release of George Fox, addressed the Quakers in Holland and Germany, carried on public controversies with Hicks, a Baptist, and Faldo, an Independent, and wrote his treatise on the "Christian Quaker and his Divine Testimony Vindicated," the "Discourse of the General Rule of Faith and Practice," "Reason Against Railing," (in answer to Hicks), "Counterfeit Christianity Detected" and a "Just Rebut to One-and-Twenty Learned Divines" (an answer to Faldo and to "Quakerism no Christianity"). His last public controversy was with Richard Baxter, in 1675, and in which each party claimed a victory. During this year Penn's active sympathies were enlisted on behalf of the imprisoned Quakers at Aberdeen.

Circumstances having turned his attention to the New World, he, in 1681, obtained from the Crown, in lieu of his monetary claim upon it, a grant of territory now forming the State of Pennsylvania. Penn desired to call the colony Sylvania, on account of the forests with which

Brown's Building. Wood Building. Western National Bank.

the region was covered; but the king (Charles II.) good-humoredly insisted on the prefix Penn. The dominant motive of the great Quaker was to establish a home for his co-religionists in the distant West, where they might preach and practice their convictions in unmolested peace. At this point his connection with America begins.

The province of New Jersey, comprising the country between the Hudson and Delaware rivers, on the east and west, had been granted in March, 1663-64, by Charles II., to his brother; James, in turn, had, in June of the same year, leased it to Lord Berkeley and Sir George Carteret in equal shares. By a deed, dated March 18, 1673-74, John Fenwick, a Quaker, bought one of the shares—that of Lord Berkeley—in trust for Edward Byllinge, also a Friend. This sale was confirmed by James, after the second Dutch War, on August 6, 1680. Disputes having arisen between Fenwick and Byllinge, Penn acted as arbitrator; and then being in financial difficulties and compelled to sell his interest in order to satisfy his creditors, Penn was added, at their request, to the two of themselves, as trustee. The disputes were finally settled by Fenwick receiving ten out of the hundred parts into which the province was divided, with a considerable sum of money, the remaining ninety parts being afterwards put up for sale. Fenwick sold his ten parts to two other Friends, Eldridge and Warner, who thus, with Penn and the other two, became masters of West Jersey, West New Jersey or New West Jersey, as it was indifferently called. The five proprietors appointed three commissioners, with instructions dated from London, August 16, 1676, to settle disputes with Fenwick (who had bought fresh lands from the Indians) and to purchase new territories, to survey and divide them, and to build a town—New Beverley (Burlington) being the result.

For the new colony Penn drew up a constitution, under the title of "concessions," which he himself thus describes: "There we lay a foundation for after ages to understand their liberty as men and Christians, that they may not be bought in bondage but by their own consent; for we put the power in the people." The greatest care is taken to make this constitution conform "as near as may be convenient to the primitive ancient and fundamental laws of the nation of England." But a democratic element is introduced and the new principles of perfect religious freedom—"that no men nor numbers of men upon earth hath power or authority to rule over men's consciences in religious matters"—stands in the first place. Such a constitution, which is in marked contrast with Locke's aristocratic one for Carolina, settled eight years previously, soon attracted large numbers of Quakers to West Jersey.

It was shortly before the events just related that William Penn inherited through his wife the estate of Worthinghurst, in Sussex, whither he removed from Rickmansworth.

In 1678 the Popish Terror came to a head, and to calm and guide Friends in the prevailing excitement Penn wrote his "Epistle to the Children of Light in this Generation." A far more important work was "An Address to Protestants of all Persuasions, by William Penn, Protestant," in 1679. This was succeeded at the general election which followed the dissolution of the pensionary parliament, by a political manifesto "England's Great Interest in the Choice of this New Parliament," Next came "One Project for the Good of England," which was perhaps, the most pungent of his political writings.

Nor were his efforts on behalf of the cause to which he had devoted himself confined to the pen. It is uncertain to what extent Penn retained his interest in West and East Jersey, or when the same ceased. The two provinces were united under one government in 1699, and Penn was proprietor in 1700. Two years later the government of New Jersey was surrendered to the Crown.

By the charter of Pennsylvania William Penn was made proprietary in the province. He was supreme governor; he had the power of making laws, with the advice, assent and approbation of the freemen, of appointing officers, and of granting pardons. These laws were to contain nothing contrary to British law, with a saving to the Crown and the English Council in case of appeals. Parliament was to be supreme in all questions of trade and commerce; the right to levy taxes and customs was reserved to England; an agent to represent William

HISTORICAL AND COMMERCIAL PHILADELPHIA.

ON THE WISSAHICKON.

Penn was to reside in London; neglect on the part of Penn was to lead to the passing of the government to the Crown (which event actually took place in 1792); no correspondence might be carried on with countries at war with great Britain.

A clause added at the last moment illustrates curiously both the strength and the jealousy of the Anglican church at the time. The importunity of the bishop of London extorted the right to appoint Anglican ministers, should twenty members of the colony desire, thus securing the very thing which Penn was anxious to avoid—the recognition of the principle of the Establishment.

Having appointed Colonel Markham, his cousin, as deputy, and having, in October, sent out three commissioners to manage affairs until his arrival, Penn proceeded to draw up proposals to adventurers, with an account of the resources of the colony. He negotiated, too, with James and Lord Baltimore, with the view, ultimately successful, of freeing the mouth of the Delaware. He offered conciliatory terms to the Indians and encouraged the formation of companies to work the infant colony, both in England and Germany, especially the "Free Society of Traders in Pennsylvania," to whom he sold 20,000 acres, absolutely refusing, however, to grant any monopolies. In July he drew up a constitution for the government of the colony.

It was in the midst of his extreme activity that Penn was made a Fellow of the Royal Society. Leaving his family behind him, Penn sailed with a hundred comrades, from Deal, in the *Welcome*, on September 1, 1682. His "Last Farewell to England," and his letter to his wife and children contain a beautiful expression of his pious and manly nature. He landed at New Castle, on the Delaware, on October 27, his company having lost one-third of their number by smallpox during the voyage. After receiving formal possession, and having visited New York, Penn ascended the Delaware to the Swedish settlement of Upland, to which he gave the name of Chester.

The Assembly at once met, and on December 7 passed the "Great Law of Pennsylvania." The idea underlying this law is that Pennsylvania was to be a Christian state on a Quaker model. Only one condition was made necessary for office or citizenship, viz.: Christianity. The constitution was purely democratic; all offices, for example, are elective. In many other provisions Penn showed himself far in advance of his time, but in none so much as where the penalty of death was abolished for all offences except murder. Lawsuits were to be superseded by arbitration—always a favorite idea with Penn. An act was passed uniting under the same government the territories which had been granted by feoffment by James, in 1682.

William Penn's connection with the Indians was one of the most successful parts of his management, and he gained at once and retained through life, their intense affection. At his death they sent to his widow a message of sorrow for the loss of their "brother Onas," with some choice skins to form a cloak which might protect her "while passing through the thorny wilderness without her guide."

Penn now wrote an account of Pennsylvania from his own observation for the "Free Society of Traders," in which he showed considerable of artistic description.

Tales of violent persecution of the Quakers and the necessity of settling disputes which had arisen with Lord Baltimore, his neighbor in Maryland, carried Penn back to England in 1684. Within five months after his arrival in England, Charles II. died and Penn found himself at once in a position of great influence. His close connection with James, dating from the death of his father, was rendered doubly strong by the fact that, from different causes, each was sincerely anxious to establish complete liberty of conscience.

In 1686, when making a third missionary journey to Holland and Germany, Penn was charged by James with an informal mission to the Prince of Orange, to endeavor to gain his assent to the removal of religious tests. In 1687 James published the "Declaration of Indulgence," and Penn probably drew up the address of thanks on the part of the Quakers.

At the Revolution Penn behaved with courage. He was one of the few friends of the king who remained in London, and when twice summoned before the council, he spoke boldly in his

HISTORICAL AND COMMERCIAL PHILADELPHIA.

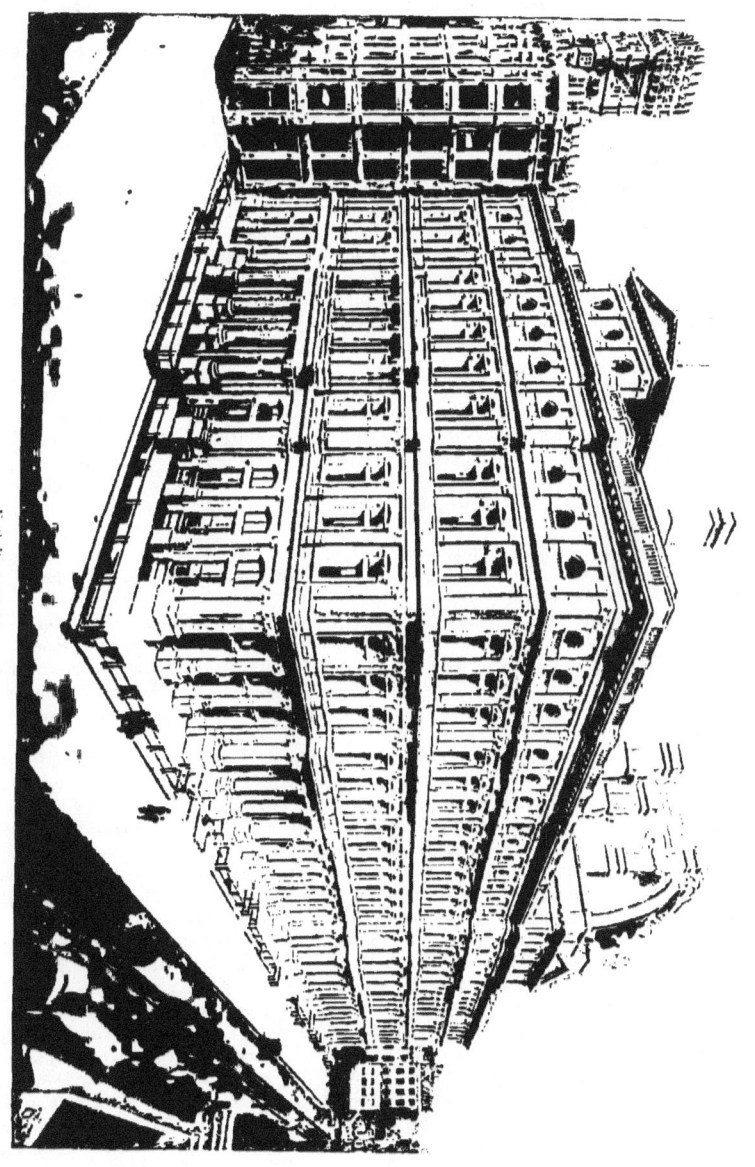

U. S. Post Office.

behalf. He admitted that James had asked him to come to him in France; but at the same time he asserted his perfect loyalty.

During the absence of William, in 1890, Penn was proclaimed by Mary as a dangerous person, but no evidence of treason was forthcoming. It was now that he lost by death two of his dearest friends, Robert Barclay and George Fox. Again, in 1691, a proclamation was issued for the arrest of Penn and two others, as being concerned in Preston's Plot. He might, on the intercession of Locke, have obtained a pardon, but refused to do so. He appears to have especially felt the suspicions that fell upon him from the members of his own body.

In 1692 he began to write again, both on questions of Quaker discipline and in defense of his sect. This year he published "Just Measures in an Epistle of Peace and Love," "The New Athenians" and "A Key Opening the Way to Every Capacity."

Meantime matters had been going badly in Pennsylvania. No sooner had Penn, by a skillful compromise, settled matters, than the colony was torn by schism, caused by George Keith. On October 21, 1692, an order of the Council was issued, depriving Penn of the governorship of Pennsylvania and giving it to Colonel Fletcher, the governor of New York. To this blow was added the illness of his wife and fresh accusations of treasonable correspondence with James.

In 1694 his wife, Gulielma, died. He consoled himself by writing his "Account of the Rise and Progress of the People Called Quakers." About two years later he again married. His second wife was Hannah Callowhill, a Bristol lady. The same year he wrote his work "On Primitive Christianity," in which he argues that the faith and practices of the Friends were those of the early Church. In 1697 Penn removed to Bristol, and during the year 1698 was preaching with great success, against oppression in Ireland, whither he had gone to look after property in Shaunagary. The following year he was back again in Pennsylvania, landing near Chester, on November 30.

Affairs once more demanded his presence in England. The king had, in 1701, written to urge upon the Pennsylvanian government a union with other private colonies for defense, and had asked for money for fortifications.

A bill was introduced into the House of Lords to convert private into Crown colonies. The accession of Anne appears to have put an end to the bill in the Lords, and to Penn's troubles on this score. He once more assumed the position of leader of the Dissenters, and himself read the address of thanks for the promise from the throne to maintain the Act of Toleration.

He now took up his abode again at Kensington, and while here published his "More Fruits of Solitude."

In 1703 he went to Knightsbridge, where he remained until 1706, when he removed to Boentford, his final residence being taken up in 1710 at Field Ruscombe, near Twyford.

In 1704 Penn wrote his "Life of Bulstrode Whitelocke." He had now much trouble from America. Moreover, pecuniary difficulties came heavily upon him, while the conduct of his son William, who had become the ringleader of all the dissolute characters in Philadelphia, was another and still more severe trial. He was harassed, too, by troubles with his government of Pennsylvania. Fresh disputes arose with Lord Baltimore, the owner of Maryland, and Penn felt deeply, what seemed to him, the ungrateful treatment which he met at the hands of the Assembly. He, therefore, in 1710, wrote in earnest and affectionate language an address to his "old friends," setting forth his wrongs. So great was the effect which this produced, that the Assembly, which met in October of that year, was entirely in his interests.

Penn now, in February, 1712, being in failing health, proposed to surrender his powers to the Crown. Before, however, the matter could go further, he was seized with apoplectic fits, which shattered his understanding and memory. A second attack occurred in 1713, and from that time until his death his powers gradually failed, although at times his intellect was clear and vigorous. He died May 30, 1718, and was buried along with his first and second wives, at Jourdan's meeting-house, near Chalfaut St. Giles, in Buckinghamshire. He left issue by both marriages.

It has finally to be mentioned that in 1790 the proprietary rights of Penn's descendants

DRINKING FOUNTAIN, FAIRMOUNT PARK.

were bought up for a pension of £4,000 a year to the eldest male descendant by his second wife, and that this pension was finally commuted for the sum of $335,000.

Upon the Penn controversy, it is unnecessary to enter; and besides, writers on this subject differ very widely. We refer our readers to Macauley's "History of England," Hepworth Dixon's "Life of William Penn," Paget's "Inquiry into the Evidence of the Charges Brought by Lord Macauley Against William Penn," and Stoughton's "William Penn."

In return for this important grant, Penn acknowledged satisfaction of a claim for £16,000 in which the British government was indebted to his father's estate. As soon as the formal steps were completed which fully established Penn's rights of proprietorship he immediately took steps to assume control of his new property and to make the necessary preparations for its development. He wasted no time in delay. Within a month from the day that the royal seal was affixed to the charter which made him proprietor of the new country beyond the Delaware, Penn had prepared and had circulated among the people of England a prospectus of the lands with a glowing enthusiasm of description that may well be envied by the ablest real estate dealers of the present day. It is worthy of note, however, in this connection, that of the hosts of people who were led by the promises thus held out to cast their fortunes in the New World, not one ever complained of misrepresentation. They found all things that were promised them and more. They found a beautiful and fertile country, with a salubrious climate and every natural facility for the happiness and prosperity of a resourceful people.

The first real estate boom in the lands to be occupied by the future city of Philadelphia, which has more than fulfilled the promise of its founder, was of a permanent nature and its logical results are seen in the development of the Philadelphia of to-day, which after a growth of more than two hundred years offers inducements for residence and for business many thousand-fold greater than those afforded by the then New World which Penn pictured in such attractive colors. The results of Penn's appeal for colonists were at once manifested in the hearty response of a large number of enthusiastic colonists of the better class. The majority of these were attracted as much by the strong personality of Penn, in whom they placed an implicit confidence which they never had reason to regret, and by the plan of government which he had outlined, as by the natural advantages claimed for the province. The whole New World was to the people of those days a veritable *El Dorado* of nature, and the questions of government, of religious liberty and of the restrictions to be placed upon the enjoyment of the fruits of individual industry were of paramount importance to intending colonists. With his firm belief in the faith and principles of the Quakers, prominent in which was a belief in individual liberty of conscience and a political equality, Penn's first act after acquiring the title to his province was to issue a statement in which he laid down the principles on which his colony was to be founded. Briefly summarized, his plan was for the foundation of a colony on the principles of brotherly love and good-will among men—a free commonwealth with equal rights to all men of good character, whatever their race, color or religion. In further compliance with the peaceful proclivities of the Quakers, he announced his intention of living on friendly terms with the Indians, and avoiding conflicts with the red men by adhering strictly to every promise made. He appealed to the patriotism of his fellow-countrymen by picturing the luster which a colony founded on such principles would add to the glory of Great Britain. This declaration of plans and principles attracted hundreds of intelligent and respectable colonists, and it should be borne in mind that the troubles and dissentions into which the colony was plunged in later years were caused by the failure of those in control to adhere to the principles laid down by Penn with such keen foresight as the foundation of its government.

As his representative in the new colony until he should come in person to take possession of his grant, Penn commissioned William Markham as deputy governor. Markham came over with the first colonists and had been thoroughly instructed by Penn in the line of policy which he should follow and the work which he should do to carry out the plans of the proprietor.

HISTORICAL AND COMMERCIAL PHILADELPHIA.

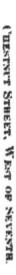

CHESTNUT STREET, WEST OF SEVENTH.

Meanwhile Penn busied himself in arranging the details of his departure, in further presentation of the advantages of the new province for intending colonists, and in the disposal of lands. So encouraging were the reports which came from the earlier colonists, so faithfully were Penn's instructions followed by his representatives at the head of the colony, and so enterprising was Penn himself in the prosecution of his plans, that by June 1st, 1682, it is recorded that Penn had sold 565,500 acres and the colony had already assumed an appearance of substantial prosperity, and the solid foundations of its future growth were laid.

Meanwhile Penn had sent to the Indian tribes a personal assurance of his good-will and desire to live on friendly terms with them, and had sent to the Swedes who were already established in the province, his assurance that they would be secure in their homes and lands and would be accorded the same rights and liberties as the new colonists.

His first care after receiving his grant was to draw up a plan of government for his province, and in this he showed a high order of statesmanship and a liberality that was the outgrowth of his broad views and his firm adherence to the principles of the Quakers. For, though the terms of his grant gave him absolute proprietorship and an opportunity for amassing enormous wealth from the revenues he could levy, his desire to found a great and flourishing colony was higher than any desire for private gain, and he framed a liberal constitution that was a further incentive to emigration to the new colony. The name Pennsylvania had been given to the territory in the royal grant.

In the fall of 1682, Penn's preparations were completed and he sailed to take formal possession of his province. On the 20th of October, 1682, accompanied by a large party of colonists, he arrived at New Castle, where he received an enthusiastic greeting from the people already established in the new land who had come to give him welcome. There were English, Dutch and Swedes in the throng, all anxious to honor the proprietor whose liberality and kindness was already bearing fruit. To these Penn made an address in which he gave renewed assurance of the continuance of the liberal plans of government which had been already outlined in his letters, and he exhorted them to so conduct themselves as to be worthy members of such a colony by cultivating qualities of sobriety, honesty and thrift. After a journey up the Delaware, Penn visited New York to confer with the governor of that province, which adjoined his territory on the north, and then returned to Pennsylvania to take up the duties and responsibilities of his proprietorship.

Prior to Penn's departure from England, the Duke of York had given up his claim to the three reserved counties on the Delaware, which had been held by New York, and the Province of Pennsylvania then included the whole territory on the western bank of the bay and river, from Cape Henlopen on the south to the forty-third degree of latitude on the north. Penn's visit to the governor of the neighboring and older province of New York was in one sense an act of courtesy, but it served also to make Penn familiar with the boundaries of his province on the north and east, to give him a knowledge of the great waterways which would be utilized to develop the commerce of his province; and more than all else, it must be supposed that Penn profited by his visit to New York to make observations of its trade and commerce which were of value to him in the planning of his own city on the Delaware, which was destined to soon become a rival of New York in commercial importance, and, for a time at least, to surpass it in the volume of trade and to be for many years the commercial metropolis of the New World.

PENN'S TREATY WITH THE INDIANS.

With his customary prudence, Penn's first care was to guard his new province from those conflicts with the aborigines which had served so much to retard the growth and prosperity of the older colonies. His deputy, Markham, had closely followed his instructions in these particulars and had already made treaties of peace and friendship with the neighboring tribes, had purchased lands, and had attended to the many details of establishing the colony as Penn had planned

GIRARD TRUST CO.'S BUILDING.

HISTORICAL AND COMMERCIAL PHILADELPHIA.

PENN TREATY STONE.

These treaties and purchases had been made, in Penn's name, and it only remained for the proprietor to formally ratify in person the work done by his deputy, and to give to the natives his own assurance of his good-will and peaceful intentions. To this end the chiefs of all the tribes were summoned to a great conference on the banks of the Delaware, and there under a noble elm, on the spot which is now marked by a stone suitably inscribed, was held the famous council which passed into history as the most memorable conference ever held between the red man and the white on this continent. On Penn's side the conference consisted in a renewed assurance of his desire to treat the Indians with fairness and justice, to recognize them as brothers, and to live with them as neighbors on terms of friendliness and peace. There was to be no place in the policy of Penn's government for wars and bloodshed. Indeed, the principles of the Quakers forbade the use of force, and Penn's plan was to meet the Indians on terms of the closest friendship. As an outward sign of this pacific policy Penn and those who accompanied him went to the council without arms of any kind, and Penn's words and his evident sincerity of purpose impressed the red men more favorably than any show of force could have accomplished. These children of the forest, whose powers of observation were accurately trained, were accurate readers of character, and Penn's estimate of their disposition proved to be well founded. They recognized him as a man who would keep his promises, and he rightly judged that if treated fairly as men they would in turn be true to their pledges. The chiefs signified their acceptance and appreciation of the proffer of friendship, and the covenant of peace there made in the name of the Great Spirit, whom both white and red man worshipped in the simple spirit of reverence, remained unbroken through the seventy years of Quaker rule in Pennsylvania, and was only broken when in later years the descendants and successors of the early colonists departed from the wise policy of kindness, honesty and tolerance which Penn had inaugurated. But by that time the whites were firmly established as the dominant power in the land, and it is a matter of history that Pennsylvania suffered less by troubles with the Indians than any of the other colonies, and this served in a great measure to advance the interests of the colony, and more especially of Philadelphia.

The next step after the conference with the Indians was a general convention of the colony, held at Chester, on December 4, 1682, which continued three days, during which the territorial legislation was completed, and the machinery of government for the new province put in working shape. Penn next went to Maryland to confer with Lord Baltimore, his neighbor on the south, and agree on the southern boundary of his province. This business occupied a month and then Penn returned to Chester to take up what was to be the most important task of all. He had made with the Indians a compact of perpetual peace; he had settled on friendly terms with his neighbors to the north and to the south, the often troublesome question of boundaries, and with no fear of encroachments from New York on the north, or Maryland on the south, or of conflicts with the Indians within his province, his mind was free to take up his long-cherished project—the planning of his city. And this brings us to the first great epoch in our history.

DREXEL BUILDING.

THE FOUNDING OF PHILADELPHIA.

In this work, again, the master-mind of Penn shows itself. His city was not planned merely for his own day and generation, but for all time, and if Penn could have lifted the veil of the centuries and looked into the future with prophetic vision, he could not have made his plans better.

In many ways, Penn was, perhaps, better qualified than any man of his day for the founding of a great city. In his youth, his father, Admiral Penn, who was a man of prominence in his day and a friend of the king, had sent him to the continent, in the hope of breaking off his growing belief in the doctrines of the Quakers. This effort was not successful, for Penn's mind was so firmly held by the teachings of Fox, that his travels only tended to confirm him in his belief, and he returned to England only to become, himself, a Quaker preacher, instead of a diplomat or a courtier, as his father had hoped. This adherence of Penn to the cause of the Quakers cost his father a peerage and himself a title, for with a son in the line of succession who openly espoused the cause of the "seditious Quakers," the gallant admiral could not be granted the token of royal favor which was the highest reward of faithful service to the Crown. This course of Penn's was a source of profound sorrow and bitter disappointment to the ambitious admiral, but he lived to appreciate the force of his son's character and give him his blessing in his chosen work.

The years of Penn's life thus spent in a conflict between the parental desires and the inclinations of his own heart and conscience were now to bear fruit. He was naturally of an observing turn of mind and in his knowledge of men, measures and places was essentially a man of the world—not of worldly desires in a selfish sense, but of worldly knowledge in its broadest sense. He was a thorough diplomat, as his treatment of the Indians and of his white neighbors of different races shows; he was a shrewd man of business, as his energetic and enterprising methods of building up his province prove; and above all he was a far-seeing man of ideas. With the simplicity and modesty of a Quaker he had the master-mind of the born leader and ruler of men, and this, his city on the Delaware, is a lasting monument.

During his visits to the great capitals of Europe he had carefully noted their plans and their lines of development, and he had the opportunity of studying the results of centuries of growth. Even then Penn had in mind the founding of a community on the principles of the Quakers, and it was with the firm conviction that neither England nor the continent afforded a suitable site for the planting of such a community, that he turned his attention to the New World. Thus, with a practical knowledge of the sources of municipal development, a firm faith in the promise of the future, and a mind and purpose wholly devoted to the welfare of the community, Penn devoted himself to the task of laying out his city. He had already decided on its name and had chosen one which was typical of the ruling spirit of his ideal community—Philadelphia, the City of Brotherly Love. It was not a new name, nor was his a new idea. Centuries—yes, ages before—men of master-minds had been imbued with the same or a very similar idea of an ideal community, typical of the highest civilization of their day, where brotherly love should rule, and history records the founding of at least two cities to which the name Philadelphia was given. But neither was the time ripe for the successful carrying out of such a plan nor was the man at hand to give it a permanent foundation. It was reserved for Penn's time to furnish in the persons of the Quakers the people whose principles and practices rendered feasible the almost Utopian dreams of the greatest minds of Grecian civilization, in the New World the ideal site for the planting of the perfect commonwealth, and in Penn himself the master-mind and hand to devise and direct the plans which, under such fortuitous circumstances, should result in establishing a permanent city of Philadelphia.

THE LOCATION OF THE CITY.

In tracing the rise and development of the city of Philadelphia through more than two

MANUFACTURERS' CLUB HOUSE.

centuries of commercial progress, it is fitting that we should, in the first place, consider its commanding location, as this has ever been and is to-day an important factor in its growth and prosperity. History gives us hundreds of instances where great cities were founded and grew to commanding prominence in population, in wealth and in commerce, and then in the course of time declined, decayed, and at last either disappeared entirely from the face of the earth—and that not through war, or pestilence, or through famine, or from any outward cause, but simply and solely because they lacked in themselves the essential elements of permanent success. The fortune of cities is not won by favor, but by the superior attractions of natural and material advantages. Trade is an exacting servant and a most tyrannical master. It builds a city and it rules it; it cherishes and protects it and makes it a magnet for the peoples of the earth, just as long as the city serves its purpose best; but just so soon as there appears elsewhere the promise of a larger prosperity and a more enduring growth trade leaves the city it has built and fostered and seeks its more attractive rivals.

We need not delve among the buried ruins of the Old World for illustrations of this well-established fact; our own land, still in its centuries of youth, will furnish abundant illustration of cities which have been founded on a mistaken idea, which have had a mushroom growth and left only a memory of disappointed hopes—the graveyard of a boom collapsed. The cities that have had a permanent and enduring prosperity have ever been and are to-day those which have offered superior facilities for trade—and one foremost among these is Philadelphia.

Where the waters of the Schuylkill meet those of the Delaware, the two great rivers approach each the other, the one from the north and west and the other from the northeast, and between them, northward from their confluence, stretches a neck of land irregular in its outline and rapidly broadening toward the north. On this neck of land, beautiful in its native verdure and the rich autumn foliage illumined by the soft rays of an October sunlight as Penn sailed up the Delaware from New Castle to survey the new domain of which he was proprietor, he planned to found his city.

It seemed as if Nature herself, in following out the law that all things are created for a purpose, had fashioned this neck of land and its embracing arms of water as the very site on which to place a commercial metropolis of the New World—and to-day the city planted there owns but one rival in commercial importance, and that is New York, to which even in many special features of advantage of residence and business Philadelphia can justly claim superiority. By reason of her favorable location Philadelphia trade and Philadelphia industry furnishes an important factor of New York's trade.

Taking Philadelphia as the center of a circle with a radius of 136 miles, we find that the territory embraced within this convenient distance includes Washington, which is 136 miles to the southwest; New York, eighty-seven miles to the northeast; Baltimore, ninety-eight miles away; Harrisburg, 106 miles distant; Brooklyn and the populous suburbs of New York City, the entire States of New Jersey and Delaware—a country teeming with a busy population that is within convenient reach of Philadelphia by many splendidly equipped lines of railroad, besides the natural waterways. As a center of trade and a convenient shipping port either by water or rail, Philadelphia has to-day many advantages of superiority that are becoming better appreciated every year, and have especially since the centennial celebration of 1876, been brought prominently to the attention of the nation.

A CITY MAGNIFICENTLY PLANNED.

While nature had thus liberally endowed the site with innumerable advantages, to Penn belongs the credit of a keenness of appreciation of the facilities thus afforded, and he alone, perhaps, of all men of his day, had the genius sufficient to plant thereon a city worthy of the magnificent work of nature. It is well to note here that of all the cities of the continent, Philadelphia was the first to be laid out on a definite and comprehensive plan—a plan so broad in

its conception, so enduring in its nature, that Philadelphia stands to-day as it has stood for more than two centuries, preëminent among the cities of the world as the one city whose original model has proven adapted to the needs of the growing capacities and intelligence of succeeding generations. The other great cities of the country owed their plan and their conformation largely to chance. This was notably the case with New York and Boston, and can be seen to-day in the older parts of those cities that were built up even so recently as the last generation. A single street often sufficed for the nucleus of a colonial city, and at best the colonists only had a thought for their immediate needs. As the villages grew into cities the natural and irregular paths made by men and animals in their journeyings to and fro across unbroken fields or through the primeval forests served first as country highways and next as village streets, to be preserved in all their tortuous windings as the cramped and congested arteries of a busy city's trade. Great conflagrations have served in other cities to compensate for their destruction of property by affording an opportunity of revising the street plans, while in America and Europe to-day great municipalities and rich and powerful governments are striving with enormous expenditure of labor and money to rebuild great cities to meet the growing necessities of modern times, and correct the errors of early builders who saw not beyond the conditions of their own day. Not so with Philadelphia. The far-seeing mind of her great founder grasped with intuitive force the essential requirements of the ideal city, and the Philadelphia of to-day is still the city of Penn—the broad plans of its founder have met the requirements of two centuries of growth, and a development along the plans made by Penn in 1683 will meet the needs of centuries to come. There were no narrow and tortuous streets permitted in Penn's plan. Broad highways laid out at right angles were its essential features, and the underlying principle of the whole system was a desire to avoid the unwholesome crowding of population which Penn had observed to be one of the greatest evils of European cities. To this end each householder in the new city was given a generous sized plot of ground and was urged to build in the center that there might be at the front and on either side a wide space for gardens, for green lawns and spreading trees, and, above all, for an abundant circulation of pure air. The essential features of this wise plan have been preserved through the centuries since, and Philadelphia is to-day a city of the most beautiful and healthful homes that can be found on this continent, or, indeed, in the whole world. The necessities of trade have here, as in all other cities, forced a concentration of trade in certain localities where similar lines of business find an advantage in proximity to neighbors, but the outlying growth of the city has been one of broad and liberal expansion, and there are more important business houses that find a thriving trade in contributing to the needs of their respective districts than can be found in any other great city of the land.

As originally platted by Penn's surveyors the city extended from river to river east and west, and from Cedar Street on the south to Vine Street on the north. This territory was laid out in two hundred blocks, with broad streets intersecting at right angles, and the streets were so planned by Penn's instructions that they could be extended from the water front into the country beyond as the city grew. It truly was a conception of a master-mind and so faithfully executed that the growth of the city to-day is still progressing on this same wise plan of rectangular blocks which serves in a great degree to give the city that appearance of neatness and of perfect order which is one of its most striking characteristics. The territory thus mapped out by Penn was of such generous dimensions that for nearly a century it sufficed to encompass the growth of the city. When we reflect that during this period Philadelphia had become the superior of New York as a commercial center, we can the better appreciate the comprehensiveness of Penn's plans.

Later on the development of the city was, as Penn had correctly judged, mainly in the country districts to the north, within convenient distance of the main city, which steadily grew in this direction and in time absorbed these suburban districts, which being laid out on the same rectangular plan as the older city, now form a part of a symmetrical whole. The

streets are to-day laid out according to Penn's original design, fifty feet in width, and run from river to river—east and west and from north to south, intersecting at right angles. The latter streets are numbered in numerical order, and Market Street, which is one hundred feet wide, divides the city into two districts north and south.

THE GROWTH OF COMMERCE.

Philadelphia was from the beginning a city of commercial importance, and it was Penn's design to make it such. Very early in its history it became a formidable rival of New York, and soon outstripped her. The new colony so favorably planted attracted to itself all the elements of progress and strength. Within two years after the founding of the city, or 1683, a printing-office was established, and this was before a printing-office was located in New York. The printing-office was the unerring sign of a prosperous community; and in the following year, or within three years after its foundation, Philadelphia had outstripped New York.

This wonderful growth of the new city was the result of its favorable location for commerce. Situated at the head of navigation on the Delaware, it afforded a safe and convenient harbor for trading vessels. The Delaware was navigable for the largest ships clear to Philadelphia. The distance from the ocean by bay and river was 120 miles, and for smaller vessels the river was navigable as it is to-day—for sloops, thirty-five miles farther or to the falls at Trenton, while above the falls there was depth of water enough for boats of eight or nine tons burden for about one hundred miles, thus affording ample facilities for trading with the interior. On the western side of the city the Schuylkill afforded navigable waters for boats of 400 tons burthen, and there is to-day a depth of about fourteen feet of water at the wharves on that side of the city.

In later years these natural resources of navigation were increased by succeeding generations. The Delaware and Hudson Canal was built from a point on the Delaware near the mouth of Lackawaxen Creek to Rondout Kill on the Hudson River, and the Morris Canal was built from a point on the Delaware opposite Easton to Jersey City. These canals were rendered necessary by the demands of the coal trade and form important lines of transportation to-day.

There were also improvements made in the navigation from the ocean. Forty-two miles below Philadelphia, at Delaware City, a canal fourteen miles in length unites the Delaware with the Chesapeake and is navigable to vessels of considerable size.

To make a safe harbor in Delaware Bay the national government has built at an expense of two and one half million dollars an immense breakwater at Cape Henlopen, which now affords shelter to large fleets of vessels with valuable cargoes and is an important protection to coastwise trade. Plans are now under way, inaugurated by the Board of Trade, for the further improvement of the wharf facilities of the city for these alone of all the natural advantages of Philadelphia have proved inadequate to meet the pressing needs of the commerce of to-day.

As in the early history of Philadelphia her facilities for ocean commerce and coasting trade made her the commercial metropolis of the country, so to-day the failure of these facilities to develop in proportion to the demands of trade have been the sole reason for her decadence in commercial supremacy. But while the shipping trade of Philadelphia has not kept pace with the times, the growth of the city in other lines of industry and trade is a marvelous one and furnishes a striking proof of the energy and resources of her people. The great lines of railroad which center in Philadelphia afford direct and rapid communication with all parts of the continent, and the accommodations which are offered for freight and passenger traffic alike are unsurpassed. These liberal advantages have borne fruit in recent years in the rapid development of Philadelphia as the most important manufacturing center of the country, a feature which will be considered more in detail in succeeding pages of this work.

The supremacy over New York in commerce and trade which Philadelphia so quickly

HISTORICAL AND COMMERCIAL PHILADELPHIA.

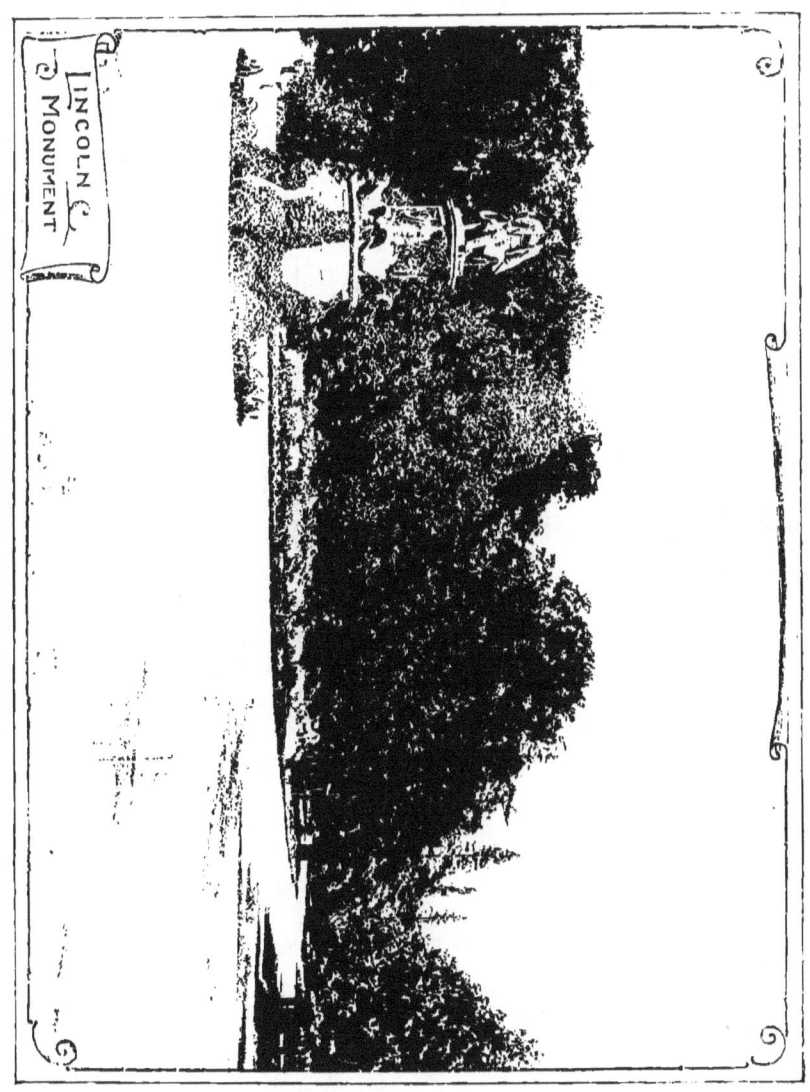

Lincoln Monument

HISTORICAL AND COMMERCIAL PHILADELPHIA.

gained was maintained until 1825, when the completion of the Erie Canal restored to New York its lost prestige, and that city has since then been the commercial center of the nation.

OLD SWEDE'S CHURCH

PHILADELPHIA IN THE REVOLUTION.

At the time of the Revolution Philadelphia was the largest and most important colonial city, and this fact, together with its convenience of location, made it the center of government. In Philadelphia, the Continental Congress met; there Washington received his commission; the Declaration of Independence was signed, and the Constitution of the United States was formulated. No city in the country is richer in historic relics of this great period in the nation's history. Her people were intensely patriotic and vigorously opposed to every form of oppression. Long before the tea episode in Boston Harbor, they had declared their opposition to the Stamp Act by no less effective though perhaps not so demonstrative action as the New England patriots. In the stirring years that followed the people of the city took a most distinguished part, and the name of Philadelphia is closely allied with the most important incidents of the Revolution and the birth of the new nation. In fact, she has been most appropriately termed the "Cradle of Liberty."

THE CENTENNIAL CELEBRATION.

With such a record in history Philadelphia was selected without any hesitation as the site of the centennial celebration of the birth of the Republic in 1876, a celebration that has passed into history as the grandest exposition of the resources of civilization that the world has ever witnessed. Every nation was represented and people from all lands came to share in the demonstration. The Exposition gave to Philadelphia a name and fame not exceeded by any city on earth. Visitors from afar were impressed with the magnificent plan of the city and its wonderful resources, and the people of Philadelphia saw the great possibilities that their city afforded for an extension of commerce and trade, and the reclaiming of the former commercial supremacy of Philadelphia was begun. During the last decade the development of Philadelphia's trade has been steady and sure.

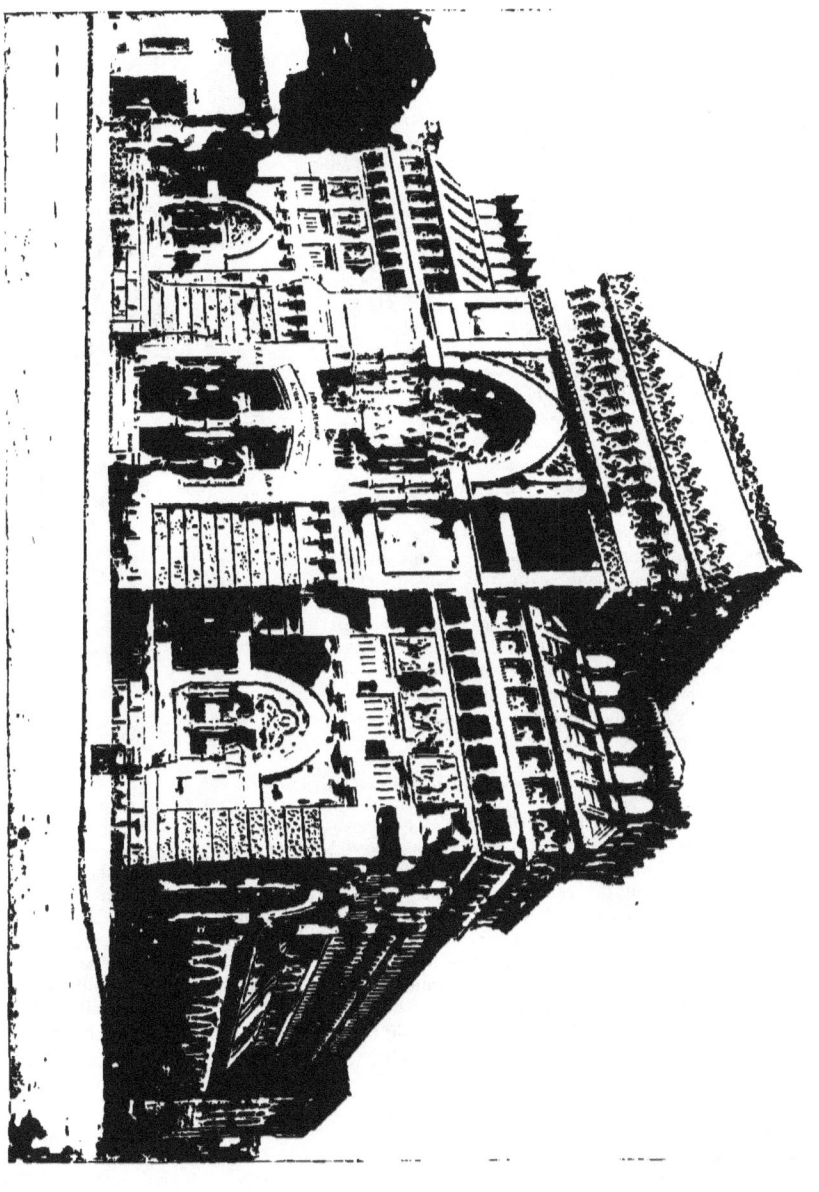

PENNSYLVANIA AVENUE AND THE POST OFFICE

HISTORICAL AND COMMERCIAL PHILADELPHIA.

THE PHILADELPHIA OF TO-DAY

is one of the most flourishing cities of the continent. The original two square miles first laid out by Penn have been added to on the south to the junction of the rivers, on the north they have extended beyond what were once suburban villages, and the city has crossed the Schuylkill and taken in a considerable area on the western bank. The present area of the city is about one hundred and thirty square miles, nearly one-sixth of which lies west of the Schuylkill.

For many years, until Chicago annexed many miles of the broad prairies of Illinois, Philadelphia was the largest city in the United States in area, and second only to London in the extent of territory within its corporate limits, and it was the second city in the United States in population. The population of Philadelphia, according to the census of 1890, was 1,046,964, and there are about 200,000 people besides whose work or interests are in Philadelphia who make their homes in neighboring towns. There are over 1,200 miles of streets, including 765 miles of paved and about forty of macadamized roadway. During the last five years a great improvement has been made in the condition of the streets and nearly two hundred miles of new pavement have been laid, the old-fashioned cobble-stone pavements being replaced by modern pavements of granite blocks, asphalt, and other improved materials. There are over fifteen hundred miles of sidewalks, of which five-sixths are built of brick. The streets are nearly all of generous width and the main streets are not less than fifty feet wide.

FOREIGN COMMERCE.

The foreign commerce of Philadelphia is now greater than it ever was before. Its steady increase in recent years and the improvements now being made in the channel of the Delaware, which have already been referred to, give reason to believe that before many years Philadelphia will again lead the commerce of the nation. The value of the exports from the port of Philadelphia has increased during fifty years from $5,152,500 in 1841, to $36,178,544 in 1890, and the value of the imports increased from $10,346,698 in 1841, to $56,057,013 in 1890. Among the causes which have contributed to this steady increase in commerce and which give promise of a still greater increase in the future are the admirable railroad facilities of Philadelphia, which are constantly being improved; and the convenience of shipment, lighterage being unnecessary, as the largest vessels can approach the wharves. Another important factor in the growth of commerce is the steady increase in manufacturing.

PHILADELPHIA AS A MANUFACTURING CENTER.

The most notable and important feature of the development of Philadelphia has been its remarkable growth as a manufacturing center. Its growth in this line has been most rapid during the last ten years. In that time it has outstripped New York and ranks to-day as the leading manufacturing city in the United States, and in the world. This position has been

CHESTNUT STREET, BELOW FIFTH

HISTORICAL AND COMMERCIAL PHILADELPHIA.

gained by the number and variety of its manufactures and by their commercial value, and the result shows the boundless possibilities of Philadelphia's growth. The range of manufactures is the most comprehensive of any city in the world. There is scarcely an article numbered among the necessities or the luxuries of mankind that is not included in the list of products made in Philadelphia.

REYNOLDS MONUMENT

The iron and steel manufactures of Philadelphia and its immediate vicinity are of immense value, and the great iron and steel plants located here are unsurpassed in the world. The magnificent new navy, the pride of the nation, was practically constructed here. The quantity of tools manufactured annually reaches an enormous aggregate. In the one item of

HISTORICAL AND COMMERCIAL PHILADELPHIA.

Chestnut St above Eighth St

saws alone Philadelphia leads the world. The manufacture of locomotives has here reached its greatest perfection, and the annual production of locomotives in Philadelphia exceeds the total product of any other place on earth.

Philadelphia has for years been the acknowledged center of the woolen goods trade, and here are manufactured every variety of clothing, which is sold all over the United States.

In the carpet trade Philadelphia stands preeminent and turns out over one-half the carpet product of the entire country.

Its immense sugar refineries turn out a product which is nearly the most valuable in the world. The mammoth breweries are among the finest in the country and their aggregate product is exceeded by only one or two other cities.

In almost innumerable lines of manufacture—in confectionery, in chemicals, in medical and surgical instruments, and in countless products that enter largely into commerce and trade—Philadelphia occupies a position among the leaders. There is one feature of her manufactures which is deserving of special notice, and that is in all her manufactures—whether great or small—the quality of the Philadelphia products is unsurpassed and goods of Philadelphia make have a world-wide reputation for reliability.

WEALTH AND POPULATION.

The city planted by Penn had a population of six hundred in 1683. In the year 1700 this had grown to five thousand. The Philadelphia of the Revolution had in 1776, at the date of the Declaration of Independence, a population of forty thousand souls. At the beginning of the present century the population was over eighty thousand, and before 1860 it had passed the half million mark. Estimated on the basis of the census of 1890 its present population is in excess of one million one hundred thousand people.

The growth of the city's wealth has kept pace with the increase of population. The assessed value of the taxable property of the city has grown from $153,369,048 in 1856 to $713,902,842 in 1891. The annual revenue and expenses of the municipal administration have increased from between five and six millions, in 1856, to the neighborhood of twenty-five millions, in 1891.

WATER SUPPLY AND SEWERAGE.

In the development of a city its water supply and its system of sewerage are factors of prime importance, exercising an immense influence on the question of health and making the city either desirable or not as a place of residence. In both these elements the city of Philadelphia is particularly favored. The question of a water supply adequate to the growing needs of the city early engaged attention, and Philadelphia was the first of the large cities of the country to provide itself with an adequate system of water-works. The Schuylkill was taken as the source of supply and the original works at Fairmount were the marvel of the day. They still form a part of the water works system which has been developed with the growth of the city. The great portion of the supply is still taken from the Schuylkill, but a part is now drawn from the Delaware at Lardner's Point. There are ten reservoirs, including one now being completed, with a total storage capacity of more than one billion gallons. The average daily consumption is 132 gallons *per capita* of population.

The system of drainage has been vastly improved during the last few years, and as now planned Philadelphia will soon be the best sewered city in the United States. Since 1854 nearly four hundred miles of sewers have been built at a cost of nearly ten million dollars, and

PROVIDENT LIFE AND TRUST CO'S BUILDING

there are now about four hundred and thirty-five miles of sewers, of which eighty are main sewers, some of which are 20 feet in diameter, or big enough to drive a horse and carriage through, and three hundred and fifty-five miles of branch sewers, which form part of a comprehensive plan that will in time afford thorough drainage to the entire city.

POLICE AND FIRE DEPARTMENTS.

In these two important features of municipal administration, Philadelphia is well favored and the systems for the preservation of order and the protection of property are not surpassed by any city in the country.

Philadelphia is essentially a law abiding city, and her people are most admirably protected from any outward annoyance. The police force, which consists of nearly two thousand men, is next to the largest in the country and is under perfect discipline. The entire city is under police protection and a mounted force patrols the suburban districts.

The fact that for many years Philadelphia has suffered no devastating conflagration is largely due to the efficiency of its fire-department. There are now over five hundred men in the department, and all the apparatus is of the latest and most approved pattern.

PARKS AND PLEASURE-GROUNDS.

One of the most notable features of Philadelphia is its admirable system of parks and pleasure-grounds. The laying out of many of these beautiful breathing-spots was included in Penn's original plan of the city, for his observation had taught him how important a system of public pleasure-grounds and breathing-places were to the healthy development of a city. The idea thus planted by Penn in the minds of the early colonists has borne fruit in one of the finest public park systems in the world.

HISTORICAL AND COMMERCIAL PHILADELPHIA.

MORTON McMICHAEL STATUE.

HISTORICAL AND COMMERCIAL PHILADELPHIA.

Fairmount Park is unquestionably the most beautiful pleasure-ground in the United States and one of the finest in the world. Its inception was the result of the establishing of the water-works system in 1811. The water-works were located at Morris Hill, otherwise known as Fairmount, where the city had purchased five acres of land. Crowds of people went out to view the water-works, and the place became so frequented that the authorities were impressed with the advantages afforded for making a public pleasure-ground and the Fairmount Gardens were laid out and opened to the public in 1825. From that time on the development of the park has continued by purchase and by gift of additional land, until now it includes a territory of more than twenty-eight hundred acres, or over three times the area of Central Park, New York. Under the direction of the Philadelphia Park Commission this magnificent park has been admirably laid out in drives, footwalks and bridle-paths, and its natural beauty has been enhanced by the planting of trees, shrubs and flowers.

The "Fairmount Park Art Association," an organization composed of a number of public-spirited citizens, has also contributed largely to enhancing the beauty of the Park by placing many handsome and appropriate groups, statuary, etc. Fairmount Park furnished an adequate and an appropriate site for the great Centennial Exposition of 1876.

Besides Fairmount, Philadelphia has fifteen smaller parks in different parts of the city, which bring the total park area to over three thousand acres.

FINANCE AND BANKING.

The first bank in America was established in Philadelphia, in 1781, by Robert Morris, the financier of the Revolution. This bank, known as the Bank of North America, continues in existence to-day. From the beginning Philadelphia has maintained its position as a prominent financial center, and is to-day one of the leading financial centers of the country. In fact for more than half a century, until the growth of the country and the establishing of the national banking system resulted in the increase of banking interests to accommodate the business of different sections of the country, Philadelphia ruled the finance of the nation. In 1791, Alexander Hamilton established in Philadelphia the first Bank of the United States.

Here also was located the second Bank of the United States, with a capital of thirty-five million dollars, with which President Andrew Jackson had the memorable controversy that is part of the financial and political history of the nation. The building erected for the original Bank of the United States, in 1791, still stands on Third Street, below Chestnut, and is now occupied by the Girard Bank. There are now forty-nine banks doing business in Philadelphia, with an aggregate working capital of nearly forty million dollars.

ANTHONY J. DREXEL.

The surplus of nine of these banks is in excess of their capital, a condition which is

Chestnut Street, above Fourth.

a conclusive proof of the sound and conservative methods which characterizes the banking system of Philadelphia. Many of these banks have had a long and honorable financial career. The present national banking system had its birth in Philadelphia, the pioneer of the system being the First National Bank, chartered on January 10, 1863.

The record of the Philadelphia Clearing House shows an increase of over one hundred per cent. in the volume of business, during the twenty years from 1870 to 1890. The figures for the former year were $1,803,941,184, and the latter year $3,710,248,015.

Philadelphia is also the great center of the system of Building and Loan Associations, which have here reached a higher development and a greater financial strength than in any other city in the country.

Philadelphia has over fifty trust companies which form an important part of the financial system, and do a large and flourishing business, besides a number of private banking houses, some of which have a world-wide reputation.

TRANSPORTATION FACILITIES.

The admirable transportation facilities which Philadelphia enjoys have ever been an important factor in the development of the city as a commercial and manufacturing center. The natural advantages of water transportation, which formed such a feature of her early prosperity, have already been referred to.

No less important in the development of the commerce of to-day is the great network of railroads of which Philadelphia is the center, and which with their various connections, put the city in close communication with every part of the country. During the present year these facilities are being extended and improved on a plan which will give the people of Philadelphia advantages for the transportation of passengers and freight that are not surpassed in the world. Among the features of this plan are the new terminal station of the Reading Railroad, at Twelfth and Market Streets, the extension of the great station of the Pennsylvania Railroad at Broad and Market Streets, the construction of a Belt Line that will give adequate facilities to all lines desiring to enter the city, the development of a comprehensive system of elevated roads, and the extension of the trolley and cable systems.

One of the most important of these is the extension of the Reading Railroad to the heart of the city and its magnificent new station at the corner of Twelfth and Market Streets. This work, undertaken and carried out at an immense outlay of money, will not only benefit the railroad but the city as well. It affords a direct system of rapid transit that brings into close communication with the city a large and populous territory, and it has already effected an enormous increase in real estate values. The new station is a massive structure of architectural beauty. The main building is eight stories high with a frontage of 266 feet on Market Street, and a depth of 100 feet. The sheds extend from the main building back to Arch Street. The first four stories are of pink granite and the upper stories are of light brick and terra cotta. The main entrance is on a level with the street and on the first floor are the ticket-office, baggage-rooms and a spacious lobby for passengers. The general waiting-room, 100 x 75 feet, is on the second floor, and at the Market Street front is a balcony overlooking the street. At one side of the main waiting-room is a ladies'-room, 44 x 56 feet, and at the other side are the dining-room and restaurant. In every appointment, the comfort and convenience of passengers has been carefully studied, and no expense has been spared to make this the finest railroad station in existence. The basement of the main building is arranged for stores, and under the train sheds in the rear is the new Market House.

During the year ending June 30, 1891, the number of passengers carried in and out of Philadelphia by the various lines of railroad entering the city was nearly seventy-five millions, or a daily average of more than two hundred thousand. During the same year the amount of freight hauled in and out of the city reached the enormous aggregate of over seventy million tons.

HISTORICAL AND COMMERCIAL PHILADELPHIA.

ARCHITECTURAL BEAUTY OF THE CITY.

In the architectural beauty of its public and private buildings Philadelphia is not exceeded by any city in the land. Her public buildings, from the venerable structures of historic associations to the palatial edifices of modern construction, represent the highest architectural skill of their day. The great business structures are typical of the solidity of the commercial houses which they shelter, and the residence districts are filled with those handsome structures that make Philadelphia a city of beautiful homes.

THE NEW CITY HALL.

Foremost among the great architectural structures of the city is the new City Hall, which has the distinction of being the largest building in the United States, not even excepting the Capitol at Washington. This magnificent structure is located in Penn Square on Broad and Market Streets. It covers an area of nearly four and one-half acres exclusive of a courtyard in the center two hundred feet square. The north and south fronts are each 470 feet long and the east and west fronts have each a length of 486 feet. Altogether the building has over seven hundred and fifty rooms. The crowning feature of the building is the grand tower which rises from the north side of the central courtyard to a height of nearly five hundred and fifty feet, making it the highest and most massive tower in the world. The summit of this tower will be crowned with a statue of William Penn, thirty-seven feet high.

The first stone of the foundation was laid on the 12th of August, 1872, the corner stone was laid with Masonic ceremonies on the Fourth of July, 1874, and the last block of marble in the tower was set in place on May 7, 1887.

The style of architecture is the French *renaissance* and the whole exterior is bold and effective in detail and rich in outline. The cost of the building has thus far been in excess of twenty million dollars.

GIRARD COLLEGE.

From its earliest history Philadelphia has been an important center of learning and is to-day the seat of many prominent institutions. One of the most famous of these is Girard College, which was founded over sixty years ago by Stephen Girard. A sailor in his early life, he first came to Philadelphia as captain of a trading ship. Later on he settled in Philadelphia and became the most successful merchant of his day, being at the time of his death in 1831, one of the richest men in the country. By his will all his vast property, with the exception of a few personal bequests, was left to the city. The various charitable institutions of the city were remembered, and he made large bequests for the improvement of the river front, for the reduction of taxes, and to increase the efficiency of the police system. But his most important bequest was two million dollars to establish a college for the education of orphan boys. The institution was to be open to white males between the ages of six and ten years who were to be supported and educated until they reached the age of sixteen years and then apprenticed to some good trade or useful employment.

He designated the site on Ridge Avenue. There on a tract of forty-five acres on Ridge Avenue, Nineteenth Street and Girard Avenue, the city erected the college which stands to-day a monument to the philanthropy of Stephen Girard. On July 4, 1833, the corner stone was laid, the buildings were completed in 1847, and on January 1, 1848, the institution was opened. The grounds are surrounded by a wall 10 feet high, and one of the explicit conditions of the bequest was that no "ecclesiastic, missionary or minister" should ever hold any office in the college or should ever be admitted within its walls, even as a visitor.

The college buildings are magnificent specimens of architecture. The main building is of marble, in the form of a Greek temple in the Corinthian style. It is surrounded by colonnades which comprise thirty-six massive marble columns, 6 feet in diameter and 55 feet high. The structure has a length of 218 feet and a width of 160 feet and a height of 90 feet. It has three stories, each divided into four rooms with vestibules, and is surmounted by a roof of massive marble tiles. The remains of the founder rest in the lower vestibule, beneath a marble statue. Four other buildings, also of marble and each 52 feet wide by 125 feet long, were built at the same time, and others have since been added until now the college has accommodation for more than thirteen hundred boys.

The property left by Mr. Girard has increased in value, until now it is worth more than fifty millions.

VIEW FROM CHAMOUNIX DRIVE.

UNIVERSITY OF PENNSYLVANIA.

At the corner of Thirty-fourth and Pine Streets stands the University of Pennsylvania, the most extensive educational institution in the State. It was first chartered in 1753, as the "Academy and Charitable School of the Province of Pennsylvania." Two years later its name was changed to "The College and Academy of Philadelphia."

The University of Pennsylvania was incorporated in 1779, and the college and university were united in 1791. The University embraces all departments of higher education and professional schools. Its medical school, established in 1764, is the oldest in the country.

ACADEMY OF NATURAL SCIENCES.

The Academy of Natural Sciences, at the corner of Nineteenth and Race Streets, is the oldest institution in America devoted to the natural sciences, and it still retains precedence by virtue of its wealth of specimens, its collections in several important departments being the most complete in the world. This institution was incorporated in 1817.

OTHER EDUCATIONAL INSTITUTIONS.

In its wealth of educational institutions, both public and private, Philadelphia is not surpassed by any city in the land. These embrace an admirable public school system and numerous academies and higher institutions of learning, together with many valuable institutions for the education of the unfortunate and the helpless.

NEWSPAPERS AND LITERATURE.

As already stated a printing-office was established in Philadelphia soon after the city was founded, and ever since then the city has occupied a prominent place as a literary center and also in the printing trade. The first type foundry in America was established in Germantown, then a suburb of Philadelphia, in 1735, and the first Bible printed in America was published here in 1743.

To-day the city has a number of excellent and enterprising newspapers of national reputation, and is the home of the great penny papers. One of the characteristic features of the Philadelphia papers is the absence of sensational features. They are essentially newspapers for the home, and as such are not surpassed by those of any city in the country. There are also several magazines and other publications of a high literary standard issued from Philadelphia offices.

THE FUTURE OF PHILADELPHIA.

With its commanding situation and the indomitable energy of the people the future of Philadelphia is one of glorious promise. Its commerce, its resources and its facilities for trade were never greater or better than they are to-day, and the spirit of the people was never more progressive. New industries are springing up on every side and old-established ones are being enlarged and extended to meet the fast growing requirements of trade.

The commerce of Philadelphia reaches to the uttermost parts of the earth. Her ocean trade is again fast approaching that of New York, and the completion of the improvements now under way in the Delaware will leave the city with facilities for affording wharfage to large vessels that will make this the most convenient shipping port in the country. Her coastwise trade, large and important to-day, is steadily growing in magnitude, and the fleets of magnificent steam and sailing vessels which ply from Philadelphia north and south along the coast and to the West Indies and adjacent islands, receive new accessions every year. More than all, the splendid fleet of armed and armored vessels, the new navy of the United States, the pride and the glory of the nation, carries to all climes and seas under the stars and stripes, a magnificent and glorious testimony of the commercial prestige of Philadelphia. For the world will recognize that the city where those splendid ships were built is one of the commanding seaports of a great maritime province.

In her domestic trade Philadelphia enjoys a prestige well earned and well maintained. Her salesmen cover the entire country and cross the borders to Canada on the north and to Mexico and the Central and South American States to the south. Philadelphia-made clothing is worn by the people of every State in the Union. Philadelphia carpets are found in the homes of rich and poor all over the land, and goods of Philadelphia manufacture, infinite in variety and sterling in quality, are accepted all over the country as the product of experienced and honest workmanship.

The railroads which make Philadelphia one of the great railroad centers of the country extend their arms of steel in every direction, bringing to the city all the products of the land and taking out in exchange an infinite variety of manufactures.

In the great marts of commerce which minister particularly to the home trade the observer finds massive and eloquent monuments to the prosperity, the comfort and the good taste of the people. These massive buildings which shelter the retail trade of the city are the direct outgrowth of the increasing demands of the great home trade of the people of the city.

New buildings going up on every side, massive and magnificent triumphs of architectural skill in the business center, residences, beautiful and inviting, in the outlying districts, prove the prosperity and the healthful growth of Philadelphia. The great churches whose tapering spires rise heavenward, the school-houses equipped with every modern improvement for the healthful education of the young, tell of the religious and intelligent character of the people. Palatial club houses and spacious temples of amusement tell of their social nature. The splendor and magnificence of the public buildings are evidence of the public spirit which is such an important element of the permanent growth of a great city.

With her growing commerce and her immense manufacturing and industrial interests, Philadelphia is more than all else a city of homes, and no city in the world affords within its corporate limits such splendid inducements for residence and business alike. With the completion of the comprehensive system of rapid transit already under way, the outlying districts will be put in close and direct communication with the business center, and the city will afford facilities of transportation that are unrivaled in their way. These improvements have already given a wonderful impetus to real estate, and this is the surest test of a city's real growth. The facilities which have been afforded to people of moderate means to build and own their own homes through the medium of the Building and Loan Associations and kindred organizations have greatly aided in building up the city, and Philadelphia has a larger proportion of householders than any of the other great cities of the land. This is one of her proudest distinctions and the most staple feature of her growth.

With a record of more than two centuries of steady progress which are part of the history of the nation, Philadelphia closes the first decade of the third century of her existence with a record that fills the future with a glorious promise. So great is her capacity for further development that the grandest dreams and most glowing pictures are likely to fall far short of the reality. The spirit of her founders is alive to-day in her people. They are earnest, energetic, self-reliant and honest. Those who come from abroad to make their fortunes here are like the early colonists, who were attracted to Penn's province, men of sterling character who form useful and valued members of the community.

No barriers of nature hinder the growth of the city. The site so well chosen by Penn will suffice for the needs of millions yet to come. The city so grandly planned by the Quaker proprietor of colonial days was founded on an enduring basis and was planned not for the narrow needs of a day or a generation but to meet the growth of ages, and it will perpetuate the memory of its founder through countless generations yet to come.

The men of the present who by their industry and energy are aiding to develop the great resources of Philadelphia, are engaged in making a history that in its relations to the future is not less important than the glorious record of the two centuries that have passed. On their talent, their energy and their faithfulness the future of the city rests. Their records show that there is no danger of the great trust being abused. The future of Philadelphia is secure in the hands of her merchants and mechanics, her artisans and tradesmen, her manufacturers and financiers, and the great army of intelligent business men who direct her commercial affairs.

The succeeding pages of this work is a record of the men of to-day and the great enterprises which they control. It is a record of energy well directed and of industry and integrity rewarded.

REPRESENTATIVE
BUSINESS HOUSES OF PHILADELPHIA.

HE SECOND NATIONAL BANK OF PHILADELPHIA, at Frankford.—This city has long been pre-eminent as a financial center, and all the indications are that she is bound to maintain supremacy in this respect. Solidity and stability of our fiscal and fiduciary institutions are justly a source of pride to Philadelphians. And while on the subject under review, it is a pleasure to direct attention to the staunch and substantial Second National Bank of Philadelphia, at Frankford, which occupies a niche in public esteem and favor accorded to none other in this section. It is one of the soundest and most ably managed corporations of the kind in the city, and its popularity and prosperity are certain to endure and increase. The "Second National" was organized and commenced business in 1864, and its history during the twenty-eight years since intervening, has been an unbroken record of progress. The secret of its success is not far to seek, however, for the bank has always been conducted on sound and conservative business principles, and its management characterized by sagacity, energy and ability, coupled with the strictest integrity. The capital stock of the institution is $280,000; it has a surplus of $135,000, and undivided profits amounting to $35,932.68, and the deposits reach the handsome sum of over $1,400,000. The investments and connections of the bank, too, are of a most desirable character, the business affords evidence of steady and material increase, and, altogether, the affairs of the "Second National," are in condition highly gratifying alike to its officers, stockholders and clients. The bank building is an imposing structure, and the offices are commodious and elegantly appointed. There is a well-equipped safe deposit department in connection, also, and private rooms, and an efficient staff is employed, everything here bespeaking order and excellent management. The Bank of the Republic, Philadelphia, and the First National Bank, New York, are its correspondents. A general banking business is transacted, including discounts, loans and  deposits, and accounts are opened with banks, bankers, merchants, manufacturers, etc., on the most favorable terms. Collections are made on all points at lowest rates, and telegraphic transfers are made also on any city in the United States. Foreign and domestic exchange is bought and sold, drafts are issued on Great Britain, Ireland, and countries of Continental Europe, while letters of credit, etc., available anywhere, are sold. In short, all classes of business comprehended in legitimate banking operations, are engaged in by this institution, and clients are assured of liberal and honorable treatment in every instance. Mr. B. Rowland, who has been president of the Second National since 1877, and a director of the same from its inception, is one of Frankford's leading business men and most respected citizens, and Mr. Charles W. Lee, who prior to becoming cashier, in 1889, had held a responsible position in the bank since its organization, is accounted one of the most able and trustworthy financiers in the community. The board of directors, than which a more representative body of citizens it would be difficult to find, is composed of Messrs. Benjamin Rowland, George W. Rhawn, John H. Webster, Watson Bavington, William Bault, David C. Nimlet, Amos C. Shalleross, Jos. L. Kinkerter, Sam'l. W. Evans, Jr.

HISTORICAL AND COMMERCIAL PHILADELPHIA.

ENJAMIN W. GREER, Bellevue Worsted Mills, Wister Station, Germantown.—In the great Philadelphia industry of cloth manufacturing a decided success has been achieved by Mr. Benjamin W. Greer, proprietor of the Bellevue Worsted Mills, located at Wister Station, Germantown. Mr. Greer began business three years ago, and has since then built up a splendid trade throughout the United States and won a reputation for his goods of a high character that any manufacturer might take pride in. He began business at his present address, where he has a finely-equipped plant, and grounds six acres in extent. The works proper are comprised in a four-story building, 150 x 200 feet in dimensions, and it is fitted with 180 looms, a 150-horse power engine and all required machinery and appliances. Employment is found for 200 experienced operatives in the various departments. Their operations are carefully supervised by competent foremen, while the proprietor personally directs all the affairs of the establishment. Mr. Greer manufactures cotton and worsted cloth for the clothing trade, turning out new and handsome designs continually, and his goods are unexcelled for finish, quality and uniform excellence. His trade extends to all parts of the country, and those who enter into business relations with him are sure to receive decided advantages.

ENNSYLVANIA STEEL COMPANY, Luther S. Bent, President; Edmund N. Smith, Secretary and Treasurer; Office, No. 208 South Fourth Street.—The Pennsylvania Steel Company has achieved an international reputation for the superiority of its product, which includes steel rails, and steel in bars, sheets and strips, and also frogs, switches, slabs and billets. This corporation is one of the wealthiest, best-equipped and most perfectly organized in the steel industry of the country, and its works at Steelton, Pa., are the largest of their kind in the State and give employment to 5,000 hands. The main offices of the company are located at No. 208 South Fourth Street. The present vast industry dates its inception back to 1865, when the Pennsylvania Steel Company was incorporated, with a capital stock of $200,000, which has since been increased to $5,000,000, and the present officers and directors are as follows, viz.; President, Luther S. Bent; vice-president, Eben F. Barker; secretary and treasurer, Edmund N. Smith; directors, Luther S. Bent, Edmund Smith, H. H. Houston, William M. Spackman, Eben F. Barker, Wayne MacVeagh and Charlemagne Tower. The plant of the company at Steelton covers an area of 150 acres, and the works are thoroughly organized and are models of their kind. The buildings are roomy and substantial, the equipment is thoroughly modern and of the greatest capacity. Numerous actual tests of the steel rails of this company in comparison with those of other makers of foreign countries and of the United States, upon some of the trunk lines, have demonstrated the superior wearing qualities of the "P. S. Co." rails, and, with their long experience in the manufacture of steel rails, this company have no hesitancy in assuring their patrons that their first quality of rails shall be unexcelled. Their "T" rails will be found to embrace the very latest productions of engineering skill in approved shapes and to present good wearing surface with due regard to a proper distribution of the metal and conforming to the improved rail fastenings. Their rails are used preferentially by the Pennsylvania, the Philadelphia & Erie, the Philadelphia, Wilmington & Baltimore, the Baltimore & Ohio, the Boston & Lowell, the Philadelphia & Reading, the Northern Central, the New York, Ontario & Western, the New York, West Shore & Buffalo, the Troy & Greenfield, the Boston, Hoosac Tunnel & Western; the Cumberland & Pennsylvania, and various other railroads throughout the United States. Their switches are also used extensively all over the country, as are likewise their frogs, switch stands and crossing frogs. The attention of railway managers is especially directed to their very complete system of interlocking switch and signal apparatus for operating signals and switches at junctions, terminals, crossings, draw-bridges, etc., which they are prepared to furnish at moderate prices, under fullest guarantees, both as to successful operation and protection from demands on account of patents. This company are now producing 300,000 tons of steel rails per year, as well as vast quantities of other steel specialties, while no labor strike has ever occurred at their works, and in view of the liberality of the management, it is safe to predict that none will ever take place and that the continued success and permanent prosperity of this great enterprise is well assured. Its executive officers are gentlemen of the highest repute in commercial and financial circles, of large experience and commanding ability, whose standing in the business world is such as to place them far beyond the requirements of any praise which these pages could bestow.

OHN DORFNER, Steam Dyeing and Scouring Establishment, No. 516 Race Street, Works, No. 515 Cresson Street.—There is certainly no place of the kind in Philadelphia where a better class of work is done than the dyeing and scouring establishment of John Dorfner, at No. 516 Race Street. The works, which are at No. 515 Cresson Street, are perfectly equipped for the purposes intended, and a number of expert hands are employed. The facilities here are first-class in all respects, and ladies' and gentlemen's clothing are cleaned and dyed in accordance with the most approved process, without the slightest injury to woof or warp. The most delicate fabrics are thoroughly cleansed and colored in the most superior manner, and at short notice, and goods are called for and delivered at any part of the city free of extra charge. The prices prevailing here, too, are extremely moderate, while the utmost satisfaction is assured in every instance, all work done being fully warranted, and all orders receive immediate attention. Mr. Dorfner is a man of about forty and a native of Bavaria, where he learned his art. He is a thoroughly skillful dyer, of over a quarter of a century's experience, and is an expert in his line. He started in business in this block thirteen years ago, and from the first has enjoyed an excellent patronage, his trade steadily growing.

HISTORICAL AND COMMERCIAL PHILADELPHIA.

ISTORICAL PUBLISHING COMPANY, Nos. 3941-43-45 Market Street.—The largest bookmaking plant in the United States is that owned and operated in this city by the Historical Publishing Company, at Nos. 3941-43-45 Market Street. This is the most extensive concern in the country conducted by private individuals, the only one larger than it being the binding and bookmaking department of the United States Printing Department at Washington, D. C. The business was founded upon a small scale, in 1886, at No. 120 North Seventh Street, by the present proprietors and officers of the company, H. S. Smith, president; Chas. R. Graham, secretary. After staying at that address six months they removed to the corner of Sixth and Arch Streets, and a year ago they took possession of their present mammoth quarters. Here they occupy a building having seven floors, a cellar and subcellar, the whole affording a floorage area of 110,000 square feet. The basement is devoted to press work, electroplating, etc.; first floor, pressroom for book and show work, in the rear of the bookkeepers' offices, etc.; second floor, compositors' rooms; third floor, lithographers, designers,

engravers, and printing appliances. The remaining floors of the building are given up to bookmaking in all its branches, from the folding of the printed pages to the final pressing off of the volume, and making the packing boxes and shipping the goods. The company publish books in many different languages, but mostly in the English, German, Spanish and Swedish, and they can turn out 5,000 volumes a day. Their trade extends to all parts of the world. Among the notable successes of books published by the house are Talmage's "Life of Christ," entitled "From the Manger to the Throne," "Footprints of the World's History," "Story of the Wild West," "The Living World," "The New Beautiful Story," "Sea and Land," "Heroes of the Dark Continent," "Russia and Siberia," "Savage World," "The World's Wonders," "Heroes of the Plains," "Sunlight and Shadow of America's Great Cities," "Health, Wealth and Happiness," "Memorial Volume to Jefferson Davis," "History of the French Revolution," "Path to Wealth," "Our Father's House," "Christ in the Camp," "Columbus and Columbia," etc., etc. Descriptive circulars are sent free on application. Mr. Smith is a native of Chester County, Pa., Mr. Graham of Kansas. Both are imbued with unlimited pluck, energy and enterprise, and the phenomenal success they have won in the publishing world is one in which they may justly take pride.

HISTORICAL AND COMMERCIAL PHILADELPHIA.

HE WM. CRAMP & SONS SHIP AND ENGINE BUILDING COMPANY, Beach and Ball Streets.— The name of Cramp will ever be associated with the construction of the strongest, most efficient and serviceable war and merchant vessels, the largest and fastest steamships and the handsomest steam yachts that plough the waters of the Atlantic. The late William Cramp contributed more to the perfect development of the modern cruiser and pleasure steamer than any other builder or designer in the United States, and leaves as an invaluable heritage to his sons the great reputation and the fruits of the success thus achieved. He established himself as a shipbuilder here in 1830, with a capital saved from his earnings as a journeyman ship carpenter, and won a prominent success from the start. To natural inventive genius he joined marked mechanical skill and soundest judgment, and was always on the alert to introduce improvements in models, style of construction and upper works. As a result his business grew in volume and importance, necessitating enlarged facilities to meet the demands of patrons, which were ably provided, and in 1872 the Wm. Cramp & Sons Ship and Engine Building Company was duly incorporated with a capital of $500,000, the present capital being $5,000,000. The company as at present organized comprises the names of ten descendants of the honored founder, the executive officers being as follows, viz.: Chas. H. Cramp, president; H. W. Cramp, secretary and treasurer; Edwin S. Cramp, superintendent and engineer; Lewis Nixon, naval architect. They have the finest manufacturing plant of the kind in the country, where are the most perfect facilities for the manufacture of steam-engines, steam pumps, and all the structural work for the largest war and naval vessels.

CHARLES H. CRAMP, PRESIDENT OF THE W. C. & S. S. & E. B. CO.

The main works have a frontage of 1,000 x 700 feet on the Delaware River, which together with the adjacent Port Richmond Iron Works, recently purchased of the I. P. Morris Company, make this one of the largest shipbuilding yards in the world. The company also has a marine railway and one of the largest dry docks in the country, located at the foot of Palmer Street, having a basin that permits the entrance of vessels 450 feet long and a draft of twenty feet, with centrifugal pumps capable of discharging 120,000 gallons per minute and emptying the basin in forty-five minutes. Over 3,600 hands are here employed, including 300 shipwrights, 500 riveters, 300 joiners, 80 riggers, 450 machinists, 700 blacksmiths and helpers and general iron workers, 65 draughtsmen, and 35 clerks, while the pay roll averages over $30,000 per week. The company has recently built the following war vessels, to wit: the U. S. S. " Baltimore," the U. S. S. " Yorktown," the U. S. S. " Vesuvius," the U. S. S. " Philadelphia," and the U. S. S. " Newark "; also the following merchant vessels, to wit: the " Monmouth," for the Central Railroad of New Jersey; the " Iroquois," for W. P. Clyde & Co.; the " El Mar," for the Southern Development Co.; the " Caracas," for Atlantic and Caribbean Steam Navigation Co; the " Venezuela," for New York and Venezuela; the " Henry M. Whitney," for the Metropolitan S. S. Co.; the " Essex," for Merchants' and Miners' Transportation Co.; the " Algonquin," for Wm. P. Clyde & Co.; the " El Sol," for the Pacific Improvement Co.; and is now building the following vessels for the U. S. Navy, viz.: the armored cruiser U. S. S. " New York," the battle ship U. S. S. " Indiana," the battle ship U. S. S. " Massachusetts," " Cruiser No. 12," (the U. S. S. " Columbia,") and " Cruiser No. 13," the triple screw cruisers. The Cramps also built the " Cetus," " Perseus," " Pegasus " and " Taurus," all iron steamers, running between New York and Coney Island; the " Mariposa " and " Alameda," running between San Francisco and Sydney, Australia; the " Kinau " for the Wilder Steamship Co., of Honolulu; the " San Pablo " and " San Pedro," for the Pacific trade between San Francisco and Panama; the steam yacht " Corsair," for Chas. J. Osborn; the " Stranger," for Geo. Osgood, of New York; the steam yacht " Atalanta," for Jay Gould; and such well-known steamships as the " Ohio," " Indiana," " Illinois," and " Pennsylvania," for the American Steamship Co. The demand for their skill and genius as shipbuilders comes from all over the two Americas, and the same is met with unexampled promptness and brilliant success. Apart from steamer and

HISTORICAL AND COMMERCIAL PHILADELPHIA.

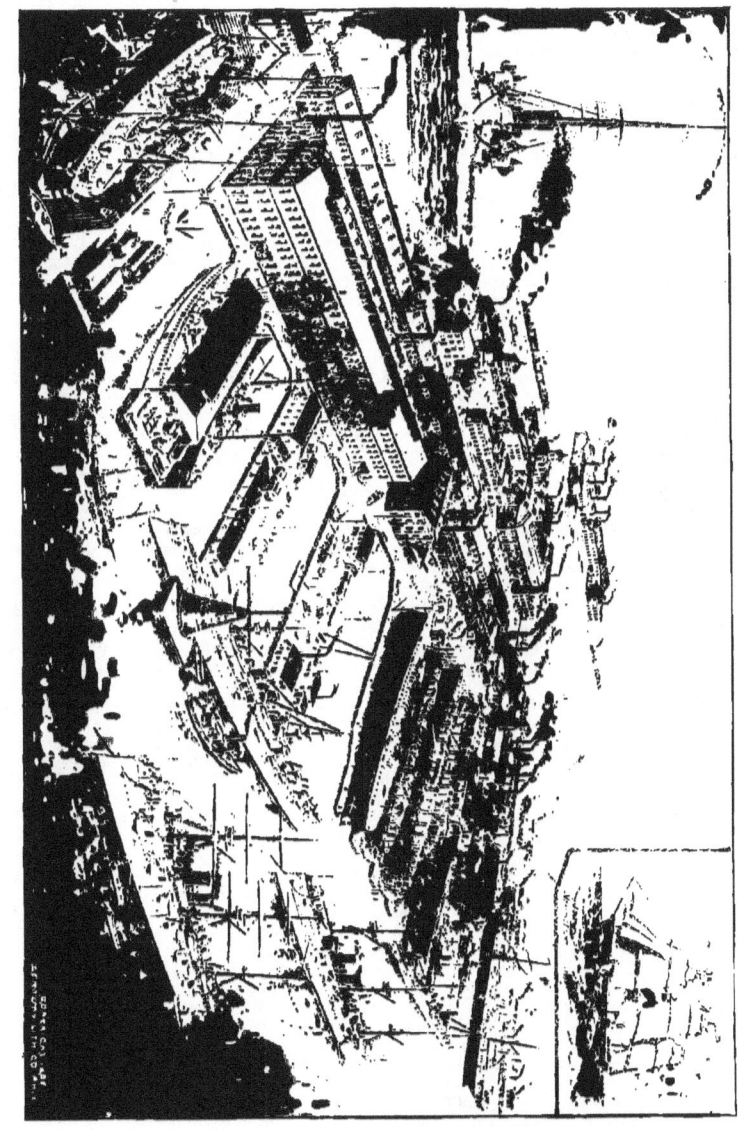

The Wm Cramp & Sons Ship and Engine Building Company's Plant.

HISTORICAL AND COMMERCIAL PHILADELPHIA

vessel work, this company has an established reputation for producing the strongest and most serviceable steam-engines on the market, which can be secured here of all sizes and at short notice. The Messrs. Cramp are all expert and practical shipbuilders, having been brought up in the industry, and are also prominent in financial and commercial circles, well equipped and perfectly prepared to maintain to their honored house its signal reputation and unequalled facilities for the production of the best ships afloat.

B. CRAMP & CO., Brass Founders, Manufacturers of American Manganese Bronze, York and Thompson Streets.—The most recent addition to the plant of the Wm. Cramp & Sons Ship and Engine Building Company is the brass and bronze foundry of Messrs. B. H. Cramp & Co., which is known and honored as the largest industrial establishment of its kind in the United States and which is eligibly located at York and Thompson Streets. This extensive business was founded in 1885, by Messrs. B. H. and H. Cramp, the present style being adopted in 1888. The works comprise several two and three-story buildings, and a foundry which covers a ground area of 87 x 137 feet, all splendidly equipped with modern machinery and appliances, including fifty-two crucible furnaces, which will melt 25,000 pounds of brass in two and one-half hours, three times per day if required, thus giving a daily capacity of 75,000 pounds. The foundry is supplied with one 15-ton jib crane, one 10-ton and two 1½-ton jib cranes, and one 1½ and one 3-ton traveling crane. As brass founders the firm of B. H. Cramp & Co. have executed many very important contracts on government work for the Wm. Cramp & Sons Ship and Engine Building Company, including the main condensers for the United States cruiser "Baltimore," which contained six castings of the combined weight of 12,004 pounds; also the main air pumps for the same cruiser, forming a single brass casting weighing 1,517 pounds. They have lately received a contract from the Morgan Line for thirty-two blades of manganese bronze, weighing on the average 1,000 pounds each, and they are also deservedly prominent as having made the blades for most of our war vessels, and some of the most prominent steamships in the United States, such as the "Caraccas" and the "Venezuela" of the Red D Steamship Line. This firm are also deservedly prominent as manufacturers of the highest grade of manganese bronze, known as the "American" grade, which is used exclusively for screw propellers by the navies of the United States, England, Russia, Spain, Germany, France and Italy. This is a non-corrosive alloy, and is in heavy increasing demand in all parts of the world, giving this house a prestige and popularity second to that of no other house in this line. The copartners, Messrs. Benj. H. and Courtland D. Cramp, are native Philadelphians, sons of Mr. Chas. H. Cramp, who is president of the Wm. Cramp & Sons Ship and Engine Building Company of this city. They possess large practical experience in the art, personally supervising all operations of these works, and in all departments they enjoy special facilities not elsewhere obtainable.

PROVIDENT BOND AND INVESTMENT COMPANY, Principal Office, No. 530 Walnut Street.—The most important question for those to decide who have funds to invest is safety. Assured of their investment, rate of interest divides their attention with permanency. The Provident Bond and Investment Company, having its headquarters at No. 530 Walnut Street, offers a securer method of investing small sums than either life insurance, building associations or savings funds. They are the successors to the Mutual Savings and Distribution Fund Association, of New York, the original tontine investment bond association in America. The company was organized under its present title in March, 1891. It has a capital of $100,000 and is officered as follows, viz.: J. H. Durland, president; Harrison Johnson, vice-president; R. A. Babbage, second vice-president; D. J. Sandham, secretary; R. H. Taylor, treasurer. Directors: J. H. Durland, D. J. Sandham, R. H. Taylor, Robert Anderson, I. E. Cochran, Jr.; William H. Emerick, Harrison Johnson, R. A. Babbage, William Lewis, Frank Powel, M. D.; George W. Elliott, W. T. Shoemaker, D. H. Sleem, M. D. This company offers unequaled advantages to investors, while pledging unquestionable security for carrying out its undertakings. It has in effect a safe system of collections and presents the best paying investment before the public in their monthly redemption bonds. These bonds embody the surest principle of gain to the persistent, give the quickest returns upon outlay, and guarantee the maximum of profit for the minimum of risk of any investment principle extant. There are many points in which the plan of this company differs profitably to their bondholder, from all other financial enterprises, while the earnest invitation of the managers to all investors to carefully investigate their plans, principles and methods of doing business, betokens a conscious strength that is certain to secure to them a continuance of the liberal patronage already bestowed. The conservative management of the company, coupled with its financial strength, has led to its recognition as one of the foremost investment mediums in this city. On August 1, 1892, it had a capital and reserve surplus amounting to over $170,000; against which surplus there is not one dollar of matured liability. If absolute security, convenience, regular income, permanency and freedom from care count for anything in an investment, these bonds more nearly meet the wants of the investing public than any other security now to be had. Of this a thorough investigation will convince the most skeptical or conservative investor, to whom patient courtesy is always shown by the officers in charge. President Durland is a well-known citizen of New York, the founder of the "Tontine Investment Bond" system and the organizer of this company. The remaining officers of the company are prominent Philadelphians and gentlemen of experience and ability, with whom it is always a pleasure to do business.

H. M. SCIPLE & CO.,
BOILERS, ENGINES, ETC.,
Third and Arch Sts.

A leading headquarters in Philadelphia for boilers, engines, shafting, sawmills, pumps and power plants is the establishment of Messrs. H. M. Sciple & Co., located at the corner of Third and Arch Streets. This representative house has been in successful operation since 1879, and none engaged in this important line of mercantile activity in this country maintains a higher standing in the trade, and few enjoy a larger measure of recognition, its annual sales reaching a very handsome figure. The business is conducted on the soundest and most progressive principles, and its management is characterized by energy, sagacity and judicious enterprise, coupled with strict integrity. All persons having dealings with this house are certain to find the same of the most satisfactory character. The boilers and engines handled by this firm are of every style, size and variety, and bear such a character for utility, reliability and superiority, as to command universal attention and general patronage. Contracts for supplying complete power plants are promptly and satisfactorily filled to the letter,

and among the patrons supplied by this house may be named the Pottsville Electric Light Company, Shenandoah Electric Light Company, Shamokin Electric Light Company, Frackville Electric Light Company, and the Salem Electric Light Company, Salem, Or.; while corporations and individuals throughout Pennsylvania, New Jersey, Delaware and the South largely depend on this house for their supplies, being attracted by the honorable methods in force, the substantial inducements offered, and the prompt and satisfactory manner in which all their orders are fulfilled. Prices are at bed-rock, and, quality considered, are the cheapest quoted by any similar concern in the land. Purchasers in this line will save money and obtain better service through this house than by dealing with any other in the country. The members of this firm are Messrs. H. M. Sciple, J. M. Gillespie and H. P. Sayford. All are experienced and practical exponents of this line of trade, possessing a foundation understanding of all its details and requirements, and eminently popular in meeting all its demands.

A. R. KELLER COMPANY,

Patentees and Manufacturers of the

PHILADELPHIA PATENT FLEXIBLE BACK FOR BLANK AND INVOICE BOOKS,

Ridge Avenue,
Noble and Eleventh Streets.

A house whose trading title would be found high up on the list of those engaged in blank book manufacturing and bookbinding, if such a list were made with the names arranged according to merit, stability and extent of operations is the A. R. Keller Company, successors to the John Y. Huber Company, located at the junction of Ridge Avenue, Noble and Eleventh Streets. This company are prominent as patentees and manufacturers of the Philadelphia patent flexible back for blank and invoice books, while they operate three separate departments for publishing, blank book manufacturing and bookbinding. The business was founded in 1855, and is under the sole management of Mr. A. R. Keller. The business premises comprise an entire five-story building, 101 x 50 feet, provided with all the latest machinery and devices designed to make skilled labor most effective, and, as steam-power is freely used, the force of 250 to 300 hands is to all intents and purposes many times multiplied. In scope, the business is all-embracing, everything proper to its line being promptly undertaken and accomplished in a manner doing the fullest credit to present-day styles of work, and giving the most complete satisfaction to the large and influential patronage. This company has issued such important publications as "The Supreme Court of the United States, its History and Centennial," prepared by the Judiciary Centennial Committee, and upon which, by written permission, the seal of

the Supreme Court was placed—an honor never before conferred upon any publication; "Acres of Diamonds," by Russell H. Conwell; and "Bradley's Atlas of the World;" also "Mitchell's Atlas" and maps of all the South American countries. The company's patent flexible back for blank books has been adopted by the United States Government and is recognized by experts as the acme of perfection; and by the aid of a machine lately invented, they are now able to produce these patent flexible backs without any additional cost over the old style. In their blank book manufactory this company turn out some of the finest work known to the trade. The fullest extent of artistic possibility signalizes their numerous productions, while their well-tested merits and marked appreciation by a critical public is their best possible recommendation, their only needed endorsement. Orders by telephone No. 2211, by telegraph or mail, receive immediate and careful attention, and prices are placed upon a fair and equitable basis. The business extends to all parts of the United States and Canada, and is yearly increasing in volume. Mr. Keller, the manager, devotes his energies and talents most untiringly to the business, insuring only reliable work and winning the esteem and confidence of a widespread and critical trade.

THOMAS DELAHUNTY, Marble and Granite Works, Established 1855, Ridge Avenue, Opposite North Laurel Hill Cemetery.—The trade represented by the establishment of Thomas Delahunty, whose marble and granite works are on Ridge Avenue, opposite North Laurel Hill Cemetery, is second to no other of its class which may fairly claim to combine with a manual handicraft the richest embellishments of art. The perfection now attained in this direction may be plainly seen in the work turned out by Mr. Delahunty, and at his works may be found a large variety of designs in monuments, headstones, etc., which evince a combination of taste and skill rarely seen in domestic manufactures of the kind. The cemeteries of Philadelphia are specially noticeable for the elegance and taste displayed in their costly and massive monuments, many of which are the product of the skill of the subject of this sketch. Mr. Delahunty was born abroad, but has resided in this city 46 years. In 1855 he established business here and has since built up a large, widespread, and influential trade. Among the notable work done by him may be mentioned the Wilson, and Kitchenman monuments in South Laurel Hill Cemetery, the Alexander Campbell, Henry Huddy and Jas. W. Queen monuments in North Laurel Hill Cemetery, the Florida monument at Tallahassee, monument to the unknown Confederate dead at Winchester, Va., which is 80 feet in height, and surmounted by the figure of a soldier standing "at rest;" the Germantown Soldier's Monument, and monuments, sepulchres or sarcophagi for Chief Justice Mercur, Walter Lippincott, James Simpson, B. F. Clyde, P. F. Morey of Portland, Oregon, and many others. Mr. Delahunty's marble and granite works are the largest in the city. The yard and buildings cover an area of 100 x 40 feet, and are completely appointed in every respect. Employment is found for forty expert workmen and all orders given Mr. Delahunty are executed in the most workmanlike and satisfactory manner.

HANSON BROTHERS, Electrotypers, No. 704 Sansom Street.—The electrotyper occupies an important position in the industrial world, and fills a niche that would otherwise be a lamentable void. The oldest house in the Quaker City engaged in this industry is that which forms the subject of this sketch. This establishment was founded in 1857 by Mr. Thomas H. Mumford, and in the year following Mr. G. L. Hanson was admitted to partnership, the firm-name becoming Mumford & Hanson. The latter's sons are now proprietors. The copartners, Messrs. G. Hanson, C. Hanson, H. Hanson, E. M. Hanson and E. H. Hanson, are natives of Philadelphia, and have had from fifteen to twenty years' experience in their vocation. They are thoroughly conversant with all its requirements, and exercise care to maintain their establishment at the highest standard of efficiency. As a result of the superiority of the work turned out, the firm have a large active trade, extending to all parts of the United States, and they also have customers in England. The business premises consist of a five-story building, 25 x 150 feet in dimensions. The equipment includes the most improved machinery, driven by steam-power, and employment is afforded from sixty to seventy hands. Electrotyping is executed in all its branches, in first-class style, at lowest cost, and all orders are promptly and satisfactorily filled.

GUTEKUNST, Photographer, Clayton S. Harris, Mgr., No. 1700 Broad Street.—There is not perhaps in the domain of the arts any line in which more notable progress has been made during the past few decades than in photography. What with invention, improvements and sustained effort, the advance made in the direction indicated since Daguerre discovered the process of retaining negative impressions by the aid of light on sensitized surfaces is truly marvelous. The work turned out by some of our leading portrait artists is a distinct triumph of science and skill; and in this connection special complimentary mention is due to the magnificent studio of F. Gutekunst, located at No. 1700 Broad Street, northwest corner of Columbia Avenue, and which enjoys a reputation second to none in Philadelphia. It is one of the oldest as well as foremost exponents of the art in this city and has a very large high-class patronage, the pictures leaving his establishment being noted for fidelity, beauty of design, delicacy of shading and elegance of finish. Mr. Gutekunst is an expert photographer of long and varied experience, and a thorough master of the art in all its branches. His business has been established since 1850, and has always maintained the first place in the foremost rank in the profession. The studio occupies two floors, each 125 x 50 feet in dimensions, with luxuriantly furnished reception-room and ladies' parlor and well-equipped operating department and employs a large staff of prominent artists. Mr. Gutekunst makes a specialty of faithful portraits of our most prominent citizens and is conceded to be the most successful photographer in Philadelphia. The establishment is provided with all the latest improved appliances and appurtenances, and is by general assent the finest and best-equipped photographic studio in the city—perhaps in the United States—over $10,000 being expended in the fitting up of the place alone. Fine photography in all its branches is executed here in the highest style of the art, and satisfaction is assured in every instance, life-sized cabinet portraits being a specialty. Pictures are finished in oils in the most superior manner, and particular attention is given to crayons, watercolors and pastels, the very best work being guaranteed, while the prices charged here are of the most reasonable character withal. This gallery is under the able management of Mr. Clayton S. Harris, who has devoted a lifetime in perfecting himself in his profession and has filled many prominent positions in Boston and other large cities. His reputation as an artist is too well known to need further comment.

ISAAC A. SHEPPARD & CO., Excelsior Stove Works, Northeast Corner Fourth Street and Montgomery Avenue.—American stoves, ranges and furnaces are recognized the world over as unequaled for economy in the consumption of fuel and for general efficiency, while they are the embodiments of mechanical workmanship of the highest order of perfection. This reputation has been won by the enterprise and skill of our leading representative houses, of which the Excelsior Stove Works, at Fourth Street and Montgomery Avenue, form a fitting illustration. These works are conducted under the enterprising proprietorship of Messrs. Isaac A. Sheppard & Co., and are among the largest and best equipped in the country. The foundation of the business was laid in 1859, by Messrs. Isaac A. Sheppard, James C. Horn, Jonathan Boddie, William B. Walton and John Sheeler, at Marshall Street and Girard Avenue, and in 1872 a removal was made to the present site. Eventually Mr. Sheppard became the sole proprietor, and in 1879 Mr. Franklin L. Sheppard, his son, was admitted to partnership, followed by the admission of another son, Mr. Howard R. Sheppard, in 1887, thus forming the firm as at present constituted. The works at the address above named cover an entire block, and comprise a series of two and three story buildings, splendidly equipped for the manufacture of ranges and furnaces, and giving steady employment to 250 skilled hands; while the firm also operate works in Baltimore for the production of stoves and hollow-ware, which occupy an entire square and furnish employment to 125 workmen. All the products of this firm are duly protected by patent, and have served to give the house a prestige and popularity with the trade shared by but few of its contemporaries in the country. The "Excelsior," the "Carroll" and "Patrol" cook stoves are all of improved patterns, and include many exclusive improvements which insure the greatest efficiency with the lowest consumption of fuel, coupled with convenience, durability and beauty. They also manufacture the "Royal Ranges," which, with the "New Franklin," "New Washington," "New Columbia," "Jewel," "New Magic," "Ruby," "Saxon" and "Stratford" ranges, are models in trimmings, finish and adaptation to the exacting requirements of families in all circumstances. Their "Fidelity" ranges, which are illustrated in the accompanying engraving, and their famous "Excelsior" ranges are recognized by the trade as the best sellers of the present time. Their Paragon Steel Plate Furnace, with equalized draft, patented August 5, 1890, embodies the great principles of perfect ventilation, thorough combustion, ease of management, and magnificent heating capacity, and is in satisfactory use in some of the finest residences. The development of the business of this house has had few parallels in the trade, and is largely due to the fact that the proprietors are practical stove founders, know what the public most desire, and are enabled to supply the same by reason of their large resources and perfected facilities. They have solved the most difficult problems involved in the construction of stoves, ranges, and furnaces; and their productions stand without successful rivals for valuable improvements, perfect operation and excellence of workmanship and finish. The honored senior partner was born in New Jersey, and for upwards of thirty years has been prominent in the industrial, political and financial circles of this city and State. He served three terms as a member of the Legislature during the war period, being chairman of the Ways and Means Committee in the House of 1861, and had full charge of the measures of legislation for sustaining the government at that critical period; while for a large part of one session he acted as Speaker *pro tem*. He also deserves credit as one of the originators and the chief promoter of the "Building Association Bill," which has since operated so beneficially in making Philadelphia "a city of homes." He is still a power in the commercial and financial circles of this city, as president of the National Security Bank, and a director of the Northern Safe Deposit and Trust Company and the Northern Liberties Gas Company; and since January, 1880, has been president of the Board of Education. The sons are native Philadelphians, trained in this branch of industry from their early boyhood, and combine their energy and ability with the ripe experience of their father to form a firm of commanding influence, wide popularity and solid worth.

ILVER KING MINING AND MILLING COMPANY, Office, No. 234 South Fourth Street.—There are numerous indications that the present boom in mining operations, especially for precious metals, is of the most permanent and conservative character. The newly-formed companies have entered the field upon the most substantial basis, headed by experienced mining experts and capitalists, not overstocked, but formed to develop some of the richest and most extensive ore leads yet discovered. The Silver King Mining and Milling Company, whose office is located at No. 234 South Fourth Street, is a favorable example of a corporation organized to conduct legitimate mining operations. Incorporated in 1888, with a capital of $1,000,000, it acquired ownership of the richest silver-bearing territory in Idaho, located in Alturas County, where they have located twelve claims and have already three openings. They have made all the necessary arrangements for conducting business under the most favorable conditions and upon a grand scale, and are securing a steady output of silver ore of the finest quality, which they are selling to smelters in large quantities. The ore assays very rich, thus placing the company upon a secure dividend-paying basis, and is to be congratulated upon a favorable prospect before it. The stock is held by prominent Philadelphians, whose interests are entrusted to safe hands. The president of the company, Mr. Henry Lewis, is one of our best-known citizens and representative business men; prominent as an iron broker for many years, and also president of the Decatur Coal Company. The secretary and treasurer, Mr. W. S. Wylie, holds a similar position in the Decatur Coal Company and is an able official.

EYSTONE HORSESHOE COMPANY, Manufacturers of Bar, Guide and Hoop Iron, also Special Sections of Iron or Steel, (Hoop Iron Can be Furnished in Lengths of 100 feet;) Seventeenth and Clearfield Streets, Stations Germantown Junction, P. R. R., Sixteenth Street Station, P. & R.—There are many extensive establishments in Philadelphia engaged in the iron industry, and prominent among such should be named that of the Keystone Horseshoe Company, located at Seventeenth and Clearfield Streets. This company are extensive manufacturers of bar, guide and hoop iron, and special sections of iron or steel; while they make a leading specialty of skelp iron for manufacturing wrought-iron water and gas pipes. The company was organized in 1884, with ample capital, and had as its president the Hon. Geo. H. Boker, until his lamented death, in 1890. This vacancy has never been filled, the present officers being Wm. Gerhard, secretary and treasurer; W. G. Howell, superintendent. The main building covers a ground area of 80 x 220 feet, and is supplied with four heating furnaces, two trains of rolls and a full complement of improved machinery, operated by a steam-engine of 250-horse power, and employment is given to seventy skilled hands. The facilities of this company for manufacturing the best quality of goods are not excelled anywhere, while the guarantee that goes with all products is proof of the care in workmanship and the reliability of stock used in manufacture. The reputation of this company's skelp iron has become inseparably connected with the city of Philadelphia, and this result is the natural outgrowth of the uniformly equitable policy that has dominated the operations of the house, and warrants the remark that in its particular line of manufacture there is no concern in the country that we can more readily endorse as affording their customers both general and special advantages not easily duplicated elsewhere. The company are now producing 12,000 tons per year, selling direct to pipe manufacturers in quantities to suit, and have attained a national reputation for the excellence of their products and their perfect adaptability to the purposes for which they are used. Mr. Gerhard, the secretary and treasurer, is a native Philadelphian, a member of the Manufacturers' Club and prominent in business and trade circles; while Mr. Howell, the superintendent, was born in France, and has resided in this country for twenty-five years. Both gentlemen give the benefit of their time and talents to the promotion of the interests of the company, and thus insure its continued success and permanent prosperity.

HE LINK-BELT ENGINEERING COMPANY, Successors to Burr & Dodge, Link Belting and Link-Belt Appliances, Nicetown.—In this age of machinery and where progress is the order of the day, as regards new inventions of every kind of machinery for nearly every purpose, the enormous demand for belts and belting has rendered their manufacture a prominent industry in the United States and one which is continually on the increase; competition only serving to increase the skill of American manufacturers. The Link-Belt Engineering Company, whose office and works are located at Nicetown, fills a niche in this branch of industry peculiarly its own. This company are internationally famous as manufacturers of the Ewart detachable link-belting and link-belt appliances; the Dodge chain, sprocket wheels, shafting, pulleys, improved appliances for handling any material in bulk or package, and are likewise prominent as engineers, founders and machinists. The business so successfully conducted by them was originally established in 1875, by Clarke & Burr, who were succeeded in 1884, by Burr & Dodge, and in 1889 their interests and those of the Link-Belt Machinery Company of New York, were consolidated under the present name, with James M. Dodge, president and chief engineer; S. Howard-Smith, vice-president and treasurer; Edward H. Burr, secretary. The plant of the company covers four acres of ground, and comprises a machine-shop, 80 x 410 feet, built of brick in the most substantial manner; a wrought-iron shop, 70 x 180 feet, and a drop-forge shop, 40 x 50 feet, both iron buildings; and a stable and storage shed, 100 x 25 feet. The equipment embraces a compressed air plant for burning oil fuel, and for operating riveting machines; an hydraulic plant for operating two cranes of two tons capacity each; a complete fire service, and three steam-engines of 100 aggregate horse power, while steady employment is given to 150 skilled and expert hands. This is one of the finest-equipped shops in Philadelphia. Link-belting has taken a prominent place among the necessities, and is very extensively employed in the handling of coal and in the equipment of flour-mills, grain elevators, breweries, malt-houses, paper and pulp mills, sugar refineries, phosphate works, tanneries, etc. The principal value of link-belting as a power transmitter lies in the nature of its construction. Being composed of links and used with sprocket wheels, it forms a positive belt, doing its duty with no waste of power from slipping and the minimum loss of power through journal friction, which latter is a large factor of loss in all flat-belt transmissions. This loss of power by friction and slippage of leather or rubber belts costs thousands of dollars in large concerns, in the consumption of coal and wear and tear on the machinery. Link-belting is successfully used for driving rotary furnaces, and for transmitting power under water, as it is uninjured by being used in hot and damp places. Under favorable circumstances link-belting can be run at a speed of 1000 feet per minute, while as high a speed as 2000 feet per minute has been accomplished. Aside from its use for transmission of power, link-belting has attained prominence as a medium for elevating and conveying material of almost any kind, which is accomplished by inserting at suitable intervals in the belt special links called attachments. This company built the coal-handling machinery used in the coal storage plants at Port Richmond; Rondout, N. Y.; Salem, Mass.; Plainfield N. J.; and South Amboy, N. J.; also for the Lehigh Avenue round-house of the Philadelphia & Reading R. R. Co., and others of immense capacity. Their coal-handling machinery is in use by the Philadelphia & Reading R. R. Co., the Pennsylvania R. R. Co.; the Cross Creek Collieries, Lehigh Valley Coal Co., and other noted corporations. This house is now making a special feature of rope sheaves. The sheaves are made in two forms: one used only for idlers having a rounded groove of but little greater radius than that of the rope employed, the other having the "V" grooved rim required for driving sheaves. Numerous experiments have been made to determine the best angle for the sides of this groove, the object being to attain the maximum grip without making the angle acute enough to cause the rope to wedge in the groove or to wear by sliding into place. The bottom of the groove is round and the sides smooth, to prevent abrasion of the rope. They have so perfected the manufacture of their sheaves that all grooves of the same nominal size have exactly the same pitch diameter, and are strictly interchangeable. This is of vital importance in a multiple-grooved sheave. If there is any inequality, the rope will travel in the groove of larger diameter at increased speed, thus causing the several ropes to pull against each other, and throwing the strain of the transmission on less than the whole number of ropes. Nothing has so militated against the general employment of rope driving in this country as the use of imperfect multiple-grooved sheaves; those constructed of wood having proved especially faulty. In the sheaves, each groove is cast separately. Some grooves have arms and hub, while others are plain rings. They all have a slight projection on one side and corresponding recess on the other, with bolt holes at the circumference, so that a multiple-grooved sheave is quickly built up by bolting together the requisite number of arm sections and ring sections. The projecting bead fits into the recess in the adjoining ring, and brings each groove accurately to one pitch surface. The joint is not perceptible, and the finished sheave presents as smooth and unbroken a surface as a single casting. This method of construction enables them to make a light and very strong sheave by placing the metal where it will be most effective. A heavy rim is avoided and the requisite strength given by introducing the proper number of arm sections. Another and most important advantage it offers is, that extra grooves can be added to an existing drive at any subsequent time when more power is needed. No other make of sheave is capable of this extension. They keep a large stock of arm and ring grooves constantly on hand, so that sheaves with any number of grooves can be furnished promptly. Other products include Emery & Garland's patent lumber trimmer, gang slab slashers, automatic fuel feeders, patent safety boots, elevator buckets, Norway iron elevator bolts, the Cockrell scouring case, Caldwell's conveyor, swivel spouts, the "L. B. M. Co." clutch, an improved hub-friction clutch, manilla rope, and leather, rubber and cotton belting. This company's business is immense and influential throughout all parts of the United States, and also extends to South America and other foreign nations. A branch office is operated at No. 49 Dey Street, New York, and the trade and consumers everywhere are supplied at short notice and on fair and equitable terms. The western connection of this company is The Link-Belt Machinery Co., of Chicago, which has an equally large and well-equipped plant.

THE JOHN C. MILLER BREWING COMPANY, Lager Beer Brewery, Ale, Porter, Brown Stout, Northwest corner Wakefield and Ashmead Streets, Germantown, Pa.—The opinion once prevailed among certain classes of the community that first-class beer, ale and porter could not be brewed in America. This sentiment is now confined solely to Anglomaniacs, who obtain their clothes from Europe, and all they possibly can of what they eat and drink. The skill and energy of American brewers have been brought to bear with such brilliant success that beer, ale and porter are now produced in this country equal in quality and purity to the best brewed in Germany, or by Bass or Guinness in Great Britain and Ireland. The John C. Miller Brewing Company, of this city, affords, in their career and by their productions, an excellent illustration of the truth of this statement. They are extensive brewers of lager beer, ale, porter and brown stout, with headquarters at Wakefield and Ashmead Streets, Germantown. The business was founded in 1865, by Mr. John C. Miller, who placed the enterprise upon a solid and substantial basis, and was succeeded in 1887 by his son, Mr. Geo. J. Miller. The present company was incorporated on the first of January, 1892, under the laws of the State of Pennsylvania, with a capital of $300,000, and with Geo. J. Miller, president, A. J. Miller, secretary and treasurer. The plant covers three-fourths of an acre of ground, and the brewery is a splendid four-story structure, equipped with all modern appliances, apparatus and machinery known to the trade, including a 200-barrel brew kettle, a 75-ton ice machine, with storage capacity for 14,000 barrels, and a productive capacity of 80,000 barrels per year. The brewery is a model of order, neatness and good management, and in these respects it has no superior in the country. The best malt and hops that can be purchased are utilized, and these are handled in such a careful and scientific manner as to result in the production of a class of goods that for purity, fine flavor and uniform excellence are unexcelled in this or any other market. An inferior grade of beer, ale or porter is never permitted to pass the gates of this establishment; hence its excellent reputation with retailers, families and the general public. Orders are filled with promptness and care, and terms and prices are made invariably satisfactory to buyers. The Messrs. Miller, Geo. J. Miller and his cousin, A. J. Miller, are well-known Philadelphians, expert and accomplished masters of the brewers' art, and recognized leaders in their special branch of industry. As to their productions, one might as well attempt to paint the lily or gild refined gold as to praise Miller's beer, ale and porter.

HENRY LEVIS & CO., Engineers, Dealers in Material for Railway and Ship Construction; Office, No. 234 South Fourth Street.—A renewed era of prosperity has made its approach, and the great railroads of the country are beginning to indicate the beneficial effects of greater activity in trade. New railroads are being projected, and nowhere can their promoters so satisfactorily negotiate for iron and steel rails and other equipments as here in Philadelphia. The extensive interests centered here as the headquarters for many of the largest railroads, render this city an especially desirable location for dealers in rails and supplies, and representative among the number is the firm of Messrs. Henry Levis & Co., who occupy eligible office quarters at No. 234 South Fourth Street. This firm are recognized as leading authorities in regard to the most perfect forms of railway and ship construction, bringing to bear vast practical experience, coupled with an intimate knowledge of the requirements of railroads and of the best sources of supply. They handle iron and steel rails, fastenings and spikes, scrap iron, bituminous coal, and plate, boiler, ship and tank iron, both as dealers and brokers, and are agents for the Paxton Rolling Mills of Harrisburg, selling largely on commission, and contracting with railroad companies for large lines of supplies. The business was established in 1873 by Messrs. Levis & Kimball, who were succeeded by the present firm in 1882. Under able and honorable management the business has been developed to proportions of great magnitude and the firm have sold many thousand tons of rails to railway and construction companies and have afforded universal satisfaction in regard to the strict fulfillment of every contract. Directorates desirous of being honorably and faithfully served at the lowest current rates will find it to their advantage to place their orders here. The firm is composed of Messrs. Henry Levis, Walter M. Gorham and Howard Siddell. Mr. Levis is one of the oldest and most expert iron brokers in Philadelphia and is prominent also as president of the Decatur Coal Company and as a director of the Silver King Mining and Milling Company of Idaho; a well-known Philadelphian who stands deservedly high in commercial and financial circles.

DECATUR COAL COMPANY, Office, No. 234 South Fourth Street.—The city of Philadelphia has long been recognized as the great coal center of the Union, and it is here that the wealthiest firms and companies have their offices and an enormous business is being carried on daily. One of the old-established and best-known houses engaged in the business is that of the Decatur Coal Company, whose offices are located at No. 234 South Fourth Street. This company are miners and shippers of semi-bituminous coal, owning 600 acres of land in Clearfield County, eligibly located on the Pennsylvania Railroad, and have a colliery which turns out 75,000 tons. The company was incorporated in 1864, under the laws of the State of Pennsylvania, with a capital of $200,000, and is officered as follows, viz.: Henry Levis, president; W. S. Wylie, secretary and treasurer. They ship by the car or cargo in quantities to suit to any point desired at the shortest possible notice. Their coal is especially adapted for use by steamships, rolling mills, locomotives, glass works, and all kinds of smithing and steam-generating purposes where intense heat is required. Many of the largest coal consumers and purchasers in all this section of the country are numbered among the constant customers of the house, and entire satisfaction is assured in all its transactions. President Levis is a well-known Philadelphian, one of the oldest iron brokers in the city, and also President of the Silver King Mining and Milling Company. Mr. Wylie, the secretary and treasurer, holds a like position in the Silver King Mining and Milling Company.

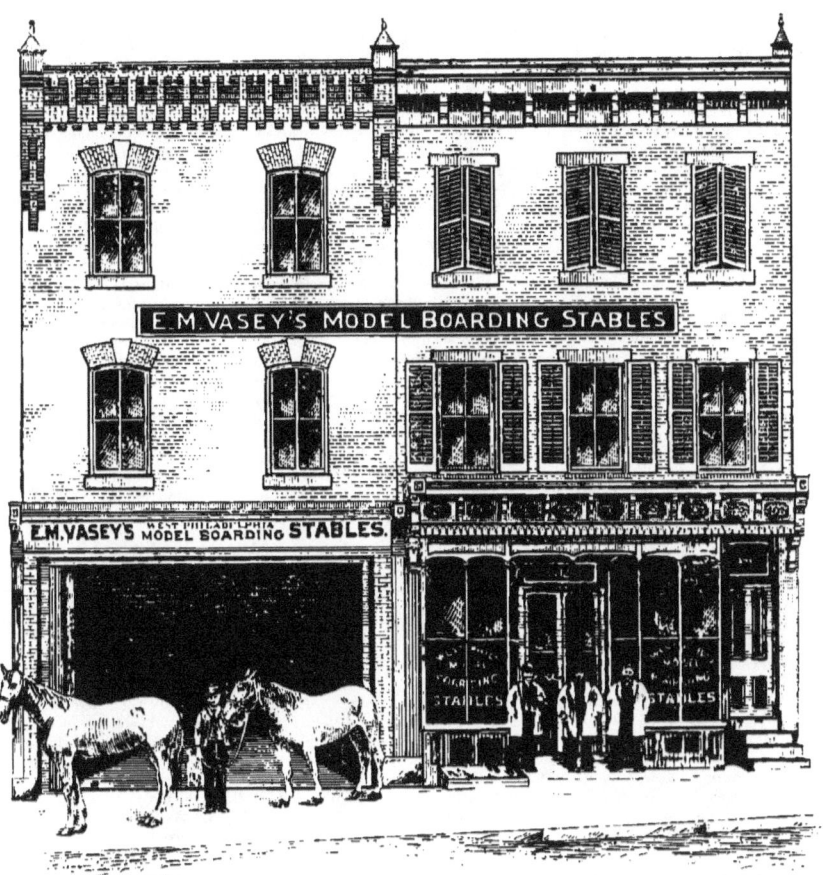

E. M. VASEY'S, West Philadelphia Model Stables, Nos. 3712 and 3714 Market Street.—One of the most complete and stylish livery stables in the city, and a leading representative of this branch of industry is that of the West Philadelphia Model Boarding Stables, located at Nos. 3712 and 3714 Market Street. There are few men, if any, in this business who are better known or more highly esteemed than the proprietor, Mr. E. M. Vasey. Mr. Vasey established business in Philadelphia nineteen years ago, and a year and a-half ago erected the splendid stables since occupied by him. The building is architecturally perfect. It has three floors, each 42 x 240 feet in dimensions, and the place is finished in hard pine. The drainage, ventilation and light are perfect. At night electric lights are used. An elevator leads to the carriage rooms on the second and third floors. There are nineteen box stalls, and the stable has comfortable accommodations for sixty-seven horses. A fine stock of road horses also gentle horses, for ladies' driving, is owned by Mr. Vasey, and a splendid variety of carriages, broughams and road wagons. Special attention is given to driving and saddle horses, and all patrons are certain to be well pleased with any horse or team hired from or boarded at these stables, while the prices charged are uniformly reasonable. Mr. Vasey is a native of Philadelphia, recognized as one of its most progressive business men, and bears an excellent reputation for honorable methods in his transactions. He is a stockholder in the Belmont Driving Club, and the Philadelphia Driving Park Club, and is a life member and one of the founders of the Turf Club.

JOHN B. STETSON COMPANY, Fine Soft and Stiff Felt Hat Makers, Fourth Street and Montgomery Avenue.—The facilities afforded to the public to gratify their tastes for the beautiful, the reliable and the perfect in their attire, have year by year enlarged the field and created a constantly increasing demand for the best and most truthful exposition of the current styles and of fashion's mandate. A notable illustration is afforded in the career of the John B. Stetson Company, the representative American hatters, whose distinctive qualifications have become universally recognized, and whose great skill and sterling spirit of enterprise lead the trade in fine soft and stiff felt hats and receive that silent homage, the imitation of would-be competitors. The factory of this company, located at Fourth Street and Montgomery Avenue, is the largest in the world devoted to its line of production. The business was founded in 1865, by Mr. John B. Stetson, in a small shop at Seventh and Callowhill Streets, with but two assistants and no capital but energy and pluck. The growth of the business from humble proportions to an honored and matured magnitude has been promoted and secured by an assiduous application of business tact and enterprise of a high order, and by a diligent observance of those principles of punctuality and integrity without which no enterprise can be placed upon a firm and lasting foundation. Through all the vicissitudes, all the inflations and depressions of trade which followed the war period, Mr. Stetson, in the language of President Lincoln, "kept pegging away," lengthening and strengthening his stakes, enlarging his commercial relations, extending his business premises, increasing his facilities for production, and expanding his popularity with all classes of the trade, until he gained the pre-eminence in his industry which he now so deservedly enjoys. The firm of John B. Stetson & Company was organized in 1867, and in 1891 the present company was incorporated, with a paid-up capital of $2,700,000, to which many of the employes subscribed, and with John B. Stetson, chairman; Wm. F. Fray, vice-president and general manager; Robt. M. Smith, treasurer; J. Howell Cummings, secretary. The manufacturing plant occupies a triangular space, fronting 162 feet on Montgomery Avenue, 365 feet on Fourth Street and 398 feet on Cadwalader Street; the main building being six-stories high, while directly across Cadwalader Street is a new six-story structure, connected by a bridge, and both built of brick in the most substantial manner, splendidly equipped with new and improved machinery, ample steam-power, and electric-light plant and other modern conveniences, while steady employment is given to 1100 skilled hands, the wages to pay whom aggregate some $10,000 per week. The output averages 2,000 felt hats per day, and every hat bearing the imprint of this company is a gem of art and taste. They are decidedly the best hats worn to-day, while that indefinable element, style, is always imparted, and so well understood is this fact that they are typical in every city in the Union. All that is best and most reliable is embodied in their production. Jobbers and the trade are supplied in quantities to suit at the shortest possible notice. Their New York salesrooms are situated at No. 750 Broadway. Mr. Stetson is not only successful as a manufacturer, but eminent as a philanthropist. He takes a personal interest in the welfare of his employes, and is the founder of the John B. Stetson Beneficial Association, which provides a benefit for the employes in case of death or sickness. Each employee under eighteen years of age is assessed fifteen cents per month and each one over eighteen years, twenty-five cents per month. In case of sickness they receive three dollars and five dollars, respectively, per week, and in the event of death $75.00 and $100.00 respectively is paid. The November statement of this association for 1891, shows 141 employees who through sickness have received amounts varying from three to twenty-five dollars, and six deaths having occurred the amount of $100.00 each has been paid to the families and relatives of five of the deceased, and $75 in the other case, the employee being under the age of eighteen. During the year this association paid for sick benefits $2029.00, and they still have a balance in their treasury of $622.69. The report is as follows: Balance on hand last report, $433.54; amount received from dues $2884.00; amount paid for sick benefits as below, $2029.00; amount paid to John B. Stetson Assessment Fund, $350.00; physician's services (one year), $390.00; printing and stationery, $15.85; balance in treasury, $622.69; total, $3317.54. Assessment Fund:—balance on hand last report, $48.84; amount received from assessments, $222.80; amount received from John B. Stetson beneficial fund, $350.00; amount paid for death benefits, as follows: 1. Wm. Coulter, $100.00; 2. Jno. McGinnis, $100.00; 3. Samuel Egelton, $100.00; 4. Ed. Major, $75.00; 5. H. R. Kendall, $100.00; 6. John M. Davidson, $100.00; total, $575.00; balance in treasury, $46.64; total, $621.64. There is also a Building and Loan Association, with a ten-year period and with ten series still in operation, two having expired, with a profit of $68.19 accruing to each share. The report for 1891, showed a total profit of $107,216.37. There is likewise a library for the free use of the employees; a Sunday-school room with a regular membership of 2,000 scholars, and where certain evenings of the week are devoted to Biblical study; while noon prayer meetings are held, a kindergarten school is organized, besides a social union, a beneficial organization, a well-equipped gymnasium, and an association whose members pledge themselves against the use of tobacco and liquors. Mr. Stetson is now rising sixty years of age, is a director in various financial institutions, and has built up an enterprise in our midst that is a monument to his perseverance, commanding ability, and love for humanity. Mr. Fray came into the house in 1869, Mr. Smith in 1868, and Mr. Cummings in 1884, and combine to form one of the thoroughly representative manufacturing enterprises of America.

(See cut of works on opposite page.)

HISTORICAL AND COMMERCIAL PHILADELPHIA.

John B. Stetson Company's Plant
See article on opposite page.

HISTORICAL AND COMMERCIAL PHILADELPHIA.

EDMUND D. SMITH & CO., Iron and General Commission Merchants, No. 208 South Fourth Street.— It need scarcely be stated that the iron and steel interests in the United States are of great importance, constituting one of the chief departments of industrial and commercial activity. Philadelphia is an important center of this industry, the transactions assuming great magnitude in the course of a year and the amount sold through the medium of manufacturers' agents and commission merchants reaches extensive proportions. A leading iron and steel firm in the city is that of Messrs. Edmund D. Smith & Co., who occupy eligible office quarters at No. 208 South Fourth Street. This firm do a general commission business in iron ores, pig iron, steel and railroad supplies, and have been established since 1881. They are the sales agents for the Sigua Iron Company, (importers of Cuban iron ore,) Buena Vista Iron Company, Salem Furnace Company, Max Meadows Iron Company, Graham Iron Company, (manufacturers of pig iron,) also the Cleveland-Cliffs Iron Company, of Cleveland, Ohio, (dealers in Lake Superior ores,) and are general handlers of pig iron and iron ores of all descriptions. They also do a commission business in steel products and in railroad equipments, such as freight cars, iron bridges, structural shapes, etc. Brief mention is made below of the several companies represented by this firm. The Sigua Iron Company was organized under the laws of the State of West Virginia, March, 1890, with a capital of $5,000,000, and is officered as follows:—President, Clarence M. Clark; secretary and treasurer, J. S. Singer; directors: E. W. Clark, B. Frank Clyde, George F. Tyler, Thomas H. Graham, David H. Thomas, Samuel Dickson, Edmund D. Smith, E. E. Denniston, Clarence M. Clark, S. H. Chauvenet, Stuart Wood and A. J. Dull. These gentlemen are well-known and influential Philadelphians, whose names are a tower of strength to any enterprise with which they may be identified. The property itself is located on the south side of the Island of Cuba, some twenty-five miles to the eastward of Santiago de Cuba. It comprises 60,000 acres of land, containing immense deposits of the highest grade of Bessemer ore; a railroad some ten miles long has been built, a harbor enclosed by breakwaters constructed; an ore pier, capable of shipping some 3,000 tons of ore a day, built in the most substantial manner by the well-known firm of contractors, Messrs. Anderson & Barr, of Jersey City; and attractive towns laid out at the coast and at the mines with sufficient accommodations to care for quite a colony. The ore is shipped from Sigua by means of English and American steamers, and the most approved methods for economical and quick dispatch have been provided, that will favorably compare with any ore-shipping point in the world. When it is remembered that there are no known deposits of Bessemer iron ore of any importance in the United States east of the Alleghany Mountains, from which the general trade can draw their supplies, this enterprise will be recognized as being of the first importance for the further development of the steel industry in all its forms along the Atlantic coast. Messrs. Edmund D. Smith & Co. act as sales agents for the ore, and as transportation agents, supplying the necessary steam tonnage to bring the ore to American ports. The Buena Vista Iron Company, Salem Furnace Company, Graham Furnace Company and Max Meadows Iron Company have blast furnaces located in the southwestern part of the State of Virginia, and are manufacturers of a high-grade foundry pig iron and a gray forge mill iron that has met with great success in the markets tributary to Virginia. The interests controlling these furnaces are also largely interested in many of of the principal ore mines in Virginia, as also in the manufacture of coke, hence are provided with a supply of the raw material from their own resources, that enables their making a standard iron at a cost only permissible where furnaces are located convenient to the ore and coke supply, and fitted with all the appliances of the most modern furnace practice. Companies situated as these are, are generally able to hold their own in a depressed state of the iron market and admirably placed to conduct a prosperous business during its normal condition. All of the foregoing may be considered as strictly Philadelphia interests, representing Philadelphian capital, enterprise and brains in a highly creditable way.

THE CONNECTICUT MUTUAL LIFE INSURANCE COMPANY, of Hartford, Conn. H. O. Chapman, General Agent, Room No. 327, Drexel Building.—The Connecticut Mutual Life Insurance Company, of Hartford, Conn., began business in 1846, and in all the essentials of good management and financial stability is not excelled by any similar institution in America or Europe. The policies issued by this company are the embodiment of simplicity, equity and every excellence which the experience of nearly half a century has shown to be of value in a life insurance contract. Under their new 'Life and Limited Life Policies,' the insured capitalizes a portion of his income to be returned when his business and family interests no longer need protection. At the end of ten, fifteen, twenty, twenty-five, etc. years, the insured can, if desired, surrender his policy for cash, the amount of such cash surrender values being stated in the policy. Dividends are declared annually and can be used in reducing the annual payments or left with the company to accumulate at compound interest, to be drawn when desired. The "Life Rate Endowments" issued by this company have similar cash values guaranteed and mature at ages 60, 65, 70, and 75. The actual cost of legitimate insurance in the Connecticut Mutual has averaged, during its entire history of forty-six years, as low, at least, as that of any other company and its business is founded upon so conservative a basis, that it is likely to maintain its present relative position. This company has issued over 200,000 policies upon residents of the United States and had on January 1, 1892, solid assets to the amount of $59,738,480, surplus of $6,650,000, and insurance in force to the amount of $155,013,655. It has managed its business at an average expense of 8.54 per cent. The Connecticut Mutual is represented in Philadelphia by H. O. Chapman, General Agent, with headquarters at Room No. 327, Drexel Building.

QUITABLE LIFE ASSURANCE SOCIETY, Reginald L. Hart, Manager, No. 277 Bullitt Building.—The three generations of the American public mingling in the mortal arena—the young man just across the threshold of the business world, the man in his prime who has about gauged the extent of his capacities, and the elderly man whose increasing years and lessening strength warn him that life's day has a limit—all are equally interested in the mighty problems involved in life insurance. This age finds the community largely one of thoughtful, intelligent men, who have a full knowledge of the value and benefit of life insurance, educated up to the duties inherent on them to protect their families, but who become bewildered as to which is the company and scheme best adapted to meet their requirements. Of all the companies whose methods and plans have been examined, the Equitable Life Assurance Society offers the most substantial inducements. Duly incorporated in 1859, it numbers among its directors the leading capitalists, philanthropists and business men of New York City, and is doing the largest business of any life insurance company in the United States. Its Philadelphia office is eligibly located at No. 277 Bullitt Building, and under the management of Mr. Reginald L. Hart, who is agent for the Philadelphia Metropolitan District. This society issues policies on carefully selected lives for any amount between $1,000, and $100,000. The cheapest and simplest form of free tontine policy is on the "life plan." If you assure at the age of thirty-five the annual premium for a $10,000 policy will be $271.00, and in the event of death at any time after the delivery of the policy and the payment of your first premium your family will receive $10,000. Under the old-fashioned policy, if your life is prolonged for many years, you would find the premium a burden during old age, but the free tontine policy provides that at the end of a term of years the policy may be returned to the society and its full value (including the entire reserve on the policy) drawn in cash. Moreover, the free tontine policy gives you a choice of no less than six ways of arranging or settling your assurance, thus guaranteeing to every policy-holder a satisfactory adjustment, no matter how his circumstances may change from year to year after his policy is issued. This policy is unrestricted after one year, incontestable after one year, and guarantees a full share of the surplus earned, and, being issued by a society holding a larger surplus than any other assurance company, may be expected to show larger profits than the policies of any other company. The Indemnity Bond of this society forms a secure and profitable investment combined with life assurance. This bond is backed by a surplus, over all liabilities, of $26,000,000; while the success with which the business of this society has been conducted, its surplus earning power, and the profits paid in the past, indicate that this bond will realize liberal profits. It may be purchased in easy installments, and at any time after three years may be exchanged for a paid up bond for an amount equal to the sum of the annual installments paid. At maturity the bond is either payable in cash or may be extended. In the latter case it will bear interest annually from the date of its extension. The annual statement of this society made December 31, 1891, shows total assets of $136,198,518.38; total paid policy-holders, $14,800,026.37; new assurance written in 1891, $235,118,331.00; total outstanding assurance, $804,894,557.00. These figures speak more eloquently than words as to the condition of this society. Manager Hart is a recognized authority as to all matters pertaining to life insurance, and a gentleman of marked executive capacity and thorough reliability, with whom it is always a pleasure to do business.

PEDRICK & AYER, Manufacturers of Universal Milling Machines, Richards' Patent Open-side Planing and Shaping Machines, Special Tools for Railway Repair Shops, Portable and Stationary Cylinder Boring Machines, Universal Grinding Machines, Office and Works at Nos. 1001 and 1003 Hamilton Street, and Nos. 1002 and 1004 Buttonwood Street.—One of the representative and most successful of the manufacturing establishments of Philadelphia is that of Messrs. Pedrick & Ayer, manufacturers of Universal milling machines, Richards' Patent open-side planing and shaping machines, special tools for railway repair shops, portable and stationary cylinder boring machines, Universal grinding machines, and other specialties, located at Nos. 1001 and 1003 Hamilton and Nos. 1002 and 1004 Buttonwood Street. This firm established their business here in 1856, and from small beginnings it has continued to grow at a rapid ratio, by reason of the superiority of the machinery and tools produced and the enterprise and skill displayed in the management. Their new and perfected plant comprises a mammoth brick structure, four stories high, fronting seventy-five feet on Hamilton Street and extending through the block 200 feet to Buttonwood Street. The equipment of machinery and tools is the best obtainable, and ample steam-power, fire-escapes, electric-lights and other modern improvements are provided, while steady employment is given to from 75 to 150 skilled hands, according to the condition of business, the factory being operated both day and night. This firm have solved every problem connected with iron-working, milling, planing, shaping, and grinding machinery, and now offer a class of specialties that insure superior and accurate work and which are unequaled in many important respects. Their Universal milling machines have merits and advantages possessed by no other make, and their great strength and capacity, as well as their adaptability to an almost endless variety of work, combine to make them superior in every way to any other Universal miller built. They are in satisfactory use by the Pennsylvania Railroad Company, by the Inman and International Steamship Companies, by the Manhattan Elevated Railroad Company, the Northern Pacific Railroad Company, and at the U. S. Navy Yard at Washington, D. C.; also, by the T. C. Dill Machine Company, L. Power and Company, U. S. Mine Signal Manufacturing and Supply Company, Philadelphia Water Department Shops, Link Belt Engineering Company, Girard College, and elsewhere in Philadelphia, and throughout other parts of the world. Richards' patent open-side planer and shaper is a very superior machine, and is warranted in every way in regard to efficiency, true working, rigidity and cutting power. It is used by such well-known Philadelphia houses as those of Powers & Weightman, Barr Pumping Engine Company, Chas. Scott Spring Co., Moore & White Company, Geo. V. Cresson, Bichle Bros., S. L. Allen & Company, and Steel, Van Rossum & Company; also at the United States Mint, and by Midvale Steel Company, Nicetown; Herring Safe Company, New York City; Jos. Clarkson & Sons, Baltimore, Md.; American Brake Company, St. Louis, Mo.; Eames Vacuum Brake Company, Watertown, N. Y.; Defiance Machine Works, Defiance, O.; Huntington & Broad Top Railroad Company, Saxton, Pa. These and other specialties of this firm are in use, not only in all parts of the United States, but also in Canada, Japan, Russia, Mexico, Cuba, South America and the Sandwich Islands. The proprietors are recognized authorities on all details of manufacture in this line, while they have exceptional facilities at command for meeting promptly every requirement of their widespread and critical trade. The copartners, Messrs. D. W. Pedrick and H. C. Ayer, are both expert and practical machinists, members of the Manufacturers' Club, and popular business men; while Mr. Ayer is also president of the Climax Cigar Bunching Machine Company, and president of the Mexican International Steamship Company.

(See cut on opposite page.)

See article on opposite page.

HISTORICAL AND COMMERCIAL PHILADELPHIA.

 THE INTERNATIONAL NAVIGATION COMPANY.—This company is too well known, both to Philadelphians and strangers, to make anything more than a passing illusion necessary. As a Philadelphia company, managed by Philadelphia brains and representing Philadelphia capital, its position is one of which the community should be proud. The head offices of this company are at Nos. 305 and 307 Walnut Street, with branch offices at No. 6 Bowling Green, New York, and No. 32 South Clarke Street, Chicago, Ill.

This company owns and controls the Inman Line, between New York and Liverpool; the Red Star Line, between New York, Philadelphia and Antwerp; and the American Line, between Philadelphia and Liverpool.

The history of the company is both interesting and instructive. Organized and managed by its president, Clement A. Griscom, it has from its infancy shown the spirit of energy and enterprise that has at last given it the finest fleet of steamers in the world. It is owing to Mr. Griscom's courage and keen foresight that the company deserted the old type of passenger ships and built the floating palaces "City of Paris" and "City of New York." Picture of the former we show on the opposite page. These boats are the pioneers in a new era of shipbuilding. Aside from the comfort and luxury enjoyed by the passengers of the boats, equaled by no hotel in Europe or America, they contain many features, until their advent, new to shipbuilding. Although twin screws had been tried on small boats, it was not deemed possible to introduce them in a large ocean-going steamer until the "City of Paris" proved the success of the experiment, which she has since emphasized by making the wonderful trip from Europe to America in 5 days, 14 hours and 24 minutes, which has never been approached by any other steamship. Her twin sister, the "City of New York," also holds the record for the fastest eastbound passage ever made, 5 days, 19 hours and 57 minutes.

Probably the most striking feature in these ships is the fact that it is an impossibility to sink them. Their construction is such that no matter what happens to them, they cannot sink, being divided both transversely and longitudinally into innumerable watertight compartments.

The American Line from Philadelphia, with a sailing every Wednesday, offers to the public an unsurpassed freight service. With its usual enterprise, this company meditates increasing this service with large and fast cargo boats, as much in advance of cargo boats of the present day, as the "City of Paris" and the "City of New York" surpassed the passenger boats which preceded them.

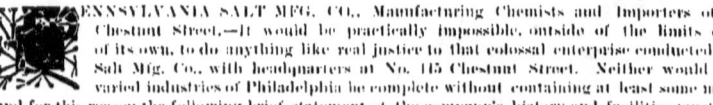 PENNSYLVANIA SALT MFG. CO., Manufacturing Chemists and Importers of Kryolith, No. 115 Chestnut Street.—It would be practically impossible, outside of the limits of a special volume of its own, to do anything like real justice to that colossal enterprise conducted by the Pennsylvania Salt Mfg. Co., with headquarters at No. 115 Chestnut Street. Neither would any account of the varied industries of Philadelphia be complete without containing at least some mention of the house, and for this reason the following brief statement of the company's history and facilities must be taken in place of what we should prefer to be a complete history of the business. The company was chartered by the Legislature of Pennsylvania, September 25, 1850, and is now governed by the following gentlemen, who constitute the Board of Directors, viz.: Theo. Armstrong, president; Francis P. Steel, vice-president; and James W. McAllister, R. Dale Benson, Thos. W. Sparks, Jno. Story Jenks, and J. Tatnall Lea, with Austin M. Purves, secretary and treasurer; Philip A. Bour, general manager of Mercantile Department. The company are the largest manufacturers in the world in their line, and their specialties include sulphuric acid, soda ash, caustic soda, sal soda, bi-carbonate of soda, saponifier or concentrated lye, Glauber's salt, alum, copperas, chloride of calcium, nitric and muriatic acids, nitrate of lead, Epsom salts, among many other chemical compounds, etc., besides metallurgy—copper, precious metals and iron, all produced at Natrona. The main works of the company are located at Natrona, on the line of the Pennsylvania railroad, about twenty-four miles from Pittsburg. In the works, mines and quarries there are employed upwards of 1200 men. A branch of these works is located in this city, where acids, alum and the famous Lewis lye are produced. This Lewis lye is powdered and perfumed, and packed in cans for family use. On account of the great expense of preparing soda compounds by the old methods, this company in 1864 directed its attention to the importation of the mineral "Kryolith," which is composed of sodium aluminum and fluorine. It is found in Greenland, and lies in a solid mass 600 feet long, 200 feet wide and upwards of 400 feet deep. For the purpose of bringing this valuable mineral to this country, this company run eight sailing vessels, fortified against ice and ably manned, between Greenland and Philadelphia, bringing thousands of tons of kryolith here every year. The great enterprise conducted by this company on land and sea, in city and country, at home and abroad, employs the energies, directly and indirectly, of 5000 people. Their Natrona works comprise over fifty acres under roof, the Philadelphia works twenty-two acres. Their unequaled products are in preferential demand by wholesale druggists, wholesale grocers and manufacturers throughout the entire United States. The largest orders are filled with unexampled promptness, and the wants of the trade are ministered to with eminent satisfaction and success in all cases. The name of this company, while talismanic as regards the enormous development of America's commerce and industry, bears equally pleasing relations to the material and educational welfare of the people employed at their works and also to the population of the great centers where their business is carried on. With their great connecting industries, securing to this community the preponderating influence in this branch of trade, this company forms the great leading factor in bringing to our shores the most valuable mineral known for its special uses, and in securing to Philadelphia the wealth and prosperity incident to being the manufacturing and purchasing center for these useful compounds.

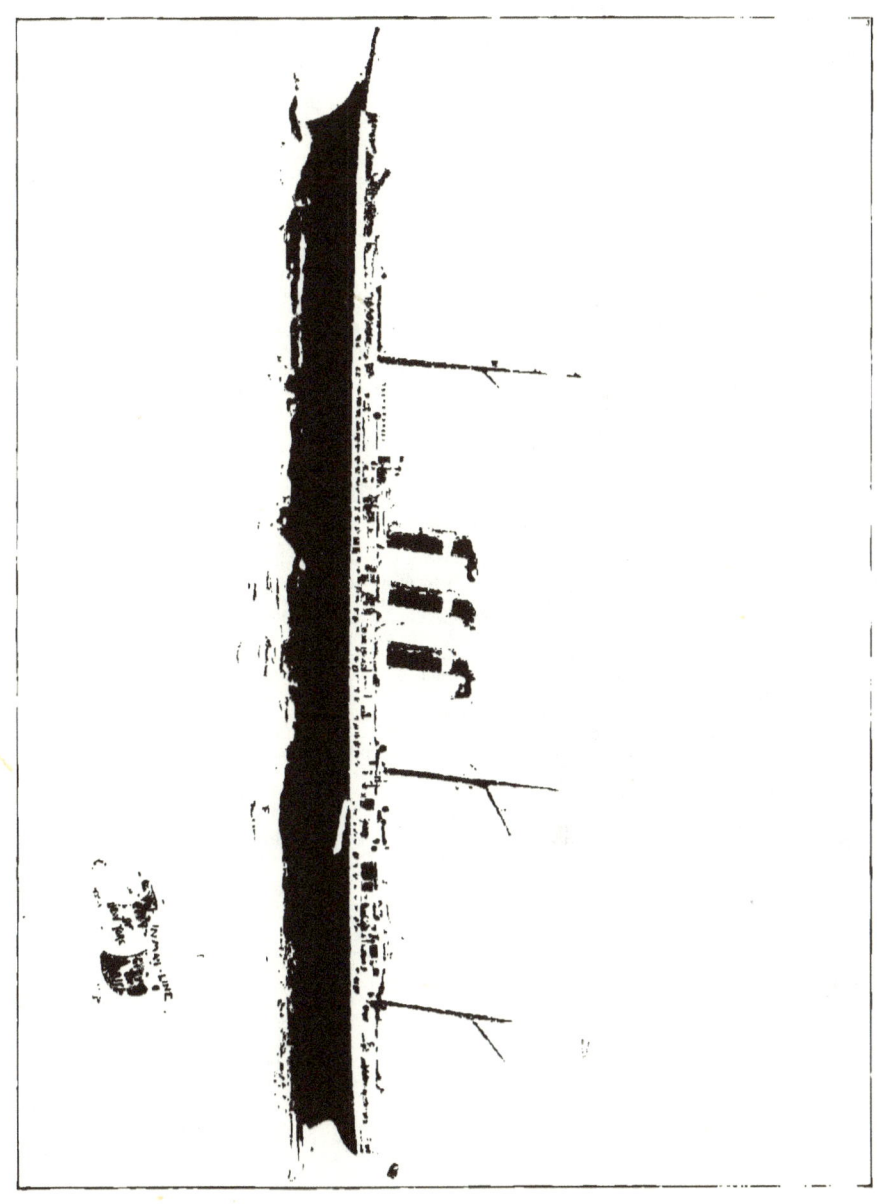

HISTORICAL AND COMMERCIAL PHILADELPHIA.

UNITED STATES CREDIT SYSTEM COMPANY, [Incorporated 1888,] Guaranteeing against Excess Losses Arising From Bad Debts, Home Office, Newark, N. J., William A. Whittick, General Agent for Eastern Pennsylvania and Delaware, No. 541 Drexel Building.—Credit underlies the fabric of the commerce of modern society. It is a necessity and in its proper sphere highly beneficial, yet, like everything else that is good, liable to abuse—as evidenced by the millions of dollars annually lost by bad debts in this country. The best remedy and guarantee that the merchant can avail himself of is that afforded by the United States Credit System Company, whose home office is in Newark, N. J., with a branch in this city at the above address, under the management of Mr. William A. Whittick, as general agent for Eastern Pennsylvania and Delaware. This company guarantees against excess losses, arising by reason of bad debts, and under its system a merchant knows in advance that if the worst should happen as to losses, he cannot lose more than he can well afford, and this fact alone is sufficient to induce him, upon sound business principles, to pay the small amount it costs to have that feeling of security that the guarantee furnishes. This company started in business in June, 1889, and has already done over thirty-three million dollars of business and issued certificates of guarantee against excess losses to importers, jobbers and manufacturers doing a business of at least three thousand millions of dollars. Its success is without parallel in the history of insurance or guarantee companies. Its cash assets on July 1, 1892, amounted to $519,445.86. It has paid in excess losses to that date $312,374.18. It has offices in Chicago, Boston, St. Louis, Baltimore, Cincinnati, San Francisco, New Orleans, Louisville, Memphis, St. Paul, Milwaukee and Detroit, and its ramifications extend to all parts of the Continent. The company holds letters from many leading firms of the United States, testifying to the prompt and equitable settlement of claims for excess losses. The new building of the company in Newark is one of the handsomest and best located structures in that city. Its officers are well-known citizens of New Jersey:—The Hon. William H. F. Fiedler, president, is ex-congressman and ex-mayor of Newark; Hon. Gottfried Krueger, vice-president, is president of the German Savings Bank; Fred M. Wheeler, the secretary, is a young man of conspicuous ability; and Hon. Julius Stapff, the treasurer, is cashier of the State Banking Company, of Newark. Its board of directors embraces names well known in Eastern business circles, such as Jerome Taylor, Esq., of Taylor & Seeley, New York City, and Henry Untermeyer, of Keller & Untermeyer, of New York City. The actuary of the company, L. Maybaum, Esq., is the main originator of this system, which is an enduring monument of his ingenuity and skill. The system of the company (its means of guarantee) is patented, and its various forms protected by copyright. Its business in Philadelphia is of an important and influential character, as shown by its list of certificate holders, which includes many of our largest and wealthiest mercantile and manufacturing concerns. Mr. Whittick, the manager in this city, is a native of England, a resident of this country since 1868, and a gentleman of large business experience, wide acquaintance and high repute, eminently fitted for the successful direction of this responsible agency.

WM. A. WHITTICK.

E. HEID, Maker of Fine Cloth Hats and Caps, No. 510 Market Street.—This house has been established for over thirty years and is to-day the largest in its line in the United States. The business was founded in 1861 by Bochel & Heid, the second member of the firm being Mr. John M. Heid, the father of the present proprietor. This firm was dissolved in 1884, and Mr. Heid succeeded to the business, which he carried on until his death in 1885, when he was succeeded by his son, Mr. E. Heid, the present proprietor, who has been in the house since 1882. The premises occupied for business purposes include the four upper floors of a five-story building, 25 x 70 feet, and a freight elevator for the delivery of goods. The machinery, which includes a large and thorough equipment, is run by steam-power, and employment is given to over one hundred work-people. Four traveling salesmen are employed, and the trade extends all over the United States. The concern manufactures fine goods only, and makes its own exclusive designs. The most popular and stylish shapes in the new so fashionable cloth hats and caps worn in all parts of the country, are the invention and make of this concern, which easily leads all the trade in the style as well as in the quality of its goods. Mr. E. Heid, the proprietor of this thriving business, is one of the younger business men of Philadelphia.

THOMAS SHORE & SON, Hosiery Press and Pump Works, Mill and Cumberland Streets, Germantown.—For more than a quarter of a century the hosiery press and pump works of Thomas Shore & Son have been in successful operation at the present location. The establishment is one of the oldest and leading concerns of the kind in this section of the city. The business was started in 1866 by the senior member of the firm, who conducted it alone up to about a year ago, when he admitted into partnership his son, Maurice Tasker Shore. The shop is a 60 x 125 feet structure, and is equipped with ample steam-power, improved machinery, appliances and tools, while eight to ten skilled hands are employed in the works. Besides hosiery presses and pumps, the Messrs. Shore also manufacture all kinds of iron railings, both in plain and artistic designs, and do machine blacksmithing generally. Belt-geared pumping machines for supplying boilers are built by them in the most superior manner, at short notice, and repairing in all branches is executed with skill and dispatch, jobbing being a specialty. All work done is warranted to be first-class. Mr. Shore, the elder, is an expert mechanical engineer and machinist of nearly half a century's experience, and his son, who is a young man, is also a thoroughly skilled mechanic. They make a specialty of designing and building mill machinery to order, and the trade, which is very large, extends throughout the Middle States.

ENGLISH & SONS. [Late Agnew & English.] Ladies' Cloaks, Suits and Furs, Seal Sacques, Wraps, and Dolmans, Fur Lined and Fur Trimmed Mantles, No. 1021 Chestnut Street, Directly Opposite Chestnut Street Opera House.—If the American ladies are the most neatly and tastefully dressed of any in the world, as is conceded by all intelligent travelers and foreigners, it is in no small degree owing to the fact that those industries engaged in producing their garments have attained such a remarkably high degree of perfection as compared with almost any other branch of commercial industry. The wholesale manufacture and sale of these goods has long been centered in Philadelphia, and one of the oldest as well as largest houses engaged therein, and which has been foremost in promoting the standard of elegance in dress, is that of Messrs. B. English & Sons, located at No. 1021 Chestnut Street, directly opposite Chestnut Street Opera House. This firm are extensive manufacturers of ladies' cloaks, suits and furs, seal sacques, wraps and dolmans, fur lined and fur trimmed mantles, and maintain the highest of reputations in consequence of their high-class, artistic and fashionable productions, and for honorable and reliable treatment of customers. The premises occupied are admirably fitted up with special reference to both business and manufacturing purposes, and the main store is 25 x 235 feet in size, the floor of which is laid with 700 yards of handsome carpeting, while all the arrangements and appointments are attractive and in good taste. The different departments embrace dressmaking, cloakmaking, tailoring and fur manufacturing, all of which are ably managed, and in the season some 150 skilled hands are employed therein. In the show rooms will be found at all times a full and complete assortment of everything in the line of ladies' cloaks, jackets, sacques, dolmans, and every kind of outside manufactured wrap, all of the very latest and most fashionable styles, which reveal the fact upon inspection that they are made of the very best productions of foreign and American looms, elegantly and suitably

trimmed by the most skillful designers and workmen, while the finer grades are fully equal to the same class of goods made to order by ladies' tailors. The fur department is packed with every sort and sample of the furriers' art, including sealskin sacques and wraps enough to supply a battalion of beauty one thousand strong, at prices which make an inquirer a purchaser every time; while furs of all kinds are promptly made to order. The elaborate finish, the perfect cut and symmetry of all work emanating from this house is justly celebrated, and the management is inspired with the determination to excel and to give the best value of any furriers in America. The business of this house was founded in 1860, by Messrs. Wm. Agnew and B. English, as Agnew & English, and in 1880, Mr. B. English succeeded to the sole control, the present firm being organized in 1886, by the admission of Messrs. J. W. and F. W. English to partnership. The honored senior partner was born in England, and came to this city in 1847; while the sons are Philadelphians by birth, trained in the business from their early youth, and members of the Union League Club, the Schuylkill Navy, the West Philadelphia Boat Club and other organizations. This firm have their permanent customers in Japan, in Asia, in France, in Canada and other parts of the globe, while shipping regularly to all sections of the United States, and are eminently popular with their host of patrons both at home and abroad.

C. SCATTAGLIA & CO., Artists and Decorative Painters; Studio; No. 1020 Chestnut Street.—One of the foremost representatives of the art decorative in this country is Mr. L. C. Scattaglia, trading under the name of L. C. Scattaglia & Co., who has had thirty years' experience in his profession, in Europe and this country, and for six years was a student at the Academy of Fine Arts, at Venice. He came to the United States nineteen years ago, landing at New York, where he remained some time, afterward removing to Baltimore, and for the past thirteen years he has lived in Philadelphia. Mr. Scattaglia is an artist and decorative painter, executes fresco painting in all its branches, and makes a leading specialty of Catholic church decorations, altar pieces, emblematical and allegorical characters and figures of the highest order. He has performed much notable work in various parts of the country, his efforts being marked with artistic excellence of the highest order of merit. Among other work done by him the following may be mentioned: Cathedral, Philadelphia; Cathedral, Scranton, Pa.; St. Ann's Church, East Lehigh Avenue, Phila.; St. Augustine's Church, Fourth Street, above Race, Phila.; St. Malachi's Church, Eleventh Street, above Master, Phila.; St. Agatha's Church, Thirty-eighth and Spring Garden Streets, Phila.; St. James' Church, Thirty-eighth and Chestnut Streets, Phila.; Church of St. Philip Neri, Queen and Second Streets, Phila.; Church of the Sacred Heart, Third and Reed Streets, Phila.; Church of the Annunciation, Tenth and Dickerson Streets, Phila.; St. John's Church, Thirteenth Street, above Chestnut, Phila.; St. John's Church, Baltimore, Md.; St. Paul's Church, Wilmington, Del.; St. Augustine Church, Washington, D. C.; St. Mary's Church, Wilmington, Del.; St. Joachim's Church, Frankford, Pa.; St. Thomas d'Aquina Church, Archbald, Pa.; St. Mary's Church, Dunmore, Pa.; St. Mary's Church, Lancaster, Pa.; Senate Chamber, Harrisburg, Pa.; St. Patrick's Church, Hyde Park, Scranton, Pa.; St. Mary's Church, Wilkesbarre, Pa.; St. Patrick's Church, Twentieth and Locust Streets, Phila.; St. Joseph's Church, below Fourth and Walnut Streets, Phila.; Sacred Heart of Jesus Chapel, Conewago, MacSherrystown; Chapel at St. Joseph's Hospital, Philadelphia, Chapel at St. Agnes' Hospital, Philadelphia; Chapel at Sacred Heart Convent, Eighteenth and Arch Streets, Phila.; Cathedral Chapel, Philadelphia; Chapel at Seminary, Overbrook, Pa.; Chapel at Convent of Good Shepherd, Philadelphia; Chapel at Sisters of Mercy Convent, Philadelphia; Chapel at St. Mary's Academy, Philadelphia; St. Patrick's Chapel, Hyde Park, Scranton, Pa.; Church of the Assumption, Twelfth and Spring Garden Streets, Phila.; Church of the Visitation, Front and Lehigh Avenue, Phila.; St. Aloysius Church, Pottstown, Pa.; St. Paul's Church, Tenth and Christian Streets, Phila.; St. Bridget's Church, Cleveland, O.; etc. Mr. Scattaglia is prepared to furnish estimates at shortest notice for work of all kinds in his line, and in every instance where his services are engaged the most satisfactory results may be expected.

HISTORICAL AND COMMERCIAL PHILADELPHIA.

DUNLAP & CO., Hats, No. 914 Chestnut Street, Branch of Fifth Avenue, New York.—An establishment which has gained a more than national fame for the elegance of its productions, is that of R. Dunlap & Co., manufacturers of gentlemen's hats, whose headquarters are in New York, and who have branch stores and agencies in all parts of the United States. This business was established in New York thirty-five years ago, and through the uniform superiority of the output, the demand for the firm's goods has steadily increased from the outset. R. Dunlap & Co. manufacture everything in the way of hats for gentlemen's wear, including silks, operas, cassimeres, soft and stiff felt and straw goods. The retail stores are at Nos. 178–180 Fifth Avenue, New York; No. 181 Broadway, New York; Palmer House, Nos. 171–179 State Street, Chicago; No. 914 Chestnut Street, this city. The branch in this city was opened twelve years ago, and is conducted under the management of Mr. A. H. Lamson, who has been with the firm for five years. Mr. Lamson is a native of Michigan, and is a popularly known business man, who possesses a thorough knowledge of the trade in which he is engaged. The store occupied is 25 x 135 feet in area, handsomely fitted up, and it contains a large, complete stock of the famed Dunlap hats also imported silk and felt hats, also a fine line of umbrellas. Five assistants are employed, and all customers are waited upon promptly and courteously.

B. SHEPPARD & SONS, Curtains, Linens, Flannels and Blankets, Embroideries, Ladies' Underwear, Infants' Outfits, No. 1008 Chestnut Street. Philadelphia can point with pardonable pride to the great emporium of J. B. Sheppard & Sons, at No. 1008 Chestnut Street, as a representative and exponent of what the dry goods trade has come to under the stimulating effects of distinguished enterprise, business capacity of the highest order, and unremitting energy and industry. This is the oldest and best-known dry goods house in Pennsylvania. It was founded in 1826, by Messrs. Sheppard & Van Harlingen, who were succeeded by Messrs. Sheppard & Arrison, and in 1884, the present style was adopted. For forty years the business has been carried on upon the present site, and steady enlargement has characterized the operations in all departments. The building occupied entire for trade purposes contains five floors and a basement, 30 x 235 feet each, in which every modern improvement has been introduced for the comfort and convenience of patrons. This is one of the few establishments in the city that is complete in all the various departments of dry goods, ladies' and children's furnishings, curtains, upholstery, flannels and blankets, linens, embroideries and infants' outfits. This house has long been headquarters for muslin and lace curtains, Nottinghams, Brussels, Cluny, Irish point, antique, renaissance, silk damask and other popular styles; also portieres, including silk shells and figured double-faced velours; China silks in new designs and colorings, made expressly for mantel draperies, bookcases, bed canopies, screen panels and sash curtains, upholstery goods and trimmings, fringes, cords, tassels and gimps. In linens this firm show everything in bleached damask, double satin damask, cream damask, bleached table cloths, bleached napkins, fringed lunch cloths, doilies, tray cloths, carving cloths, Turkey red damask, fancy tabling, cardinal damask, linen sheeting, pillow-case linen, crumb cloths, damask towels, stair linens and crashes. In ladies' underwear and infants' outfits nothing has been too fine or fashionable for this firm to import and display. So, too, as regards blankets and flannels, laces and embroideries and handkerchiefs. The establishment is one of the busiest in its line in the city, its counters being thronged daily by the leaders of fashion, and from 100 to 150 hands find employment here. Each department is complete within itself under an expert manager. This house commands the direct patronage not only of the people of Philadelphia and the surrounding cities and towns, but its mail order department affords a ready means for people in all parts of the country to satisfy their wants. The fame of the house is so familiar to the general public that further comment on our part would be superfluous. The proprietors, Messrs. A. M., E. L., W. B. and J. B. Sheppard, Jr., are sons of the honored senior member of the original firm, and were trained in the business from their early youth. Mr. A. M. Sheppard, is a director of the Market Street National Bank, and all the partners stand deservedly high in the commercial, financial and social world.

THE CHAPMAN DECORATIVE COMPANY, (Limited), No. 1322 Chestnut Street. There is no firm in their line in Philadelphia more widely or more favorably known than The Chapman Decorative Company, (Limited), No. 1322 Chestnut Street, and they fully sustain their reputation. The house is a leading and a thoroughly reliable one, and has a very large and high-class patronage. It was established in 1887 by Joseph Chapman, who continued the business until 1889, when the present limited partnership was formed. Mr. R. J. Chapman, president; Mr. J. F. Huneker, vice-president, and Mr. F. J. Torchiana, treasurer, are all gentlemen in the prime of life and natives of this city. They are all men of energy and enterprise, of thorough business experience, and are subscribers to the "Bourse." They occupy the whole of the four-story and basement building, at No. 1322 Chestnut Street and three doors at No. 1318, and have a four-story structure also at No. 1308 Drury Street used for manufacturing purposes, etc. The various departments are well ordered and thoroughly equipped, and from 125 to 150 hands are employed. The warerooms are spacious, commodious and handsomely appointed, and an exceedingly fine stock can always be found here, including antique and modern furniture, in unique design and of exquisite workmanship; rich and beautiful effects in interior hard-wood decorations, screens, mantels, etc., superb mirrors, stands and cabinets, artistic wall paper, borders, dadoes and kindred articles, also elegant draperies, curtains hangings and art stained glass. All goods sold by the Chapman Decorative Company, (Limited), are fully warranted, and purchasers are assured of getting the very latest styles and newest effects in this establishment, and courteous attention and satisfactory treatment. Plain and ornamental painting, frescoing and mural art decorating generally are done in the most superior manner, and furniture is made to order in any desired design, at short notice. All work executed is guaranteed to be strictly first-class, and all orders receive immediate attention, while the prices charged by this firm are of the most reasonable character. This firm, through their superior and artistic designs, were successful in securing the decorations of the Pennsylvania State Building at the Columbian Fair, Chicago.

THEO. W. MYERS & CO., Stock Brokers, No. 114 Custom House Street. The stock brokerage establishment of Theo. W. Myers & Co. is one of the most prominent of the kind in the United States, and since its inception, a quarter of a century ago, its career shows one continued and unbroken record of good fortune, achieved upon a basis of honorable dealing. The headquarters are on New Street, New York, the Philadelphia office at No. 114 Custom House Street, in the basement of the Drexel Building, and the firm has correspondents in all the principal cities of the country. The firm holds membership in the New York Stock Exchange, and the Chicago Board of Trade. The head of the house, Mr. Theo. W. Myers, is Comptroller of the City of New York, elected to that position at the last election held in the metropolis. Mr. Myers is a capitalist who holds an interest in scores of enterprises, and he is recognized as one of New York's leading citizens. The branch office in this city was opened fifteen years ago, and has from the first been conducted under the management of Mr. Eugene Harvey. Mr. Harvey is a Cincinnatian by birth, and has resided in Philadelphia the past twenty years, during which period he has become very popularly known in the community. The firm conduct a general business as stock brokers, on a strictly commission basis; have private wires to New York, this city, and Chicago, and buy and sell bonds and stocks for cash, or on margin. All facilities are possessed for the prompt transaction of business, and customers have their interests promoted in the most careful and intelligent manner.

HISTORICAL AND COMMERCIAL PHILADELPHIA.

LUBURG MANUFACTURING COMPANY, Manufacturers and Jobbers; Bicycles, Children's Fine Carriages, Adjustable Reclining Chairs, Invalid Appliances and Wheel Chairs, Safety Bicycles, Tricycles, Etc.; Office and Library Desks, Refrigerators and Ice Chests, Folding and Combination Beds, Fancy Chairs, Rockers, Etc., Etc., Office and Salesrooms Nos. 321, 323, 325 North Eighth Street, Shipping and Receiving Department, Nos. 324 and 326 Franklin Street.—It is now but a dozen years or so since the Luburg Manufacturing Company was organized in this city, yet these few years have made their name as familiar to city people and country folk as Shakespeare and Robinson Crusoe. From small beginnings, the management has, by energy and push, placed a comparatively new industry upon a basis firm and permanent. The company are manufacturers of children's fine carriages, safety bicycles and tricycles, the Luburg improved adjustable reclining chair, invalid appliances and wheel chairs, office and library desks, sanitary commode chairs, folding and combination beds, refrigerators and ice chests, fancy chairs, rockers and kindred specialties. Their main office and salesrooms are located at Nos. 321, 323 and 325 North Eighth Street, with shipping and receiving department at Nos. 324 and 326 Franklin Street. The company was incorporated in 1880, with a capital of $150,000, and is officered and managed by C. E. Luburg as president; A. J. Luburg as secretary and treasurer. To these gentlemen is due the remarkable success of an enterprise which started out on a comparatively unknown sea of American manufacture. They have held the business tiller with firm and steady grasp, until they have not only steered the young ship into still waters, but have covered it with the iron-plates of certainty and success. They occupy a new six story building, fronting on North Eighth and extending back 300 feet to Franklin Street, divided into manufacturing and sales departments and finely finished throughout in polished oak, and perfect in convenience of arrangement for rapid production and the transaction of business upon a large scale. The riding of bicycles is steadily growing more popular among business men, for it furnishes a rapid means of conveyance, and gives a pleasure and exhilaration which only the wheelman can realize and no words can describe. The safety bicycles made by this company are beautiful machines, in the construction of which have been placed all the skill and experience attainable. It is light, easy-running, staunch, swift, safe and durable. The fine workmanship and excellent materials used, have made this wheel the finest in the world, and its name is fast becoming a household word. From ocean to ocean and over the ocean its fame has spread, and shipments are now made regularly to England, Australia, South America, Mexico Canada, China and other foreign lands. In children's carriages this company makes a greater variety than any other house. The display of new designs and popular styles in this line is one of the attractions of this great emporium, and is admired by hosts of visitors daily. The Luburg improved adjustable reclining chair has fifty changes of position and is unequalled in utility, convenience comfort and elegance. A complete line of appliances is here shown for the sick-room, each article possessing some merit peculiarly its own. All the specialties of this enterprising company are fully warranted, and distance competition as regards both quality and price. They are supplied to the trade in this country and in foreign lands in quantities to suit at the shortest possible notice, and wherever introduced they practically supplant all similar productions by reason of their great salability and unapproachable merits.

HEXTER BROTHERS, Manufacturers of Summer Clothing Exclusively, No. 675 Broadway, New York; Nos. 132 and 134 Market Street.—In all branches of business the specialties are coming to the front. This is as true of the clothing trade as of other commercial pursuits, and a particularly striking illustration of this is the success which has been met with by the well-known firm of Hexter Brothers. This firm, whose reputation is not excelled by any house in the clothing business in Philadelphia, was established on January 1, 1881, by Messrs. Alexander and Samuel Hexter. These two enterprising gentlemen saw in the clothing trade an opportunity for the development of a special field, and that field was the manufacture of summer clothing. They devoted themselves especially to this field, with the result that they were crowned with success from the start and they have continued in their special field with such intelligently directed enterprise that they have long honored a commanding position in the trade. Mr. Alexander Hexter died in November, 1890, and the business has since been conducted by Mr. Samuel Hexter alone under the old firm-name, a name which had become so well known that it is in fact a trade-mark, certifying that the goods sent out under it are in every way as represented and are not excelled by any manufactured. This is a high guarantee, because of all the branches of the clothing trade the requirements of summer clothing are more exacting. The style, quality, cut and fit of summer clothing are more carefully looked after by purchasers than those of garments worn at other seasons of the year. There is a greater variety of style and of fabrics, and to gain and hold a commanding position in the manufacture of summer clothing indicates a fertility of resource, and a persistent enterprise, together with an intuitive knowledge of what will best meet the popular taste. All these qualities are possessed to a high degree by this house and have contributed to its success. The business occupies commodious quarters, which are in themselves indicative of the magnitude of the enterprise. The main building at Nos. 132 and 134 Market Street is a five-story structure, 40 x 120 feet. Even this great building is not large enough to afford room to handle the immense stock and the five upper floors at the corner of Fifth and Market Streets are also occupied. These are each 18 x 100 feet. Inside and outside these premises the force employed numbers 600 people. Eight traveling salesmen are employed and the trade of the house covers the entire country. The New York headquarters are at No. 675 Broadway. Mr. Hexter was born in Minersville, Schuylkill County, Pa., and is an honored resident of Philadelphia.

HISTORICAL AND COMMERCIAL PHILADELPHIA.

EORGE P. CONNER, Continental Pharmacy, No. 830 Chestnut Street.—One of the most extensive retail drug and prescription businesses in the entire city of Philadelphia is that conducted by Mr. George P. Conner, located at the corner of Ninth and Chestnut Streets, under the Continental Hotel. This well-known establishment—which is open day and night every day in the week—was first opened in 1870 by Mr. A. L. Helmbold, and came into the hands of the present proprietor on February 1, 1892, he having been for twenty years with the house and for the last fifteen its manager. In addition to dispensing absolutely pure, fresh and potent drugs, chemicals, medicines and family remedies, the pharmacy is extensively patronized by private residents and others for the full line of high-grade pharmaceutical compounds, tinctures, cures and other first-class proprietary articles that are made and put up on the premises, among them being the popular CREME ANTOINETTE for softening the skin, promoting freshness and adding beauty to the complexion. Ladies consider CREME ANTOINETTE an indispensable auxiliary to the toilet and bath, acting as a tonic and styptic to the skin, imparting a velvety condition which no other preparation has ever done. It is entirely a vegetable preparation, containing no mineral or poisonous substances. It prevents the ravages of old age, and keeps the skin fresh and blooming with radiant beauty; it positively prevents wrinkles; the Grecian and Roman ladies used such philters of beauty, hence the rhapsodies of poets and authors as to their complexion. It allays instantly the smarting caused by sunburn and cures chapped hands. This valuable crème is prepared only by Mr. George P. Conner, and is a general favorite wherever once introduced. This pharmacy is held in especially high repute for the scrupulous care that is observed in the preparation of physicians' prescriptions and miscellaneous recipes, popular prices prevailing in each department. The pharmacy itself is one of the handsomest in this city of pharmacies; the floor is laid with marble and mosaic tiles, the counters are marble, and general fixtures are of a rich hard wood, and a conspicuous ornament of the whole is the soda fountain, put in at a cost of $3,000. Ten duly qualified assistants are in regular attendance upon customers, and the heavy and carefully selected stock carried includes every possible requisite for the systematic conduct of a large drug, prescription and family trade. Mr. Conner is a native of Philadelphia, where he has resided all his life, and where he is esteemed not only as a citizen of solid worth but an accomplished and skilled pharmacist and honorable business man.

ILSON BROTHERS & CO., Civil Engineers, Architects and Consulting Engineers, Drexel Building, Room No. 1036.—With the vast increase of population, refinement and wealth in the United States, there has arisen not only a growing demand for the blending of the artistic and the beautiful with the utilitarian in modern architecture, but likewise a need for professional services disconnected from and independent of the business of building or contracting. This need and demand is met to the fullest extent in this city by the eminent civil engineers, architects and consulting engineers, Messrs. Wilson Brothers & Co., who occupy eligible office quarters in the Drexel Building. This firm are neither builders nor contractors, but act strictly in a professional capacity. Having a large staff of assistants trained in their respective specialties, they are prepared to design and superintend the execution of any kind of engineering and architectural work. The firm originally began business here on the first of January, 1876, while previous to that time the copartners had been engaged for over fifteen years in the active practice of their professions, in the service of leading railroad companies. The firm was reorganized in 1888, and is now comprised of the following partners, to wit: John A. Wilson, civil engineer; Joseph M. Wilson, civil engineer and architect; Henry W. Wilson, civil engineer; Charles G. Darrach, civil and hydraulic engineer; Henry A. Macomb, architect. Mr. John A. Wilson graduated as civil engineer at the Rensselaer Polytechnic Institute, Troy, N. Y., in 1856, and in 1857 he was appointed topographer, under Mr. John C. Trautwine, on surveys in Central America for the Honduras Inter-Oceanic Railway. In 1858 he entered the service of the Pennsylvania Railroad Company, as assistant engineer, becoming principal assistant engineer in 1860, chief engineer of the Junction Railroad in Philadelphia in 1861, chief engineer of the Pennsylvania Railroad Company, lessee of the Philadelphia & Erie Railroad, in 1864; chief engineer of maintenance of way on the main line in 1868, and, from 1870 to '75, was chief engineer in charge of construction of the Low Grade Division of the Allegheny Valley Railroad, and of branch roads for the Pennsylvania Railroad Company. Mr. Joseph M. Wilson graduated from the Rensselaer Polytechnic Institute in 1858, and, after a special course of study for two years in analytical chemistry, entered the service of the Pennsylvania Railroad Company, as assistant engineer, in 1860. In 1863 he became resident engineer on the Middle Division of the Pennsylvania Railroad, and in 1865 was appointed principal assistant engineer on the main line of the road in special charge of bridges. The title of his position was afterwards changed to that of engineer of bridges and buildings, which position he has held continuously to the present time. He was connected with the designing and construction of the most important buildings of the Centennial Exposition, in 1876, and has made two visits to Europe, where he made a special study of hospital and prison construction, railway stations, bridges, etc. All the members of this firm have had long and thorough training in all the various details of their profession, and have become eminent in it practice. They are prepared to make surveys for railroads, and to furnish plans and specifications for roofs, railway and highway bridges, railway stations, machine-shops, engine-houses, factories, private dwellings, churches, stores, offices, prisons, hospitals and other public institutions, water works, sewerage systems, wharves, piers, and all classes of engineering and architectural work, while construction of work is promptly attended to, and examinations are made of railway, mining and other properties. Their designs have become widely and justly celebrated, and their fame rests upon a long and successful career. During the years of their practice here, they have been largely engaged in designing and supervising the erection of the most advanced classes of public and private buildings, among which are hotels, hospitals, churches, schools, private mansions, summer homes, villas and cottages in this and other metropolitan centers and fashionable resorts of the country. It is needless to particularize in regard to the work of such a nationally famous firm as is this, but it is of interest to note among their creations in this city such magnificent specimens of architecture as the Times Building, Edison Electric Light Company Building, Trust Company of North America Building, the Drexel Building, the Drexel Institute, Philadelphia & Reading Terminal Railroad Station, Pennsylvania Railroad Stations at Broad Street, at Thirty-second and Market Streets, at Centennial Grounds, at Girard Avenue, and at Fifty-second Street; Office of Baldwin Locomotive Works, St. Andrew's Protestant Episcopal Church, New County Prison, Presbyterian Hospital, Germantown Dispensary Hospital, Educational Home, Pennsylvania Industrial Home for Blind Women; and residences for B. K. Jamison, Esq., Hon. John Scott, Jos. D. Potts, J. J. Martin, Thomas W. Sparks, David D. Elder, W. H. Wilson, F. G. Thorn, Edward H. Williams, Theodore C. Engel, Thos. B. Shriver, and many others; likewise, the State Hospital for the Insane, Norristown, Pa.; State Industrial Reformatory, Huntingdon, Pa.; Astronomical Observatory for U. S. Military Academy, West Point, N. Y.; Trinity Protestant Episcopal Church, Williamsport, Pa.; Seaside Memorial Chapel, Beach Haven, N. J.; German Reformed Church, Altoona, Pa.; Baptist Church, Raleigh, N. C.; Protestant Episcopal Church, Goldsboro, N. C.; Bryn Mawr Hotel, Bryn Mawr, Pa.; Renovo Hotel, Renovo, Pa.; The Mountain House, Cresson Springs, Pa.; The Sagamore, Lake George, N. Y.; The Baldwin, Beach Haven, N. J., among other prominent structures throughout the country. The firm have also done much important work in designing railway stations for the Pennsylvania, the New Jersey Central, the Philadelphia & Trenton, the Northern Central, the Philadelphia & Erie, the Allegheny Valley, the Baltimore & Potomac, the Belvidere Delaware, the Philadelphia & Long Branch, the Cumberland Valley, the New York, West Shore & Buffalo, and other railroads; also, passenger stations for the New York Elevated Railway, and many machine, shops, factories and car shops, for the leading railroads of the country. In the building of railroad bridges, this firm stands without a peer, and as regards highway bridges they are equally successful. They are also largely engaged in electric light work, boiler heating and electric light engineering in all its branches. They attend faithfully to all details, their plans are carefully studied and well digested, and they are fully prepared to design and supervise the erection of any building, not only promptly, but with that intelligent apprehension of design which has ever caused their efforts to be so highly appreciated.

HISTORICAL AND COMMERCIAL PHILADELPHIA.

UNION CENTRAL LIFE INSURANCE COMPANY, of Cincinnati, Ohio, J. W. Woods, Agent, Drexel Building.—The Union Central Life Insurance Company, of Cincinnati, Ohio, was incorporated in 1867, and is represented in Philadelphia by Mr. J. W. Woods, as general agent for the New England and Middle States, Maryland and the District of Columbia, with headquarters in the Drexel Building. This gentleman has been at the head of the agency here since 1885, and for fifteen years previously was agent for the company for the State of Pennsylvania. Under his expert and enterprising guidance, the affairs of the company are steadily prospering in this important territory. Among the elements that have contributed to the substantial growth of the Union Central and to its increasing favor among insurers, are its liberal contracts and generous dealing with policy-holders, together with the issuance of all safe and desirable forms of policies. The fact that large accessions are being made to its business without resort to other than the most legitimate measures is conclusive evidence of the high estimation in which this staunch and ably managed institution is regarded by the public, and proves that prudent and far-seeing men are becoming more and more generally convinced that insurance in such a company as the Union Central affords not only the safest, but also one of the most profitable, investments that can be made. This company has a cash capital of $100,000, while its assets at the close of the year 1891 amounted to $8,003,822.91. It issues endowment policies at life rates and all non-forfeitable and liberal forms of policies, while there is no investment safer, surer or more desirable and profitable than a ten, fifteen or twenty annual payment life rate endowment policy in this company, which its officers and agents confidently submit to the careful examination of all moneyed men. The officers of this company are among Cincinnati's best-known citizens and leading business men, whose names are a tower of strength to any undertaking with which they may be identified. The list is as follows, viz.: John M. Pattison, president; R. S. Rust, vice-president; E. P. Marshall, secretary; J. R. Clark, treasurer; W. L. Davis, cashier; Wm. B. Davis, M. D., medical director; C. W. Davis, M. D., assistant medical director; Ramsey, Maxwell & Ramsey, counsel; Directors, John M. Pattison, president Union Central Life Insurance Company; Wm. B. Davis, M. D., Cincinnati; Prof. W. G. Williams, LL.D., Ohio Wesleyan University, Delaware, O.; Wm. M. Ramsey, Ramsey, Maxwell & Ramsey, Cincinnati; Richard Dymond, of William Glenn & Sons, Cincinnati; R. S. Rust, LL.D, vice-president Union Central Life Insurance Company; J. R. Clark, treasurer Union Central Life Insurance Company; Peter Murphy, banker, Hamilton, O.; E. P. Marshall, secretary Union Central Life Insurance Company; A. J. Sage, D. D., Cincinnati; Sanford Hunt, D. D., agent Methodist Book Concern, New York. Mr. Woods, the agent here, was born in Cumberland Valley, and is a life resident of this city and a gentleman whose statements and representations are always thoroughly reliable.

T. JACKSON & CO., Real Estate Brokers, No. 711 Walnut Street.—Among the firms identified with the extensive business transacted in Philadelphia in real estate and loans, there is none more favorably known than that of J. T. Jackson & Co., which firm has been actively engaged in business for the past sixteen years as real estate brokers, buying and selling on commission. They have spacious and well-appointed offices on the first floor of the building No. 711 Walnut Street, where they transact a general real estate business, looking after details with efficiency and rendering experienced service in connection with the purchase, sale or renting of real estate, taking the entire charge of property for residents and non-residents, owners and estates; securing desirable tenants, collecting rents and interest, and making a leading specialty of the negotiation of mortgage loans, for which department of this business their connections and facilities are specially advantageous. The firm has acted as brokers in many of the largest deals on Chestnut and Market Streets within the past few years. They have on hand at all times for sale or lease, desirable lots and tracts, improved and unimproved, in the city and suburbs, and they make a prominent specialty of Lawnton, Oak Lane, Chelten Park, Melrose Ogontz, and Jenkintown building lots, being agents for these subdivisions, which contain several hundred acres, located along the P. & R. R. R. Mr. Jackson, who is now the sole proprietor of the business, is a native of Chester County, Penn., and is himself the owner of large real estate interests. The business was established sixteen years ago by him and the present style was assumed in 1881 on taking in a partner. The partnership expiring by limitation the title is still retained. Besides their business as above, they are general agents for the American Security and Trust Company of Washington D. C., capital $1,250,000 full paid, also for the International Loan and Trust Company of Kansas City, Mo., capital $1,000,000 full paid, and sell largely of their guaranteed first mortgages and interest bearing bonds in this market. Mr. Jackson is at all times prepared to offer attractive inducements to those desiring to invest in real estate and real estate securities, and his long experience, wide acquaintance, and efficient personal attention, has added steadily to the volume of his patronage and has secured for him a prominent place among the real estate brokers of this city.

CAMBRIA IRON COMPANY, Powell Stackhouse, President; W. S. Robinson, Secretary and Treasurer; John Fulton, General Manager, Offices No. 218 South Fourth Street. The wonderful development of American manufacturing interests has attracted the attention of the entire civilized world, and the State of Pennsylvania has great cause for congratulation that she is the principal center of the iron and steel industry of the nation. The natural advantages of this State are unequaled for securing to manufacturers the utmost facilities, while the liberal investment of capital is noticeable in the many extensive and magnificently equipped works all through the State, which are eligibly located for receiving the necessary materials, coal and iron ores. The representative and most progressive corporation in the iron and steel industry is recognized to be the Cambria Iron Company, whose offices are located at No. 218 South Fourth Street. This company was organized in 1852, with an authorized capital of $5,000,000, and operate at Johnstown, Pa. The works are equipped with thirteen Siemens furnaces, twenty-nine reverberating heating furnaces, one 24-inch two-set and one 21-inch three-set rail mill, two 21-inch three-set bar mills, one 12-inch four-set splice bar mill, one 16-inch three-set merchant mill, one 22 inch four-set puddle mill, one ten-set rod train, one 48-inch and one 40 inch blowing mill, making a total of thirty-four sets. The steel works were originally built in 1871, and have two 11-ton converters, with a capacity of $325,000 net tons ingots and two additional converters are nearly completed; three 30-ton open hearth furnaces and one 15-ton Krupp washer, with a capacity of 30,000 tons ingots. In the manufacture of steel rails this company has long held a leading position in the United States. The heavy importations of steel rails from Great Britain were greatly reduced through the energy and enterprise of this corporation, whose steel rails are fully equal in quality, strength and reliability to those of the most eminent foreign manufacturers. The tracks of many of the principal railroads of the United States have been laid wholly or in part with rails of this company's manufacture, and the works have a capacity of 225,000 tons of steel rails, besides 100,000 tons of steel in other shapes. At their Gautier steel department, originally built in 1878 and rebuilt in 1889, they have seven reverberatory heating furnaces, six train rolls and a full complement of other machinery, and produce merchant bar steel of all sizes for all purposes, making a specialty of tire, spring tuyere bars, etc., and producing 75,000 tons per year. The works of this department are now being very extensively enlarged. This company also operate six blast furnaces, which are supplied with ores from Michigan and which have a productive capacity of 350,000 tons of Bessemer pig and Spiegeleisen iron per year. The processes by which the manufacture of these specialties are conducted in the mills of this company are of the most perfect character, while the utmost care is exercised by the officers and managers to maintain the highest standard of excellence, so that the company's products are in heavy and constantly increasing demand in all parts of the country. The officers of the Cambria Iron Company are as follows, viz: Powell Stackhouse, president; Jno. W. Townsend, vice-president; J. Lowber Welsh, second vice-president; Wm. S. Robinson, secretary and treasurer; Harvey Ellis, assistant treasurer; A. P. Robinson, assistant secretary; C. S. Price, general manager; Cyrus Elder, solicitor and general agent; Fred. Krebs, superintendent Gautier steel department. These gentlemen are well and widely known as experienced iron and steel manufacturers, whose connection with the Cambria Iron Company gives it a leading position with the largest manufacturing corporations in America or Europe.

HISTORICAL AND COMMERCIAL PHILADELPHIA.

THE TRACY WORSTED MILLS CO., No. 2500 Spring Street.—The manufacture of worsted yarns may acceptably be denominated one of the leading industries of Philadelphia, and a vast amount of capital is invested in this line, and employment is furnished a large force of workmen. Among the oldest of the most prominent houses engaged in the trade, special mention should be made of the Tracy Worsted Mills Company, situated at No. 2500 Spring Street. This enterprise was founded in 1867 by Messrs. Griswold & Co., who became succeeded by Tracy & Co., and on March 3, 1880, the present company was organized, and incorporated under the State laws of Pennsylvania, with ample capital and the following officers: President, J. V. McCollum; secretary, R. C. Binder; treasurer, Chas. C. Roberts. These gentlemen have all had long and valuable experience in the yarn manufacturing industry, Mr. McCollum having been connected with this mill since it started, while Mr. Binder's experience covers a period of 25 years, Mr. Robert's 12 years, or an aggregate experience of 72 years; Mr. Joseph A. Perkins, the assistant superintendent and manager, has been 23 years in the trade, thus making a grand total of 92 years, or almost a century's experience that is brought to bear in the management of these mills. The plant is an extensive one, covering about an acre, on which are erected buildings of two, three and four stories each. The mechanical equipment includes 6,000 spindles, 13 cards and 18 combs, which are driven by a 500-horse power engine, and employment is found for 500 experienced operatives. The works have a productive capacity of 3500 pounds of yarn a day. The company manufacture a general line of worsted yarns for the production of cassimere cloths, which they sell to manufacturers of those fabrics. They also produce fancy yarns for handwork. The yarns are kept up to a high uniform standard of excellence, and sustain a first-class reputation in the trade.

UNITED FIREMEN'S INSURANCE CO., Office, No. 419 Walnut Street. Of the successful fire insurance corporations having their headquarters in Philadelphia, few are so well appreciated as the United Firemen's Insurance Company, whose home offices are located at No. 419 Walnut Street. This company was incorporated in 1860, under the laws of the State of Pennsylvania, and the following year it entered upon a career of usefulness which has been continued with increasing prosperity to itself and fully justifying the reliance placed upon it by the public. It has a capital stock of $200,000, and is officered as follows, viz: Robert B. Beath, president; Joseph L. Caven, vice-president; Dennis J. Sweeny, secretary; directors, Henry Bumm, William M. Singerly, Chas. M. Lukens, Alfred Moore, Holstein De Haven, Henry B. Tener, Geo. B. Bonnell, William Wood, Jacob F. Ridgway. This company writes insurance on dwellings and contents, manufactories and their products, elevators, warehouses, grain, merchandise and business property of all kinds, taking risks in all parts of the United States. It has local agents in all parts of the country, who report direct to the home office, and are doing a large and safe business in the States of Pennsylvania, New York, New Jersey, Maine, Vermont, Massachusetts, Rhode Island, Connecticut, Delaware, Maryland, Ohio, Michigan, Wisconsin, Minnesota, Iowa, Indiana, Illinois, Tennessee, Kentucky, Missouri, Kansas and California, as well as other parts of the Pacific Slope. General agents are established at San Francisco. Conservatism rather than haste, carefulness rather than impulsiveness, final profit rather than present volume of business, have been the leading mottoes of its insurance creed, and by a conscientious adherence to them its managers have made a record which mark them as among the successful insurance men of the country. The statement of the company made January 1, 1892, shows assets amounting to $1,190,614.49 and a net surplus of $84,115.27; while its business is constantly increasing owing to the moderation of its rates, the liberal character of its policies and the reliability of its management. Its present strength and efficient direction are sufficient guarantees of its future solidity, and it stands to-day a pillar of security to the insured. Its board of officers and directors presents an array of business talent and financial solidity which commands the unbounded respect and confidence of the entire community. The president, Mr. Beath, was secretary eleven years, and was elected to his present position in 1891; while the present secretary, Mr. Sweeny, has been engaged in the insurance business for a period of twenty years. The vice-president, Mr. Caven, was formerly president of the corporation, and is now president of the Real Estate Title and Trust Company of Philadelphia. Under such experienced guidance, the United Firemen's is writing some $350,000 in risks per year, and is recognized as one of the financial bulwarks of the city.

JOHN LYNCH & BRO., Flour Commission Merchants, No. 112 North Delaware Avenue. Among the various commercial enterprises that rank high in the material resources of Philadelphia, the trade in flour may be rightly classed as one of the first. This city has long occupied a prominent position in the trade as a distributing point for this food staple, and her wholesale commission merchants enjoy a widespread reputation for the facilities they have introduced, by means of which fresh and choice goods are furnished the trade. A foremost house annually handling an immense quantity of flour is that of John Lynch & Bro., located at No. 112 North Delaware Avenue. This enterprise was organized ten years ago by Messrs. John and Hugh Lynch, under the existing firm-name, and since then they have developed a large, first-class trade throughout Pennsylvania, New Jersey, Delaware and the South. The premises occupied comprise a store 25 x 150 feet in dimensions, and goods are also stored in two public warehouses. Consignments are received in carload lots from the West and Northwest, and the special brands handled are "Pillsbury's Best," "Purity," "Sea Foam," "White Frost," and others equally well known. The Messrs. Lynch handle goods direct from the mills and producers, on commission; and their connections with shippers are such as to enable them to fulfill orders promptly, and to the entire satisfaction of all concerned.

THE COMPOUND SPRING POWER COMPANY, (Incorporated), Business Office, No. 1014 Arch Street.—Prominent among the ingenious and valuable inventions of this modern utilitarian age may be named the spring power machines invented by Mr. D. M. Pfautz, of this city, and now owned and manufactured by the Compound Spring Power Company, whose business office is located at No. 1014 Arch Street. This company was incorporated December 18, 1890, with a capital of $300,000, and is officered as follows, viz: D. M. Pfautz, president and treasurer; A. H. Bryant, vice-president; E. B. Schuder, secretary. The company manufacture the compound spring sewing machine motor, which saves the labor of treading the machine and has no rival for simplicity of operation, the large amount of work it will perform in a day, and its perfect labor-saving qualities; the compound spring general motor, a more powerful machine, taking the place of any other small motor, to run grocers' coffee mills, printing presses, ventilating fans, etc.; the compound spring dynamo motor, which will drive a dynamo to produce the electric light for every house and store, every one having control of his own lights; and the compound spring quadricycle, a four wheeled cycle, running by spring power, would while running, under perfect control of the rider and able on a good road to run thirty miles per hour, creating a veritable revolution in the bicycle business. These machines are all found running at the company's office, and ladies, as well as gentlemen, will find a visit there both pleasant and profitable. The inventions are attracting the attention of capitalists and business men everywhere, and are sent to all parts of the country. Mr. Pfautz is now engaged in constructing his new patents for street car propulsion, which promise to excel all present systems in street cars, and also his spiral motors for propelling boats. The president, Mr. Pfautz, is a native of Lancaster, Pa., who came to this city in 1868 and has given the subject of spring power the study of a lifetime. His ideas are thoroughly practical, based on natural laws, and his success is as well merited as it is decisive and pronounced. Mr. Bryant, the vice-president, was born in Buffalo, N. Y., and has resided here for the past twenty-five years, while the secretary, Mr. Schuder, is a Philadelphian by birth and education, and belongs to one of the oldest families in the city, and his ancestors were among the leading men in the Masonic Fraternity of this city. All the officers devote close personal attention to the advancement of the interests of the company, and assure its permanent prosperity by their intelligent enterprise and honorable methods.

Chestnut Street, looking West from Ninth Street. 1880.

HISTORICAL AND COMMERCIAL PHILADELPHIA.

ILLIAM C. MORGAN & CO. General Stock Brokers, No. 421 Drexel Building.—Among the leading and reliable bankers and brokers of Philadelphia is the firm of William C. Morgan & Co. This prosperous house was established in 1863 and now is one of the oldest firms on the street. They bring to bear a wide range of practical experience coupled with intimate knowledge of values, and number among their permanent customers many wealthy capitalists, stock operators and business men. They buy and sell strictly on commission all stocks, bonds and miscellaneous securities. They have every facility for obtaining the earliest information affecting any security, and faithfully serve the best interests of customers. They make a specialty of first class investment securities, such as State, city and county bonds, etc., and those in need of financial aid will find them prepared to make the most liberal terms, making advances on approved collateral. They are widely known in financial circles for their ability and integrity, and can be recommended to our readers as well qualified to give sound and reliable information as to all classes of securities either for investment or for speculative purposes. Their correspondents in all the principal cities keep them fully posted on all that is going on in the financial world. Mr. Morgan, the head of the firm, is a Philadelphian by birth. His long experience in his special line has brought him a host of patrons, who have learned to appreciate his valuable and efficient services.

ORRIS, TASKER & CO. (Incorporated), Manufacturers of Boiler Tubes, Oil Well Tubing and Casing, Wrought Iron Pipes and Fittings, Iron Founders, Gas Engineers and Machinists, City Office, Nos. 222 and 224 South Third Street.—The magnitude of the vast manufacturing interests centred and represented in Philadelphia has long rendered her the leading industrial emporium on this continent. There are various causes for the supremacy thus maintained, among which are its near proximity to inexhaustible supplies of ores, coal and natural gas, its unexampled transportation facilities by rail and water, and the distinguished enterprise and ample resources of its leading manufacturers and business men. The great representative house in its line, and the pioneer in several of the most difficult branches of the iron industry, is that of Morris, Tasker & Co. (Incorporated), who have a reputation and a trade coextensive with the limits of the country as extensive manufacturers of boiler tubes, oil well tubing and casing, wrought iron pipes and fittings, and as iron founders, gas engineers and machinists, with office and warerooms at Nos. 222 and 224 South Third Street. This corporation are proprietors of the Delaware Iron Company's Mills at New Castle, Del., and of the Pascal Iron Works in Philadelphia, and give employment to from 1,500 to 2,000 workmen. The foundation of this great enterprise was laid in 1821 by Mr. S. P. Morris, who in 1831 admitted his brother, Henry Morris, and Mr. Thomas T. Tasker, his former superintendent, to partnership under the firm name of Stephen P. Morris & Co. The business grew to proportions of great magnitude, and eventually the head of the firm retired, being succeeded by his brother, Wistar Morris, the firm then becoming Morris, Tasker & Morris. This firm erected the Pascal Iron Works here in 1836, on the square bounded by Tasker, Morris, Fourth and Fifth Streets, and in 1846 added a large mill fronting on Morris Street. Mr. Wistar Morris subsequently retired, and Messrs. Charles Wheeler and Thomas T. Tasker, Jr., were admitted under the now so familiar style of Morris, Tasker & Co. Mr. Henry Morris retired in 1856 in favor of his son, Stephen Morris, and in 1858 Mr. Thomas T. Tasker, Sr., retired, his interest being divided between his sons, Thomas T., already a member, and Stephen P. M. Tasker, now admitted. Mr. Charles Wheeler retired in 1864, followed by the retirement of Mr. Henry G. Morris, and on the death of Mr. Stephen Morris his interest was purchased by the surviving partners, Messrs. Thomas T. Tasker, Jr., and Stephen P. M. Tasker. In 1876 Mr. Thomas T. Tasker, Jr., disposed of his interest, and Messrs. Charles Wheeler and T. Wistar Brown being admitted, a joint stock company was formed, composed of Messrs. Stephen P. M. Tasker, Charles Wheeler and T. Wistar Brown. In 1883 occurred the decease of Mr. Wheeler, and on February 8, 1888, the term of the limited partnership having expired, a corporation was duly organized under the present name, with a capital of $500,000, and with the following officers—to wit, Andrew Wheeler, President; Jonathan Rowland, Vice President; T. Wistar Brown, Treasurer; Stephen P. M. Tasker, Consulting Engineer; H. C. Vansant, Secretary. The Pascal Iron Works form a very important factor in the industrial activity of this city. The plant covers two city blocks, spacious and splendidly equipped mills and shops, and every modern facility for the rapid and perfect production of gas works' outfits, retorts, holders, etc., all kinds of heavy castings, wrought iron pipe of all sizes, and fittings and extra lap welded tubes for boilers. The output here averages 25,000 tons of finished work per year, and large contracts are taken for the erection of gas and water works complete. The works at New Castle, Del., were designed and constructed under the management of Mr. Stephen P. M. Tasker, and are the model of the kind, including a rolling mill, a lap welded pipe mill, furnaces, etc., which turn out from thirty-six to forty thousand tons of finished pipe, ranging from one-eighth up to twenty-two inches in diameter, annually, and for which there is always a great and growing demand. The capacity of the works owned and controlled by Morris, Tasker & Co., the industrial forces employed and the ample capital invested, all characterize this concern as the leader in its line in America, and one whose superior products are in universal demand by the trade and consumers. The material and workmanship are both subjected to the closest inspection and guaranteed, and municipal corporations, gas and water companies the country over largely use these products in preference to all other brands. The facilities of the works are as perfect as its connections are widespread and influential; the largest orders are filled immediately on terms and prices which are not to be duplicated elsewhere, while the principles that regulate the business policy of the house are such as entitle it to general respect and confidence, while the great extent of its operations has made its position one of national prominence and placed its officers and managers in the front rank of Pennsylvania's industrial representatives. President Wheeler resides at Bryn Mawr, and is a member of the firm of Morris, Wheeler & Co., in the same line of industry; also a Director of the Central National Bank and the Delaware Insurance Company, one of the original promoters of the Philadelphia Bourse, and a prominent member of the Board of Trade. Mr. T. Wistar Brown, Treasurer of the company, is also Vice President of the Provident Life and Trust Company, a Director of the Central National Bank, a member of the dry goods manufacturing firm of John Farnum & Co., besides being identified with many other local institutions and enterprises, and resides at Valla Nova. Vice President Rowland is a well known citizen of Holmesburgh, while Messrs. Tasker and Vansant reside in Philadelphia, and are promoting the interests of this corporation with zeal, discrimination and brilliant success.

EO. D. WETHERILL & CO., Importers and Dealers in Drugs, Chemicals, Etc.; Manufacturers of White Lead, Colors, Putty and Calcite, Atlas Ready Mixed Paints; No. 56 N. Front Street.—One of the oldest and best known houses in the manufacture of paints in this country is that of Messrs. Geo. D. Wetherill & Co. This firm are extensive importers and dealers in drugs, chemicals, etc., and manufacturers of paints, white lead, colors, putty and calcite, making a specialty of Atlas Ready Mixed Paints. The business was founded in 1807 by John Wetherill & Co., and in 1816 the senior partner retired and the present name and style was adopted. The present members of the firm, Messrs. Geo. D. and Thomas Wetherill, are brothers, and sons of Christopher Wetherill, who died in 1891, after being in the firm for a period of fifty years. The works comprise five buildings, of four stories each, and are equipped with forty paint mills, four putty mills, and the latest improved machinery, operated by a steam engine of 400 horse power. The store of the firm is five stories in height, 18x125 feet in size, and every department is kept stocked to repletion at all times. The firm have long enjoyed a national reputation, and built up a trade coextensive with the limits of the country, as manufacturers of the celebrated Atlas Ready Mixed Paints. These paints are always uniform and reliable, unrivalled in appearance, unexcelled in durability, unparalleled in economy, unequaled in convenience, unprecedented in reputation, and undisputed in the broad claim of being the best article of the kind on the market. They are easily applied, and are unapproached and unapproachable in any feature of merit, effectiveness and beauty. This firm are also selling agents for John L. Whiting & Sons, brush manufacturers, of Boston. The Messrs. Wetherill are well known Philadelphians, honored members of such organizations as the National Wholesale Drug Association, the Philadelphia Drug Exchange, the Manufacturers' Club, the Trade League, the Philadelphia Bourse, the Board of Trade and the Philadelphia Paint Club.

HISTORICAL AND COMMERCIAL PHILADELPHIA.

URK & McFETRIDGE, Printers, Lithographers and Publishers, Nos. 306 and 308 Chestnut Street.—A leading firm of printers, lithographers and publishers here are Messrs. Burk & McFetridge, who occupy the very spacious and eligible quarters at Nos. 306 and 308 Chestnut Street. This firm was organized and began business September 15, 1877, having purchased from W. W. Harding the "Inquirer" book and job printing establishment, which they have since conducted with marked ability and steadily increasing success. The premises occupied comprise four floors, 75 x 80 feet each, splendidly equipped with new and improved presses and machinery, and ample steam-power, and constant employment is here provided for 100 skilled and expert hands. This firm are widely known for their many important publications of books, newspapers and periodicals, while they do a very large and influential business as commercial printers and lithographers with corporations, firms and individuals all over the United States. They are especially prominent as publishers of "Reciprocity," a semi-monthly journal devoted to the enlargement of domestic trade and the extension of international commercial reciprocity, and which has a wide circulation throughout the United States, Great Britain, Germany, France, Mexico, Central and South America, China, the East Indies, Australasia, and other parts of the globe; subscription price $3.00 per annum. This firm also publish "Philadelphia and New York Securities," a book full of all necessary information regarding investments, and whose scope makes it at once a directory, blue book and statistical manual combined; comprising as it does detailed information respecting the financial, banking, trust, insurance, railway, mining, telegraph, telephone, steamship, storage and manufacturing companies. Much of the data found in this work is absolutely exclusive, being nowhere else obtainable, and in the two years of its existence his work has become the authorized and recognized authority in Philadelphia financial circles, while it is used in all the principal cities of the Union, and commands appropriate recognition upon the London Stock Exchange. Under the enterprising methods of Messrs. Burk and McFetridge, this house has not only become one of the best-patronized printing establishments in the city, but from its history and literary prestige, a place of special interest to public and professional men. Here are wont to gather many of those most conspicuous in literature, politics and finance, for the interchange of information upon congenial topics. Orders and communications by telephone No. 710, by telegraph or mail, receive immediate attention, and in every department, as publishers, printers, lithographers, editors and compilers, the house is a type of true American enterprise and literary genius and skill. The copartners, Messrs. Wm. M. Burk and John R. McFetridge, are native Philadelphians, who have given their business a life study.

UPPLEE HARDWARE COMPANY, Manufacturers, Importers and Dealers in Hardware, Cutlery, Lamps, Etc., Nos. 503 Market and 4 and 6 North Fifth Streets. A thoroughly important and representative establishment in Philadelphia and one which materially adds to its facilities as the best purchasing point in the United States, is that of the Supplee Hardware Company, located at Nos. 503 Market and 4 and 6 North Fifth Streets. This company are extensive manufacturers, importers and dealers in hardware, cutlery, lamps, etc., and theirs is the oldest as well as the largest house in its line in the city. The business was founded in 1830, by Conrad & Walton, sale place in 1867 to Lloyd, Supplee & Walton, and they in turn, in 1881, to the Lloyd & Supplee Hardware Co., the present company being incorporated in 1889. It has a capital of $500,000, and is officered as follows, viz: William W. Supplee, president; Newton F. Cressman, secretary; William D. Supplee, treasurer. The business qualifications of these gentlemen are of a very high order, their methods are prompt, honourable and equitable, and they have ever retained the confidence and esteem of leading commercial and financial circles. The premises occupied for trade purposes comprise five floors and a basement, 50 x 150 feet each, with ell, 45 x 50 feet, and an additional warehouse on North Street. Here is emphatically a vast depot for hardware, tools, and builders' supplies, where can at all times be found the fullest and most comprehensive stock of hardware, also table and pocket cutlery from the most famous manufacturers of Europe and America, lamps and lamp goods in brilliant array, and many specialties peculiar to this house. To attempt an enumeration of the articles displayed by this company would be to present our readers with an immense catalogue, suffice it to say, "they keep everything." Among prominent specialties which they control are the "Pennsylvania," the "Quaker City" and "Continental" lawn mowers, which stand ahead of all competitors in this or any other country. As manufacturers they also make specialties of meat cutters, and saw-sets, and many other articles which are in heavy and influential demand in this and foreign countries. Their "Pennsylvania" lawn-mowers were awarded the only premium given in this line at Paris, in 1889. Price and quality combined are beyond successful competition by any other first-class house in the trade, and the business is immense and influential throughout all the Middle, Southern and Western States, requiring in its transaction the services of eighty assistants and twenty-four salesmen upon the road. The officers of the company are native Philadelphians, who have pushed their way, by force of energy and character, to a commanding position in the mercantile world, and are recognized as worthy exponents of the hardware trade of this country. President Supplee is a well-known member of the Trades' League, the Commercial Exchange, the Manufacturers' Club, the Union League and the Philadelphia Bourse. Secretary Cressman has been identified with the house for twenty years, and Treasurer Supplee, a son of the president, was trained in the business from his youth up, and all are promoting the interests of the company with zeal, discrimination and brilliant success.

ANAYUNK TRUST COMPANY, No. 4340 Main Street, Manayunk.—The Manayunk Trust Company is the only institution of this kind in Manayunk, and was chartered in 1890. It occupies spacious and elegant quarters in its own building, at No. 4340 Main Street, and is liberally patronized by our best citizens. This company acts as administrator, executor, guardian and trustee to receive and execute trusts of all kinds; while loans are made on mortgages on the installment plan, mortgages are bought and sold, and a general real estate business is transacted. Every description of realty is bought and sold, rents are collected, property is leased and rented, and estates managed for absent owners, while the latter go to enjoy travel and European life for years at a time. The company's cash department is a thoroughly organized banking institution, where interest is paid on deposits, at the rate of two per cent. on checks at sight and three per cent. on deposits subject to ten days' notice; while trusts and indemnity certificates are issued for one year, bearing four per cent. interest, interest payable every six months. If you wish to buy a house or invest your money in a mortgage, this company will make you absolutely safe against defective titles and incumbrances. If you intend building, this company will, for a small price, draw the agreement with your builder and see that he fulfills it; pay the mechanics and material men and insure you against liens. If you are the owner or holder of a mortgage and would like to have the title examined, and if a defect or incumbrance is discovered have the same removed, this company will attend to the business for you. A thorough system of organization pervades the whole of the departments, and the prompt and efficient manner in which this extensive business is transacted is in the highest degree creditable to the management. The officers and directors of the company are as follows: President, Richard Hey; vice-president, Graham J. Littlewood; secretary and treasurer, Thomas H. Ashton; attorney-at-law and trust officer, Francis S. Cantrell. Directors, Richard Hey, of Richard Hey & Son, manufacturers; Graham J. Littlewood, of G. J. Littlewood & Co., dyers; John G. Morris, of Morris & Ott, manufacturers; Ben Kenworthy, of B. Kenworthy & Co., wool; Charles W. Klauder, coal and feed; Henry Fitzmann, merchant; William Bernard, coal; George W. Bromley, of G. W. Bromley & Co., civil and topographical engineers; James Z. Holt, of Baker, Holt & Co., manufacturers; John J. Foran, real estate agent; Edward Foster, of E. Foster & Bro., hardware; Charles J. Webb, of C. J. Webb & Co., wool; Joseph H. Kenworthy, of T. Kenworthy & Bro., wool; P. P. Liebert, of Liebert & Obert, brewers; J. H. Birkmire, stone yard. The executive officers are gentlemen with whom it is always a pleasure to do business, while the board of directors presents an array of talent and solidity that commands the respect and confidence of the entire community.

HISTORICAL AND COMMERCIAL PHILADELPHIA.

W. KURTZ & CO., Bankers & Brokers, Bullitt Building, No. 131 South Fourth Street.—One of the leading bankers and brokers of Philadelphia is Mr. W. W. Kurtz, carrying on operations under the firm title of W. W. Kurtz & Co. He was born in Gettysburg, Pa., but has resided in this city for many years. In business and financial circles he bears an unsullied reputation. In 1865, in company with a partner, he established business as a banker and broker, the firm name being Kurtz & Howard, but on the retirement of Mr. Howard, Mr. Kurtz adopted the present firm title. For the past twenty-two years he has been a popular member of the Philadelphia Stock Exchange, and was once honored by being elected to the presidency of that institution. Employing a staff of efficient assistants, Mr. Kurtz carries on a splendid business, receiving deposits, making investments of capital, and buying, selling and carrying on margin stocks and bonds of all kinds. Herzfeld & Co. are his New York agents, and the latest financial news may always be had at his office.

HOWELL & BROS., LIMITED, Manufacturers of Wall Papers, Washington Avenue and Twenty-first Street.—This house has the distinguished honor of being the oldest in the wall paper industry in the United States, and has long been a recognized leader in the trade. The founder of the business, John B. Howell, father of Mr. Zophar C. Howell, came from England in 1793, and started in the manufacture of wall paper in this city the same year. He subsequently moved to New York City, and from there to Albany, where he admitted Mr. Lemuel Steel to partnership, as Howell & Co. In 1817 the business was transferred to Baltimore, and in 1825 was permanently located in Philadelphia. Five sons of Mr. Howell became engaged in the business, and in 1885 the firm name of Howell Bros. was adopted. The present proprietors are Messrs. Zophar C. Howell and Zophar L. Howell. The senior partner is a son of the founder, and was born in Albany, N. Y., on January 31st, 1811, becoming a member of the firm in 1839. The present manufactory was built for the purpose in 1865, and the main building is 214x396 feet, which, with the other premises and grounds occupied by the firm, comprise an entire square. The equipment is perfect and complete in all departments, every improvement and modern appliance being in use to facilitate production, including improved machinery operated by a Corliss engine of 150 horse power, and steady employment is given to 250 operatives. The firm have secured the services of a corps of original and tasteful designers, who are expert judges of shades and effects, and are eminently successful in producing patterns that will best serve the purpose of harmonious designs in house decoration. Gold and highly colored parlor and drawing room papers, with beautiful dadoes and friezes to match; also rich library paperings, in imitation of leather, carved oak and walnut; and plain and embossed flocks, are all manufactured here in great variety, and extremely rich and pleasing effects are produced in comparatively inexpensive goods. The output averages 10,000,000 pieces per year. The proprietors are gentlemen with whom it is always a pleasure to do business. The honored senior partner is President of the Camden National Bank, and has been a contributor to the Franklin Institute since its organization, and long prominent in commercial and financial circles. Mr. Z. L. Howell was born in this city, is a director of the Camden National Bank, and combines his energy and ability with the ripe experience of his father to form a firm of commanding influence and solid worth.

THOS. THOMPSON, SONS & CO., Manufacturers and Importers of Upholstery Goods, Cabinet Hardware, and Railroad Car Supplies, No. 242 South Second Street.—The leading representative house engaged in this branch of business is generally regarded as that of Messrs. Thos. Thompson, Sons & Co. This extensive business was founded in 1858 by Thomas Thompson, who embarked in the manufacture and importation of upholstery goods, cabinet hardware and railroad car supplies, with every resource and facility at command for those early days, and soon developed widespread trade connections. The firm name of Thos. Thompson, Sons & Co. was adopted some forty years ago, and the business is now conducted by Messrs. Thomas M. and Lewis A. Thompson. The honored senior partner and founder of the business died in 1878, and his sons have since continued the enterprise without change in the firm name. Their operations cover every branch of the upholstery goods trade, as well as that pertaining to cabinet hardware, while they are likewise prominent as manufacturers of elastic car seat springs of unequalled strength and elasticity, besides everything in the line of railroad car supplies. They steadily retain the foremost place in the trade, in the introduction of many exclusive novelties in styles, textures, patterns and shades of upholstery goods. They occupy a splendid five story building, 35x130 feet in dimensions, finely equipped and admirably arranged in every department. Here the firm display a very heavy stock of goods, the most extensive and valuable of any in the city, including high art fabrics of every description, inclusive of the popular Renaissance styles; silk damasks, velours and raw silks in vast variety; brocatels, sateens, plushes and satins; gimps, fringes and trimmings; and all shades of decorative silks and fabrics; besides cabinet hardware of the best brands. The trade of the house is thoroughly national in extent, and Philadelphia is to be congratulated upon having permanently located in her midst such a representative house in its line as that of Thos. Thompson, Sons & Co. Hon. Thomas M. Thompson is the present comptroller of the city, elected from January 1, 1891; while he was for years on the Finance Committee in the City Council, has been President of the Furniture Board of Trade, and is a prominent member of the Union League, and honorably identified with the commercial growth and financial prosperity of the city. Mr. Lewis A. Thompson is also an honored member of the Union League, and an active member of Grace Episcopal Church. Both are native Philadelphians.

J. J. MOHR, Anthracite and Charcoal Pig Iron, Coke, Car Wheels, Muck Bar, Bullitt Building, No. 131 South Fourth Street.—Mr. J. J. Mohr established his business here in 1870, and handles foundry and forge pig iron, muck bars, coke, car wheels, etc.; being especially prominent as agent for the E. & G. Brooke Iron Company, receiving the entire output of six furnaces, the Sheridan, Leesport, Mt. Laurel, Mill Creek, Brooke and Joanna having a combined capacity of 3,500 tons per week, and also a part of Temple furnace. He ships direct from the furnace, and also handles Connellsville and Gallatin coke, old car wheels, and the Brooke muck bars as a specialty. With his exceptional connections and facilities this gentleman is in a position to offer special inducements, quoting bottom prices and supplying the best quality, and relations once formed with him are reasonably certain of leading to an enduring business connection. The trade of the house extends to all parts of the United States, and the supplies furnished invariably give satisfaction and command an immense sale wherever once introduced. Mr. Mohr is a native Pennsylvanian, a merchant for some years previous to engaging in his present trade, and a gentleman of large business experience, wide acquaintance and sterling personal worth.

WM. H. WIGMORE, Manufacturer, for the Trade Exclusively, of Gold, Silver and Plated Surgical Instruments, No. 107 S. Eighth Street.—The only manufacturer of surgical instruments for the trade exclusively, is Mr. Wm. H. Wigmore. For the past thirteen years this gentleman has been conducting active operations in this field of enterprise. He established the business through his own thrift, ability, earnest and untiring work, and to him belongs the credit of its success. The works are comprised in two commodious floors, 30x87 feet in dimensions, and the mechanical equipment includes special machinery driven by electric power. Employment is found for twenty-seven skilled hands, and under the personal guidance of Mr. Wigmore are manufactured gold, silver, and plated surgical instruments of every variety, many of them being of Mr. Wigmore's own invention. The goods are finely finished and thoroughly reliable in every particular. A complete stock is carried, wholesale orders only are given attention, and the trade of the house extends all over the United States. Mr. Wigmore was born at Red Bank, N. J., and has lived in Philadelphia twenty years. Mr. Wigmore is also an authority and specialist on poultry and cattle specialties, including caponizing, and manufactures instruments largely for this line, and is the author of a treatise on how to make poultry pay.

HISTORICAL AND COMMERCIAL PHILADELPHIA.

HE ALDINE HOTEL, S. Murray Mitchell, Proprietor, W. F. Perry, Manager, Rates $4.50 to $5.00 per Day, Parlor and Baths Extra, Chestnut Street above Nineteenth.—Philadelphia has among her valued facilities and advantages, the magnificent Aldine Hotel, one of the finest modern structures of the kind in the United States, and by far the most luxurious, elegant and comfortable hotel in the city. Mr. S. Murray Mitchell, the enterprising proprietor, has been in control since 1879, and has become widely recognized as an expert authority on the difficult science of modern hotel keeping. Numerous additions have since been made to its capacity and accommodations, and the house is now seven stories in height, 125 x 225 feet in dimensions, and contains 235 rooms for guests, many of them being en suite. The building was specially planned to secure the utmost of light, air and ventilation, and was constructed in the most substantial manner, and in a handsome style of architecture. It represents a very large investment both in the premises and in the rich character of the furniture and decorations, in which has been brought into play the highest art and skill of the designer, upholsterer, cabinet-maker and furnisher. The public halls, parlors, reception-rooms, dining halls and other apartments are elegant in appearance and outfit, and nowhere outside of the largest capitals of the world can such a happy combination of elegance, taste and comfort be found. All the modern improvements have been introduced, including fire-escapes, steam heat, electric lights, passenger elevator, annunciators, telegraph office, billiard parlors, barber-shop, and a well-managed bar, stocked with the finest of wines and liquors. The steam-engine and boiler are located entirely outside of the premises, under the pavement on Sansom Street; the laundry is also isolated, and the culinary department is in the fireproof basement, with ventilating shafts which carry all odors to the roof. There is a fine courtyard in the center of the lot, with sparkling fountain and fragrant flowers, and everything in the surroundings suggests the refining influences of a quiet and pleasant home. The house is conducted strictly on the American plan, and nowhere can families, tourists excursion parties, public men and private individuals be better accommodated. The main dining hall is a noble apartment, 25 x 144 feet, where many public dinners and notable banquets have been held, and the house is as widely celebrated for its cuisine and bills of fare as for the elegance of its accommodations and the excellence of its management. The service is perfect, and guests dine a la carte at this hotel in a manner unrivaled on the continent. The house holds the patronage of the best classes of society, and its registers are filled with the names of eminent capitalists, professional and public men, foreign tourists and visitors, who find here strictly high-class hotel accommodations. The situation of the hotel, on Chestnut Street, just above Nineteenth, is thoroughly central and desirable, and no luxury to be found in any hotel in the country is lacking at the "Aldine." Mr. Mitchell is a native of Harrisburg, and has been a resident of this city since 1869. He is ably assisted by Mr. W. F. Perry, as manager, and has won success and wide celebrity, as a hotel man, by honestly deserving it.

W. JOHNS MANUFACTURING COMPANY, Philadelphia Branch, Nos. 170 and 172 North Fourth Street, Main Office, No. 87 Maiden Lane, New York; Eastern Branch, Nos. 119 and 121 Federal Street, Boston; Western Branch, Nos. 240 and 242 Randolph Street, Chicago.—Until within a few years comparatively, mineral asbestos, which has now proved so invaluable for structural and mechanical purposes, was almost totally unknown, except to the chemist and a few others who were happily possessed of more than ordinary knowledge of the subtle sciences. The leading manufacturer in this line in this country is the H. W. Johns Manufacturing Company, whose principal office is at No. 87 Maiden Lane, New York, with a branch at Nos. 170 and 172 North Fourth Street, Philadelphia. This company is renowned the world over as a manufacturer of asbestos, and materials for structural, mechanical and electrical purposes. The business was established in 1858, by Mr. H. W. Johns, who is the inventor of nearly all the practical uses of asbestos and also of the materials and special processes made and used by this company, and the enterprise was continued by him until 1870, when, in consequence of its rapid increase, it was duly incorporated into the company bearing his name, since which period it has obtained a widely extended patronage, owing to the unequaled facilities afforded for manufacturing and the unsurpassed quality, utility and durability of its asbestos and other materials. The branch office in this city was established in 1876, and is now under the management of Mr. D. T. Dickson, who came into control on July 1, 1891, as successor to Mr. J. G. Granbery, who had been made treasurer of the company. The building here occupied for trade purposes contains five floors and a basement, 40 x 100 feet each, giving ample accommodations for supplying the most extensive demand. The leading specialties sold here at both wholesale and retail are paints and colors, roofing and building materials, steam pipe coverings, steam packings, fireproof cements, asbestos fabrics, tubes, blocks, etc., and "Vulcabeston." The latter article is patented, and is composed of asbestos, India rubber and other vulcanizable gums combined with materials for special requirements, adapting it for fire and acid proof articles, steam packings, electrical insulators, etc. It is superior to any other material yet discovered for similar purposes, on account of its permanent resistance to heat and immunity from injury by acids, gases, moisture, etc. It can be made in any desired form, is practically indestructible, will not shrink, expand or warp, and is the most perfect electrical insulator known. The liquid paints made by this company are strictly first-class, composed of pure linseed oil and the highest grade of pigments. They are combined by processes exclusively the property of the company, and are unequaled by any in richness, permanency of color and durability, and are now generally regarded as the standard paints for structural purposes, of which this company is the most extensive manufacturer in the world. Their asbestos roofing is practically fireproof and the acknowledged standard for roofing purposes. The trade and consumers are supplied in quantities to suit the shortest possible notice and terms and prices are made invariably satisfactory to buyers.

ALFRED HUMBERT, (The National Watch Case and Jewelry Manufacturing Company,) Manufacturer of High-grade Gold Watch Cases, Diamond Mountings, Jewelry, Fancy Rings, Solid Seamless Wrought Gold Rings, Sole Eastern Agent Rockford Silver Plate Company, Nos. 715, 717, 719 Arch Street. The leader in this city in the important lines of diamond mountings, watch case and gold ring manufacturing and jewelry repairing, is acknowledged by expert judges to be Mr. Alfred Humbert, whose headquarters are located at Nos. 715, 717, and 719 Arch Street. This representative house was founded in 1838, by Mr. Gustavus Gigon, and, after some changes, Mr. Humbert became sole proprietor in 1876, and again succeeding to the business of the National Watch Case and Jewelry Manufacturing Co., in 1890. The manufacturing plant covers an area of 65 x 300 feet, and is splendidly equipped with new and improved machinery and ample steam-power, while steady employment is given to between sixty and seventy-five skilled and expert hands. The high-grade gold watch cases manufactured are of the very finest and most artistic description, suited to the requirements of the best class of American made and imported Swiss watches, and in heavy and appreciative demand by the trade. Mr. Humbert turns out only the highest grade of goods in all departments, and his solid seamless wrought gold rings are the acme of perfection. In diamond mounting, watch case and jewelry repairing, Mr. Humbert is prepared to guarantee the finest and most reliable service. He is also sole Eastern agent of the Rockford Silver Plate Company. There have been numerous patents granted for so-called improved imitation diamonds, under various names, but all are defective as they are either coated on the back with metal which washes off or are transparent at center, usually styled in the trade "fish-eyed," and it does not matter how fine the paste is, it always betrays itself at center, being at that spot transparent, like glass. With the "Monarch Brilliant," of this house this trouble is entirely overcome; it is the nearest approach to a diamond, and is creating a sensation in the trade wherever presented; it is the coming leader in the trade over all imitation diamonds yet placed on the market. The factory at this date is overwhelmed with orders; it is a red letter year with the house, the amount of trade on that article alone proving almost phenomenal. A corps of expert salesmen represent the interests of the house upon the road, and all orders and commissions are promptly and perfectly fulfilled at terms and prices which are invariably satisfactory to the trade. Mr. Humbert is a native of New York city, and a recognized expert and connoisseur in the manufacture of watch cases, gold jewelry, and the setting of diamonds.

114   HISTORICAL AND COMMERCIAL PHILADELPHIA.

PHILADELPHIA KNITTING MILLS CO., Sixteenth Street and Indiana Avenue. Though but a comparatively short time established, the Philadelphia Knitting Mills Co., Sixteenth Street and Indiana Avenue, has built up an exceedingly large business. They are manufacturers of silk and cotton hosiery of a distinctly superior quality, and their productions command extensive sale throughout the United States. The plant is perfectly equipped in every respect, the facilities being unsurpassed, and the trade of the concern affords evidence of steady and substantial increase. The Philadelphia Knitting Mills Co., of which Wm. H. Bilyeru is president and treasurer, G. H. Frazier, secretary, and Charles Möller, manager, was organized in 1890, and the signal success that has attended the venture from its inception amply attests the wisdom that inspired the enterprise, to say nothing of the merit of the goods. The mill is a three-story, 50 x 100 feet brick structure, with a spacious one-story brick building in connection, used for weaving, and the concern is fitted up with full steam-power and the latest improved machinery, etc. There are three hundred knitting heads of various kinds in operation here, and upward of one hundred and twenty operatives are employed in the establishment. The company manufactures a complete line of ladies' and gentlemen's full fashioned silk and cotton hose in fine grades and in a great variety of pretty designs, styles and shades, and carry a very large and elegant stock. They sell direct to the largest jobbing and retail houses in the United States, and are in a position to offer liberal inducements, the prices quoted being notably low, superiority of production considered. The gentlemen above named are all Philadelphians by birth, and men of standing in the community, prominent and esteemed in business circles and in social life.

JOSEPH PARKER'S SONS, "Combination Stores," No. 1823 Germantown Avenue. A review of Germantown's noteworthy mercantile houses would hardly be complete without more than passing mention of Joseph Parker's Sons' "combination stores." This is the oldest and the largest establishment of the kind in this section of the city, and for above forty-one years has been steadily growing in popularity and patronage. The business was established in 1851 by Joseph Parker, who conducted the same up to about two years ago, when it passed into control of his sons and successors, Hiram T., John T. and William V., who under the firm-name that heads this sketch have since continued it with uninterrupted success. The place of business has always been on this street, and has been at the present location since 1872. The premises occupied here comprise three spacious floors, and are neatly fitted up and well arranged throughout. There are eight different departments, and seven or more clerks are in attendance, the proprietors themselves exercising immediate supervision over the entire concern. A vast and varied stock is constantly kept on hand here, and includes stationery and fancy goods of all kinds; hosiery and gents' furnishing goods, trunks and traveling bags; baseball, cricket and tennis outfits; toys, games and novelties in great variety; also pocket and table cutlery, housekeeping hardware, china and glassware, crockery, kitchen specialties and a large assortment of baby carriages, express wagons, wheelbarrows, velocipedes, etc., etc., together with a multifarious collection of useful and ornamental articles of a household nature. The prices charged here are notably low, exceptional bargains being offered in housekeeping specialties, while every article is warranted to be as represented, and shoppers are always assured of finding courteous treatment, as well as honorable dealing in this old-time and popular emporium. The Messrs. Parker, who are gentlemen in the prime of life, born here in Germantown, are all men of thorough business experience, active and energetic, and unless all the signs are greatly at fault, the popularity and prosperity of the establishment are bound to increase and endure under their efficient management.

GLOVER BROS., Iron Foundry and Hardware Works, Mill Street and Penn. R. R., Frankford. The iron foundry and hardware works of Glover Bros., Mill Street and Penn. R.R., were established in 1885 by the firm named. They were formerly located at Kensington Avenue and Green Street, and removed to the present place about a year ago. The premises here occupied cover one and a half acres of ground, and the plant is thoroughly equipped. The main building is a commodious two-story brick structure provided with ample steam-power and all needed appliances and appurtenances, and fifty-five in help are employed. Light and medium castings and hardware specialties are turned out to order here at short notice, and perfect satisfaction is assured, the facilities being of a superior character. Patterns are called for and castings delivered in the city daily, and all orders receive prompt and personal attention, while all work done is warranted to be strictly first-class. Messrs. Thomas and John H. Glover, the proprietors, are gentlemen in the prime of life, active and energetic, and are natives of this city. They are both men of thorough practical skill and many years' experience, and exercise immediate supervision over all work executed in their establishment. They learned their trade with Morris, Tasker & Co., both occupying responsible positions in that house until the time they established business for themselves.

NEWELL & RIDGWAY, (Successors to Newell & Bro.) Importers of Wines and Liquors, Dealers in Fine Old Whiskeys, Store, No. 43 North Front Street. About forty years ago the house now controlled by Messrs. Newell & Ridgway, importers of wines and liquors, at No. 43 North Front Street, was founded by Messrs T. P. and T. C. Newell, under the firm title of Newell & Bro. In 1865, Mr. T. C. Newell died, and in 1870 the firm became Newell & Ridgway. On July 26, 1891, Mr. T. P. Newell died, and the present proprietors are Messrs. Harry Newell and Charles S. Ridgway, Mr. Newell being a son of Mr. T. P. Newell. Mr. Ridgway entered the house in 1885, five years before being admitted to partnership. Both gentlemen are natives of New Jersey, and members of the Wholesale Liquor Dealers' Association. The premises occupied consist of a six-story building, 20 x 40 feet in dimensions, and every convenience has been provided for the transaction of business. Messrs. Newell & Ridgway are direct importers of the choicest foreign wines and liquors, and make a speciality of fine old whiskeys. An immense stock is at the control of the firm, and all orders meet with prompt fulfillment, while bed-rock prices prevail. None but the most reliable goods are handled, and everything sold is guaranteed to be exactly as represented. The trade supplied extends through Pennsylvania, New Jersey, Delaware and Maryland. Splendid whiskeys may be had from Messrs. Newell and Ridgway, and all goods may be depended upon to be exactly as represented.

WOODCOCK BROS., Manufacturers of Hosiery and Knit Goods, Nos. 109 and 111 Jefferson Street, Germantown. Within the lifetime of a generation the hosiery and knit goods industry has grown from comparatively insignificant proportions to vast magnitude here in Germantown, and the improvement in the productions has fully kept pace therewith. The goods turned out by some of our leading firms in the line indicated have a national reputation, and in this connection special mention is due Woodcock Bros., whose mills are located at Nos. 109 and 111 Jefferson Street. They are manufacturers of hosiery and knit goods of a distinctly superior character, and their productions command extensive sale throughout the United States, high standard of excellence being maintained by them. Messrs. T. J. and John F. Woodcock, who compose the firm, are gentlemen in the prime of life and natives of England, but have been in this city since childhood. They are both men of practical skill and many years' experience, active and energetic, and are thoroughly conversant with the wants of the trade. They occupy three 40 x 125 feet floors and the basement, and their establishment is equipped with ample steam-power and perfect facilities, including one hundred different kinds of knitting machines, while upward of one hundred hands are employed. The firm manufacture a general line of hosiery and knit goods, the productive capacity being from 500 to 1,000 dozen pairs per day, according to style of goods, and the output is handled by Watson, Ball & Co., selling agents, No. 62 White Street, N. Y. This flourishing enterprise had inception in 1875, when the business was established in a very modest way by Thos. Woodcock & Son, the firm consisting of Messrs. Thos. Woodcock and his son, T. J. Woodcock. This firm conducted the business up to 1880, when the senior partner admitted his other son, John F. Woodcock, to partnership. In 1888 the senior partner retired and the present firm-name was adopted, steam-power and machinery being introduced into the establishment in this year.

MARKET STREET, EAST OF SIXTH STREET.

INDSAY, MINES & CO., Iron, Steel, Ores, Coal, Coke, Nos. 411 and 413 Walnut Street.—By reason of its contiguity to the great coal and iron regions, together with its exceptional transportation facilities by land and water, Philadelphia has attained and is bound to maintain supremacy, as the chief distributing center for the products indicated. The importance of the coal and iron interest represented in this city today can scarcely be overestimated. The growth of this trade has been especially notable during the past few decades, and many substantial merchants have come to the front in the line within recent years. Among these may be mentioned Lindsay, Mines & Co., whose office is at Nos. 411 and 413 Walnut Street. They handle iron, steel, ores, bituminous coal and coke and are doing an extensive business, their total annual sales reaching a handsome figure. Messrs. A. A. Lindsay and J. Lansing Mines, who compose the firm, are gentlemen in the prime of life and natives of this state. They are men of thorough experience and of energy and enterprise, well and favorably known in commercial circles, and are subscribers of the Bourse. The firm was established in 1888, and from the start has been highly prosperous, selling extensively to dealers and large consumers throughout Pennsylvania, New Jersey and Delaware. They handle large quantities of iron and steel scraps, making a specialty of pig iron, furnace ores and bituminous coal and coke, and can fill orders for anything in their line on the most favorable terms. They ship direct from the mines and producers in car lots and are in a position to offer substantial inducements, quoting bottom prices.

EBER & PETZOLDT, Continental Carpet Mills, Manufacturers of Ingrain Carpets, Southeast Corner of Mascher and Putnam Streets, Nos. 2121-2123 East Dauphin Street.—The products of the carpet looms of today are veritable works of art, while they are no longer confined to the homes of the opulent, as the economy of steam production has placed them within the means of all classes of people. Philadelphia has long been noted as the leading center of production in this line, and among the enterprising and progressive firms engaged therein is that of Messrs. Weber & Petzoldt, proprietors of the Continental Carpet Mills, at the southeast corner of Mascher and Putnam Streets. This firm are extensive manufacturers of ingrain carpets, including extra super, C. C. super and seven and nine pair Union in all the latest designs and patterns. The business was established in 1870, by Mr. Edward Weber, and in 1891 the present firm was organized by the admission of Mr. L. Petzoldt to partnership. The manufacturing plant comprises two floors, 50 x 80 feet each, splendidly equipped with fourteen power and four hand looms and all necessary machinery operated by steam-power, and steady employment is given to thirty-five skilled and expert hands. The goods here manufactured are of a fine quality, and after many years' trial, have thoroughly substantiated every claim made for them and have given unbounded satisfaction wherever used. The output averages fifty-five rolls of carpeting, 130 yards to a roll, per week, and the retail trade is supplied direct from the mills in quantities to suit at the shortest possible notice and at terms and prices which are safe from successful competition. Orders are received from all sections of the United States, and are filled with eminent satisfaction and success in all cases. The copartners are both natives of Germany, expert and practical carpet-weavers, and useful, honorable and reliable business men, with whom it is always pleasant and profitable to deal.

WILSON BISCUIT WORKS, Biscuit Manufacturers, J. R. Strachan, Manager, Nos. 210 to 214 North Front Street. One of the greatest revolutions effected in the methods of any industry the past quarter century is that which has taken place in the production of crackers and all kinds of plain and fancy biscuits. This radical change has been brought about by the introduction of machinery and improved methods by which large houses have to a degree obtained control of the business, minor rivals, great numbers of them being bakeries only in name, being supplied daily with their goods by the larger concerns. One of the largest and most progressive houses in the United States engaged in this line of industry is that of the New York Biscuit Company, whose principal office is in the American Express Company Building, Chicago, and which have branches in the principal cities of the Union. The Wilson Biscuit Works was originally founded by Theo. Wilson, who was succeeded by his son, Walter G. Wilson, who afterward formed the Walter G. Wilson Co., which later changed to the Wilson, Cass Co.; still later to the Wilson Biscuit Co., and in 1889 the present company was organized. The Philadelphia factory, which supplies the trade throughout Pennsylvania, New Jersey and Delaware, is known under the name of the Wilson Biscuit Works. It is conducted under the management of Mr. J. R. Strachan, who was formerly with the Vandeveer & Holmes Biscuit Co., of New York, and has had 15 years' experience in the trade; consequently understands perfectly all its requirements. The New York Biscuit Company was organized under the State laws of Illinois, with a capital of $10,000,000, and is a consolidation of thirty biscuit manufactories in the United States. The officers are: President, W. H. Moore, attorney, of Chicago, Treasurer, G. P. Johnson, of New York; Secretary, George E. West, of New York. The works in Philadelphia are the largest in the city. They comprise two spacious four story buildings, equipped with six tile and five reel ovens. Employment is found for 200 hands, 125 barrels of flour are used daily, and the cakes and biscuits turned out cannot be excelled for wholesomeness and excellence.

CENTENNIAL NATIONAL BANK, Thirty-second and Market Streets.—The city of Philadelphia has in the Centennial National Bank a most substantial and ably conducted institution, one which has largely aided the development of the mercantile and manufacturing interests of this community. It was organized January 17, 1876, and during the same year completed and occupied its fireproof structure at Thirty-second and Market Streets. It has a paid up capital of $800,000, and is officered as follows—viz., President, Clarence H. Clark; Vice President, H. M. Lutz; Cashier, J. M. Collingwood; Directors, Clarence H. Clark, H. M. Lutz, G. E. Pugh, John Scott, Jos. J. Martin and F. S. Kimball. The banking rooms of the institution have every convenience for the prosecution of business, being also provided with two vaults of the Farrell make, and every security against loss. The Centennial National is a bank of issue, deposit and discount; negotiating loans, handling first class commercial paper, issuing drafts, dealing in foreign exchange, and making collections on all available points through its numerous correspondents, who include the First National Bank of New York, the Suffolk National Bank of Boston, the Merchants' National and the Traders' National Banks of Baltimore. Its investments and operations have been so successful that a snug surplus of $380,000 has been accumulated, with undivided profits of $25,015.75, while its individual deposits average $1,880,000, and its loans and discounts $1,350,000. Its safe deposit vaults are a notable feature of it, and an inspection of the vaults in this bank will demonstrate how absolutely this citadel of safety holds one's effects beyond the reach of any class of meddlers. The immovable compartment safe, of which you have the only keys, has the environment of colossal steel vault work unsurpassed, as well as bars and bolts, time locks, secret safeguards, inviolable privacy, untiring vigilance by day and night, experienced management, provision for any exigency, police service constant and at command. The ten dollar safe will hold a good fortune in stocks and bonds. It will retain your family jewels, relics, souvenirs, private papers, and your will; and to it you have the freest resort upon every business day of the year. Boxes can here be rented for from $5 to $10, according to size, while these vaults have few equals in construction and thorough equipment. There is also a savings department connected with this bank, where deposits of $5 and upwards are received, on which interest is allowed at the rate of 3 per cent per annum. The executive officers of this bank are all well known gentlemen in both financial, commercial and social life.

BANNER THOMAS, Manufacturer of the Celebrated Excelsior Cotton and Linen Netting, Importer of Silver Gray Gilling Twine and Hemming's Fish Hooks; Store, No. 117 Market Street; Factory, Nos. 3116 to 3120 Frankford Road. An old established house in this branch of industry, and one which has for many years enjoyed a first class reputation for superior work, is that of Mr. Banner Thomas. He is the sole manufacturer of the celebrated "Excelsior" Cotton Banding, for woolen, worsted and cotton mills; also Patent Hook Bands, for worsted spinning. He is also the sole manufacturer of the famous "Excelsior" Separator Belts for the creameries. These belts are acknowledged by all who have used them to be far superior to all others in use. We would refer all parties interested in separator belts to A. W. Preston, Esq., Secretary of the Solebury Dairymen's Association, of Solebury, Bucks County, Pa., for reference as to quality. This business was established in 1847 by Mr. Robert Thomas, the father of the present proprietor, who conducted a rope and cordage manufactory at Nos. 3116 to 3120 Frankford Road. In 1877 this factory was enlarged, and a department for the manufacture of the celebrated "Excelsior" cotton and linen netting of every description was added by the present proprietor. He also established in 1857 a store having four floors, each 20x100 feet in dimensions. Here he sells all goods of his own manufacture, and keeps on hand a full stock of netting, silver grey gilling twine and Hemming's fish hooks. He is also agent for Carter's oiled clothing. An extensive trade is carried on at both wholesale and retail in Pennsylvania, New Jersey, Delaware and the Southern States principally, and scattering throughout other sections of the Union. The best houses in the trade handle his products, and he uses only the best materials for manufacturing purposes, quality being his first consideration. The ample resources and the facilities of this house enable it to offer inducements to the trade, as regards liberality of terms and prices, which add materially to the popularity of the establishment. Mr. Thomas is a native of Philadelphia, and is about sixty-three years of age.

HISTORICAL AND COMMERCIAL PHILADELPHIA.

JOSEPH POTTER, Successor to Potter Bros., Manufacturer of Straw Goods, Nos. 529 and 531 Arch Street; New York office and Salesroom, No. 88 Prince Street. Managed by Jas. Williams. The gentleman whose name heads this sketch is one of the leaders in this line in Philadelphia. He has excellent facilities, turns out a superior class of goods and his trade is constantly growing. He was formerly of the firm of Potter Bros., established some twenty years ago, and in 1888 succeeded the same as sole proprietor. Mr. Joseph Potter is a gentleman of middle age and a native of England, but has been in this country for many years. He is a man of practical skill and thorough experience, active and energetic, and is well known in the business. He manufactures ladies', misses' and children's straw hats, and sells to jobbers throughout the United States. The premises occupied by him at Nos. 529 and 531 Arch Street are spacious and commodious, comprising the whole of a 40 x 300 feet floor, reached by elevator, and are equipped with steam-power, machinery, etc. Upward of fifty help are here employed and several salesmen represent the house on the road. A very large and fine stock is always kept on hand and all orders are promptly and carefully filled, while the lowest prices are quoted. Mr. Potter has an office and salesroom also in New York, at No. 88 Prince Street, and is represented there by Jas. Williams.

HALL & CARPENTER, Importers of Tin Plate and Metals, No. 709 Market Street.—The elements of commercial success are seldom found in happier combination than in the case of the house of Hall & Carpenter, the well-known importers of tin plate and metals, at No. 709 Market Street, who have secured for the goods imported and manufactured by them such wide celebrity coupled with a trade of great and growing magnitude. It was on the first of February, 1867, that the above-named firm was organized and commenced business, and in 1883, by the decease of Mr. Carpenter, Mr. Augustus R. Hall became the sole proprietor, continuing the business under the old and honored firm-name. The business premises comprise an entire five-story building, 22 x 255 feet, extending through the block to Filbert Street, where is carried the largest and most valuable stock of the kind in the city. This firm long ago secured the recognition and patronage of the best class of the trade throughout the United States, and the substantial inducements offered as to both quality and price may be said to have had their natural result. This house handles the best tin plate and metals in the world; also tinsmiths' and stovemakers' supplies, sheet copper and ingot copper, black and galvanized sheet iron, corrugated conductors, spiral pipe, registers, Kalemein sheet iron, zinc and japanned wares, wire nails and rivets, and many patented articles of which this house has the exclusive sale. These are all standard products that competition fails to keep up to in many cases, and they invariably commend their own superior merits to the confidence and patronage of critical and discriminating buyers. This firm are also widely prominent as exclusive manufacturers of the "Crown Specialties." The long experience of Mr. Hall in this branch of trade gives him superior advantages, while his high reputation is a sufficient assurance that all orders will receive faithful attention and will prove satisfactory to patrons in every instance. Mr. Hall was born in Paterson, N. J., being a direct descendant of Robert Hall, who came from Westminster, England, and settled in Pennsylvania in 1682. Mr. Hall came to this city in childhood, and becoming of age was admitted into the house of W. N. &  G. Taylor, becoming a partner in 1862 under the name and style of the N. & G. Taylor Co., as importers of tin plate, withdrawing therefrom to found the present house. He was one of the foremost promoters of the movement for the formation of a direct steamship line from Philadelphia to Liverpool, and has long been a prominent member of the Maritime Exchange, Commercial Exchange, Board of Trade, Manufacturers' Club, Franklin Institute, Union League, Art Club, the F. and A. M. and the Historical Society of Pennsylvania, and an honorary member of the First Regiment Veteran Corps. He is an expert authority upon tin and terne plates, and "Hall's G. D. C. Ternes" are typical in every State in the Union.

J. PÉQUIGNOT, Diamonds, Watches, Jewelry, No. 804 Chestnut Street.—A leading headquarters in Philadelphia for diamonds, watches and fine jewelry is the establishment of Mr. Z. J. Péquignot. This representative house was established in 1854 by Messrs. C. and A. Péquignot, who were succeeded by the present proprietor in 1874. The store is spacious in size, and forms one of the attractions of this popular shopping thoroughfare. The display made in gems and precious stones at this house is truly magnificent. Mr. Péquignot is a connoisseur and expert of wide celebrity, and as an importer of diamonds, watches and fine jewelry he is a recognized authority in all the details and intricacies of the business. In gems and stones of worth, the selections here displayed are among the largest and choicest to be found in the city. Diamond and emerald, ruby, and beryl, opal and pearl, sard and peridot, jacinth and spinel, topaz and turquoise, sapphires and cameos, intaglios and sardonyx, rock crystal and amethyst, are all fittingly represented. Diamonds are here displayed of all conceivable shapes, of unsurpassed clearness, and absolute faultlessness—"gems of purest ray serene;" rivere solitaire, cluster and pendant, pianche and aigrette, necklace and bracelet chains, earrings and chatelaines—in fact, every article esteemed for its genuineness and suited for personal adornment here greets the eye and delights the sight. The line of fine Swiss and American watches is rarely excelled anywhere, while everything in the shape of fine jewelry can here be secured at the lowest prices. The constant aim and ambition of Mr. Péquignot is the purchase of articles of novelty, beauty, and merit, and his patronage is large and influential with the élite of the city, and with the most critical and discriminating buyers throughout the State. Mr. Péquignot was born in Switzerland, but has resided here since childhood, is still in the active prime of life, and recognized as an authority in the jewelry trade, and as an enterprising, progressive and reliable business man.

HISTORICAL AND COMMERCIAL PHILADELPHIA.

ROBERT GLENDINNING & CO., Bankers and Brokers, No. 101 South Fourth Street.— One of the principal houses engaged as bankers and brokers in this city is that of Robert Glendinning & Co. The copartners, Mr. Glendinning and George A. Huhn, have had mature experience in their vocation, and are recognized authorities on all questions pertaining thereto. The establishment was founded in 1864 by Mr. Glendinning, who in the same year became a member of the Philadelphia Stock Exchange and in 1868 purchased a seat in the New York Stock Exchange. In 1881 Mr. Huhn, who had been of the firm of W. H. Tevis & Co., became Mr. Glendinning's partner. Mr. Huhn has been a member of the Philadelphia Stock Exchange since 1869, and of the Chicago Stock Exchange the past four years. The firm have direct wires to their correspondents, J. and S. Wormser and H. B. Hollins & Co., of New York, and Jamieson & Co., of Chicago, and are in constant receipt of the latest intelligence regarding the financial world. Messrs. Glendinning & Co. receive money on deposit and for investment, and are general brokers in stocks, bonds and investment securities of all kinds.

WILLIAMSON BROS., Engineers, Machinists and Boiler Makers, Corner Richmond and York Streets.—The firm of Williamson Bros., the well known engineers, machinists and boiler makers, established their business here in 1866, and make a specialty of patent hoisting engines, ship steering engines, winding engines and locomotive steam cranes, while they also manufacture stationary engines, boilers, tanks and general machine work. Founded upon a substantial basis of skill, energy and integrity, the business has had a remarkable growth, and is one of the best illustrations of industrial progress in the State. The copartners are close students of the progress made in steam engineering, and have included in their engines every improvement that conduces to economy in running and increased horse power. The best of material only is used, and every part is fashioned and put together with the greatest accuracy and care. Every engine is severely tested before shipment, and is guaranteed to give satisfaction, while prices are at bed rock, and, quality considered, are the cheapest quoted by any engine builders in the land. The designs and patterns of this firm in hoisting engines include spur geared hoisters with cone friction drum, link motion and positive clutch drum, or clutch on crank shaft, used for dock, warehouse, ship and builders' use, as well as the finest types of frictional geared hoisters in existence, intended for fast hoisting, quick handling, and to avoid risks of breakage; which are in use on most of the principal steamships running out of New York and Philadelphia, also on the Great Lakes and vessels in foreign countries, while for coal purposes they have Williamson Bros.' Patent Frictional Geared Fast Hoisting Engine, which hoists half a ton of coal to a height of sixty feet at the rate of 700 feet per minute, and handles fifty tons per hour with each drum. This is the fastest type of hoisting engine made, and is used at the Reading Railroad Co.'s coal depots at Philadelphia, Brooklyn, New Bedford, Newburyport and Salem, and by many private firms in different cities. Their ship steering engines have the improved worm gear of the Allaro Hambley style, and are most ingeniously connected to the steering wheel and rudder chains, either as sole motors or detachable. They are vastly superior to any other style, and are used in preference to all others by the Pennsylvania Railroad in their ferry boats on New York Harbor, and also by the United States Navy, all the great American ocean steamship lines, the finest lake steamers, and in use preferentially all over the world. These engines may justly be described as unequalled in utility, unprecedented in reputation, and undisputed in the broad claim of being the finest steam steering engines under the sun. The firm is composed of Messrs. G. W., J. D. and W. C. Williamson, the two first named being natives of the Kensington district of Philadelphia, while the last named was born in Brandywine, Del. Messrs. J. D. and W. C. Williamson were formerly engineers in the American Navy, and are active members of the American Society of Naval Engineers and the American Society of Mechanical Engineers. All are in the active prime of life, and are expert and practical engineers and machinists.

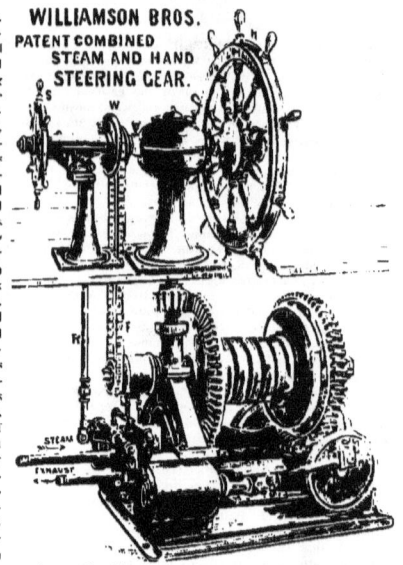

WILLIAMSON BROS. PATENT COMBINED STEAM AND HAND STEERING GEAR.

THE HOWE SCALE COMPANY, No. 508 Market Street.—The Howe Scale Company, of Rutland, Vermont, stand at the head in their line, both as regards experience, facilities, and the wonderful record of their scales for uniform accuracy and reliability. The Philadelphia house has been in operation for some thirty years, and since 1888 has been under the management of Mr. E. R. Austin, who has been connected with the company for many years, who supplies the trade throughout Eastern Pennsylvania, Southern New Jersey, Delaware, Maryland and New York State. He occupies spacious and well equipped premises. A heavy and complete stock is constantly carried of the Howe scales, in all sizes and of every variety; also coffee mills, trucks, grocers' sundries, etc., while special trucks are promptly made to order. The merits embodied in the construction of the Howe track scale are acknowledged by the highest authority of civil engineers. They are used in preference to any other make by the leading railroads of the country; also by leading coal mines and manufactories throughout Pennsylvania, Ohio, New York, Illinois, Missouri, Michigan, Massachusetts, Kansas, Iowa, Alabama, Georgia, Colorado, Wisconsin, Texas, and other States. Mr. Austin, the manager, is a native Philadelphian, and a gentleman of large business experience and thorough reliability, with whom it will be found both pleasant and profitable to deal.

JOS. WARRINGTON, Builder of Fine Carriages, Nos. 2200 and 2202 North Broad Street. Mr. Jos. Warrington makes carriages, buggies, phaetons, victorias and sleighs, equal in style, finish and workmanship to any contemporary establishment in the city. He makes a leading specialty of top buggies, and for excellence in this line received the first premium medal in 1880, at the fair of the Pennsylvania State Agricultural Society. Mr. Warrington was born in New Jersey, but has resided in Philadelphia since boyhood. In 1876 he established business here, and has met with well earned success, acquiring an enviable reputation and building up a trade that comes from all parts of the United States. Mr. Warrington turns out a line of fine carriages, etc., made in any of the approved modern styles which the skill of the present day can produce, using none but the very best materials. The manufacturing facilities of the house embrace a commodious and spacious factory, in which all the operations of wood and iron working, trimming, upholstering and painting are carried on under the personal supervision of the proprietor.

HISTORICAL AND COMMERCIAL PHILADELPHIA.

THOS. J. MARTIN, JR & BRO., Attorneys at Law, Patent Attorneys, Real Estate, Etc., No. 708 Walnut Street. The several ramifications of the business of Messrs. Thos. J. Martin, Jr. & Brother, located in this city at No. 708 Walnut Street, constitute, as a whole, a connection of considerable volume and significance, the chief components of which are the professions of attorneys-at-law, patent attorneys (with an influential practice among patent solicitors, attorneys and inventors all over the United States) conveyancers and real estate agents and brokers. The business received its inception eight years ago at the hands of the present copartners, Mr. Thomas J. Martin, Jr., attorney-at-law and patent attorney, and Mr. Frank P. Martin conveyancer, and by the continued exercise of a sound judgment and scrupulous care in the fulfillment of all they undertake, the firm have gained the confidence and perpetual support of a large and influential clientele composed of trustees, property owners, executors, investors, capitalists, commercial and financial houses, etc. In addition to a general practice as attorney-at-law and patent attorney, the chief lines undertaken are the preparation, execution and detailed examination of titles, deeds, leases, trusts, wills and other legal instruments, the settlement, transfer and entire management of estates, the purchase, sale and exchange of all kinds of real estate, particularly fine residential property in the suburbs, the collection of house and ground rents and interest, the letting of premises in general, and the speedy negotiation of loans upon bond or mortgage at the fairest rates of interest on behalf of either borrower or lender. Handsomely appointed offices are maintained on the first floor at the location named, and among the several facilities there kept for the systematic conduct of the business, are registers of valuable and eligible properties on hand for sale, rent or exchange. The Messrs. Martin are young men of Quaker City birth and Mr. Thos. J. Martin, Jr. originally studied law under George Northop, Esq.

READING PAPER MILLS, Geo. F. Baer, President; James N. Mohr, Vice-President; J. Bushong, Treasurer; No. 134 South Fourth Street Philadelphia, the home of the printer's art in America, has ever been celebrated as headquarters for the wholesale paper trade and a leading house represented here is that of the Reading Paper Mills, located at No. 134 South Fourth Street, in the Bullitt Building. This company was organized in 1884, under the laws of the State of Pennsylvania, and own and operate three paper mills at Reading, Pa. The Reading Mill is equipped with two 1100 and two 1000 pound Umpherston and one Jordan engine and one 80-inch Fourdrinier, operated by steam-power, and has a capacity for turning out 12,000 pounds of book paper per day. The Packerack Mill has three 800, three 600-pound and one Kingsland engine, one 73-inch Fourdrinier and ample steam-power, and turns out 10,000 pounds of book paper per day. The Tulpehocken Mill is supplied with two 500, one 850 and one 1000-pound engine one Kingsland engine and one 62-inch Fourdrinier, together with both steam and water power, and produces 8000 pounds of manilla and rope paper per day. The company early achieved an enviable reputation for the superiority of their product, and the management in this city brings to bear every possible qualification for the successful carrying on of this difficult branch of trade. They have developed a business of great and growing magnitude in all parts of the United States, and are prepared to promptly fill the largest orders for all descriptions of book plate, litho, manilla and rope paper. The absolute perfection of their paper is guaranteed, and terms and prices are made invariably satisfactory to the trade. The officers of this company are as follows, viz.: Geo. F. Baer, president; James N. Mohr, vice-president; Jacob Bushong, treasurer. These gentlemen are well-known Pennsylvanians, experienced and practical paper manufacturers, and of excellent repute and standing in commercial, financial and trade circles.

JOHN D. EMACK, Slate Blackboards, Miner and Shipper of Roofing Slate, No. 411 Walnut Street; Yard, Slatington, Pa. Of all the details which are in popular use in the art of building or construction there is scarcely any one which is more important than slate, and, indeed, as it is the top and finishing crown of all the rest, it may, in this sense, be considered the most important. Vast quantities of slate for roofing are always in demand in the building trade, besides what is required for use in the interior of buildings, such as for mantels and other accessories and also for school blackboards and slates, while slate is, likewise, largely used for tiling, as it is superior to marble and outwears it, there being no friction; also, for steps to modern houses and for wainscoting, both plain and marbleized. The leading miner and shipper of this indispensable article in Philadelphia is Mr. John D. Emack, whose offices are eligibly located at No. 411 Walnut Street. This gentleman handles all sizes and shapes of roofing slate as well as slate blackboards, mantels, etc., and is one of the largest shippers in this line in the United States. The business was established at Slatington, Pa., in 1875, by Messrs. Caskie & Emack, the present proprietor succeeding to the sole control in 1887. He contracts with quarries for their entire yearly output, and is prepared to supply Lehigh, Bangor, Penn Argyle, Delta, Vermont, Chapman and Slatington slates, in quantities to suit, at the shortest possible notice. He supplied the slate for the Philadelphia postoffice, the temple at Broad and Berks Streets, the House of Refuge, at Glenn Mills, Pa.; and government buildings at Portland, Ore.; Chattanooga, Tenn.; Birmingham, Ala.; Washington, D. C.; Huntsville, Ala.; Las Vegas, N. M., and other places. Roofers and contractors are promptly supplied to the full extent of their wants, and terms and prices are made invariably satisfactory to all parties. The business is conducted exclusively at wholesale and sales average over 50,000 squares per year. Mr. Emack is a resident Philadelphian, in the active prime of life, a recognized authority in the slate trade, a member of the Master Builders' Exchange, and a gentleman of marked business ability, wide acquaintance and eminent popularity.

JAMES NASSAU, Formerly of the firm Nassau & Kuhn, Proprietors of the Chas. C. Phillips Company, Manufacturer of Varnishes, Japans, and Surfacers, No. 218 South Fourth Street.—The most enterprising, practical and successful manufacturer of varnish and kindred preparations in the world today is undoubtedly Mr. James Nassau, formerly of the late Chas. C. Phillips Company, and now an extensive manufacturer of varnishes, japans and surfacers, at No. 218 South Fourth Street. The business so successfully conducted by Mr. Nassau was founded in 1855, by Mr. Chas. C. Phillips, and in 1865 Mr. Nassau became a partner under the style of Chas. C. Phillips & Co. Mr. Phillips died in November, 1886, and Mr. Nassau continued with the Chas. C. Phillips Company until January, 1892, when he became sole proprietor. The present works were built in 1890, and cover nearly an entire block. The different departments are splendidly equipped, ably managed and thoroughly organized, every modern facility being at hand for insuring rapid and perfect production, and employment is given to a large force of skilled and expert hands. The output comprises all grades of varnishes and japans, while the leading specialties of the house are Nassau's Vitrealba for ivory white, Nassau's Ambrolio finishes, Nassau's Opalite surfacers, Nassau's primer, Nassau's wood finish, and all grades of cabinet, car and coach varnishes. Mr. Nassau is a manufacturer of a class of goods of exceptional merit, and they have secured distinct recognition throughout the civilized world owing to the uniformly high standard at which the same are maintained. These varnishes are adapted for use in every season and climate, and are noted for their brilliancy, rapidly drying properties, reliability and durability, and are notably economical. They are, in short, the ne plus ultra of coach and hard wood varnishes, and the best and cheapest on the market. Every article sold is fully warranted, while the prices quoted are remarkably low and the most liberal inducements are offered to the trade. Sales are immense in all parts of the United States, and a fine growing export trade is enjoyed with Germany, France and other European countries. Orders by telephone No. 1174, by telegraph or mail, receive immediate and careful attention, and all transactions are placed upon a fair and equitable basis. Mr. Nassau is a native Philadelphian, an expert and practical varnish manufacturer, endowed with a genius for discovery and improvement, and an ambition to excel; a member of the Pennsylvania Association of Master Painters and Decorators, and the Philadelphia Bourse; and an enterprising, progressive and popular business man.

Independence Hall.

HISTORICAL AND COMMERCIAL PHILADELPHIA.

HE WEST PHILADELPHIA REAL ESTATE AGENCY, Clayton W. Peirson, Proprietor, No. 3818 Lancaster Avenue.—The handsomely appointed office of the West Philadelphia Real Estate Agency, located on the first floor at No. 3818 Lancaster Avenue, is the centre of an extensive and influential real estate and insurance business in this section of the city, and it is now resorted to by property owners, trustees, capitalists and others for the execution of commissions in all branches of the profession. The agency is popularly regarded as one of the most reliable and expeditious mediums for the purchase, sale and exchange of property of all kinds, more especially residences in the Twenty-fourth, Twenty-seventh and Thirty-fourth Wards; while it is held in high repute for making prompt and accurate settlements, as also for the scrupulous care that is exercised in the fulfillment of all transactions. In addition to the transfer of real estate, the agency is a headquarters for the speedy negotiation of loans upon bond or mortgage for both borrower and lender, the collection of house and ground rents and interest, the examination of titles, etc., the transfer, settlement and entire management of estates and the letting of premises in general; while especial facilities are possessed for directing all desirable fire risks into the hands of the most responsible corporations at the lowest current rates of premium. The business was established in July, 1887, by the present sole proprietor, Mr. Clayton W. Peirson, who was formerly of Peirson, Baldwin & Yare. Mr. Peirson, who is a gentleman of middle age, was born in Philadelphia and is subagent for the Buffalo German Insurance Co, of Buffalo, the American and the Continental of New York, the Security of New Haven and the Westchester of New York. The firm also conducts a large business in rare works of art, and the lovers of art will find at the above address a large assortment of paintings, embracing fine art productions; this latter comprehending almost every description of art work extant, the chief line being foreign and American oil paintings as the leading specialty, water color sketches, landscapes, crayons, pencil pieces, etchings, engravings, oleographs, etc. The distinct success of this enterprise is largely attributed to the fact that the manager, Mr. Clayton W. Peirson, is a connoisseur and astute judge and he selects the stock with a scrupulous care born of long experience. The show room is on the second floor, and a large and handsome collection is kept on hand.

EORGE BRANSON & CO., Manufacturers of Hosiery, N. E. Corner American and Jefferson Streets.—The eminent and enterprising house of George Branson & Co. has by reason of its able policy and skilful management secured to Philadelphia the most important trade in hosiery in this section of the country. Their factory, at the northeast corner of American and Jefferson Streets, is the largest and most complete of its kind in Pennsylvania, comprising three immense brick buildings, three and five stories high, fully equipped with steam knitting, carding and spinning machinery of the latest improved pattern, operated by a steam engine of 100 horse power; and steady employment is given therein to some 500 skilled hands. The house long ago achieved national celebrity for the superiority of its product, and developed a trade and connection of the most desirable and extended character. It was in 1859 that this enterprise was inaugurated, by Messrs Thomas Branson and Benjamin Schofield. In 1875 Mr. Thomas Branson died, after placing the business upon a solid foundation, and his son, Mr. George Branson, succeeded to his interest. Mr. Schofield retired in 1883, and Mr. Branson completed the new mill the following year, which is the model of its kind in America to-day. Mr. Branson died in 1889, after an eminently useful and honorable business career, since which date the house has been under the active management of his son-in-law, Mr. Wm. W. Finn, Jr. Both as regards ample resources, perfected facilities and character and magnitude of its product, this house stands unrivalled on the continent, and the best class of trade has so decided. The daily output is 2,880 dozen of Branson's seamless half hose, ladies' hosiery and cut goods in a great variety of styles, while 10,000 pounds of yarn are made per week. The soundest judgment is exercised in the manufacture of their various yarns, while they lead the trade in originating new styles and patterns, and their colors and shades are remarkably brilliant, and their dyes are absolutely fast. The highest standard of excellence is maintained in workmanship and finish, and the goods are eagerly sought after by leading jobbers and retailers throughout the country. The largest orders are filled promptly, and terms and prices are made invariably satisfactory to the trade. Mr. Finn, the managing partner, is a native Philadelphian, a member of the Manufacturers' Club, and a young man of experience and ability, who has won a reputation in the industrial world highly creditable to his skill and integrity, while retaining to Philadelphia the supremacy in this staple branch of industry.

HE MUTUAL FIRE INSURANCE COMPANY, of Germantown and its Vicinity.—A time honored, prosperous and popular home institution is that of the Mutual Fire Insurance Company of Germantown and its Vicinity, which was founded in 1843, being incorporated under the State laws of Pennsylvania. The board of management has been noted for ability, commendable conservatism and reliable methods. The officers and managers are as follows: President, Jabez Gates; Secretary and Treasurer, Wm. H. Emhardt; Managers, Jabez Gates, Charles Otto, Edward T. Tyson, Horatio G. Jones, Reuben V. Salida, Henry B. Bruner, Benjamin Allen, John Allen, Charles W. Schaeffer, Peter B. Hinkle, Thos W Wright, M. L. Finkel, Daniel B. Rufe or, A. B. Kerper and Wm. D Dounton. These gentlemen are prominently identified with the financial and commercial progress of Germantown, and enjoy the esteem of all their fellow citizens. The company is in a most flourishing condition, and its funds are invested in the most judicious manner. The total amount of risks in force June 30, 1891, was $16,379,749, while the amount for reinsurance, reserve, and for claims of every description was $396,946.80. The company write policies in Bucks, Montgomery, and Philadelphia counties only. Insurance is effected at lowest premium rates, to any amount, and all losses that occur are promptly and satisfactorily settled.

EOPLE'S FIVE YEAR BENEFIT ORDER, J G. Howard, General Deputy for Eastern Pennsylvania, Office No, 702 Chestnut Street.—The best record made by any beneficiary organization is that achieved by the People's Five Year Benefit Order, which was incorporated March 22, 1889, under the laws of Massachusetts, and is the first and largest five year benefit order in America. It agrees to pay each member, lady or gentleman, $50 in five years from date of membership, and from five to twenty dollars per week in case of sickness or accident. It paid $130,000 to the sick during the first eighteen months of its existence, while the cost of membership last year was only nineteen assessments of $1.50 each. The objects of the order are to unite in the bonds of protection, prudence and peace all acceptable persons between thirteen and sixty nine, of good moral character, industrious habits, sound bodily health, respectable calling, and who believe in a Supreme Being. There is connected with the order a Relief Fund, divided into four classes, from which each individual member shall be entitled to draw a sum, as he may elect, of $500, $400, $300 or $200, on which he is to pay from $1.50 to 60 cents on each assessment. The laws of the order provide that $300 can be drawn in sick or accident benefits on a certificate of $500 during five years' membership; not more than $20 per week for five weeks in one year. Assessments as needed will be called on the first of each month into the Relief Fund to pay sick, accident and maturity benefits. This order is attracting the best citizens to its ranks, and in every city and town where it has been introduced it has met with decided popular favor. It is already so solid that competition does not come near it, and as an organization for the mutual assistance of members in the line of sick and endowment benefits it stands unexcelled, while the annual expense of carrying a membership is within the reach of all. It had written 23,500 certificates up to June, 1892, and had accumulated $1,000,710.13 in assets. All money is deposited with the State Treasurer of Massachusetts, and the headquarters of the order are in Boston. The Philadelphia office is under the management of Mr. J. Griffith Howard, as General Deputy for Eastern Pennsylvania This gentleman is a native of Pennsylvania, a resident of this city for the past ten years, a graduate of the Philadelphia College of pharmacy, and was formerly in the drug business in this city.

HISTORICAL AND COMMERCIAL PHILADELPHIA.

R. SEIDEL, Philadelphia Black Lead Crucible Works, Nos. 1324 to 1344 Callowhill Street.—One of the thoroughly representative manufacturing enterprises of Philadelphia is that known far and near as the Philadelphia Black Lead Crucible Works, conducted under the proprietorship of Mr. R. B. Seidel, at Nos. 1324 to 1344 Callowhill Street. This house has been in successful operation since 1866, and the proprietor has deservedly won a high reputation as an extensive manufacturer of superior black lead crucibles for melting steel, brass and other metals; also, any size or shape made for chemical, assaying and refining purposes; black lead stoppers, etc., for Bessemer steel makers; fine plumbago for lubricating and stove polish manufacturers; also, superior hammered charcoal iron of different sizes and shapes. The plant is very extensive, comprising several two and three-story buildings, fully equipped with new and improved machinery and ample steam-power, and steady employment is given to from fifty to sixty skilled workmen. A leading specialty is made of the article known as the black lead stopper, for Bessemer steel makers, in which department these works are recognized as excelling all others in the country. The finest plumbago known in the world for lubricating and stove polish is also made here, and the superior black lead crucibles for melting steel, brass and other metals, produced at these works are widely preferred to any other brand, on account of their reliable quality, care in workmanship and uniform excellence. The Henry Disston saw works used over $30,000 worth of these crucibles last year. They are in heavy and influential demand on their merits, not only in all parts of the United States, but also in France and Belgium. The output averages 100,000 steel and 50,000 brass crucibles per annum, and all the products are guaranteed to stand exposure to the highest temperature without alteration. Orders, of whatever magnitude are filled with the utmost promptness and care, and terms and prices are made invariably satisfactory to the trade. Mr. Seidel is a native of Reading, Pa., and was engaged in the iron business from his youth until 1866. He is still proprietor of the Exeter Steam Forge, at Exeter Station, Pa., where he manufactures superior hammered charcoal iron, and is accounted among the representative manufacturers of Pennsylvania. He is ably assisted by his son, Mr. E. B. Seidel, who is general manager of the crucible works and an expert authority upon all matters relating thereto. This house is, unquestionably, the oldest and most representative concern of its kind in Pennsylvania, the forefathers of the proprietors originally coming from Sweden. They supply many of the largest and best concerns in Philadelphia and other large cities. Their goods being conceded to be the finest in the market. Their European trade is rapidly extending, the quality of their goods winning universal praise. Quality of material used and the general excellence of their products has given this house a reputation second to none in this industry.

JOB G. MITTON, Jr., Manufacturer of Stonecutters' Tools, Thirtieth and Walnut Streets.—The growing demand for an improved class of stonecutters' tools, etc., so noticeable of late years, has, in the nature of things, resulted in marked improvement being made in these implements. Some of our Philadelphia toolmakers in the particular line indicated have a widespread reputation, and among these can be named Job G. Mitton, Jr., corner Thirtieth and Walnut Streets. He is one of the foremost and best known in the business in this city, and his productions command extensive sale, owing to their exceptional merit. Mr. Mitton is a gentleman of middle age, active and energetic, and was born in Pottstown, Pa. He is a man of thorough practical skill and many years' experience, and is an expert toolmaker, steel worker and machinist. He has been established in the business since 1875 and was formerly located at No. 3146 Chestnut Street, whence he moved to Thirty-first and Ludlow Streets, occupying the present quarters about seven years. His shop is ample and perfectly equipped, three fires being in operation here, and a number of skilled mechanics are regularly employed. Mr. Mitton manufactures hammers, drills, crowbars, jumpers, chisels, points, wedges and stone tools of every description, and is prepared to make anything in this line to order, at shortest notice. Every article turned out by him is warranted as to workmanship and material, and repairing and sharpening are attended to also in the most prompt and excellent manner. His prices, too, are very moderate, and his trade, which is large, extends throughout Pennsylvania, Delaware, New Jersey and, practically, all over the country.

HENSON BROTHERS, Manufacturers of Knit Goods, No. 125 Main Street, Germantown.—The house of Henson Brothers, in Germantown, is recognized far and near as the most enterprising and progressive of any in the knit goods industry. They manufacture a full line of ladies' high-class knit goods, such as capes, hoods and jackets, turning out only the finest class of work and ranking as leaders in their line of industry in this country. The foundation of this business was laid in 1852, by Mr. William Henson, in a modest and unpretentious way, making his own machinery and steadily developing his business on the substantial basis of merit. He was, emphatically, a pioneer in the knit goods industry in this section, and his sons received a thorough training in the art of manufacture under his careful tuition and guiding hand. The two oldest sons, Messrs. F. W. and F. S. Henson, succeeded their father, and on their retirement, in 1890, their younger brothers, Messrs. A. A. and J. B. Henson, became the proprietors, under the present name and style. The main mill is a three-story structure, 50 x 150 feet, supplied with new and improved machinery, operated by a steam engine of 35-horse power and the output is one of great magnitude and variety. This firm is famous for the introduction of novelties in ladies' knit goods that should and have proved remarkably attractive and popular. The firm are constantly studying on new designs and fresh novelties, and theirs is the house above all others for new goods and taking novelties made up from knitted fabrics. All their goods are noticeable for beauty of design, first-class materials and artistic workmanship and are in heavy and increasing demand by leading retailers in New York, Philadelphia, Chicago, Boston, St. Louis, New Orleans, San Francisco, Baltimore, Washington, Cincinnati, Cleveland, Detroit, Milwaukee, St. Paul, Minneapolis, Omaha, Kansas City, Louisville, Atlanta, Richmond, Wilmington, Newark, Jersey City, Pittsburg, Buffalo, Providence and other trade centers throughout the country. Orders are given prompt and perfect fulfillment, and terms and prices are made eminently satisfactory to the trade. The sales agents in New York City are Messrs. Kitso, Chaffee & Co. The sound judgment and executive capacity of the proprietors is generally recognized, and the favorable prospects for this house indicates the permanent retention to Philadelphia of the supremacy in this most important branch of skilled industry.

TEMPLE GLENN, Jobbing Bricklayer, No. 1031 Sansom Street, Residence, No. 1519 Tasker Street.—The brick contractor occupies a most important position in the industrial world, as very extensive operations are constantly going on in bricklaying and in building. One of the oldest Philadelphia houses engaged in the trade is that of Mr. J. Temple Glenn, whose office is at No. 1031 Sansom Street, and his residence at No. 1519 Tasker Street. This establishment was founded in 1855 by Mr. John E. Glenn, and in 1879 he admitted to partnership his son, Mr. J. Temple Glenn, the firm-name of John E. Glenn & Son being adopted. Eleven years ago Mr. J. Temple Glenn succeeded to the sole control. He has had eighteen years' practical experience in his vocation, and has amply proved his executive ability and trustworthiness in the fulfillment of contracts. He carries on a general business as a jobbing bricklayer, executing bricklaying in all its branches, building and contract work, and makes a leading specialty of boiler and engine work. Over fifty hands are employed, and the trade is derived from all parts of the city and its vicinity. Among the important contracts fulfilled by the firm was the building of the Central Theater, the brick foundation of the Edison electric light plant, storehouse at Forty-ninth and Sansom Streets, schoolhouse at Frankford Avenue and Ontario Street, six large boilers for Forder's Glazed Kid Works, Frankford Avenue and Wheatsheaf Lane; twelve 300-horse power boilers, Edison electric light works; Lansdowne Mills; iron foundry, Twenty-second and Ontario Streets; the Rowe residence, Thirty-second and Columbia Avenue, and many others. Estimates are furnished at short notice and all work done under the supervision of Mr. Glenn is certain to give satisfaction.

HENRY ALLEN & CO., Bankers and Brokers, No. 129 South Fourth Street, Bullitt Building.—One of the most prominent firms operating on the stock exchanges of this country is that of Henry Allen & Co., whose headquarters are at No. 31 New Street, New York, and who have branches at Chicago, Philadelphia and Buffalo, their office in this city being at No. 129 South Fourth Street. The proprietors, Messrs. Henry Allen and E. L. Norton, are members of the New York Stock Exchange, the New York Produce Exchange, the New York Cotton Exchange and the Chicago Board of Trade. They have been a long time established, and now command a very extensive, influential clientèle. The manager of the Philadelphia branch is Mr. J. C. Gray, who has been operating in this line for the past four years. On the opening of an office on April 25, 1892, in this city, Mr. Gray was appointed manager, a position his experience well qualifies him to satisfactorily fill. The firm carry on an active business as bankers and brokers, on a strictly commission basis. They buy and sell bonds and stocks for cash, or on margin, and special attention is given to the promotion of solid and substantial enterprises, and they also buy and sell grain, cotton and provisions. All facilities are possessed for the prompt transaction of business, and all customers have their interests advanced in the most careful and intelligent manner.

AVIL PRINTING CO., Printers and Lithographers, Nos. 3991-5 Market Street.—Lithography is the art of drawing or engraving upon stone designs, from which impressions can be taken on paper. It is a branch of engraving and a very important one, since it has to a great extent superseded engraving on steel and copper, while its comparative cheapness, the cost being about one-third that of engraving upon metal, commends it to general use. The largest and leading printers and lithographers in Philadelphia are the Avil Printing Company, who operate an immense establishment at Nos. 3991 to 3995 Market Street. This extensive business was founded in 1878, by John D. Avil, at No. 1012 Market Street, with one cylinder and two job presses and a fifteen-horse power engine. The business developed at a rapid ratio, and in 1883 a new building was erected by Mr. Avil which he was obliged to enlarge the following year; and in 1889 they built a seven-story addition in the rear, adding a four-story building in 1891, with two floors adjoining and a large vault for the storage of plates, etc. The premises now occupied exclusively for their business comprise two floors measuring 40 x 190 feet, three floors, 40 x 180, one floor 40 x 157, one floor 40 x 87 and two floors 40 x 60 feet, the remainder of the property being rented to other parties. The equipment is thorough and complete, embracing thirty-five presses, three being lithograph power and three lithograph hand, besides twenty-one cylinder and eight job presses, and six wire stitchers, four paper cutters, two folders and pasters and 650 fonts of type. There is a complete electrotype foundry connected, while the firm also manufacture their own printing ink, and employment is given to two hundred skilled and expert hands, the motive power being furnished by a 60-horse power steam-engine. The fine facilities of the company enable them to execute in the most workmanlike and artistic manner and without any delay the largest contracts. The arrangements which they have perfected with artists and designers are such that they can furnish every variety of illustration, and in the department of lithography the company are the recognized leaders in this section of the country. All branches of commercial and job printing are given prompt and skillful attention, such as letter, note and bill heads, checks, drafts, notes, receipts, bills of exchange, certificates of stock, and all kinds of fine printing and lithographing. Large orders are received from all quarters of the globe, and the house has its permanent patrons in New York City and London, in Chicago and Paris, in Boston and Berlin, in Montreal and Madrid, in San Francisco and St. Petersburg, in the City of Mexico and the little islands scattered over the ocean. Its field is the world. Trade depressions in local places do not affect it. Its daily output is larger than that of any competing concern here, while it turns out better work than any of its rivals, and can claim with mighty England that the sun never sets upon the products of its industry. The Avil Printing Company was incorporated in 1886, and is officered as follows, viz: John D. Avil, president; H. S. Smith, vice-president; Frank S. Hobby, treasurer; Charles H. Clark, secretary. President Avil is an expert and practical printer of vast experience and established reputation; the owner of the company's immense business premises, which cost in the neighborhood of $150,000, and a useful, public-spirited citizen. Vice-President Smith is president of the Historical Publishing Co. The treasurer, Mr. Hobby, has been with the house since its first inception, and both he and the secretary, Mr. Clark, are accomplished and faithful officials.

CYRUS BORGNER, Successor to Borgner & O'Brien, Manufacturer of Fire Brick and Clay Retorts, Twenty-third Street, Above Race.—The facilities possessed by Mr. Cyrus Borgner as a manufacturer of fire brick and clay retorts at Twenty-third Street, above Race, for producing the best quality of goods are not excelled anywhere, while the guarantee that goes with all products is proof of the care exercised in workmanship and the reliability of all stock used. The reputation of the products has caused a heavy demand in all parts of the world, and this gratifying result is attributable not only to the superior quality of the goods but also to the uniformly equitable policy that has dominated the operations of the house, warranting the remark that in its particular line of manufacture, there is no concern in the country that we can more readily endorse as affording their customers both general and special advantages not easily obtainable elsewhere. The business was originally established in 1870, by Messrs. Borgner & O'Brien, the present proprietor succeeding to the sole control in 1891. The plant includes an extended water front and direct railway connections, with a two-story brick building, 80 x 205 feet, and an addition measuring 75 x 150 feet, while the equipment is thoroughly complete and perfect. The house is headquarters for fire brick and clay retorts of every description; also for tiles, fire clay, fire mortar, ground brick, circle brick and blocks in great variety, while brick and tiles of any shape are promptly made to order. An immense stock of standard sizes is constantly carried and the house is in a position to guarantee the prompt and perfect fulfillment of all orders and to place all transactions upon a substantial and satisfactory basis. Shipments are made to every quarter of the globe and the goods are as highly appreciated in Paris as in Philadelphia, in London as in New York, in Vienna, Berlin and Hamburg as in Chicago, Boston and Baltimore. Mr. Borgner is a native Philadelphian, a member of the Board of Trade, a charter member of the Builders' Exchange, a director of the Bourse, and accounted as one of those active, energetic, public-spirited business men, who build up great enterprises in every avenue of commerce and trade.

TOWNSEND WHELEN & CO., Bankers and Stock Brokers, No. 309 Walnut Street.—One of the principal firms engaged as bankers and brokers in this city is that of Messrs. Townsend Whelen & Co., whose business quarters are located at No. 309 Walnut Street. This representative house was established in 1837 by Messrs. Charnley & Whelen, who were succeeded in 1860 by Edward S. Whelen & Co., and on July 11, 1865, the present style was adopted. Messrs. Townsend Whelen & Co. carry on general operations as bankers and brokers, receiving deposits subject to check at sight, allowing interest on daily balances, buying and selling all classes of stocks and bonds on commission, and carrying the same on margins on the most favorable terms, and their ample resources and influential connections enable them to satisfactorily meet all the requirements of those with whom they have dealings. The latest stock news is constantly being received, and the fullest information regarding the movements of the market is available to customers. The New York correspondents of the firm are Messrs. Tillinghast & Griffin, of No. 11 Wall Street, while they are authorized agents for the city of Pittsburgh, the city of Allegheny, the Allegheny Valley Railroad Company, the Richmond, Fredericksburg & Potomac Railroad Company, the New England Loan and Trust Company, of Des Moines, Iowa, and other corporations. They execute large orders for business houses and private parties from all sections of the United States, and the character of their clientage abundantly demonstrates their energy, ability and influence. Appraisements of estates are made free of charge, and the facilities possessed by this firm for covering every branch of their business are unsurpassed and rarely equalled by any of their contemporaries in Philadelphia or New York. The individual members of this firm are Messrs. Henry Whelen, William N. Whelen, Henry Whelen, Jr., and Charles S. Whelen. Robert Coleman Drayton and J. Hunter Ewing, who have been in the employ of the Messrs. Whelen for many years, have an interest in the business. The firm are well known members of the Philadelphia and New York Stock Exchanges, and financiers of large experience, wide acquaintance and high repute.

G. W. PATTON & CO., Foreign and Domestic Wool, No. 38 North Front Street.—There is no interest of greater importance among the commercial resources of Philadelphia than the trade in wool, the aggregate annual transactions in this staple being of immense magnitude. Among the many houses engaged in this line none are more favorably known than that of G. W. Patton & Co., whose headquarters are at No. 38 North Front Street. This firm was organized ten years ago, and in 1891 Mr. C. J. Bigley, Mr. Patton's partner, retired. Mr. Patton is a native Philadelphian and has for many years been identified with the wool industry. He was for twelve years a partner in the firm of Wm. Hall & Co. His thorough experience, therefore, has given him an expert knowledge of wool, its values, and all the requirements of the trade, and how best to meet the demand. The warehouse occupied has four floors, each 25x125 feet in dimensions, and Mr. Patton also has a warehouse at No. 31 North Water Street, having five floors, each 25x225 feet in area. Heavy stocks are carried at both places. Mr. Patton is an importer of foreign wools, also of worsted and mohair yarns, and is a general dealer in all grades of foreign and domestic wool, woollen rags and shoddy. He has a large shoddy factory at Clifton Heights, Delaware County, Pa., which is equipped with three picker machines and six double sets of cards. The trade of the house is large, active, and extends all over the country, but is particularly heavy in Pennsylvania, New Jersey, Delaware, New York and New England, and Mr. Patton is prepared to meet orders at lowest current quotations.

JAMES E. DINGEE, Brick Manufacturer, Principal Office, Twenty-sixth and York Streets.—In the manufacture of building brick a leading and representative position in this city is occupied by Mr. James E. Dingee, whose office and brick yard are at the junction of Twenty-sixth and York Streets, and his residence at No. 1707 Master Street. This is a time honored concern, having been established in 1832 by the father of the present proprietor, Mr. Edward Dingee, by whom it was directed up to 1844, when his son, Mr. James E. Dingee, succeeded to the ownership. These brick works are probably the largest in the city. The property occupied covers an area of eighteen acres. The mechanical equipment is of the most complete, approved character. There are twelve large kilns, two boilers of 100 horse power each, two steam power presses having each a daily capacity of 140,000 brick, and two brick machines of 30,000 brick capacity a day each; then there are twenty-five hand made gangs, twenty-eight teams, and employment is found for about 350 hands. The output amounts to $2,000,000 brick a year, a leading specialty being made of pressed brick, and these are all disposed of in Philadelphia and vicinity. The products are all of a superior, uniform, reliable character, and a heavy stock is carried to meet the active demands of the trade. Mr. Dingee is a native of this city, a member of the Master Builders' Exchange and several fraternal societies, and he sustains a first class status in the business and financial world.

GEMMI BROS., Manufacturers of Pearl and Vegetable Ivory Buttons of Every Description, Nos. 123 and 125 North Fifth Street.—The designing, ornamentation and production of the finer class of buttons enlist the services of the best talent available in several of our large manufacturing cities. Buttons are of two kinds, those which are to be sewed to the garment through holes drilled in the button itself, and those which have a shank by which they are attached to the garment. A representative house in Philadelphia engaged in the manufacture of pearl and vegetable ivory buttons is that of Gemmi Bros., located at Nos. 123 and 125 North Fifth Street. The business was established in 1890 at the present location, and a liberal, permanent and influential patronage has already been built up. It is one of the largest establishments in its line in the city, and employment is furnished to from one hundred to one hundred and twenty-five skilled and experienced workmen. The premises occupied comprise a floor, 10x100 feet in dimensions, fully equipped with all improved machinery, operated by steam power. The pearl and vegetable ivory buttons manufactured by this house are unrivalled for quality, design, elegance, reliability and excellence by those of any other first class house in the trade in this country or Europe. The goods are general favorites with jobbers and retailers, and command a ready sale wherever introduced, while the prices quoted are the lowest in the market. The house has the capacity of producing from four thousand to five thousand gross per week, and is prepared to fill orders of any magnitude promptly. Its trade extends all over the United States, and is being constantly increased under the efficient efforts of a corps of competent traveling salesmen. Mr. Barton Gemmi, the active member of the firm, is an enterprising and reliable business man, and has had fifteen years' experience in this business. The house has developed an extensive industrial interest of a very beneficial and useful character, in every respect a credit and a source of strength to the city.

ARCHIBALD HOLMES, Manufacturer of Extra Superfine Ingrain Carpetings, Hancock Street above Lehigh Avenue. An old established house holding a popular place in the carpet trade is that of Archibald Holmes. This establishment was founded in 1872, on Taylor Street, by the present proprietor, who began with sixteen hand looms. Success following his efforts, he afterwards removed to Trenton Avenue, where he put in twelve power looms. Prosperity continuing to attend him, he in 1887 removed to the present address, where the equipment comprises twenty looms, all run by steam power, and having a productive capacity of one hundred and forty rolls of carpet per month, each roll having one hundred and forty yards, or a grand total of nearly twenty thousand yards monthly. Employment is found for thirty-five experienced hands. Mr. Holmes has had mature experience in his vocation, possesses an expert knowledge of all its details, and personally looks after the labors of his assistants. He manufactures extra superfine ingrain carpetings in a large variety of handsome designs. He is constantly introducing new patterns, and the goods are always kept up to the highest standard of excellence. Mr. Holmes was born abroad, but has lived in Philadelphia for the past forty-five years. He has built up a splendid trade as a manufacturer, selling direct to leading jobbers in New York, Chicago, St. Louis, and other prominent cities.

OWENS BROTHERS, Manufacturers of Fine Cloth Hats and Caps, Factory, Palmyra, N. J.; Office, No. 620 Arch Street. That the manufacture of fine cloth hats and caps is one of great magnitude is sufficiently evidenced by the operations of this prominent old house alone. The spacious factory it occupies at Palmyra, N. J., is equipped with a great number of the most perfect machines, but despite the productiveness which these facilities, regular work is found for forty trained operatives. Cloth hats and caps of the finest description are made in an infinite variety of styles, shapes and sizes, and a stock of great bulk is at all times carried. Owens, Roemich & Co., were the founders of the business, in 1880, and the business has been carried on for five years under the present title. The present firm consists of Harry H. and Frank T. Owens, both experienced and honorable young men. The trade extends all over the United States and goods are shipped direct to purchasers. The Messrs. Owens were born in New Jersey. They are young men occupying a foremost position in the front ranks of their industry.

ARCH STREET, WEST OF SIXTH STREET.

SEARLE, VANNEMAN & CO., Importers and Jobbers of Hosiery, White Goods, Notions, Men's Furnishing Goods, No. 731 Market Street. A new aspirant for the favor and patronage of the trade in hosiery and notions made its appearance in Philadelphia in 1890, upon a basis of substantial equipment, ample resources, magnificent facilities, and a wide and valuable experience, such as no other firm could command at its inception. We refer to the popular and flourishing house of Messrs. Searle, Vanneman & Co., located at No. 731 Market Street. They are extensive importers and jobbers of hosiery, white goods, notions and men's furnishing goods, and carry at all times an immense stock of both foreign and domestic products. The building occupied for trade purposes contains four floors and a basement, 40 x 150 feet each, with an annex floor of the same size, all arranged to the best advantage for the adequate display of goods. As importers, this firm possess facilities unsurpassed by those of any of their contemporaries, and are constantly offering a large and varied assortment of the choicest fabrics and latest styles and novelties, culled from the best markets of the world to enrich the salesrooms of American dealers. The specialties embrace ladies' fast black cotton hosiery, ladies' colored cotton hose, ladies' Lisle hose, unbleached Balbriggan hose, opera hose, ladies' silk hose, children's cotton hosiery, children's Lisle hose, infants' hosiery, children's silk hosiery, gentlemen's solid colored cotton half hose, genuine Irish Balbriggan half hose, black and colored bright silk half hose, merino half hose and bicycle hose, double satin damasks, cream damask, bleached table cloths, tray cloths, cardinal cloths, linen sheeting, fancy Turkish towels, huckaback toweling, men's white shirts, night shirts, flannel and neglige shirts, silk outing shirts, linen collars and cuffs, waterproof and celluloid collars and cuffs, silk scarfs, white lawn ties, plain and fancy silk suspenders, hose supporters, sporting outfits, gentlemen's pajamas and fine underwear, fine quality neck ruche, ruffling, skirt plaitings, tourist ruffling, made-up laces, children's lace collars, veilings, black laces, white real laces, white imitation laces, web laces, silk and linen handkerchiefs, Hamburg embroideries, aprons, buttons, tidies, pin cushions, and white goods and notions in great profusion and variety. Buying in large quantities from the most celebrated manufacturers at home and abroad, this firm have become widely and deservedly noted for their splendid array of goods and the liberality of their terms and prices. They supply the leading retailers throughout the country, being represented on the road by a corps of expert salesmen, and are in a position to guarantee the prompt and perfect fulfillment of all orders. The copartners, Messrs. O. H. Searle and T. H. Vanneman, are both in the active prime of life, subscribers to the Bourse, and merchants of thorough enterprise and marked executive ability.

HISTORICAL AND COMMERCIAL PHILADELPHIA.

HENRY KELLY, Public Accountant, No. 58 South Third Street, (Northwest Corner Third and Chestnut Streets).—In making reference to the more prominent public accountants in Philadelphia, more than a passing mention should be made of the business conducted by Mr. Henry Kelly, of No. 58 South Third Street, (northwest corner Third and Chestnut Streets,) which, albeit of an extensive and comprehensive nature, has a direct and by no means unappreciable influence upon the best interests of finance, trade and commerce here. Mr. Kelly's operations, while largely centered in Philadelphia and the adjacent districts, extend, nevertheless, throughout the United States, and comprise a general accountancy business. The keeping and closing of books, the preparation of balance sheets and manufacturers' cost accounts, of which latter he makes a specialty, and the periodical auditing of books and accounts for any kind of financial, manufacturing, trade or mercantile, house are matters for which Mr. Kelly's services are largely sought. But he devotes more especial study and attention to what may be designated the higher walks of the profession, the arrangement, adjustment and final settlement or determination of partnerships, the apportioning of claims where several interests are involved, the detection of defalcations, the adjustment of systematic discrepancies or faulty accounts and the preparation and arrangement of delicate and intricate accounts, as well as the adjustment of estates and complicated interests upon recognized rules and usages of law and equity. Mr. Kelly has been established here since January 1, 1884, and he has since gained the highest reputation for the masterly skill with which he deals promptly and decisively with any matter he takes in hand, while as to accuracy it need scarcely be said that without it he could not have survived the first twelve months, there being but one result in accountancy, and that the correct one. Mr. Kelly has twenty-five years' practical experience at his command and is a Fellow of the American Association of Public Accountants. He was born within the city of London, in 1847, and he has been a resident of Philadelphia since he reached the United States in 1882. Mr. Kelly is frequently called upon to examine properties of all kinds, including large industrial enterprises, with a view to placing them on the market.

STANDARD SEWING MACHINE COMPANY, No. 923 Arch Street.—The "Standard" rotary shuttle sewing machine is acknowledged to be the most wonderful invention of the age in its line, and is pronounced superior to any other in the world. It is manufactured by the Standard Sewing Machine Company of Cleveland, Ohio, and is sold in Philadelphia by Mr. T. D. Brown as the company's manager for Eastern Pennsylvania, Southern New Jersey, the District of Columbia and the States of Delaware and Maryland, with headquarters at No. 923 Arch Street. The Standard shuttle is wheel-shaped and revolves upon its own center. It does not cease its motion while the machine is in operation. The old-style shuttles start and stop twice at every stitch. This causes great friction, strain, noise and unsteadiness, when rapidly run. The Standard runs as easy, smooth and quiet at 1500 stitches per minute as others do at 700. The Standard is self-threading throughout, except the needle. The needle is the shortest used in lock-stitch machines. Finer needles with the same size thread or silk can be used than in any old-style shuttle machine. The needle is self-setting; no change of tension required for different thicknesses of goods. There is no necessity for holding the thread at the beginning of a seam to prevent it from being drawn down; no change of tension required for different lengths of stitch. The first stitch is perfect, without holding the ends of thread. The tension is entirely released when taking out the goods by a simple device peculiar to the Standard. These unexcelled machines are made in several different styles for families, dressmakers and manufacturers. They are to be found on sale in all parts of the country, and are highly endorsed by users everywhere. Mr. Brown has a stock of one thousand of these machines on hand in this city, to the end that no delay may be experienced in the filling of orders, and gives steady employment to 125 assistants in this agency. Mr. Geo. W. Hindermyer has charge of the retail department, and will be found prompt and efficient in meeting every demand of the public. Mr. Brown is a native of Wilmington, Del., with the Domestic Sewing Machine Company for eighteen years, and a young man of wide experience, eminent popularity and sterling personal worth.

JOHN D. PESSANO, Real Estate Broker, No. 907 Walnut Street.—For the past two years, Mr. John D. Pessano, located at No. 907 Walnut Street, has been prominently identified with the improvement and development of real estate in Philadelphia and the suburbs, and his name is now closely associated with some of the most successful realty investments on record. Of these may be noted the suburb of Berlin, which when opened up had one thousand lots, and now has but one hundred and forty left; the present value being far in advance of the original purchase price, also sixty-three beautiful houses at Fifty-second Street Station, and others at Mount Airy near Chestnut Hill. Although established on his own account but two years, Mr. Pessano has taken a long course of law studies and possesses a wide range of practical experience in the profession, extending over a period of fifteen years, thirteen years of which were spent with one of the most influential real estate firms in this city, added to which he exercises sound judgment and scrupulous care in the fulfillment of all he undertakes. Thus, he has gained the confidence and perpetual support of a large number of influential property owners, capitalists, trustees, investors and others in and around the city, for whom he transacts a general real estate business, buying, selling, renting and exchanging all kinds of realty on commission, collecting house rents at three per cent commission and ground rents and interest at one per cent commission, settling, transferring and taking entire charge of estates and negotiating loans upon bond or mortgage at the fairest rates of interest; also undertaking the preparation and detailed examination of titles, deeds, leases, wills, trusts and similar legal instruments, together with the several other branches of practical conveyancing while he possesses especial facilities for directing all desirable fire, life and accident insurances into the hands of the best and soundest corporations at the lowest current rates of premium. Mr. Pessano was born in this city in 1864 and is held in warm regard, as much for his sterling integrity as for his recognized professional attainments.

D. S. WILTBERGER, Wholesale Druggist and Dealer in Paints, Oils, Glass and Patent Medicines, No. 233 North Second Street.—An old-time and prominent Philadelphia wholesale drug house is that of D. S. Wiltberger, No. 233 North Second Street. It is one of the oldest and foremost in the city, being in existence for eighty-odd years, and has always maintained a high reputation in the trade. This business was established in 1812, by Thomas Wiltberger, who was succeeded by his son Alfred Wiltberger, who died in January, 1872, when his brother, D. S. Wiltberger, assumed control, and has since conducted it with uninterrupted success. He is a general wholesale druggist and dealer in paints, oils, glass and patent medicines, and is proprietor of Barlow's indigo blue, a preparation of exceptional merit, which has been on the market now for over forty years. His trade, which is large, extends throughout Pennsylvania, New Jersey and Delaware. The business premises occupy four spacious floors and are well ordered and excellently arranged in every department. The office is connected by telephone (No. 179), the facilities, altogether, are first-class and a dozen to fifteen are employed in the establishment. The stock, which is of a comprehensive character, is very large and carefully selected and includes everything in the line of pure drugs, chemicals, acids, extracts, tinctures, etc., all the standard proprietary remedies and patent medicines, seeds, spices, roots, barks and herbs, soda, saleratus and kindred products, and mineral waters, toilet articles, perfumery, soaps, sponges, chamois skins, medicated paper and druggists' sundries in great variety; also a full line of paints, oils, window glass and painters' supplies generally. The trade is supplied on the most favorable terms, the lowest possible prices being quoted, and all orders are filled in the most prompt and trustworthy manner. Mr. Wiltberger is a gentleman past middle age and was born in this city. He is a man of entire reliability in his dealings, as well as business ability and experience, and is a member of the Philadelphia Drug Exchange, the Board of Trade, the Trade League and the Bourse.

HISTORICAL AND COMMERCIAL PHILADELPHIA.

THE GUARANTEE COMPANY OF NORTH AMERICA, A. F. Sabine, Resident Secretary, No. 506 Walnut Street.—The Guarantee Company of North America, whose head office is at Montreal and whose Philadelphia office is located at No. 506 Walnut Street, is the original company in the United States, the oldest and largest of its kind in America, and the second largest purely guarantee company in the world. The business of this company is solely that of granting bonds of suretyship for employees of approved character, guaranteeing the faithful discharge of their duties in positions of trust. Its bonds are accepted and generally preferred by leading banks, railways and commercial institutions, while its contracts are amply secured by assets and resources of over $1,100,000, and an annual revenue of over $410,000. It also retains ample balances at its several branches. The Philadelphia office was opened in November, 1881, and has been under the constant management of Mr. A. F. Sabine as resident secretary, and as manager for Pennsylvania, New Jersey, Delaware and Maryland, with local agencies at Baltimore and Pittsburg. This office alone issued bonds in the year 1891 to the amount of nearly $8,000,000, and the records and facilities of the company are at the service of its patrons, enabling it to surround employers with safeguards not to be afforded by any other means. This is the only guarantee company in America which confines its business exclusively to guaranteeing officers and employees of financial and commercial corporations, preferring experienced methods and continued solvency rather than an increased revenue, accompanied by the hazards and divided attention of a mixed surety or casualty business. Its extensive ramifications and channels of correspondence throughout the world afford important means of protection to employers against the retention or admission to service of persons of doubtful integrity, and have often been of material aid to employers in recovering losses in excess of amounts covered by the company's bonds. It has repaid to employers over $800,000 for losses sustained by the infidelity of employees without contest at law, while the prevention of defaults by thorough investigation and subsequent revision of employees is made a special point in this company's service. Its rates are based upon experience and practical knowledge of the business, and they are the lowest consistent with efficient service and security. It has a paid-up capital of $310,000 with a surplus to policy-holders of $500,581.80 and total resources for security of policy-holders amounting to $1,119,916.50. The officers and directors of the company are as follows, viz.: President, Sir Alexander T. Galt; E. S. Clouston, general manager Bank of Montreal; Geo. Hague, general manager Merch Bank, Canada; D. S. MacDougall, MacDougall Bros., financial agents; T. G. Shaughnessy, vice-president Canadian

Pacific Railroad; E. C. Smith, president Central Vermont Railroad, St. Albans; Wm. Wainwright, assistant general manager Grand Trunk Railroad; Wm. J. Withall, vice-president Quebec Bank, Montreal; vice-president and managing director, Edward Rawlings. The Philadelphia directors consist of the following well-known and substantial citizens: Benjamin B. Comegys, president Philadelphia National Bank; J. Livingston Erringer, president Philadelphia Trust Company; Amos R. Little, director Pennsylvania Railroad; Thos. DeWitt Cuyler; Alfred M. Collins, A. M. Collins, Sons & Co.; John C. Sims, Jr., secretary Pennsylvania Railroad Company; C. Hartshorne, vice-president Lehigh Valley Railroad; G. R. W. Armes, assistant treasurer Norfolk & Western Railroad; Geo. M. Troutman, president Central National Bank. Mr. Sabine, the resident secretary, is a native of England, who was connected with the insurance business for a period of thirty-six years and is a gentleman of large experience, eminent ability and sterling worth, with whom it is always a pleasure to do business.

THE WRIGLEY MANUFACTURING COMPANY, Sixteenth Street and Erie Avenue.—One of the representative corporations of Philadelphia is the Wrigley Manufacturing Company, known and honored both at home and abroad as the proprietors of Wrigley's Mineral Scouring Soap, whose headquarters are located at the above address. This company was organized in 1870 by Mr. William Wrigley, and under his energetic and capable management its career has been remarkably successful, while the steadily increasing demand for the product indicates how perfectly it has met the wants of the public. The factory is a two-story building, 40 x 100 feet in size, splendidly equipped with the latest improved machinery and ample steam-power, while the work is conducted under the personal supervision of Mr. Wrigley, whose large practical experience and known progressive enterprise are evidenced in the superior qualities of the soap bearing the company's imprint. To clean, scrub, scour and polish, Wrigley's Mineral Scouring Soap is emphatically the best and cheapest soap extant, and is rapidly taking the place of more expensive articles. It is the most effective soap in the world for cleaning painted wood-work, floors, windows, oil cloths, woolenware, glass and crockery, marble floors and bath tubs; for scouring and polishing tin, iron or brass ware, knives and forks, stair rods, brass spigots, and all metal surfaces, and for removing rust from machinery, surgical and dental instruments, etc.; also for washing hands. With less application of strength, and in a brief time it produces a lasting and brilliant finish on all metallic surfaces, while it is death to dirt in any and every form, is perfectly harmless to the skin and will not injure the hands. Its sales are constantly on the increase, the trade finding it very desirable to handle, selling readily to the public, and, once introduced, creating for itself a permanent future demand. It has, in fact, leaped at once into the line of staple products, and become a familiar household word. Wrigley's "Up to Date" laundry soap is perfectly pure, softens hard water, and will not injure hands or fabrics. The cakes are thicker and larger than the "Ivory" soap, and are sold at five cents. It will float, and can be used just as you like. These goods are in heavy and growing demand, not only in all parts of the United States but in many European countries. A branch house is operated at No. 157 Kinzie Street, Chicago, which supplies the Western trade. Mr. Wrigley, the founder and moving spirit of this enterprise, is a native Philadelphian, who served with honor and credit throughout the Civil War as captain of Company H, 95th Pennsylvania Infantry, and who is past commander of Post No. 2, G. A. R., and also very prominent in Masonic circles.

HISTORICAL AND COMMERCIAL PHILADELPHIA.

HARLES O. STRUSE, Dealer in Lehigh and Schuylkill Coal, Lime, Kindling Wood, and Builders' Supplies in General, Cement, Sand, Stone, Brick, Chimney Tops, Drum Pipe, Kindling Wood by Box or Load, Yard, Shur's Lane, Manayunk. Among the best known of the most successful houses in Philadelphia engaged in handling coal and building supplies special mention should be made of Mr. Charles O. Struse, whose yard is located at Shur's Lane, Manayunk. Mr. Struse established business eight years ago, at the above address, and has since built up a large trade throughout the city and its vicinity. The extensive yard occupied covers an area of 75 x 256 feet, has numerous coal pockets, and is connected by a siding with the Philadelphia & Reading Railroad, which conveys the coal directly to the pockets. These have each a storage capacity of 200 tons, and a stock of 1800 tons of coal is always kept on hand. Mr. Struse handles the best grades of Lehigh and Schuylkill coal, and also deals in kindling wood, lime, cement, sand, stone, brick, chimney tops, drum pipe, and builders' supplies in general. Mr. Struse is assisted in the management of the business by his two sons, who are twins. Four teams are run, and an active trade is supplied. The house sustains an excellent reputation wherever known. Mr. Struse was born in Manayunk, and is a stone mason by trade, having had an experience of thirty-five years in this line. He is also a builder, and does a large business in building and selling houses. During the war he enlisted in the 119th Regiment, Pennsylvania Volunteer Infantry, but was returned as too young. Toward the end of the war, however, he joined the 73d Pennsylvania Volunteer Infantry, and took part in the campaign. He is a member of Post No. 12, G. A. R., also of the Masonic Order, and enjoys the esteem of all his fellow-citizens.

HE HASTINGS TRUSS CO., Manufacturers of Indestructible Hard Rubber Trusses, Leather Covered and Elastic Trusses, Supporters, Shoulder Braces, Etc., No. 221 South Ninth Street. The Hastings Truss Company, No. 221 South Ninth Street, are the largest producers of indestructible hard rubber and leather covered trusses, belts, supporters, etc., in the world. Established in 1872, under the name of Hastings & Garson, their signal success is a triumph of that necessary combination of intelligence, mechanical skill and untiring energy. From Buenos Ayres to Puget Sound, from Quebec to antipodal Australia, their trusses are kept on sale by druggists and surgical instrument dealers generally. In their special application department orders to meet particularly difficult cases are frequently received from the principal cities of South America, Spain, Portugal, and even British India, Japan and China. The United States government, through the Marine Hospital Service, the army and the Indian departments,

has favored this company with orders for large quantities of their apparatus. The various hernial lesions, often threatening the life of the patient, are successfully treated by the expert fitters in their application department. To the Philadelphia public The Hastings Truss Company is very popularly known through extensive advertising of cut prices in their appliances, trusses are fitted at such low charges that the best appliances are within the purchasing capacity of the poorest sufferer. The present head and front of this thriving business is Major William H. Hastings, manager and treasurer of the company, a well-known and popular citizen, and an elder brother of General D. H. Hastings. The equipment of The Hastings Truss Company's factory is unsurpassed, the machinery and appliances being of the most modern and improved patterns. Employment is given to from sixty to one hundred employees. The capacity of the factory is one million instruments per annum.

W. G. ELLIS & CO., Manufacturers of the Star Seamless Hosiery, Nos. 115, 117 and 119 Race Street. The manufacture of ladies', gents', misses', and children's hose is carried on in this city upon the most extensive scale by the firm of W. G. Ellis & Co., whose establishment is located at Nos. 115, 117 and 119 Race Street. This firm are deservedly prominent as manufacturers of the Star Seamless Hosiery, and have been established in the business here since 1882. They bring to bear ample resources and splendid facilities, as an inspection of their large factory abundantly demonstrates. It comprises three floors, 50 x 100 feet each, equipped with 125 seamless knitting machines, fifty rib frames, ten looping machines, and five sewing machines, operated by steam power, and steady employment is given therein to from one hundred and seventy-five to two hundred operatives. The productive capacity of the factory is 600 dozen per day, and these goods find a ready sale and a permanent demand among jobbers in all parts of the United States. Quality is ever the first consideration, and the management is not only able and experienced, but the most progressive of any in the knit goods industry, continually introducing to the trade with marked success various novelties and valuable specialties which sell rapidly and take with the public wherever introduced. The hosiery here manufactured is preferred by many dealers to any other make, on account of its great salability, the uniform excellence and solid merits, while terms and prices are made invariably satisfactory to buyers. Shipments are regularly made to the great centers of New York, Chicago, St. Louis, Boston, Baltimore, Cincinnati, New Orleans, San Francisco, Kansas City, St. Paul, Minneapolis, Milwaukee, Detroit, Louisville, Atlanta, Savannah, Charleston, Richmond, Pittsburg and other points, and the trade is steadily on the increase. Mr. Ellis, the active member of the firm, is a native of Bucks County, Pa., for some years with Ellis, Ayers & Co., jobbers in hosiery and notions, and an expert and talented business man, whose sound judgment and executive capacity is generally recognized.

HARLES CHIPMAN & SON, Manufacturers of Hosiery and Underwear, No. 1649 Wakefield Street, Germantown. To say that the hosiery and knit-goods interests in Germantown constitutes a factor of surpassing importance in the sum of industrial activity of Philadelphia hardly conveys an adequate idea of the great extent thereof. Within a quarter of a century it has grown from comparatively limited proportions to vast magnitude, and it is worthy of remark, too, that the improvement in the productions has fully kept pace with the growth of the industry. Distinctly notable among the big concerns in the line indicated is that of Charles Chipman & Son, manufacturers of hosiery and underwear, No. 1649 Wakefield Street. This is the largest and best-equipped plant of the kind in the city, and the facilities are of a most superior character. The Messrs. Chipman manufacture an excellent article of cotton hosiery and underwear, and their goods command an immense sale throughout the country. This flourishing enterprise had inception in 1881, when the business was established by the senior member of the firm, who conducted it alone up to 1888, when he admitted into partnership his son, Frank L. Chipman. The factory, which was built expressly for the purpose some three years ago, is a spacious four-story structure, with a T-extension dyehouse, etc., in connection. There is in service a 150-horse power engine, 318 knitting machines of various kinds, eighty sewing machines and all the latest improved appliances, and upward of 300 hands are employed. The productive capacity is 300 dozen pairs per day, and the output is sold to the trade through jobbers all over the country. The Messrs. Chipman are Philadelphians by birth, and trace their ancestry back to 1683 in this city, their forefathers being among the earliest settlers hereabouts. Mr. Chipman the elder is also interested in several other mills in Schuylkill County.

HISTORICAL AND COMMERCIAL PHILADELPHIA.

ARTHUR W. HOWE, Iron Commission Merchant, Iron, Steel and Ores, No. 607 Drexel Building.—One of the most successful and active commission merchants in the line of iron, steel and ores in this city is Mr. Arthur W. Howe. Though only established a little over two years he has in that time, by strict attention to business, developed an extensive and growing trade throughout New England and the Middle States. Among the companies represented by Mr. Howe are the New Jersey and Pennsylvania Concentrating Works, of Ogden, N. J., producers of concentrated ore; the Delaware Rolling Mills, of Phillipsburg, N. J.; the Princess Furnace, Glen Wilton, Va.; and the Muirkirk Furnace, Muirkirk, Md., etc. He has also a large and valuable trade in black furnace and foundry coke and bituminous coal. Mr. Howe's office is conveniently located at No. 607 Drexel Building, where he is prepared to execute with promptness and care any business with which he may be intrusted.

CROFT & ALLEN CO., Manufacturers of Confections, Chocolate and Preserved Cocoanut, Market and Thirty-third Streets.— One of the most striking instances of successful business development in Philadelphia is that afforded by the Croft & Allen Company, manufacturers of confections, chocolate and preserved cocoanut, at Market and Thirty-third Streets. The foundation of the business was laid in the sixties by Samuel Croft, and subsequently the firm of Croft & Wilbur was organized, succeeded in turn by the firm of Croft, Wilbur & Co., in 1870, and Croft & Allen in 1885; and on the first of January, 1891, the present company was incorporated under the laws of the State of Pennsylvania, with a capital stock of $100,000, and with Samuel Croft, president; Geo. W. Allen, vice-president; V. W. Walter, treasurer; & F. Roberts, secretary. The present premises have been occupied since 1889, and comprise five immense floors, having a frontage of 230 feet on Market, 315 feet on Lancaster Avenue and 208 feet on Thirty-third Street, all fitted up with new and improved machinery, operated by a steam-engine of 250-horse power and four boilers of 400-horse power, and employment is given to a force of 600 skilled hands. There is an arc and incandescent electric light plant, a De La Vergne refrigerating plant for the chocolate cooling room, together with two elevators, automatic sprinklers and other modern improvements. The company are large importers of the cocoa bean and cocoanuts, and manufacture chocolates, lozenges, marsh-mallows, preserved cocoanut, cream chocolates and fine imperial work, all in immense quantities. Their fine chocolate goods proved at once a gratifying revelation to the trade, and have spread into widespread popularity and a growing demand. Their confections include all the rare, exquisite flavors so difficult to obtain in their pristine excellence elsewhere. The management has shown marked enterprise in widening the field of their styles and novelties in flavors, combinations and importations, and confectioners handling their goods can meet every taste and fancy in pure and wholesome confectionery. They have always believed in giving the public the best only. They consequently use only the purest and choicest of chocolates, sugars, flavors, extracts and vegetable colors, all manipulated in the most cleanly and scientific manner, by their own processes, with the result that purchasers accept this company's trade-mark as proof of quality and demand it in preference to all others. Although now the largest manufactory of the kind in the United States, the company are contemplating an addition which will make it 50 per cent. larger, and own the property opposite, which will be eligible for the extension. They send out a corps of talented salesmen on the road, and fill the largest orders with promptness and scrupulous care. Their trade extends to all parts of the United States, Canada, England, and South America, and their field of usefulness is constantly enlarging. The officers are all well-known Philadelphians, expert and practical confectioners, members of the National Confectioners' Association, the Philadelphia Bourse, Board of Trade and Grocers' and Importers' Exchange, and honored and esteemed in the business world.

B. A. HERTSCH & CO., Manufacturing Chemists. Sole Makers of the B. A. Hertsch Brand Prepared Glue, No. 1161 Germantown Avenue, Nicetown.—There is no vocation so fraught with responsibility as that of the apothecary, for upon his accuracy human life itself depends. Fatal mistakes are constantly being made, a fact well-known to newspaper readers, and therefore the greatest care should be exercised, when drugs are needed, to secure them from an establishment whose reputation is sans reproche. Such an establishment is that of B. A. Hertsch & Co., of Nicetown, and it is the largest and leading house of the kind in this section of the city. The business was founded in 1889 by the present active proprietor, Mr. B. A. Hertsch. This gentleman was born in Germany, but has resided in the United States twenty-three years. He graduated from the Philadelphia College of Pharmacy in 1891, is a member of its Alumni, and also of the State Pharmaceutical Association. He is prominently identified with the Masonic Fraternity, being a member of Mitchell Lodge, No. 296; Germantown R. A. Chapter, No. 208; Phila. Commandery, K. T. No. 2; Phila. Consistory, 32°; of Philadelphia, and Lulu Temple, A. A. O. N. M. Shrine. Mr. Hertsch is a thoroughly skilled pharmacist and manufacturing chemist, and he gives special attention to the compounding of physicians' prescriptions, accuracy being assured in every instance. The premises occupied comprise a store and two upper floors, each 20 x 50 feet in dimensions, the store being finely finished in oak, and appointed with show cases, a handsome soda fount, and attractive shelfware. An immense stock is carried of pure drugs and chemicals, proprietary medicines, sponges, perfumes, toilet goods, confections, roots, herbs, fancy articles, cigars, acids, dye stuffs, white lead, oils, turpentine, varnish, glass, putty and a general line of painters' supplies. The firm are agents for the Pixto Cough Cure, Pixto Liver Pills, Pixto Plasters, Bender's Rheumatic Remedy, Jackson's Cholera Drops, Jackson's Sarsaparilla, and Mrs. Evans' Soothing Syrup. A leading specialty is made of B. A. Hertsch's Brand Prepared Glue, which is put up in large and small bottles, and is sold very extensively, especially in the West. The firm commands a large, active trade, and their patronage is steadily growing in volume.

G. J. LITTLEWOOD & CO., Albion Dye and Bleach Works, Main Street, Below Shur's Lane, Manayunk, City Office, No. 132 Chestnut Street, Main Office and Works.—The Albion Dye and Bleach Works of this city have been in active operation since 1868, when they were founded by Mr. G. J. Littlewood, who adopted the firm-name of G. J. Littlewood & Co. The main works are on Main Street, below Shur's Lane, Manayunk, while for the convenience of customers a city office is maintained at No. 132 Chestnut Street. Mr. Littlewood was born in England, but has resided in this city the greater part of his life, having come here some fifty years ago when a young man eighteen years of age. Since then through energy and industry he has become one of the most prominent citizens, and now holds the office of vice-president of the Manayunk Trust Company, besides being sole owner of a most prosperous business. The Albion Dye and Bleach Works cover an area of 100 x 250 feet, and are equipped with the most approved appliances incidental to the business. Employment is furnished seventy-five operatives, and an active business is done in dyeing cotton yarn, warps, wool and raw stock in general for mills in all parts of the United States, but especially in Virginia and North Carolina. The resources of the establishment enable it to fill all orders at shortest notice, no matter how large they may be, and in the matter of prices the firm can successfully meet all competition.

HISTORICAL AND COMMERCIAL PHILADELPHIA.

ALEX. KERR, BRO. & CO., Importers and Dealers in all Kinds of Salt, Pier 8, North Wharves. The oldest as well as the largest importers and dealers in salt of all kinds in this country are Messrs. Alex. Kerr, Bro. & Co., of this city, whose headquarters are located at Pier 8, North Wharves, and who are also owners of the Kerr Salt Company, manufacturers of all kinds of salt, at Rock Glen, Wyoming County, N. Y. The business was established here in 1849 by Alexander Kerr, the present firm being organized in 1877, composed of the founder of the house and Messrs. Frank Kerr, his brother, and Samuel T. Kerr, his son. In 1886 they established the Kerr Salt Company, and have opened up salt wells 2,000 feet deep. They handle all kinds and grades of salt in car, cargo, and smaller lots, exclusively at wholesale, and possess unequalled facilities for conducting the business upon a grand scale. The connections of the house with salt manufacturers abroad places it in a position to command every favorable opportunity of the foreign market and to offer inducements to the trade in quality and prices of goods which challenge comparison and defy successful competition. This firm is prepared to supply salt which is considered superior to any other in the market for the curing of provisions of all kinds, fish, pickles, and for many other purposes, also the best coarse salt, rock salt, and the finer grades for the dairy, table and culinary purposes. The business is broadly distributed throughout the entire United States, and an office is operated at No. 303 Exchange Place, Baltimore, Md. The Messrs. Kerr are accounted among the best known business men of Philadelphia, closely identified with the commercial growth and prosperity of the city. They are members of the Importers' and Grocers' Exchange, the Board of Trade, the Commercial Exchange, and the Maritime Exchange, and possess an expert knowledge of the various qualities and kinds of salt, and are recognized authority in their special branch of trade.

EDWARD MEEKS, Publisher, No. 1012 Walnut Street. Philadelphia has ever been a leading centre of the publishing interests of the world, and the works issued by its leading houses go to all parts of the globe. Much capital is invested in this intellectual industry, as well as the time and energies of some of our most talented business men. One of the successful establishments in the trade is that of Mr. Edward Meeks, whose office and stockroom is at No. 1012 Walnut Street. Mr. Meeks is a native of Philadelphia, has arrived at the meridian of life, and has been engaged in the book business since youth; consequently he possesses an expert knowledge of all its requirements. He was with the houses of J. B. Lippincott & Co. and Claxton, Remsen & Co., and left their employ to establish business on his own account. In this venture he has been thoroughly prosperous, winning a large, steadily growing patronage, and shipping his publications to all parts of the civilized world. Mr. Meeks publishes only high class standard works, including volumes of poetry, volumes on literary subjects, works of science, practical hand books for engineers and others, and the "Avon" edition of Shakespeare. A catalogue giving full information as to titles, authors, prices, etc., is mailed to any address on application, and any book ordered will be sent to the address designated, free of postage, at the price indicated by the catalogue.

H. R. RAIGUEL, JR., Superintendent of the Prudential Insurance Company, No. 139 South Seventh Street. The Prudential Insurance Company of America, whose home offices are located in Newark, N. J., was the first to introduce industrial insurance into America, the first to issue an incontestable industrial policy, and the first to give dividend additions to its industrial policies. It now offers the most liberal industrial policy in this country. The Prudential is represented in Philadelphia by Mr. H. R. Raiguel, Jr., as superintendent of the first district, with headquarters at No. 139 South Seventh Street. The company established its business here in 1879 with one office, and it now operates five offices in different sections of the city. The Prudential insures every member of a family between one and seventy years of age, if in good health. It issues small policies with correspondingly small premiums to suit every condition of life. It makes premiums payable weekly, thus dividing even the small annual premium into fifty two parts, so as to make it possible for the poorest to carry an insurance policy. It issues endowment policies for small weekly premiums, and paid up policies in exchange for any policy issued by the company after premiums have been paid for five years from January 1, 1892. It now has a larger membership than any other company in the world of the same age, and a greater ratio of assets to liabilities than is shown by the largest life insurance companies in the United States. It has paid up to the year 1875 the sum of $9,000,000 in death claims, and had 1,400,000 policies in force, with assets of $6,883,671.32, and a surplus to policy holders of $1,149,067.06. Its Philadelphia offices alone collect $30,000 per week, and give employment to over three hundred people. Mr. Raiguel has been with the company for the past ten years, and is an accepted authority in industrial insurance.

HALL ROHRMAN & SON, Tinwares, Nos. 155 to 161 North Front Street. This is one of the oldest and largest concerns of the kind in the city, and has been in operation for nearly half a century. The firm are manufacturers of tinwares of every description, and are wholesale dealers in iron and agate hollow ware, tea caddies, coffee mills, coolers and kindred grocery store supplies. They do an immense business, and their trade extends throughout the United States. The factory occupies four 75x75 foot floors, and is equipped with full steam power, machinery, etc., while fifty to seventy-five hands are employed. The office and sales department are at No. 55 North Second Street, and the premises there comprise four 30x90 foot floors. A vast, varied and complete stock is constantly kept on hand, and half a dozen salesmen represent the house on the road. With unequalled facilities this firm can offer exceptional inducements to the trade, quoting rock bottom prices. This widely known house was established in 1846 by J. Hall Rohrman, who was succeeded by J. Hall Rohrman & Son. Mr. Rohrman the elder was removed by death, and the business was conducted the business alone up to 1889, when he retired, and R. W. Birdsall became sole proprietor. Mr. Birdsall, who has since continued the business under the old firm name with uninterrupted success, is a gentleman of middle age and a native of Lancaster County, Pa. He is a director of the Camden National Bank, and a member of the Mercantile Beneficial Association.

J. L. SMITH'S MAP ESTABLISHMENT, No. 27 South Sixth Street. The history of the career of Mr. J. L. Smith's Map Establishment for twenty years has been a plain record of prosperity. His business embraces the preparation of maps of every conceivable order and variety; also atlases, globes, spring rollers, map cases, drawing papers, tracing cloth, engineers' supplies, etc. Special attention is given to job work, and every facility is at hand for mounting in all styles drawings, plans and maps on spring rollers, in cases, on cloth, on stretchers, and cut to fold. He carries a splendid line of maps, both mounted and in pocket form; including a railroad and commercial map of the United States and Canadas, the most reliable railroad map ever made; maps of the world in various sizes and styles; indexed pocket maps of the various States and Territories; library and office maps of the different countries of the world; maps of Philadelphia, London, Paris, Montreal, Mexico, Chicago, Cincinnati, New York, and other cities; post route maps of the States, used in the postal service; large scale maps of the States and Territories, school maps, guide books, Johnston's illustrative charts, indexed maps, sectional State maps, new railroad and business atlas, atlases of the world, metric charts, globes, spring rollers, etc., and the trade is both wholesale and retail, extending to all parts of the United States. Mr. Smith is a native Philadelphian, and enlisted in '62 as a drummer boy in the 118th Pennsylvania Infantry, serving three years, and becoming a corporal. He is the author of the "History of the Corn Exchange Regiment" (Antietam to Appomattox), which is a thoroughly interesting and readable work of 780 pages, profusely illustrated, and has a wide sale. He is a well known member of the Veterans' Association.

HISTORICAL AND COMMERCIAL PHILADELPHIA.

ILLIAM PENN HOTEL AND SALE STABLES. Wm. D. Althouse, Proprietor, Nos. 3809 to 3835 Market Street, West Philadelphia.—The most extensive sale and exchange stables in this city are owned and conducted by Mr. Wm. D. Althouse, proprietor of the William Penn Hotel, and whose hostelry and stables are situated at Nos. 3809 to 3835 Market Street. The stables were originally conducted by B. Jacobs & Sons, and seven years ago the present proprietor succeeded to the control. Mr. Althouse was born in Berks County, Pa. He has been in the horse trade for the past thirty years and formerly had a sales stable at Reading, Pa. He is, therefore, thoroughly acquainted with horse flesh and a good judge of all that goes to make a sound and desirable animal. The stables are very large, admirably drained, lighted and ventilated and can accommodate 40 horses at one time. Horses are received from the East and West and sold or exchanged at low rates of commission, with a view to the best interests of the patrons of the house. Auction sales are held on Tuesdays and Fridays, and are always well attended. The William Penn Hotel, run in conjunction with the stables by Mr. Althouse, is comprised in a four-story structure and contains fifty cleanly-kept rooms. All modern conveniences have been provided. The rates are $1.50 a day and visitors to the city will find this a most comfortable stopping-place.

RANKFORD MUTUAL FIRE INSURANCE COMPANY OF THE COUNTY OF PHILADELPHIA, John Shallcross, President; No. 1510 Frankford Avenue.—No fire insurance corporation in Philadelphia has made such solid progress or proved such a reliable factor in the vast field of underwriting as the old and popular Frankford Mutual Fire Insurance Company of the County of Philadelphia. It was organized fifty years ago, at a time when the field was in need of strong and ably managed corporations, and speedily took, and has ever since maintained, a representative position. Its enviable record of solvency and integrity has rendered it remarkably popular with the public and enabled it, under wise management, to select its risks with due regard to safeguards and surroundings. It takes risks in the counties of Philadelphia, Bucks and Montgomery only, and it controls the insuring of the most desirable lines of business and residential property throughout that territory. On December 31, 1891, it had risks in force amounting to $4,195,307.03, with assets of $182,070.51, and a surplus of $117,181.69. These figures are more eloquent than words and reflect the greatest credit on the executive officers. Its assets are most judiciously invested in real estate, bonds, mortgages and other good investments. All just claims are promptly paid in full and its business is constantly on the increase. Its founders were men who had the rare foresight to recognize the possibilities of such an institution and who laid the foundations sufficiently strong and deep to bear any superstructure that time, experience and wealth might rear. They builded well and their successors have been eminently worthy of the succession. Under its present wise and conservative management, this company is doing a large and safe business, all its movements being marked by prudence, caution and honorable business methods, and it is universally recognized as one of those solid, ably-conducted corporations, whose record reflects credit alike upon its officers and the community where its influence is felt. Its executive officers are as follows, viz.: John Shallcross, president; H. St. Clair Thorn, secretary; William Overington, treasurer. The president, Mr. Shallcross, has been a director of the company for the past fifteen years and was elected to the presidency on January 1, 1892, bringing to bear special qualifications for the discharge of its duties. The secretary, Mr. Thorn, has held that position since 1882, and is known as an expert and talented underwriter, whose judicious and conservative policy has secured to the company a continuance of a very large business with an unusually small proportion of losses. The treasurer, Mr. Overington, has been continuously in office for forty-nine years and enjoys the warmest regard of policy-holders and the public for his long and honorable business career, while the board of directors commands the unbounded respect and confidence of the entire community.

BROAD STREET, LOOKING NORTH FROM PUBLIC BUILDINGS.—1889.

HISTORICAL AND COMMERCIAL PHILADELPHIA.

BUREAU BROTHERS, Bronze Statuary, Architectural Works, Fountains, Railings, and Castings, Etc., S.W. Corner Twenty-first Street and Allegheny Avenue. In the designing and execution of bronze statuary a signal success has been achieved by the firm of Bureau Brothers, whose works are situated at the southwest corner of Twenty-first Street and Allegheny Avenue. This house was established in 1864 by Mr. Achille Bureau, continuing under his control until 1888, when his sons, Messrs. Edmund W. Bureau and Edouard S. Bureau, succeeded to the management, choosing the firm name of Bureau Brothers. Both gentlemen are natives of Philadelphia, and practical bronze workers of thorough experience and artistic talent. They have performed much excellent work, among other productions being the admirable equestrian statue of General Reynolds, which stands in front of the Public Building, this city; the "Puritan" statue at Springfield, Mass., and the Ottawa Indian monument in Lincoln Park, Chicago, Ill. These works are speaking witnesses to the ability of the Messrs. Bureau. The works cover an area of 100x115 feet. The foundry is a 25x80 feet brick building, and the finishing shop, also of brick, is 35x55 feet in area. Employing upwards of twenty hands, the firm possess all the latest improvements for art bronze and bronze casting in all its various branches. Estimates are furnished at shortest notice, original designs supplied, and satisfactory, artistically finished work is assured in every instance.

W. GILBERT & CO., Carriage Goods and Saddlery Specialties, Wagon Hardware and Wheel Stock, No. 108 North Third Street. Although established not longer ago than February 8, 1892, this firm has already built up a large trade throughout Pennsylvania, New Jersey, Delaware and New York. The members of the firm, Messrs. T. Woolsey Gilbert and Charles L. Dowler, are both natives of this city, and have had long and thorough experience in their vocation, the former having been engaged therein eleven years, the latter nine years. Mr. Gilbert was formerly with Kennedy, Willing & Co., and Mr. Dowler with C. B. Day & Co. The business premises comprise four floors, each 20x60 feet in area, and a heavy stock is always carried of wagon hardware and wheel stock, carriage goods and saddlery specialties. The firm are agents for the Snowflake Axle Grease, Nichols' Wagon Cushions, and Wm. Harlan & Son's Colors. A general jobbing trade is carried on, and all orders are met upon the most favorable terms.

THE DR. BOSANKO MEDICINE COMPANY, No. 329 Arch Street.—The Dr. Bosanko Medicine Company are manufacturing and supplying the people of the United States with a number of valuable remedial agents, whose efficacy and beneficent effects have been amply proven, and their virtues testified to by physicians and private individuals alike. The company was organized May 1, 1879, at Piqua, Ohio, and on October 1, 1890, a removal to this city was effected. The proprietors, Messrs. E. C. Deweese and K. E. Hafer, are sole manufacturers of Dr. Bosanko's Pile Remedy, Dr. Bosanko's Pile Syringe, Dr. Gunn's Onion Syrup and Dr. Gunn's Improved Liver Pills. These remedies are sold in all parts of the country. They have proved efficacious and thoroughly satisfactory in every case where they have been used, and hundreds of testimonials could be given describing the cures effected. Dr. Bosanko's Pile Syringe is sold for 50 cents, Dr. Bosanko's Pile Remedy for 50 cents, Dr. Gunn's Onion Syrup, for coughs and colds, 50 cents, and Dr. Gunn's Improved Liver Pills at 25 cents a box, or six for $1.25. The Bosanko Medicine Company occupy two commodious floors, each 20x125 feet in dimensions, and fifteen assistants are employed in manufacturing the company's specialties.

BAKER, HOUSEHOLDER & LEONARD, Engineers and Machinists, No. 628 Cherry Street.—In no branch of industry, science or art has the march of progress left such imprints during the past twenty years as in the sphere of activity devoted to the construction of machinery of all kinds. Of those who have made a reputation for skill and ability in the manufacture of machinery and general mechanical engineering in Philadelphia, none stands higher than the firm of Baker, Householder & Leonard, of No. 628 Cherry Street. These gentlemen have had fifteen years' practical experience in this line, and are well known as expert general machinists. They occupy one floor, 25x100 feet in dimensions, fully equipped with all improved machinery and appliances operated by steam power, and manufacture anything to order in the line of special machinery, including perforating machinery for use in manufacturing toilet paper, book binding and printing machinery, being experts in this branch, having a national reputation; and special attention is given to repairing this class of machinery at reasonable rates. Designs and plans for machinery of every kind are executed in the highest style of the art, while estimates for all classes of work are promptly furnished on application. The members of the firm, Mifflin J. Baker, D. W. Householder and T. P. Leonard, are all natives of Philadelphia and are endowed with inventive genius of a high order and remarkable energy. They have won a name and fame in this line of constructive enterprise which proves their commanding ability and skill, and of which they have every reason to be proud.

GEORGE W. BECKETT, Sanitary Plumber, No. 2036 Pine Street and S. W. Corner Twenty-second and Pine Streets. During the six years of his establishment as a sanitary plumber, Mr. George W. Beckett, has succeeded in building up a large and fast developing connection among regular patrons throughout the city and suburbs and he has been intrusted with some highly important and valuable contracts, such as the work on the Bethany Church, the residence of J. Parker Norris, 2122 Pine Street, and those of leading men of the immediate neighborhood. A specialty is made of house drainage, in addition to which a general line of jobbing and repairing is undertaken, as well as contracts for new work, including the supply and fixing of water closets, urinals, bath tubs, showers, bath boilers, basins, wash bowls, cisterns, pumps, hydrant work, etc. The store, at Twenty-second and Pine Streets, which has been occupied for the last five years, is fully equipped and stocked with a carefully chosen line of sanitary appliances and supplies of the latest styles and make; six skilled artisans being employed. Mr. George W. Beckett has had twenty-five years' practical experience in the trade, and personally directs the prompt fulfillment of all orders. He is a middle aged gentleman, a native of Dublin, Ireland, whence he came to the United States in 1881, settling in Philadelphia the following year, when he took out his papers and became a citizen of the United States.

HALEY & BAKER, Blank Book Manufacturers and Paper Rulers, No. 321 Chestnut Street.—A prominent and old standing house engaged in this city as blank book manufacturers and paper rulers is that of Messrs. Haley & Baker, carrying on their operations at No. 321 Chestnut Street, who now control an extensive trade among the best regular customers throughout the city and adjacent country, and enjoy a high reputation for fine work, expedition and moderate prices. The enterprise was established in 1861 by Mr. James Haley and Mr. Sloan, as Messrs. Haley & Sloan, and on the decease of the latter, in 1864, the present firm was formed by Mr. Haley admitting into partnership Mr. Joseph A. Baker. The firm have every possible facility at their command, in the matter of modern machines and appliances, for turning out the most satisfactory work and enabling them to compete with other responsible houses; and thus a heavy demand is made upon their resources for the manufacture of all kinds of blank books, paper ruling, perforating, eyeletting and the ruling and binding of account books to order, either to ordinary or special pattern; while particular care and attention are devoted to ruling, binding and paging for the trade. This heavy and regular volume of business necessitates the regular employment of some fourteen skilled assistants, and the premises utilized for the same purposes comprise the fifth floor at the address noted, 25x90 feet in area, furnished with a full equipment of hand and foot power machinery of that very complete nature already hinted. The firm undertake orders from any distance, and already have many regular patrons in Chicago, Ill., and Louisville, Ky.

HISTORICAL AND COMMERCIAL PHILADELPHIA.

FRANKLIN A. SMITH, Manufacturer and Dealer in Yellow Pine Flooring, For the Trade Only, Thirtieth and Locust Streets.—A house that is carrying on extensive transactions in a special department of the lumber industry is that of Mr. Franklin A. Smith, whose office and yard are located at the junction of Thirtieth and Locust Streets, where he also has a large wharf. This has been a lumber yard for the past twenty-five years or more. Mr. Smith first established business in 1879 at the Spruce Street wharf, where he continued up to five years ago, when he removed to his present address. He has a thorough practical knowledge of the lumber industry, having, it may be said, been raised in a sawmill in Maine, the Pine Tree State, where he was born. Through this knowledge, and his ability as a business man, he has built up a large, influential trade, and now has permanent patrons in all parts of Pennsylvania, New Jersey, Delaware and New York City. The yard covers an area of two acres, and is connected with the Pennsylvania Railroad by two switch lines. The planing mill has five of the latest planing machines, driven by steam power, and the output capacity is 50,000 feet of lumber a day. Employment is given thirty-five workmen. Mr. Smith is a manufacturer and dealer in yellow pine flooring for the trade only, and receives his timber from Florida, both by rail and water. His sales for 1891 amounted to 8,000,000 feet of lumber. A heavy stock is always carried, and the wants of the trade are met upon the most liberal terms. Mr. Smith is a member of the Lumber Exchange, the Philadelphia Bourse, and is also prominent in the Masonic Fraternity.

HUGHS, COOK & CO., Hides and Tallow of All Kinds, No. 3935 Market Street.—One of the representative establishments, which convincingly demonstrates the commercial supremacy of Philadelphia, is that of Messrs. Hughs, Cook & Co., dealers in hides and tallow, at No. 3936 Market Street, and exporters of oleomargarine oil, with factory at No. 1700 Lancaster Avenue. The oleo factory was established in 1877, by Messrs. Owen Hughs and John Cook, and in 1882 the business now conducted was started by the consolidation of the interests of Owen Hughs & Son and John Cook's Sons. The premises occupied are spacious and commodious, and every modern convenience and facility is at hand for the transaction of a large and active business, no similar concern in the city being better prepared for taking proper care of its extensive and still growing business. The house commands all the advantages naturally accumulated by long years of identification with a special branch of trade, and, in the handling of green hides, the rendering of tallow and the manufacture of oleo oil, the firm are in a position to supply the trade with the best quality of goods at short notice, in quantities to suit and at terms and prices which are safe from successful competition. Their resources are ample and abundant, their facilities are unsurpassed and the connections are widespread and influential both at home and abroad, and the substantial inducements offered to the trade are of a character to enable the firm to place the house in the front rank of the trade. One of the largest houses in its line in the country, it exercises a commanding influence upon the commerce of the city, and its business extends to all parts of the United States and Europe. The copartners, Messrs. Wm. D. Hughs, John H. Cook and Edwin F. Cook, are well known Philadelphians, trained in the business from their youth up, members of the Manufacturers' Club, and young men of large practical experience, wide acquaintance and sterling personal worth.

DR. JAEGER'S SANITARY WOOLEN SYSTEM COMPANY, No. 97 Franklin Street, New York; Philadelphia Depot, No. 1104 Chestnut Street, Samuel C. Hancock, Manager.—Dr. Jaeger's Sanitary Woolen System Company, whose Philadelphia depot is eligibly located at No. 1104 Chestnut Street, has very appropriately introduced to the American public many articles new and foreign to our use, but entirely practicable and really essential to our perfect comfort and health. Dr. Jaeger's sanitary woolen underclothing is made in shirts, night dresses, chemises, drawers, or in combination garments of shirts or chemises and drawers, in one piece, for both sexes. In appearance and feeling these fabrics are very similar to spun silk, and it may be confidently asserted that no garments hitherto made are so agreeable to the wearer. They are perfectly soft, made of the finest wool and will adapt themselves to the body in the most graceful manner. They may be worn through the heat of summer with comfort, and in colder weather they maintain as much warmth as the heavier flannel clothing. The stockinet, from which this clothing is manufactured, is also for sale here by the yard. The bedding department contains the following-named articles: camel's-hair pillows, blankets, comfortables, sleeping-sacks, mattresses, pillow-cases and sheets. The camel's-hair pillows are filled with pure camel's-hair and are covered with a thick, soft, woven material of the same. The sheets and pillow-cases are made of very fine, durable, white cashmere and will not shrink in washing. The blankets and bed-coverings are made of the finest quality of undyed natural brown camel's-hair or sheep's-wool. Sanitary woolen hats are subject to special treatment in manufacture, as compared with ordinary felt hats, whereby their sanitary value is increased, They are much lighter than the ordinary hat; and the usual strip of leather at the place where the hat fits round the head is replaced by a strip of wooden felt especially manufactured for the purpose. The difference in point of comfort, especially when the forehead is perspiring, is very great. The sanitary woolen boots and shoes have wooden materials inside, with and without leather protection. From a sanitary point of view, the latter are preferable, and can be used not only in dry weather, but also where the soil is not heavy in wet weather. These boots and shoes either completely cure or greatly mitigate the complaint of excessive perspiration of the feet, constant coldness, gout, etc. Weak feet are hardened, the joints are strengthened, corns and other troubles are prevented. Tourists are particularly recommended to use Dr. Jaeger's boots and shoes. The miscellaneous articles comprise stockings and socks, ladies' corsets and corset covers, ladies' petticoats, dressing-robes, camel's-hair shawls, men's smoking jackets, knitted garments, lawn tennis shirts, children's night-dresses, white woolen handkerchiefs, natural brown laces, Tyrolese belts, suspenders, belt bandages for stomach troubles, ladies' dress goods and gentlemen's suitings, trouserings and overcoatings. Mr. Samuel C. Hancock, manager of the Philadelphia depot, is a native of this city and well and favorably known in its business and social circles. He occupies spacious and attractive quarters, where he displays a splendid line of these celebrated goods, and is a gentleman with whom it will be found both pleasant and profitable to deal.

WITHOUT THIS TRADE MARK.

HENRY STUTZ, JR., Contractors' Supplies, Dynamite, Powder, Fuse and Caps, Exploders, Blasting Machines, Sledges and Hammers, Jumpers and Churn Drills, Bull Points and Wedges, Pinch and Crow Bars, Nos. 4806-1811 Germantown Avenue, Germantown.—The leading depot for contractors' supplies in Germantown is the well-known establishment of Henry Stutz, Jr., which has been in existence for the past thirty years. The business was started in 1862 by Henry Stutz, the elder, who carried on the same up to 1870, when he was succeeded by Henry, Jr. The store is commodious and well ordered, and several assistants are in attendance. A large and first-class stock is constantly kept on hand here, including the articles above mentioned, rock tools generally, and everything comprehended in contractors' supplies; also a full line of glass house-furnishing goods. There is, likewise, a yard in connection for the storage of grindstones and other articles. Mr. Stutz was born in Germantown, and is a man of entire reliability in his dealings. He is a member of the Knights of the Golden Eagle, the U. O. of A. M., and other societies.

HISTORICAL AND COMMERCIAL PHILADELPHIA.

JACOB HOFFMANN & SON, Manufacturers of Pearl Buttons and Novelties, Nos. 217 and 219 New Street.— One of the oldest exponents of artistic pearl working in the entire Keystone State is the well known and responsible firm of Jacob Hoffmann & Son, carrying on their operations in this city at Nos. 217 and 219 New Street. The manufactures of this house consist of pearl buttons of various kinds, sizes, shapes and styles, sleeve links, studs, solitaires, brooches, head and dress ornaments, articles for jewelry mounting, and a full line of fancy novelties, also views, scenes and frames, made in the most artistic manner. These productions from first to last are of the finest description, both from an artistic and a practical standpoint; their patterns and styles are original and unique, their make is the best, and their finish is clean, accurate and of the highest order of merit, while the pearl used is selected with the utmost care and procured at first hand from the leading sources of supply. The business was founded in 1862 by Messrs. Hoffmann and Bauman, the latter subsequently retiring; in 1860 Mr. Jacob Hoffmann admitted his son, George Hoffmann, into partnership, and the house has been owned and conducted in detail by Mr. George Hoffmann since the decease of his worthy father in 1879. The permanent, substantial trade controlled reaches to all parts of the United States, and its volume furnishes regular employment for twenty skilled operatives. No pains or expense are spared in order to maintain the productions of the house at a uniformly high standard of excellence, and thus the factory, 20x40 feet in area, is provided with a very complete equipment of lathes, pearl cutters, boring machines, polishers and other improved machinery and appliances pertaining to this special line of industry, steam power being the motive force used. Mr. George Hoffmann was born in Germany in 1847, has resided in this city since 1854. He is thoroughly practical, and is an expert worker in this line of trade, and has been engaged with the house since its foundation in 1862.

REDSTONE OIL, COAL AND COKE COMPANY, Office, No. 201 Walnut Place.— The Redstone Oil, Coal and Coke Company occupy a foremost position among the representative business houses of Philadelphia, while the works are at Grindstone P. O., Fayette County, Pa., on the Monongahela division of the Pennsylvania Railroad. The company was organized six years ago, being incorporated under the State laws of Pennsylvania, with ample capital, and the following prominently known gentlemen as officers: President, Jacob E. Ridgway; Vice President, J. I. Bishop; Treasurer, Geo. W. Dohnert; directors, Jacob E. Ridgway, William K. Brown, M D, James McKay, Caleb S. Ridgway, A. L. McFarlane. The company deal in gas and steam coals and coke, selling the products of their own mine. The property is between 3,000 and 4,000 acres in area. A deep shaft has been built, employment is found for a large force of hands, and the output is a very heavy one. The mechanical equipment is perfect in every respect. Thirty coke ovens are kept in operation. The trade supplied extends all throughout the Western and Northwestern States. Mr. Jacob E. Ridgway is also Chairman, and Mr. J. I. Bishop Treasurer and Secretary, of the Ridgway Supply Company, Limited, who conduct a general merchandise establishment at Grindstone P. O. They have a capital of $5,000, all paid in, carry a heavy stock, and command a large, steadily growing trade. Messrs. Jacob E. and Caleb S. Ridgway and John I. Bishop also compose the Ridgway-Bishop Coal Company, who control 2,000 acres in Washington Co., Pa.; on the Bridgeville Branch of the P. C. & St. L. Ry.

THE GEO. A. SMITH MACHINERY COMPANY, Manufacturers of and Dealers in Boot and Shoe Machinery, Etc., Nos. 415 and 417 Arch Street. About the most widely known depot for boot and shoe machinery in Philadelphia is the spacious and well ordered establishment of the Geo. A. Smith Machinery Company. The company are manufacturers of and dealers in boot and shoe machinery, duplicate parts, leather and findings; and their trade, which is very large, extends throughout the United States. The house was established in 1881 by Geo. A. Smith, who conducted the same alone up to July, 1891, when this business was incorporated under the laws of the State of New Jersey, and the present name adopted. The capital stock is $75,000, and the President of the company is Geo. A. Smith, the Vice President is Harry L. Herron, the Secretary, Richard Mengert, and the Treasurer, R B. Rittersbach. Besides the 30x150 foot store on Arch Street, they occupy four 20x120 foot floors in the rear, at No. 417 Appletree Street, which are equipped with ample steam power and machinery for manufacturing purposes. The facilities are of a superior character altogether, and a large force of skilled workmen are employed, while four representatives are kept on the road. The stock, which is of a comprehensive character, includes sole sewing machines, second lasting machines, tacking and nailing machines, heeling machines, heel breasting, scouring and burnishing machines, edge trimming, edge setting and sand papering machines, buffing machines, rolling and splitting machines, all sizes and kinds; dyeing and moulding machines, stiffening skiving machines, and kindred appliances in great variety; also jacks for all branches, belting, etc., etc., superior burnishing inks, flexible insoling, bottom stain of all colors, shoe tools, leather, findings and shoe manufacturers' supplies generally; and rebuilt machines are always kept on hand, at greatly reduced prices. The trade is supplied on the most reasonable terms, and all orders are promptly and carefully attended to, while shoe factories are fitted up complete with machinery and shafting in the very best manner.

WILLIAM D. WILSON, General Insurance Broker, Forrest Building, No. 119 South Fourth Street.— This is one of the old and well established insurance houses that does credit to the city. It dates its foundation back to April 27, 1867, on which date its doors were first thrown open. Mr. Wilson is a native of Delaware, but has resided in this city since infancy, a period of over forty years. Mr. Wilson is prepared to effect any and every kind of insurance, fire, marine, life, accident, plate glass, boiler or indemnity, in any of the staunch and reliable companies, at the very lowest current rates of premium; and is not only retaining his old business, but is steadily including new customers, and now controls the insuring of many of the largest and most desirable lines of business and residence property, ships and vessels, hulls and cargoes, yachts, stocks of merchandise, grain and household effects in the city. His policies are clearly worded, explicit contracts; his rates are the lowest commensurate with absolute security; and, as is well known to hundreds of his customers, all losses are promptly paid as soon as they are adjusted. Mr. Wilson's record is one of the most creditable character, and by permission he refers to such representative business men and firms of this city as Henry Disston & Sons; Frank W. Henson, of No. 4427 Germantown Avenue; Philip Jagode & Co., Nos. 12, 14 and 16 Letitia Street; Thos. Beardwood & Bro., No. 1640 North Sixth Street; John Forrest (Keystone Mills), Twenty-fifth and Callowhill Streets; and Burk & McFetridge, Nos. 306 and 308 Chestnut Street, among others.

CHICAGO VARNISH COMPANY, No. 142 North Fourth Street, E. S. Gellatly, Resident Manager.— There is, perhaps, no single article used by carriage and furniture manufacturers to which more importance attaches than varnish. Of the various products now on the market, there are none superior to the goods manufactured by the Chicago Varnish Company, whose Philadelphia branch, E. S. Gellatly, resident manager, is at No. 142 North Fourth Street. Their varnishes and japans are noted for brilliancy, durability and general excellence, and command extensive sale. They are, in fact, preparations of exceptional merit, and are in widespread and growing demand all over the United States. The Chicago Varnish Company was established in 1865, and has branches in New York and Boston, the Philadelphia office controlling the trade in Pennsylvania and the Southern States. They are manufacturers of a general line of varnishes and japans, and their products are maintained at a uniformly high standard, while the prices quoted are notably low, quality of goods considered. Mr. Gellatly, the company's representative in this city, is a man of thorough experience, being engaged in this line for fifteen years. He has been manager here since the branch was established, and has built up a large and flourishing business. The trade is supplied on the most favorable terms, and all orders for anything in varnishes and japans, from a quart can to a barrel or car load, are filled in the most prompt and trustworthy manner.

HISTORICAL AND COMMERCIAL PHILADELPHIA.

ILLIAM A. HAINES, Manufacturer of Fancy Leather Goods, Pocketbooks and Bags, Nos. 133, 135 and 137 North Seventh Street. This flourishing business was established in 1878 by William A. Haines, under whose management it has since been conducted with eminent success. The goods turned out here are noted for beauty of design, excellence of make and elegance of finish, and are productions of a distinctly superior character, and command extensive sale throughout the United States. The premises occupied as office and factory at Nos. 133-137 North Seventh Street, comprise three 55 x 100 feet floors, and are equipped with ample steam-power and the latest improved machinery, etc. The facilities are first-class in all respects, and seventy-five to ninety hands are employed in the concern, while half a dozen salesmen represent the house on the road. Mr. Haines manufactures exquisite novelties in ladies' satchels, portmonnies, reticules, music rolls, fancy leather bags, pocketbooks, and everything in this line, and every article is warranted as to workmanship and material. An exceedingly fine assortment is constantly carried in stock. Mr. Haines is a man of thorough experience in this line, and gives close attention to every detail of the business.

ERRY & ORTON COMPANY, Atlantic Works, Manufacturers of Machinery for Working Wood, Twenty-third and Arch Streets, New York, No. 136 Liberty Street. The rapid strides made in the perfection of every description of wood-working machinery by the Berry & Orton Company, of this city, have elicited the closest investigation and widespread patronage of the woodworking trade of the world, necessitating enlarged facilities on the part of this enterprising house. The foundation of their immense business was laid in 1869, by Messrs. Richard Thorn & Co., and in 1888 the present company was incorporated, with L. H. Berry, president; L. O. Orton, treasurer; H. W. Thorn, secretary. They occupy new premises known as the Atlantic Works, at the corner of Twenty-third and Arch Streets, which was built expressly for the company, at a cost of $100,000, and is the finest and best-equipped of the kind in the country. The main building is of brick, five stories high and 150 x 200 feet in dimensions, splendidly fitted up with a perfect and comprehensive equipment of the latest improved machinery, operated by a steam-engine of 150 horse power, and steady

employment is given to from 150 to 200 skilled hands. The officers are constantly engaged in noting results of their important improvements and experimenting on others, and each season sees something new in unison with the ever-growing demands for labor and material saving wood-working machinery of the most perfect type. They manufacture all kinds of wood-working machinery from original designs and most improved patterns, including timber planers, mortising, matching, tenoning, boring, gaining and sawing machinery. Band saw machinery employed in cutting both curved and straight lines from the most delicate fretwork to the huge logs of the Pacific Coast with greater speed and less waste than possible with other kind of saws. The advances made in band sawmills and planing machines by this company have placed their productions far beyond competition, and they are found running and giving the most admirable service in the largest car shops, moulding, flooring and planing mills in this country. Quality has ever been the first consideration of the management, and their claims to merit are based on the severest tests of everyday use in all kinds of woods for all purposes. The triumphant record of their machinery and its ever-widening use are ample sufficient guarantees that purchasers can do best here. Orders of whatever magnitude are filled with promptness and scrupulous care, and a branch office is operated at No. 136 Liberty Street, New York. The president, Mr. Berry, is in charge of the manufacturing department; the treasurer, Mr. Orton, is the general manager of the business, and the secretary, Mr. Thorn, presides over the office. All are able business men, and the company under their expert and talented direction, worthily maintains the supremacy in the manufacture of wood-working machinery of the most advanced and perfect type. This company was awarded a certificate at the Philadelphia Centennial Exhibition on their work for the excellence of its construction, simplicity and solidity of parts, also for power of machines and points of ingenuity and originality of design.

HISTORICAL AND COMMERCIAL PHILADELPHIA.

LIVERIGHT, GREENEWALD & CO., Manufacturers of Clothing, No. 1013 Market Street. Philadelphia's supremacy in the wholesale manufacture of clothing is assured by the possession of such an eminent and enterprising house as that of Messrs. Liveright, Greenewald & Co., located at No. 1013 Market Street. This firm are extensive manufacturers of men's, boys' and youths' clothing, and the sound judgment, marked executive capacity and perfect facilities of its founders and promoters have secured for the fine clothing of this house the national reputation of being fully equal to custommade. The business was established in 1871 by Messrs. Max Liveright, Simon Liveright, Morris Liveright and B. F. Greenewald, as Liveright & Greenewald, and subsequently Messrs. Marcus Dreifus and Morris Lang were admitted to partnership, forming the firm as at present constituted. Requiring larger premises and increased facilities for their rapidly extending trade, the building at No. 1013 Market Street was erected for them, to which they have lately removed. These premises comprise an entire six-story building 28 x 210 feet in dimensions, with a cellar and subcellar, and 350 hands are kept busy the year round in making the clothing sold by this firm. These goods are all distinguished for some excellence peculiarly their own, while the finer grades are recognized as equal in every respect to the best custom work, in fit, finish, elegance and fashion. The proprietors exercise sound judgment and the greatest enterprise in the selection of their woolens and suitings, and are first to secure all the new shades, patterns and textures in both American and foreign fabrics, while their styles are invariably correct. Their business has attained proportions of great and gratifying magnitude, growing up on the sound basis of the best clothing of every grade at the lowest prices commensurate with honest workmanship. A corps of twelve talented salesmen represent the interests of the house upon the road, and the largest orders are filled with dispatch and satisfaction in all cases. The members of the firm are all well known Philadelphians, and under their expert and successful guidance this house has few equals anywhere for all those qualifications that insure efficiency and thorough excellence.

MARKET STREET, FROM TWELFTH STREET.

THOMAS GREAVES, Manufacturer of Cardigan Jackets, Nos. 1663, 1665, 1667 Wakefield Street, Germantown. For upward of a quarter of a century Thomas Greaves, successor to Greaves & Thurman, manufacturer of cardigan jackets, Nos. 1663-67 Wakefield Street, has been extensively engaged in the line indicated here in Germantown. He was formerly the junior member of the firm of Greaves & Thurman, established in 1867, and succeeded the same as sole proprietor January 1, of the present year. He is one of the leaders in this branch of industry in the country, and his productions command extensive sale throughout the United States. Mr. Greaves is a gentleman of middle age and was born in England, but has been in this city since 1858. He is a man of thorough practical skill and many years' experience, active and energetic, and exercises close personal supervision over every detail of the business. His factory is a three-story building, 30 x 125 feet in dimensions, and is perfectly equipped in every respect. There are forty knitting machines, a number of sewing machines and all the latest improved appliances in operation in the establishment, and fifty hands are employed. Mr. Greaves manufactures cardigan jackets of every size, style and variety, both plain and fancy, and of a distinctly superior quality, and turns out about one hundred dozen per week. He keeps on hand always a large and first-class stock, and can fill the largest orders at short notice, and on most favorable terms, and sells direct to the trade, to which he quotes rock-bottom prices.

HISTORICAL AND COMMERCIAL PHILADELPHIA

 W. RULON & SONS, Importers of East India Goods, Indigo, Drugs, Spices, Etc., No. 31 North Front Street.—The oldest establishment in the United States engaged in the importation of drugs and East India goods is that of J. W. Rulon & Sons, which was founded in 1824 by J. W. Rulon, who sailed from this port with cargoes of American products to the East Indies, and returned with goods produced in that country. In 1844 he admitted to partnership his sons, Messrs. S. A. and J. W. Rulon, Jr., thus organizing the firm of J. W. Rulon & Sons. In 1872 the senior member died, after a very lengthy and highly honorable mercantile career; in 1877 his son, J. W. Rulon, Jr., retired, and Mr. S. A. Rulon has since remained in sole control. This gentleman was born in the Quaker City and is a foremost member of the Board of Trade. He has a staff of agents in London, Calcutta, Singapore and Colombo, is a direct importer, has a trade extending all over the United States, and receives shipments of goods to this city, New York and Boston, three-fourths of the shipments being made to New York. Mr. Rulon imports tapioca, senna, rhubarb, gums, spices, copal, India teas, indigo, shellac, Persian rugs, and plumbago and cocoanut oil from Ceylon. In the four story warehouse on North Front Street a heavy stock is carried.

 TYNDALE & MITCHELL COMPANY, China, Glass, Pottery, Etc., No. 1217 Chestnut Street.—Among the few leading houses engaged in Philadelphia in the direct importation of china, glass, crockery and ceramics in general, a first place is occupied by the old established undertaking now widely known as Tyndale & Mitchell Company, carrying on extensive operations at No. 1217 Chestnut Street, who by virtue of their long standing relations with the leading manufacturers in Europe and elsewhere are enabled to place upon the American market the finest descriptions of goods at the lowest trade prices; and as a consequence they now control a business of the largest proportions. This veteran undertaking was founded about eighty years ago, and the present proprietors are Mr. Joseph S. Perot and his two sons, Mr. Thomas L. Perot and Mr. John Perot. Their arrangements embrace every facility for purchasing goods in France, Italy, Germany, England, etc., to meet the demands of their customers. The choicest descriptions of china, glass and crockery are extensively dealt in, embracing everything in the line, of the finest patterns and designs, and a leading specialty is made of rich cut glass, bric à brac and art ceramics, procured from all over the world. The salesroom and store, 30x155 feet in area, are handsomely appointed in every detail, and contain a magnificent display of goods, which number among

the largest and finest collections of china, glass, crockery, bric à brac and art ceramics, terra cotta ware, etc., in Philadelphia; dinner, tea and toilet sets of the latest patterns and designs being especially heavy and choice assortment. An adequate staff of competent assistants is in regular attendance upon patrons and visitors, to whom is always extended every courtesy and attention. The three proprietors are all natives of the Quaker City and interested in the Philadelphia Bourse enterprise.

 ISAAC LOCKHART, Manufacturer of Standard Ingrain Carpets, N. W. Corner Hancock and Somerset Streets.—This establishment bears an excellent reputation in the trade, and its goods are noted for their uniform excellence. The business was founded six years ago by Lockhart Bros. at the present address, and a year ago Mr. Isaac Lockhart became sole proprietor, his brother retiring. The premises occupied have dimensions of 50x100 feet, and are equipped with sixteen looms, which are operated by steam power, and employment is found for twenty-five expert workmen. Mr. Lockhart personally directs their labors, and manufactures ingrain carpets of superior quality and in handsome designs. The output amounts to thirty rolls per week, each roll containing 130 yards. The goods are always maintained at the same high standard of excellence. Mr. Lockhart was born abroad, but has resided in Philadelphia the past thirty years. He is esteemed as a reliable business man and public spirited citizen.

 C. STARK & CO., Memorial Cards, No. 706 Chestnut Street.—" In the midst of life we are in death," is a true apostolic saying, and one whose truth is recognized by all. But death is not pleasant to dwell upon. We hear with perfect equanimity of the deaths of strangers, but not until those personally beloved are taken from us does the full significance of the upgiving of life reveal itself. When this mournful and unavoidable event occurs, it is the manifest duty of the survivor to observe the occasion with every possible exhibit of feeling and ceremony. In this connection we wish to win the attention of our readers to the establishment of Edw. C. Stark & Co., whose fine memorial goods have acquired so much favor throughout the United States and Canada. This house was founded seven years ago, by the present sole proprietor, Mr. E. C. Stark, under the title of the Memorial Card Company, and two years since he adopted the existing firm name. Mr. Stark is a native of Hoboken, N. J., came to this city in 1873, and has had eighteen years' practical experience as a printer. He is a pioneer in his present line, and has achieved a well deserved success. Mr. Stark turns out a very fine line of memorial goods, including memorial cards, prayer cards, satin puffs, verses, prayers, frames, etc. Illustrated circulars, including verses, prices, and all information, are sent free on application.

HISTORICAL AND COMMERCIAL PHILADELPHIA.

IAMOND ELECTRIC COMPANY, Light and Power, Seventeenth and Clearfield Streets. There is no science or industry of the present day that has made such wonderful progress as the electric, and this may well be termed the "Electric Age." Thus is all the more remarkable when we consider that electrical science is but yet comparatively in its infancy. In this connection special mention should be made of the Diamond Electric Company, corner of Seventeenth and Clearfield Streets, this city, one of the most prosperous electrical concerns in the city, engaged in furnishing light and power. The company was chartered in 1891, with a capital stock of $250,000, and the following prominently known gentlemen as officers: President, Chas. A. Porter; secretary, John B. Stauffer; superintendent and manager, H. A. Eckman; directors, Chas. A. Porter, David Martin, Wm. B. Doxey, Wm. A. Latta, Geo. A. Castor. The company's plant is splendidly equipped. The main building has two floors, each 100 x 150 feet in dimensions. The building is of brick, with terra cotta trimmings, and the offices are handsomely appointed with brass fixtures, tiled floor and attractive furnishings. The mechanical outfit includes five boilers each of 200-horse power, two engines of 100-horse power each, a 250-horse power engine, four dynamos of 60 arc light capacity each, and three incandescent light dynamos, having a total capacity of 3,000 lights. The company supply light and power for public and private use over a radius within three miles of their station. A staff of skilled hands is employed, the service is first-class in every respect, while the charges are uniformly reasonable in character. This company in establishing their plant have spared no expense to make it the model electrical station in America, no innovation is made in electrical science that they do not at once avail themselves of, and it is par excellence the most modern and at the same time most complete institution of its kind to be found in the present age.

UARANTEE TRUST AND SAFE DEPOSIT COMPANY, No. 316 Chestnut Street. That bank vaults or private safes do not afford that entire security which can be obtained in the vaults of a well-managed and successful safe deposit company is clearly proven by the fact that fifteen millions of dollars have been stolen from banks and private vaults during the past few years, while no safe deposit company has ever been robbed and no attempt by burglars has ever been made. This shows emphatically that the precautions taken by these companies have been absolutely successful. The Guarantee Trust and Safe Deposit Company, at Nos. 316, 318 and 320 Chestnut Street, was incorporated May 31, 1876, as the "Granite Insurance Trust and Safe Deposit Company," its present title being adopted in 1872. Its magnificent building is a credit to the company and an ornament to the city. It has a frontage of 57 feet on Chestnut Street and 198 feet on both Hudson Street and Carpenter's Court. It is a genuinely fireproof structure, planned expressly with a view to affording the best attainable facilities for the security and safe keeping of valuables of every description, wills, deeds, insurance policies, savings bank books and other papers; coupon, registered and other bonds; certificates of stock, plate, jewelry, clothing and other personal effects. The foundations of this splendid building are of stone from 8 to 12 feet deep and 4 feet thick. The basement walls are 3 feet thick,

of hard brick laid in cement. The walls above the main floor are 2 feet 3 inches thick, and the interior and partition walls are also of brick. The floors are of iron beams with brick arches and are laid with concrete and encaustic tiles. It would be difficult to suggest anything either in location, material of construction, which could render it more se- cure or indestructible. The massive fire and burglar-proof vaults of the company are six in number and constructed of the most superior hardened iron and steel plates, securely welded together and impenetrable to the finest tem- pered steel drills, and enclosed on all sides with massive walls of dressed granite blocks, weighing several tons each, all laid in cement and se- surely clamped and dow- eled together. The en- ers over the top are nine ormous blocks of granite, each weighing from eight to thirteen tons. Over two thousand safes have been put in for the immediate use of renters, while there is room for four thousand more. They are fitted with combination and permu- tation locks of the best tation construction known. They are rented at from $5 to $125 per annum, according to size and location and are opened only with the keys held by the renters. The offices are patrolled day and night by armed watchmen and the watch on the vaults never ceases day or night, Sundays or holidays. These with other safeguards, which for pru- dential reasons are not made public, serve to ren- der the vaults of the Guar- antee Trust and Safe De- posit Company the most se- cure in the world. This com- pany also receives deposits of money at interest, paya- ble by check on demand, or on certificate payable on presentation; acts in the capacity of executor, ad- ministrator, guardian, as- signee, committee, re- ceiver, agent, attorney, etc.; and executes trusts of every kind under ap- pointment of states, courts, corporations or individ- uals; collects interest or income, and transacts all other business authorized by its charter. This com- pany acts as agent for the management of estates, as well as the collection of income and many of the largest estates in this city and vicinity are placed in its hands, while their own- ers go to enjoy travel and European life for years at a time. Its capital is spe- cially pledged by the terms of its charter for the faithful discharge of all trusts committed to its care, while it has ever been the policy of this famous company to keep pace with the times, and by adding every improvement which experience can suggest to increase the security of its fire and burglar proof vaults. It is open for general business from 9 A. M. to 4 P. M., for deposits of money and payment of checks from 9 A. M. to 3 P. M. The officers and directors of this company are as follows, viz.: President, Richard Y. Cook; vice-president, George H. Earle, Jr.; treasurer, Harry J. Delany; secretary, John Jay Gilroy; trust officer, Richard C. Winship; directors, Edward C. Knight, John J. Stadiger, W. Rotch Wister, Alfred Fitler, J. Dickinson Sergeant, Aaron Fries, Charles A. Sparks, Joseph Moore, Jr., Richard Y. Cook, George H. Earle, Jr., Jay Cooke, Jr., Conyers Button. These gentlemen are all honored and esteemed in the financial world for their ability and integrity, and the success achieved by this corporation is justly a source of pride to every citizen of the "City of Brotherly Love."

HISTORICAL AND COMMERCIAL PHILADELPHIA.

THE SAVING FUND SOCIETY of Germantown and its Vicinity, Corner of Main and School Streets. One of the most solid, prosperous and popular financial institutions in the city is the Saving Fund Society of Germantown and its vicinity, whose banking is at the corner of Main and School Streets. This society was chartered in 1854, and it has been successfully directed from the outset and ever enjoyed the fullest confidence of the public. The following prominently known gentlemen are the officers and board of managers: president, Isaac C. Jones, Jr.; vice-president, James M. Aertsen; secretary Elliston P. Morris; treasurer, Charles A. Spiegel; managers, Ellison P. Morris, Samuel Morris, J. L. Erringer, Jas. M. Aertsen, James S. Jones, Philip C. Garrett, William G. Spencer, Isaac C. Jones, Jr., Joseph S. Harris, William W. Justice, Francis B. Reeves, Justus C. Strawbridge, William Hacker, John J. Henry, Tatnall Paulding. Mr. Jones has been president the past four years and prior to that was vice-president seven years. Mr. Aertsen, who has been vice-president the past four years, has been with the society since 1854. Mr. Morris has been secretary since 1854, while Mr. Spiegel, with the bank twenty years, has been treasurer the past twelve years. The business was formerly conducted at the corner of Main Street and Chelton Avenue, but in 1883 the society built the handsome quarters since occupied by them. The affairs of the society are in a most flourishing condition, as the following summary of the statement, presented Jan. 1, 1892, will show: Received from depositors in 1891, $4,134,007.58; interest credited and paid in 1891, $69,965.37; total, $4,203,972.95, paid to depositors in 1891, $4,188,912.76; showing a gain in deposits $75,060.25; total received from depositors since organization, $48,111,655.04; total paid to depositors since organization $45,916,963.40; showing balance due January 1, 1892, $2,494,691.64; total interest paid to depositors since organization, $867,863.61; whole number of accounts opened, 39,863; whole number of accounts closed, 27,496; whole number of accounts now open, 12,487. The managers serve without compensation or direct personal advantage, and neither they nor any officer or agent of the Saving Fund can directly or indirectly borrow money, nor by note, bond or mortgage or other obligation, become in any way indebted to it. The deposits range from ten cents upwards, and when they reach $5.00 bear interest.

THOMAS SHAW, Mechanical Engineer and Manufacturer of Engineers' Special Appliances, Patentee of the United States Standard Mercury Steam Gauge, Offices, No. 915 Ridge Avenue, Works, No. 1015 Ridge Avenue. One of those reputable and reliable houses that have added so materially to the influence of Philadelphia as a source of supply is that so ably conducted by Mr. Thomas Shaw, the eminent mechanical engineer, at No. 915 Ridge Avenue. This gentleman is a native Philadelphian, who established himself in business here in 1872, and has achieved world-wide renown as the inventor of Shaw's United States standard mercury gauges, vacuum, gas and blast gauges; Shaw's mercury tank indicator, Shaw's patent governor for tank-pumping engines, Shaw's mine signal machine, etc.; also as a manufacturer and designer of special tools, machinery and engineers' supplies, hydraulic machinery, pressure gauges, etc. He has taken out 111 patents on eighty-six different subjects, while his specialties are unequaled for faultless construction, perfect accuracy and thorough adaptability to the requirements of the trade. His gauges are in preferential use all over the world. Shaw's mercury gauge, invented by him in 1880, has been adopted as the standard in the United States Navy and by many leading railways. Shaw's mercury blast gauge records the pressure of natural gas or air for blast furnaces, cupolas, forge fires, etc. Shaw's patent governor for tank-pumping engines controls the engine by the height of the water; while his latest invention, the mine signal machine, is used for testing dangerous gases, and is already adopted in Pennsylvania and by the chief mine inspector of Ohio. Shaw's mercury tank indicator has been in use several years in prominent buildings, giving perfect indication of amount of water in tanks. It saves excess of pumping, overflowing the tanks, or the danger of having the tanks empty, and the trouble of sending parties to note the amount of water in the same. It is a valuable instrument that pays for itself in a short time, in the advantages derived from its use. Mr. Shaw occupies a four-story building, which is fully equipped with new and improved machinery and ample steam-power, and employment is given therein to some twenty-five skilled assistants. He is thus prepared to meet all demands of a trade that is world-wide in extent, while he is also general manager of the United States Mine Signal Manufacturing and Supply Company of Philadelphia, and stands at the head of the mechanical engineering profession of this country.

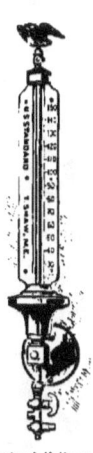

PHILADELPHIA MARBLE COMPANY, Representing Vermont Marble Company, Producers of Rutland, Sutherland Falls and Mountain Dark Marbles, No. 201 South Thirtieth Street.—In this brief sketch of the Vermont Marble Company, as represented here by the Philadelphia Marble Company, at No. 201 South Thirtieth Street, we introduce to our readers the largest marble quarrying concern in the world, ranking first in quality and foremost in the volume of its production. The Vermont Marble Company has its quarries, mills and works at Proctor, Center Rutland and West Rutland, in Rutland County, Vermont, and has been represented here by Mr. Samuel Williams as manager since 1879. He carries a full line of finished work for both building and monumental purposes, and his house is the recognized leader in its line in the city. His yard has a frontage of 175 feet on the river, and is connected by switch with the Pennsylvania Railroad. He is prepared to supply dealers and contractors with the famous Rutland, Sutherland Falls and Mountain Dark marbles, in quantities to suit at the shortest notice, while he gives special attention to orders for monumental work. Fabrication of memorial work has become an art requiring originality of conception, technical training, patient and intelligent application, and the very acme of expert workmanship, to secure an artistic totality of admirable and enduring qualities. To fully meet these essential requisites, the efforts of the Philadelphia Marble Company are unremitting. Their premises are replete with a varied and complete assortment of designs, suited to the tastes and means of all, and values are here offered which cannot be duplicated elsewhere. All work proves as represented, is guaranteed in every respect, and every statement in letter and spirit is fully substantiated. In both memorial designs, ideal and realistic carving, and in the selection of materials, this company stands preëminent in the trade. The fullest extent of artistic possibility has signalized their many productions. Their well-tested merits and marked appreciation in every cemetery in this city and throughout the country is their best possible recommendation, their only needed endorsement. For the execution of building work no house in the marble business is so well adapted for success. The Sutherland Falls marble is undoubtedly the strongest, most durable and in general effect most satisfactory for this class of work. It is not a pure white, but slightly clouded or vari-gated; is a fine, hard and close-grained stone and so does not absorb the impurities of the atmosphere, but retains its bright and clear appearance after continued exposure. Not being a dead white, it blends so nicely in an entire front as to be especially pleasing and harmonious. It is peculiarly adapted for buildings requiring large pieces, as blocks of almost any size can be quarried. When a dark stone is required, nothing can be found any handsomer than the Rutland Blue or Mountain Dark. Rock-faced it presents the finest effect of any known material. The business of the Philadelphia house extends throughout Pennsylvania, New Jersey, Delaware, Maryland and the South, and is annually increasing under enterprising and reliable management. Mr. Williams, the manager, has been connected with the marble business for a period of thirty years, is an expert authority in the selection of materials and eminently popular and successful in meeting every demand of a widespread, high-class trade.

HISTORICAL AND COMMERCIAL PHILADELPHIA.

W. R. McGLENN, Marble and Brownstone Works, Lehigh Avenue, above Kensington Avenue.—The number of fine business and residential buildings that are constantly being erected in Philadelphia, has resulted in making the trade in building stone one of the most important industries in the city. One of the foremost houses engaged in the business is that of Mr. W. R. McGlenn, whose marble and brownstone works are located on Lehigh Avenue, above Kensington Avenue. Mr. McGlenn is a Philadelphian by birth. In 1886 he established business at the corner of Front and Norris Streets, where he is now erecting a handsome building for store and hall purposes, having removed the stone works to Lehigh Avenue in March, 1892. His present residence is at No. 2456 North Seventeenth Street. The premises occupied for business purposes are amply large, excellently equipped, and employment is found for twenty-five workmen. Mr. McGlenn executes building and cemetery work and general jobbing to order, making a leading specialty of building stone work. Among the important contracts he now has on hand may be mentioned the furnishing of stone for residences for Mr. Langham, corner Seventeenth and Cumberland Streets, and Mr. Hagan, Second and Oxford Streets, and Second and Indiana Avenue. Estimates for anything in his line are promptly furnished by Mr. McGlenn, and all orders are filled carefully upon liberal terms.

MARSHALL BROS., Bobbin and Spool Makers, For Cotton, Woolen and Silk Factories, Corner Frankford Avenue and Adams Street, Frankford.—For a quarter of a century the bobbins and spools made by Marshall Bros., corner Frankford Avenue and Adams Street, have been in use all over this country. The productions of this firm have a reputation second to none, and are in extensive and growing demand. The Messrs. Marshall manufacture bobbins and spools of every size and description for cotton, woolen and silk mills, and turn out a class of work of a very superior character. They have excellent facilities, and can execute orders for anything in their line at shortest notice and upon the most favorable terms. Their factory is a 40 x 125 feet two-story structure, and is equipped with ample steam power and the latest improved machinery, while twenty hands are employed in the concern. The firm is composed of James and John Marshall, and their nephew, William Marshall, who succeeded to his father's interest in the business about two years ago. The Messrs. Marshall are natives of England and have been in this city for the past twenty-seven years. They are all men of practical skill and thorough experience, and are well known in the cotton, woolen and silk industry throughout the United States.

R. S. REED, Real Estate, Etc., Northwest Corner Thirty-third and Chestnut Streets.—The real estate market of Philadelphia is one of the most substantial, active and flourishing to be found in the entire country, and the high standard to which it has been raised must be credited to the honorable methods and public-spiritedness of our real estate agents and brokers. One of the oldest, best-known and most prominent among those extensively engaged in this field of enterprise is Mr. R. S. Reed, whose headquarters are at the northwest corner of Thirty-third and Chestnut Streets, and his branch office at No. 184 Darby Road. He established at the former address eighteen years ago, meeting with the best of success, and he has always commanded a large, active and most desirable patronage. The branch office was opened about a year since. Mr. Reed has been a notary public for fourteen years, and attends to all the duties of that position. He was born in Lancaster, Pa., and has resided in Philadelphia 50 years; before engaging in his present line he was identified for many years with the wholesale grocery trade. Employing four assistants, Mr. Reed carries on a general business in buying and selling property of all kinds, making a leading specialty of residences in the Twenty-fourth and Twenty-seventh Wards. He also negotiates loans and mortgages, assumes the management of estates, effects fire insurance, collects rents, secures tenants, and profitably invests capital for investors. His judgment is invariably sound, his advice reliable and judicious, and those who require anything in his line will do well to secure his services.

GEO. F. CREUTZBURG & SON, Importers, Manufacturers and Dealers in Fine Cutlery, Pocket Cutlery, Scissors and Shears, Cooks' Carving and Butcher Knives, Razors, Hones, Strops, Etc., also Repairers of all Kinds of Cutlery, Concaving Razors a Specialty, No. 119 North Sixth Street.—An old-established and widely-known Philadelphia cutlery firm is that of Geo. F. Creutzburg & Son, No. 119 North Sixth Street. This is one of the oldest and leading houses in its line in the city, and for forty-odd years has been conducted at the present location with uninterrupted success. They are importers, manufacturers and dealers in fine cutlery, turning out and handling only high-grade goods. They do both a wholesale and retail business, and their trade, which is very large, extends throughout the United States. The quarters occupied for manufacturing purposes, etc., are commodious and well equipped, and are fitted up with ample steam-power and the latest improved machinery, appliances and tools. The facilities are first-class in all respects, and twenty skilled hands are employed. The firm occupies a 25 x 60 feet store and basement, and the third and fourth floors besides, where can always be found an extensive and complete assortment, and is represented on the road by several salesmen. The stock comprises fine pocket cutlery, scissors and shears, cooks', carving and butcher knives, razors, hones, strops and barbers' supplies generally in this line, and cutlery of all kinds is repaired here in the most superior manner at short notice. This house also manufactures and makes a specialty of the Eagle brand of razors. Razors, scissors, knives, etc., are ground also, and special attention is given to the concaving of razors. All work done is guaranteed to be first-class, perfect satisfaction being assured, while every article sold is warranted to be exactly as represented. The prices, too, are always the lowest, liberal inducements being offered to the trade, and all orders are promptly and carefully attended to.

GEO. W. DEVINNY, Masonic Marks and Society Badges, No. 1030 Chestnut Street.—The vast membership of the numerous societies and fraternal organizations of the United States, has caused the building up of several business callings, each of importance and steadily increasing value. One of these is represented by the manufacturer of masonic marks and society badges. The leading house in the Quaker City, engaged in this line, is that of Geo. W. Devinny, whose salesroom and factory are at No. 1030 Chestnut Street. Mr. Devinny established business six years ago, bringing thorough experience to bear, having followed the trade for the past quarter century. He has won a large trade throughout Pennsylvania and vicinity, and acquired an enviable reputation for the superior merits of his products. Mr. Devinny is a native of Philadelphia, and now in the middle age of life. During the war he enlisted as a private in Company I, 90th Regiment, Pennsylvania Volunteer Infantry, serving for two years with the Army of the Potomac, taking part in five important engagements, and was appointed 2nd U. S. Invalids by President Lincoln. He is a member of the Society of the Potomac, and also of George G. Meade Post, No. 1, G. A. R., being Past Commander of this post, which is the largest in the city. He is also prominent in fraternal orders, being Past Grand of Chosen Friends Lodge, No. 100, I. O. O. F.; Past Commander of Holy Cross Commandery, No. 22, Knights of Malta; Deputy Supreme Commander of the Knights of Malta; trustee of Perkins Lodge, No. 602, F. and A. M., and a member of the Knights of Pythias, Red Men, Knights of the Golden Eagle, American Mechanics, Knights Templar, etc. Mr. Devinny employs a staff of expert assistants and manufactures masonic marks and society badges of every variety, executing gold and silver work only. The goods are all of the choicest character, artistically finished, and those who order anything in his line from Mr. Devinny are certain to receive the best of satisfaction.

HISTORICAL AND COMMERCIAL PHILADELPHIA.

ANAYUNK NATIONAL BANK, No. 4375 Main Street.—Manayunk owes much of its present prosperity and is under great obligations to the Manayunk National Bank, which under able and progressive management, has fostered and promoted various mercantile and manufacturing interests in this entire community. It was duly incorporated in 1870, and its stock was promptly subscribed for by leading citizens of Manayunk and vicinity. From the start this bank had the confidence and patronage of the commercial and industrial world, and has carried increasingly large lines of deposits, the majority representing active accounts, while its loans and discounts represent sound business transactions of the larger houses. It has a capital stock of $300,000, and is officered as follows, viz.: President, David Wallace; cashier, John J. Foulkrod; directors, John J. Foulkrod, David Wallace, C. J. McGlinchey, A. Platt, John Flanagan, Harmon Johnson, Leander M. Jones, Wm. Rice and Wm. H Nixon. This bank transacts a regular legitimate banking business in deposits, loans, collections and exchange; receives the accounts of banks, bankers, corporations, individuals and firms on the most favorable terms; discounts first-class commercial paper and makes loans on approved collateral; deals in foreign exchange, issues sight drafts and makes collections on all available points through its numerous correspondents, who include the Hanover National Bank of New York and the National Bank of the Republic of Philadelphia. It has accumulated a surplus fund of $100,000 with undivided profits of $51,304.26, while its deposits average $778,000 and its loans and discounts $775,000. The bank's total assets now amount to $1,211,977.60, which is abundantly indicative of the wise and liberal policy ever animating the officers and the directorate. No fiscal institution in the city has achieved more deserved popularity, none has a better system or more ably advances its customers' best interests and none is more worthy of confidence. President Wallace has been at the helm since 1881 and a director from the inception of the bank. The cashier, Mr. Foulkrod, was elected to that position in 1871, having previously been connected with the Second National of Frankford and the Bank of the Republic of Philadelphia, and in the banking business constantly since 1867, and both gentlemen are thoroughly trained financiers, whose opinions are of weight in banking circles.

HE S. S. WHITE DENTAL MANUFACTURING COMPANY, Founded by Samuel S. White in 1844, Incorporated in 1881; Chestnut Street, Corner of Twelfth.—The name of S. S. White has been so long and so prominently identified with the manufacture of the finest classes of dental instruments that it represents what a trade-mark does in other branches of business. The industry founded by Dr. Samuel S. White in 1844 has become the largest in its line in the whole civilized world. There is no city so densely populated, no island so remote, but the name of this house is coupled with the prosperity and well-being of its people. Dr. White died in 1879, but his name and fame survive and The S. S. White Dental Manufacturing Company, which was incorporated in July, 1881, with a paid up capital of $1,000,000, now makes more than three-fourths of all the dental goods used in the United States. The Philadelphia office of the company (the headquarters) is eligibly located on Chestnut Street, corner of Twelfth, and is under expert and successful management. The premises here occupied comprise a splendid five-story marble front building, 45 x 235 feet in dimensions, divided into manufacturing and sales departments, in which are employed some 300 persons. A complete stock of the company's specialties is here constantly carried, comprising the latest improved dental chairs, and every known instrument of merit for extracting, filling and cleaning teeth; also electric motors, all the best tools and equipments for the manufacture of sets of teeth, as well as full supplies of porcelain teeth; and gold, silver, rubber and other materials. The company has a plant at Frankford, Pa., for the manufacture of fine steel instruments, where employment is given to 200 hands; and another plant on Staten Island, for making dental chairs and heavy goods, where 100 employees are engaged. One hundred and eight first premiums have been received at the great expositions throughout the world, and the business relations of the company are practically universal. Branch offices are operated in New York, Brooklyn, Boston, Chicago and Atlanta, with its main office in this city. Here is published the "Dental Cosmos," the leading dental magazine of the universe, founded in 1859. The executive officers of the company are as follows, viz.: Henry M. Lewis, president; W. H. Gilbert, general manager; J. Clarence White, secretary; Samuel T. Jones, treasurer. All have been trained in the business for years, are eminent in the world of manufactures and of the highest repute in the business community. Their field is practically unlimited, and they can claim with mighty England that the sun never sets upon the products of their industry.

. F. WELLS & SON, Carpenters, Contractors and Builders, Office, No. 260 South Eighth Street, Shop, No. 520 Buckley Street.—In no part of the world is the constructive art, in all its numerous ramifications, of greater importance than in Philadelphia, where buildings of all kinds, large and small, are in constant progress in every part of the city. Among houses that have been for some years established in this branch of commercial and industrial activity in this city is that of C. F. Wells & Son, whose office is located at No. 260 South Eighth Street. They also occupy a two-story building for workshop at No. 520 Buckley Street. This firm began business in 1886 for themselves under the present style, Messrs. C. F. Wells and W. C. Wells being the proprietors of the business. They bring vast practical experience to bear as well as good sound judgment and ample resources, and the buildings constructed by them are noted as being reliable and beautiful in exterior and perfect and elegant within, while the prices asked are the lowest consistent with the best workmanship. They have built numerous houses in the city and suburbs, all planned and supervised with the greatest care and fitted with the very latest improvements. They built the "Colonial Hotel" and numerous residences, etc., in the city as well as a great many residences in Germantown. Mr. C. F. Wells has had a practical experience of forty years. They are natives of New Jersey and have been residents of the city for a number of years. Mr. C. F. Wells is a prominent member of the I. O. O. F. W. C. Wells, his son and partner, is a young man and has been brought up in the business. They give employment to a competent staff of mechanics and workmen.

HISTORICAL AND COMMERCIAL PHILADELPHIA.

 DAVID HOFFER, Wholesale Dealer in Dressed Beef, Southwest Corner Twenty-ninth and Market Streets, also Nos. 1722-24-26 Fairmount Avenue, Philadelphia has ever been celebrated for its home dressed beef, the excellence of which affords the Western beef no chance for favorable comparison. A foremost house engaged in the wholesale handling of city dressed beef is that of Mr. David Hoffer, whose headquarters are located in the Philadelphia Market, southwest corner Twenty-ninth and Market Streets, and who has a retail branch at Nos. 1722 1724 1726 Fairmount Avenue and Nos. 251 253 Warren Street, Jersey City. The establishment has telephonic service, the calls being: Market Street, No. 278, W. P.; Fairmount Avenue, No. 6338. Mr. Hoffer is a native of Philadelphia and one of our most prominent citizens, and thoroughly identified with the city's best interests. He is a member of the Philadelphia House, the Maritime Exchange, and the Marketmen's Association. In 1855 Mr. Hoffer began business as a retail dealer in meats, in the Girard Street Market, afterward removing to Fairmount Avenue, and seventeen years ago he added a wholesale department. In March, 1891, Mr. Hoffer opened his wholesale store in the Philadelphia Market. The present extent of the business demands the employment of twenty-five hands. The cooling-room is equipped with an overhead railway, and has a storage capacity sufficient for forty-eight head of cattle. The sales amount to from 70 to 100 head of cattle weekly. First-class beef only is dealt in, and the trade is supplied at lowest prevailing market prices.

 GEORGE CARELESS, Manufacturer of Fine Silver Plated Ware, No. 611 Arch Street.—One of the oldest-established houses in the entire city of Philadelphia, engaged as a manufacturer of fine silver plated ware, is that of George Careless, located at No. 611 Arch Street. This responsible undertaking was founded in 1858 by Messrs. Careless and Furnare, the latter retiring in 1863 and since the decease of Mr. George Careless, three years ago, the business has been managed in detail by his son, Mr. William Careless. The basis of the operations of the house consists in the manufacture to order for the trade, of a general line of electro-silver plated tableware, such as mugs, center ornaments, sugar bowls, milk and cream jugs, tongs, tea and coffee pots, urns, salvers, and everything in tableware, in addition to which anything in fine silver plate is made to order to any design from the plainest to the most richly artistic and elaborate and chased, engraved, figured, etc., to any pattern, while also, repairing, gilding and replating are promptly executed. The factory, 25 x 125 feet in area, on the third floor at the address named, is furnished with a complete modern equipment of machinery, appliances and accessories pertaining to the industry, ample electric-power being provided and ten skilled workers there regularly employed. The able and experienced manager, Mr. William Careless, was brought up to this line of trade and is now forty-three years of age. He is a native of Birmingham, England, but was brought to this city when only three months old and is a member of the Knights of Pythias, the Independent Order of Odd Fellows, the Knights of the Golden Eagle, the Independent Order of Red Men, the Legion of the Red Cross and the Home Builders.

 MILTON A. CRESSMAN & CO., Produce Commission Merchant, Nos. 66 and 68 North Water Street.—That branch of mercantile industry designated under the head of commission merchants, is a very important business in Philadelphia, and a powerful auxiliary in expanding and building up the general interests of the city. By alluring produce and other goods to this city, direct from the producer, not only do our citizens procure their food supplies at a minimum cost, but a considerable trade is attracted to Philadelphia, that, under other conditions, would seek a market where the producer sold his produce. A prominent house engaged in the trade is that of Milton A. Cressman & Co., whose establishment is at Nos. 66 and 68 North Water Street. This business was inaugurated three years ago by the present proprietors, Messrs. Milton A. Cressman and A McF. Dunne, both of whom have been with John Jamison & Co., and in the produce commission trade fifteen and eighteen years respectively. Both are natives of this city, and members of the Philadelphia Produce Exchange, and National Cheese, Butter and Egg Association. The premises occupied comprise a four-story building, 20 x 40 feet in dimensions, equipped with two large cooling-rooms, and all facilities. The firm make a leading specialty of butter, eggs, and cheese, receiving the entire products of creameries in Pennsylvania, New York, Ohio, and the West, and their trade extends through Pennsylvania, New Jersey, Delaware, and the South. A single consignment of goods on the part of the producer, or a survey of Messrs. Milton A. Cressman & Co's. stock and facilities, will prove the liberality and reliable character of the establishment.

 JAMES STAFFORD, Star Woolen Mills, Manufacturer of Blankets, Woolen Goods and Yarns, Church Street, Manayunk. In the production of blankets, woolen goods and yarns, a marked success has been achieved in this city by Mr. James Stafford, proprietor of the Star Woolen Mills, located on Church Street, corner of Wood. Mr. Stafford was born in England, but came to Philadelphia forty-five years ago, when but ten years old, his parents having emigrated to this country. Thirty years ago, opposite the site he now occupies, he assisted in establishing the foundation of the business which has since grown to such great magnitude. Ten years were passed at that address, when a removal to the present location was effected. The lot occupied is large in extent. The mill buildings are of stone, have three and four floors respectively, and are furnished with a first-class mechanical equipment, which includes thirty-four broad power looms, four sets of sixty inch wide cards, and the most improved textile machinery, all driven by a 70-horse power engine. There is also a large dyehouse attached thereto. Employment is found for ninety-six hands. Mr. Stafford has had thirty-five years' experience in his vocation, and sees to it that his mills are always maintained at the highest point of efficiency. He manufactures blankets, woolen goods and yarns, also linings for dress goods. The output is a heavy one, employment regular, the goods of first quality, and the trade extends to all parts of the United States. Mr. Stafford is president of the Real Estate Syndicate of Manayunk and Wissahickon, which is actively engaged in buying up land and opening lots in this section for sale for residential purposes. The rapid growth of the city is quickly enhancing the value of property on all sides, and the first investors are those who gain the most. Full particulars can be learned on application to Mr. Stafford.

 GEORGE WM. OTTO, Agent. Manufacturer of all Kinds of Pure Soda Waters, and Bottler of Bergner & Engel's Tannhauser Beer, No. 530 Bainbridge Street.—Probably the oldest bottling establishment in active operation in the city of Philadelphia is that owned by George Wm. Otto, and situated at No. 530 Bainbridge Street. This enterprise was founded in 1835 by Eugene Roussel, and in 1866 the present proprietor succeeded to the control of affairs. Owing to the thorough knowledge brought to bear by him, together with his prompt, energetic and liberal policy, the large trade now commanded has been built up. The works were formerly located at No. 536 Locust Street, but owing to the growth of the industry, a removal to the present spacious quarters was effected ten years ago. The premises consist of two floors, each 60 x 100 feet in dimensions, and the place is equipped with a large generator and first-class machinery, driven by steam-power. Mr. Otto employs twelve hands, and owns thirteen horses and ten wagons. He manufactures all kinds of soda waters, his products being noted for their purity, flavor, and uniform excellence. Mr. Otto also bottles ales, porter, and lager, also Philip Zaum's Weiss beer, and makes a specialty of Bergner & Engel's Tannhauser beer. He disposes of over six thousand barrels of beer yearly, selling to families and dealers. Mr. Otto was born in Germany, and came to this city twenty-six years ago, since then becoming a well-known and popular citizen. He is a member of the Masonic Order, also of the National Bottlers' Association, and has ably served as secretary of the latter organization.

HISTORICAL AND COMMERCIAL PHILADELPHIA.

ALFRED M. HERKNESS & CO., Horse and Carriage Bazaar, Ninth and Sansom Streets.—This famous horse and carriage bazaar was originally founded in 1817 by Mr. Alfred M. Herkness, who adopted the firm name of Alfred M. Herkness & Co. This gentleman was born in Scotland, but has resided in this city for the past sixty years, coming here from the "Land of the Heather" when a lad of fourteen years, and has risen to prominence through his own exertions and industry. In 1870 Mr. Herkness admitted to partnership his son, Mr. A. Morris Herkness, and in 1882, a second son, Mr. Walter W. Herkness, also came into the firm. These young men are native Philadelphians, and are possessed of sound business ability. They are popularly known in business and social life. The extensive premises occupied consist of a five story building, 150x235 feet in dimensions, and five stories in height. There is ample storage capacity for about 300 carriages, and there are stalls for 150 horses. Among the conveniences is a riding ring around the auctioneer's stand for the display of the horses offered for sale. Public sales are held on Wednesdays and Saturdays, which are always well attended, and private sales are held daily. The Messrs. Herkness receive horses from all over Pennsylvania, and the sales amount to over 125 head weekly. Carriages and wagons of all kinds are also dealt in.

DANIEL B. RUFFNER, Dealer in Lehigh and Schuylkill Coal, Lime, Cement, Etc.; and RUFFNER & DUNN, Manufacturers of Nut Locks and Tube Cleaners; Norristown Railroad and Bowman Street.—The Philadelphia coal trade has one of its foremost representatives in Mr. Daniel B. Ruffner, whose extensive yard is located at the junction of the Norristown Railroad and Bowman Street, East Schuylkill Falls. Mr. Ruffner was born in this city, in the Twenty-eighth Ward, on January 1, 1875, and he has long been prominently known in fraternal, business and social circles. He is a director of the Mutual Fire Insurance Company of Philadelphia, a member of the firm of Ruffner & Dunn, and sole proprietor of the large coal yard at the address already indicated. He established this business in 1872. The yard has an area of 75x220 feet, and a storage capacity of 15,000 tons of coal. Six men and three teams are kept busy, and Mr. Ruffner carries on a general business as a dealer in the best

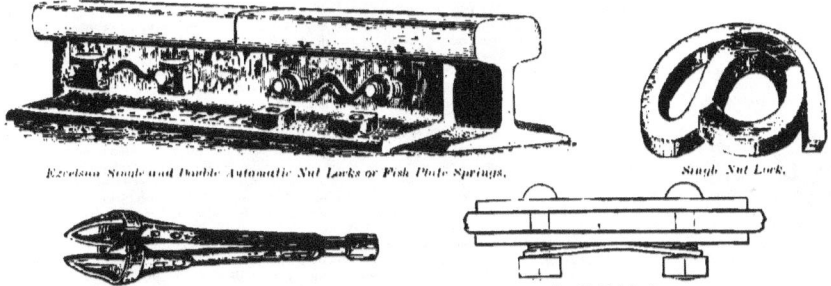

Excelsior Single and Double Automatic Nut Locks or Fish Plate Springs. *Single Nut Lock.*

Excelsior Steel Tube Cleaners. *Double Nut Lock.*

grades of Lehigh and Schuylkill coal, and also handles masons' materials, such as lime, cement, etc. Both a wholesale and retail trade is carried on, and all orders are filled at lowest market prices. In 1877, with Mr. Wm. Dunn, the firm of Ruffner & Dunn was established for the manufacture of tube cleaners. In 1889, on the admission to partnership of Mr. G. S. Bolton, the firm name became Ruffner, Dunn & Co., for the manufacture of nut locks. In 1890 Mr. Bolton retiring, the firm style again became Ruffner & Dunn. The plant owned by Mr. Ruffner is comprised in buildings and grounds 100x130 feet in dimensions, and the place is equipped with the most improved machinery, while employment is given to about twenty-five workmen. The works are in charge of Mr. Dunn, who is a skilled practical mechanic. He was born abroad, but has long resided in this city. The firm are patentees and sole manufacturers of the Excelsior Steel Tube Cleaners and the Excelsior Single and Double Automatic Nut Locks or Fish Plate Springs. These inventions are the best, for the purposes for which they were devised, now to be found in the market, and they are in demand in all parts of the country. Illustrated circulars, giving full details, are sent free on application.

J. B. STANGER & BROS., Furnishing Undertakers, No. 4346 Frankford Avenue.—One of the oldest established furnishing undertakers in Frankford is the responsible firm of J. B. Stanger & Bros., located at No. 4346 Frankford Avenue, who are well known for promptitude in the fulfillment of all orders, and for making fair and reasonable charges. The business was founded in 1857 by Mr. Jacob S. Stanger, who was succeeded in 1887 by his three sons, the present proprietors, Mr. John B. Stanger, Mr. Adam C. Stanger and Mr. Joseph A. Stanger; the latter having graduated in 1891 at the United States School of Embalming, and being a member of the Undertakers' Association. The firm manufacture their own caskets, coffins, etc., and supply everything appertaining to a funeral, including the hearses, carriages, coffins, caskets, palls and sundries, from the plainest to the most elaborate; while they also undertake embalming by the latest approved scientific methods, as well as all the duties and preliminaries incidental to interment. The premises utilized have been occupied since 1857, and are the firm's own property. They comprise a finely furnished office, wareroom, and a fully equipped two story building in the rear used as shop. The three proprietors, who are natives of this city, are thoroughly practical in this line, and were brought up to the business. They all take active part in the fulfillment of orders, and employ three competent assistants besides.

J. C. KELLY, Carriage Builder, No. 4695 Main Street, Germantown.—The largest and best equipped carriage factory in Germantown is that of Mr. J. C. Kelly. The operations of the house are confined exclusively to the highest grade of work, and the prices range from $350 for a road wagon, and finer vehicles in proportion. Nevertheless, in view of the quality of the work turned out, these charges are eminently fair and reasonable, and each customer may be sure of receiving a substantial *quid pro quo* for the amount paid, for the work turned out from first to last materially upholds the old saying that "the best is the cheapest." The materials selected are chosen with the utmost care from the finest the market affords, every consideration being had for durability and lightness combined with strength, while the carriages, etc., are made by only experienced hands upon the most approved principles of construction. This important and progressive enterprise was established in 1872 by Messrs. Weirman & Kelly and in 1885 it came under the sole control of the present proprietor, who possesses a practical experience in the trade dating back to 1869. The experienced proprietor, Mr. J. C. Kelly, was born in Ireland, but has been in the United States since infancy.

HISTORICAL AND COMMERCIAL PHILADELPHIA.

EORGE REDLES, Bobbin and Spool Manufacturer, No. 4543 Wakefield Street, Germantown.—For close upon half a century, George Redles, the well known bobbin and spool manufacturer, No. 4543 Wakefield Street, has been in business at the present location. He commenced as a chairmaker in 1845, and in 1865 embarked in the branch of industry in which he is now engaged. He is the oldest in this line in the city and has a large trade. He turns out a very superior class of work and his productions are in widespread and growing demand, sending bobbins and spools all over the country. Mr. Redles, who is a gentleman of full middle age, was born in Strawberry Alley, Phil., in 1821, and is one of Germantown's oldest and best-known residents. He is a man of thorough practical skill, as well as long and varied experience, active and energetic, and gives close personal attention to every detail of the business. His factory is a 30 x 100 feet two-story building and is equipped with steam-power, latest improved machinery, etc., while a dozen or more in help are employed here. Bobbins and spools of every description are manufactured and made to order by Mr. Redles. Stocking, shirt and drawer boards are made to order likewise at short notice and satisfaction is assured. Every article leaving this establishment is warranted as to make and material, while the prices charged are of the most reasonable character and all orders receive immediate attention.

AUCH, RUETSCHLIN & CO., (Successors to Rauch, Hawlk & Co.,) Wholesale Grocers and Flour and Tea Dealers, No. 231 North Third Street.—Few among Philadelphia's wholesale grocery firms are more widely or more favorably known than that of Rauch, Ruetschlin & Co., No. 231 North Third Street. This is one of the most prosperous houses in the line indicated, in the city, and its trade, which is very large, extends throughout Pennsylvania, Delaware, Maryland, District of Columbia and the adjoining States. An immense quantity of flour is handled, the firm being millers' agents, and shipments of the latter in car lots are made to all parts of the country. This popular and reliable house was established in 1881 by Kline, Hawlk & Rauch, who were succeeded by Rauch, Hawlk & Co., the present firm-name being adopted about two years ago. They occupy the whole of a 30 x 125 feet five-story building with complete facilities, and employ a large staff on the premises, while five salesmen are kept on the road. A heavy stock is constantly kept on hand, and includes fine teas and coffees, pure spices, syrups, molasses, sugar, rice, dried fruit, canned goods and ta-ble delicacies, choice butter, cheese, prime lard, hams, bacon, etc., best brands of family flour, the house being sole agents for White, Gold and Imperial brands of flour, oatmeal, corn meal, barley, beans, peas, salt, vinegar, oils, soda, saleratus, baking powder, soaps, starch and everything in staple and fancy groceries. All orders by telephone, (No. 2112) mail or otherwise are filled in the most prompt and trustworthy manner, quality and quantity being guaranteed, and the prices quoted are invariably the lowest, the trade being supplied on the most favorable terms. Messrs. Samuel Rauch, H. Ruetschlin and H. W. Dorward, who compose the firm, are gentlemen in the prime of life and natives of this city. They are all men of energy and enterprise and of thorough business experience, well-known in the trade.

EO. W. KELLEY, Marble and Granite Works, Opposite Ridge Avenue Depot.—One of the most noteworthy marble and granite works in Philadelphia is that of Mr. Geo. W. Kelley, situated at the junction of Ridge and Susquehanna Avenues, opposite the Ridge Avenue Depot, and which is well supplied with every appliance necessary for the business. Mr. Kelley has had a long experience as a marble and granite cutter, and is consequently thoroughly conversant with every detail of the business, while he enjoys a reputation for first-class work at reasonable prices, second to no other in the city. In 1872 he began business on Eighth Street and removed to his present location in 1880, since acquiring a large and most desirable trade. The works and yard cover an area of two acres, and are equipped in the most complete manner. A heavy stock of superior marble and granite is carried, also of house trimmings of all kinds in stone. Specialties are made of all kinds of building, monumental and cemetery work, and marble, granite and brownstone work in general; statuary, slabs, railings, headstones, footstones, etc., which is promptly done and in the best manner. Mr. Kelley has gained a substantial reputation for his skill in the production of monuments, tablets and memorials and has erected many of the finer and more artistic specimens which are to be seen in the cemeteries of Philadelphia. The trade is extensive and increases with each current year.

WEN D. ROBERTS, Real Estate, No. 241 South Fifth Street. One of the successful real estate men in Philadelphia is Mr. Owen D. Roberts, of No. 241 South Fifth Street, real estate agent, broker and conveyancer. Mr. Roberts started in this business five years ago and by his ability and his thorough knowledge of the profession soon gained a good share of business in the profession. He has a large local business and handles all kinds of real estate, attending to all branches of the business. He is a native of Philadelphia and though a young man has already shown himself the possessor of more than ordinary ability.

ERMANTOWN WOOLEN MILLS, Chas. H. Topham, Proprietor, Manufacturer of Wool and Merino Shoddies, Wool Scouring, Willowing, Etc., Corner of Ashmead and Wakefield Streets, Germantown. The Germantown Woolen Mills, Chas. H. Topham, proprietor, corner of Ashmead and Wakefield Streets, is one of the most complete and best equipped concerns of the kind in Philadelphia. The facilities are first-class in every respect and the products command extensive sale throughout the United States. Mr. Topham manufactures wool and merino shoddies of a very superior quality and his goods are not only in widespread, but growing demand, owing to the uniformly high standard of excellence at which the same are maintained. Wool scouring, willowing, etc., are attended to here also in the most excellent manner in short notice, and perfect satisfaction is assured, all orders for the trade receiving immediate attention. The mill is a 45 x 100 feet two-story structure, with ample steam power and latest improved machinery, etc., and twenty five in help are employed. The products include everything in the line above indicated, and a large stock of wool and merino shoddies is constantly kept on hand to meet the requirements of a steady and increasing demand. Mr. Topham, the proprietor, is a gentleman of about thirty five, born in Germantown. He is a man of practical skill and thorough experience, and is fully conversant with the wants of the trade. He established this flourishing business about seven years ago, and was formerly located at Wister Street and Reading Railroad, moving to the present place about a year ago. He is assisted by his brother, a young man of push and energy, who is foreman of the mill.

BISSINGER & SON, Importers of Tailors' Trimmings, No. 528 Market Street.—This business, which was established eighteen years ago by Mr. M. Bissinger, has steadily grown until the house ranks among the first in Philadelphia engaged in the importing trade, and it covers a big territory, which includes the States of Pennsylvania, Ohio, New Jersey, Virginia, Delaware and New York. Three years ago Mr. Harry Bissinger, son of the founder of the business, was admitted as a partner. He had already acquired a practical knowledge of the business, and proved himself a capable business man. The firm occupy the second and fourth floors, each 30 x 110 feet, at No. 528 Market Street, where they always carry a complete line of tailors' trimmings. They make a specialty of the finest imported goods, and import many of their goods direct. They have a special arrangement with some of the leading houses on the other side by which they are enabled to secure the first importations of many of the leading fashionable novelties, and they are always prepared to furnish the latest styles in trimmings from London or Paris. For eighteen years this reliable house has been a leader in its special line, and it is today better equipped than ever to supply the demands of an exacting trade. Two travelling salesmen are in the employ of the house. Both the members of the firm are natives and residents of Philadelphia.

GERMANTOWN REAL ESTATE, DEPOSIT AND TRUST COMPANY, Corner Main Street and Chelten Avenue; Chestnut Hill Office, Opposite Pennsylvania Railroad Station.—This company was duly incorporated in 1889, and from its inception has secured the endorsement of all classes, and become a favorite place of deposit for large as well as small sums. It has a capital of $300,000, full paid, and is officered as follows: President, Samuel Mason; Secretary and Treasurer, Samuel G. Jones; Real Estate and Trust Officer, Jay Gates; Directors, Henry L. Davis, Frank J. Firth, Wm. G. Foulke, Philip C. Garrett, Chas. F. Gummey, Samuel Mason, John B. Morgan, Wm. H. Scott, Joseph M. Shoemaker; Advisory Committee of Stockholders, Samuel Emlen, Josiah F. Jones, Calvin Pardee, Francis B. Reeves, Benj. H. Shoemaker, Wm. G. Warden, Wm. H. Haines, R. C. McMurtrie. The banking rooms of the company are eligibly located in their own building, corner Main Street and Chelten Avenue, Germantown, and every possible facility is afforded for the prompt and safe transaction of business. This company receives deposits on the most favorable terms, paying interest at the rate of two per cent per annum upon deposits subject to check at sight, and three per cent upon deposits that are made payable on two weeks' notice. Special deposits of large amounts are received for stated periods of time, for which the company issues its certificate of deposit. Collections are promptly made on all available points, and money is loaned on approved collateral. Safes in fire and burglar proof vaults are rented from $5 to $30 per annum, and a storage vault is also provided, which is specially adapted for the safe keeping of trunks or boxes containing silver plate, jewelry or other valuables. Bonds, certificates of stock and other valuable papers received for safe keeping at a moderate charge. This company also accepts trusts of every description by appointment of court or otherwise, acting as executor, administrator, guardian, receiver, committee, agent, assignee, trustee, etc. Wills are receipted for and safely kept without charge. Titles to real estate are insured, giving purchasers an absolute guarantee that the title to the property bought is good and marketable. Deeds, mortgages, agreements, bonds and all other legal papers are carefully prepared. Sales of realty are negotiated, money is advanced to builders, mechanics' liens are insured against, houses are rented, and rents, interest and income are collected and promptly remitted. Money is safely invested, and can be drawn on brief notice. If allowed to remain it earns a handsome rate of interest.

TAYLOR FAUNCE, Auditor and Public Accountant, No. 707 Drexel Building.—The rapid growth of the enormous corporations and large firms with their increasing complexity of accounts and transactions render it absolutely necessary for such concerns to avail themselves of the abilities of the trained public accountant, in order to keep proper track of their business, of their profits and losses, and to avoid the ever present danger of defalcations by trusted employees. In this connection we desire to direct special attention to Mr. Taylor Faunce, of the Drexel Building, who, as an auditor and public accountant, has won a well deserved reputation throughout our leading financial and public circles by his undoubted ability and thoroughness of work in the handling of accounts. He is a native of Philadelphia, where he has served a lengthy apprenticeship—extending over sixteen years, in almost every branch of mercantile and financial business, as clerk, bookkeeper, secretary, etc., which has given him a wide range of experience that fully fits him for his present duties. In January, 1892, Mr. Faunce opened his present office, and is prepared to undertake special auditing, examinations and investigations of all descriptions of accounts, and of the most difficult sets of books. He has already executed important commissions for leading concerns in the most eminently satisfactory manner. He devotes most patient care to unravelling entangled accounts, rectifying errors and securing to companies and firms a balance sheet which shows just where they stand or whether they have made or lost during the preceding year. Mr. Faunce can be relied upon to promptly execute all orders, and is moreover a gentleman of sterling integrity and soundest judgment; one in whom every confidence can be reposed, no matter how onerous or extensive the trust. Mr. Faunce has had fourteen years' experience as a bank clerk with the national banks of Philadelphia, v z., The Union, Mechanics', Northern Liberties and Northern National. He was appointed by the Court of Common Pleas in January, 1891, as examiner of savings banks for Philadelphia County, in association with J. Quincy Hunsicker. The office was abolished at the last session of the Legislature, by the passage of a bill creating the office of Superintendent of Banking. For a short term Mr. Faunce assisted the Bank Examiner of the District of Philadelphia. He also examined on behalf of District Attorney and Committee on Insolvent Institutions, the Shackamaxon Bank, Bank of America, American Life Insurance Company, was chairman of committee of investigation of the city treasurer's accounts; and was employed by the United States Treasury Department in the Keystone Bank examination until it was discontinued, owing to the appropriation running out.

F. W. LEYPOLDT, Manufacturer of Scarificators, Spring Lancets and Patent Button Hole Cutters, No. 243 North Fifth Street.—The gentleman whose name heads this sketch enjoys the distinction of being the only manufacturer of scarificators in the United States. He also manufactures spring lancets, patent button hole cutters, press tools, special tools, and specialties; also executing repairs, etc., and his establishment is the oldest in this line in the country. His productions, too, are of a distinctly superior character, and are in widespread demand, being sold to the trade all over the country. This business was established in 1847 by F. C. Leypoldt, who was succeeded in 1889 by his son, Frederick W., the present proprietor, who has since conducted it with uninterrupted success. The factory, at No. 243 North Fifth Street, is commodious and well equipped, and several expert workmen are employed here. The scarificators and spring lancets manufactured in this shop are made in various styles and designs, and every one is fully warranted as to workmanship and material. Scarificators are made to order on agreement at short notice and in the most superior manner, perfect satisfaction being assured. F. C. Leypoldt's patent button hole cutter is also a device of exceptional merit, and is adapted for tailors, shoe, dress and shirt makers, and for family use. This instrument, which has been on the market for over twenty-six years, cuts the lightest and heaviest fabrics, and is conceded to be, in all respects, the most excellent button hole cutter ever invented. A full stock is constantly kept on hand, and all orders receive prompt and personal attention. The trade is supplied on the most favorable terms, and the very lowest possible prices are quoted. Mr. Leypoldt is a man of practical skill and ingenuity, and is an expert in his line. He is well and favorably known in social life as well as in business circles, and is a prominent member of the I. O. O. F. (encampment), the Knights of the Golden Eagle, and other societies.

WILLIAM LOESCH, Graduate in Pharmacy, N. E. Corner Eleventh and Somerset Streets.—The pharmacy of Mr. William Loesch, located at the northeast corner of Eleventh and Somerset Streets, controls a liberal share of the best trade hereabouts, conducted with private residents and medical practitioners, and it is now well known as a reliable dispensary for absolutely pure, fresh and potent drugs, chemicals, medicines and family remedies. The business was established in 1884 by Mr. T. A. Walker, and in 1891 it came into the hands of the present proprietor, who is a graduate of the Philadelphia College of Pharmacy (1890) and is a member of its Alumni Association. A large number of proprietary articles are made and put up on the premises, the specialties are Loesch's Liver Granules, Loesch's Plasters, Loesch's Tooth Wash, Loesch's Hydrobromate of Caffeine, Loesch's Neuralgia and Headache Powder, Loesch's Worm Syrup, Loesch's Worm Lozenges, Loesch's Worm Powders, Loesch's Laxative Fig Syrup, Loesch's Soothing Syrup, Loesch's Bronchial Lozenges, Loesch's Sarsaparilla, and the trade for these reaches all over the city. In addition, particular care and attention are devoted to the preparation of physicians' prescriptions and miscellaneous recipes, and the finest drugs are alone used. The store, 18x30 feet in area, occupying a prominent corner position, is finely furnished and contains a large and carefully selected assortment of pure drugs, confections, cigars, perfumes, toilet articles, and everything usually to be found in a first class drug and prescription store. Mr. Wm. Loesch is a young man of Philadelphia birth, and is a member of the Independent Order of Odd Fellows, and other leading societies.

HISTORICAL AND COMMERCIAL PHILADELPHIA.

F. TAYLOR & CO., Lumber and Millwork, Broad Street, above Lehigh Avenue.—One of Philadelphia's oldest and leading lumber firms is that of B. F. Taylor & Co., whose office, yard, etc., are located on Broad Street, above Lehigh Avenue. The concern has been in existence for close upon half a century, and has passed through three successive generations of the same family. This flourishing business was established in 1845 by B. B. Taylor & Co., who was succeeded, in 1872, by B. F. Taylor (son of B. B.) The latter conducted it alone up to 1883, when he admitted into partnership his son, F. W. Taylor, and under the firm-name that head this sketch it has since been continued with uninterrupted success, although the senior member was removed by death in 1894. The business premises were formerly located at No. 1011 North Delaware Avenue, and were moved to the present place in 1888. The yard here is 400 x 300 feet in area, and is conveniently situated, the rear being on the line of the Pa. R. R. Supplies come direct from all the lumber regions of the country, and an immense stock is constantly kept on hand. This includes rough and dressed lumber of every variety, hard woods, sash, doors and blinds, door and window frames, moldings, posts, pickets, shingles, lath and everything in builders' supplies; also best grades of Lehigh and other coals, for factory and family use. Sixteen to eighteen in help are employed, and nine teams are in regular service, an exceedingly large trade being done. All orders, wholesale and retail, are promptly attended to, and the prices quoted by the firm are the very lowest consistent with quality and quantity purchased, substantial inducements being offered to builders, contractors and large consumers. Mr. F. W. Taylor, who is now sole proprietor, is a gentleman in the prime of life and a native of this city. He is a young man of energy and excellent business ability, as well as thorough experience, and is a member of the Lumbermen's Exchange.

HENRY GOLDNER, Machine and Boiler Works and Blacksmithing, Tasker Street Wharf. For thoroughly excellent all-around work in machine and boiler construction and blacksmithing, or for promptness and reliability in executing orders, none in the line indicated in this city enjoy a better reputation than Henry Goldner, whose shop is on Tasker Street Wharf. He has been established at the present location since 1885, and has acquired an extensive patronage. His works, which were rebuilt by him in 1889, are spacious, commodious and perfectly equipped, the facilities being first-class in every respect. The concern is provided with ample steam-power, the latest improved lathes, shears, punches, vises, etc., and thirty-one skilled hands are here employed. Mr. Goldner, whose trade extends throughout Pennsylvania, New Jersey, Delaware and the adjoining States, is a gentle man of middle age and a Philadelphian by birth. He is an expert boiler-maker and general mechanic, of many years' experience, a thorough master of his art in all its branches, and prior to going into business for himself had been employed by the Messrs. Cramp, the shipbuilders, for a number of years. He is prepared to furnish estimates on anything in his line, upon application, and guarantees perfect satisfaction, while his prices are most reasonable. Machinery and boilers for all purposes are built to order, at short notice, and tank and sheet iron work generally is done in the most prompt and superior manner. Steamship and boiler repairs are a specialty, while blacksmithing and jobbing of every description are executed with skill and dispatch, all orders receiving immediate attention.

BONSALL BROS., Conveyancers, No. 116 North Ninth Street. It is but rendering a just tribute to accord to the firm of Messrs. Bonsall Bros., of No. 116 North Ninth Street, Philadelphia, the credit and distinction of being the leading and the oldest house of its class in the vicinity. The business was established in the year 1857 by Messrs. Ellwood and Sterling Bonsall, which latter gentleman died in 1880, leaving the existing conditions. The business is that of conveyancers, the house engaging in every department of the calling. The operations of the concern embrace the purchase and sale upon commission of real estate mortgages and ground rents, the loaning either in the capacity of parties or as agents sums of money upon mortgage of realty; the making or valuations of property, real and personal, and the undertaking of the custody of estates and the collection of rents and interest. An important department of the business comprises the investment of moneys for persons upon all classes of real estate securities as ground rents, etc., and the house is identified with several of the prominent trust companies of the city. These gentlemen come from an old and distinguished family that came from Derbyshire, England, in 1683, and the family have all been residents of this State since. The grandfather of Mr. Ellwood Bonsall, Mr. Edward Bonsall, was the first man in Philadelphia to enter into the business of conveyancing, which he did in 1774, the family having followed the business ever since. He was also a land surveyor in this city and was prominent in his day in both these fields of industry. The management of the business evinces a creditable example of systematic harmony and precision and the office hours of the concern are from 9 A. M. to 3 P. M. The proprietors of the business are Mr. Ellwood Bonsall, a gentleman of middle age and his son, Mr. Ellwood W. Bonsall. They are among the ablest and most respected of the city's business men and Mr. Ellwood Bonsall is the president of the Philadelphia Conveyancers' Association.

WM. MacNEECE, Manufacturer of Art Furniture, Antique Work a Specialty, No. 933 Locust Street. Prominent among the various houses of enterprise and refinement in the city of Philadelphia, successfully engaged in the manufacture of art furniture, and in the reproduction of antique work, stands that of Mr. Wm. MacNeece, located at No. 933 Locust Street. This gentleman established his business here in 1886, bringing to bear a practical experience of forty years in this line, coupled with a perfect knowledge of the growing wants and requirements of the times. He occupies spacious and commodious premises, supplied with improved machinery and ample steam-power, and gives steady employment to a large force of skilled workmen. He manufactures a general line of art furniture to order, much of which is made from the rarest of woods, including mahogany, cherry, American and English oak, French walnut, ebony and rosewood, which, from their fine grain and richness of color always sustain the highest finish. Antique furniture, making a specialty in artistic clock cases and antique chairs, clocks and other kindred specialties, are also furnished at short notice, and the house is liberally patronized by the élite of this city and vicinity when in search of the rich, rare, and the unique.

JOHN W. HEPWORTH & CO., Manufacturers of Knitting Machinery, Lehigh Avenue and Mascher Street. In the domain of the mechanical arts there is perhaps no line in which more progress has been made of late years than in the construction of textile machinery, and these remarks apply in an especial manner to knitting machines, in which a degree of excellence akin to perfection has been attained. Some of our Philadelphia firms engaged in the branch of industry above indicated have a world wide reputation, and among these may be named John W. Hepworth & Co., whose shop is located at Lehigh Avenue and Mascher Street. They are manufacturers of knitting machinery of a distinctly superior character, and their productions are not only in extensive use all over the United States, Canada and Mexico, but also in South America and Europe. They have been established since 1889, and were formerly located on Germantown Avenue, moving to the present place about seven years ago. The premises here occupied are spacious and commodious, and are equipped with steam-power lathes and all the latest improved appliances while twenty-five to thirty hands are employed. The productions include small and large Balmorals, looping machines and all kinds of machinery and accessories for knitting mills. Knitting machines are built to order and also repaired by this firm in the most superior manner at short notice, all orders receiving prompt attention, and perfect satisfaction is assured, while their prices are of the most reasonable character withal. Mr. Hepworth, the head of the concern, is a gentleman of middle age and a native of this city. He is a practical machinist and a man of exceptional skill in his line, and exercises close personal supervision over all work executed in his establishment.

ERCHANTS' TRUST COMPANY, Nos. 611 and 613 Chestnut Street.—The Merchants' Trust Company, at Nos. 611 and 613 Chestnut Street, is unquestionably one of the conservative financial corporations of Philadelphia, and exercises a most beneficial influence in its important sphere of operations. It was incorporated in 1889, with a capital of $500,000.00, and is officered as follows, viz.: President, Joseph R. Rhoads; vice-president, John F. Lewis; secretary and treasurer, Robert Morris Early; trust officer, Wm. B. Lane. Directors: Nicholas Brice, Howard Butcher, A. Graham Elliot, Thomas R. Gill, Thomas A. Gummey, Charles S. Hinchman, Spencer M. Janney, John F. Lewis, John B. Love, John Lucas, S. Davis Page, Joseph R. Rhoads, Edward S. Sayres, E. Cooper Shapley, J. Bolton Winpenny. The company thus has the benefit of the soundest, most conservative management, and has enjoyed from the outset a large and growing patronage. It executes trusts, receives deposits, rents safes, insures titles, acts as registrar, issues searches, makes loans, collects income and becomes surety. Its charter gives it special powers to act as executor, guardian, trustee, or in any other fiduciary capacity; it is a legal depository for money paid into court, and a designated depository for the funds of those acting as executors, trustees, guardians, receivers, etc. It acts as registrar or transfer agent of stocks and bonds, and as trustee for railroad and other corporation mortgages. The company's safe deposit vaults are absolutely fire and burglar proof, and are guarded night and day by watchmen under the supervision of the American District Telegraph Company. Boxes are rented therein at moderate prices, also safes of various sizes. The company transacts a general banking business, receiving deposits subject to check and allowing interest at two per cent on daily balances; while it also has a well-patronized savings fund department, which is open from 9 A. M. to 4 P. M., and where deposits are received from $1.00 up to any amount, payable on ten days' notice and with interest at three per cent. In all its departments, this company offers perfected facilities to the public. Its assets are of a secure and remunerative character, and it is unquestionably a model institution, well meriting the large measure of trust and confidence it has inspired.

FAIRMOUNT WATER WORKS.

WILLIAM A. FLANAGAN, Dealer in Wool, Hair, Wool Waste, Woolen Rags, Etc., No. 106 North Front Street. Few among the many substantial merchants engaged in the wholesale handling of wool, hair, waste, etc., in this city, are more widely or more favorably known than William A. Flanagan, whose office and warehouse are at No. 106 North Front Street. He has been established about fifteen years and has built up an extensive trade throughout Pennsylvania, New Jersey, New York and New England. Mr. Flanagan is a gentleman in the prime of life and is a native of Philadelphia. He is a man of thorough experience in this line, as well as of energy and enterprise, and prior to going into business on his own account had been with William Johnston, shoddy manufacturer, for a number of years. He occupies four spacious floors and employs an efficient staff of assistants. Mr. Flanagan is a general dealer in foreign and domestic wool, hair, cotton waste, woolen rags, shoddies, etc., and carries a very large and complete stock. He can fill orders for anything in the line indicated upon the most favorable terms, and relations once formed with him are reasonably certain of leading to an enduring business connection. All orders are attended to in the most expeditious and trustworthy manner, and communications by telephone (No. 164) will receive prompt response.

HISTORICAL AND COMMERCIAL PHILADELPHIA.

ELAPLAINE & CO., Hatters' Goods, No. 19 North Third Street.—A prominent and noteworthy Philadelphia firm engaged in the wholesale handling of hatters' goods is that of Delaplaine & Co., No. 19 North Third Street. The house is a leading and representative one, and has a large trade which extends south as far as New Orleans and west to California. They sell extensively to hatters in this city, New Jersey and Connecticut, the total annual sales reaching quite a handsome figure. The business was established in 1875 by Sherman & Delaplaine, who conducted the same up to about a year and a half ago, when it passed into control of the present firm. It has since continued with eminent success, and all the indications are that the prosperity of the house is bound to endure and increase under the efficient management of Mr. Delaplaine, who has been connected with the hat trade for many years, is of extended business experience, is well up in the needs of the trade, and well known personally throughout the United States. He is a New Yorker by birth. The quarters occupied as office and salesrooms are compact and well ordered. Imported goods only are handled, and a full and fine stock is constantly kept on hand, including a general assortment of hatters' specialties. All orders are attended to in the most prompt and reliable manner, and the most liberal inducements are offered to manufacturers, bottom prices being quoted, while every article sold is warranted.

ARMERS' NEW HAY MARKET HOTEL, Jos. M. Jones, Proprietor, Jack Richardson, Superintendent, Phil. Dilling, Boss Stableman, Twelfth and Cambria Streets.—The Farmers' New Hay Market Hotel, Twelfth and Cambria Streets, was first opened to the public January 9, 1860, by David Campbell, and in July of the same year came into control of Jos. M. Jones, the present proprietor, under whose efficient management it has since been conducted with uninterrupted success. This is in all respects a well-kept and an excellent hostelry, and receives a substantial patronage. It is conveniently located, and is fitted up in the best manner, and the business of the house affords evidence of steady and gratifying increase. It is a favorite resort for farmers, and has first-class accommodations for the traveling public. The hotel building is a 50 x 100 feet three-story brick structure, and contains seventy-five rooms. It is finely furnished throughout, is lighted by the electric system and is thoroughly heated. The house is perfectly ventilated, too, the sanitary arrangements being exceptionally good, and the best stabling is provided for 225 horses. The yard, which is paved, covers three acres of ground, and there are in connection three capacious hay sheds, with weighing scales, etc. Mr. Jack Richardson, formerly of the Old Hay Market, is superintendent of this establishment, and Mr. Phil. Dilling is the boss stableman. The sleeping apartments are commodious, airy and comfortable, the fare is tip-top, and the service is all that could be desired. Twenty-five in help are employed, there is an excellent café and reading-room in connection, and the bar is stocked with the finest brands of wines, liquors, ales, beer and cigars. The rates are certainly very reasonable, everything considered, the terms being $1.00 to $1.50 per day, and, altogether it would not be easy to find such accommodations, comfort and attention at the same figures as are provided for his guests by mine host of the Farmers' New Hay Market Hotel. Mr. Jones is a gentleman of middle age and was born in Montgomery County, Pa. He is a man of energy and good business qualities, untiring in his attention to his patrons, and all the indications are that his popularity and prosperity are bound to endure and increase.

eKIEFFER & CANNING, Importers and Jobbers of Drugs and Druggists' Specialties, Southeast Corner Twenty-second and Market Streets. Philadelphia is prominent as the "home of pharmacy," and the term is well applied, not only on account of its many establishments, but also because of the superior qualifications of those who are engaged in the business and profession. A leading importing and jobbing house in this line is that of Messrs. DeKieffer & Canning, located at the southeast corner of Twenty-second and Market Streets. This firm are extensive manufacturers of standard proprietary remedies, importers of drugs and druggists' specialties, manufacturers in paints, oils, varnishes and glass. The business was founded some fifty years ago, by John W. Sames, and in 1891 the present firm succeeded to the control, bringing to bear every qualification as manufacturing pharmacists and expert business men. The building occupied contains four floors and a basement, 30 x 110 feet each, supplied with a well-equipped laboratory and all modern conveniences for the business, and steady employment is given to some twenty skilled and expert assistants. This firm believe that honest goods and reliable formulas, faithfully followed, soon obtain recognition and appreciation from a conscientious and discriminating profession. They recognize in the retail druggist himself their most serious competitor, and invite from them a scrutiny of prices, formulas and output, convinced that the verdict will be that the firm can serve them with mutual profit and satisfaction. The business is conducted at both wholesale and retail, and goods are sent to all parts of the United States. Physicians' prescriptions and doctors' orders are promptly filled, while the stock here carried includes everything in demand by the live retail druggist. The copartners, Messrs. Otto DeKieffer and James M. Canning, are native Philadelphians. The former is a graduate of the Philadelphia College of Pharmacy, while Mr. Canning devotes his entire time and attention to the paint and varnish department. They are subscribers to the Bourse, and accomplished pharmacists and enterprising, progressive and responsible business men, who are winning a grand success by honestly deserving it. This firm have added extensively to their paint manufacturing plant by the introduction of new machinery and latest appliances and are now better able than ever to cater to the wants of their patrons in their specialties of fine coach and painters' colors, wood fillers, etc.

A. FURBUSH & SON MACHINE CO., No. 224 Market Street.—There are certain enterprises carried on in Philadelphia which cannot be regarded as of secondary importance to the continued growth and prosperity of this city in an industrial or commercial sense, and, among the number, that conducted by the M. A. Furbush & Son Machine Co., as makers of wool and worsted machinery of every description, at No. 224 Market Street, commands our attention at this time. The business was originally established in 1859, by Mr. M. A. Furbush, who was succeeded in 1863 by Messrs. M. A. Furbush & Son, and in 1883 the present company was incorporated, under the laws of the State of New Jersey, with a capital of $300,000, and with Mr. M. A. Furbush, president. After a long and most honorably successful business career, Mr. Furbush died in 1887, since which time his place has been ably filled by Mr. Charles H. Knowlton, who for a great many years has been superintendent of the shops at Twelfth and Market Streets, Camden, N. J., where the company employs from 300 to 400 skilled workmen. In 1892, Mr. M. A. Furbush, the younger son of the founder of the business, became treasurer of the company, and Mr. Edwin C. Grier, who for many years has been connected with the office in Philadelphia, was elected secretary. Paying close and undivided attention to the excellence of their productions rather than to the amount of sales or monetary returns, their trade has steadily enlarged until they have reached a preëminence in their industry of which they have every reason to be proud. Endowed with a genius for invention, and an ambition to excel, the officers of the company have devoted themselves with ardor to the production of a class of machinery which should not only vie in excellence with both domestic and foreign productions, but should, when once introduced, be preferred to all other makes. That they have succeeded in their laudable endeavor there is no longer any doubt, as the superiority they have attained is such as to have created a permanent and constantly increasing demand for machinery of their manufacture, and the business of the company now extends to all parts of the United States, Canada and Mexico. The greatest success of the company has been attained by the manufacture of the Murkland Ingrain carpet loom, of which they have the exclusive control and have built upwards of 5000. They carry a large and complete stock of machinery on hand and are prepared to fill all orders promptly and at terms and prices which are invariably satisfactory to buyers, and their long reputation for excellence together with the strictest integrity which has ever been followed out as established by the founder, recommends the company to consideration by any one interested in the textile industry.

HISTORICAL AND COMMERCIAL PHILADELPHIA.

FRANKFORD REAL ESTATE AND SAFE DEPOSIT COMPANY, No. 4314 Frankford Avenue.—The Frankford Real Estate and Safe Deposit Company commenced business on the 11th of February, 1888, and has since made rapid and substantial progress. It combines a general banking business with departments devoted to real estate transactions. Its business in each of these departments is now larger than ever before, indicating the increasing confidence reposed in it by the general public. It receives accounts, both large and small, active or otherwise, and allows interest at the rate of 2 per cent on check account and 3 per cent on saving fund account. It loans on real estate and collateral security, it handles much of the choicest commercial paper drawn in this section of the city, and makes collections and clearances through the Penn National and Second National Banks of Philadelphia. The company has at all times a large number of desirable properties for sale, and is prepared to take the entire management of estates, buy and sell property of all kinds, invest money in mortgages, and to attend to all business usually done by trust companies. The loans of the company are all well secured, and, in addition to its paid up capital of $50,000, it has accumulated assets amounting to $198,000. The management is deservedly popular, and new accounts are being opened daily. The officers and directors of this company are as follows, viz:—Wilson Stearly, President; John B. Lennig, Vice President; John T. Crankshaw, Secretary; Charles T. Holme, Treasurer; William H. Peace, Solicitor. Board of Directors: John B. Lennig, Wilson Stearly, William H. Peace, Amos Pennypacker, Joseph Noel, Emmett O'Neill, Harry B. Yerger, Charles B. Siner, William Horrocks, Harry F. Schlater, William B. Allen, E. H. Middleton, Samuel Christian. The executive officers are obliging and efficient in all their dealings, and add materially by their own individuality to the popularity of the company, while the Board of Directors comprise much of the solid business element of this community.

JOHN S. PALMER, Manufacturer of Paper Boxes, No. 35 Wister Street, Germantown.—Like all other branches of manufacture, notable progress has been made in the paper box industry of late years. What with invention, improvements and sustained effort, the productions of our leading manufactures in the line indicated are almost perfection. And in this connection special mention is due John S. Palmer, whose office and factory are at No. 35 Wister Street, who turns out a distinctly superior class of work. His facilities are at once ample and excellent, and his trade, which extends throughout this vicinity, very large. Mr. Palmer, who is also head of the firm of John S. Palmer & Son, Hosiery Mills, 68 Wister Street, is a man of middle age, active and energetic, and was born in Delaware County, Pa. He started in the paper box line about ten years ago, and from the first has been highly successful, his business rapidly growing. The premises occupied here comprise two spacious floors, equipped with full steam power, latest improved machinery, etc., and twenty to thirty to help are employed in the establishment. Mr. Palmer manufactures various styles and patterns in boxes of every size, shape, style and variety, keeping on hand always a large stock, and can turn out anything in this line to order, at shortest notice, while his prices are exceptionally low. The hosiery mills, which are situated at Nos. 68 to 72 Wister Street, were established some five years since by the present proprietors, and are a perfectly equipped plant where employment is given to from twenty to thirty hands. The firm of John S. Palmer & Son are manufacturers of hosiery of excellent quality, and their production is knit goods commands extensive sale throughout the country. Their capacity is 2,000 dozen per week, and their goods are in great demand by many of our leading houses. This branch of the business is under the immediate supervision of Mr. William Palmer, eldest son of John S. Palmer, who brings to bear an experience of over five years in this industry.

WALTER DOUGLASS, Patents and Patent Causes, No. 914 Walnut Street.—One of the well known solicitors and counsellors in patent matters and causes located in Philadelphia is Mr. J. Walter Douglass, who occupies commodious and well equipped offices at No. 914 Walnut Street, with offices also in New York and Washington. This gentleman has been engaged in the active practice of his profession since 1885. His legal education was received under the preceptorship of the late Henry Baldwin, Jr., who was widely known as an eminent solicitor and counsellor in patent matters and patent causes and with whom he spent ten years. His practice embraces attention to the preparation and prosecution of applications for letters patent in this country and all the foreign countries, the registration of trade marks and labels, the preparation of caveats and design patents, the reissuing of defective patents, the making of searches as to the patentability of unprotected inventions and as to the scope and validity of letters patent in litigated causes, the conducting of interferences, litigations and appeals before the Patent Office and courts, the negotiation of patented inventions, the formation of companies and syndicates to develop and introduce patents and inventions, and he is in touch with most of the large manufacturing and introduction companies and concerns in this country and the foreign countries. He has direct correspondence and business connections in all the foreign countries, and has a large international patent business. His fees are moderate and the inventions of persons in moderate circumstances are prosecuted upon weekly payments. His aim is to see that the interests of each patron are carefully guarded and intelligently promoted and protected. The crude ideas of the inventor are also developed in his offices and protected, as well as machinery in all its details planned out for buildings or manufacturing and introducing purposes. Mr. Douglass is a Philadelphian by birth, and a young man of standing in the profession and also in social circles.

ARTHUR E. PAIGE, Mechanical Expert, No. 711 Walnut Street. A well known mechanical engineer, draughtsman and all-round expert engaged in this city, fully meriting a prominent mention in this work, is Mr. Arthur E. Paige. Mr. Paige first embarked in the profession here in 1882, and started practising for his own account in 1885, since which time he has built up a large and influential connection among patent attorneys, inventors and others. Mr. Paige's operations are bounded only by the confines of the Union. His practical experience is of a wide and diversified nature, and his acknowledged talents embrace a full and concise knowledge of mechanical engineering and engine and machine construction, statics, dynamics, drawing and designing, and a fecundity of inventive genius. A few of the chief matters he undertakes are the preparation of detailed drawings for the Patent Office, machine building, ornamental designs, the rendering of valuable aid to inventors in perfecting uncompleted inventions, examining the practical working of mechanical patents, supervising the construction and erection of engines, machines and models, the reconstruction and development of mechanical devices and appliances, and a general line of consultation relative to engineering and machinery matters. Mr. Arthur E. Paige is a young gentleman of New Jersey birth, and came to Philadelphia in 1881.

SCOTT PAPER COMPANY (Limited), Paper, Nos. 25 and 27 North Sixth Street; Factory, Nos. 526 and 528 North Street.—For the past quarter century the house now controlled by the Scott Paper Company (Limited) has been a valued factor in the development of Philadelphia's commerce. The enterprise was founded in 1867 by E. Seymour Scott & Bros. It remained under that management up to 1879, when the present company was organized and incorporated under the State laws of Pennsylvania, with a capital of $24,000, and the following gentlemen as officers: Chairman, E. Irwin Scott; Secretary and Treasurer, C. W. Scott; while Mr. John P. Onderdonk, a capitalist of this city, is a stockholder in the concern. The Messrs. Scott reside at Swarthmore. The company has developed a large, first class, steadily growing trade, and now has patrons in all parts of the United States. Their salesroom is comprised in a store and basement, 24x90 feet in dimensions, and it is filled with a heavy stock of paper of all kinds. The company manufacture toilet paper, of which a leading specialty is made, and their mill, at Nos. 526 and 528 North Street, is a five story building, 30x90 feet in dimensions. The place is equipped with first class steam power machinery, and the wire loop toilet paper made here includes many brands. Forty hands are employed in the city, and on the road the house is represented by seven salesmen. Orders of any magnitude are filled and shipped to any point without delay.

HISTORICAL AND COMMERCIAL PHILADELPHIA.

EST PHILADELPHIA BANK, Isaac W. Hughes, President, Fleming Parke, Cashier, No. 3938 Market Street.—Philadelphia affords, as it has for a lengthy period, one of the most desirable and profitable fields for legitimate banking in the United States. The present prosperous era finds her leading financial institutions, better prepared than ever to meet all demands of trade, and to handle satisfactorily the vast business that is offered. Representative among her banking houses stands the West Philadelphia Bank, so indispensable to the citizens of that section of the city, and eligibly located at No. 3938 Market Street. It was originally organized in 1857, as the West Philadelphia Savings Fund, and was reorganized under its present name in 1869. It has a paid up capital of $100,000, and its officered as follows, viz: President, Isaac W. Hughes; vice-president, Samuel Lloyd; cashier, Fleming Parke; directors, Isaac W. Hughes, Samuel Lloyd, B. Frank Pierson, J. H. Dungan, E. M. Willard. The present building was erected by the bank in 1874, and is constructed of stone, thoroughly fireproof, and finely finished in its interior with hard woods and elegantly appointed. The bank transacts a general business in deposits, loans, collections and exchange, and has the accounts of leading merchants and manufacturers in this vicinity, as well as banks, bankers, corporations and individuals out of town. From its inception it has enjoyed the confidence of the public in the highest degree. Its founders were men who had the care foresight to recognize the possibilities of such an institution, and who laid the foundation sufficiently strong and deep to bear any superstructure that time, experience and wealth might rear. They builded well, and their successors have been eminently worthy of the succession. Under its present wise and conservative management, this bank is doing a large and safe business, all its movements being marked by prudence, caution and honorable business methods, and it is generally recognized as one of those solid, ably conducted institutions that reflect credit alike upon their officers and the community where their influence is felt. Although founded upon a rock it has each twelve months been raised above the level of the year before, and has now accumulated a surplus fund of $41,728.59, with undivided profits of $6,177.79; while its individual deposits average nearly half a million, and its resources aggregate about $600,000. Its loans and discounts represent safe and legitimate transactions in the best lines of commercial paper and loans on choice collateral and its capital stock is held at a high premium as a most desirable and remunerative investment. It issues drafts, makes telegraphic transfers of money and collects on all points. This bank has a safe deposit, department where safe deposit boxes in its impregnable vaults can be rented at from $5 to $15 per annum. The boxes now number 300, and afford a great convenience to capitalists and business men. The executive officers of this bank are gentlemen with whom it is always a pleasure to do business. President Hughes is a well-known practicing physician and has filled this position since 1869, with honor and credit. The cashier, Mr. Parke, has held that responsible post since 1878, and is a financier of large experience, wide acquaintance and high repute. This bank was originally started with others by the late Thos. A. Scott, ex-president of the Pennsylvania Railroad. Ex-Chief Justice Ellis Lewis of the Supreme Court of Pennsylvania was also a director for several years.

RADWAY & JOCHER, Insurance Agents and Brokers, Office, No. 136 South Fourth Street. Messrs. Bradway & Jocher have long been connected with the insurance business and are exceptionally well versed in the strong and weak points of the insurance management and policy, and the firm do a large business, both as agents and brokers. They are sole agents in this city for the National Fire Insurance Company, of Hartford, Conn., and the Guardian Assurance Company, of London, Eng., and in addition do a general brokerage business. The Guardian is noted as having the largest paid-up capital of any company, doing a fire business in this country. Absolute protection is, therefore, guaranteed to its policy holders, while its record for prompt and equitable settlement of honest claims is unsurpassed. The National has a cash capital of $1,000,000, a net surplus of $578,674.37, and total assets on January 1, 1892, amounting to $2,901,736.80. It is thus seen that this firm represents some sound concerns and represents them worthily. They control the insuring of large lines of the choicest business and residential property in this city and vicinity, and are eminently and deservedly popular with all classes of property owners on account of their promptness, courtesy and thorough reliability. The members of this firm are Messrs. William L. Bradway and John C. Jocher, Jr. Mr. Bradway is a native Philadelphian and an underwriter of thirteen years' experience, while Mr. Jocher has had an experience of nineteen years in the insurance business and for seven years was local agent for the Girard Insurance Company, of Philadelphia. Both are members of the Fire Underwriters' Association, of Philadelphia, and authorities in their calling.

YE & TREDICK, Manufacturers of Plain and Automatic Circular Rib Knitting Machinery, No. 628 Arch Street. This firm established their business here in 1885, and have steadily extended its scope, and developed a trade connection of the most desirable and widespread character. Their patent automatic circular rib knitting machines, two feeds, are adapted for knitting all kinds of plain and ribbed hosiery, leggings, gaiters, etc., in ladies', misses' and children's sizes, of any gauge and number of needles desired. These machines are made in the most thorough manner, both as to workmanship and material used. All parts are interchangeable and perfect, and perform their work automatically in every respect, making an unlimited number of desirable designs in solid colors as well as in two colors, in blocks, checks and stripes. They are complete with automatic stop-off, and needle protector and all the latest improvements, producing from six to eight dozen pairs of hose legs per day of ten hours. Their patent automatic welt top cuff and shirt border machines are adapted for making ribbed tops for half-hose, cuffs for shirts and drawers, and bottoms for plain undershirts; making the slack course for transferring, and a course near the welt to cut off by; also for producing plain ribbed legs for ladies', misses' and children's sizes in seamless hosiery, also makes a valuable style in legging. This machine is also made in the best manner and guaranteed, and all parts are interchangeable. A one-feed welt top machine produces from twenty-five to thirty dozen tops per day. Particular attention should also be called to their large automatic four and eight feed fancy rib knitting machines, adapted for the production of ladies', misses', children's and infants' plain and fancy ribbed underwear, skirts, jackets, jerseys, caps, etc., in various desirable designs; also men's ribbed underwear. They are equally adapted for knitting cotton, woolen, worsted, Lisle thread or silk. These machines are made in the best and most careful manner, and guaranteed; and are arranged so that broken needles, butts, shanks, etc., can be taken out readily without difficulty. All parts are interchangeable and perfect, having all the latest improvements in this class of machinery, including slack course and stop-off needle protector, improved roller dogs, which make only a slight tension necessary for drawing down the work, automatic oilers, etc. Their automatic circular sleevers, two feeds, to go with above-mentioned machines, are complete for making sleeves for cardigan jackets, ladies', misses', children's and infants' ribbed underwear, jerseys, jackets, etc., also men's underwear and jacket sleeves, including cuffs finished with a full close welt, equal to any single feed welt made. They also make a line of plain ribbed knitting machinery, four, eight and twelve feeds, built in the same manner and up to the standard of their automatic fancy machines, being uniform with them in every respect, excepting that they do not have the automatic fashioning attachment. This firm are also agents for the Keystone seamless knitter for knitting plain hosiery and footing ribbed hosiery; and also sells the best makes of loopers, winders, steam presses, trimmer sewing machines, button-hole machines, hosiery and shirt boards, etc., at manufacturers' prices. The business of the firm is immense and influential throughout the United States, Canada, Mexico, Europe, Australia and South America and their field may be said to be the world. Their main office and salesrooms, at No. 628 Arch Street, are stocked to repletion at all times with new and improved machines, while their factory at Wilmington, Del., gives steady employment to seventy-five skilled hands. The copartners, Messrs. Geo. E. Nye and Edward Tredick, are natives of New Hampshire, endowed with the inventive genius of the typical Yankee, and honored and esteemed both at home and abroad.

HISTORICAL AND COMMERCIAL PHILADELPHIA.

ILLIAM J. BENNERS & SONS, Wholesale Dealers and Shippers of Hard Wood Lumber, Walnut, Ash, Oak, Cherry, Hickory, Poplar, Etc., Thirtieth Street, Below Walnut.—A foremost exponent of the hard wood lumber trade in this city is the house of William J. Benners & Sons, whose yard is located at Thirtieth Street, below Walnut. The trade of this establishment extends all throughout Pennsylvania, New Jersey, New York and Delaware, and the yearly sales amount to from 7,000,000 to 8,000,000 feet of lumber. The business was founded twenty-six years ago by Mr. William J. Benners, and fifteen years ago he admitted to partnership his sons, Messrs. H. H. and A. E. Benners, the present firm-name being adopted. All three are natives of Philadelphia and are popularly known in financial and business circles. Extensive premises are occupied at the address named, and a very large stock is at all times carried. The Messrs. Benners are wholesale and retail dealers in hard wood lumber, and keep on hand the best grades of walnut, ash, plain oak, quartered oak, cherry, chestnut, poplar, maple, plain sycamore, quartered sycamore, hickory, butternut, hazel, black birch, etc., making a leading specialty of same for interior finishing uses. They receive the entire products of a number of Western and Southern mills and their connections and facilities are of so excellent a character that all orders are promptly filled at the lowest market quotations.

ATIONAL METAL EDGE BOX COMPANY, Patented Paper Box Machinery, Metal Edge Boxes and Novelties; Paper Mills, Readsboro, Vermont; Nos. 621 and 623 Cherry Street.—During the past few years many noteworthy manufacturing enterprises, have had their inception in Philadelphia. Among these there is, perhaps, not any more worthy of special mention in this review than that of the National Metal Edge Box Co., located at Nos. 621 and 623 Cherry Street, which is the only concern in its line in the city and it is one of the largest and best-equipped establishments of the kind in the United States. The company are manufacturers of patented paper box machinery, metal edge boxes and novelties, and their productions command an immense sale. They have paper and pulp mills at Readsboro, Vermont, which are the largest of the kind in the United States, and possess exceptional facilities in the way of water-power and natural supplies for manufacturing purposes. They turn out fifteen tons of finished stock daily; this stock is supplied to the lessees of their machinery throughout the country. They manufacture everything that can be made from paper pulp board, including plaques, photograph holders, cigar cases, matched boxes, collar boxes, glove cases, picture frames, fans, baskets, office file boxes, advertising specialties and artistic novelties in great variety, all in unique and pretty designs, and these are in widespread and rapidly increasing demand. The patent paper box machinery manufactured by them is conceded to have no equal, being by universal assent the most ingenious, perfect and effective for the purposes intended ever invented, too. Their metal edge boxes, which are the leading specialty, are articles of exceptional excellence. They are neat in design, strong, durable and handy, and every one is warranted as to make and material. The National Metal Edge Box Company, of which Moses Newton, (Holyoke, Mass.), is president, and Benj. Wolf, (Philadelphia,) treasurer, was organized about three years ago; it was incorporated under the laws of the State of New Jersey with a capital stock of $500,000. From the start the enterprise has been a signal success, the business growing and extending, until it has become exceedingly large. The factory occupies the whole of a six-story structure, 60 x 150 feet, and is equipped with full steam-power and the latest improved machinery, appliances and appurtenances, while upward of one hundred hands are here employed.

OHN G. FORD, Real Estate, Mortgage and Fire Insurance Broker and Notary Public, No. 713 Walnut Street.—Prominent among those gentlemen well-known in the real estate world should be named Mr. John G. Ford, the real estate, mortgage and fire insurance broker, and notary public, whose office is eligibly located at No. 713 Walnut Street. He established his business here in 1889, and as a result of his large acquaintance, sound judgment and wide range of experience, he is enabled to execute with consummate skill the purchase, sale and transfer of real estate of all kinds, and conducts other commissions, intrusted to his care in connection with the negotiation of loans upon bond or mortgage, to the complete satisfaction of clients, alike in the matter of charges, terms and conditions. The business of this house, although local in its character, is of the most important nature, and embraces a general line of real estate transactions, for property owners, large operators and investors of the most representative types. In addition to a general line of city and suburban property, Mr. Ford also handles Southern and Southwestern lands, including large tracts in Virginia, West Virginia and Florida, and offers rare bargains in manufacturing sites, orange groves and farm property. He is likewise prominent as agent in Eastern Pennsylvania for the Guaranty Savings and Loan Association, of Minneapolis, Minn., which is one of the oldest and wealthiest national organizations of the kind, with an authorized capital of $40,000,000. Its plan as now perfected stands preëminently at the head as regards safety, equity and profit. Mr. Ford is also special agent for the American Fire Insurance Company, of Philadelphia, and is prepared, both as agent and broker, to promptly place the largest risks, distributing the same among staunch and reliable companies, quoting the lowest rates of premium, and guaranteeing a speedy and liberal adjustment of all losses. Mr. Ford is a native of Maryland, who came to this city forty years ago, and for thirty-five years was connected with the Philadelphia Inquirer as cashier and business manager. He has a wide acquaintance with men and things in Philadelphia, and is a gentleman of reliability and integrity, with whom it is always a pleasure to do business.

. J. MURRAY, M. D., Druggist, No. 3286 Ridge Avenue and Thirty-fifth Street and Sunnyside Avenue, Falls of Schuylkill.—The neatest and best-appointed drugstores in the Falls district are those of B. J. Murray, No. 3286 Ridge Avenue and Thirty-fifth Street and Sunnyside Avenue. They are in all respects first-class pharmacies, where physicians' prescriptions and family recipes are compounded in the most careful and accurate manner, from strictly pure and fresh ingredients, and at extremely moderate prices. Dr. Murray, the proprietor, is a gentleman of courteous manners, in the prime of life, and was born in this city in 1859. He is a graduate of the Philadelphia College of Pharmacy, class of '80, also a graduate of the Medico-Chirurgical College, as a physician and surgeon. He is a member of several societies, both professional and social, and is a young man of energy and enterprise, as well as of skill and reliability. Dr. Murray has been established for the past twelve years, as a pharmacist and druggist, and was formerly located at No. 3356 Ridge Avenue, whence he moved to the present location in 1891, opening a branch store at Thirty-fifth Street and Queen Lane the same year, which was removed to his large and handsome store under America Hall, Thirty-fifth Street and Sunnyside Avenue. Both places are finely fitted up and well equipped, and a large, complete stock is always kept on hand at each, including carefully selected drugs, chemicals, tinctures, extracts, etc., of every description, all the standard patent medicines, proprietary remedies, herbs, barks, roots, seeds, etc., also a full line of toilet articles, perfumery, soaps, sponges, chamois, and druggists' sundries generally. In connection with his drug department, he also carries a full line of paints, oils, glass, varnishes, and all kinds of brushes. He also manufactures a full line of proprietary articles, which has quite an extensive sale, among which are Murray's Liver and Dyspeptic Pills, Compound Sarsaparilla Mixture for the Blood and Nerves, Worm Mixture, Cough Mixture, Electric Liniment, Antiseptic Tooth Wash. Several competent assistants are in attendance at these two popular and excellent pharmacies, and night-bell calls receive prompt response, prescriptions being a specialty.

DONALDSON IRON COMPANY, Manufacturers of Cast Iron Pipe and Special Castings for Water and Gas, also Flange Pipe, Emaus Pipe Foundry, Emaus, Lehigh County, Pa.; John Donaldson, President; No. 136 South Fourth Street. The great representative concern in the United States in the manufacture of cast iron pipe for water and gas is the Donaldson Iron Company, proprietors of the Emaus Pipe Foundry at Emaus, Lehigh County, Pa., with offices at No. 136 South Fourth Street, in this city. This company has a reputation and a trade co-extensive with the limits of the country, and has been in successful operation since 1880. The capacity of the works, the industrial forces employed and the ample capital invested, all characterize this foundry as the leader in its line in America, and one whose superior products are in universal demand by the trade and consumers. The company make two, three, four, six, eight, ten, twelve, fourteen and sixteen inch pipe, both material and workmanship being subjected to closest inspection and guaranteed; and municipal corporations, gas and water companies the country over largely use these pipes in preference to all other brands. Here is headquarters for extra and double extra strong cast iron pipe in constant use by contractors and oil producers, and special castings of any size for gas and water piping. The facilities of the works are thoroughly perfect, enabling the production of three-fourths of a mile of pipe per day, and the largest orders are filled immediately on terms and prices which are not to be duplicated elsewhere. The company are now engaged on a contract for supplying sixty-five miles of pipe to the city of Philadelphia, and the patronage they enjoy is of a character that speaks volumes for the reliability and superiority of their product. The Donaldson Iron Company was organized in 1880, under the laws of the State of Pennsylvania, and is now governed by the following board of directors, viz: John Donaldson, president; George Ormrod, treasurer and general manager; H. F. Donaldson, secretary; and M. Shimer, Thomas Whitaker, H. A. Stiles, who is vice-president of the Penn. Gas Coal Company, and Harry Peacock. President Donaldson is a well-known Philadelphian, long and prominently identified with the iron and coal trade; while the general manager, Mr. Ormrod, resides at Allentown and is an expert in this branch of skilled industry. The management of this company has served to make its position one of national prominence and places its founders and promoters in the front rank of Pennsylvania's industrial representatives.

DELAWARE RIVER, BELOW SOUTH STREET.

HARLES M. BURNS, Architect, No. 717 Walnut Street. For some of its finest structures erected within the past quarter century, Philadelphia is indebted to the skill and good taste of Mr. Charles Marquedent Burns, architect, whose offices are at No. 717 Walnut Street. This gentleman was born in the Quaker City and his choice of vocation in life was that of the architect. In this line he studied under able mentorship, and having gained a thorough knowledge of the profession established business twenty-five years ago. Natural ability, combined with the valuable experience gained in the pursuit of his calling, enabled Mr. Burns to achieve a marked success, and to win a large, influential patronage, while he has won fame for the originality of his designs, their architectural beauty, and the perfection noticeable in every detail. Among the most important of Mr. Burns' architectural creations were the group of conventual buildings erected by Miss Drexel at Andalusia, Pa.; the Church of the Advocate, Philadelphia; Church of St. Peter, Uniontown, Pa.; Church of St. Stephen, Wilkesbarre, Pa.; Church of the Redeemer, at Bryn Mawr; the Church of the Saviour, West Philadelphia; the Astor Memorial Cathedral of St. Augusta, Sioux Falls, Dakota, etc., etc. These edifices are distinctive ornaments of the sections in which they are erected. Mr. Burns is at all times prepared to furnish estimates, plans and specifications for work of all kinds in the constructive line, and all his designs are made with a view to the conservation of space and to furnish the maximum of accommodation, solidity, and effect. He is an active member of the business world and enjoys the esteem of the entire social and business community.

HISTORICAL AND COMMERCIAL PHILADELPHIA.

ROBERT WILDE'S SONS, Carpet Yarn Manufacturers, Leverington Avenue and Hamilton Street.—One of the foremost representative houses of those engaged in the production of carpet yarns in this city is that of Robert Wilde's Sons, whose mills and grounds, covering an area of two and a half acres, are located at the junction of Leverington Avenue and Hamilton Street. This property is owned by the firm. The business of the establishment was inaugurated twenty-two years ago by Mr. Robert Wilde, a business man of enterprise and sound ability, and he justly met with the most substantial success. In 1884 he was succeeded by his sons, Messrs. Isaac and Thomas B. Wilde, who adopted the present firm style of Robert Wilde's Sons, thus perpetuating the name of their honored father. Mr. Isaac Wilde was born in Covington, Ky., his brother in England, and they have resided in Philadelphia the past thirty-eight years. They were raised to a practical knowledge of their business under the mentorship of their father, and being apt pupils mastered all its details. The mills are comprised in a stone building, 60x140 feet in dimensions, and the mechanical outfit is first class in every particular. It includes 1,200 spindles, and all requisite machinery, and it is driven by a 100 horse power engine. The Messrs. Wilde employ fifty experienced operatives, and manufacture carpet yarns of all grades, turning out 25,000 pounds per week. They have permanent customers in the leading carpet manufacturers of the city, and supply an active, steady demand.

LENMORE WORSTED COMPANY (Limited), Germantown Avenue and Tenth Street.—This company was organized in 1884, and is under the management of Lewis A. Rommel, Secretary and Treasurer; Samuel A. Wood, Superintendent. The main mill is three stories high and 80x200 feet in dimensions, with a two story annex, 40x120 feet, splendidly fitted up with the latest improved machinery and appliances for the Bradford system of spinning, including 5,000 spindles, and steady employment is given to 300 skilled operatives. The concern is a model in its line, thoroughly organized, ably managed, and producing goods which are leaders with the best class of trade. These yarns are used mostly for fine worsted coatings, suitings, ladies' dress goods, as well as for fine knitting purposes. They are manufactured to order for fabric mills, and are recognized everywhere as standard productions, having no superior in the market as regards quality, finish, uniformity and general excellence. The average output is 1,500 lbs. per day, and shipments are regularly made to all parts of the United States. Mr. Rommel, the Secretary and Treasurer, was formerly a member of the firm of Croft, Midgeley & Rommel, of Camden, N. J., previous to the organization of this company, and is a native Philadelphian, of excellent standing in business circles. Superintendent Wood has had an experience of forty years in this line of manufacture, and is promoting the interests of this company with distinguished ability and decided success.

MOSHANNON COAL COMPANY, Room No. 407, Drexel Building.—The Moshannon Coal Company was incorporated in 1864, under the laws of the State of Pennsylvania, with a capital of $100,000, and is officered as follows, viz.: Daniel Brittain, President; Frank Mitchell, Secretary and Treasurer. The company own and control nearly one thousand acres of coal land in Clearfield County, Pa., and produce the finest grades of soft coal in the State. This land and the mines thereon the company lease to coal operators on shares, and the product is warranted to maintain the highest standard of excellence, being mined by expert superintendents who are noted in the coal regions for the care taken in getting rid of all impurities, thereby making the product as near perfect as coal can be produced. It ignites readily and has good lasting qualities. A specialty is made of supplying gas works, dealers and large buyers in cargo lots, and the company are in a position to promptly fill the largest orders and to guarantee satisfaction in every particular. The prices quoted are always regulated by the market. President Brittain is a native of Bloomsburg, N. J., a resident of this city for the past forty years, and prominently identified with the coal trade since 1849. Mr. Mitchell, the Secretary and Treasurer, has been connected with the coal trade for a period of thirty-nine years and with this company since 1880.

JOHN W. CALVER & CO., Manufacturers of Bonnet and Hat Frames, Nos. 727 and 729 Arch Street.—The establishment of John W. Calver & Co., manufacturers of bonnet and hat frames, at Nos. 727 and 729 Arch Street, occupies a foremost position in its industry. This is a house of standard reputation, the quality of the goods manufactured, their excelling merit, and the high and honorable record of the concern being beyond reproach. The business was originally founded in 1840 by W. G. Calver, and twenty-six years later, in 1866, he was succeeded by his son, John W. Calver, who has since remained sole proprietor, continuing business under the firm name of John W. Calver & Co. He is a native of Philadelphia, a member of the Board of Trade, and for standing in the mercantile world is of the most creditable character. The spacious store occupied has an area of 25x150 feet, and is admirably equipped, while employment is found the year round for sixty skilled hands. Bonnet and hat frames are turned out in vast quantities in an endless variety of styles, and the active demand enjoyed comes from all parts of the United States. In addition to the above business, Mr. Calver, in company with his son, Mr. C. P. Calver, also carries on business in the production of society goods. The firm name is John W. Calver & Son. This enterprise was inaugurated in 1889.

ENTERPRISE DYEING AND FINISHING WORKS, Joseph Hanson, Agent, Mascher and Somerset Streets.—A branch of enterprise contingent upon the great yarn manufacturing industry of Philadelphia is that of dyeing and finishing. One of the most successful concerns of the kind is that of the Enterprise Dyeing and Finishing Works. The business is conducted under the management of Mr. Joseph Hanson, who is agent for the owner. Mr. Hanson is a native of this city, is thoroughly skilled in the dyeing industry, and he started in business about twenty years ago, beginning upon a small scale. Meeting with success, he built works at his present address, and they were further enlarged in 1881. Two years ago the establishment became the property of his mother, Mrs. E. Hanson, for whom he has since acted as agent. The premises occupied are comprised in a lot, 96x200 feet in area, upon which are a large three story building, a two story building, and a one story building. The place is equipped with the best machinery adapted to the industry. It is driven by steam power, and employment is found for twenty experienced hands. Mr. Hanson dyes and finishes yarns of all kinds, making a leading specialty of hosiery yarns, and the works can dye and finish 7,000 pounds daily. Many leading Philadelphia yarn manufacturers are among Mr. Hanson's permanent customers.

M. HARLEY & CO., Oils, Nos. 52 and 54 North Water Street.—This thriving business was established in 1886 by Messrs. J. M. Harley and E. T. Foster. The latter gentleman retired in May, 1892. Mr. Harley also deals in canned and bottled goods, grocers' sundries, etc., which he added in 1889. He is a native of Montgomery County, and has had an experience of forty years in the general merchandizing business, having kept stores in this line in Lexington, Pa., for ten years, in North Wales for eleven years, and three years in Skippack Tp., Pa. He is the sole proprietor of the justly celebrated "Star" cylinder, engine, spindle, wool and harness oils, put up in quarts and pint cans, and sold by the dozen. These oils are warranted pure, containing no acid or alkali to corrode, or grit to wear out the material. All his lubricant oils are in steady consumption in many leading mills and factories in different parts of the country. He also does a large wholesale trade in superior compounds and greases, and various supplies for mines and rolling mills. Here too can be found the finest grades of lamp oils, high test burning oils, naphtha, gasoline, benzine and everything in the line of lamp goods; also full lines of salt, cider and vinegar. Mr. Harley's trade is widely extended and still growing.

154 HISTORICAL AND COMMERCIAL PHILADELPHIA.

THOMAS DEPUY, Carpetings, Matting, Oil Cloth, Etc., No. 35 North Second Street.— An old established and leading house in its line in this city is that so successfully conducted by Mr. Thomas Depuy, located at No. 35 North Second Street. The business was established in 1845 by Stephen C. Fonlke, who was succeeded by Allen Scott & Co. The present proprietor has been engaged in this business for twenty-two years, and now commands the favor and patronage of all who value reliable service and the widest range of first class goods from which to make selections. The name of Depuy is one well known in Philadelphia as the oldest in the carpet trade of the city, Mr. Thomas Depuy being the son of Mr. J. Stewart Depuy. The premises occupied comprise a store and basement, 30x185 feet in dimensions, the two upper floors being 30x50 feet. A large stock of carpetings, including Brussels, Axminster, tapestry, moquettes and ingrain, is constantly carried, also a fine assortment of mattings, oil cloths, etc. Imported as well as domestic goods are freely carried, and Mr. Depuy has all his arrangements perfected for securing the freshest and choicest novelties as soon as they are ready for the trade. He is in constant receipt of consignments from the great manufacturing centres of the country, and the relations he sustains with importers and producers are of the most favorable kind, and he is prepared to give his customers advantages in goods and prices rarely offered elsewhere. Four clerks are employed. Mr. Depuy is a gentleman in the active prime of life, and held in the highest esteem in this community for his integrity and personal worth. He is a member of the Columbia Club and the Philadelphia Bourse, and for the past 25 years has been an active member of the F. and A. M., and the success he has achieved is well merited. In 1891 he purchased the building he now occupies, and no facility is lacking whereby the convenience of patrons and the interests of the house may be enhanced.

WM. SOWDEN, Meat Market, No. 3143 North Thirty-fifth Street.— A first class and admirably conducted meat and provision market in Falls of Schuylkill is that of which Mr. Wm. Sowden is the proprietor, located at No. 3143 North Thirty-fifth Street. Mr. Sowden, who is an Englishman by birth, came here to reside in 1887, and four years later embarked in his present enterprise, which has since fairly bounded into popular favor and patronage, and filled a long needed want in this community. The store, 20x40 feet in dimensions, is nicely fitted up, in the most modern approved style, with all the necessary facilities and conveniences for the handling of the stock and systematic conduct of affairs, and three competent and efficient assistants and a team are engaged in constant service. Here is at all times found everything in the line of prime beef, veal, mutton, lamb, pork, salted, smoked and cured meats of all kinds, etc., together with poultry and game and the different variety of fresh fruits and vegetables, all in their respective seasons. For quality and freshness these products are unsurpassed in the market, and the prices which rule are so low as to defy successful competition. All orders are promptly filled, and delivered free of charge, and a large and highly desirable family custom is constantly entered to, while the business continues to show a steady and firm growth. Mr. Sowden is a young man of pronounced ability, who fully understands the requirements of the trade, and his future success is assured.

G. WENDEROTH, Boot, Shoe and Trunk House, No. 4570 Germantown Avenue.— A leading, well patronized and representative city house in the boot, shoe and trunk trade is that of Mr. J. G. Wenderoth, located in this section, at No. 4570 Germantown Avenue. In 1886 this flourishing business was originally established by the present proprietor, and has since been conducted by him with great success and prosperity. The premises occupied comprise a large and commodious store, 20x50 feet in dimensions, handsomely and conveniently appointed throughout with special reference to the business; and in the attractive plate glass show windows and upon the shelves a fine display is made of everything in the line of footwear. In the general complete assortment carried will be found boots, shoes, slippers and rubbers in all sizes, widths, styles and grades, for men, women and children, all of the best makes, and guaranteed to give entire satisfaction in durability, quality, perfect fit and price. A specialty is also made of trunks, grips, travelling bags, etc., and in each department of the store the goods have been most carefully selected from the best manufacturers in the country. Particular attention is here given to fine custom made boots and shoes, all orders for which are promptly and reliably executed, and the workmanship of these is unsurpassed in the trade. From two to three competent salesmen are in constant attendance, and prompt and courteous treatment is accorded to all patrons. Mr. Wenderoth, who is a native of this city, is a thoroughly experienced, able and progressive business man, and the recipient of a large, highly desirable and permanent patronage. He is a member of the Red Men and Knights of Malta.

J. ROBBINS, Practical Paper Hanger, Main Street, Chestnut Hill.— In this age of the increase of material wealth and the progress indicative of the present century, the demands of all classes are more exacting than ever before. This fact is self evident in every branch of trade, and more particularly so in the art of interior decoration and adornment of our houses. A representative and thoroughly reliable house devoted to this special line of work is that of Mr. H. J. Robbins, on Main Street, which is the only business of this character conducted in Chestnut Hill. The enterprise was established in 1878 by the present proprietor, Mr. Robbins. The store is of ample dimensions, compactly arranged and admirably fitted for the advantageous display of a full line of rich and pleasing effects in drawing room, library, parlor paperings, etc., window shades of every description and a full line of Lincrusta Walton and felts. Besides making a specialty of wall papering and interior decorating in all its branches, frescoing in copied or original designs is undertaken at reasonable prices, when the high character of the work is taken into consideration. Mr. Robbins employs four skilled assistants, is a young man, and a prominent member of the Knights of the Golden Eagle.

F. STUCKERT, Architect, No. 524 Walnut Street.— Mr. Stuckert is a native and life long resident of Philadelphia. He studied his profession partly at the Franklin Institute of this city, and since he began business has received a most substantial and flattering patronage. Among the churches that have been erected from his designs are the following: Princeton Presbyterian, corner Powelton Street and Saunders' Avenue; Fourth Baptist, corner Fifth and Buttonwood Streets; Baptist Chapel, corner Buttonwood and Chatham Streets; Third Baptist, corner Wakefield and Wistar Streets; First Congregational, corner Seymour and Lynch Streets; Hebrew Temple, " Adath Jeshurun," corner Seventh Street and Columbia Avenue; St. Luke's Lutheran, corner Seventh Street and Montgomery Avenue; Reformed Presbyterian, corner Seventeenth and Bainbridge Streets; Church of the Transfiguration, Woodland Avenue, near Walnut Street; Clinton Avenue Baptist, Trenton, N. J.; Pennington Presbyterian, Pennington, N. J.; Flemington Presbyterian, Flemington, N. J.; St. Michael's Lutheran, Germantown; St. Paul's German Reformed, Wharton and Ward Streets; Methodist, corner Wharton and Eighteenth Streets; Snyder Avenue Baptist, corner Seventh Street and Snyder Avenue, etc. Among the factories built from Mr. Stuckert's plans were the following, owned by prominent business men of the city: Factory, southwest corner Third and Cumberland Streets; weave shed and factory, southeast corner Huntingdon and Jasper Streets; " Star and Crescent Mills," northwest corner Lehigh Avenue and Front Street; " Rainbow Dye Works," northwest corner Lehigh Avenue and Howard Street; factories, northeast corner Sixth and Master Streets; southwest corner Seventeenth and Dickinson Streets; Wayne and Bristol Streets; factory and store, southwest corner Sixth Street and Girard Avenue; Tannery and store, Third Street north of Willow; tannery, northwest corner Front Street and Fairmount Avenue; two factories on Sixth Street near York; factories, Frankford Avenue near Wellington Street; northwest corner Huntingdon and Hancock Streets; Naunam Street west of Twentieth; Ice works, Fifth Street near Berks; factory with fire proof floors, Fourth Street near Montgomery Avenue.

HISTORICAL AND COMMERCIAL PHILADELPHIA.

HE AMERICAN TRUST, LOAN AND GUARANTEED INVESTMENT COMPANY, Broad Street and Ridge Avenue.—One of the most important and beneficial financial institutions of Philadelphia is that of the American Trust, Loan and Guaranteed Investment Company, which was incorporated in 1886, under the laws of the State of Pennsylvania, with a capital of $250,000, and is officered as follows, viz: President, A. H. Fracker; secretary and treasurer, Chas. F. Kolb. Directors: V. W. Walter, John S. Newman, J. J. Barker, A. Lichten, Andrew Kaap, Simon L. Bloch, E. D. Banzher, B. F. Greenewald, A. H. Fracker, R. Brunswick, J. H. W. Chestnut, M. D., Thomas C. Else, George W. Nock, I. L. Shoemaker, Joseph K. Gamble; solicitor, Geo. S. Graham. In 1890 the company took possession of their elegant new stone building, which is unexcelled for safety, elegance and general utility. Every possible safeguard is thrown around the spacious vaults, three in number, constructed on the most approved principles, absolutely fire and burglar-proof, guarded by night and day, while the doors are fastened with Yale time locks. There is a capacity for 1500 safe deposit boxes, and these are rented at reasonable rates, while the steady growth in the number of renters shows how widely these vaults are appreciated. The company receives and guarantees the safe-keeping of securities and valuables at a nominal sum per annum. A general banking business is also transacted, interest being allowed on deposits, loans are made on approved collateral, and collections are promptly made all over the country. The company acts as agent for the registration or transfer of stocks and bonds of corporations and in the payment of coupons, or interest on registered securities, and issues bonds of suretyship. A most popular and much availed of feature of the company's business is acting as attorney for the treasurers or trustees of churches, schools, colleges, charitable societies, etc., keeping their books, supervising their investments, collecting income and rendering accounts when required. As interest is paid on all balances lying idle, it is of manifest advantage to secure the services of such a responsible fiduciary agent. Its trust department, under the provisions of its perpetual charter, executes trusts of every description. Added to these features is its guaranteed investment department. On September 8th, 1892, its total assets amounted to $150,761.99. The executive officers of the company are all well-known Philadelphians who bring to bear every qualification, and are in every way representative of a sound policy and integrity of management.

. E. ARCHAMBAULT & SON, Fine Carpetings. Northeast Corner Eleventh and Market Streets.—One of the oldest retail houses in Philadelphia, and the largest in its line is the well-known house of V. E. Archambault & Son. Established in 1842, by Mr. V. E. Archambault, the high reputation and immense trade of this house have been earned by half a century of reliable dealing. The massive building which forms the headquarters for its trade stands a magnificent monument to fifty years of progressive business methods. These premises comprise seven entire floors, each with an area of 2,000 square feet. These acres of floor space are piled high with every conceivable kind of floor covering. Here are miles upon miles of carpetings—Brussels, ingrain, velvets, in fact every style and texture that is manufactured. Here are the best products of domestic carpet manufacture and the richest importations from foreign lands, which represent in their rich colorings the results of generations of the most patient and expert carpet weaving. There are rich and beautiful rugs from the Orient; there are floor coverings of every sort to suit every taste and need. There are goods for those of moderate means who want the most durable article at a moderate cost, and there are goods for those of ample means and luxurious taste. Being large buyers and direct importers, the house has the very best facilities for handling the very best goods at the very lowest prices. The house has always catered to the city trade, and its enormous business gives employment to forty-five hands the year round. The firm consists of Mr. V. E. Archambault, the honored founder of the house, whose half century of active business life makes him one of the veteran merchants of Philadelphia, and his son, Mr. Victor E. Archambault, Jr., who was taken into partnership by his father in 1882. Both are natives and residents of Philadelphia.

. N. FRANK & CO., Standard Cloak Company, No. 830 Arch Street.—Though but a comparatively young firm, H. N. Frank & Co., the "Standard Cloak Company," No. 830 Arch Street, have already attained a position in the forefront rank in their line. They are manufacturers and importers of ladies', misses' and children's cloaks, and they turn out a distinctly superior class of goods, while their productions command an extensive sale throughout the United States. The garments made by this widely-known firm are noted for beauty of design, style, finish and fabric, and are maintained at a uniformly high standard of excellence. The cloaks leaving their establishment are not, in fact, surpassed in a single feature of merit by anything of the kind on the market, and the demand therefor is rapidly growing all over the country. The house was established in 1891 by H. N. Frank, who is the sole proprietor (the "Co." being nominal). The premises occupied comprise four spacious floors, and are perfectly equipped in every department, the facilities being unexcelled. The salesroom, which is 25 x 180 feet in dimensions, is handsomely fitted up and tastefully arranged, the display being exceptionally attractive, and everything bespeaks order and excellent management. The firm are direct importers of fine cloakings, and every garment sold by them is of their own manufacture, all goods being warranted as to make and material. An immense stock is always kept on hand, upward of one hundred expert operatives and a number of skilled designers and cutters being regularly employed, in addition to an efficient staff of clerks and salesmen, and eight representatives on the road. The assortment embraces stylish and elegant cloaks in a great variety of pretty patterns and of latest designs in every size, shape and style. Mr. Frank is a native of this city, and is well endowed with the qualifications that lead to success.

OSEPH LOUCHHEIM & CO., Manufacturers of Clothing, New York Office, No. 704 Broadway, Nos. 314 and 316 Market Street. —A widely-known and noteworthy Philadelphia firm engaged in the wholesale clothing line is that of Joseph Louchheim & Co. They are manufacturers of men's and boys' wear of all kinds and in all grades, and their productions command extensive sale throughout the United States. They make a specialty of fine and medium grade suits, and their goods are maintained at a uniformly high standard of excellence, every garment leaving their establishment being warranted as to workmanship, trimming, finish and fabric. The house was established in 1865 by the present senior member of the firm, who conducted the business alone up to 1886, when he associated with him in partnership Louis L. Eliel, and on Jan. 1, 1892, he admitted his son, Mr. Harry F. Louchheim, to partnership. They occupy two five-story buildings, each 50 x 150 feet in dimensions, equipped with freight elevators and all conveniences, and upward of sixty in help, including cutters, etc., are employed on the premises, in addition to several hundred hands outside and thirteen representatives on the road. An immense stock is constantly kept on hand, and includes clothing for men, boys, and children, in every style, size, shape and variety, juvenile attire being a specialty. Mr. Louchheim is one of Philadelphia's solid citizens, prominent and esteemed in commercial and financial circles, and is a director of the Seventh National Bank, and is connected with many charitable organizations.

HISTORICAL AND COMMERCIAL PHILADELPHIA.

 S. FAUSSETT, Wholesale Dry Goods, No. 533 Arch Street.—A house whose enterprise, energy and marked ability has placed it in the front rank of the wholesale dry goods trade of Philadelphia is that of Mr. H. S. Faussett. This gentleman established business in this line at the present location in 1889, and has met with almost unparalleled success. He occupies a commodious office and salesroom of ample dimensions, and a large stock of dry goods, the products of the best manufacturers, is kept constantly on hand. The trade of the house is largely with the dealers of Philadelphia, but is being rapidly extended throughout the State and through the Southern States under the efficient efforts of a corps of competent travelling salesmen. The enterprise and energy of this house is proverbial, and its methods, resources and facilities insure to it a continuance of growth and a prosperous career. Mr. Faussett is a native Philadelphian, and a merchant of high standing.

 OTTO MARTIN & CO., Manufacturers of Lithographic Printing Inks, No. 130 North Fourth Street.—This is one of the oldest and foremost houses in the line indicated, and for upward of a quarter of a century has maintained an A1 reputation in the trade. The house was established in 1867, and for the past twenty years the business has been conducted at the present location. There has never been any change in the style or personnel of the firm. They are manufacturers of a superior class of lithographic printing inks, and are direct importers of lithographic stones and materials, also bronze powder, gold, silver and metal leaf. The goods made and handled by them are all of excellent quality and their trade, which is very large, extends throughout the whole of the United States. The business premises occupy an entire four story, 30x80 foot, building, with first class facilities, and an efficient staff is employed in the establishment, while two salesmen represent the house on the road. A very large and fine stock is constantly kept on hand, and comprises everything in the lines above indicated. The trade is supplied on the most favorable terms, bottom prices being quoted. Mr. Otto Martin, who is and has always been the sole member of the firm, was born in Germany, and has been in this country thirty years or more, coming to Philadelphia in 1867.

 KOENIG & CO., Manufacturers of Musical and Mathematical Instrument Cases; Office, No. 737 Walnut Street.—Though only a year or so established, J. Koenig & Co., manufacturers of musical and mathematical instrument cases, have built up an extensive business. The firm was formerly located at No. 711 Sansom Street, and removed to the present quarters in May last. They occupy a 30x80 foot (third) floor here, with complete facilities, and employ a dozen or more expert hands. They manufacture elegant cases for musical and mathematical instruments, etc., in plush, velvet and morocco; cases for jewelry and silverware in beautiful designs and exquisite finish, and sell to the trade. The productions are unsurpassed for fine workmanship or durability, and every article is warranted as to make and material. A large and splendid assortment is constantly kept in stock. Mr. Koenig, the head of the firm, is a gentleman in the prime of life, born in Germany, and has been in this city for a number of years. He is a man of thorough practical skill and twenty years' experience, active and energetic, and is a member of the Knights of the Golden Eagle, the Red Cross, and several German societies.

 WILLIAM DEVINE, Agent, Manufacturer of Window Shading and Wall Papers, Shades and Fixtures; Store and factory, No. 125 North Second Street.—This enterprise, which holds an important position in the mercantile community, was inaugurated by William Devine in 1862, and was very successfully conducted by him until July, 1891. After his death, which occurred at this time, the widow, who is the present proprietor, succeeded to the control. The management of the house has from the beginning been energetic and judicious, and the liberal policy pursued towards dealers and consumers has resulted in the accumulation of a widely extended and influential patronage. Here is manufactured not only window shades, but the cloth from which they are made, a specialty being the beautiful dado shades. A large stock of cord and tassels, roller ends, racks, brackets and wall papers is kept constantly on hand. The paper hangings are brought from the most noted manufactories of Europe and America, and the display is of the richest and most elegant character. Employment is furnished to twenty five skilled hands, and in the busy season forty five dozen shades per day are produced. The trade of the house is with the dealers and jobbers all over the United States, but is principally in the States of Pennsylvania, New Jersey and Delaware.

 SOUTHWARK PAINT WORKS, Joseph Lawless, Proprietor, Manufacturers and Dealers in Paints, Oils, Glass, Putty, Varnishes, Coach Painters' Materials, Sponges, Etc., No. 1119 Passyunk Avenue.—The Southwark Paint Works, Joseph Lawless, proprietor, No. 1119 Passyunk Avenue, were established about two years ago by the gentleman above named, and from the start the venture has been a very prosperous enterprise. Mr. Lawless manufactures a superior class of mixed paints, and deals in all kinds of painters' and varnishers' supplies. He does a large business, and his trade gives evidence of steady increase. The quarters occupied as factory and store are commodious and well equipped, the facilities for grinding, mixing, etc., being ample and excellent, and a number of hands are regularly employed here. A large and first class stock is always carried, and includes paints of every description, oils, glass, putty, varnishes, colors, coach painters' materials, sponges, brushes, emery, sand paper, etc., etc. All orders are promptly and carefully attended to, and the lowest prices prevail, the trade and public being supplied on the most favorable terms. Mr. Lawless, who is a gentleman in the prime of life, born in this city, is a man of entire reliability in his dealings, as well as of push and energy, and, unless all signs fail, his success is bound to endure.

 WILLIAM A. CUSHING, Real Estate Broker, Room No. 4, 126 South Fourth Street.—A leading representative of this business in Philadelphia is Mr. Wm. A. Cushing, who has been established as a real estate broker here since 1880. He conducts a general real estate business, buying, selling and exchanging property of all kinds, negotiating mortgages, loaning money on approved collateral, managing estates, collecting rents, and handling Philadelphia realty of every description. He has made a study of real estate in all its branches, is thoroughly informed as to present and prospective values, and can be engaged with perfect confidence in all matters relating thereto. Mr. Cushing is a native Philadelphian with an experience of eighteen years in the real estate business.

 NATHAN MILLER, Manufacturer of Ingrain Carpets, Mascher Street, Below York.—The history of this concern is one of steady progress, and of the deserved reward of perseverance and energy. The enterprise was founded in 1878, on Rosehill, by Mr. Miller, who began operations with four hand looms, his capital being small. Owing to the excellence of his products, however, his success was continuous, and he frequently enlarged his facilities, and made several moves, each time into larger quarters. In 1887 he began the use of power looms, and in 1889 took possession of his present quarters. Here the premises occupied have dimensions of 50x120 feet, and are equipped with sixteen looms, driven by steam power, while employment is found for thirty skilled operatives. Mr. Miller manufactures all grades of ingrain carpets, in extra supers and unions, making a leading specialty of the finer qualities. The output amounts to one hundred and forty rolls of carpet a month, and the jobbing trade is supplied direct upon the most favorable terms. Mr. Miller was born abroad, but has resided in the United States since 1876. He has had twenty-two years' practical experience as a carpet man, and the successful business career he has led is one reflecting the highest credit upon his ability and methods.

HISTORICAL AND COMMERCIAL PHILADELPHIA.

IXTH NATIONAL BANK, Corner Second and Pine Streets.—There are but few, if indeed any at all, among the many solid and substantial financial institutions for which Philadelphia has long been noted that maintain a higher reputation for integrity and stability than the Sixth National Bank, corner Second and Pine Streets. This is by universal assent one of the soundest and stanchest in the city. It is an ably managed and thoroughly trustworthy institution, conducted on strict business principles, and has secured firm hold on public confidence and favor. The "Sixth National" was incorporated March 29, 1864, and during the twenty-eight years since intervening has enjoyed an uninterrupted career of prosperity. Its history has been an unbroken record of progress, and all the indications are that its popularity is bound to increase and endure. The bank has a capital stock of $150,000, the surplus fund amounts to $150,000, and the undivided profits are upward of $18,000, while the deposits reach almost $1,000,000. The connections and investments of the institution are of the most desirable character, the business grows steadily apace, and altogether, the affairs of the bank are in a condition highly gratifying alike to its stockholders, directors and clients. The Sixth National Bank building is a handsome three-story structure, and the banking offices, which are conveniently located on the first floor, are commodious, timely fitted up and well equipped in every respect. An efficient clerical staff is employed, and everything bespeaks order and excellent management. A general banking business is transacted, including loans, discounts and deposits, and accounts are opened with banks, bankers, merchants, manufacturers, etc., on the most liberal terms consistent with sound and conservative methods. Collections and telegraphic transfers are made on all cities and towns of the United States, at lowest rates; foreign and American exchange is bought and sold, while drafts are issued on Great Britain, Ireland and countries of continental Europe. Bills of exchange and letters of credit, available anywhere, are sold, also approved commercial paper, and securities are negotiated; and in short, all classes of business comprehended in legitimate operations in this line are engaged in. The correspondents of the bank are the Ninth National and the Importers' and Traders' National Banks of New York. The officers of the Sixth National Bank of Philadelphia are Jonathan May, president; William D. Gardner, vice-president; Robert B. Salter, cashier; the board of directors being composed of Messrs. Jonathan May, Wm. D. Gardner, Daniel Baird, David H. Bowen, Henry D. May, William S. Emley, H. Shetzline, Robert D. Salter and James Wilson. The gentlemen named are all men of standing in the community, well and favorably known in commercial and financial circles and prominent in business life.

RIFFIN, GRAHAM & CO., Importers and Retailers of Fine Carpetings, No. 1620 Chestnut Street.—Although of comparatively recent establishment, Messrs. Griffin, Graham and Co., importers and retailers of fine carpetings, are already the center of a large connection, and they are speedily becoming a leading source of supply for Pennsylvania, New Jersey, Delaware and Maryland. This distinct success cannot fail to be regarded as a true index of the firm's ability to meet the many requirements of retail buyers by placing upon the market a full line of floor coverings, of both foreign and American origin, at rockbottom figures. The firm handle every description of floor coverings of all grades and of the latest introduction as to patterns, styles and make; and they draw their supply from various countries in Europe and Asia, besides dealing in American manufactures. The first floor, at the address named, 25 x 150 feet in area, is used as main salesroom, and is handsomely furnished and very efficiently lighted with skylights running its entire length, everything being quite new; the two floors above, each 25 x 80 feet in size, are also utilized, the second story as salesroom and third story as upholstering-room. Here are to be seen an immense, though carefully selected stock of everything in the way of floor coverings; a few of the chief lines being Axminster, Wilton, body Brussels, choicest tapestries, and best ingrain carpets, many of rich and artistic designs; elegant Turkey squares and druggets, Smyrna and other rugs; mats in great variety; oilcloths of all grades, linoleum, mattings, crumb cloths, etc. This flourishing enterprise was initiated early in 1892, by the present copartners, Mr. N. O. Griffin and Mr. John W. Graham, who are young men of good standing.

EFORMED CHURCH PUBLICATION HOUSE, Booksellers and Stationers, No. 907 Arch Street.—The leading and representative Reformed Church Publication House, Rev. Chas. G. Fisher, D.D., proprietor, was established in 1864 by the Reformed Church Publication Board. In 1888 Mr. Fisher, who had been superintendent, secretary and treasurer of the Board, became sole proprietor. He handles a large stock of theological works, Sunday-school libraries, reward cards, pulpit and family bibles, miscellaneous books, stationery of all kinds, etc.; also the German publications of the Church are kept on hand. The house publishes "The Reformed Church Messenger," "The Reformed Quarterly Review," "The Missionary Guardian," (monthly), "The Sunday-school Treasury," "Sunshine," (weekly), Heidelberg Teacher," (quarterly), "Scholar's Quarterly," (quarterly). "Lesson Papers," (advanced and primary). The spacious store occupied is handsomely fitted up and contains at all times a complete stock. As three per cent. of the gross receipts have to be paid each year to the Publication Board, church people should patronize the house liberally. Mr. Fisher is a native of Pennsylvania.

HE F. A. DAVIS COMPANY, Medical Publishers, Main Office, No. 1231 Filbert Street.—The medical profession, as well as humanity in general, have found the printing press an able assistant. The benefits of medical discovery and research are directly proportioned to the means given for communicating them to the members of the profession. To the average man, the life of a physician of large practice seems rather unattractive. Always subject to a call from any patient, his time is never his own; and how the doctors are able to do the necessary reading and study to keep them abreast with the advance made by the master-minds in the profession is a problem which appeared, until the last few years, to be almost an impossible one to solve, but it has been solved. The F. A. Davis Company, whose principal office is at No. 1231 Filbert Street, are the publishers of the "Annual of the Universal Medical Sciences," which might appropriately use the sub-title, the "Problem Solved." The" Annual of the Universal Medical Sciences" is to the medical profession, what the "Law Reports" are to the legal profession, the "Statesman's Year Book" to the statesman. It gives the progress of medicine from January to January of each year, separating from the vast amount of material, contributed by its 300 editors and correspondents, simply the progress of the year, repeating nothing old, giving no space to vaporing theories, but giving to the profession a reliable guide to what is new in medicine and surgery. Among its contributors are and have been such men as the late D. Hayes Agnew, the late Joseph Leidy, Dr. Wm. Pepper, Dr. J. William White, Dr. James C. Wilson, Dr. William Goodell of Philadelphia, and equally prominent doctors in New York, Chicago, Cincinnati, Boston, Baltimore, Washington, St. Louis, etc., and some of the great men in Europe. This work, now in its fifth year of publication, has the largest subscription list ever attained by any medical work. Of it, the "London Lancet" (perhaps the greatest medical authority in the world) remarks, "Its circulation must, if it maintains its present standard of excellence, become as world-wide as the information which it contains." It is something of which Philadelphia should justly be proud, that the acknowledged greatest medical work in the world, should have been conceived and brought forth in this city. This house was founded in 1879 by Mr. F. A. Davis, and has continued under the name of "F. A. Davis," until November 19, 1891, when the present company was organized and incorporated under the laws of the State of Pennsylvania. In addition to the "Annual of the Universal Medical Sciences" and its attendant monthly journal, the "Satellite," this company publishes "The Medical Bulletin," (a montly journal of medicine and surgery). The combined circulation of these two journals, it is stated, averages about eighteen thousand copies per month. They also publish such standard works as "Diseases of the Nose and Throat," by Sajous; "Diseases of the Nervous System," by Ranney; "Materia Medica and Therapeutics," by Shoemaker; "Principles of Surgery," by Senn; "The Physician Himself," by Cathell; "Practical Gynæcology," by Goodell, etc., etc.

HISTORICAL AND COMMERCIAL PHILADELPHIA.

OBERTS & ANDREWS, Produce Commission Merchants and Dealers in Foreign and Domestic Fruits, No. 119 Callowhill Street. The wholesale commission trade in produce and fruits has long been a prominent feature of Philadelphia's commerce, and a valuable factor in the upbuilding of the city's business fame and prosperity. A house in this line enjoying an excellent status is that of Roberts & Andrews, of No. 119 Callowhill Street, corner of New Market Street. This establishment was founded four years ago by the present proprietors, Josiah Roberts, Jr., and B. D. Andrews. Both are natives of New Jersey, having been raised on farms in that State, and they reside in Camden. Mr. Roberts was for twenty-one years a member of the firm of Roberts & Brother, commission merchants, this city, and Mr. Andrews was bookkeeper for the firm eight years. The premises occupied by Messrs. Roberts & Andrews, built exclusively for their use, in 1888, comprise a four-story building, 25 x 75 feet in dimensions, and it is furnished with all appliances and conveniences for the storage and safe preservation of stock. The firm employ twenty-one assistants and are general produce commission merchants and wholesale dealers in foreign and domestic fruits of all kinds. Consignments are solicited, the sales are active, and large shipments are made daily. Messrs. Roberts & Andrews are members of the Produce Exchange, also the Fruit Buyers' Union. They attend personally to the interests of their patrons, and their record is of a character to command for them the esteem of all their fellow-citizens.

STAND PIPE—FAIRMOUNT.

OVER INK COMPANY, No. 145 North Sixth Street.— It is now more than a half a century since the Hover inks were first placed on the market, and during the entire period they have been steadily growing in popular favor. They have long been noted for their general excellence, and are maintained at a uniformly high standard. The writing fluids manufactured by the Hover Ink Company, whose office and factory are at No. 145 North Sixth Street, are made on scientific principles, in accordance with a regular formula, from the very best available ingredients, and are used extensively in banks, mercantile houses, railroad offices, etc., throughout this city and State. They are, in short, preparations of a distinctly superior character, and are handled by the trade all over the country. Besides high grade writing fluids, the Hover Ink Company manufactures other inks of every color, shade and tint; also mucilage of an excellent quality, and keep on hand always a large, first-class stock. They occupy the whole of a commodious three-story building, with complete facilities, and employ an efficient staff of help. They are prepared to supply dealers and large consumers on the most favorable terms, quoting bottom prices to the trade, and all orders will be promptly and carefully filled. These inks, which were awarded a prize medal at the American Institute and International Exhibition, and also received a diploma at the Franklin Institute, are fully warranted, and are exceptionally profitable goods to handle. This concern had inception in 1841, when the business was established by Joseph E. Hover, who carried on the same until 1886, when he was succeeded by Charles P. Brooks. Something over a year ago C. A. Worrall became manager for the estate, and as such has since conducted the establishment with uninterrupted success.

RANK BROS, & CO., Manufacturers of Fine Clothing, No. 51 North Third Street.—This is an old and honored house, and was founded in 1858 by Messrs. Frank Bros. & Co., and the same name and style has been retained by the present proprietors. The building occupied contains five floors and a basement, 35x80 feet each, in which fifty skilled hands are employed, while three hundred work people are kept busy outside. They use only the choicest woolens and suitings of foreign and domestic make, selected with the utmost care, examined thoroughly for imperfections, sponged and shrunk, and cut by leading experts to the actual latest fashionable styles. The finish will be found thoroughly elegant, and no more stylish or durable clothing can be obtained in the United States. The goods embrace all grades, and the house commands the permanent patronage of the best class of retailers from Boston to Colorado. The rarest inducements are offered to the trade. The members of this responsible firm are Marx B. Loeb, Jacob S. Frank, Horace Loeb and Jacob F. Loeb. The senior partner became a member of the original firm in 1867; Mr. Frank came into the firm in 1870, while Messrs. Horace and Jacob F. Loeb, sons of the senior partner, were admitted to partnership in 1889.

. & R. WISTER & CO., Brokers and Commission Merchants in Foundry and Forge Pig Irons, Iron, Steel, Metals, Fire Bricks, Etc., No. 257 South Fourth Street.—A prominent and widely known Philadelphia iron and steel firm is that of L. and R. Wister & Co. They are brokers and commission merchants, and are agents for the Sterling Coal Company. They handle everything in the line indicated, including foundry and forge pig irons, plate, boiler, bar and iron generally; also steel, metals, fire bricks, ores, etc., and deal extensively in all kinds of scrap iron, coal and coke. The business transacted is exceedingly large, the annual reaching upward of 100,000 tons, and the trade of the firm is constantly growing. The house was established about twelve years ago, and under the present firm name has always been conducted, although some changes have taken place in the personnel of the copartnership, which originally consisted of Messrs. L. and Rodman Wister and J. N. M. Shimer. Mr. Jones Wister acquired an interest in the concern about eight years ago, and Mr. L. Wister was removed by death in 1891. The office is well appointed and connected by telephone (No. 308), and several clerks are employed. The firm make a specialty of pig irons, and handle the following brands: "Dunbar," "Bushong," "Kemble," "Tuscarawas," "Edge Hill," "Weysbrooke," "Liberty," "Heck," "Silver Spring," "Ferguson," the Lickdale Iron Company's steel blooms, slabs and ingots, and silver gray carbonizing iron. They are prepared to execute orders for anything in the line of iron, steel, metals, etc., on the most favorable terms, quoting bottom prices. The members of the firm, who are all Philadelphians by birth, are men of long and thorough experience in the trade.

UTTER BROS., Importers and Packers of Leaf Tobacco, Nos. 155 and 157 Lake Street, Corner La Salle Street, Chicago; No. 43 North Third Street.—Messrs. Sutter Bros. are importers and packers of the finest grades of leaf tobacco from Cuba and Sumatra, and also handle immense quantities of Pennsylvania, Connecticut and Wisconsin growths. The building occupied here for trade purposes contains five floors and a basement, 25x298 feet each, appropriately fitted up with every convenience for storage, assorting and packing of the large and valuable stock. The firm have very superior connections with growers and shippers, both at home and abroad, and are prepared to lay before manufacturers the most desirable leaf at prices not easily found elsewhere, and have a large and influential trade not only in all parts of the United States, but also in England, Germany, France, Spain, Canada, and other foreign ports, their business aggregating $1,750,000 yearly. The firm of Sutter Bros. is composed of five brothers, Messrs. Louis P., Adolph, Jacob, Edward A. and John E. Sutter, all of whom were born in Detroit, Mich., and are well known citizens of Chicago, except Mr. John E. Sutter, who resides in Philadelphia. Mr. M. Louis, the manager in this city, is specially intimate with the buying and selling markets, and is a sound judge of the value of leaf tobacco.

EIL & TAWS, Importers and Dealers in Drawing and Artists' Materials and Mathematical Instruments, No. 814 Chestnut Street.—Messrs. Weil & Taws are importers and dealers in drawing and artists' materials and mathematical instruments. They are both young men, abreast of the times in every particular, and possess a thorough knowledge of all the requirements of their business. Their business has received a great impetus lately, and they are now doing a thriving retail and wholesale trade. Their commodious premises are heavily stocked with a large and superior stock of artists' and draughtsmen's materials, art novelties, etchings, paintings, both of foreign and American production. They have influential foreign connections and import directly themselves from all parts of Europe full lines of goods. They also handle a complete variety of all kinds of mathematical and scientific instruments, and sell at the lowest possible prices. Mr. J. H. Weil is a Hungarian by birth, and a resident of the city for about six years. He is an accomplished linguist, speaking fluently seven languages. Mr. H. M. Taws is a native Philadelphian, descended from ancestors whose line reaches back to colonial times.

. S. DUNMORE, Fancy and Staple Groceries, House Furnishing Goods, Etc., Main Street, above Union Avenue, Chestnut Hill.—One of the leading grocery and house furnishing businesses in Chestnut Hill is that conducted by Mr. R. S. Dunmore, located on Main Street, above Union Avenue. This responsible house is now well known here for handling exclusively the most reliable grades of goods in each line at fair and reasonable prices, for making exact representations and for rigidly adhering to other business principles that alone insure a permanent success. The enterprise was established at the same location in 1891 by Mr. Dunmore and a Mr. Duncan, and for the past five years its continued prosperity has been solely attributable to the personal endeavors of Mr. Dunmore himself. The large and carefully selected stock carried includes a full assortment of house furnishings and staple and fancy groceries, a few of the chief lines being choice China and Japan teas, Java and Mocha coffees, family flour, biscuits, the standard brands of canned and bottled goods, jellies, dried and crystallized fruits, preserves and a superior line of imported table delicacies; three competent clerks being in regular attendance upon customers, and a wagon retained for the collection and delivery of orders. Mr. R. S. Dunmore, who is a gentleman of middle age, was born in Chester County, Pa., coming to Chestnut Hill twenty-six years ago, and is a member of the Knights of Pythias and the Knights of the Golden Eagle.

. NEWELL & SON, Landscape and Business Photographers, No. 633 Arch Street.—There is no branch of industry, art or science in which such marked advances have been made during recent years as in photography. Notwithstanding all that has been attained, much depends upon the skill and judgment of the operator in obtaining favorable and desirable results. Among the old established and prosperous houses engaged in business in Philadelphia, that of R. Newell & Son, located at No. 633 Arch Street, has always maintained a most enviable reputation for superior workmanship and liberal business methods. Mr. R. Newell established business here in 1855, and in 1872 his son was admitted to partnership. The firm work for the trade in Pennsylvania and vicinity, employing five competent assistants. They occupy three floors, 20x100 feet in dimensions, fitted up with every convenience and appliance known to the profession, including the best light and accessories. The establishment is fully equipped for indoor or outside work, landscapes, buildings and country seats being photographed at short notice. Their interior work is exceptionally fine, having made a special study of this particular branch. Special arrangements have been made for photographing groups. The ground floor is provided with a skylight for the photographing of merchandise of every description, and photography in all its branches is executed in the highest style of the art at reasonable prices. Messrs. Robert and Harry Newell, are gentlemen of enterprise, ability and high artistic attainments, honorable in their dealings and highly respected in social and commercial circles.

HISTORICAL AND COMMERCIAL PHILADELPHIA.

CRANE IRON COMPANY, Office, No. 221 South Fourth Street.—Considered as a factor in the sum of commercial activity in this city, the importance of the pig iron and kindred interests can hardly be overestimated. The transactions in the products indicated here in Philadelphia in the course of a year reach vast magnitude and represent millions, while the volume of trade grows apace. Notable among the concerns represented here is the Crane Iron Company, whose works are located at Catasauqua, Pa., with an office at No. 221 South Fourth Street, in this city. This company manufacture both foundry pig, open hearth and Bessemer pig iron, and their leading brands are "Crane," "Castle," and "Mohican." The works were built in 1839, 1842 and 1846, with present furnaces in 1856, 1867 and 1884, while the first iron was made July 4, 1840. The company was incorporated in 1839, under the laws of the State of Pennsylvania, and now has a capital of $1,500,000, with the following officers and managers, to wit ; H. W. Hazard, president; James M. Hodge, secretary and treasurer; Leonard Peckett, superintendent; David Davis, cashier. This company was the first in the United States to make pig iron by the use of anthracite coal, and they now use anthracite coal and coke, and New Jersey, Pennsylvania, Lake Superior and foreign ores. They operate four blast furnaces, two measuring 75 x 18 and two 60 x 16 feet, one having iron stoves and the others three Whitwell stoves each, and having a combined annual capacity of 150,000 tons net. The company have also operated the Macungie furnace since 1899, which turns out 17,000 tons of Bessemer pig iron per annum. The processes by which the specialties of this company are manufactured are of the most perfect character, a uniformly high standard of excellence being maintained, so that their brands are rapidly increasing in demand in all sections of the country. The resources of the company are ample and abundant, their facilities for rapid and perfect productions are rarely equaled, and the largest orders are therefore guaranteed prompt and satisfactory fulfillment in all cases. Such a house as this proves of inestimable value to a great commercial center like Philadelphia, and by its operations conduces greatly to the activity of trade. The officers of the Crane Iron Company are gentlemen of ripe experience in the iron industry, whose standing in business and trade circles places them far beyond the requirements of any praise which these pages could bestow.

LANG, BERNHEIMER & CO., Distillers and Wholesale Dealers in Fine Pennsylvania Whiskeys, Sole Proprietors of the Centennial Club Whiskey, No. 118 North Front Street.—One of the oldest-established, and a leading house actively engaged in the wholesale trade in whiskeys, is that identified with the honored name of Lang, Bernheimer & Co., whose warehouse is at No. 118 North Front Street. The business was founded in 1850 by Messrs. Louis Lang and G. Bernheimer, who continued together until their pleasant co-partnership was broken by the death of Mr. Bernheimer, and Mr. Lang has since directed affairs under the original firm-title of Lang, Bernheimer & Co. The premises occupied comprise a four-story warehouse, 25 x 100 feet in dimensions, filled with a heavy assortment of foreign and domestic wines and liquors. Only the standard class of liquors are dealt in and as a consequence each year has witnessed an increase of stock and facilities and a corresponding enlargement of trade, which extends throughout Pennsylvania, New Jersey, Delaware and the New England and Southern States. The goods are sold free or in bond, and are received direct from the producers. Mr Lang is a distiller and rectifier, and makes a leading specialty of fine Pennsylvania whiskeys, being sole proprietor of the celebrated " Centennial Club Whiskey," which is unrivaled for flavor and purity. Mr. Lang is a member of the Pennsylvania and Philadelphia Wholesale Liquor Dealers' Associations, the Manufacturer's Club and National Cattle Feeders' Association. By the exercise of great commercial ability this house has achieved a reputation for square dealing and reliability accorded only to those whose transactions have been based on the strictest principles of mercantile honor.

ROBERT J. WALKER, Star Finishing Works, No. 2335 Hamilton Street.—For the past forty years Robert J. Walker, whose well-equipped "Star Finishing Works" are located at No. 2335 Hamilton Street, has been established in business. He is the oldest and foremost representative of the branch of industry indicated in Philadelphia, and has an extensive patronage. His facilities for finishing all kinds and qualities of cotton fabrics, or for napping, calendering, etc., are unsurpassed, and the work done by him is of a distinctly superior character. Mr. Walker, who is a gentleman somewhat past the meridian of life, but active and energetic, was born in the South, and has resided in this city since 1847. He is a man of thorough practical skill, as well as of long and varied experience, fully conversant with every feature and detail of the business, and was the first in the city to start a finishing shop alone. He started in 1852 on Edward Street, in a very modest way, and after a number of changes of location, moved to the present quarters in March, 1876. The premises occupied by him here are spacious and commodious, and are fitted up with ample steam-power and the latest improved machinery, appliances and appurtenances known to the industry, while twenty-five to forty in help are employed. Mr. Walker is prepared to finish cottonades, jeans, cheviots, ticking, ginghams, dress fabrics, and cotton and worsted goods of every description in the very best manner, guaranteeing perfect satisfaction, and all orders are executed at short notice. All goods are prepared for finishing by a trimming machine of exceptional merit, patented by Mr. Walker, and which is for sale on application to him, who is the manufacturer. All varieties of goods are napped, calendered, re-dressed, re-finished and packed in the most expeditious and superior manner, likewise, at the lowest prices, and all goods in this establishment are fully insured. Mr. Walker is also a patentee of great renown in this class of machinery, and is the proprietor of some of  the most valuable patents used in finishing. Mr. Walker also has a safety device for use on elevators which can be seen in operation at his works at No. 2335 Hamilton Street. It is of exceptional merit, and is worthy of the attention of the public, being the simplest and most effectual safeguard ever devised. State rights are for sale on application to R. J. Walker. Mr. Thos. Sermendinger is the manager of these works.

HISTORICAL AND COMMERCIAL PHILADELPHIA.

F. HAMELL & CO., Established 1857, Rope and Twine Manufacturers, Agents of the Penn Cordage Co., Dealers in Ship Chandlery, Naval Stores, Fishermen's and Boatbuilders' Goods, No. 16 North Delaware Avenue.—A house which occupies a leading position in its special department of commerce is that of Messrs. F. E. Hamell & Co., rope and twine manufacturers and ship chandlers, at No. 16 North Delaware Avenue, telephone No. 518. This establishment was founded in 1857, by John S. Lee & Co., who were succeeded by Richard B. Williams, and seventeen years ago Messrs. F. E. Hamell and Geo. L. Stubbs became the proprietors. On June 1, 1892, Mr. Stubbs retired, and Mr. Hamell remains sole proprietor, trading as F. E. Hamell & Co. The premises used for business purposes comprise two floors, each 30 x 150 feet in dimensions, and they are equipped with every convenience for the handling of an active trade. A heavy stock is carried of rope and twine of all kinds, ship chandlery, naval stores, and fishermen's and boatbuilders' goods. Mr. Hamell is president of the Penn Cordage Co., agent for Walter Coleman & Sons' blocks, and keeps a full supply of these superior goods. A staff of six to eight clerks is employed, and all orders are promptly filled at rock-bottom prices. Mr. Hamell is a native of New Jersey, and entered the house, of which he is now proprietor, in 1869. He is a live, progressive business man, and enjoys the fullest confidence of the mercantile community.

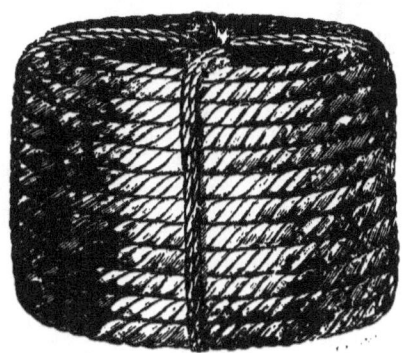

UNION NATIONAL BANK, Third and Arch Streets.—One of the live financial institutions of Philadelphia to which our business men can look with confidence and pride is the Union National Bank, whose banking rooms are located at the corner of Third and Arch Streets. This bank commenced business as a State institution in 1858, and was reorganized under the national banking laws in November, 1864. It has a paid-up capital of $500,000 and is officered as follows, viz.: President, David Faust; vice-president, E. G. Reyenthaler; cashier, W. H. Carpenter; directors: David Faust, E. G. Reyenthaler, C. F. Stadiger, William S. Reyburn, W. H. Carpenter, I. J. Dohan, Aaron Gans. Swinging a heavy capital, controlled by founders and promoters of unquestioned ability and integrity, it has not only proved a pillar of strength in time of great financial necessity and fear, but has upheld and fostered the material interests of the entire mercantile and manufacturing community. Its watchwords have been prudence and economy—prudence in investments, economy in expenses of handling business—and from these two walls of strength has sprung a solid arch of prosperity and profit. A bank so long established and having gone so far in its career with ever-growing success is naturally an assurance of permanency, but there is more than mere "solidity," as the word goes, which has contributed to its prosperity and popularity. Although founded upon a rock, it has each twelve months been raised above the level of the year before, and now has a surplus fund of $350,000, with undivided profits of $18,017.22, while its individual deposits average upwards of $1,500,000, and its loans and discounts over $2,000,000. The Union National does a regular legitimate banking business in deposits, loans, collections and exchange, receiving the accounts of banks, bankers, corporations, firms and individuals on the most favorable terms; discounting choice commercial paper, making loans on approved collateral, dealing in foreign exchange, issuing drafts and letters of credit, handling first-class securities and making collections on all available points through its numerous correspondents, who include the Chemical National, First National and Hanover National Banks of New York; and the National Bank of Illinois, of Chicago. A valuable and increasing list of patrons is drawn to its counters, the ability of the management and the high standing of the officers and directors giving every guarantee of the intelligent conservation of all interests committed to its care. The executive officers are gentlemen with whom it is always a pleasure to do business. President Faust has filled that position with honor and credit since 1864, and is known and esteemed as one of our solid, substantial citizens and most experienced business men. The cashier, Mr. Carpenter, has been in the banking business for a period of twenty-eight years, being with the Penn National Bank previous to connecting himself with this institution, in 1883, and is a financier of tried ability, wide acquaintance and high repute, while the board of directors commands the esteem and confidence of the entire community.

A. F. RIESER, Specialist in Butter, and Sole Agent for Ritter's Creamery Butter, No. 115 New Market Street.—In the whole range of commercial enterprise as exhibited in the business resources of Philadelphia, there is no department of more importance than that devoted to the commission trade in country produce, and among the most enterprising of the houses engaged in this line is that of A. F. Rieser, situated at No. 115 New Market Street. Mr. Rieser began business five years ago on Callowhill Street, and has been at his present address since 1889. The premises are provided with cold storage and all requisite facilities, and a large, superior stock is at all times carried. Mr. Rieser is sole agent for Ritter's butter and cream, the creamery being at Hamburg, Berks County, Pa.; he is also agent for many other creameries throughout the State. A leading specialty is made of butter and eggs, the choicest the market affords being kept for sale. An active demand is supplied and all orders are filled at lowest current rates. Mr. Rieser is a native of Berks County, Pa., but has long resided in this city. He holds a membership in the Produce Exchange, maintains an excellent position in the produce commission trade, and as a business man of integrity and enterprise is well qualified to hold his position in the commercial world.

WM. T. WATERS & CO., Steam Broom and Whisk Works, No. 37 North Water Street.—The Steam Broom and Whisk Works of Wm. T. Waters & Co., at No. 37 North Water Street, is one of the oldest representatives of this industry in the Quaker City, and its superior products are shipped to all parts of Pennsylvania, New Jersey, Delaware, and the South, while some goods are exported to Scotland. The business was founded in 1842, by Wm. Cody & Co., the Co. being Mr. Waters. Mr. Cody retired in 1878, when the present firm was organized. Mr. Waters is a native of Trenton, N. J., and resides in Camden. The works are comprised in a five-storied building, 20 x 75 feet in dimensions, and they are equipped with first-class machinery and labor-saving appliances, operated by steam-power, and employment is furnished a large force of hands. The firm manufacture all varieties of brooms, whisks and brushes, the goods all being made in the best and most durable manner. They also are general dealers in woodenware, broom handles, broom corn, wire, twine, cordage, etc., and are agents for Milliken's Parlor Pride " Enamel." A large stock is always kept on sale, and the trade is supplied at lowest prices.

D. V. BROWN, Wholesale and Manufacturing Optician, No. 734 Sansom Street.—Success in any department of business depends to a very great extent upon the intelligence proficiency and ability which are brought to bear upon it. This is more particularly true and applicable to the fine and intricate branches of trade such as that in which Mr. D. V. Brown is engaged. This gentleman established an office in this city, at No. 734 Sansom Street, in October, 1891. He has had twenty years' practical experience in the business, and is an expert manufacturer of optical goods. He grinds lenses and manufactures optical goods, representing also the Julius King Optical Company, of Cleveland, Ohio, and San Francisco, who also have a branch in Mexico, and wherever known enjoys the highest reputation for first class work. The premises utilized comprise two floors, supplied with all necessary machinery operated by steam power, and a corps of expert workmen is constantly employed. The trade of the house is wholesale exclusively, and dealers in this line should not fail to examine the goods and prices of this reliable manufacturer before leaving orders elsewhere. His goods are just what he represents them to be and are popular wherever introduced, as is evidenced by the fact that this house is noted for retaining its customers for many years, when it is once given a fair trial. Special optical and retail work is done to order, Mr. Brown making it a personal duty to see that all work leaving his establishment is optically correct, and he has on his list of patrons many prominent oculists throughout the country. Mr. Brown is a native of Massachusetts, but has been a resident of this city nine years, having been identified with the optical profession for twenty years, and is highly esteemed for his honorable manner of conducting all transactions and for his marked ability as an optician.

A. W. STRAUB & CO., Manufacturers of Grinding Mills, No. 3741 Filbert Street—A responsible and well known house engaged in Philadelphia as manufacturers of grinding mills is that of A. W. Straub & Co., a name that has for several years past been closely associated with one of the best, most durable and efficient implements, known as the Quaker City Grinding Mill, "for grinding corn cobs, feed and table meal," now on the market. These mills were invented and patented by Mr. Straub, and they have stood the severest practical tests for some ten years, holding their own against all other makes, and steadily growing in popularity and favor with all classes of users. 1. The double reduction grinding disks used in this mill are cast of steel, cheaply renewed; perfectly interchangeable by any one in ten minutes. They are divided into three portions: 1st, the saw toothed inner edge of eye, upon which are located the conveyor flights to draw in between the disks cool air and grain, crowding them through the mill. 2d, the bosomed space between the disks, which approach each other as they pass from the centre, is filled with furrows, running their knife edges front to cut the grain into fine sandy meal with the least power possible. 3d, the second reduction is produced upon the flat outer portion, which is covered with furrows running their inclined side front, causing the hard sandy meal to roll back between the inclines of the furrows on opposite disks, causing a mashing, crushing or mellowing action upon the meal, already cut fine, like corrugated rolls running at different speeds, thus producing a cooler, finer and softer meal than any iron mill we have ever seen. 2. The crushing saws are formed on a sleeve cast fast to the spindle with lead. No bolts to rattle out and pass through the mill. 3. The grinding case is cast in two halves; they each have a babbitted journal bearing cast fast to it; a cone shaped projection at front end contains the cob cutting saws, and a recessed space at the back end is provided with an eccentric to damsel the feed shoe. There are three discharging openings - one upon either side and one downward. But one half of the case is bolted to the legs, leaving the other free for quick removal to examine or renew the grinding disks. 4. The framing-ring is turned true on face side, and has the bed disk bolted to it. The ring is upon a universal joint, free to move every way except revolve with the running disk; hence the grinding faces are always returned in perfect line to each other. 5. The spindle is of steel, with button between its hardened end and the temper screw. It has a cutter head (which carries the running disk), cob cutting saws, eccentric, pulley and fly wheel. 6. The bridge tree is provided with a spring at one end to yield and allow the disks to separate if an iron spike, by accident, should enter the mill. 7. The three discharge spouts are provided with tin covers, allowing the desired one to be opened either side or downward. 8. The legs support the front half of case only, leaving back half free for removal. 9. The damsel is formed with a malleable casting and two steel plates, between which the eccentric works to shake the feed shoe at the top end of bar. 10. The hopper has a valve in front to control the quantity of grain fed into the mill by the feed shoe. 11. The pulley is overnecked, allowing the belt to approach from any angle and be removed without unlacing. 12. The cob crushing hopper has a sliding apron in front and a perpendicular back, to cause the cobs to fall at one end and slide at the other into the crushing chamber without bridging. 13. The anti-friction metal button has an oil hole through which the oil circulates to cool it end and end of spindle. 14. The temper screw, to regulate the degree of fineness required. 15. The jam nut lever, to secure the temper screw after properly set. 21. Jam between the crushing chamber and grinding disks to regulate the flow of cobs to suit the power used. 22. Eccentric to shake the feed shoe. The firm was established twenty-five years ago by the present proprietors, who are thoroughly practical mechanics. Mr Straub is the inventor and manufacturer of Straub's Sub-aqueous Tunnel (patented April 2, 1889), for water pipes, pedestrians, vehicles and steam or other railways. The premises, situated at No. 3741 Filbert Street, are spacious and well arranged, and are fully equipped with improved mechanical appliances and accessories pertaining to this special branch of industry, a large force of skilled workmen being there regularly employed. At the World's Columbian Exposition they will exhibit in the Agricultural Building their mills grinding grain, and invite all to call and investigate who are interested in the state of the art. They have also asked for permission to exhibit by drawings and models Straub's system of "Sub-aqueous Tunneling," also their "Improved Metal Railroad Cross Ties," for full investigation. No trouble to show them to any interested party; please call upon them for further particulars.

JACOB RUBENSTONE, Diamond Setter, Manufacturer of Fine Diamond Mountings and Fancy Rings, No 118 South Seventh Street. The gentleman whose name heads this sketch is a manufacturer of the finest diamond mountings and fancy rings of various and unique designs and of the very best quality; and all orders placed with this flourishing firm are certain to be handled in the most judicious and thoroughly capable manner. Though Mr. Rubenstone is comparatively a young man, he has had sound, practical experience in all branches of the trade, extending over a period of some eighteen years. A large amount of business is transacted with the trade, society badges are made to order, and a large amount of jobbing of all kinds is carried on by a corps of experienced and competent workmen. The raised art trade receiving special attention at his hands. The business has been established eight years, and the large patronage recorded is a valuable tribute to the popularity of the concern; trade relations being maintained throughout the whole Middle and Southern States. Mr. Rubenstone was born in Germany and has resided in Philadelphia about fifteen years.

HISTORICAL AND COMMERCIAL PHILADELPHIA.

GEO. W. CROUCH, Successor to J. Becher, Horse Collar Manufacturer and Dealer in Neat's-foot Oil, Etc., No. 245 Race Street.—The oldest establishment of the kind in the Quaker City is that of Mr. Geo. W. Crouch, manufacturer of horse collars and harness, at No. 245 Race Street. This house was originally founded in 1840 by Jas. Becher. The firm later became Becher & Albright, and after that Becher & Shume, who continued at the head of affairs up to 1880, when Mr. Crouch succeeded to the control. Mr. Crouch entered the house thirty-five years ago, when a lad eleven years old, and he learned his trade here. He was born at West Farms, New York State, but has resided in this city for the past forty years, and is well and favorably known in the community. He is prominently identified with numerous organizations, being Past Sachem of Pequod Tribe, I. O. Red Men; Past Grand Chancellor of Pennsylvania, Aurora Lodge, Knights of Pythias; Past Grand Chief St. George Castle, State of Penn-sylvania, Knights of the Golden Eagle; member Schuyler Council, 1174, American Legion of Honor, Past Officer Crescent Council No. 9, Legion of the Red Cross; Secretary of the Lehigh Building and Loan Association; Junior Warden Phila-delphia Consistory, A. and A. S. Rite; Phila-delphia Conclave No. 8, K. of R. C. of C.; Kensington Lodge, No. 5, K. of B.; Lu Lu Temple, A. A. O. N. of M. S.; Past Master A. Y. M. Richmond Lodge, No. 230; Past High Priest of T. B. Freeman Chapter, No. 249, R. A. R.; Past Eminent Commander of St. John Commandery No. 4, Knights Templar, and Past Grand Cohocksink Lodge, No. 383, I. O. O. F. He is also a member of Post 63, G. A. R. During the war he served with the 213th Regt., Penn. Volunteer Infantry. The premises occu-pied for business purposes consist of a four-story and basement building, 25 x 100 feet in dimensions, which is admirably equipped with all conveniences. Mr. Crouch employs about twenty hands, and manufactures a general line of harness, making a leading specialty of horse collars. He also deals in neat's-foot oil, etc. A heavy stock is at all times carried of first-class goods, and orders of any magnitude meet with prompt fulfillment.

CHAS. W. LYNDELL, Glazed Kid Maker, Cuckoo Kid; Works, Fox and Collins Streets, Branches at Boston, Rochester and New York; Office and Salesrooms, Nos. 144 and 146 North Fifth Street.—Within a comparatively recent period, the manufacture of glazed kid leather has grown to be an extensive and highly important branch of industry in this city; and it may be observed, too, that marked improvement has been made in the goods produced of late years. The products of some of our leading manufacturers have a national reputation, and in this connection special mention is due Chas. W. Lyndell, the widely-known glazed kid maker, whose office and salesrooms are at Nos. 144 and 146 North Fifth Street, with works at Fox and Collins Streets. The "Cuckoo Kid" manufactured by this gentleman is an article of exceptional excellence, and is noted throughout the country. It is made from carefully selected and best available skins, in accordance with the most approved process, and is unsurpassed for elegance of finish or durability. The works cover half an acre of ground, and are perfectly equipped. The facilities are first-class in all respects, and upward of 150 hands are employed at manufacturing. The quarters occupied on North Fifth Street are spacious and commodious, and a very large and fine stock is always kept on hand here to meet the requirements of the trade, which extends all over the United States. The house is represented on the road by four or more salesmen, and has branches in New York, Boston and Rochester. This flourishing business was established in 1888. Mr. Lyndell, who is a gentleman in the prime of life, was born in this city, is a man of energy and enterprise, as well as of skill and experience, and has a thorough knowledge of the wants of the trade.

SCHOENEWALD & STILLMAN, Manufacturers of General Brass Goods, No. 11 North Seventh Street.—This firm began business four years ago, and have since met with such substantial success that the trade that has been built up now extends all over the country. The co-partners, Robert Schoenewald and Thomas C. Stillman, are thoroughly experienced business men. Mr. Stillman attends to the office work of the establishment, and Mr. Schoenewald, who is a brass founder and metal worker of eighteen years' experience, supervises the mechanical department. The premises, which comprise two floors, each 30 x 100 feet in dimensions, are equipped with steam-power machinery, and employment is afforded twenty-five skilled workmen. As founders the firm turn out bronze and brass castings of every description, and execute brass finishing and metal spinning in all its branches. They also manufacture faucets for refrigerators and water-coolers, and metal spun toys of all kinds.

FRANK McNAMARA, Fashionable Hatter, Nos. 1619 and 1621 South Street.—The largest hat and cap business on South Street is that conducted from Nos. 1619 and 1621 by Mr. Frank McNamara, who is the only retail hatter in the entire city of Philadelphia that manufactures on the spot the whole of the goods sold, with the exception of straw hats. Thus, at least, one profit is saved, and the greatest satisfaction ensured alike as to reasonable prices, correct styles, fine quality, and thorough reliability, and, as a consequence, the house is now widely and favorably known for the genuine quality and satisfactory nature of its goods, and for strictly honorable methods in all transactions. The business was established at the same location by Mr. Michael McNamara in 1872, and two years ago it came into the hands of his son, the present proprietor, who was brought up to this line of trade, and owns the building, Nos. 1619-1621 South Street. The store, 30 x 46 feet in area, is handsomely appointed in every detail, and contains a large and very select stock of the finest grade of silk, stiff and soft felt, straw and other hats, and caps of the correct styles for the existing season. The factory, in the rear, consists of a three-story building, fully equipped for making all kinds of hats and caps, as well as for blocking, ironing and general repairing, six skilled hands being regularly engaged and ten during the busy season. Mr. Frank McNamara is a native of this city, and still a young man.

NICHOLAS J. GRIFFIN, Successor to A. J. Gallagher & Son, and The Hamilton Distilling Company, Manufacturer of Alcohol and Cologne Spirits, Nos. 307 and 309 North Second Street.—The house now owned and directed by Mr. Nicholas J. Griffin has for the past two decades held a prominent place in its special branch of commerce. The business was founded twenty years ago by A. J. Gallagher & Son, who were succeeded by the Hamilton Distilling Company, and in 1888 Mr. Griffin became proprietor. His thorough experience, added to his sound business ability, has enabled him to greatly enhance the trade of the house and to increase its popularity with first-class dealers. The premises occupied comprise a double building, having five floors and basement, 45 x 125 feet in dimensions. Mr. Griffin is one of the distributors of the product of The Distilling and Cattle Feeding Company, distillers and rectifiers of alcohol and spirits, of which he makes a specialty. The active trade supplied extends to all parts of Pennsylvania, New Jersey, Delaware, New York, the South and the New England States. Orders are met at such liberal terms as to prove entirely satisfactory. Mr. Griffin is a member of the Drug Exchange of Philadelphia, a director of the Philadelphia Warehousing and Cold Storage Company, Board of Trade, Philadelphia Bourse, and other organizations. It should be mentioned that Mr. Griffin is also sole agent in the State of Pennsylvania for the "Orient" brand of pure rye whiskey, which is justly famed for its purity and general excellence. Mr. Griffin deals largely in all the other leading brands of Eastern Rye Whiskey, both in bond and free—the goods being handled in bulk and sold only to wholesale dealers.

N. GREENLUND, Watches, Clocks and Jewelry, Eyeglasses, Spectacles, Etc., No. 3258 Ridge Avenue.—A first-class and thoroughly reliable city establishment that at once secured an enduring hold on the people of this community is that of Mr. B. N. Greenlund, dealer in watches, jewelry, etc., located at No. 3258 Ridge Avenue. This store was opened by the present proprietor in 1891, and from the first attracted attention and drew to itself a patronage both substantial and influential, while it has been unremittingly increasing its custom since. The salesroom, 20 x 40 feet in dimensions, is neatly and admirably arranged, being fitted up with elaborate show-cases, counters, etc., and made attractive by the elegant manner in which the fine stock is displayed, while in permanent attendance will be found two courteous and experienced assistants. In the large and valuable assortment handled will be shown everything in the line of gold and silver watches, of both foreign and domestic production, clocks of all kinds, diamonds and other precious stones, jewelry in the greatest variety of useful and ornamental articles, sterling silver and plated ware, eyeglasses, spectacles and optical goods generally. In each department the stock has been most carefully selected from the best manufacturers, and in every instance is representative of all the latest novelties of the day in fashionable and desirable goods, while the prices quoted are placed at the lowest figures consistent with fair and equitable dealings. A specialty is made of repairing American, English and French watches and clocks, also of all kinds of jewelry and silverware, and the work of this house is neatly and promptly executed in the highest style of the art. Mr. Greenlund, who is a native of Warren, this State, has resided in Philadelphia since 1889, and is a practical and experienced watchmaker and jeweler of the highest standing in the trade, whose permanence and prosperity stand assured.

ARCH STREET, WEST OF THIRTEENTH STREET—1889.

WOLTEMATE BROTHERS, Greenhouse and Bedding Plants, No. 4648 Germantown Avenue.—The headquarters for greenhouse and bedding plants in this section of the city are at No. 4648 Germantown Avenue, the well known establishment of Woltemate Brothers. This is the oldest and leading floral depot in Germantown, and has been in existence for the past forty-four years. The firm are growers of and dealers in plants and shrubs, general florists and landscape gardeners, and their patronage is of a substantial and influential character. This business was established in 1848, by Henry C. Woltemate, on whose death, November, 1874, his widow assumed control and conducted it up to 1887, when it passed into the hands of her sons, Albert and William Woltemate. At this period the present firm-name was adopted, and under this style it has since been continued without change, although one of the brothers (William) was removed by death, in 1891. The quarters occupied as office, store and greenhouses are commodious, finely fitted up and perfectly equipped, and a large staff of help is employed. A general stock of greenhouse and hothouse plants is constantly on hand, a good stock of orchids being the firm's latest acquisition. Bedding plants, shrubs, etc., are furnished and planted by careful, competent men, cut flowers being supplied to order. Floral emblems are made to order in appropriate designs at short notice, and decorations are furnished for all occasions, while landscape gardening is attended to in the most prompt and superior manner. All orders receive immediate attention and the prices charged by the firm are most reasonable, everything considered, satisfaction being assured.

HISTORICAL AND COMMERCIAL PHILADELPHIA.

ILLIAM HALL & CO., Manufacturers of Shoddy and Dealers in Woolen Rags and Shoddy Material; Office, No. 25 North Front Street; Warehouse, No. 31 North Front Street; Factory, West Fernwood, Delaware County, Pa.—The largest and foremost representative of that important industry—the manufacture of shoddy—in Philadelphia, is the well-known house of William Hall & Co., whose office and salesroom is at No. 25 North Front Street. The splendid reputation which this establishment bears is sufficient to entitle it to special notice in any work bearing on the commercial resources of the Quaker City. The business was founded in 1867 by Mr. William Hall, under the firm-name of William Hall & Co., which is still continued. Nine years ago his sons, Messrs. T. C. and John H. Hall, were admitted to partnership, and they are now the proprietors, their father having died in 1888. Both gentlemen are natives of Philadelphia, active members of the Trades' League, and are favorably known in financial and business circles. The quarters occupied are comprised in a four-story building, 25 x 91 feet in dimensions. The firm also have a warehouse at No. 31 Front Street, a five-storied structure, 25 x 91 feet in area. At West Fernwood, Delaware County, Pa., they have a shoddy factory. The plant is a large one, equipped with first-class machinery, including seven pickers and eighteen carding machines, and steam supplies the driving power. The Messrs. Hall are manufacturers of shoddy, and dealers in woolen rags and shoddy material, and they command a heavy trade in Pennsylvania, New Jersey, Delaware, New York, and New England. The heavy stock at all times carried, and their long-established facilities, enable the firm to meet all orders at exceptionally favorable terms.

M. KAUPP, Steam-power Book and Job Printer, No. 208 New Street.—A leading and successful printing house in this busy locality is that which is under the efficient management and direction of Mr. J. M. Kaupp, located at No. 208 New Street. Twelve years ago this business was originally founded by the present proprietor, who has since sustained a well-deserved reputation for the superior excellence of the work turned out, both in the English and German languages and prompt and reliable methods of dealing. For three years past the present apartment in this building has been occupied and this, which has the dimensions of 20 x 30 feet, is equipped in the most approved manner, the outfit embracing three job presses driven by steam-power, all the latest styles in type, etc., and employment is afforded a force of five experienced hands. Everything in the line of books and job printing is here executed in the most prompt, accurate and careful manner, the facilities of this house for doing all kinds of work being of the best, and are equal to all demands that are made upon it. Satisfaction is guaranteed in every instance, and all orders receive immediate attention, while the most reasonable rates consistent with the superior style of the workmanship at all times prevail. Mr. Kaupp's trade extends throughout this entire city, and is both permanent and influential in character, while business relations established with him cannot fail to be satisfactory in every instance, as in dealings with customers he has ever been found prompt, reliable and decisive. He is a member of the F. and A. M., and a member of German social organizations. A native of Germany, Philadelphia has claimed him as a resident for the past fifteen years.

ALTIMORE AND PHILADELPHIA STEAMBOAT COMPANY, Office No. 28 South Delaware Avenue.—One of the most popular water routes for excursionists from Philadelphia is that furnished by the Baltimore and Philadelphia Steamboat Company, (Ericsson Line), to Baltimore via the Chesapeake and Delaware Canal. This is the oldest propeller line in the world, having been in operation for a period of fifty-five years, and has its offices at No. 201 Light Street, Baltimore; and No. 28, South Delaware Avenue, Philadelphia. The company own five steamers, to wit: the "General Cadwallader," "Rich Willing," "Elizabeth," "H. L. Gow," and "John S. Shriver." All have large and greatly improved passenger accommodations, affording every comfort to their patrons, and are lighted throughout by electric lights and heated by steam, while choice meals with all substantials and delicacies are served in fine style. These steamers leave Philadelphia and Baltimore every day at 5 P. M., except Sundays and holidays, arriving at each port the following morning. Weather permitting, landings will be made at Betterton (both ways) daily, and on Mondays, Thursdays and Saturdays (both ways), at Reybold's Wharf, and Town Point Wharf. Betterton is the best fishing-ground in the country. Anglers can here take the succulent white perch and other choice fish during the months of July, August and September. Its fishing facilities are inexhaustible, while it is also a very pleasant place for a picnic or a holiday or vacation sojourn. It has a fine hotel, and plenty of boats, fishing tackle and experienced guides are furnished at short notice. Scores of parties and clubs were organized this season for trips to these and other Maryland fishing and hunting grounds, via the Baltimore and Philadelphia Company's line. Excursion tickets to Baltimore or to Betterton from this city are sold for $2, good for ten days; while excursion tickets are also for sale to and from all way landings and special excursion rates are given to parties and clubs by applying at the office. The trip takes one into a great region for wild duck and terrapin, and as wild geese and turkeys also abound here plentifully the sport of gunning, next to fishing, is practiced by the hundreds of visitors. Freight and baggage are called for and delivered to all parts of the city by applying at this office, and orders by telephone, No. 822, receive immediate and careful attention. Mr. F. S. Groves, the agent in charge, succeeded to the control on the death of his father, A. Groves, Jr., in 1891, and is thoroughly conversant with all the wants and requirements of the public.

AWYERS & CO., Fruit and Produce Commission Merchants. Peaches, Pineapples, Raspberries, Florida Oranges, Strawberries; York State Grapes a Specialty in their Season. No. 121 Callowhill Street.—No commercial interest of the Quaker City is of more paramount importance than that of the fruit and produce trade, in which immense operations are carried on. An old, established concern engaged in this line is that of Sawyers & Co., situated at No. 121 Callowhill Street. This house was founded seventeen years ago, by the senior proprietor, Mr. James Sawyers, at the corner of Second and Poplar Streets, from whence he moved to Nos. 331 and 333 Water Street, and from the latter place to the present address six years ago. Here the premises consist of a three-story building, provided with all conveniences for the satisfactory conduct of the trade in hand. Messrs. Sawyers & Co. are general commission merchants and wholesale dealers in foreign and domestic fruits and produce of all kinds, and are in constant receipt of consignments from New Jersey, Pennsylvania, Delaware, Maryland, Virginia, Ohio and Indiana, receiving goods in carload lots. Liberal advances are made to consignors, when required, and promptness and reliability are assured in every instance. Mr. Sawyers is a native of England, but has resided twenty years in this city, while Mr. John C. Cook, who has been a member of the firm for the past two years, was formerly in the employ of Mr. Sawyers and is conversant with all the details of the trade. They receive goods direct from first hands, and their experience and comprehensive knowledge of the wants of this market, prove of invaluable benefit to both producers and consumers.

OBERT WAREHAM, (Late Foreman for Edmund Draper, Deceased), Manufacturer of Engineers' and Surveyors' Instruments, No. 402 Locust Street.—Mr. Robert Wareham has a national as well as a local reputation for the manufacture of instruments for engineers and surveyors. The business was established by Edmund Draper over fifty years ago. Mr. Wareham entered the employ of Mr. Draper in his boyhood and was with him for nearly forty years. He gained a thorough knowledge of the business and for many years was foreman of Mr. Draper's establishment. On Mr. Draper's death in 1882, Mr. Wareham succeeded to the business, which he still carries on. He has a large local trade besides filling orders from all parts of the United States. He makes all kinds of instruments for engineers and surveyors and gives particular and prompt attention to repairing. An important specialty of his manufacture is the Philadelphia Levelling rod, Draper's pattern, which is known to surveyors all over the country.

HISTORICAL AND COMMERCIAL PHILADELPHIA.

R. HOBENSACK'S MEDICAL INSTITUTE, No. 206 North Second Street.—From earliest times the art that alleviates and removes pain and heals the afflicted has been justly regarded as among the highest and noblest of human functions. And in connection with these observations, it will not be amiss to refer to Dr. Hobensack, the widely known and skillful physician of this city, who has accomplished many marvelous cures at his offices, No. 206 North Second Street. These offices were established in 1850 by Dr. J. N. Hobensack, an eminent physician, who practiced the healing art till 1870, when his son, Dr. J. B. Hobensack, became his assistant, and father and son worked together till the death of the former, which occurred in 1875. Since that time Dr. J. B. Hobensack has become famous for his unequalled success in the cure of disease. He is a graduate of the University of Pennsylvania, Philadelphia, and of the Eclectic College of Medicine at Cincinnati, as M.D. He is a member of the Cincinnati Eclectic Medical Association from which he received a gold medal for investigating syphilis. He is preceptor of this association, with the members of which he is very popular. He successfully treats special diseases, for which he receives patients from all over the United States. He treats personally and by mail, and all curable cases are guaranteed. A staff of experienced physicians, surgeons and specialists are always in attendance. Dr. Hobensack is ably assisted by Dr. R. M. Booker, a graduate of Jefferson Medical College, class of 1888, with the degree of M.A., and of Central High School. He is a young man of rare ability and skill, and has had a wide experience in the laboratory and in his profession as a physician. Dr. Hobensack deals in all kinds of trusses, abdominal supporters, silk elastic hose, and all kinds of frames for correcting deformities, and surgical instruments of every description. He is a middle aged gentleman, and one of the most famous physicians in the United States. He is a member of the Philadelphia County and Pennsylvania State Medical Society.

LONG VALLEY COAL COMPANY, Office, No. 201 Walnut Place.—No industrial interest of Pennsylvania is of greater value and importance than that of coal mining, the quality of the best grades finding a ready and growing market all over the country. Prominent among the miners and shippers of semi-bituminous coal stands the Long Valley Coal Company, whose mines are at Long Valley, Bradford County, Pa., on the Barclay Railroad, near Towanda, with offices at No. 201 Walnut Place, in this city and Towanda. This company was incorporated in 1879 under the laws of the State of Pennsylvania, with a capital of $125,000, and is governed by the following board of directors—viz., J. Raymond Claghorn, President; Andrew Wheeler, H. C. Davis, H. D. Wilson, Anthony Taylor, C. R. Claghorn with E. O. Macfarlane, Superintendent, Treasurer. The company's property comprises 3800 acres of land, situated on the Barclay Railroad, and their mines have an annual output of 100,000 tons of coal. The mines have been developed in the most approved and systematic manner, and shipments are made all along the lines of the Reading system. The quality of the coal here mined is equalled by few, and no fuel proves more satisfactory or more economically sustains the processes of combustion. The lowest market prices are always quoted, and the coal gives entire satisfaction whenever introduced and tested. President Claghorn is also President of the State Line and Sullivan Railroad Company, and eminently fitted by experience and ability to successfully direct the affairs of this enterprising corporation. The treasurer, Mr. Macfarlane, is a well known citizen of Towanda, Pa., superintendent of the Barclay Railroad, and an efficient and popular official.

ENRY ROHNER, Successor to A. Kiesewetter & Co., Dealer in Fine Groceries, all Kinds of Foreign and Domestic Cheese; Foreign Delicacies a Specialty; N. E. Corner Fifth and Race Streets. Philadelphia is not behind any city in the world in the extent and magnitude of its grocery business, and the enterprise which characterizes her representative firms in this branch of commerce is not excelled by any other city in the United States. One of the most reliable and popular houses engaged in this business is that of Henry Rohner, whose establishment is located at northeast corner of Fifth and Race Streets. This house stands at the head of the list in the fine grocery line in the city. The business was established in 1875 by A. Kiesewetter & Co., the present proprietor, who had been with the house fourteen years, succeeding to the control in 1889. The house has long been recognized by the best families in the city as dealing in the choicest foreign and domestic groceries and table luxuries brought to America, and no inferior goods are allowed to be sold. The premises occupied comprise two buildings and a basement, 20x100 feet in dimensions, elegantly equipped, which are stocked with an assortment of staple and fancy groceries, table luxuries, etc., which have no superiors in this country or Europe, while the prices quoted are always regulated by the market. Ten experienced and efficient assistants are employed, and all orders are promptly filled. Goods are delivered to all parts of the city free of charge, two wagons being employed for that purpose. The facilities of the house are in every way unsurpassed and the business has ever been conducted on the enduring principles of equity. Mr. Rohner is an extensive importer of foreign table delicacies, including all kinds of foreign cheese. His trade, both wholesale and retail, is large and constantly increasing.

OBERT W. MARIS, Apothecary, N. E. Corner Spruce and Tenth Streets.—An important branch of the drug trade of Philadelphia is the establishment of Robert W. Maris, located at the northeast corner of Spruce and Tenth Streets. This well known house was first opened to the public in 1831 and has been controlled by Joseph C. Turnpenny, Samuel S. Bunting and Howard Knight, the present proprietor succeeding to the control in 1890. The store occupied is one of the handsomest and best equipped in this section of the city, and has long been regarded as popular headquarters for all who esteem purity and excellence of stock, and enterprise and reliability of management. A large and valuable stock is carried, consisting of pure drugs, chemicals, standard proprietary and family medicines, dyes and colors, essences and extracts, surgical appliances, toilet goods and perfumery, fancy articles and holiday presents, besides that multitude of supplies coming under the head of druggists' sundries. The purest and most reliable goods are handled, and Mr. Maris puts up a line of specialties, makes his own tinctures, and is prepared at all times, day and night, to give special attention to the filling of physicians' prescriptions. Mr. Maris is a graduate of the Philadelphia College of Pharmacy, class of '88, is a member of the alumni association of the same, and has had several years' experience in this business previously to taking control of this house. All those favoring him with their patronage can be assured of receiving reliable goods and equitable prices.

TELLER BROS., Packers of and Wholesale Dealers in Seed Leaf Tobacco and Importers of Havana and Sumatra; Warehouse, Lancaster, Pa.; Store and Office, No. 117 North Third Street. The oldest concern in this city devoted to the wholesale trade in leaf tobacco is that of Teller Bros. This house was founded in 1840 by Raphael Teller, who, a term of years later, admitted to partnership his brothers, Sol and David Teller. The senior member of the firm, Raphael Teller, retired six years ago; Messrs. Sol and David Teller retired the first of January, 1892, and they were succeeded by Lewis Teller, son of Sol. Teller, and Jacob Teller, son of Raphael Teller. Both are natives of this city, and active members of National Tobacco Dealers' Association and the Philadelphia Tobacco Trade Association. Mr. Lewis Teller has been in the firm twenty years, Mr. Jacob Teller the same, and they consequently possess a sound knowledge of the leaf tobacco trade in all its branches. The warehouse occupied has four floors, 39x125 feet in dimensions. The firm also have a large packing house in Lancaster, Pa. They carry on an extensive business as packers and wholesale dealers in seed leaf tobacco, and importers of Havana and Sumatra. One of the firm visits Havana twice a year, where they have an extensive warehouse at No. 64 Cuba Street. A very heavy stock of Havana tobacco is at all times to be found there. The trade of the house extends all over the United States. The trade of the Western States, as well as the whole of that of New York State, is ably represented by Mr. Samuel Alexander, who has been connected with the firm for seven years. The Messrs. Teller Bros. possess such superior facilities that they are enabled to meet all orders upon the most satisfactory terms.

HISTORICAL AND COMMERCIAL PHILADELPHIA.

COATES & MATHIAS, Quaker City Whisk Broom Works, Also Manufacturers of Plush Novelties and Triplicate Mirrors, Nos. 5, 7 and 9 Arch Street.—The Quaker City Whisk Broom Works occupy a representative place among the industrial enterprises of this great trade center, and command an influential trade, extending over a widespread territory. The business was established fifteen years ago by R. H. Eastburn, and on January 1, 1892, the present proprietors came into possession, the copartners being J. K. Coates and Wm. Mathias. Mr. Coates has had twenty years' experience in his vocation, and Mr. Mathias has followed the business since boyhood. Both were formerly with the establishments of David Fell, and Fell & Eastburn. The business premises comprise a four-story building, 50 x 100 feet in dimensions, and it is splendidly equipped with the most improved machinery, driven by steam-power. Employment is found for forty-five expert operatives, and the works have a weekly output capacity of 350 gross of whisk brooms. In addition to whisk brooms the firm manufacture a general line of plush novelties and triplicate mirrors, turning out a large variety of superior goods in these lines. A heavy stock is at all times kept on hand, and orders invariably meet with prompt fulfillment. Messrs. Coates and Mathias have won a measure of popularity, confidence, and respect in the commercial community second to no other in the same line, and their present high standing in the trade renders further comment upon our part superfluous.

THE INTEGRITY TITLE INSURANCE, TRUST AND SAFE DEPOSIT COMPANY, Southwest Corner of Fourth and Green Streets. Real estate title insurance has passed beyond the field of debate and is now accepted by the public as an absolute necessity and one of the greatest value, affording the utmost security to owners of real estate and enabling them to buy, sell or effect loans with a degree of promptitude and satisfaction before unknown. The leading representative of this line of business in Philadelphia is The Integrity Title Insurance, Trust and Safe Deposit Company, whose offices are eligibly situated at the southwest corner of Fourth and Green Streets. This company was incorporated May 20, 1887, with an authorized capital of $500,000 and is officered as follows, viz.: President, Jacob Rech; first vice-president, Frederick A. Poth; second vice-president and title manager, Chas. F. Ehrenpfort; secretary and treasurer, Herman Wischman; solicitor, Albert S. Letchworth; board of directors, George W. Vogler, physician; Frederick A. Poth, brewer; Philip Doerr, of Philip Doerr & Sons, carpet manufacturers; Chas. F. Ehrenpfort, conveyancer; Thomas Y. England of England & Bryan, leather dealers; Frederick Ortlemann, milk dealer; Jacob Roth, merchant tailor; George Nass, lumber merchant; Philip Spaeter, cooper; Charles Mahler, shoe manufacturer; Charles Herbst, of Jacob Berges & Co., dyers; Jacob Rech, carriage builder; John F. Rau of Snowdon & Rau, coal merchants; Albert S. Letchworth, attorney-at-law; Chas. Roesch of Chas. Roesch & Sons, butchers; Chas. G. Berlinger, of Berlinger Bros., butchers; C. J. Heppe, pianos; Lewis Kramer, notions and hosiery; Philip Zaun, brewer; George Kessler, builder; Frederick Mayer, No. 431 Reed Street; C. Theis Weger, brewer; Levi H. Bell, of Samuel Bell & Sons, flour merchants; Wm. H. Rookstool, butcher; Albert Hellwig, of A. Hellwig & Co., dyers. These names speak for themselves, being those of representative citizens and leading business men, under whose sound and enterprising guidance this company is reaping a suitable reward in the development of a business of great magnitude and widespread influence. This company is perfectly prepared to examine and insure titles to real estate, the examinations being made by a well-organized law department with a board of eminent counsel at the head, and promptly attends to all the details pertaining to the buying, selling and renting of real estate; acts as surety, administrator, trustee, etc.; collects rents, dividends, interests, etc.; loans money on mortgages and on good collateral, payable in installments, and keeps the choicest of first mortgages on hand for sale. No company is so thoroughly prepared to promptly examine and guarantee the title to realty, while its guarantee is one of hard cash and honorable management. It may truly be said that the company has revolutionized the methods of real estate transfer and so simplified the question and thrown such positive safeguards around the titles to all realty on which it issues policies that transactions therein can now be effected with as much ease and at as little expense as those in stocks or bonds. This company also operates a thoroughly organized banking department and a savings bank; receives money on deposit in the one, subject to check on sight and allowing two per cent. interest, and in the other any amount from $1 upward at three per cent. It likewise rents boxes for the safe keeping of valuables, in burglar and fire-proof vaults, guarded by latest improved time locks, for $5 upwards yearly. The company is solidly prosperous, having a surplus fund of $69,000 with undivided profits amounting to $34,797.53, while their deposits average over $800,000 and resources aggregate $1,300,000. The secretary and treasurer, Mr. Wischman, gives his entire time and attention to the promotion of the company's interests and is an accomplished and faithful official, a native Philadelphian and deservedly popular with the patrons of this representative institution.

GEO. FRESHELL, Druggist, No. 3526 Haverford Avenue.—An old-established and thoroughly trustworthy house engaged in the drug business on Haverford Avenue, which has always maintained a most enviable reputation for superior goods and service, and honorable business methods, is that of Mr. Geo. Freshell. This establishment has been in successful existence for a most extended period of time, and thirteen years ago the present proprietor succeeded Dr. H. W. Siddell in the management and direction of its affairs. The commodious and well-appointed store occupied is neatly and handsomely fitted up with oak fixtures, electric-light, plate-glass show cases and windows, etc., and at all times it presents one of the most attractive features of this neighborhood. It is fully stocked with a large and first-class assortment of pure and fresh drugs and chemicals, pharmaceutical preparations, proprietary remedies of established merit, mineral waters, liquors, surgical instruments, toilet and fancy articles, perfumery, etc.; in short, everything to be found in a well-regulated metropolitan pharmacy. Special attention is given to the compounding of physicians' prescriptions and family recipes, and all the best appliances have been provided to secure accuracy and precision in their preparation, which is performed at all hours of the day or night, and two reliable assistants are employed in constant service. Mr. Freshell is a thoroughly competent, experienced and legally registered pharmacist, who has been identified with this profession for nearly a quarter of a century, and his patronage is extremely large and of the most influential character. He was born at Portsmouth, Ohio, but has long been a resident of this city and has attended the Philadelphia College of Pharmacy and is a member of the Apothecaries' Union here.

HISTORICAL AND COMMERCIAL PHILADELPHIA.

ARTHUR HAGEN & CO., Manufacturers' Agents for the Sale of Tobacco, Etc., No. 64 North Front Street.—Twenty-five years of uninterrupted prosperity sums up in brief the history of the well known firm of Arthur Hagen & Co., manufacturers' agents for the sale of tobacco, etc., No. 64 North Front Street. This is one of the oldest houses of the kind in the city and maintains an excellent reputation in the trade. It was established in 1867 by Arthur Hagen, who conducted it alone up till about 1872, when he took into partnership H. C. Ellis. They are general agents for S. W. Venable Tobacco Company, Petersburg, Va., and Harry Weissinger Tobacco Company, Louisville, Ky., and sell to jobbers throughout Pennsylvania, New Jersey, Delaware and adjacent States, doing a large business. They occupy four floors and employ three clerks and salesmen. A large stock of plug tobacco constantly kept on hand here. The firm is prepared to fill orders for anything in the line indicated on the most favorable terms, quoting manufacturers' prices; and relations once formed with this old and reliable house are likely to lead to an enduring business connection. Messrs. Hagen and Ellis are members of the Board of Trade and also of the Bourse.

WILLIAM KING & CO., Wholesale Grocers, Nos. 247 and 249 North Second Street, and Nos. 138 to 142 New Street.—The wholesale trade in multifarious food products comprehended under the general head of groceries constitutes, as it scarcely need be said, an extensive and highly important branch of commercial activity in this busy metropolis. Engaged in the line indicated, Philadelphia has a number of solid and substantial firms, prominent among them being that of Messrs. William King & Co., whose establishment is eligibly located at Nos. 247 and 249 North Second Street, and Nos. 138, 140 and 142 New Street. This is the oldest as well as the largest house in its line in this section of this city, having been founded in 1857 by William King, the present firm being organized in 1880 by the admission of Mr. Woolson Brown to partnership. The business premises comprise a three-story building, 20x100 feet in dimensions, and a four-story warehouse, of the same size, every department being complete and well ordered and splendidly stocked at all times. A vast, varied and exceptionally fine assortment of goods is here displayed, including a fine selection of staple and fancy groceries and specialties; prominent among the varied lines the direct importation of Private Growth Old Government Java coffee and their famous brand of King's Choice Corn, choice California fruits, canned, dried and evaporated. Only strictly first class goods are handled, every article sold being fully warranted, while the prices quoted are the very lowest consistent with quality, the most liberal inducements being offered to the trade, and the business of the house is brisk and lively in Pennsylvania, New Jersey, Delaware and adjoining States. Mr. King came to this city in 1854 and is a true type of the energetic, persevering, self made men who have done so much to build up the commerce of this community. Mr. Brown is a native Pennsylvanian, connected with this house since 1869, and both are members of the Wholesale Grocers' Association, and the Grocers' and Importers' Exchange, and expert authorities in this special branch of trade.

FRANK W. STANTON & CO., Importers and Commission Merchants in Foreign and Domestic Fruits; Bananas a Specialty; No. 14 Vine Street.—The remarkable growth of the wholesale commission trade in fruits in Philadelphia during the past twenty years has placed it in a position and given it a prominence that is a matter for most favorable comment, and demands the fullest consideration in this volume. A recently established house engaged in this branch of industry is that of Frank W. Stanton & Co., located at No. 14 Vine Street. Mr. Stanton inaugurated his enterprise in January, 1892, but prior to that had had ten years' experience in the trade, having been connected with such prominent banana importers as the Baltimore Fruit Company, of which he was the secretary and treasurer, and was also manager of the Merchants' Fruit Company, and was also connected with Messrs. Warner & Merritt for some time. Since beginning operations on his own account he has met with the most substantial success, building up within a short time a large, rapidly growing trade throughout Pennsylvania, New York and New Jersey. Consignments are received largely from Pennsylvania, New York, New Jersey, Delaware, Jamaica, Central America, and the South generally. Mr. Stanton is an importer of and commission merchant in foreign and domestic fruits, making a leading specialty of bananas, of which he is a very heavy shipper; also of oranges and lemons, and is a direct importer of cocoanuts. The premises used for business purposes consist of a four story and basement building, 25x100 feet in dimensions. The basement and second floor contain banana ripening rooms. A large stock is carried, and orders from the trade are promptly met at satisfactory terms. The elements of success exhibited in the growth of this business are clearly indicated in the personal characteristics of the proprietor, whose natural capabilities have found an admirable outlet in the prosecution of a work in which he has already acquired an enviable reputation.

M. L. SNYDER, Rubber Goods, No. 25 South Second Street.—The well known house of M. L. Snyder was established by that gentleman fourteen years ago, and after a time his brother was admitted to partnership, but retired in 1891. The premises utilized for the business comprise a floor and basement, 20x100 feet in dimensions, and a large stock of rubber goods received direct from the best manufacturers is kept constantly on hand, which includes rubber, leather and cotton belting, for driving, conveying and elevating; rubber, cotton and linen hose, for water, steam and acids, and rubber, plumbago and asbestos packing for pistons and joints. The firm are agents for Metropolitan Injectors, the simplest, cheapest and best in the market; also for the Brooklyn Leather Belting Company, manufacturers of short lap oak leather belting only; for the Keystone Raw Hide Lace Leather, cut and in sides; Taper Sleeve Pulley Works, solid and split wood pulleys; the Peerless Vitrified Emery Wheels, the best in the market; and other specialties are added from time to time as they are placed on the market. Several competent assistants are employed. Mr. Snyder is a native of Philadelphia, and an honorable and reliable gentleman.

JAMES MORONEY, Importer and Wholesale Dealer in Fine Wines and Liquors, Nos. 317 and 319 Walnut Street.—For close upon half a century the well known house of James Moroney, importer and wholesale dealer in wines and liquors, Nos. 317 and 319 Walnut Street, has been in existence, and has always maintained an excellent reputation in the trade. It is one of the oldest and most reliable establishments of the kind in Philadelphia, and for the past forty-seven years has been conducted at the present location with uninterrupted success. The business was established in 1845 by John Elliott, who carried on the same up to 1874, when he died and was succeeded by the present proprietor, Mr. Moroney, who is a gentleman of middle-age, active and energetic, and was born in Ireland, but has been in this city for many years. He is a man of thorough experience in this line, well and favorably known in the trade, and has been connected with this time honored house since 1858. Mr. Moroney imports direct handling the finest goods, and has a large and flourishing business throughout Pennsylvania, Southern New Jersey, Delaware and the States adjoining. He occupies commodious premises and keeps on hand always a large, first class stock, which includes pure, finest choice imported and domestic wines, brandies, gins, whiskeys, rums, cordials, bitters and everything in the line of liquors, fine old native whiskeys being a specialty. Goods are bottled to order, also, and quality and quantity are guaranteed. Dealers and large consumers are supplied on the most favorable terms, the lowest possible prices being quoted to the trade, and all orders are promptly and carefully filled.

HISTORICAL AND COMMERCIAL PHILADELPHIA.

GUENTHER, General Upholsterer, Fine Furniture, Curtains, Window-Shades, Etc., Nos. 3529 and 3531 Lancaster Avenue.—Among the representative and enterprising business men of this community, special mention should be made of Mr. F. Guenther, general upholsterer and manufacturer of furniture, etc., who enjoys an enviable reputation throughout the trade. In 1877 Mr. Guenther first embarked in this business for himself on Thirty-seventh Street, but twelve years ago he took up his stand on this popular thoroughfare, where he occupied one store up to 1886, when the necessities of the trade becoming such as to require more room, he also took possession of the premises next door. This commodious and well-appointed establishment, which comprises three floors and a basement, is provided with all the requisite appliances, tools and facilities for the successful prosecution of the work engaged in, and steady employment is furnished to four skilled and experienced workmen. A specialty is here made of fine upholstered furniture of every description to order, also of curtains, window-shades, etc., while particular attention is also given to upholstering and repairing of all kinds, and only first-class work is executed here, being invariably performed in the highest style of the art at the lowest consistent prices. All orders are promptly and reliably filled, and the fullest satisfaction is guaranteed in every instance, while a splendid patronage is enjoyed, so that the general business transacted by Mr. Guenther amounts to a most prosperous annual aggregate. Born in Germany, he has resided in Philadelphia for the past twenty-one years, and he is widely known as a thoroughly practical and experienced upholsterer, being a master of all branches of the trade.

SOUTH BROAD STREET.

SHERIDAN'S CANTON TEA STORE, No. 3950 Lancaster Avenue.—Among the most conspicuous and reliable business houses of its kind in Philadelphia, that known as Sheridan's Canton Tea Store is particularly worthy of special recognition in the trade. This business was originally inaugurated by Mr. Thos. F. Sheridan in 1883 at the present address and has since been conducted by him with uniform success and prosperity. This store, 30 x 50 feet in dimensions, is attractively appointed throughout and appropriately arranged with every convenience and facility necessary for the handling of the stock and systematic conduct of affairs, while the working force comprises six efficient assistants and a delivering team. This is, undoubtedly, one of the most popular and best patronized houses of the kind in this section and it has achieved a wide reputation for the superior character and uniform excellence of its goods, which embraces the finest importations of all kinds of teas put upon the market, also fragrant coffees and spices, of which commodities this establishment makes a leading specialty. The proprietor is an excellent judge of the various articles dealt in, and he is always prepared to offer the best inducements to his patrons in the way of reliable goods, at fair and reasonable prices, successfully competing with any other merchants in the city. All orders receive immediate attention, being promptly filled and delivered, free of charge, and a large permanent and flourishing trade has been developed. Mr. Sheridan has been actively identified with this business for the past twenty-five years, and he is well and favorably known throughout the city of his adoption as an upright, honorable and responsible tradesman. He is a popular member of the Retail Grocers' Association of Philadelphia.

HISTORICAL AND COMMERCIAL PHILADELPHIA.

 J. B. LEE & SON, Wholesale and Retail Drygoods, Notions, Trimmings, Ladies', Gents' and Children's, Furnishing Goods and Clothing, Hats, Caps, Umbrellas and Wet Weather Garments, Nos. 4017, 4019, and 4051 Lancaster Avenue, No. 666 Preston Street, West Philadelphia.—The extensive drygoods establishment of Messrs. J. B. Lee & Son, situated at the address given above, conspicuous by its turret, staff and flag bearing the word "Lee's," is freely recognized as headquarters hereabouts for the most reliable grades of quality at fair and reasonable prices in each of the several lines of goods dealt in, and it is now the center of a retail trade of considerable volume and significance. This important and progressive enterprise was initiated by Mr. J. B. Lee and his son, Mr. Preston B. Lee, in 1876, in one small store at the corner of Thirty-seventh Street and Haverford Avenue, and since the decease of the worthy senior in March, 1880, Mr. Preston B. Lee has had entire control of affairs. Ever since its inception, the house has enjoyed an unbroken record of prosperity and steadily increasing patronage, which is mainly attributable to the sterling principles of fair and honorable trading rigidly adhered to, the sale of genuine and reliable goods at commensurate prices being the chief characteristic. Thus, in 1882 the increased trade necessitated more commodious quarters and a removal was effected to Nos. 3925 to 3927 Lancaster Avenue, and in 1889 the present handsome emporium was erected. The whole premises now occupied consist of four spacious double stores and the entire basement, 66 feet on Lancaster Avenue, 25 feet on Preston Street and 160 feet deep; the latest improvements being provided, such as patent cash railroad system, electric-lights, and every facility for the systematic conduct of the business; twenty-five competent hands being regularly employed on the spot. The stock carried is in itself a positive wonder of comprehensiveness, and each department is complete and self contained, with a full and rich assortment of goods of the latest styles and of the newest introduction; the chief lines being drygoods, dress materials from the finest silks, cassimeres and woolen fabrics to good cottons and prints, notions, trimmings, millinery of direct importation, ladies', gentlemen's and children's furnishing goods, ladies', misses' and children's cloaks, jackets, wraps and outdoor garments, hats, caps, umbrellas, wet weather garments and household linen, blankets, curtains, etc.; while in the basement is to be found a very superior stock of ready-made clothing. The able and energetic proprietor, Mr. Preston B. Lee, is a native of Philadelphia and is a gentleman now of middle age.

 **R. A. SHETZLINE & SONS,** Wholesale Fruit and Produce Dealers and Shippers, No. 1 Vine Street, Corner Delaware Avenue.—To say that the wholesale fruit and produce interest constitutes a factor of surpassing importance in the sum of trade and commerce in this city hardly conveys an adequate idea of its extent. The quantities of oranges, lemons, and foreign produce alone disposed of daily in the produce district reaches enormous proportions. Among those contributing most extensively to the commercial activity in the wholesale trade in green and dried fruits and produce may be mentioned the well-known and responsible firm of R. A. Shetzline & Sons of No. 1 Vine Street, corner of Delaware Avenue, who enjoy a high reputation in the trade. This firm are wholesale dealers and shippers in all kinds of green and dried fruits and produce, and have a widespread and substantial business connection. This is one of the largest houses in this line in Philadelphia, and a specialty is made of handling carload lots of these perishable articles, which are shipped in such prime condition and with such care that they always arrive at their destination as sound and attractive as when they are loaded, and all orders are attended to with promptness and dispatch. The business was established in 1861 by Leibfreid & Shetzline, who were succeeded by R. A. Shetzline, then by R. A. Shetzline & Co., and in 1892 by R. A. Shetzline & Sons, the firm being now composed of Messrs. R. A. Shetzline, and his sons, D. W. and R. A. Shetzline. These gentlemen have all had a long practical experience in this line, and are fully conversant with every want and requirement of the trade. They attend personally to the examination of cargoes and the disposition of the fruits and produce handled. The premises occupied comprise a building with four floors, 25 x 75 feet in size, which presents a bustling and busy scene at all times with fifteen employees handling immense quantities of fruit and produce both in the receipt and shipment. They receive from North Carolina, Delaware, Pennsylvania, Virginia and Maryland, and all through the South, while they ship throughout Pennsylvania, New Jersey, New York, and throughout the Western and Northwestern States, and have, by their enterprise and honorable business methods, built up a trade and connection with buyers and producers that is not rivalled by any other similar house in the trade. Promptness, liberality, and square and honorable dealing has marked the history of this house from its foundation, and its brilliant success is but the just reward of merit, and relations once established with the firm will not only prove pleasant but profitable. The telephone connection is No. 2911.

 FRANK P. STREEPER, Pharmacist, Corner of Main and Evergreen Streets, Chestnut Hill.—The finely appointed and newly furnished pharmacy of Mr. F. P. Streeper is a model of elegance in its admirable arrangement. Every modern convenience is at hand for the comfort of patrons, and to facilitate the transaction of business. The enterprise was established a few months ago by Mr. Streeper, who is a graduate of the Philadelphia College of Pharmacy, being number three in the class of 1888, and also a member of its Alumni Association. He has had ten years' practical experience in the business, and prepares and puts up for sale a line of compounds, tinctures and fluid extracts. The store has an area of 20 x 30 feet, and is heavily stocked with a carefully selected line of drugs, medicines and chemicals, extracts, herbs, barks and pharmaceutical specialties, minerals, standard proprietary remedies, sanitary preparations, toilet articles, perfumery, soaps, sponges, chamois, and druggists' sundries in great variety. The store is open day and night, four competent assistants being regularly employed. Special attention is given to the compounding of physicians' prescriptions and family recipes, and punctual and courteous service is accorded to all patrons.

 DAVID S. WOODRUFF, Provision Dealer, Fresh and Salt Meats, No. 1614 Spruce Street.—The provision business now carried on by Mr. David S. Woodruff was established thirty-five years ago and has been conducted by its present proprietor over a quarter of a century. It was founded by Warner & Myers, and Mr. Woodruff, who had been in the employ of that firm for seven years, succeeded to the business in 1867. The store is 25 x 100 feet, and is always filled with the best line of produce in the market. A specialty is made of home-made preserves and the finest country produce. He handles the best fresh and salt meats, poultry, butter, eggs, oysters, terrapin and game in season, vegetables and fruits. He employs from eight to ten hands and two teams. His trade is mainly in the city and suburbs. He supplies the best hotels, restaurants and families and caters especially to the best family trade. Mr. Woodruff is ably assisted in his extensive business by his two sons, Mr. Isaac N. Woodruff and Mr. David S. Woodruff, Jr., both of whom inherit their father's talent for the business. Mr. Woodruff was born in New Jersey, but has long been identified with the business interests of Philadelphia and is a member of Crescent Lodge No. 493, F. and A. M.

HISTORICAL AND COMMERCIAL PHILADELPHIA.

T. E. WESCOAT, Fruit and Produce Commission Merchant, No. 333 North Water Street; Residence, No. 1019 West Dauphin Street.—One of the leading fruit and produce commission merchants is Mr. T. E. Wescoat, whose heavy dealings and extensive trade in this line have materially advanced the general commercial activity of Philadelphia. He is a large handler of general lines of farm produce, oranges and lemons, domestic fruits of all kinds, but makes a specialty of berries of which he receives the largest and choicest consignments from the best fruit growing sections of the country. He brings to the business mature experience and intimate knowledge of all the details of the trade, he having been in the trade for twelve years or more, three of which he was connected with the house of F. D. Myers, and five years of Kerns & Wescoat. He established his present place of business at No. 333 North Water Street in 1886 and has made a signal success in face of the keenest competition. He is a middle aged gentleman of rare business talent and of proved integrity, strictly reliable in all his transactions and enjoying the most implicit confidence of his numerous patrons. He is a resident of Philadelphia, but originally came from New Jersey, in which State he was born and reared. His energy and push have made him a favorite in the trade, doing a steady and increasing business with the largest shippers and producers, always giving satisfaction for quickness of sales and promptness of returns. It is greatly due to the characteristic efforts of men of his stamp that Philadelphia is taking on unusual, rapid and sound development and is gradually becoming the central commercial metropolis of the finest agricultural region in the country. Mr. T. E. Wescoat's business career has been rewarded not only by the esteem of his patrons, but also by the substantial pecuniary recognition of their permanent custom. In 1888 he opened a branch house in Mantua Market, West Philadelphia, and a year later admitted his brother to partnership therein. He is a member of the Encampment of the I. O. O. F., and widely esteemed for his sterling integrity.

JOS. E. BOWEN & SON, Commission Merchants in Produce, Oysters, Fish, Eggs, Terrapin and Game, No. 2, Pier 17, North Delaware Avenue.—Prominent in the staple branches of the produce commission trade, the house of Mr. Jos. E. Bowen & Son at No. 2, Pier 17, North Delaware Avenue has developed influential and widespread connections of the most desirable character, and is regarded as a leader in its line in the city. A constant supply of vegetables and produce is received daily from the best farms in New Jersey and elsewhere, the resources and facilities employed being admirable for reaching a desirable class of buyers. An extensive wholesale and commission trade is also transacted in oysters from the States of Delaware, New Jersey, Virginia and Maryland; only the finest qualities of bivalves being handled. An extensive and flourishing trade is also operated in fish of every variety, eggs, terrapin and game of all kinds throughout the surrounding States, with a large local patronage also. Consignments are solicited, and returns for the same promptly made, while all orders for the city or country receive immediate attention from the proprietor and a corps of experienced assistants. The business was originally located at the foot of Vine Street and was established by Mr. Bowen thirty-five years ago, removing to its present eligible location in 1872. Mr. Bowen is a gentleman in the prime of life, was born and resides in Philadelphia, and is a member of the Masonic order.

J. P. MOYER & CO., Wholesale Commission Merchants in Eggs, Poultry, Game, Live Stock, Domestic Fruit and Vegetables in Season, No. 309 North Front and No. 308 North Water Streets.—One of the leading and best known wholesale produce commission merchants in Philadelphia is the responsible house of J. P. Moyer & Co., located at No. 309 North Front and No. 308 North Water Streets, who are permitted reference by courtesy to a number of prominent financial and other houses in this part of the country. As receivers and shippers of eggs, butter, poultry, game, sheep, lambs, calves, hogs and live stock, fresh and dried domestic fruits of all kinds in season, vegetables and produce, the firm control an extensive and soundly based trade reaching on the one hand among wholesale consumers all over the city and adjacent country, and, on the other, with growers, dealers and producers located throughout the West as far as Indiana and South to Florida. Heavy and regular consignments are received direct and are disposed of in the most speedy and satisfactory channels with a skill born of long experience; accurate account sales are rendered and prompt returns made. The enterprise was established fifteen years ago by the present sole proprietor, Mr. J. P. Moyer, and under his able and experienced direction it has ever since been attended by a steadily increasing trade and reputation. The premises utilized, fronting on both streets, consist of a building of five floors, each 25x50 feet in area, well fitted and equipped throughout for the successful conduct of the important business carried on, a heavy and very select stock of each of the various lines of goods in season being always carried. Mr. J. P. Moyer was born in Montgomery County, Pa., is a resident of this city and an esteemed member of the Philadelphia Produce Exchange.

THE J. M. ARMSTRONG COMPANY (Frank L. Armstrong, Manager), Music Typographers, No. 710 Sansom Street.—The J. M. Armstrong Company, music typographers, lithographers, printers and electrotypers, No. 710 Sansom Street, is an industry of recognized importance. This is the largest and leading enterprise of its kind in Philadelphia, and is doing a large and flourishing business. There are in Philadelphia many establishments which are the oldest in their lines in the United States, and the fact speaks volumes for the solidity and permanence of this city's commercial and industrial institutions. An instance in point is found in The J. M. Armstrong Company, which has been in existence almost a century, the foundation of which was conceived by L. Johnson, a type founder, in 1794. This branch was supplemented by the addition of music typography, electrotyping, printing and binding, and these latter departments were purchased in 1867 by the late Mr. J. M. Armstrong. This gentleman achieved a most distinct success in his venture, and is acknowledged to be the genius for many improvements in bringing the art of music typography to its present state of perfection, and his death, by the cruel hand of an assassin, thirteen years ago, after having built a large and influential trade extending throughout the United States, Canada, Mexico, West Indies and South America, is to be deplored. At his death, which occurred in 1878, the business was continued by his two sons, Frank L. and Thomas M. Armstrong, and his widow. Mr. Frank L. Armstrong is the business manager for the estate. He is a native of this city, was raised in his present line of business, and possesses an expert practical knowledge of all its branches. The premises occupied are spacious in size, the mechanical equipment embraces all the latest and best methods and appliances for the purpose, and employment for a large force of skilled workmen. This house is prepared to electrotype and engrave music of every kind, also titles, in the highest style of the art. At the International Exhibition in 1876 this establishment was the only one awarded a medal and diploma for the production of music plates, thus demonstrating the superiority of the work over that of all others. An unrivaled assortment of material, added to their acquaintance and experience with music typography, enables this company to claim that nowhere else can be so fully met the requirements of those desiring plates for sheet music, masses, and music of every description in round notes, character notes, or Gregorian style, and in any language. They also give special attention to titles, letter press, and lithography, in one or more colors. Having recently improved their facilities, this company are now prepared to execute all orders speedily, and at prices the most reasonable for artistic productions.

HISTORICAL AND COMMERCIAL PHILADELPHIA.

ANCE BROTHERS & WHITE, Manufacturing Chemists and Pharmaceutists, Northwest Corner Callowhill and Marshall Streets. One of the leading representative firms of manufacturing pharmaceutical chemists in the United States is that of Messrs. Hance Brothers & White, whose headquarters occupy the block bounded by Callowhill, Marshall, Seventh and Willow Streets. It is also one of the oldest-established, having been in existence for about forty years, and has steadily maintained the highest of reputations for the superiority of its products and the ability and equity of its business methods. The plant occupies an entire block, comprising twelve buildings specially erected for their purposes, from two to five stories high with connecting basements and vaults. All are admirably fitted up with the most improved apparatus and machinery, having ample steam-power, while steady employment is given to about two hundred skilled hands. This firm are extensive manufacturers of medicinal fluid and solid extracts, powdered extracts, sugar and gelatine coated pills and granules of the pharmacopœia, compressed tablets and

lozenges, elixirs of all kinds, spread and roll plasters, fruit juices and essences, preparations of mercury, seidlitz and compound powders, confections, tinctures, ointments, solutions, etc.; also Podophyllin, Leptandrin and other resinoids; oleoresins and the various other vegetable preparations used in medicine; absorbent and medicated cottons; Hance's conical plate drug-mill, Hance's non-wasting, percolating and filtering apparatus; and many other valuable specialties. The house has achieved international celebrity for the elegance and integrity of its standard pharmaceutical preparations, made especially for the apothecaries' dispensing counter, which are favorite brands with the medical profession generally. Their fruit juices have earned special fame since their first introduction, in 1888, when they were pioneers in this country, a domestic article of this class having never before been produced here. Their advent made new possibilities for the soda fountain, which has now, in all parts of the country, come to be recognized as the refreshing and healthful fount for quenching thirst and gratifying the palate. They carry at all times a thoroughly comprehensive line of galenical preparations, representing thousands of items which are constantly being added to. All the departments are under the superintendence of educated chemists and pharmacists; substantial inducements are offered to the trade as regards both quality and prices. The goods are in heavy and permanent demand in all parts of the United States and branch houses are operated by this firm in New York, Boston, Chicago and Pittsburg. The proprietors—Messrs. Edward H. Hance, Joseph C. Hance, Anthony M. Hance and Edward H. Hance, Jr.—are native Philadelphians, and both by reason of their vast practical experience and high order of professional attainments are eminently fitted for meeting the exacting requirements of the medical profession. They are noted for their care in the selection of crude drugs and other materials entering into the vast list of the preparations they supply, and which cover every branch of the materia medica, and are worthy of the marked appreciation accorded by their wide circle of intelligent patrons.

HOMAS HAWKINS, Manufacturer of Ornamental, Cut, Stained and Leaded Glass, Northeast Corner Thirteenth and Cumberland Streets. The growth of artistic taste in the decoration of both public and private buildings has caused the manufacture of ornamental, cut and stained glass to become a steadily developing industry. A most worthy Philadelphia house engaged in this line is that of Thomas Hawkins, situated at the northeast corner of Thirteenth and Cumberland Streets. The business was founded in 1885 by Mr. Hawkins, who had passed a thorough experience in the ornamental glass industry, and since starting for himself has built up a large, first-class trade, permeating the entire country. The works are comprised in a commodious, two-story building, affording a superficial area of 5,000 square feet. The equipment is most thorough, all approved appliances having been provided, and the machinery is driven by steam-power. Employment is found for from seventeen to twenty hands. Mr. Hawkins personally directs their labors and manufactures ornamental, cut, stained and leaded glass of every description, including glass signs, decorated cut glass for windows and doors, in latest designs, and makes a leading specialty of leaded and stained glass for private houses. Particular attention is also given to repairing stained and leaded glass. Only the finest class of work is turned out, as an inspection of the large stock carried will show. Any design desired can be obtained here at shortest notice, and first-class work is guaranteed in every instance. Mr. Hawkins was born in Philadelphia in 1856. He is a member of the Knights of the Golden Chain and the United Friends, and is popular as an able, conscientious and enterprising business man.

HISTORICAL AND COMMERCIAL PHILADELPHIA.

NATIONAL BANK OF GERMANTOWN, Main Street, Corner of School Street.—Foremost among the live financial institutions in this section of the city, to which our business men look with confidence and pride, is the old, reliable National Bank of Germantown, whose handsome bank building, erected two years ago, is located at the above address. This flourishing fiscal corporation was founded in 1811, as the Germantown Bank, and in 1864 it became a National Bank. Its financial history, during its eighty years of existence, is one long story of enduring prosperity, achieved as the reward of able and skillful management, and of the constant maintenance of the most rigid principles, having for their vital element, honor and integrity. The character of the business undertaken by the bank is of a general order; the institution being conducted upon a basis of conservatism, appropriately tempered with progressiveness to suit the exigencies of an enterprising commercial country. Following is the bank's report, presented Sept. 30, 1892. Resources. Loans and discounts, $1,516,563.02; over drafts, $555.11; United States bonds to secure circulation, $50,000.00; other stocks, bonds, and mortgages, $124,275.00; due from approved reserve agents, $138,880.91; due from other National Banks, $98,265.23; due from State banks and bankers, $20,000.00; real estate, furniture and fixtures, $100,000.00; other real estate and mortgages, $25,959.87; current expenses and taxes paid, $15,533.68; premiums paid, $5,508.32; specie, United States and National bank notes, $207,540.80; Total, $2,363,272.38. Liabilities.—Capital stock paid in $200,000.00; surplus fund, $200,000.00; undivided profits, $18,102.59; National bank notes outstanding, $42,100.00; dividends unpaid, $4,082.00; individual deposits subject to check, $1,578,755.31; due to other National banks, $41,255.48; Total, $2,363,272.38. The correspondents of the National Bank of Germantown are the Importers' and Traders' National and Central National Banks of New York, and the First National Bank of Chicago. The officers and directors of the bank are as follows: President, W. W. Wister; cashier, Canby S. Tyson; vice-president, C. W. Otto; directors, W. Wyman Wister, W. Wynne Wister, Jr., C. W. Otto, Jabez Gates, Conyers Button, J. E. Jones, Joseph Bosler, Daniel Williams, William W. Johnson, M. D., C. J. Wister, J. R. Gates, Benjamin Allen, C. S. Tyson. Mr. Wister has been president for the past thirty years; Mr. Otto has been with this bank for the past forty years, and virtually fills the position of president, and Mr. Tyson has held the office of cashier the past seven years, prior to which he was for fifteen years a teller in the Farmers' and Mechanics' National Bank. The bank is ably officered, and it deservedly commands the confidence of the entire community.

C. W. Otto, Vice-President.

D. K. BORCKY, Practical Copper, Tin and Sheet Iron Worker, No. 2736 Germantown Avenue.—For all the best makes of gas, gasolene, oil and coal stoves, ranges and heaters, silver and agate-iron ware, kitchen utensils and house furnishing goods, Mr. D. K. Borcky, located at No. 2736 Germantown Avenue, is held in high repute as being a reliable dealer, handling genuine qualities of goods at the lowest prices. Mr. Borcky is also well known as the patentee and sole manufacturer of the celebrated "Genuine" washing-machine, which has many points of superiority over all others. In addition, a full line of copper, tin and sheet iron work is undertaken, including roofing, gutters, piping, flues, etc.; bath tubs are re-lined, refrigerators, gas, gasolene and oil stoves are repaired and a specialty is made of repairing and painting tin roofs. Mr. Borcky did the mill work for Ivins, Dietz & Magee, on the iron carpet mill at Lehigh Avenue and Marshall Street, and also the mill work for the Reading Screw Works at Hope Street near Lehigh Avenue. He also did the heater work for Dennis Mahoney in his residence at Tenth and Westmoreland Streets, and on many other mills, stores and residences in the city and vicinity. The enterprise was established on November 1, 1889, by the present proprietor, who possesses twenty-one years' practical experience in the trade and personally conducts every detail of the business; selecting the stock and materials with the utmost care, accurately and promptly fulfilling all orders, etc. Of the several kinds of goods made and dealt in, an abundant assortment is always on hand for customers to choose from; the store, 17 x 26 feet in size, is well arranged and the heavy trade controlled, reaching all over the city, furnishes regular employment for six skilled assistants. Mr. D. K. Borcky was born in Berks County, Pa., and is now thirty-eight years of age.

POTTER & SEYMOUR, Real Estate and Conveyancing, No. 1851 Main Street, Germantown.—For several years past Messrs. Potter & Seymour, located at No. 1854 Main Street, have been prominently identified with the progress and development of real estate interests in Germantown and vicinity. The firm are held in high repute for the expeditious transaction of all commissions, for making prompt and accurate settlements, and their services are now called into requisition for all branches of the profession; more particularly, however, for the purchase, sale and exchange of realty throughout this section, the letting of premises, the collection of house and ground rents and interest, the examination and preparation of titles, deeds, leases, and similar legal instruments, and the settlement, transfer and entire management of estates, while the firm's facilities are systematic and complete for the speedy negotiation of loans upon bond or mortgage upon the most favorable terms. The business was established under the same name in 1872, at the present location by Mr. Joseph K. Potter and Mr. E. B. Seymour, and in 1875 the former gentleman was succeeded by his brother, Mr. W. F. Potter, he and Mr. Seymour being now the copartners. In addition to the lines already noted, the several duties incidental to the office of notary public are undertaken. Mr. W. F. Potter was born in this city, while Mr. F. B. Seymour, who possesses twenty-six years' practical experience in the profession, is a native of Virginia, whence he came to Philadelphia in 1872.

HISTORICAL AND COMMERCIAL PHILADELPHIA.

 IRD BROS., Wholesale and Retail Cash Grocers, S. E. Corner Second and Moore Streets. A well known and enterprising firm of wholesale and retail grocers in South Philadelphia is that of Messrs. Bird Bros., located at the southeast corner of Second and Moore Streets, who possess every facility for filling large or small orders promptly and satisfactorily, alike as to genuine and reliable quality and rock bottom prices. A full line of staple and fancy groceries is handled, including, among other things, choice China and Japan teas of direct importation, Java and Mocha coffees in original packages, pure spices, the standard brands of family and biscuit flour, canned and bottled goods of every kind, and a rich assortment of imported table delicacies. The trade controlled, reaching all over this section of the city, is conducted partly at wholesale, although retail is the specialty, and two wagons are kept constantly busy in the collection and delivery of orders. This flourishing business has steadily accrued during the eight years that it has been conducted under the skilful direction of the present proprietors, Messrs. Wm. O. and Geo. A. Bird, who are thoroughly practical grocers of long and varied experience. The premises utilized consist of a floor and basement, each 20x100 feet in area, containing a heavy and carefully chosen stock of the several lines of goods dealt in; five competent assistants being regularly employed. The Messrs. Bird are young gentlemen of Irish birth, and have resided in Philadelphia for a number of years.

 AGEE ART COMPANY, Manufacturers of Art Novelties, Christmas and New Year Cards, Valentines, Easter and Birthday Souvenirs, Etc., No. 1006 Walnut Street.—Since Mr. Geo. V. Magee inaugurated this enterprise he has built up a large, superior trade all through the United States and Canada, and he has achieved a first class reputation for the superior character of his productions. The business premises comprise a four story building, 25x90 feet in dimensions. Every facility and convenience has been provided for the successful conduct of affairs, and employment is found for from twenty-five to thirty skilled hands. Mr. Magee manufactures a general line of art novelties, Christmas and New Year cards, valentines, Easter and birthday cards, photo holders, silk, celluloid and paper novelties, sachets, bags, etc., and deals in etchings, oil paintings, engravings and handpainted articles. He turns out from eight hundred to nine hundred different varieties of art novelties, and fancy stationery, the goods all being of excellent workmanship and finish. A heavy stock is at all times kept on hand, and both a wholesale and retail trade is supplied. The house is represented on the road by six travelling salesmen, and a branch office is maintained in New York. Mr. Magee is a native of Philadelphia where he is well and favorably known.

 W. MONTGOMERY, Fruit and Produce Commission Merchant, No. 9 Vine Street.—A well known and very successful fruit and produce commission merchant in Philadelphia, controlling a heavy and regular wholesale and retail trade of a local nature, is Mr. R. W. Montgomery. During the four years of his establishment Mr. Montgomery has experienced a steady and continuous success, until he now receives large regular consignments of fresh fruits of all kinds in their respective seasons, produce and vegetables direct from many of the best growers throughout Pennsylvania, New Jersey, Delaware, Maryland, Virginia and the Southern States, for disposal upon this market, and thus he is enabled to offer to consumers some liberal inducements, as to price, fresh quality, rock bottom prices, and the prompt fulfillment of all orders. A specialty is made of staple produce, such as potatoes, onions, cabbages, etc., which are always kept in stock in sufficient quantities to meet all but special demands without delay. A spacious floor and basement are occupied, and every facility is at hand for the successful conduct of the business. Mr. R. W. Montgomery, who has been engaged in this line of trade for the past ten years, was born in Delaware and is a resident of Camden.

 ARRIS, FULLER & SMITH, Stock Brokers, No. 402 Library Street.—Among the leading stock brokers of Philadelphia may be mentioned Mr. Wm. C. Smith, who is a member of the firm of Harris, Fuller & Smith of No. 402 Library Street. Mr. Smith has been established as a stock broker in this city since 1885, and the present firm was organized in Feb., 1892. He was formerly of the firm of Lee & Smith, and was for several years with E. W. Matthews. This firm are in possession of the best possible facilities for the purchase and sale of all kinds of railroad and mining stocks, bonds and investment securities, either for cash or on a margin, on commission. Orders are made at once, and transfers executed together with all business of this nature as readily as could be done in New York, this office being connected by wire with the New York office of Harris & Fuller at Nos. 44 and 46 Broadway. All business trusted to this firm is dealt with promptly and in a manner which secures the greatest advantage to customers. Mr. Smith is a native of New York State, but has been for many years a resident of Philadelphia. He is a member of the Stock Exchange of Philadelphia, and is a man of excellent standing in financial circles. They also do an extensive business at the New York office.

 CURDY & HALLOWELL, Conveyancers, Real Estate and Insurance Brokers, No. 731 Walnut Street and No. 677 North Fifteenth Street.—There are numbers of our citizens who pursue the occupation of real estate brokers with credit and success, and earn a well merited reputation for the conscientious and efficient manner with which they conduct affairs intrusted to their charge. Prominent among the number thus referred to is the firm of McCurdy & Hallowell, whose offices are located at No. 731 Walnut Street and No. 677 North Fifteenth Street. This business was established in 1890, and the firm have gained an influential and liberal clientage, numbering among their patrons many wealthy investors, large property owners and active operators. The firm conduct a general business in the sale, purchase, exchange and letting of real estate. They promptly negotiate loans on bond and mortgage, and invest money for clients on first class security. Fire insurance policies in first class companies are also procured at lowest rates, and a specialty is made of the care and management of estates. Messrs. McCurdy and Hallowell are each recognized as an authority as regards both present and prospective values of the residential and business property of Philadelphia and its suburbs, while their extensive and influential connections afford excellent facilities for the immediate disposal of any realty placed in their hands. Both members of the firm are natives of this city, and are regarded as among our most enterprising and reliable young business men.

 NOCH T. ROBERTS, Coal, Flour and Feed, No. 4931 Main Street.—The oldest and most popular enterprise engaged in the handling of coal, flour and feed in Germantown is that conducted by Mr. Enoch T. Roberts, whose office and store are situated at No. 4934 Main Street. This responsible house has long been a leading source of supply hereabout for the finest grades of anthracite and bituminous coal, carefully selected, picked and screened for private families, bakers and other retail consumers; and the extent of its operations may be fairly gauged from the fact that the annual sales of coal aggregate more than twelve thousand tons. In addition, an extensive business is controlled in feed of all kinds and the standard brands of flour, the daily sales amounting to a carload lot. As in coal, so in flour and feed the facilities are complete for procuring shipments direct from the best sources of supply upon the most advantageous terms, and the house is thereby enabled to place its customers upon the fairest basis, alike as to price, quality and prompt delivery. The yard, situated on Cumberland Street, covers an area of one and a half acres, and is provided with sheds, bins, coal pockets, and every facility for the conduct of the business. A heavy stock of hard and soft coal, fine flour and feed is always on hand; four competent assistants are regularly employed around the premises, and three wagons are retained for delivery purposes. Two railroad sidings run into the yard, so that cars direct from the mines, as also cars of flour and feed, are enabled to unload right on the spot. The business was established twenty-seven years ago by the present proprietor, Mr. Enoch T. Roberts, who was born in Germantown, as also were his ancestors for generations back.

HISTORICAL AND COMMERCIAL PHILADELPHIA.

OBERT L. M. CAMDEN, Jr., & BROTHER, Designers, Artists, Illustrators, No. 729 Walnut Street.—One of the leading designers, artists and illustrators in Philadelphia is the responsible firm of Robert L. M. Camden, Jr., & Brother, located at No. 729 Walnut Street, who enjoy the highest reputation for the excellence of their productions, the originality and beauty of their designs, and the accuracy of their work. The firm's operations consist for the most part in a general line of commercial work, such as the preparation and supply of wood, steel, photo and other engravings of all kinds, pictorial, artistic, special and copper plate work, for illustrated catalogues, pamphlets, certificates, bonds, elaborate letter heads, etc.; this and a large quantity of more or less similar work is executed either to furnished designs, sketches or drawings, or to original designs of the firm's own creation, from the plainest to the most richly artistic and elaborate. Engravings, etchings, blocks, etc., are also prepared

from photographs, from the objects themselves, or from any kind of picture or illustration, the size required, whether larger or smaller than the original, being quite immaterial, and in all these matters the results are of the finest description; a true reproduction of the finest finish and of clear and accurate delineation. The business was established at the same location seven years ago by Mr. Robert L. M. Camden, Jr., who in 1891 admitted his brother, Mr. Horace P. Camden, into partnership, and the large, permanent trade now controlled reaches among regular patrons throughout all sections of the United States. A suite of five rooms on the third floor at No. 729 Walnut Street is occupied and a full equipment of improved tools, materials, appliances and accessories is at hand for the systematic conduct of the business, four expert artists and engravers being there regularly employed. Of the talented proprietors, who are both young men, Mr. Robert L. M. Camden, Jr., was born in California, but has lived in Philadelphia for the past thirty years, while Mr. Horace P. Camden is a native of this city.

OHN SHARP & SON, Wholesale Grocers, No. 15 Market Street, No. 1 North Front and No. 2 North Water Streets.—The oldest active representative of the wholesale grocery trade in Philadelphia is Mr. John Sharp, the venerable head of the firm of John Sharp & Son, whose warehouse is at No. 15 Market Street, No. 1 North Front and No. 2 North Water Streets. Mr. Sharp was born in 1805, on the high seas, and since 1823 has lived in this city. He has now attained his eighty-seventh year, and has long been known as a most estimable, public spirited citizen, and a representative, honorable merchant. He began business in 1836, and has always been located at the same address. In 1864 he admitted to a partnership interest his son, Mr. Samuel R Sharp, when the present firm name was adopted. Mr. Samuel R. Sharp is a native Philadelphian, entered his father's establishment at an early age, and is a thoroughly experienced business man of sound executive ability. The business premises comprise five spacious floors, and they are stored with a very heavy assortment of foreign and domestic groceries of every variety, also clover and timothy seed. The trade supplied extends through this State, New Jersey, Delaware and Maryland. The firm employ two traveling salesmen. Many of the patrons have been customers of the house for a long term of years. The liberal policy followed by the firm assures the fulfilment of orders upon the most satisfactory terms. Messrs. Sharp are members of the Grocers' and Importers' Exchange, and the Philadelphia Bourse, and they command the unbounded respect and confidence of the entire mercantile community.

AXSON, COMFORT & CO., Funeral Supplies, Nos. 529 and 531 Arch Street.—In comparison with the business done in the line of funeral supplies by the house of Messrs. Paxson, Comfort & Co., at Nos. 529 and 531 Arch Street, and Nos. 521, 526 and 528 Cherry Street, all other similar institutions pale in importance and magnitude. Theirs is the largest establishment of the kind in the world, and in its character a monument of commercial greatness. The business premises comprise a splendid seven story building, 40x300 feet in dimensions, with an extension of 40 feet in rear on Cherry Street, and the facilities for production are on the most extensive scale. The supplies manufactured and handled by this firm embrace every conceivable description of wood, metal and cloth covered caskets, burial robes, shrouds and burial case linings, coffin hardware, trimmings, and undertakers' supplies generally; while they also deal in horses, carriages and hearses. They manufacture their own trimmings, and handle the products of half a dozen manufactories in the lines indicated. In every pattern and style shown, the variety of which is as wide as the possibilities of the industry will admit, the greatest taste and elegance obtains, and the beauty and finish of the work stands unrivalled in the market and distances competition. Under the system prevailing, each branch of the business represents an establishment in itself, the organization being so thorough that even the smallest detail is subject to the influence of well defined order and method. The firm justly merit the title of "leader in funeral fashions." It places upon this market entirely new and original styles of burial robes, made adjustable to the form, close fitting, accurate in detail, and presenting the appearance of costumes made to measure. The trade of the house extends to every part of the United States, and continues to increase in extent and importance, shipments being also made to South America, Mexico and other foreign ports. With their immense resources this demand is readily met, and the facilities enjoyed give peculiar advantages which inure to the benefit of dealers. A force of 110 skilled hands is employed in the factory, and a dozen talented salesmen represent the interests of the house upon the road. The individual members of this firm are Messrs. Moses Paxson, Howard Comfort and E. T. Comfort, all of whom are natives of Bucks County, Pa. Mr. Paxson started a general country store at Newton, Pa., on April 10, 1852, came to Philadelphia, and embarked in the dry goods business as a member of the firm of Paxson, Shubert & Co. In 1874 the present business was established in a small way on Church Street, and in 1883 the firm moved into their new building. Mr. Howard Comfort is a graduate of Haverford College, and a trustee of that college, and also of the Insane Hospital at Frankford, and the Lincoln Home for the Colored Race. All the partners are expert authorities in their line of trade, and employ every legitimate and honorable means to further the commercial and industrial interests of Philadelphia.

HISTORICAL AND COMMERCIAL PHILADELPHIA.

ONPAREIL VEST MANUFACTURING COMPANY, M. J. Cohen, Manager, No. 501 Market Street. The Nonpareil Vest Manufacturing Company, though less than two years old, has displayed such intelligent enterprise and built up such a large and important business that it now ranks with the leading concerns in the city engaged in the manufacture of clothing. The business was established in January, 1891, by Hexter Bros., and in July of the same year it passed into the hands of its present manager, Mr. M. J. Cohen. The specialty of the house is the manufacture of white and fancy vests for the wholesale trade, and from the start the goods have had a large sale with the leading wholesale dealers in Philadelphia and New York. The goods are made in the best manner of carefully selected materials, and in style, finish and general workmanship they are not excelled by any in the trade. The plant and warerooms occupy the four upper floors of a six-story building, which are equipped with every improved appliance for the manufacture of goods and the handling of an immense stock. Power is furnished by an electric motor and a freight elevator conveys the goods from the different floors. A force of 250 people find employment in the different departments of the business. Mr. M. J. Cohen, to whose enterprise and sagacity the success of this thriving business is due, is a native of Germany, but was raised in England and has been in the United States for the last thirteen years.

EWIS L. BAILEY & CO., Manufacturers of Ladies' and Children's Cloaks, No. 507 Market Street. The success which has attended this house furnishes a striking illustration of what enterprise, sagacity and honorable business methods can accomplish. Mr. Lewis L. Bailey established the business here in 1877, under the present firmname, and, by observing a straightforward policy in all his dealings, his business has grown step by step to its present magnitude. He occupies three floors, 20 x 120 feet each, and gives employment to fifty skilled hands in the house and to some two hundred outside. Confining himself to the manufacture of ladies' and children's cloaks and producing a stylish and well-made garment at a very reasonable cost, his output is in great and increasing demand wherever once introduced, and he now sends goods to all parts of the United States. He buys his materials in vast quantities direct from the manufacturers on terms which smaller competitors cannot command, and, having superior facilities for the production of a high order of goods, he is always in the forefront with the latest changes in fashion, and permits no garment to leave his establishment which will not bear comparison with the best custom-made article. A corps of expert salesmen represent the interests of the house upon the road, while a branch office is in operation in Chicago. Mr. Bailey is a native of Philadelphia, and an experienced and talented manufacturer.

HARLES E. ZANE, Importer of Kid Gloves, Fabric Gloves and Silk Mitts, No. 731 Arch Street. Mr. Charles E. Zane is a direct importer of kid gloves, fabric gloves and silk mitts, handling the highest grades of goods of both foreign and home production, and making a leading specialty of the finest kid gloves in the market. He established his business here in 1879, and has built up a trade connection co-extensive with the limits of the entire country. The specialties in kid gloves which Mr. Zane is now offering to the trade are the most famous in the brilliant capitals of Europe, and renowned for their durability, fitting qualities, elasticity, pliability and fine finish. He carries at all times an immense stock of all colors and sizes for both ladies and gentlemen, the leading shades for evening wear including white, pearl, lavender, flesh, cream, lemon, fon, fawn, drab and light slate; for ordinary wear the darker shades embrace dark slate, dark stone, plum, olive brown, tan, dark brown, and navy blue. Each and every one of these gloves is warranted to be accurate in fit, of fast colors, and of the best general construction and make. They will be found to be the best gloves in this country or Europe. A corps of sixteen talented salesmen represent the interests of the house upon the road. Mr. Zane is a native of New Jersey, an expert authority in the glove trade, and a young man of large business experience.

RED. L. FOSTER & SONS, Boot and Shoe Makers and Rubber Shoe Brokers, Etc., Nos. 128 and 130 Market Street. One of the most progressive of the leading houses engaged in this field of commerce is that of Messrs. Fred. L. Foster & Sons. This widely-known establishment was founded in 1862 by Messrs. Foster, Meixell & Co., and was continued under that management up to 1885, when the firm of Fred. L. Foster & Sons was organized, the copartners being Mr. Fred. L. Foster and his sons John B. and Fred E. Foster. Two years ago Mr. Conrad F. Clothier, Jr., was also admitted to partnership. Mr. Fred. L. Foster, senior member of the firm, was born in Portsmouth, N. H., and his sons are natives of Pottsville, Pa., while Mr. Clothier was born in this city. The business premises occupied comprise two connecting buildings, each four stories in height, and having dimensions of 20 x 124 feet each. They are lighted by electricity, have a freight elevator, and every facility is possessed for the receipt, storage, and handling of goods. The firm control the products of several large factories, and are general boot and shoe makers and rubber shoe brokers. Their house is the Philadelphia headquarters for Goodyear's India Rubber Glove Manufacturing Co., of New York. An immense stock is carried, and an active trade is supplied throughout the Middle States, south to Georgia, and west as far as the new State of Washington. A number of salesmen represent the firm on the road. The firm has opened up a large trade throughout the entire country and has sold some export orders through its unique and novel system of advertising which has culminated in an exposition of their entire line in a handsome catalogue, which they have appropriately styled " Foster's Little Quaker." They request the trade to send for the catalogue. "The Little Quaker" will do the rest.

AWSON & ADAMS, Real Estate and Mortgage Brokers, No. 2712 Germantown Avenue, Tenth and Lehigh Avenue. There are perhaps not any among Philadelphia real estate men who are better known or stand higher in public esteem than Dawson & Adams, whose office is at No. 2712 Germantown Avenue. They have been established since 1884, and have a large patronage, numbering in their clientele some of the most prominent property owners in the community. Messrs. A. M. Dawson and Jno. P. Adams, who compose the firm, are Philadelphians by birth. They are general real estate brokers, buying, selling and exchanging city and suburban property of every description on commission, and carry on their books a number of choice building lots and residences which they offer for sale on the most favorable terms, on easy payments. Particular attention is given to the collection of rents and interests, and prompt returns are made for the same; and estates are taken in charge and judiciously managed. Mortgages are negotiated, also, and money is procured on real estate, at lowest rates of interest. Conveyancing in all its branches is attended to, likewise, and insurance placed with first-class fire companies; and all business intrusted to this reliable firm is certain to be handled in the most careful, capable and satisfactory manner. Mr. Dawson is a prominent Mason and Mr. Adams is active as a member of the Royal Arcanum, Girard Council No. 1017.

cKAY & KAHLER, Terra Cotta Sewer Pipe, Vitrified Paving Brick, Etc., Broad and Glenwood Avenue, Germantown Junction, P. R. R. This thriving and prosperous business was established in 1888, by George McKay, who conducted it up to about two years ago, when he took into partnership Oscar A. Kahler. The firm are dealers in terra cotta sewer pipe, vitrified paving brick, fine ornamental building brick, fire brick, chimney tops, flue lining, lawn vases, and all other clay products. They also deal in various brands of imported and domestic cements, etc., and their trade, which is very large, is steadily growing. Their yard, which is conveniently situated at Broad and Glenwood Avenue, Germantown Junction, P. R. R., covers an acre of ground and the facilities are first-class in every respect. A big stock is constantly kept on hand here, and an efficient staff of help is employed, while several wagons deliver throughout the city. Mr. McKay, the senior member, was born in Ireland; and Mr. Kahler, his partner, is a man in the prime of life and a native of this city.

HISTORICAL AND COMMERCIAL PHILADELPHIA.

CHARLES BROSSMANN, Thirty-eighth Street and Powelton Avenue.—Of the many finely equipped stables of which Philadelphia may justly boast, one in the western section of the city which deserves more than passing mention in these pages is that conducted by Mr. Charles Brossmann, at No. 8 North Thirty-eighth Street. This genial establishment is devoted to the boarding, sale and exchange of fine horses, and is popularly regarded by horsemen as the most reliable hereabouts. As a boarding-stable it is complete and self-contained for the efficient care and comfort of the horse, more particularly for fine road stock; any kind of horse being taken in by the day, week or under contract. The finest qualities of provender and bedding are used, an ample supply of pure, fresh water is at hand, and sick horses are promptly attended to by an experienced veterinary surgeon. The establishment is, however, most favorably known as a speedy and trustworthy medium for the purchase, sale and exchange of trotters, road and saddle horses; and a large number of high-bred saddle stock is always on hand, together with trained harness horses. The stable consists of two commodious floors, divided into stalls, loose boxes, etc., accommodating many horses; every provision is made for efficient light, uniformity of temperature, ventilation, facility of cleansing and ample water supply and drainage; and a full equipment of stable requisites and supplies is furnished. Mr. Charles Brossmann is also the proprietor and director of the Powelton Riding Academy, at the corner of Powelton Avenue and Thirty-eighth Street, initiated September, 1890. This fashionable academy, is much frequented by ladies, gentlemen, misses, youths and children, and a large number of proficient equestrians have received their initial lessons here. There is a ring of oval shape, 40 feet across one way and 80 the other, and several docile tractable horses are kept in constant readiness. Mr. Charles Brossmann, who is a thoroughly practical and expert equestrian, is a native of Germany, and has been engaged for many years in the horse business, and is acknowledged to be the best and most successful trainer of horses and teacher of horsemanship in Philadelphia.

JOHN HOHENADEL, Brewer, Corner Queen Street and Norristown Railroad, Falls of Schuylkill.—The brewery of Mr. John Hohenadel was established in 1860 by Mr. John W. Hohenadel, and at his death, in 1888, he was succeeded by his son, Mr. John Hohenadel. This gentleman was born in this city, is prominently known in fraternal and social circles, and is a skilled, practical brewer. The plant covers an area of 300 by 400 feet, upon which are erected a number of brick buildings especially adapted for the business. The products include lager beer and porter, and the output amounts to 5,000 barrels yearly. A leading specialty is made of lager. Only the finest malt and hops that can be procured are used, and they are handled in such a thoroughly scientific manner as to result in the production of a pure, finely flavored, and sparkling beer that really has no superior.

WALTER L. LEWIS, Paper Hangings, Frescoing and Interior Art Decorations, No. 2012 Pine Street.—A representative house in the line of frescoing and interior art decorations in Philadelphia is that of Mr. Walter L. Lewis, located at No. 2012 Pine Street. This gentleman established his business here in 1890, and has won a high reputation for the artistic merits of his work. He carries a large and well-selected stock of paper hangings, which commend their own merits to the confidence and patronage of the most critical and discriminating buyers, while he makes a specialty of general interior decorating in fresco work, wall tinting, etc., and his work in churches, residences and public buildings is greatly admired by experts, and forms the best possible recommendation, his only needed endorsement. He did the frescoing, papering and painting in the building of the Society for the Prevention of Cruelty to Children, and also the interior work of the Mirvis Building, No. 715 Arch Street, the walls of which were done in Boston felt, and the ceilings in china gloss paints, and a fine sample of his work may be seen in the frescoing and papering of the residence of Police Captain William Brown, No. 1719 Pine Street. His services are in important and increasing demand throughout the city and surrounding country, and are rendered in such a manner as to add materially to his popularity and insure his continued success. Mr. Lewis is a native Philadelphian, a thorough master of his art in all its branches, and an enterprising, progressive and reliable young business man who is winning success by honestly deserving it.

J. M. HESS, Manufacturer of and Dealer in Stoves, Heaters and Ranges, No. 2432 Germantown Avenue.—Beyond question the business conducted by Mr. J. M. Hess, located at No. 2432 Germantown Avenue, as a manufacturer of and dealer in stoves, heaters and ranges and a general sheet metal worker, is the oldest of the kind in Philadelphia, for it was established as far back as 1757, by Mr. F. M. Hess, and, in 1840, it came into the hands of his son of the same name, who died December 25, 1873, at the advanced age of eighty-eight years. At that date the business was assumed by his son, Mr. J. M. Hess, who had started for himself in 1862, and died in 1886, when his son, the present proprietor, succeeded. All kinds of tin, zinc, copper and sheet-iron work are executed in the best style to order, tin roofing, conductors, spouting and guttering are undertaken, roofs are painted and repaired, boilers are set and jobbing in all branches receives prompt attention; while stoves, heaters and ranges are made, supplied and fitted up complete with all piping and connections. The trade controlled reaches all over the city and adjacent districts, and its volume furnishes regular employment for several skilled assistants. A large stock of stoves, heaters, ranges, trade requisites and supplies, tinware and kitchen utensils is always on hand, and the popular prices command ready sales. Mr. J. M. Hess is thoroughly practical in this line and takes an active part in the prompt and accurate fulfillment of all orders, whether sent by mail or otherwise. He was born in Philadelphia, on December 14, 1862, and is a member of the Knights of the Golden Eagle, the Red Men and the Independent Order of Odd Fellows.

G. W. & W. D. HEWITT, Architects, Bullitt Building, No. 133 South Fourth Street.—The subjects of this sketch, Messrs. G. W. and W. D. Hewitt, are architects of whom Philadelphia and the country at large may well be proud. Monuments significant of their ability and legitimate architectural taste, stand pre-eminent in the shape of magnificent buildings, which go far toward making this city one of the most beautiful, as a whole, in the world. Both have had long and valuable experience. Mr. G. W. Hewitt first studied under the mentorship of John Notman, this city, and afterward was for eight years a member of the firm of Furness & Hewitt. Mr. W. D. Hewitt studied with the latter firm, afterward studying abroad for a year and a-half. Twenty years ago the Messrs. Hewitt organized the present copartnership and have since won a flattering reputation. The buildings erected under their supervision include the Bullitt Building, in which Messrs. Hewitt have their office; the Episcopal Hospital, Hahnemann Hospital, Devon Inn, Wissahickon Inn, hotel at Tacoma, Washington; Stratford Hotel, Holy Trinity Parish building, Pennsylvania Trust Company's building, at Reading; Wistar Museum of Anatomy, at the University of Pennsylvania, etc. The success attained by the firm has been the result of diligent study and natural ability, combined with a straightforward system of honorable dealing

HISTORICAL AND COMMERCIAL PHILADELPHIA.

HILADELPHIA SUPPLY COMPANY (Canby & Costello), Manufacturers of Steam and Hydraulic Packing of Every Description, also Rubber Goods, No. 235 North Front Street.—This company are manufacturers of steam and hydraulic packing of every description, also rubber goods of various kinds, and established their business here in 1889. They occupy an entire four story building, supplied with new and improved machinery, and possess every facility for conducting the business under the most favorable conditions and upon the largest scale. Their packings are recognized as absolutely unrivalled for quality, durability, utility and uniform excellence, having no superiors in the European or American markets. They supply many of the largest manufacturers in Philadelphia, and also furnish engineers' supplies of every description in quantities to suit at the shortest possible notice. They also handle Turner's Traction Belt Grease and Leather Preservative, for rubber, leather and canvas belting. This softens and preserves the leather, counteracts moisture, prevents slipping and stretching, removes glazing from rubber, and prevents fraying of edges. It is used preferentially by the leading mills, foundries, iron works, machine shops, flour mills and manufactories of every large city in the Union. The proprietors, Messrs. Chas. Canby and Geo. M. Costello, are native Philadelphians and young men of large practical experience, who are destined to attain great success in their vast and fertile field of usefulness.

ENNSYLVANIA OPTICAL COMPANY (Limited), Manufacturers of All Kinds of Optical Goods, Sole Owners and Manufacturers of Bellati's Adjustable Offset Guard, No. 1018 Chestnut Street.—The Pennsylvania Optical Company (Limited) was initiated at the same location three and a half years ago, and was duly incorporated under the laws of the State of Pennsylvania, the officers being Mr. F. Bachman, President (a physician practising in the city), and Mr. A. J. Bellati, Secretary and Manager, under whose able and experienced direction every detail of the business is conducted. The company's operations include the manufacture of all kinds of optical goods, the grinding and polishing of pebbles for spectacles, eyeglasses, lenses, etc., every description of repairing incidental to the trade, and as a specialty the accurate fulfilment of oculists' prescriptions, while they are sole owners and manufacturers of Bellati's adjustable offset guard, the "Marvel," for which Messrs. Williams, Brown & Earle are selling agents. This eyeglass guard is a most ingenious though simple contrivance, and can be attached to any of the old forms of eyeglasses. The heavy and permanent trade controlled by the company reaches all over the United States, and its volume furnishes regular employment for five expert opticians in the manufacturing department. Mr. A. J. Bellati, who learned the trade in Connecticut and has eighteen years' practical experience at his command, was born in Italy and has resided in Philadelphia for the past nine years.

MAENE, Sculptor, No. 309 Griscom Street, Between Fourth and Fifth, Spruce and Pine.—The demand for decorations in architecture in this country is a growing one; and it is well represented in this city by Mr. E. Maene, whose office and works are at No. 309 Griscom Street, between Fourth and Fifth, Spruce and Pine Streets. This gentleman was born in Belgium, where he first studied his profession, which he has followed for the past twenty-four years. He came to this country ten years ago, coming to Philadelphia two years later, and seven years ago he established business here, meeting with excellent success. He employs from twenty to twenty-five assistants, occupies a two story building, 40x100 feet in dimensions, and executes designs for ornamental and statuary work of all kinds. He has done a large amount of carving for residences and public buildings, including the Jewish Temple, Keystone Bank, Bank at No. 927 Chestnut Street, etc. His trade extends all over the country. All of Mr. Maene's products bear the stamp of artistic excellence and the imprint of the master's hand. The city is to be congratulated upon the accession to her industries, than which no more praiseworthy institution exists within her boundaries.

HE STAR ENGRAVING AND PRINTING COMPANY (Limited), No. 118 South Seventh Street.—The Star Engraving and Printing Company (Limited), located at No. 118 South Seventh Street, rank as one of the leading engravers and designers in Philadelphia, and they now control a trade and connection of large proportions, reaching throughout the whole of the United States, East of the Mississippi River. Original designs of any sort are furnished upon application, as also estimates for all classes of work in this branch of art, and the two chief kinds of engraving executed are wood engraving and photoengraving, a specialty being made of line and stipple effects by zinc etching or photoelectrotyping, and half tone effects by copper etching. By these two latter processes, an exact representation is ensured of photographs, brush drawings, nature, and any sort of copy or pen drawings, wood cut or lithographic prints, etc., being particularly suitable for plans, maps, architects' drawings, portraits, buildings, interiors, landscapes, machinery, bill and letter heads, book work, newspapers, catalogues, etc. Every facility is possessed for executing equally the finest book work or that for the coarsest newspaper. Twenty-two artists and others are regularly employed. The company was incorporated and commenced operations at the same location three years ago, the manager being Mr H. Fischler, who has at his command five years' practical experience in the trade. Mr. Fischler is a gentleman of German birth, and has resided in the Quaker City for over twenty years. This company is now building a new plant for themselves on Centre Street near Sixth, in order to accommodate their largely increasing trade.

ENRY, BAYARD & CO., Manufacturers and Dealers in Lumber; Office and Yard, No. 2931 North Broad Street.—The transactions in lumber daily here in Philadelphia reach enormous proportions, and the volume of sale grows steadily. Notable among the representative firms contributing to the sum of activity in the line indicated is that of Henry, Bayard & Co., whose office and yard are located at No. 2931 North Broad Street, their telegraph and shipping address being Germantown Junction. They are manufacturers and dealers in lumber generally, shipping direct from mills in Pennsylvania, and make a specialty of hemlock in dimensions. They transact a wholesale business entirely, and have an exceedingly large trade, shipping throughout Pennsylvania, New Jersey, New York, Delaware, Maryland, Ohio and West Virginia. The firm's facilities, both in respect of sources of supply and for shipping, enable them to execute the largest orders at short notice. The premises occupied on North Broad Street are spacious and commodious, and a stock of hemlock, pine and oak lumber is constantly kept on hand, the total annual sales reaching many millions of feet. The house can supply hemlock lumber of all descriptions in special bills, to order, in the promptest manner. The firm is composed of Messrs. Chas. W. Henry, James Bayard, Mark D. Sproul, and John J. Henry, gentlemen of middle age and Philadelphians by birth, and are well and favorably known in lumber circles. They have been established as at present since 1867.

M. BETZ, Watches, Diamonds and Jewelry, No. 631 Chestnut Street.—An important and well known house engaged in this city as a manufacturer and dealer in fine watches, diamonds and jewelry is that of H. M. Betz. The business was established by the present proprietor ten years ago, since which time it has steadily developed in both its volume and scope. Fine watches, diamonds and plain and fancy jewelry are manufactured on the premises to order, and the goods of leading makers and importers are extensively handled, and are supplied at both wholesale and retail; a specialty being made of the sale of goods on easy terms of payment to suit the purchaser; only a nominal interest being charged on the net trade price. Branch offices are maintained throughout the Keystone State at Frankford, Chester, Easton, Reading and Altoona; and the headquarters in this city comprise a spacious room furnished with every facility, including a safe of large proportions for the efficient keeping of the choice and costly stock always on hand. Four competent assistants are regularly engaged, and a staff of ten travelling salesmen watch the best interests of the house among customers. The worthy proprietor, Mr. H. M. Betz, is a native of Frankford, Pa.,

HISTORICAL AND COMMERCIAL PHILADELPHIA.

 A. DOUGHERTY'S SONS, Distillers, No. 1136 North Front Street.—Recent improvements in the processes of distillation assure the production of spirituous liquors that are of the highest standard both in quality and purity. The oldest, largest, and most noted distillers in Philadelphia are J. A. Dougherty's Sons, whose headquarters are located at No. 1136 North Front Street. This house enjoys an international reputation and patronage for its special brand of fine whiskey, "Dougherty's Pure Rye," highly esteemed by the trade and first-class retailers, both at home and abroad, for its absolute purity, superior excellence, evenness of quality, natural flavor and fine tone properties, while it is sold under a guarantee to give perfect satisfaction. The brand of this house is widely noted for its particular merits, and is a prime favorite wherever introduced. The goods are distilled in the most careful and systematic manner, and are in every way the standard with the best class of consumers. This firm sell their own products only, and have built up a fine growing export trade with Germany and South America, while their whiskey is a standard favorite in Philadelphia, New York, Chicago, St. Louis, Baltimore, New Orleans, Washington, Atlanta, Louisville, Omaha, Denver, San Francisco, and throughout the whole country from Maine to Oregon. The works of the firm comprise a series of four and five story buildings, on each side of the street, covering a ground area of several acres; while they have their own bonded warehouse with a storage capacity of 31,000 barrels, a grain elevator holding 50,000 bushels of grain, and well-equipped cooper-shops; while the distillery has a productive capacity of 13,000 barrels annually. The prices quoted are invariably fair and equitable. The products of this house are invariably sold ahead, the demand gaining immensely each year. The house was founded in 1841 by Mr. J. A. Dougherty, who died in 1866, after placing the business upon a sound and healthy basis, and was succeeded by his sons, Messrs. C. A. Dougherty, W. H. Dougherty, and J. A. Dougherty Sr. W. H. Dougherty being deceased the firm is now composed of Messrs. C. A. Dougherty, J. A. Dougherty, E. V. Dougherty and W. H. Dougherty, the last two being sons of Mr. C. A. Dougherty. These gentlemen were all reared in the business, and have a foundation understanding of its minutest details and the requirements of the trade. All the partners are worthy exponents of this important industry, and the widespread reputation of their house has been acquired and is solely maintained on the basis of the merit of its product and the equity and integrity of its business policy.

 A. SCHWARZ, Importer of German, French and English Toys and Fancy Goods, Fancy Chinaware, Music Boxes, Etc., No. 1006 Chestnut Street.—Few persons outside of those immediately concerned have anything like an adequate idea of the extent of the wholesale and retail toy trade in this city. The growth of the important branch of mercantile activity indicated has been especially notable during the past decade or two, while the volume of business grows apace. The oldest as well as the largest house engaged in this line in Philadelphia is that of Mr. G. A. Schwarz, located at No. 1006 Chestnut Street. This house has been in successful operation since 1859, and enjoys a prestige and patronage thoroughly national in extent and eminently creditable in character. Mr. Schwarz is widely and deservedly prominent as an extensive importer of and wholesale and retail dealer in German, French and English toys, fancy chinaware, music boxes, etc. The business premises comprise an entire five-story building, 25 x 245 feet in dimensions, and unequaled facilities are at hand for conducting all operations under the most favorable auspices and upon the largest scale. The immense and valuable stock contains everything desirable in the toy line, including doll carriages, skin horses and teams, tricycles, velocipedes, express wagons, sulkies, boy carts, wheelbarrows, toys' and girls' sleds, toboggans, Edison phonographic dolls, doll houses and furniture, pianos, xylophones, zitherns, metallophones, musical boxes, symphoniums, folding board games, card games, parlor bagatelle boards, lotto games, playing cards, soldier equipments, pewter soldiers, mother goose trains, savings banks, jumping ropes, tin toys, building blocks, kindergarten occupations, school bags, roll top desks, scholars' companions, paint boxes, painting books, clothes wringers, toy knitters, hand sewing machines, tin kitchens, pewter tea sets, Punch and Judy theaters, jugglers' tricks, universal spelling boards, Christmas tree ornaments, amateur photograph outfits, telephones, electric motor and battery, printing presses, the People's typewriter, baby swings, tourist cameras, archery goods, fishing tackle, field croquet, lawn tennis, puzzles, tops, etc., etc. Importations are received direct from all the chief points in Europe and all the freshest novelties and most unique inventions are received as soon as they are ready for the trade. Mr. Schwarz is a native of Germany, a resident of this city for the past thirty five years, and one of Philadelphia's most extensive importers and representative business men.

 H. LENTZ & CO., COÖPERATIVE NICKEL PLATING COMPANY, No. 207 Quarry Street.—The Coöperative Nickle Plating Company, of the firm of W. H. Lentz & Co., was originally founded about a year ago under the above style, and under the efficient and able management and direction of Mr. Lentz, the active member of the firm, it has gained an enduring hold in the trade, and keeps steadily pushing its way to still greater popularity and recognition. The premises occupied are commodious in size, and are equipped in a first-class manner with all the best improved machinery, steam power, etc., while seven experienced and skillful hands find permanent employment therein. The range of work includes grinding, polishing and nickle plating in all its branches, which are done in the most expeditious and excellent manner for the trade. A specialty is made of sharpening clippers, and all orders receive immediate attention, while the charges are invariably placed at the lowest figures. A large and desirable class of patronage has already been developed. Mr. Lentz, who is a native of this city, is thoroughly experienced in all branches of this industry, and all his transactions are characterized by promptness, care and reliability.

 CHRISTIAN PFLAUM, Jr., Wholesale and Retail Confectionery, Southwest Corner of Fourth and Vine Streets.—Probably no line of manufacture has had a more rapid growth in the United States during the past few decades than that of fine confectionery, and it can be truthfully stated that the products of our manufacturers at the present day are fully equal to those of France, which country for many years enjoyed the reputation of producing the finest and best of these toothsome delicacies. This result has been accomplished through the energy, enterprise and skill of the leading houses engaged in the business. A decidedly prosperous, popular and reliable house engaged in this line in Philadelphia, deserving of more than passing notice in these pages in consequence of its superior goods and liberal business methods, is that of Mr. Christian Pflaum, Jr., whose fine establishment is located on the southwest corner of Fourth and Vine Streets. This well-known concern was founded originally by Mr. John Yungker, at this address in 1867, and was conducted by him with excellent success until 1884, when it passed into the control of the present proprietor. Mr. Pflaum is a native of this city and was raised in this house, having been connected with it continuously ever since 1872, and under his management of its affairs the trade has grown to its present proportions, principally wholesale and extending throughout the Middle, Eastern and Southern States, requiring the constant services of four traveling salesmen. The premises occupied are amply spacious and commodious, comprising a finely appointed store and basement, the latter being used for factory purposes, and is fully equipped with the latest improved machinery, tools and appliances, and steady employment is given to a full force of skilled and experienced hands. The range of products embraces the very choicest grades of confectionery, such as caramels, fine creams, roast and smooth almonds, fine chocolates, French fruit glacés, bonbons, French nougat, glazed chocolates, lozenges, Boston chips, penny goods, mixed candies, etc., etc. These are made fresh daily of the very purest refined cane sugar, in which none but unadulterated fruit and other extracts are used for flavoring, while the greatest caution is exercised by the proprietor that no deleterious substances are permitted to be used in his establishment, and the very lowest prices are quoted to the trade. Mr. Pflaum is a young man of superior business ability, honorable and upright in his dealings, and justly merits the success he has achieved by his perseverance and straightforward dealings.

HISTORICAL AND COMMERCIAL PHILADELPHIA.

JOSIAH BRANT, House and Sign Painter, No. 219 Arch Street.—One of the very oldest established houses of its kind in this city, is the reliable and well known concern of Josiah Brant, house and sign painter, of No. 219 Arch Street. The foundation of this flourishing business dates back many years, and was originally inaugurated by the firm of Hunsicker & Brant, who conducted it most successfully up to about fifteen years ago, when the partnership having been dissolved, the present proprietor assumed the sole control and direction of its affairs. These premises have been occupied since 1844, and comprise a commodious store, especially adapted and arranged for the purposes of the business, and stocked with a large and first-class assortment of painters' supplies of every description. As many as twenty to forty skilled and experienced workmen are employed, and the proprietor is always found prepared to execute all orders and commissions for anything in the line of painting, in all its branches, at the very lowest rates consistent with superior workmanship and fair and equitable dealings. Particular attention is given to house and sign painting of all kinds, and all the work executed is performed in the most artistic and finished manner without any unnecessary delay, satisfaction being guaranteed in every instance. Mr. Brant, who is a practical and experienced business man of entire probity in all his dealings, is widely recognized as an expert and progressive exponent of this branch of skilled industry, and his extensive trade is of the most influential and permanent character.

EDWARD J. ETTING, Iron Broker and Commission Merchant, Foreign and American Pig Iron Bars, Blooms, Scrap, Old Rails and Railroad Supplies, No. 222 South Third Street.—This gentleman has been established in this business here since 1861 and has built up a reputation and a patronage thoroughly national in extent. He is a large buyer of foreign and American pig iron bars, blooms and scrap, old rails and railroad supplies, and attends to the marketing of the product of some of the most celebrated furnaces in the United States. He is agent for the Trenton Iron Company, for the sale of wire and wire rope; is exclusive agent for the Union Mining Company, for the sale of "Mount Savage" fire brick, for Eastern Pennsylvania, West New Jersey and Delaware, and handles foundry and forge iron of different brands in large quantities. He has a storage yard at Pier No. 57 South, which is connected by track with the Pennsylvania Railroad, and where a very large and complete stock is constantly carried. Negotiable warehouse receipts are issued, and iron is weighed, stored and delivered. The proprietor numbers among his permanent customers the leading mill men of this city and State, and also has a large and influential trade throughout the United States. Those interested either here or in any part of the United States in the purchase or sale of iron and steel will find every facility afforded them by this enterprising house. Mr. Etting is a native Philadelphian and known and honored as a gentleman of sterling merit.

JOHN ROEHM, Bavarian and Lager Beer Brewer, (Telephone.) Office, No. 831 North Fourth Street; Brewery, Nos. 811-851 Charlotte Street.—The leader in the brewing of Bavarian and lager beer in Philadelphia is by common consent Mr. John Roehm. This gentleman is an expert and practical brewer of large experience and high reputation, and established his business here in 1886. The brewery is a substantial brick structure six stories high and 149 x 114 feet in dimensions, and is splendidly equipped with all the modern apparatus, machinery and appliances known to the trade. A force of twenty-five skilled assistants contribute to the satisfactory operations of the house, and the annual product averages 50,000 barrels. Only the very best malt and hops that can be purchased are utilized, and these are handled in such a scientific and careful manner as to result in the production of beer, both light and dark varieties, that really has no superior in this country for quality, purity, fine flavor and uniform excellence. It is a prime favorite with connoisseurs and large dealers in this city and throughout Pennsylvania, New Jersey and Delaware, and is highly recommended by the medical fraternity as a healthful beverage. Orders by telephone, telegraph or mail receive immediate and careful attention, and goods are delivered at terms and prices which are invariably satisfactory to consumers and the trade. Mr. Roehm is a native of Germany who came to this country in 1865. He is recognized as a useful and responsible citizen, as well as an authority in the brewing industry and is a member of the Manufacturers' Club, the F. and A. M., the Turners and other German societies.

ROBT. L. LATIMER & CO., Dealers in Bolting Cloth, and Flour Mill Supplies, No. 21 North Front Street.—Among the old established houses in this city a time-honored and widely-known one is that of R. L. Latimer & Co., dealers in bolting cloth and flour mill supplies, at No. 21 North Front Street. This business was established away back in 1835, by a Jacob B. Ritter, succeeding him came Messrs. J. M. Latimer & Co. The present firm was established in 1886, Mr. J. M. Latimer having retired. Mr. Robert L. Latimer has been connected with the house in all sixteen years, and is intimately conversant with every detail of the business. He is a native Philadelphian, a man of sound judgment and superior business ability. He has made a specialty of the celebrated Improved Genuine Dutch Anchor bolting cloth, handled by this house since 1835. He is also prepared to take orders of any magnitude for flour mill machinery, furnishing complete outfits from top to bottom. All kinds of patent mill machinery and mill supplies are carefully packed and promptly shipped to any desired point, such as roller mills, mill-stones, portable mills, middling mills, cotton, leather and gum belting, elevator buckets, conveyor digits, smut machines, bran dusters, purifiers, centrifugal reels, bolting chests, bolting cloth, etc. Mr. Latimer can point with pride to a magnificently developed trade in these articles all throughout the Southern and Western States, and Pennsylvania, Delaware, Maryland, and New Jersey, all of which is the fruit of honorable efforts well directed, and of studious interest in always selling the best goods at a margin of profit mutually fair to both buyer and seller. By these methods the firm has gained its present splendid reputation.

STRATTON ICE WORKS, Ice, Wholesale and Retail. For Table Use a Specialty, Made From Distilled City Water, No. 2610 Callowhill Street.—The best ice in the world is undoubtedly that made by the Improved Absorption Ice Machine invented by Mr. H. D. Stratton, proprietor of the Stratton Ice Works, at No. 2610 Callowhill Street. These works are the only manufacturers of ice from condensed water that has not passed through the engine, doing business in Philadelphia, and deals in ice at both wholesale and retail, made from distilled city water, a specialty being made of supplying ice for table use. Mr. Stratton, the inventor of this process of artificial ice manufacture and refrigeration, established himself in the business originally at Columbus, Ga., in 1878, removing to this city in 1890 and building his present plant, where he has two of his machines in operation and is making 120,000 pounds of ice per day, which is used by the principal hotels in Philadelphia and is supplied to ice dealers here and elsewhere. This ice is perfectly transparent and is made 11 inches thick and in 200-pound blocks. With his process of distilling water, Mr Stratton frees it from all impurities and he feels perfectly safe in making the claim that the ice made by his machines is equaled by the ice made in no other machine. Over one hundred are in use in the Southern States, and their sales are rapidly increasing in all parts of the country. They are used and endorsed by leading ice companies and large consumers in New Orleans, La.; Pittsburg, Pa.; Louisville, Ky.; Springfield, Ill.; Charleston, S. C.; Mobile, Ala.; Chattanooga, Tenn.; Savannah, Ga.; Jacksonville, Fla.; Wilmington, N. C.; Birmingham, Ala.; Galveston, Tex.; Richmond, Va.; Atlanta, Ga.; Richmond, Ind., and other places, and Mr Stratton controls the ice business in Jacksonville, Fla., and also at Pensacola, Fla. Mr. Stratton is a native Philadelphian, of excellent repute and standing in mercantile and social circles, and may be accounted among that class of energetic, public-spirited business men who build up great enterprise in every avenue of commerce and trade.

HISTORICAL AND COMMERCIAL PHILADELPHIA.

OHN JAMISON, Commission Merchant, Water and Market Streets.—The remarkable growth of the commission business of late years has placed it in a position, and given it a prominence that is assumed by very few other industries in the great city of Philadelphia. One of the houses that have exerted a large influence in promoting the status of this branch of commerce, is that of John Jamison, whose warehouse stands at the corner of Water and Market Streets. The members of this flourishing firm are thoroughly experienced in the business, to which they devote their closest attention and care, and have shown a commendable perception of the wants of the trade. The business was founded in 1849, by John Jamison, and through the energy and ability exercised he soon forged to the front, and became the acknowledged leader in his line. His death occurred in 1886, after a long, most honorable career, and he was succeeded by his sons, Messrs. John and Samuel Jamison, who were raised from youth in the business, and were amply qualified to continue the success achieved by their revered father. They are natives of this city, and members of the Fruit and Produce Exchange, National Cheese, Butter and Egg Association, and the Philadelphia Bourse. The business premises occupied comprise a five-story and basement building, 25 x 100 feet in area, and a large building adjoining. Cooling-rooms and all modern conveniences are at hand, and the public warehouses are also drawn upon for the storage of stock. This is the largest butter, egg and cheese establishment in Philadelphia, the annual sales amounting to upward of a million dollars. The Messrs. Jamison are sole agents for a number of creameries, taking their entire products, and they carry on an active business as commission merchants in butter, cheese, eggs, lard, pork, hams, canned meats, and other provisions. Consignments are received from all sections of Pennsylvania, New York, Ohio, Indiana, and the West, and the trade supplied extends through this State, New Jersey, Delaware, and the South. The activity and enterprise of this reliable firm need not be recounted, since its merits have been fully recognized in the community, and the city may well be congratulated on the possession of such a monument of commercial success.

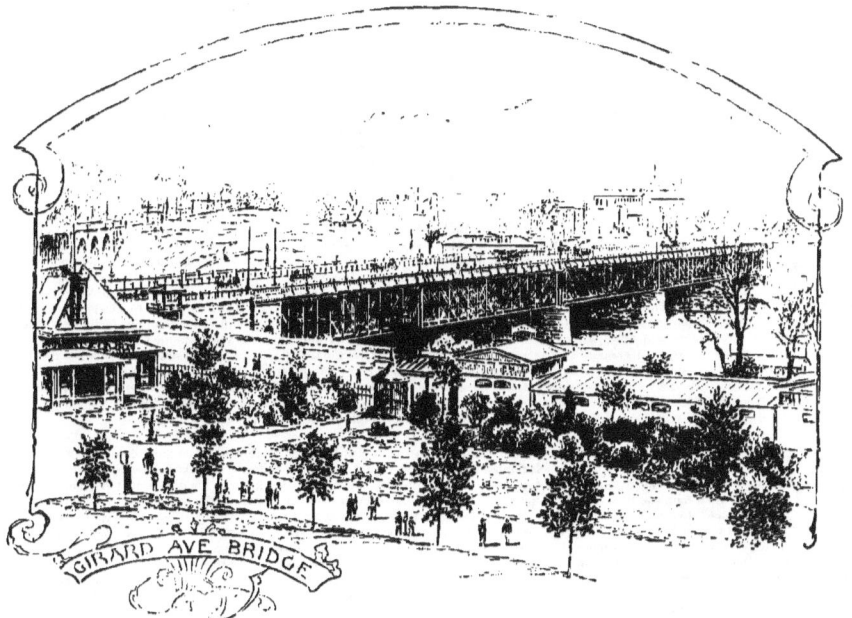

GIRARD AVE BRIDGE

M. S. RHODES & COMPANY, Curves, Crossings, Frogs, Switches, Joint Plates, all Sizes of Knees, Cable, Street Railway and Builders' Iron Work, Machinery and Heavy Castings of all Descriptions, Twenty-third and Wood Streets.—The firm of Wm. S. Rhodes & Co. (who are successors to the Way Foundry Co.), Twenty-third and Wood Streets, was established about three years ago. They are manufacturers of machinery, and heavy iron castings of every description, and can execute orders for anything in this line, at shortest notice, their facilities being of a very superior character. They turn out an excellent class of work, and have a large and rapidly growing business, producing five or ten tons of castings a day. The foundry, which is an old and well-equipped one, is provided with two large cupolas and all the latest improved appliances, and seventy-five to one hundred hands are employed in the concern. The firm are prepared to give estimates on cable, street and builders' iron work, and guarantee perfect satisfaction. Curves, crossings, frogs, switches, joint plates, all sizes of knees, etc., are turned out in the most expeditious manner, and gray castings of every size and description are made to order here at short notice, all orders receiving immediate attention, while the lowest consistent prices are quoted. The copartnership consists of Mr. Wm. S. Rhodes and C. S. Bement, the last-named gentleman being the senior member of the firm of Bement, Miles & Co., machinists. Mr. Rhodes, who is the active manager of the concern, is a man of thorough practical skill in this line, as well as of many years' experience, and exercises close personal supervision over every detail of the business.

HISTORICAL AND COMMERCIAL PHILADELPHIA.

ALKER BROS. & CO., Founders and Machinists, No. 2227 Ward Street. This house was founded in 1867 by Messrs. Thomas, William and James Walker, and William Anderson, under the present firm style. Mr. James Walker died about fifteen years ago, and in 1889 Mr. Wm. Walker died, the business now being conducted by Messrs. Thomas Walker and Wm. Anderson. Both gentlemen are natives of Philadelphia, and are practical machinists of thorough skill and mature experience. They were formerly connected with the Bushill Iron Works. The plant includes ground and buildings covering an ample area, and includes foundry, blacksmith shop and pattern shop. The main building has two floors, each 30x125 feet in size. The mechanical equipment is first class in every respect, and employment is found for some twenty-five experienced workmen. The firm carry on a general business as founders and machinists, melt about 15,000 pounds of iron every week, and make a leading specialty of the manufacture of gold and silver mining machinery. The goods are all of superior excellence, and the large trade supplied extends all throughout the United States, Chili, Mexico, Cuba and Canada.

ICHAEL J. BROWN, Wool, No. 105 Chestnut Street.—Although established but two years on his own account as a wool broker, Mr. Michael J. Brown has been actively engaged in the wool trade for the past twenty-eight years, and for twenty-five years was prominently identified with Messrs. Gregg Bros., Gregg, Green & Co., and W. H. Gregg & Co., successively. Thus Mr. Brown has at his command a long and varied practical knowledge of the various qualities and grades of wool, especially domestic wool, their respective application and suitability for different manufactures, and the tendency and probable course of the market at any time as regulated by supply and demand. It will therefore be understood that Mr. Brown is entitled to meet the exact requirements of consumers of every class at rock bottom prices, while on the other hand his established connection with manufacturers places him on a distinct vantage ground in the speedy disposal of wools. Mr. Michael J. Brown, who was born in the Quaker City, is secretary of the Building Association League of Pennsylvania, and is a newspaper man of recognized attainments, being editor of the Building Society column in the "Public Ledger," and the "Press," and tariff matters in the "North American."

OHN L. JORDAN, Receiver and Dealer in Butter, Eggs, Cheese, Poultry, Game, Etc., No. 306 North Front Street.—One of the most active and enterprising receivers and dealers in butter, eggs, cheese, dried fruits, poultry and game is Mr. John L. Jordan, who has been established in the business here since 1868. He long ago developed a desirable and growing trade with buyers in this city and vicinity, and has manifested special abilities in the securing of the choicest of supplies for this market. He occupies an entire four story building, supplied with a cooling room and all modern facilities for handling and preserving the stock, and is in daily receipt of supplies fresh from the hands of producers in Pennsylvania, Ohio, Indiana, Iowa, Illinois, New Jersey, Delaware and New York. He is the receiver of the product of several celebrated creameries in New York and the West, which is in heavy demand by the choicest trade in this city; while he also handles the finest factory bran's of cheese direct from New York markets, as well as fresh eggs, dried fruits, and the best poultry and game in season. Mr. Jordan is a native of New Jersey, in the active prime of life, a member of the Philadelphia Produce Exchange and the National Butter, Cheese and Egg Association.

H. JONES, Manufacturer of Sash, Doors and Mill Work in General, Office Fixtures, Etc.; Prompt Attention to Planing and Sawing; Factory, rear, Nos. 2923 and 2925 North Broad Street.—The enterprise so successfully conducted by Mr. J. H. Jones as a manufacturer of sash, doors and mill work in general in the rear of Nos. 2923 and 2925 North Broad Street was originally established in 1891 by Messrs. Jones and Clymer, Mr. Jones succeeding to the sole control in the fall of that year. The business premises comprise a two story building, 40x80 feet in dimensions, fully equipped with the latest improved wood working machinery, operated by a steam engine of 15 horse power, and giving employment to a large force of skilled workmen. The principal business to which attention is devoted is the execution of all kinds of mill work to order, including the manufacture of office fixtures, doors and window frames, and a valuable line of inside and outside finish, suited to the requirements of the trade and public, and which by reason of its superior excellence in both material and workmanship is in heavy and influential demand throughout the city. The facilities here possessed for the prompt execution of orders and commissions are of the most complete and perfect character, while prices are placed at the lowest point of moderation, and success, which is well deserved, has crowned the efforts of the proprietor in catering to the demands of his patrons in this direction of trade. Mr. Jones is a native of Montgomery County, Pa., in the prime of life, a member of the Knights of Pythias and Knights of the Golden Eagle, and a reliable and substantial business man.

M. A. SIMPSON & SON, Insurance, No. 339 Walnut Street.—No firm has legitimately achieved more deserved prominence in national fire insurance circles in Philadelphia than Messrs. Wm. A. Simpson & Son. The business was founded in 1856 by Messrs. Wm. A. and B. Mitchell Simpson, as insurance brokers, and, on the death of the honored senior partner in 1888, Mr. B. Mitchell Simpson became sole proprietor, continuing the business without change in the firm name. He represents here in Philadelphia such famous and powerful corporations as the Phœnix, of Brooklyn; the British America, of Toronto; the Broadway, of New York; the Spring Garden, of Philadelphia; and the Washington, of Cincinnati, while he also transacts a general brokerage business in fire insurance. Under his management and through his energy this agency not only retains its old customers, but is steadily including new ones, and now controls the insuring of many of the largest and most desirable lines of business and residential property in this city and vicinity. The policies of this firm have always been clearly worded, explicit contracts; their rates are the lowest commensurate with absolute security, and, as is well known to hundreds of their customers, all losses are promptly adjusted and paid. There are few, if any, firms here who exceed them in the annual volume of their business as agents and brokers; their record is one of the most creditable character, and their enterprise and honorable, liberal methods have deservedly secured an extensive and desirable circle of patronage, and they are in every way representative of the vast insurance interests of the United States. The companies they represent are worthy of every confidence. The Phœnix has assets amounting to $5,187,267.60, with a cash capital of $1,000,000; the British America has assets in its United States branch of $791,878.05; and the Washington gives special attention to insuring store buildings, dwellings and household goods for a term of one, two, three or five years, at a material reduction on yearly terms, aiming to do a small, well selected business, at rates equivalent to the hazard. Mr. Simpson is a native Philadelphian, a member of the Philadelphia Fire Underwriters' Association, and an expert and talented underwriter and adjuster.

CHAS. MURTHA, Brick Manufacturer, Germantown Avenue, above Broad Street.—This enterprise was founded in 1860 by David Murtha, an able business man, who foresaw the extent to which this industry would expand in the Quaker City, and he remained at the head of affairs up to 1886, when his son, the present owner, came into the control. The plant comprises thirty acres of clay land, equipped with four large kilns, the most improved machinery, driven by steam power, and the working force includes sixty men and fifteen teams. Mr. Murtha manufactures hand and machine pressed bricks for building purposes, and the works have a yearly output of 10,000,000 bricks. The product is of a uniformly superior quality, as the trade is well aware, and builders and contractors are supplied upon the most liberal terms. Mr. Murtha is a member of the Order of Odd Fellows, an organization he strongly supports, and he is popularly known in his native city.

HISTORICAL AND COMMERCIAL PHILADELPHIA.

 JAMES KERR, Rectifier and Wholesale Dealer in Pure Old Rye Whiskeys, Brandies, Wines, Gins, Etc., No. 1628 Market Street.—In the great liquor traffic of Philadelphia the house of James Kerr, located at No. 1628 Market Street, has for several years past been widely known as a leading source of supply for all the best brands of foreign and domestic wines and spirits, and the extensive trade now controlled reaches throughout Pennsylvania and New Jersey, and consists mainly in selling to jobbers and large retail houses, although a number of private families are supplied at wholesale prices. This important undertaking was founded in 1869 by the present proprietor, who receives valuable aid at the hands of his son, Mr. D. J. Kerr, to whom are entrusted the clerical duties and office management. Of the various kinds of whiskeys, rums, brandies, gins, wines, etc., handled, the house deals largely in the finest brands of Pennsylvania whiskey, and makes a specialty of Gibson's Pure Rye, while several choice lines in both wines and liquors of foreign and domestic origin, are selected with the greatest care for family trade and medicinal purposes. The business was conducted for twenty years at Nos. 1709-1711 Market Street, but owing to recent developments those premises were found to be inadequate, and in 1889 a removal was accordingly effected to the present location. Here four floors and a basement are utilized, each 25 x 125 feet in size, well fitted and fully equipped throughout for the most satisfactory handling of the heavy and regular shipments received and dispatched, seven duly qualified assistants being regularly engaged on the spot, and two travellers throughout the country among customers. A heavy and choice assortment of wines and liquors, especially whiskeys, is here always carried, duty paid, and a large bulk is also kept in bonded warehouses. James Kerr was with the house of Gibson, Son & Co., for twelve years, from whom he received his training in this line, and had charge of their floors for nine years of that time. He is a member of the Liquor Dealers' Association, while his son is of Philadelphia birth, and still a young man.

 JOHN A. ENGLISH, Dealer in Salt and Fresh Oysters, Nos. 314 and 316 South Delaware Avenue.—The most extensive house in Philadelphia engaged in the industry is that of Mr. John A. English. Mr. English has an expert and valuable knowledge of the oyster business, in which he was literally raised from boyhood. In 1863 he established operations on his own account on South Delaware Avenue, and for the past thirty years has been located at his present address. Mr. English enjoys the highest esteem of his compeers for his many fine qualities, and in the trade his reputation for integrity and upright business methods have given him a popularity from which has accrued an ever-increasing patronage. Mr. English is an oyster planter, owning large oyster beds at Morris Cove, on the east shore of the Delaware River, from which shipments are made via the West Jersey railroad and boats. The finest oysters in the country are raised at this cove, and connoisseurs can testify to their lusciousness. Mr. English also owns an equal interest in the West Shore oysters of Delaware Bay, bed., and owns some thirty sailboats. He employs 200 hands at the beds in the oyster season, and thirty hands at the store in this city. About half a million oysters are shipped daily to all parts of the United States in winter. The oysters are sold shucked and in the shell. Only first-class fresh and salt water oysters and clams are handled, and the trade is supplied upon the most satisfactory terms.

 GEORGE L. FLICK, Manufacturer of Steamship Ranges, Galley and Cabin Stoves, Etc., No. 141 North Front Street.—Forty odd years of uninterrupted prosperity marks the business career of George L. Flick, manufacturer of steamship ranges, galley and cabin stoves, etc., No. 141 North Front Street. He is one of the oldest and foremost in his line in the United States, and has a large patronage. He turns out a superior class of work, including side lights, anchor lights, ventilators, deck irons, deck plates and kindred articles, also tin, copper, iron and brass ware of every description for vessel use. Floors are laid with tile, brick, iron or zinc, at short notice, likewise, and satisfaction is assured in every instance. Mr. Flick is manufacturer of the celebrated "Keystone" caboose, which is conceded to be in all respects the most excellent article of the kind produced in the country, and which is steadily growing in favor, owing to its exceptional merit. The quarters occupied as shop, etc., are commodious and well equipped, and several competent workmen are employed. A first-class stock is constantly kept on hand, outfits for new vessels being a specialty, and all orders for anything in the line above indicated will receive prompt and personal attention, while the prices charged here are of the most reasonable character. Mr. Flick, who is a gentleman somewhat past the meridian of life, but active and energetic, is a man of thorough practical skill as a general metal worker, being an expert in the fitting out of galleys and cabins, and is master of his art in all its branches.

 WATSON, PARKER & CO., Foreign Fruits and Produce, No. 204 North Delaware Avenue.—A recently established house that is achieving a most marked success in the trade, is that of Watson, Parker & Co. The firm began operations in May, 1892, and through the thorough knowledge gained by long experience, the copartners, Messrs. R. J. Watson and H. B. Parker, have quickly forged to the front, and are acquiring a rapidly extending patronage. Both gentlemen are natives of Virginia, but have long lived in the Quaker City. Mr. Watson was formerly with the Hart Steamship Company, of Philadelphia, and J. D. Hart & Co., of Baltimore. Mr. Parker was with the Baltimore Fruit Company, of this city, and C. M. Taylor & Co., and Hart & Co., of Baltimore. The firm occupy a spacious store, 25 x 250 feet in dimensions, in which is a banana ripening room with a storage capacity for from seven thousand to eight thousand bunches of bananas. They carry on a general business as commission merchants in foreign fruits and produce, making a leading specialty of bananas and cocoanuts, large consignments being received from South America, Central America and the West Indies. A large stock is at all times kept on hand. In all their business transactions Messrs. Watson & Parker have evinced, in a marked degree, the sterling qualities and equitable methods incident to a successful mercantile career.

 ASHLAND HOTEL, European Plan, Oliver Sproul, Sole Owner and Proprietor, Seventh and Race Streets.—One of the very best among Philadelphia's popular priced hotels is the Ashland Hotel, Seventh and Race Streets, opposite Franklin Square, of which Mr. Oliver Sproul is the sole owner and the proprietor. This is a favorite resort for commercial travelers and professional people, and occupies a niche in the esteem of the traveling public accorded to few establishments of the kind in this city. The "Ashland" is centrally located, being convenient to the principal business thoroughfare, and is easy of access to all points of interest, horse-cars for all sections of the city and suburbs passing in the immediate vicinity of the house. The hotel building is a substantial five-story brick structure, containing 110 rooms, and is handsomely furnished throughout. It is well lighted, thoroughly heated and perfectly ventilated, and is provided with ample safeguards against fire and accident. The sleeping apartments are commodious, airy and comfortable, the accommodations are tip-top in every particular; the fare is of a superior character, the service and attendance are all that could be desired, and the bar is stocked with the finest brands of wines, liquors, cigars, etc. The house is conducted on the European plan, being open for the reception of guests at all hours. The prices range from fifty cents to two dollars per day, for single rooms, and upwards for suites. The dining-room is spacious, neat and inviting, there are well-appointed sample and billiard-rooms connected with the hotel, which has two commodious entrances, and the office is conveniently situated on the ground floor. Altogether everything is first-class, and the guests of mine host of the "Ashland" are assured of the best treatment and most superior "creature comforts" the city affords at the terms here prevailing. Mr. Sproul, by whom this deservedly popular and flourishing hostelry was established in 1870, is a native of Europe, and a man of pleasing and courteous manners, as well as good business qualities. Mr. Sproul has had many years' experience in this line, and prior to coming to this country had been engaged in the business in England for some time.

HISTORICAL AND COMMERCIAL PHILADELPHIA.

AROLD GODWIN, Architect and Engineer, Office, No. 905 Walnut Street.—The gentleman whose name heads this sketch is one of the most skilful and best known among the younger architects and engineers of Philadelphia. Mr. Godwin, who has a well equipped office, where he employs several competent assistants, is a comparatively young man and was born in Roxborough, Philadelphia. He is a thoroughly practical draughtsman, all round architect and civil engineer, of ample experience in his profession, and is master of his art in all its branches. He has been established about six years, and has acquired a large and flattering patronage. He is prepared to make plans for all classes of buildings, giving particular attention to mills, factories and business structures generally, and guarantees the utmost satisfaction. Designs, specifications, etc., are furnished at short notice, while construction is personally supervised. Mr. Godwin, who is now engaged in putting up the Forest Laundry, Twelfth Street and Columbia Avenue, has built a crematorium at Germantown, and the Maternity Hospital of Pa., and many notable structures in and around Philadelphia, including a number of manufacturing establishments, store and office buildings, school houses and institutions, besides 1,000 or more private residences.

REENHALGE & WADSWORTH, Plush Manufacturers, Corner Somerset and Palethorp Streets.—The plush manufacturing industry is well represented in Philadelphia by the house of Greenhalge & Wadsworth. The members of the firm, Messrs. Robert C. Greenhalge and Jackson Wadsworth, both possess a thorough, practical knowledge of their calling, and therefore, when they established business fifteen years ago, they were amply qualified to win the substantial success that has since followed. The premises used cover an area of 40x150 feet, and the equipment consists of twenty-four looms, steam power, and all apparatus applicable to the industry. Forty hands are employed when the factory is running full. Messrs. Greenhalge & Wadsworth manufacture plush of all grades, making a specialty of the finer lines, and their goods are all of a uniform excellence that assures their guarantee value to the trade. The output amounts to about twenty-five forty-yard cuts per day, and the goods are sold direct to jobbers in all the principal cities of the country. Mr. Greenhalge was born in Philadelphia, Mr. Wadsworth is English, but he has resided in this city twenty-eight years, and they sustain an excellent reputation in the industrial world.

. S. CHANDLER, Tobacco Commission Merchant, No. 65 North Front Street. One of the oldest Philadelphia houses engaged in this line is that of W. S. Chandler, whose establishment was founded twenty-five years ago by W. S. Chandler & Co., but for the past five years Mr. Chandler has been in the sole control. He is agent for the Greenville Tobacco Company of Louisville, Ky.; J. N. Wylie & Co., of Danville, Va., and Larus & Bro., of Richmond, Va. The Greenville Tobacco Company's brands are: "On the Square," "Monitor," "Lemon Pie" and "Brandy;" Wyllie's brands: "Stonewall," "Uncle Remus," "Happy Hunter," and "Old Dominion;" Messrs. Larus & Co.'s brands; "Peyton & Co." and "Jones & Son's Cavendish." He sells by sample on commission, having influential connections with manufacturers, and has permanent customers in all parts of Pennsylvania, New Jersey, Delaware and Maryland. All goods are shipped direct from factory. Mr. Chandler is a native of Delaware, and has resided a lengthy term in this city.

ARRY SWAIN, Druggist, Second Street and Snyder Avenues and No. 1829 South Second Street. One of the most successful pharmacists in this section of Philadelphia is Mr. Harry Swain, who operates two stores, one at Second Street and Snyder Avenue, that he inaugurated two years ago, under the same name, and another at No. 1829 South Second Street, also established by him seven years ago. The stores are ample and commodious, neatly arranged, furnished and equipped with all modern conveniences for the skilful performance of the work. A full and complete display of pure fresh drugs and chemicals is shown, together with all kinds of proprietary remedies, druggist's sundries, physicians' requisites, toilet requirements, fancy articles, etc. All goods may be relied on as being the best, and no expense is spared to maintain both of these establishments at the highest standard of excellence. A specialty is made in the compounding of fluid extracts, compounds, and tinctures, of Mr. Swain's own superior preparation, and the dispensing of physicians' prescriptions and family recipes by a corps of skilled and competent assistants at fair and reasonable prices. Mr. Swain, who is an active young business man, and studied with Dr. S. D. Marshall, is a native of Georgetown, Del., and a graduate of the Philadelphia College of Pharmacy and a member of the Alumni Association.

cKEAIGE & McCOMB, Wholesale Commission Merchants in Poultry, Eggs, Fruits and Produce, No. 333 North Front Street. Among the better known and more substantial wholesale produce commission merchants engaged in the Quaker City, a prominent place is occupied by the responsible firm of McKeaige & McComb, who are receivers of heavy and regular consignments of poultry, eggs, butter, fresh and dried domestic fruits and all kinds of vegetables in season, produce, calves, sheep, lambs, hogs and other live stock, for disposal upon this market, from many of the best growers, raisers and producers throughout Pennsylvania, New Jersey, Delaware and Maryland. These consignments, in the firm's skilful and experienced hands, find speedy and safe channels of consumption among retail dealers and other wholesale consumers hereabouts; accurate account sales are rendered, prompt settlements made, and every facility is extended to patrons. This old and reliable house came into the hands of the present firm in 1891, the copartners being Mr. A. McKeaige and his son in law, Mr. James McComb. A spacious floor and basement are utilized and are well fitted and equipped for the receiving, handling, packing and despatching of consignments in the most expeditious and satisfactory manner. Of the experienced proprietors, Mr. McKeaige was born in Ireland and came to Philadelphia about forty years ago, while Mr. McComb is a native of this city.

LDINE LIVERY STABLES AND RIDING ACADEMY, Twenty-Second Street above Pine, T. Riddle & Co., Proprietors. Equestrianism, or horse-back exercise, is one of the most healthful forms of recreation, and is every year coming more and more into popular favor. Riding schools are to be found in all large cities, where one may gain a knowledge of the art. One of the best conducted establishments of the kind is that of the Aldine Riding Academy, on Twenty-second Street above Pine, T. Riddle & Co., proprietors. They also conduct a general livery and boarding stable business. This academy is the most complete and largest in the city for educating ladies, gentlemen, and children in horsemanship. It is thoroughly ventilated, lighted, and open day and evening nine months of the year, from October 1st to June 30th. Every convenience and comfort has been introduced for patrons, and the greatest attention is given to correct and thorough teaching and the best care for children. The terms are reasonable, and special classes are held for gentlemen and ladies. The premises occupied comprise a two-story and basement building, 80x125 feet in dimensions the upper floor being used as a riding academy. In addition to the riding school, the firm conduct a general livery and boarding stable, let private turnouts, make a specialty of saddle horses, and special attention is paid to furnishing complete establishments for conveying parties to and from churches, weddings, balls, parties, etc., shopping, park driving, etc. The stable has ample accommodations for 140 horses, and forty horses and rigs are kept at the disposal of the public. The sole proprietor of the establishment, Mr. T. Riddle, was born abroad, but has resided in this city the greater part of his life, having come here in 1850. He is a sound judge of horseflesh, and is popular with all who know him.

HISTORICAL AND COMMERCIAL PHILADELPHIA.

SAMUEL W. BROWN & CO., Platinum Enlargements by Electric and Solar Light, Office and Printing Rooms, No. 915 Sansom Street.—The work turned out by some of our leading photographers in the line indicated above is certainly a triumph of science and skill, in which connection special mention is due Samuel W. Brown & Co., than whom none in the business in Philadelphia sustain a higher reputation. The platinum enlargements by electric and solar light made in this establishment are unsurpassed in a single feature of excellence, and are noted for fidelity and execution. The facilities are first-class in all respects, all the latest improved appliances and appurtenances being in service, and the work done here is of a notably superior character. Mr. Brown, who is the sole proprietor, is a native of this city, and a young man of exceptional skill, and is an expert in his line. He started in business in December, 1883, and from the first has been highly prosperous, acquiring a large patronage throughout the United States, with some also in the West Indies and South America. He occupies two spacious floors, which are perfectly equipped for the purposes intended, and employs several competent assistants. All classes of work in the line above indicated are done here in the most expeditious and excellent manner, and satisfaction is guaranteed in every instance, all orders receiving prompt and personal attention. Mr. Brown is a member of the F. and A. M., K. of G. E., American Mechanics, Knights of Birmingham and other societies.

GREAVES' MACHINERY DEPOT, No. 109 North Front Street.—The well-known textile machinery depot of Charles E. Greaves, No. 109 North Front Street, was established about twenty-two years ago by the present proprietor. It is ac   known and best-patronized concerns of the kind in this city. The quarters occupied here are commodious and well arranged, and a large, first-class stock is always kept on hand. The assortment includes new and second and hosiery, wool and worsted machinery of every description, lathes, twisters, winders and spooling frames, spools, cards, and, in short, everything in this line, both for hand and steam-power. Every article sold here, too, is fully warranted, while the prices charged are distinctly low, and all orders are attended to in the most prompt and careful manner. Mr. Greaves is a gentleman of middle age, and was born in England, but has long been a resident of this city. He is a man of practical skill, as well as of many years' experience in this line, thoroughly reliable in his dealings, and gives close personal attention to every detail of the business.

JOHN H. KENNEDY, Contractor and Practical Furniture Finisher in all its Branches, No. 119½ North Second Street.—This well-known house was established in '81 and its career has been one of steady development, while its management has been marked with prudence, energy, ability and liberality. The premises occupied contain 10,000 square feet of floor surface, supplied with all appliances necessary for the successful prosecution of the business. Furniture of every description is finished and refinished in any shade or color desired by experienced workmen, who are also sent to all parts of the city and country at   ort notice. Special inducements are offered to manufacturers and dealers by the single piece or car load, and estimates are promptly furnished upon applica ion. A large trade has been established, which is steadily increasing, and large contracts are being continually finished for the leading manufacturers of this and other cities. Mr. Kennedy is a native of Virginia, and has been at times manager of the finishing departments of extensive manufactories in Boston, New York and Baltimore. He is thoroughly experienced in his business, and a reliable, responsible business man, and we would commend the house to furniture dealers and manufacturers as being well worthy their attention.

GRIENDLING'S SONS, Barbers' Chairs, Supplies, Furniture and Interior Decoration, No. 213 North Second Street.—The well-known establishment of J. Griendling's Sons, manufacturers of, and dealers in barbers' furniture and supplies, was inaugurated by J. Griendling in 1852. This gentleman, after a long, honorable and successful career, retired in 1887, and his sons continued the business. The premises occupied comprise three floors, 30 x 75 feet in dimensions, fully equipped with everything necessary for the successful prosecution of the business. The firm are prepared to fit up any style of barber-shop, from the smallest to the largest, with chairs, mirrors, mug-cases, washstands, poles, etc., also deal extensively in razors, hones, straps, brushes, combs, etc. The elegance of their productions are unsurpassed, and are the best that money, talent, and skilled labor can produce. A specialty of the house is cup decorating, and they turn out some of the finest and richest barber s mugs in the country. The trade of the house extends throughout Pennsylvania, New Jersey, and Delaware, and is large and constantly increasing. The members of the firm are C. Griendling and J. Griendling, Jr., both natives of Philadelphia, and of excellent standing in business circles.

F. SWEENY & SONS, Engravers of Signs in Brass, Copper, Nickel and Silver Plate, No. 709 Sansom Street.—The well-known representative house of J. F. Sweeny & Sons was established by Mr. J. F. Sweeny in 1857. He moved to Philadelphia fifteen years ago, and in May 1892, his two sons Jos. F., Jr., and James E., were admitted to partnership. The firm are engravers of brass, copper, nickel and silver paste signs. They also engrave memorial tablets, name plates for engines and machinery, door plates, etc. Mr. J. F. Sweeny has had thirty-six years' practical experience in the business, and his sons have been trained to this business from childhood. Two spacious rooms are occupied, fully equipped with special machinery, tools, and appliances, and a force of skilled and e   erience workmen is constantly employed. Designs and estimates are cheerfully furnished, and the prices in all cases are extremely modera e. Sweeny's engraved brass and silver signs may be seen in all parts of the United States, and the demand for them is steadily increasing. The members of this reliable firm are all natives of New York City, but have been residents of Philadelphia for the past fifteen years.

EDWARD McGETTIGAN, Importer of Fine Wines and Wholesale Liquor Dealer, Southwest Corner Eleventh and Bainbridge Streets.—Prominent among the leading houses engaged in the wholesale liquor trade in Philadelphia is that of Mr. Edward McGettigan, located at the southwest corner of Eleventh and Bainbridge Streets. This gentleman is an extensive importer of fine wines and a wholesaler of domestic and imported liquors of the finest grades. He established his business here in 1865, and his facilities for the prosecution of the trade are equaled by but few houses in this section of the country. Cash pur chases, direct importations, long experience and a thorough knowledge of the business in all its branches, together with progressive and liberal methods of management have enabled this house to compete successfully with its largest contemporaries in city or country. Mr. McGettigan in all things keeps fully abreast of the age. His order is flashed over the cable to the vintners of Germany, France and Spain and the goods are received and put on sale in his fin establishment the succeeding week. He is widely noted as a direct importer of the famous products of the Rhine valley, the champagne, Burgundy and Medoc districts of France, and the Malaga and other Spanish vineyards, including special dry sherries of great age and perfect bouquet, the best ports from Oporto, and Madeira and Hungarian wines, French cognac brandies, Holland and London Dock   ins the finest old Irish and Scotch whiskeys, English ales and porter. Connois seurs will recognize here the finest products of the Old World, while in Bourbon and rye whiskeys, the assortment is equally compre hensive, a specialty being made of the celebrated Dougherty and Gibson whiskeys. These brands are noted for their ma chless qualities and have achieved a popularity second to none in the market. They are absolutely pure, contain no fusel oil, and whether for social indulgence or medicinal purposes they have no superior. Two thousand barrels are ke t in bond and orders for all grades of goods handled receive prompt and careful attention. Mr. McGettigan controls the very best class of hotel and retail trade in this city, is a member of the Whole sale Liquor Dealers' Association of Philadelphia, an expert and practical rectifier and an honorable, reliable and self-made man.

HISTORICAL AND COMMERCIAL PHILADELPHIA.

GEO. P. BROWN, Wholesale Commission Merchant, Butter, Eggs, Cheese, Poultry, Etc., No. 2927 South Street.—Among the leading and responsible butter, egg, cheese and poultry wholesale commission merchants in this vicinity is Mr. George P. Brown who established his enterprise in 1889. The store occupied is commodious, ample and neatly kept, ruling market prices prevail, while a heavy and fine stock is constantly kept on hand, embracing the choicest of creamery butter, fresh laid eggs, prime cheese and poultry, and game in their respective seasons. Daily consignments of these goods are regularly received from the most reliable sources of rearing and production, and such are the facilities of the house, expanding as they naturally have, that Mr. Brown is enabled to guarantee that everything emanating from the establishment shall be of first class character. An extensive suburban and city trade is enjoyed of both wholesale and retail character. Mr. Brown is a young man, and a native of Chester County, Pa.

DW. A. PHILLIPS, Burial Casket and Coffin Manufacturer, N. W. Corner Tenth and Lombard Streets. One of the largest manufacturers of burial caskets in the entire city, if not the largest, is Mr. Edward A. Phillips, carrying on his operations at the northwest corner of Tenth and Lombard Streets. This responsible and progressive enterprise is the centre of a trade of considerable magnitude and significance, reaching throughout New Jersey, Pennsylvania, Maryland, Delaware, Virginia and other adjacent States, and it now enjoys a wide reputation for turning out the finest and most uniformly reliable work. Caskets and coffins of all kinds are manufactured to order and for stock to any pattern or design, from the simplest to the most elaborate and detailed instructions are rigidly adhered to, and plans, drawings or ideas are accurately interpreted. In addition, the house is a dealer at both wholesale and retail in every possible requisite for the undertaker and funeralist; the list of such goods being far too lengthy and comprehensive to give here; suffice it to say that the house possesses every facility for meeting the full requirements of the best trade houses promptly and at rock bottom prices. The business was established in 1876 by the present proprietor, who possesses a practical experience in this line dating back to 1858. The premises utilized consist of a four story building, 18x110 feet in dimensions, well fitted throughout, and fully equipped for the due prosecution of the trade; a large and handsome collection of coffins, caskets, and undertakers' requisites is always on view, and nine skilled assistants are regularly employed. Mr. Edward A. Phillips, who was born in this city, is a member of Post No. 5 of the Grand Army of the Republic, and served from 1862 throughout the late war, as private in the 118th Pennsylvania Volunteer Infantry.

GEO. W. C. BAKER & CO., Real Estate and Insurance, No. 4019 Lancaster Avenue. Although of comparatively recent establishment, Messrs. George W. C. Baker & Co., located at No. 4019 Lancaster Avenue, have already succeeded in building up an extensive connection as real estate and insurance brokers and agents, and their clientele now includes a number of prominent capitalists, property owners, trustees and others hereabouts. Thus the firm's services are largely sought for all branches of the profession, more particularly for the purchase, sale and exchange of real estate, especially residential property in the twenty-fourth, twenty-seventh and thirty-fourth wards, the collection of house and ground rents and interest, the letting of premises, the preparation and careful examination of titles, deeds, leases and similar instruments, the settlement, transfer and entire management of estates, and the speedy negotiation of loans upon bond or mortgage; while as insurance brokers they are enabled to cover all desirable risks at the lowest current rates of premium, obtaining policies from any responsible corporation desired. The sole proprietor, Mr. George W. C. Baker, who was born in San Francisco, California, has brought his Western push with him, is sub agent for the Royal Assurance Co. of Liverpool, and was formerly engaged with the building firm of Nicholson and Michaelson.

FRED. W. HEERMANN, Importer and Wholesale Dealer in Wines and Liquors, Fine Whiskies, Brandies, Etc., No. 3726 Haverford Street. A well known and very successful wholesale wine and liquor dealer in West Philadelphia is Mr. Fred. W. Heermann, carrying on his operations at No. 3726 Haverford Street, who is held in high repute for handling the most reliable and satisfactory grades of goods and for strictly honorable dealings in all transactions. All kinds of imported and domestic wines and liquors are handled, both bottled and in bulk, including fine whiskies, brandies, gins, rums, European wines, and, as a specialty, California wines. The house is a direct importer of Rhine wines, and has always on hand a full assortment of pure rye and Bourbon whiskies, brandies, gins and wines specially selected for family use and for medicinal purposes. Moreover, a heavy stock of all kinds of imported and domestic wines and liquors is always carried, both duty paid and in bond; three competent assistants being regularly employed on the premises. Mr. Fred. W. Heermann established himself in 1882 in the retail liquor business, which he gave up in favor of the wholesale in 1887. He is a native of this city, now of middle age, and is a member of the Wholesale Liquor Dealers' Association of Philadelphia.

W. F. VAN GUNDEN, Marble and Granite Dealer, No. 1410 Fairmount Avenue.—Mr. W. F. Van Gunden, marble and granite dealer and worker, located at No. 1410 Fairmount Avenue, although established as recently as 1891, has already succeeded in working up a trade of large proportions, which necessitates the regular employment of some twenty skilled mechanics. This pronounced success is largely attributable to the wide range of practical experience possessed by the proprietor, who was for twenty-four years with Van Gunden & Young, as workman and salesman, and his father, of that firm, was a marble worker for over fifty years. Mr. W. F. Van Gunden undertakes, for an influential patronage throughout the city and country, the manufacture of all kinds of cemetery work in the marble and granite, such as monuments, tombs, headstones, columns, etc., including the best descriptions of carving and ornamentation; and designs and estimates are at all times cheerfully furnished upon application. The yard has an area of 50x100 feet, and besides being fully equipped with all tools and appliances pertaining to the trade, contains a fine display of work executed on the spot. All orders are sure of receiving prompt and accurate fulfilment under the close personal supervision of the able proprietor, who is a native of Philadelphia, and now of middle age.

H. FAIRLAMB & CO., Shippers of Portland and Rosendale Cement, "Red Beach" Calcined Plaster, Land Plaster, White and Bar Sand; Office and Wharf, Nos. 115 to 121 South Thirtieth Street. A foremost house engaged in the shipment of cement and plaster is that of P. H. Fairlamb & Co., whose office, warehouse and wharf are at Nos. 115 to 121 South Thirtieth Street; telephone 471, W. P. This enterprise was founded ten years ago, under the present firm style, by Mr. Fairlamb, and two years ago he admitted Mr. B. F. Smedley to a partnership interest. Both are natives of this city, and business men of thorough experience, who follow a cost policy, and are equitable and honorable in all their dealings. They are members of the Builders' Exchange. The firm occupy extensive premises, possess all requisite facilities and conveniences, and carry a heavy supply of Alsen Portland cement, Dyckerhoff Portland cement, Excelsior Portland cement, Diamond Portland cement, S. & H. Portland cement, Dongan Portland cement, Saylor's Portland cement, Improved Anchor cement, Improved Union cement, Hoffman Rosendale cement, Rock Lock Rosendale cement, Shield Brand Rosendale cement, Red Beach calcined plaster, land plaster, plastering hair, Chester Valley lime, mortar colors, marble dust, etc., and special attention is given to shipments of fine and coarse white sand and bar sand by the carload or barrel. In 1891 Messrs. Fairlamb & Co. disposed of 30,000 barrels of cement, and this year expect to sell 50,000 barrels, and perhaps greatly exceed that figure, as their trade is rapidly increasing.

HISTORICAL AND COMMERCIAL PHILADELPHIA.

MOORE, KELLY & Co., Wholesale and Retail Dealers in Choice Lehigh and Schuylkill Coal, Etc., No. 1528 Washington Avenue. Residence No. 2223 Catherine Street.—A very successful firm of coal-merchants in the southern section of Philadelphia is that of Messrs. Moore, Kelly & Co. at No. 1528 Washington Avenue, who handle the finest grades of Lehigh and Schuylkill coal for manufacturers' and family use, bituminous coal for blacksmiths, genuine 72-hour Connellsville coke, and kindling wood by the cord, load or box. The trade controlled reaches throughout the city, and in coal and coke is conducted at both wholesale and retail; large regular consumers being supplied in car-load lots at substantial inducements as to prices and terms, delivering and qualities. The premises have been employed as a coalyard for the past twenty years, and in September, 1891, the present firm took possession, the copartners being Mr. Robert Moore and Mr. Thomas Kelly. The yard, 80 x 100 feet in size, has a railroad siding running into it, so that cars direct from the mines can unload on the spot; sheds, bins, etc. are provided, and every convenience is at hand for keeping the coal dry, under cover, as also for carefully picking and screening the heavy stock carried. The retail trade aggregates twenty-five hundred tons annually and several competent hands and patent wagons are kept constantly employed. Of the energetic proprietors, Mr. Robt. Moore was born in this city in 1861; while Mr. Thomas Kelly, was born in Ireland in 1867, coming to the United States (New Egypt, N. J.) in 1882, and settling in this city six years ago.

JAMES L. WILSON, Painting in all its Branches, No. 518 South Ninth Street.—There is little doubt but that the oldest-established painting and decorating business in the entire city of Philadelphia is that conducted by Mr. James L. Wilson, located at No. 518 South Ninth Street, for it was founded as far back as 1832 at the same location by Mr. James Wilson, who was succeeded in 1872 by his son, the present proprietor. In face of such a long standing, it needs scarcely to be said that a high reputation attaches to the house for executing the finest and most reliable work in each branch of the trade at fair and reasonable prices, and a large local business is now controlled, the volume of which furnishes regular employment for upwards of twenty skilled workmen. All kinds of painting are equally undertaken, including fine sign writing and lettering, plain and ornamental work on exteriors and interiors, fresco, panel and other artistic painting to any design from the simplest to the most elaborate, tinting, gilding and general decorating; and among the many important contracts undertaken may be noted the work on the United States Warehouse, the Arsenal and a number of residences all over this section. The shop, 20 feet square, is fully equipped and contains a large and carefully selected stock of requisites and supplies. The experienced proprietor, Mr. James L. Wilson, is a native of Philadelphia, and was brought up to this line of trade.

S. W. GOODMAN, Printing House, Designing and Engraving, Blank Books, No. 116 North Third Street.—For over twenty-seven years S. W. Goodman has been established, and has conducted business at the present location since 1865. He turns out a very superior class of work, is prompt and reliable in executing orders, and his prices are exceptionally low. Mr. Goodman was born in Germany, but has resided in this city a long time. He is a practical printer himself, master of the art in all its branches, and gives close personal attention to every detail of the business. The quarters occupied by him are commodious and the facilities are first-class. There are two cylinder presses, four jobbers and an excellent outfit of type in service here and fifteen to twenty hands are employed. Mr. Goodman is prepared to give estimates on all classes of book and job work, fine commercial printing being a specialty, and guarantees perfect satisfaction. Designing and engraving are attended to also, while blank books are made to order in any desired size and style.

PELEG A. DYER, First-class Boarding Stables, Nos. 2715-2717 and 2719 Germantown Avenue.—The boarding stables of Peleg A. Dyer were established by the present proprietor in 1888, and in consequence of the honorable, just methods he employs in the conduct of the business, his success from the outset has been of the most pronounced character. The building occupied is a commodious two-story structure, 50 x 130 feet in dimensions, fitted up with all the modern facilities and conveniences for the purposes of the business, and both the front and rear are provided with fire escapes. The entire main floor is devoted to the stabling department and this is well lighted, thoroughly ventilated and drained, and perfect as regards sanitary arrangements, while in winter the stables are cut off from the cold by partitions. Accommodation is here afforded for fifty head of stock, and the proprietor makes a specialty of boarding horses by the day, week or month, in fact, for any length of time, at the most reasonable rates, and all animals intrusted to his keeping receive the very best of care, food and treatment. Mr. Dyer has in his care at all times horses belonging to many of our most prominent merchants and private citizens. He is a native of Bucks County, Pennsylvania, and has resided in this city twenty years.

CHARLES P. LAWRENCE, Sailmaker, No. 16 North Delaware Avenue.—The business of this prosperous concern was founded in 1865 by Mr. Charles Lawrence, the father of the present proprietor, who was one of the most successful sailmakers in this city. In 1890 the present proprietor, Charles P. Lawrence, succeeded, and has ably sustained the high reputation of the house which was so by his father. The premises occupied comprise the third, fourth and fifth floors of No. 16, each 50 x 75 feet in dimensions, and are equipped in the most improved manner for business operations. Mr Lawrence manufactures all kinds of sails of every size, style, and variety, flags, tents and awnings. He makes a specialty of large sails and of supplying Philadelphia yachts with sails and other rigging in this line. Sails and flags are made to order in the most expeditious and excellent manner, and a fine assortment of goods may also be found on hand at all times. Mr Lawrence does a large trade with all seaports of the United States. He understands his trade thoroughly, having been brought up to the business with his father from a boy. All his work is noted for its durability, accuracy and thorough finish. Mr. Lawrence is a native of Philadelphia and is a young man of push and energy, and all the go-ahead qualities that make up the successful business man.

M. B. ALLEBACH, Watchmaker, Jeweler, and Importer of Watches, also Dealer in Diamonds, No. 136 North Second Street.—This business was established eighty years ago by Theo. Dubosq, who was succeeded by Mr. Seginise, and he by Mr. Arose. In 1859 Mr. Allebach bought out the business and has continued it ever since. The quarters occupied are well fitted up and handsomely appointed and were the first in Philadelphia to have plate glass windows. Mr. Allebach was born in Bucks County, Pennsylvania, and lived, during his youth, in Schuylkill County, Pennsylvania, becoming identified with his trade early in life. He learned the art of watchmaking and soon achieved an enviable reputation for the superiority of his work. This establishment attracts marked attention by reason of the excellent work executed. Mr. Allebach is a manufacturer of high-case clocks and in this branch of business he has had twenty years' experience. His workroom is equipped with all machinery, dies, etc., for the manufacture of watches and clocks, and also for repairing. Mr. Allebach also deals largely in diamonds and imported watches. He selects his diamonds with great care, giving particular attention to the color, cutting, shape and brilliancy. These he keeps either in parcels or mounted and sells them at remarkably low prices. The building which he occupies is one of the oldest in Philadelphia and is famous for its parlor in which Washington once danced.

HISTORICAL AND COMMERCIAL PHILADELPHIA.

M. H. COLLISSON, Jr., Plumbing, Steam and Gas Fitting, No. 1855 Germantown Avenue.—The well known house of Wm. H. Collisson, Jr., was established in 1862 by Messrs. Schriver & Collisson, the present proprietor, a son of Mr. Collisson, succeeding to the control in 1882. The premises occupied comprise a store and shop, 25 x 80 feet in dimensions, and eight of the most skilled and experienced workmen to be found are constantly employed. The large well-selected stock of the various commodities incident to this line of trade is complete in every department, and the work performed, which embraces plumbing, steam and gas fitting, and general job work is noted for its superior excellence. Specimens of Mr. Collisson's work may be seen in any of the fine residences in this section, and he has also fitted up mills and factories. Modern methods of building have made steam heating a necessity, and in this work Mr. Collisson excels. He accepts contracts for the complete piping of houses for gas, placing chandeliers and putting in fixtures. He does all grades of plumbing, puts in sinks, basins, and fits bathrooms in the finest and most modern styles. All work in the line of sanitary plumbing is done in the most scientific manner, and satisfaction is guaranteed in every instance. Mr. Collisson is a practical workman, and sees to it that every contract that is carried out is to the utter satisfaction of his patrons. Mr. Collisson is a native of Germantown, a prominent member of the American Mechanics, the A. O. of United Workmen, and is highly esteemed as an honorable, reliable business man.

NINTH STREET, SHOWING POST OFFICE.

UGUST WERNER, Maker of Fine Shoes, No. 1023 Walnut Street.—Among the makers of fine shoes in this city few if any enjoy a better reputation than August Werner. He has been established here about two years, and has a large and growing patronage. He has a well-appointed store, with shop in connection, and employs ten experienced workmen. Mr. Werner is a gentleman of thirty-six, born in Germany, and has been in Philadelphia since 1874. He is a man of practical skill and thorough experience, and is master of his art. Mr. Werner, who was for thirteen years with Benkert & Son, prior to going into business for himself, makes ladies' and gentlemen's boots and shoes to order, and guarantees satisfaction in every instance, making a leading specialty of fine custom work. His prices are very reasonable, too, quality of material and character of workmanship considered, while perfect fit is assured. He keeps on hand a first-class stock, all of his own make.

TEPHEN A. BICKHAM, Leaf Tobacco; Packing House, Churchtown, Lancaster Co., Pa.; No. 163 North Second Street.—Mr. Stephen A. Bickham was of the firm of Martin Bickham & Bro., from May 1889 to Dec. 1891, at which time the partnership was dissolved and the business continued by Mr. Stephen A. Bickham alone. The premises occupied comprise three floors 25 x 75 feet in dimensions, conveniently fitted up, and containing at all times a large stock of domestic cigar leaf of all grades. Mr. Bickham supplies a large number of cigar manufacturers in this and other cities with the finest domestic leaf in large or small quantities. He deals principally in Connecticut, New York State, Wisconsin, Ohio and Pennsylvania leaf. He has always on hand an extensive stock of all grades of both foreign and domestic leaf. The trade of the house is wholesale and retail, and extends throughout the United States. Mr. Bickham is a native of Lancaster Co., Pa., was born on a farm, and is a practical tobacco dealer, being an excellent judge of the weed. His business is conducted upon a policy of strict integrity and liberality.

HISTORICAL AND COMMERCIAL PHILADELPHIA.

JOHN W. BONNER, Agent, Manufacturer of Fine Dress Shirts, No. 810 Walnut Street.—One of the oldest-established houses in the city engaged in the manufacture of fine dress shirts is that of which John W. Bonner is agent. The enterprise was inaugurated in 1866, and the house enjoys a high reputation for the excellence of its productions and has customers in all parts of the United States. The store and shop occupied are of ample dimensions and the finest facilities are at hand for manufacturing shirts to order, and employment is furnished to a large force of skilled hands. The goods are made of the best material and warranted to give satisfaction as to fit and workmanship. Mr. Bonner is a native of Ireland but has been a resident of this city for forty-two years. He is a thorough master of his art, honorable and reliable in all business transactions and eminently popular with his numerous patrons.

STANTON & LEWIS, General Blacksmiths, No. 318 Branch Street, above Race Street.—Messrs. James P. Stanton and William Lewis, who compose this firm, are both men in the full prime of life and natives of this city. They are thoroughly skilled general blacksmiths, of twenty-five and thirty years' experience respectively, and are masters of their art in all its branches. They have been established here at No. 318 Branch Street (above Race Street) since 1880, and have built up a large and growing trade. They have a spacious and well-equipped shop with two fires, and employ half a dozen hands. Blacksmithing in all its branches is executed by this firm in the most superior manner at short notice, and forgings of every description are turned out by them, steel work being a specialty. Chasers for printing machinery, etc., are manufactured, likewise, and jobbing generally is done with skill and dispatch. All orders receive prompt and personal attention, and all work is warranted to be first-class, while the prices charged here are of the most reasonable character.

H. MEDICKE, Manufacturer of Heaters and Ranges, No. 1231 Vine Street.—A very successful sheet metal worker in this city is Mr. J. H. Medicke. The chief lines undertaken are the sheet iron work for heaters and ranges, and putting them up in working order with all piping and connections, hot air work, a general line of copper, zinc, sheet iron and tin work and tin roofing as a specialty; while particular care and attention are devoted to all kinds of bricklaying, repairing and jobbing. The business was established in 1873, by the present proprietor, who is thoroughly practical in this line and maintains a close scrutiny over the prompt and accurate fulfillment of all orders undertaken. The trade reaches throughout the city and suburbs and furnishes regular employment for six skilled mechanics. The store, 20 x 40 feet in area, is well fitted and arranged, and contains a carefully chosen stock of the standard makes of ranges, heaters and stoves; efficient and economical. The shop in the rear is fully equipped and every facility is at hand for turning out the best work on short notice. Mr. J. H. Medicke, who is a gentleman of middle age, was born in Germany, reached the United States in 1863, and is a member of the Free and Accepted Masons.

JOHN OGDEN & CO., Apothecaries, Walnut and Thirteenth Streets, and Arch and Nineteenth Streets.—A leading establishment in Philadelphia for drugs, chemicals and medicines, is the elegant and reliable pharmacy of Messrs. John Ogden & Co., located on the corner of Walnut and Thirteenth Streets and Arch and Nineteenth Streets, the former being established over fifty years and the latter some twenty years ago. Both are handsomely and attractively fitted up and will always be found to contain a full and complete stock of pure drugs and chemicals, the rarest and latest preparations, all the standard proprietary medicines, surgical instruments, sick-room appliances, physicians' requisites and druggists' sundries. The firm is one which pays the strictest and most careful attention to the compounding of physicians' prescriptions, using nothing but the purest ingredients from the best-known houses of this country and Europe, and the house has the utmost confidence of leading physicians. This firm also manufactures the celebrated Remington Still, used for fluid extracts, etc.; while they also put up a valuable line of tonics and remedies. The firm is composed of Messrs. John Ogden and W. S. Harvey. Mr. Ogden, the active member of the firm, is a native of New Jersey, a graduate of the Philadelphia College of Pharmacy, a member of the American Pharmaceutical Association and is an accomplished and popular business man.

THE PHILADELPHIA STORAGE AND UPHOLSTERING COMPANY, Lewis King, Proprietor, No. 1928 Pine Street.—The Philadelphia Storage and Upholstering Company was established in 1889, by King & Myers, and under this firm-name was conducted up to about a year ago, when Lewis King, the present proprietor, assumed sole control. Mr. King was born in Florida, and has been in this city fourteen years, and is a man of practical skill and thorough experience in his line. The building occupied by him is a commodious two-story structure, with ample facilities, and half a dozen in help are employed. A large and fine stock of antique furniture can always be found here, and every article sold is fully warranted, while the prices prevailing are exceptionally low. Cabinet-making and upholstering are done in the highest style of the art. Repairing is neatly done, likewise, and interior decorating is executed in the most superior manner, all work being warranted first-class. Furniture, household effects, china and valuables are carefully packed, stored and shipped, and moving is attended to with care and dispatch, at reasonable rates.

R. PANCOAST, Building Stone, Main Street, Near Highland Avenue.—The largest and most successful dealer in granite, blue stone, limestone, and other stone adapted for building purposes in Philadelphia, is Mr. S. R. Pancoast. The business was founded here in 1883, by Mr. J. N. Keach, the present proprietor becoming a partner in 1887, and succeeding to the sole control in 1891. The business premises cover an acre of ground and every facility is at hand for systematic and successful work in all branches of the business. A large force of competent workmen is constantly employed under the personal supervision of the proprietor. Mr. Pancoast is prepared to furnish estimates for the construction of buildings of all kinds, and many of the finest buildings and private residences that grace this section of the city have been erected in whole or in part by this house. A large and valuable stock of stone and granite is kept on hand which is cut to order at short notice. Mr. Pancoast is a native Philadelphian, who has been connected with this branch of business for the past sixteen years.

JOHN F. WALSH'S SONS, Wall Paper and Interior Decorations, No. 216 South Eighth Street. The reliable house of John F. Walsh's Sons, No. 216 South Eighth Street, has long been known to every one in Philadelphia who has had occasion to think of beautifying a home. The business was established by Mr. John F. Walsh in 1866, and at his death, Messrs. Andrew A. and Thomas C. Walsh succeeded to the control and have been eminently successful in keeping up the excellent reputation that the house has for years enjoyed. These gentlemen are widely known as expert fresco painters and general interior decorators and their services are in great demand by those of refined tastes. The premises occupied by the firm comprise a store and basement, 24 x 60 feet in dimensions, handsomely furnished and containing a large stock of wall papers in all the latest styles. Specimens of their work may be seen in the City Court House, Eden Hall and in most of the convents of the city, beside many fine private residences, business houses and banks. From ten to twenty workmen are employed and all orders are promptly filled. All work is under the personal supervision of one of the firm and satisfaction is guaranteed in every instance both as regards workmanship and prices. We would recommend those desiring truly artistic workmanship in this line to leave their affairs in the hands of this firm.

HISTORICAL AND COMMERCIAL PHILADELPHIA.

H. WALMSLEY (Limited), Opticians and Photographic Stock Merchants, No. 1022 Walnut Street.—This company was duly incorporated and commenced business at the same location in 1889, the officers being Charles Brealy, Esq., Chairman, and J. W. Delany, Esq., Secretary and Treasurer. A specialty is made of the accurate preparation of oculists' prescriptions, the lenses, etc., being ground and polished on the premises; and, moreover, the company are retail dealers in all kinds of optical goods, spectacles, eyeglasses, lorgnettes, lenses, microscopes, objectives of all powers, as well as a full line of photographic supplies and requisites for amateurs and professionals, the latest improved cameras being a special feature. Of the whole a large and very complete stock is carried, representing the finest manufactures in each line, obtained direct in every instance from the leading sources of supply upon the most advantageous terms. The store, 20x40 feet in area, is handsomely furnished and well appointed in detail, and the factory, in the same building, is fully equipped, ten skilled assistants being regularly employed. Chas. R. Brealy and J. W. Delany were both born in this city.

M. H. GODSHALL, Carriage Builder, Main Street and Highland Avenue.—The specialty of this house consists of a rich class of work of the highest finish, such as landaus, coupés, broughams, victorias and fine buggies, all of which are modelled upon the latest approved principles of construction, according to the correct style; and the materials used, from the axles and wheels right through to the paint, lacquer and varnish, are of the finest quality the market affords. Moreover, anything in the form of a vehicle is manufactured to order, and detailed instructions are rigidly adhered to; repairing, painting, trimming and jobbing of all kinds are neatly executed and promptly attended to, and vehicles of any sort are taken on storage. The enterprise was established in 1884 down in the city by the present proprietor, who has been actively engaged in this line of trade since 1871, and removed the seat of his operations to his present location five years ago. Here a lot, 73x200 feet in area, is utilized, having upon it a building of three floors, each 35x62 feet in dimensions, furnished throughout with a full equipment of machines, fires, forges, appliances, tools and accessories for fine carriage and wagon building, from A to Z; ten mechanics being regularly employed, all skilled in their respective departments. Mr. William H. Godshall is a young man, a native of Bucks County, Pa., and came to Philadelphia in 1874, having been an esteemed resident of Germantown for the past ten years.

RUTHERFORD & BARCLAY, Miners and Manufacturers of Rutherford's Metallic Paint; Office, No. 517 Drexel Building; Works, Lehigh Gap, Pa.—Messrs. Rutherford & Barclay, as miners and manufacturers of "Rutherford's Metallic Paint," established their business in 1886, and have won a high reputation. They are now turning out 6,000 tons of paint per year, while they make but one color—brown. It is extensively used in all climates for painting railroad cars, bridges, oil barrels, metal roofs, vessels, brick walls, shingle roofs, fences, out buildings, machinery, iron railings, gas holders, etc. It is manufactured from magnetic iron ore, possesses peculiar properties not found in any other paint, and is always uniform and reliable, is unexcelled in durability, and is the very best coating for iron, tin and wood in the market. It is largely used for painting cottages and hotels at all sea-side resorts, as it is not affected by salt air as other pigments are. Shingle roofs painted with two coats of Rutherford's metallic paint will not warp or crack, and will be preserved for years. It outwears all lead paints and costs only one quarter as much. It is warranted fire proof and free from adulteration; requires no drier, contains no sediment, and has greater spreading capacity than any other paint. It is in use throughout the United States, Canada, and many portions of Europe. The copartners, Messrs. Henry Rutherford and Charles Barclay, are native Philadelphians.

GEORGE H. WEST & SONS, Wholesale Dealers in Boots and Shoes, No. 21 North Third Street.—An old half a century of uninterrupted prosperity marks the history of the well known house of George H. West & Sons, wholesale dealers in boots and shoes, thus making it one of the oldest and leading establishments of the kind in Philadelphia. The firm handle everything in the line indicated, and their business, which extends throughout the Middle States and the principal portion of the South, is very large, the total annual sales reaching a handsome figure. The building occupied as office and salesrooms is a commodious five story and basement structure, equipped with freight elevator and complete facilities, and eight of a staff are here employed, in addition to seven representatives on the road. An extensive and first class stock is constantly kept on hand, and includes foot wear of all sizes, widths, shapes and styles, in both fine and medium grades, ladies', misses' and children's low cut shoes being a specialty. Every pair sold by this reliable firm are warranted as to make and material, no inferior goods, whatever, being handled, while the very lowest consistent prices are quoted, the most liberal inducements being offered to the trade, and all orders are filled in the most prompt and trustworthy manner. This time tried and deservedly popular house was established some fifty odd years ago by H. F. & W. Rodney, and later passed into control of West, Southworth & Co., who were succeeded in 1878 by George H. West & Sons, under which firm name the business has since been conducted with eminent success, although the senior member was removed by death in January, 1890. Messrs. Pemberton B. West and Henry F. West, sons of George H., who now compose the firm, are gentlemen in the prime of life and natives of this city. Mr. Pemberton B. West is a prominent Mason and is also an active member of other societies.

EDWARD FADIN, Fruit and Produce, No. 310 North Delaware Avenue.—One of the most successful and prominent, as well as the oldest, dealers in fruit and produce in this city is Mr. Edward Fadin who has been established in trade since 1856. Mr. Fadin is a native of Philadelphia and resides in Camden. His business has attained a large development through the able management he has given to it since the retirement of his partner, Mr. Austin, about twelve years ago, at which time he moved to his present stand. He handles all kinds of country produce, vegetables etc., and also deals extensively in fruits, such as lemons, oranges and lemons. His large banana room at all times contains a choice variety of that product. In domestic fruits also he does an enormous trade and acts as general purchasing agent. He has a liberal patronage on all lines, having numerous buying customers among dealers and large consumers. The house is one of the best and most widely known in the city, and to all his dealings Mr. Fadin has the reputation of being one of the most honorable men in the trade and has gained hosts of friends during his long business career.

DANIEL DOREY, Importer and Manufacturer of Hat and Cap Leathers and Springs, No. 235 Race Street.—Among the representative staunch houses in its special line in Philadelphia, the pioneer concern and the one best known is that of Daniel Dorey, importer and manufacturer of every variety of hat and cap leathers and springs. It is the oldest house in this trade in the United States, and enjoys an immense patronage among the leading hat manufacturers. It was established in 1846 by Mr. Dorey, and was originally located on Market Street, and remained there nineteen years; then Mr. Dorey moved to Third Street, and after stopping there twenty years, took up his quarters in his present place, at No. 235 Race Street. In this building, which he owns, Mr. Dorey occupies two large floors, each twenty feet wide and one hundred feet deep, containing every necessary appliance for the speedy turning out of large stocks of goods. He employs half a dozen expert hands, and supplies the trade principally in the Middle and Southern States. Mr. Dorey's present preëminence is no more than the just reward properly due to efforts rightly directed. He is a native of Philadelphia, an old and honored resident, and a man widely respected for his splendid business talents.

HISTORICAL AND COMMERCIAL PHILADELPHIA.

CHRISTIAN MILLER, Importer and Bottler of all Kinds of Malt Liquors, Alaconda, Natural Mineral Water and Aerated Waters. Prompt Attention to Orders by Mail, Nos. 14 to 20 East Chelten Avenue, Germantown.—The oldest established and largest bottling house in Germantown is that of Mr. Christian Miller, located at Nos. 14 to 20 East Chelten Avenue. The business premises occupied comprise a building, 71 x 70 feet in dimensions, and three stories in height, fully equipped with all the latest improved machinery operated by steam-power. Employment is furnished to twelve experienced hands and orders are promptly filled. Mr. Miller is an extensive bottler of all kinds of malt liquors, natural mineral water and aerated waters; he also bottles Bergner & Engel's Premium lager beer, porter, ale and brown stout, India pale ales, etc. The house has secured a large family and general trade in this section and Philadelphia, and five wagons are kept busy delivering goods. Orders by mail or express are given the promptest attention and goods are delivered at the shortest notice without delay. Mr. Miller is a native of Bucks Co., Pa., but has been twenty years a resident of this city. He is a member of the Knights Templar of the F. and A. M., the Knights of Birmingham, and the Red Men. He is thoroughly acquainted with all the demands of the trade in which he is engaged and is honorable and reliable in all transactions.

C. J. BIDDLE, Drugs, No. 3418 Market Street.—One of the most prominent and valuable retail drug establishments in Philadelphia is that of Mr. C. J. Biddle, located at No. 3418 Market Street. This concern was founded by Mr. Heathcote, and since his time has been controlled by several different proprietors, Mr. Biddle taking possession in Oct., 1879, as successor to Ben Shoemaker, Jr. Mr. Biddle has, by skill and energy, built up a large and influential patronage and maintained a popularity vouchsafed to but few of his competitors. The store occupied is handsomely fitted up with cherry fixtures and every facility is provided for the prompt and accurate transaction of business. The stock embraces pure drugs, chemicals, and standard proprietary remedies of every description, the assortment containing nothing but the freshest and finest goods. The display of toilet and fancy specialties is rich and attractive and comports admirably with the reputation of the house for handling only the choicest productions that can be obtained. A specialty is made of the compounding of physicians' prescriptions, and the preparations, for safe and responsible service, are unsurpassed. Mr. Biddle is a native of Bucks County, Pa. He graduated from the Philadelphia College of Pharmacy in 1874, and is a member of the Alumni Association of the same. He spent five years in the Philadelphia Hospital and learned this business with Bullock & Crenshaw. He employs two experienced assistants, is thoroughly qualified to successfully conduct the affairs of the business and is highly regarded as one of the most capable and trustworthy gentlemen in his profession in the city.

A. VANIER, House, Sign and Fresco Painting, Plain and Decorative Paper Hanging, No. 9 South Sixteenth Street.—Twenty years of successful, steadily-growing business is a record to be proud of. That is the record of Mr. A. Vanier, whose store at No. 9 South Sixteenth Street, has one of the finest lines of wall paper in the city. Twenty years ago Mr. Vanier started in business as a painter, and, in 1890, he added the wall paper business. He has a neat store, 25 x 40 feet, where he carries an immense stock, which includes a full line of American wall papers. His main business is house and sign painting and he makes a specialty of interior decorating. His shop is at No. 1731 Barker Street. He employs from 25 to 40 men and turns out a high class of work, being one of the leaders in his line in the city. He is himself a practical worker, a fine designer, and an artist of rare skill. His business is mainly in the city and suburbs and he caters for a high-class trade, for which he has fine facilities. Mr. Vanier is a native of Boston, but he has been here since his boyhood. He is a member of the F. and A. M., Knights Templar, I. O. O. F. and other organizations.

CHARLES A. EBEL, Teamster, Residence, No. 1827 North Twentieth Street, Office, No. 1003 Sansom Street.—One of the best-known, most popular and enterprising business men of Philadelphia in this special line of activity is Mr. Charles A. Ebel, teamster, whose office is most eligibly located at No. 1003 Sansom Street. Mr. Ebel, who was born in Germany, came to this city to reside twenty years ago, and two years later embarked for himself in his present business, of which he has since made such a pronounced success, and his popularity as a careful and reliable teamster is widespread. He has in his employ five experienced and efficient workmen and owns four of the largest wagons, and he is always found prepared to undertake all kinds of teaming, truck loads of anything, no matter what weight or size, being conveyed to any required distance in the most careful and safe manner. He promptly fills the largest orders, and proper attention in every instance is given to all transportations entrusted to his care, while his charges are invariably placed at the most reasonable rates consistent with fair and just dealings. A large, permanent and extensive trade has been developed throughout this city and the general business transacted amounts to a most prosperous annual aggregate. Mr. Ebel is thoroughly experienced in every branch of this business and all those entering into business relations with him will find it to their advantage in every way. He is well known in social as well as mercantile circles, being a member of the I. O. O. F.

JAMES A. LOUGHNEY, Plumber, Gas and Steam Fitter, Office, No. 1043 Lancaster Avenue.—One of the most popular and extensive plumbing and gasfitting businesses in Philadelphia is that conducted at No. 1043 Lancaster Avenue, by Mr. James A. Loughney, who has been entrusted from time to time with the fulfillment of some highly important and significant contracts, among others being the whole of the plumbing of sixty-five houses on Thirty-eighth and Broom Streets, the building at Fortieth and Spring Garden Streets, Twenty-eighth Street and Fairmount Avenue; sixty-five houses on Forty-second and Baring Streets, the building at Twenty-first and Parrish Streets and seventeen houses on Forty second and Baring Streets. Thus, Mr. Loughney's ability to execute the finest work at reasonable prices is soundly established upon actual results, and since he initiated his business twelve years ago, he has succeeded in working up a large trade in this section of the city, the volume of which furnishes employment for upwards of thirty skilled mechanics. All kinds of sanitary and ordinary plumbing, gas and steam fitting are undertaken, including jobbing and repairing in all branches of the trade, contracts for new work, drainage, ventilation, piping, connections, the supply and fixing of water-closets, urinals, bath-tubs, cisterns, tanks, pumps, bath boilers, washbowls, chandeliers, gas brackets, radiators, etc. The workshop is spacious and fully equipped and every convenience is at hand for turning out the best work on short notice. Mr. Loughney, who is still a young man, is a thoroughly practical plumber, having learned the trade with Messrs. Hare, Kite & Bros., and personally directs the prompt and accurate fulfillment of each order with which he is entrusted.

HISTORICAL AND COMMERCIAL PHILADELPHIA.

JOHN HUGGARD, Importer 4-4 White Linens, Linen Specialties, L. C. Handkerchiefs, Nos. 36 and 38 Strawberry Street.—One of the oldest and most extensive importers of this class of goods is Mr. John Huggard, who imports direct from Belfast, Ireland, 4-4 white linens, shirting linens and other specialties, linen cambric handkerchiefs, etc., and carries a full stock in all lines. The business premises comprise salesroom and basement, each 25x40 in area, with an L used for shipping purposes. Two travelling salesmen are employed, and a large business is transacted in Pennsylvania, New York and New Jersey. Mr. Huggard established this business in 1864 and has occupied his present place since 1870. He was born in this city, and is an active, energetic and enterprising man of business.

HENRY C. FORNER, Conveyancer and Real Estate Broker, No. 325 South Fourth Street.—Although established as recently as January 1st, 1892, Mr. Henry C. Forner has already built up a large and fast increasing connection as a conveyancer and real estate broker. For fourteen years Mr. Forner studied conveyancing in the law office of Charles Henry Jones, and thus he is enabled to bring a thorough and practical knowledge to bear upon the fulfilment of any matter relative to the conveyance of property, exercising a scrupulous care in the settlement, transfer and entire management of estates, the preparation of titles, deeds, leases, trusts, wills and similar instruments, as well as their minute and detailed examination. Moreover, he transacts a general real estate business, devoting particular attention to the collection of house and ground rents and interest, the purchase, sale and exchange of city, suburban and country property of every sort, the letting of premises in general, and the speedy negotiation of loans upon bond or mortgage. Mr. Forner is a young Philadelphian and is warmly esteemed.

ALEX. GALLAGHER, Manufacturer of Stone Cutters' Tools, Thirtieth and Walnut Streets. There is perhaps not one in his line in this city who has a better reputation for skill and reliability than Alex Gallagher, manufacturer of stone cutters' tools, Thirtieth and Walnut Streets. He turns out a very superior class of hammers, chisels, points, wedges, drills and everything in the line indicated, and enjoys an excellent patronage. Mr. Gallagher, who is a gentleman in the prime of life and a Philadelphian, is a thoroughly expert workman of many years' experience. He has been established at the present location since 1885 and from the start has been highly prosperous, his trade steadily improving. He has a well equipped shop, with two fires, and employes several skilled hands. Mr. Gallagher is prepared to make all kinds of stone cutters' tools to order, and every article turned out by him is warranted as to workmanship and material. Tools are repaired also in the most superior manner, at short notice, and perfect satisfaction is assured in every instance, all orders receiving prompt and personal attention, while the prices charged for tools and jobbing are of the most reasonable character.

THOS. H. McCOLLIN & CO., Dealers in Photographic Supplies, No. 1030 Arch Street. This reliable and representative house was founded in 1858 by Mr. B. L. Dubbs, who was succeeded in 1874 by Mr. Thos. H. McCollin, and in 1887 the present firm was organized by the admission of Mr. A. E. Maris, to partnership. The business premises comprise three floors, 25x186 feet each, giving ample accommodations for supplying the most extensive demand. This establishment is a great emporium from which professionals and amateurs alike can obtain complete outfits or supplies of any kind. The firm deal in all kinds of photographic apparatus, including the most approved cameras, lenses of all powers and sizes, from the most famous makers; full lines of chemicals, and the various necessaries to the working outfit. They are especially prominent, however, as sole importers of the Orthoscope lens, the Berlin vignetting paper, and the endless roll crayon paper; and as manufacturers of the famous compound Blitz pulver, which eclipses all other inventions in the production of flash light for photographing at night. The brilliant results achieved by its use in securing pictures of dark mines and caverns, as well as in most exquisite portrait work, have made it widely popular. This house also leads all others in the line of blue process paper for builders' plans, etc.; while another specialty is McCollin's outfit for photography with the microscope. Messrs. McCollin and Maris are both native Philadelphians, and experts in their branch of trade.

TAYLOR & CO., Dealers in Lehigh and Schuylkill Coal; Yard, Huntingdon and American Streets.—For several years past Messrs. Taylor & Co. have been an important factor in the great coal supply of Philadelphia. They handle the best grades of Lehigh and Schuylkill coals, and the trade controlled consists in the supply of factories, etc., in carload lots, and private families throughout the city for retail quantities; the latter being the speciality of the business. Four wagons are retained for delivery purposes, and eight competent hands find regular employment around the premises. Every facility is possessed for obtaining shipments direct from the mines upon the most advantageous terms, and thus the firm is enabled to charge rock bottom prices for each quality. The supplies are received by the Philadelphia and Reading Railroad, a branch track from which runs right through the yards, so that the cars unload on the spot. The yards, together with sheds, stables, offices, etc., cover an area of 80x113 feet, and have a capacity for storing a thousand tons of coal, properly screened. The enterprise was established in 1875 by the present sole proprietor, Mr. Henry Taylor, who was born in Canada and came to the United States in 1865, and is a member of the Philadelphia Coal Exchange.

LUTNER BROS., Wagon Builders Nos. 34 to 40 Tasker Street.—An old established house and one that has long enjoyed an enviable reputation for first class work in the line of wagon building is that of Lutner Bros., located at Nos. 34 to 40 Tasker Street. This prosperous business was established in more than twenty-five years ago by Mr. Thos. E. Lutner, who retired in 1888 and was succeeded by his sons, the present proprietors. The premises occupied comprise a brick building, 61x60 feet in dimensions, equipped with all the latest improved machinery, tools and appliances known to the trade. The firm keep five fires running, and are prepared to do the iron work in a satisfactory manner, making a specialty of heavy work. Their productions are unsurpassed for strength and ease of draft and are the embodiments of mechanical workmanship of the highest order of perfection. Wherever introduced, these wagons are general favorites, and are without exception the best in the market. A visit to this factory will satisfy purchasers and their friends that the productions of this house are without rival and justly merit the commendations bestowed upon them by the trade and public. From eight to ten skilled workmen are employed, and all orders are promptly filled. The members of the firm are Messrs. Thomas and James Lutner, natives of Philadelphia and gentlemen of ability and experience. Thomas is a practical wood worker and James is an engineer, and both are highly esteemed in the community for their strict integrity.

T. F. HUTCHISON, Tin Roofing, Galvanized Iron Work, No. 5156 Germantown Avenue. The house of Mr. T. F. Hutchison, dealer in stoves, ranges, tin ware and kitchen goods, was established in 1887 and has gained a position in the front rank of the trade in this city. His business premises comprise a store, 20x89 feet in dimensions, with a two-story shop in the rear and unsurpassed facilities are at hand for conducting all branches of the enterprises. In his splendid warerooms can be found everything needed in the line of stoves, ranges and furnaces, tin ware, and kitchen furnishing goods. Mr. Hutchison is a genuine tin and sheet iron worker, making a specialty of hot air work, putting heaters in residences, and everything in this line. He keeps the heaviest coated roofing tin made, of which over 600,000 square feet have been used without a single complaint. A large force of skilled and experienced workmen are employed. Mr. Hutchison is a native of Pennsylvania and has been a resident of this city for twenty years. He is honorable and reliable in all transactions, and merits the success he has gained.

HISTORICAL AND COMMERCIAL PHILADELPHIA.

EORGE MOLLENKOF, Undertaker and Embalmer, No. 4502 Main Street, Germantown.—An experienced, popular and first-class furnishing undertaker and embalmer, in Germantown, is Mr. George Mollenkof, who is widely recognized here as a leader in his profession. He has been established in this business for the past four years, in which he has since attained a front rank position, and in May last removed his main warerooms from No. 5041 Main Street, his original location, to No. 4502, although his branch office is also on this thoroughfare, one door below his former place of address. Both as an embalmer and general undertaker, Mr. Mollenkof has displayed marked ability, having a natural adaptation for this vocation, and being considerate of the feelings of bereaved relatives and friends. In conducting this business he makes no unseemly display, while by faithful and efficient service to those who employ him he has gained the esteem and good-will of the whole community. The premises which he occupies are 30 x 40 feet in dimensions, and include handsomely appointed office and warerooms, with a factory in the rear used for manufacturing purposes, and three competent assistants are required in regular employment. A fine assortment of caskets, coffins and funeral requisites of every description, of the proprietor's own make, is here displayed, and he is always prepared to furnish everything that is desired for funerals, including hearses and carriages, at the most reasonable rates. All calls, day or night, receive prompt attention, and the large and influential trade developed extends throughout this city and the adjacent districts. Mr. Mollenkof, who is a cabinet-maker by trade, and a native of Germany, has resided in this country for the past quarter of a century, and is a popular member of the Knights of the Golden Eagle, the I. O. O. F. and Red Men.

H. DOERLE, Conveyancer and Real Estate Agent, No. 737 South Third Street.—Prosecuting a successful business as a conveyancer, real estate agent and insurance broker, we find Mr. P. H. Doerle, with headquarters at No. 737 South Third Street. He established his business here in 1880 and has always enjoyed a liberal patronage derived from leading capitalists and substantial property owners in this city and vicinity. He is thoroughly experienced in the knowledge of laws and customs of real estate and may be consulted upon all such matters with the utmost confidence. He has at all times on his lists eligible business premises, dwelling-houses and building lots for sale and to rent, and investors will always find his office a useful medium through which to obtain their wants. Conveyancing in all branches is given prompt attention, while a specialty is made of the collection of rents and interest. Insurance is also effected in first-class companies at the lowest rates of premium and the prompt payment of all losses is guaranteed. Mr. Doerle is a native Philadelphian and a young man of large practical experience, wide acquaintance and sterling worth.

USTUS D. DICKINSON, Manufacturer of Fine Harness, Main Street, below Highland Avenue, Chestnut Hill.—The leading house in the manufacture of fine harness in Chestnut Hill is that of Justus D. Dickinson, situated on Main Street, below Highland Avenue. The business was established in 1885 by the present proprietor, Mr. Dickinson, and removed to the premises now occupied in May, 1892. He is a thoroughly practical workman, having had five years' experience as superintendent of the shop of John McLeod. In addition to the manufacture of harness of every kind and description in single or double, coupé and track, a special feature is made in the production of fine coach house goods. The premises occupied are spacious and commodious, admirably appointed, and comprise a finely fitted workshop, fully equipped, while regular employment is furnished a number of skilled workmen to meet all demands of the trade. The house also produces a line of rich and high-grade class of work in turf goods, besides handling whips, robes, rugs, and every requisite necessary for the coach house, stable or carriage-room. Mr. Dickinson is a man of middle age, born on Chestnut Hill, and is prominently identified with the Independent Order of Odd Fellows' Encampment, Knights of Pythias and Knights of the Golden Eagle.

H. KOLB, Gents' Furnisher and Clothier, No. 4889 Main Street. Germantown.—This popular and well-known house was established in 1877, by Mr. Edward Kolb, and, in 1887, the firm-name was changed to J. H. Kolb & Co., the present name and style being adopted in 1891. The attractive store occupied is 25 x 125 feet in dimensions, and fitted up with tasteful appointments throughout. The counters and shelves are burdened with a very extensive assortment of superior ready-made clothing for men, youths and boys, in all the latest fashions and illustrating the current demand. These goods are made from the very best materials, display the best workmanship, and are stylish in cut, fit and finish and in appearance, while in the matter of prices, this house cannot be excelled by any other establishment in the city. In the rear of the store is kept a full line of ready-made clothing, including gents' and boys' suits in all the popular shades and patterns, which in fit, finish and general appearance are equal to the best tailor-made suit. The firm also carry at all times a full and complete line of goods embraced in gents' furnishings. The firm mark all goods in plain figures, selling at one price and for cash only. Mr. J. H. Kolb, the active member of the firm is a native of Germantown, and during his career as a business man has established a large and influential trade.

OBERT H. MURROW, Boot and Shoe Store, Northeast Corner Nineteenth and South Streets.—For a period of forty years the house of Mr. Robert H. Murrow has been a leading source of supply for boots and shoes of a thoroughly reliable quality. It was founded in 1852, by Mr. James Murrow, who was succeeded by his nephew, the present proprietor, in 1884. The store is spacious in size, attractive in all its appointments and perfect in convenience of arrangement for display, inspection and sale. The stock embraces boots, shoes, rubbers and slippers for men and boys, ladies, misses and children, and in all the various styles, sizes and grades, while the prices are the lowest in the market for this quality of goods. Boots and shoes are also made to order, and in all cases the finest workmanship, the latest style and perfection in fit are guaranteed. Repairing is also neatly and promptly executed. Mr. Murrow is a native Philadelphian, who served the United States Government as a letter carrier in this city from 1875 to 1885, and is a young man of sterling personal worth.

MITH & PYLE, Lapidists, No. 711 Sansom Street.—The business represented by Smith & Pyle, lapidists, was established by Mr. Smith, January 1, 1862, and the following June Mr. Pyle was admitted to partnership. The talent and thorough practical knowledge of the firm soon brought their work into active and increasing demand. The premises utilized for the business comprise two rooms at No. 711 Sansom Street, ample in dimensions, provided with an abundant outfit of the best machinery, appliances and devices that can be made available, and admirably equipped in every other respect for an extensive and meritorious production. The work of this firm on precious stones displays the skill, accuracy and precision of the lapidary in their highest development, the very best standard of artistic excellence being maintained. None but skilled workmen are employed. The firm number among their patrons many of the most noted manufacturing jewelers of Philadelphia and vicinity. Their trade is being rapidly extended to all parts of Pennsylvania and the South. The members of the firm are Messrs. H. W. Smith and Abraham Pyle, both graduates of Girard College and natives of Philadelphia. Mr. Pyle was for six years a clerk in the Mechanics' National Bank and now has charge of the office work, while Mr. Smith is the lapidist and has had six years' practical experience in the business. He is a popular member of the American Mechanics.

HISTORICAL AND COMMERCIAL PHILADELPHIA.

WASHINGTON POWELL, Conveyancer, Real Estate Broker and Collector, Office, Southwest Corner Tenth and South Streets.—Mr. G. Washington Powell has been established in business here for a period of thirty years, and enjoys a deservedly high reputation for business ability and sound judgment. He transacts a general real estate business in the city and vicinity, buying, selling, leasing and exchanging property of all kinds, attending to the management of estates, collection of rents, the negotiation of loans on bond and mortgage, and effecting insurance in reliable companies. He makes a specialty of handling residence property in the First, Second, Third, Twenty-sixth and Thirtieth Wards of the city, and is a recognized authority as to the present and prospective values of realty in those wards. All advice given or transactions effected through him can be relied upon as absolutely safe, and his charges are invariably moderate. Deeds, bonds, mortgages, leases, wills, powers of attorney, articles of agreement, and all other legal instruments of writing are drawn with accuracy and dispatch. Titles are examined and briefs prepared, registers of property for sale or to let are open for the inspection of those interested, while particular attention is paid to the collection of rents, interest, etc. As an insurance broker, Mr. Powell is prepared to place risks in any insurance company desired, quoting the lowest rates of premium, and guaranteeing a prompt and liberal adjustment of all losses. He numbers among his permanent patrons many of the largest and wealthiest capitalists, investors and property owners in Philadelphia. Mr. Powell is a native Philadelphian, and has been a notary public since 1880.

FREAS & SON, Family Grocers, Main Street and Washington Avenue, Germantown.—The oldest-established house in its line in the city is that of Messrs. H. Freas & Son, which was opened to the public in 1827, and enjoys a high reputation for the excellence of the goods carried. The building occupied is 75 x 125 feet in dimensions, and is filled to repletion with a carefully selected stock of family groceries, hardware, garden implements, furnishing goods, wines, liquors, etc. Here will at all times be found fresh crop teas, select coffees, pure sugars, spices and condiments, the best grades of patent fancy flours, all kinds of farinaceous goods, green and dried fruits, and one of the choicest stocks of canned goods, etc., in Germantown. The firm handle only those brands which are put up by honorable and responsible packers and guarantee quality. The goods in all departments are purchased in immense quantities from producers, and the firm, conducting a heavy trade, can put prices where they are a positive attraction to the public. Mr. H. Freas is a native of Montgomery Co., Pennsylvania, but has been a resident of this city since 1827. Though now eighty-one years of age he is still actively engaged in business, and is highly esteemed in financial circles for his excellent methods and sound judgment. He owns the hotel opposite his place of business, the Washington House, and also about $300,000 worth of real estate in this section.

WALTER K. BILES, Wall Papers, Etc., and Painting in all Branches, No. 1520 Frankford Avenue.—An old and reliable wall paper house in Frankford is that of Mr. Walter K. Biles, which was established at the same location in 1872 by Mr. Gilbert H. Blaker, and in March, 1892, it came into the hands of the present proprietor, who possesses seven years' practical experience in this line. In addition to the sale of the imported and domestic wall papers, shade cloth and window-shades, a full line of plain and decorative painting is undertaken, including fresco, panel and relief work to any design, from the simplest to the most elaborate, tinting, gilding, varnishing, polishing, hardwood filling, fine sign writing and lettering in the latest styles. The store, 20 x 50 feet in size, is well arranged, and a large and carefully selected stock is always on hand, affording an ample choice in all kinds of wall papers, shade cloth and window-shades, as well as various interior decorations, upwards of ten skilled hands being regularly employed. Mr. Walter K. Biles is a native of Philadelphia, and still a young man.

DAVID B. McMENAMIN, Agent for Soaps, Front and Market Streets.—Mr. David B. McMenamin is the duly accredited representative here for Messrs. Schulz & Co., of Zanesville, Ohio, manufacturers of soaps, whose most popular and best brands are the "Star," "Fatherland," "Irish," "Scotch," "Montag" and "Duck" family and laundry soaps. Although established in this line of commerce for only one year, Mr. McMenamin has a practical experience at his command ranging over a period of eight years, and he has succeeded in building up an extensive trade with jobbers throughout this section of the Union. All orders receive prompt attention, and are shipped direct from the factory at Zanesville. Mr. McMenamin is a young gentleman of Philadelphia birth, and was formerly engaged for seven years with his father in the canned goods business.

WATSON & ROBINSON, Wood Working Mill, Manufacturers of Frames, Doors, Sash, Shutters, Stair Work, Nos. 32 to 46 Queen Street.—One of the oldest-established and most extensive wood working mills in Germantown is that owned and conducted by Messrs. Watson and Robinson. This progressive undertaking was founded in 1867 at the same location by Mr. S. E. Hughes, who in 1877 was succeeded by the present firm, composed of Mr. Alfred C. Watson and Mr. John Robinson, under whose skilled and experienced direction every detail of the enterprise is conducted. A full line of wood work for the building, carpentering, cabinet-making and furniture trades is undertaken, including frames, doors, sash, shutters, stair work, newel posts, scrolls, blinds, brackets, finish, trimming, molding, match and sheathing, grooving, sawing, turning of all kinds and planing, and the firm's operations, reaching all over the city and adjacent districts, are of considerable magnitude and significance, for they work, cut up and otherwise use nearly one million feet of lumber annually. The mill, although occupied ever since the initiation of the business, is strictly "up to date," with regard to the mechanism and machinery employed, for the firm have adopted from time to time all the latest improved appliances and methods as they have been introduced, and thus are enabled to make a special feature of the finest work, in fancy hard woods of a superior finish and make. The mill itself comprises a substantial structure of three stories, having an area on each floor of 100 x 125 feet, furnished with an elaborate plant of improved sawing, planing, grooving, beading, molding and other machines, lathes of the latest construction and all necessary appliances and accessories pertaining to the industry; a 50-horse power steam-engine being the motive force used and from fifty to sixty skilled mechanics employed. In addition to the mill, extensive lumber yards are utilized, covering one and a half acres, and a heavy and select stock of well-seasoned hard and soft woods is always on hand. Of the able proprietors, Mr. Alfred C. Watson is a native of Germantown; while Mr. John Robinson was born in Belfast, Ireland, and has resided in this city since 1846.

J. RICE, Commission Merchant in Butter, Eggs, Poultry and all kinds of Live Stock, Nos. 323 and 325 North Water Street.—This responsible house was established in 1881 by the present proprietor and under his able and skillful direction a heavy volume of wholesale trade is now controlled reaching throughout the city and suburbs, while, also, a sound reputation is enjoyed for handling only prime and fresh goods in each line at rock-bottom prices, for the speedy disposal of consignments and for making accurate returns daily. Consignments and shipments are constantly arriving of dairy produce, poultry, calves, sheep, lambs and hogs, from raisers and producers in Delaware, Maryland, Pennsylvania, New Jersey and Ohio, for disposal upon this market, and the very choice, fresh butter handled is received from three of the best creameries. This live stock and produce find ready sale on the premises, which latter comprise a spacious floor, 25 x 165 feet in area, well fitted and equipped for the most expeditious handling and dispatch of shipments. The experienced proprietor, Mr. C. J. Rice, who is a young man of energy and sound business ability, was born near Harrisburg, Pa., raised in Delaware, and is a resident of Philadelphia.

ZOÖLOGICAL GARDEN - RUSTIC BRIDGE - YAKS

HARRY R. HAGEN, Conveyancer, Real Estate and Insurance Broker, Notary Public, No. 1136 Germantown Avenue.—Of the many solid citizens of Germantown who have come to the front in the realm of realty within recent years, few, if any, have been more successful than Harry R. Hagen, whose office is at No. 1136 Germantown Avenue. He has been engaged in this line about two years, and has acquired a large and desirable patronage. Mr. Hagen, who is a conveyancer, real estate and insurance broker and notary public, is a gentleman of middle age and a native of this city. He is a man of strict integrity, active and energetic, and is well and favorably known in the community both in business circles and in private life. He buys, sells and exchanges city and suburban property of every description on commission, and gives personal attention to the management of estates. Rents and interests are collected in the most prompt and trustworthy manner, mortgages are negotiated and loans are procured on collateral security; risks are effected in first-class fire companies, at lowest rates, and investments are judiciously placed; also, titles are examined, and conveyancing in all its branches carefully attended to, while deeds, mortgages, affidavits and other legal papers are accurately drawn up. In short, all classes of business pertaining to the purchase, sale, care and transfer of realty and the placing of insurance are attended to by Mr. Hagen, and those having dealings with this gentleman are assured of finding the same of an eminently satisfactory character.

WILLIAM BICHY, Apothecary, Established 1885, No. 5557 Main Street, Opposite Carpenter Street, Germantown.—One of the finest and most complete drugstores in this vicinity is the commodious, finely-appointed, and in all respects first-class establishment of William Bichy, where physicians' prescriptions and family recipes are compounded in the most vigilant and accurate manner. A laboratory where all of the important preparations, fluid extracts and tinctures are manufactured is attached to the store, to secure fresh and pure drugs. The business was inaugurated in 1885 at No. 5561 Main Street, and was removed to present location in 1890. The premises occupied consist of a store, 20 x 60, a handsome soda fountain being a feature. A large and carefully selected line of drugs, medicines and chemicals, perfumery, soaps, toilet articles, stationery, mineral waters, cigars and tobacco, physicians' requisites, and druggists' sundries, all derived from the most reliable sources of production, are offered for sale at the lowest prices. Mr. Bichy has had ten years' practical experience, was regularly graduated from the Philadelphia College of Pharmacy and is a member of its Alumni Association. He was born in Buffalo, is a young man and an expert master of every branch of the pharmaceutical profession.

WILLIAM B. DIXEY, Plumber and Sanitary Engineer, Etc., No. 3826 Market Street. A well-known and very successful licensed plumber, gasfitter and sanitary engineer in West Philadelphia is Mr. William B. Dixey, located at No. 3826 Market Street, whose ability to execute the best and most reliable work is amply attested by the several important and significant contracts with which he has been intrusted from time to time, notably the plumbing and gasfitting in the Palace Hotel, Goshen, Va.; the police station and patrol house, at Sixty-first and Thompson Streets, here; Terry Building, Roanoke, Va.; Randolph, Macon Academy, Front Royal, Va.; and the Court House at Sixth and Chestnut Streets. The business was established in January, 1879, by Mr. William B. Dixey. All kinds of sanitary plumbing and gasfitting are undertaken, both jobbing and repairing, and contracts for new work, including drainage, piping, ventilation, the supply and fixing of water-closets with all the latest improved sanitary appliances, urinals, bath-tubs, washbowls, tanks, pumps, sinks, cisterns, gas brackets, chandeliers, etc., particular attention being devoted to sanitary engineering. Ten to thirty-two skilled artisans are employed and each order undertaken is executed accurately and promptly, under the direct supervision of Mr. Dixey, who is a young man of Philadelphia birth and is a registered and thoroughly practical plumber.

HISTORICAL AND COMMERCIAL PHILADELPHIA

METHODIST EPISCOPAL BOOK ROOM, Philadelphia Conference Tract Society, F. B. Clegg, Agent, No. 1018 Arch Street.—While in the main this work will be found descriptive of the mechanical industries and commercial interests of the great city of Philadelphia, it is not only just, but necessary, to do justice to those establishments that have done and are still doing so much to elevate society by the dissemination of the products of the printing press. The religious publications are especially worthy of mention, as they are in a great measure the safeguards of public morals and deserve the recognition and respect of every citizen in the country. A very prominent, prosperous, and ably-managed house of this character is that of the Methodist Episcopal Book Rooms, located at No. 1018 Arch Street, whose productions are of great interest to a vast number throughout the United States. The business of this house was founded in 1866 by the Philadelphia Conference of the Methodist Episcopal Church, which was done for the purpose of circulating all endorsed publications bearing upon the doctrines inculcated by the precepts of the Methodist Episcopal Church, and from the date of its inception has been very successful in its mission. The premises occupied are very spacious and commodious and are admirably adapted to the wants of the business and every convenience is provided for the comfort of patrons and visitors, while every facility is at hand for the prompt filling of all orders. The trade extends all over the United States and is constantly increasing. A full and complete stock of every publication pertaining to the Methodist Episcopal Church is to be found here, also a fine line of other religious works, miscellaneous books, theological commentaries, tracts, Church and Sunday-school periodicals, also mottoes, catechisms, hymn books, Sunday-school libraries, reward cards, pulpit, family and pocket Bibles and New Testaments, certificates and stationery of all kinds. The office of the "Philadelphia Methodist" is also here, for which subscriptions and advertisements are received, and all books are sold here at the lowest prices. The business of the house is conducted by an agent who is elected by the board of managers. The present agent, Mr. F. B. Clegg, has been with the concern ever since it was established and has filled his present position ever since 1884. He is a native of this city, a gentleman of middle age, energetic and courteous, and is highly respected by all with whom he has any social or commercial relations.

THE MOORE & WHITE COMPANY, Fifteenth Street and Lehigh Avenue, Huntingdon Street Station, P. & R. R.R., Germantown Junction, P. R. R.—This company are prominently and honorably identified with the wonderful progress and improvement made in the erection of paper mills and the perfection of paper mill machinery, while they are expert general machinists and engineers, and the owners and manufacturers of the "Moore & White" patent friction clutch pulleys, cut-off couplings, shafting, pulleys, gearing, etc. The business was established in 1885 by Messrs. John W. Moore and J. Atwood White, the present style being adopted in 1887, with the above-named gentlemen as proprietors. The plant covers one and one-half acres of ground, on which are erected a machine-shop, 60 x 330 feet, a pattern-shop, 60 x 60 feet, and a blacksmith-shop, 10 x 50 feet, all splendidly equipped with new and improved machinery, operated by a steam-engine of 50-horse power, and steady employment is given to one hundred skilled hands. This company makes a specialty of paper machinery and are widely recognized as experts in all matters pertaining to the build and practical working value of the same; while as designers and inventors they have made many of the most valuable improvements known to the industry. They contract for the erection and equipment of paper mills throughout, design and construct all machinery for the same, and are prepared to fit up paper mills in any part of the United States, Canada or South America. Their patronage comes from the best class of manufacturers in those countries, and no house stands higher in the esteem of the trade, or is better able to meet promptly and successfully every emergency incident to the business. Their methods are thoroughly enterprising and progressive. They are constant investigators in this field of skilled industry, and the splendid achievements already effected by them indicate that they will continue to maintain the supremacy in their special field of labor. Their patent friction clutch is everywhere recognized as a superior article without objectionable features. They are in use doing all kinds of work, such as driving electric-light machinery, wood and iron working machinery, paper machinery, cotton and woolen machinery, etc., and give perfect satisfaction under all circumstances. Among prominent parties using them in Philadelphia may be named: Hon. John Wanamaker, The Neafie & Levy Ship and Engine Building Co., A. A. Jewett & Co., Lehigh Valley R. R. Co., Hensel Silk Mfg. Co., the United States Mint, J. B. Avil Printing Co., Diamond Mills Emery Co., H. Disston & Sons, Spreckels Sugar Refinery Co., Manayunk Paper Co., McDowell Paper Mills, American Bank Note Co., Megargee Paper Mills, Berry & Orton Co., H. B. Smith Machine Co., Wm. M. Singerly, Gen. V. Cresson, Wm. Sellers & Co., Baldwin Locomotive Works, Philadelphia Textile Machinery Co., Pennsylvania Iron Works, Bement, Miles & Co., Jacob Naylor, among many others; also Connecticut River Paper Co., Holyoke, Mass.; Hudson River Pulp and Paper Co., Palmers Falls, N. Y.; Cliff Paper Co., Niagara Falls, N. Y.; Great Bend Paper Co., Great Bend, N. Y.; Port Leyden Pulp and Paper Co., Port Leyden, N. Y.; Ticonderoga Pulp and Paper Co., Ticonderoga, N. Y.; Taggart's Paper Co., Felt Mills, N. Y.; Watertown Paper Co., Watertown, N. Y.; Clarion Pulp and Paper Co., Johnsonburg, Pa.; Pennsylvania Pulp and Paper Co., Lock Haven, Pa.; Dilworth Paper Co., Pittsburgh, Pa.; York Haven Paper Co., York Haven, Pa.; American Straw Board Co., Chestertown, Md.; Lynchburg Pulp and Paper Co., Lynchburg, Pa.; Richmond Paper Mfg. Co., Richmond, Va.; Stockton Paper Mills Co., Segal Mfg. and Paper Co., Blair Mfg. Co., United States Napping Machine Co., Camden, N. J., and other mills all over the country. Mr. Moore is a native of Laurel, Del., who acquired his trade in Wilmington, and commenced its practice in 1870. Mr. White was born in Chester County, Pa., and has been steadily at work in this line since 1872. Both are thoroughly practical and accomplished manufacturers.

BLANKLEY BROS. & CO., Manufacturers of Machinery Castings, in Loam, Green and Dry Sand, Twenty-second Street and Allegheny Avenue.—Though but a comparatively short time established—since March, 1891—Blankley Bros. & Co., manufacturers of machinery castings, in loam, green and dry sand, Twenty-second Street and Allegheny Avenue, have acquired a reputation and a patronage second to none in the business in Philadelphia. The firm have exceptional facilities, the plant being capacious and perfectly equipped, and all orders are executed at shortest notice. The general partners are J. B. Blankley, J. H. Blankley, G. Blankley, Jr., and C. M. Blankley, and the special partner is Mrs. H. B. Way, who is a sister of the gentlemen named. The Messrs. Blankley, who are Philadelphians by birth, are all men of thorough practical skill and many years' experience. They occupy spacious premises, including foundry, cleaning shed, pattern-shop, engine and boiler house, etc., and the establishment is provided with full steam-power, and all the latest improved appliances, while over fifty hands are regularly employed here. The firm are prepared to give estimates on all classes of machinery castings, both light and heavy, and guarantee the utmost satisfaction, while workmanship and material are warranted to be strictly first class in every respect.

HISTORICAL AND COMMERCIAL PHILADELPHIA.

TT & NICOUD, Pharmacists, Southwest Corner Fifth and Lombard Streets.—Prominent among the drug houses in Philadelphia enjoying an excellent reputation for handling and preparing the best goods is that of Messrs. Ott & Nicoud. This business was inaugurated by G. Krause, 1861, who sold out to H. Weinger, in 1866, Mr. Emil Ott succeeding in 1885, Mr. Nicoud entering the firm in 1886. The store occupied is 20 x 40 feet in area, finely fitted and arranged throughout for the successful prosecution of the work. A special feature of the trade is the compounding of physicians' prescriptions and family recipes, for which purposes special arrangements have been made for their dispensing in the most accurate manner at lowest prices, and none but competent assistants are employed. The stock comprises pure fresh drugs and chemicals, proprietary remedies, pharmaceutical preparations of their own superior production, and which have attained a wide reputation for their curative qualities, and a general line of miscellaneous articles usually found in a first-class pharmacy. Mr. Ott and Mr. Nicoud are highly intelligent and courteous gentlemen, and are both graduates of the Philadelphia College of Pharmacy in the classes of 1879 and '81 respectively.

AMUEL E. GARDINER, Conveyancer, Real Estate, Notary Public, Insurance, Southeast Corner of Seventh Street and Washington Avenue. Mr. Samuel E. Gardiner has been established about ten years in the handling of realty and has built up a brisk business. He was born in Medford, N. J., and came to Philadelphia in his youth, and is thoroughly conversant with every detail connected with the purchase, sale and transfer of realty and kindred interests. He is a conveyancer and notary public and is a member of the Conveyancers' Association of Philadelphia. He is a general real estate broker and is local agent for the Insurance Company of Pennsylvania. Mr. Gardiner, who makes a specialty of the sale of property in the First, Second, Third, Twenty-sixth and Thirtieth Wards, gives personal attention to the collection of ground rents and interests and to the management of estates. He is prepared to place fire insurance at lowest rates, also, while loans and mortgages are negotiated by him on the most favorable terms. Legal documents are carefully drawn up, likewise; titles are searched and conveyancing in all its branches is promptly and reliably attended to.

IRK & NICE, Furnishing Undertakers, Main Street and Washington Avenue.—The largest undertaking establishment in Philadelphia and the oldest in the United States is that of Messrs. Kirk & Nice, which was founded in 1766, or 123 years ago, when the country was under English rule. The business has always been carried on at the same address. Many of the soldiers killed at the battle of Germantown were taken there, coffined and buried from the place. In 1828, Messrs. John and Samuel Nice succeeded to the ownership. They afterwards separated, Samuel Nice continuing alone up to 1865, when he was succeeded by his son, William J. Nice, and son-in-law, B. Frank Kirk, who have since conducted affairs under the firm-name of Kirk & Nice. Both are natives of the Quaker City and generally esteemed as citizens of integrity and ability. In 1879 they tore down the old buildings and erected their present spacious quarters, which have a floorage area of 13,080 square feet. A large stable is connected. The firm own three fine hearses, three dead wagons, five carriages and sixteen horses. They manufacture all the caskets, coffins, and burial cases used in their business, six men being constantly kept busy in this department exclusive of drivers. Funerals are taken entire charge of, embalming done and satisfactory services assured in every instance.

OUIS J. MEYER, Gilder, Electro Silver Plater, No. 705 Sansom Street.—Mr. Louis J. Meyer established this business here in 1882, and has obtained a liberal patronage from the trade. The premises occupied comprise a floor of ample dimensions, fully equipped with the latest improved electro-plating machines and other appliances. Several experienced operatives are employed and the machinery is driven by electric power. Mr. Meyer is a thoroughly practical and scientific plater, having learned the trade with Samuel Lakens, Jr. He was employed by him for eight years previous to establishing this business and is prepared to turn out in the highest style of the art, gold, silver and nickel plating and gives his attention to oxydized metals and platina. He is prepared to skillfully execute all work in his line, guaranteeing perfect satisfaction in every instance. The trade of the house extends throughout the Middle States and South to North Carolina. Mr. Meyer is a native of Philadelphia.

OHN McWILLIAMS, Fine Tailoring, No. 902 Walnut Street.—The tailoring business conducted under the name of John McWilliams, was established about eight years ago by the gentleman above named. Mr. McWilliams died in October, 1890, when his widow, Mrs. M. C. McWilliams, became proprietress, and, with Mr. F. W. Melhuish as manager, has since continued the business with uninterrupted success. Mr. Melhuish, who is a comparatively young man, active and energetic, is a practical tailor and cutter, of thorough experience, master of the tailoring art in all its branches, and has been connected with Mr. McWilliams for a number of years. The store is compact and neatly fitted up, and an elegant assortment of imported woolens is here displayed. The stock embraces all the latest novelties and newest designs in cloths, cassimeres, cheviots, serges, checks, stripes and fashionable suitings, and fifteen hands are employed. Every garment made in this establishment is warranted as to style, cut finish and fabric, while perfect fit is assured, and the prices charged are extremely moderate, quality of material and character of workmanship considered.

ONRADT ART METAL INDUSTRY, Charles Conradt, Proprietor, No. 224 Vine Street.—For thoroughly excellent all-around work in the line of silver and nickel plating, and kindred branches, or for promptness and reliability in executing orders, none in the business in Philadelphia sustains a better reputation than the time-honored house of the Conradt Art Metal Industry. Established in 1820 by G. L. Conradt, the concern is the oldest one in the United States, and the foremost of its kind in the city. Mr. Charles Conradt, the present proprietor, succeeded his father in 1867, having been born and raised in the business. The house has been located for nineteen years at its present site, No. 224 Vine Street. Mr. Conradt does a flourishing trade in the city and vicinity, turning out none but high-grade work at the lowest possible prices, which the ample facilities and modern improvements of his shop render a comparatively easy task. Plating and finishing in every style is done; metal wares, soda fountains and fixtures of all kinds are renewed and refinished in the highest style of art, and guaranteed to be first-class work. Mr. Conradt's lifelong experience in his business has made him a past master in all its branches, and has secured for him a steady patronage among those who know a good thing when they see it and cling to it.

DWARD F. KLAISZ, Ornamental Painter, No. 134 North Fifth Street.—This house turns out a distinctly superior class of work, and has a large patronage. The proprietor, Mr. E. F. Klaisz, does all kinds of ornamental painting, and makes a specialty of flags, banners, transparencies, etc. The business conducted by him was established in 1865 by N. W. Bittens, and in 1884 came into control of Mr. Klaisz. He occupies commodious quarters here on the second floor, and employs a number of hands. Estimates are given on all classes of work in the line indicated, and all orders are executed in the most expeditious and excellent manner. Particular attention is paid to original and artistic designs, and satisfaction is assured in every instance, while the prices charged are of the most reasonable character. Mr. Klaisz, who is a young gentleman born in this city, is a thorough practical workman himself, and an expert in this special branch of art. He is well and favorably known, and is a member of the F. and A. M. the K. of G. E., and other societies.

HISTORICAL AND COMMERCIAL PHILADELPHIA.

M. BOVARD & SON, Watches, Clocks, Jewelry, Silverware, Etc., Repairing a Specialty, No. 4389 Cresson Street, Manayunk.—One of the leading and oldest-established watch clock and jewelry businesses in Manayunk, is that conducted by Messrs. M. M. Bovard & Son, located at No. 4389 Cresson Street, who enjoy a reputation second to none here for handling the most reliable grades of goods in each line, for making exact representations and for rigidly adhering to other honorable methods, that have been largely accountable for the distinct, progressive success attained. Mr. M. M. Bovard, who is a thoroughly practical watchmaker and jeweler, initiated the business in 1869, and in 1882 he admitted his son, Mr. William H. Bovard, who was brought up to this line of trade. The store is of ample dimensions, finely fitted up and contains a handsome display of gold, rolled and plated jewelry of all kinds, novelties in silver and gold, the standard makes of American watches and clocks in great variety, and a choice collection of sterling and plated silverware; the repairing of watches, clocks and jewelry being a specialty. The worthy senior is a native of Chester County, Pa., coming to Philadelphia in 1852, and is a member of the Independent Order of Odd Fellows, as also of Post 45 of the Grand Army of the Republic, having served for three years during the late war as private in the Ninety-fifth Pennsylvania Volunteer Infantry. Mr. Wm. H. Bovard was born in Manayunk and is a member of the Free and Accepted Masons and the Independent Order of Odd Fellows. He is also a director of the National Retail Jewelry Association of Philadelphia and of the Glen Willow Ice Manufacturing Company.

A. FERRIS, Dealer in Flour, Feed, Baled Hay, Straw, Salt, Land Plaster, Peruvian Guano, Etc., Nos. 3388 and 3410 Ridge Avenue.—One of the oldest-established and most popular mercantile houses of Philadelphia devoted to the trade in flour, feed, hay, straw, etc. is that which is under the able management and direction of Mr. M. A. Ferris. This flourishing business was originally founded more than a quarter of a century ago by Mr. John R. Ferris, who conducted its affairs up to his death in 1876, when he was succeeded by his son, the present proprietor. The premises occupied comprise appropriately and conveniently fitted up buildings for storage purposes, and salesroom, and the services of three efficient assistants and three teams are required in constant employment to meet the demands of the trade. The finest brands of family flour, grain and feed of all kinds, meal, baled hay, straw, salt, etc., are handled, and the stock is selected from the most reliable sources, while patrons of this house have learned by experience that nothing of an inferior quality, or that is adulterated, will be sold to them. Mr. Ferris is agent in this section for Baugh's phosphate, and he also deals in land plasters, Peruvian guano and kainit for fertilizing purposes, while upon all consignments he is always prepared to make liberal cash advances, and prompt and satisfactory returns are guaranteed in every instance. All orders receive immediate attention, and the prices which govern are the very lowest in the market. Mr. Ferris is the recipient of an extensive trade throughout this city, and the large wholesale and retail business he transacts amounts to the most prosperous annual aggregate. He is a native of Philadelphia, and is widely recognized as a leader in his important line of trade, besides enjoying great popularity in social circles as well, being a member of several different organizations here.

WHITE, HENTZ & CO., Sole Proprietors of Trimble Whiskeys, Nos. 222 and 224 North Second Street.—The recognized importance of Philadelphia as a great centre of the wholesale wine and liquor trade of the United States is the result of the efforts put forth by such representative houses as that of Messrs. White, Hentz & Co., at Nos. 222 and 224 North Second Street. This is the oldest and one of the most eminent houses engaged in this department of commerce in Philadelphia, and one of the oldest in the world. It was founded in 1786, by Philip Wager, and subsequent changes occurred as follows, viz: 1819, Van Syckel & Garrison; Van Syckel & Sons; 1849, White & Hentz; 1885, White, Hentz & Co. The distinctive features of enterprise and push for which this house became early distinguished have been abundantly exemplified by the successors and present co-partners, whose resources are ample, facilities perfected, and connections of the most widespread and influential character. They now occupy two large buildings, three and four stories high respectively, fronting on both North Second and Broad Streets, and measuring 200 feet in depth. The site is the same as that occupied in 1734, and the house is therefore one of Philadelphia's most familiar landmarks, surrounded by pleasant memories and historic associations. The firm are internationally famous as sole owners of the celebrated Trimble whiskeys, and are also extensive importers of wines, gins, brandies and liquors of every description. The Trimble whiskeys have distinctive features as to purity, flavor and medicinal tonic properties, that are recognized by leading experts and connoisseurs, and they are sold not only by prominent druggists but by the trade generally. The stock in store is always of great magnitude, and dealers are supplied in quantities to suit at the shortest possible notice. It is a matter of record that the best whiskeys, those which appeal to the most refined palates and are most highly prized on account of their age and health giving properties, are very difficult to obtain in ordinary trade. The average dealer is not an expert, and it requires the sound judgment and vast practical experience of such a firm as White, Hentz & Co., to insure to the buyer prime quality, as is found in Trimble whiskey. This brand is exceptionally pure and choice, and is used in many of the hospitals in this city and State and for fine bar trade, for family use and for the medical profession there is none superior. This firm are also direct importers and representatives in America of the leading brands of sherries, ports, madeiras, and other wines, likewise fine brandies, gins, etc. The vintages kept in stock are of the most rare quality, and predominately meet the tastes of the best critics. The facilities of this firm are not excelled by any contemporary concern in America. Cash purchases, direct importations, long experience and a thorough knowledge of the business in all its branches, with progressive and liberal views characterizing the management, enable this house to compete successfully with the largest houses in any part of the world. They keep in all things fully abreast of the age. Fine goods are a specialty of this old and honored house, and its character and standing is national in extent, while as regards business capacity and true American enterprise it justly merits the excellent reputation it has permanently maintained during its exceptional career of nearly one hundred years. The individual members of this representative firm are Messrs. J. Henry Hentz, J. P. Robinett and J. Henry Hentz, Jr. The senior partner came into the house in his early youth, and was admitted to partnership in 1849. He is a gentleman of broad culture, wide observation and eminent popularity, and is emphatically one of the leading representatives in his line in America. Mr. Robinett has also been connected with the house from his youth, and came into the firm in 1885. Mr. J. Henry Hentz, Jr., is a graduate of the Pennsylvania University, and has been a member of the firm since 1885. All are Philadelphians by birth and training, experts in the wine and liquor trade, and well-known members of the National, the Philadelphia and the Pennsylvania Wholesale Liquor Dealers' Associations; the Trades' League and the Philadelphia Bourse. The operations of the firm extend not only to all parts of the United States, but frequent shipments are also made to Europe. Branch houses are operated at Nos. 17 South William Street, New York; and Nos. 617 Twelfth Street, N. W., Washington D. C.; while the name and fame of the firm are recognized and familiar in all parts of the world.

HISTORICAL AND COMMERCIAL PHILADELPHIA.

GEORGE H. RUTH & CO., Manufacturers' Agents, Importers and Decorators of Crockery and Glassware, Lamps and Fancy Goods, No. 519 Market Street.—This firm are importers, manufacturers' agents and decorators of crockery and glassware, lamps and fancy goods. Their immense warerooms are filled with a most extensive stock, which includes the finest specimens of these goods that the world can produce. By means of its extensive connections abroad, the house is enabled to afford its customers an early opportunity to make selections from the latest novelties to be found in the great capitals of Europe, and it acts directly as manufacturers' agents for some of the finest goods that are produced, either in this country or abroad. In the line of decorated goods its display is especially large, varied and complete. The premises occupied comprise a five-story building. Each of the five floors is 20 x 120 feet in dimensions and each is filled with an immense stock, including the finest Dresden and Sevres ware, tea and dinner sets in endless variety, cut glass and plain glassware of every kind, for use and ornament; decorated ware of every description and a multitude of fancy goods. The lamp department embraces every style, size and variety. The house numbers among its customers the leading dealers in Pennsylvania, Delaware, Maryland, South Carolina, North Carolina and Georgia. This territory is covered by five travelling salesmen. This business was founded eighteen years ago by Fisher, Son & Ruth, who were succeeded two years ago by the present firm of George H. Ruth & Co. This firm consists of Mr. George H. Ruth and Mr. E. F. Albrecht. Both these gentlemen are natives and residents of Philadelphia.

ROBERT THOMAS & SON, Lumber Merchants, Main Street and Mount Airy Avenue, Germantown.—This well-known firm deal in lumber and building material of all kinds, carry a stock of 500,000 feet of lumber and sell about 1,100,000 feet a year. Lumber is planed and sawed at shortest notice and at most reasonable prices. This establishment was founded in 1858, by Robert Thomas, and in 1867 his son, Abraham W. Thomas, was admitted to partnership. In 1862 Mr. Thomas, Jr., left his business to go to the war, enlisting in the 15th Pennsylvania Volunteer Cavalry, and serving until the close of hostilities in 1865. He was at the front in many important battles, was captured by the Confederates and kept a prisoner for sixteen months, nine months of which were passed amid the horrors of Andersonville. He is a member of Post No. 6, G. A. R., also of the Masonic Order, and is universally esteemed in this, his native town. Mr. Robert Thomas was also born in Germantown and is a gentleman of advanced years, being now seventy-six. He has taken a prominent part in the affairs of the community, having been a justice of the peace, councilman and alderman, and is now a notary public. He enjoys the respect of all his fellow-citizens. Mr. A. W. Thomas is also postmaster of Station No. 11, since October, 1890, when it was first opened, and prior to that was for six years assistant postmaster in the Germantown post office.

C. H. GARDEN & CO., Hats, Caps, Furs, Straw and Millinery Goods, Nos. 606 and 608 Market Street.—This immense business was founded in 1841, by Mr. C. H. Garden, who soon developed most important and far-reaching connections for those days. The firm of Garden & Brown was subsequently formed, and in 1848 the present style was adopted. The building now occupied for trade purposes was built in 1865, and contains seven floors and a basement, 40 x 120 feet each, the arrangements and conveniences of which are complete and perfect, and where is displayed the largest stock in this line in the country. This firm enjoy the finest opportunities in the markets of both America and Europe. Their stock always includes the newest styles, the freshest novelties and most desirable shades and patterns in straw and fur goods, the latest Parisian novelties in flowers, feathers, ornaments, trimmed and untrimmed hats and bonnets, and fine millinery merchandise of every description. A corps of sixteen talented salesmen represent the interests of the house upon the road, and the trade extends from New York to California and from the St. Lawrence to the Gulf of Mexico. The goods are in preferential demand by first-class dealers throughout this immense territory and are standard in the United States. The individual members of this firm are Messrs. C. Henry Garden, Daniel Donovan, Joseph Tierney, James L. Hugh and William Morton Garden. The honored senior partner and founder of the house was born in Philadelphia and now resides in New York City, where he is prominent in business and financial circles as vice-president of the Ninth National Bank. Mr. Donovan came into the firm in 1852, and is one of Philadelphia's representative merchants, also a director of the Mechanics' National Bank, the Equitable Trust Company, and the Beneficial Savings Association. Messrs. Tierney and Hugh have been in the firm since 1861, while Mr. William M. Garden, a son of the senior partner, was admitted in 1872.

ALBERT SCHENCK, Importer of China and Glassware, No. 27 North Fifth Street and Nos. 417, 419 and 421 Commerce Street.—The well-known house of Mr. Albert Schenck, importer of china and glassware, has for years occupied a commanding position in its line of trade. This house was established by Mr. Albert Schenck and Mr. J. E. F. Zieh, in 1872, which remained until January 1, 1886, when the firm dissolved and was continued by Mr. Schenck under the present style of Albert Schenck. Mr. Schenck was born in Germany, but came to the United States in his boyhood, forty-five years ago, and has since made his home in the city of Philadelphia. He is ably assisted in the conduct of his business by his manager, Mr. F. H. Herzog, who is also a native of Germany and came to this country thirteen years ago. He then entered the employ of Mr. Schenck and devoted himself to the business with such energy and fidelity that seven years ago he was appointed manager and has since then so well discharged the duties of his important position that the trade of the house has grown and its reputation has increased. The business occupies three buildings, each of which has four spacious floors, each 25 x 80 feet in dimensions, and on each floor is displayed an immense stock of china and glassware, which includes the finest goods that are produced, embracing beautiful novelties in china, tea and dinner sets, superb vases, exquisite porcelains, delicate Sevres and Dresden ware and glassware in great variety, including the choicest designs for table use and for ornament, and a multitude of the most beautiful house-furnishing specialties, together with hotel and bar glassware in endless variety. The house imports direct from England, France, Germany and Austria. The trade of the house covers a wide area of country, extending as far south as San Antonio, Texas, and as far west as Dakota, and employs three traveling salesmen the entire year on the road covering this territory.

WILLIAM D. LELAR, Real Estate and Collection Agency, Notary Public, No. 731 South Third Street.—During the two years of his establishment in the real estate profession, Mr. William D. Lelar has succeeded in securing a large and influential connection in this section of Philadelphia in the purchase, sale and exchange of all kinds of real estate in any part of the city and suburbs, the letting of premises in general, the collection of house and ground rents, interest, and outstanding accounts, the settlement, transfer, and entire management of estates, the examination of titles, deeds, leases, and other legal instruments, and the speedy negotiation of loans upon bond or mortgage; while as a notary public he takes acknowledgments and affidavits, depositions, etc. Moreover, Mr. Lelar is an insurance broker, and is thereby enabled to direct all desirable fire risks into the safest channels at the lowest current rates of premium. Mr. Lelar, who is a middle-aged gentleman of Philadelphia birth, has been a notary public since 1890, and was formerly a magistrate for five years. He is a member of Post No. 46, of the Grand Army of the Republic, and served during the late war from 1861 to December, 1862, as private in Company H, of the 90th Pennsylvania Volunteer Infantry. He served with much gallantry, and had the misfortune to lose his leg at the battle of Fredericksburg.

This Style Machine $25.00 Delivered.

C. SAWYER, Manufacturer and Dealer in Sewing Machines, Needles and Oil, No. 201 South Eleventh Street. Mr. C. Sawyer, the well-known manufacturer and dealer in sewing machines, needles and oil, established business in Philadelphia in 1873, and has been engaged in this business continuously, in this place and in Cleveland Ohio, since 1865. His factory, located at Nos. 217 and 219 Quince Street, is admirably equipped. Twenty skilled mechanics are employed. At the salesroom, No. 201 South Eleventh Street, is kept a large stock of machines of Mr. Sawyer's manufacture, also needles and oil. The "Favorite" sewing machine manufactured here embodies every desirable quality, and has won the admiration of all who have seen it in operation at home and abroad. It is the simplest, strongest and best adjusted sewing machine in the world. It is the perfection of mechanism for hemming, felling, trimming, binding, cording, seaming, braiding, embroidering and other purposes too numerous to particularize, and the price is no higher than is demanded for inferior machines. It is sold extensively all over the United States. Mr. Sawyer is a native of Massachusetts, but has been a resident of Philadelphia since 1873, and is honored and respected in all the various walks of life.

HARTFORD STEAM BOILER INSPECTION AND INSURANCE COMPANY, Hartford, Conn., Corbin & Goodrich, General Agents, No. 132 Walnut Street. This company is represented in Philadelphia by Messrs. Corbin & Goodrich, as general agents for Eastern Pennsylvania, Southern New Jersey and the State of Delaware. The company was organized and incorporated in 1866, with a capital of $500,000, and with a perpetual charter. The policy of insurance which this company issues covers damage to boilers, buildings, stock and machinery; also from loss of life, permanent total disability and accident to persons arising from explosion, and is a guarantee that the work of inspection has been thoroughly done. No inspection can be so careful and complete as one where the party making it has a pecuniary interest. This company imposes no arbitrary conditions, it is interested in no patented boilers or boiler appliances, nor is it interested in insurance schemes entirely foreign to the business of steam boiler inspection and insurance, but on the receipt of the proposal for insurance the boilers are thoroughly inspected and classified and are accepted at a proper rate per cent., unless they are found, on inspection, absolutely unsafe, in which case the applicant is furnished with a written statement of their condition. The rates for risks are very reasonable in character, and all losses that occur are promptly paid. The affairs of the company have been very ably and successfully managed from its inception, and the corporation is recognized everywhere as a pillar of strength and security to the insured. The general agents, Messrs. E. A. Corbin and H. G. Goodrich, are natives of Connecticut, representing this corporation here since 1868, and eminently popular and respected as expert underwriters, for both boiler and fire insurance, members of the Philadelphia Underwriters' Association and the Philadelphia Bourse and enterprising and reliable business men.

GARRETT & BUCHANAN, General Paper Dealers, and Manufacturers of Tissue, Heavy Manilla and Wrapping Papers in Rolls and Sheet, Also Waxed Papers of all Kinds, Nos. 3 and 5 Decatur Street. Especially progressive and representative, in the truest and best sense, of the Philadelphia houses engaged in handling tissue, heavy manilla and wrapping papers of all kinds, in roll and sheet, also waxed papers, is that of Messrs. Garrett & Buchanan, located at Nos. 3 and 5 Decatur Street. This firm control the products of these Pennsylvania paper mills, and their ripened experience with all that relates to the paper trade, either in its technical or commercial branches and in connection with every kind and grade, adapted to whatsoever purpose has served to give them a deservedly high prestige throughout the country. The business was established in 1856, by Mr. C. S. Garrett, who was succeeded in 1864 by the firm of C. S. Garrett & Bro., who in turn gave place to the firm of C. S. Garrett, Bro. & Co., in 1873, and in 1876 the present firm was organized by Messrs. Sylvester Garrett and Alex. S. Buchanan. The business premises comprise two buildings, containing four floors and a basement, 10 x 60 feet each, with an additional floor on Market Street, thus giving ample accommodations for supplying the most extensive demand. The partners are possessed of a very thorough and versatile knowledge of the qualities and kinds of paper manufacture and of their market values. They have moreover the advantage of an extensive connection with mills, and are in a position to offer special inducements to business men. Favored by this and their own energy and persistent application, as well as their earnest endeavor to supply exactly what patrons require, they have built up a widespread and influential connection not only in all parts of the United States, but also in Australia, while the same is developing naturally in appreciation of the honorable system of business pursued. A corps of talented salesmen represent the interests of the house upon the road, and all orders receive immediate and careful attention. Mr. Garrett is a native of Chester County, Pa., and a resident of Swarthmore. He is a director of the Quaker City National Bank and the Swarthmore Land and Improvement Company, and is well and favorably known in commercial and financial life. Mr. Buchanan was born in Ireland, and came to this country in 1847. He served during the war as first-lieutenant in the 10th Missouri Infantry and as aide-de-camp on General Sullivan's staff, and was stationed at General Grant's headquarters during the siege of Vicksburg. He is a member of the Loyal Legion, and highly esteemed in military and social circles.

. WHITE & SON, Flour and Feed, Nos. 4002-4004 Lancaster Avenue.—A popular and reliable mercantile house in this section of Philadelphia, devoted to the trade in flour and feed, is that of the well-known firm of A. White & Son, of Nos. 4002 and 4004 Lancaster Avenue. This flourishing business was originally established here fourteen years ago by Mr. A. White, who conducted it most successfully for seven years alone, after which time his son was admitted into the partnership, under the above style. The premises here occupied consist of three floors in a commodious building, and these are finely equipped throughout for the purposes of the business, and perfect in convenience of arrangement for the handling and storage of the stock. This firm make a specialty of the Melbourne Mills flour, and they deal in all the very best grades of the different varieties of this staple commodity, together with feed of all kinds, while they particularly recommend the celebrated Washburn, Crosby Co.'s "Gold Medal" flour, which is guaranteed to be the very best produced, and stands unequaled in the market, without a rival. The exigencies of this business are such as to require the services of six efficient assistants, and three teams are constantly employed, and all orders, of any magnitude, receive prompt attention, while the trade secured by this house is large, permanent and extensive, and of both a wholesale and retail character. Both members of this firm are noted for the promptness, honor and reliability which characterize all their business transactions. Mr. White, Sr., was born in Bucks County, this State, while his son is a native of this city.

. EYNON & SON, Saw and Planing Mill, Wholesale and Retail Dealers in Hickory, Oak and Pine Wood, Etc., Nos. 4048 and 3050 North Broad Street.—This firm established their business here in 1885, and quickly secured a large and influential support. Their plant covers a ground area of 50 x 140 feet, and includes a brick mill, fully equipped with the latest improved wood-working machinery and ample steam-power, while employment is given to a large force of skilled workmen. A specialty is made of planing and sawing to order for lumber dealers and builders, in which branch of work this firm enjoys excellent facilities and can always quote satisfactory prices. They are also prominent as wholesale and retail dealers in hickory, oak and pine wood, which is received in immense quantities and sold by the cord or by the box to suit the requirements of all classes of buyers. A large business is done in supplying bakers with cord wood and families with split wood and fine kindling for kitchen use; while hard wood for open grates is cut to order at short notice. Mr. T. J. Eynon was born in Wales, and came to this country in 1844, while his son, Mr. David G. Eynon, was born in Norristown, Pa., and is a member of the Knights of the Golden Eagle, United American Mechanics' and Red Men. Both partners devote all their energy to the management of their business.

OHN O'BRIEN, Coal, Northeast Corner American and Somerset Streets.—A successful, well-known and popular coal dealer of this section of the city is Mr. John O'Brien. He is a native of Philadelphia, has been identified with the coal trade for the past eighteen years, and in 1889 he established himself in business at the above address, having for three years previous to this been a partner in the firm of Mulholland & O'Brien. He deals here exclusively in the best qualities of hard and soft coal for domestic and steam purposes at retail, and his yard, which is connected by a switch with the Philadelphia & Reading Railroad, has a storage capacity for such large quantities as to enable him to meet every demand of the public with promptness and satisfaction. All orders, either large or small, receive immediate attention, and a sufficient force of competent hands contribute to the satisfactory operations of the house, while four teams are in permanent service. Mr. O'Brien is an experienced and reliable business man, and those trading with him once, finding it to their advantage, remain his patrons always. He is a member of the Coal Dealers' Association of this city.

JOHN A. ADDIS, Undertaker and Embalmer, No. 211 North Fourth Street. Foremost among the leading and best known undertakers and embalmers in this community stands Mr. John A. Addis, whose office and warerooms will be found eligibly located at No. 211 North Fourth Street. Eight years ago he embarked for himself in this business, and his success from the outset has been of the most gratifying character, a large and influential trade of considerable magnitude having been developed throughout this city. For the past three years the present desirable premises have been occupied, the original establishment having formerly been located across the street, and these comprise a store and basement, each 20x30 feet in dimensions, which are tastefully and attractively appointed and especially arranged for the purposes to which they are devoted. A complete stock is at all times carried, and everything in the line of caskets, coffins, shrouds, robes and funeral requisites of every description

may be obtained here, while the proprietor is always prepared to take entire charge of funerals at all times, and all calls, day or night, receive his prompt attention. His stable and wareroom being in close proximity, No. 324 Wood Street, enables Mr. Addis to fulfill orders with promptness and despatch. He is a practical and experienced embalmer, being a graduate of Dr. Deicker's class of embalming, as well as a general furnishing undertaker, and the considerate and efficient manner in which he performs all the duties incident to his vocation cannot fail to recommend him to afflicted families, who may feel assured that in engaging him all the services will be most satisfactorily carried out. Mr. Addis is thoroughly experienced in all branches of his profession for which he has a natural adaptation, and his reputation is widespread throughout this his native city. He is a member of the Philadelphia Undertakers' and also Funeral Directors' Associations, besides the A. O. Hibernians and C. Knights of America.

WILLIAM H. LAIR, Ornamental Glass Cutter, No. 207 Quarry Street. The foundation of the reputable and time honored house of William H. Lair, ornamental glass cutter, occurred about 1862, and it enjoys the distinction of being the oldest of its kind in the city. Mr. Lair, the founder, is a native of Philadelphia, a business man of rare ability, and the fortunate possessor of a splendid and flourishing business attained through the highest standard of workmanship and fair dealings with patrons. He undertakes the cutting of glass to any size, and the beveling of the same to order; also vestibule, transom and car lights, gas globes and glass signs. The premises where the work is done are spacious and adequately equipped with steam power and all the machinery necessary for the turning out of perfect work. He makes a specialty of bevelled plate glass. The shop contains three bevelling mills, five grindstones and one polisher.

HISTORICAL AND COMMERCIAL PHILADELPHIA.

CHARLES H. HOWELL & CO., Paint, Color and Varnish Makers, Ajax Paint, All Colors and White, Nos. 212, 214, 216 Race Street.—The house of Messrs. Charles H. Howell & Co. at Nos. 212, 214 and 216 Race Street, is prominently and popularly identified with the production of the highest grade of paints, colors and varnish known to the trade, and its name has become recognized as a veritable trade-mark for purity, durability and superior excellence in these lines of goods. The firm established their business here in 1876, occupying a five-story double building at the address above mentioned, and a varnish factory at Kensington, all supplied with new and improved machinery and ample steam-power, and giving steady employment to a large force of skilled hands. This firm are especially prominent as manufacturers of Ajax mixed and marine paints, while their output also embraces damp wall paint, steel color, wood filler, iron filler, fine putty, roof paint, car and coach colors in Japan and varnish, house and fresco colors, dry, moist and in oil; marine black paint, marine bronze green, Hatteras copper paint, Howell's red deck paint, marine seam paint, and marine cement. Their marine paints are always uniform and reliable, unrivaled in appearance, unexcelled in durability, unparalleled in economy, unequaled in convenience, unprecedented in reputation, and undisputed in the broad claim of being the best marine paints in the world. The Ajax ready-mixed paint is not only the best, but also the cheapest, for ships, while the marine black paint introduced by this firm, has replaced lamp black and boiled oil, and has been generally adopted by the better class of vessels, whose masters realize that a vessel protected with the best paint not only lasts longer and looks better, but in dull times charters quicker than one that looks shabby and run down. The trade of the house is immense and influential throughout the entire United States, and has been built up on the legitimate basis of superior goods and liberal, honorable business methods. An agency is operated at No. 79 Maiden Lane, New York. Mr. Charles H. Howell, the active member of the firm, is a native Philadelphian, a well-known member of the Paint Club, and an expert authority in the paint, oil and varnish trade.

BAILY & TRUSCOTT, Architects, No. 138 South Fourth Street.—The firm of Baily & Truscott, the well-known architects, at No. 138 South Fourth Street, have elevated the plane of modern building to a high degree of symmetry and perfection. In fact, there are few contemporaries of theirs, here or elsewhere, who strive to maintain that standard by which they plan, construct and finish every house they build. The copartners, Messrs. W. L. Baily and Arthur Truscott, are both thoroughly experienced in the profession, having made it a life-study, and organized the present firm in January, 1891. Their methods are thoroughly characteristic. They approach the erection of a house after a careful study of the location, the preparation of the most elaborate plans and the infusion of great artistic beauty and harmony into their architectural designs. With their large practical experience and perfected facilities, they endeavor to prepare plans and specifications in the promptest manner, adopting the most economical construction, and erecting their buildings under their personal supervision when desired. They designed alterations for Queen & Co.'s store on Chestnut street; the building for the Hurley estate, at Seventeenth and Chestnut Streets; the Home for Deaf Children at Bala; a residence for Mr Fox at Bryn Mawr and one for Wm. S. Blakeley, Chester, Pa; the Taylor Building, and a number of handsome residences on Cooper Street, in Camden; and a number of others in the vicinity of Philadelphia, and their services are in constant and important requisition in this city and elsewhere. Mr. Baily is a native Philadelphian, was Professor of Architecture at the University of Pennsylvania, and studied his profession with T. P. Chandler, Jr., Addison Hutton, Cope & Stewardson and Wilson Brothers, supplemented by a year of travel and study in Europe; and is a member of the Academy of Natural Sciences and the Art Club, while both he and Mr. Truscott are members of the American Institute of Architects, the Philadelphia Society of Architects, and the T-Square Club. Many of his sketches have been exhibited and published. Mr. Truscott was born in England and since 1876 has studied with T. P. Chandler, Jr., Wilson Brothers and Cope & Stewardson, and was in the practice of his profession for two years in Columbus, Tenn., where he was architect of the United States Arsenal and was established in this city two years previous to the formation of this firm, during which time he built the New Jersey Trust and Safe Deposit Building, St. Paul's Episcopal Church, the main court-room of Court House, Broadway School and St. Paul's Chapel, all in Camden. Mr. Truscott has few superiors as a draughtsman and is recognized by the best talent of the country for his originality and feeling.

G. W. BUTTERWORTH, (Succeeding Butterworth & Prentis.) Wholesale Fruit and Vegetables, Nos. 829 to 833 North Second Street.—In referring to the fruit and produce commission trade of Philadelphia, its magnitude cannot fail to convince our readers that no opportunity has been lost by merchants to avail themselves of the advantages that appertain to the city for the receipt and distribution of goods in this line. A representative house engaged in the trade is that of G. W. Butterworth, succeeding Butterworth & Prentis, situated at Nos. 829 to 833 North Second Street. This establishment was founded in the 60's, by Joseph Wilkins. He was succeeded by Fling, Shrively & Co., who continued together up to 1887, when Butterworth & Prentis bought the business. Mr. George W. Butterworth is a native of this city, a member of the Philadelphia Produce Exchange and prominently known in the commercial world. The premises occupied comprise two four-story buildings at the address named, each 25 x 100 feet in dimensions, and a warehouse to the rear of this house, having four large floors used for the storage of fruit, and which holds 20,000 barrels of apples. Mr. Butterworth is a wholesale dealer and commission merchant in foreign and domestic fruits and vegetables, a heavy exporter of apples and an extensive importer of potatoes and onions. A large stock is carried to meet the active demand, fresh consignments are always solicited, and prompt returns guaranteed in all cases. The prosperous career of the house from its establishment is the best evidence that it is founded on a basis of general usefulness and popularity which must insure its future maintenance and prosperity.

WILLIAM SCHOELGENS, (Successor to F. Brecht & Co.,) Grower and Dealer in the Best Brands of California Wines and Brandies, Office and Vaults, No. 625 Arch Street.—An old-established Philadelphia house engaged in the trade is that of William Schoelgens, successor to F. Brecht & Co., grower and dealer in the best brands of California wines and brandies, whose office and vaults are at No. 625 Arch Street. This business was founded in 1866, by A. F. Brecht & Co., and, in October, 1891, Mr. Schoelgens, who had been a member of the firm seven years, succeeded to the sole control. Before that he conducted a large vineyard for eleven years, in Los Angeles, Cal. Mr. Schoelgens is a native of Germany, but has resided in the United States twenty-three years. He is a thoroughly practical wine grower, having learned the business in the Fatherland, and his goods are noted for their flavor, purity and general excellence. He owns an extensive vineyard and wine-making plant in California, and it turns out a large product annually. In Mr. Schoelgens' fine vaults over 35,000 gallons of wine and brandy are stored in wood, and some of the goods have lain here since 1872. The white wines handled include hock, Riesling, Chasselas, Guttedel, Traminer, 1867; and mountain, 1867; the red wines, claret, Zinfandel and Burgundy; and the sweet wines, port, sherry, muscatel, Tokay, Angelica, Madeira, Malaga. A full line of German wines and liquors of all kinds is kept on hand and orders from any part of the United States are filled without delay.

HISTORICAL AND COMMERCIAL PHILADELPHIA.

GEO. D. WOODSIDE & CO., Proprietors of Big Elk Dairies and General Commission Merchants, Dealers in Butter, Eggs, Poultry, Game, Etc., No. 22 South Water Street.—Of the immense bulk of butter, eggs, poultry and game which the great West pours into the lap of Philadelphia, no inconsiderable portion finds its way to No. 22 South Water Street, the site of the establishment of Messrs. Geo. D. Woodside & Co., the well known commission merchants in this line. The business so successfully conducted here was originally established in 1882 by Messrs. Madison Lovett & Co., on South Fifteenth Street. In 1889 the present firm succeeded to the control, and a removal was made in January, 1892, to the present premises, which include a cooling room, having a capacity for one thousand butter tubs. The firm are especially prominent as proprietors of the Big Elk Dairies, six in number, located in Chester County, and receive the entire output of the same, which in 1891 amounted to two hundred and seventy thousand pounds. They carry in stock some three thousand pounds of butter, as well as large quantities of eggs, cheese, poultry and game, which is received on commission from all parts of New York, Pennsylvania and the West. For the judgment displayed in the execution of these commissions and the strict integrity of all transactions, as well as the great promptitude with which its patrons' requirements are filled, the house has an enviable fame attaching to it throughout Pennsylvania, New Jersey and Delaware. All consignments are promptly acknowledged and handled with profit to the shipper, while prompt returns are invariably made. The members of this firm are Messrs. Geo. D. and John W. Woodside, son and father. The latter is the owner of the Big Elk Dairies, and one of the founders of this house. Mr. Geo. D. Woodside is a well known Philadelphian, a member of the Produce Exchange and the National Butter, Cheese and Egg Association, and combines his energy and vigor with the ripe experience of his father to form a firm of commanding influence.

F. GUTEKUNST, Photogravure, Phototype Specialties; Works, Ninth Street and Girard Avenue; Office, No. 712 Arch Street.—In making suitable reference to the house of Mr. F. Gutekunst, at No. 712 Arch Street, we introduce to our readers the best photograph, photogravure and phototype establishment in this country, South America and the continent, ranking first in quality and second to none in the volume of production. The proprietor is noted as an artist, and as the leader in photogravure and phototype specialties. Mr. Gutekunst has been established in the business since 1856, and unquestionably stands at the head of his profession in America. He occupies an entire five story building, 83x140 feet in size, and also operates a plant for photo-mechanical work at Ninth Street and Girard Avenue. He makes a specialty of fine work for illustrated journals, while he photographs everything in the line of machinery, landscapes and views, and his portrait work is recognized as the acme of perfection. Mr. Gutekunst gives employment to some forty skilled assistants the year round. His work is in constant and influential demand in all parts of the United States and the continent, and his talents, taste and judgment are everywhere recognized and appreciated. An immense stock of portraits and art specialties is here displayed, while the house keeps pace with the growing demands and refinements of the times. Mr. Gutekunst is a native Philadelphian, a member of the Academy of Natural Science, and a life member of Franklin Institute.

J. M. ZOOK, Real Estate; Office, No. 319 Walnut Street.—For some few years past Mr. J. M. Zook has been identified with the handling of real estate in Philadelphia. For five years Mr. Zook was established in business in association with Mr. Chase, and for the past six months he has been operating for his sole account. He devotes especial attention to conveyancing, undertaking with scrupulous care the settlement, transfer and entire management of estates, the preparation and minute examination of titles, deeds, leases, trusts, wills and similar instruments; while his facilities are complete for the speedy negotiation of loans upon bond or mortgage—either for borrower or investor. Moreover, Mr. Zook transacts a general real estate business, buying, selling and exchanging city, suburban and country real estate of every sort, finding desirable tenants for premises in general, and collecting house and ground rents, interest and outstanding accounts. Mr. Zook is a young gentleman of Chester County, Pa., birth and is well known for his expeditious transactions and prompt and accurate settlements. His specialty is property on the main line of the Pennsylvania road, and in Chester and Delaware counties, Pa.

THOS. S. WATSON, Agent; Manufacturer of Iron and Wire Work, No. 18 North Front Street.—For over fifty-six years the East End Wire Works, Thos. S. Watson, Agent have been conducted at the present location. This is one of the oldest and largest concerns of the kind in Philadelphia. It was established by Thomas Watson, who died in April, 1886, when his son and successor, Thomas S., assumed control of the business. He turns out a class of iron and wire work of exceptional excellence, and his productions not only command extensive sale throughout Pennsylvania, New Jersey, Delaware and the Southern States, but are exported quite largely also to Central and South America. The works occupy four 30x100 foot floors, and are thoroughly equipped. The facilities are first class, and a large number of expert hands are employed. Mr. Watson, the younger, was born in this city, and is a man of practical skill himself and of many years' experience, and is conversant with the business in its every detail. He manufactures iron, brass and copper wire, cloth, wire sieves, coal and sand screens, wire and iron window guards, elevator and bank guards, and is also one of the only manufacturers of iron elevator cars, a comparatively new industry, brass and bronze grills, wrought iron railings, fire escapes, iron bedsteads, woven wire mattresses, builders' and general iron work, and is prepared to give estimates on anything in the line indicated.

CHARLES FREDERICKS, Manufacturer and Dealer in Hatters' Specialties, No. 12 North Seventh Street.—For some twenty-one years Charles Fredericks, manufacturer of and dealer in hatters' specialties, No. 12 North Seventh Street, has been established in business, and has built up a large patronage, sending goods all over the country. He started in 1871, and was formerly located at Fifth and Market Streets, moving to the present place last year. The quarters here occupied by him as shop, etc., are ample and well equipped, and half a dozen skilled hands are employed. Mr. Fredericks turns out a very superior class of work, manufacturing springs, corrugated trimmings, linings, etc., and keeps on hand always a large and first class stock of hatters' specialties. Mr. Fredericks is a native of this city, and is a man of practical skill as well as many years' experience, and is thoroughly conversant with the wants of the trade.

ENTERPRISE PLATING AND SILVERWARE MANUFACTURING CO., F. H. Hyde, Proprietor, No. 35 North Eleventh Street.—The Enterprise Plating and Silverware Manufacturing Company has achieved a high reputation in its line of work. The enterprise was inaugurated here in May, 1890, by Mr. F. H. Hyde, under the above title, and a specialty is made of plating for the trade in gold, silver, nickel, copper, brass, bronze, oxidized silver, oxidized nickel, oxidized brass, Japanese bronze, ormolu dipping, lyinc coloring, pearl finish, satin finishing, brainow coloring, brass finishing, polishing, lacquering, dipping and black dipping for brass, particular attention being given to platinum plating. The business premises comprise three spacious floors, thoroughly equipped with modern machinery, operated by an electric motor, and steady employment is given to a large force of skilled and expert hands. Orders and commissions are filled for the trade or private parties with promptness and dispatch, while a large business is done in the manufacture of silverware to order. A fine sample stock is carried, and everything in the line of metal goods for household use is here produced in the highest style of the art. They also make a specialty of silver plating flowers, wreaths, and other trimmings for the millinery and hat trade—an entirely new industry in this country. Mr. Hyde is a native of Massachusetts, an expert designer and accomplished workman, and a young man of large business experience and sterling personal worth.

HISTORICAL AND COMMERCIAL PHILADELPHIA.

THOMAS B. DALE, Plumber, Gas and Steam Fitter, No. 20 Manheim Street, near Main Street, Germantown.—Among the better class of practical plumbers and gas and steam fitters in Germantown, a leading place is occupied and fully maintained by Mr. Thomas B. Dale, located at No. 20 Manheim Street, whose operations consist largely of a fine line of residential work all over this vicinity. Mr. Dale personally directs the prompt and accurate fulfillment of each order with which he is entrusted, and with thirteen years' practical experience at his command he is enabled to ensure the best and most satisfactory results, alike as to the materials used and the workmanship employed. All kinds of sanitary and ordinary plumbing and gas and steam fitting are undertaken; both jobbing and contracts for new work, including drainage and ventilation as a specialty, the supply and fixing of water-closets, urinals, cisterns, bath-tubs, bath boilers, tanks, washbowls, lift and force pumps, etc. Mr. Dale has had a long and practical experience, having been engaged in this business since 1874. He was engaged in the business for five years under the style of Smith & Dale before starting out for himself, and in 1885, with characteristic energy he commenced business at the present location under the present style. The store and shop in the rear, 20 x 60 feet in area, which have been occupied since 1886, contain a large and carefully selected stock of improved sanitary appliances and the finest plumbers' requisites and supplies, as well as a full equipment of tools and appliances for turning out the best work at short notice; a force of from fifteen to twenty picked mechanics being regularly employed. Mr. Dale, who is now thirty six years of age, is a member of the Free and Accepted Masons, the United American Mechanics and the Independent Order of Odd Fellows.

DEVLIN & BROTHER, Oakdale Oil Works, Oils, No. 2726 Germantown Avenue.—The Oakdale Oil Works of Messrs. Devlin and Brother are a prominent source of supply for lubricating, burning and other oils, at the lowest trade prices. The chief kinds of oils dealt in are high fire test, cylinder, engine and machinery oils, spindle oil, paraffine, wool, car and linseed oil, screw cutting oil, coal oil, benzine, torch, cottonseed and signal oil, lard, neat's-foot and whale oil, sperm and olive oil, fish oils, castor oil, roll neck grease, axle grease, lubricating compounds, tallow oil and refined tallow; while a specialty is made of headlight oil which is largely supplied to oil dealers and stores, and is one of the finest illuminating oils on the market. These various kinds of oils and greases are either manufactured by the firm or procured direct from the leading independent refineries of Western Pennsylvania, thereby enabling the house to offer to all classes of consumers substantial inducements. The enterprise was established in 1878 by Mr. Anthony V. Devlin, who in 1883 admitted his brother, Mr. Philip J. Devlin, into partnership. The premises at the address named consist of office and wareroom, 38 x 90 feet in area, containing a large and carefully selected stock of the several kinds of oils, greases, etc., dealt in. The storage and barreling department, 50 x 80 feet in size, situated at No. 3100 Germantown Avenue, is well equipped for the several purposes of the business, and six competent assistants are there regularly employed. The trade controlled by the firm reaches throughout the city and State, and five wagons are maintained to serve oil to the trade, etc. Of the able proprietors, Mr. Anthony V. Devlin was born in Wilmington, Del., while Mr. Philip J. Devlin is a native of the Quaker City; and both gentlemen are prominent members of several fraternal orders.

GEO. C. BOWKER, Notary Public, Real Estate, Conveyancing, Money Loaned, Rents Collected, Main Street, Next to the Bank Manayunk; Girard Trust Building, Broad and Chestnut Streets.—A liberal share of the best real estate business in Manayunk is controlled by Mr. George C. Bowker, located on Main Street, next to the bank, with a Philadelphia office in the Girard Trust Building at Broad and Chestnut Streets. During the three years that he has been practicing here as a conveyancer, notary public and real estate agent, Mr. Bowker has gained the confidence and support of a number of property owners, trustees, capitalists and others, and he is now freely recognized as a cautious investor, a reliable and expeditious medium for the purchase, sale, rent and exchange of real estate of all kinds, and the speedy negotiation of loans upon bond or mortgage, and as a careful and trusty agent for the collection of house and ground rents and interest; while as a conveyancer and notary public his services are largely sought for in the examination and preparation of titles, deeds, leases, trusts, wills and similar legal instruments, the settlement transfer and entire management of estates, taking depositions and acknowledgments, etc. Mr. Bowker graduated this year from the Law School of the University of Pennsylvania and is now a member of the Philadelphia Bar. He is a member of the Law Academy of Philadelphia, the American Academy of Political and Social Science and of other learned societies.

LEMUEL Z. SHERMER, Harness and Horse Collar Manufactory, No. 5680 Germantown Avenue.—Shermer's harness and horse collar manufactory is one of the oldest houses of the kind in the entire city. The undertaking was founded in 1846, by Mr. Wm. Shermer and Mr. L. Zell, who dissolved partnership in 1868. Subsequently Mr. Shermer resumed business in this city, with his two sons, Messrs. Lemuel Z. Shermer, and Wm. H. Shermer. Mr. L. Z. Shermer is a thoroughly practical harness-maker, having been actively engaged in this line for thirty-one years, while Mr. Wm. H. Shermer has followed the manufacture of collars for twenty-four years. All kinds of light and heavy, plain and fancy, single and double harness, horse collars, saddles, bridles, etc., are manufactured to order and for stock, and the repairing of harness and trunks is undertaken. The workshop, store etc., 20 x 32 feet in area, are fully equipped for turning out the finest hand work, and a large and fine grade stock is always on hand; seven skilled assistants being regularly employed on the spot. Mr. Wm. Shermer, whose practical experience dates back to 1836, besides being the oldest harness-maker in this section, is, with but one exception, the oldest in the whole State of Pennsylvania. His son, Mr. Lemuel Z. Shermer, was born in this block where the business is carried on, is now forty-seven years of age and is a member of the United American Mechanics and the Independent Order of Odd Fellows, and Mr. Wm. H. Shermer is a member of the Junior Order of United American Mechanics. Mr. Wm. Shermer was in business in 1869 with Jos. Becher at No. 245 Race Street, making a combination of two of the oldest practical men in the business.

SIDEBOTHAM & LEVER, Fire Insurance, Real Estate Brokerage, No. 4318 Frankford Avenue.—A very successful and well-known firm of insurance agents and real estate brokers in Frankford is that of Messrs. Sidebotham & Lever. Of the two main branches of the firm's affairs, fire insurance constitutes the leading specialty, they handling many of the largest manufacturing interests in Philadelphia and acting as the resident agents for the Fire Association of Philadelphia, the Phœnix Assurance Company, of London; the Royal Insurance Company, of Liverpool; the Pennsylvania Insurance Company, of Philadelphia and the Hamburg-Bremen, of Germany. Thus they are enabled to direct all desirable fire risks into the hands of some of the wealthiest and most powerful institutions in the world; freely recognized, alike for the equity of their policies and the liberality of their settlements, while the rates of premium are as low as the lowest. The business was established at the same location seven years ago, by the present copartners, Mr. John Sidebotham and Mr. G. Frank Lever, who are owners of considerable real estate in Frankford and vicinity and conduct a general realty business over this part of the city, buying, selling, renting and exchanging property and premises of all kinds; collecting rents and interest, negotiating loans on bond or mortgage and taking entire management of estates. A well-appointed suite of rooms is maintained on the first floor. The proprietors are both natives of the Quaker City and Mr. John Sidebotham, in addition to his active interest in this house, is also a manufacturer of wick goods, etc., in Frankford. Mr. G. Frank Lever was connected with the Philadelphia & Reading Railroad for eight years as traveling special agent.

HISTORICAL AND COMMERCIAL PHILADELPHIA.

 F. SABIN, Manufacturer of and Dealer in Ranges, Heaters, Stoves, Etc.; No. 146 North Second Street.—In the business of plumbing, roofing and sheet metal work, and in the sale of ranges, heaters and stoves, the establishment of Mr. F. Sabin, known as the Calorie Stove Works, at No. 146 North Second Street, occupies a prominent position in this city. The business was founded twenty years ago by Mr. Wm. H Stiles, the present proprietor succeeding to the control in 1887. The thoroughly all round utility which has characterized the house under the management of Mr. Sabin, in meeting the requirements of patrons in the matter of plumbing, ventilation, drainage, roofing, spouting and general heater work, as regards the scrupulous care and technical knowledge displayed in all work, has been potent in building up a widespread and influential connection in city and country. The business premises comprise three floors and a basement, 20x100 feet each, which are fitted up with the best and modern appliances for prompt and efficient work, while a splendid stock of goods is also carried therein. Mr. Sabin is agent for the Thomas, Roberts, Stevens & Company, the well known stove founders, and handles their celebrated productions, which include the "Challenge Siphon Furnace," the latest invention in this line, on an entirely new principle, and whose durability is unequalled. Twenty five per cent more heat is guaranteed with the same amount of coal over any furnace made. Mr. Sabin also keeps a full line of the celebrated gauze door goods on hand, and repairs for all kinds of stoves, ranges and heaters. First class workmen are sent to all parts of the city and country, and metal roofing and spouting in all its branches is executed with promptness and care, the N & G. Taylor's tin being used for roofing; while orders for plumbing and heater work receive immediate and skilful attention, and estimates, plans and specifications are cheerfully furnished. Mr. Sabin is also agent for the Kline Furnace Company's steel range, of Rochester, N. Y.; and for the Chicago and Erie Stove Company's steel ranges, of Chicago and Erie. Mr. Sabin is a native Philadelphian, an expert plumber and metal worker, and an enterprising, progressive and reliable business man, with whom it is always pleasant and profitable to deal.

 ST. CLOUD PHARMACY, N. E. Corner Seventh and Arch Streets; Consultation Free; Dr. B. L. Brown. Of the many excellent drug stores in this part of the city, none maintains a higher reputation than the St. Cloud pharmacy, northeast corner Seventh and Arch Streets. This is a first class place, where physicians' prescriptions and family recipes are compounded in the most careful and accurate manner from strictly pure and fresh ingredients. The prices charged here, too, are most reasonable, being, in fact, exceptionally low, while consultations are given free by Dr. B. L. Brown, the proprietor, having his office on the premises. The store is commodious, neat and well appointed, and a large, complete stock is always kept on hand, including, in addition to drugs, chemicals, tinctures, acids, extracts, etc., pharmaceutical preparations of every description, all the standard patent medicines and proprietary remedies; also a full and fine line of toilet articles, perfumery, soaps, sponges, chamois, and druggists' sundries to great variety. Several qualified assistants are in attendance, and night bell calls receive prompt response, prescriptions being a specialty. This popular and excellent pharmacy was established about a quarter of a century ago, and in 1891 came into control of the present proprietor, who has since conducted it with uninterrupted success. Dr. Brown, who is a gentleman of twenty seven, is a practicing physician, graduating in 1891 as an M D from the Jefferson Medical College, and is a thoroughly competent pharmacist of eight years' or more experience.

 CENTRAL CYCLE COMPANY, Frank R. Evans, Manager, Dealers in Bicycles, Tricycles, Sundries and Sporting Goods, No. 707 Arch Street and Nos. 1724 and 1726 North Broad Street. Though but a comparatively short time established, the Central Cycle Company, Frank R. Evans, manager, have secured a hold on popular favor second to none in the line indicated in this city. They are dealers in bicycles, tricycles, sundries and sporting goods, and have a very large and high class patronage. Every wheel, device and accessory sold by them is fully warranted as to make and material, while all work executed is guaranteed to be strictly first class, having the largest and best equipped repair shops in Philadelphia. The warerooms are commodious and well arranged, and a splendid assortment is constantly kept on hand, the stock embracing over 300 bicycles and tricycles of the finest makes; also the world renowned Cleveland sundries and sporting goods. They have a spacious and excellently appointed school in connection, likewise, with the most complete and perfect facilities, and employ, all told, a staff numbering upward of twenty. There are private parlors and dressing rooms for ladies, special attention being given to teaching beginners to ride, for which purpose several experts are in attendance, while bicycles and tricycles in great variety are rented at very moderate rates. Mr. Evans is a native of this city, and is a man of thorough experience, as well as of energy and enterprise, and is conversant with every feature and detail of the business. He is a member of the F. & A. M., and several other societies.

 SAMUEL VAN SCIVER, Conveyancer and Penman, No. 918 Drexel Building. Among the leading professional penmen of the United States is Mr. Samuel Van Sciver of the Drexel Building. He is a native of New Jersey and still resides in the beautiful town of Westmont in that State. He has had a wide range of commercial experience, having traveled through the country as an expert for wholesale firms and for the appraisement and purchase of real estate for a syndicate of this city, and also in the paint and tobacco line. The remarkable beauty of his penmanship has elicited the warmest encomiums wherever it has been seen. His services are constantly in demand in drawing up testimonials and important documents. Since 1889 he has devoted all his time to professional penmanship and to the business of conveyancing. He was formerly located in Fourth Street, but moved to his present central office in 1890. His specialty is in drawing up resolutions for framing, and preparing official documents for societies, clubs, etc. His work is like copper plate, and is conceded to be ahead of the finest engraved work in point of symmetry and beauty. Mr. Van Sciver has also won an enviable reputation as a conveyancer, preparing deeds, bonds and other legal documents for Philadelphia's most prominent attorneys and real estate companies. His unvarying accuracy, perfect legibility, coupled with neatness of appearance, render his work unrivalled, so that it is much preferred by leading lawyers, notaries, institutions, societies, etc., here and elsewhere.

 JOSEPH HYDE, Plumber, Gas Fitter and Sheet Metal Worker, Nos. 103 to 105 Division Street.—One of the best known and most reliable plumbers and sheet metal workers in Manayunk is Mr. Joseph Hyde, located at Nos 103 and 105 Division Street, who now enjoys an established reputation for executing really good work in each branch of the trade, at just and reasonable prices. Of the several kinds of work undertaken, a few of the leading are; tin and sheet iron work in general, all sorts of sheet metal specialties for mill use to order, hot air work, stoves, heaters and ranges, piping, flues, the relining of bath tubs, copper work of all kinds, tin roofing, spouting and guttering, steam and gas fitting, chandelier, radiator and steam heating work with pipes, etc., and a full line of ordinary and sanitary plumbing, such as drainage, ventilation, sanitary engineering, boiler and hydraut work, etc., while every description of jobbing and repairing incidental to the trade are equally undertaken. The business has been established for the past fifteen years under the able direction of the present proprietor, who possesses twenty-five years' practical experience in this line, and gives his personal attention to all orders. A two story building, 30x60 feet in area, is utilized, and all tools and appliances are at hand for turning out the finest work on short notice; six skilled mechanics being regularly employed. Mr. Joseph Hyde is a native of England, now of middle age, and has resided in Philadelphia for the past twenty-three years.

HISTORICAL AND COMMERCIAL PHILADELPHIA.

H. NARAMORE, Agent, Importer of Tailors' Trimmings, No. 22 Bank Street.—Mr. G. H. Naramore, agent and commission merchant in tailors' trimmings, has been established since October, 1890. He acts as the duly-accredited representative for the Saugatuck Manufacturing Company of Connecticut, manufacturers of suspender and covered buttons, and the Globe Button Works of Newark, N. J., manufacturers of oborine, composition buttons; and for these two standard makers he has succeeded in establishing a large and ever-increasing connection among the best trade houses and other wholesale consumers, throughout the city and surrounding country. In addition to the articles named, all kinds of tailors' trimmings are handled, such as plain and fancy braids, tapes, hooks and eyes, cloth buttons, linings, fasteners, etc.; all of which emanate from leading manufacturers either at home or abroad. The salesroom contains a large sample stock of the several kinds of trimmings dealt in. Mr. Naramore is a native of Vermont and has resided in Philadelphia since 1871.

E. CLARK & CO., Fine Furniture and Interior Decorations, No. 1803 Chestnut Street.—One of the leading houses in Philadelphia engaged in the handling of fine upholstered furniture and interior decorations, is that of Messrs. W. E. Clark & Co. The enterprise was initiated in 1888 by Mr. W. E. Clark, who in 1889 admitted Mr. S. D. Hecht into partnership; both being expert workers in this line and designers of rare intuitive taste and ability. The house is now in the center of a heavy volume of retail trade, carried on with an élite patronage, and largely confined to the city and adjacent districts, although extending in rather less degree all over the United States. All kinds of the finest upholstered furniture are dealt in; such as dining and parlor suits, lounges, settees, couches, stools, ottomans, etc., in rich plush, velvet tapestry and fancy fabrics in all colors; interior decorations of a superior order are made and put up, also draperies and fancy novelties. Contracts are undertaken for the complete furnishing of residences throughout, ready for occupancy; while a specialty is made of the most elaborate upholstery and drapery in the latest styles and designs. A branch is maintained at Bar Harbor, conducted under the direct supervision of Mr. W. E. Clark. The premises in this city comprise a three-story building, 25 x 10 feet in area, with a fully equipped workshop in the rear. An immense stock of the most careful selection is always carried, comprising a handsome display of upholstered furniture, and a magnificent line of draperies, curtains and interior decorations generally; regular employment being furnished on the spot for twenty-five competent assistants. Mr. Clark and Mr. Hecht are both young men of Philadelphia birth, and Mr. Clark was formerly engaged for eighteen years with Mr. John J. DeZouche, of this city.

THOMPSON, FOUST & CO., Manufacturers' Agents and Commission Merchants in Hosiery, Underwear, Small Wares, Cardigan Jackets, No. 9 Bank Street and No. 12 Strawberry Street.—Thirty odd years of uninterrupted prosperity marks the history of the widely-known house of Thompson, Foust & Co., manufacturers' agents and commission merchants for the sale of hosiery, small wares, cardigan jackets, etc., which is one of the oldest and most prominent concerns of the kind in Philadelphia and whose trade extends throughout the United States. This solid and responsible house was established by Wilcox Brothers, who were succeeded by E. R. Thompson & Son, who were in turn succeeded by John W. Lynch & Co., by whom it was conducted to about three years ago, when the present firm was organized. The premises occupied as offices and salesrooms comprise a store and basement and fourth floor in a 30 x 127-foot building, and are well ordered and excellently arranged. An efficient staff of clerks, salesmen, etc. are employed here, while some half a dozen representatives are kept on the road, and the proprietors exercise immediate supervision over the entire business. The firm handle a general line of hosiery, knit goods and small wares, on commission, and are agents for Justus Koch & Co., manufacturers of hosiery, No. 4 Moyer Street, this city; Justus Koch, manufacturer of cardigan jackets, Frankford Road, and several knitting mills in and around Philadelphia. Messrs. L. W. Thompson and H. H. Foust, the individual members of the firm, are natives of this city, and maintain an excellent standing in commercial circles.

WOLF BROTHERS, Manufacturers of Paper and Envelopes, New York Office, Nos. 121 and 123 Leonard Street, Corner Elm Street, Nos. 500 to 510 Minor Street.—This house was originally established in 1877, by Messrs. Clarence and Benjamin Wolf, and in 1889 Mr. Louis Wolf was admitted to partnership, followed, on the first of January, 1890, by the admission of Mr. Albert Wolf, thus forming the firm as at present constituted. They control the products of four immense paper mills, and handle paper of all kinds at their headquarters in this city. The business premises here comprise five mammoth structures, five stories in height and 60 x 140 feet, supplied with steam-power and all modern facilities. Here is carried at all times a magnificent stock of news, book, writing and manilla papers, envelopes and open end bags for all purposes, which are offered to the trade at the lowest ruling market prices. This firm are in a position to handle the best and most desirable grades of goods in immense quantities, and to guarantee the prompt and satisfactory fulfillment of all orders of whatever magnitude, and their success in this respect is evidenced by the large and influential trade they have built up among the largest and closest buyers in the country. The Messrs. Wolf are all native Philadelphians, and gentlemen of large business experience and sterling enterprise.

ESTEY, BRUCE & CO., Estey Organ, Estey Piano, Etc., No. 18 North Seventh Street.—In making reference to the famous Estey organs and pianos, space will not admit of our doing the subject adequate justice, and therefore, it must suffice to give a few brief remarks in order that those interested may seek the fullest information and details from Messrs. Estey, Bruce & Co., located in this city at No. 18 North Seventh Street, who are the eminent firm's duly-accredited representatives for the Keystone State, Delaware and Western New Jersey. The Estey organs and pianos, now in almost universal use, are generally conceded to be the finest instruments of the kind on the market, alike for volume, purity and sweetness of tone, delicate, even and elastic touch, light and quick action and for durability of construction, handsome appearance and elegant and artistic finish. The annual output is such that no fewer than five hundred workmen have to be employed at the manufactory. The representation here was founded about thirty-three years ago by Mr. E. M. Bruce; the present style having been assumed in 1883, and this firm—now the first of its kind in Philadelphia—are at all times glad of the opportunity of extending to visitors every courtesy and the fullest possible information concerning the Estey organs and pianos and their many points of superiority. The warerooms are a landmark in this part of the city, and consist of three spacious floors, each 20 x 50 feet in area. Sales are effected either for cash or on the easy purchase system by monthly installments; thus placing the Estey organs and pianos within easy reach of all.

WILLIAM YOUNG, Real Estate Agent and Conveyancer, No. 725 South Second Street.—Mr. William Young succeeded Mr. Vanatta, who established this business in 1883. Mr. Young was with Mr. Vanatta nine years, and since obtaining control of the house, has by faithful, conscientious zeal for the best interests of his customers gained the confidence of the community and secured a very superior clientele. He is familiar with both present and prospective values of realty in and around the city and has always on his books many desirable bargains, including business, residential and manufacturing sites, for sale, to let or exchange. He, however, makes a specialty of property in Wards 1 and 4, and the line which he handles is absolutely perfect as regards its title, and all realty dealt in through him may be relied upon as a safe investment. Mr. Young possesses unsurpassed facilities for the prompt negotiation of loans on bond and mortgage. Mr. Young is a native Philadelphian. He studied with Mr. Snyder, one of the oldest conveyancers of the city, and is a prominent member of the Conveyancer's Association of Philadelphia.

DOCK STREET FROM WALNUT STREET

ILLIAM C. RANDOLPH, Manufacturer of Bone Rings for Decorating Harness, Nos. 213 and 215 Arch Street.—For a period extending over thirty-four years, William C. Randolph, manufacturer of bone rings for decorating harness, Nos. 213 and 215 Arch Street, has been engaged in this branch of industry. He is one of the oldest in his line in Philadelphia and his productions are sold to the trade all over the United States. He was formerly of the firm of Lounsbury & Randolph, established in 1878, and for the past twenty-eight years has conducted the business alone with uninterrupted success. Mr. Randolph is a gentleman of full middle age and was born in New York, but has been in this city since boyhood. He is a man of practical skill himself, active and energetic, and gives close attention to every detail of the business. His shop, which is on the fifth floor here, is equipped with steam-power and machinery, and a number of expert hands are employed. Besides bone rings for the purposes above indicated, Mr. Randolph manufactures a variety of other articles in bone, ivory, horn and kindred substances, and keeps on hand always a large and fine assortment of these goods. Turning and carving are done for the trade, likewise, and the work executed here is of a distinctly superior character. Every article is warranted as to make and material, while the prices quoted are notably low, excellence of productions considered, and all orders are promptly and carefully attended to.

V. SICKEL, Pension and Claim Attorney, Branch Office, No. 612 F. Street N. W. Washington, D. C.; No. 729 Walnut Street.—The gentleman whose name heads this sketch is one of Philadelphia's best-known pension and claim attorneys. He has been engaged in this branch of practice since 1881 and has acquired a large patronage, his clientele extending throughout the United States. He occupies a well-appointed suite of rooms on the first floor of No. 729 Walnut Street, and has a branch office also at No. 612 F. Street, N. W., Washington, D. C. Mr. Sickel was born in this city. He is a thoroughly competent attorney of many years' experience and is an expert in matters pertaining to United States Government pensions and other claims. All classes of business in the line indicated are engaged in by him and all interests intrusted to this gentleman are certain to be attended to in the most careful, capable and trustworthy manner.

HISTORICAL AND COMMERCIAL PHILADELPHIA.

CHAS. E. READ, Manufacturer of Gent's and Boys' Fine Footwear, No. 5006 Main Street, Germantown.—Conspicuous among the leading and best known mercantile establishments of Germantown, stands that which is under the efficient management and direction of Mr. Chas. E. Read, manufacturer of gentlemen's and boys' fine footwear. In 1877 this business was originally founded by Mr. Jos. Read, who conducted it up to 1888, when he was succeeded by his two sons under the style of Jos. Read's Sons, but this partnership having been dissolved about a year and a-half ago, the present proprietor has since assumed sole control of its affairs with marked ability and success. The premises occupied at No. 5006 Main Street are spacious, commodious and of ample dimensions, and these are perfectly equipped with all the necessary facilities and appliances for the successful prosecution of the business, while permanent employment is afforded five experienced and skilled hands. The work of this reliable house is all executed by hand, and the boots and shoes manufactured are made from the very best quality of leather obtainable in the most thorough style of workmanship, and are pronounced perfect in fit and finish, correct in style and appearance, and durable in wearing qualities. All orders for anything in the line of footwear receive immediate attention, and regardless of all kinds is also promptly and skillfully executed in the highest style of excellence. In the salesroom will be found a superior assortment of gentlemen's and boys' boots, shoes and slippers in all sizes, widths, styles and grades, of Mr. Read's own manufacture, a specialty being made of durable bicycle shoes, and these never fail to give entire satisfaction to the most discriminating class of purchasers, while substantial inducements are offered in the way of price. Mr. Read is a practical and experienced business man of reliability, whose large and permanent trade extends throughout this, his native city, and its vicinity.

CHAS. S. KALBACHER, Nos. 15 to 19 Wister Street, Germantown.—Foremost among the substantial business men of this community, of wide-spread popularity, stands Mr. Chas. S. Kalbacher, bottler of J. C. Miller's "Munchenser" lager beer, whose establishment is desirably located at Nos. 15 to 19 Wister Street. The foundation of this flourishing business dates back sixteen years, and has always been under the efficient management and direction of its present proprietor, who is a practical, experienced and reliable merchant, wide awake to the interests of his customers, and from the outset he has enjoyed a most prosperous and successful career. The large and commodious premises occupied comprise a bottling department, having the ample dimensions of 30 x 100 feet, together with a store, 20 x 30 feet in measurement, and a stable in the rear, while employment is furnished to three skilled hands, and two teams are also required in constant service. All the latest improved facilities, appliances and conveniences are in use in this building, which has been recently erected for the purposes of the business, and Mr. Kalbacher makes a specialty of bottling the celebrated J. C. Miller's "Munchenser" lager beer, which is put up in pint bottles and is acknowledged to be the best, most superior and refreshing beverage of the kind produced and highly recommended by physicians. It commands a large sale in this city and vicinity, particularly in Germantown and Chestnut Hill. All orders are promptly filled at short notice, and goods are delivered free of charge. Mr. Kalbacher caters to a fine family trade and to all those in search of a delicious and excellent beer we heartily recommend this put up in his establishment, as it is guaranteed to give entire satisfaction to the most expert judges. Born in Germany, Mr. Kalbacher has resided in this city for the past twenty-two years, and has since become well known among our successful and representative business men.

A. G. C. WELDEN, Butter, Eggs and Poultry, No. 2550 Germantown Avenue.—One of the most popular and successful among the younger produce dealers doing business in this section of the city is Mr. A. G. C. Welden, whose establishment is located at No. 2550 Germantown Avenue. Mr. Welden, who is an enterprising and reliable young business man of sterling qualities, was born in Bucks County, this State, but for the past twelve years he has resided in this metropolis, and in 1887 embarked in his present enterprise at No. 2546, four doors from his present address—and in 1891 removing to his present commodious quarters. After starting in business he soon established himself in public favor and confidence, owing to his promptness and straightforward methods of dealing, and he quickly built up a large and flourishing patronage. A neatly appointed and well-ordered store is occupied, which is perfect in convenience of arrangement for the handling of the stock and systematic conduct of affairs; and the services of three competent assistants and a delivery wagon are required in constant employment. A large stock is at all times carried, including everything in the line of farm produce, a specialty being made of prime butter, of which he handles large shipments from Chester, Lancaster and Bucks Counties, fresh every week; eggs and poultry in season, and fresh invoices are constantly received direct from the hands of the producers. All orders are promptly filled and delivered at the lowest ruling market prices, and the trade of this house, already large, gives evidence of constant and gratifying increase.

E. M. PLATT, Druggist, Sansom and Thirty-sixth Streets.—An old-established and leading pharmacy in this section of the city, conducted upon the highest standard of professional skill and ability, by a practical and experienced chemist, is that of Mr. E. M. Platt. This well-patronized store has been in successful existence for the past seventeen years, and in 1891 it came under the control of the present efficient proprietor, who is the successor to Mr. W. H. Koons. The salesroom is neatly and handsomely furnished, being appropriately fitted up with all the modern adjuncts of convenience and attractiveness, and contains a full and general assortment of pure and fresh drugs and chemicals, proprietary remedies of acknowledged merit, surgical instruments, toilet and fancy articles, soaps, perfumery, etc., in fact, the usual complement of the first-class pharmacy. Patrons will, in the future as in the past, find every element of satisfaction both in the variety and high standard quality of the stock, and reasonable prices charged. Especial care is here exercised in the compounding of physicians' prescriptions and family recipes all of which are promptly prepared with accuracy and precision, from the most reliable ingredients obtainable. Mr. Platt puts up the following preparations which are in extensive demand all over the city and suburbs: Myrrh-Rosa, a deliciously refreshing mouth and tooth wash; Bouquet Glycerine Jelly, which is an efficient remedy for chapped hands and sunburn; Flowers of America cologne, a delightful toilet article, and Violet Water and Lilac Blossoms, both fragrant toilet waters. The large and liberal trade secured comes from far and near, and is derived from many of the leading families and physicians of this community. Mr. Platt is a competent, reliable and vigilant druggist, a graduate of the Philadelphia College of Pharmacy of the class of '87, and a member of its Alumni Association. He is a native of Chambersburg, this State, in which place he studied the business, previous to taking up his abode in this city.

S. P. CRANSTON, Real Estate and Fire Insurance, No. 5933 Lancaster Avenue.—For a number of years Mr. S. P. Cranston has been prominently identified with the handling of real estate in West Philadelphia, making a specialty of residential property in the Thirty-fourth, Twenty-fourth and Twenty-seventh Wards. He has constantly on hand a large quantity of real estate in that locality for sale, rent or exchange. Mr. Cranston is well known for promptitude in all transactions; for making accurate settlements, and for exercising a scrupulous care in all he undertakes, and by these means he has gained the confidence and support of a number of property owners, trustees and investors in this section of the city. His services are now largely sought for in all branches of the profession, including the purchase, sale and exchange of city and suburban building lots and realty in general, the letting of premises, the collection of rents, interest and outstanding accounts, the transfer, settlement and entire management of estates, the examination of titles and the negotiation of loans upon bond or mortgage. Mr. Cranston is also an insurance broker and local agent for the Girard Fire Insurance Company here, and he is thereby enabled to direct all desirable risks into the safest channels at the lowest current rates of premium. The business was established in 1888. Mr. Cranston is a native of this city.

HISTORICAL AND COMMERCIAL PHILADELPHIA.

HOMAS H. GRIGG, Drug Store Fixtures, Factory, No. 3824½ Lancaster Avenue and No. 3829 Warren Street.—One of the leading houses in West Philadelphia engaged in the manufacture of drug store fixtures is that of Thomas H. Grigg. Of the excellent principles which govern the detailed working of this responsible house, more particularly with regard to the work turned out, a few of the chief are originality of design, superior workmanship, judgment in construction, the best materials only, fine taste, true harmony, neatness and excellent finish. The enterprise was established at the same location by the present proprietor twelve years ago, and the factory now occupied was erected specially for the purpose in 1885. Drug store fixtures are made to order from original designs, as also specialities in art furniture, such as cabinets, etc.; antique furniture is repaired and beautifully finished in the best style, and particular attention is devoted to repairing furniture and household articles of every description, while a perfect, neat and reliable drawing board is made, being superior to any in the market, and sought after by the first designers in the country. The operations of the house have embraced the complete fitting up of several of the finest drug stores in West Philadelphia, and twelve picked mechanics are kept busily employed. The premises comprise a building of three floors, each 30x70 feet in area, provided with a full equipment of improved machinery pertaining to the trade, steam power being the motive force used. The able proprietor is thoroughly practical in this line of trade, and takes particular care that none but the finest work is turned out. He is a middle aged gentleman of Maine birth, and reached Philadelphia twelve years ago.

OHN WHY, Jr., & BRO., Bicycles and Accessories, Nos. 5 and 7 W. Chelten Avenue. The responsible firm of John Why, Jr., & Bro. are agents for the Hart Cycle Company and A. G. Spalding Bros. Co., whose goods they handle largely, as also the recognized standard makes of bicycles of the latest pattern. A speciality of the business consists in repairing of all kinds, more particularly high grade wheels. The store, 25x40 feet in area, is well arranged, and a full display of the best known kinds of bicycles is here to be seen, as also a complete assortment of accessories and supplies, including saddles, pneumatic tires, bells, spanners, lamps, oils, oil cans, etc. The individual partners are Mr. John Why, Jr., and Mr. Joseph Why, who are young men of Philadelphia birth, and are members of the Wissahickon Wheelmen and the League of American Wheelmen.

M. C. WHEELER, Printer, Corner Market and Strawberry Streets. Mr. William C. Wheeler has earned a well deserved reputation for reliability, and now controls a connection reaching to all over the United States. Every description of fine printing is undertaken, from a newspaper to a card; and including, as leading lines, book, pamphlet, job and mercantile printing in all branches, society and private work, wedding cards, ball and concert programmes, menus, etc., in gold, silver or illuminated, and in plain, medieval and fancy types. For the several purposes of the business, premises are occupied at the address named, consisting of a well appointed office on the second floor and a spacious press room on the fourth floor, the latter being furnished with a complete modern equipment of cylinder and job presses and other machines and accessories; steam power actuating the whole, and an average staff of ten skilled assistants engaged. Although the business of the house is of a truly national character, it is largely centred in the city, and include's fine book, pamphlet, job and commercial printing for several of the leading financial and mercantile institutions, trade houses, etc., in Philadelphia. The enterprise has been established for the past six years, and during the whole of that time has been conducted under the skilful and successful direction of the present proprietor, Mr. William C. Wheeler, who is a native of New York City, a resident of Palmyra, N. J., and has at his command an experience in this line extending over a period of eighteen years.

HOMAS B. LOVATT, Auctioneer, No. 430 South Street and No. 607 Passyunk Avenue.—One of the oldest established auctioneering businesses in the entire city of Philadelphia is that conducted at No. 430 South Street by Mr. Thomas B. Lovatt, whose services are now fully occupied with one or other of the several branches of the profession. About sixty five or seventy years ago one George W. Smith commenced operations as an auctioneer in this vicinity, and he continued in business up to 1870, when he was succeeded by Messrs. J. Daly & Co., who, however, retained control of affairs for only three years, and in 1873 they retired in favor of Mr. Thomas B. Lovatt. Mr. Lovatt has succeeded in building up a business of the largest proportions, and he is now held in high repute for the plain, straightforward and equitable methods to which he rigidly adheres, while he possesses all the attributes necessary to the successful pursuit of this most arduous of avocations. Sales at private residences receive special attention; farm sales are undertaken, including real estate, personal effects, live stock and "tools of trades," and on consignments of goods liberal advances are made. Moreover, at headquarters sales take place every weekday, and a full line of furniture and household goods, as well as pawnbrokers' unredeemed pledges, are disposed of without reserve. The premises utilized comprise a brick structure of three and four floors, 25x100 feet in area, and an L, 50 feet, provided with elevator and every comfort and convenience for the accommodation of buyers and visitors, seven competent assistants being there regularly employed. Mr. Lovatt was born in Philadelphia, and is a gentleman now of middle age.

ORELL & BRO., Commission Merchants in Butter, Eggs, Poultry, Etc., No. 232 Callowhill Street. A very successful house in this city engaged as commission merchants and wholesale dealers in butter, eggs and poultry is that of Messrs. J. and W. E. Morell. The business was established during the present year by the present proprietors, Messrs. Morell & Bro. They have been connected with the business for a number of years. A speciality is made of Pennsylvania eggs, which, with the other lines of produce handled, are guaranteed strictly fresh; and if not as represented, goods can be returned, and the money will be refunded. Consignments and shipments of prime poultry, butter and eggs are constantly arriving direct from creameries, dairies and farms in Pennsylvania, New Jersey and elsewhere, for disposal upon this market, and a fine choice stock in each line is usually carried on the premises. These latter consist of three floors, each 20x40 feet in area, well fitted and equipped for the successful conduct of the business. Live and dressed poultry are both largely dealt in, and the relative prices in each line are as low as the lowest. The able proprietors, Messrs. J. and W. E. Morell, were born in Philadelphia, and have been residents in this city since birth.

HARLES BETZ, Carriage and Wagon Builder, Nos. 1825 to 1829 North Sixth Street. Mr. Charles Betz is a German by birth and has been a resident of this city since 1856. He began at his trade at the bottom round of the ladder, as an apprentice, and after years of close practical experience in all its branches, he established himself in business on Frankford Avenue in 1866, and at once built up a trade that soon grew to such proportions that he was compelled to provide better facilities in order to meet its demands, and in 1888 he moved to his present location. The premises occupied are very spacious, comprising a substantial two story building, 51x80 feet in dimensions, with ample yard and shed accommodations for the covered storage of lumber, iron and other materials required in the business. The factory is admirably arranged for the various branches of the trade, while a fine repository is provided for the exhibition and sale of the various kinds of vehicles manufactured. The range of products embraces every kind of vehicle, such as heavy road wagons, drays, trucks, carts, furniture vans, express, grocers' and milk wagons, also the carriages of every description, embodying all the very latest improvements for comfort and pleasure, sleighs, road and track sulkies, brewers' and bottlers' wagons, etc. These vehicles are all made of the very best seasoned woods, finest quality of steel, iron and other material. Mr. Betz is a member of several social and benevolent organizations.

HISTORICAL AND COMMERCIAL PHILADELPHIA.

HENRY A. W. SMITH, Plumber, Steam and Gas Fitter, No. 4812 Germantown Avenue.—A prominent and reliable house engaged in sanitary plumbing and gasfitting, in Germantown, is that of Henry A. W. Smith, located at No. 4812 Germantown Avenue, where he occupies a commodious store and carries a fine assortment of plumbers' supplies, including bath tubs, closets, washbowls, faucets, lead and iron pipe, gas fixtures, chandeliers, brackets and other specialties pertaining to the line. Mr. Smith is prepared to furnish estimates and enter into contracts of any magnitude for the plumbing, ventilating, lighting and heating of public buildings and private residences in the city and vicinity. Being a thoroughly expert sanitary engineer, his work, when once completed, remains perfect for years and satisfaction is guaranteed to patrons in every respect. No house in this section of Philadelphia stands higher in the esteem of its patrons or is better prepared for prompt, efficient and satisfactory work. Prices are placed at the lowest point consistent with first-class work and his patronage is large and active at all seasons of the year. Mr. Smith is a man in the prime of life and of excellent standing in social and business circles. He numbers among his customers many of the most prominent citizens of Germantown and is a man deserving of the most implicit trust and confidence in any contract he may undertake, the best work and fairest dealing being assured. He uses nothing but the best materials and is thorough and expert in all branches of his trade.

H. McCANN, Conveyancer and Real Estate Agent, No. 3841 Lancaster Avenue.—For several years past Mr. F. H. McCann has been prominently identified with the progress and development of real estate interests in West Philadelphia. He makes a specialty of residential property, more particularly in the Seventh, Eighth, Ninth, Tenth, Twenty-fourth Twenty-seventh and Thirty-fourth Wards, and at the well-appointed office on the first floor at the address named registers are kept of a large quantity of valuable and highly eligible real estate of this nature, on hand for sale, rent or exchange, two competent clerks being there regularly employ d. Mr. McCann has been established in the profession since 1861, and he possesses a ripe experience ranging over a period of thirty-two years. He is sub-agent for the United Firemen's Insurance Company of Philadelphia, and the Mechanics' of Philadelphia, and thus he is enabled to cover all desirable fire insurance risks at the lowest current rates of premium, besides conducting business in all branches of the real estate profession, buying, selling, renting, collecting, negotiating loans and conveyancing. Mr. McCann is a gentleman of middle-age, and was born in Southwark, Pa.

PULASKI & CO., Manufacturers and Dealers in Picture Frames, No. 724 Chestnut Street. Branch, No. 1619 Columbia Avenue. —This is one of the largest and leading houses in its line in the city. The firm does both a wholesale and retail business, and its trade extends all over Pennsylvania and throughout the adjoining States. The premises occupied comprise an entire 25 x 150-foot four-story and basement building, with complete facilities for manufacturing. The establishment is excellently equipped in all departments and thirty in help are employed here. The firm manufactures elegant picture frames of every description, and keeps on hand always a very large and splendid assortment. The stock, which is exceedingly fine, includes artistic picture frames and mouldings in exquisite designs and superb finish, art novelties, etchings, engravings, paintings water-colors, pastels, photogravures and pictures in great variety, and frames are made to order, likewise, in the most superior style at short notice. All work done here is guaranteed to be first-class. Dealers are supplied on the most favorable terms, special inducements being offered to the trade. This enterprising firm, which is composed of F. Pulaski and E. Titlebaum, was established about ten years ago, and has a branch store at No. 1619 Columbia Avenue. The proprietors, who are natives of Austro-Hungary, but many years in this country, are men of energy and business ability, and have a drygoods' store at Cuthbert, Ga., which is under the management of Mr. Titlebaum.

F. HEACOCK, Dealer in Grocers', Butchers' and Confectioners' Fixtures, No. 51 North Second Street.—For all kinds of grocers', butchers' and confectioners' fixtures and tools of trade, it would, indeed, be difficult to find a more reliable house than that of Mr. H. F. Heacock, where may always be found a large and carefully chosen assortment of goods of the best and most reliable and serviceable make in each line. These goods include the grocers' favorite "Imperial" tea and spice caddies, scales of many different kinds, spring balances, coffee mills, ordinary tea and spice caddies, funnels, candy jars, scoops, knives, steels, hatchets, Koch's adjustable-reversible patent shelf brackets, Coles' pulverizing-granulating coffee mills, ice cream freezers, patent tills, cash registers, etc., etc., as well as the various manufactures of the Southwark Scale Company, for whom the house acts as agent. The business was established by that company in 1882, and three years ago it came into the hands of the present proprietor. The trade is conducted at both wholesale and retail. The premises occupied consist of a store and basement, each 20 x 50 feet in area, well ordered and fitted throughout for the due conduct of the business. Mr. Heacock is a young gentleman of Philadelphia birth and was formerly engaged for six years with the Southwark Scale Company, and for a like period with the Southwark Hardware Company.

CHARLES MATTHIAS & CO., Manufacturer of Horse Collars, No. 110 North Third Street.—It might appear to the ordinary superficial observer that the particular make of a horse collar is of comparatively little importance, but those who are posted and are acquainted with the needs of the horse know full well the absolute necessity of so manufacturing and fitting a collar that it shall not gall and chafe the animal. To this end special skill and experience are required. The firm of Charles Matthias & Co. are leaders in this line of work, though yet a young house, comparatively, having been founded in the latter part of 1891. They can produce scores of testimonials from owners of horses as to their eminent fitness for producing superior collars. All their work is guaranteed and they pay special attention to repairing. They manufacture to order at shortest notice, and at extremely reasonable prices, all kinds of kay, patent leather, Irish, Scotch, wagon and short straw horse collars of the best grades. Mr. Charles Matthias, the head of the firm, is a practical man, a native of Philadelphia, where he learned his trade, being connected at one time with Mr. Kiehl.

WILLIAM J. LLOYD MANUFACTURING COMPANY, Successors to American Manufacturing Company, Manufacturers of Hardware Specialties, Twenty-second Street and Washington Avenue.—One of the most widely-known and most noteworthy concerns in Philadelphia devoted to the production of hardware specialties is that of the Wm. J. Lloyd Manufacturing Company, which is one of the largest and leading establishments in its particular line in the country. This flourishing enterprise was started in 1874, by the American Manufacturing Company, who were succeeded about three years ago by the present firm. They are manufacturers of the Great American meat cutter, the Great American stuffer attachments, Charlton's detachable meat hooks, Lloyd acme saw sets, the Leopold patent saw sets, the Leach improved saw sets, the Bonney hollow augers, Weston pattern bench hooks, Smith pattern bench hooks, improved spoke trimmers, American saw filers' vises, Excelsior can openers and a number of other patented articles, and are constantly adding new inventions to their catalogue. The productions of this company are noted for their exceptional merit and are not only in extensive and growing demand throughout the United States, but are exported quite largely, also. The factory is equipped with ample steam-power, the latest improved machinery and all needed appliances, while upward of fifty in help are employed at manufacturing. A large and complete stock is constantly kept on hand. Mr. William J. Lloyd, who is the sole proprietor, is a gentleman of middle-age, well-known to the jobbing trade, having been connected with it for years, a native of this city and a man of skill and ingenuity, as well as of many years' experience.

HISTORICAL AND COMMERCIAL PHILADELPHIA.

 HOPPE, Real Estate Broker and Notary Public; Offices, S. E. Corner Second and McKean Streets, and No. 304 Drexel Building.—Few among the responsible real estate brokers of Philadelphia have a higher reputation than Mr. F. Hoppe, whose offices are located in the Drexel Building and at the southeast corner of Second and McKean Streets. He is a general real estate agent, and has developed an influential connection, carrying through successfully many important transactions in city realty. He buys, sells and rents property, collects rents, effects insurances in first class companies at lowest rates, and undertakes the entire management of estates. He also negotiates loans on bond and mortgage. He also attends to the sale of country property, making a specialty of Pennsylvania lands. He is a popular notary public and possesses a thorough knowledge of the laws relative to the transfer, etc., of real estate. Mr. Hoppe is a man of middle age, was born in Germany, but has resided and done business in Philadelphia for upwards of ten years. He established his present business in 1889 and has brought it to its present large proportions by his unremitting attention to his patrons, by his sterling integrity, his sound common sense, and his rare discrimination in matters requiring careful judgment.

 AS. A. McGRANE, Hardware and House Furnishing Goods, Locksmith and Bellhanging, No. 518 South Twenty-first Street.—Although not yet quite two years in existence, the hardware and house furnishing goods house of James A. McGrane has already attained the lead in its line. The premises occupied comprise a commodious store and shop, eligibly located, while every convenience is at hand for the successful prosecution of the work, and for the attractive display of the large and superior class of goods handled. The stock embraces general hardware for both builders' and mechanics' use, table and pocket cutlery, tin and sheet iron ware, and a general line of house furnishing goods, and kitchen ware in great variety. A specialty is also made in repairing bells, locks, etc., putting up speaking tubes and in electrical work. Courteous clerks and assistants are regularly employed, and popular prices prevail. Mr. McGrane is a native of Philadelphia, and has had a practical experience of seven years in his line.

 OHN D. JOHNSON & Co., Manufacturers of and Dealers in Plumbers' Supplies (Columbian Iron Works); Office, Nos. 139 and 141 North Seventh Street.—The manufacture of plumbers' supplies is a most important modern branch of industry, and has been developed to a high standard of perfection. A leading house in Philadelphia engaged in this line is that of John D. Johnson & Co., proprietors of the Columbian Iron Works, located at Hainesport, N. J., and wholesale room is at Nos. 139 and 141 North Seventh Street, this city. This establishment was founded in 1857 by Mr. John D. Johnson, who continued at the head of affairs up to sixteen years ago, when he died, and was succeeded by his son, John D. Johnson, who had been raised in the business and was well qualified to continue the success won by his progenitor. Three years ago Mr. Benjamin Deacon, who had been in the house eight years, was admitted to a partnership interest. Both gentlemen are natives of New Jersey, and are popularly known in trade circles as business men of honor and ability. The works at Hainesport cover an area of two acres, are equipped with the finest steam power machinery, and one hundred men are employed there. The firm manufacture a general line of sinks, stands, traps, soil pipe, and iron work of all kinds used by plumbers. At the store in this city a heavy stock is carried, and a large trade is supplied, extending all over the Middle and Southern States. The superiority of the goods handled by the firm is well known, and all orders are met at lowest prices.

 M. PROCTER, Jr., CO., Apothecaries, Ninth and Lombard Streets.—The Wm. Procter, Jr., Co., located at the corner of Ninth and Lombard Streets, conduct one of the largest apothecary businesses in this section of Philadelphia, and they are, perhaps, best known as the manufacturers of a number of pharmaceutical compounds, cures, tinctures and proprietary articles, including Vinum Digestivum, Pepsin, Fortior and Saccharated, Compound Syrup Hypophosphites, etc. The extensive connection controlled is permanently established upon many years of successful trading, for the business was founded in 1844 at the same location by Mr. William Procter, Jr., and came under the control of the present proprietor, David Preston, in 1874. He first entered the store in 1861 as an apprentice, grew up in the business, and graduated in 1865 at the Philadelphia College of Pharmacy, being now a member of its Alumni. The store itself, 20x60 feet in area, is handsomely appointed with soda fountain, plate mirrors and other superior fixtures, and a heavy and very complete stock is always carried of pure and fresh drugs, chemicals, medicines, and everything requisite to the systematic conduct of a drug, family and prescription business. David Preston was born in Maryland, came to this city in 1861, and is a member of the American and of the Pennsylvania Pharmaceutical Associations.

 EORGE M. CHRISTMAN, Germantown Junction Coal Yard, Nos. 2923 and 2925 North Broad Street and Pennsylvania Railroad.—This house has been in successful operation since 1883 and conducts a large business in Lehigh, Schuylkill and other superior grades of coal at both wholesale and retail. The yard covers a ground area of 50x285 feet, situated on the line of the Pennsylvania railroad, with every convenience for the shipment of supplies and for the storage of the immense stock that is constantly carried. All coal purchased of this responsible house is guaranteed to maintain in every respect the highest standard of excellence, and holds the front rank as regards the care in its preparation for the market, coming as it does from the best equipped collieries in America. The resources of the house are such, that orders can be filled with the utmost promptness at wholesale by the car load, or at retail by the ton. Sales aggregate from 15,000 tons per year, and the business is steadily increasing. Mr. Christman is a native of Montgomery County, Pa., and a resident of Philadelphia for the past twenty-five years, and is a member of the Coal Exchange.

 HILIP DAVEY, Photographer on Wood, No. 706 Chestnut Street.—The leading photographer on wood in this city is Mr. Philip Davey, who established his business here in 1886 and makes a specialty of photographing machinery, horses, and other subjects for the wood engraving trade. The excellence of his work and its fidelity to every detail demonstrates a true conception of the artist's mission, and places Mr. Davey in the front rank of his profession. The services of Mr. Davey are in constant and important requisition throughout the city and surrounding country. Mr. Davey is a native of Philadelphia, a resident of Laurel Springs, New Jersey, and a young man of marked artistic ability, a member of the American Mechanics and the Knights of the Golden Eagle.

 EO. HAGY & BRO., Patent Lime, Etc., Opposite Wayne Junction Depot, Stenton Avenue.—This firm are manufacturers of the best quality Whitemarsh Patent Lime, and dealers in coal, lime, cement, coke, and masons' materials of all kinds. The business was founded twenty-seven years ago, at Manayunk, by the present owners, Messrs. George and Lewis Y. Hagy, both of whom are natives of this State, having been born in Montgomery County. They have built up a large, first class trade, and now have permanent patrons in all parts of the country. Their lime kilns and quarries are located on Hagy's Siding, Plymouth Railroad. The property is a valuable and extensive one, and provided with a large number of lime kilns and all facilities for perfect production. The premises in the city cover an area of 160x170 feet, and the place is amply protected by shedding. This is the largest coal yard in Germantown. There are twenty-five coal bins in it, each with a storage capacity of 300 tons of coal. A very heavy stock is at all times carried, and both a wholesale and retail trade is supplied, carload lots of lime being shipped direct from the kilns.

HISTORICAL AND COMMERCIAL PHILADELPHIA. 213

CLAPP & MATTIS, Meats and Provisions, No. 1950 Main Street.—A prominent and popular meat market and provision store in this section of the city is that conducted by Messrs. Clapp & Mattis, No. 1950 Main Street, Germantown. The business was established in 1884 by the present proprietors, Christian Clapp and A. Wesley Mattis, who have had twenty years' experience in this line of trade. Both gentlemen are enterprising and progressive, and their good business management has gained the store an excellent reputation and wide patronage. Their large and handsomely fitted market is 25x60 feet in dimensions, and is thoroughly stocked with a choice and select line of goods, including the best grades of fresh and salt meats, a full line of provisions, fresh vegetables and game in season. A specialty is made of the celebrated "J. B." butter, which is received in large invoices twice a week. The trade is heavy, and extends among the best class of residents of this vicinity, requiring the services of six skilled and polite assistants, while four wagons are required in the delivery department. Both gentlemen are natives of Philadelphia and prominent members of the Retail Grocers' Association, and are men well and favorably known in mercantile circles. Messrs. Clapp and Mattis are members of the United American Mechanics and the Tonti Society.

GLOVER & REEP, Artistic Paper Hangings, Interior Decorations, No. 3949 Lancaster Avenue.—Among the leading, most popular and skilful of the representative paper hangers and decorators of this vicinity, special mention should be made of the firm of Glover & Reep, who have won an enviable reputation for promptness and reliability. This business was founded by these gentlemen two years ago, and from its inception a large and substantial patronage has been received, which still keeps steadily increasing in magnitude and importance yearly. In the commodious and neatly appointed salesroom will be found a large and comprehensive stock of the most artistic wall papers of every description, from the plainest to the most elaborate designs and styles of both imported and domestic patterns, and so varied is the assortment, the most fastidious patron cannot fail to make suitable selections here. From four to six skilled and experienced workmen are given regular employment, and the range of work includes paper hanging, frescoing, kalsomining, tinting, etc., in fact, interior decorations of all kinds, all of which are executed in the highest styl of the art at reasonable rates. This firm enters into contracts for all classes of work, and all orders receive immediate attention, while many fine residences in this section owe much of their beauty and artistic effect to the workmanship of this house. Mr. Glover, the active member of this firm, is thoroughly familiar with every branch of this business, and previous to embarking for himself was with A. G. Miller of this city. Mr. Reep is actively engaged in the grocery business, and both of these gentlemen are natives of Philadelphia.

F. B. KRELL, M.D., Druggist, No. 743 South Third Street.—The extensive business conducted at Dr. F. B. Krell's pharmacy is in itself substantial proof that the house enjoys a wide reputation as a reliable dispensary for absolutely pure, fresh and potent drugs, chemicals, medicines and family remedies. Not by any means less freely recognized is the prescription department and laboratory, which are liberally patronized for the careful and accurate preparation of physicians' prescriptions and miscellaneous recipes, as also for the several high grade pharmaceutical compounds, cures, tinctures and other proprietary articles made and put up on the spot. The pharmacy itself is finely fitted up and carefully stocked with everything requisite to the systematic conduct of a large drug, prescription and family trade. Dr. F. B. Krell, graduated in March, 1884, at the Philadelphia College of Pharmacy, also at the Jefferson Medical College in 1889, as a fully qualified physician, and in 1888 he bought his present store of Mr. Wm. Danheran. Dr. Krell was born in Mahoney City, Pa., where he studied medicine with Dr. Bissel, and pharmacy with Mr. Haas. Dr. Krell is a member of the Philadelphia County and the Pennsylvania State Medical Societies.

PINKSTONE, Watches, Clocks and Jewelry, N. E. Corner Twentieth and South Streets.—The leading and most extensive retail jewelry establishment in this section of Philadelphia is unquestionably that of Mr. P. Pinkstone, located on the northeast corner of Twentieth and South Streets. The business was inaugurated in 1872 by the present proprietor, who two years ago removed to the present location. The store, 20x86 feet in area, is handsomely furnished and richly stocked with a full and complete line of watches, clocks, jewelry, silverware, diamonds, art novelties, spectacles, etc. Mr. Pinkstone has had thirty years' practical experience at the trade, and is one of the most expert watchmakers and jewelers in the city, and a complete master of the art in all its branches. All engraving, repairing of jewelry, or adjustment of fine watches and clocks is promptly and skilfully executed at prices consistent with first class work. Mr. Pinkstone is a gentleman of middle age, a native of England, and a prominent member of the Independent Order of Odd Fellows, the Foresters, and the Retail Jewelers' Association.

FRANK ROSATTO, Manufacturer of Billiard and Pool Tables, No. 515 South Eighth Street.—A successful house in this city engaged in the manufacture of billiard and pool tables is that of Mr. Frank Rosatto. Mr. Rosatto was born in the sunny land of Italy in 1851, but has resided in this city since childhood, having come here in 1857 with his parents, and was educated in the public schools. Sixteen years ago Mr. Rosatto established business here, and he has since built up a large, first class trade, extending to all parts of the country. The factory is equipped with fine machinery, driven by steam power, and employment is given a force of skilled workmen. At the handsome salesroom on South Eighth Street Mr. Rosatto displays a large stock of the elegant tables made by him. He also carries a full assortment of billiard and pool cloth, billiard and pool balls, cues, racks, and general supplies of all kinds in this line and careful attention is given repair work.

ISAAC WOLF, Insurance, Nos. 136 and 138 South Fourth Street.—Mr. Isaac Wolf has been established in this business here for a period of twenty years, and as a practical and experienced underwriter is prepared to offer the most substantial inducements to the insured, including low rates and liberally drawn policies, while all losses sustained are equitably adjusted and promptly paid. He has the entire confidence of leading insurance corporations, and takes the entire charge of insurance of property, dwellings, stores and stocks of merchandise, placing and distributing risks among sound companies only, renewing policies when expired, and generally relieving the business community of all care and trouble in this important respect. Mr. Wolf is a native of Germany, a resident of this city since 1860, and a member of the Fire Underwriters' Association of Philadelphia.

J. J. ATKINSON, Wholesale Commission Merchant and Dealer in Fruit and Country Produce, No. 304 South Front Street.—Among the long established and prominent houses engaged in this field of enterprise, that of Mr. J. J. Atkinson holds a foremost place. Since its inception this house has done much in influencing the shipments of products to this city, and in attracting attention to the many advantages Philadelphia possesses as a primary market for country produce. Mr. Atkinson began business in 1872, and has been at his present address, No. 304 South Front Street, the past five years. Here he occupies a three story and basement building, 20x40 feet in dimensions, and provided with all required conveniences. Mr. Atkinson employs a staff of assistants and conducts a general business as a wholesale commission merchant and dealer in fruit and country produce of all kinds. Mr. Atkinson was born in New Jersey, and resides in Paulsborough, that State, being a heavy property owner and prominent citizen there. He is an active member of the Order of Odd Fellows, Knights of Pythias, Red Men, and Whippoorwills.

HISTORICAL AND COMMERCIAL PHILADELPHIA.

MAURICE H. POWER, Printer, No. 907 Chestnut Street.—Undertaking equally all branches of fine printing, Mr. Maurice H. Power is held in high repute for the accuracy and artistic finish of his productions. The business was established four years ago by the present proprietor, who is a thoroughly practical man in this line. All kinds of fine printing, from a visiting card to a newspaper, are undertaken, including book, pamphlet, circular mercantile and general job printing, society and private work, etc., such as ball and concert programs and tickets, menus, certificates, and similar work; which are executed in plain, fancy or mediaeval types, in gold, silver and various colors; no pains being spared to ensure a high finish, an artistic appearance and unique style. For these several purposes, a spacious printing office is maintained on the third floor of the "Evening Bulletin" Building, 30 x 120 feet in measurement, furnished with a cylinder press, Gordon presses and a full equipment of machines and accessories pertaining to the industry; steam-power being the actuating force employed, and an average of nine competent assistants engaged on the spot; while a large number of fonts of modern type is at hand for executing every description of printing in the best and most satisfactory manner, and a heavy assortment of cards and paper, both plain and tinted, is kept constantly in stock, suitable for all purposes. The experienced proprietor is a native of Massachusetts.

JAMES B. RAMSEY & SON, Paper Manufacturers, No. 14 Decatur Street.—This is a time-honored house, having been founded thirty-four years ago by Messrs. Wells & Buckman, the firm afterward becoming Chas. Wells & Co. Mr James B. Ramsey being the "Co." On the death of Mr. Wells in 1882 Mr. Ramsey purchased the interest of the estate of Charles Wells, and he continued alone up to January 1, 1892, when he admitted to partnership his son, Mr. James Bradford Ramsey, Jr., and adopted the present firm-title. Both gentlemen are natives of Philadelphia, and have always resided here, and they sustain an A1 status in the business and financial world. The Messrs. Ramsey are owners of the Cecil Mills, located at Rising Sun, Md., and the Valley Mills, near Oxford, Pa. These mills are equipped with first-class machinery, afford employment to fifty-five workmen, and are constantly turning out large quantities of manillas of superior quality. The firm's warehouse in this city is a five-storied building 18 x 60 feet in size. The trade supplied is especially large in Philadelphia, New York and Baltimore, but a scattering patronage is also had from all the Middle States and the West.

STAMM & CO., Manufacturers of Pantaloons, No. 39 North Third Street.—Messrs. S. Stamm & Co. are manufacturers of pantaloons for men, youths and boys, and turn out an immense quantity of goods of all grades, in every variety of material. They employ skilled cutters and experienced operatives, and have gained an excellent reputation with the trade. They occupy the three upper floors of the building at the above location, each 20 x 80 feet in area. The cutting is done on the premises, and the garments are made up by a large force of outside operatives. Several traveling salesmen are employed, and a large volume of trade is carried on with dealers in Pennsylvania, Maryland, New Jersey and Delaware. The business of this concern was established in 1880 by Bacharach and Stamm. On the 6th of October, 1890, Mr. S. Stamm became the sole proprietor, and on December 1, 1891, the present firm was organized by the admission of Mr. H. W. Hirnheimer to partnership. Mr. Stamm is an elderly gentleman, a native of Germany, and came to the United States in 1866. Mr. Hirnheimer is a young man, also born in Germany, and has lived in this country since 1872.

H. STEPHEN & CO., Iron and Steel, Nos. 416-420 Walnut Street.—Messrs. H. Stephen & Co. are commission merchants and brokers, and are agents for the Etna Iron and Steel Co. of Bridgeport, O.; Pottstown Band Iron Mill, of Pottstown, Pa., and other manufacturing concerns. They handle everything in the line indicated, including "Star" boiler and bridge rivets, wrought iron plate washers, Woodbridge fire bricks, tiles, clays, etc., iron and steel bars, cold rolled strip steel, band iron, coil and crane chains, railroad chains, dredging chains, stud chains, wrought and cast iron, scraps, bolts and nuts, wire solder, cast iron and gas pipes, castings, forging, angles, beams, channels, tees, rails, nails, spikes, etc., also tire, cast tool steel, black and galvanized sheet iron, horseshoe iron, toe-calk and machinery steel, cold rolled shafting, nickel plated steel gongs, planished machinery steel, etc., etc. They also handle fireproof lumber, fire bricks of all kinds and shapes, blocks and kindred articles, and special work of every description. The trade of the firm extends all over the United States. They occupy a commodious office (Room No. 63), and employ several clerks. All orders for anything in iron, steel, etc., are executed upon the most favorable terms, the firm being in a position to offer liberal inducements to dealers, manufacturers and large consumers. This business was established in 1884 by Messrs. H. Stephen, E. H. Dieffenbach and David B. Yerger, although the senior partner retired some three years ago. Messrs. Dieffenbach and Yerger are now the sole members. They are natives of this city, men of thorough experience, and business ability.

WM. BERGER Germantown Monumental Marble Works, No. 5101 Main Street, Germantown; Branch Yard, Adjoining Ivy Hill Cemetery.—As a designer and dealer in monuments Mr. Wm. Berger holds a leading position in this city. The house was founded in 1859 and is the oldest in its line in the city. The premises occupied comprise a building, 28 x 80 feet in dimensions, situated on a lot 25 x 125 feet in area. The concern is supplied with every modern convenience and facility. Mr. Berger is at all times prepared to furnish marble and granite monuments of any grade desired from the plainest to the most elaborate, devoting particular attention to cemetery and memorial work of all kinds. He imports largely of Italian marble for statuary work, also Scotch granite, and handles the best grades of light, dark and red granite from the quarries of Massachusetts, Vermont and Virginia. Specimens of his artistic handiwork exhibit decided genius, not only in execution but also in design and can be found in all the cemeteries of this vicinity. Artistic designs are furnished on application. Cemetery lots are enclosed with marble or granite posts of the latest design, and house work and jobbing receive prompt attention. Besides the main establishment, which is located at No. 5141 Main Street, Mr. Berger also has a yard adjoining Ivy Hill Cemetery. The advantages of the concern for turning out the finest memorial work are rarely equaled. Mr. Berger is a native Philadelphian and is an accomplished master of his art. He is popular in business and social circles and is a member of the Knights of Pythias.

JOHN B. HAMMER, Heater and Range Work, No. 5101 Main Street, Germantown.—There is certainly not one among Germantown's general sheet metal workers who enjoys a better reputation or a more substantial share of patronage than John B. Hammer. He is the leader in his line in this vicinity and does the work of seven estates. The business conducted by him was established in 1862 by Benjamin Fife, who was succeeded by his brother-in-law, John Gavin, and in 1876 came into control of the present proprietor. Mr. Hammer was born here in Germantown and is a man of thorough practical skill and twenty years' experience. The quarters occupied by him as store and shop are commodious and well ordered and nine or ten able help are employed. A large stock is constantly kept on hand, and includes stoves of every description, ranges and heaters, tinware, kitchen specialties, etc. Mr. Hammer is prepared to attend to all classes of work in the line indicated, including tin roofing and repairing, and guarantees perfect satisfaction. Estimates are furnished, special attention being given to hot air heating of residences and to heater and range work generally. Jobbing is executed with skill and dispatch and all work done is warranted to be first class, while the prices charged are very moderate. Mr. Hammer is a member of the P. and A. M., the I. O. O. F., the K. of P., the Royal Arcanum, the K. of G. E., the A. O. U. W., and the Junior Order of American Mechanics.

HISTORICAL AND COMMERCIAL PHILADELPHIA.

  H. MARKLEY, Engravers on Wood, Nos. 416-418-420 Walnut Street.—One of the largest and finest wood-engraving businesses in Philadelphia is done by a woman. This is A. H. Markley, who is a Philadelphian by birth, a practiced wood-engraver not excelled by any in the city. She started in business twelve years ago and has occupied the present offices for the last two and one-half years. The business gives employment to ten hands and the workshop is at No. 542 Walnut Street. A specialty is made of engraving machinery for catalogue work, etc. The reputation of the house for prompt and excellent work is first-class. In work which requires accuracy as well as artistic excellence it has no superior.

CHESTNUT STREET, LOOKING EAST FROM ELEVENTH.

 R. WM. REUSS, Druggist, No. 833 South Second Street.—No department of commercial enterprise in Philadelphia is of more direct value and importance to the community than that in which the practical manufacturing and dispensing pharmacist brings to bear his professional skill and experience. The representative and progressive house of Dr. Wm. Reuss, located at No. 883 South Second Street, was established by this gentleman in 1856 at No. 501 South Second Street, and was recently removed to the present location. The premises occupied are spacious and attractively fitted up and contain a large stock of the finest drugs and chemicals, proprietary medicines of acknowledged merit and reputation, fancy toilet articles, perfumery, mineral waters, surgeons' and physicians' requisites, and indeed every article that may be thought of in connection with a first-class pharmacy. There is no branch of the drug business so important as the careful, conscientious and intelligent compounding of physicians' prescriptions and family receipts, and this branch holds a paramount position in this establishment. All modern appliances have been provided to secure accuracy, and no person more fully appreciates the responsibility that rests upon him than Dr. Reuss. The patronage of this reliable house is large, first-class and influential. Dr. Reuss is of German nativity, and is a graduate of the University at Giessen. He has been a resident of this city thirty-eight years and is of excellent standing in the profession and in social circles.

 A. NILSON, Pianos and Organs, No. 5007 Main Street, Germantown.—Mr. P. A. Nilson, the popular and well-known music dealer, located at No. 5007 Main Street, established business in this city in 1877 and has done much to foster and promote a love for music in this community. The premises occupied by him comprise three floors, 20 x 60 feet in dimensions, and a large stock of first-class pianos and organs, together with a full line of musical merchandise is kept constantly on hand. Mr. Nilson is agent for A. Nilson & Company's pianos and handles other makes also. He is also agent for several leading makes of organs, and keeps violins, guitars, banjos, accordions, harmonicas, auto-harps, etc., constantly on hand, also all kinds of strings, frames, pictures, art decorations, fancy wares, novelties, mirrors, etc. His store is recognized as headquarters for this class of goods, and musicians, musical students and choristers make it their chief rendezvous. We would earnestly recommend any of our readers in want of goods in this line to give this reliable house a call before leaving orders elsewhere. Tuning and repairing are given prompt attention, and the trade of this house in the city and its vicinity is large, first-class and influential. Mr. Nilson is a native of Sweden, but has been a resident of this city for the past twenty years, and has gained an enviable reputation as an honorable, reliable business man.

HISTORICAL AND COMMERCIAL PHILADELPHIA.

JOHN A. R. McLEOD, Fine Harness, No. 4842 Main Street.—Without doubt, the leading manufacturer of fine harness in Germantown is Mr. John A. R. McLeod. This business was established twenty years ago, and has been conducted at the same location for the past eighteen years, having all along been directed by the present proprietor. Coach harness and dog cart and four and six in hand harness constitute the specialties of the business, in addition to which any kind of light or heavy single or double harness is manufactured to order. The premises utilized comprise a building of three floors, each 20x80 feet in area, fully equipped for turning out the best work on short notice. A handsome display of harness, saddles, bridles and horse equipments is here to be seen, and the large city and vicinity trade controlled furnishes regular employment for twelve skilled assistants. Mr. McLeod was born in Londonderry, Ireland, coming to this city in 1861, and he has been actively engaged in this line for the past thirty years. He is a member of Post No. 6 of the Grand Army of the Republic, and served for three years during the late war as private in the 92d Pennsylvania Volunteer Infantry.

ALBERT A. ARDIS, Jr., Bricklayer and Builder; Residence, No. 1122 South Sixth Street; Shop, No. 705 Sansom Street.—For reliable work at fair and reasonable prices it would be difficult to find a better bricklayer and job builder in the Quaker City than Mr. Albert A. Ardis, Jr., who has at his command a wide and varied practical experience in this line, ranging over a period of a quarter of a century; and he has succeeded in working up a large permanent trade during the five years of his establishment. His operations consist for the most part of all kinds of repairing and jobbing work, alterations to old buildings, laying sidewalks, erecting foundations, walls, etc., while special attention is given to heaters, ranges and furnaces. Several skilled artisans are regularly employed. Mr. Ardis was born in this city, and is a member of the Knights Templars, of the Free and Accepted Masons, as well as of the Independent Order of Odd Fellows.

GILBERT & SON, Fine Shirt Manufacturers and Gents' Furnishers, No. 620 Chestnut Street.—These gentlemen have achieved a success in this line second to none other in the city. In every sense of the word they are fine shirtmakers, handling also a general line of gentlemen's fine furnishings. Their business was established some twenty years ago by the present senior partner, who continued it alone up to April 1, 1891, when he admitted his son, Mr. Leon H., to an interest in the business, and adopted the present firm name. The premises occupied, covering an area of 25x80 feet, are fitted with elegant show cases and display windows. The heavy stock is attractively arranged and displayed, nothing comprised under the head of gentlemen's furnishings being lacking to make it complete in every line. Five salesmen are employed to cater to the wants of the purchasing public. Both members of the firm are natives of this city. The honored senior partner is a member of the Loyal Legion and the G. A. R. At the outbreak of hostilities during the late war he enlisted in the 91st Pennsylvania Regiment and went to the front, serving altogether three years and eleven months, during which time he was in many fierce engagements and was wounded four times, though not dangerously. For his bravery he was promoted to captain, and he retired from the field in 1865. His son is a young man with many sterling qualities.

JOS. C. NORTH & SONS, Coal, No. 417 Washington Avenue.—The coal business conducted by Messrs. Jos. C. North & Sons now ranks among the oldest established in this section of Philadelphia, and the firm are widely and favorably known for giving fully 2240 lbs. to the ton, for handling the finest grades of coal at the lowest commensurate prices, and for filling all orders promptly and accurately. The enterprise was initiated in 1860 by Mr. Joseph C. North and his sons, Mr. Jos. S. North and Mr. Alonzo North, the worthy senior retiring in 1886. The trade controlled consists in the supply of Lehigh, Schuylkill, and other fine anthracite coal for family use, and bituminous steam coal for manufacturing and trade purposes, each kind being procured direct from the mines and carefully packed, screened, and kept dry under cover. The yard, having a capacity for storing a thousand tons of coal, is provided with bins, coal pockets, sheds, etc., and a side track from the Pennsylvania Railroad enables cars to unload right on the spot. Some ten competent hands are regularly employed, three wagons are retained for delivery purposes, and the annual sales aggregate seven thousand tons. The Messrs. North are natives of Philadelphia.

JOHN H. SCHELDER, Fine Custom Tailoring, No. 1931 South Street.—There is not one among the younger custom tailors in Philadelphia that sustains a higher reputation than Mr. John H. Schelder. Mr. Schelder has had twenty-one years' practical experience in the business, and established the present enterprise ten years ago, and during the intervening period it has enjoyed an unbroken record of progress. The premises occupied comprise a store, 20x70 feet in area, well fitted and carefully stocked with a fine display of superb foreign and domestic novelties, embracing suitings, trouserings, vestings, etc., in all the new and popular styles and at the lowest prices. An influential patronage has been gained from many who appreciate good fitting, fashionable, well made custom clothing. Mr. Schelder, who is a native of Germany and came to this country in 1871, is a prominent member of Keystone Council No. 14, Legion of the Red Cross.

M. S. BONSALL'S SONS, Practical Metal and Slate Roofers, Heaters, Ranges, Etc., No. 3841 Market Street.—One of the oldest established metal and slate roofing businesses in Philadelphia is that of Messrs. Wm. S. Bonsall's Sons. From time to time the firm have been intrusted with the execution of several very important and significant contracts, such, for instance, as the roofing, etc., for the Lincoln Institute Educational House, the Presbyterian Hospital, the Pennsylvania Railroad Depot, the Presbyterian Home for Aged Women, and Martin, Fuller & Co.'s abattoir, thus clearly indicating their ability to turn out the finest and most durable work. The chief lines undertaken are tin, copper, zinc, and corrugated iron roofing, spouting, leaders, gutters, slate and tile roofing, heater, range and furnace work complete with all fines, piping and connections, metal chimney pots and cowls, and a general line of sheet metal work, while jobbing and repairing in all branches of the trade receive every care and attention. The business was founded in 1841 by Mr. William S. Bonsall, and was successfully conducted by him up to the year of his death, 1887, when his sons, Messrs. Thomas and William S. Bonsall, succeeded, they being both thoroughly practical in this line. The workshop, 72x120 ft. in area, is fully equipped with tools and appliances of the latest improved pattern for turning out the best work at short notice, and regular employment is furnished for upwards of twenty skilled mechanics. The Messrs. Bonsall are young men of Philadelphia birth.

MANSFIELD BROS., Printers, No. 721 Sansom Street.—For the past two years this enterprise has been in successful operation, and under the efficient management and direction of its practical and experienced proprietors the business continues to show a rapid and firm growth. The apartment occupied on the second floor of the building has dimensions of 20x40 feet, and is perfectly equipped for the purposes of the business, ample steam power, three job presses, complete outfit of type and every necessary facility being in service, while ten expert hands are employed. Book and job work in all their branches are done in the most expeditious and excellent manner, at the most reasonable prices. Fine commercial printing and that for publishers being a specialty. All orders receive immediate attention. Messrs. Wesley W. and Frank W. Mansfield are both practical and expert printers themselves, of long and varied experience in the exercise of their art. They are natives of this city, and popular members of the United American Mechanics' and the F. & A. M.

HISTORICAL AND COMMERCIAL PHILADELPHIA.

ANDREW G. ELLIOTT, Dealer in Stoves, Heaters and Ranges, Tin Plate and Sheet Iron Worker, Tin Roofing and Spouting, No. 5570 Main Street, Germantown.—A well-known and enterprising house engaged in the handling and sale of stoves, heaters and ranges, and in tin plate and sheet iron working and tin roofing, is that of Mr. Andrew G. Elliott, located at No. 5570 Main Street, Germantown. Having had sixteen years' practical experience at the business, he inaugurated this establishment six years ago. The premises occupied consist of a building, 20 x 60 feet, comprising a store in front, with two floors in rear of 25 x 40 feet in area, for working purposes, fully equipped with all the necessary tools, machinery and appliances for manufacturing and repairing purposes, and employment is given a number of skilled and experienced workmen. The stock in store is a full and complete line of parlor and cooking stoves, heaters, ranges, furnaces, grates, also oil and gas stoves of all the latest patterns from the leading manufacturers in the country, which are offered at the lowest market prices and guaranteed to be as represented. Mr. Elliott is also prepared to do all kinds of work pertaining to the setting up of hot air and ventilating work in buildings. A specialty is also made in tin and sheet-iron work at low prices. He is a young man, a native of Germantown, and a member of the Knights of Pythias and the Free and Accepted Masons.

HENRY T. HAYHURST, Graduate in Pharmacy, Registered Pharmacist, No. 5111 Germantown Avenue, Corner Herman Street, Germantown.—One of the leading and best patronized drugstores in this section of the city is that of Mr. Henry T. Hayhurst, which was established by him November 1, 1890. This gentleman has had twenty years' experience in this line, having formerly been manager of Davis' drugstore in this city. The store is handsomely furnished, spacious and commodious, and presents at all times an attractive appearance. Patrons of this establishment always find goods as represented and prices at the bottom notch. All the manufactured drugs are from the best known manufacturing chemists of Europe and America and his own laboratory is kept busy preparing prescriptions for the medical fraternity and his other patrons. He puts up a general line of compounds, makes his own tinctures, etc. and keeps constantly on hand a fine stock of druggists' sundries, imported and domestic perfumes, combs, sponges, hair and tooth brushes, and a full line of toilet articles which are offered to customers at most reasonable prices. Mr. Hayhurst is a native of New York, but has been a resident of Germantown for eighteen years, and is highly esteemed in professional and social circles. He graduated at the Philadelphia College of Pharmacy in 1876.

GEORGE T. SORBER, Real Estate, Conveyancing, Insurance and Collection Agency, No. 108 East Chelten Avenue, Germantown.—Mr. George T. Sorber established business here in 1872 and has for years been the recipient of a very flattering and remunerative patronage. He occupies a very neatly equipped office, which is furnished with every convenience for the speedy transaction of business and reliable information for investors. Mr. Sorber is a recognized authority in regard to value of residential and business property throughout the city and has brought to a successful issue many important transactions, and intending investors, who rely upon his sound judgment and judicious advice in purchasing property, will secure not only a steady income, but likewise a prospective increase of value. He also makes a specialty of negotiating loans on bond and mortgage and is very popular with those property owners in need of financial assistance. He is prepared to place insurance in reliable companies, being agent for the Union Fire Insurance Company, also the Mutual and the United Firemen's, and owners of city and suburban buildings can obtain lowest rates. He makes a specialty of handling real estate in Germantown and Chestnut Hill. Mr. Sorber is a native Philadelphian.

H. C. NOLAN & CO., Manufacturers of High-grade Cigars, No. 117 North Fifth Street.—The high-grade cigars manufactured by H. C. Nolan & Co. are noted for choice flavor, superior quality and excellent make, and command extensive sale throughout the United States. These goods are strictly hand-made, no molds, whatever, being used, and are manufactured from carefully selected, first-class tobacco, by expert workmen. The factory is a 25 x 100 feet four-story building, with complete facilities, and upward of one hundred hands are employed here. The output is upward of about five million cigars a year, and these are all sold to the jobbing trade. Messrs. H. C. Nolan and R. D. Sorver, who compose the firm, are men of thorough experience, active and energetic, and during the five years they have been established in business here, have been signally successful.

GEORGE BUTTERWORTH, Beamer of Plain and Fancy Warps, Mascher and Somerset Streets.—The well-known house of Mr. George Butterworth, beamer of plain and fancy warps, was established at Ninth and Dauphin Streets in 1886, and is now on the corner of Mascher and Somerset Streets, where he occupies a most desirable location. The premises occupied for the business comprise a floor 30 x 130 feet in dimensions, equipped with six beaming frames and one splitting machine, and every modern facility is at hand for conducting all operations under the most favorable auspices and upon the largest scale. Mr. Butterworth has been trained in this branch of industry from his youth up and possesses a fundamentary understanding of all the details of the business and the requirements of the trade. He supplies both cotton, wool, mohair and silk yarns, all of which are of the finest quality and thoroughly adapted to meet the most exacting requirements of manufacturers, while orders and commissions are given prompt and perfect fulfillment. Mr. Butterworth is a native of England, and has been a resident of this country since 1883.

CHARLES M. GHRISKEY, Hardware Commission Merchant, No. 508 Commerce Street.—Few firms are so highly respected or so universally popular as this. The inception of the enterprise dates back to 1849, the founders being Messrs. Colwell & Ghriskey. In January, 1859, the copartnership was dissolved, and since then Mr. Ghriskey has remained in the sole control. He employs a staff of traveling salesmen and commands an excellent trade, extending throughout Pennsylvania, Maryland, Virginia, West Virginia and west to Ohio, Indiana and Illinois. The premises occupied are comprised in a building having five stories and basement, a frontage of 18 feet and depth of 90 feet. The building has a freight elevator and is equipped with all other requisite conveniences. A very large stock is always carried of hardware of all kinds, and Mr. Ghriskey makes leading specialties of the following, for which he is Philadelphia agent:—Chapin's rules and planes, Disston's saws, Wellington's emery, Butcher's chisels, Chesterman's tapes, Hammond's & Beatty's edge tools, Coe's wrenches, etc. Mr. Ghriskey is a native of Philadelphia, has always resided here and is one of our best known merchants.

HUNTER & DICKSON, Pipe, Fittings and Brass Goods for Gas, Steam and Water, Nos. 213 and 215 Arch Street.—A successful firm occupying a representative position in this industry is that of Hunter & Dickson, located at Nos. 213 and 215 Arch Street, where they occupy a store and basement, each 25 x 110 feet in dimensions. This firm was organized eleven years ago, the copartners being T. C. Hunter and D. F. Dickson. Both are native Philadelphians and were formerly employed with Morris, Tasker & Co. and Pancoast & Maule. Their many years' practical experience has given them an expert knowledge of the trade in which they are embarked and they successfully meet all its requirements. Employing twelve hands, Messrs. Hunter & Dickson carry on an active, steadily increasing business as general dealers in pipe, fittings and brass goods for gas, steam and water, keep on hand a full assortment of supplies of every description in this line and they meet a large demand, which comes from all sections of this State, New Jersey and Delaware. Messrs. Hunter and Dickson are held in the highest estimation and their career has been a prosperous one.

HISTORICAL AND COMMERCIAL PHILADELPHIA.

ROWAN & PARKER, Rectifiers, Wholesale Liquor Dealers and Importers, No. 529 South Second Street. Perhaps no firm engaged in the wholesale wine and liquor trade in Philadelphia is more widely or more favorably known than that of Rowan & Parker, whose establishment is located at No. 529 South Second Street. The house is one of the oldest and one of the most responsible establishments of the kind in the entire city, having been in existence since 1842, and fully sustains today its old time reputation for a superior quality of goods and honorable dealing. The business was established by J. McMullen, who had a distillery in the rear of the store. The present firm succeeded to the business in 1882, but have dispensed with the distillery. The premises occupied comprise a store and basement, 25x80 feet in dimensions, commodious and handsomely appointed, the place being fitted up and equipped in first class style throughout. A very heavy and complete stock is constantly kept on hand, including California, Ohio, Virginia and other American wines of all grades kinds and prices, also French, Spanish and Rhine wines of every description, imported and native brandies, gins, rums, whiskeys, all the prominent brands, free and in bond, cordials, bitters, liquors generally, case goods and mineral waters. The prices quoted here are reasonable for the quality of goods carried, and all orders of whatever magnitude receive prompt attention, satisfaction being guaranteed in every instance, and orders by mail are filled and securely packed for shipment in the most expeditious and trustworthy manner. The trade of this reliable house extends throughout Pennsylvania, Delaware, New Jersey and Maryland. The members of the firm are Wm. F. Rowan and Thomas Parker, natives of Ireland, but residents of this city since 1867 and '66 respectively. Both gentlemen are thoroughly experienced in this business, Mr. Parker having been employed by the wholesale liquor house of Walden & Co. for twenty years previous to establishing this business. They are well and favorably known in the community alike as citizens and merchants. Mr. Parker is a prominent member of the F. & A. M. No. 3.

ALBERT HAAS, Gents' Furnishing Goods, Stationery, Tobacco and Sugars, No. 5701 Germantown Avenue. The only store in the Mount Airy section of Philadelphia, engaged in the sale of gentlemen's furnishing goods, stationery, tobacco and cigars, is that conducted by Mr. Albert Haas. An agency of the Forrest Laundry is maintained here, and orders for fine family coat are received and promptly executed direct from a nearby yard. The business was established by the present proprietor in 1880 on the same street in this locality, and two years ago the store now occupied was removed to. This latter, 30x60 feet in area, is well fitted, and a large and carefully selected stock is always on hand, the chief features of which are a complete assortment of gentlemen's furnishings of the latest styles, plain and fancy stationery and supplies, baseball and tennis goods, the standard brands of smoking and chewing tobaccos, a very choice line of imported and domestic cigars and smokers' requisites in abundant display. Mr. Albert Haas is a young man of Philadelphia birth and is a member of the United American Mechanics, the Red Men and the I. O. of O. F.

CHARLES F. SEITTER, Hardware, No. 3514 Kensington Avenue. Mr. Seitter first embarked in this business for himself in 1891 at the above address, and from its inception he has been steadily winning his way to public favor. The large and commodious store, 20x60 feet in dimensions, is neatly fitted up with special reference to the business, every facility and convenience being at hand for the handling and display of the large stock carried and two competent assistants are in attendance. In the extensive and excellently selected assortment will be found everything in the line of builders', shelf and fancy hardware, table and pocket cutlery of all kinds, mechanics' tools in great variety, agricultural implements, agate ware, kitchen utensils and housekeepers' supplies of this character generally, all of which are offered for sale at the lowest prices consistent with first class goods and fair and equitable dealings. Mr. Seitter, who is a native of this city, is a practical and experienced young business man, and he spares no efforts to please his numerous patrons in every particular. He is a member of the Sons of America.

THEODORE BECK, Manufacturing Jeweler and Diamond Setter, No. 618 Chestnut Street. — The gentleman whose name heads this sketch is a native of this city and a manufacturing jeweler and diamond setter of thorough experience. The business of which he is the able proprietor was established under the firm name of Schmidtman & Beck in June, 1880, and by them continued until April 18, 1891, when the partnership was dissolved, Mr. Beck succeeding to the sole control, and during the period since intervening has been steadily winning his way to popular favor and patronage. His work rooms are thoroughly equipped with all necessary tools and appliances, and a large annual business is transacted, extending throughout the city, while some out of town trade is also enjoyed, jobbing for the trade forming the greater part of the business. Diamond jewelry is manufactured to order, or for the trade in the highest style of the art and in the newest, most artistic and handsome designs, while the precious gems are also mounted and set in a manner unexcelled in any style or design of setting, or when desired, in mountings made from original designs by Mr. Beck.

JOHN G. RUFF, Carpenter and Builder, No. 619 Cherry Street. — For over a quarter of a century John G. Ruff, the well known carpenter and builder, has been established in business. He is one of the oldest and foremost in his line in this section of the city, and does a large amount of work. He enjoys an A1 reputation for skill and reliability, and has built many handsome structures in and about Philadelphia. Mr. Ruff is a gentleman of middle age, active and energetic, and was born in Baltimore, Md. He is a thoroughly practical carpenter and builder of some forty odd years' experience, and is master of his art in all its branches. He is well and favorably known in fraternal circles and in social life, and is a member of the F. and A. M., the I. O. O. F., the K. of P., the Red Men, the A. L. of H., and the P. O. A. M. Mr. Ruff employs thirty five hands or more, as occasion demands, and is prepared to furnish estimates on all classes of buildings, giving particular attention to residences, and does the masonry and woodwork, plumbing and everything. Houses are altered and remodeled, also, stores and offices are fitted up, and repairing and jobbing are executed in the most excellent manner at short notice. All work done by Mr. Ruff is warranted to be first class, and all contracts undertaken by him are certain to be performed in the most expeditious as well as most competent and satisfactory manner. He makes a specialty of buying land in the city and suburbs, and putting up dwellings thereon, for sale on easy terms, and has built upwards of seven hundred houses.

N. F. TOMLIN, Real Estate, Insurance, Conveyancing, Etc., No. 2737 North Fifth Street. One of the most reliable and best known real estate and insurance brokers in this part of the city is N. F. Tomlin, who has been engaged in the line indicated for the past seven years. Mr. Tomlin is a Philadelphian by birth, and a man of thorough experience in the handling of realty and risks, and is Secretary of the Co-operative Land Association of Franklinville, Conveyancer of the New Feature Building and Loan Association, and President and Conveyancer of the Clinton Street Land Association. Mr. Tomlin, who is a qualified notary public, buys, sells and exchanges city and suburban property of every description. He is prepared to assume the management of estates, and to give personal attention to the collection of rents, interest and debts, making prompt returns for the same. Mortgages are negotiated, also, on favorable terms, and loans are procured on collateral security. Insurance is placed with responsible fire companies at lowest rates, and deeds, affidavits and other legal documents are carefully drawn up, while conveyancing in all its branches is attended to in the most trustworthy manner. N. F. Tomlin is a member of the Common Council of this city, having been elected in February, 1891, to represent the Thirty-third Ward.

HISTORICAL AND COMMERCIAL PHILADELPHIA.

ROBERT ANDERSON, Real Estate Broker and Conveyancer, Corner Forty-fourth Street and Lancaster Avenue. Residence No. 418 North Fortieth Street.—A well-known and very successful real estate broker and conveyancer in West Philadelphia is Mr. Robert Anderson, located at the corner of Forty-fourth Street and Lancaster Avenue, who now enjoys the confidence and enduring support of a large number of prominent capitalists, trustees, property owners, investors and others in this section of the city. Mr. Anderson has been practicing as a real estate broker, conveyancer and insurance agent for the past seven years, and he is now held in high repute for exercising a scrupulous care, sound judgment and mature discretion in the fulfillment of all commissions entrusted to him, as well as for making prompt and accurate settlements. His services are now called into requisition for the purchase, sale and exchange of realty of all kinds—more particularly residential property in the Twenty-fourth and Thirty-fourth Wards—the collection of house and ground rents and interest, the letting of premises, the entire management of estates, the careful examination of titles, deeds, leases and similar instruments, and the speedy negotiation of loans upon bond or mortgage; while as sub-agent for the Girard Fire Insurance Company and the United Firemen's, he is enabled to direct all desirable risks into the safest channels, at the lowest current rates of premium. Mr. Anderson's chief business lies in advances to builders. He furnishes land for building purposes and advances the money for building on them. Mr. Anderson was born in this city and resides at No. 418 North Fortieth Street.

H. VALDIVIA, Leaf Tobacco, No. 225 North Third Street.—Although of comparatively recent establishment, three years ago, the house of J. H. Valdivia already stands well in the front ranks of the trade in leaf tobacco. The honored proprietor possesses an experience in this line extending over twenty years. He is an importer, jobber and packer of the finest grades of foreign and domestic leaf. In domestic goods he packs immense quantities of Wisconsin, Ohio and Connecticut leaf, making a particular specialty of the latter. His goods are in large and extensive demand all throughout the Eastern and Middle States, and wherever introduced are preferred by buyers to all other packings on account of their uniform quality and careful selection and curing. At the warerooms a large stock is constantly carried. The prices quoted and terms given are in all cases at the lowest ruling market figures, quality of goods considered. Mr. Valdivia is a native of New York, but for the past three years a resident here, and the success he has already achieved is well deserved.

GEO. HARTEL, Merchant Tailor, No. 1035 Walnut Street.—Though only a few years established, George Hartel, the well-known merchant tailor, has already acquired a large and high-class patronage. The garments leaving Mr. Hartel's place are noted for being A1 in every respect, alike in style, cut, finish and fabric. Perfect fit is assured, and his prices, too, are certainly very reasonable, quality of material and character of workmanship considered. He is a direct importer, making a specialty of uniforms and liveries, and shows an elegant assortment of foreign and domestic cloths. He has a large and finely appointed store, with work-room in connection, and employs upward of twenty hands. The stock, which is extensive, includes all the newest designs and latest novelties in fancy cassimeres, cheviots, checks, stripes, plaids, serges and fashionable suitings in a great variety of patterns from which the most fastidious in dress can make selection. Mr. Hartel is a native of this city, as was also his father before him. He is a thoroughly practical tailor and cutter, of some thirty-five years' experience, and prior to going into business for himself was with Wanamaker & Brown for over twenty-one years.

PH. DOFLEIN, Manufacturer of Soap and Bottle Molds, No. 1 Clyde Place.—This important business was founded by the present proprietor, Mr. Ph. Doflein, forty years ago, and under his skillful and experienced direction it has ever since steadily and continuously developed. All kinds of soap and bottle molds are made, and particular attention is devoted to fancy work. The premises utilized consist of a building of three floors, each 20 x 30 feet in area, furnished with a complete modern equipment of machinery, appliances and accessories pertaining to the industry; steam-power operating the whole and several skilled hands being there regularly employed. The worthy proprietor, Mr. Doflein, was born in Germany, but has resided in Philadelphia for over fifty years.

D. DOUGHERTY & CO., Bedding, Wholesale Exclusively, Nos. 329 and 331 North Second Street.—This firm are widely and deservedly prominent as manufacturers of iron and brass bedsteads, mattresses, feathers, spring beds, etc. The business was originally established thirty-five years ago, by Morgan & Co., who were succeeded by the present firm in 1891. The business premises comprise two separate buildings, four stories high and 25 x 125 feet each, fully supplied with new and improved machinery and ample steam-power, and steady employment is given to forty skilled and expert hands. This firm display the largest line of brass and enameled bedsteads in Philadelphia, while in this department of manufacture they have no rivals in this country as regards superior finish and substantial elegance. These bedsteads are rapidly superseding the old styles, and no handsomer or better made goods are to be seen here, in Paris or London. The woven-wire mattresses made here are the acme of perfection, and are preferred over all other makes wherever introduced. Estimates are cheerfully furnished, feathers are cleaned by steam and hot air process, and catalogues are mailed on application. Mr. Dougherty, the active member of the firm, is a native Philadelphian, who was connected with the house of Morgan & Co., for twelve years previous to succeeding to the control.

THE DAISY SUSPENDER COMPANY, No. 501 Market Street.—The Daisy Suspender Company has for several years past been widely known in the trade as a manufacturer of suspenders. This important enterprise has been established now for the past fifteen years. Mr. S. Oppenheimer is thoroughly practical in this line of industry. Suspenders of every description are manufactured both for stock and to special instructions, and in addition to possessing every facility and modern appliance for ensuring the most satisfactory results, the company exercise the greatest care in selecting the materials, used employing only such fabrics, buckles, fasteners and inventions as are best calculated to form a really good, durable suspender of neat and stylish appearance. The factory is on the second floor at the location noted above, 18 x 80 feet in area, and is provided with machines and incidental appliances of the complete nature already hinted; an average of ten skilled operatives being engaged and a heavy stock always carried. The proprietor, Mr. Oppenheimer, is a native and resident of this city and is very popular.

C. KRAUS, Real Estate, Conveyancing, Collections, Insurance, Notary Public, No. 518 South Fifth Street.—During the seven years of his establishment in this profession, Mr. Kraus has gained the well-earned confidence and support of many well-known property owners, capitalists, trustees and others in this section of the city. He is largely resorted to for the purchase, sale, rent and exchange of city and suburban realty of all kinds, the collection of house and ground rents and interest, the preparation and examination of titles, deeds, leases and similar instruments, the speedy negotiation of loans upon bond or mortgage, and the covering of real and personal effects against loss by fire, while as a notary public he takes depositions and acknowledgments, attests affidavits, etc. His office, 20 x 30 feet in size, is the headquarters of the firm of Kraus & Sudeko, dealers in choice Lehigh coal, with yards at No. 1236-40 North Ninth Street. Mr. Kraus has been a partner in this firm for the past few months. He was born in this city in 1865, is a graduate of the Philadelphia High School, auditor of the Randall Building and Loan Association, and represents the Home Insurance Company of New York.

HISTORICAL AND COMMERCIAL PHILADELPHIA.

AVIS & GALT, Silversmiths, No. 750 Sansom Street.—The establishment of Davis & Galt, the well known silversmiths of this city, represents one of the most prominent institutions of the kind in this section. The business was established by Mr. Davis in 1875, and May 17, 1888, the present firm was organized. The premises occupied comprise a three-story building, 20x100 feet in dimensions, fully equipped with all necessary machinery, operated by steam power, and employment is furnished to thirty-five skilled workmen. The firm have, with characteristic enterprise, availed themselves of every late and meritorious device for perfecting the operations of the house, and a heavy and valuable stock is constantly carried, the trade of the house extending to all parts of the United States. The display made in the handsome salesroom of the house is worthy of the inspection of connoisseurs in this line, as it is unequalled in this section of the country for beauty and originality of design and artistic workmanship. The goods are recognized as standard in all markets of the country. Nowhere can a finer stock of solid sterling silverware be found than at this establishment. Mr. J. H. Davis is a native of Virginia, but has been a resident of this city forty years, and has had thirty-five years' experience in this line. Mr. C. E. Galt is a native of the District of Columbia, and came to this city in 1888. He was for ten years connected with the firm of M. W. Galt & Co., of Washington, D. C.

EWITT C. WILLIAMS, Bromide Enlargements, and Printer for Amateur Photographers, No. 909 Arch Street.—The leading artist in Philadelphia engaged in photographic printing for amateurs is Mr. DeWitt C. Williams. Mr. Williams initiated his operations in this important profession in 1877, and the business which has since accrued is of the most representative nature, and reaches to all parts of the city and suburbs, its volume necessitating the regular employment of six skilled photographers. In addition to printing for amateur artists, the house undertakes bromide enlargements for the leading city galleries, and the processes employed in both branches of the art are of the latest approved nature. Every modern appliance and facility is at hand for insuring the most satisfactory results. The fourth floor at the address noted, 25x50 feet in area, is occupied, and here is to be seen a handsome display of copies and enlargements executed on the spot. Mr. Williams is a native of Pittsburgh, Pa., and is a photographic artist of the highest attainments. He has resided in Philadelphia for the past twenty-five years, and is a member of the Royal Arcanum, the Knights of Pythias, the Order of the Golden Eagle, the American Legion of Honor and the Ancient Order of United Workmen.

OOLEY & GEIGER, Pharmacists, Corner Germantown Avenue and Cambria Street.—The neatly appointed and well equipped pharmacy of Cooley & Geiger, corner Germantown Avenue and Cambria Street, is one of the finest and best appointed in this quarter of the city. It is in all respects a first class drug store, and physicians' prescriptions and family recipes are here compounded in the most accurate and reliable manner, from strictly pure, fresh ingredients. The firm prepare their own tinctures and fluid extracts, and also put up some proprietary remedies of a meritorious character. They enjoy a large patronage, and their trade affords evidence of steady increase. This business was established in 1878, at No. 2732 North Eleventh Street, by William C. Gill, and, after several changes in proprietorship, in 1891 came into control of H. C. Cooley, who conducted it alone up to September, 1892, when he took into partnership George L. Geiger and removed to the present location. The store is commodious and very handsomely fitted up, and everything about the place bespeaks order and admirable management. A large, carefully selected and complete stock can always be found here, and includes, besides drugs of all kinds, chemicals, extracts, acids, etc., all the standard patent medicines and pharmaceutical preparations, pure medicinal wines, liquors, mineral waters, etc., also a choice assortment of toilet articles, perfumery, soaps, sponges, chamois skins and druggists' sundries generally. Particular attention is given to prescriptions, and night calls receive prompt response, while the prices charged are exceptionally moderate. Mr. Cooley, the senior member of the firm, is a young man and a native of New Jersey, residing in Philadelphia since 1883. He was graduated from the Pennsylvania College of Pharmacy in 1887, and also from the Powers College of Pharmacy in 1892. He is an ex-apothecary of the U. S. Navy, and holds the position of Demonstrator to the Professor of Chemistry and Toxicology, in the Powers College of Pharmacy. He stands high in his profession, and is a member of the F. & A. M, and other societies. Mr. Geiger, his partner, is also a young man, born in this State. He is a graduate of the Powers College of Pharmacy, too, class of '90, and is a thoroughly competent and experienced pharmacist.

. H. HAINES, Fruit and Produce, No. 322 North Front Street.—Although only established a few months, the fruit and produce house of C. H. Haines is one of the most popular in the city. Mr. Haines was formerly in business with his father—who is extensively acquainted with the trade—and has had twelve years' practical experience, having been raised on a farm in New Jersey. His business connections are of a most influential character, and he enjoys an enviable patronage in and around the city. He is a commission merchant and handles all kinds of country produce, receiving large consignments daily from farms in New Jersey. He has ample facilities for judiciously handling all consignments, and makes immediate and satisfactory returns therefor. Mr. Haines is a native of New Jersey, and lives in Wenonah, where he is highly connected.

EORGE MANDER, Builder, Etc., No. 509 West Lehigh Avenue.—Mr. George Mander has been established about five years, and has a large and growing business. Mr. Mander is a Philadelphian by birth, and is a man of practical skill and thorough experience, and gives close personal attention to business. He employs fifteen to twenty men, and is prepared to furnish estimates on all classes of buildings, giving particular attention to residences. Houses are re-modeled and reconstructed in the most superior manner, and jobbing generally is properly attended to. Mr. Mander, who builds houses in the Twenty-eighth and Thirty-third Wards for sale on easy time payments, does heater and range work of all kinds, hot air heating being a specialty. All work executed by him is warranted to be first class, while its prices are of the most reasonable character, and those having dealings with him are assured of finding the same both pleasant and profitable.

. H. PIPER & CO. Sole Miners and Shippers of Sonman White Ash Bituminous Coal and Coke; General Office, Nos. 11 and 413 Walnut Street.—The superiority of the original Sonman white ash bituminous coal, mined only by W. H. Piper & Co., has been abundantly attested by observation, comparison and experiment, as well as by chemical analysis. It is the purest fuel for steam and forging uses, and is conceded to be in all respects the most effective and most excellent product for the purposes indicated now upon the market. The firm above named own some 1,500 acres of coal lands at Lilly, Cambria County, Pa. and operate four mines there. They have ample transportation facilities, the Pennsylvania Railroad running through the tract for a distance of two miles, while they have shipping wharves also at Greenwich Point, Philadelphia; South Amboy, N. J., and Baltimore, Md. They employ a large force of help at the collieries, producing over 500,000 tons a year, and can put out 1,800 tons a day. The firm also operate twenty coke ovens, and produce between 7,000 and 8,000 tons of coke annually. They have recently spent $20,000 for a rope hauling plant to take the place of mules, formerly used, and its power is supplied by steam. This flourishing enterprise had inception in 1877, when the business was started by Dysard & Co., who were succeeded about two years later by the present proprietors. The firm is composed of Messrs. W. H. Piper, and John H. Lowers, and the senior member was formerly the "Co." of Dysard & Co. They are prepared to fill orders for Sonman white ash bituminous coal and coke by the cargo or car load, on the most favorable terms, selling to dealers and large consumers, and ship throughout Pennsylvania, Delaware, New Jersey, New York, New England and the Southern States.

HISTORICAL AND COMMERCIAL PHILADELPHIA.

W. KANOUSE, Successor to William H. Chandler, Dealer in Fine Groceries, Nos. 102 and 104 East Chelten Avenue, Germantown.—Energy and enterprise seldom fail to produce successful results in any branch of commercial industry, and when well directed, almost invariably lead to success in all the walks of life. As a noteworthy example of this we would call attention to the establishment so successfully conducted by Mr. H. W. Kanouse. This gentleman was for twenty-five years employed by the Phœnix Iron Works Company, at Phœnixville, Pa., in the latter part of the service acting as superintendent of the bridge department. He has displayed the same enterprise, energy and ability in conducting the present business that won the confidence and esteem of his employers in years past and is determined to win success by honestly deserving it. This prosperous enterprise was inaugurated by Mr. William H. Chandler, in 1875, the present proprietor succeeding to the control in 1890. The house is eligibly located at Nos. 102 and 104 East Chelten Avenue, is spacious and conveniently fitted up for the business, and a large, carefully-selected stock is constantly carried, which includes the best brands of family flour, superior butter, fresh eggs, produce, provisions, the very freshest new crop Young Hyson, Oolong, Souchong, imperial, gunpowder, English breakfast and Japan teas; choice fragrant South and Central American Java, Mocha and Arabian coffees, cocoas, chocolates, spices; select brands of hermetically sealed goods in tin and glass, table delicacies, sauces, relishes, condiments; foreign and domestic fruits and everything usually found in a first-class establishment in this line. The house is the largest in its line on the street and enjoys a large trade. A corps of competent assistants is employed and all goods are promptly delivered, two wagons being in constant service for this purpose. Mr. Kanouse is a native of Montgomery County, Pa., and went to Phœnixville twenty-five years ago, where he remained, as has been mentioned, until about two years ago. He is a prominent member of the Knights of the Golden Eagle, the Knights of Pythias, and is highly esteemed as a business man of excellent ability.

L. BLITZSTEIN & CO., Passage Tickets, Money Exchange, No. 131 South Fourth Street.—This agency was established in January, 1891. Tickets to and from England, Germany, Russia, France and Continental Europe, and, in fact, all parts of the globe with which steamship communication is maintained, are sold at the lowest current rates, this firm being passage agent for the American-Hamburg Packet and other steamship lines. Drafts and money orders are issued to all parts of the world. This office has become a notable money exchange for foreigners and European travelers in this city and throughout the State. Mr. Blitzstein, the active member of the firm, is a native of Russia, who came to this city in 1888. He is an expert manufacturer of fine Turkish and Russian tobacco, and is also a jobber in tobacco at manufacturers' prices, with business premises at South west corner of Fourth and Lombard Streets.

JAMES S. PRIEST, Manufacturer of Tin, Sheet-iron and Copper Ware, Novelty Steam Boilers, Corner Gay and Cresson Streets.—For more than a quarter of a century, or, to be exact, since 1865, James S. Priest, manufacturer of novelty steam boilers, metallic roofer, plumber, etc., has been established in business at the present location. Mr. Priest was born in Montgomery County, Pa., but has been in this city some thirty years. He is a man of thorough practical skill and thirty-five years' experience and gives close personal attention to every detail of the business. He occupies compact quarters as shop and store, keeping on hand always a full stock of heaters and ranges, novelty steam boilers, tin, sheet-iron and copper ware, etc., and employs half-a-dozen in help. Mr. Priest does all kinds of sheet-metal roofing and tin and sheet-iron work generally. He makes a specialty of steam-heating, and attends also to gasfitting and plumbing. Heaters and ranges are repaired and reset in the most superior manner and roofs are repaired and painted, while jobbing in all branches is executed with skill and dispatch.

WILLIAM H. McMAHEN, Wholesale Bedding Supplies, No. 115 South Second Street.—About the most successful and most noteworthy among the younger men engaged in the production and wholesale handling of bedding supplies in Philadelphia is William H. McMahen, whose office, factory and warehouse are located at No. 115 South Second Street, and does a very large business, his trade extending throughout the Middle and Southern States. He occupies for business purposes the whole of a 25 x 125-feet five-story building, with complete and excellent facilities, and employs fifteen in help in the establishment, while two representatives are kept on the road. The productions include mattresses, pillows, bolsters, curled hair and bedding supplies generally, and a big stock is constantly carried on hand here. This embraces iron bedsteads, cots, spring mattresses of woven wire etc., bed springs, live geese feathers, and, in short, everything in this line; and mattresses, etc., are made to order likewise, at short notice. All orders receive immediate attention, and every article leaving the establishment is fully warranted, while the most liberal inducements are offered to the trade. Mr. McMahen is a gentleman of about twenty-six and was born in this city. He is a young man of energy and enterprise, as well as of thorough experience, and during the five years he has been established here his business career has been marked by uninterrupted prosperity.

NATIONAL LAW AND COLLECTION ASSOCIATION, D. H. Showers & Co., General Managers, No. 337 Drexel Building.—The National Law and Collection Association of this city is preëminent. Starting out in 1875, this concern has steadily won its way in the favor of the business community until it stands to-day a monumental example of how much can be done when it is done well and done in the right way. Its representatives may be found in every part of this country, in Canada, Europe—in fact, in all parts of the civilized world. Its mission is to collect doubtful debts and protect its members against incurring losses. The association also litigates causes anywhere and everywhere, makes prompt reports and returns on claims, and speedily effects compromises of financially embarrassed parties. A specialty is made of city collections. Besides this the association will negotiate mortgages and loans and will undertake the sale for cash of extensive manufacturing or business plants. The fees charged for these extremely valuable services are almost absurdly low, compared with their arduous nature and the difficulty of carrying them to a successful issue. Mr. D. H. Showers, the general manager, who so ably conducts this useful bureau, is a native of Pennsylvania. He carries on the complex affairs of this splendid organization with a smoothness and ease characteristic of a master mind that excites general admiration.

MANAYUNK STEAM LAUNDRY, M. and J. Metzler, Proprietors, Nos. 108 and 110 Levering Street, Manayunk.—The Manayunk Steam Laundry of M. and J. Metzler is in all respects the leading and best-appointed establishment devoted to the branch of industry indicated hereabouts. The building occupied by the Messrs. Metzler is a commodious three-story structure, and is equipped with ample steam-power, latest-improved machinery and all needed appliances, and about forty hands are employed. The firm have a number of agencies in various parts of the city, and in all suburban parts within a radius of sixty miles, and goods are called for and delivered free of charge, three wagons and the railroad express companies being in service. Lace curtains, laces, fine textile fabrics, ladies' underwear, bed spreads, pillow cases, shams, sheets, table linens, napkins, towels, etc., are made up in the most superior manner; also shirts, collars and cuffs, undershirts, drawers, jackets, coats, vests and pants, and satisfaction is assured in every instance, particular attention being paid to lace curtains. Family washing is a specialty. The Messrs. Metzler, the proprietors, during the six years they have been established in business, have been highly prosperous. They are members of the F. and A. M., the I. O. O. F. and the United American Mechanics.

HISTORICAL AND COMMERCIAL PHILADELPHIA.

AMES ROBERTSON, Manufacturer and Commission Merchant, of Buckskin, Kid and Sheepskin Gloves and Mittens; Office, No. 16 Bank Street; Mills, Gloversville, N. Y.—The gentleman whose name heads this sketch has been engaged in the line above indicated for more than a quarter of a century. He is a manufacturer of and commission merchant in buckskin, kid and sheep skin gloves and mittens; also skirtings, skirts, hosiery and converters of cotton goods and has an extensive trade selling to jobbers throughout the United States. He is interested in mills at Gloversville, N. Y., where he has gloves and mitts manufactured by contract and handles a general line of goods as above noted. The premises occupied as office and salesrooms at No. 16 Bank Street comprise an entire 20 x 80 four-story and basement building, with freight elevator and complete facilities, and six or more of a staff are employed here while three salesmen represent the house on the road. A very large and first-class stock is constantly kept on hand and all orders receive prompt attention. Mr. Robertson was born in New York State, but has long been a prominent merchant in this city, residing at Stratford.

PUBLIC LEDGER BUILDING.

QUAKER CITY WATCH CASE COMPANY, Louis A. Buchy, Proprietor, Manufacturers of Solid Gold, Gold Filled and Silver Watch Cases, No. 316 Griscom Street.—The Quaker City Watch Case Company, carrying on their operations at No. 316 Griscom Street, is one of the most successful and progressive enterprises of the kind in Philadelphia, and they are now the center of an extensive connection among jobbers, dealers, watchmakers and other trade houses all over the United States. The basis of the company's operations consists in the manufacture, for stock and to order, of solid gold, gold filled and silver watch cases, to any pattern or style, and either engine turned, plain or engraved in all designs, both original and furnished, from the simplest to the most richly artistic and elaborate; while solid gold rings and various kinds of jewelry are also manufactured, old gold and silver are bought and a specialty is made of repairing in all branches of the trade. The undertaking was established four years ago by the present sole proprietor, Mr. Louis A. Buchy, who has at his command a wide and varied experience in this line of trade ranging over a period of ten years. The factory comprises the second and third floors at the address named, each 20 x 60 feet in area, containing an elaborate plant of improved machinery, appliances and accessories pertaining to the industry; a steam engine being the motive force used and regular employment is furnished twelve skilled workers. A traveling salesman is constantly out in the interests of the house and a large and choice stock is always on hand sufficient to meet all but the biggest orders without delay. Mr. Louis A. Buchy is a native of this city and now twenty-five years of age.

SAMUEL K. REICHNER, Real Estate Broker and Conveyancer, No. 1361 Passyunk Avenue. A very successful real estate agent, conveyancer and insurance broker in South Philadelphia is Mr. Samuel K. Reichner. During the ten years that he has been established in the profession, Mr. Reichner has gained the confidence and support of a large number of property owners. While dealing in all kinds of realty, Mr. Reichner makes a specialty of residential property in the First, Second, Third, Twentieth and Thirtieth Wards, and at his well-appointed office registers are kept of several highly eligible and valuable properties on hand for sale, rent or exchange, two competent clerks being there regularly employed. In addition Mr. Reichner conducts a general conveyancing and fire insurance brokerage business and collects house and ground rents and interest; possessing, also, especial facilities for the speedy negotiation of loans upon bond or mortgage. Mr. Reichner is a young man of Philadelphia birth and is local agent for the Pennsylvania Insurance Company.

HISTORICAL AND COMMERCIAL PHILADELPHIA.

LEVELAND BAKING POWDER CO., Chas. F. Warner, Manager, No. 123 Chestnut Street.—The Cleveland Baking Powder Company, whose Philadelphia office is located at No. 123 Chestnut Street, is one of those institutions that do credit to the city. The headquarters of the company are at Nos. 81 and 83 Fulton Street, New York, where the business was originally established in 1879, by Cleveland Bros., the present company being organized in 1890, with branches in Philadelphia, Boston, Chicago and San Francisco. The reliability and superiority of Cleveland's Superior Baking Powder is so thoroughly appreciated and understood by the trade that it practically supplants all similar productions wherever introduced. The manager here brings to bear upon the business the widest range of practical experience, coupled with an intimate knowledge of the wants and requirements of the trade, and the largest orders are filled promptly direct from the factory. The company have their baking powder factory at Brooklyn, N. Y., and also own and operate at Jersey City, N. J. the largest cream tartar works in the United States. The executive officers of the company are as follows, viz: C. N. Hoagland, president; Geo. P. Tangeman, vice-president; Chas. O. Gates, treasurer; N. Cleveland, secretary. President Hoagland is an expert chemist, formerly president of Royal Baking Powder Co., for twenty years, and the organizer of that company and its formula. The management is thoroughly experienced in all departments, and the success enjoyed has been honestly won and is well deserved.

HOTEL WAVERLY, European Plan, Northeast Corner Fifteenth and Filbert Streets.—This hotel was originally opened in 1886, by Mr. D. Bergen, and later came into the control of A. A. Allison, as proprietress; with T. J. Victory and J. H. Kern, as managers. The building is built of brick, four stories high, and 75 x 100 feet in dimensions, and constructed in modern style with due regard to the comfort, convenience and safety of guests. There are fifty elegantly furnished rooms, all pleasantly situated, light and airy, while guests will find here every convenience and all modern improvements that art and science can invent, including steam heat, electric light, annunciators, and bathrooms on every floor. Conducted strictly on the European plan there is associated with the Hotel Waverly one of the finest cafés in the city. The management secures its table supplies from the most reputable sources. All the delicacies that can possibly be obtained are served in liberal abundance. Any dish is cooked to order in the best manner, and at moderate prices, while there is a first-class bar attached, where the finest brands of champagnes, wines, brandies, whiskeys, beer and ales are served to suit the customer. The hotel has been under the sole management of T. J. Victory since July 12. It has been refurnished, refitted and improved and is in every way neat and attractive. Mr. Victory, the popular proprietor, is a native of Philadelphia.

ATANACH & PETERSON, Real Estate Brokers and Conveyancers, Notaries Public, No. 3331 South Second Street.—During the two years of their establishment as real estate brokers and conveyancers, the responsible firm of Catanach & Peterson have transacted a general real estate business. The individual partners—Mr. David N. Catanach and Mr. J. Frank Peterson—have long been prominently identified with real estate interests in the city and are recognized authorities on all matters respecting the transfer, valuation and settlement of property and estates. Mr. Catanach has for several years been a partner of Simpson & Catanach at Nineteenth and Wharton Streets, and Mr. Peterson has conducted a separate office at No. 629 Walnut Street since 1882. Among the firm's several operations may be noted the purchase, sale, rent and exchange of all kinds of property in Philadelphia, more especially residences, the collection of house and ground rents and interest, the settlement, transfer and entire management of estates, the speedy negotiation of loans upon bond or mortgage and the preparation and careful examination of titles, deeds, leases and other instruments; as also the taking of depositions and acknowledgments and the several other duties incidental to the office of notary public; while as insurance brokers the firm possess every facility for directing all desirable fire risks into the safest channels at the lowest current rates of premium. Messrs. Catanach and Peterson are young men of Philadelphia birth and are sub agents for the Pennsylvania Insurance Company.

M. T. ZINN, Designer and Engraver on Wood, No. 723 Walnut Street.—The enterprising and reliable house of Mr. Wm. T. Zinn, wood engraver, was established in this city in 1883, on Sansom Street, and moved to the present location four years ago. This gentleman has had a thorough and well-rounded training and education in this business. The preparation for the satisfactory prosecution of affairs is complete, a full equipment having been provided of all the tools and devices that can be profitably employed and such additions made to the facilities as have been suggested by the judgment of the proprietor. Mr. Zinn devotes his talents to every branch of the business, such as cuts of machinery, stores, landscapes, portraits, views of buildings, newspaper headings, catalogue and book illustrations, letter headings, business cards, book covers, monograms, colored labels, and letterings of every description, etc. Only high-class work is done. The proprietor is entirely original in his designs, endeavoring to ascertain the customer's idea and to carry it out in the most artistic manner. In order to obtain the greatest accuracy, all photographs, designs, drawings, etc., are submitted for approval. A corps of experienced assistants is employed. The trade extends to all parts of the United States. Mr. Zinn is a native of Philadelphia and is a prominent and popular member of the Mercantile Beneficial Society and the A. O. of United Workmen and several other societies.

OYCE BROTHERS, Importers and Grocers, Southwest Corner Walnut and Thirteenth Streets.—The firm of Boyce Brothers is a leading house in its line. It was established in 1879, by Mr. Robert M. Boyce, Mr. William Boyce and Mr. Thomas W. K. Boyce. The premises occupied comprise a three-story brick building, each floor 25 x 100 feet, filled with an immense stock of everything in the grocery line. The store is handsomely fitted with hard wood fixtures and ranks among the most attractive in the city. The firm are large importers and confine their dealings strictly to the highest grade of goods procurable and allow nothing to enter into their stock that is not considered first-class. They are the sole agents in the United States for the celebrated "Perfection perforated and self-waste consuming" candles, the famous Colerraine Farm genuine Irish bacon and hams, Taylor's Coleraine Irish malt whiskey, same as supplied to the House of Commons; Burt's English malt extract, an appetizing and invigorating tonic endorsed by physicians; Diamond B. B. Bottling Bass & Co.'s pale ale, the most perfect ale on the market; Diamond B. B. Bottling Bass & Co.'s Burton ale, Bass & Co.'s imperial stout and Guinness's Dublin brown stout, finest brewings; the La Royale boneless sardines, besides controlling all goods put up under the Diamond B. B. brand, which is a guarantee of their extra fine quality, such as B. B. brand, Sublime olive oil, B. B. cream Lucca oil, B. B. maccaroni, vermicelli, and spaghetti, B. B. French vegetables in glass and in tins, B. B. olives and capers, B. B. Mexican chilli, B. B. flour, Special tea, Special coffee, domestic vegetables of all kinds, flavoring extracts, seasoning herbs spices, bay rum, cologne water, clarets, etc. They are also agents for Mrs. McCready's pickles, preserves, jellies and brandied fruit; Moravian candies, made at the Sister's House, Bethlehem, Pa.; Brae Brook Farm hams, bacon and lard; Chesterfield's Old Plantation Virginia hams, bright brine, table and dairy salt; Brown's London Meltonian liquid blacking, in jars; Castaing's Black Diamond blacking and russet dressings and lots of other specialties that are not to be found elsewhere. In connection with their line of fine groceries they carry a very complete assortment of fine liquors, their wine cellar containing over 200 kinds of the finest liquors for table and medicinal use that are to be found; and to supply the demands of their trade for cigars they are compelled to keep about 450 varieties, ranging from $30 to $700 per thousand. Although their main trade is in the city and suburbs, they have a large trade throughout Pennsylvania, New Jersey, Delaware and Maryland and are constantly receiving orders for their specialties from all parts of the United States.

HISTORICAL AND COMMERCIAL PHILADELPHIA.

LBERT E. BURNS, Agent for The Trenton Lamp Co., Fine Cheap Decorated Lamps; The Mayer Pottery Manufacturing Co., Square Shapes and Gold Band Ware; The D. E. McNicol Pottery Co., C. C. and Rock and Yellow Ware; The Empire Pottery Co., Fine Decorated Toilet and Tea Ware, Salesroom, Nos. 111 and 113 North Seventh Street. Although established only since February of this year, A. E. Burns, representing manufacturers and importers of majolica and china ware, glassware, crockery, etc., etc., has already built up a flourishing business. He is agent for the Trenton Lamp Company and the Empire Pottery, and represents several other big concerns. He handles everything in the line indicated, making a specialty of fine goods, and sells to jobbers and retailers in Philadelphia and throughout the adjacent States. Mr. Burns, who is a gentleman in the prime of life, is a man of energy and thorough experience, and is well known in the trade. He was raised in the business, and for several years was a traveling salesman for some of the leading jobbing houses in Philadelphia. He has a compact office and salesroom on the second floor of Nos. 111 and 113 North Seventh Street and carries a splendid sample stock, which includes elegant imported and American productions in china and glassware, superb majolica ware, Barbatine ware, bisque figures, magnificent decorated lamps, exquisite tea sets, fancy vases, chamber and dinner sets, Rockingham and yellow ware, W. G. and C. C. ware, bric-a-brac, art novelties, toys and kindred articles. He can fill orders for anything in the line indicated at manufacturers' prices, shipping direct from factories, and is in a position to offer substantial inducements to jobbers and dealers.

HAS. RUMPP, Manufacturer of Fancy Leather Goods, Portemonnaies, Pocketbooks and Satchels, No. 47 North Sixth Street.—This prominent undertaking was founded in 1852 by Mr. Charles Rumpp and his cousin, Mr. C. F. Rumpp, but that partnership only lasted for six years and for the past thirty-four years the business has been skillfully directed in every detail by the present proprietor. The chief lines of manufacture are portemonnaies, pocketbooks, satchels, sample and traveling trunks, purses, card cases, cigar cases and a large variety of fancy leather novelties which are made for stock and supplied at both wholesale and retail to regular patrons throughout Pennsylvania, New Jersey, and west to Ohio. In addition a specialty is made of any kind of fancy leather goods, bags, etc., to order to any particular pattern or style; a branch of the business in which more than usual satisfaction is invariably rendered. The manufacturing department consists of a building of four floors, each 20 x 60 feet in area, furnished with a complete equipment of machines, tools, appliances and facilities pertaining to the industry, a large force of expert workers being there regularly employed. The worthy proprietor is a native of Germany and reached the United States when only two and a-half years old.

LBERT P. REGER, Manufacturers' Agent for Sheet Brass, Brass and Copper Wire, Etc., No. 302 Drexel Building.—Among the rising young business men of the city may well be mentioned the name of Albert P. Reger, who although lately established, is already developing a keen business ability that is bound to bring him speedily to the front. He is the sole agent for the Bridgeport Brass Company, whose full line of goods in their specialty cannot be excelled either in variety or excellence. Mr. Reger sells to the trade, on order, in all parts of the United States, and has already drummed up a phenomenal business during the short time that he has been engaged in this special line. He is a young man, a native of this city, and a typical representative of the hustling, busy, go-ahead business man of the present day. The productions which Mr. Reger specially represents are sheet brass, brass and copper wire, seamless brass and copper tubes, brass and copper rods, rivets and burrs, copper electric wire, etc. His uniform courtesy, energy, tact and general attention to the wants of his patrons have won for him universal favor.

. GOLDSMITH & SONS, Fine Summer Clothing, No. 336 Market Street.—The firm of A. Goldsmith & Sons, manufacturers of fine summer clothing, have been able, in the short space of four years, to establish a trade in these goods extending from the New England States to Florida and westward to the Missouri. The making of the clothing is an art little understood by the great army of consumers, but the wide distinction and difference between properly made clothing and hastily constructed, ill-fitting garments are readily seen and appreciated. It was with a thorough understanding of this fact that the Messrs. Goldsmith started to make a somewhat finer trade than the ordinary of men's clothing and overcoats in 1888, and have since maintained their high standard, their goods rivaling in appearance and workmanship the best custom made clothing. The firm occupy the whole building, 18 x 65 feet, five stories high. They employ 315 hands—the larger portion of these doing their work outside the building. An unusually heavy stock is carried, and four salesmen are constantly on the road selling the goods. The firm comprises Mr. A. Goldsmith, who is a native of Germany, but has been forty-two years in the United States, and his sons, Milton and Edwin M. Goldsmith, both of whom are natives of Philadelphia, and all are residents of the city.

EORGE MACLEAN, Agent, Stained and Mosaic Glass for Churches and Dwellings, No. 319 Walnut Street.—Among the ablest and most successful manufacturers of stained glass in Philadelphia is Mr. George Maclean, carrying on his operations at No. 319 Walnut Street. No more cogent argument and conclusive proof of the ability of this responsible house to turn out the finest and most elaborate work can be adduced than are evidenced by the many important contracts that have been fulfilled; these include upwards of twenty recently completed, entirely of the house's own designing and manufacture, as well as a long list of work all over the country, executed under the direct personal supervision of Mr. Maclean, excelling in thoroughly harmonious schemes of color and in designs of character and originality. He founded and was the first president of the Century Stained Glass Company. All kinds and descriptions of stained, leaded and mosaic glass for churches and dwellings, as well as memorial windows are manufactured. Original designs and estimates are cheerfully furnished upon application and plans and drawings, specifications, etc., provided by patrons are rigidly adhered to and faithfully interpreted, whether of the plainest description or of the most richly artistic and elaborate.

HARLES S. HIRST, Maker of Fine Jewelry and Diamond Mountings, Importer of Diamonds and Precious Stones, No. 631 Chestnut Street.—The well-known and responsible house of Mr. Charles S. Hirst was initiated by the present proprietor six years ago, and the volume of trade now controlled is of a heavy and ever-increasing nature and reaches to all parts of the city and adjacent districts, as well as in a lesser degree throughout the Middle States, mostly wholesale and also at retail to the many patrons which have constantly dealt with the house for years. The house is a direct importer of diamonds and precious stones and an extensive dealer in all kinds of fine jewelry and diamond mountings, while facilities are possessed for making these two latter kinds of goods to order to special pattern or design, the best materials and workmanship being guaranteed in each instance. A neatly-fitted and well-arranged office is maintained on the second floor at the address noted and is furnished with a large safe, with Holmes' electric protection attached, for the safe keeping of the choice and costly stock always kept on hand. The able proprietor, Mr. Hirst, who is a native of the Keystone State and still a young man, has a long and versatile experience of the trade at his command and personally superintends every detail of the business. He had for ten years previous to going into business, been connected with the well-known house of Bailey, Banks & Biddle.

HISTORICAL AND COMMERCIAL PHILADELPHIA.   225

LIJAH CUNDEY, Wayne Junction Wood Turning Mills, Corner Wayne and Roberts Avenues.—For more than a quarter of a century, or, to be exact, since 1865, Elijah Cundey, the well known wood turner, whose mills are at Wayne Junction, has been in business. He is one of the oldest established and foremost in this line indicated in this city and has a very large patronage, his trade extending throughout Philadelphia and sections of the States of Pennsylvania and New Jersey. He turns out a very superior class of work, and his facilities are unsurpassed. Mr. Cundey was born in this city and is a man of thorough practical skill and many years' experience, and is master of his art in all its branches. He bears a highly creditable war record, too, having served at the front during the "late unpleasantness" from 1861 to 1865. He is a prominent member of G. A. R. Post 94, and is colonel of Encampment No. 2 of the Union Veteran Legion, and belongs to several other societies. Mr. Cundey occupies a 60x100 foot shop, equipped with steam power, the latest improved wood working machinery, tools and appliances, and employs forty to sixty skilled hands. Wood turning in all its branches is executed to order here at short notice, and jobbing of every description for the manufacture of textile fabrics is done with skill and dispatch. Heavy timber is sawed to order, likewise, and bobbins and spools are manufactured in any desired size or design for cotton, woolen, silk and hosiery machinery. Mr. Cundey also manufactures wringing sticks, condensing spools, swifts, skewers and kindred articles, and repairs the same, and is prepared to supply wooden ware and fancy stores with anything in his line, keeping on hand always a large assortment of Indian clubs, dumb bells, croquet, base ball bats, tops of box and other woods, mallets of lignumvitae and dogwood, tenpins and balls, shelf and stair balusters, newel posts, brush and duster handles, file handles, etc.

OHN E. BAKER, Wholesale and Retail Dealer in Grain, Flour, Feed, Hay and Straw, Nos. 715 and 717 Fitzwater Street.—Among the many establishments in this section of the city engaged in the grain and feed line, none enjoys a higher reputation than that of Mr. John E. Baker. The business was established in 1867 by Mr. Samuel Baker, who retired in 1894, and was succeeded by his son, Mr. John E. Baker, the present proprietor. A warehouse, 50x100 feet in area, is occupied for the transaction of the work. Ample storage facilities are possessed, and all the necessary conveniences are at hand for the successful prosecution of the business, and employment is furnished four hands and teams in filling orders, and the patronage extends throughout the entire city and vicinity. A full supply of flour and feed, embracing oats, meal, corn, straw, etc., is carried, the stock always being selected with great care by Mr. Baker, and the trade is of both a wholesale and retail character. The house is almost daily in receipt of large consignments from the best farming sections of the country, and are therefore in a position to offer them to customers at the lowest market prices. Mr. Baker is a young man, a native of Philadelphia, and was raised in the business.

AVID H. BOWEN & SON, Undertakers, No. 813 South Second Street.—The business so successfully conducted by Messrs. David H. Bowen & Son was established by the senior partner in 1837. In 1870 Clement R. Bowen was admitted to partnership and the present firm name adopted; then five years later another son, Chas. H. Bowen, became a member of the firm. These gentlemen are accomplished masters of their vocation, and are eminently qualified in every way to render the most satisfactory service. The firm furnish everything required for the plainest or most imposing ceremonies, and take charge of the dead and superintend every detail of the last sad rites of burial, and the afflicted have always a melancholy pleasure in securing the professional services of these considerate gentlemen, who are both practical embalmers, skilful and precise, and preserve bodies entrusted to their care for any required period. Their charges are always reasonable and just. They have a large first class patronage in this city. Mr. David H. Bowen, the founder of the business, is not an active member of the firm, but his two sons, Messrs. Clement R. and Chas. H. Bowen, have charge of the business. These gentlemen are natives of Philadelphia, well known and highly esteemed in the business and social circles of the city. Mr. Clement Bowen is a graduate of the Renard School of Embalming, and Chas. H. is also a practical embalmer. The success which has attended the efforts of these reliable gentlemen has been well merited.

BRAHAM ENGARD, Confectionery and Ice Cream, No. 4962 Germantown Avenue.—This gentleman established his business twenty-two years ago, and his patronage has extended to such large proportions as to require the services of ten skilled assistants and three wagons in the delivery department. Mr. Engard makes a specialty of manufacturing ice cream and enjoys the reputation of making the most delicious article found in this section of the city. His establishment is the largest and most complete store of the kind in Germantown and is literally patronized by the best class of residents of the vicinity. Mr. Engard makes a specialty of supplying weddings, parties and picnics with refreshments, and likewise does an extensive business by wholesaling to families. He makes all his ice cream by hand machinery and can hardly supply the large demand for his superior goods. His lines of confectionery include all kinds and flavors of fruit and plain candies and leave nothing wanting. Mr. Engard is a native of Philadelphia and is a thoroughly reliable merchant.

ENRY OGDEN & SON COMPANY (Limited), Furniture, Carpets and Bedding, Nos. 2119 and 2121 South Street.—The furniture, carpet and bedding business conducted by the Henry Ogden and Son Company, Limited, is the largest of the kind in this section of Philadelphia, and a reliable headquarters for the latest styles of fine furniture and carpets, as also for the most reliable grades of bedding. In the furniture department is to be found a handsome display of artistic drawing room furniture, richly upholstered in velvets, satins, plushes, etc., of various colors, antique furniture, fancy tables with marble tops and gilt frames and legs, ornamental whatnots, etc.; substantial dining room and parlor suits and tables in all the finest hardwoods, bureaus, boudoirs, hall chairs and stands, bedroom and chamber furniture of original designs, desks, and many other superior lines. An elegant display of carpets is also on view, comprising the newest patterns in Brussels, ingrain, Axminster and tapestry, as also Turkey druggets, Smyrna and other rugs and mats; all of the best qualities, while everything in mattresses, feather beds and bedding in general is likewise kept in stock in ample assortment. The business was established in 1876 by Mr. Henry Ogden; in January, 1891, it became Henry Ogden & Son, and on March 1, 1892, it was duly incorporated under its present style; Mr. Henry Ogden being chairman and Mr. Henry H. S. Ogden, secretary and treasurer. Sales are effected for cash only, and a heavy volume of local trade is controlled. The premises utilized comprise a building of three floors and basement, each 50x70 feet in area, well fitted and fully equipped throughout, seven courteous assistants being in regular attendance upon customers. The worthy chairman is a native of England, whence he came to this city thirty-five years ago, and is a member of the Knight Templars of the Free and Accepted Masons. His son was born in Philadelphia.

R. JAMES P. MILNER, Pharmacist, N. E. Corner Sixth and Lombard Streets.—The popular pharmacy of Dr. James P. Milner has been a noted and successfully conducted one since it was established ten years ago by the present proprietor, who originally entered into business twenty-three years ago, and during the entire term has been located in this immediate vicinity. The store occupied is 20x30 feet in dimensions, and is neatly fitted up in modern style, perfectly equipped and admirably arranged for the purposes of the business. The extensive stock carried embraces a complete assortment of fresh pure drugs and chemicals, family and proprietary remedies, toilet goods, fancy articles, perfumery, surgical appliances, physicians' supplies and druggists' sundries in general, all derived from the most reliable sources of production. Particular attention is given to compounding physicians' prescriptions and family recipes, and every care is taken to preclude the possibility of error. The doctor was born in the city, and is a graduate of the Philadelphia College of Pharmacy and the University of Pennsylvania.

HISTORICAL AND COMMERCIAL PHILADELPHIA.

THOMAS SCOTT & CO., Grocers, Tea and Produce Dealers, No. 128 Market Street.—Forty-one years of uninterrupted prosperity marks the history of the well-known house of Thomas Scott & Co., grocers, tea and produce dealers, which was established in 1851 by Thomas Scott, and under the present firm-name has always been conducted; Thomas J. Scott, son of the senior member, being admitted into partnership in January last. The business was formerly carried on at Second and Race Streets, and in 1861 was removed to the spacious quarters now occupied. The premises here comprise four 20 x 75 feet floors, and eight in help are employed. An extensive and carefully selected stock is always kept on hand, and includes fine teas and coffees, pure spices, condiments and table delicacies, canned goods, green and dried fruits, and country produce generally, best brands family flour, choice dairy butter, cheese, eggs, lard, hams, bacon and prime provisions; also sugar, syrups and molasses, fish, salt, vinegar, beans, peas, rice and everything in staple and fancy groceries, select teas and coffees being a specialty. Both a wholesale and retail business is done by the firm, and the trade and public are supplied on the most favorable terms, substantial inducements being offered to dealers and large consumers. Mr. Scott, the elder, is a gentleman of full middle age, and a native of Ireland, but has been in this city for forty-six years. He is a member of the Grocers' and Importers' Exchange and a subscriber to the Bourse.

E. BORDA & SON, Coal, No. 336 Walnut Street.—This firm are shippers of anthracite and bituminous coal, and are also prominent in the trade as agents for Philadelphia & Reading Railroad Company's coal, and Davis Coal & Coke Company's Cumberland coal. The honored senior partner, Mr. E. Borda, has been established in the coal business here for a period of forty years, and in 1877 the present firm was organized by the admission of Mr. Charles A. Borda to partnership. This firm ship from Greenwich and Port Richmond, in Philadelphia; Port Liberty and Perth Amboy and Elizabethport, N. J.; and Canton piers, Baltimore, and, with their ample resources and influential connections, they are now doing a large business, mostly in the Eastern and Southern States. The sales of this house are over 250,000 tons per year, forming an important item in the commerce of this city and State. Mr. E. Borda, although born in Paris, France, is recognized as one of the pioneers in the development of the coal industry in this State. He was for years an operator in the Schuylkill coal regions, manager for the Heckscher estate, and an owner as well as manager of various collieries until 1877, since which date he has been known principally as an agent and commission merchant, deservedly prominent in the coal trade and as an esteemed citizen of Philadelphia. Mr. Charles A. Borda is a native of Schuylkill Co., Penn., and combines his energy and vigor with the ripe experience of his father to form a firm of commanding influence, wide popularity and solid worth.

EDISON'S MIMEOGRAPH, W. M. Abbey, Agent, No. 802 Walnut Street.—Edison's "Mimeograph" is one of the "Wizard's" greatest achievements. While not so publicly dazzling as the "electric light," nor so prominent as the "telephone," not as bewildering as the "phonograph," not as ambitious as the "sea signalling apparatus," yet it is one of the most useful devices for business men. Although invented not longer than four years, yet to-day over 80,000 mimeographs are in use, and the demand for them is rapidly increasing as their value becomes better known. Edison's mimeograph is to-day recognized as the standard duplicating device for autographic or type-written work, by the commercial, educational, and religious world. It is simple in construction and operation, is not affected by climatic changes, is reasonable in price, and durable, and will produce over 3,000 autographic, and over 1,500 type-written copies from one original, on any kind of paper. The Philadelphia agent for the mimeograph is Mr. W. M. Abbey. He has excellently-appointed quarters, and carries a full line of machines and supplies. This agency was established in 1888, and has been under the present management over four years. Mr. Abbey is a native of New York, and he has developed a success in his present position in which he may well take pride.

JOHN H. SCOTT, Conveyancer, Real Estate No. 808 Walnut Street.—A foremost representative of the real estate interests of Philadelphia and vicinity is Mr. John H. Scott, conveyancer, whose office is at No. 808 Walnut Street. Mr. Scott has been established for the past twenty-five years, and has developed a large, permanent trade of strictly first-class character, bringing expert practical experience to bear, coupled with an intimate knowledge of the merits of the various residential and business sections of the city. Mr. Scott can be relied upon by the investing public to afford them judicious advice, and the benefit of his sound judgment in effecting purchases that will not only afford a steady income, but likewise almost a certainty of increased value in the near future. His connections are of a superior character, including, as he does, many of our leading capitalists, merchants and operators among his permanent customers, and he has carried through to a successful issue many heavy transactions. Most of the realty handled by Mr. Scott is owned by himself. It includes lots and land on Clear View, Sharon Hill, Cloverdale, Woodburn Heights, Buttonwood, and Delaware Park, the whole comprising some 3000 acres. Mr. Scott is a native of this city, where his ancestors have resided for nearly 200 years past, and he enjoys the fullest confidence and respect of all his fellow-citizens.

RIDGWAY HOUSE, American and European Plan, Delaware Avenue and Market Street.—The Ridgway House is conducted on the American and European plan, and the terms are most reasonable, the rates being $2.00 per day, with rooms at 50 and 75 cents. The house is pleasantly located, and is convenient to ferries, railroad depots and business centers, and street cars pass in the immediate vicinity to and from all parts of the city. The hotel building is a handsome and substantial six-story brick structure, and contains one hundred rooms. It is finely furnished throughout, steam heated, excellently lighted and perfectly ventilated, and is provided with electric bells, fire escapes, and all modern appliances for the convenience and safety of guests. The dining-room is spacious, clean and inviting, and the sleeping apartments are commodious, neat and airy. There are in connection, also, a first-class bar and café, and the liquid refreshments are of the finest brands. The "Ridgway" is an old and well-known hostelry, and for sixty years has been steadily growing in popular favor. The house was formerly conducted by J. B. Butterworth, father of the present proprietor, for twenty years, the son assuming control in 1882. Mr. Butterworth, the younger, is a Philadelphian by birth, and has been for years associated with his father in the management of the hotel. Mr. Butterworth was also proprietor of the La Pierre House, of this city, for eleven years. He is a member of the National Hotelmen's Association.

H. RUTHERFORD, Manufacturer of Heaters and Ranges, Tin and Sheet Iron Worker, Plumbing, Tin Roofing and Gasfitting, No. 1703 Pine Street.—For over thirty-six years H. Rutherford, manufacturer of heaters and ranges, tin and sheet-iron worker, etc., No. 1703 Pine Street, (north side), has been established in business at the present location. He is one of the oldest in this line in the city, and has an excellent patronage. Mr. Rutherford, who is a gentleman of about sixty-seven, was born in Ireland, but has resided in Philadelphia since early infancy. He is a man of entire reliability in his dealings, as well as practical skill and many years' experience, and is one of the best known citizens in the community. His son, Charles, is now associated with his father in the business. The quarters occupied as store and shop are spacious and commodious, and a large stock is always kept on hand here, including heaters, ranges and stoves of all kinds and best makes of tin and sheet-iron ware, kitchen specialties, etc. Four competent workmen are employed, and sheet metal work generally is done to order, at short notice. Tin roofing, plumbing and gasfitting are attended to, also, in the most superior manner, while repairing and jobbing are executed with skill and dispatch. All orders receive prompt attention, and all work done is warranted to be first-class, while the prices charged by Mr. Rutherford are of the most reasonable character.

AMES SHORE & CO., Steam and Hot Water Heating, Sanitary Plumbing, Ventilating, No. 8 East Chelten Avenue, Germantown. This representative house was founded in 1866 by Mr. James Shore, and in 1886 the present firm was organized by the admission of Mr. Herbert H. Hurst to partnership. The firm occupy commodious and well appointed quarters for store and workshop, and keep on hand a complete assortment of lead, water, steam and gas pipe, fittings of every description, steam and hot water heating apparatus, ventilators, sinks, water closets, wash stands, pumps and sanitary devices. Estimates are furnished on all classes of work in the lines above indicated, including heating and ventilating, house drainage, water service and sanitary plumbing, and satisfaction is guaranteed in every instance. Repairing and remodeling are also executed in the most expeditious and excellent manner, while jobbing generally receives immediate attention, and a large and influential business is transacted in fitting up residences throughout all this section of the country, requiring the constant services of a large force of skilled workmen. Mr. Shore is a native Philadelphian, Mr. Hurst was born in Germantown, and is a plumber of sixteen years' practical experience. Both are members of the United American Mechanics and the P. O. Sons of America, while Mr. Shore is also a member of the Protestant Association of America, and Mr. Hurst is an Odd Fellow.

ALLAGER & FEUSHT, Granite and Marble Works, No. 3108 Chestnut Street.—Messrs. Robert Gallager and George Feusht, who compose this firm, are practical granite and marble workers and thorough masters of their art. They started in business some four years ago, and have built up an excellent trade. The quarters occupied by them at No. 3108 Chestnut Street are commodious and ample, with complete facilities, and several competent workmen are employed. The firm keeps on hand always a large and fine stock of granite and marble, rough, squared and wrought, and is prepared to give estimates on all classes of granite and marble work, both for monumental and building purposes, and guarantees perfect satisfaction. Monuments, headstones, tablets, bases, pedestals, coping, railings, etc., are manufactured in the most superior manner at short notice, cemetery work being a specialty. A specialty is also made of sculpture work, either from designs furnished or from those drawn by the firm. This firm executed the equestrian monument erected by the 8th Pennsylvania Cavalry at Gettysburg.

A. BOWMAN, Livery Stables, No. 1308 and 1310 Girard Avenue.—The carriages furnished by the livery establishment of Mr. A. A. Bowman are not excelled by any other in the city. Mr. Bowman owns twenty-five first class carriages of various descriptions, and is prepared to furnish conveyances for use at weddings, parties, funerals, etc., or for pleasure riding; and in this department of his business has a large, high class patronage. He also has superior boarding accommodations and gives especial attention to the care of valuable animals. The stables are 40x175 in dimensions, two stories in height, built of brick, and are finely fitted up with all the modern sanitary improvements, particular care having been bestowed upon the important matters of light, ventilation and drainage. The accommodations are sufficient for the stabling of sixty horses and the storage of nearly one hundred carriages. Ten persons are employed, including several experienced drivers; and through telephonic communication orders receive prompt attention. This business was established in 1880 by Wm. Leitch, Jr., and passed into the present proprietorship in 1892. Mr. Bowman is a native of this State.

ARRY D. BENNER, "Acme" Meat and Provision Market, No. 4517 Main Street, Germantown.—Enterprising and progressive business measures will accomplish much, and by their practice Mr. Harry D. Benner has risen to prominence and success. He is the energetic and popular proprietor of the "Acme" Meat and Provision Market. Mr. Benner established his business four years ago, and his enterprise at once received a liberal public support. His store is one of the largest and best fitted up on the street, and his stock of goods is at all times complete and of the choicest the market affords. He carries a varied first class stock of fresh and salt meats, a full line of provisions, fish and game in season, while his refrigerating facilities for keeping the same in excellent order are perfect. His large and constantly increasing trade requires the services of six expert assistants and four delivery wagons. Mr. Benner was born in Germantown and is an active and popular member of the Knights of Pythias, United American Mechanics and P. O. Sons of America, and a gentleman well known by everybody.

B. MORSE, Druggist, N. W. Corner Seventeenth and South Streets.—This business was established several years ago, and after passing through several changes came into the hands of Mr. H. B. Morse, the present proprietor, who brings to bear upon the work nine years of practical experience. He is a graduate of the Philadelphia College of Pharmacy and a member of its Alumni Association, and is thoroughly familiar with the medicinal properties of drugs, compounds and prescriptions, and prepares medicines and a line of pharmaceutical compounds, fluid extracts and tinctures with accuracy and promptitude. The store is tastefully fitted up with plate glass show cases and ornamental counters and shelving, and well equipped for all the purposes of the trade. The stock includes a large and complete assortment of pure drugs, fresh chemicals, and all standard proprietary remedies, toilet articles, perfumes, soaps, etc. Prescriptions are filled night and day, and a beautiful soda water fountain forms a portion of the equipment. Mr. Morse is a native of Kentucky, coming to this city six years ago.

EORGE JAEGER, Photographer, No. 829 Arch Street.—One of the leading photographers for first class work in this city is Mr. George Jaeger, located at No. 829 Arch Street, whose productions are renowned for their excellence of style, finish, clearness and accuracy of portraiture. The services of the house are now regularly sought by patrons all over Philadelphia and the suburbs for all branches of the photographer's art; landscapes and general outside work being equally undertaken with interiors of buildings, machinery, statuary and other objects, as well as portraits in all styles and sizes, while illuminating and crayon work together with fine photography constitute the leading specialties of the business. The enterprise was initiated by Mr. Jaeger in 1880 at No. 106 North Eighth Street, whence it was removed in 1887 to the premises now occupied. These latter comprise office, waiting and show rooms, studio, etc., on the second floor, 25x75 feet in area, well fitted and appointed throughout, and a full equipment of appliances of the latest pattern being provided for executing the highest grades of fine photography. Five competent artists are regularly engaged under the close supervision of the able proprietor, who is, himself, an expert photographer with twenty-five years' experience at his command. He is a native of the Quaker City.

EST END DRUG STORE, No. 3712 Market Street.—This thriving business dates its foundation way back to 1847, and for a number of years the house was known as the "Weigand's Pharmacy." During the current year it came under the control and direction of its present owner, who became the successor to Mr. J. M. Bourke. The commodious and well arranged salesroom is fitted up in a style which represents a happy combination of convenience and attractiveness, and it is completely stocked with a large and first class assortment of fresh drugs and chemicals, of standard strength and purity, proprietary remedies of established reputation, pharmaceutical specialties, druggists' sundries, toilet and fancy articles, extracts, perfumes, etc., all of which have been most carefully selected from the most reputable sources of supply. Physicians' prescriptions and family recipes of all kinds are here compounded in the most skillful and accurate manner. The West End Drug Store is under a strong and competent management, with competent and courteous pharmacists to attend to every detail of the business.

HISTORICAL AND COMMERCIAL PHILADELPHIA.

 POEHLMANN, Groceries and Provisions, Corner Broad and Cumberland Streets.—This thriving business was originally founded in 1865 by Mrs. M. E. Poehlmann, who conducted it most successfully up to 1889, at which time her sons, Messrs. W. and J. Poehlmann, became her successors; but the year following this partnership was dissolved on account of the death of the latter member, and the present proprietor assumed sole control of its affairs. The commodious and well appointed store, 20x40 feet in dimensions, is perfect in convenience of arrangement for the successful prosecution of the business, and the services of three competent assistants and a team are required in permanent employment. Everything in the line of staple and fancy groceries, teas, coffees, canned goods, fruits and vegetables of all kinds in season, butter, eggs, cheese, flour—a specialty being made of the popular "Blue Vein" brand—provisions, fresh, salted and smoked meats, poultry and country produce generally, is found here in a fresh and wholesome condition, all of which have been most carefully selected. Orders are called for and goods are delivered free of charge at any given residence. Mr. Poehlmann is the recipient of a large and liberal trade extending throughout the city.

 McGARRIGLE, Flour, Feed, Hay, Grain and Straw, Nos. 4712 and 4514 Main Street.—One of the largest livery stable businesses in Germantown is that conducted by Mr. P. McGarrigle. A full line of light carriages, landaus, hacks, coupés, victorias, etc., is kept in constant readiness at all hours of the day and night, suitable for balls, parties, weddings, pleasure driving, funerals, ladies out shopping or making calls, etc., and some hundred and fifty different rigs, both new and second hand, are here for sale or to let. The enterprise was established by the present proprietor eight years ago, and in addition to the extensive livery business already alluded to, one of almost equal volume and significance is conducted as a wholesale and retail dealer in the finest grades of flour, feed, straw, all kinds of grain, salt, and the standard brands of roller patent flour for families and bakers, two teams being retained for delivery purposes and ten competent assistants regularly employed. The premises utilized, which are Mr. McGarrigle's own property, are situate on a lot 80x290 feet in area, and comprise a residence and feed store on the street front, and a fine two story stable in the rear, furnished with stalls and loose boxes capable of accommodating seventy horses, besides having ample storage room for the several fine carriages already alluded to. The worthy proprietor, Mr. P. McGarrigle, was born in Ireland, whence he came to the United States in 1871, settling in this city three years later.

 THOMAS C. RAYNOR, Veterinary Surgeon, No. 21 West Chelten Avenue, Germantown.—Mr. Thomas C. Raynor, veterinary surgeon, has been established in that profession here for the past two years. Dr. Raynor's services are now called into requisition by owners of poor horses, cattle, etc., in all parts of this section of Philadelphia, and he has yet to hear of the first instance of any patron of his being other than amply satisfied with his treatment of the respective animals with which he has to deal. Dr. Raynor is especially expert in treating sick or lame horses, and his cures are invariably of an enduring nature, thus demonstrating clearly his sound ability and wide research in veterinary matters in general. Fair and reasonable charges and prompt response to all summonses are his essential characteristics, and he is to be found at his well appointed office daily from 8 to 10 A.M. and from 3 to 6 P.M. Dr. Raynor is but twenty-six years of age, and bids fair to become a distinct light and ornament in the profession. He is a graduate of the class of 1890 at the Veterinary Department of the University of Pennsylvania, and his father and several relatives are actively engaged in this eminently useful calling.

 THE JOHN HANCOCK MUTUAL LIFE INSURANCE COMPANY, OF BOSTON, MASS., No. 418 Saunders Avenue.—Since its organization under the laws of the commonwealth of Massachusetts in 1862, the John Hancock Mutual Life Insurance Co., of Boston, Mass., has ingratiated itself with all classes throughout the Eastern, Northern and Middle States. The institution is no "infant prodigy" or "phenomenon," but is a steadily progressive undertaking that has developed from a comparatively modest beginning. Its success was won upon the equitable and straightforward conditions of its policies, its liberality in making settlements and dealing with lapses, and the low rate of its policies. Some forty principal industrial offices are maintained, each one of which is the centre of a large force of local agents and an extensive business with the working classes; policies being issued for weekly payments of from five to fifty cents. In this city three of these offices are maintained, and that in West Philadelphia situated at No. 418 Saunders Avenue, is intrusted to the able and distinctly successful direction of Mr. George H. Lukes, the superintendent, who initiated the branch in 1888. An especially large connection is controlled from here, and its volume calls for the constant employment of thirty-seven local agents. Mr. George H. Lukes has been with the John Hancock Co. for the past eight years, and he was formerly engaged with the Metropolitan Co., of New York. He is thoroughly practical in all insurance matters, and is a recognized authority on the respective merits and demerits of the various forms of policies now before the public.

 RUSSEL T. BLACKWOOD, Druggist and Pharmacist, S. E. Corner Fifteenth and Thompson Streets.—Foremost among the oldest established and leading pharmacies of Philadelphia stands that which is under the proprietorship of Mr. Russell T. Blackwood, eligibly located corner of Fifteenth and Thompson Streets. This flourishing business dates its foundation back as far as 1850, at which time it was originally established by Mr. Chas. Stark, who carried it on most successfully up to 1870, when he was succeeded by Wm. Weber, who was followed by Mr. Blackwood, March 1, 1892. The premises occupied, which are 20x40 feet in dimensions, are provided with all the necessary conveniences and facilities for the satisfactory prosecution of the business, the salesroom being a model of neatness, order and elegance, and two efficient clerks are in constant attendance. The stock handled is always full and complete, and embraces the purest and freshest drugs and chemicals, proprietary remedies of admitted merit, pharmaceutical preparations, druggists' sundries, toilet and fancy articles, etc., also a fine line of choice cigars and confectionery. Particular attention is here given to the compounding of physicians' prescriptions and family recipes, in the preparation of which only the best and most reliable drugs are used, while every precaution is taken to insure perfect accuracy. Mr. Blackwood, who is a thoroughly competent and experienced druggist and pharmacist of many years' practical experience in the largest pharmacies of this city, is the recipient of a large, permanent and influential trade extending throughout this his native city. Mr. Blackwood puts up many valuable preparations, including "Blackwood's Fifteen Minute Headache Cure," "Blackwood's Dentiform," which is a delightfully fragrant and healthful tooth wash, also "Blackwood's Compound Syrup of Sarsaparilla." All these preparations are extensively used and are general favorites with the public. He is a graduate of the Philadelphia College of Pharmacy, and a popular member of several social organizations.

 GEO LINDLEY, Machinist, Nos. 45 to 50 Wakefield Street, Germantown.—Mr. Geo. Lindley established his business here in 1879, and makes a leading specialty of the manufacture and repairs of knitting machinery of all kinds, while executing general machinists' work and making special machinery to order. In all this class of work Mr. Lindley has the reputation of turning out results which can only emanate from long practical experience and thorough theoretical knowledge of the machinists' trade. Orders are constantly being received from all parts of Pennsylvania, Delaware, New Jersey and New York, and every modern facility is at hand for insuring rapid and perfect production. The workshop is under the superintendence of Mr. Joseph North, who has been in the house since 1879 and is an expert and practical master of his trade. Mr. Lindley was born in Philadelphia, and has had thirty-two years' experience in the machinists' trade. He is a member of the F. & A. M. Commandery, the Red Men, and the Sons of St. George.

HISTORICAL AND COMMERCIAL PHILADELPHIA.

R. WM. DELKER, Druggist, No. 1030 South Second Street.—This flourishing business was originally founded in 1867 by Dr. Andrew Nebinger, and for the past decade it has been under the efficient management and direction of its present proprietor, who learned the business with his preceptors Drs. Andrew and Robert Nebinger, and was graduated from the Philadelphia College of Pharmacy in 1873. The present desirable store was taken possession of about Oct., 1887, and during the erection of the new building now occupied, and which was built expressly for the business, the store was located directly across the street. This store is commodious in size, fitted up with all the modern adjuncts of convenience and attractiveness, and perfectly arranged for the purposes of the business, while two registered pharmaceutical assistants are in constant attendance. The large and comprehensive stock is displayed to the best advantage, and embraces pure and fresh drugs and chemicals, proprietary remedies of standard worth, physicians' and surgeons' supplies, pharmaceutical preparations of every description, toilet and fancy articles, perfumery, soaps, sponges, etc. A specialty is here made of compounding physicians' prescriptions and family recipes, and the laboratory is supplied with all the requisite appliances and facilities for securing accuracy and precision in their preparation. Dr. Delker enjoys a large and extensive practice throughout the city as a physician. In 1884 he was graduated from the Jefferson Medical College as an M.D., and is a member of its Alumni Association, besides the American and Pennsylvania Pharmaceutical Societies, the Apothecaries' Union and the Philadelphia and State Medical Associations. He is a native of Ashland, Pa.

ILLIAM K. STOCKLEY, Commission Sales Stable, Coach, Driving and Saddle Horses, No. 322 North Broad Street.—For some few years past this commission sales stable has been a well known market for the purchase and disposal of horses of all kinds, more especially high bred stock. The business was established eight years ago by Mr. Baney, who was succeeded in October, 1891, by the present proprietor, Mr. William K. Stockley, under whose close supervision its every detail is conducted. Mr. Stockley has had a practical experience with horses ranging over a period of thirty five years, being an astute judge of the points of the animal, and skilled in veterinary matters; and the reputation of the establishment above alluded to, is substantially upheld and augmented by the strictly honorable principles to which he rigidly adheres. All classes of horses are bought, sold and exchanged on commission, and a select assortment of coach, driving and saddle stock is constantly on hand, as also draught horses of various kinds. The stable is spacious, and was especially constructed with every regard for efficient light, ventilation, drainage, heat, water supply, etc. Stalls and loose boxes are provided and comfortable quarters are furnished for fifty head. Mr. William K. Stockley was born in Sussex County, Del., and formerly owned a stable for eleven years at the corner of Thirty-ninth and Market Streets.

KULP & SON, Hardware, House Furnishing Goods, Cutlery, Tools, Etc., No. 4162 Germantown Avenue, Nicetown.—This flourishing business was inaugurated by the present proprietors in 1885, and has since been conducted by them with uniform success and prosperity. The premises occupied comprise the first floor and basement, each 20x50 feet in dimensions, which are fitted up in the most appropriate style, while from three to four competent assistants and a delivery team are employed in constant service to meet the demands of the trade. This firm handles a remarkably fine stock, embracing hardware, carpenters', builders' and mechanics' tools, garden implements, shelf goods, table and pocket cutlery of all kinds, and all those various articles coming under the head of house furnishing goods, in great profusion. These goods are representative of all the best and most reliable makes put upon the market, and they are offered for sale at the lowest consistent prices. Special attention is given to all kinds of jobbing in this line of trade, all of which work is promptly executed in the best manner at such rates as are compatible with first class service. Messrs. G. and Wm. A. Kulp, who compose this firm, are both practical and experienced business men who, by their well directed management and upright methods of dealing, have reared an enterprise which places them among the leading and prosperous merchants of this their native city.

OUTHWARK ICE COMPANY (John R. Carpenter, Proprietor; Residence, No. 419 Dickinson Street); Office and Depot, Moyamensing and Washington Avenues.—Ice was formerly little used, but within a comparatively recent period it has become a staple commodity and a household necessity. Few families are so poor that they do not patronize the iceman during the heated term, and large quantities are used by the breweries, packing houses, hotels, etc. Prominent among the leading houses engaged in this useful and growing industry in the city of Philadelphia is that of the Southwark Ice Company, Mr. John R. Carpenter, proprietor. This business was established by Mr. John H. Bevens twenty five years ago, and has been controlled by the present proprietor since 1874. Mr. Carpenter employs eight assistants and has seven wagons and ten horses in his service. His storehouse has a capacity of five hundred tons, and during the past year his sales have amounted to three thousand tons. Great care is taken in securing the ice to have it perfectly pure, thick and clear, and the liberal patronage bestowed upon this house shows that the proprietor has been eminently successful in meeting the wants of his patrons. The trade of the house is both wholesale and retail, and the lowest prices at all times prevail. Mr. Carpenter is a native of Salem, N. J., but has resided in Philadelphia for twenty five years. His great great grandfather came to this country with William Penn. Mr. Carpenter is now in the active prime of life, and as a business man maintains an excellent reputation for honorable and straightforward dealing.

OUIS SPOERHASE, Jeweler, No. 4078 Lancaster Avenue.—An old established and reliable jewelry house in West Philadelphia is that of Mr. Louis Spoerhase, who is well known hereabouts for handling the finest qualities of goods and for strictly honorable dealing in all transactions. The business was established by the present proprietor at the same location in 1869. The chief kinds of goods dealt in are solid, rolled and plated gold and silver jewelry, both plain and fancy; stone goods, mountings and settings, diamonds of direct importation, the best standard makes of American watches, silverware in great variety, clocks, and a full line of optical goods. A separate department is maintained for the repair of jewelry, silverware, watches, etc., and for the cleaning and adjustment of complicated timepieces; regular employment being furnished for three skilled assistants. The store is neatly fitted and well ordered, and the large and carefully chosen stock carried makes a handsome display. Mr. Louis Spoerhase is of German birth, and is a thoroughly practical jeweler and watchmaker.

P. CORBIN & CO., Commission Merchants in Oysters, Fruit, Produce, Etc., No. 310 South Delaware Avenue.—Among the old established and representative houses of Philadelphia engaged in handling oysters, fruit and produce at wholesale and on commission, none is better known than that of L. P. Corbin & Co. This house was founded in 1868 by Simpson & Corbin, who were succeeded by Corbin, Whiton & Co., the latter by Corbin & Swing, and afterward Mr. L. P. Corbin became sole proprietor, remaining alone up to two years ago, when Mr. Edw. Clayville was admitted to partnership. The premises occupied comprise a store, 20x60 feet in area, and it is furnished with all modern facilities for the prompt fulfillment of orders; employment being found in its operations for three assistants. Consignments are received from the best productive centres in the Middle, Southern and Western States, and the trade of the house extends throughout Pennsylvania, New Jersey and Delaware. Mr. Corbin was born in Maryland, and has resided in Philadelphia thirty years, of which twenty eight years have been spent in his present line. He is a member of the I. O. O. F., A. O. U. W., and Knights of Honor. Mr. Clayville, also a native of Maryland, came to this city twelve years ago, and entered Mr. Corbin's employ. He is a member of the Order of Odd Fellows, Red Men, and P. O. Sons of America.

JOHN M. SHARPLESS & CO., Importers, Manufacturers and Dealers in Dye Stuffs and Chemicals, Nos. 20 and 22 North Front Street.—The stability of Philadelphia as a commercial field is shown in the great number of old mercantile concerns still in existence here, and still expanding their facilities and resources. Some of these houses were founded before the town of American independence was sounded. An establishment that has been in existence for more than a half century is that of John M. Sharpless & Co., whose office and warehouse are at Nos. 20 and 22 North Front Street. This business was founded in 1835. The present proprietors are Messrs. Thomas Scattergood and John W. Pepper, both native Philadelphians, and prominently known in the business and financial world. Mr. Scattergood has been a member of the firm since January, 1868, and Mr. Pepper for the past fourteen years. The former is a director of the Delaware County National Bank, of Chester, Pa., and Mr. Pepper is a mem-

VIEW OF WORKS OF J. M. SHARPLESS & CO., FROM RIVER FRONT

ber of the Manufacturers' Club, the Trades League, and the Philadelphia Bourse. The firm's warehouse is a five story and basement building 25x100 feet in dimensions, and it contains a very heavy stock of dye stuffs and chemicals of all kinds, both of foreign and American production. The firm have a large, finely equipped factory on the Delaware River front, at Chester, Pa., with ample wharf facilities and railroad connections direct with Pennsylvania, Philadelphia & Reading, and Baltimore & Ohio railroad systems where they manufacture a general line of dye wood extracts and dye woods. They have a splendid trade with tanners, textile mills, soap makers, etc., in various parts of the United States, and also export a large quantity of goods. The fifty-seven years of continuous existence of this reliable house has given it unexcelled facilities and advantages, and the firm can furnish the best goods at bottom quotations.

J. H. STROUP & CO., Druggists, No. 3243 Market Street.—Among the popular and reliable druggists of this community stands the firm of J. H. Stroup & Co., whose finely appointed Market Street Pharmacy was established here more than two years ago, but not until quite recently did it come under the control and direction of its present efficient proprietor, Mr. Stroup, who is the active member of this firm. The commodious store occupied is handsomely and conveniently fitted up with special reference to the business, and at all times presents that inviting and attractive appearance associated with a first class establishment of this character. The large, complete and carefully selected stock carried embraces everything in the line of pure and fresh drugs and chemicals, all the standard proprietary remedies, pharmaceutical preparations, liquors, mineral waters, physicians' and surgeons' requisites, druggists' sundries, toilet and fancy articles, soaps, sponges, perfumery, etc., all of which have been obtained from the most reputable sources of supply. A specialty is here made of compounding physicians' prescriptions and family recipes, all orders being promptly prepared with accuracy and dispatch, and in every instance from the best and most reliable ingredients obtainable. A large and influential trade has been developed. Mr. Stroup is also proprietor of "Donty's Beef, Iron and Wine," which is a valuable stimulating tonic composed of Liebig's Extract of Beef, a valuable Salt of Iron and Sherry Wine. He is also proprietor of "Donty's Tonic Root Beer," which makes five gallons of sparkling, refreshing summer drink, and also of "Donty's Concentrated Extract of Vanilla" for flavoring ice cream, custards, jellies, pastry, etc. Mr. Stroup, who is a native of Minersville, this State, is a duly qualified and legally registered pharmacist, practicing under a certificate issued by the State Pharmaceutical Board.

CHAS. S. McNALLY, Paints, Oils, Glass, Etc., Nineteenth and Callowhill Streets.—Among the fully responsible houses of its kind in this section of the city, special mention should be made of that of Mr. Chas. S. McNally, manufacturer and dealer in paints, oils, varnishes, etc. Mr. McNally, who is a native Pennsylvanian, assumed control of this thriving business in 1889, as successor to the well known Tully Paint and Varnish Company of Tullytown, Bucks County, this State, who conducted this house as a branch of their main works for many years. He had been in the employ of this company for ten years, previous to assuming the proprietorship of this store, and is thoroughly experienced in and familiar with the business in all its branches. The salesroom is ample and well ordered, being appropriately arranged and fitted up with special reference to this line of trade, and a requisite stock is at all times handled. In the assortment will be found everything in the line of painters' supplies, including all kinds of dry and mixed paints ready for use, colors, oils, varnishes, glass, putty, etc., of both imported and domestic goods, and the same are sold in any desired quantity at the most reasonable rates. He also keeps in stock a fine line of paints for finishing iron work, and enters into contracts for doing all kinds of work of this character. He has now a contract on hand for furnishing the materials for finishing the Ice Plant machinery at the World's Columbian Exposition at Chicago. Mr. McNally is the recipient of a large and substantial retail trade throughout this city, in which he is so well and favorably known.

HISTORICAL AND COMMERCIAL PHILADELPHIA.

EORGE W. MANNING, All Kinds of Sewing Machines, Needles and Parts for all Machines, No. 1015 Christian Street.—Mr. George W. Manning keeps his store open for the supply of all the recognized standard makes of sewing machines. He possesses a wide and varied experience in this line, and is at all times glad to extend to patrons the full benefit of his opinion and practical knowledge to aid them in a wise selection of a machine to meet precisely their respective requirements. The stock he carries is as complete as can be found in any part of the entire city, and conspicuous among the handsome array of highly finished sewing machines are the "Singer," "Howe," "Standard," "Home" and "Household;" needles and parts for all machines, as well as patterns, etc., etc., are also to be found here in abundant assortment. The repairing department is a special feature of the business, and its chief characteristics are fine work, promptitude and moderate charges. Sales are effected either for cash or on the instalment plan of easy purchase, and a heavy volume of trade is controlled throughout the city. Mr. Manning is a young man of Michigan birth, and has been engaged with the Singer Company for seven years, as also with the Remington Company. He first established his business in 1870 at Cleveland, Ohio, afterwards removing to Buffalo, N. Y., and sixteen years ago he transferred these at of his operations to Philadelphia.

M. & E. SWEENEY, Wholesale Dealers in Fine Liquors, No. 1641 Ridge Avenue.—This business was established as a retail store by B. M. Sweeney in 1881, a brisk trade being enjoyed from the start, which soon assumed such proportions that a wholesale and retail business was inaugurated, under the firm name and style of Sweeney Brothers Mr. B. M. Sweeney retiring in 1889 it has since been successfully conducted by the present proprietor. The premises occupied are commodious, well arranged and fully fitted up with every appliance. The assortment includes the choicest brands of ports, sherries, clarets, champagnes, Irish and Scotch whiskeys, brandies, gins, rums, cordials, etc., which are unsurpassed for quality, purity and flavor, and are sold bottled or in bulk, imported and domestic; and whiskeys can be obtained free or in bond, at fair and reasonable prices. A speciality is made in California wines and brandies, including Zinfandel Red Wines, at $1.00 per gallon, put up in stone jugs. Mr. Sweeney is a young man and a native of Philadelphia.

HARRY CHURCH, Wholesale and Retail Dealer in Butter, Eggs and Poultry, No. 103 Pine Street; No. 15 Washington Street, Cape May, N. J.; N. W. Corner Bond Street and Bangs Avenue, Asbury Park, N. J.—This prosperous business was established in 1886 by Kehr & Church, the present proprietor succeeding to the control in 1891. Mr. Church is an extensive wholesale and retail dealer in butter, eggs and poultry, large consignments of which are daily received from all States A store and basement, 30x60 feet in dimensions, is occupied, affording ample and complete storage facilities; and a large stock is kept constantly on hand, and all persons having dealings with this concern are assured of satisfactory treatment. The trade of the house is both wholesale and retail, and in both branches is large and steadily increasing. Mr. Church is a native of New Jersey, but has been a resident of this city for seven years, and is an active and energetic young business man and a prominent member of the I. O. O. F.

ACOB WINDOLPH, Flour, Feed, Grain, Hay and Straw, Main Street and Gravers Lane, Chestnut Hill.—One of the oldest merchants in this section is Mr. Jacob Windolph, who is engaged in the handling of flour, feed, grain, hay and straw. Mr. Windolph established the business in 1852 on Chestnut Hill. The store occupied is commodious, neatly furnished and fitted up with every convenience for the successful prosecution of the work. The stock carried is large and well selected, and embraces the best brands of family flour, corn and oat meals, grain of all kinds, ground feed, baled hay, straw, etc. Mr. Windolph was born in Germantown, and when twenty-one years of age was a member of the old Volunteer Fire Department.

W. BOERNER, Broad Street Floral Emporium, Nos. 521, 523 and 525 South Broad Street.—One of the best known and most popular florists in this section of Philadelphia is Mr. A. W. Boerner. The enterprise was established three years ago by the present sole proprietor, who has since continued it with an unbroken record of progress. The premises occupied comprise a one story building, with extensive greenhouses and grounds, in addition to a store 60x60 feet in area, finely furnished, and equipped with all materials and requisites for the artistic arrangement of floral decorations and emblems for weddings, parties, funerals, etc., elaborate centre pieces, choice bouquets and boutonnières, and for the general and successful prosecution of the brisk trade carried on. Popular prices prevail. Five skilled assistants are regularly employed Mr. Boerner, who was born in Germany and is a skilled florist by trade, came to this country forty five years ago. He has had fifteen years' practical experience at his present business, and is a member of the Free and Accepted Masons, Williamson Lodge, No. 369, Penn.

AMUEL McNICHOLL, Fine Harness, No 4737 Main Street.—This thriving business was established here by the present proprietor in 1881. The premises occupied comprise a two story building having the dimensions of 20x40 feet, fully equipped in the most complete manner and perfect in convenience of arrangement for the purposes of the business, while the demands of the trade are such as to require the services of nine experienced assistants in constant employment. A large and complete stock is at all times carried in the salesroom, including all kinds of single and double, light and heavy harness, saddles, bridles, halters, etc., together with a fine assortment of trunks, bags, grips, valises, etc., all of which are made from the best quality of materials, are guaranteed to be strictly first class in every respect, and are offered for sale at the lowest prices consistent therewith A specialty is made of coach harness, and in the manufacturing of anything in this line of trade the very finest class of work only is executed, and all orders receive immediate attention, while repairing of every description is also neatly and satisfactorily done at short notice. Mr. McNicholl, who is a practical harness maker of long experience in the business, is highly regarded for his skill, industry and integrity. Born in Ireland, Germantown has claimed him as a resident for the past eighteen years, and he has since become a popular member of several fraternal orders here.

DWARD WHITEHILL, Dealer in Artistic Furniture, Carpets and General Household Goods, Nos. 1024 and 1026 South Street.—One of the oldest and most thoroughly representative furniture and carpet houses in this section of Philadelphia is that of Edward Whitehill, situated at Nos. 1024 and 1026 South Street. The enterprise was first established by Mr Whitehill in a modest way with one storeroom. By paying strict attention to the wants of customers, handling only first class articles, and confining himself to sound business principles, a large and permanent trade was developed, which has been steadily increasing ever since. In 1889 it became necessary to obtain more room, and the store next door was added. The premises now occupied consist of three floors, each 40x100 feet in area, well stocked and equipped throughout for the successful prosecution of the business. A full and complete line of furniture and carpets of artistic and modern designs, together with a miscellaneous stock of general household goods, constitute the principal feature of the house's operations. Goods being obtained in large quantities direct from the manufacturers, Mr. Whitehill is enabled to offer them at reasonable prices for cash, or at easy terms on the instalment system Mr. Whitehill employs six competent assistants, is a young man and a native of Philadelphia.

HISTORICAL AND COMMERCIAL PHILADELPHIA.

 M. H. THOMAS & CO., Importers and Jobbers in Dry Goods Specialties, No. 622 Market Street.—The leading house of Wm H. Thomas & Co. was established in February, 1891. They import and sell the finest grade of dry goods specialties to be purchased anywhere within the city limits. In their commodious salesrooms Mr. Thomas, who has carried on the business since its establishment, has constantly on hand a most extensive and varied stock in his line. The premises occupied are 40x25 feet in area, which are fitted up with special reference to the business, and a large and varied stock of dry goods specialties of all kinds in the richest fabrics and in all the new and beautiful designs and shades which are picked from each country's best productions is constantly carried in stock and sold to wholesale dealers all over the country east of the Mississippi. Mr. Thomas is upon the road a great part of the time and picks up bargains in dry goods whenever chance offers anything new and original, or sends a representative to pick it up at the highest marketable value, and this departure has been an important factor in the success which has always attended this house.

 M. KOLB, Corn and Feed Mills, White and Yellow Corn Meal, Cracked Corn, Feed Meal, Ground Oats, Bran, Etc., No. 3047 Chestnut Street.—The corn and feed mills of Wm. Kolb have been in operation for about twelve years. They were built and started by the present proprietor and are the largest in their line in the city and in addition to the milling business they conduct a large general commission business in flour of all kinds, grain, hay, straw, etc. The concern is a commodious three story structure, and is provided with two runs of stones and complete facilities for grinding, etc. All kinds of mill feed are ground to order here at shortest notice. A large and first-class stock is constantly kept on hand, and includes white and yellow corn meal of an excellent quality, cracked corn, feed meal, ground oats, bran, and everything in this line. An efficient staff of help is employed, while several wagons deliver to customers, all orders receiving prompt attention, and the prices charged here are exceptionally low, quality of goods considered. Mr. Kolb is a gentleman of middle age, active and energetic, and was born in Chester County, Pa. He is a man of entire reliability in his business relation, and is a member of the Commercial Exchange. His son, Mr. Horace Kolb, is in full charge of the mills.

 GEORGE H. LUCKMAN, Rag Carpets Woven to Order, Brussels, Ingrain and Rag Carpets for Sale, No. 4424 Main Street.—The carpet house of Mr. George H. Luckman is well known for handling the most reliable grades of goods and for charging fair and reasonable prices. Brussels, ingrain, and rag carpets of the latest styles and designs are largely dealt in and kept in stock in rich and heavy assortment, as also oil cloths, Smyrna and other rugs, carpet sweepers, etc., while carpets are laid and relaid on short notice by experienced hands. The specialty of the business, however consists in the weaving of rag carpets to order, the latest approved methods and appliances being adopted. The enterprise was established at the same location two years ago by the present proprietor, Mr. George H. Luckman, who has been actively engaged in rag carpet making here for the past thirty years, and personally superintends the prompt and accurate fulfillment of all orders. The premises occupied consist of a well-fitted store, 20x60 feet in size, and a shop in the rear, fully equipped with three looms and other appliances pertaining to rag carpet manufacture, several skilled operatives being there regularly employed. Mr. George H. Luckman is a native of this city.

 JOHN C. LEWIS, Heaters, Ranges and Stoves, Tin Roofer and Sheet Iron Worker, Nos. 2216 and 2218 Germantown Avenue.—An old established and reliable sheet metal worker and dealer in stoves, heaters and ranges is Mr. John C. Lewis. Stoves, heaters and ranges are made, supplied and set up in thorough order; stove and range connections, piping, flues, etc., are made, also tin roofing, spouting, guttering and a full line of tin and sheet iron work; while all kinds of jobbing and repairing incidental to the trade receive every care and attention. The business was established in 1876 by the present proprietor who takes active part in the prompt and accurate fulfillment of all orders with which he is intrusted, about fourteen skilled mechanics being regularly employed. The premises utilized consist of three floors, each 32x40 feet in area, furnished with a full equipment of tools, accessories and supplies for turning out the best work on short notice. Mr. John C. Lewis was born in Ohio and came to this city in 1850. He is a member of Gen. E. D. Baker Post, No. 8, of the Grand Army of the Republic, and served for three years during the late war in the 39th Iowa Volunteer Infantry, Company A.

 EDGAR P. PARIS & CO., Apothecaries, Corner Main and Coulter Streets.—This business was originally established in 1864 by D. A. Jones, and was next conducted by C. A. Daniels, and in 1876 the present enterprising proprietor assumed control, since which date the volume of business has rapidly increased. The store, 20x40 feet in size, is well arranged and thoroughly stocked with a complete line of drugs, chemicals, toilet articles, patent medicines, etc., while a handsome soda fountain has also been introduced. Special attention is given to the compounding of physicians' prescriptions, and this department of the business is personally attended to by the proprietor. Three polite and expert clerks are employed, and the place receives a liberal support from the residents of this section of the city. Mr. Paris entered the store as a clerk, and through his ability and business capacity worked himself to the head of the enterprise. He is a native of this city, and is an active and prominent member of the Knights of Pythias, I. O. O. F., and United American Mechanics. His methods are strictly reliable and honorable.

 FRANK B. HEINS, Practical Plumber, Gas and Steam Fitter; No. 2113 South Street.—Mr. Frank B. Heins established this business three years ago in a basement, in a small way, but owing to constantly increasing patronage, larger and more commodious facilities became necessary for the prosecution of the work, and the present premises were assumed which comprise an appropriately fitted store stocked with a complete assortment of plumbers', steam and gas fitters' supplies. Everything in the way of plumbing, ventilating, steam and gas fitting is undertaken, contracts are entered into, and the complete fitting up of buildings of all kinds is satisfactorily accomplished. A specialty is made in sanitary engineering and underground drainage. Mr. Heins has had ten years' practical experience and has executed the plumbing work in many large buildings and private residences, among them being the plumbing and sanitary work in the residence of Mr. George A. Dunning, Mount Airy. Mr. Heins also carries in stock a general line of plumbing materials, including bath tubs, basins, boilers, faucets, lead and iron piping, etc., and regular employment is furnished five journeymen. He is a native Philadelphian, and a prominent member of the Independent Order of Odd Fellows.

 JAMES DILKS, Musical Instruments, Stationery, Etc., No. 1923 South Street. The establishment of Mr. James Dilks was inaugurated nineteen years ago by the present sole proprietor. The premises occupied embrace a store, 20x30 feet in area, well fitted and equipped for the advantageous display of a large and carefully selected stock of musical instruments of all kinds and descriptions, including pianos, organs, banjos, mandolins, guitars, cornets, harmonicas, drums, and a miscellaneous assortment of all articles pertaining to this line of merchandise, while stationery in great variety is kept for sale in any quantity at the lowest market prices. A specialty is the handling of old violins, which are bought, sold, repaired or exchanged, and for which Mr. Dilks has achieved a widespread reputation, extending throughout Pennsylvania and adjoining States. Polite clerks serve customers and popular prices prevail. Mr. Dilks is a native of New York but has been a resident of this city forty-five years.

HISTORICAL AND COMMERCIAL PHILADELPHIA.

CHAS. S. ROBBINS, Fashionable Hatter; Gloves and Umbrellas, No. 41 North Second Street.—The oldest established house in its line in Philadelphia is that now so successfully conducted by Mr. Chas. S. Robbins. This gentleman succeeded Mr. Thomas M. Seeds, who had controlled the business for more than thirty years. Since January 1, 1892, the business has been conducted by Mr. Robbins, who has been eminently successful in gaining many new customers and retaining old ones. He had been with the house for thirteen years previous to assuming control of affairs, and was well known and popular with its permanent patrons. The premises utilized for the business comprise one floor, 20x100 feet in dimensions, and a very heavy stock is carried of hats and caps in all fashionable shapes, also a fine assortment of gloves and umbrellas, embracing all the styles demanded by the trade. The house numbers among its regular customers many of the first class citizens and prominent business men of the city who have been its liberal patrons for many years. Mr. Robbins has been a resident of this city for many years, and is highly respected for his good qualities as a man and merchant.

SEXENNIAL PRINTING HOUSE, General Job and Commercial Printing, No. 110 North Tenth Street.—This concern is of comparatively recent formation, the business having been established September 15, 1891, by Mr. John A. Devine and Mr. E. W. Pitner, under the above title. The premises comprise the second floor, 25x50 feet in dimensions. They have a well equipped plant, embracing one cylinder press and four job presses, a fine assortment of new type, plain and fancy, in all the latest styles, together with all the general appliances for turning out anything in the line of printing, from a businesscard or circular to the finest book work. They use electric power, employ from seven to nine experienced hands, and do a general job printing business, making a specialty of commercial and society printing. The work turned out is strictly A1, and they have a large city and suburban trade. Both members of the concern are skilled practical printers. Mr. Devine was born in this city; Mr. Pitner in Danville, Pa. They are both members of the Order of Sparta and the Sexennial League. They do the printing required by the last named organization.

JOHN MEADOWS, Electro Plater, No. 132 South Tenth Street.—The reliable and representative house of Mr. John Meadows, of No. 132 South Tenth Street, was first established by Mr. John Meadows in 1852, and in 1890 Mr. Henry Klineberg was admitted to partnership. The premises occupied comprise one floor, 25x90 feet in dimensions, fully equipped with all the latest improved dynamo electric and other plating machines and appliances necessary for the successful prosecution of the business. The machinery is operated by steam power, and seven experienced workmen are employed. Gold and silver plating in all its branches is here executed in the highest style of the art. Excellence of workmanship, durability of finish, and prompt attention to orders are the characteristics of all work executed at this establishment. Mr. Meadows is a native of England, but has been a resident of this city for forty years, and is a thoroughly practical man of forty years' experience, and thoroughly versed in all the secrets of the art. Mr. Klineberg is a native Philadelphian, and has over fifteen years' experience in the business. This firm were victims of the disastrous fire of April 27, 1892.

O'MALLEY & WALSH, Coal Dealers, Nos. 626 and 628 Washington Avenue.—This business was initiated by the present proprietors, Messrs. O'Malley & Walsh, in May, 1891. The firm make a specialty of handling large consignments of Lehigh and Schuylkill coal, and being in direct communication with the Pennsylvania railroad by a switch running into the yards, are constantly receiving shipments of all grades and kinds of coal direct from the mines, thereby enabling them to offer the same to regular consumers at the lowest cash prices. Their business methods are fast becoming known for giving full weight, making accurate settlements, and promptly delivering all orders entrusted to their care. Several teams and competent hands are employed, and a brisk trade is carried on. Messrs. O'Malley and Walsh are both native Philadelphians, and prior to embarking in this enterprise, Mr. O'Malley was a collector and Mr. Walsh a dry goods clerk, and were well known in trade circles.

W. W. COLLINS, Dry Goods and Notion House, No. 4168 Germantown Avenue.—For twenty-one or more the well known dry goods and notion house of Wm. W. Collins has been steadily growing in popularity. It is the leading and best stocked establishment of the kind in Nicetown. Goods are sold at rock bottom figures, exceptional bargains being offered in wash fabrics, underwear, domestics, etc., and every article is warranted to be exactly as represented. The store is spacious, neatly fitted up and well arranged, and half a dozen assistants are in attendance. A very large and first class stock is constantly kept on hand, and comprises handsome silks, velvets, plushes and cashmeres, elegant shawls, suits, cloaks and wraps, jackets, jerseys, etc.; pretty patterns in fancy calicoes, ginghams and prints, laces, embroideries, ribbons, dress trimmings, gloves, hosiery and notions in great variety. The assortment also includes a fine line of millinery goods, ladies' and gents' furnishings, table and household linens, cottons, flannels, sheetings, towelings and staple dry goods generally. Mr. Collins the proprietor was born in this city, and is favorably known as a merchant and a citizen.

S. MILHE, Paper Hangings, Successor to A. D. Hackman, No. 2556 Germantown Avenue.—This business was originally founded here in 1888 by Mr. A. D. Hackman, who conducted it for two years and then sold out to Mr. L. S. Milhe, who, in turn, during the passing year, was succeeded by his brother, the present proprietor. The commodious and well ordered store, 18x24 feet in measurement, is appropriately fitted up for the handling and display of the stock and systematic conduct of affairs. The comprehensive and varied assortment at all times found here embraces everything in the line of wall paper, friezes, borders, dados, etc., from the plainest to the most artistic and elaborate designs, in both imported and domestic patterns, all of which are representative of the most fashionable styles of the day, and the most fastidious purchaser cannot fail to make suitable selections here. Paper hanging and interior decorations of every description are done in the most expeditious and excellent manner at reasonable rates, from six to eight experienced hands being constantly employed, and the proprietor, who enjoys a reputation for skill and reliability second to none in the trade, exercises close supervision over all work executed. Mr. Milhe is an energetic, progressive business man, who is untiring in his efforts to please. He is a native of Bucks County, Pa., and a member of the K. of G. E.

CHAS. TODD, Druggist, No. 4403 Main Street, Manayunk.—The old established pharmacy conducted by Mr. J. Charles Todd is one of the leading here. Besides being well known as a reliable dispensary for absolutely pure, fresh and potent drugs, chemicals, medicines and family remedies, it is freely recognized for the scrupulous care and accuracy that are exercised in the preparation of physicians' prescriptions and miscellaneous recipes, while the laboratory is held in high repute, also for the several high grade pharmaceutical compounds, tinctures, cures and other first class proprietary articles that are made and put up on the spot. The business was established in the same vicinity in 1864 by Dr. W. C. Todd, who was succeeded in 1886 by his son, the present proprietor. The store, which is of ample dimensions, has been occupied for the past twenty years, is handsomely appointed, and contains a large and carefully selected stock of drugs, chemicals, medicines and every requisite for the successful conduct of a large drug, prescription and family trade. Mr. J. Chas. Todd, who is a native of the Quaker City and still a young man, was brought up to this profession and took two courses of study at the Philadelphia College of Pharmacy.

E. & R. G. FOSTER, Schuylkill Falls Range and Heater Works, 3115 Ridge Avenue, Corner Spencer Street.—The Falls of Schuylkill Range and Heater Works were established in 1866 by Edward Foster, who conducted the business alone up to 1888, when the present firm name was adopted. They are manufacturers of and dealers in tin, copper and sheet iron ware, stoves, ranges and heaters, and handle a general line of hardware and cutlery. They occupy commodious quarters as store and shop, keeping on hand always a large and first class stock, and employ some half a dozen in help. The Messrs. Foster are general sheet metal workers and roofers, and attend also to gas fitting and plumbing. Roofs are repaired and painted in the most superior manner at short notice; heaters and ranges are repaired and reset with skill and despatch, and jobbing in all branches is promptly attended to. All work executed by this firm is guaranteed to render satisfaction, and every article sold by them is warranted, while their prices are most reasonable, being exceptionally low, in fact. The Messrs. Foster are both men of practical skill and thorough experience.

WELSH & NAULTY, Funeral Directors and Practical Embalmers, N. E. Corner Third and Pine Streets.—Among our leading representatives of this profession in this section of the city there are perhaps not any who stand higher in popular esteem and favor than Welsh & Naulty. They have been established since January, 1877, and from the first have been highly prosperous, their business giving evidence of steady increase. Messrs. William Welsh and Charles W. Naulty, who compose the firm, are gentlemen in the prime of life, and natives respectively of Wilmington, Del., and Philadelphia. They are both men of practical skill and thorough experience as embalmers and funeral directors, conversant with every feature and detail of the business. They are members of several Catholic societies, while Mr. Naulty, who is Secretary of the Funeral Directors' Association, is councilman for the Fifth Ward. They occupy commodious quarters, connected by telephone 1761, and keep on hand always a full stock of coffins, caskets and funeral requisites. The firm have a well equipped livery stable also, at No. 122 Lombard Street, and have in service a number of first class carriages and a hearse. Remains are taken in charge any hour, day or night, and prepared for burial, and embalming is attended to in accordance with the most approved process. Interments are procured in any of the city and suburban cemeteries, and funerals are personally conducted in the best manner, everything being furnished, while the prices charged are most reasonable.

CHARLES CRAWFORD, Florist, No. 524 North Eleventh Street.—One of the leading and most popular florists in the city is Mr. Charles Crawford. He has well equipped greenhouses at Fifty-fifth Street and Woodland Avenue, where he employs seven skilled gardeners in the cultivation of a great variety of flowers, shrubs, etc. From this establishment he receives daily the finest fresh cut flowers, and makes a specialty of bouquets, baskets and flowering plants in pots for parties and weddings, also the most artistic ornamental pieces for table decoration; and furnishes to order beautiful wreaths, crosses and emblematic designs for funerals. His patronage is among high class trade in the city and suburbs, and he also fills many orders from distant localities. He is an expert practical florist, and possesses great taste in the arrangement of flowers. His present business was established in 1877, but his experience dates back to his boyhood. Mr. Crawford is a native Philadelphian, one of the third generation of his family resident here.

WM. SMITH & CO., Commission Merchants, Fruit and Produce, No. 265 North Front Street and No. 262 North Water Street.—The foundation of this establishment was laid in 1859 by Mr. Wm. Smith, and was conducted by that gentleman under the present firm style up to 1875, when he admitted to partnership his son, Wm. V. Smith. Three years ago the senior member of the firm retired from active business life, and Mr. Wm. V. Smith now continues in the sole control, though he retains the original firm title, so familiarly known to the trade. He is a native of Delaware, and a thorough, practical business man. The premises occupied consist of a four story warehouse of ample dimensions, and every facility is at hand for the prosecution of the trade. The house receives consignments from every productive centre in New York, Pennsylvania, New Jersey, Delaware, Maryland, Virginia, and the Western trade, and it ships goods to all the principal points in this State, New Jersey, Delaware and the North. The products handled include poultry, eggs, domestic fruits and general produce, and the firm prides itself upon the promptitude with which it disposes of and makes returns on consignments.

EDWARD A. GROBEN, Fish, Oysters, Clams, Lobsters, Crabs and Terrapin, No. 4936 Main Street, Germantown.—It is now about two years ago since Mr. Edward A. Groben established his oyster and fish market at No. 4936 Main Street, since which date his place has become a well patronized headquarters for fresh oysters, fish, clams, lobsters, crabs and terrapin. The proprietor brings four years' practical experience to bear in the management and conduct of his business, and to his knowledge and experience of the trade may be attributed his success. A full line of the above mentioned sea and fresh water food is constantly kept on hand, and orders for the same are delivered with promptness and despatch. His store, 25x60 feet in area, is handsomely fitted and contains excellent refrigerating facilities for the preservation of the goods handled. The market is extensively patronized by the best class of residents of this section of the city. Mr. Groben is an active member of the I. O. O. F. and the United American Mechanics, and a man well and favorably known.

A. H. GUMPERT, Proprietor, Belmont Laundry, No. 1011 Lancaster Avenue.—The Belmont Laundry, which is under the efficient management and direction of Mr. A. H. Gumpert, was originally established four years ago by the present proprietor. The spacious premises are well arranged and perfectly equipped with all the newest and best improved methods and appliances for the purpose, operated by ample steam power, which was introduced here about a year ago, and employment is afforded to six experienced and competent assistants. Everything in the line of laundry work is done in the best possible manner, a specialty being made of collars and cuffs, shirts, underwear, pillow shams, table linen, etc., in fact, both the plainest and coarsest goods and those of the finest fabrics, and in every instance these are done up without tearing or injury, at short notice. All orders receive immediate attention, and goods are called for and delivered at any residence free of charge. Mr. Gumpert is a native of Philadelphia. He has two agencies established here, and is a popular member of the Laundrymen's Association.

CHAS. P. REESE & CO., Wholesale Dealers in Mutton, Lamb and Veal, Philadelphia Market Thirtieth and Market Streets; also Abattoir, Thirtieth and Race Streets. In the great wholesale trade in meats, a foremost leader in his special line is Mr. Chas. P. Reese, trading under the firm name of Chas. P. Reese & Co. He originally established his enterprise at the corner of Fortieth and Market Streets, removing from there in May, 1887, to the abattoir, corner Thirtieth and Race Streets, and a year and a half ago he opened a branch at the Philadelphia Market, corner Thirtieth and Market Streets. He deals at wholesale exclusively, handling Western and Pennsylvania stock and he deals only in the choicest mutton, lamb and veal, for which he has a large and steadily growing trade. At the abattoir Mr. Reese has a cooling room with a storage capacity of 700 head, and also has a large cooling room in the market. The sales amount to some 650 head weekly, and a large stock is always carried to meet the wants of the trade. Eleven hands are employed. Mr. Reese is a native of Philadelphia, where he has long been favorably known as an expert practical butcher and a trustworthy business man.

HISTORICAL AND COMMERCIAL PHILADELPHIA.

ILLIAM BARRY, Looking Glass and Picture Frame Gilder, No. 737 Sansom Street.—The reputation of the popular and reliable establishment of Mr. William Barry, looking glass and picture frame gilder, began with the foundation of the enterprise six years ago, and from the first has been steadily growing. The premises occupied comprise a commodious second floor, equipped with all the necessary appliances and facilities, and perfect in convenience of arrangement for the successful operation of the work engaged in; and two competent and experienced assistants are employed in constant service. Mr. Barry's specialty is the regilding of looking glass and picture frames of every description, which are touched up in such a thorough and superior manner as to make them look equal to new. All work of this class is done for the trade in the highest style of the art. In the general restoring of oil paintings, etc., to which particular attention is also devoted, the work is most accurately and faithfully done, and perfect satisfaction is guaranteed. Mr. Barry is a thorough master of his art in all its branches, having been actively identified with the business since 1880. He was brought up in this city, coming here fifty years ago.

OHN F. MANN & BRO., Wholesale and Retail Dealers in Veal, Nineteenth Street Market; and the Abattoir, Thirtieth and Market Streets. Messrs. John F. Mann & Bro., are wholesale and retail dealers in veal, who butcher and have their wholesale department at the abattoir corner Thirtieth and Market Streets, while for retail department they occupy four stalls in the Nineteenth Street Market. The firm deal only in Pennsylvania raised stock, which they personally select from the most reliable sources, and they kill some 300 calves a week. The business was established by the present proprietors twenty-five years ago, at the Nineteenth Street Market, and they did their killing at Nineteenth and Berks Streets up to May, 1892, when they removed to the abattoir at Thirtieth and Market Streets. Here they have a cooling room with a storage capacity of 500 head, and a heavy stock is at all times carried to meet the active demands of the trade. The members of the firm, Messrs. John F. and David Mann, are natives of this city. They are skilful, practical butchers, employ ten competent assistants, and are progressive, reliable business men.

. S. DUNSHEE, Artistic Photographer, No. 1330 Chestnut Street. Opposite U. S. Mint.—Among the prominent and ably conducted establishments engaged in this business is that of Mr. E. S. Dunshee, which has always sustained a most excellent reputation for high class productions. Mr. Dunshee is a native of Bristol, Vermont, and for many years was engaged in this interesting industry in Boston, Mass., and desiring to operate in a larger and more important field he came to this city and founded this establishment in 1880, which at once became the centre of a very large and substantial patronage. The premises occupied comprise an entire second floor, easy of access, and include a handsomely furnished office, reception room and toilet, while the operating, finishing, printing and other rooms are all on the same floor, being the only establishment of its kind in the city having all its business on the same floor. The operating departments are thoroughly equipped, and the very latest improved devices, mechanical and scientific appliances known to the profession are to be found here in successful operation, and employment is given to none but thoroughly skilled artists and assistants. He is prepared to execute photography in all its branches and in the most artistic style, producing true to life pictures in any size from life to the miniature portrait for the locket. Using the dry plate and instantaneous process, he is especially successful with groups and children. Old pictures are copied, enlarged or reduced in size, equal to the original, and a specialty is made of portraits in oil, water colors, India ink and pastel. He also has a branch establishment in Frankford, this city, where equally fine work is produced. Mr. Dunshee has followed the business the longest of any now engaged in it, and is highly esteemed in commercial circles.

AMUEL H. MAYBERRY, Wholesale and Retail Grocer and Tea Dealer, No 3846 Ridge Avenue.—This flourishing business was originally founded in 1870 by the present proprietor. The large and commodious store occupied has the dimensions of 50x75 feet, and is neatly and attractively appointed throughout, while the services of from three to five competent assistants and two teams are required in constant employment to meet the demands of the trade. Everything comprehended in the line of staple and fancy groceries is carried in stock, including the purest and finest teas, coffees, sugars, spices, canned goods in infinite variety, table delicacies, sauces, cereals, flour, condiments, dried fruits, pure cider vinegar, molasses, syrup, prime butter, cheese, eggs, household specialties, hams, fruits and vegetables of all kinds in their respective seasons, etc. The proprietor makes a specialty of the "Gold Medal," "Pride of the West" and "Ambrosia" flour; also "Aunt Sally" baking powder, and F. J. Heinz's pickles, mustard and catsup. For quality, quantity and variety these supplies cannot be surpassed in the market, having been most carefully selected in each department, and the prices quoted are placed at the lowest point, and goods are delivered at residence without delay, free of charge. Mr. Mayberry, who was born in Ireland, has resided in this country since 1867, and is a member of the A. P. A.

ILEY & WALLACE CO., Manufacturers of Pharmaceutical Specialties, No. 123 North Seventh Street.—Messrs. Wiley & Wallace Co., manufacture a general line of pharmaceutical specialties, such as beef, iron and wine, pills and various proprietary remedies, which are put up in the name of the druggists for whom intended, and their preparations are of a highly meritorious character. They are also manufacturers of pure fluid extracts, tinctures chemicals and all compounds used in prescriptions, and their products not only command extensive sale throughout the United States, Canada and Mexico, but are exported largely to South America, some also to England. The premises occupied as laboratory and factory comprise five spacious floors, and are perfectly equipped. The facilities are first class in all respects and twenty-five or more are employed in the establishment. A very large and complete stock is constantly kept on hand here, and all orders are promptly and carefully filled. This flourishing business was established in 1865 by Spencer & Thomas, who were succeeded by Thomas & Giwiney, and these were succeeded in turn by Thomas & Schiedt, J. A. Schiedt & Co., and Wiley & Wallace in 1892. Under the last firm name the house was conducted up to about three years ago, when the present copartnership was formed, Jacob A. Schiedt being President, and W. T. Wallace, Secretary and Treasurer of the company, which was duly incorporated. Messrs. Schiedt and Wallace are natives of this city, and maintain an A1 reputation in wholesale and retail drug circles.

ENRY C. COATES Printer, No. 1211 Market Street.—This is in all respects an enterprising, reliable house and was established in 1862 by John Coates, father of the present proprietor, who succeeded to control in 1866. The quarters occupied for business purposes comprise a second floor, 40x40 feet in size, used for office purposes, and a third floor, 25x100 feet, used for plant. This comprises eight job presses and one cylinder, and a multifarious assortment of all the newest and best faces of type, borders, etc., which is constantly being added to as occasion requires or novelties appear, while a force of from twelve to fifteen in help is employed the year round. All kinds of work from a card to a quarto volume are printed here in the highest styles of the art, at prices which are as low as the lowest, and satisfaction is guaranteed; a specialty, however, being made of fine catalogue and mercantile work. The trade extends all over the United States. Mr. Coates is a thoroughly practical printer of many years' experience, and master of his art in all its branches. He is a native of Philadelphia, and was reared in the business. He served during the Civil War with the First Minnesota Regiment, taking part in all of its principal engagements, and is a member of the G. A. R., Post 100, Department of Pennsylvania. He is assisted in the office details by his son Fred, who is a young man and a native here.

HISTORICAL AND COMMERCIAL PHILADELPHIA.

 J. DEVLIN, Furniture and Upholstery, No. 921 Pine Street.—An old established and reliable manufacturer of fine furniture and upholstery and dealer in antiquities in Philadelphia is Mr. C. J. Devlin, carrying on his operations at No. 921 Pine Street. The specialty of this business consists in upholstering and repairing, and includes everything in the line to order, such as the upholstering and reupholstering of fine furniture in the richest materials, the making of mattresses and bedding, draperies, curtains and interior decorations in general, while the operations of the house also include the purchase and sale of antique furniture, and the making of fine furniture of any pattern or style to order. The enterprise was established by the present proprietor in this locality in 1862, and a trade has since steadily developed, reaching all over the United States, its volume furnishing regular employment for ten skilled hands. The premises utilized comprise a well fitted store, 20x80 feet in size, and a shop in the rear fully equipped for turning out the finest work and for executing all orders promptly and accurately, a large and carefully chosen stock being always on hand of fine furniture, antiquities and an elegant display of upholstered goods. The experienced proprietor, Mr. C. J. Devlin, was born in Ireland in 1828, coming to Philadelphia in 1849, and has been actively engaged in this line of trade for the past thirty-five years.

 NUTTALL & SON, Hardware, House Furnishing Goods, Stoves, Heaters and Ranges. Nos. 1501, 1503, 1505 South Second Street.—The house of Messrs. R. Nuttall and Son is one of the representative establishments in this line and the largest in its section of the city. It was founded in 1869 by Mr. R. Nuttall, Sr., and in 1872 the present firm was organized by the admission of Mr. J. Nuttall to partnership. The firm are wholesale and retail dealers in hardware, house furnishing goods, stoves, heaters and ranges, while giving prompt attention to locksmithing, bell hanging and general jobbing. The premises occupied comprise three storerooms and a basement, 70x80 feet each, and two floors for stock rooms, 40x80 feet. The firm carry a very large line of fine shelf hardware, table and pocket cutlery, machinists' and mechanics' tools, including every novelty and desirable specialty in these lines, and both in prices and quality of merchandise this house is known to excel. Their goods speak for themselves and the wants of all classes of buyers are ministered to with success and satisfaction. The Messrs. Nuttall are native Philadelphians, and eminently successful as leaders in their line of trade.

 S. C. MARKLE, General Furnishing Undertaker, No. 1509 Frankford Avenue.—One of the oldest established furnishing undertakers in Frankford is Mr. S. C. Markle. The business was founded in 1848 by the present proprietor, who, with a practical experience at his command ranging over a period of half a century, is enabled to meet the exact requirements of all classes, alike as to coaches, hearses, coffins, caskets, and a full line of equipments and accessories, while he also executes embalming by the latest approved scientific methods, and undertakes all the duties incidental to interment, thereby relieving his patrons of the many harassing details and preliminaries in the distressing hour of bereavement. His well appointed office has been occupied for the past twenty-five years. Mr. S. C. Markle, who is a native of Roxbury, Pa., has resided in Frankford for the past forty-four years, and is a member of the F. and A. M., the Undertakers' Association, and the Sovereign Patriotic Knights.

 SAMUEL IFILL, Livery and Boarding Stable, No. 5157 Germantown Avenue.—The leading representative of the livery and boarding stable interest in its section of the city is the house of Mr. Samuel Ifill. This house was established in 1840 by Fred Johnson, the present proprietor succeeding to the control in 1887. The present building was erected by Mr. Ifill and occupied by him on the 1st of January, 1894. It is built of brick, in the most substantial manner, contains two floors, 104x62 feet each, and has first class accommodations for fifty-seven horses. The stable is well drained, ventilated and lighted, has a number of box stalls and ample room for the storage of carriages and supplies, and every care and attention is given to the animals intrusted to the proprietor. Mr. Ifill has some of the most stylish and elegant equipages to be seen in the city and a stock of superior thoroughbred driving horses, which can be hired for business or pleasure, night or day, on the most reasonable terms. Among the vehicles are included coaches, coupés, landaus, barouches, and hacks for calls, shoppings or weddings. The boarding branch of the business is liberally patronized, and an extensive business is done in the livery department. Orders by telephone No. 102 receive immediate response, and the wants of all classes of patrons are ministered to with eminent satisfaction and success. Mr. Ifill is a native Philadelphian and a young man of large experience and thorough reliability.

 CHARLES L. EBERLE, Pharmacist, Monument Square, Corner Mill Street, Germantown.—This flourishing business dates its foundation way back to 1830, at which time it was originally established. Dr. Rex conducted it up to 1859, when he was succeeded by the present proprietor and manager. For the past twenty-eight years the present desirable premises have been occupied at the corner of Monument Square and Mill Street, and these comprise a store of ample dimensions, which is handsomely fitted up in the most convenient manner for the purposes of the business, and at all times presents one of the most attractive features of this vicinity. It is completely stocked with a carefully selected assortment of pure and fresh drugs and chemicals, all proprietary remedies of well known merit, physicians' and surgeons' requisites, mineral waters, liquors, druggists' sundries of all kinds, perfumes, soaps, sponges, toilet and fancy articles, etc., in fact, everything pertaining to a first class and well regulated pharmacy. Mr. Eberle makes his own tinctures, tonics, lotions, extracts, etc., and puts up a general line of pharmaceutical compounds, also devotes special attention to the compounding of physicians' prescriptions and family recipes, which are prepared in the most accurate and careful manner from the purest and best ingredients obtainable. Mr. Eberle's ample and first class patronage is enjoyed, and the popularity of the house throughout all classes of the community is at once recognized. Mr. Eberle is a competent, vigilant and trustworthy pharmacist, who brings to bear upon this business more than forty years of practical experience, having started out in life at the early age of fourteen years, and in 1859 he was graduated from the Philadelphia College of Pharmacy, and is now a member of its alumni association. He is a native of Germantown, and for several years has taken an active part in educational and other municipal affairs.

 WM. ROBINSON, Men's and Boys' Clothing, No. 4180 Germantown Avenue.—A popular and successful exponent of the clothing trade in Nicetown is Mr. Wm. Robinson. Mr. Robinson, who is an Englishman by birth, came to this city to reside in 1873, and more than a dozen years ago embarked for himself in his present enterprise. The premises occupied include a large and commodious corner store, 32x10 feet in dimensions, which is fitted up in the most attractive and convenient style for the purposes to which it is devoted, and from three to four courteous and efficient clerks are in constant attendance. Mr. Robinson deals in every description of ready made clothing for men, youths and boys, in all grades, styles and patterns of fashionable and seasonable goods, together with hats and caps of all kinds in the latest shapes and styles, and gentlemen's furnishings in profuse variety. From the first he has made it his aim to keep none but the best and most reliable goods, and those representing the latest novelties, while his prices are always placed at the lowest point consistent with fair and equitable dealings. A specialty is here made of fine custom made garments, all orders for which are promptly filled, and these productions are guaranteed to give entire satisfaction in every feature of merit, in cut, fit, style, material and workmanship. Mr. Robinson is untiring in his efforts to please those who favor him with their patronage. He is a member of the Knights of Malta and the I. O. O. F.

HISTORICAL AND COMMERCIAL PHILADELPHIA.

RCH STREET HOUSE, American and European Plan (Theo. K. Batt, Proprietor), N. W. Corner Delaware Avenue and Arch Street.—Among the several old-time hostelries for which Philadelphia is so justly famed, a leading place is occupied by the Arch Street House, situated at the foot of Arch Street. This well known hotel is patronized by all the best classes of the traveling public—congressmen, officials, legal functionaries, commercial men, tourists, pleasure seekers and private families—and has been standing for the last seventy-five or a hundred years, coming into the hands of the present proprietor and host, Mr. Theo. K. Batt, three years ago. Its management is experienced, liberal and able, each department is in the hands of a competent manager, and the whole comes under the direct administration of the proprietor. The hotel has everything in its favor for making it a popular resting place or temporary abode for all travelers, combining the comforts of home life with every luxury and modern convenience that science and art can suggest. Its location, too, is most desirable, being central, close to the wharves and steamboat landing, as also the railroad ferries, while street cars pass right by the door; it is conducted on both the American and European plan, the rates for the former being $2 per day. The Arch Street House, although of such old standing, is second to none in the city in its service and appointments, and was refurnished and newly decorated throughout early in 1892; it comprises a brick structure of six floors and basement, and contains eighty-five rooms, including spacious sleeping apartments, an elegant dining hall capable of seating a hundred guests, ladies' parlor of sumptuous appointments, reading room, gentlemen's smoking and news room, entrance hall, office, and a well fitted café in the basement. The excellence of the catering is only equalled by the culinary department and the cuisine, which latter is a noteworthy feature of the Arch Street House, and is fully maintained by the close care and skill of the experienced and well known chef, Lewis Thompson. The premises are provided with fire escapes, ample lavatories, baths, etc., and there is a fine refreshment bar on the first floor. The popular proprietor, Mr. Theo. K. Batt, was formerly engaged in the grocery trade, and is a member of the National Hotelmen's Association.

IMLEY & SEIDLE, Importers and Wholesale Dealers in Foreign and Domestic Fruits, Bananas, Oranges, Lemons and Apples, in Car Lots only, a Specialty, No. 405 New Market Street, and Nos. 340 and 342 North Water Street.—To say that the wholesale fruit trade of this city forms an interest of surpassing importance hardly conveys an adequate idea of the extent thereof. The transactions in bananas, oranges and lemons alone in the course of a year reach vast magnitude, and the volume of sales grows apace. Among the Philadelphia merchants contributing most extensively to the general commercial activity in the line indicated can be named Kimley & Seidle, No. 405 New Market Street, and Nos. 340 and 342 North Water Street. They are importers of and dealers in foreign and domestic fruits of every variety, making a specialty of California products, and are doing an exceedingly large business. They are receivers and shippers, and their trade extends throughout Pennsylvania, Delaware, New Jersey, New York, the States adjoining, and to Canada. The firm is the leading one in its line in this city, and are now the heaviest banana handlers in Philadelphia, Pennsylvania, New York and Maryland, and the heaviest jobbers wholesale in foreign fruits, and their trade is increasing every day and maintains an A1 standing. The house has unequalled facilities for placing consignments of fruits to advantage, and guarantees prompt returns in every instance, being thoroughly responsible in all its financial obligations, as reference to the National Bank of Northern Liberties or the Dun and Bradstreet Commercial Agencies will attest. The business premises are very spacious and commodious, there being six floors devoted to oranges and lemons, and two floors and basement to bananas, and a staff of competent help is employed. An immense stock can always be found here, and all orders are promptly and carefully filled, while the house, with its exceptional advantages, is in a position to offer substantial inducements to the trade. Messrs. George Kimley and William Seidle, the members of the firm, are gentlemen in the prime of life and natives of Philadelphia. They are men of energy and enterprise, thoroughly conversant with the business, and all the indications are that the signal success that has attended their efforts during the seven years they have been established is bound to endure. They are members of the Produce Exchange and the Fruit Buyers' Union. The firm was formerly Kimley, Seidle & Dastwyler, but on August 16, 1892, Mr. Dastwyler retired, and Messrs. Kimley & Seidle continue the business on a purely wholesale basis.

S. JOHNSON, Tin, Slate, Gravel Roofing, No. 16 North Seventh Street; also Successor to V. W. Walter, Nos. 144 and 146 North Sixth Street.—One of the oldest established and best known roofing and sheet metal working businesses in the entire city is that of Mr. T. S. Johnson, established and located by him twenty-one years ago at No. 16 North Seventh Street, and who in March, 1891, bought the large business of Mr. V. W. Walter, at No. 146 North Sixth Street, established twenty-five years before, and now conducts both enterprises. All kinds of tin, slate and gravel roofing are executed in the best style, as also the repair and painting of old roofs as a specialty, in addition to which a full line of tin and sheet iron work is undertaken, including pipes, flues and connections for hot air heating, stove, heater and range work in all branches, the relining of bath tubs, the making of kitchen utensils to order, gutters, leaders, chimney tops, ventilators, etc., together with all kinds of jobbing and repairing. The house enjoys an established reputation for turning out only the best and most reliable work at fair and reasonable prices, and a large, permanent trade is controlled, reaching all over the city and adjacent districts, furnishing regular employment for a number of skilled mechanics the year through. The premises located at No. 16 North Seventh Street, and at Nos. 144 and 146 North Sixth Street, are both fully equipped with improved machines, tools and appliances for insuring the prompt and satisfactory fulfilment of orders. The proprietor, Mr. T. S. Johnson, who is a middle aged gentleman of Philadelphia birth, is a member of the Volunteer Firemen's Association, having formerly been actively connected with one of the old companies under the volunteer system, with which he is still identified.

AREY & CO., Fine Carriage Lamps, Etc., No. 343 Arch Street.—For more than a quarter of a century, or, to be exact, just twenty-six years. Carey & Co., manufacturers of fine carriage lamps, etc., have been established in business. They are one of the oldest and most widely known firms in the line indicated in Philadelphia, and have a large trade. They turn out a distinctly superior class of work, and their productions are in extensive demand all over the United States. The quarters occupied as factory by the firm are on the fourth floor, and are ample and well equipped. The facilities are first class, and a number of expert workmen are employed here. The firm manufactures elegant carriage lamps and kindred articles of every style and variety in beautiful designs and superb finish, and every one is fully warranted as to workmanship and material, while repairing is attended to also with skill and dispatch. Mr. E. R. Carey, who is the sole proprietor, is a native of this city, and is a thoroughly practical workman and a man of exceptional skill in his line.

KEHRWEIDER COMPANY, Studio, No. 4905 Main Street, Germantown. The Kehrweider Company has gained an enviable reputation for artistic work. This company was organized in 1885 and has occupied the present location for the past four years. The premises utilized for the business comprise two floors, 20x40 feet in dimensions. This company are prepared to take views, and outdoor pictures of groups, buildings, residences and landscape scenery, also to enlarge small pictures, photographs, daguerreotypes, ambrotypes or drawings, while in crayon work and pastel the productions of this house are particularly fine. Six skilled and experienced assistants are employed, and all orders are promptly filled. The members of the company are: Alexander, Mr. H. and Mrs. C. Kehrweider, all of whom are thoroughly experienced in the business and have in every way kept pace with the rapid advancement of the photographic art.

MORRISON PLUMBING COMPANY, No. 3919 Lancaster Avenue.—The Morrison Plumbing Company has won an enviable position in its line of trade. This business was originally founded in 1876 by Mr. Charles R. Morrison, who conducted it up to the passing year, when the present company became his successor, although he still remained as general manager of its affairs. The present desirable premises were also taken possession of quite recently, and these comprise a store, especially equipped with all the necessary conveniences and facilities for the purposes to which it is devoted, while it contains at all times a heavy stock of plumbers' supplies of every description. Sanitary work and all branches of plumbing, steam and gas fitting are given prompt attention, and from eight to twelve skilled artisans are given constant employment, while Mr. Morrison, who is a practical, experienced and licensed plumber himself, exercises a close surveillance over every department of the business, so that full reliance may be placed upon his satisfactorily executing all work intrusted to the care of this house. The building located at Nos. 3905 to 3909 Baring Street has just been completely fitted out by this concern. A large, permanent and first class trade has been developed. Mr. Morrison, the manager, is a native of Philadelphia.

MILLER & MELVILLE, Printers, No. 113 North Twelfth Street.—Though but a comparatively short time established, Miller & Melville, printers, No. 113 North Twelfth Street, have acquired an excellent patronage. They turn out first class work, are prompt and reliable in executing orders, and their prices are of the most reasonable character. The firm do a large amount of printing for secret societies, this being their specialty, and their trade is rapidly growing. They started in business in 1891, and were formerly located at No. 1018 Chestnut Street, moving to the present place in January last. The quarters here occupied are ample and well equipped, and half a dozen hands are employed. Job printing of every description is done in the most superior manner. Messrs. H. D. Miller and J. H. Melville are both practical printers, of thorough experience in the exercise of their art. Mr. Miller, who was born in Massachusetts, but has lived in this city since boyhood, is a prominent member of the F. & A. M and the I O. O. F., Right Eminent Grand Recorder for the United States of the Knights of Malta, and for ten years was superintendent of the Drifton Hospital at Drifton, Pa., also connected with the Penn Hospital for three years; while Mr. Melville, who is a Philadelphian by birth, is also a member of the Knights of Malta, and several other societies.

JOHN W. SIDLE, Optician, Mechanician, and Maker of Instruments of Precision, Etc., No. 1029 Filbert Street.— One of the most skilful opticians and mechanicians in this city, and the leader in his special line of work, is Mr. John W. Sidle. He manufactures instruments of precision, perfect in workmanship; and is the inventor of the " Acme " microscope, the superiority of which is well known to scientific professors. He also makes telescopes and optical instruments of every description, physical apparatus, etc. His leading specialty is the manufacture of photographers' apparatus of the most improved and perfect character. His workshop is 20x40 feet in dimensions, supplied with electric power and equipped with machinery and appliances of the very finest description. Six skilled mechanics are employed. Mr. Sidle is a native of Chester County, Pa., and has been established at his present business since 1888 in Chestnut Street, and removed to his present quarters in 1891. He is a member of the Order of Odd Fellows and the Knights of the Golden Eagle.

THOMAS McGIRR, Painting, No. 113 North Seventh Street.— Mr. Thomas McGirr has been established since 1888, and has built up a large trade, his patronage steadily improving. Mr. McGirr is a Philadelphian by birth. He is a man of thorough practical skill and twenty-five years' experience, and is master of his art in all its branches. He occupies ample and compact quarters as store and shop, keeping on hand always a complete stock of paints, oils, varnishes, white lead, glass, brushes, etc., and employs sixteen in help. Mr. McGirr is prepared to do all kinds of interior and exterior painting, and gives particular attention to hall and ceiling work. Sign painting is executed also in the most artistic manner, and gilding on glass, hard wood finishing, staining, graining, etc., are done in first class style at short notice.

Dr. J. H CANTRELL, Druggist, No. 1000 South Second Street. Among the time honored and reliable pharmacies of Philadelphia, that which is under the able management and direction of Dr. J. H. Cantrell takes a position as third among the oldest established houses of its kind in this city. It dates its foundation way back to 1828, when it was originally opened by Mr. Jno. A. Cantrell, who carried on the business most successfully up to his death in 1873, from which time on his widow controlled its affairs for four years, and then sold out to her son, the present proprietor. He occupies a commodious and well appointed store at No. 1000 South Second Street, which is handsomely and attractively fitted up with ornamental fixtures, plate glass windows, electric light, etc. It is completely stocked with a first class assortment of everything comprehended in the line of drugs and chemicals, all of standard strength and purity. Special attention is here given to compounding physicians' prescriptions and family recipes in the most prompt and accurate manner at all times, this department being most carefully and efficiently directed. An extensive and flattering patronage is enjoyed. Dr. Cantrell, who besides being an accomplished and vigilant pharmacist, was also graduated in 1856 from Jefferson Medical College as a physician, and he has a fine practice extending throughout this his native city. He is a member of the Americus Club and Young Men's Democratic Association.

JAMES AXFORD, New and Second Hand Furniture, Stoves and Bedding, Storage, Carpets and Oil Cloths; No. 4960 Main Street. —An important commercial pursuit is followed by Mr. James Axford, proprietor of the furniture, carpet and storage establishment No. 4960 Main Street, Germantown, Philadelphia. On January 1, 1886, this gentleman established his business on this thoroughfare, and in 1886 moved to his present address, where he occupies a four story building, 24x175 feet in area, which is attractively fitted and well stocked with a superior line of furniture, stoves, carpets, oil cloths, bedding, etc. The premises furnish ample storage capacity, and household goods are stored at reasonable rates, while moving is a special department of the business, drays and moving vans being kept for that purpose. Upholstering in all its branches is executed at short notice, and the work is performed in first class style. Mr. Axford was born in England and came to Philadelphia in 1851, where he has since resided and become a substantial merchant and a public spirited citizen.

HISTORICAL AND COMMERCIAL PHILADELPHIA.

JOHN REESE, Ship Chandler and Grocer, Dealer in all Kinds of Ship and Steamship Supplies, No. 217 Lodge Street.—A reliable source of direct supply for all kinds of ship chandlery, etc., in this city, is that afforded by the responsible house of John Reese, located opposite the Maritime Exchange. This house confines its operations exclusively to the supply of steamers and sailing vessels with stores of all kinds; the chief lines being chandlery, groceries, deck, cabin and engine stores, and the "Genuine Rahtjens Composition" of Messrs. M. Holzapfel & Co., of Newcastle-upon-Tyne, for whom the house acts as the sole agent in Philadelphia. The business was established in 1854 by Capt. Charles Hoyer, who was succeeded ten years ago by the present proprietor, Mr. John Reese, under whose skilful and successful direction every detail is conducted. A commodious store and basement are utilized and are well arranged. The worthy proprietor is a native of Philadelphia and is very popular among vessel owners, masters and others.

SPERRY, Bookbinders' Stamp and Letter Engraver, Manufacturer of Brass Type, Etc., No. 622 Arch Street.—The operations of this house consist largely in the engraving and making of bookbinders' stamps and letters, which are characterized by their accuracy of detail, clearness of outlines, and by their durability, and are made in any patterns or designs from the plainest stamp to the most ornamental and elaborate. In addition the house manufactures brass type and all kinds of brass letters, dies, stamps and moulds to order for the trade, the best results being insured, alike as to material and high finish. Mr. J. Sperry established himself in this line twenty-five years ago in England, and removed the seat of his operations to this city in 1880. The third floor at the location named is occupied, and is fully equipped with machines, appliances, tools and necessories pertaining to the industry; three skilled mechanics being there regularly employed. Mr. Sperry was born in England, and has been an esteemed resident of this city for the past twelve years.

JOS. L. KINKERTER, Dealer in Building and Housekeeping Hardware, Heaters, Stoves and Ranges, No. 4669 Frankford Avenue.—There is little doubt but that the largest hardware house in Frankford is that conducted by Mr. Joseph L. Kinkerter, now well known for handling the most satisfactory grades of goods in each line. The heavy and comprehensive stock carried includes among other things a carefully selected assortment of building and housekeeping hardware, paints, oils, glass, belting, wire, rivets, carpenters' and machinists' tools, pumps, roofing felt, lamps, burners and chimneys, granite and tin ware, table and floor oil cloth, the standard makes of heaters, stoves and ranges, table and pocket cutlery, etc. In addition to the sale of these goods, a general line of tin and sheet iron work is undertaken, the fitting up of stoves, heaters and ranges complete with all piping and connections, hot air work, flues, etc., and jobbing and repairing in all branches of the trade. The premises utilized comprise a spacious store and basement, each 60x80 feet in area. The enterprise was established at the same location in 1876 by the present proprietor, Mr. Joseph L. Kinkerter, who owns the building he occupies.

THOMAS THE TAILOR, No. 4743 Main Street.—The superiority of tailor made clothing is too marked and well known to need mention herein. An enterprising advocate of this system of making clothes is Mr. Wm. B. Thomas, merchant tailor, No. 4743 Main Street, Germantown, Philadelphia, who is well known for his skill and knowledge of the art of tailoring. When a boy of fifteen this gentleman started business on this street, and three and a half years ago moved to his present address, where he occupies a finely fitted and thoroughly stocked store. His line of goods includes all the latest patterns and styles in foreign and American goods, which are made to order at reasonable prices. Mr. Thomas's work is conspicuous for exactness of fit, superior workmanship and durability. His trade is large and extends to all parts of the city, and requires the services of from ten to fifteen expert assistants. He makes a speciality of dyeing, scouring and repairing clothes, and performs work promptly. Mr. Thomas is a young man of enterprise and good business judgment. He is a native of this city, and is a prominent member of the Red Men, Knights of Malta and United American Mechanics. He enjoys an excellent reputation for practising reliable and fair dealing business measures.

FRANCIS J. LAMMER, Apothecary, No. 1701 Dauphin Street.—One of the handsomest as well as best conducted drug stores in this section of Philadelphia is that which is under the skilful and efficient management of Mr. Francis J. Lammer, who graduated under the preceptorship of Messrs. John Wyeth & Brother, and is eligibly located at the corner of Dauphin and Colorado Streets. This business was originally founded here in 1889 by Messrs. Francis J. and J. S. Lammer, who conducted it together for about a year, when partnership was dissolved and the latter member retired, from which time on the present proprietor assumed sole control of its affairs. He is a native of this city, a graduate of the Philadelphia College of Pharmacy, with honorable mention, of the class of 1886, and a young man of more than ordinary business tact and ability; and we would refer to his work in the "U. S. Dispensary" (pp. 516). The well arranged salesroom, 16x30 feet in dimensions, is fitted up in a style which represents a happy combination of modern elegance and convenience. The assortment of drugs, chemicals, medicines, proprietary remedies, fancy articles, cigars, etc., embraces all of the purest and freshest class of goods to be found at a first class family drug store. Two competent assistants are employed in constant attendance, and physicians' prescriptions and family recipes of all kinds are skilfully and accurately compounded. Mr. Lammer's reputation as an experienced and responsible druggist and apothecary is of the very highest.

BEWLEY'S BOARDING AND LIVERY STABLE, No. 3850 Lancaster Avenue. The foundation of this flourishing business dates many years back, and in August, 1891, came under the control and direction of its present efficient proprietors, Messrs. William M. and Harry Bewley, who were successors to Mr. Robert Walters. The premises occupied have an area of 30x180 feet, and consist of a two story building, equipped with an elevator and all the latest modern improvements, besides being well lighted, ventilated and drained, and perfect as regards sanitary arrangements. Besides many carriages, there are accommodations for thirty horses, and those taken to board, by the day, week or month, receive the best of food, care and attention in every instance from the competent hostlers employed in constant service. Special attention is given to gentlemen's road horses. Horses, carriages, buggies, coupés, light wagons, etc., are also kept for hire, and for comfort, fashionable style and elegance the equipages furnished here are unsurpassed, and all orders are promptly attended to without any unnecessary delay. Both members of this firm are natives of Philadelphia, and enterprising and honorable young business men.

C. W. SCHUMACHER, Dealer in Wall Paper and Window Shades, No. 4411 Main Street, Frankford.—The oldest established wall paper house in Frankford is, beyond question, that of Mr. C. W. Schumacher. The business was founded in the same locality in 1859 by the present proprietor, who has been actively engaged in this line for the past forty years. In addition to the sale of all kinds of imported and domestic wall coverings and window shades, the house undertakes contracts and accepts orders for paper hanging, window shade making to any size, interior decorating of every sort, fresco, panel and ceiling painting to any design from the plainest to the most elaborate interior and exterior painting, fine sign writing and lettering, etc. The store, 20x70 feet in area, which has been the headquarters of the house for the past twenty years, is well fitted and conveniently arranged for the due conduct of the business. A large and select stock of wall papers of all kinds, shade cloth, rollers and window shades complete is always on hand, and five competent assistants are regularly employed. Mr. Schumacher is a native of Philadelphia.

HISTORICAL AND COMMERCIAL PHILADELPHIA.

LEWIS H. QUAY, Frescoing, Paper Hanging, House, Sign and Decorative Painting, No. 5228 Germantown Avenue.—This house has been in active operation over thirty-three years, being located twenty years in Wilmington, Del., twelve years in Chester County, Pa., and one and one half years in present premises. By strict attention to business, coupled with a just system of dealing, Mr. Quay has built up an influential and permanent trade. He occupies a very neatly and appropriately fitted up store, fully equipped with every necessary convenience for the attractive display of the large and handsome stock of goods on hand. Mr. Quay does all kinds of house, sign and decorative painting, frescoing, and all kinds of plain and fancy decorating, at prices consistent with first class work. A brisk general jobbing business is carried on, and from five to ten first class workmen are regularly employed. Mr. Quay is a native of Chester County, Pa., and a member of the Free and Accepted Masons. He is an artist of no small merit both as a landscape and portrait painter, many of his pictures having elicited the warmest praise. His crayon work is second to none and has given the most complete satisfaction wherever introduced. Mr. Quay is prepared to execute all kinds of banner work and transparencies at shortest notice and undertakes any work that comes within the province of an artist and painter.

WILSON WOODS & BRO., General Upholsterers, No. 4769 Main Street.—Nothing adds more to the beauty and elegance of a house than rich draperies and artistically upholstered furniture. Nothing adds more to the comfort and health of a home than clean carpets and bedding. A prominent house in Germantown engaged in general upholstering is that of Wilson Woods & Bro., located at No. 4769 Main Street. This prosperous business was established by the present proprietors in 1878, and a successful and desirable trade has been established among the first families of this city. They make a specialty of custom work, giving particular attention to the arrangement of curtains, draperies, etc., fine upholstered furniture in great variety, veranda awnings, window shades, etc. They make, alter and lay carpets, repair and polish furniture. They have on the premises their own plant for renovating and purifying hair mattresses and feather bedding removing, all dust and odor from same by a special process of their own; also have their own machinery for cleaning customers' carpets and rugs. The spacious store occupied is conveniently fitted up for the business, and a large stock of goods is kept on hand, including all the latest and most desirable patterns in draperies and upholstering goods. Ten experienced assistants are employed, and all orders are promptly and satisfactorily filled, while the most reasonable prices at all times prevail. The copartners, Messrs. Wilson and Samuel Woods, have had many years' experience in this business, and are possessed of a complete understanding of all its details and requirements. They are both prominent members of the I. O. O. F., and are held in high esteem in the business and social circles of the city.

EDWARD WENDELL, Wholesale Manufacturer of Mouldings and Picture Frames, Mirrors, Wall Pockets, Easels, Engravings Etc., No. 711 North Second Street.—Mr. Edward Wendell, the wholesale manufacturer of mouldings and picture frames, mirrors, wall pockets, easels, etc., has been established in business for the past fifteen years, and during this period has succeeded in building up a trade of great magnitude, extending throughout the States of Pennsylvania, New Jersey and Delaware. From the inception of the business it has always been located on this street, and for the past seven years has occupied the present premises. These comprise three floors, 20x110 feet in dimensions, and are fitted up and supplied with all the latest improved labor saving machinery adapted to this line of manufacture, and furnished with steam power; a force of from sixteen to twenty hands being constantly employed. The goods are manufactured by a process which prevents any chipping or cracking of the overlay. A full line of the products of the manufactory is constantly on hand, and orders of whatever size are promptly filled. The proprietor was born in Ireland, but for twenty-three years has been a resident of this city, and is a thoroughly practical and expert manufacturer.

JOHN C. WILSON, Manufacturer of Cracked Corn and Feed Meal, Wholesale and Retail Dealer in Flour, Feed, Grain, Hay, Straw, Salt, Etc., Nos. 1118 and 1120 South Seventh Street—A reliable and enterprising house in South Philadelphia engaged in the handling of flour, feed, grain, hay, etc., is that of Mr. John C. Wilson. This reliable house is headquarters for the finest grades in each line of goods dealt in. These latter include family and bakers' flour, mill and other feed, grain of all kinds, hay, straw, salt, etc., in addition to which cracked corn and feed meal are manufactured on the premises. The enterprise was established at the same location by the present proprietor twenty years ago, and the distinct success that has since been achieved is largely attributable to the fact that the goods in each line are procured direct from the best sources of supply upon the most advantageous terms, thereby enabling the house to place its customers upon the fairest basis, alike as to price, quality and prompt delivery. The premises occupied are spacious and well equipped with steam power, roller for mill feed and every facility for the due conduct of the business; four skilled hands being there regularly employed. Mr. John C. Wilson was born in Philadelphia, and is a member of the Commercial Exchange.

THOS. COMFORT & SON, Manayunk Brass Foundry, Main Street below Washington Street.—This responsible enterprise is governed by the dictates of long and varied practical experience, which results in the high reputation now enjoyed for turning out the finest and cleanest castings in brass, copper or bronze, strictly accurate according to template, drawing or specification. The business was established as an iron foundry in 1857 by Mr. Thomas Comfort, who in May 1892, gave up iron castings for his present operations and admitted his son, Mr. John Comfort, into partnership; they having been actively engaged in this line for thirty-four years and ten years respectively. The foundry itself, contained in a two story building 29x10 feet, in area, is fully equipped for turning out all kinds of fine crucible work at short notice; two furnaces and all tools and appliances being at hand, and three skilled workmen regularly employed. Of the able partners, the worthy senior was born in Trenton, N. J., in 1831, coming to Philadelphia fourteen years ago from Norristown, where he served his time for four years; while Mr. John Comfort is a native of Manayunk and now twenty-nine years of age.

WOTHERSPOON & SON, China, Glass and House Furnishing Goods, Wooden and Willow Ware, No. 2123 South Street.—This important and enterprising house was established twenty four years ago by Mr. William Wotherspoon, and in 1885 the present firm succeeded, composed of Mrs. Emma Wotherspoon and her son, Mr. James R. Wotherspoon. A special feature of the business consists in the manufacture of Wotherspoon's Watering Pot and the Eureka Fumigator; this latter is a most ingenious contrivance for effectually exterminating bugs and other insects in greenhouses, and the firm are going to exhibit it at the World's Fair. The store, 25x100 feet in area, is finely furnished and most conveniently arranged for the systematic conduct of the business; and customers are promptly and intelligently waited upon by five courteous assistants. The heavy stock carried is complete, and comprises imported and domestic china, glassware, crockery and ceramics of the finest grades of quality, a choice assortment of lamps and lamp supplies, an elegant display of chaste bric à brac, a full line of tinware, kitchen utensils and house furnishing goods, a careful selection of wooden and willow ware, oil stoves of the standard makes, baskets in great variety, garden hose, oil cloth, screens and many other lines far too numerous to mention. Mrs. Emma Wotherspoon is a native of England, and with her son, Mr. James R. Wotherspoon, who was born in Connecticut, reached Philadelphia in 1867.

HISTORICAL AND COMMERCIAL PHILADELPHIA.

P. GROVES' SONS, Furniture, Carpets, Stoves, Oil Cloths, Store Fixtures, Nos. 4218 and 4220 Lancaster Avenue.—This business was established by Mr. G. P. Groves in 1857. Since his death, which occurred in 1886, the business has been very successfully conducted by Messrs. Jas. P., Geo. P., W. P. and John M. Groves, under the above name and style. The business was first located at corner of Forty-third Street and Lancaster Avenue, but has occupied the present desirable location, Nos. 4218 and 4220 Lancaster Avenue, since 1867. The premises comprise three floors, 20x125 feet in dimensions, and the arrangement is convenient and attractive, the stock being so disposed as to afford every advantage to customers. The firm deal largely in furniture, carpets, stoves, oil cloths, store fixtures, etc., all of which are displayed in the greatest variety, embracing all grades from the plainest to the most costly. All the latest and best designs are shown, it being the rule of the house to offer patrons the latest patterns in every department, and to name such prices as bring them within the reach of all. The establishment is handsomely fitted up, lighted by electricity, and presents at all times a brilliant appearance. A corps of competent salesmen is employed. The members of the firm, Messrs. Jas. P., Geo. P., W. P. and John M. Groves, are all natives of Philadelphia, and thoroughly understand the art of pleasing their patrons.

J. & G. F. LIVEZEY, Painting and Painters' Supplies, No. 4699 Main Street, Germantown.—This responsible firm are held in high repute for executing the finest and most reliable work in each branch of the trade, strictly in accordance with instructions, plan, design or specification, whether of the plainest or the most artistic and elaborate; while original designs for ornamental work together with estimates, are cheerfully furnished upon application. The enterprise was established on Main Street in 1872 by the present copartners, Mr. J. J. Livezey and his brother, Mr. G. F. Livezey, who possess a wide range of practical experience in this line ranging over a period of twenty-three years and twenty years respectively. While undertaking all kinds of painting and decorating, the firm's work is seen to the greatest advantage in fine fresco, panel and relief painting, tinting, gilding, ornamentation, sign writing and lettering in the latest styles. The firm have been intrusted from time to time with the fulfillment of some highly important and significant contracts, notably the beautiful interior work on the Market Square Church, the Germantown Club House, the Mannheim Cricket Club House, the Lehigh Valley Building, and a general line of fine residential work all over this section, eighteen skilled painters being regularly employed. The store, which has been occupied for the past five years, is the centre of a large volume of wholesale and retail trade in paints, oils, varnishes, glass and a full line of painters' supplies. Messrs. J. J. and G. F. Livezey were born here in Germantown in 1851 and 1854 respectively, and the former gentleman is a member of the United American Mechanics.

NEWTON WILLARD, Druggist and Apothecary, Corner Main and Cotton Streets, Manayunk.—One of the oldest and best known pharmaceutical establishments in Manayunk is that conducted by Mr. T. Newton Willard. The specialty of the house consists in the preparation of physicians' prescriptions and miscellaneous recipes, which are dispensed with scrupulous care, and only pure, fresh and fully potent drugs and medicines used. Moreover, a large number of high grade pharmaceutical compounds, tinctures, cures, family remedies and other first class proprietary articles are made and put up on the spot, and go to swell the otherwise complete stock always carried. This important business was founded at the same location in 1857 by Mr. S. W. Brown, and for the past four years its continued prosperity has been solely attributable to the sustained efforts of the present proprietor, who graduated at the Philadelphia College of Pharmacy in 1882, and is a member of its alumni. The store itself is of ample dimensions, handsomely furnished, and the carefully selected stock carried embraces every requisite for the successful conduct of a large drug, prescription and family trade. Mr. T. Newton Willard, who has been actively engaged in the profession for sixteen years, is a young man of Pennsylvania birth, and came to Philadelphia ten years ago.

JOHN S. KENNELLY, Furnishing Undertaker, Office and Livery Stables, Nos. 212-220 Queen Street.—The undertaking business of Mr. John S. Kennelly, whose livery and boarding stables are situated at Nos. 212-220 Queen Street is one of the oldest of the kind in this section of Philadelphia. The facilities possessed by this responsible and progressive house are complete for providing any kind of funeral, from the plainest to the most elaborate, at short notice, including the hearses, coaches, carriages, coffins, caskets, palls, shrouds, accessories and all matters incidental to interment, while embalming is also undertaken and executed by the latest approved scientific processes. This business was established at the present proprietor in 1870 on Moyamensing Avenue, whence three years ago it was removed for want of more commodious quarters to the premises now occupied. While enjoying a high reputation as an able funeralist and general undertaker, Mr. Kennelly is held in scarcely less repute for the care he exercises with horses taken in to board by the day, week, or under contract, and for the handsome turnouts he provides, suitable for all occasions. The stables consist of a two story brick building of ample proportions, furnished with loose boxes and stalls capable of accommodating thirty-five horses; efficient light, heat, ventilation, facility of cleansing and perfect drainage being maintained, and every comfort for high bred stock provided. Eighteen horses and several carriages are kept in constant readiness at all hours, and six competent assistants are employed. The worthy proprietor, Mr. John S. Kennelly, was born in Ireland, whence he came to Philadelphia forty-five years ago. He is now a wealthy man, prominent and esteemed in both business and social circles, and is a member of ten different fraternal orders and societies, as well as of the National Funeral Directors' Association, the Philadelphia Funeral Directors' Association, and the Liverymen's Association of Philadelphia.

HARRISON TRYON, Photographer of Machinery, No. 1617 Spring Garden Street.—The business so successfully conducted by Mr. Harrison Tryon was originally established in 1881 by Messrs. Haumer & Tryon, the present proprietor succeeding to the sole control in 1889. He occupies spacious and well equipped premises, and possesses every modern facility for the prompt and efficient execution of all kinds of mercantile work, making a leading specialty of machinery. Several experienced assistants are employed, and everything pertaining to this branch of photography is executed in the highest degree of artistic and mechanical excellence. Mr. Tryon counts among his numerous patrons many leading manufacturers and business men of Philadelphia and vicinity, and is regarded as the leading artist in his line. Mr. Tryon is a native Philadelphian, who received a thorough training with Hemple, the photographer, and who has built up a reputation second to none in the profession.

JOHN J. O'ROURKE, Undertaker and Embalmer, S. W. Corner Tenth and Tasker Streets.—Mr. John J. O'Rourke enjoys a high reputation throughout this section of the city for his thorough ability to meet the requirements of all classes by furnishing funerals complete, from the simplest to the most elaborate. During the eight years of his establishment in this line, Mr. O'Rourke has enjoyed a steady and continuous prosperity, and during 1891 he conducted three hundred and sixty funerals. He provides everything incidental to burial, including the coffins, caskets, hearses, coaches, palls, shrouds and accessories; and, moreover, he undertakes embalming by the latest approved scientific methods, being thoroughly practical in this line. The office, which has been occupied for the past two years, is handsomely fitted, and all orders sent or left there are sure of prompt fulfillment, it being open day and night. The able and energetic proprietor was formerly travelling salesman for a chemical house and pursued a course of studies at the Philadelphia College of Pharmacy. He is a native of this city, and is a member of twenty-two different orders and societies.

HISTORICAL AND COMMERCIAL PHILADELPHIA.

MERINO & CO., Importers and Wholesale Dealers in Wines and Liquors, Nos. 134 and 136 Market Street.—The wholesale trade in liquors has reached a high state of development in Philadelphia, and is one of the leading commercial features of the city. One of the time-tried and honored houses engaged in the business is that of A. Merino & Co., situated at Nos. 134 and 136 Market Street. This widely known establishment, which commands an influential trade and employs four traveling representatives, was founded in 1851 by Mr. A. Merino, and under the firm title of A. Merino & Co. was conducted by him with steadily increasing success up to March 9, 1891, when his death occurred, after a lengthy, useful and honorable mercantile career. He was succeeded by his son, Mr. A. J. Merino, who had been a partner with his father for eight years, and consequently had become fully conversant with all the requirements of the business. The enterprise was first founded at No. 110 South Front Street, a removal afterward being made to No. 128 South Front Street, and the present quarters have been occupied the past year and a half. The premises consist of a five story and basement building, 25x75 feet in dimensions, and it contains a heavy stock of the choicest foreign and domestic wines and liquors, none but strictly first class goods being handled. The firm are sole agents for and make leading specialties of Dr. Harter's Wild Cherry Bitters, "Belle of Bourbon" Famous Sour Mash Whiskey, Walker's Canadian Club Whiskey, and Dr. J. G. B. Siegert & Sons' Genuine Angostura Bitters. Both a wholesale and family trade is supplied, goods are sold free or in bond, in bulk or bottled, and orders are met upon only such liberal terms as an old established house as this only could warrant.

L. HUFF & CO., Dealers in Paper and Paper Bags, Twines and Wooden Dishes, No. 507 North Second Street.—This firm is widely known as wholesale and retail dealers in paper and paper bags, twines and wooden dishes. This prosperous business was established in 1876 by Mr. Geo. Willett, who was succeeded by David Miller, the present firm succeeding to the control in 1890. The spacious store occupied is admirably arranged for the reception and preservation of the immense stock carried, which embraces wrapping paper, paper bags, straw boards, binders' boards, printers' and stationers' supplies, and all those specialties usually handled by a house of this kind. The stock is invariably large and complete, received direct from the most reputable manufacturers. Heavy shipments are made to permanent patrons all over this and adjoining States. The members of the firm are Messrs. C. L. Huff and Edwin U. Haverstick, who were both formerly with the Ide & Haverstick Company. Mr. Huff is a native of New Jersey, and Mr. Haverstick of Philadelphia. These gentlemen are widely esteemed for their abilities as business men, and their success is well merited.

E. HAENCHEN, Pharmacy, No. 3844 Haverford Avenue.—A well known and old established pharmacy in West Philadelphia is that conducted by Mr. C. E. Haenchen. The business was initiated here twenty years ago by Mr. Haenchen, who formerly conducted a similar store for six years at Ninth and Callowhill Streets. A specialty is made of the preparation of physicians' prescriptions and miscellaneous recipes, besides which a number of tinctures, emulsions and proprietary articles are compounded on the premises. The store is spacious and finely fitted up; the heavy and carefully selected stock carried embraces a full line of everything usually to be found in a first class drug and prescription store, and two only qualified assistants are in regular attendance upon customers. Mr. C. E. Haenchen, who is a middle aged gentleman of German birth, is a graduate of the Universities of Munich and Erlangen, is a registered pharmacist in this city, and a member of the Philadelphia College of Pharmacy and of the American Pharmaceutical Society.

EZRA MOLL, Cash and Credit House (G. G. Heiserman, Manager), No. 2320 Germantown Avenue, Third Door below York Street.—A well known and reliable cash and credit house in the northern section of Philadelphia is that of Mr. Ezra Moll, dealer in Brussels and ingrain carpets of the latest styles and designs, floor and table oil cloths, window shades of all sizes, hanging and other lamps in great variety, rugs, mats, matting, floor cloths, wash wringers, carpet sweepers, clocks for the mantelpiece, hall, etc., looking glasses, blankets, quilts, counterpanes and household linen; a large and carefully selected stock being always on hand, affording an abundance of choice in each line. The enterprise was established in 1881 by Messrs. E. and J. D. Moll, and since 1889 Mr. Ezra Moll has been sole proprietor. The active management of affairs is intrusted to the able direction of Mr. G. G. Heiserman, a young man of Philadelphia birth, who has held this position for the past three years. The premises utilized comprise a well fitted store, 20x50 feet in size, and two floors above of like dimensions; three competent assistants being regularly employed. Mr. Ezra Moll was born in Berks County, Pa., and is a member of the United American Mechanics.

ANDREW BLUM, Tailor, No. 4808 Main Street.—One of the leading merchant tailors in Germantown is Mr. Andrew Blum, who has long been held in high repute for turning out garments which for style, material, fit, finish and correct fashion for the existing season of the year are at least equal to those of any other house throughout the entire city. The business was established in 1868 on Main Street by the present proprietor, who is a practical tailor with forty-six years' varied experience at his command, and as a cutter and designer is a recognized expert. The active management of affairs is intrusted to his son, Mr. Joseph A. Blum, who executes a large proportion of the cutting, and has been actively engaged in this line of business since he was fifteen years of age. The trade controlled reaches all over this section of the city, and fourteen skilled operatives are kept busily engaged the year round. The store, 25x40 feet in size, which has been occupied for the past eighteen years, is finely furnished and conveniently arranged; and here is always to be found a large and select stock of imported and domestic woolens, worsteds, etc., affording an ample choice for each kind of garment required. The worthy senior, Mr. Andrew Blum, was born in Germany in 1832, and reached Philadelphia in 1853, having come to the United States in 1851. The able manager, Mr. Joseph A. Blum, is a native of this city and now thirty-one years of age. Mr. Andrew Blum is a member of the Independent Order of Odd Fellows, and his son is a member of the Republican Club, as also of the German Maennerchor.

GEORGE S. ROWBOTHAM & SONS, Dry Goods, Notions, Boots, Shoes and Clothing, Nos. 4212, 4214 and 1216 Lancaster Avenue; Branch Store, No. 5152 and 5154 Lancaster Avenue.—This business was established at No. 4212 by Geo. S. Rowbotham in 1876. His two sons, Messrs. J. P. and Geo. W. Rowbotham, being admitted to partnership, the present firm name was adopted in 1886. In 1891, owing to the rapid increase of business, branch stores were opened at Nos. 5152 and 5154 Lancaster Avenue. In 1892 the establishment at No. 4212 was rebuilt and elegantly fitted up. It is lighted by electricity and supplied with a cash carrier. The fine assortment of dress goods in silks, satins, velvets, woolens and cottons, embraces all the latest styles, and designs of both European and American production. In linens and muslins, hosiery, underwear, laces, ribbons, embroidery, edgings, etc., the stock is particularly attractive, as are also the trimming, notion and glove departments where the latest novelties are shown at the very lowest prices. The firm also keep a large stock of boots, shoes and rubbers, received direct from the best manufacturers; also a full and complete line of ready made clothing. Twenty clerks and salesmen are in attendance. The premises comprise three floors, having 75 feet front on Lancaster Avenue, and the display of elegant goods in the large plate glass windows as well as in the spacious interior attracts crowds of sightseers as well as regular customers. The firm is composed of Messrs. Geo. S. Rowbotham and his two sons, J. P. and Geo. W. The senior partner is a native of England, but came to America when but nine years of age, while the sons are natives of Philadelphia.

HISTORICAL AND COMMERCIAL PHILADELPHIA.

HULTZ BELTING COMPANY, No. 129 North Third Street.—The supply of belting is one of the most important in connection with mechanical work, and forms any individual industry of leading value in the business world. One of the largest concerns in the United States engaged in the trade is the Shultz Belting Company, whose main office and factory are at St. Louis, Mo., while branches are maintained at New York, Boston, Chicago, Philadelphia, San Francisco, Mobile, New Orleans, etc., etc. The branch at Philadelphia is conducted by Mr. James Garnett and Mr. A. M. McComb, both practical business men, well versed in the knowledge of belting manufacture and the uses of belting. The establishment here is a four-story building at No. 129 North Third Street, where a full stock of the Shultz Belting Company's goods is carried. They are also sole agents for the sale of Bavdick's stove supplies, Caldwell's conveyors, all kinds of perforated metals, corrugated steel fasteners, elevator buckets and bolts, oak tanned, cotton and rubber belting, and general mill supplies. They are the manufacturers of the National Pulley Covering, and only from them can this covering be obtained. They give personal and prompt attention to all orders and correspondence, and will cheerfully attend to any business intrusted to them, although it may not be in their regular line. The reputation throughout the country of the Shultz Belting has been fairly won and steadily maintained, and it stands to-day without an equal for any class of work. Their woven leather belting for dynamos and generators in electric power stations has largely superseded other link belts. Taken all in all, the Shultz Patent Fulled Leather Belting is the very best that has ever been placed on the market. Parties needing a first-class belt will serve their interests best by sending their orders to No. 129 North Third Street, Philadelphia, James Garnett, manager.

INNERTY, McCLURE & CO., Wholesale Druggists and Manufacturing Chemists, No. 112 Market Street.—The wholesale drug establishment of Messrs. Finnerty, McClure & Co., of No. 112 Market Street and No. 7 Letitia Street, occupies a foremost position in the trade, and its management is characterized by ability, enterprise and energy. The business was founded in 1890 by the present copartners, Messrs. E. J. Finnerty, Jr., David McClure, F. H. Heritage, and L. D. McClure, under the existing firm-title. They bring thorough experience to bear. Mr. David McClure was for five years a member of the firm of Budd, Butterworth & McClure, and Mr. Heritage was also connected with that establishment. Mr. Finnerty was for a year the leading member of the firm of E. J. Finnerty Jr. & Co. Messrs. E. J. Finnerty, Jr. and L. D. McClure are graduates of the Philadelphia College of Pharmacy. The firm are members of the Philadelphia Drug Exchange. Mr. Heritage is a native of New Jersey, and his colleagues were born in this city. The premises occupied comprise a four-story and basement building, 20x100 feet in dimensions, which is filled with a large and superior stock of drugs, chemicals and pharmaceutical preparations of all kinds, perfumery, patent medicines, roots, herbs, barks, paints, oils, glass, etc. The firm are proprietors and manufacturers of Finnerty's W. C. & H. Expectorant, Finnerty's Sarsaparilla, Finnerty's Beef Iron and Wine, Finnerty's Cramp and Diarrhœa Mixture, Finnerty's Liver Granules, Penn's White Liniment, Horn's Eye Ointment, Brewster's Horse and Cattle Powder, McClure's Magic Liniment, Champion Root Beer, Champion Gold Paint. They are also sole agents for Michener's German Dyspepsia Lozenges, Nichol's Balm and Fir Balsam and Arnica Plasters, Japanese Pile Cure and Dr. E. C. West's nerve and brain treatment. The firm employ fifteen assistants and three traveling salesmen, and are prepared to meet all orders upon the most liberal basis.

MERICAN MANUFACTURING COMPANY, M. T. Maguire & Co., Proprietors, Sole Manufacturers of "Oleite of Iron," A Superior Dressing for Harness, Buggy Tops, Etc., Office and Factory, No. 431 Race Street.—A superior article—known under the name of "Oleite of Iron"—has its source of production in this city, being made by the American Manufacturing Company, whose office and factory are at No. 431 Race Street. "Oleite of Iron" is the invention of Mr. M. T. Maguire, who is a native of this city, popularly known in social and business circles. It is now two years since he introduced the preparation to the attention of the public, and during that time it has steadily come into use in all parts of the United States and Canada and the demand continues to steadily grow in volume. "Oleite of Iron" is a superior leather dressing in paste form, is not a soap, and is guaranteed never to get hard in frosty weather or soft in warm weather. It is put up in one pound and smaller size cans, handsomely labelled, with full directions for use, and retails at twenty-five and fifty cents a can. It contains nothing to injure leather, being free from turpentine, lampblack or acid. By one application harness, buggy tops, carriage curtains, satchels, etc., are oiled, dyed and polished and rendered soft and pliable and look like new. It does not soil the hands, horse's skin or blanket. In this one respect alone it shows its great superiority over other dressings on the market; such as black harness soap, lye preparations, greases, etc., no necessity to use soaps of any description, black or white. The peculiar properties possessed by "Oleite of Iron" renders the gloss or polish produced more lasting and will not fade or tarnish by handling. "Oleite of Iron" can also be used on horse's and cow's hoofs to prevent them from cracking and to cure cracked hoofs; also on belting, gum or leather; patent leathers, etc., and is absolutely waterproof. One pound box of "Oleite of Iron" is sufficient to dress from fifteen to twenty-five sets of harness, whether they are old or new, coarse or fine; then they are oiled, dyed and polished all at one time, making it the best and cheapest dressing on the market. "Oleite of Iron" has never failed to give entire satisfaction in every case all over the United States and the Dominion of Canada. Please send for a sample box, or for a dozen boxes, in order to convince yourself of the superior qualities of "Oleite of Iron." Manufactured and sold in any desired quality by the American Manufacturing Company, No. 431 Race Street. Agents wanted in every city and town in the United States and Canada. A force of from 300 to 400 hands is engaged in the manufacture of this article, their labors being supervised by the general superintendent, Mr. W. H. Kinkel. The output is a heavy one, a large stock is carried and all orders, large or small, alike meet with the same fulfillment. The American Manufacturing Company buys and sells for cash only; therefore they sell their goods at bottom prices—terms, cash. Thousands of testimonials from all parts of the United States and the Dominion of Canada can be procured at the office and will be mailed free to any person who desires to see them.

HISTORICAL AND COMMERCIAL PHILADELPHIA.

EO. C. MASON & SON, Architects, Office, No. 1010 Drexel Building.—Among the best known firms engaged as architects in the United States is that of Geo. C. Mason & Son, whose headquarters are at Newport, R. I., and who have a Philadelphia office at No. 1010 Drexel Building. The firm is certainly a responsible one, and receives a highly flattering measure of recognition, its patronage extending throughout Rhode Island, New York, New Jersey and Pennsylvania. The business was established at Newport in 1858 by Mr. Geo. C. Mason, In 1865 his son, Geo. C. Mason, Jr., entered his office and, when he had mastered the profession, was in 1871 admitted to a partnership interest. Both gentlemen are natives of Newport, R. I., and are favorably known to architects in all parts of the country. Mr. Mason, Jr., is a director of the American Institute of Architects, and is First Vice President of the Philadelphia Society of Architects. The branch in this city was opened by the Messrs. Mason in 1885. The firm are prepared to make plans for buildings of every description, giving special attention to residences, business blocks, church edifices and high class structures, and guarantee the utmost satisfaction. Designs, specifications, etc., are furnished at short notice, while construction is personally supervised, and all work undertaken by these gentlemen is certain to be performed in the most expeditious, careful and superior manner. One of the latest important works done by the Messrs. Mason was the building of the U. S. Naval War College at Newport. They have also built residences in all sections of the States above mentioned, and in every instance their services have given the utmost satisfaction.

DWARD MULLIGAN, Fine Rye Whiskeys, S. W. Corner Tenth and Christian Streets.—Among the many undertakings engaged in the great liquor traffic of Philadelphia, a prominent place is occupied by the old and responsible house of Edward Mulligan, located at the southwest corner of Tenth and Christian Streets. The facilities possessed by this house for procuring the finest qualities of imported and domestic wines and liquors direct in each line are complete, and thus purchasers are placed upon the fairest basis, alike as to price, quality and prompt delivery. By these means a heavy volume of a wholesale trade has accrued, reaching throughout Pennsylvania and New Jersey among retailers, hotels, clubs, restaurants and a legion of private families, and the house now enjoys a wide reputation for the uniform reliability of the liquors, etc., handled, and for straightforward methods in all dealings. The business was established at the same location in 1861 by the present proprietor, who is agent for the Star and Crescent Distillery Company, of Peoria, Ill., and himself travels periodically among customers. The heavy and carefully chosen stock carried—both duty paid and in bond—comprises as leading lines fine old rye and Bourbon whiskeys, gins, brandies, rums, California wines, and the standard brands of bottled beers, as also a full line of European wines and spirits; while an especially selected assortment of wines, liquors and beers is always on hand, in bottle, etc., suitable for invalids and for family use. The premises utilized comprise three spacious floors, each 20x100 feet in area, well arranged and fully equipped for the systematic conduct of the business. The worthy proprietor, Mr. Edward Mulligan, is a native of Ireland, and a member of the Wholesale Liquor Dealers' Association of Philadelphia.

EORGE C. PRICE, Expert Watchmaker, No. 720 Sansom Street.—As an expert watchmaker and repairer of fine watches, Mr. Geo. C. Price has no superior in this city. He has been engaged in the business here since 1861, and has built up a high reputation and a large and influential patronage throughout Pennsylvania, New Jersey, Maryland and the District of Columbia. He gives special attention to the repairing of fine watches and clocks for the trade. He alters watches from slow to quick rate, adjusts them to the changes of heat and cold, and guarantees his work. He occupies both spacious and commodious quarters, employing a number of skilled assistants. Mr. Price is a native Philadelphian, who has given constant attention to his trade since 1861, and is known and honored as a leader in his line and a member of the F. & A. M.

. M. WALKUP, Carpenter and Builder, Office and Shop, No. 825 Filbert Street.—The many important operations in which Mr. A. M. Walkup, carpenter and builder, has been engaged from time to time are abundant testimony of his thorough ability to undertake any branch of this leading industry, and to faithfully and accurately interpret architects' plans and designs, whether for heavy or light construction. The business was established in 1882 by Mr. A. M. Walkup, who possesses a thoroughly practical and technical knowledge of the business and is, moreover, a talented designer, most of his own plans being of his own creation and execution. The trade now controlled reaches throughout the State of Pennsylvania, and although all branches of building and carpentering are equally undertaken, from the erection of a church to general jobbing and repairing, a leading specialty is made of the finest descriptions of hardwood working, such for instance as the complete fitting up of banks, offices, counting houses, stores and business premises generally, a line in which Mr. Walkup is enabled to render more than usual satisfaction. The office and shop, 25x75 feet in area, are well equipped with the finest facilities and appliances pertaining to the industry, and many skilled mechanics are regularly employed. In addition to this flourishing business, Mr. Walkup acts as the duly accredited Philadelphia representative for Messrs. C. D. Gottschalk & Brother, mill workers, whose plant and factory are at Lansdale, Pa. Mr. Walkup is a native of the Quaker City, and is a member of the Free and Accepted Masons, and the Independent Order of Odd Fellows.

. N. ALEXANDER, Manufacturer of Stained Glass, No. 320 Harmony Street.—A reliable and very successful house engaged in this city in the manufacture of stained and other glass is that of Mr. S. N. Alexander. All kinds of stained and leaded glass for churches and residences, as well as memorial and figure windows, are manufactured in the best styles, to any design, from the simplest to the most richly elaborate, and a specialty is made of bevelled plate for dwellings. The enterprise was established five years ago by the present proprietor, who is thoroughly practical in this line of trade, and personally directs the prompt and accurate fulfilment of all orders, and the faithful reproduction of plans and designs. The premises utilized comprise three spacious floors, furnished with a kiln and a full equipment of machines and appliances, of the latest improved pattern, pertaining to the industry. Special designs and estimates are prepared and furnished for any kind of work upon application, and the prices charged are at all times fair and reasonable. Mr. Alexander is a native of this city and learned his trade here.

HAS. F. HOSER, Electric Power Printer, No. 1958 Main Street.—The largest mercantile and job printing office in Germantown is that owned and conducted by Mr. Charles F. Hoser. A specialty is made of magazine printing for any number of weekly or monthly copies, in addition to which the operations of the house include job work of every description, mercantile printing, stationery and blank book manufacture, binding in the latest styles, numbering, perforating, tableting, ruling, bronzing, engraving and lithography; the printing being executed with modern fonts of type to any design and in all colors. The business was established in 1877 by Mr. J. M. Whitby, who was succeeded in 1887 by Messrs. Hoser Brothers, and in March, 1891, it was assumed by the present proprietor, he having been actively engaged in the trade for the past ten years. The printing office, occupying the second and third floors at the location named, is furnished with three largest size job presses, using electric power, and other machines and appliances pertaining to the industry, four skilled assistants finding regular employment there. Mr. Charles F. Hoser was born in Germantown in 1868, was educated at the public schools here, and is a member of the Sons of Temperance, the Ancient Order of Foresters, the Junior Order of United American Mechanics, and the Independent Order of Odd Fellows.

HISTORICAL AND COMMERCIAL PHILADELPHIA.

ILSON & RAUGHLEY, Wholesale and Retail Flour, Feed, Grain, Hay, Straw, Etc., No. 4241 Germantown Avenue, Nicetown.—Although but recently founded, within the past year, by the above gentlemen, this business has secured an enduring hold on the people of this community, and is rapidly developing a large and extensive trade throughout this section of the city, as well as Germantown and the adjacent districts. The premises occupied comprise two floors in a large and commodious building, 28x100 feet in dimensions, and this is perfect in convenience of arrangement for the handling and storage of the large stock at all times carried, while the exigencies of the business are such as to require the services of three assistants and two teams in constant employment. A specialty is here made of the very best grades of family flour, including the patent roller process, also feed of all kinds, grain, hay, straw, etc. All orders receive immediate attention, and hay is sold by the bale or carload, the business of this house being of both a wholesale and retail character, and continues to show a steady and firm growth. Messrs. Wilson and Raughley are worthy leaders in this line, and are both natives of Delaware, but have resided in this city for the past two years.

J. & W. JONES, Dyers and Scourers, Main Office and Works, No. 2108 Germantown Avenue; Offices, Ninth and Vine Streets; No. 1018 Columbia Avenue. There is little doubt but that the oldest established dyeing and scouring business in the whole United States is that conducted by Messrs. J. & W. Jones. This veteran undertaking was founded as far back as 1840 by Mr. Edward Jones. In 1859 his sons, Messrs. J. and W. Jones, succeeded; in 1890 Mr. W. Jones died, and the following year Mr. J. Jones retired in favor of his son, Mr. William Jones, the present sole proprietor. The firm undertake a general line of dyeing and cleaning, such as that of the Staten Island Dye House. Fabrics of various kinds are dyed in the piece in any color; garments of every description, feathers, trimmings, etc., are also dyed and cleaned, and a specialty is made of dress goods for men and women. The house enjoys an established reputation for turning out the finest and most reliable work promptly and at reasonable prices. The dyes, chemicals and other compounds employed are selected with scrupulous care, so as to produce fast, bright colors and the most efficient cleaning without undue injury to the fabric. The premises at No. 2108 Germantown Avenue comprise two floors, each 33x82 feet in area, with a handsomely furnished office in front. The works are fully equipped with improved machinery, appliances and accessories pertaining to the industry, a twenty horse power steam engine being the motive force used and fourteen skilled operatives are regularly employed. The trade controlled reaches throughout the city and adjacent districts, and three wagons are kept busily engaged in making deliveries. Mr. Wm. Jones is a thoroughly practical dyer of long and varied experience. He is a native of the Quaker City and is a member of the Free and Accepted Masons.

H. BALLANTINE, M.D., Pharmacy, S. W. Cor. Tenth and Morris Streets. The old established pharmacy of Mr. C. H. Ballantine, situated at the corner of Tenth and Morris Streets, is the centre of a permanent, substantial business conducted largely with private residents throughout this section of the city, and it is now freely recognized as a reliable and efficient dispensary for pure, fresh and potent drugs, chemicals, medicines and family remedies. The store was first opened twenty years ago by a Mr. Bell, and since 1882 it has been conducted under the able and very successful direction of the present proprietor, who graduated at the Philadelphia College of Pharmacy in 1880, and at the Jefferson Medical College in 1882, the preceptors being Mr. George M. Ward and Prof. Rogers, to the latter of whom Mr. Ballantine acted as assistant in chemistry at the Jefferson College for four years. The specialty of the business consists in the preparation of physicians' prescriptions and miscellaneous recipes, and the handsomely appointed store, occupying a commanding corner position, contains a very complete and select stock of everything necessary to the systematic conduct of a large drug, prescription and family trade, toilet requisites and perfumes being in especially fine assortment. The talented proprietor is a middle aged gentleman of Philadelphia birth, a member of the Knight Templars and of the Free and Accepted Masons.

F. P. SHERRY, Painters' Supply House, N. W. Corner Twenty-first and South Streets.—Among the many responsible houses engaged in Philadelphia in the handling of painters' supplies that of F. P. Sherry, although not one of the largest, is nevertheless held in high repute for handling exclusively the most reliable grades of goods in each line. The trade is conducted at both wholesale and retail with painters, dealers and other consumers. This progressive enterprise was established five years ago by the present proprietor, who was brought up to this line of business and possesses fifteen years' practical experience. A full line of painters' supplies as well as other goods are kept in stock, chief among the whole being dry and ready mixed paints in abundant assortment, paint pigments, oils, brushes, varnishes, castile soap, gold paint, ammonia, witch hazel, sponges, chamois and glass and artists' materials. A store 20x30 feet in area is occupied, as also a basement for storage purposes. Mr. F. P. Sherry, who was born on Lombard Street, in this city, is still a young man and a member of the Knights of Pythias and the Independent Order of Odd Fellows.

R. WOLLENBERGER, One Price Merchant Tailor and Clothier, S. E. Corner Eleventh and South Streets.—The well known and popular one price merchant tailoring and clothing establishment of R. Wollenberger is one of the oldest in this section of Philadelphia. The business was established by the present proprietor in 1867 with one store, but eighteen years of energetic and persistent attention to the development of the trading connection necessitated the enlargement of his facilities and accordingly in 1885 the store at No. 85 was taken in; thus the premises now occupied comprise two commodious stores, 40x50 feet in area, with two stories above of the same dimensions. Ten courteous assistants are regularly employed and the stock carried embraces a carefully selected line of fine imported and domestic woolens, suitings, and trouserings, in accord with the prevailing popular fashion. Mr. R. Wollenberger is a native of Germany, a man of middle age, and came to the United States in 1849. He is a thoroughly practical tailor, and possesses correct taste and judgment in the cutting and fashioning of clothing, and a member of several German societies.

S. B. LENHERT, Livery and Boarding Stable, Nos. 3470 and 3872 Lancaster Avenue.—One of the best equipped livery and boarding stables in West Philadelphia is that conducted by Mr. S. B. Lenhert, which is well known for affording comfortable quarters for all kinds of horses, particularly fine road stock. The stables are still better known, however, as a headquarters for fine turnouts for all occasions; nine horses are kept in constant readiness at all hours, as also broughams, landaus, victorias, etc., suitable for funerals, weddings, parties, shopping, making calls and park driving; each vehicle being accompanied by a competent coachman attired in a neat and attractive livery. Everything around the stables is strictly first class; they were erected by the present proprietor in 1889, and were specially constructed with every regard for ventilation, uniformity of temperature, drainage and facility of cleansing, and they are provided with electric lights, concreted floor and a full equipment of stable requisites, elevator, etc. The whole premises, which front on both streets, comprise three floors, each 35x180 feet in dimensions, containing stalls and loose boxes capable of accommodating forty horses, two harness rooms, carriage repository, office, ladies' waiting room and storage for fodder. Mr. S. B. Lenhert is a native of Lancaster County, Pa., still a young man, and is a member of the Philadelphia Liverymen's Association.

TEXTILE MACHINE COMPANY (Limited), Builders of Textile Machinery, Nos. 2300 to 2308 North Eighth Street.—This flourishing enterprise had inception in 1883, when the business was established by the Lemaire Feeder Company, who conducted it up to 1888, when the present limited copartnership was organized. The Textile Machine Company, Limited, of which George Remsen is chairman, J. L. Kendhart, secretary, and G. Himelspark and W. T. Leech, managers, is an incorporated concern, and has a cash capital of $75,000. The gentlemen above named are all men of practical skill and thorough experience in the line indicated, and are experts in the construction of machinery for cotton, woolen and carpet mills. They are builders of textile machinery of every description, and their productions are in extensive use throughout the United States and Canada. The machinery turned out by this company is of a distinctly superior character, their specialty,

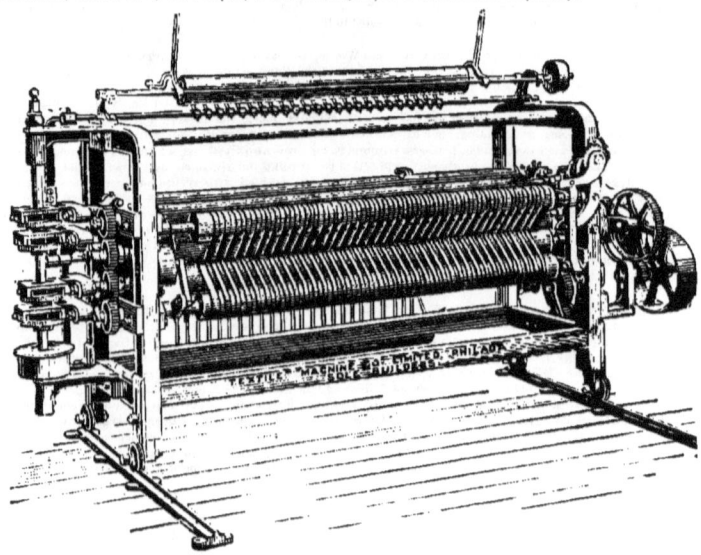

The Bolette Condenser.

The Bolette Condenser, being an appliance of exceptional merit, constituting the best dividing and rubbing motion known. They are sole manufacturers of the Bolette Condenser. These condensers are now so well and favorably known that comment on their merits is superfluous. They are now an acknowledged success, and the majority of the leading mills of the United States are using them. They are furnishing large numbers to mills located in every State in the Union. The numerous improvements that have from time to time been suggested in practice are all embodied in the machines of their late manufacture, making them less complicated, stronger and more easily handled. Those they are now building are so perfected (the result of long experience) that they are universally acknowledged to be superior to any machine of the kind on the market. Their latest patent consists of an appliance for giving the blades a backward and forward movement and side motion at the same time. Another improvement is their new eccentric, which enables them to run the condenser at a much greater speed, thus giving all the rubbing required for any grade of stock. The one doffer system is now coming largely into use, its many advantages securing for it a very general adoption. For this system the Bolette Condenser is preëminently suited, giving as is well known, a uniform quality of roping, no such distinction known as tops and bottoms being produced, necessarily making better yarn, better spinning, and increased production with less waste.

The Ingraham Harness Motion is a novelty lately manufactured by this company. This new harness motion is now being introduced to the trade, and is known as the Ingraham Harness Motion, and is built especially to be fitted on old looms, making them practically fancy machines, at a very small investment. It has been submitted to the most severe tests, always with entire satisfaction, and we take pleasure in calling the attention of manufacturers to its adaptability for all kinds of work. The Ingraham motion is positive in its action, moving the warp up and down by the action of the jacks, requiring no springs or weights to form part of the shed. It is an open shed machine, hence easier on the yarn, as it only changes that portion of the warp required for each pick. It has a leveling attachment which brings the warps all up to the top of the shed, and facilitates taking out broken picks and mending broken threads the loom can then be started without any further adjustment of pattern chain or other parts and without losing a pick. It is easier for inexperienced hands to run than any other harness motion, because of its simple construction, and its being impossible to break any part by a backward motion of the loom. Each jack has an independent automatic lock which is not dependent on any other part of the motion. The manufacturers using them have found these machines capable of very superior work; even on plain goods, they find that it covers better than the roller loom, and saves its cost in strapping and labor on the fancier weaves of the latter. It is easily attached and adjusted to almost any make of loom. There are now in use about six hundred of these motions on eleven different makes of looms, varying in reed space from thirty-two inches to one hundred inches, and they can be made from sixteen harness up to any number the loom can accommodate. It has fewer parts and greater wearing surface than any other harness motion on the market. It has been in use for over a year by some of the largest and most progressive manufacturers in the country, giving them entire satisfaction, as it will weave the finest silk as well as the heaviest woolen or worsted goods. The builders have this motion attached to a loom, and will be pleased to show the machine in active operation to any one calling at their works.

HISTORICAL AND COMMERCIAL PHILADELPHIA.

The Kershaw Feeding Machine for second breaker and finishing cards, which is not surpassed by anything of the kind produced in this country, is also made a specialty of, and all their productions are in widespread and growing demand. The Textile Machine Company, Ld united, is prepared to build all classes of machinery and accessories for cotton, woolen and carpet mills, on the most favorable terms, and guarantee the utmost satisfaction, having first class facilities, and all orders are executed in the most expeditious and trustworthy manner. The works occupy two 50x100 foot floors, at No. 2300 North Eighth Street, and are thoroughly equipped in every respect, while thirty-five to forty skilled workmen are employed in the establishment.

We wish to call attention to the New Kershaw Feeding Machine for Second Breaker and Finisher Cards, which we have recently placed upon the market, being an entirely new and far superior feed to any heretofore built. This machine, we claim, will save from five to ten per cent of the stock, by preventing a large portion of the waste ends, and on some work entirely dispensing with same; this claim we are prepared to substantiate by actual tests. It prevents the bunching in of the stock, and feeds it evenly in a *flat* condition to the board. The improvement which does this work can readily be placed upon Apperly Feeds now in use. The following description of the machine will convey to practical readers some notion of the method of its operation: The feeding is received from the second breaker in a traversing apron about four inches wide. This carries the material to the draw rolls, which receive it and press it into a condition so that it will hold its own weight while being carried up by the overhead rigging to the feed. In this process the stock is a flat web about four inches wide, and very loose and open, having had nothing to solidify it but the pressure of the draw rolls. The traverse rolls now take the web. These rolls are usually six inches long, and they lay the stock diagonally across the machine. While the rolls traverse in a diagonal manner they are in fact held at about right angles with the carding cylinder. The precise angle at which they are placed will be regulated by the character of the stock being worked. The object aimed at is to have the edges of the feed as nearly as may be in a straight line. Set in any other manner, there would be a serious loss of stock in the waste ends, and this machine proposes to prevent such waste to a degree hitherto difficult to attain. The machine is remarkable for the evenness of the stock delivered from the finisher. The stock is taken from the second breaker doffer just as fast as it is delivered, and in the same condition, and it is placed positively upon the feed board without the least particle of tension. Any given number of inches of the web occupy the same number of inches on the board, and every part of the board is covered alike, and the material is carried to the feed rolls in the same manner. There is no drawing from one side to the other, caused by the action of the licker in drawing the stock through the feed rolls, which always causes one side to be heavier or lighter than the other in the delivery from the doffers. In the operation of this machine all parts are delivered alike, and it is practically impossible to get an uneven delivery. The condition of the stock thus passing under the feed rolls is necessarily superior. It is always loose and open, not rolled by the doffer and passed through the tube to be twisted like a rope. The saving of labor and trouble thus effected will be appreciated by every practical man. This process gives perceptibly better carding with smaller effort, and this, of course, means better spinning and better yarn. There is no lumping in from the feed rolls where this machine is used. Where small lickers in are used to prevent this, long stock ordinarily cannot be properly handled. But with this machine even a small licker in will give better results, although the best results are secured with a licker in of, say, eight inches. This machine is nowgiving entire satisfaction in the mills where it has been introduced. We shall be pleased to show it to any one interested at any time, either at our works or in the mills in operation.

The Acme Doffer Comb has an even stroke, without vibration; in consequence breaking of sliver or web is overcome, being a feature long sought for, and as yet possessed by no other make of comb, and has the following valuable points: 1. A comb is set for a two inch stroke; it will not overreach and make a two and one half inch stroke, either above or below the adjustment. This is an improvement that cannot be over estimated, making the comb adaptable to all kinds of work, whether for wool, cotton, silk or worsted. 2. "The Acme Doffer Comb" is the only comb that can be successfully applied to either a woolen, cotton, silk or worsted card, a self-recommending feature. 3. A noiseless doffer comb has long been a want with manufactures, and although several makes of combs have been put on the market for which this has been claimed, the "Acme" is the only one that fills the bill. 4. The accuracy with which the "Acme Comb" can be adjusted to doffer, and then remaining in position after months of wear, is another point of which too much cannot be said. 5. All lost motion is taken up by means of set screws, which are easily and rapidly adjusted. 6. The speed of the comb, to which particular attention was given by the inventor, embodies the sum and substance of the different good points claimed for this comb. They also make a special line of iron doffers, with steel shaft two and three sixteenths inches diameter, running all the way through the cylinder.

M WEINERT & CO. Successors to GILBERT & WEINERT, Commission Merchants and Dealers in Fruit and Produce, S. W. Corner Front and Vine Streets. There is no doubt that the commission business of Philadelphia, in its several departments, presents a field for the exercise of business enterprise second to no other commercial industry, and that the energy displayed by those engaged in this line has done much toward developing the commercial importance of the city. A representative house engaged in the fruit and produce branch of the trade is that of Wm. Weinert & Co., at the southwest corner of Front and Vine Streets. This establishment was founded eight years ago by Messrs. Wittig & Gilbert, who were succeeded by Messrs. Gilbert & Weinert, and in May, 1891, Mr. Weinert, who had formerly been manager for the founders, became sole proprietor, adopting the trade name of Wm. Weinert & Co. He is a native Philadelphian and has had an experience of some twenty years in the fruit and produce trade, which has made him fully conversant with all its details and requirements. He receives consignments from New York, New Jersey, Pennsylvania, North and South Carolina, Georgia and Florida, and supplies an active demand that comes from all sections of this State, New Jersey, New York, Delaware and New England. The premises occupied consist of a four story and basement building, is conveniently arranged for the prompt transaction of business. Mr. Weinert is a general commission merchant and wholesale dealer in foreign and domestic fruits of all kinds, and makes a leading specialty of pineapples and New York State small fruits. Not the least of the advantages accruing to shippers of goods to this house lies in the fact that no quantity is too large for the firm to handle, and all consignments may be immediately drawn against, while the policy governing Mr. Weinert's management has always been characterized by making the interests of the trade identical with his own.

LOUIS S. FISKE & CO., Commission Wool Merchants, No. 31 South Front Street and No. 35 Letitia Street.—In this historical review of the great commercial interests of Philadelphia special attention has been devoted to the details of the rise and progress of the wool commission trade, and to the securing not only of accurate statistical facts, but likewise of the interesting details of the growth of the representative houses, to which the city is so greatly indebted. One of the prominent representatives of the trade is the firm of Louis S. Fiske & Co., with warehouse at No. 31 South Front Street, extending through to No. 35 Letitia Street, and four other warehouses. The active proprietors are Messrs. Louis S. Fiske and Frank H. Keen, while Mr. John Dobson, of the famous carpet manufacturing firm of John & James Dobson, this city, is a special partner. Mr. Fiske has been in the wool trade since 1808; Mr. Keen since 1877. The firm of Louis S. Fiske & Co. was organized in 1882, and under its able management has advanced to a foremost position among its contemporaries, and acquired influential connections, as well as a large, steadily growing trade. The five spacious warehouses occupied are of large dimensions, and a large corps of hands is employed in the handling of stock. The firm are commission dealers in domestic wools, receiving consignments from all the States and Territories, and a large active demand is supplied. All grades are handled and orders of any magnitude are promptly met at fair quotations. The firm are members of the Manufacturers' Club, Union League, and other organizations, and they have ever given a conscientious support to all measures best calculated to advance the permanent welfare and prosperity both of the trade and the community at large.

HISTORICAL AND COMMERCIAL PHILADELPHIA.

BRONSON & CO., Commission Merchants and Dealers in Broom Corn, Manufacturers' Supplies and Machinery, No. 233 North Water Street.— One of the oldest houses in the country engaged in this trade is that of Bronson & Co., which is an offshoot of an establishment founded in 1828, in Montgomery County, New York State, by Mr. Geo. W. Bronson, who, at his death was succeeded by his sons, three in number. One of these, Mr. E. D. Bronson, retired from the copartnership in 1878, came to this city, and with his two sons, Messrs. W. T. and E. A. Bronson, organized the firm of Bronson & Co. The copartners are all natives of Montgomery County, N. Y., but reside in Philadelphia. The business premises comprise four floors, each 25x250 feet in dimensions and equipped with all conveniences for the storage and manipulation of stock. The Messrs. Bronson are commission merchants and general wholesale dealers in broom corn, receiving the same from Illinois, Iowa, Nebraska, Kansas and Missouri, and they handle from 800 to 1,000 tons a year. The firm also deal in manufacturers' supplies and machinery, and in all the departments of their business are prepared to offer to the trade the most substantial advantages.

MATTHEW McCAULEY, Fashionable Boot and Shoe Maker, Stores, No. 1631-33 South Street.—The well known and reliable boot and shoe house of Mr. Matthew McCauley is not only the oldest on this busy thoroughfare, but ranks among the oldest in the entire city, for it was established by the present proprietor in 1858. A high reputation now attaches to the house for the genuine and uniformly reliable nature of the whole of the footwear sold, alike as to style, lateness of fashion, fit, comfort, durability and reasonable prices; and the heavy and carefully selected stock carried embraces an ample choice in the finest grades of ladies', gentlemen's, misses', youths', boys' and children's boots, shoes, slippers, rubbers, gaiters and sundries. In addition, custom boot and shoe making to order to exact measure is undertaken and every care and attention is paid to all branches of fine repairing. The premises comprise a handsome double store, 30x60 feet in area, well arranged for the systematic conduct of the brisk trade carried on; three competent assistants being in regular attendance upon customers. Matthew McCauley, who is a thoroughly practical shoe maker, was born in Ireland, came to Philadelphia forty years ago and now owns the whole building in which his stores are located.

JAMES W. BEW, Furniture, Carpets, Bedding, House Furnishing Goods, Wall Papers and Window Shades, No. 3351 and 3353 Ridge Avenue.— Mr. Bew embarked in this business for himself in 1880. The large and commodious double store occupied has the dimensions of 50x100 feet, and is attractively appointed throughout and perfect in convenience of arrangement for the handling and display of the immense stock at all times carried, while three courteous and efficient salesmen are in constant attendance. In the comprehensive assortment will be found parlor, library, hall, bed and dining room furniture from the plainest to the most expensive and elaborate styles and designs, also everything in the line of carpets of all grades in all the latest and most fashionable patterns of the day, bedding, window shades, oilcloths, lamps, hardware, wall papers in the greatest variety of artistic designs, and house furnishing goods of every description. In each department of the store the entire stock has been most carefully selected from the latest novelties in the market. Mr. Bew is a man of entire probity in all his dealings.

Mrs. MARY A. HAROLD, Dry Goods and House Furnishing Goods, No. 917 Passyunk Avenue.— This business was established twenty-two years ago by Francis Harold, at No. 949 Passyunk Avenue, and has since his death been continued by his widow, the present proprietor. The premises occupied were erected in 1888, and consist of three floors and a basement, each 20x75 feet in area, well fitted and arranged for the due prosecution of business. A large and carefully selected stock of dry and fancy goods, together with a full line of house furnishing goods of every kind and description, are offered for sale at prices that compare favorably with those of other responsible dealers, either for cash or on the system of easy weekly payments. Mr. J. S. Harold, who is a son of the proprietor, is responsible for the able and efficient management of affairs.

L. A. TREICHLER, Apothecary, Main and Penn Streets. Mr. L. A. Treichler has been identified with the apothecary business since 1865. Twenty years ago he first embarked in this line of professional industry on his own responsibility at Reading, this State, but in 1874 he removed to this city, where he has since been located. His store, 15x40 feet in measurement, is conveniently appointed and perfectly equipped throughout with special reference to the business. In the large and complete stock handled will be found a carefully selected assortment of pure and fresh drugs and chemicals, proprietary remedies of acknowledged worth, pharmaceutical preparations, toilet articles, soaps, sponges, perfumery, all the requisites used by physicians, etc., and all of the very highest standard character. Mr. Treichler puts up a general line of pharmaceutical compounds himself, makes his own tinctures, tonics, fluid extracts, etc., and devotes special attention to the prescription department, every care being given to the compounding of physicians' orders, and also to the filling of difficult formulas. He is a vigilant and responsible druggist and apothecary of the highest standing in the profession, a native of this State, and a graduate of the Philadelphia College of Pharmacy, besides being a member of its Alumni Association and the State Pharmaceutical Board.

JOHN G. SCHULER, Carpenter and Builder, Haines and Watson Streets.— One of the oldest established carpenters and builders in Germantown is Mr. John G. Schuler, whose operations consist largely in the erection of residences. Jobbing and repairing in all branches of this trade receive the promptest and most careful attention, also in addition to which the fitting up of offices, stores, saloons and other business premises is equally undertaken and executed in the best possible manner, in all the fancy hardwoods, to any style or design, from the plainest to the most artistic and elaborate. The business was established at the same location by the present proprietor forty years ago, and the trade now controlled necessitates the regular employment of ten skilled mechanics. The workshop, 40x60 feet in dimensions, is fully equipped for the execution of fine work on short notice, and among the various contracts undertaken may be mentioned the addition to the Germantown Poor House. Mr. John G. Schuler was born in Germany in 1827, whence he came to this city forty-two years ago, and is a member of the Free and Accepted Masons, the Independent Order of Odd Fellows and other prominent societies.

C. A. BROBST, Paints, Oils, Varnishes, Glass, Etc., No. 2830 Germantown Avenue. This flourishing enterprise was established by the present proprietor in 1888, and it has since steadily and continuously developed in both the volume and scope of its operations, until it is now regarded as the headquarters hereabouts for the best and most reliable qualities of dried and mixed paints, oils, varnishes, paint pigments, French and American window glass, artists' materials, gilders' and painters' supplies, brushes, etc. The handsome double bulk store, 30x60 feet in area, is finely fitted up with electric lights and other superior fixtures; a heavy and carefully selected stock is always on hand, affording an ample choice in each line, and the prices charged are at all times fair and reasonable. Mr. C. A. Brobst is a gentleman of middle age, was born in Pennsylvania, and is a thoroughly capable man in his business. He has had about thirty-five or forty years' experience both as a practical painter and artist, and has had charge of the painting department of the North Penn. and B. B. division of the Philadelphia and Reading railroad, also the Woodruff Palace Car Company's painting department, etc.

HISTORICAL AND COMMERCIAL PHILADELPHIA.

ONAWAY & CO., Commission, Butter, Eggs, Poultry, Game, Live Stock, Green and Dried Fruits, Apples, Potatoes, Onions and Hay, No. 310 North Front Street.—Among the representative firms contributing to the activity of the produce commission industry of Philadelphia is that of Conaway & Co., whose office and warehouse are at No. 310 North Front Street. The business of this house was inaugurated in 1881 by the present proprietor, Mr. Wm. B. Conaway, who has had twenty-one years' experience in the commission trade, and the thorough knowledge of the same possessed by him, together with his business ability and energy, has naturally resulted in the upbuilding of a large, active, and permanent, first class trade. The building used for business purposes has four floors, each 20x75 feet in dimensions, and is equipped with an elevator. Mr. Conaway is agent for the Farmers' Alliance of Pennsylvania, Maryland and New York State, and carries on general transactions as a wholesale commission merchant in butter, eggs, poultry, game, live stock, green and dried fruits, making a leading specialty of apples, potatoes, onions and hay. Consignments are received from New York, Pennsylvania, New Jersey, Delaware and Maryland. All interests placed with this time tried and reliable house are certain to be handled in the most judicious and trustworthy manner, while all orders are promptly and reliably executed. Mr. Conaway was born in Maryland, but has resided in Philadelphia twenty-five years. He is a member of the Fruit and Produce Exchange, and enjoys the confidence and good will of the entire business community.

LYON, LICHTEN & CO., Manufacturers of Fine Glazed Kid. Salesroom, No. 31 North Fourth Street; Factory, Orthodox Street and Frankford Creek.—The manufacture of leather has long been one of Philadelphia's prominent trade industries, and has attracted the time, capital and ability of some of the city's most progressive business men. A representative house engaged in this field of usefulness is that of Messrs. Lyon, Lichten & Co., whose office and salesroom are at No. 31 North Fourth Street. This establishment was founded twelve years ago by J. P. Matthews & Co., the firm later changing to Paschall. Lichten & Co., next to Paschall, Lichten & Lyon, and in September, 1891, the present firm was organized, the copartners being Gustave Lyon and Jonas Lichten. The former is a native of France, the latter of Philadelphia, and they are well known in commercial and financial circles, while in the leather trade they sustain an A1 status. Their products go to all points lying between Massachusetts and Missouri. The factory, located at Orthodox Street and the Frankford Creek, is equipped with all requisite machinery and appliances, and employment is found for 150 experienced workmen. Messrs. Lyon, Lichten & Co., manufacture fine glazed kid, and the output is a very large, as well as a very superior one. A heavy stock is at all times carried, and business relations established with this firm are certain to prove profitable to patrons.

JOHN T. PALMER, Book and Commercial Printer, No. 406 Race Street.—In this review of the industrial and commercial enterprises of Philadelphia, special mention should be made of the enterprising and reliable establishment of Mr. John T. Palmer, located at No. 406 Race Street, which was established by the present proprietor in 1880. This gentleman has had many years' experience in this business and is prepared to execute all work in the line of book and commercial printing in a highly satisfactory manner. The premises occupied comprise a floor, 65x115 feet in dimensions, equipped with five cylinder and ten job presses, and employment is furnished to forty expert hands. Everything in the line of book, job and mercantile printing is executed in the very best style of the art at short notice, special attention being given to fine catalogue work. Having a complete pamphlet bindery in connection the proprietor is able to keep prices at a minimum, while he exercises close personal supervision over every feature and detail of the business, a postal card being promptly answered and, altogether, Mr. Palmer receives an extensive and flourishing patronage. Mr. Palmer is a native Philadelphian and a gentleman of enterprise, energy and entire probity in his dealings, as well as of practical skill, and is in fact largely endowed with the qualities that bespeak success in all the walks of life.

JOSEPH McKEE, Manufacturing and Dispensing Chemist, No. 4032 Lancaster Avenue.—The pharmacy of Mr. Joseph McKee, situated at No. 4032 Lancaster Avenue, has speedily come to be recognized as a reliable dispensary for all kinds of drugs, chemicals, medicines and family remedies; for it was opened to the public as recently as August 6, 1891, and now controls a liberal share of the best trade hereabouts. The store is handsomely appointed in every detail, with oak fixtures, soda fountain, mirrors and other superior fittings; four fully qualified assistants are in regular attendance upon customers, and the carefully selected stock carried embraces a full line of everything usually to be found in a first class drug and prescription store. A branch is maintained at Twenty-third and Callowhill Streets, initiated in 1888, and is conducted on the same excellent lines as those which govern the parent establishment. Mr. Joseph McKee, who is a young man of New Jersey birth, originally studied with Mr. H. F. Seeley here, graduated at the Philadelphia College of Pharmacy, and is a member of its alumni association, as also of the Apothecaries' Union of Philadelphia.

J. SUMMERS, Dry Goods, Trimmings, Boots, Shoes and Trunks; also a full line of Ladies' and Children's Trimmed Hats, Nos. 3322 and 3324 Germantown Avenue.—The foundation of this reliable house dates back to 1862, at which time it was established by Mr. John Summers, who conducted it up to 1888, when he retired, and his son, the present proprietor, succeeded to the control of the business. The large and commodious premises occupied comprise a store of ample dimensions, devoted to the dry and fancy goods department, also a salesroom, covering an area of 20x40 feet, for the handling of trunks and fine foot wear, and employed in constant attendance are from three to five competent and polite assistants. The large and comprehensive stock is displayed to the best advantage, and embraces everything in the line of dry and fancy goods in all the newest styles, fashionable designs and novelties of the day, also trimmings, ladies' and gentlemen's furnishings of every description, trunks, traveling bags, etc., and boots and shoes in all sizes and grades, together with rubbers and slippers. A specialty is also made of ladies' and children's trimmed bonnets and hats of all the most fashionably correct styles. Mr. Summers is also agent for the "New Home" sewing machine and McCall's patterns, of which he carries a complete stock. He is a native of this city and a reliable and responsible young business man.

W. HELFFRICH, Boarding Stables, at the Intersection of Powelton Avenue, Thirty-eighth and Warren Streets.—Five years ago Mr. Helffrich first established himself in this business on Lancaster Avenue, but in the mean time, having built his present stables, he took possession of them in 1890, and his career from the outset has been one of steady progress and success. This large and commodious building, which comprises two floors, is fitted up in the most modern style with all the latest improvements, and affords ample capacity for sixty head of horses, besides ample accommodations for carriages, etc., while the services of a large force of experienced and efficient stablemen are required in permanent attendance. He has also in connection with his boarding stables a first class livery, where all the latest styles of equipages, in light, family vehicles, are for hire, with courteous and attentive drivers always in attendance, at reasonable rates. Open night and day. It also contains an elevator, and the stables are thoroughly drained, lighted and ventilated, and perfect as regards sanitary arrangements. A specialty is here made of boarding horses, by the day, week or month, and in every instance these animals invariably receive the best of care, food and attention from the grooms in attendance, and the rates charged are always the most fair and reasonable. Born in Berks County, this State, Mr. Helffrich has resided in Philadelphia for several years past. He is an expert judge of horses and thoroughly experienced in all branches of this business.

HISTORICAL AND COMMERCIAL PHILADELPHIA.

GEORGE HEYSER, Clothing, Nos. 1828 and 1830 Lancaster Avenue. Heyser's large clothing house is freely recognized as the cheapest and most reliable establishment of the kind in West Philadelphia. The business is divided into two main departments; one for the merchant tailoring, and the other for the sale of ready made clothing. The former comprises the making to order of a very superior line of fashionable garments, of superfine imported and domestic fabrics, of the highest finish and of the correct style for the existing season of the year; the changes made being as low as stock prices elsewhere. These garments are guaranteed equal in all respects to the best turned out by any other responsible house, and are particularly suitable, on account of their low cost, for clerks, salesmen, drummers, and others whose respective positions demand a neat and stylish appearance upon limited means. In the ready made department is always to be found a rich assortment of spring, summer, fall or winter clothing, according to the season, of the latest styles, for gentlemen, youths, boys and children; men's nobby all wool suits costing $10, light and heavy overcoats, spring goods, blazers, hunting suits, sporting jackets, breeches, etc., being offered at equally reasonable prices; while Fauntleroy jackets and pants are made to order to exact measure from $2.50 to $5.00. This important and progressive enterprise was established in 1888 by the present sole proprietor, Mr. George Heyser, who in that year erected the building known as the Music Hall, of which he occupies the first floor and basement, each 40x160 feet in dimensions. A stock of foreign and American cloths and trimmings is always on hand, suitable for any kind of garment being worn at the time. An elegant display is also made of fine grade clothing of the newest styles and patterns. Rock bottom prices are the salient feature of the establishment, and eight courteous salesmen are in constant attendance upon customers. Mr. George Heyser is a native of Maryland, whence he came to Philadelphia sixteen years ago.

ISAAC TOWNSEND, Manufacturers' Agent for Silver Lake Company's Steam Packing and Solid Braided Sash Cord, No. 263 North Third Street.—Both as an industrial art and as a commercial pursuit, the manufacture of window sash cord, etc., is of such prominent importance as to call for a favorable notice in a work of this kind. This class of goods is so generally used, that an industry engaged in turning out a line of goods surpassing all those on the market is essentially worthy of mention. A representative and noteworthy house extensively engaged in the manufacture of braided window sash cord, metal tent slips, swivels for flag halyards, and a general line of cordage, is that known as the Silver Lake Company, whose office and salesroom in Philadelphia, under the able and careful management of Mr. Isaac Townsend, the selling agent, are located at No. 263 North Third Street. This was established in 1871 at No. 112 North Third Street, but has been in the present place since 1874, and consists of a commodious store, of ample dimensions. The salesroom is well equipped, and fully stocked with the company's goods. These goods are unrivalled for quality, finish, durability and excellence, and have no superior in the American market, while the prices quoted are as low as the lowest. An extensive trade is carried on in selling large quantities of cordage, etc., to jobbers in the city and vicinity. Mr. Townsend has a patent swivel for flag halyards. The swivel was patented in 1880, and is a great improvement on the old way, having clamps for the head and foot of flags, preventing the twist in halyards, and allowing the flags to shift in changing winds. Mr. Townsend is a native of New Jersey, and has resided in this city for the past fifty two years.

S. W. GADD, M.D., Druggist, No. 1155 South Eighth Street. The pharmacy conducted by Dr. S. W. Gadd, at the corner of Eighth and Federal Streets, is one of the oldest established and best patronized in this section of Philadelphia, and it is now freely recognized alike by private residents and the medical profession as a reliable store for absolutely pure, fresh and potent drugs, chemicals, medicines and family remedies. Moreover, Dr. Gadd's eminent position and qualifications as a fully qualified physician insure the compounding of prescriptions and miscellaneous recipes in an accurate and satisfactory manner, while the several cures, proprietary articles of the late Dr. Burden, and pharmaceutical preparations which he makes and puts up in his laboratory are held in high repute for their efficacy and genuine reliability. The store was first opened in 1857 by Dr. Andrew M. Burden, and since 1884 its continued prosperity has been wholly attributable to the sustained efforts and skill of the present proprietor, who graduated at the Philadelphia College of Pharmacy in 1880 and in medicine at the University of Pennsylvania in 1885, his preceptors being Drs. Judson Daland, and A. C. Deakyne. The finely furnished pharmacy contains a large and especially complete stock of everything necessary to the successful conduct of a first class drug, prescription and family trade, and two duly registered clerks are in regular attendance upon customers. Dr. Gadd now controls an extensive and influential practice in this section of the city, and his wide research and thorough mastery of the profession are constantly exercised to the permanent benefit of all those who seek his aid and advice. Dr. Gadd is a native of England, but is a naturalized citizen of the United States, and member of the Independent Order of Odd Fellows, as well as of the alumni associations of the college and university from which he was graduated.

HENRY M. WEAVER & SON, Manufacturers of Fine Cigars, and Jobbers in Chewing and Smoking Tobacco, No. 155 North Sixth Street. The old established and popular house of Henry M. Weaver & Son, located at No. 155 North Sixth Street, was founded by Henry M. Weaver in 1876. In 1883 the son was admitted to partnership and the present firm name adopted, and they have occupied the present desirable location since 1876. The firm are jobbers of chewing and smoking tobacco and manufacturers of fine cigars. Buying only the finest grade of leaf, and buying it only when suited to their trade, enables the house to turn out a superior grade of goods and thus keep up its reputation. The superior brands manufactured here are in great demand by the trade and are so well known that they sell themselves. The house has every facility for turning out fine goods, employing only skilled workmen and using only good material, which has been properly cured and correctly put through all the processes that go to make good tobacco. The firm pay particular attention to their hand made Havana stock. Every leaf is examined before it is worked, and the very finest results are obtained, all of which has helped to place the concern where it is, among the leaders. The members of the firm, Messrs. Henry M. and Geo. W. Weaver, are both natives of this city and enjoy an excellent reputation for industry, integrity and correct business principles and methods.

J. P. SULLIVAN, Conveyancer and Real Estate Broker, Etc., No. 4825 Germantown Avenue. Mr. J. P. Sullivan, the well known conveyancer, real estate and insurance broker, is among the most popular in this line in this section of the city. Mr. Sullivan, who is a native of Philadelphia, first embarked for himself in the real estate business here in 1886, and has since met with the most gratifying results. The accessible office is very tastefully and neatly furnished with all the necessary conveniences, and the transactions of this concern include all the departments of a general real estate and insurance business, such as the buying, selling, renting and leasing of property of all kinds, or management of estates, the collection of rents and other incomes, conveyancing, the negotiation of loans in bond and mortgage and the investment of funds. Upon the books will be found all classes of property throughout Philadelphia, Germantown and Nicetown, a specialty being made of that in the Twenty eighth and Thirty third Wards, and Mr. Sullivan's long experience, coupled with his intimate knowledge of the values of residential and business property throughout this section, render his advice and judgment particularly valuable to intending investors. He is always prepared to draw up deeds, mortgages and other legal instruments in the most careful and satisfactory manner, and is a commissioner for the State of New Jersey, as well as a notary public, which he was made in 1891. Being also a licensed insurance broker, and sub-agent for the Ætna Insurance Company, he carries on a most extensive business in this line, effecting risks on all classes of insurable property immediately, at the lowest rates compatible with safety, and all trusts committed to him are discharged with great fidelity and to the complete satisfaction of all concerned.

HISTORICAL AND COMMERCIAL PHILADELPHIA.

M. L. CLOWER, Germantown Market House, No. 4807 Main Street.—For the period of twenty-five years intervening between 1867 and the present time the name of Wm. L. Clower has been conspicuously prominent as one of the representative merchants of Germantown, his "Germantown Market House," being the largest establishment of the kind in this section of the city. Mr. Clower was born in England, but has resided in Philadelphia the past thirty-five years. He is a member of several mercantile associations, and is popularly known in the community. The premises occupied comprise buildings and lot covering an area of 40 x 250 feet. The neatly kept store is 40 x 60 feet in size. To the rear of this are the ice machines for cooling the basement, which is used for cold storage purposes, while back of the ice machines is the slaughter house, all the meats sold by Mr. Clower being killed on the premises, and he handles only the finest stock raised in the State. In the proper season from fifty to one hundred hogs are cut up daily, and a large business done in curing hams and shoulders, and making sausage, lard, and other hog products. Employing from fifteen to twenty assistants, and running five wagons, Mr. Clower conducts a wholesale and retail trade as a dealer in prime meats of all kinds, also poultry, game, vegetables, butter and eggs. The trade extends all over the city and vicinity, and customers have their wants supplied at the very lowest prices.

WEED & JESSON, Machinists' Die and Press Tool makers and Manufacturers of the Acme Button Fasteners, Thermometer Fittings, Clock Wheels, Umbrella Springs, Etc., No. 208 New Street.—Messrs. J. K. Weed and J. B. Jesson, who compose this firm, are gentlemen in the prime of life, active and energetic. The former is a native of this city, and the latter was born in England. Both are practical mechanical engineers, machinists and toolmakers, of some thirty odd years' experience, and are masters of their art in all its branches. They have been established since 1885, and were formerly located on Third Street, removing to No. 208 New Street about three years ago. The shop, which is on the first floor, is 30 x 100 feet in dimensions, and is equipped with ample steam-power, improved lathes, drills, shapers and all needed appliances. The facilities here are first-class, and half a dozen skilled workmen are employed. The firm are manufacturers of Acme Button Fasteners, thermometer fittings, clock wheels, umbrella springs, etc., and their trade, which is large and constantly growing, extends throughout the United States. Special machinery is designed and built to order, and machinists' die and press tools are made for jewelers, silversmiths, opticians and metal workers in general. All work turned out in this establishment is warranted to be strictly first-class, satisfaction being assured in every instance, while the prices charged are of the most reasonable character, and all orders receive prompt and personal attention.

GEORGE W. SUNDERLAND, Real Estate Broker, No. 432 South Sixth Street.—Choice and eligibly located properties have always been and will continue to be sought after as the safest and most profitable form of investment for capital, and the trade in realty in this city is one of vast magnitude and importance. Prominent among the real estate brokers stands Mr. George W. Sunderland, whose office is eligibly located at No. 432 South Sixth Street. He has been engaged in this business since 1882, and brings to bear a wide range of practical experience and an intimate knowledge of the various sections of the city. He has always upon his books descriptions of the most available bargains in houses, stores and building lots, and is prepared to effect purchases, sales, and exchanges of real estate on commission, while procuring loans at the lowest rates upon bond and mortgage, collecting rents, securing good and responsible tenants for stores and dwelling-houses, and also cares for numerous properties on behalf of the owners, either resident or non-resident, giving them the benefit of his skill and experience. Mr. Sunderland is a native Philadelphian and a young man of high social and business standing, whose connections are of the most superior character, and whose efforts to serve the best interests of his patrons have resulted in the development of a large and permanent patronage.

FERDINAND KELLER, Importer and Dealer in Foreign and Domestic Antiques, Manufacturer of Hand-made Furniture in Antique Styles; Salesrooms, Nos. 216 and 220 South Ninth Street; Factory, No. 311 Griscom Street.—Within the last half century or so has grown a public demand on the part of people of refinement for antique furniture, for the original productions where such were available, and also for reproductions of the same. In the eighteenth century the art of furniture making had reached the acme of perfection; royalty and wealth had encouraged the industry until perfect marvels of workmanship were produced. With the decline of royalty and the advent of the "People," these rich creations fell into disfavor, and at the beginning of the present century specimens of antique work could be had for a mere nominal price. These same specimens now command almost fabulous prices. One of the foremost Philadelphia houses engaged in handling goods in this line is Mr. Ferdinand Keller, whose salesrooms are at Nos. 216 and 220 South Ninth Street and his factory at No. 311 Griscom Street. Mr. Keller was born in Germany, where he first learned the cabinet-making trade, under his father's guidance, and he has ever made a study of art in furniture. In 1880, he came to this city and established business here. In this venture he has met with well-deserved success, winning a reputation of enviable character, and building up a select trade all over the United States, while he has also filled orders received from the Sandwich Islands. Mr. Keller is proficient in the English, German and French languages, and annually he pays a visit to Europe, searching the markets for goods for his establishment, and he never fails to return with a choice assortment. Mr. Keller is an importer and general dealer in foreign and domestic antiques and manufacturer of hand-made furniture in antique styles. His salesrooms are well worthy a visit. They contain thousands of antiques, including from an Indian tomahawk, an old flint-lock gun, to a full suit of armor of the sixteenth century. There is much to please and interest here. Mr. Keller gives employment to sixty hands, and all who visit him are certain to be courteously received, and to carry away pleasant recollections.

HISTORICAL AND COMMERCIAL PHILADELPHIA.

DIAMOND GLASS COMPANY, Bottles and Vials, Office and Salesroom, No. 235 Race Street; Works, Royersford, Pa. The manufacture of glass bottles and vials in this State is an industry second to none in importance, and in point of capital invested and amount of labor employed it ranks among the highest. The fragile nature of the product necessarily compels a large output to fill the large demand for these goods. For thoroughly first-class work in this line, promptness in executing contracts and general reliability, the Diamond Glass Company of Royersford, Pa., with an office and salesroom in Philadelphia, is without a peer in the State. This prosperous business was established in 1882 and is now a model of its kind. The copartners, six in number, bring great practical experience to bear upon this industry, their practical knowledge of every detail thus enabling them to meet the requirements of the most exacting and critical customers. Their vast works cover about five acres of ground, and present an animated appearance when in full blast. Three hundred hands are employed, eighty of whom are first-class glass blowers. The output of these works challenges rivalry. They manufacture largely every imaginable kind of bottle or vial, special designs and private mold ware being made to order at the lowest market prices, and all goods are guaranteed to rank with the best in elegance, finish and durability. At the Philadelphia office and spacious salesroom, at No. 235 Race Street, can be seen a full line of the concern's manufactured wares. This depot has been established since 1891, the company's growing trade rendering it imperative. Messrs. I. M. Schellinger and A. A. Murray, two members of the firm, are in charge of the works. The other four, Messrs. Charles Raiser, J. A. Fredricks, J. W. Hiller and W. J. Ralston, are active at the works at Royersford. The Philadelphia branch supplies the Eastern Virginia and Southern trade, while shipments are made direct to other parts of the country from factory. The Diamond Company is rapidly gaining fame and fortune and it is earning all it gets through strictly legitimate business methods.

ALBERT A. REDIFER & BRO., Successors to John J. Redifer, Last Manufacturers, No. 210 New Street. An old and time-honored house in this city and one that has gained widespread popularity is the firm of Albert A. Redifer & Bro., successors to John J. Redifer, manufacturers of boot and shoe lasts. The history of the concern reaches back to 1835, when it was established by John J. Redifer, the father of the present members. Albert A. succeeded to the business in 1888, and, in the early part of 1891, he admitted his younger brother, Oscar L. They are both young men and were born in Philadelphia. The senior partner, Albert, has been identified with the house for seventeen years; in fact he was raised in it and learned his trade there practically and thoroughly. The extent of his social acquaintance may be judged when it is stated that he is prominently connected with no less than fourteen or sixteen societies—among them the Order of Red Men, of which he is the past great sachem for the State of Pennsylvania and the Order of the Golden Eagle, of which he is past chief knight. He also occupies a high and honorable standing in the lodges of the Odd Fellows, Free Masons, Knights of Pythias and in the Legion of the Red Cross. Upon succeeding to the business the young Messrs. Redifer found a large and established trade. With characteristic energy they were not willing to stand upon this. They infused new blood into the business and galvanized the old concern with new life, gradually increasing their trade until they are now receiving orders from all parts of the United States. They have fully maintained the past reputation of the house, turning out none but the best work, superior in quality and of the most approved pattern. Their factory occupies three floors of the building, No. 210 New Street. Each floor is 20 x 50 feet in dimensions, and supplied with steam-power and the latest modern machinery. Fifteen men are employed who turn out about 300 finished lasts a day.

FRANCIS P. ROGERS & SON, Tin, Iron and Copper Ware Manufacturers, Southwest Corner of Ninth and Locust Streets. The manufacture of tin, iron and copper ware has developed a great activity in this city within a few years and now takes an important position among the other industries. An old, well-known and successful house in this line is that of Francis P. Rogers & Son, at the southwest corner of Ninth and Locust Streets. This business was founded at No. 937 South Sixteenth Street, away back in 1857, by Mr. Rogers, who can now point to a flourishing trade built up to its present large proportions through his experience ranging nearly forty years. He does all kinds of furnace work, fireplace heaters, etc., sets up and repairs heaters, paints and points old roofs, and attends to all kinds of jobbing. Mr. Rogers does an extensive manufacturing business in tin, iron and copper ware, dairy fixtures, metallic roofing and patent rain spouting. He has well-equipped and commodious workshops, including three floors, each 20 x 50 feet in dimensions. None but skilled assistants are employed, who are afforded every facility, in the way of improved machinery, for turning out first-class work. The proprietor is a practical mechanic and personally supervises all the details of the business. At the Centennial Exposition he drew the first premium for the best exhibit in his line on dairy fixtures, having no competition.

HORACE T. POTTS & CO., Iron and Steel, No. 215 North Second Street.—Among the firms engaged in the handling of iron and steel in Philadelphia this is one of the oldest and foremost in its line in the city, and maintains an excellent reputation. It was established about eighty years ago, by William L. Potts, who was succeeded by his son, Thomas I. Potts, and then by Horace T. Potts, who, some ten years since, took into partnership Walter W. Cook. In January, 1892, Harrison J. Potts, son of the senior member, acquired an interest in the business, as did also at the same time Adam J. O'Hara. The firm are commission merchants and manufacturers' agents, and sell extensively to blacksmiths and wagon-makers throughout Pennsylvania, New Jersey, Delaware and the States adjoining. They represent the Diamond State Horse Shoe Company, the Frontier Steel Works and other concerns, and handle a general line of merchant iron and steel, Norway iron being a specialty, and they do both a wholesale and retail trade. They occupy a 25 x 125 feet floor and employ an efficient staff. A heavy stock is constantly kept on hand here, and all orders receive prompt attention, while the prices charged are invariably the lowest. Mr. Horace T. Potts, the head of the firm, is a prominent member of the Iron Merchants' Association of Philadelphia and also of the Bourse.

HISTORICAL AND COMMERCIAL PHILADELPHIA.

THOMAS BUCK & CO., Manufacturers of Plain and Fancy Hosiery, Southwest Corner Mascher and Somerset Streets.—The growth of the hosiery industry in this section of the city has been especially notable during the past decade, and a number of noteworthy firms have come to the front in the line indicated hereabouts within recent years. Among these there is none more worthy of special mention than that of Thomas Buck & Co., whose well-equipped factory is situated on southwest corner of Mascher and Somerset Streets. They are manufacturers of plain and fancy cotton hosiery of a superior quality, making a specialty of ladies' wear, and their productions are in extensive and growing demand. They have first-class facilities, and turn out a very excellent class of goods, which are handled by jobbers in Philadelphia, New York, Chicago and the principal cities in the West. This enterprising and prosperous firm was established in 1889, and was formerly located at Fourth Street, above Somerset, moving to the present place about two years ago. The premises here occupied are spacious and commodious and are provided with ample steam-power, 270 knitting machines, 35 sewing machines, etc., while 130 hands are employed. Mr. Buck, the head of the firm, is a young gentleman, and a Philadelphian by birth. He is a man of thorough practical skill and many years' experience in this line, active and energetic, and exercises close personal supervision over the entire business.

REIFSNEIDER BROS., Manufacturers of Parlor Furniture, Couches, Etc., No. 138 North Second Street.—This firm is by general assent a prominent and responsible one, manufacturing a class of medium and cheap grades of furniture of exceptional excellence. Messrs. W. O. and Geo. F. Reifsneider are young men and natives of this city, the former being a thoroughly practical upholsterer of long and varied experience. They established business in 1885 as retail dealers in this line, but two years ago discontinued that branch and began manufacturing for the trade. For the purposes of business they occupy four floors at the above address, each 25 x 60 feet in area, fully equipped for turning out a line of furniture of any quality. They are prepared to turn out all classes of work required by the trade, of the highest quality of excellence, at short notice and at prices safe from successful competition. Messrs. Reifsneider Bros. are able to place their output on the market with the assurance that it is the best of its grade which thorough system and expert workmanship can turn out, while in style and design it is unexcelled. Messrs. Reifsneider are to be congratulated on the success they have achieved by their efforts.

CALLOWHILL BEEF COMPANY, Receivers and Commission Merchants in Swift's Chicago Dressed Beef and Mutton, H. A. Wood, Manager, Corner of Callowhill Street and Delaware Avenue.—Swift's Chicago dressed beef is now so well known to the trade and public in general that its merits are universally recognized and the demand for the products handled by this great Chicago concern is steadily increasing. The Philadelphia branch of the house was established seven years ago, and has been in the management of Mr. H. A. Wood, who conducts operations under the firm-name of the Callowhill Beef Company, and occupies a building at the corner of Callowhill Street and Delaware Avenue. The premises are in direct communication with the railroad and from seventeen to eighteen car loads of beef are landed here every week. The premises are equipped with an overhead railway and cold storage facilities and five car loads, or 150 head of cattle can be stored here. A large stock of Swift's famed Chicago dressed beef and mutton is at all times carried, and the trade supplied, which is exclusively wholesale, extends throughout Pennsylvania, New Jersey and Delaware. Sixteen hands are employed and orders of any magnitude are filled at lowest market quotations. Mr. Wood, who resides in this city, is a thoroughly practical butcher and expert judge of meats, and also a business man of energy, enterprise and ability. He has built up a large, superior trade, and in the business circles of the community he is known and esteemed for his liberal policy and sterling personal worth.

H. CATON, Manufacturer of Barrels, No. 106 East of No. 401 Vine Street.—The oldest and leading house engaged in the cooper's trade in Philadelphia is that conducted by Mr. J. H. Caton, who is a manufacturer of barrels and an extensive buyer and seller of the same. The business was founded over one hundred years ago by Mr. Hugh McGee, the present proprietor succeeding to the control in September, 1872. The building owned and occupied by him was built 125 years ago and contains three floors, 30 x 60 feet each, all well equipped for the business and supplied with every facility for conducting all operations upon a large scale. An extensive and complete stock of barrels and cases is kept on hand, from which the trade is supplied in quantities to suit at the shortest possible notice. Barrels are bought and sold, cases are strapped to order and the largest contracts are executed with the utmost dispatch. Mr. Caton is a native Philadelphian, a member of the Red Men, the I. O. O. F., and the A. O. U. W., F. and A. M., Druids and Shields of Honor, and an experienced and practical cooper who has built up an extensive patronage in this city and throughout the United States.

McFARLAND, Steam Packing Box Manufacturer, Nos. 12, 13 and 14 Fetter Lane.—Among those who have gained an excellent reputation in this line of business may prominently be mentioned Mr. A. McFarland, the steam packing-box manufacturer of Nos. 12, 13 and 14 Fetter Lane. This business was established in 1888, when it was known under the style of McFarland & Kees, and so continued until March, 1892, when Mr. McFarland assumed sole control. Being untrammeled, he has since then given the business a great impetus and has added new prosperity to an already prosperous concern. All sorts of packing-boxes are manufactured by him, but his specialty lies in the making of the largest sizes. For this work Mr. McFarland has every facility at his commodious workshops, which occupy three large floors, furnished with steam-power and fitted up with the best and most approved machinery, rendering it an easy matter to fill at short notice the largest orders. Ten experienced workmen are employed and have plenty to do to keep pace with the steady demand for boxes. He has always on hand a heavy stock of second-hand cases which can be bought at very moderate prices. Besides this Mr. McFarland does a large jobbing trade. He is a middle aged man, a native of Ireland, is also a prominent member of F. and A. M., also I. O. O. F. of this city, and has been a resident of Philadelphia since 1873. He is a practical workman and his success is mainly due to the careful supervision of all goods and work turned out from his shop.

HONGLER & BREADY, Cotton and Wool, Noils, Worsted, Woolen and Cotton Waste, No. 111 Arch Street.—In this utilitarian age when everything may be used to advantage, the trade in cotton and wool has become a most important feature of commerce. One of the most important Philadelphia houses engaged in this line is that of Messrs. Hongler & Bready, whose warehouse is at No. 111 Arch Street. The enterprise was inaugurated three years ago by Mr. Wm. C. Hongler, who brought his thorough experience to bear, having for eight years prior to that been with Burr Bros. & Co., and for a year being a member of that firm. Mr. Chas. R. Bready was formerly connected with the firm of E. N. M. Search & Co., dealing in wool, noils, etc., and for several years was junior member of that firm. Messrs. Hongler & Bready have met with a substantial success fully exceeding their anticipations and now command an increasing foreign and domestic trade. They deal in domestic cotton and wool, and cotton and wool stocks of all kinds. The warehouse is a four-story building and is provided with all the facilities for the transaction of business, and at all times contains a good stock of all grades in this line. The highest cash prices are paid for cotton and woolen stocks, and manufacturers are supplied with any desired quantity upon the most liberal basis. Messrs. Hongler & Bready are both natives of Philadelphia, and are young men of energy and progressive methods. By industry and an honorable business policy they have attained success and are highly esteemed by all who know them. Daniel M. Stuart, Esq., No. 634 Drexel Building, is attorney and counselor for the firm.

HISTORICAL AND COMMERCIAL PHILADELPHIA.

EITEL & KINSLER, Manufacturing Jewelers, Sixth and Chestnut Streets. The well-known and liberally patronized house of Messrs. Beitel & Kinsler was established in 1860 by Beitel & Shantz on Dock Street. The present firm was organized in 1872, and the present location has been occupied since 1876. The factory of this favorite manufacturing house is located in the Ledger Building, and it is equipped with the best mechanical appliances known to the trade. The firm manufacture watches, clocks, jewelry, and execute all kinds of ornamental work, engine turning, engraving, chasing, etc. Any kind of jewelry is made to order, and a special feature is the execution of difficult work at reasonable prices. Messrs. Beitel & Kinsler are Philadelphians by birth and training, and expert practical engine turners.

HE READ & STANTON COMPANY, (Limited,) Importers and Grinders Spices and Mustards. Proprietors of Chéf Sauce; Main Office, No. 47 North Front Street; Sauce Factory, No. 231 Race Street. The sauce manufacturers of the United States are but limited; Philadelphia can boast of one whose goods are known to both this and the European continent. The Chéf Sauce now manufactured by the Read & Stanton Company, (Limited,) was first put up in Philadelphia some ten years ago, by an Englishman who had spent his lifetime in the manufacture of condiments, sauces, etc.; it was little anticipated that at the time of placing it upon the market it would so quickly reach the public favor. Four years ago the Chéf Sauce proprietorship was bought of the Grocers' Supply Company, by the present owners, since which time it has advanced more rapidly than before. Orders have been filled for parties in Sweden, France, England, Canada, West Indies, and the United States in general. The Read & Stanton Company, (Limited,) consists of H. Read, chairman, and H. Stanton, secretary and treasurer, with main office at No. 47 North Front Street, Sauce Factory at No. 231 Race Street, and branch offices in New York and Baltimore. That Chéf Sauce has become so popular in comparatively a short space of time, is undoubtedly to be attributed to its excellent quality and moderate price. The imported sauces at twenty-five cents a bottle are too high in price to meet the desire of hotels, or the majority of the public, and when as good an article can be had for ten cents, it is but a matter of time before it displaces the others. True it is that there are and will always be a certain class of people who will buy the imported goods simply because they are imported, but they do not constitute the majority. Chéf Sauce has been improved upon considerably since it has been with its present owners, and numbers of people daily use it in hotels believing they are using an imported and higher priced article, and the hotel-keeper doubtless believes with the poet that "where ignorance is bliss 'tis folly to be wise."

OODMAN & BROTHER, Produce Commission Merchants, and Packers and Shippers of Fruits and Vegetables, Nos. 316 North Front Street; Branch Stores: Mahanoy City, Penna., Shenandoah, Penna.—Great though the produce commission market of Philadelphia has been in the past, its future is still more bright with promise; immense as the transactions heretofore have been, they are rapidly increasing in volume, and new houses are constantly springing up to compete for patronage in this great branch of commerce. Among these one of comparative recent inception is that of Goodman & Brother, whose headquarters are at No. 316 North Front Street, and who have branch stores at Mahanoy City and Shenandoah, Pa. They began business in this city October, 1890, and prior to that had kept a grocery in Mahanoy City, their native place. The copartners, Messrs. O. H. Goodman and Grant Goodman, are thoroughly experienced in their present line of trade, and are winning a large, first class trade throughout Pennsylvania, as reliable produce commission merchants, receivers, and shippers of fruits, produce, etc. Mr. O. H. Goodman is in charge of the branches at Mahanoy City and Shenandoah, while Mr. Grant Goodman assumes the management in this city. Consignments are received from New Jersey, Delaware, Maryland, New York, Ohio, and the Southern States, which are quickly disposed of at advantageous rates. In all their dealings, the firm aims to advance the best interests of their customers, and their permanent success is fully assured. For reference as to this firm's standing the Dun or Bradstreet Commercial Agencies.

ARRISON SAFETY BOILER WORKS, Germantown Junction.—There are numerous manufacturing enterprises in Philadelphia that maintain an active trade and do a large annual business in their respective lines of goods, but it is only here and there that we find a great representative concern, alert to avail itself of every method and every invention which can in any way tend to improve the quality or extend the field of usefulness for their goods. The growth and development of such concerns cannot be gauged by the general run of trade. They are on a different plan, and fill a sphere of usefulness of the widest extent with the largest consumers of their specialties. An apt illustration of this class of houses is afforded by the Harrison Safety Boiler Works, which are located at Seventeenth and Clearfield Streets, Germantown Junction. These works are famous for the production of the celebrated Wharton-Harrison safety boiler. In 1863 Mr. Joseph Harrison, Jr., having witnessed a terrible boiler explosion while engaged in important engineering work for the Russian government, constructed the first practical and successful safety boiler. His business steadily increased until his lamented death in 1874, when the works lay idle until the organization of the present company in 1880. The present proprietors, by persistent attention to all details of construction, by a continual series of scientific and practical tests, have since secured many important improvements in design, form of setting and material employed, resulting in a product unsurpassed for uniformity, reliability, durability and economical working, and which ranks as the safest practical steam generator for general use. When the friction of competition rules more closely than ever, it is only those who have full confidence in their resources who can possibly come to the front. Unquestionably the success of this house is due to the complete knowledge possessed by its proprietors concerning all details and processes of manufacture. They are experts in the business, and give it the benefit of their close personal attention. Their plant covers a ground area of 150 x 400 feet, and the equipment is of the finest and most elaborate character for insuring rapid and perfect production, while employment is given to from seventy-five to one hundred skilled workmen. The Wharton-Harrison safety boiler is theoretically and practically safe from all destructive explosions, even when carelessly used. It is constructed upon a system or series of uniform parts, few in number, easily made, and easily put together or taken apart, and not of costly material. Its strength is in no respect dependent upon any system of stays or braces, whereby the inefficiency or rupture of one of these braces or stays can cause greatly increased strain upon the others, thereby endangering the whole structure. In churches, colleges, banks, stores, residences, greenhouses, electric lighting stations and manufacturing establishments, the favorable record of these boilers established during twenty-five years' use, and attested by repeated orders, stamps it without a peer for efficiency and safety. These boilers are preferentially used and warmly endorsed by such well-known Philadelphia houses as the Philadelphia Saving Fund, Provident Life and Trust Co., City Trust Safe Deposit and Surety Co., Girard Life Insurance, Annuity and Trust Co., Pennsylvania Co. for insurance on lives and granting annuities, Insurance Co., of the State of Penn., Penn. Mutual Life Insurance Co., Philadelphia National Bank, Real Estate and Trust Co., Germantown Real Estate Deposit and Trust Co., Bement, Miles & Co., S. S. White Dental Manufacturing Co., Tatham & Bros., Phosphor-Bronze Smelting Co., Midvale Steel Works, Empire Chain Works, Philadelphia Inquirer, Saturday Night, Evening Call, Evening Bulletin, Frederick Brown Building, Forrest Building, Haines Building, Benj. H. Shoemaker, Coffin, Altemus & Co., Continental Brewing Co., Hon. John Wanamaker, among many others; also by parties in New York City, Chicago, Baltimore, Providence, Fall River, New Orleans, Atlanta, Cincinnati, St. Louis, Minneapolis, and other prominent commercial and manufacturing points throughout the country. The proprietors, Messrs. Jos. S. Lovering Wharton and William S. Hallowell, are native Philadelphians, expert and successful manufacturers, members of the Manufacturers' Club, and other local organizations, and of high repute in the business world.

HISTORICAL AND COMMERCIAL PHILADELPHIA.

HAS. J. DITTESS & CO., Power Printers, No. 118 North Sixth Street.—This house has been in successful operation since 1860, and is doing a large and influential business in all parts of the city and surrounding country. The office is finely equipped with cylinder presses and five jobbers operated by steam power, and the finest work in the line of job printing is turned out in the most expeditious manner and at reasonable prices. Employment is given to a dozen or more skilled assistants and everything is printed from a card to a newspaper. Mr. Dittess, the active member of the firm, is a native Philadelphian and has had a practical experience of twenty-two years in the art of printing, and is a young man of marked business ability, wide acquaintance and sterling personal worth.

DWIN BENNER, Successor to Samuel Tiller, Plate Printer, Music Plates and Titles Engraved, No. 202 South Ninth Street.— Probably the oldest established house in the country in the line of engraving and printing music plates is that now controlled by Mr. Edwin Benner. He is a successor to the business started in 1822 by Samuel Tiller, who died in 1880, leaving Mr Benner in sole possession of a thriving business which he has since greatly improved by superior ability and workmanship. Mr. Benner employs five workmen, who are constantly busy turning out a high grade of handiwork in plate music printing for all kinds of musical instruments, and in the tasteful engraving of title pages. He supplies the publishing trade all over the United States and has been eminently successful in maintaining the reputation which the house has enjoyed for so many years. The working premises cover a floor area of 20 x 60 feet, fully equipped with the best machinery. The press work is all done by hand, producing a neatness and finish of detail that never can be attained by fast steam presses. Mr. Benner is a man of middle age, a native of Philadelphia and well qualified to lead, as he does, in his special line.

L. LAMB & SON, Commission Merchants, Butter, Eggs, Poultry and all Kinds of Fruit and Produce, No. 339 South Front Street.—This house, which is a thoroughly reliable one, and does a large and flourishing business, was established in 1882 by the present senior member, who conducted it alone up to May last, when he took into partnership his son, William W. Lamb. They have a compact, well arranged store and part of the building, and employ several assistants. The firm are general commission merchants, handling butter, cheese, eggs, poultry, and all kinds of fruits and produce. They keep on hand always a large and first class stock and can fill orders for anything in their line at lowest market rates. They receive from all parts of the country, and have unexcelled facilities for placing consignments to advantage, while returns are promptly made in every instance. The Messrs. Lamb are natives of New Jersey, and reside in Camden. They are men of thorough reliability in their dealings, and are well and favorably known in the trade. Mr. Lamb, the elder, is an active member of the F. & A. M., the Red Men and other societies.

ATON & REANEY, Printers, No. 110 North Sixth Street. For thoroughly first class all round work in the typographical line, or for promptness and reliability in executing orders, no firm in the business in this quarter of the city sustains a better reputation than that of Eaton & Reaney. These enterprising young business men have had nine years' experience in this line, and established business at the present location in 1890. They occupy an office, 25x100 feet in dimensions, fully equipped with all necessary machinery, including job and cylinder presses operated by steam power, employ ten expert printers, and are prepared to execute book, job, and commercial printing in the highest style of the art at reasonable prices. The members of the firm are Messrs C. J. Eaton and B. J. Reaney. Mr. Eaton is a native of Boston, Mass., and has been for eleven years a resident of this city. Mr. Reaney was born in Chester, Pa., and still resides there. He is a popular member of the United American Mechanics and is sergeant of Company B, 6th Infantry, N. G. P.

ILLIAM P. IRELAND, Wholesale Fruit and Produce Commission Merchant, No. 115 Callowhill Street. One of the flourishing concerns in this line is that of William P. Ireland. Mr. Ireland established business on his own account in 1885, previous to which he had been for a year a partner in the firm of Crew & Ireland. He was originally at No. 309 North Front Street, but removed to the present address three years ago. Here, with the best of facilities at command he carries on a general business as a wholesale fruit and produce commission merchant, dealing in all kinds of fruits and vegetables in season, also live and dressed poultry, butter and eggs, and consignments are received from Maryland, Pennsylvania, New Jersey, Delaware, the Carolinas, and Florida. A heavy stock is always carried, owing to the large number of consignments that are constantly coming in, but as these are quickly disposed, the stock is always fresh and of superior quality. Mr. Ireland was born in Maryland, where he was raised on a farm, and early gained a knowledge of farm products. He is a member of the Fruit and Produce Exchange, and enjoys the good will of all with whom he has had dealings.

r. F. A. GENTH, Analytical and Practical Chemist and Mineralogist. No. 111 South Tenth Street.—The oldest established and best known exponent of this profession is Dr. F. A. Genth, who was born in Germany and came to this city in 1850. He has actively and successfully conducted an ever growing business since that date, and for sixteen years of the time was head of the chemical department in the University of Pennsylvania. In the analysis, assay of gold, silver, lead, copper and other ores, his certificates are eagerly sought for and have afforded the basis for the sale and working for many of the most celebrated mining properties on the continent. His large practical experience and scientific knowledge eminently qualify him to afford accurate and beneficial guidance, and his services are in widespread requisition in the erection of chemical works and the regulation of those already in existence. He has acted as an expert in many patent causes pertaining to all branches of mineralogy and chemical science, while he is constantly promoting the twin causes of science and industry, and by means of his accurate analysis is affording his patrons a perfect knowledge of the constituents of any substance submitted to his investigation. Dr. Genth is personally popular in both professional and commercial circles.

ANIEL W. LOOSE, Sign Painter, N. W. Corner Ninth and Filbert Streets. The well known artistic sign painter, Mr. Daniel W Loose, established business in Philadelphia in 1887 at No. 437 Arch Street, moving to the present location, northwest corner of Ninth and Filbert Streets, in July, 1892. The house has from the date of its foundation always received a liberal patronage. The premises occupied are spacious and commodious, fitted up for the trade in the best possible manner, and are thoroughly equipped with all the appliances required in the business. Lettering in all its branches is finely executed, a specialty being made of enameled letters. Signs of every description—wire, board, brass, nickle, and embosse I glass signs, are finely painted, also much canvas and banner work is artistically executed. The satisfactory manner in which all work is done by Mr. Loose has brought him a very extensive trade, which is rapidly increasing, and he numbers among his customers very many of the largest business houses throughout the city. Tradesmen who desire first class work should not fail to visit this house. Mr. Loose is a native Philadelphian, has had ten years' practical experience in this business and is an energetic, clear headed business man and a popular member of the Knights of Pythias.

HISTORICAL AND COMMERCIAL PHILADELPHIA.

T. A. ROGERS & SON, Planters and Wholesale Dealers in Fresh and Salt Oysters, Nos. 324 and 326 South Delaware Avenue.—The planting of and wholesale trade in oysters forms a leading staple industry of Pennsylvania, and numerous houses are engaged upon an extensive scale in this line. One of the oldest and most prominent representatives of the trade is the house of T. A. Rogers & Son, whose office and salesroom are at Nos. 324 and 326 South Delaware Avenue, telephone, No. 1551. This well known establishment was founded in 1860, on the same street, by the senior member of the firm, Mr. Thomas A. Rogers. In 1885, on the admission to partnership of his son, Mr. Maurice A. Rogers, the present firm name was adopted. Mr. Rogers, Sr., is a veteran in the oyster trade, possesses an expert knowledge of all its requirements, and he enjoys an enviable record as an honorable, progressive business man. He was born in New York, but resided in Michigan from the age of three years till he was twenty years of age, while Mr. Maurice A. Rogers was born in Philadelphia, but both for many years past have resided in Camden. Mr. Rogers is very prominently identified with the interests of that city, having represented the district the past two years as State Senator, previous to which he had held many municipal offices of trust. He is a statesman of force and ability, and gives his constituents an able representation. The firm own valuable oyster beds at Morris Cove, also on the West Shore in Delaware, the shipping station being at the Cove, from whence shipments are made via the West Jersey Railroad to all points in the Middle and Eastern States. In the season the firm employ from 100 to 150 men, run 20 sailboats, and handle from one to two carloads of oysters daily. The oysters handled are the choicest to be found in the market, and the trade is supplied upon the most liberal terms.

J. S. QUIRK & CO., Practical Designers and Engravers on Wood, Nos. 609 and 611 Chestnut Street.—It would be impossible to overestimate the excellence of the productions which emanate from the reliable firm of Messrs. J. S. Quirk & Co., practical designers and engravers on wood, located in this city at the above address and as a fair average illustration of the class of work they turn out, may be taken their own business card, which in itself is a gem of wood carving, and to an experienced eye is an embodiment of artistic talent, sound ability, originality of design, good taste and delicacy and clearness in the blending of colors, light and shade, etc. The business was established in 1884 by the present sole proprietor, Mr. J. S. Quirk, who has fifteen years' experience at his command, and is unquestionably possessed of rare talent and creative genius as a designer. Engraving on wood in all its branches is undertaken for an influential patronage throughout the city and suburbs, and in a smaller volume in New York and Baltimore, and it needs scarcely to be said that the house fully merits the confidence and liberal support accorded it, by executing really good work with promptitude and at the lowest prices. Four competent assistants, skilled in wood engraving, are regularly engaged under the direct surveillance of the experienced principal, and the workshop and offices on the third floor at the location indicated above are replete with tools, appliances and all modern facilities for turning  out work of the highest order of merit. The worthy proprietor is a native of Keokuk, Iowa, still a young man, has resided in Philadelphia since 1884, and is a member of the Free and Accepted Masons, the Knights of Pythias and the Order of the Mystic Shrine.

H. L. COOPER, Wool, No. 8 North Front Street.—In that branch of trade devoted to the handling of wool, a representative house is that conducted by Mr. H. L. Cooper, who controls a trade of the largest proportions at wholesale chiefly throughout Pennsylvania, New Jersey, Delaware, New England, although extending in rather less volume to the remoter parts of the Union. The foundation of this business was laid in 1887 by the present proprietor, and the subsequent development to its now existing proportions is attributable in the main to the ripe experience and thorough knowledge of the wool trade which Mr. Cooper possesses and continuously exercises in each department of the house; he has been actively engaged in this line for a consecutive period of twenty-four years, is an expert judge of the staple product and its suitable application in its several qualities to various lines and departments of wooden goods manufacture, and, moreover, he exercises a keen discrimination in the selection of his supplies, buying at the right time in the right markets, and securing heavy quantities for cash direct from growers. Thus he is enabled to meet the exact requirements of wooden manufacturers with the kind and grade of domestic wool suited to their respective needs at rock bottom prices, and largely by these means he has attained the distinct success already alluded to. The house handles equally all kinds and grades of the domestic product, as well as tolls, and keeps on hand a heavy stock to ensure the prompt fulfilment of orders. The premises utilized consist of a five-story building, 20x100 feet in area on each floor, well fitted and arranged throughout for the successful and systematic conduct of the large business there transacted. Mr. H. L. Cooper is a gentleman of Philadelphia birth, and was for ten years a member of the firm of I. Reifsnyder & Co.

WM. BOOTHBY, Wholesale Dealer and Shipper of Choice Oysters, No. 307 South Front Street.—Representative in the wholesale oyster trade is the widely and favorably known house of Wm. Boothby, whose headquarters are located at No. 307 South Front Street, and who, in connection with Mr. Kugler, is owner of the oyster houses and restaurants at No. 1235 Chestnut Street, Nos. 810 and 812 Vine Street, and Nos. 1718 Ridge Avenue. These houses have no equal in the city. The public here are great consumers of oysters, but their tastes are educated and their requirements are exacting, so that only the choicest growths find an extended market here. Realizing this fact, Mr. Boothby has steadily devoted himself to handling the best grades of oysters, and will handle nothing else. He sells the trade in shell and bulk in quantities to suit, and makes regular shipments to customers in every part of the United States. No house in Philadelphia is so well prepared to fill the largest orders at the shortest notice with the freshest, finest and choicest oysters as is this reliable concern. The Philadelphia trade is of the greatest magnitude, including leading dealers, the largest hotels, restaurants and other prominent consumers, and the proprietor is known everywhere to deal in the best qualities of stock, quoting the lowest market rates. He gives employment to between two hundred and three hundred people, receiving oysters in the shell from Virginia, Maryland, New Jersey and New York, and forming an important factor in the commercial activity of this city. Mr. Boothby was born in England, and came to this city fifty-three years ago, when a lad of three. He chose the life of a sailor, and before reaching his majority had become master of a vessel, and earned an enviable reputation as an expert navigator. When the war broke out he was captured and imprisoned in Castle Thunder, and his escape from Salisbury in company with others was one of the exciting episodes of "the times that tried men's souls." Mr. Boothby is a Past Sachem of Idaho Tribe of Red Men, and a member of the Knights of Birmingham, F. & A. M., the I. O. O. F., the United Workmen, and other social clubs and organizations, and a true type of the self made man.

HISTORICAL AND COMMERCIAL PHILADELPHIA.

ANDREYKOVICZ & DUNK, Importers of Aniline Dyes, Dyestuffs and Chemicals. Manufacturers of Extracts of Indigo. Nos. 58 and 60 North Front Street.—The trade in dyestuffs and chemicals has greatly increased in volume during the past generation. The very eminent and responsible firm of Andreykovicz & Dunk has not only been closely identified with the business during the past thirty-five years, but has become one of the leading firms engaged in its importation and supply. The business was founded in the year 1854 by the present firm, who are large wholesale dealers and importers of aniline dyes, chemicals and extracts of indigo. They formerly owned a factory and did their own manufacturing, but of late years have given it up, importing all their goods. Foreign products are procured direct from the most reliable European houses, and the mercantile department is organized and directed in the most active manner. The house commands a business of very considerable volume in all the goods specifically named, and the list of goods it handles coming under the heading of "dyes" and "chemicals" are very numerous. Soluble extracts are the specialty of the house, and in this department the firm is most highly famed for the choice character of its goods. Mr. Andreykovicz is a skilful chemist, and is well versed in the quality of the merchandise he handles, and generally informed as to the exact purpose to which each kind and grade is adapted. The firm has a fine four-story building, 50 x 100 feet in dimensions, and very heavily stocked in each line. A very extensive trade is drawn from the dyers and textile mills throughout all the United States, and the efforts of the house are to supply only the best goods. Mr. Andreykovicz is a native of Poland, and has lived in Philadelphia since 1850. His partner, Mr. Dunk, is a Philadelphian by birth. They are members of the Bourse.

WILLIAM S. ADAMS, Importer and Jobber of Cigars, No. 17 North Front Street.—One of the most successful jobbers in imported and domestic cigars of all grades is Mr. Wm. S. Adams, whose establishment is eligibly located at No. 17 North Front Street. This enterprising and thoroughly reliable gentleman established business here in January, 1892. He has had ten years' practical experience in the cigar trade, being with D. D. Hanna of Philadelphia, and possesses a thorough knowledge of all the details of the business. A heavy and first-class stock is kept constantly on hand, comprising imported and domestic cigars of all grades, a specialty being made of the following brands: "Adams' Puffs," "Adams' Royal," "Adams' Excelsior," and "Adams' Wanita," and all orders for anything in the lines indicated are filled in the most prompt and reliable manner at exceptionally favorable prices. Mr. Adams is a native of Philadelphia, but was raised in New Jersey, and is now a resident of Collingswood, N. J. He is a man of energy, enterprise and experience, who has been eminently successful in developing a trade which extends throughout Pennsylvania, New Jersey and Delaware, and is constantly increasing under the efficient efforts of several experienced commercial travelers.

F. D. MYERS & CO., Fruit and Produce, No. 331 North Water Street.—The splendid advantages enjoyed by Philadelphia as a city best adapted to the manipulation of the farm products of the country, have tended to the promotion of transactions in this line of the greatest magnitude and importance, and to the establishment of numerous houses, whose aggregate annual business is simply prodigious. An eminently prosperous concern engaged in the trade is that of Mr. F. D. Myers & Co., whose office and store are at No. 331 North Water Street. This enterprise was founded in 1876 by Mr. Myers, and from 1885 to 1888 he had a partner, the firm being Myers & Smith. In the latter year the firm was dissolved, and Mr. Myers has since remained in sole control, trading under the firm-name of F. D. Myers & Co. He is thoroughly acquainted with all the requirements of the trade, and has developed a large business throughout this State and New Jersey. While handling a general line of domestic fruits and produce, as a commission merchant, Mr. Myers makes a leading specialty of New York potatoes, of which last year, he received 300 carloads; shad is another specialty, while large quantities of Florida oranges and lemons are handled. Consignments of goods are received from Pennsylvania, New Jersey, New York, Maryland, Delaware and the South, and from Canada. Those shipping fruits and produce to this market will find no more reliable, energetic, or liberal house anywhere than the subject of this article, whose systematic arrangements and large transactions enable him to handle goods to the best advantage and in the shortest possible time.

C. P. POOLE & CO., Manufacturers of Tin Cans for Paint, Putty, Lard, Preserves, Fruit, Etc. Etc., Square Varnish Cans, Candy Boxes, Etc., Nos. 253, 255, 257 and 259 North Front Street.—The house of C. P. Poole & Co. is a very important one in this line and the largest in Philadelphia devoted to the manufacture of tin cans. It was established eleven years ago, by its present proprietors, since which time a large and growing trade has been acquired, which extends throughout Pennsylvania, New Jersey, New York, and the New England States. The manufacturing plant comprises five buildings, each having four floors, and dimensions of 70 x 100 feet. The works are equipped with fourteen power presses, two pedal presses, and improved tinsmiths' machinery and tools, and employment is found for a force of one hundred hands in the various departments. The products of the house consist of round and square tin cans of all kinds, square varnish cans, candy boxes, cracker boxes, lard pails, and cans for paint, putty, preserves, fruit, etc. Notwithstanding the unsurpassed facilities of the house for production, the factory is driven to its utmost capacity to fill orders, a gratifying state of affairs which shows the liberal methods followed by the management. The members of the firm are Messrs. Chas. P. Poole, and Jas. Forrester. These gentlemen are thoroughly experienced business men, and sustain an excellent reputation in the commercial world. Mr. Poole opened a house in Boston at Nos. 42 to 48 Batterymarch Street, February 1, 1892, in connection with Mr. E. W. Frost, for the purpose of supplying the New England trade.

TRUMBAUER & SON, Produce Commission Merchants, Choice Grades Solid and Creamery Print Butter, and Penn'a Eggs a Specialty, Northwest Corner Front and Pine Streets.—A well-known and old-established firm of produce commission merchants, efficiently representative of the better class of such houses in Philadelphia, is that of J. Trumbauer & Son, located at the northwest corner of Front and Pine Streets, who control a permanent substantial trade reaching among dealers and other wholesale consumers all over the city and adjacent country. This responsible house was founded in 1868 by the present senior proprietor, Mr. John Trumbauer, and after the retirement of a Mr. Wauer, with whom he was for some little time associated, his son, Mr. Harry Trumbauer, was admitted into partnership four years ago. Heavy consignments are daily arriving from the best farming districts all over the United States, consisting of cheese, butter, eggs, live and dressed poultry, game in season, sheep, lambs, calves, hogs and other live-stock, green and dried fruits of all kinds, a specialty being made of choice grades of solid and creamery print butter and Pennsylvania eggs. These consignments are speedily disposed of with a skill and judgment indicating ripe experience and a thorough knowledge of the trade, and, moreover the firm enjoy an established reputation for exercising a scrupulous care in the handling and keeping of goods, for rendering accurate account sales, making prompt returns and for safeguarding the best interests of their patrons in every way. The premises utilized, which were occupied in May, 1892, owing to largely increased business, consist of a building of four floors, each 25 x 50 feet in area, well fitted and equipped throughout for the successful conduct of a large and brisk business, four competent clerks being there regularly employed. Mr. John Trumbauer and his son, Mr. Harry Trumbauer, were both born in Bucks County, Pa., and have resided in Philadelphia since 1865. The worthy senior is a gentleman of middle age and is a member of the Philadelphia Produce Exchange, as also of the Order of Tonti and the Guardians.

HISTORICAL AND COMMERCIAL PHILADELPHIA.

E. DITSON & CO., Music Publishers and Dealers in Sheet Music, Music Books and Musical Instruments (Fred E. Spear, Manager), No. 1228 Chestnut Street.—It is generally conceded in the musical world that Messrs. J. E. Ditson & Co., located at No. 1228 Chestnut Street, lead the trade in Philadelphia as music publishers and dealers in sheet music, music books and musical instruments; and the extent and volume of their operations, their sound business methods, and the class of goods they handle, are abundant testimony to the same effect. The trade controlled, while chiefly centred in Pennsylvania and the Southern States, reaches to all sections of the Union, more especially in sheet music, of which the firm publish ever one hundred thousand of the latest pieces. In music books the great masters and the modern composers are alike represented, and orchestras, musical societies, choirs, schools, etc., are supplied on the most advantageous terms. The firm's headquarters are situated at No. 151 Washington Street, Boston, and the establishment in Philadelphia, inaugurated fifteen years ago, has since 1880 been intrusted to the skilful and distinctly successful direction of Mr. Fred E. Spear, the firm's manager here. The premises which it is found necessary to maintain consist of a building of four floors, each 25x150 feet in area, and three floors in the adjoining building, of like dimensions. Each floor is completely stocked with sheet music, music books, small musical instruments of all kinds for band and orchestra, and musical merchandise in general, more than forty competent assistants being regularly engaged, and two active travelers to attend to the outside duties. The store, on the first floor, is handsomely appointed. The experienced manager, Mr. Fred E. Spear, is a native of Boston, and now of middle age.

GENTZSCH & SONS, Plain and Fancy Paper Box Manufacturers, Sample Cards and Shelf Boxes a Specialty, Fine Confectioners' Boxes, No. 126 North Fourth Street.—For the past thirty five years the paper box factory of A. Gentzsch & Sons has been in operation. The business was started by the present senior member of the firm, who conducted it alone up to 1888, when he took into partnership his sons, August, Albert, William and G. A. Gentzsch. They occupy four 30 x 100 foot floors, equipped with ample steam power, and the latest improved machinery, tools, etc., and upward of seventy-five hands are employed. The Messrs. Gentzsch are manufacturers of plain and fancy paper boxes of every description, and in all sizes, shapes and designs, including fine confectioners' boxes, sample cards and shelf boxes being a specialty. Paper boxes are made to order at shortest notice and at lowest rates, the prices charged by this firm being notably low, while every article is warranted as to make and material. All orders are attended to in the most expeditious manner, and all communications by telephone receive prompt response. Mr. Gentzsch, the elder, is a gentleman of mature age, but active and energetic, and was born in Germany. He has lived in this city a long time, is well and favorably known both in business and social life, and is a member of the German Gun Club and several societies.

JOSEPH ZENTMAYER, Optician, Manufacturer of Microscopes, Spectacles and Eye Glasses, No. 209 South Eleventh Street.—The famous house of Joseph Zentmayer was founded in 1853 by the late Joseph Zentmayer, who built up this business by his genius and perseverance to proportions of great and gratifying magnitude, and at his lamented death in 1888 he was succeeded by his two sons, Messrs. Frank and Edward Zentmayer, who have since continued the business under the honored name of the founder. They are extensive manufacturers of microscopes, microscopic apparatus and optical instruments, spectacles and eye glasses, and give special attention to dentists' prescriptions. Their large experience in the manufacture of microscopes, microscopic apparatus, etc., enables them to offer to the public the most improved and perfect instruments in construction as well as workmanship. The fame of their instruments has spread to all parts of the civilized globe. No city so densely populated, no island so remote, but what has felt the influence of this old and honored house. By the introduction of suitable machinery, and by a division of labor, the Messrs. Zentmayer have secured the highest finish of workmanship at a moderate price, and they are thus enabled to battle on even terms with their most formidable competitors in any part of the world. In regard to the quality of their instruments, they refer to any first-class microscopist, university or college. All their microscope stands have undergone a reconstruction, and are provided with their patented arrangement of swinging the sub-stage and mirror, having the object as its centre, without which no instrument can be considered complete. Their leading specialties embrace Zentmayer's American Centennial Stand, Zentmayer's New Model United States Army Hospital Stand, Zentmayer's Histological Stand, Zentmayer's American Continental Stand, Zentmayer's American Student Stand, Zentmayer's Clinical Stand, Zentmayer's Pocket Microscope, Zentmayer's Botanical Dissecting Microscopes, Zentmayer's Modified Abbe Condenser, pocket magnifiers, achromatic object glasses, Ryder's automatic microtome, the oxy-hydrogen lantern, Zentmayer's lens and mounting material and accessories of every description. Catalogues are mailed free on application. The Messrs. Zentmayer are native Philadelphians, members of the Academy of Sciences and the Franklin Institute, and trained in the optician's art under the tuition of their father—the foremost optician of his time.

DAUGHERTY BROS., Wholesale Dealers in Oysters, Clams, Terrapin, Etc., No. 16 Spruce Street.—Although only little more than a year established, Daugherty Bros., wholesale dealers in oysters, clams, etc., No. 16 Spruce Street, have already built up a large and flourishing trade. The secret of their prosperity is not far to seek, however. Enjoying exceptional advantages in respect of sources of supply, with excellent shipping facilities at Maurice Cove, on the West Jersey Railroad, and handling only choicest quality mollusks, the Messrs. Daugherty have been enabled to achieve the distinct success that has attended their well directed efforts. The firm are interested in oyster beds at Maurice Cove, Delaware River, and Pleasantville Cove, and have six boats in service. They employ forty to fifty hands in season, and ship throughout the Middle and Eastern States, handling about 150,000 oysters a day on an average. Consignments are solicited, and all interests placed with this reliable firm are certain to be disposed of to the best advantage, while prompt returns are assured in every instance. They have a commodious, well arranged store on Spruce Street, and keep on hand here always a large and first class stock of oysters, clams, crabs, lobsters, terrapin, etc. All orders for anything in this line are filled in the most careful and expeditious manner, and the lowest market prices are quoted. The firm have both a double and single horse wagon, upon which three men are constantly employed, and they do all their own carting. Messrs. C. S and F. S. Daugherty are gentlemen in the prime of life and natives of New Jersey, residing in Camden. They are men of energy and enterprise, thoroughly conversant with the wants of the trade, and their business is rapidly growing. Mr. C. S. Daugherty has had thirteen years' experience in mining and prospecting in the West. Mr. F. S. Daugherty is connected with several fraternal societies, including the United Friends, Sons of Temperance, and Brotherhood Union and the Red Men.

A. G. LAURENT, Druggist, No. 736 South Third Street.—The pharmaceutical establishment of Mr. A. G. Laurent is popularly regarded as one of the most reliable dispensaries in this section of the city, and it is held in high repute for the careful and accurate preparation of physicians' prescriptions and miscellaneous recipes. The store itself is finely fitted up and contains a large and select stock of drugs, medicines and everything requisite for the systematic conduct of a drug, prescription and family trade. Mr. A. G. Laurent is of German birth and reached Philadelphia in 1850. He first established himself in business in 1857 at Camden, N. J., and continued there up to 1861, when he engaged in the war as surgeon's steward, on board the steamers "Flag" and "Vicksburg," until 1865. In 1870 he started a pharmacy in this city at No. 302 South Fourth Street, and in February, 1888, removed to his present location. He is a member of Post 91 of the Grand Army of the Republic, the Union Veteran League, Camp 2, and the Naval Veteran League, and originally studied pharmacy at Charleston, S. C.

HISTORICAL AND COMMERCIAL PHILADELPHIA.

HE AMERICAN MARINE AND CANAL PROPELLER COMPANY, Room No. 743 Drexel Building.—One of the important inventions of the present day is that now being introduced by the American Marine and Canal Propeller Company, of this city, whose office is located at Room No. 743 Drexel Building. This company own the patents issued for the Bender Propeller in the United States, Canada, England, Belgium, France, Italy, Russia and Germany; and have had several experimental trials of their 30 feet launch, each of which has been most satisfactory in demonstrating all that they claim for their system of propulsion, both in speed and power. (See "New York Recorder" of Oct. 24th and Nov. 8th and 10th, 1892; "Buffalo Courier," Oct. 21st, 1892; "Lockport Sun," Oct. 19th, 1892; "Philadelphia Evening Call," Nov. 1st, 1892). The motive power consists of two paddle wheels hidden from view in two brass drums, on either side of the craft amidships. Each wheel is composed of four paddle-blades, 12 inches long and 4 inches wide. The drums are air-tight and open one-quarter of their diameter at the bottom of the vessel, under the water, when it is running. On the interior of the drums, on either side of the opening, are abutments, which prevent the water from running into the drum and consequently prevent the churning of air and water together. The paddle-wheels are one-twelfth less in diameter than the inside

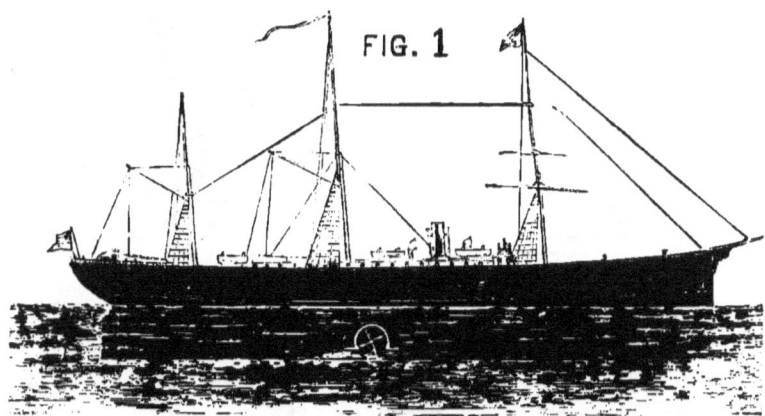

of the drum, and allow the air within the drum to pass from the ends of the paddles. The wheels are connected with a shaft, which in turn is directly connected by a crank to the engine. The boat runs without vibration and without creating any wash. This is the chief merit claimed for this construction of propeller, while in addition they have greater towing power than any other form of boat, and the principle can be applied to the largest steamships in the world at a great saving of machinery and fuel. The Bender Propeller moves through the water with much greater steadiness than is the case with any other propelling power, thereby increasing the comfort of passengers and safety of freight; while, the propelling power being at all times in the water, no matter how much the ship shall be pitched by a storm, the wheels can never be out of water, thus greatly saving power and doing away with the necessity of a marine governor, and racing and slip being unknown. This company was incorporated in 1887, under the laws of the State of West Virginia, and is officered as follows, viz.: A. D. Markley, president; W. W. H. Davis, vice-president; Theo. Rumel, treasurer; Jos. I. Morris, manager. The company has a capital stock of $500,000, whose par value is $10 per share, and is rapidly extending its business to all parts of the world. Their boats are being manufactured at McKeesport, N. Y., and a steam model can be seen at the Philadelphia office. The management of the affairs of the company is in able, enterprising and experienced hands. President Markley is a well-known Pennsylvanian, State Senator for Montgomery County. Vice-President Davis was a general in the army, and is now the publisher of the Doylestown "Democrat." Treasurer Rumel is prominently known in the financial world as auditor for Drexel & Co.; while Manager Morris is at the head of the ship-building firm of Morris & Mather in Camden, and an expert authority on all matters connected with this branch of industry. The permanent prosperity and brilliant success of this enterprise is thus well assured.

ILSON & ROGERS, Boneless Meats and Provisions, Tenderloins a Specialty, Nos. 234, 236 and 238 North Water Street.—A house in this city that can be recommended with every confidence as an able, expeditious and reliable source of supply for the finest qualities of prime boneless meats and provisions, is that of Wilson & Rogers, located at Nos. 234, 236 and 238 North Water Street, whose reputation is soundly based upon several years of very successful and satisfactory trading. This responsible undertaking is governed in detail by a policy which, while essentially enterprising, partakes largely of the sterling principles of old-time trading, a scrupulous care, upheld by thorough knowledge and ripe experience, being exercised in the selection of supplies and in the fulfillment of all orders, whether sent by mail or otherwise. The basis of the firm's operations consist in the handling at wholesale, of boneless meats, choice cuts of beef, hams, lard, pork, bacon, and a full line of prime provisions, tenderloins being a speciality. These fine quality edibles are procured at first hands from raisers and other leading sources of supply throughout the Western States, in large quantities for cash upon the most favorable terms, thereby enabling the firm to cater to the highest class of trade, supplying the finest viands at the lowest relative prices and meeting the requirements of the trade promptly and accurately. The firm's customers consist largely of hotels, restaurants, clubs, public institutions, colleges, vessels, steamboats, steamship companies, etc., and are located throughout the Keystone State, Virginia, New York, Delaware and New Jersey. At No. 236 North Water Street are maintained a well-appointed office on the second floor, a cooling-room and three storerooms, each 20 x 50 feet in area, well fitted and fully equipped throughout for the successful conduct of a large business of this nature. This well-known representative house was established seven years ago by the present partners, Mr. Joseph A. Wilson and Mr. H. V. Rogers, of whom the former gentleman is in the business in Washington, D. C., while Mr. Rogers has charge of affairs in this city.

HISTORICAL AND COMMERCIAL PHILADELPHIA.

WILLIAM MEYER, Steam Packing-box Manufacturer, Nos. 214 and 216 Quarry Street.—The steam packing-box manufactory of Mr. William Meyer, located at Nos. 214 and 216 Quarry Street, is the oldest and best-known establishment of its kind in the city. It was founded in 1842, by Martin Meyer, the grandfather of the present proprietor, who succeeded to the business upon the death of his father in 1889. Mr. Meyer is a native of Philadelphia and has occupied his present quarters at Nos. 212 and 214 Quarry Street for a year past. Previous to that the establishment was at No. 129 Bread Street and No. 217 Quarry Street. The equipment of the factory, occupying two floors, each 30 x 80 feet, is very complete, and care is taken to use only well-seasoned and sound lumber. The planing machines, saws and machines, etc., are driven by steam power. Packing-boxes of all sizes, shapes and thicknesses of material are here turned out in great quantities by a force of ten thoroughly trained workmen, and sold at the lowest rates compatible with the good quality of the work. Mr. Meyer does a driving business, principally local in character, and also a large trade in first-class carpenter work, shelves and fixtures, of which he makes a specialty, and for getting out which he has special facilities.

THE RAWSON MANUFACTURING COMPANY, Manufacturers of the Rawson Step-ladder Chair, Ladies' Sewing Tables, Patent Combined Porcelain Lined Water Cooler and Refrigerator, Spring Beds, Woven Wire Mattresses, Wood, Canvas Wire and Upholstered Cots, Cribs, Cradles, Camp Stools, Etc., Factory, North Twenty-first Street, above York.—Among the more noteworthy industrial enterprises which have had inception in Philadelphia in recent years may be mentioned that of the Rawson Manufacturing Company, whose factory is located on North Twenty-first Street, above York. This is a big concern and is the largest of the kind in the city. It has been in existence since 1890, and from the start the venture has been a signal success. The company are manufacturers of the Rawson step-ladder chair, which possesses many advantages over the old style chair, having a drop seat and bent back, its construction being of round pieces instead of the sawed out square chair as formerly made by them; ladies sewing tables, patent porcelain-lined water cooler and refrigerator, spring beds. This company are the manufacturers of two special springs that are meeting with universal acceptance, which are placing said firm among the first manufacturers of this line of goods. This firm also runs several automatic wood turning machines, making a variety of turnings for themselves and the trade; also their patent crib and cradle is a pronounced success, woven-wire mattresses, wood, canvas, wire and upholstered cots, cribs, cradles, camp stools, etc., and their productions command extensive sales. They turn out a distinctly superior class of articles and sell to the trade throughout the United States. The plant is a capacious and excellently equipped one, and the facilities altogether are first-class. The factory is a three-story brick structure, 150 x 60 feet, ample yard in connection, and is provided with full steam-power, latest improved machinery, etc., and seventy-five hands are employed. An exceedingly large stock is constantly kept on hand, and includes besides the articles above indicated, also a number of specialties of a highly meritorious character. Dealers and jobbers are supplied on the most favorable terms, bottom prices being quoted, while all goods are warranted as to make and material, and all orders are filled in the most prompt and reliable manner. The president of the company is Jos. W.

Crawford; W. S. Plummer is vice-president; and J. S. Keller is secretary and treasurer. These three gentlemen are all men of energy and enterprise, and are well known in business circles. The P. O. address of the Rawson Manufacturing Company is Twenty-first Street, above York, and the freight address is Germantown Junction.

THE EASTON & McMAHON TRANSPORTATION COMPANY. Established 1860, Incorporated 1884; Offices: No. 18 South Delaware Avenue, Philadelphia; No. 2 Coenties Slip, New York; No. 4 Post Office Avenue, Baltimore.—The leading freight carriers by barges and steam tugs having their headquarters in Philadelphia are The Easton & McMahon Transportation Company, who operate offices at No. 18 South Delaware Avenue, Philadelphia; No. 2 Coenties Slip, New York; and No. 4 Post Office Avenue, Baltimore. This company take freight to and from New York, Philadelphia, Baltimore, Newport News, Troy, New Haven, and intermediate points, via. the Delaware and Raritan and Chesapeake and Delaware Canals. The business was originally established in 1860 by Messrs. Easton & McMahon, and in 1884 the present company was incorporated under the laws of the State of Delaware, and is officered as follows, viz.: John L. Brady, president; James T. Easton, vice-president; Henry Easton, treasurer; F. W. Commiskey, secretary. The company own two steam tugs and fifty barges and lighters, and enjoy the best possible facilities for shipping bulky and heavy freight speedily and at the lowest rates, while much of the valuable commerce of the harbor of Philadelphia passes through their experienced and responsible hands. They rank among the very first carriers and lighterers in this section, and are prepared to furnish barges for lightering and steam tugs for towing at the shortest notice and on the most reasonable terms. They are also agents for the American Steamship Company, and prominently represented in the Maritime Exchange and the Philadelphia Bourse. President Brady is a well-known Philadelphian, who succeeded to this position in January, 1891, on the death of his father, Owen Brady. The Messrs. Easton and Secretary Commiskey reside in New York City, and all stand deservedly high in maritime and shipping circles.

JAS. G. LINDSAY & CO., Iron and Steel Factors and General Dealers in Iron Ship and Bridge Builders' Materials and Railway Track Material, No. 133 South Fourth Street.—One of the most prominent houses in the United States engaged in the sale of iron ship and bridge builders' materials and railway track material is that of Messrs. Jas. G. Lindsay & Co., located in Bullitt Building, No. 133 South Fourth Street. This firm are general dealers and commission merchants in this line, and enjoy a reputation and a trade thoroughly national in extent and eminently creditable in character. The business was originally established in 1882 by Lindsay, Parvin & Co., the present firm succeeding to the control some years later. They handle iron and steel plates for all purposes, boiler tubes and wrought iron pipe, steel and iron angles, beams and channels, plain and corrugated sheet iron and sheet steel, iron and steel forgings, pipe coils, cast iron pipe, rails, fish plates and spikes, frogs and switches, wheels and axles, car and locomotive bearings, passenger and freight cars, plate girders for bridges and buildings, and make a specialty of ship and bridge material. Contracts are placed for iron and steel structures, and the firm have contracted for all the material used by Cramp & Sons in building Cruiser No. 13, as well as a large portion for several of the other cruisers built by the Cramps, and have supplied the metal for nearly all the yachts built for the various millionaires of the country. The resources of the house are ample and abundant, its connections are perfect, and its facilities are unrivalled. Such a house as this proves of inestimable value to a great commercial centre, and by its operations conduces greatly to the activity of trade, affording substantial advantages to both seller and buyer. Orders by telephone No. 2712, by telegraph or mail, receive immediate and careful attention, and contracts are made for delivery in any part of the United States. Mr. Lindsay is a native of Pennsylvania, was with iron ship builders in Wilmington, Del., for over twenty years, and has been connected with the iron trade nearly all his life. He is therefore recognized as an authority in his business. He has also been interested in some important railway projects involving a great deal of money, which have been carried forward to successful termination, as well as in other business enterprises, and is a gentleman of ability and integrity, abundantly worthy of the large measure of success attending his well directed efforts.

THE CENTRAL BOARDING AND SALES STABLES, No. 826 Filbert Street, R. S. Reeve, Manager.—One of the leading concerns of the kind in this city, and probably the oldest, is the Central Boarding and Sales Stables at No. 826 Filbert Street, established fifty years ago as sales stables exclusively. In 1889 Mr. R. S. Reeves became manager, and added the boarding department. The premises comprise two floors, each 60x150 feet in dimensions, affording comfortable quarters for 100 horses, with ample room for carriages, supplies, etc. The lighting, ventilation and general sanitary arrangements are first class, and horses receive the best feed and care at the hands of about ten reliable employés. Attached to the stables is a well equipped blacksmith shop, in charge of a skilled mechanic. Mr. Reeves makes a specialty of buying and selling horses on commission, and always has a good assortment of home bred and western horses for all purposes. He also deals in horses on his own account, and gives special attention to gentlemen's road horses. He is an expert judge of all the points of a fine animal, and his experience of many years makes him an authority upon all matters pertaining to horses. He was born in New Jersey, and resides in that State.

MORRIS & RICHTER, Electricians, Hardware and Electrical Supplies, No. 2349 North Fifteenth Street.—Mr. R. Walter Morris is an electrician and dealer in electrical supplies, and has been established in business since the year 1890, and in January, 1892, formed a partnership with Mr. Edward Richter under the present firm style, and moved to their present location in March, 1892. The firm undertakes all kinds of electrical work from the fitting of a bell to the equipment of a complete plant, their specialty being electric wiring. Their connection is drawn from the better element of the locality, and they guarantee all work intrusted to them. The premises occupied comprise an excellently equipped store and shop covering a superficial area of 20x40 feet, wherein is carried a varied and complete assortment of electrical supplies, a staff of eight assistants being maintained. Mr. Morris is a native of Philadelphia and a young man, having a thorough and practical acquaintance with the complexities of the electrician's art, his experience of the same covering a period of ten years. He exercises an important influence upon the prosperity of his profession, and is a prominent member of that worthy organization, the Sons of Veterans, while Mr. Richter is a native of Germany, but has resided in this city for some time.

HUEY & CHRIST, Wines and Liquors, No. 1207 Market Street.—One of the oldest and most eminent houses in this department of commerce is unquestionably that of Messrs. Huey & Christ, located at No. 1207 Market Street. This establishment is headquarters for the choicest vintages and brands of champagnes, ports, sherries and all other imported wines, as well as the highest grades of domestic whiskeys. The business was founded in 1837 by Messrs. Kryder & Bailey, and in 1867 the firm became Kryder & Co., Messrs. Huey & Christ being partners therein and succeeding to the sole control in 1874. This firm are recognized as pioneers in introducing to the American public a class of wines not previously duplicated, while they make a specialty of Bailey's pure rye whiskey, and handle the finest domestic liquors in the market. The building occupied for trade purposes contains four stories and a basement, 23x90 feet each, giving ample accommodations for supplying the most extensive demand, while they also have large wine cellars at Norristown, Pa., where they can store 1,700 barrels. This firm are direct importers and representatives of the most famous brands of brandy in existence, such as E. A. Magnier & Co's., E. Remy Martin & Co's., and the Vineyard Proprietors Company's, while they are now making a leader of Eugène Perré & Co's. Tres Sec champagne, which is rapidly coming to the front strictly on its merits. The firm has steadily increased the sales of their champagnes until they are staple articles of consumption in the best hotels, restaurants and private tables in Philadelphia, New York, Chicago, Boston, Baltimore and other large cities of the Union. The vintages kept in stock are of the rarest and most exquisite quality, and preëminently meet the tastes of the most refined connoisseurs. It is abundant demonstration of the fact to state that the leading bars, hotels and private cellars in Pennsylvania, New Jersey, Delaware, Ohio, Indiana, Michigan and adjoining States are regularly replenished from the stocks of Messrs. Huey & Christ. This firm control a two-thirds interest in the Florida Wine Company, and they likewise handle the best Cognac brandies, long specially in demand for medicinal use, as well as rums, gins, cordials and bitters. Their specialty in whiskey has distinctive features as to flavor, purity and medicinal tonic properties that are readily recognized by experts and druggists. Hotel men and dealers sell Bailey's pure rye very largely in preference to all other brands. A corps of talented salesmen represent the interests of the house upon the road, and orders of whatever magnitude are filled promptly, while terms and prices are made invariably satisfactory to the trade. The copartners, Messrs. William M. Huey and Amos H. Christ, are well known Philadelphians, members of the Whiskey Dealers' Association, and first subscribers of the Bourse, and young men of large business experience, wide acquaintance and eminent popularity.

HISTORICAL AND COMMERCIAL PHILADELPHIA.

 GEO. R. FLEMING & CO., Piano and Organ Warerooms, No. 1229 Chestnut Street.—With the steady increase of material wealth, refinement and culture among our people during the last quarter of a century, there has been created a demand for those surroundings in the home circle that not only add to its comforts, but its happiness and pleasure. Foremost among these surroundings is the piano or organ, and in no other country in the world is there to be found so many of these promoters of pleasure and happiness as in America—which speaks volumes for the progress of our people. To those contemplating the purchase of a pianoforte or organ, much of the bewilderment caused by the conflicting claims of manufacturers may be avoided by following the unbiassed opinion of those who are responsible and reliable dealers in such merchandise. A prosperous, popular and responsible house engaged in this business in Philadelphia, well worthy of more than passing comment in these pages, is that of Messrs. Geo. R. Fleming and Company, eligibly and centrally located at No. 1229 Chestnut Street. This business was founded by Mr. Fleming in 1888 under the present firm title, and at once secured a very liberal and substantial trade, and the establishment has acquired a most deservedly high reputation in consequence of its high-class productions and honorable, straightforward business methods. He is a thoroughly experienced man in the business and handles none but the best grades of instruments, and being an excellent judge of them he has no hesitation in expressing his views and opinions upon the various qualifications of the productions of different makers. His warerooms are very spacious and commodious, comprising an entire first floor and basement, each 25x200 feet in dimensions. The store is handsomely furnished and provided with every facility for the transaction of business and the advantageous display of his large and valuable assortment, while every convenience is afforded patrons desiring to test and select an instrument. The stock carried embraces a full line of grand, square and upright pianos from the celebrated factories of Messrs. Behr Brothers, Kimball, Newby & Evans, Robert Cable and Vose & Sons, while his parlor, church and school organs are of the Kimball manufacture. The well known reputation of these instruments has been demonstrated by their universal popularity among those who have used them. They are unsurpassed for quality, richness and volume of tone, construction and superior finish. They are sold either for cash or on the instalment plan, the latter arrangement allowing those of comparatively limited means to acquire one of these valuable instruments on the most liberal terms of payment. A specialty is the rebuilding, repairing and tuning of instruments, for which purpose none but the most skilful workmen and assistants are employed, while the prices are very reasonable. Mr. Fleming is a native of Michigan and has been a resident here since 1884. He is a very active, enterprising and industrious young man, prompt, reliable and honorable, and is held in the highest estimation in social and commercial circles.

 F. C. ROWLEY, Wholesale Dealer in Oysters, Clams, Terrapin and Crabs, No. 18 Spruce Street. Among the leading industries of the day that contribute most to Philadelphia's general prosperity and commercial importance, the wholesale trade in oysters, clams, etc., has assumed a prominent place, and is daily assuming larger proportions. A house in this particular line, enjoying high repute for its thoroughly responsible character, its reliability and promptness in all transactions, is that of Mr. F. C. Rowley, of No. 18 Spruce Street, one of the leading wholesale dealers in oysters, clams, terrapin and crabs. This enterprising concern was established by its present able proprietor in 1877, and has been located in the present commodious premises for the past two years. Here may be found at all times a heavy and well assorted stock of the most luscious bivalves, and a tempting array of other shell fish. Every convenience is supplied for the proper care of the stock, which is always kept at a proper temperature both while in storage and in course of shipment. Mr. Rowley uses at times a ton of ice daily in packing and shipping goods, which gives one a fair idea of the booming business he is doing. His trade, which is principally done through the Middle States, is of a most substantial character, reaching the best class of permanent patronage. Mr. Rowley has oyster beds in all the Southern waters, and ships direct to wholesale dealers in any part of the United States. He is a Marylander by birth, where he is widely known and highly esteemed. Mr. Rowley's fair dealings and the unvarying excellence of his stock have served to advance him quickly into public recognition. His wide experience in the trade enables him to efficiently serve the best interests of his patrons. He is always among the foremost with the first offerings of the season in his line of goods, and his extended facilities enable him to offer to customers the most substantial inducements.

 C. SAWYER, Manufacturer and Dealer in Sewing Machines, Needles and Oil, No. 201 South Eleventh Street. Mr. C. Sawyer, the well known manufacturer and dealer in sewing machines, needles and oil, established business in Philadelphia in 1873, and has been engaged in this business continuously, in this place and in Cleveland, Ohio, since 1865. His factory, located at Nos. 217 and 219 Quince Street, is admirably equipped. Twenty skilled mechanics are employed. At the salesrooms, No. 201 South Eleventh Street, is kept a large stock of machines of Mr. Sawyer's manufacture, also needles and oil. The "Favorite" sewing machine manufactured here embodies every desirable quality, and has won the admiration of all who have seen it in operation at home and abroad. It is the simplest, strongest and best adjusted sewing machine in the world. It is the perfection of mechanism for hemming, felling, trimming, binding, cording, seaming, braiding, embroidering and other purposes too numerous to particularize, and the price is no higher than is demanded for inferior machines. It is sold extensively all over the United States. Mr. Sawyer is a native of Massachusetts, but has been a resident of Philadelphia since 1873, and is honored and respected in all the various walks of life.

 HARKNESS & DERING (Successors to Ellwood Shannon & Son), Teas, Coffees and Spices, No. 214 Chestnut Street. It is a pleasure to call attention to the house of Messrs. Harkness & Dering, the well known dealers in teas, coffees and spices. This is the oldest house in its line in the city, having been established in 1843 by Mr. Ellwood Shannon. In 1868 the firm became Ellwood Shannon & Son, who were succeeded by the present proprietors in 1886. The establishment is spacious in size and a leading factor in the mercantile activity of this busy thoroughfare. The trade is conducted at both wholesale and retail, and the stock carried is the largest and choicest of its kind in the city, embracing leading brands, fresh from the original chests as imported, such as the finest fragrant Foochou tea, the finest Young Hyson, Imperial, Gunpowder, Orange Pekoe, Formosa, English Breakfast, Japan, Assam and Ceylon teas. These goods are pure and unadulterated, commending their own merits to the confidence and patronage of critical and discriminating buyers, while hotels, boarding houses, restaurants, institutions and the trade are supplied at wholesale rates. Goods are delivered in the city or sent securely packed to any part of the country, C. O. D., no chinaware, tea sets, watches, dictionaries or spoons, and no misrepresentation to effect sales. The trade is large, first class and influential in Philadelphia, New Jersey and Delaware, and is increasing under enterprising and reliable management. The copartners, Messrs. V. R. Harkness and E. M. Dering, are well and favorably known in this city.

HISTORICAL AND COMMERCIAL PHILADELPHIA.

JOHN E. EYANSON & SON, Practical Plumbers, No. 207 South Tenth Street.—In the important business of plumbing, together with gas and steam fitting and all kinds of electrical work for lighting purposes, the firm of John E. Eyanson & Son, at No. 207 South Tenth Street, has secured a well-earned reputation and their establishment has long been recognized as one of the most reliable of its kind in Philadelphia. It was founded in 1850 by Mr. John Philbin with whom Mr. J. E. Eyanson served an apprenticeship of five years. At Mr. Philbin's death, (Dec., 1867,) the business was continued by his son, Stephen R. Philbin and John E. Eyanson until December, 1874, when Mr. Philbin retired from business, Mr. Eyanson succeeding to the sole control, and admitting his son, Mr. J. Edward Eyanson, to partnership in 1885. The premises occupied are spacious in size and are fully stocked with a well-selected and complete assortment of plumbers', gasfitters' and electrical supplies of every description. Everything in the way of sanitary plumbing and ventilating, gas and steam fitting, and electric-lighting is executed by this firm in a thoroughly first-class and reliable manner. Contracts for the complete fitting of buildings of all kinds are satisfactorily performed at the lowest possible prices consistent with the best materials and superior workmanship, and among the contracts executed by this firm, may be mentioned the fitting up of the Drexel building, the University of Pennsylvania and Swathmore College. Their services are in constant and important requisition in city and country, requiring the constant employment of from twenty to thirty skilled workmen, while the proprietors give the business the benefit of their close personal supervision. Orders by Bell telephone No. 3920, by telegraph or mail receive immediate and careful attention. The senior proprietor is a native of Philadelphia, Pa., and a resident of this city, while his son was born in Baltimore, Md., and both are members of the Master Plumbers' Association, Master Builders' Exchange and of excellent repute in business and social circles.

HENRY E. KRAM & CO., Wholesale Grocers, No. 104 North Third Street.—This business was established in 1861 by David Bruner & Co., who were succeeded in 1885 by Kram & Snyder, who had been interested in the business many years previous to this, Mr. Kram having been connected with the house for the past thirty years. When Messrs. Bruner & Co. retired in 1885, the firm of Kram & Snyder took charge of the business with its steadily increasing trade, ably sustaining its old-established reputation. The firm of Henry E. Kram & Co. succeeded, August 31, 1892. The firm occupy a fine four-story building, covering an area of 20 x 60 feet. This is suitably fitted up with all conveniences for the business to which it is devoted. The stock is very full and complete, and is carefully selected. It consists of fine staple and fancy groceries, choice teas, pure spices, hermetically sealed canned goods, in tin and glass, pickles, jams, sauces, and the many articles usually found in a first-class grocery store. The firm make a specialty of cigars, which are manufactured by a house in the First District, of which they are part owners. The favorite brands are K. & S. 104, Kram's Special and others. An extensive trade is carried on with Pennsylvania, New Jersey, Delaware, Maryland, Virginia, New York, and all parts of the United States, these goods being all of first quality and sold at moderate prices, are in great demand. Mr. Kram is a native of Bucks County, and a member of the Wholesale Grocers' Association.

BOSTON LAUNDRY, Thomas E. Houston, Proprietor, Nos. 236 and 238 New Street. The Boston Laundry, of which Mr. Thomas E. Houston is proprietor, was started in a small way sixteen years ago by Mr. Houston at the present location, and from this humble beginning it has grown and prospered and extended its field of usefulness until now a three-story structure, 40 x 100 feet in size, is occupied, supplied with fourteen machines operated by steam-power and employing thirty hands. Agencies are established on the outskirts of the city as well as throughout New Jersey, and altogether a large and expanding trade is enjoyed, requiring six teams in the delivery and collection services. The work turned out from here is of the highest order of merit—thoroughly washed and ironed. Mr. Houston is a thoroughly expert laundryman, and gives his entire time and attention to overseeing every department of his enterprise. He is a native of this city, a member of the C. K. of A., Catholic Beneficial Societies, also Sons of Veterans, and of the Merchants' and Salesmen's Association.

C. R. SMITH & SON, Established 1837, Jewelers, Diamond Importers and Makers of Fine Watches, No. 1018 Chestnut Street.—One of the oldest and most prominent houses in this industry is that of C. R. Smith & Son, which has been in active operation for more than a half century. The founder of the establishment, Mr. C. R. Smith, began business in 1837, continuing alone up to 1883, when his son, Mr. C. E. Smith, became his partner, the firm-name of C. R. Smith & Son being then adopted. In 1889 the senior member of the firm died, his decease closing a long life and most honorable mercantile career. During the present year his son admitted to partnership Mr. J. H. Bailey, who had been in the house since boyhood. Mr. Bailey was born in Ohio, and has resided here eighteen years. Mr. Smith is a native Philadelphian, and is prominently known here. The firm are diamond importers, jewelers and makers of fine watches, importing direct from the leading European houses, and making a leading specialty of diamonds, unset or handsomely mounted. The factory is 25 x 100 feet in dimensions, and equipped with superior machinery, driven by steam power, and thirty skilled hands are employed. The salesroom is on the first floor, has a frontage of 25 feet, and a depth of 80 feet, and is appointed in elegantly tasteful style, while the stock carried is one of the choicest and most valuable to be seen on Chestnut Street. A splendid trade is carried on, derived from all sections of Pennsylvania and vicinity.

McCOWAN & LONGAKER, Safety Lighting Devices, Office and Factory, No. 3230 Germantown Avenue.—The grandest achievements in the production of safety lighting devices are those which are now being introduced by Messrs. McCowan & Longaker, whose office and factory are located at No. 3230 Germantown Avenue. This firm are manufacturers and sole agents for the United States of the "Consecutive Safety Lighting Devices," consisting of self-lighting lamp burners, self-lighting lantern burners, self-lighting gas burners, self-lighting pocket lights, self-lighting boudoir lights, and self-lighting hand lights. They established their business here in 1892, on the substantial basis of merit, and it has had a remarkable growth, forming one of the best illustrations of industrial progress in the city. The firm occupy a fine three-story factory, 30 x 100 feet in dimensions, fully equipped with new and improved machinery and appliances, and affording employment to some seventy-five skilled hands. In placing the consecutive safety lights before the public, this firm does so with the knowledge that in them they have an article that stands to-day unequalled by any other means of lighting ever invented or discovered. As a preventative of calamity by fire through the careless use of matches, it is without a rival and will supersede anything of the kind ever placed upon the market. It greatly reduces the liability of damage by fire in mills, factories or any manufacturing concern having a large number of employees, while, as regards the self-lighting hand lamp, it will not blow out by wind or in carrying it, can always be relied upon, does not get out of order, and the price is within the reach of all. The burners will light 100,000 times and are warranted to be as represented. They can be carried in the pocket, or attached to any lamp or lantern or to the gas burner. They are for sale by the leading storekeepers in all parts of the country, and an immense stock is carried by the firm, to the end that no delay may be experienced in the filling of orders. The copartners, Messrs. A. T. McCowan and R. R. Longaker, are natives of Pennsylvania, and gentlemen of enterprise, pluck and public spirit, who have learned the value of printers' ink, and are winning success by honestly deserving it. Mr. I. M. Rose, the inventor of the safety lighting devices, is a silent partner in the firm while giving the business the benefit of his expert knowledge and sound practical advice.

MATHIEU BROTHERS & CO., Produce Commission Merchants, No. 123 Callowhill Street. Among the many houses engaged in the great produce supply of Philadelphia, none enjoy a higher and more soundly established reputation for all-round reliability, expeditious and honorable dealing than do Messrs. Mathieu Brothers & Co., located at No. 123 Callowhill Street, who, as commission merchants and wholesale dealers, control a trade of large proportions, reaching among dealers and other wholesale consumers throughout the city and suburbs. This responsible undertaking was founded a number of years ago by Messrs. J. L. Clymer & Co., and in 1883 it came into the hands of Messrs. Mathieu Brothers & Co., the present proprietors being Messrs. H. A. Mathieu and J. William Mathieu. The house enjoys the confidence and perpetual support of a large number of growers, raisers and producers in Pennsylvania, Virginia, Maryland, West Virginia, Ohio, Indiana, Iowa, Michigan and Illinois, from whom heavy and regular consignments are constantly arriving, including butter, eggs, live and dressed poultry, game in season, and dried fruits of all kinds. These consignments are speedily disposed of with a skill and judgment sure indicating ripe experience and a thorough knowledge of the trade; accurate account-sales are rendered, prompt returns made, and such facilities extended to patrons for the protection and promotion of their best interests that it would be difficult for any other responsible house to excel; while, on the other hand, some liberal inducements are offered to wholesale consumers as to price, quality, freshness and prompt delivery. The premises utilized consist of three floors, each 20 x 60 feet in area, furnished with a cooling-room, an elevator and every other convenience for the most successful conduct of a large business of this nature, six competent clerks being regularly employed. Mr. H. A. Mathieu, who is a young gentleman of energy, tact and sound ability, was born in the Quaker City and is a member of the Philadelphia Produce Exchange, and the National Butter, Cheese and Egg Association, besides being prominently identified with the Masonic Fraternity.

CHAS. F. SCHOELL, Merchant Tailor, No. 133 South Tenth Street. One of the most accomplished merchant tailors of Philadelphia is Mr. Chas. F. Schoell, who is a popular caterer to first-class custom and enjoys an enviable patronage. His business was established in 1870 and has occupied the present desirable location for the past twenty years. The elegant parlors are 20 x 40 feet in dimensions and a large stock of foreign and domestic cloths is displayed in all the latest shades and patterns, from which the most fastidious can not fail to find something to suit. Mr. Schoell makes a specialty of fine clothing, and is a skilled and thorough exponent of the art, and in cut, finish, and general excellence the reputation of the house is a credit to its director. Special attention is given to scouring and repairing. Mr. Schoell is a native of Germany, but has been a resident of this city for twenty-eight years, and is highly esteemed in business and social circles, and a popular member of the Merchant Tailors' Exchange.

HEAD IT OFF!
Don't Wait 'til it takes hold.

WAMPOLE'S
Tasteless Preparation of Cod Liver Oil,

Heads off Consumption, Cures Colds and Coughs, Checks Waste, Makes Fat.

SOLD BY DRUGGISTS THROUGHOUT UNITED STATES AND CANADA.

MR. H. LEFEVRE, JR.,

lately representing the house of E. O. Murdock of New York City, in Philadelphia, has now accepted a position to represent the house of U. C. GRAVES & CO., (of Fifth Street, Philadelphia) in New York City, in Paints, Varnishes, &c.

Address, 104 John St., N. Y. City,

Care J. H. Lyles.

THE READING ROLLING MILL COMPANY,

OFFICE,
257 South Fourth Street.

The Reading Rolling Mill Company, whose office is at No. 257 South Fourth Street, was organized in 1890. It was duly incorporated under the laws of the State of Pennsylvania with a capital stock of $300,000, all paid in. The plant, which is located at Reading, Pa., is leased from the Philadelphia & Reading Railroad Company, and the lease is perpetual. There are fifteen double puddling furnaces, ten heating furnaces, seven forge fires and four trains of rolls $\frac{3}{4}$ and $\frac{7}{8}$ inch in operation. The mill is perfectly equipped, the facilities there being first-class in every respect, and a large force of help is employed. The company manufactures all kinds of structural iron work for bridges, buildings, etc., and can turn out 48,000 tons a year. They are prepared to give estimates on anything in the line above indicated, and are in a position to execute the largest orders at short notice. The president of the Reading Rolling Mill Company is Jos. H. Cofrode, the secretary and treasurer is P. R. Foley, J. L. Rake is the general manager and William Brazier is superintendent of the mill. The directors are Jos. H. Cofrode, Geo. W. Bush, Francis H. Saylor, William Nolan, Daniel R. Cofrode, J. F. Bailey and Chas. A. Sterling. Mr. Jos. H. Cofrode is president of Cofrode & Saylor (incorporated), engineers and contractors, and owners of the Philadelphia Bridge Works. Mr. Foley is treasurer of the Philadelphia Bridge Works; Mr. D. R. Cofrode is of Cofrode & Evans, contractors; Mr. Saylor is of Cofrode & Saylor (incorporated) and a director of Philadelphia Bridge Works, and Mr. Nolan is of Nolan Bros., contractors; Mr. Bailey is of J. F. Bailey & Sons, selling agents for the Reading Rolling Mill Company and general commission merchants in iron and steel. Mr. Chas. A. Sterling is the president of the National Storage Company.

Duquesne Coal Company,

—— DEALERS IN ——

Honey Brook Lehigh Coal,

SAND,
LIME,
HAIR,
PLASTER,
CEMENT, &c.

No. 2927 North Broad Street.

No interest in the range of industrial and commercial activity is of more importance to Philadelphia than that of coal, both as regards capital invested and the direct benefits derivable therefrom to all classes of the community. One of the enterprising houses of Philadelphia engaged in this line is that of the Duquesne Coal Company, located at No. 2927 North Broad Street. This company are dealers in Honey Brook Lehigh coal; also Rambo's lime, and the best qualities of plaster, cement, hair, sand, etc. They established their business here in 1891, and their connections with the largest miners and shippers are such as to place them upon a par, so far as competition is concerned, with any of their contemporaries, whether dealing by the car load or at retail by the ton. Their yard embraces an acre of ground and is supplied with coal pockets, storage capacity for 1500 tons of coal and direct connections with the Pennsylvania R. R., so as to insure prompt receipt and delivery of supplies. They always have in stock the best products of the anthracite mines and guarantee quality and weight in all cases, while selling at the lowest market prices. A specialty is made of Rambo's lime, which commends itself to the confidence and patronage of every discriminating purchaser. Orders are promptly filled and the trade of the house is brisk and lively throughout the city and surrounding country. The proprietors, Messrs. Geo. S. Thompson, Byron S. Eastburn and William M. Vantier are native Philadelphians and young men of large experience and eminent popularity, whose future success seems well assured.

CLYDE STEAMSHIP CO.,

This company own and control a large number of steamships, steamboats, etc., their lines running between BOSTON, NEW YORK, PHILADELPHIA, BALTIMORE and WASHINGTON, NORFOLK, NEWBERNE, RICHMOND, TROY, ALBANY, WILMINGTON, N. C., GEORGETOWN, S. C., CHARLESTON, S. C., and JACKSONVILLE, FLA., and on the St. John's River between JACKSONVILLE, FLA., PALATKA, SANFORD and intermediate landings, also from NEW YORK to TURKS ISLAND, HAYTI, SAN DOMINGO and other West India ports. It was founded by Mr. Thomas Clyde, the father of Messrs. Wm. P. and B. F. Clyde, composing the well-known shipping firm of Wm. P. Clyde & Co., the largest individual steamship owners in this country, who have continued the policy of the Clydes as inaugurated by their father, they being the leaders in practically all the improvements made in steamships in this country during the last fifty years.

In 1844 Mr. Thomas Clyde built the Steamer "JOHN S. McKIM," the first twin-screw propeller steamer built in the United States for commercial purposes, thus recognizing and practically applying nearly fifty years ago this method of obtaining speed with economy. This steamer was used successfully as a transport for troops, and in 1846 carried Col. Jefferson Davis' regiment of Mississippi Volunteers to the Mexican War from New Orleans, and it is a remarkable coincidence that another of Mr. Clyde's steamers, the "REBECCA CLYDE" in 1865 brought Jefferson Davis as a prisoner from Savannah to Fortress Monroe.

The Messrs. Clyde, though building and owning every variety of steamships and steamboats, have always given the preference to the screw propeller, and have used it wherever practicable. They experimented upon and demonstrated the practicability of the propeller for shallow harbors and rivers where others believed nothing but the more expensive side-wheel steamers were advisable. They have made and adopted many improvements both in model and machinery of steamers.

In 1871 they built the first compound engine constructed in this country and placed the same in the "GEO. W. CLYDE."

In 1886 they constructed the first large triple expansion engine built in this country, and placed it in the steamer "CHEROKEE."

In 1888 they built the steamer "IROQUOIS," the first steel steamer ever built in this country for commercial purposes.

In the fall of 1886 Messrs. Wm. P. Clyde & Co. started their direct line of steamers between New York and Jacksonville, Fla., commencing the service with the two steamers "CHEROKEE" and "SEMINOLE," of over 2000 tons burden each, constructed upon a model specially designed by the Messrs. Clyde, and which enabled them to successfully cross the St. John's Bar and go up the St. John's River to Jacksonville, when, before that time, the largest vessel which had crossed the St. John's Bar was considerably less than 1000 tons. This service has been continued since its inauguration with the utmost regularity. Larger steamers have since been built for and placed on the Jacksonville Line, the "IROQUOIS," 3000 tons, in 1888, and the "ALGONQUIN," 3000 tons, in 1890.

WM. P. CLYDE & CO., GENERAL AGENTS.

No. 5 Bowling Green, New York.   No. 12 So. Delaware Ave., Philadelphia, Pa.

STANLEY G. FLAGG & CO.

Malleable Iron, Gray Iron and Steel Founders,

MANUFACTURERS OF

MALLEABLE IRON, CAST IRON AND STEEL FITTINGS

For connections of Wrought Iron or Steel Pipe for conveying Gas, Steam, Oil, Water, Ammonia, Etc., Etc.

FINISHING AND MACHINE SHOPS,

North Nineteenth Street, Pennsylvania Avenue and Hamilton Street,
PHILADELPHIA, PA.

A most important establishment and one that secures to Philadelphia the most advanced methods and perfect facilities for the manufacture of Malleable Iron, Gray Iron and Steel Castings, as also Fittings for Gas, Steam, Water, Etc., is that of Stanley G. Flagg & Co., the well-known founders and manufacturers, situated at North Nineteenth Street, Pennsylvania Avenue and Hamilton Street. The business was founded in 1856, by Mr. Stanley G. Flagg, at Frankford, in a very small way, and was steadily developed on the basis of merit and skill, and in 1870 the present premises were erected. Mr. Stanley G. Flagg, Jr. was admitted to partnership in 1880, followed by the admission of the junior partner, Mr. George Flagg, in 1882, thus forming the firm as at present constituted. The partners bring to bear vast practical experience, coupled with energy and ability, ample resources and a thorough knowledge of the wants of the trade. Their plant has a frontage of 440 feet on Nineteenth Street, 250 feet on Pennsylvania Avenue and 130 feet on Hamilton Street, and comprises several buildings, one to four stories in height, thoroughly equipped with a costly and elaborate outfit of machinery and appliances, and steady employment is given to from 350 to 400 skilled hands. The foundry has two cupolas, melting from fifteen to twenty tons per day, also a reverberatory furnace, erected purposely for the manufacture of light and medium weight steel castings by a process especially their own, while the firm also operate a foundry for gray iron castings, at Nos. 1109 to 1119 Front Street, having one cupola melting five tons per day. The proprietors exercise a personal supervision over all the details of the work, and maintain an enviable reputation for the perfection and durability of all mechanism leaving their works. They use only the best grades of iron and steel, and all workmanship is strictly first-class. The firm have successfully coped with the most difficult problems in the course of their business, and turn out a class of castings second to none in the world for smoothness, softness, quality of metal and adaptability to the purposes intended, while their iron pipe fittings are recognized by experts as a superior article. A specialty is made of small steel castings under one hundred pounds, in which department this firm is known to excel. The business of the house extends to all parts of the United States, and is annually increasing under liberal and reliable management. The Messrs. Flagg are all founders and manufacturers of large experience and established reputation, members of the Manufacturers' Club, the Philadelphia Bourse and the Trade League, and highly regarded in industrial and trade circles for their commanding ability and sound business principles.

JOHN BLOOD & CO.;

MANUFACTURERS OF

HOSIERY

—AND—

JERSEYS,

Northwest corner Seventh and Somerset Streets.

No branch of the manufacturing industries of the city has been conducted with greater vigor and discretion, and with more substantial results, than that of the production of textile goods. The aggregate capital invested is immense, and the morale of the firms engaged in the business unexcelled in commercial circles. The foremost house in its special line is that of John Blood & Co., manufacturers of hosiery and jerseys, whose mills are at the northwest corner of Seventh and Somerset Streets. This great enterprise was founded sixteen years ago by John Blood & Co., at the corner of Third and Master Streets, was afterwards removed to the corner of Adams and Emerald Streets, and lastly to the present address. The firm are closely connected and identified with the manufacturing prosperity of Philadelphia, energy add very materially to its commercial development. Their connections extend throughout the United States, their goods bearing a standard reputation in the trade. The present works were built by the firm six years ago. The building is a brick structure, having three floors and basement, 45 x 200 feet in dimensions. It is equipped with the finest machinery, driven by steam-power. The plant includes 600 knitting machines, 100 sewing machines, and all requisite appliances. The extent of the operations carried on demands the employment of 500 skilled operatives. The firm manufacture hosiery and jerseys of all sizes, grades and varieties, constantly introducing new patterns and designs. The output is a very heavy one, while the goods are all made in the best form of workmanship, from the choicest materials. These goods are shipped to all parts of the United States. The members of the firm are Messrs. John Blood and John Diggle. The former was born in Ruddington, England, is now in the middle age of life, and has worked in a mill since seven years of age. He has resided in this city the past twenty-eight years. Mr. Diggle is a native of Germantown, born of English parentage, and has been connected with mill-work since boyhood. Both gentlemen are well known in financial and commercial circles, and are esteemed for their integrity and honorable methods.

270

O. F. ZURN & CO.,

408 to 418 Vine St., Cor. of Crown St., PHILA., Pa. High Grade Oils Exclusively.

Manufacturers ROYAL DYNAMO and ROYAL CYLINDER OILS

now in use by scores of Central Electric Lighting Companies throughout the U. S. and Canada. Correspondence solicited from parties desirous of overcoming present Lubricating difficulties, to all such we say "no charge until we show satisfactory results."

The history of American manufactures has never been fully written; in fact the data for such a work are not available. The noble efforts which have contributed to the stupendous results now attained are not generally a matter of record. It is interesting, however, to note those firms whose history is also that of the development of the various industries in which they are engaged.

A house occupying a foremost position in the oil manufacturing industry of this city is that of O. F. Zurn & Co., located at the above-noted address. This establishment has been in active operation since 1882. The founders are men of large experience in their line, and three years ago the present firm succeeded to the ownership, the copartners being O. F. Zurn, J. M. Zurn, J. D. Kelley and C. J. Curran, all young business men of energy and progressive policy. They employ quite a number of traveling representatives and have a trade extending to all sections of the Union, also South America and Europe. Their present quarters, the largest building in the city devoted exclusively to their line of business, is a four-story structure, 100 x 160 feet in dimensions, and contains a number of handsome offices and a complete stock of high-grade oils for all purposes, including the famous "Royal" brands of cylinder, dynamo, engine and machinery oils.

Some years since after careful experimenting upon the steam-boilers at their own plant the firm of O. F. Zurn & Co., were induced to place upon the market a number of "compounds" intended to prevent the formation of scale in steam-boilers, and to remove same, when already in existence.

Their method of determining remedy required is to analyze the scale or water in use, a fully equipped laboratory and a competent chemist being employed for the purpose. While making no pretensions to having discovered a universal cure-all, yet their success in this line has been remarkable. Concerning the standing of a house so long and favorably known to the trade, we may not presume to make comments. In conclusion, however, it is but just to say that its business is conducted upon those principles of fairness and liberality without which no permanent success such as theirs is possible.

JOHN T. DOHAN. WM. H. DOHAN

DOHAN & TAITT,

Importers of Havana and Sumatra.

PACKERS OF LEAF TOBACCO.

WAREHOUSES:
LANCASTER, PA.
BALDWINSVILLE, N. Y.
JANESVILLE, WIS.

Manufacturers' Agents for Plug Chewing Tobaccos.

107 Arch Street.

The oldest representative of the leaf tobacco industry in Philadelphia is the house of Dohan & Taitt, whose headquarters are noted in these headlines and who also have large warehouses at Lancaster, Pa., Baldwinsville, N. Y., and Janesville, Wis. The house was founded on Water Street, in 1855, by M. J. Dohan and John T. Taitt, under the existing firm-name of Dohan & Taitt, and they remained together up to 1874, when Mr. Taitt's death occurred. In October, 1894, Mr. Dohan's decease also took place, after a long, useful and highly honorable mercantile career. His sons are now proprietors of the establishment. These young men, Messrs. John T. Dohan and William H. Dohan, are natives of this city, and were brought up from youth to a knowledge of the leaf tobacco industry, consequently they are amply qualified to continue the success achieved by their predecessors. They hold membership in the National Tobacco Dealers' Association and the Philadelphia Tobacco Board of Trade. The warehouse in this city is a six-story building, 20 x 125 feet in dimensions, and it is at all times filled with a superior stock of Havana and Sumatra leaf, also Pennsylvania, New York and Wisconsin leaf tobacco, a leading specialty being made of tobacco from these States. The firm are agents for plug chewing tobaccos, and carry a complete supply of these goods, as well as of leaf tobacco, and orders from any point in the United States are carefully filled at lowest quotations.

CRAVEN & DEARNLEY,

SPINNERS OF

WORSTED,

WOOLEN,

AND MOHAIR

✳ YARNS, ✳

Eighth and Somerset Streets.

A feature of Philadelphia's industries entitled to special mention is the manufacture of yarns, and among the worthy houses engaged in this line, a foremost, honored and representative position is occupied by Messrs. Craven & Dearnley, whose mills are at the corner of Eighth and Somerset Streets. This prosperous establishment was founded in 1881, by the present proprietors, Messrs. Wm. Craven and John H. Dearnley, both of whom possess an expert knowledge of the trade in which they have achieved such a signal success. Mr. Craven is probably the oldest active exponent of the yarn manufacturing industry in the city, as he has been identified with the trade for the past sixty years. He is veritably the Nestor of his calling. Mr. Dearnley, who is a young man, has had eleven years' experience, and is, moreover, a business man of push and enterprise. The premises occupied comprise a three-story building, 200 x 68 feet, and a three-story and basement brick building, 200 x 45 feet in dimensions. It is fitted with A1 machinery, including twenty-six worsted spinning frames, having a daily capacity of 3,000 pounds, also four sets of woolen machinery having a total capacity of 1,000 pounds per day. The driving force is supplied by a 300-horse power engine, and employment is found for 325 experienced operatives. Messrs. Craven & Dearnley are spinners of worsted, woolen and mohair yarns of all grades. The goods are sold to knitters and weavers in all parts of the United States, and the splendid facilities that have been developed by this firm enables them to offer the most advantageous terms and prices.

LEHMAN HOUSE

SALE and EXCHANGE STABLES,

ELI KINDIG, Jr., Proprietor.

3919 MARKET STREET.

The trade in horses is an important department of business in Philadelphia, and has engaged in its prosecution most energetic and enterprising business men. One of the leaders among the number is Mr. Eli Kindig, Jr., proprietor of the Lehman House Sale and Exchange Stables, located at No. 3919 Market Street. There are few men, if any, in the business better known or more highly and widely esteemed than Mr. Kindig. He was born in York, Pa., and was raised from youth to a personal knowledge of horse flesh. He is an expert judge of the noble animal as to soundness, beauty, disposition and speed, and knows also what his wants are and how to provide for them. Nineteen years ago he came to this city and established the business that has since been directed by him with such prosperous success. The stables are large, well drained and ventilated, and have accommodations for 200 horses. Mr. Kindig deals in Western stock mostly, selling horses and mules of all values, at private sale, and he disposes of some 1,500 head a year. A large stock of horses of all grades is constantly kept on hand, making a specialty of coach, road and saddle horses, handling more than any other dealer in the State in that class of horses, and any one requiring first-class value for their money will do well to call upon Mr. Kindig, who will extend them every courtesy.

THE WARDEN

Manufacturing Company,

Germantown Junction.

Philadelphia has no manufacturing establishment whose products are in greater request or of more practical utility and value than those of the Warden Manufacturing Company, whose works are located at Germantown Junction, near Seventeenth and Clearfield Streets. This company are extensive manufacturers of boilers, tanks, stacks and water works stand pipes; while making prominent specialties of the Manning vertical boiler, the Warden patent purifier, the Atkinson feed water heater, the Cycle filter, the Heine safety boiler, and all kinds of boiler work to order. The business was established in 1883, by Mr. Henry Warden, the present company being organized in 1891. The plant covers six acres of ground, and the main building measures 100 x 200 feet, while there is a blacksmith-shop and boiler-room, 100 x 100 feet, and all are splendidly equipped with new and improved machinery and ample steam-power, while steady employment is given to 200 skilled workmen. The Manning vertical boilers are recommended as unusually economical in the use of fuel, while their great popularity and success are due to the boilers being internally fired and having a high furnace, to the correct ratio between the diameter and length of the tubes being maintained, and to the covering of the boiler with first-class non-conducting material, thereby reducing the loss of heat due to radiation to a much greater degree than is possible in brick set boilers. They are used and endorsed by such great manufacturing concerns as the Amoskeag Manufacturing Co., and the P. C. Cheney Co., Manchester, N. H.; Merrick Thread Co., Holyoke, Mass.; Goodyear's Metallic Rubber Shoe Co., Naugatuck, Conn.; Sawyer Woolen Mills, Dover, N. H. The Warden patent purifier, owned by this company, uses heat as the precipitating agent for preventing the formation of scale in boilers, and is the only purifier based on this method in which a settling chamber is used of such size as to insure the water remaining in it a sufficient length of time to settle the salts precipitated; and it is also the only one in which the settling chamber is outside the boiler. The device is of such a simple design and construction that the cost of operation and repair is reduced to a minimum. The Atkinson patent feed water heater is without doubt the best appliance made for heating water by means of exhaust steam. The heaters are thoroughly well made, and the cylinders are of ample capacity. The Cycle filter is thoroughly self-cleansing, and is entirely controlled by one valve, requiring only three motions of the valve to cleanse the same; while it is simple in construction, uses the minimum amount of wash water per million gallons filtered, and costs less per million gallons capacity. Plans and estimates are furnished for any sized plants. These and other specialties of this company are in heavy and influential demand throughout the United States and South America, and add materially to the prestige and popularity of the house by their inherent and superior merits. Illustrated catalogues are mailed to any address, and orders and communications receive immediate and careful attention. The moving spirits of this company are expert and successful manufacturers, who have achieved a position in the industrial world that affords the best possible proof of their genius and commanding skill.

Star and Crescent Mills Co.,

Manufacturers of

TURKISH TOWELS, TIDIES, TERRY CLOTH, TURKISH CLOAKINGS, ETC., ETC.,

FRANK LEAKE, President.   DOUGLAS LEAKE, Secretary and Treasurer.

OFFICES: New York, No. 83 Leonard St.; Boston, No. 78 Chauncey St.; San Francisco, No. 119 Bush St.; Philadelphia, Lehigh Avenue and Hancock St.

One of the notable concerns in this city engaged in the production of textile specialties is that of the Star and Crescent Mills Company, manufacturers of Turkish towels and terry fabrics, whose plant is located at Lehigh Avenue and Hancock Street. This house was founded in 1882, by Frank Leake & Co. at No. 1643 Hancock Street, where they continued until 1885, when the growth of the business justified the purchase and enlargement of the present mills. In 1889 the firm added a bleachery to their plant, which has gained for the house the reputation of the "Best Bleach."

The present company was incorporated in 1888, with a capital stock of $200,000. The president, Mr. Frank Leake, was for five years selling agent for the Fairfield Mills (John Rothwell & Son,) which plant he purchased in 1885, thus forming the basis for the present plant. He is a member of the Philadelphia Bourse, the Trade League and the Manufacturers' Club.

This plant is one of the finest in the city, occupying the block bounded by Lehigh Avenue, Somerset, Hancock and Mutter Streets.

The Philadelphia "Ledger" of January 22, 1892, says of these mills and their business: "Odd as it may seem, Turkish towels are not made in Turkey except in limited quantities, but chiefly in the United States, and the largest manufacturers of them in this country are in this city. The Star and Crescent Mills Company are the largest, it is claimed, in the world. Mr. Frank Leake, the president of the company, stated yesterday that they now export goods to Europe and Canada and have recently opened up a trade with South America which promises much. During November twenty shipments of goods were made to various South American houses. In December four shipments were made. While a considerable quantity of goods are shipped to England, none of the staple line of goods, in which competition with the foreign manufacturers is almost impossible, are exported to that country, but to Canada and South America all classes are sent. Since the passage of the new tariff act, Mr. Leake states, greater opportunities have been given them, and increased attention is now being directed toward the development of a trade for the better class of goods. The business of these mills is not entirely devoted to the manufacture of towels, although they are manufactured from the size of a doily to that of a small sheet. Bath robing, tidies, dusters or wash-rags and toweling cloth are also woven. Some idea of the extent of the manufacture may be had by mentioning that ten miles of goods are woven each day. There are always four and a-half tons of toweling in the vats in the bleach-house. There are 190 looms in constant operation, and, owing to their construction, it is claimed that their products are equal to that of about 250 ordinary looms. Something should be said of the designs and colorings of these goods, which are equal in many respects and superior in others, to the foreign goods. In variety there are about 500 designs now being woven, and new ones being constantly introduced. Of this number 200 figures are in bath robing alone. The colors and materials which contribute to the color effects number nearly 150."

This company sell their products direct from the mills to jobbers and large retailers in all parts of the country

KEYSTONE KNITTING MACHINE MFG. CO.,

BUILDERS OF THE CELEBRATED

Keystone Seamless ✺
✺ Knitting Machine,

1716-20
NORTH FIFTH ST.

Agents for all Classes of Machinery for Seamless Hosiery and Underwear.

A branch of industry of a very important and meritorious character represented in Philadelphia is that of the manufacture of knitting machinery, and a leading exponent thereof is the Keystone Knitting Machine Manufacturing Company, whose headquarters are located at Nos. 1716 to 1720 North Fifth Street. This company enjoy an international reputation and trade as builders of the celebrated Keystone Seamless Knitting Machine, and also as agents for all classes of machinery for seamless hosiery and underwear. The business was first established in 1886, by Thomas A. Pearce, and in 1891 the present company was incorporated with a capital stock of $100,000, with J. C. Egly, president; W. G. Dillmore, vice-president; Thomas A. Pearce, secretary and treasurer. The works of the company are at Wilmington, Del., and comprise a building 200 x 300 feet, fully equipped with new and improved machinery and ample steam-power, and steady employment is given to 110 skilled hands. The premises occupied in this city comprise an office, stockroom and repair-shop, and ample space is here afforded for the large and valuable stock that is constantly carried. The Improved Keystone Seamless Knitter has met with unbounded praise wherever shown or used. It is believed by experts and good judges to be better adapted to the use of hosiery manufacturers than any other machine ever offered. The materials and workmanship used are of the very best, the parts are all interchangeable, and it is without exception the simplest, most substantial and durable machine built. Every machine is thoroughly tested before leaving the shops, when delivered has a complete stocking knit on it, and is guaranteed perfect in every respect. It knits a firm even web, does not cut or strip the yarn, and makes a perfect heel and toe, the gore being closer and more even than the goods knit on other machines. It is capable of producing goods equal to those imported, and at prices that enables the manufacturer to successfully compete with the foreign manufacturer, and is equally well adapted to the coarse or heavy grades. This company are also agents for Hepworth & Company's loopers, single or double stitch, or both combined; also cop and skein winders, steam presses, hosiery boards, bobbins, etc. They make a specialty of fitting up and starting new mills and are prepared to furnish foremen and skilled operators to parties purchasing machinery. Orders are filled at extremely low prices, and the trade is broadly distributed over the United States, Canada, South America and Europe. President Egly is a native of Germany, who came to this country twenty-five years ago; Vice-President Dillmore is a well known Philadelphian; and Mr. Pearce, the secretary and treasurer and founder of the business, is also proprietor of the Penn Hosiery Mills, a member of the Manufacturers' Club, and an enterprising, progressive and successful business man.

Long Distance Telephone Connection.

J. W. HOFFMAN & CO.,

IRON AND STEEL MERCHANTS.

333 & 335 WALNUT ST., PHILADELPHIA.

JOHN W. HOFFMAN,
ERNEST LAW.

Dear Sir:—

The Iron and Steel interests and kindred industries centred in Philadelphia, as a distributing market, are represented by a number of merchants whose standing and business energy have made this city the headquarters for buyers throughout the entire country, and the most desirable point for foreign houses to establish connections for the intelligent and economical execution of export orders. It is quite certain that the United States is on the eve of a large and rapidly increasing export trade, and that it will be to the interest of foreign buyers to place the execution of their commissions for **purchase at lowest prices and careful and prompt shipment**, in the hands of **well-informed**, as well as responsible firms. The coming Columbian Exhibition will certainly bring to this country a large number of visitors who will take advantage of the opportunity to establish business connections, and to these gentlemen, particularly the ones interested in iron or steel in all forms, or their products in the shape of **cars, bridges, structural work, etc.**, we would extend a most cordial invitation to visit **our office in Philadelphia**, and to make the acquaintance of our representative at Chicago, having arranged for a constant attendance there during the Exposition. Established in business for twenty-five years, and having intimate connections with all the **leading manufacturers in the country** we can readily satisfy as to our ability to serve our correspondents with intelligence, and to their advantage, and we are prepared to give such **bankers' references** as may be desired as to the standing and responsibility of our firm. Our business connections with the terminal companies in New York and Baltimore, enable us to deliver goods for export, when required at either of these ports, with as much satisfaction and certainty as the local merchants. We should be much pleased to have correspondents address us in advance of their visit, and will give prompt and careful attention to any inquiries, placing our services and information at their disposal.

Faithfully Yours,

J. W. HOFFMAN & CO.,

IRON AND STEEL MERCHANTS.

Iron and Steel Boiler Plates, Tank Iron and Steel, Black and Galvanized Iron and Steel Sheets, all Grades, Pig Iron, Boiler Rivets, Bolts, Nuts, Washers, Etc., Angles, Tees and Shapes, Bar Iron and Steel, Steel Castings, Forgings, Cars and Railroad Equipments.

Nos. 333 and 335 Walnut Street, Philadelphia.

GEORGE EVANS & CO.,

~Tailors~

AND MANUFACTURERS OF

✴ ✴ UNIFORMS, ✴ ✴

No. 132 North Fifth St.

The oldest and most noted Philadelphia firm engaged in the manufacture of uniforms is that of George Evans & Co., whose establishment is at No. 132 North Fifth Street, and it is the only one exclusively in the particular line indicated in the city. This is a thoroughly reliable and widely-known house, and its trade, which is very large, extends all over the United States. Every garment made here is warranted as to material and workmanship, and perfect fit is assured, likewise. Mr. Evans, the head of the firm, is a gentleman of mature years, active and energetic, and was born in Wales, but has long been a respected resident of this city. He is a man of thorough practical skill and some forty odd years' experience, and is master of the tailoring art in all its branches. He established this flourishing business in 1860, and was formerly located on Market Street, removing to the present commodious quarters in 1880. The premises here occupied by the firm comprise three spacious floors, with ample and excellent facilities, and from seventy-five to one hundred hands are employed, including a number of expert designers and cutters. An extensive and elegant stock is always kept on hand here and embraces all the latest novelties and finest productions in imported and domestic cloths for military, naval, band, police and society uniforms, including a line of high-grade fabrics from which the most fastidious in dress can make selection. The firm of George Evans & Co. are tailors and manufacturers of uniforms of every description and have a national reputation for first-class work and fine goods. They are prepared to give estimates on anything in their line and quote the very lowest possible prices, while all orders are certain to be attended to in the most expeditious and thoroughly satisfactory manner. They make a specialty of inventing and introducing new and unique designs and patterns of ornamentation in gold and other braids, and issue an illustrated catalogue which is presented free upon application. Their assortment of military caps, hats, helmets, epaulettes, accoutrements and equipments generally is very large, varied and complete.

SCOTT & WILLIAMS,

Successor to JOS. HEGINBOTHOM MACHINE COMPANY,

Builders of Knitting Machinery,

No. 2079 East Cumberland St.

The greatest success in the manufacture of knitting machinery was achieved by the Jos. Heginbothom Machine Company, whose productions acquired a widespread celebrity as the embodiment of inventive genius and the perfection of mechanism, and whose office and works were located at Nos. 2077 to 2081 East Cumberland Street. The business so successfully conducted by them was established in 1865 by Mr. Joseph Heginbothom, and in 1883 the company was incorporated under the laws of the State of Pennsylvania, and was officered by L. N. D. Williams, president; Robert W. Scott, treasurer and general manager. It is now under the name and proprietorship of Scott & Williams who are successors to the Jos. Heginbothom Machine Company. The works comprise a three-story building, 150 x 75 feet, also a two-story building, 175 x 50 feet in dimensions, fully equipped with new and improved machinery, operated by a steam-engine of 80-horse power, and steady employment is given to 125 skilled hands. Those who are in any way acquainted with the bygone methods of manufacturing hosiery and knit goods will readily admit that the genius of the inventor and the skill of the mechanic have had great obstacles to contend with in the manufacture of machinery for accomplishing the work originally performed by the slow and tedious process of hand labor. This conviction will be greatly strengthened by a visit to the works of this company, or to any of the numerous mills where the machinery made here is in operation; for, while in the former they would be struck with the wonderful means used to remove all mechanical difficulties, in the latter they would be still more astonished by the inconceivable rapidity and mathematical accuracy resulting from the use of these machines. In the prosecution of their work this firm's main object has been to construct such mechanism as should be durable, rapid and perfect in its operation, and at the minimum of cost; and in this laudable endeavor they have attained a brilliant success, as is well proven by the career of the house and the great popularity of its products both at home and abroad. Their Automatic Ribbed Shirt Machine is used by leading manufacturers almost exclusively, possessing many points of excellence, and is without doubt the most efficient and best built machine for the manufacture of ribbed underwear in the market. Their Circular Ribbed Border Machine is specially built for making ribbed borders for the bottoms of shirts, drawer bottoms or shirt cuffs, and will make plain, welt and tuck work, all changes being made automatically. Hard, forged steel cylinders and dials are used in all these machines, and the workmanship is first-class in every particular. They also make a looper that will not break the needle nor injure the brass between the points, being made with a flexible or yielding needle-arm; and are built in two styles, one adapted for single stitch only, and usually used for closing the toes of seamless hosiery; the other for double stitch, used for underwear or in any other connection where great elasticity and strength are required. These and other specialties bearing the imprint of this company are so perfect and exact in construction and operation as to reduce the work of making knit goods to a simple mechanical operation, and they are in heavy and influential demand throughout the United States, Canada and South America. Catalogues are mailed on application. Messrs. Scott & Williams are well-known Philadelphians, who have achieved a position in the industrial world that entitles them to universal respect, and merits for them the entire confidence of the trade here and elsewhere. This house is undoubtedly the representative concern in this country as builders and patentees of knitting machinery, their trade extending to Europe and other countries.

BULL'S HEAD HORSE and MULE BAZAAR

COACHERS, DRIVERS AND SPEED A SPECIALTY.

Auction Sales every MONDAY and THURSDAY.

WEBER & SULLIVAN, Proprietors.

Nos. 3730 to 3738 Market Street,

West Philadelphia.

The horse market of Philadelphia has been developed to proportions of great magnitude, and there are numerous houses extensively engaged in this branch of trade. One of the best known and most popular among the number is the Bull's Head Horse and Mule Bazaar, of which Messrs. Weber and Sullivan are proprietors, and which is located at Nos. 3730 to 3738 Market Street. This is an old-established business. It was run for nineteen years by S. S. Phipps, and on February 1, of the present year, he was succeeded by the present owners, Messrs. Charles Weber and M. M. Sullivan. Mr. Sullivan has had a sales stable in the next block for the past thirteen years and has done business with leading business men of Philadelphia and surroundings. Both gentlemen have been familiar with horses since their youth, and are expert judges of all that is desirable in a first-class animal. Their stables are excellently lighted, drained and ventilated, and can accommodate 250 horses. A very large business is constantly carried on in the buying and exchanging of horses and mules. This is forcibly shown when we state that the sales from February 1 to July 15 amounted to 5,000 head. Auction sales are held on Mondays and Thursdays, during the year, and are always well attended. A leading specialty is made of Western stock. Horses and mules are received for sale daily on commission, and consignors are assured the best market prices and prompt returns. Mr. Weber has been shipping horses for the past eleven years and is well known throughout the Western and Eastern States as a thoroughly reliable dealer whose honor can always be relied upon in any transaction in which he is engaged, both as to qualities and worth of the animals. Messrs. Weber and Sullivan devote personal attention to their patrons, are straightforward business men, liberal in all their dealings, and enjoy a well-deserved popularity.

SPAETH, KRAUTTER & HESS,

Anchor Brewery,

Germantown and Lehigh Avenues.

The brewing interests of Philadelphia have attained proportions of great magnitude, enlisting as they do ample capital, superior equipments and sterling enterprise. In the item of lager beer especially are the achievements of our leading brewers worthy of special mention, and prominent among the number stand the firm of Spaeth, Krautter & Hess, proprietors of the Anchor Brewery, at Germantown and Lehigh Avenues. This brewery was built in 1885, when the present firm was organized. The brewery is a substantial brick building, four stories high, and supplied with a steam kettle holding 200 barrels, a Consolidated ice machine of thirty-five tons capacity, and every modern appliance tending to facilitate rapid and perfect production. The storage accommodations of this brewery are so extensive that the lager is not hurried from the vats to the consumer, but is retained in cool cellars till of proper age. The lager beer here brewed is recognized by leading experts to be of the best possible quality and standard, the ingredients used being of the best grade obtainable, and the product is preferred by thousands in this city and elsewhere to that of any other brand, on account of its superior quality, perfect purity, fine flavor and uniform excellence. The sales of the firm now aggregate some 40,000 barrels per year, and the business is steadily increasing as an inferior grade of lager is never permitted to pass its gates: hence its great popularity with retailers, families and the general public. The copartners, Messrs. John Spaeth, Louis Krautter and Harry Hess, are all natives of Germany, expert and practical brewers of large experience and established reputation, members of the United States and the Philadelphia Brewers' Associations, and eminently and deservedly popular in business circles for their enterprise, skill and thorough reliability.

THOMAS W. FLING & BRO.,

Manufacturers of

FANCY AND SEAMLESS HOSIERY,

68-76 Wister Street, - Germantown.

One of the oldest and most prominent houses engaged in the manufacture of fancy and seamless hosiery in Philadelphia is that of Messrs. Thomas W. Fling & Bro., located at Nos. 68 to 76 Wister Street, Germantown. This house was established in 1843, by Mr. Geo. Fling, who was succeeded in 1883 by his son, Mr. Thomas W. Fling, and in 1890 the present firm was organized by the admission of Mr. Charlton G. Fling to partnership. The partners bring to bear ample resources and splendid facilities, as an inspection of their factory abundantly demonstrates. The equipment embraces fifty different kinds of knitting machines and twenty sewing machines, all operated by steam-power, and having a productive capacity of 500 dozen per day. The goods comprise a general line of cotton hosiery, both plain and fancy, while quality is ever the first consideration, and the management is not only able and experienced but the most progressive of any in the knit goods industry, manufacturing and introducing to the trade with marked success new and beautiful designs and patterns, which sell rapidly and are in growing demand everywhere. Jobbers throughout all parts of the United States are supplied in quantities to suit at the shortest possible notice, while terms and prices are made invariably satisfactory to the trade. The sound judgment and executive capacity of the management is generally recognized, and the prospects of the house for the future are of the most favorable character, indicating the permanent retention to Philadelphia of the supremacy in this branch of skilled industry. The Messrs. Fling are natives of Germantown, trained in the art of manufacture from their early youth, enterprising and alert to meet the most exacting demands of customers, and reliable and responsible in all their dealings.

New Philadelphia
PLANING MILL CO.,

W. H. KLINE, Proprietor.

No. 2711 North Broad Street.

A flourishing industry in this section of the city is that of the New Philadelphia Planing Mill Co., at No. 2711 North Broad Street. This enterprise was founded in 1882 by Mr. Geo. M. Miller, and in 1890 he was succeeded by Messrs. Kline & Hogeland. The latter retired the same year and Mr. W. H. Kline has since remained in sole control. The premises occupied comprise a mill and lot covering an area of 105 x 205 feet. The mill is a one-story building having dimensions of 40 x 60 feet, and it is equipped with first-class woodworking machinery, driven by a fifty-horse power engine. Employment is found for eighteen skilled workmen. Mr. Kline is a thoroughly experienced woodworker, personally directs the labors of his assistants, and he manufactures a general line of house trimmings, including window-frames, door-frames, shutters, blinds, brackets, hothouse sash, moldings, scroll work, etc., and he also executes sawing and planing to order. A large stock of building lumber is at all times kept on hand, and orders are filled at lowest prices. Mr. Kline was born in Dauphin County, Pennsylvania, and is now a gentleman of middle age. He served in the late war with the Pennsylvania Reserve Corps, under General Meade, and is a member of Bryson Post, No. 225, of which he is past commander. He is also a member of the Royal Arcanum and the Ancient Order of United Workmen, and is thoroughly respected in business and social circles.

JOHN ADAMS,
WOOD MANTELS, WARDROBES AND INTERIOR DECORATIONS,
DOORS, SASH, BLINDS, MOLDINGS,
Lumber and Mill Work of All Kinds,

Seventeenth Street and Indiana Avenue, Sixteenth Street Station, Philadelphia and Reading R. R., Germantown Junction, Pennsylvania R. R.

Few, if any, among the number engaged in the lumber and mill work line in this section of the city, enjoy a more substantial patronage than John Adams, Seventeenth Street and Indiana Avenue. His facilities are first-class in every respect, and his trade, which is very large, is steadily growing. He manufactures everything in the line of doors, sash, blinds, moldings and kindred builders' supplies, and turns out a superior class of work in hardwood finish and interior decorations. Mr. Adams, who is a gentleman of middle age and a native of New Jersey, but has been a resident of Philadelphia since 1877, is a man of practical skill and many years' experience, and is thoroughly conversant with the business in all its branches. He has been established here about twelve years, and from the start has been highly prosperous. The premises occupied by him as planing-mill, etc., are spacious and commodious, and include a 45 x 205-feet two and three story structure, equipped with ample steam-power, improved machinery, etc., while twenty-five to thirty in help are employed. The concern is conveniently situated, being close by the Sixteenth Street Station of the Philadelphia & Reading R. R. and the Germantown Junction, Pennsylvania R. R. An extensive stock is constantly kept on hand, and includes rough and dressed lumber, doors, sash, blinds, door and window frames, moldings, wood mantels, etc., and sawing, planing and turning are done for the trade, at short notice. Sash, doors, blinds, mantels, etc., are made to order, likewise, in any desired size or design, and estimates are given on all kinds of mill work. All orders are promptly attended to, and the lowest consistent prices are quoted, special inducements being offered to builders, contractors and large consumers.

FRANK EDWARDS,

English, Irish and Australian

WOOLS, MOHAIR, ETC.,

Nos. 32 and 34 Strawberry Street.

The gentleman whose name heads this sketch is agent for the sale of English, Irish and Australian wools. He also handles mohair, and foreign carpet wools and does a large business, selling extensively to mills throughout the United States. He represents Francis Willey & Co., of Bradford, England, one of the leading firms in their line in the world, and for thirty years prominent in the trade. Mr. Edwards is a gentleman in the full prime of life, born in England, and has been in this city since May, 1894. He is a man of many years' practical experience in this line, active and energetic, and is thoroughly conversant with the trade. The premises occupied as office and warehouse, at Nos. 32 and 34 Strawberry Street, comprise the whole of a commodious five-story and basement building, equipped with freight elevator and complete facilities, and an efficient staff of help is employed here, while a heavy stock is always kept on hand. Mr. Edwards is prepared to execute orders for foreign wools of every variety and all grades, also for mohair, and anything in this line on the most favorable terms, quoting the lowest prices consistent with quality of goods; and relations once formed with him are reasonably certain of leading to an enduring business connection.

THE NONPAREIL CEMENT COMPANY, Incorporated.

Successors to ROBERT COANE & CO.,

Manufacturers and Importers of PORTLAND CEMENTS,

Main Office and Warehouse, Ninth and Oxford Streets.

The ever-increasing magnitude of building operations throughout the United States has created an active demand for the highest grade of cement, which is consumed in enormous quantities. A leading house engaged in this branch of trade in Philadelphia is that of The Nonpareil Cement Company, whose main office is located with warehouse at Ninth and Oxford Streets, and works at Coplay, Pa. This company is extensively engaged in the manufacturing and importing of Portland cements. The business was originally established in 1890 by Robert Coane & Co., and in 1892 the present company was organized, with Robert Coane, president; George W. Sullivan, secretary and treasurer. The management brings to bear all the advantages derived from long years of identification with this line of industry, perfected facilities, influential connections, both at home and abroad, and a thorough knowledge of the wants of buyers, in all the different sections of the country. The company are manufacturers of Nonpareil Portland, Monarch Portland and Acme Improved Rosendale cements, and are importers of high-grade Belgium, German and English Portland cement, and also represent some of the leading factories making enamel and vitrified brick, and are extensive dealers in builders' materials, while they are, likewise, prominent in the trade as agents for terra cotta and fire clay products. The company operates quarries on the Lehigh Valley Railroad, where they have modern facilities at hand for producing a first-class article with great expediency. They have lately made a new departure in the cement trade, that of barreling and grinding carefully-selected Portland clinker at home, thereby enabling them to sell a first-class article in competition with spurious grades of imported and domestic cements. They have the latest improved machinery and splendid railroad connections to their warehouse and mill and are in a position to fill all orders with despatch, being located in the heart of the city, on the great Philadelphia & Reading Railroad System. This company has a shipping capacity, both from its own and other works in its control, of nearly two thousand barrels per day, domestic cements alone, and have at all times large quantities on hand of German, English and Belgium cements, at the following ports, viz: New York, Philadelphia and Baltimore. Cements manufactured and handled by this company are now specified by the leading architects and engineers over the country, and can be used with safety in all submarine operations, buildings and engineering works where great strength of rock-like solidity are necessary. The economy of using Nonpareil Portland, which is the company's leading brand, has been successfully demonstrated, and it is now generally conceded that concrete made from this brand, on account of its strength, etc., is cheaper and better than when made from other brands of cement.

J. F. RAUSENBERGER,
Bee Hive Meat Market,
COR. MAIN AND JOHNSON STS., GERMANTOWN.

The largest meat, poultry, provision, vegetable and general market in Germantown is that conducted by Mr. J. F. Rausenberger, known as the Bee Hive, located at the corner of Main and Johnson Streets. This reliable market controls the lion's share of the best family trade here, and it is freely recognized as headquarters for the choicest qualities of viands and edibles in each line. These include prime beef, mutton, pork, veal and lamb, fresh eggs, butter, poultry and provisions, a full assortment of canned and bottled goods of the standard brands, vegetables and fruits of all kinds in season. The business was established here in 1890 by the present proprietor, who has been actively engaged in this line for thirty years—formerly on Columbia Avenue in the city. The store, 35 x 70 feet in size, contains a rich and tempting display of goods tastefully arranged all around, and the brisk business carried on constitutes the establishment a veritable beehive. Popular prices prevail in each line. Six wagons are kept constantly busy in making deliveries, and thirteen competent hands are regularly employed. Mr. Rausenberger was born in Philadelphia in 1847, and is a member of the Knights Templar of the Free and Accepted Masons, and Baker Post of the G. A. R., having served for three years in the Sixth Pennsylvania Cavalry under General Sheridan, enlisting in the sixteenth year of his age, and took part in every engagement of his regiment.

SULLIVAN,

PHOTOGRAPHER,
Branch of Superior Portrait Co.,
No. 1705 South Street.

The flourishing local trade controlled by Mr. Charles M. Sullivan, as a high-art photographer, located at No. 1705 South Street, constitutes the business the largest in this section of Philadelphia, and it has all accrued during the four years of its establishment at the same location, under the able and skillful direction of the present proprietor, who possesses a practical experience in the profession ranging over a period of fourteen years. All kinds of art photography are undertaken and executed in the finest style by the latest approved processes and appliances; the chief lines being portraits of various sizes in inks, oils, watercolors, crayons, pastels, etc., enlargements, developing for amateurs and others, groups, figures, statuary, interiors, objects in motion, and a full line of fine photography; while a specialty is made of copying and photographing of deceased persons, and every facility is possessed for executing large or small orders on the shortest notice. The whole of the building, No. 1705 South Street, is occupied for residence and business, with studio, operating rooms, and reception rooms on the first floor, art gallery, skylight, etc., on the second floor, three skilled artists being there regularly employed. Mr. Charles M. Sullivan is a young man of Philadelphia birth and is a member of the Ancient Order of Foresters as well as of several clubs and societies.

GEO. V. CRESSON COMPANY, Manufacturers of Power Transmitting Machinery, Shafting and all its Appurtenances, Main Office and Works, Eighteenth Street and Allegheny Avenue.—The great and important strides made by the Geo. V. Cresson Company of this city in the manufacture of power transmitting machinery and all its appurtenances, have elicited the closest investigation and widespread patronage of the industrial world. The main office and works of the company are situated at the address given above, with a branch office at No. 136 Liberty Street, New York City. The company make a specialty of transmission of power by vertical shafting, also by rope driving, and their name has become a veritable trade-mark for all machinery in their line. The business was established in 1859, by Mr. Geo. V. Cresson at Fifteenth Street and Pennsylvania Avenue. In 1864 he erected a machine shop at Eighteenth and Hamilton Streets where his business was continued until 1888, when material enlargements were needed for the growing demands of the business and the present plant was erected. On the 22d of July, 1892, the Geo. V. Cresson Company was incorporated under the laws of the State of Pennsylvania, with the following officers: Geo. V. Cresson, president and treasurer; Antonio C. Pessano, vice-president and general manager; E. Oscar Haempture, assistant treasurer; Morris W. Rudderow, secretary and business manager. The plant of the company covers an area of about five acres and comprises a machine shop 500 x 50 feet, with basement 250 x 50 feet; a machine shop, 244 x 108 feet; a foundry for heavy work, 200 x 55 feet; a foundry for light work, 100 x 65 feet; a foundry for brass, phosphor bronze and steel castings, 34 x 65 feet; with a carpenter shop, pattern shop, pattern and storage house, 100 x 55 feet; engine room, 36 x 28 feet; boiler room, 36 x 30 feet; cupola house, 34 x 25 feet; foundry storehouse with a capacity for storing 1,000 tons of molding sand, 200 tons of coke, 300 tons of coal and 1,500 tons of pig iron. The entire works have a perfect and comprehensive equipment of improved machinery operated by a steam-engine of 400-horse power, and steady employment is given to some three hundred skilled workmen. The company take contracts for complete power plants of any kind and act as mill engineers, making drawings and superintending construction; they possess improved facilities for the manufacture of shafting, pulleys, hangers, etc., and having a full line of patterns, are enabled to meet every want of the public promptly, while in cases where their standard patterns do not answer all requirements they are prepared to make necessary changes at short notice. Parting or split pulleys receive special attention and a very large stock of all sizes is constantly kept on hand; they make machine molded gearing of any size and are prepared to cut bevel and spur gears of any diameter and width face. From the most improved patterns are also furnished mule and guide pulleys for belts from two to twenty inches wide, adjustable in any direction; parting hangers which can be applied to any point on the line without taking down the shaft, also patent adjustable loose pulley arrangements, wall boxes, wall plates, wall brackets, clamp boxes, friction clutch pulleys and couplings of all sizes. All shafting manufactured here is coupled together as ordered, tried and tested, so that no imperfections may be found when erected. The management are constantly adding to their large stock of pulley patterns and are prepared to furnish a greater variety of sizes than there can be found anywhere; they are continually at work noting results of their important improvements and experimenting upon additional ones, and each season sees something new in unison with the ever growing demand for power transmitting machinery of the most advanced type. The improvements made in their specialties have placed them far beyond competition and they are found in satisfactory use in the largest manufacturing and electric light plants, not only throughout the United States but also in Canada, South America, Mexico, Germany and other foreign countries. Quality has ever been the first consideration with the management, and their claims for merit are based on the severest tests of every day use in the mills and shops throughout the land. The triumphant record of their machinery and its ever widening use are alone sufficient guarantees that purchasers can do best here. Medals have been received at United States Centennial Exhibition, the Franklin Institute, the Novelties Exhibition and the World's Fair at Paris in 1878; a fine exhibit will be made at the World's Fair in Chicago in 1893. Illustrated catalogue mailed on application and prices furnished upon receipt of specifications. President Geo. V. Cresson, the honored founder of the enterprise, is one of the best known and most successful engineers and machinery manufacturers in the country, and in connection with the other officers of the company, each of whom is a skilled expert in his line, worthily maintains the supremacy in power transmitting machinery of the most advanced character throughout the world.

TO BE HELD IN

CHICAGO, ILLINOIS, U. S. A.,

MAY 1st TO OCTOBER 31st, 1893.

SUPPLEMENT TO

"HISTORICAL AND COMMERCIAL PHILADELPHIA."

—NOTE—

In presenting to our subscribers these supplemental pages we offer at once complete views of the more prominent buildings in Jackson Park, designs for which have been made and accepted and which are now in course of erection.

Presented collectively, as in the pages that follow, we believe them both instructive and interesting to the public, and a medium which will serve to show the elaborate preparations now being made to make the COLUMBIAN EXPOSITION of 1893 the best of its kind ever before attempted.

In every building erected the architect and the builder have combined the highest talents of their arts to attain perfection, and the exhibitor at this Fair is assured of having his displays exhibited in buildings whose every detail, architectural and constructional, are the acme of perfection.

THE PUBLISHERS.

VIEW LOOKING SOUTH OVER THE LAGOON.

(SEE OPPOSITE PAGE.)

This view is taken looking south over the lagoon which lies between the buildings for Manufactures and Electricity. This lagoon crosses the great basin and terminates beyond the second bridge at the obelisk and fountain.

On the extreme right of the picture a portion of the east front and one of the towers of the Electrical building are visible. Beyond and opposite the building across the basin is seen part of the palace of Machinery, its eastern façade crowned with domes and towers.

On the extreme left is seen a corner of the west front of the Manufactures building, and opposite this and across the basin the building for the Agricultural exhibit. This building is connected with the palace of Machinery by the long colonnade in the center background, forming a great portico entrance to the live-stock grounds farther south, and at the same time completing the monumental group on the south of the great basin. A triple arch bridge spans the lagoon in the foreground, affording communication between the Electrical and Manufactures buildings. It is only one of many such bridges which will be built in other parts of the grounds. Notice to the right or the left the manner of terracing. From the water rises a sea wall whose coping guards access to the first terrace. In this wall gates and jetties will be arranged so that landings can be effected from the small boats of the park. The first terrace is the domain of the landscape gardener, and will be devoted to flowers, shrubbery and gravel walks. Some four feet above this terrace is the great paved platform serving as a base to the buildings. This platform is finished with balustrades, vases and statuary, and approach to it from the first terrace is gained at intervals by monumental flights of steps.

This view, looking as it does down the lagoon toward the great basin, represents a part of the grounds where the buildings are most thickly clustered, where distances are at the minimum, and where the perspective is least extended. Picture then the grand scale on which the scheme is being worked out, the care and attention that has been given to produce imposing effects and magnificent vistas; and the enticement offered to architects and artists to create masterpieces. Surely the plan is incomparable, and its culmination will close an epoch in the history of art.

View Looking South Over the Lagoon.

ADMINISTRATION BUILDING.

This building is the gem of all the architectural jewels of the Exposition. Constructed of material to last but two years, it will cost $650,000. Although it covers a space but 250 feet square, yet it is one of the noblest achievements of modern architecture. It will occupy the most commanding position on the exposition grounds. The building consists of four pavilions, 84 feet square, one at each of the four angles of the square of the plan, and connected by a great central dome, 120 feet in diameter, and 260 feet high. In the center of each façade is a recess, 93 feet wide, within which is a grand entrance to the building. The first story is in the Doric order, of heavy propor-

tions. The second, with its lofty colonnade, is in the Ionic order. Externally, the design is divided into three principal stages. The first stage consists of the four pavilions, corresponding in height with the buildings grouped about, which are 65 feet high. The second stage is of the same height, and is a continuation of the central rotunda, which is 175 feet square. The third stage is the base of the great dome, 40 feet high, and octagonal in form, and the dome itself rising in graceful lines, richly ornamented with heavily molded ribs and sculptured panels, and having a large glass skylight. The interior effects will be even more gorgeous than the exterior, resplendent with carvings, sculptures and immense paintings.

AGRICULTURAL BUILDING.

With the exception of the Administration building, the Agricultural building will be the most magnificent structure on the Exposition grounds. In size it is 800 by 500 feet, severely classic in style. It is almost surrounded by lagoons. The features of this building are its five pavilions, one at each corner and one in the center. The corner pavilions are 64 by 48 feet square. The grand entrance is on the north. It is 60 feet wide, leading

into a vestibule 30 feet deep and 60 feet wide. At the entrance are Corinthian columns 5 feet in diameter and 40 feet high. Beyond these massive columns is the rotunda, 100 feet in diameter, surmounted by a glass dome 130 feet high. There are eight minor entrances 20 feet wide. The roof will be principally of glass.

GOVERNMENT BUILDING.

The Government building is 420 by 350 feet in size. It is two stories high, and covers about four acres. The building is of iron, brick and glass, and classic in design. From the center an octagonal dome rises 150 feet. The building will front to the west. It will have rooms for exhibits of the State Department, Smithsonian Institute, the Interior Department, Fish Commission, Postoffice Department, Agricultural Department, War Department and the Department of Justice. A large area adjacent to the building will be devoted to field hospitals, life-saving

stations, lighthouses, etc. The building will probably be connected with the State Fisheries Exhibit by a bridge and terrace, and steps will let down to the lagoon. The government display will be most interesting. The War Department will show all the machinery required to manufacture small arms, and will make cartridges on the grounds. The Postoffice Department will show a model postoffice, and will handle all the Exposition mail. The Treasury Department will coin silver, and print silver and gold certificates. Congress has appropriated $400,000 for the construction of this building.

MINES AND MINING BUILDING.

The style of architecture of the Mines building is classic, and its dimensions are 700 by 350 feet. The height to the main cornice is 65 feet. There is an entrance on each side of the building, the grand entrances being at the north and south end. These are 110 feet high and 32 feet wide, each opening into a vestibule 88 feet high

and elaborately decorated. At each corner of the building there is a pavilion, 68 feet square and 90 feet high, surmounted by a dome. A balcony, 60 feet wide and 25 feet high, encircles the building, and leading to it are eight stairways. The roof is of glass, 100 feet from the floor. The cost will be $350,000.

FISH AND FISHERIES BUILDING.

This cut shows the central portion of the Fisheries building. Excluded from the view are two smaller polygonal buildings, connected with the main building on either end by arcades. The extreme length of the building over all is 1,100 feet, and the width 200 feet. It is built on a banana-shaped island, and the building is subdivided into three parts, to conform to the shape of the site. In the central portion will be the general fisheries exhibit.

In one of the polygonal buildings will be the angling exhibit, and in the other the aquaria. The exterior of the building is Spanish-Romanesque, and will contrast agreeably in appearance with the classic style of all the other buildings.

ELECTRICAL BUILDING.

The building covers a space of 700 by 350 feet, or more than five and one-half acres. Like most of the other buildings, the style of architecture is Italian renaissance. It is 60 feet high, and ornamented with designs suggestive of the department. It is one of the handsomest of the grand central group, and will cost $650,000. There

will be four entrances to the building, the main one on the south. It will be built of a material resembling granite in color. A statue of Franklin will rise conspicuously before the south entrance.

WOMEN'S BUILDING.

This building is 200 by 400 feet in its general dimensions, and is two stories high, with an attic containing committee-rooms and general offices. On the end of the pavilion are roof gardens, protected from the sun by awnings, and commanding beautiful views of the surrounding grounds. It is located on the west side of Jackson Park,

directly opposite the Midway plaisance. On the east and west fronts are spacious loggias 200 feet long and 20 feet wide, surmounted by open balconies, accessible from the second floor. In the center is the great hall, about 80 feet wide by 200 feet long and the full height of the building, surrounded by corridors which open upon the central hall by a series of arches or colonnades, and giving access to various exhibition, committee and reception rooms, ladies' parlors, etc.

MANUFACTURES AND LIBERAL ARTS.

Is designed by Mr. George B. Post of New York City. It is much the largest building in the Exposition in extent and area. It is 800 feet wide and 1,700 feet long. The southerly end of the building faces on the great court directly opposite the Agricultural Hall, and on the north end faces the Government building; on the west side faces the Electricity building, and on the east Lake Michigan. In form it is rectangular, with an exhibition hall extending about a great interior court. This exhibition hall receives light from both sides and from the top, and each section is composed of a great central arch 100 feet wide, open to the roof, and 80 feet high, with galleries 50 feet wide on either side. Directly in the center is the great dome, which has a clear open space of 260 feet in diameter, with a surrounding gallery 50 feet wide in addition. The roof of this dome is supported by great arched trusses of iron, and is 175 feet high from the floor to the apex of the roof.

The galleries are approached upon the main floor by 30 great staircases, the flights of which are 12 feet wide each. There are four great entrances, one in the center of each façade. These are designed in the manner of triumphal arches, the central archway of each being 40 feet wide and 80 feet high. Surmounting these portals is the great attic story, ornamented with immense sculptured eagles, 18 feet high, and on each side above the side arches are great panels with inscriptions, and the spandrels are filled with sculptured figures in bas-relief.

At each corner of the main building are pavilions forming great arched entrances, which are designed in harmony with the great portals.

The long façades of the great hall surrounding the building are composed of a series of arches, filled with immense glass windows. The lower portion of these arches, up to the level of the gallery floor and 25 feet in depth, is open to the outside, thus forming a covered loggia, which forms an open promenade for the public, and will provide a very interesting feature, particularly on the east side where it faces the lake. It is intended to locate here a number of cafés, where the great crowds can loiter at their ease and enjoy the breezes and cool shadows of the afternoon.

The spandrels of these arches are decorated with great shields, which contain the coats of arms of the states of the Union.

In the great open courts of this building, north and south of the great dome, are to be placed annexes, which can be used for the music hall and for the shoe and leather exhibit. Each of these annexes covers about 100,000 square feet in area, and taken in conjunction with the great area of the dome in the center, will form an unrivaled suite of great halls.

In the department allotted to glass work, each manufacturer will have an opportunity to display his work in a separate window.

MACHINERY HALL.

The main Machinery building measures 850 by 500 feet. It is spanned by three arched trusses, and the interior will present the appearance of three railroad train houses, side by side, surrounded on all the four sides by a 50-foot gallery. The trusses are to be built separately, and so that they can be taken down and sold for use as railroad train houses, and it is hoped to have iron trusses instead of cheaper ones, which may, however, be necessary. In each of these three long naves there is to be an elevated traveling crane, running from end to end of the building. These will be useful in moving machinery, and when the Exposition opens platforms will be placed on them, and visitors will view from these the entire exhibition, at a great saving of tramping.

Shafting for power will be carried on the same posts which support these traveling bridges. Steam-power will be used throughout this main building, and this steam will be supplied from a main power house adjoining the south side of the building. The exterior toward the stock exhibit and the railroad is to be of the plainest description. On the two sides adjoining the grand court, the exterior will, however, be rich and palatial. All the buildings on this grand plaza are designed with a view to making an effective background for displays of every kind, and in order to conform to the general richness of the court, are enriched with colonnades and other architectural features.

The design follows classical models throughout, the detail being borrowed from the renaissance of Seville and other Spanish towns as being appropriate to a Columbian celebration. As in all the other buildings on the court, an arcade on the first story permits passage around the building under cover; and as in all the other buildings, the fronts will be formed of "staff," colored to an ivory tone. The ceilings of the porticoes will be emphasized with strong color.

A colonnade with a café at either end forms the connecting link between Machinery and Agricultural halls, and in the center of this colonnade is an archway leading to the exhibits. From this portico there will be a view nearly a mile in length down the lagoon, and an obelisk and fountain placed in the lagoon between the two buildings, Agricultural and Machinery, will form a fitting southern point to this vista.

The machinery annex will be placed in the rear of the Administration building and in the loop formed by the railroad tracks. It will be entered by tunnels or subways, as well as by bridges, from Machinery hall and the buildings for Administration, Mines and Transportation. It is to be a very large but very simple building. While in the main Machinery building a railroad train house is the type, in the annex a mill or foundry will be considered the model for construction. It is all to be built of wood in the most simple and economical manner. Its shape, however, is peculiar. It is to be annular in form, the outer diameter being 800 feet, and the inner diameter 400 feet. The building will have a nave 100 feet wide, with a 50-feet wide lean-to in one story on the inside, and a 50-feet wide lean-to on the outside.

TRANSPORTATION BUILDING.

The Transportation building is one of the group forming the northern or picturesque quadrangle. It is situated at the southern end of the west flank, and lies between the Horticultural and Mines buildings. Its axial relation is with the Manufactures building on the east side of the quadrangle, the central feature of each of the two buildings being on the same east and west line.

The Transportation building is exquisitely refined and simple in architectural treatment, although it is intended to make it very rich and elaborate in detail. In style it savors much of the Romanesque, although to the initiated the manner in which it is designed on axial lines, and the solicitude shown for fine proportions and subtle relation of parts to each other, will at once suggest the methods of composition followed at the Ecole des Beaux Arts.

Viewed from the lagoon, the cupola of the Transportation building will form the effective southwest accent of the quadrangle, while from the cupola itself, reached by eight elevators, the northern court, the most beautiful effect of the entire Exposition, may be seen in all its glory.

The main entrance to the Transportation building will consist of an immense single arch, enriched to an extraordinary degree with carvings, bas-reliefs and mural paintings. The entire feature will form a rich and beautiful yet quiet color climax, for it will be treated entirely in leaf, and will be called the Golden Door.

The remainder of the architectural composition falls into a just relation of contrast with the highly wrought entrance, and is duly quiet and modest, though very broad in treatment. It consists of a continuous arcade, with subordinated colonnade and entablature. Numerous minor entrances are from time to time pierced in the walls, and with them are grouped terraces, seats, drinking fountains and statues.

The interior of the building is treated much after the manner of a Roman Basilica, with broad nave and aisles. The roof is therefore in three divisions; the middle one rising much higher than the others, and its walls are pierced to form a beautiful arcaded clere-story. The cupola, placed exactly at the center of the building, and rising 165 feet above the ground, is reached by eight elevators. These elevators will of themselves naturally form a part of the transportation exhibit, and as they will also carry passengers to galleries at various stages of height, a fine view of the interior of the building may easily be obtained. The main galleries of this building, because of the abundant placing of passenger elevators, will prove quite accessible to visitors.

The main building of the transportation exhibit measures 960 feet front by 256 feet deep; from this will extend westward to Stony Island Avenue a triangular annex covering about nine acres, and consisting of one-story buildings sixty-four feet wide, set side by side. As there will be a railway track every sixteen feet, and as all these tracks will run east and west, these annex buildings may be used to exhibit an entire freight or passenger train, coupled with its engine. It is likely that the display of locomotive engines will be quite stupendous.

HORTICULTURAL BUILDING.

The accompanying cut presents the front elevation of the Horticultural Hall, designed by W. L. B. Jenney, of Chicago. The building is situated immediately south of the entrance to Jackson Park from the Midway plaisance, and faces east on the lagoon. In front is a flower terrace for outside exhibits, including tanks for nympheas and the victoria-regia. The front of the terrace, with its low parapet between large vases, borders the water, and at its center forms a boat landing.

The building is 1,000 feet long, with an extreme width of 286 feet. The plan is a central pavilion with two end pavilions, each connected to the center pavilion by front and rear curtains, forming two interior courts, each 88 by 270 feet. These courts are beautifully decorated in color and planted with ornamental shrubs and flowers. The center pavilion is roofed by a crystal dome 187 feet in diameter and 113 feet high, under which will be exhibited the tallest palms, bamboos and tree ferns that can be procured. There is a gallery in each of the pavilions.

The galleries of the end pavilion are designed for cafés, the situations and surroundings being particularly well adapted to recreation and refreshment. These cafés are surrounded by an arcade on three sides, from which charming views of the grounds can be obtained.

In this building will be exhibited all the varieties of flowers, plants, vines, seeds, horticultural implements, etc. Those exhibits requiring sunshine and light will be shown in the rear curtains, where the roof is entirely of glass and not too far removed from the plants. The front curtains and under the galleries are designed for exhibits that require only the ordinary amount of light. Provision is made to heat such parts as require it.

The exterior of the building is in staff or stucco, tinted a soft warm buff, color being reserved for the interior and the courts. The appropriation for this building is $400,000. It will probably be built for something less than this sum.

the entire building are galleries 40 feet wide, forming a continual promenade around the entire structure. Between the promenade and the nave are the smaller rooms devoted to private collections of paintings and the collections of the various art schools. On either side of the main building will be one-storied annexes, which will be divided into large and small galleries, capable of expansion if a demand for space should warrant. The annexes will be 120 by 200 feet wide. The main building is entered by four great portals, richly ornamented with architectural sculpture, and approached by broad flights of steps. The walls of the loggia of the colonnade will be highly decorated with mural paintings, illustrating the history and progress of the arts. The frieze of the exterior walls, and the pediments of the principal entrances will be ornamented with sculptures and portraits in bas-relief of the masters of ancient art. The general tone or color will be light gray stone.

The construction, although of a temporary character, is necessarily fire-proof. The main walls will be of solid brick, covered with staff architecturally ornamented, while the roof, floors and galleries will be of iron. All light will be supplied through glass skylights in iron frames. The building will be located at the south side of the improved portion of the park, with the south front directly on the north of the lagoon. It will be separated from the lagoon by beautiful terraces ornamented with balustrades, with an immense flight of steps. From the main portal there will be a landing for boats. The north front will face the wide open lawn and the group of state buildings. The immediate neighborhood of the building will be ornamented with groups of statues, replicas and ornaments of classic art, such as choragic monuments, the "Cave of the Winds," and other beautiful examples of Grecian art. The ornamentation will also include statues of heroic and life-size proportions. The probable cost of the building will be between $500,000 and $600,000.